POETS

Great Writers of the English Language

Poets

Novelists and Prose Writers

Dramatists

POETS

EDITOR

JAMES VINSON

ASSOCIATE EDITOR

D. L. KIRKPATRICK

ST. MARTIN'S PRESS
NEW YORK

All rights reserved. For information write:
ST. MARTIN'S PRESS
175 Fifth Avenue
New York, New York 10010

ISBN 0-312-34640-9
Library of Congress Catalog Card Number 78-78299

Typeset by Computacomp (UK) Ltd.,
Fort William, Scotland

CONTENTS

EDITOR'S NOTE

The selection of writers included in this book is based on the recommendations of the advisers listed on page ix.

The entry for each writer consists of a biography, a complete list of his published books, a selected list of published bibliographies and critical studies on the writer, and a signed critical essay on his work.

In the biographies, details of education, military service, and marriage(s) are generally given before the usual chronological summary of the life of the writer; awards and honours are given last.

The Publications section is meant to include all book publications, though as a rule broadsheets, single sermons and lectures, minor pamphlets, exhibition catalogues, etc. are omitted. Under the heading Collections, we have listed the most recent collections of the complete works and those of individual genres (verse, plays, novels, stories, and letters); only those collections which have some editorial authority and were issued after the writer's death are listed; on-going editions are indicated by a dash after the date of publication; often a general selection from the writer's works or a selection from the works in the individual genres listed above is included.

Titles are given in modern spelling, though the essayists were allowed to use original spelling for titles and quotations; often the titles are "short." The date given is that of the first book publication, which often followed the first periodical or anthology publication by some time; we have listed the actual year of publication, often different from that given on the title-page. No attempt has been made to indicate which works were published anonymously or pseudonymously, or which works of fiction were published in more than one volume. We have listed plays which were produced but not published, but only since 1700; librettos and musical plays are listed along with the other plays; no attempt has been made to list lost or unverified plays. Reprints of books (including facsimile editions) and revivals of plays are not listed unless a revision or change of title is involved. The most recent edited version of individual works is included if it supersedes the collected edition cited.

In the essays, short references to critical remarks refer to items cited in the Publications section or in the Reading List. Introductions, memoirs, editorial matter, etc. in works cited in the Publications section are not repeated in the Reading List.

We would like to thank the advisers and contributors for their patience and help.

ADVISERS

Walter Allen
F. W. Bateson
Bernard Bergonzi
Earle Birney
Ruby Cohn
Allen Curnow
Warren French
John C. Gerber
Roma Gill
Daniel Hoffman
C. Hugh Holman
Louis James
A. Norman Jeffares
Lewis Leary
David Lodge

W. H. New
Roy Harvey Pearce
George Perkins
John M. Reilly
H. Winston Rhodes
Pat Rogers
Gāmini Salgādo
C. K. Stead
James Sutherland
Derek A. Traversi
Gerald Weales
Margaret Willy
James Woodress
Judith Wright

CONTRIBUTORS

Peter Alcock
M. J. Alexander
Walter Allen
W. E. K. Anderson
David Astle
Alvin Aubert
T. Bareham
Samuel Irving Bellman
Alice R. Bensen
Bernard Bergonzi
Gabriel Bergonzi
Francis Berry
David Blamires
Walter Bode
Margaret Bottrall
Mary Weatherspoon Bowden
Laurel Brake
J. S. Bratton
Lawrence J. Broer
Ashley Brown
Cedric C. Brown
Lloyd W. Brown
Terence Brown
P. H. Butter
Richard J. Calhoun
Ian Campbell
Guy A. Cardwell
Geoffrey Carnall
Frederic I. Carpenter
Paul Christensen

William Claire
John R. Clark
Leonard Clark
Garth Clucas
A. O. J. Cockshut
William J. Collins
Neil Corcoran
T. W. Craik
Greg Crossan
Richard H. Crowder
Curtis Dahl
William Daniels
Walter R. Davis
Dennis Davison
Elizabeth Story Donno
Wilfred S. Dmwden
Charles Doyle
Victor A. Doyno
R. P. Draper
Rhodes Dunlap
Brian Elliott
Frank Fabry
Peter Faulkner
Ian Fletcher
Margaret Forey
Edward Halsey Foster
John Wilson Foster
G. S. Fraser
Jane S. Gabin
Sally M. Gall

John C. Gerber
Winifred Gérin
D. B. Gibson
Roma Gill
Clarence A. Glasrud
Duncan Glen
Ian A. Gordon
Lois Gordon
Desmond Graham
Dorothy Green
Roger Lancelyn Green
Joan Grundy
Andrew Gurr
Harlan W. Hamilton
Maurice Harmon
Donald M. Hassler
John Heath-Stubbs
Geof Hewitt
Daniel Hoffman
Jonathan Holden
C. Hugh Holman
Derek Hudson
Robert N. Hudspeth
Ruth Hughey
A. Norman Jeffares
Robert K. Johnson
M. K. Joseph
Nancy C. Joyner
Martin Kallich
Bruce Kellner
Richard Kelly
Peter Kemp
Burton Kendle
Keneth Kinnamon
G. A. Lester
James A. Levernier
Peter Lewis
Maurice Lindsay
Dorothy Livesay
Bruce A. Lohof
John Lucas
A. W. Lyle
E. D. Mackerness
Allan H. MacLaine
Matthew P. McDiarmid
F. M. McKay
Earl Miner
Gail Mirza
H. A. Mirza
Jerome Mitchell
George Monteiro
Catherine E. Moore
Rayburn S. Moore
J. E. Morpurgo

Kenneth Muir
John M. Munro
Bruce Nesbitt
Alastair Niven
Brady Nordland
J. Norton-Smith
Thomas F. O'Donnell
B. C. Oliver-Morden
Bridget O'Toole
C. A. Patrides
Derek Pearsall
John J. Perry
Margaret Perry
Kirsten Holst Petersen
John B. Pickard
F. B. Pinion
Joan Pittock
Arthur Pollard
John Press
Hilary Pyle
Peter Quartermain
C. J. Rawson
David Ray
E. H. Redekop
Thomas Dillon Redshaw
Joan Rees
James Reeves
Samuel J. Rogal
Pat Rogers
Eric Rothstein
Earl Rovit
Glenn Richard Ruihley
James E. Ruoff
Daniel Rutenberg
Carol Lee Saffioti
Gāmini Salgādo
A. J. Sambrook
George Brandon Saul
Daniel R. Schwarz
Brian W. M. Scobie
Catherine Seelye
Roger D. Sell
Brocard Sewell
Raymond C. Shady
William E. Sheidley
Helena Mennie Shire
Alan R. Shucard
Jon Silkin
Peter Simpson
Amritjit Singh
M. Sivaramakrishna
Floyd Skloot
Ian C. Small
A. J. M. Smith

Elton E. Smith
Stan Smith
Harry M. Solomon
Hilda D. Spear
Jon Stallworthy
Donald E. Stanford
Kay Stevenson
Graham Storey
Joseph H. Summers
Wesley D. Sweetser
Donald S. Taylor
Myron Taylor
Ned Thomas
Anthony Thwaite
Anne Tibble
Derek A. Traversi
Richard C. Turner
William M. Tydeman

Raymond B. Waddington
Linda W. Wagner
Alan Wall
George Walsh
Marcus Walsh
William Walsh
Alan Warner
J. R. Watson
Harold H. Watts
Gerald Weales
Robert Welch
Thomas Wheeler
John Stuart Williams
Margaret Willy
George Woodcock
James Woodress
T. D. Young

POETS

Lascelles Abercrombie
Conrad Aiken
Mark Akenside
William Alabaster
William Allingham
A. R. Ammons
Christopher Anstey
John Armstrong
Matthew Arnold
John Ashbery
Margaret Atwood
W. H. Auden
Alfred Austin
Margaret Avison
Sir Robert Ayton

Philip James Bailey
Anna Barbauld
John Barbour
Alexander Barclay
Richard Harris Barham
George Barker
Joel Barlow
Barnabe Barnes
William Barnes
Richard Barnfield
Blanche Baughan
James K. Baxter
James Beattie
Sir John Beaumont
Joseph Beaumont
Thomas Lovell Beddoes
Hilaire Belloc
Stephen Vincent Benét
William Rose Benét
Edward Benlowes
Louise Bennett
Beowulf Poet
John Berryman
Mary Ursula Bethell
Sir John Betjeman
Laurence Binyon
Earle Birney
Elizabeth Bishop
John Peale Bishop
Sir Richard Blackmore
Robert Blair
William Blake
Robert Bloomfield
Edmund Blunden
Wilfrid Scawen Blunt
Robert Bly
Louise Bogan
William Lisle Bowles

Anne Bradstreet
Edward Brathwaite
Christopher Brennan
Nicholas Breton
Robert Bridges
Emily Brontë
Rupert Brooke
Gwendolyn Brooks
Sterling Brown
William Browne
Elizabeth Barrett Browning
Robert Browning
William Cullen Bryant
Basil Bunting
Robert Burns
Guy Butler
Samuel Butler
John Byrom
Lord Byron

Charles Stuart Calverley
Alistair Campbell
Roy Campbell
Thomas Campbell
Thomas Campion
Thomas Carew
Bliss Carman
William Ellery Channing
George Chapman
Thomas Chatterton
Geoffrey Chaucer
Thomas Holley Chivers
Charles Churchill
Thomas Churchyard
John Clare
John Pepper Clark
Austin Clarke
John Cleveland
Arthur Hugh Clough
Samuel Taylor Coleridge
William Collins
Padraic Colum
William Combe
Henry Constable
Ebenezer Cooke
Richard Corbett
Charles Cotton
Abraham Cowley
William Cowper
George Crabbe
Hart Crane
Richard Crashaw
Isabella Valancy Crawford
Robert Creeley

Countée Cullen
E. E. Cummings
John Cunningham
Allen Curnow
Cynewulf

Samuel Daniel
George Darley
Erasmus Darwin
Donald Davidson
John Davidson
Donald Davie
Sir John Davies
W. H. Davies
C. Day Lewis
Walter de la Mare
Sir John Denham
Lord de Tabley
Aubrey De Vere
William Diaper
James Dickey
Emily Dickinson
Richard Watson Dixon
S. T. Dobell
Austin Dobson
Rosemary Dobson
Alfred Domett
John Donne
Hilda Doolittle
Earl of Dorset
Gavin Douglas
Keith Douglas
Ernest Dowson
Joseph Rodman Drake
Michael Drayton
William Drummond
John Dryden
Stephen Duck
Eileen Duggan
Paul Laurence Dunbar
William Dunbar
Robert Duncan
Geoffrey Dutton
Timothy Dwight
John Dyer

Richard Eberhart
T. S. Eliot
Ebenezer Elliott
Ralph Waldo Emerson
William Empson

A. R. D. Fairburn
William Falconer

Kenneth Fearing
Sir Samuel Ferguson
Robert Fergusson
Eugene Field
Edward FitzGerald
Robert D. FitzGerald
James Elroy Flecker
Giles Fletcher, the Elder
Giles Fletcher, the Younger
John Gould Fletcher
Phineas Fletcher
Stephen Collins Foster
Philip Freneau
John Hookham Frere
Robert Frost
Roy Fuller

Sir Samuel Garth
George Gascoigne
David Gascoyne
Gawain Poet
John Gay
Manmohan Ghose
Mary Gilmore
Allen Ginsberg
Denis Glover
Sidney Godolphin
Oliver St. John Gogarty
Oliver Goldsmith
Barnabe Googe
John Gower
James Grainger
Robert Graves
Thomas Gray
Matthew Green
Horace Gregory
Sir Fulke Greville
Louise Imogen Guiney
Thom Gunn
Ralph Gustafson
Ramon Guthrie

William Habington
Joseph Hall
Fitz-Greene Halleck
Thomas Hardy
Sir John Harington
Charles Harpur
Blind Hary
Stephen Hawes
Robert Stephen Hawker
John Hay
Robert Hayden
Paul Hamilton Hayne

4

Seamus Heaney
Felicia Hemans
William Ernest Henley
Robert Henryson
Lord Herbert of Cherbury
George Herbert
Robert Herrick
Geoffrey Hill
Thomas Hoccleve
Ralph Hodgson
Charles Fenno Hoffman
Sir Richard Holland
Oliver Wendell Holmes
Thomas Hood
A. D. Hope
Gerard Manley Hopkins
Francis Hopkinson
A. E. Housman
Richard Hovey
Langston Hughes
Ted Hughes
Alexander Hume

James I, King of Scotland
Randall Jarrell
Robinson Jeffers
James Weldon Johnson
Lionel Johnson
Samuel Johnson
David Jones
Ebenezer Jones
Ben Jonson

Patrick Kavanagh
John Keats
John Keble
Henry Kendall
Sidney Keyes
Henry King
William King
Thomas Kinsella
Rudyard Kipling
A. M. Klein
Stanley Kunitz

Archibald Lampman
Walter Savage Landor
Andrew Lang
John Langhorne
William Langland
Sidney Lanier
Philip Larkin
D. H. Lawrence
Layamon

Irving Layton
Edward Lear
Laurie Lee
Denise Levertov
Alun Lewis
Vachel Lindsay
Dorothy Livesay
Frederick Locker-Lampson
Henry Wadsworth Longfellow
Richard Lovelace
Amy Lowell
James Russell Lowell
Robert Lowell
John Lydgate
Sir David Lyndsay
George Lyttelton

Hugh MacDiarmid
Kenneth Mackenzie
Archibald MacLeish
Louis MacNeice
James Macpherson
Charles Mair
David Mallet
James Clarence Mangan
Edwin Markham
Christopher Marlowe
John Marston
John Westland Marston
Andrew Marvell
John Masefield
R. A. K. Mason
William Mason
Edgar Lee Masters
James McAuley
Claude McKay
George Meredith
James Merrill
W. S. Merwin
Charlotte Mew
Alice Meynell
William Mickle
Edna St. Vincent Millay
Joaquin Miller
John Milton
Harold Monro
Lady Mary Wortley Montagu
John Montague
Alexander Montgomerie
Marianne Moore
T. Sturge Moore
Thomas Moore
Dom Moraes
William Morris

5

Edwin Muir

Sarojini Naidu
Ogden Nash
Shaw Neilson
Howard Nemerov
Norman Nicholson
Alfred Noyes

Frank O'Hara
Gabriel Okara
Christopher Okigbo
John Oldham
Charles Olson
Wilfred Owen

P. K. Page
Thomas Parnell
Kenneth Patchen
Andrew Barton Paterson
Coventry Patmore
Okot p'Bitek
Ambrose Philips
John Philips
Katherine Philips
Sylvia Plath
Edgar Allan Poe
John Pomfret
Alexander Pope
Ezra Pound
Winthrop Mackworth Praed
E. J. Pratt
Matthew Prior
Al Purdy

Francis Quarles

Kathleen Raine
Sir Walter Ralegh
Allan Ramsay
John Crowe Ranson
Sir Herbert Read
William Pember Reeves
Kenneth Rexroth
Adrienne Rich
Edgell Rickword
Laura Riding
James Whitcomb Riley
Charles G. D. Roberts
Edwin Arlington Robinson
John Wilmot, Earl of Rochester
W. R. Rodgers
Theodore Roethke
Samuel Rogers

Isaac Rosenberg
Christina Rossetti
Dante Gabriel Rossetti
Muriel Rukeyser
George William Russell

Thomas Sackville
Carl Sandburg
Siegfried Sassoon
Richard Savage
Delmore Schwartz
Duncan Campbell Scott
F. R. Scott
John Scott
Sir Walter Scott
William Bell Scott
Sir Charles Sedley
Robert Service
Anna Seward
Anne Sexton
William Shakespeare
Karl Shapiro
Percy Bysshe Shelley
William Shenstone
Sir Philip Sidney
Louis Simpson
Edith Sitwell
Sir Osbert Sitwell
Sir Sacheverell Sitwell
John Skelton
Kenneth Slessor
Christopher Smart
A. J. M. Smith
Stevie Smith
Sydney Goodsir Smith
W. D. Snodgrass
Gary Snyder
William Somerville
Charles Hamilton Sorley
Raymond Souster
Robert Southey
Robert Southwell
Bernard Spencer
Stephen Spender
Edmund Spenser
William Stafford
Thomas Stanley
C. K. Stead
James Stephens
Wallace Stevens
Douglas Stewart
Trumbull Stickney
William Strode
Sir John Suckling

Henry Howard, Earl of Surrey
Jonathan Swift
Algernon Charles Swinburne
Joshua Sylvester
Arthur Symons

Sir Rabindranath Tagore
Allen Tate
Bayard Taylor
Edward Taylor
Sara Teasdale
Alfred, Lord Tennyson
Dylan Thomas
Edward Thomas
R. S. Thomas
Francis Thompson
James Thomson
James (B. V.) Thomson
Thomas Tickell
Henry Timrod
Melvin Tolson
Aurelian Townshend
Thomas Traherne
John Trumbull
Frederick Goddard Tuckerman
Martin Tupper
George Turbervile
Thomas Tusser

Mark Van Doren
Henry Vaughan
Thomas Vaux
Jones Very

Derek Walcott
Edmund Waller

William Walsh
Ned Ward
William Warner
Robert Penn Warren
Joseph Warton
Thomas Warton
Vernon Watkins
Thomas Watson
Sir William Watson
Isaac Watts
Francis Webb
Charles Wesley
Phillis Wheatley
John Wheelwright
George Whetstone
Walt Whitman
John Greenleaf Whittier
Michael Wigglesworth
Richard Wilbur
Anne Wilkinson
William Carlos Williams
Anne Finch, Countess of Winchilsea
Yvor Winters
George Wither
William Wordsworth
Sir Henry Wotton
Judith Wright
Sir Thomas Wyatt
Elinor Wylie

William Butler Yeats
Andrew Young
Edward Young

Louis Zukofsky

ABERCROMBIE, Lascelles. English. Born in Ashton-upon-Mersey, Cheshire, 9 January 1881. Educated at Malvern College; University of Manchester, 1900–02. Married Catherine Gwatkin in 1909; three sons, one daughter. Reporter, Liverpool *Daily Courier*, 1908–10; free-lance journalist and reviewer, 1910–15; Inspector of Munitions, Liverpool, 1915–18. Lecturer in Poetry, University of Liverpool, 1919–22; Professor of English Literature, University of Leeds, 1922–29; Hildred Carlile Professor of English, Bedford College, University of London, 1929–35; Goldsmith Reader in English, Merton College, Oxford, 1935–38. Clark Lecturer, Trinity College, Cambridge, 1923; Ballard Matthews Lecturer, University College, Bangor, 1924; Leslie Stephen Lecturer, Cambridge, 1929; Lecturer in Fine Arts, Queen's University of Belfast, 1931; Turnbull Lecturer, Johns Hopkins University, Baltimore, 1935; Gregynog Lecturer, University College, Aberystwyth, 1938. M.A.: University of Liverpool; Oxford University; D.Lit.: Queen's University of Belfast; Litt.D.: University of Manchester; Cambridge University. Member of the British Academy, 1937. *Died 27 October 1938.*

PUBLICATIONS

Verse

Interludes and Poems. 1908.
Mary and the Bramble. 1910.
Emblems of Love, Designed in Several Discourses. 1912.
Twelve Idyls and Other Poems. 1928.
The Poems. 1930.
Lyrics and Unfinished Poems. 1940.
Vision and Love. 1966.

Plays

The Sale of Saint Thomas, act 1. 1911; complete version, 1930.
Deborah (produced 1964). 1913.
The Adder (produced 1913). In *Four Short Plays,* 1922.
The End of the World (produced 1914). In *Four Short Plays,* 1922.
The Staircase (produced 1920). In *Four Short Plays,* 1922.
Four Short Plays (includes *The Adder, The Staircase, The End of the World, The Deserter*). 1922.
Phoenix (produced 1924). 1923.

Other

Thomas Hardy: A Critical Study. 1912.
Speculative Dialogues. 1913.
Poetry and Contemporary Speech. 1914.
The Epic. 1914.
An Essay Towards a Theory of Art. 1922.
Principles of English Prosody. 1923.
Communication Versus Expression in Art. 1923.
Stratford-upon-Avon: A Report on Future Development, with Patrick Abercrombie. 1923.

The Theory of Poetry. 1924.
The Idea of Great Poetry (lectures). 1925.
Romanticism. 1925.
Drowsie Frightened Steeds. 1928.
Poetry: Its Music and Meaning. 1932.
Principles of Literary Criticism. 1932.
The Art of Wordsworth, edited by R. Abercrombie. 1952.
A Personal Note. 1974.

Editor, *New English Poems: A Miscellany.* 1931.

Bibliography: *A Bibliography and Notes on the Works of Abercrombie* by Jeffrey Cooper, 1928.

Reading List: *Abercrombie* by Oliver Elton, 1939.

*   *   *

T. S. Eliot reviewing the latest Georgian anthology in 1918 remarked disparagingly that "the Georgians caress everything they touch," and he called the prevailing tone "minor-Keatsian." Although Lascelles Abercrombie was a leading member of this group, his poetry is neither lyrical nor sensuous. For the most part he is a philosophical poet dealing with abstract ideas in closely-packed, complex, and often turgid style. His fundamental belief, set out in his poems and the pseudo-philosophical book *Speculative Dialogues,* is that life is a striving towards a perfect consciousness, producing an "ecstasy" or "exultation" which is the manifestation of God. In "Soul and Body," for example, Soul tells Body that he is seeking a passion beyond that which Body can give, and in "The Eternal Wedding" the poet says,

> Now all life's loveliness and power we have
> Dissolved in this one moment, and our burning
> Carries all shining upward, till in us
> Life is not life, but the desire of God,
> Himself desiring and himself accepting.

Many of the poems, called Dramatic Interludes, are set out in dramatic form, though they were not intended for staging, but he also wrote a number of verse plays which were produced. They are flawed like many of his poems by an over-inflated style. Frequently the Interludes and the plays reveal characters coming to self-knowledge or a realisation that their past actions have been caused by motives of which they were unaware: St. Thomas (in *The Sale of Saint Thomas*) is forced by the Noble Stranger to see that his waverings are the result of his lack of faith; Judith, in the poem of that name, realises "How a mere bragging was my purity," and how her defilement by Holofernes has brought her new perfection of virginity; the woman in "Blind," who has tramped the roads with her blind son seeking the man who had betrayed her many years before, finds, when her son has killed the man, that her search was not for vengeance, but for her lost love − "it was I who was blind." Paradoxical, enigmatic, or unexpected endings are common in Abercrombie's poetry and often they can seem merely contrived.

There is also at times an unnecessary dwelling on violence and horror, as, for example, in "The Olympians," *The Sale of Saint Thomas*, and *The End of the World*. More disturbingly there is often too a sense of some mysterious fear or evil waiting to pounce; so even in the by and large joyful "Marriage Song" the God of Marriages is accompanied by "the black, ravenous and gaunt" "wild hound Fear," "All frenzied fire the head − /The hunger of its mouth a hollow crimson flame/The hatred in its eyes a blaze/Fierce and green."

In spite of being only the second living poet to have his collected poems published by the Oxford University Press, Abercrombie felt his poems represented a sense of "unrealised ambition," and after the War he devoted most of his time to criticism, particularly aesthetic theory in which he was greatly influenced by Croce. His theorising is sometimes rather simplistic, but the discussions of such topics as Romanticism and Wordsworth are stimulating and acute.

—David Astle

AE.   See **RUSSELL, George William.**

AIKEN, Conrad (Potter).   American. Born in Savannah, Georgia, 5 August 1889. Educated at Middlesex School, Concord, Massachusetts; Harvard University, Cambridge, Massachusetts (President, *Harvard Advocate*), 1907–12, A.B. 1912. Married 1) Jessie McDonald in 1912 (divorced, 1929), one son, two daughters; 2) Clarice Lorenz, 1930 (divorced, 1937); 3) Mary Hoover, 1937. Contributing Editor, *The Dial*, New York, 1916–19; American Correspondent, *Athenaeum*, London, 1919–25, and *London Mercury*, 1921–22; London Correspondent, *The New Yorker*, 1933–36. Instructor, Harvard University, 1927–28. Fellow, 1948, and Consultant in Poetry, 1950–52, Library of Congress, Washington, D.C. Recipient: Pulitzer Prize, 1930; Shelley Memorial Prize, 1930; Guggenheim Fellowship, 1934; Bryher Award, 1952; National Book Award, 1954; Bollingen Prize, 1956; Academy of American Poets Fellowship, 1957; National Institute of Arts and Letters Gold Medal, 1958; Huntington Hartford Foundation Award, 1961; Brandeis University Creative Arts Award, 1966; National Medal for Literature, 1969. Member, American Academy of Arts and Letters, 1957. *Died 17 August 1973.*

PUBLICATIONS

Collections

Selected Letters, edited by Joseph Killorin.   1978.

Verse

Earth Triumphant and Other Tales in Verse.   1914.
The Jig of Forslin: A Symphony.   1916.
Turns and Movies and Other Tales in Verse.   1916.
Nocturne of Remembered Spring and Other Poems.   1917.
The Charnal Rose, Senlin: A Biography, and Other Poems.   1918.
The House of Dust: A Symphony.   1920.
Punch: The Immortal Liar.   1921.

The Pilgrimage of Festus. 1923.
Priapus and the Pool and Other Poems. 1925.
(*Poems*), edited by Louis Untermeyer. 1927.
Prelude. 1929.
Selected Poems. 1929.
John Deth, A Metaphysical Legend, and Other Poems. 1930.
Preludes for Memnon. 1931.
The Coming Forth by Day of Osiris Jones. 1931.
Landscape West of Eden. 1934.
Time in the Rock: Preludes to Definition. 1936.
And in the Human Heart. 1940.
Brownstone Eclogues and Other Poems. 1942.
The Soldier. 1944.
The Kid. 1947.
The Divine Pilgrim. 1949.
Skylight One: Fifteen Poems. 1949.
Collected Poems. 1953.
A Letter from Li Po and Other Poems. 1955.
The Flute Player. 1956.
Sheepfold Hill: 15 Poems. 1958.
Selected Poems. 1961.
The Morning Song of Lord Zero: Poems Old and New. 1963.
A Seizure of Limericks. 1964.
Thee. 1967.
*The Clerk's Journal: An Undergraduate Poem, Together with a Brief Memoir of Dean
    LeBaron Russell Briggs, T. S. Eliot, and Harvard, in 1911.* 1971.
Collected Poems 1916–1970. 1971.

Play

Mr. Arcularis (produced 1949). 1957.

Fiction

Bring! Bring! and Other Stories. 1925.
Blue Voyage. 1927.
Costumes by Eros. 1928.
Gehenna. 1930.
Great Circle. 1933.
Among the Lost People (stories). 1934.
King Coffin. 1935.
A Heart for the Gods of Mexico. 1939.
Conversation; or, Pilgrims' Progress. 1940; as *The Conversation,* 1948.
The Short Stories. 1950.
The Collected Short Stories. 1960.
The Collected Novels. 1964.

Other

Scepticisms: Notes on Contemporary Poetry. 1919.
Ushant: An Essay (autobiography). 1952.

A Reviewer's ABC: Collected Criticism from 1916 to the Present, edited by Rufus A. Blanshand.   1958; as *Collected Criticism,* 1968.
Cats and Bats and Things with Wings (juvenile).   1965.
Tom, Sue, and the Clock (juvenile).   1966.

Editor, *Modern American Poets.*   1922; as *Twentieth Century American Poetry,* 1944; revised edition, 1963.
Editor, *Selected Poems of Emily Dickinson.*   1924.
Editor, *American Poetry, 1671–1928: A Comprehensive Anthology.*   1929; as *A Comprehensive Anthology of American Poetry,* 1944.
Editor, with William Rose Benét, *An Anthology of Famous English and American Poetry.*   1945.

Reading List: *Aiken: A Life of His Art* by Jay Martin, 1962; *Aiken* by Frederick J. Hoffman, 1962; *Aiken* by Reuel Denney, 1964.

*   *   *

Characteristically, Conrad Aiken himself raises the essential critical problem in a note he wrote in 1917: "It is difficult to place Conrad Aiken in the poetic firmament, so difficult that one sometimes wonders whether he deserves a place there at all" (*Collected Criticism*). The problem is further complicated by the fact that Aiken was not only a poet, but also a respected novelist and critic. The list of his admirers is persuasive: R. P. Blackmur, Allen Tate, Malcolm Lowry all find in him one of the central voices of his age. Yet to the contemporary reader such claims are likely to seem excessive.

About the scope of his ambition there can be no doubt. Five long, complicated novels; many lengthy poetic sequences, or "symphonies," dealing with themes as varied, and as large, as the history of America (*The Kid*), the importance of his Puritan heritage ("Mayflower"), the problems of the self encountering the realities of love and death (*Preludes for Memnon* and *The Coming Forth by Day of Osiris Jones*): all testify to the courageous attempt to convey a rich, complex life in a wide-ranging, always technically experimental, art.

The centre of this art lies in the difficultly maintained balance between aesthetic purity and formal perfection on the one hand, and the menacing chaos of terrifying experience on the other. It is tempting to relate this to Aiken's very early experience as a child when he discovered the bodies of his parents after a mutual suicide pact: this moment is placed at the centre of his long autobiographical essay *Ushant*. This deeply buried memory may also have encouraged Aiken's passionate interest in Freud. The five novels show this interest everywhere: the hero of *Blue Voyage*, Demarest, is on a voyage of self-discovery through journey, quest, and dream. This novel, like *Great Circle* – which Freud himself admired – is an elaborate metaphor for the author's psychic search, the exploration of his own consciousness. At their best, the novels find a language for disturbing, hidden states of the psyche: the combination of thriller form and psychoanalytic imagery in *King Coffin* is uniquely memorable. But too often the novels slip into vagueness and imprecision. As Frederick J. Hoffman has observed, their separate parts fail *quite* to cohere. The lack of adequate characterisation, and the over-literariness of the enterprise, are at odds with our valid expectations of prose fiction. It is significant, then, that Aiken's "autobiography," *Ushant*, should seem to so many of his critics his finest achievement in prose. Here, Aiken as writer, and his literary friends, including Eliot and Pound, are at the centre of a "fictionalised" account of the author's life. Apart from its other intrinsic interests, this quite extraordinary, unclassifiable work is justified, almost alone, by the majestic sweep and lyrical seductiveness of Aiken's rhetoric.

It is this majestic rhetoric that one also recognises in the poetry: Malcolm Lowry referred to Aiken as "the truest and most direct descendant of our own great Elizabethans" (*Wake, 11,*

13

1952). This quality is immediately apparent in *Preludes for Memnon*:

> What dignity can death bestow on us,
> Who kiss beneath a street lamp, or hold hands
> Half hidden in a taxi, or replete
> With coffee, figs and Barsac make our way
> To a dark bedroom in a wormworn house?

The combination here of the common and quotidian – street lamp, taxi, coffee – with noble, "Elizabethan" cadences, is the characteristic Aiken manner. It is a manner that frequently skirts parody and pastiche, but equally often rises to a rich, solemn verbal music. In poem after poem in his enormous output, Aiken sustains a long, flowing musical line, celebrating, as in "Landscape West of Eden," the capacity of language to order the chaos of the unaccomodated self. What one misses, however, in too much of this poetry, and what contributes to a certain lack of *energy* in the verse, is any intense verbal particularity, or, often, the sense of real feeling significantly expressed. In *Time in the Rock*, one of his most ambitious pieces, there is little sense of any real pressure or urgency behind the words; they have a tendency, as it were, to slip off the edge of the page as we read; nothing seems to make it all *cohere*.

His more objective, "dramatic" poems, like *The Kid* and "Mayflower," with their incorporation of historical and legendary material and their evocations of New England landscape and geography, are perhaps more valuable, in the end, than his lyrical self-communings. The contemporary reader is also likely to be more drawn to the lighter side of Aiken: in a poem like "Blues for Ruby Matrix" the rhetoric remains, but allied now to a delightful sexiness and tenderness.

Whatever the mode, however, there is always in Aiken, even if only residually, that sense of horror, of terror, and of death – "The sombre note that gives the chord its power," as he puts it in "Palimpsest" – that gives the best poetry its capacity to hurt and wound us. When, in *Preludes for Memnon*, he defines the role of the poet, Aiken finds a definition that takes full note of this fundamental ground-bass of his own work: the poet is one who

> by imagination [apes]
> God, the supreme poet of despair ...
> Knowing the rank intolerable taste of death,
> And walking dead on the still living earth.

—Neil Corcoran

AKENSIDE, Mark. English. Born in Newcastle upon Tyne, 9 November 1721. Educated at a dissenting minister's school, Newcastle; studied theology in Edinburgh, 1739, then medicine at the University of Edinburgh (elected Member of the Medical Society of Edinburgh, 1740), and at the University of Leyden, Dr. of Physic 1744; awarded M.D., Cambridge, 1753. Practised medicine in Newcastle, 1741–43, Northampton, 1744–45, and in Hampstead, London, 1745–47; Editor, *The Museum; or, The Literary and Historical Register*, London, 1746–47; granted a pension by Jeremiah Dyson, 1747; resumed practice of medicine, 1748; appointed Assistant Physician, then Principal Physician, St. Thomas's Hospital, London, and Principal Physician, Christ's Hospital, London, 1759; created Physician to the Queen, 1761. Fellow, 1754, and gave the Gulstonian Lectures, 1755, Croonian Lectures, 1756, and the Harveian Oration, 1759, College of Physicians, London. Fellow of the Royal Society, 1753. *Died 23 June 1770.*

PUBLICATIONS

Collections

Poetical Works, edited by George Gilfillan.   1857.

Verse

A British Philippic: A Poem in Miltonic Verse.   1738; as *The Voice of Liberty,* 1738.
The Pleasures of Imagination.   1744; revised edition, in *Poems,* 1772.
An Epistle to Curio.   1744.
Odes on Several Subjects.   1745; revised edition, 1760.
Friendship and Love: A Dialogue, to Which Is Added A Song.   1745.
An Ode to the Earl of Huntingdon.   1748.
An Ode to the Country Gentlemen of England.   1758.
An Ode to the Late Thomas Edwards.   1766.
Poems, edited by Jeremiah Dyson.   1772.

Other

Dissertatio Medica Inauguralis, de Ortu et Encremento Foetus Humani.   1744.
De Dysenteria Commentarius.   1764.

Editor, *The Works of William Harvey.*   1766.

Bibliography: in *Seven 18th Century Bibliographies* by Iolo A. Williams, 1924.

Reading List: *Akenside: A Biographical and Critical Study* by C. T. Houpt, 1944 (includes bibliography); *Four Dialectial Theories of Poetry* by R. Marsh, 1965; *The Rhetoric of Science* by W. P. Jones, 1966.

*   *   *

Mark Akenside's most important poem is *The Pleasures of Imagination,* a didactic poem in blank verse. Whereas other eighteenth-century poets, such as Thomson and Young, when they attempted blank verse might be accused of writing heroic couplets without the rhymes, Akenside showed a far better grasp of the metonic style, and could weld together a blank verse paragraph by the construction of long periodic sentences and the skilful use of *enjambement.* Sometimes indeed his sentences are too long and involved, and this tends to obscure his argument. The matter of the poem derives partly from Addison's *Essays on the Imagination,* partly from Shaftesbury's *Characteristics.* It has something of a Platonic tinge, foreshadowing the idealistic philosophy of Coleridge and the other Romantics:

> Mind, mind alone (bear witness earth and heaven!)
> The living fountains in itself contains
> Of beauteous and sublime.

Some other passages in which Akenside describes the mountainous scenery of his native Northumberland have often been noted as anticipating Wordsworth. But Akenside's relation is less to Romanticism than to the development of a line of Neo-Classical writing which began in the mid-eighteenth century and ran on into the Romantic period, finding its fullest expression in the work of Landor. There are elements of it in the Odes of Keats, and such poems as Wordsworth's *Laodamia*. In the earlier period this eighteenth-century Neo-Classicism, which manifested itself most clearly in the fields of painting and architecture, should be distinguished from the dominant Augustan style, based on Roman models, by its orientation towards the Greek ideal. In poetry, the Odes of Gray and Collins belong here, as do those of Akenside. These last do not deserve their almost total dismissal by Johnson. They are rather stiff, have less musical quality than Gray's, and have much less imaginative and formal originality than those of Collins. Nevertheless some of them, such as the "Ode to the Evening Star," have considerable merit and deserve to be better known.

Akenside's "Hymn to the Naiad" is an extended blank verse lyric modelled on the Hymns of the Alexandrine Greek poet Callimachus. It represents another aspect of Neo-Classicism, the reviving feeling for Greek mythology. Of his other pieces, "The Virtuoso" is a youthful exercise in the Spenserian manner, which like many eighteenth-century poems in this vein is as much a parody as an imitation. *An Epistle to Curio* (later remodelled as an ode) is addressed to William Pulteney who deserted Walpole for the Tory side. It is a notable piece of political invective, illustrating the Radical stance which, at least in his early Nonconformist years, Akenside evinced. The short "Inscriptions" show his lapidary style at perhaps its most effective.

—John Heath-Stubbs

ALABASTER, William. English. Born in Hadleigh, Suffolk, 27 January 1568. Educated at Westminster School, London; Trinity College, Cambridge (Queen's Scholar), 1584, Fellow, 1589, M.A., 1591; ordained Anglican priest. Married Katherine Fludd in 1618. Chaplain to Robert Devereux, Earl of Essex, 1596–97. Converted to Roman Catholicism, 1597, and arrested and deprived of Anglican orders, 1598; broke parole, went to Rome and enrolled in the English College; returned to England in 1599 and was imprisoned in the Tower of London and later in Framlingham Castle, Suffolk; pardoned on the accession of James I, but was imprisoned again in 1606; travelled in the Low Countries in 1606; at the English College, Rome, 1609; imprisoned by the Inquisition, 1609, declared heretical and fled to England, where he recanted of Catholicism, then recanted his recantation, then recanted again; created Doctor of Divinity at Cambridge in 1614, and given the rich living of Therfield, Hertfordshire; later a chaplain to James I. *Died 28 April 1640.*

PUBLICATIONS

Verse

The Sonnets, edited by G. M. Story and Helen Gardner. 1959.

Play

Roxana (in Latin), from a play by Luigi Groto. 1632.

Other

Apparatus in Revelationem Jesu Christi.   1607.
De Bestia Apocalyptica.   1621.
Ecce Sponsus Venit.   1633.
Spiraculum Tubarum.   1633(?).
Lexicon Pentaglotton (Hebrew, Chaldean, Syriac, Talmudic-Rabbinic, Arabic; an abridgement of a work by V. Schindler).   1635.

Reading List: *Recusant Poets* by Louise Imogen Guiney, 1938.

*   *   *

During a decade flooded by amorous sonnet sequences, Alabaster, in prison or in hiding after his first conversion to the Roman Catholic Church, wrote some seventy religious sonnets which his modern editors place "among the earliest metaphysical poems of devotion that we have." Composed around 1594–1598 and circulated in manuscripts of which six survive, the sonnets were not printed in full until 1959, edited by G. M. Story and Helen Gardner.

His early, unfinished Latin epic *Eliaeis* and his Latin play *Roxana* were praised by Spenser and Dr. Johnson respectively; his contemporary reputation rested primarily on Latin essays in mystical theology and scriptural interpretation, such as the *Apparatus in Revelationem Jesu Christi*, which, though written in one of his Catholic periods, caused him trouble with the Inquisition. In his calmer later years, reconciled to the Anglican Church, married, made a Doctor of Divinity at Cambridge (in the same year as Donne), he continued to write learned prose, but produced no more poetry.

Like Donne in his fondness for compression, ingenious working out of imagery, colloquial vigour, and even in occasional punning on his own name (as in "This alabaster box" which he presents in "A New Year's Gift to my Saviour"), he often celebrates paradox, especially in the fifteen sonnets on that paradoxical subject, the Incarnation. At some points, in combining Biblical phrasing and homely imagery, he may suggest Herbert, or, in a sonnet uniting a survey of contemporary religious problems with anxiety about personal commitment, Milton: Sonnet 40, "To Christ (2)" rings with vigorous vocabulary as it portrays angels charged "to break the heads of heresy/Or scatter them in their apostasy,/Or against the Turkish swads to make a stand," before concluding quietly, "Lo here I am lord, whither wilt thou send me?" A recent article compares Alabaster's sonnets with those of La Ceppède, and, indeed, the associations called up by his poems may suggest whatever range of sixteenth and seventeenth century poetry one knows – on the continent or in England – and thus underline the community of devotional and aesthetic traditions of the period.

—Kay Stevenson

————————

ALLINGHAM, William. Irish. Born in Ballyshannon, Donegal, 19 March 1824. Married the artist Helen Paterson in 1874. Civil Servant, Irish Customs, 1846–70; Sub-Editor, then Editor, *Fraser's Magazine*, London, 1874–79. *Died 18 November 1889.*

PUBLICATIONS

Collections

> *Works.*   6 vols., 1890.
> *Poems*, edited by John Hewitt.   1967.

Verse

> *Poems.*   1850; revised edition, 1861.
> *Day and Night Songs.*   1854; revised edition, as *The Music Master: A Love Story, and
>   Two Series of Day and Night Songs*, 1855, 1884.
> *Peace and War.*   1854.
> *Laurence Bloomfield in Ireland.*   1864.
> *Fifty Modern Poems.*   1865.
> *Songs, Ballads, and Stories.*   1857.
> *Evil May-Day.*   1882.
> *Blackberries Picked Off Many Bushes.*   1884.
> *Irish Songs and Poems.*   1887.
> *Rhymes for the Young Folk.*   1887; as *Robin Red Breast and Other Verses*, 1930.
> *Flower Pieces and Other Poems.*   1888.
> *Life and Phantasy.*   1889.
> *Thought and Word.*   1890.
> *By the Way: Verses, Fragments, and Notes*, edited by Helen Allingham.   1912.

Plays

> *Ashby Manor.*   1883.
> *Hopgood and Co.*, in *Varieties in Prose 3*.   1893.

Other

> *In Fairy Land* (juvenile).   1869.
> *Rambles in England and Ireland.*   1873; as *Varieties in Prose 1–2*, 1893.
> *Varieties in Prose.*   3 vols., 1893.
> *A Diary*, edited by Helen Allingham and D. Radford.   1907.
> *Letters to Robert and Elizabeth Barrett Browning.*   1914.
>
> Editor, *Nightingale Valley* (anthology).   1860.
> Editor, *The Ballad Book.*   1864.

Bibliography: *A Bibliography of Allingham* by Patrick S. O'Geharty, 1945.

Reading List: *Allingham: An Introduction* by Alan Warner, 1971.

*   *   *

The work of William Allingham has never been widely known. To some extent he fell
between two stools – England and Ireland. Born and brought up in remote Ballyshannon, he

turned his eyes to literary London and wrote in the shadow of Tennyson, whom he knew and admired. He was not passionate or national enough to make an impact on Irish readers, while English readers were not deeply interested in poems about Ireland. His most popular poems, found in many Victorian anthologies, were his songs for children, "The Fairies," "The Leprechaun," "Robin Redbreast," and "Wishing"; but his long narrative poem, *Laurence Bloomfield in Ireland*, contains much finer and more masculine work. It deals with the conflict between Irish landlords and tenants; there are evictions and a land agent is murdered. The poem is written in couplets that are sometimes reminiscent of Pope of Crabbe. It is long and discursive, but there are powerful realistic scenes, and the character sketches of local landlords have a keen ironic edge. Underlying the whole is a deep compassion for the hard lives of the Irish poor.

In addition to this major work, Allingham wrote a number of successful ballads and songs. He collected popular airs and wrote them down, and he had some of his own ballads printed as broadsides and sold in the street and market-place. "Adieu to Belashanny," "Lovely Mary Donnelly," and "The Girl's Lamentation" are among the best known. These ballads follow a folk tradition, but he also wrote more personal lyrics such as "The Dream" and "The Boy from His Bedroom Window," poems that have a haunting music. In later years he turned to epigrams and short poems which he collected in a volume entitled *Blackberries*. Some of these have a piquant brevity.

He wrote prose as well as poetry. He contributed articles to *Fraser's Magazine*, which he edited for a time, and under the pseudonym of Patricius Walker he published a series of "Rambles" in 1873. But his most interesting prose work is his *Diary*, which was edited by his wife after his death. This contains many illuminating sidelights on Victorian people and places, and it reveals something of Boswell's sharp eye and ear for detail. Here is his quick snapshot of Ouida, the novelist, at a dinner party: "sinister, clever face, hair down, small hands and feet, voice like a carving knife."

Both in style and attitude Allingham has a certain Victorian primness. There is no abandonment to religious or aesthetic or erotic passion in his life or his poetry. His verse is strongly traditional, and his language followed the path of literary convention. Nevertheless, his quiet unassuming qualities as a man and a writer grow on the reader as familiarity increases.

—Alan Warner

AMMONS, A(rchie) R(andolph). American. Born in Whiteville, North Carolina, 18 February 1926. Educated at Wake Forest College, North Carolina, B.A. 1949; University of California, Berkeley, 1950–52. Served in the United States Naval Reserve, 1944–46. Married Phyllis Plumbo in 1949; one child. Principal, Hatteras Elementary School, North Carolina, 1949–50; Executive Vice-President, Friedrich and Dimmock Inc., Mellville, New Jersey, 1952–62. Since 1964, Member of the Faculty, Associate Professor, 1969–71, since 1971, Professor of English, and since 1973, Goldwin Smith Professor of English, Cornell University, Ithaca, New York. Visiting Professor, Wake Forest University, 1974–75. Poetry Editor, *Nation*, New York, 1963. Recipient: Bread Loaf Writers Conference Scholarship, 1961; Guggenheim Fellowship, 1966; American Academy of Arts and Letters Travelling Fellowship, 1967; National Endowment for the Arts grant, 1969; National Book Award, 1973; Bollingen Prize, 1975; National Institute of Arts and Letters award, 1977. D.Litt.: Wake Forest University, 1972; University of North Carolina, Chapel Hill, 1973. Lives in Ithaca, New York.

PUBLICATIONS

Verse

Ommateum, with Doxology. 1955.
Expressions of Sea Level. 1964.
Corsons Inlet. 1965.
Tape for the Turn of the Year. 1965.
Northfield Poems. 1966.
Selected Poems. 1968.
Uplands. 1970.
Briefings: Poems Small and Easy. 1971.
Collected Poems 1951–1971. 1972.
Sphere: The Form of a Motion. 1974.
Diversifications. 1975.
The Snow Poems. 1977.
The Selected Poems 1951–1977. 1977.

Reading List: "Ammons Issue" of *Diacritics*, 1974.

*   *   *

A.R. Ammons is one of the most prolific poets of his generation, amassing to date some dozen books of verse that have won him the National Book Award in 1973, for his *Collected Poems 1951–1971*, and the Bollingen Award for *Sphere: The Form of a Motion*. The earliest poems, searching boldly for a center of self from which to project his persona, achieve their best effect from his recklessly strewn imagery and the pressure of his imagination to find the edges and furthest barriers of experience. The excellent *Selected Poems* of 1968, a winnowing of all the early work, dramatizes this search with varied, often profoundly moving language.

Ammons's attention ranges from intricately detailed portraits of the landscape of upper New York state, to travels throughout the southwestern United States, and memories of his childhood growing up on a farm in North Carolina, where he is fresh and original as a lyric poet. His reminiscence of the partly mute woman who raised him as a child, "Nelly Myers," is a minor classic of the modern elegy, with its lilting rhythms and its quiet, loving tribute to her wisdom and imperfections.

Much of Ammons's poetry depends upon a texture of rapid, rambling speech that precipitates a poem within its often lush formations. The edge of his poem is not silence but the banter and commentary in which it lies embedded. This pointedly risky strategy of creating a lyric can, when it is not in control, produce tracts and harangues that run tediously on devoid of any poetry. When inspired, however, the language gives way to a charged form of words partly submerged in the verbal undergrowth. His poems are like forms half perceived lying in high grass.

His verbal felicity has, however, occasioned more dry commentary than inspired lyricism. In an experiment with writing on adding machine tape, which imposed a narrow frame on the poet, Ammons wrote a seemingly endless discourse on the minutiae of his life during the winter of 1964–65, published as *Tape for the Turn of the Year*. As a professor teaching at Cornell University and living in Ithaca, New York, the persona lacks adventure and change, and the poet's journal suffers from the uneventful pace of his days. In succeeding volumes, *Northfield Poems* and *Uplands*, the style is noticeably more clipped and abrupt, approaching Imagist concision. The poet is clearly inspired by natural phenomena, particularly in the latter volume where his attention to mountain scenery is keenly alert. In *Briefings* he continues to experiment with short, sudden articulations of feeling and momentary perceptions. But in *Sphere* the style changes again into a long sequential discourse patterned by sections of four triplets where language is only partly sculpted. *The Snow Poems* returns to the mode of shorter poems and is a large collection devoted to the poet's favourite landscape, the snow-laden terrain of the northeast.

Throughout this large canon, Ammons continues to search for a final center of self irreducible of ambiguity. In his natural landscapes he has sought the recesses of the mystery of his own nature. But in chronicling his middle years and the details of his life from day to day, he provides the fullest account of the frustrations and triumphs of the middle class American reluctant to accept his professional life as the whole of his existence.

—Paul Christensen

ANSTEY, Christopher. English. Born in Brinkley, Cambridgeshire, 31 October 1724. Educated at school in Bury St. Edmunds, Suffolk; Eton College; King's College, Cambridge, 1742–46, B.A. 1746. Married Ann Calvert in 1756; several children, including the poet John Anstey. Fellow, King's College, 1745 until he succeeded to his family estates, 1754. Moved to Bath, 1770. *Died 3 August 1805.*

PUBLICATIONS

Collections

Poetical Works, edited by John Anstey. 1808.

Verse

Elegia Scripta in Coemeterio Rustico Latine Reditta, from Gray's poem, with W. H. Roberts. 1762.
On the Death of the Marquis of Tavistock. 1767.
The New Bath Guide; or, Memoirs of the B--r--d Family in a Series of Poetical Epistles. 1766; edited by P. Sainsbury, 1927.
The Patriot: A Pindaric Address to Lord Buckhorse. 1767; *Appendix*, 1768.
Ode on an Evening View of the Cresent at Bath. 1773.
The Priest Dissected. 1774.
An Election Ball in Poetical Letters in the Zommerzetshire Dialect from Mr. Inkle of Bath to His Wife in Gloucester. 1776; revised edition, 1776.
Ad C. W. Bampfylde, Arm: Epistola Poetica Familiaris. 1776; translated as *A Familiar Epistle*, 1777.
Fabulae Selectae (in Latin), from Gay's poems. 1777(?).
Envy. 1778.
Winter Amusements: An Ode. 1778.
A Paraphrase or Poetical Exposition of the Thirteenth Chapter of First Corinthians. 1779.
Speculation; or, A Defence of Mankind. 1780.
Liberality; or, The Decayed Macaroni: A Sentimental Piece. 1788.

The Farmer's Daughter: A Poetical Tale.   1795.
The Monopolist: A Poetical Tale.   1795.
Britain's Genius: A Song Occasioned by the Late Mutiny at the Nore.   1797.
Contentment; or, Hints to Servants on the Present Scarcity: A Poetical Epistle.   1800.
Ad Edvardum Jenner: Carmen Alcaicum.   1803.

Bibliography: "A Bibliography of Anstey's First Editions" by Iolo A. Williams, in *London Mercury*, January-July 1925.

Reading List: *Anstey, Bath Laureate* by William C. Powell, 1944; *Portraits in Satire* by Kenneth Hopkins, 1958.

*   *   *

Christopher Anstey's son John, in the preface to his father's *Poetical Works*, praises his "power of originating by the natural force of his genius, new and unexpected images, with the admirable talent of combining, varying, and multiplying them at pleasure." *The New Bath Guide*, however, remains the only poem of this skillful dilettante's small but varied English output – he also wrote Latin verse – in which he used his power and talent with real success. A comfortable country squire who enjoyed the wit and learning of acquaintances in Cambridge and Bath, Anstey specialized in verse of gentle mockery. His unpretentious, graceful, sprightly style won him admiration from the other fashionable amateurs who frequented Lady Anne Miller's salon near Bath, where the guests met to hear read and to judge their own verse, dropped by each (so as to preserve anonymity) into an allegedly antique urn upon entering. With this sort of audience, Anstey aspired to little and achieved it. His elegy for the Marquis of Tavistock, his burlesque ode to the boxer Buckhorse, and his *Election Ball*, and imitation of his *New Bath Guide*, are sporadically effective; the shorter light verse is pleasant.

The New Bath Guide, a series of verse letters supposedly written from Bath by members of the visiting Blunderhead family, achieved a great vogue and stimulated such parodies and imitations as *Tunbridge Epistles* and *Poetical Epistles to the Author of the New Bath Guide*. Anstey spoofs various kinds of modern verse (odes, hymns, songs, religious stanzas) while he offers comic accounts of Bath customs and habitués (bell-ringing, medical consultations, the baths themselves; gouty lords, amorous "beaux garçons"). He also satirizes pedantry and zeal, particularly evangelistic Methodism in Letter VII and the ribald Letter XIV, where Prudence Blunderhead describes her seduction by young Roger as a visit from a divine spirit come to "fill [her] full of Love." Most of the letters use a tripping anapaestic tetrameter which, in Anstey's hands, serves well for medical jargon, colloquialism, and ironic poetic cliché, sometimes with rhymes ("her toe" / "concerto," "takes here" / "Shakespeare") that recall Butler's *Hudibras*. The metre kept its popularity for light verse through the nineteenth century. Gilbert used it for the Nightmare song of the Lord Chancellor in *Iolanthe* (1882) and, more recently, T. S. Eliot, for several poems in *Old Possum's Book of Practical Cats* (1939).

—Eric Rothstein

ARMSTRONG, John.   Scottish.   Born in Castleton, Liddesdale, Roxburghshire, c. 1709. Educated at the University of Edinburgh, M.D. 1732. Practised in London from 1735:

Physician to the London Soldiers' Hospital, 1746–60; Physician to the Army in Germany, 1760–63; returned to London on half-pay and resumed his medical practice, 1763; toured Europe with the painter Fuseli, 1770. *Died 7 September 1779.*

PUBLICATIONS

Collections

Poetical Works, with Dyer and Green, edited by George Gilfillan.   1858.

Verse

The Oeconomy of Love: A Poetical Essay.   1736; expurgated edition, 1768.
The Art of Preserving Health.   1744.
Of Benevolence: An Epistle to Eumenes.   1751.
Taste: An Epistle to a Young Critic.   1753.
A Day: An Epistle to John Wilkes.   1761.

Play

The Forced Marriage, in *Miscellanies.*   1770.

Other

Dissertation Medica Inauguralis de Tabe Purulenta.   1732.
An Essay for Abridging the Study of Physick.   1735.
The Muncher's and Guzzler's Diary.   1749.
Sketches; or, Essays on Various Subjects.   1758.
Miscellanies.   2 vols., 1770.
A Short Ramble Through Some Parts of France and Italy.   1771.
Medical Essays.   1773.

Translator, *A Synopsis of the History and Cure of Venereal Diseases,* by L. Luisini.   1737.

Bibliography: in *Seven 18th-Century Bibliographies* by Iolo A. Williams, 1924.

Reading List: "Armstrong: Littérateur and Associate of Smollett, Thomson, Wilkes, and Other Celebrities" by L. M. Knapp in *Publications of the Modern Language Association,* 1944; *George and John Armstrong of Castleton* by William J. M. A. Maloney, 1954.

*   *   *

The oldest function of poetry may indeed have been to convey information, particularly of battles or other historic events. It was, however, used notably by Ovid in *The Art of Love* for instruction in the ways of love, and by Virgil in his *Georgics* for information on horticulture, though in neither case was the conveying of information the only purpose achieved.

John Armstrong, the son of a Roxburghshire clergyman, inherited the gift of homily and had the good fortune to be a friend and fellow student at Edinburgh University of James Thomson. Armstrong thus became one of the "vast assembly moving to and fro" portrayed in the lotus-land of Thomson's *Castle of Indolence*. Himself reputedly an extremely lazy man, Thomson got Armstrong to write the last four stanzas of the first canto of *The Castle of Indolence*; those in which human diseases born of laziness are delineated. Here is how Armstrong delineates what he might nowadays term psychosomatic depression — from *The Art of Preserving Health*:

> Sour melancholy, night and day provokes
> Her own eternal wound....
> Then various shapes of curs'd illusion rise:
> Whate'er the wretched fears, creating fear
> Forms out of nothing....
>   The prostrate soul beneath
> A load of huge imagination heaves;
> And all the horrors that the murderer feels
> Will anxious flutterings wake the guiltless breast.

Armstrong was a doctor through and through. His professional skills were put to informative literary use in his poem in four books, *The Art of Preserving Health* a surprisingly lively compendium of common sense cast in blank verse, dividing the four books of his subject into air, diet, exercise and the passions. Doubtless he was aware of the difficulties of reaching the higher flights with such a theme, for of diet he remarks: "A barren waste, where not a garland grows / To bind the Muse's brow."

Armstrong's *Taste: An Epistle to a Young Critic* is in some respects a fairly conventional satire in the manner of Pope and Swift; *A Day: An Epistle to John Wilkes Esq.* provoked the virulence of Churchill, who described Armstrong's work as a repository "Where all but barren labour was forgot, / And the vain stiffness of a lettered Scot."

The "lettered Scot," however, turned his verse to a use neither vain nor stiff in his poem *The Economy of Love*, which led an apothecary, having read it, to inquire rhetorically: "How, in the name of heaven, could he ever expect that a woman would let him enter her house again, after that?" "That" was, in fact, a practical sex manual intended for the helpful instruction of newly married couples who might otherwise have been forced to rely upon the antique circumlocutions of Aristotle. Banned from reprints of Armstrong's work throughout the 19th century, with its Thomsonian periphrasis it may make us smile in the 20th. But there is vigour in the writing, and the practical doctor was no prude. One sample must suffice. Having for the first time removed his new wife's clothes, the young husband is told:

> Then when her lovely limbs,
> Oft lovely deem'd, far lovlier now beheld,
> Thro' all your trembling joints increase the flame;
> Forthwith discover to her dazzled sight
> The stately novelty, and to her hand
> Usher the new acquaintance. She perhaps
> Averse, will coldly chide, and half afraid,
> Blushing, half pleas'd, the tumid wonder view.

Dr. Armstrong could not of course foresee that a later generation of women would be taught to suffer sex and "think of England," or that many of the representatives of a still later age would not have waited until after marriage to become acquainted with each other's bodies.

In his day his work won the admiration of such divers critics as Goldsmith, Lord Monboddo, Hume and Boswell, who found it "impossible to translate into French his force of style a force remarkable even in English." He inspired Dr. Theobald to produce an Ode,

"Ad Ingenuum Virum, tum Medicis, tum Poeticis, Facultatibus Praestantum, Johannum Armstrong, M.D."

—Maurice Lindsay

ARNOLD, Matthew.   English.   Born in Laleham, Staines, Middlesex, 24 December 1822; son of the teacher Dr. Thomas Arnold, thereafter Headmaster of Rugby School. Educated at Winchester College, 1836–37; Rugby School, 1837–41; Balliol College, Oxford (Classical Scholarship; Newdigate Prize, 1843), 1841–44, graduated with second class honours 1844. Married Frances Lucy Wightman in 1851; one daughter. Fellow, Oriel College, Oxford, 1845; Master at Rugby School, 1846; Secretary to Lord Lansdowne, then President of the Council, 1847–51; Inspector of Schools, England, 1851 until his retirement in 1883 (frequently sent by government to enquire into state of education on the Continent, particularly in Germany, France, and Holland). Professor of Poetry, Oxford University, 1857–67. Lectured in America, 1883, 1886. Granted Civil List pension, 1883. *Died 15 April 1888.*

PUBLICATIONS

Collections

> *Poetical Works,* edited by C. B. Tinker and H. F. Lowry.   1950.
> *Complete Prose Works,* edited by R. H. Super, 11 vols., 1960–77.
> *Poems,* edited by Kenneth Allott.   1965.
> *Selected Poems and Prose,* edited by Miriam Allott.   1978.

Verse

> *Alaric at Rome: A Prize Poem.*   1840.
> *Cromwell: A Prize Poem.*   1843.
> *The Strayed Reveller and Other Poems.*   1849.
> *Empedocles on Etna and Other Poems.*   1852.
> *Poems.*   1853; *Second Series,* 1855.
> *New Poems.*   1867.
> *Poems.*   2 vols., 1869; revised edition, 1877, 1878, 1881.
> *Selected Poems.*   1878.

Play

> *Merope.*   1858.

Other

> *England and the Italian Question.*   1859; edited by Merle M. Bevington, 1953.

25

The Popular Education of France, with Notices of That of Holland and Switzerland. 1861.
On Translating Homer. 2 vols., 1861–62.
A French Eton; or, Middle Class Education and the State. 1864.
Essays in Criticism, vol. 3 edited by E. J. O'Brien. 3 vols., 1865–1910.
On the Study of Celtic Literature. 1867.
Schools and Universities on the Continent. 1868.
Culture and Anarchy: An Essay in Political and Social Criticism. 1869; edited by J. Dover Wilson, 1932.
St. Paul and Protestantism. 1870.
Friendship's Garland, Being the Conversations, Letters, and Opinions of the Late Arminus Baron von Thunder-ten-Tronckh. 1871.
Literature and Dogma: An Essay Towards a Better Appreciation of the Bible. 1873.
God and the Bible: A Review of Objections to Literature and Dogma. 1875.
Last Essays on Church and Religion. 1877.
Mixed Essays. 1879.
Irish Essays and Others. 1882.
Discourses in America. 1885.
Special Report on Certain Points Connected with Elementary Education in Germany, Switzerland, and France. 1886.
General Grant: An Estimate. 1887; edited by John Y. Simon, 1966.
Civilization in the United States: First and Last Impressions of America. 1888.
Reports on Elementary Schools 1852–82, edited by Francis Sandford. 1889.
On Home Rule for Ireland: Two Letters to the Times. 1891.
Letters 1848–88, edited by George W. E. Russell. 2 vols., 1895.
Note-Books. 1902; edited by Howard Foster Lowry, Karl Young, and Waldo Hilary Dunn, 1952; as *Diaries,* edited by W. B. Guthrie, 1959.
Arnold as Dramatic Critic, edited by C. K. Shorter. 1903; edited by B. Matthews, as *Letters of an Old Playgoer,* 1919.
Letters to John Churton Collins. 1910.
Unpublished Letters, edited by Arnold Whitridge. 1923.
Letters to Arthur Hugh Clough, edited by Howard Foster Lowry. 1932.
Five Uncollected Essays, edited by Kenneth Allott. 1953.

Editor, *The Great Prophecy of Israel's Restoration: Isaiah, Chapters 40–66 Arranged for Young Readers.* 1872.
Editor, *The Six Chief Lives from Johnson's Lives of the Poets, with Macaulay's Life of Johnson.* 1878.
Editor, *Poems of Wordsworth.* 1879.
Editor, *Poetry of Byron.* 1881.
Editor, *Letters, Speeches, and Tracts on Irish Affairs,* by Edmund Burke. 1881.
Editor, *Isaiah of Jerusalem in the Authorized English Version.* 1883.

Bibliography: *Bibliography of Arnold* by T. B. Smart, 1892; *Arnold's Letters: A Descriptive Checklist* by Arthur K. Davis, 1968.

Reading List: *Arnold* by Lionel Trilling, 1939, revised edition, 1955; *The Poetry of Arnold: A Commentary* by C. B. Tinker and H. F. Lowry, 1940; *Arnold* by J. D. Jump, 1955; *Arnold* by Kenneth Allott, 1955; *The Voices of Arnold* by W. S. Johnson, 1961; *Arnold and the Decline of English Romanticism* by D. G. James, 1961; *Arnold the Poet* by H. C. Duffin, 1962; *Arnold and the Romantics* by L. A. Gottfried, 1963; *Imaginative Reason: The Poetry of Arnold* by A. D. Culler, 1966; *Arnold: A Study of the Aesthetic Temperament in Victorian England* by W. A. Madden, 1967; *Arnold: The Poet as Humanist* by G. R. Stange, 1967; *Arnold, Ruskin, and *the Modern Temper* by Edward Alexander, 1973; *Writers and Their Background: Arnold* edited by Kenneth Allott, 1977.

*   *   *

The functions of the poet and of the critic are often thought of as being distinct, even opposed. Arnold, in his later years, became the eminent critic – not only of literature, but also of the society of his age – and prolonged application of his powers to critical effort checked, if it did not altogether disable, the creative power.

Even at the outset of his career as a poet the self-critical component of his personality was strong. He omitted *Empedocles on Etna* from the collection *Poems* (1853) on the grounds of the critical principles set out in the Preface to that collection. *Empedocles* is a fine and stately verse drama by Arnold the poet, modelled on Greek tragedy but the theme of a philosopher casting himself into a volcanic crater out of despair from trends of thought to which he feels alien was censored by Arnold the critic because the situation of Empedocles was one in which "no poetical enjoyment can be derived." Passive endurance, except the suicide, was no substitute for an action.

But, to Arnold, his Victorian England of industrial expansion and material progress offered no "actions" (which we can roughly define as stories or subjects) comparable, in dignity, power, or significance, with those rendered by Homer, the Greek tragedians, Virgil, or Shakespeare. And of all literary art he most admired the Greek for the sheer – but austere – strength with which it rendered such actions or stories.

When Arnold had completed his "Sohrab and Rustum," he reported "it pleases me more than anything I have done" and that he had found a story which was "a very noble and excellent one." He indeed had, according to his critical principles, good cause for his pleasure: he had constructed a heroic episode which, though in English blank verse, was in the manner of Homer. The story relates how the Persian warrior, Rustum, engaged in single combat the champion of the Tartars, his son, Sohrab, and kills him, only then discovering the identity of his opponent. Whether or not this story had "a shadowy personal significance" (hinting at Dr. Arnold's effect on his son, Matthew, or on the earlier Matthew Arnold's effect on the later Matthew Arnold), it remains a powerfully moving poem with wonderful coda which resists criticism.

Another epic episode, the subject drawn from Norse mythology, "Balder Dead," and another imitation of Greek tragedy, *Merope*, may be cited as examples of Arnold's continual struggle to find in times and places other than his own – since contemporary England afforded none – actions "possessing an inherent interest in themselves, and which are to be communicated in an interesting manner by the art of the poet."

Despite Arnold's efforts at finding worthy actions which were to be rendered in an objective way, some of his shorter poems telling, in his own person, of failure, or dissatisfaction, or despondency, are central to an understanding of his work, creative and critical, as a whole.

There is the group of poems which appeared under the title of "Switzerland," and possibly associated with this is the poem "Requiescat." They are love poems. We can deduce from the poems that Arnold had fallen in love with Marguerite, a French girl, in Switzerland; that, despite the attraction, he had desisted from embracing –

> Again I spring to make my choice;
> Again in tones of ire
> I hear a God's tremendous voice:
> "Be counselled and retire."

– for reasons of duty or loyalty owed elsewhere, or on grounds of conscience, or from being conditioned to refuse on account of his moral upbringing; that he had nevertheless continued to repine at that lost chance; but

27

> A God, a God their severance ruled;
> And bade betwixt their shores to be
> The unplumb'd, salt, estranging sea.

Then there is a case for believing the lines beginning "Strew on her roses, roses ..." to be Arnold's lament, years later, on hearing of Marguerite's death. If this touching or pathetic, though not tragic series, about an affair never consummated, bespeaks of vacillating hopes and desires, then this wavering between committal and denial is the substance of two of Arnold's greater poems, "Dover Beach" and "A Summer Night." In the former, the to and fro of the waves –

> You hear the grating over
> Of pebbles which the waves draw back, and fling
> At their return ...

– is rhythmically enacted in the verse; in the latter the – in either way – unsatisfying choice being offered to man is contemplated – "Is there no life, but these alone? / Madman or slave, must man be one?" – and both emerge from a dismayed view of the society of his day; and we recall that Arnold declared that "all poetry is at bottom a criticism of life."

The tenour of "Dover Beach" and "A Summer Night" is developed, with much other orchestrated material, in the splendid "The Scholar-Gipsy" and "Thyrsis." Both are elaborate odes. If Arnold generally tends to be deficient in rhythmical vitality and emotional engagement, these poems are the exception. "Thyrsis," an elegy for his friend Clough, is no less an indictment of the modern world for being set in the pastoral mode. "The Scholar-Gipsy," a distant precurser of the to-day's "drop-out" from the "sick disease of modern life," possesses a rich appreciation of the alternatives. Wordsworth, among the English poets, had been Arnold's most admired exemplar, but in these two odes the influence of Keats had been admitted and absorbed.

A reading of Arnold's essay "The Function of Criticism" does much to illuminate Arnold's own poetry and his reasons for turning from the writing of verse to (mainly) the writing of criticism. Finally, if the poetic production is, compared with that of other Victorian poets, small and the emotional range narrow – tending to the moods of dejection or resignation – it has been held that he has had more to say about our fate in the twentieth century than his more robust contemporaries.

—Francis Berry

ASHBERY, John (Lawrence). American. Born in Rochester, New York, 28 July 1927. Educated at Deerfield Academy, Massachusetts; Harvard University, Cambridge, Massachusetts (Member of the Editorial Board, *The Harvard Advocate*), B.A. in English 1949; Columbia University, New York, M.A. in English 1951; New York University, 1957–58. Copywriter, Oxford University Press, New York, 1951–54, and McGraw-Hill Book Company, New York, 1954–55. Art Critic, European Edition of the *New York Herald Tribune*, Paris, 1960–65, and *Art International*, Lugano, Switzerland, 1961–64; Editor, *Locus Solus* magazine, Lans-en-Vercors, France, 1960–62; Editor, *Art and Literature*, Paris, 1963–64; Paris Correspondent, 1964–65, and Executive Editor, 1965–72, *Art News*, New York. Since 1974, Professor of English, Brooklyn College of the City University of New York. Since 1976, Poetry Editor, *Partisan Review*, New Brunswick, New Jersey. Recipient: Fulbright Fellowship, 1955, 1956; Yale Series of Younger Poets Award, 1956; Poets Foundation grant, 1960, 1964; Ingram Merrill Foundation grant, 1962, 1972; Guggenheim

Fellowship, 1967, 1973; National Endowment for the Arts grant, 1968, 1969; National Institute of Arts and Letters award, 1969; Shelley Memorial Award, 1973; Modern Poetry Association Frank O'Hara Prize, 1974; National Book Critics Circle Award, 1976; Pulitzer Prize, 1976; National Book Award, 1976. Lives in New York City.

PUBLICATIONS

Verse

> *Turandot and Other Poems.* 1953.
> *Some Trees.* 1956.
> *The Poems.* 1960.
> *The Tennis Court Oath.* 1962.
> *Rivers and Mountains.* 1966.
> *Selected Poems.* 1967.
> *Sunrise in Suburbia.* 1968.
> *Three Madrigals.* 1968.
> *Fragment.* 1969.
> *The Double Dream of Spring.* 1970.
> *The New Spirit.* 1970.
> *Three Poems.* 1972.
> *The Vermont Notebook*, with Joe Brainard. 1975.
> *Fragment, Clepsydre, Poèmes Francais.* 1975.
> *Self-Portrait in a Convex Mirror.* 1975.
> *Houseboat Days.* 1977.

Plays

> *The Heroes* (produced 1952). In *Three Plays*, 1978.
> *The Compromise* (produced 1956). In *Three Plays*, 1978.
> *Three Plays* (includes *The Heroes, The Compromise, The Philosopher*). 1978.

Fiction

> *A Nest of Ninnies*, with James Schuyler. 1969.

Other

> Editor, with others, *American Literary Anthology 1.* 1968.
> Editor, *Penguin Modern Poets 24.* 1973.
> Editor, *Muck Arbour*, by Bruce Marcus. 1974.

> Translator, *Melville*, by Jean-Jacques Mayoux. 1960.
> Translator, *Alberto Giacometti*, by Jacques Dupin. 1963.

Bibliography: *Ashbery: A Comprehensive Bibliography Including the Art Criticism, and with Selected Notes from Unpublished Material* by David K. S. Kermani, 1976.

Reading List: *Alone with America* by Richard Howard, 1969; *American Free Verse: The Modern Revolution in Poetry* by Walter Sutton, 1973; "Ashbery: The Charity of Hard Moments" by Harold Bloom, in *Salmagundi,* Spring-Summer 1973.

*　　　*　　　*

John Ashbery was originally associated with the New York school of poets, whose central figure is Frank O'Hara, and whose poetic style is noted for its painterly emphasis on setting, luxurious detailing, and leisurely meditative argument. This group closely identified itself with the abstract expressionist painters and with the Museum of Modern Art; some of these poets wrote for *Art News.* Ashbery was directly connected with all three spheres, and from the painters learned a curious collage-like style of poetry made of bits and pieces of lyric phrasing. This mode of speech, lacking transition between leaps of thought and reflection, early marked Ashbery as difficult, if not impenetrable. As he remarked in a later poem,

> I know that I braid too much my own
> Snapped-off perceptions of things as they come to me.
> They are private and always will be.

The root of Ashbery's lyric style may be traced back to the Symbolists, and to the allusive poems of T. S. Eliot, whose echo is frequently heard in Ashbery's work. At his best, Ashbery can give uncanny immediacy to his language; his stance of uncertainty before life draws him to the appearance of the phenomenal world which he contemplates in a delicate, sinewy language.

Some Trees is Ashbery's first work of note, and contains one of his most anthologized poems, "The Instruction Manual." His second major book of poems, *The Tennis Court Oath,* in particular emphasizes the style of pastiche. Beginning with *Rivers and Mountains,* Ashbery introduced his specialty, the long discursive meditation running to many pages in which the effort is made to piece together the fragments of experience into a sensible whole. "The Skaters" makes up half of the book. The meditative style is pursued most fully in *Three Poems,* prose poems that are linked like the moments of dialectical reason, in which the speaker struggles to reveal the metaphysical and spiritual basis of his existence.

Much of the poetry of these books is suffused with a restrained melancholy. Ashbery is articulating the post-existential awareness, in which existence is an accepted but utterly unknowable dimension. That stance is succinctly phrased in "Poems in Three Parts":

> One must bear in mind one thing.
> It isn't necessary to know what that thing is.
> All things are palpable, none are known.

No faith or hope can fully support the speaker, and he is recurrently plunged into self-analysis to discover the purpose of his life. *Self-Portrait in a Convex Mirror* continues this self-analysis and metaphysical exploration, particularly in the brilliant long title poem and in "Grand Galop." In his recent books, there is a perceptible effort to take up subjects beyond the self, but the poems are still deeply absorbed with the absence of a philosophical and religious context in which to value or understand life. Ashbery's innovative and sophisticated humor is clear in *The Double Dream of Spring,* particularly in such surreal high jinks as his "Variations, Calypso and Fugue on a Theme of Ella Wheeler Wilcox."

—Paul Christensen

ATWOOD, Margaret (Eleanor). Canadian. Born in Ottawa, Ontario, 18 November 1939. Educated at Victoria College, University of Toronto, B.A. 1961; Radcliffe College, Cambridge, Massachusetts, A.M. 1962; Harvard University, Cambridge, Massachusetts. Lecturer in English, University of British Columbia, Vancouver, 1964–65; Instructor in English, Sir George Williams University, Montreal, 1967–68. Recipient: E. J. Pratt Medal, 1961; President's Medal, University of Western Ontario, 1966; Governor-General's Award, 1967; Centennial Commission prize, 1967. Lives in Ontario.

PUBLICATIONS

Verse

Double Persephone. 1961.
The Circle Game. 1964; revised edition, 1966.
Talismans for Children. 1965.
Kaleidoscopes: Baroque. 1965.
Speeches for Doctor Frankenstein. 1966.
The Animals in That Country. 1968.
Five Modern Canadian Poets, with others, edited by Eli Mandel. 1970.
The Journals of Susanna Moodie: Poems. 1970.
Procedures for Underground. 1970.
Power Politics. 1971.
You Are Happy. 1974.
Selected Poems. 1976.

Fiction

The Edible Woman. 1969.
Surfacing. 1972.
Lady Oracle. 1976.

Other

Survival: A Thematic Guide to Canadian Literature. 1972.

Reading List: "The Poetry of Atwood" by John Wilson Foster, in Canadian Literature Autumn 1977.

*   *   *

Margaret Atwood's poetry succeeds not by masterly technique or style but by a peculiar and highly individual force of content, by exciting transformations whereby the identities of Canadian pioneers, of forest animals, Indians, the wilderness, women, and Canada itself conduct strange traffic with one another. These identities flesh out in multiple guise the root formula of Atwood's poetry. In most of her work, Atwood concerns herself with the self's inhabitation of spaces and forms, and the metamorphoses entailed therein. In her world, extinction and obsolescence are illusory, for life is a constant process of re-formation. Metaphor, simile, and personification in her verse might therefore just as easily be explained in terms of zoomorphism, anthropomorphism, and totemism as in terms of poetic

31

convention. The self is eternally divided in its attitude to the forms and spaces it inhabits, simultaneously needing, fearing, desiring, and despising them. Hence the paranoid and schizophrenic motifs of the poetry.

Atwood's many Canadian admirers regard her as being deeply involved, at a time of cultural resurgence in Canada, with the problematic identity of her country, and to an extent this is true. As though aware of belonging to a minority culture on the North American continent, Atwood has in her poetry, particularly *The Circle Game, The Animals in That Country, Procedures for Underground,* and, above all, *The Journals of Susanna Moodie,* re-enacted her pioneer ancestors' experience in early Canada. But the metaphoric possibilities of pioneering are what interest Atwood.

Animals, for example, abound in her poetry as they did in the world of the pioneer, but they frequently embody the timeless dreads of the poet and her speakers. They are also the heraldic and mythic animals of the red men whom the settlers confronted and who still pre-empt white Canadians. The wilderness still beckons and forbids Canadians, as the novel *Surfacing* and the poetry demonstrate; it represents the interior and dangerous landscape of the mind as well as the primordiality to which all must in the end revert, as the briefly resurrected Susanna Moodie explains: "at the last/judgement we will all be trees."

Atwood's verse transformation of Mrs. Moodie's nineteenth-century pioneer journals (e.g., *Roughing It in the Bush*) is her finest volume of poetry, and offers pioneering as one extended metaphor for contemporary women's questioning of the traditional roles laid down by men for them to play. *Power Politics* explores sexual identity and relationships by means of the different metaphor of politics. Yet another and more original metaphor is the Circe episode of the *Odyssey* in the "Circe/Mud Poems" sequence of *You Are Happy,* in which the themes of pioneering, Canada and womanhood are connected.

Atwood is a prolific poet and novelist (occasionally hasty, one might feel) who seems, like her speakers, both to desire and fear escape from form. Her verse avoids rhyme and merely flirts with stanzaic pattern. Her basic unit is not the line (sense is fractured into an abundance of short lines) but the insight, and this in turn relies on the terse shock of metaphor. Yet the bones of older forms show appropriately through, to provide an uneasy counterpoint to her themes.

—John Wilson Foster

AUDEN, W(ystan) H(ugh). American. Born in York, England, 21 February 1907; emigrated to the United States in 1938; naturalized, 1946. Educated at St. Edmund's School, Grayshott, Surrey; Gresham's School, Holt, Norfolk; Christ Church, Oxford (exhibitioner), 1925–28. Served with the Strategic Bombing Survey of the United States Army in Germany during World War II. Married Erika Mann in 1935. Schoolmaster, Larchfield Academy, Helensburgh, Scotland, and Downs School, Colwall, near Malvern, Worcestershire, 1930–35. Co-Founder of the Group Theatre, 1932; worked with the G.P.O. Film Unit, 1935. Travelled extensively in the 1930's, in Europe, Iceland, and China. Taught at St. Mark's School, Southborough, Massachusetts, 1939–40; American Writers League School, 1939; New School for Social Research, New York, 1940–41, 1946–47; University of Michigan, Ann Arbor, 1941–42; Swarthmore College, Pennsylvania, 1942–45; Bryn Mawr College, Pennsylvania, 1943–45; Bennington College, Vermont, 1946; Barnard College, New York, 1947; Neilson Research Professor, Smith College, Northampton, Massachusetts, 1953; Professor of Poetry, Oxford University, 1956–61. Editor, Yale Series of Younger Poets, 1947–62. Member of the Editorial Board, *Decision* magazine, 1940–41, and *Delos* magazine,

1968; The Readers' Subscription book club, 1951–59, and The Mid-Century Book Club, 1959–62. Recipient: King's Gold Medal for Poetry, 1936; Guggenheim Fellowship, 1942; American Academy of Arts and Letters Award of Merit Medal, 1945, Gold Medal, 1968; Pulitzer Prize, 1948; Bollingen Prize, 1954; National Book Award, 1956; Feltrinelli Prize, 1957; Guinness Award, 1959; Poetry Society of America's Droutskoy Gold Medal, 1959; National Endowment for the Arts grant, 1966; National Book Committee's National Medal for Literature, 1967. D.Litt.: Swarthmore College, 1964. Member, American Academy of Arts and Letters, 1954; Honorary Student, Christ Church, 1962, and in residence, 1972–73. *Died 28 September 1973.*

PUBLICATIONS

Collections

Collected Poems, edited by Edward Mendelson.   1976.

Verse

Poems.   1928.
Poems.   1930; revised edition, 1933.
The Orators: An English Study.   1932; revised edition, 1934, 1966.
Poems (includes *The Orators* and *The Dance of Death*)   1934.
Look, Stranger!   1936; as *On This Island,* 1937.
Spain.   1937.
Letters from Iceland, with Louis MacNeice.   1937.
Selected Poems.   1938.
Journey to a War (verse sections), with Christopher Isherwood.   1939; revised edition, 1973.
Another Time: Poems (includes *Spain*).   1940.
Some Poems.   1940.
The Double Man.   1941; as *New Year Letter,* 1941.
Three Songs for St. Cecilia's Day.   1941.
For the Time Being.   1944.
The Collected Poetry.   1945.
The Age of Anxiety: A Baroque Eclogue (produced 1954).   1947.
Collected Shorter Poems 1930–1944.   1950.
Nones.   1951.
The Shield of Achilles.   1955.
The Old Man's Road.   1956.
Reflections on a Forest.   1957.
Auden: A Selection by the Author.   1958; as *Selected Poetry,* 1959.
Homage to Clio.   1960.
Auden: A Selection, edited by Richard Hoggart.   1961.
Elegy for J. F. K., music by Igor Stravinsky.   1964.
About the House.   1965.
The Twelve, music by William Walton.   1966.
Marginalia.   1966.
Collected Shorter Poems, 1927–1957.   1966.
Selected Poems.   1968.
Collected Longer Poems.   1968.

A New Year Greeting, with *The Dance of the Solids,* by John Updike.   1969.
City Without Walls and Other Poems.   1969.
Academic Graffiti.   1971.
Epistle to a Godson and Other Poems.   1972.
Auden/Moore: Poems and Lithographs, edited by John Russell.   1974.
Poems, lithographs by Henry Moore, edited by Vera Lindsay.   1974.
Thank You, Fog: Last Poems.   1974.

Plays

The Dance of Death (produced 1934; as *Come Out into the Sun,* produced 1935).   1933.
The Dog Beneath the Skin; or, Where Is Francis?, with Christopher Isherwood (produced 1936; revised version, produced 1947).   1935.
No More Peace! A Thoughtful Comedy, with Edward Crankshaw, from the play by Ernst Toller (produced 1936).   1937.
The Ascent of F6, with Christopher Isherwood (produced 1937).   1936; revised edition. 1937.
On the Frontier, with Christopher Isherwood (produced 1938).   1938.
The Dark Valley (broadcast, 1940).   In *Best Broadcasts of 1939–40,* edited by Max Wylie, 1940.
Paul Bunyan, music by Benjamin Britten (produced 1941).   1976.
The Duchess of Malfi, music by Benjamin Britten, from the play by John Webster (produced 1946).
The Knights of the Round Table, from the work by Jean Cocteau (broadcast, 1951; produced 1954).   In *The Infernal Machine and Other Plays,* by Jean Cocteau, 1964.
The Rake's Progress, with Chester Kallman, music by Igor Stravinsky (produced 1951).   1951.
Delia; or, A Masque of Night, with Chester Kallman (libretto), in *Botteghe Oscure XII.*   1953.
The Punch Revue (lyrics only) (produced 1955).
The Magic Flute, with Chester Kallman, from the libretto by Schikaneder and Giesecke, music by Mozart (televised, 1956).   1956.
The Play of Daniel (narration only) (produced 1958).   Editor, with Noah Greenberg, 1959.
The Seven Deadly Sins of the Lower Middle Class, with Chester Kallman, from the work by Brecht, music by Kurt Weill (produced 1959).   In *Tulane Drama Review,* September 1961.
Don Giovanni, with Chester Kallman, from the libretto by Lorenzo da Ponte, music by Mozart (televised, 1960).   1961.
The Caucasian Chalk Circle (lyrics only), with James and Tania Stern, from the play by Brecht (produced 1962).   In *Plays,* by Brecht, 1960.
Elegy for Young Lovers, with Chester Kallman, music by Hans Werner Henze (produced 1961).   1961.
Arcifanfarlo, King of Fools; or, It's Always Too Late to Learn, with Chester Kallman, from the libretto by Goldoni, music by Dittersdorf (produced 1965).
Die Bassariden (*The Bassarids*), with Chester Kallman, music by Hans Werner Henze (produced 1966).   1966.
Moralities: Three Scenic Plays from Fables by Aesop, music by Hans Werner Henze.   1969.
The Ballad of Barnaby, music by Wykeham Rise School Students realized by Charles Turner (produced 1970).
Love's Labour's Lost, with Chester Kallman, music by Nicholas Nabokov, from the play by Shakespeare (produced 1973).

The Entertainment of the Senses, with Chester Kallman, music by John Gardner (produced 1974).   In *Thank You, Fog*, 1974.
The Rise and Fall of the City of Mahagonny, with Chester Kallman, from the opera by Brecht.   1976.

Screenplays (documentaries, in verse): *Night Mail*, 1936; *Coal Face*, 1936; *The Londoners*, 1938.

Radio Writing: *Hadrian's Wall*, 1937 (UK); *The Dark Valley*, 1940 (USA); *The Rocking-Horse Winner*, with James Stern, from the story by D. H. Lawrence, 1941 (USA); *The Knights of the Round Table*, from a work by Jean Cocteau, 1951 (UK).

Television Writing (with Chester Kallman): *The Magic Flute*, 1956 (USA); *Don Giovanni*, 1960 (USA).

Other

Education Today − and Tomorrow, with T. C. Worsley.   1939.
The Intent of the Critic, with others, edited by Donald A. Stauffer.   1941.
Poets at Work: Essays Based on the Modern Poetry Collection at the Lockwood Memorial Library, University of Buffalo, with others, edited by Charles D. Abbott.   1948.
The Enchafèd Flood; or, The Romantic Iconography of the Sea.   1950.
The Dyer's Hand and Other Essays.   1962.
Selected Essays.   1964.
Secondary Worlds.   1968.
A Certain World: A Commonplace Book.   1970.
Forewords and Afterwords (essays), edited by Edward Mendelson.   1973.
The English Auden: Poems, Essays, and Dramatic Writings, 1927–1939, edited by Edward Mendelson.   1977.

Editor, with Charles Plumb, *Oxford Poetry 1926*.   1926.
Editor, with C. Day Lewis, *Oxford Poetry 1927*.   1927.
Editor, with John Garrett, *The Poet's Tongue: An Anthology*.   2 vols., 1935.
Editor, *The Oxford Book of Light Verse*.   1938.
Editor, *A Selection from the Poems of Alfred, Lord Tennyson*.   1944; as *Tennyson: An Introduction and a Selection*, 1946.
Editor, *The American Scene, Together with Three Essays from "Portraits of Places,"* by Henry James.   1946.
Editor, *Slick But Not Streamlined: Poems and Short Pieces*, by John Betjeman.   1947.
Editor, *The Portable Greek Reader*.   1948.
Editor, with Norman Holmes Pearson, *Poets of the English Language*.   5 vols., 1950.
Editor, *Selected Prose and Poetry*, by Edgar Allan Poe.   1950; revised edition, 1955.
Editor, *The Living Thoughts of Kierkegaard*.   1952; as *Kierkegaard*, 1955.
Editor, with Marianne Moore and Karl Shapiro, *Riverside Poetry 1953: Poems by Students in Colleges and Universities in New York City*.   1953.
Editor, with Chester Kallman and Noah Greenberg, *An Elizabethan Song Book: Lute Songs, Madrigals, and Rounds*.   1955.
Editor, *The Faber Book of Modern American Verse*.   1956; as *The Criterion Book of Modern American Verse*, 1956.
Editor, *Selected Writings of Sydney Smith*.   1956.
Editor, *Van Gogh: A Self-Portrait: Letters Revealing His Life as a Painter*.   1961.
Editor, with Louis Kronenberger, *The Viking Book of Aphorisms: A Personal Selection*.   1962; as *The Faber Book of Aphorisms*, 1964.

Editor, *A Choice of de la Mare's Verse*. 1963.
Editor, *The Pied Piper and Other Fairy Tales*, by Joseph Jacobs. 1963.
Editor, *Selected Poems*, by Louis MacNeice. 1964.
Editor, with John Lawlor, *To Nevill Coghill from Friends*. 1966.
Editor, *Selected Poetry and Prose*, by Byron. 1966.
Editor, *Nineteenth Century British Minor Poets*. 1966; as *Nineteenth Century Minor Poets*, 1967.
Editor, *G. K. Chesterton: A Selection from His Non-Fiction Prose*. 1970.
Editor, *A Choice of Dryden's Verse*. 1973.
Editor, *George Herbert*. 1973.
Editor, *Selected Songs of Thomas Campion*. 1974.

Translator, with Elizabeth Mayer, *Italian Journey 1786–1788*, by Goethe. 1962.
Translator, with Leif Sjöberg, *Markings*, by Dag Hammarskjöld. 1964.
Translator, with Paul B. Taylor, *Völupsá: The Song of the Sybil*, with an Icelandic Text edited by Peter H. Salus and Paul B. Taylor. 1968.
Translator, *The Elder Edda: A Selection*. 1969.
Translator, with Elizabeth Mayer and Louise Bogan, *The Sorrows of Young Werther, and Novella*, by Goethe. 1971.
Translator, with Leif Sjöberg, *Evening Land/Aftonland*, by Pär Lagerkvist. 1975.

Bibliography: *Auden: A Bibliography 1924–1969* by Barry C. Bloomfield and Edward Mendelson, 1972.

Reading List: *The Poetry of Auden: The Disenchanted Island* by Monroe K. Spears, 1963, and *Auden: A Collection of Critical Essays* edited by Spears, 1964; *Auden's Poetry* by Justin Replogle, 1969; *Changes of Heart: A Study of the Poetry of Auden* by Gerald Nelson, 1969; *A Reader's Guide to Auden* by John Fuller, 1970; *Auden* by Dennis Davison, 1970; *The Later Auden* by George W. Bahlke, 1970; *Auden as a Social Poet* by Frederick H. Buell, 1973; *Man's Place: An Essay on Auden* by Richard Johnson, 1973; *Auden: A Tribute* edited by Stephen Spender, 1975.

*   *   *

One of the most recurrent features of W. H. Auden's poetry is the *paysage moralisé* (an early poem is actually called this) in which the landscape becomes the emblematic topography of a spiritual condition. Auden, whose earliest reading was in geology and mining and who first thought of becoming an engineer, has always believed that the way we locate ourselves in space, in a specific lanscape we alter and adapt to, both determines and reveals our moral being, our sense of personal destiny and collective responsibility. Thus, in those fine "Horatian" *Bucolics* from the 1950's he can playfully link our neuroses with our choice of locale, as in "Mountains" –

And it is curious how often in steep places
You meet someone short who frowns,
A type you catch beheading daisies with a stick

– or prescribe the curative powers of "Lakes" (which always recall the "amniotic mere" of the womb): "Moraine, pot, oxbow, glint, sink, crater, piedmont, dimple ...?/Just reeling off their names is ever so comfy." While in "Plains" he can express his aversion to those flats "where all elsewheres are equal," "nothing points," and the tax-collector's writ is unchallengeable ("where roads run level,/How swift to the point of protest strides the crown./It hangs, it flogs, it fines, it goes"). "In Praise of Limestone" (1948) sets the tone for much of this later work, making a limestone landscape symbol of both our yearning for stability and our actual transience, beginning

> If it form the one landscape that we, the inconstant ones,
>   Are consistently homesick for, this is chiefly
> Because it dissolves in water

and ending with a wistful confession:

> Dear, I know nothing of
> Either, but when I try to imagine a faultless love
> Or the life to come, what I hear is the murmur
> Of underground streams, what I see is a limestone landscape.

The tone is more relaxed in these post-war poems, but the technique is the same as that employed in those poems of quest, pursuit, and flight which dominate his earlier writings, poems whose terrain is best described by Caliban in *The Sea and the Mirror,* that extended commentary in verse and prose on Shakespeare's *Tempest* which enables Auden to dramatize his views on the relation between life and art. Caliban, spokesman of the carnal and material, of "history," speaks with sympathy of the spirit Ariel's obligation to deliver us from "the terrible mess that this particularized life, which we have so futilely attempted to tidy, sullenly insists on leaving behind," translating "all the phenomena of an empirically ordinary world" into "elements in an allegorical landscape":

> a nightmare which has all the wealth of exciting action and all the emotional poverty of an adventure story for boys, a state of perpetual emergency and everlasting improvisation where all is need and change.

Certainly, John Buchan seems as much an influence as Marx or Nietzsche on those early poems in which the young, proud inheritor finds himself unexpectedly turned into an outsider, as in "The Watershed," "frustrate and vexed" in face of an abandoned, derelict landscape racked by depression and unemployment, "already comatose,/Yet sparsely living"; one who "must migrate" ("Missing") to become a leader, turn into a "trained spy" ("The Secret Agent"), and ("Our Hunting Fathers") "hunger, work illegally,/And be anonymous" in a world of suspicion, insecurity and betrayal, as "all the while/Conjectures on our maps grow stranger/And threaten danger" ("No Change of Place"). The Auden of these early poems, walking a dangerous tightrope between "Always" and "Never" ("Between Adventure") saw his personal anxieties bodied forth in the world at large, and found a refuge for his public-school hauteur and élitism in a communism which rationalized his contempt for an age of mediocrity, impotence and defeat. In "Family Ghosts," for example, he sees "the assaulted city" surrounded by "the watchfires of a stronger army," and it isn't possible to decide whether this is a personal allegory of love or a political poem which looks towards class-struggle as release from the "Massive and taciturn years, the Age of Ice." Christopher Isherwood, Auden's collaborator in the verse-plays *The Dog Beneath the Skin, The Ascent of F6,* and *On the Frontier,* wrote of him in these terms in 1937, speaking of Auden's love for the Norse sagas: "The saga world is a schoolboy world, with its feuds, its practical jokes, its dark threats conveyed in puns and riddles and understatements"; in *Paid on Both Sides,* Auden's early, expressionist charade, he adds, "the two worlds are so inextricably confused that it is impossible to say whether the characters are really epic heroes or only members of a school O.T.C." Stephen Spender, also one of Auden's "Gang" during this period, has written of the "schoolboy ruthlessness" and latent fascism of *The Orators,* and the once-popular plays in which Auden and Isherwood tried to explore the contemporary crisis in the terms of Ruritanian allegory, knockabout, and morality-play which rob it of all urgency, are dismissed by Spender as virtuoso exercises, "a hash of the revolutionary and pacifist thought of the 1930s, reduced to their least convincing terms," which "provide considerable evidence that one aspect of the 1930s was a rackety exploitation of literary fashions."

Letter to Lord Byron perhaps best sums up the ambivalence of Auden's mood in the 1930's. Written is a skilful pastiche of Byron's own insouciant rhythms and rhymes, it expresses an aristocratic, Byronic disdain for the cant and hypocrisy of the "well-to-do" Home Counties, with their bland, self-deceiving smugness, against which Auden sets the urgencies of a more desolate world:

> To those who live in Warrington or Wigan,
> It's not a white lie, it's a whacking big 'un.
>
> There on the old historic battlefield,
>   The cold ferocity of human wills,
> The scars of struggle are as yet unhealed;
>   Slattern the tenements on sombre hills,
>   And gaunt in valleys the square-windowed mills
> That since the Georgian house, in my conjecture
> Remain our finest native architecture.

Yet that shift in the last couplet from moral outrage to sober aesthetic appreciation, together with the easy abstraction and the typecast imagery, reveals Auden's basic remoteness from his subject; indeed, a stanza later he can confess openly to his twentieth-century delight in that landscape: "Tramlines and slagheaps, pieces of machinery,/That was, and still is, my ideal scenery."

"Journey to Iceland" (1936) explains the rationale of Auden's travelogues: "North means to all *Reject*"; but such rejection also brought with it a new perspective that extended his control of his material and made possible a larger, clearer vision, revealed in that mythic conspectus of human evolution "Sonnets from China," originally included in the travel book *Journey to a War*. After the claustrophobic, cryptic, furtive atmosphere of the earlier poems, Auden here perfected the new straightforwardness already evinced in "Spain 1937," where "the menacing shapes of our fever/Are precise and alive." Significantly, the latter's explicit commitment to communism led a censorious later Auden to excise it from the canon (those patriarchal, castrating imagos, the Censor and the Scissor Man, have made themselves felt again and again in his poetic career). His reasons are interesting. Of the last stanza of "Spain" –

> The stars are dead. The animals will not look.
> We are left alone with our day, and the time is short, and
>   History to the defeated
> May say alas but cannot help or pardon

– he has said: "To say this is to equate goodness with success. It would have been bad enough if I had ever held this wicked doctrine, but that I should have stated it simply because it sounded to me rhetorically effective is quite inexcusable." But what the poem in fact stresses is the openness of human choice and the tragic discrepancy between history and morality (success may involve "The conscious acceptance of guilt in the necessary murder"), between – in Pascal's terms – Nature and Justice. There is nothing here which belies Auden's later conversion to Kierkegaard's Christian existentialism: the belief that man is responsible for his acts, and must make his leap of faith in fear and trembling, knowing that it may be a wrong and corrosive choice. That faith is best expressed in *For the Time Being*, a "Christmas Oratorio" which recreates the Christian myth in contemporary terms (casting Herod, for example, as a well-intentioned liberal statesman whose massacre of the innocents is for the public good). History is now for Auden seen in the perspective of eternity:

> To those who have seen
> The Child, however dimly, however incredulously
> The Time Being is, in a sense, the most trying time of all.
> For the innocent children who whispered so excitedly
> Outside the locked door where they knew the presents to be
> Grew up when it opened. Now, recollecting that moment
> We can repress the joy, but the guilt remains conscious.

For Auden, who had originally identified with "Voltaire at Ferney" (1939), perennial oedipal rebel —

> Cajoling, scolding, scheming, cleverest of them all,
> He'd led the other children in a holy war
> Against the infamous grownups

— this "growing up" expressed, in terms of traditional theology, his final transfer of allegiance from the Son to the Father, effected, ironically enough, through the advent of that Child to a world at war. The transfer can be seen occurring in his fine poem "In Memory of Sigmund Freud" (1939), where that liberating discoverer of the unconscious is seen both as wide-eyed child and benevolent father who

> showed us what evil is, not, as we thought,
> deeds that must be punished, but our lack of faith,
>   our dishonest mood of denial,
>   the concupiscence of the oppressor.

The same affirmation animates "In Memory of Ernst Toller," acknowledging the great gift of both Freud and Marx to human self-understanding: the disclosure of those unconscious determinations of our identity — whether biological or socio-economic, each shaping the other — which constrain our existential freedom only when unrecognized:

> We are lived by powers we pretend to understand:
> They arrange our loves; it is they who direct at the end
> The enemy bullet, the sickness, or even our hand.
>
> It is their tomorrow hangs over the earth of the living
> And all that we wish for our friends: but existence is believing
> We know for whom we mourn and who is grieving.

For the later, Anglican, Auden, finally expatriate in an alien and yet familiar America, acknowledgment of our guilt is the ground of freedom. Rosetta, one of the four "displaced persons" lining a wartime bar in New York in *The Age of Anxiety,* at a time when "Many have perished, more will," daydreams of

> one of those landscapes familiar to all readers of English
> detective stories, those lovely innocent countrysides
> inhabited by charming eccentrics with independent means
> and amusing hobbies to whom, until the sudden intrusion
> of a horrid corpse onto the tennis court or into the greenhouse,
> work and law and guilt are just literary words.

As the 1936 poem "Detective Story" and the essay "The Guilty Vicarage" make clear, this landscape is Auden's own peculiar version of the myth of the Fall: to live in history is to accept complicity, and to accept complicity is the beginning of grace: "But time is always guilty. Someone must pay for/Our loss of happiness, our happiness itself." Each of the "travellers through time" of *The Age of Anxiety* sets out "in quest of his own/Absconded self yet scared to find it" (for it will turn out to be the culprit). In *New Year Letter* Auden resolves, in his own person, to accept responsibility for his fallen condition. History is the middle way, that Purgatory where, "Consenting parties to our lives," we may "win/Truth out of Time. In Time we sin./But Time is sin and can forgive"; in Time too we learn "To what conditions we must bow/In building the Just City now." But the world remains one in which "Aloneness is man's real condition."

What underlies all Auden's poetry, in fact, early and late, is this tension between aristocratic disdain and a humble and, at times, humiliating love for the things of this world. It is there in his love poetry, whether in the early and beautiful "Lullaby" ("Lay your sleeping head, my love,/Human on my faithless arm") or the innocuous narcissism of the last poem in his *Collected Poems* (1976), also called "A Lullaby" − "now you fondle/your almost feminine flesh/with mettled satisfaction" − but with its last line, "Sleep, Big Baby, sleep your fill," almost an epitaph. The explicit homosexual lust of "Three Posthumous Poems" that translation of *Eros* into *Agape*, of sensual into spiritual love, was no more difficult for Auden than it was for the Sufi poets. His perennial movement between renouncing and embracing, *askesis* and indulgence, is embodied in his very language, which at once delights in the rich multiplicity of an abundant world and yet keeps it at bay with a deliberate, distancing artificiality that defamiliarizes the accustomed, or calls attention to the medium itself through nonce-words and neologisms, arcane or archaic usages, portentous polysyllables cut short by sudden racy slang, magpie gauds and macaronics. By turns demotic and hieratic, shifting peremptorily in rhythm, tone, and register, skittish, hoydenish, and haughty, polyglot and jargonish, ruminative and aphoristic, shocking and coy, Auden's language corresponds in its variety to a frame of mind, to that master of disguises (Sherlock Holmes was always a hero) his poems expose from first to last. If his later poetry is more domestic and muted, full of thanksgivings and valedictions, elegies and reminiscences, it can still rise to pyrotechnic heroisms of language. But perhaps the best of these later volumes is *Homage to Clio,* a series of poems dedicated to Auden's first and last love, the matronly Muse of History:

> Madonna of silences, to whom we turn
>
> When we have lost control, your eyes, Clio, into which
>   We look for recognition after
> We have been found out....
>
>   I have seen
> Your photo, I think, in the papers, nursing
>   A baby or mourning a corpse: each time
>
> You had nothing to say and did not, one could see,
>   Observe where you were, Muse of the unique
> Historical fact, defending with silence
>   Some world of your beholding....

With this one poem alone Auden could establish his claim to be a serious and a major poet, fulfilling that specifically human vocation, the ability "with a rhythm or a rhyme" to "Assume ... responsibility for time."

—Stan Smith

AUSTIN, Alfred.   English.   Born in Headingley, Leeds, Yorkshire, 30 May 1835. Educated at school in Headingley; St. Edward's School, Everton, Lancashire; Stonyhurst College; Oscott College, Warwickshire; University of London, B.A. 1853; Inner Temple, London, 1854–57; called to the Bar, 1857. Married Hester Homan-Mulock in 1865. Practised law on the Northern Circuit, 1857–58. Conservative candidate for Parliament for Taunton, 1865, and Dewsbury, 1880. Leader writer for the London *Standard,* 1866–1896; Foreign Correspondent in Italy, 1869, and Germany, 1870 and 1884. Founder Editor, *National Review,* 1883–93. Poet Laureate, 1896. Lived in Hertfordshire, 1862–67, and at Swinford Old Manor. near Ashford, Kent, from 1867. *Died 2 June 1913.*

PUBLICATIONS

Verse

> *Randolph.*   1854; revised edition, as *Leszko the Bastard: A Tale of Polish Grief,* 1877.
> *The Season: A Satire.*   1861; revised edition, 1861, 1869.
> *My Satire and Its Censors.*   1861.
> *The Golden Age: A Satire.*   1871.
> *Interludes.*   1872.
> *Soliloquies in Song.*   1882.
> *At the Gate of the Convent and Other Poems.*   1885.
> *Days of the Year: A Poetic Calendar.*   1886.
> *Love's Widowhood and Other Poems.*   1889.
> *English Lyrics,* edited by William Watson.   1890.
> *Lyrical Poems.*   1891.
> *Narrative Poems.*   1891.
> *Fortunatus the Pessimist: A Dramatic Poem.*   1892.
> *A Betrothal.*   1893.
> *The Conversion of Winckelmann and Other Poems.*   1897.
> *Victoria, June 20, 1837–June 20, 1897.*   1897.
> *Songs of England.*   1898; revised edition, 1900.
> *Polyphemus.*   1901.
> *A Tale of True Love and Other Poems.*   1902.
> *Victoria the Wise.*   1903.
> *The Door of Humility.*   1906.
> *Sacred and Profane Love and Other Poems.*   1908.
> *Love Poems.*   1912.

Plays

> *The Human Tragedy.*   1862; *Madonna's Child,* act 2, 1873; *Rome or Death!,* act 3, 1873; complete edition, 1876; revised edition, 1889.
> *The Tower of Babel.*   1874.
> *Savonarola.*   1881.
> *Prince Lucifer.*   1887.
> *England's Darling.*   1896; as *Alfred the Great,* 1901.
> *Flodden Field* (produced 1903).   1903.
> *A Lesson in Harmony* (produced 1904).   1904.
> *Achilles in Scyros* (produced 1909).

Fiction

> *Five Years of It.* 1858.
> *An Artist's Proof.* 1864.
> *Won by a Head.* 1866.
> *The Lord of All.* 1867.
> *Lamia's Winter-Quarters.* 1898; revised edition, 1907.

Other

> *A Note of Admiration.* 1861.
> *A Vindication of Lord Byron.* 1869.
> *The Poetry of the Period.* 1870.
> *Russia Before Europe.* 1876.
> *Tory Horrors; or, The Question of the Hour.* 1876.
> *England's Policy and Peril.* 1877.
> *Hibernian Horrors; or, The Nemesis of a Faction.* 1880.
> *On a Recent Criticism of Mr. Swinburne's.* 1881.
> *Skeletons at the Feast; or, The Radical Programme.* 1885.
> *The Garden That I Love.* 2 vols., 1894–1907.
> *In Veronica's Garden.* 1895.
> *Spring and Autumn in Ireland.* 1900.
> *Haunts of Ancient Peace.* 1902.
> *The Poet's Diary.* 1904.
> *The Bridling of Pegasus: Prose Papers on Poetry.* 1910.
> *Autobiography.* 2 vols., 1911.

Editor, *An Eighteenth Century Anthology.* 1904.

Reading List: *Austin, Victorian* by Norton B. Crowell, 1953 (includes bibliography).

*   *   *

Succeeding, as he did, Tennyson as Poet Laureate, Alfred Austin, certainly no great poet, almost inevitably became something of a by-word. Tennyson had added lustre to the office: Austin's appointment, on the advice of Lord Salisbury, was, as in the case of the many neglible Poets Laureate of the eighteenth century, a matter of party political patronage. He had been a devoted follower of Disraeli and as editor of the *National Review* had served Conservative interests. "I am told that Mr. Swinburne is the greatest poet in my dominions," Queen Victoria is reported to have said, but apparently she was overruled. Swinburne's earlier work had after all been the subject of scandal, and it has been pointed out that most of the other possible candidates might be considered in one way or another as unsuitable. Morris was identified with socialism, and Yeats with Irish Nationalism; Meredith was thought to be too highbrow, and Kipling too vulgar, while Hardy as a poet was virtually unknown. So Austin, or so Lord Salisbury thought, it had to be.

He began badly in 1896 by publishing in *The Times* an Ode on the Jameson Raid, praising what soon turned out to be both a military fiasco and an embarrassment to the British Government. Most of his subsequent Laureate poems were equally unfortunate in style if not in subject. But he is probably not the author of the lines most frequently quoted as his: "Across the wires the electric message came: He is no better, he is much the same" – this from a poem on the illness of the Prince of Wales.

Yet Austin does not entirely deserve the obloquy which has been heaped upon him. His early satire, *The Season,* has considerable merit. It is written in heroic couplets, for Austin was an upholder of Augustan values at a time when they were often decried. By something of an irony, his essay on Tennyson (written during that poet's lifetime) shows considerable critical intelligence, and puts a finger on some of the real weaknesses of its subject. Of his other prose writings, *The Garden That I Love* enjoyed much popularity in its day.

—John Heath-Stubbs

AVISON, Margaret (Kirkland).   Canadian.   Born in Galt, Ontario, 23 April 1918. Educated at the University of Toronto, B.A. 1940. Recipient: Guggenheim Fellowship, 1956; Governor-General's Award, 1961. Lives in Toronto.

PUBLICATIONS

Verse

> *Winter Sun.*   1960.
> *The Dumbfounding.*   1966.

Other

> *The Research Compendium,* with Albert Rose.   1964.

Reading List: *Avison* by E. H. Redekop, 1970.

*   *   *

Throughout her life, Margaret Avison has been concerned with the nature of imaginative perception. She writes of the transcendental nature of reality, about the ability of the "optic heart" to see beyond the surfaces of things. Like many Canadian poets, she has a strong sense of the physical landscape, of earth, rock, water, of city streets and buildings which support or overwhelm man, but a close, often undefinable and dangerous, relationship links man to the world in which he lives. In many of the shorter poems of her first book, *Winter Sun,* she depicts, with acuteness and compassion, the modern city, sometimes in extraordinary vignettes, sometimes in sequences of brief scenes or images. Strange and sudden interlockings of external and internal landscapes occur; her landscape becomes multiple, an everywhere inhabited by the mind of the poet, an always in which past and present collide.

Avison believes that the forms of language, words themselves, are threatened by our inability to see things freshly. So the "deciphering heart" must take the confusion in speech between the ancient and the new and resolve it into a new imaginative order. She does this in her own language, crossing the often rigid boundaries between our newest technologies and our lagging perceptions of history, between the secular and sacred imaginations, between given poetic forms and new structures of words. In her longer poems, she moves freely back and forth between centuries and places, creating pieces of a jigsaw world which the reader must put together. The reader, in fact, must behave much like her persona of the artist, "at once Hansel and Gretel," plunging into the forests and seas of the imagination, for her diction is terse and economical, sometimes arcane, her syntax often convoluted, and her images always dense.

In the context of other contemporary poetry, some of Avison's most remarkable poems are the explicitly Christian poems in *The Dumbfounding.* Here she writes in the traditions of Donne, Herbert, and Hopkins, drawing ideas and sometimes language from each, and creating poems that are deeply personal expressions of the poet's relation to God. Many of them, although at first sight somewhat remote from the poems in *Winter Sun,* are about ways of perceiving reality, spiritual exercises of the optic heart. In poem after poem, she imagines the vision of rebirth, the moment when, like her swimmer, man recognizes the existence of the whirlpool and enters the black pit, or when Christ transcends the defining lines drawn by man. The recognition of this moment of love is for her "the dumbfounding." In a poem arising out of the first landing by man on the moon, she continues to express this "now" as the moment beyond the technical data of the moon mission – that epiphanic, dumbfounding perception of reality.

Avison's poems are both immediately recognizable and profoundly strange, because her perspectives of common, ordinary things are always unexpected. She communicates in all her poetry a strong sense of historical continuity, but the contemporary world of dams, TV, space flight, napalm, and fission is always at hand, waiting for the encounter with imagination, waiting for judgment.

—E. H. Redekop

AYTON, Sir Robert. Scottish. Born in Kinaldie, Fife, c. 1569. Educated at St. Leonard's College, University of St. Andrews, 1584–88, M.A. 1588. In Paris, 1603; thereafter a courtier of James I: served as Groom of the Privy Chamber, 1608, and Secretary and Master of Requests to Queen Anne; also went on diplomatic mission to Germany, 1609; Secretary and Master of Requests to Queen Henrietta Maria, 1626; Master of the Royal Hospital of St. Katherine, 1636. Knighted, 1612. Granted royal pension, 1611, additional pension, 1620. *Died 25 February 1638.*

PUBLICATIONS

Collections

   A Choice of Poems and Songs, edited by Helena Mennie Shire. 1961.
   The English and Latin Poems (includes letters), edited by Charles B. Gullans. 1963.

Verse

   De Foelici et Semper Augusto Jacobi. 1603.
   Basia. 1605.
   In Obitum Thomae Rhaedi, Epicidium. 1624.
   Lessus in Funere Raphaelis Thorii. 1626.

Reading List: *Song, Dance, and Poetry of the Court of Scotland under King James VI* by Helena Mennie Shire, 1969.

*   *   *

Robert Ayton was born of gentlefolk at Kinaldie in Fife, and graduated from St. Andrew's University. He was already writing verses, not only in the literary Scots of the poets under King James VI of Scotland but also in the neo-Latin of European renaissance style (Latin poems of his were included in the distinguished collection *Delitiae Poetarum Scotorum*, 1637), when he hailed King James's accession to the English throne by a Latin panegyric, printed in Paris in 1603.

The new court of King James in Westminster was hospitable to poets from the north and Ayton soon made his way there. He was knighted in 1612 and served as Secretary to Queen Anne and later to Queen Henrietta Maria. Court service was his life. A gracious and well-loved personality (Ben Jonson was happy to say that Ayton was his friend), the Scots poet composed, now in English, witty, graceful, and dignified pieces to celebrate royal occasions, glad or sorrowful. And from his "jocund muse" flowed many delightful songs of love's pleasures or pains. Tender or teasing, simply but subtly phrased, they were always finely articulate. Some were written to match tunes or songs already known, for instance an air by Campion; more were set in different song-styles by musicians such as Henry Lawes, William Blagrave, and John Wilson.

Sir Robert did not cherish his muse. His vernacular lyrics remained in manuscript, the favourites widely known and sonetimes printed in miscellany or song-book. Watson's *Choice Collection* (1706) featured a number, in tribute to a poet of Scotland. Ayton was the last of King James' "Castalian poets" of the north.

—Helena Mennie Shire

BAILEY, Philip James. English. Born in Nottingham, 22 April 1816. Educated in Nottingham; at the University of Glasgow; studied law in a solicitor's office, London, 1833–34; entered Lincoln's Inn, London, 1834, and called to the Bar, 1840, but never practised. Married twice; one son, one daughter by first wife; married Anne Sophia Carey in 1863 (died, 1896). Retired to his father's house at Basford, Nottingham, 1836, and devoted himself to writing; settled in Jersey, 1864, and thereafter frequently visited the Continent; settled in Blackheath, London, 1885. LL.D.: University of Glasgow, 1901. Granted Civil List pension, 1856. *Died 6 September 1902.*

PUBLICATIONS

Collections

    The Poets and Poetry of the Century 4, edited by A. H. Miles and others. 1891.

Verse

    Festus. 1839; revised edition, 1845,1864, 1889.
    The Angel World and Other Poems. 1850; revised edition, in *Festus,* 1864, 1889.
    The Mystic and Other Poems. 1855; revised edition, in *Festus,* 1864, 1889.
    The Age: A Colloquial Satire. 1858.
    Universal Hymn. 1867.
    Nottingham Castle: An Ode. 1878.
    Causa Britannica. 1883.

Other

    The International Policy of the Great Powers 1861.

Reading List: "A Victorian Faust" by Alan D. McKillop, in *Publications of the Modern Language Association,* 1925; "Bailey's Debt to Goethe's *Faust*" by G. A. Black, in *Modern Languages Review,* 1933; *The Victorian Temper* by J. H. Buckley, 1952; *Sunk Without Trace* by Robert Birley, 1962.

*   *   *

    Few works of literary art can have attracted so much favourable notice as Philip James Bailey's *Festus,* and then have sunk so low. When the work first appeared, in 1839, it was hailed as marking the emergence of a new, great poet, worthy to rank beside Wordsworth and Shelley. In 1845 a second, enlarged edition was called for, and critics began to claim that Bailey was Tennyson's superior. And this, it should be noted, though Tennyson's 1842 volume had brought him praise and fame. Tennyson himself allowed that *Festus* influenced him when he came to write *Maud.* Further editions of the poem, always enlarged, appeared during Bailey's lifetime, but the bubble burst during the mid-1850's, and by the time of his death Bailey was virtually forgotten. What can account for so odd an history?
    The answer is that *Festus* came at the right time. Young poets and literary men were on the look out for a poem which would carry forward the banner of the great Romantics; they wanted someone who could fulfil the role of poet as prophet and seer, fearless truthteller to the age, visionary and inspirer of the people. In *Festus,* Bailey claimed to be doing just this,

and his early readers took the will for the deed. Festus is a searcher after the truth, a Faust figure, and Bailey's hero undoubtedly owes something to Goethe. We need to recall that at this time Carlyle was trumpeting the greatness of Goethe to a growing audience, so that Goethe, together with Shelley, becomes a model to follow. In the 1839 version Festus is not a poet, although poetry is incidental to his quest for knowledge and truth. But in the 1845 version Festus *has* become identified with the poet as such. In the "Proem" to his work, Bailey claims that

> Poetry is itself a thing of God;
> He made his prophets poets: and the more
> We feel of poesie do we become
> Like God in love and power, – under-makers.
> All great lays, equals to the minds of men,
> Deal more or less with the Divine, and have
> For end some good of mind or soul of man.

The sentiments have an impeccable Romantic pedigree, but of course we are entitled to ask just *how* Bailey intends to substantiate his claims for poetry; and the fact is that he doesn't at all manage to do so. I have pointed out in *Literature and Politics in the Nineteenth Century* (1971) that "the poet is simply to be believed and belief is aided by a grand cloudiness." But such assertiveness could hardly expect to withstand close scrutiny. And as soon as W. E. Aytoun coined the word "Spasmodic" to describe the kind of poetry written by Bailey and his epigoni, Dobell, Alexander Smith, and Marston, and subjected that poetry to withering analysis, as he did in the mid-1850's, then *Festus* and its many imitations were bound to become spent forces.

It must, however, be said that Bailey had a genuine talent for spotting what the age demanded. And although he could not finally satisfy it, that is only partly his fault. For, after all, the demand that a poet be total man and truth teller is not really one that can, or perhaps ever should, be satisfied.

—John Lucas

BARBAULD, Anna (Laetitia, née Aikin). English. Born in Kibworth-Harcourt, Northamptonshire, 20 June 1743. Educated at her father's school in Kibworth, and at Warrington Academy, Lancashire. Married the Rev. Rochemont Barbauld in 1774 (died, 1808). With husband, kept a boarding school in Palgrave, Suffolk, 1774– 87. Lived in London after 1787. *Died 9 March 1825.*

PUBLICATIONS

Collections

A Memoir, Letters, and a Selection, by Grace A. Ellis.   2 vols., 1874.
Tales, Poems, and Essays.   1884.

47

Verse

> Corsica: An Ode.   1768.
> Poems.   1773; revised edition, 1792.
> Epistle to William Wilberforce.   1791.
> Eighteen Hundred and Eleven.   1812.

Other

> Miscellaneous Pieces in Prose, with John Aikin.   1773.
> Lessons for Children.   1778.
> Hymns in Prose for Children.   1781; revised edition, 1814.
> Civic Sermons to the People.   1792.
> Evenings at Home; or, The Juvenile Budget Opened, with John Aikin.   6 vols.,
>   1792–96.
> Remarks on Wakefield's Enquiry.   1792.
> Sins of Government, Sins of the Nation.   1793.
> Works.   2 vols., 1825.
> A Discourse on Being Born Again.   1830.
> Letters of Maria Edgeworth and Barbauld, edited by Walter Sidney Scott.   1953.

> Editor, Devotional Pieces from the Psalms and the Book of Job.   1775.
> Editor, The Pleasures of the Imagination, by Akenside.   1794.
> Editor, Poetical Works, by Collins.   1797.
> Editor, Selections from the Spectator, Tatler, Guardian, Freeholder.   3 vols., 1804.
> Editor, Correspondence of Samuel Richardson.   6 vols., 1804.
> Editor, The British Novelists.   50 vols., 1810.
> Editor, The Female Speaker.   1811.

Reading List: A Memoir of Mrs. Barbauld, Including Letters by Anna L. LeBreton, 1874;
Georgian Chronicle: Mrs. Barbauld and Her Family by Betsy Rodgers, 1958.

*   *   *

   Mrs. Barbauld remains a valuable writer if only because her work serves so well as a
compendium of late eighteenth-century taste. Her Poems are representative of the themes,
genres, and styles of late neoclassicism. Corsica, for example, is a meditative-descriptive
poem in blank verse which echoes Milton by way of Thomson and which espouses the rights
of man in the Corsica discovered by Boswell. Her two major satires, Epistle to William
Wilberforce and Eighteen Hundred and Eleven, are stately, declamatory, public rather than
personal, written in heroic couplets. Her couplets, like all her verses, are competent,
somewhat mechanical, yet pleasing, as these lines from Eighteen Hundred and Eleven
illustrate:

> And think'st thou, Britain, still to sit at ease,
> An island queen amidst thy subject seas,
> While the vext billows, in their distant war,
> But soothe thy slumbers, and but kiss thy shore?

As essayist, also, she followed eighteenth-century models, usually striving for the dignity and
grandeur of Johnson's balanced style, most often choosing serious subjects such as
"Education" and "Inconsistency in Our Expectations."
   But Mrs. Barbauld was more than a pale survivor of a fading culture. If she merited the

gibes of young Romantic poets, she also deserved the popular respect which lasted throughout her life. For she was a courageous woman who accepted the duty of writing for the radical dissent to which her family adhered. In political pamphlets, she wrote with tough vitality against the Corporation and Test Acts, against "Sins of Government, Sins of the Nation," or for the rights of common men in "Civic Sermons to the People." Generally free of neoclassic convention in these pamphlets, she is the plain-speaker as well as the voice of reason, the angry prophet as well as the patient teacher.

By temperament conventional, as a woman uneasy about being a published author, Mrs. Barbauld nonetheless ventured into new directions if the need were sufficient. She became a pioneer in juvenile literature because as a teacher she found no books suitable for children under six. Despite Charles Lamb's accusation that the "accursed band of Barbaulds" stifled imagination with "geography and natural history," she created in *Lessons for Children* and *Hymns in Prose for Children* a small world which still evokes the freshness and delight of a child's view of country life.

Similarly, when required to turn editor-critic for Samuel Richardson's *Correspondence* and for a collection of novels, *British Novelists*, Mrs. Barbauld wrote a group of essays which dealt seriously and perceptively with a genre not then entirely respectable, arguing always that "this species of composition is entitled to a higher rank than has generally been assigned to it."

No single work of Mrs. Barbauld's stands above the rest, except perhaps the charming *Hymns* with their rhythmical prose or, for an earlier generation, an ode entitled "Life." Rather, her importance is based upon the whole of her work: poems, essays, pamphlets, pieces for children, and critical prefaces. Taken as a whole, they not only reveal a gifted, highly intelligent, serious woman who was motivated to write by respect for reason and duty to an idealistic yet practical religion, Unitarian Christianity, but they also illuminate the literary and social milieu of that highly significant transitional period which her life spanned.

—Catherine E. Moore

BARBOUR, John. Scottish. Born near Aberdeen in 1316. May have studied at Oxford University and in Paris, and travelled extensively on the Continent. Took holy orders; Archdeacon of Aberdeen, 1357–95; also held office in the household of King Robert II: auditor of exchequer, 1372, 1382, 1384; clerk for the audit of the household, 1374; pensioned by the king, 1378. *Died 13 March 1395.*

PUBLICATIONS

Verse

  The Bruce, edited by J. Pinkerton. 3 vols., 1790.
  The Bruce, edited by W. W. Skeat. 4 vols., 1870–89.
  The Bruce, edited by W. M. Mackenzie. 1909.
  The Bruce: A Selection, edited by Alexander Kinghorn. 1960.
  The Bruce (translation), by A. A. H. Douglas. 1964.

Reading List: *The Wallace and the Bruce Restudied* by J. T. T. Brown, 1900; *Barbour, Poet and Translator* by George Neilson, 1900; *Die Nationale Literatur Schottlands* by Friedrich Brie, 1937.

*   *   *

John Barbour is the father of Scottish poetry, yet his *Bruce*, materially a chronological series of heroic narratives, derives from a native tradition of lays in the French octosyllabic couplet that is probably as old as the century of Malcolm Canmore and Macbeth. As in the lays the matter is factual, the treatment dramatic and spirited, but with a political perspective and descriptive fluency learned respectively from Scottish histories and French romances. He knew nothing of his English contemporary Chaucer.

Generally Barbour's subject is national and individual freedom – "Fredome is a noble thing,/It makis man to have liking,/He lives at ese that frely lives." His purpose is to illustrate the qualities of leadership that won freedom in the men that "deliverit thair land all free," King Robert and his captains Edward Bruce, James Douglas, Thomas Randolph, and lesser men. It is a national and not simply monarchic and aristocratic war that he delineates. He refers approvingly to Scipio's manumission in an emergency of the Roman slaves, for free men fight best for freedom, and makes a renegade Scots noble tell the English king that Scotland is invincible because its farmers and ploughmen fight as well as do its knights. He has the distinctively Scottish attitude to kingship: his hero-king is concerned for more than his feudal rights, he grieves for his people, is at home with men of all classes, greets personally each man as he comes for the fighting at Bannockburn. An effect of the author's nationalism is a very human realism that seeks to "schaw the thing richt as it wes." Thus romantic fiction is eschewed, and, though such terms as "chivalry" and "courtesy" are used, the former refers to achievements in war, "birnand, slayand and distroyand," and the latter is applied to incidents such as the king's halting his little army so that a laundress can have her baby in safety. Language is appropriately sober and simple as befits Barbour's view of his nation, "the few folk of ane symple land," and in this kind has the truly heroic manner:

> His worschip and his mekill mycht
> Maid all that war with him so wicht
> That thai mycht neuir abaysit be
> Quhill forouth thame thai mycht him se.

The "mesure" that shows in his style, emotive only at grand points, appears also in his differentiation of character, Bruce's wisdom and Douglas's "sutelte" being regularly contrasted with the alleged impulsiveness of Edward Bruce and Randolph. It has been said that Barbour's *Bruce* is more chronicle than poem, but the shaping conception is always apparent, and when the reader reaches the approving sentence, "Thir lordis dyit apon this wyis," he has been made aware of a great action worthily interpreted.

—Matthew P. McDiarmid

BARCLAY, Alexander. Scottish. Born, probably in Scotland, c. 1475. May have studied at Oxford and Cambridge universities. Travelled in Italy and France; took holy orders; Chaplain, College of Ottery St. Mary, Devon, c. 1508–11; became a monk of the Benedictine monastery at Ely, 1511, and later of the Franciscan order at Canterbury; Vicar, Great Baddow, Essex, 1546–52; Rector, All Hallows, London, 1552. *Died 10 June 1552.*

Publications

Collections

The Ship of Fools (includes *The Mirror of Good Manners* and *Eclogues*), edited by
Thomas H. Jamieson.   2 vols., 1874.

Verse

The Castle of Labour, from a work by Pierre Gringore.   1503; edited by A. W. Pollard,
1905.
The Ship of Fools of the World, from a work by Sebastian Brant.   1509.
The Life of Saint George.   1515; edited by William Nelson, 1955.
Eclogues 1–3.   1530; *Fourth Eclogue*, 1521; *Fifth Eclogue*, 1518; edited by Beatrice
White, 1928.
The Mirror of Good Manners, from a work by Dominicus Mancinus.   1523.

Other

The Life of the Blessed Martyr Saint Thomas.   1520.
The Introductory to Write and to Pronounce French.   1521; selections edited by
Alexander J. Ellis, in *On Early English Pronunciation*, 1871.
A Little Chronicle.   1525.

Translator, *The War Against Jugurtha*, by Sallust.   1520.

Bibliography: in *The Ship of Fools*, 1874.

Reading List: "Barclay: A Product of His Age" by S. Guttman, in *Papers of the Michigan Academy 35*, 1951; "Barclay and the Edwardian Reformation" by R. J. Lyall, in *Review of English Studies*, 1969.

*   *   *

To anyone expecting idyllic pastoral poetry in the tradition of Theocritus or Virgil the five *Eclogues* of Alexander Barclay must come as a decided shock. Instead of a golden world where shepherds, free from the curse of labour, can devote their time to love and song, we find a harsh, cruel rural environment, a land of storms, flood, bitter cold, hunger, and disease. The shepherds, typical English rustics despite their conventional Italianate names, can only complain about their wretched plight and take refuge in the thought that, however intolerable these physical discomforts may be, the moral pollution of the court or town is even worse.

This is the excuse, in Eclogues I, II, and III, for a lengthy diatribe against the corruptions of the court, consisting mainly of a translation of the *De Curialium Miseriis* of Aeneas Sylvius – clumsy when literal, but vigorous and homely when Barclay adapts the Latin original to his English context or adds local references ("Bentleyes ale which chaseth well the bloud," IV, 722). The satirical targets in the final two eclogues are rich men and town-dwellers, and the source here is largely Mantuan.

For all the rural realism of the pastoral framework, it is clear that Barclay's main interest is in the satire: he is fascinated by the idea of the court as an "ymage infernall,/Without fayre paynted, within uggly and vile" (I, 1260–1). This discrepancy between appearance and reality extends to the inhabitants – "oft under yelowe lockes/Be hid foule scabbes and fearfull French pockes" (I, 358–9); but worst of all is the instability of courtly life, the need to flatter, the backbiting, the informing, the capriciousness of princes – "No love, no favour, fayth not fidelitie" (I, 1005). In the face of this, who would not prefer the philosophy of stoic endurance that keeps the shepherds morally unscathed in their rural solitude?

It is worth noting that Barclay's shepherds adhere to the principal of stylistic decorum laid down in the Preface: "it were not fitting a heard or man rurall/To speake in termes gay and rhetoricall" (Prologue, 83–4). And Cornix and Coridon do indeed have at their disposal a fund of rough, colloquial speech which they deploy with gusto in describing, for example, the nocturnal inconveniences of a communal sleeping-chamber at court: "Some fart, some flingeth, and other snort and route./Some boke, and some bable, some commeth dronke to bed...Some spue, and some pisse, not one of them is still" (III, 106–110). Local references, proverbs, and rustic similes ("nimis tepidum" becomes "hote as horse pis," II, 632) all demonstrate Barclay's concern to transform the rather bald Latin of his originals into something more closely approximating the homely diction of English shepherds.

This typical combination of crude native speech in the service of satire extends to Barclay's other major work, The Ship of Fools, a translation of Locher's Latin version of the Narrenschiff by Sebastian Brant. This remarkable poem surveys the entire spectrum of late Mediaeval society and casts a satirical eye upon an enormous variety of human failings: lascivious women, decayed clergymen, obsessed bibliomaniacs, corrupt lawyers, avaricious doctors – all have their place reserved aboard the Ship of Fools, and the overall picture is one of the whole world rushing headlong to destruction in the grip of wilful vanity, stupidity, and ignorance. The tone of this complaint is perhaps sterner than that of the Eclogues – the voice of the preacher is more obviously to the fore: "Thus is this Covetous wretche so blyndly led/By the fend that here he lyveth wretchydly/And after his deth damned eternally" ("Of Avaryce," 19–21). Moreover, each section concludes with an explicitly didactic "envoy of Barklay to the Folys," usually recommending penance and self-control as a means of avoiding the "infernal pains" of hell.

But it is the vivid pictures of folly in action that remain with the reader: Barclay's homely vernacular can effortlessly bring to life characters such as the harlot, who "syttyth in the strete as past both shame and fere/Hir brestes bare to tempt them that pass by/Hir face anoyntyd blasynge abrode hir here" ("Of bodely pleasour," 15–17); or the victims of drunkenness, of whom "Some are Ape dronke full of lawghter and toyes/Some mery dronke syngynge with wynches and boyes/Some spue, some stacker some utterly ar lame ..." ("Of glotons," 111–113).

If The Ship of Fools, on account of its length and heavy didacticism, is unlikely to find much of an audience today, Barclay's Eclogues at least deserve our attention, not just because they represent the first set of eclogues written in English, but because in so many ways – their combination of pastoral and satirical elements, their adherence to stylistic decorum, their dry humour, their refusal to emulate the Arcadian escapism of the Continental eclogue – they anticipate a much greater work published more than sixty years later: it is impossible to determine whether Spenser actually read Barclay, but it is surely of considerable interest that the very qualities that have directed so much critical attention to The Shepheardes Calender are to be found in the humbler, less ambitious, but no less enjoyable Eclogues of Alexander Barclay.

—A. W. Lyle

BARHAM, Richard Harris. English. Born in Canterbury, Kent, 6 December 1788. Educated at St. Paul's School, London; Brasenose College, Oxford, 1807–10. Ordained priest,

1813; obtained the living of Snargate in Romney Marsh, 1817, and St. Mary Magdalene and St. Gregory, 1824–42; appointed priest-in-ordinary of the chapels royal, 1824; received minor canonry, St. Paul's Cathedral, London, 1821; Lecturer in Divinity at St. Paul's, 1842; Rector, St. Augustine, Watling Street, 1843–45. *Died 17 June 1845.*

PUBLICATIONS

Verse

> *Verses Spoken at St. Paul's School.* 1807.
> *The Ingoldsby Legends; or, Mirth and Marvels.* 3 vols., 1840–47 (vol. 3 edited by R. H. D. Barham); edited by D. C. Browning, 1960.
> *The Ingoldsby Lyrics,* edited by R. H. D. Barham. 1881.

Fiction

> *Baldwin; or, A Miser's Heir: A Serio-Comic Tale.* 1820.
> *Some Account of My Cousin Nicholas.* 1841.

Other

> *Personal Reminiscences by Barham, Harness, and Hodder,* edited by R. H. Stoddard. 1875.
> *The Garrick Club.* 1896.

Reading List: *The Life and Letters of Barham* by R. H. D. Barham, 2 vols., 1870; *A Concordance to The Ingoldsby Legends* by George W. Sealy, 1882; *Barham* by William G. Lane, 1968.

*   *   *

Richard Harris Barham is better known as Thomas Ingoldsby, pseudonymous author of *The Ingoldsby Legends,* published in three series, the last of them posthumously. A few of the legends (mainly in the first series) are in prose, but most of them are in verse. The legends embody a type of humour popular in the Victorian era. The starting point for their humour is the invention of the persona of Thomas Ingoldsby, Esquire, the scion of an ancient and prolific family, the heir to a traditionally haunted manor-house, Tappington Everard. The legends presented by Ingoldsby purport to stem from the "family memoranda" stored in an old oak chest, and their varying style is accounted for by their having been written by various of Ingoldsby's ancestors.

In truth the tales are humorous, but generally grotesque, stories, peppered with parodies and burlesques of other writers, chiefly, though not entirely, of Barham's near contemporaries. On the surface the world of Ingoldsby is one of nightmare horror, of violence and of mystery – ghosts and witches, hauntings and cursings, hangings, murders and suicides. All is told, however, with such verve and gaiety that the predominant emotion is not fear, but amusement. Sometimes the humorous side prevails entirely, a ghost turns out to be a somnambulist ("The Spectre of Tappington"); witches, the drunken imaginings of a lover disappointed of his tryst ("The Witches' Frolic"); a jewel thief, nothing but a frightened jackdaw ("The Jackdaw of Rheims"). When murder does, in fact, occur, it is recounted with a nonchalant humour that precludes any sense of horror, as, for instance, in "The Tragedy," when the heroine's husband murders her lover and her page:

> Catherine of Cleves   Roar'd "Murder!" and "Thieves!"
> From the window above   While they murder'd her love;
> Till, finding the rogues had accomplished his slaughter,
> She drank Prussic acid without any water,
> And died like a Duke-and-a-Duchess's daughter!

In lines such as these the romantic and heroic are mocked by the use of the inelegant word "Roar'd" and the lady's suicide is reduced to anti-climax by the cliché "without any water."

Barham was an accomplished story teller and had a gift for rollicking rhythms and absurd rhymes. Much of his humour has now become somewhat dated, but a number of his tales give pleasure to the modern reader, and his parodies, though not of the quality of those of the Smith brothers before him nor of Calverley after him, are skilful and amusing. He has a small but secure niche in the history of nineteenth-century light verse.

—Hilda D. Spear

BARKER, George (Granville). English. Born in Loughton, Essex, 26 February 1913. Educated at Marlborough Road School, Chelsea, London; Regent Street Polytechnic, London. Married Elspeth Langlands in 1964; has several children. Lived in the United States, 1940–43, and in Rome, 1960–65. Professor of English Literature, Imperial Tohoku University, Sendai, Japan, 1939–41; Visiting Professor, State University of New York at Buffalo, 1965–66; Arts Fellow, York University, 1966–67; Visiting Professor, University of Wisconsin, Madison, 1971–72, and Florida International University, 1974. Recipient: Royal Society of Literature bursary, 1950; Guinness Prize, 1962; Borestone Mountain Poetry Prize, 1967; Arts Council bursary, 1968. Lives in Norfolk.

PUBLICATIONS

Verse

Thirty Preliminary Poems. 1933.
Poems. 1935.
Calamiterror. 1937.
Elegy on Spain. 1939.
Lament and Triumph. 1940.
Selected Poems. 1941.
Sacred and Secular Elegies. 1943.
Eros in Dogma. 1944.
Love Poems. 1947.
The True Confession of George Barker. 1950; augmented edition. 1964.
News of the World. 1950.
A Vision of Beasts and Gods. 1954.

Collected Poems, 1930–1955.   1957.
The View from a Blind I.   1962.
Collected Poems 1930–1965.   1965.
Dreams of a Summer Night.   1966.
The Golden Chains.   1968.
At Thurgarton Church.   1969.
Runes and Rhymes and Tunes and Chimes (for children).   1969.
To Aylsham Fair (for children).   1970.
The Alphabetical Zoo (for children).   1970.
Poems of Places and People.   1971.
III Hallucination Poems.   1972.
In Memory of David Archer.   1973.
Dialogues etc.   1976.

Plays

Two Plays (includes *The Seraphina* and *In the Shade of the Old Apple Tree*).   1958.

Radio Plays: *The Seraphina,* 1956; *Oriel O'Hanlon* (published as *In the Shade of the Old Apple Tree*), 1957.

Fiction

Alanna Autumnal.   1933.
Janus (includes *The Documents of Death* and *The Bacchant*).   1935.
The Dead Seagull.   1950.

Other

Essays.   1970.

Editor, *Idylls of the King and a Selection of Poems,* by Tennyson.   1961.

Reading List: *Barker* by Martha Fodaski, 1969; *Homage to Barker on His 60th Birthday* edited by John Heath-Stubbs and Martin Green, 1973.

*   *   *

In the 1930's, critics had tended to think of the young George Barker as ranking, in his vivid and bewildering use of images, with Dylan Thomas and, in his awareness of the destructive effect of social privation ("It was hard cash I needed at my roots"), with Auden and what was sometimes called Auden's "school." Nobody compared him, as in his off-hand vividness he might have been compared, with Louis MacNeice. As he grew older, it became harder to range him with anybody else, and by the 1950's he was in a sense a very isolated writer, critically speaking. The 1950's saw the publication of his most personal long poem, *The True Confession of George Barker,* a poem both blasphemous and obscene in a Villonesque way, and yet, like Villon's poems, obviously the work of a born Roman Catholic. He had become the last *poète maudit,* the last conscious bohemian. In fact, when Faber, his publishers, brought out his *Collected Poems, 1930–1955,* they left out the poem, against his wishes.

By 1973, on his sixtieth birthday, that omission was generally ignored, but the event brought forth a very distinguished *festschrift*, many of the contributors to which were either unknown to or not on speaking terms with each other; but they were all united in admiration of a desperately honest and unduly neglected poet. Barker has puzzled critics because he combines a comic wit and a polished impropriety with a lyrical simplicity and an ability to express the inner agony of the obdurate Catholic sinner. All these themes can be found in the contortedly powerful prose of his partly autobiographical novel, *The Dead Seagull*. Barker is technically a very uneven poet, his feelings too often at the mercy of a facile rhetoric, but his best work will last.

—G. S. Fraser

BARLOW, Joel. American. Born in Reading, Connecticut, 24 March 1754. Educated at Moor's School, Hanover, New Hampshire; Dartmouth College, Hanover; Yale University, New Haven, Connecticut, 1774–78, B.A. 1778; admitted to the Bar, 1786. Served as a Chaplain with the Massachusetts Brigade, 1780 until the end of the Revolutionary War. Married Ruth Baldwin in 1781. Practiced law after the Revolution, also taught school and was proprietor of a bookshop in Hartford, Connecticut; Founding Editor, with Elisha Babcock, *American Mercury*, 1784; lived in Europe, 1788–1805; European Agent for the Scioto Company, 1788–89; proprietor of La Compagnie du Scioto, 1789; lived in London, a friend of Thomas Paine, 1790–92, and in Paris from 1792; became involved in French radical politics; also served as American Consul in Algiers, 1795; lived in America, at his home Kalorama, near Washington, 1805–11; American Ambassador to France, 1811–12. *Died 24 December 1812.*

PUBLICATIONS

Verse

> *The Prospect of Peace.* 1778.
> *A Poem.* 1781.
> *An Elegy of the Late Titus Hosmer.* 1782.
> *The Vision of Columbus.* 1787; revised edition, as *The Columbiad*, 1807.
> *The Conspiracy of Kings.* 1792.
> *The Hasty-Pudding.* 1796.
> *Doctor Watts's Imitations of the Psalms of David, Corrected and Enlarged.* 1785; supplement, 1785.
> *The Anarchiad: A New England Poem*, with others, edited by Luther G. Riggs. 1861.

Other

> *Advice to the Privileged Orders in the Several States of Europe.* 2 vols., 1792–93.

A Letter to the National Convention of France.   1793(?).
The History of England, 1765–95.   5 vols., 1795.
The Political Writings.   1796.
A Letter to the People of Piedmont.   1798.
To His Fellow Citizens.   2 vols., 1799–1800.

Editor, *M'Fingal: A Modern Epic Poem,* by John Trumbull.   1792.

Translator, *New Travels in the United States of America in 1788,* by J. P. Brissot de
   Warville.   1792; revised edition, 1794.
Translator, *The Commerce of America with Europe,* by J. P. Brissot de Warville.   1794.
Translator, with Thomas Jefferson, *Volney's Ruins; or, Meditations on the Revolution of
   Empires.*   2 vols., 1802.

Reading List: *Life and Letters of Barlow* by Charles Burr Todd, 1886; *The Early Days of
Barlow, A Connecticut Wit: His Life and Works from 1754 to 1787* by Theodore Albert
Zunder, 1934 (includes bibliography); *The Connecticut Wits* by Leon Howard, 1943 (includes
bibliography); *A Yankee's Odyssey: The Life of Barlow* by James Woodress, 1958; *Barlow* by
Arthur L. Ford, 1971.

                              *   *   *

Although Joel Barlow had hoped to be remembered as an epic poet, only one mock-epic
poem and a short bitter piece of satiric verse give him what enduring interest he has as a poet.
At the same time, however, he holds a secure place as a political pamphleteer in the early
national period and as a minor figure in American history. He is a character of considerable
interest, for his life touches many of the significant historical events between the Revolution
and the War of 1812, and he stands as a representative figure of the American
Enlightenment.

Going from a Connecticut farm to Yale on the eve of the Revolution, Barlow versified his
way through college, and, after serving as a chaplain in Washington's army, he set about
writing his epic, *The Vision of Columbus,* a poem in nine books of heroic couplets celebrating
the history of America, past, present, and future. The poem was a considerable success in its
day, but it seems unreadable in the 20th century. Twenty years later Barlow brought out an
expanded and revised version that he called *The Columbiad.* It appeared as a large quarto,
leather bound and handsomely illustrated, the most beautiful book yet produced in America –
but still unreadable.

The Hasty-Pudding, on the other hand, is a delightful piece of mock-heroic verse
occasioned by Barlow's visit to Savoy in 1793 when he was running unsuccessfully for the
French National Assembly. It was inspired by his being served a dish of corn meal mush
(polenta, hasty pudding), which reminded him of his Connecticut boyhood. This poem has
been reprinted many times and is often anthologized. The other notable piece of verse,
"Advice to a Raven in Russia," was occasioned by Barlow's sharp reaction to Napoleon's
campaign in Russia in 1812. It was written in the last month of Barlow's life when he had
gone to Vilna as American Minister to France in an effort to negotiate a treaty with Napoleon.
To a Jeffersonian American the slaughter and carnage all about him evoked bitter criticism,
and in a sense Barlow himself some days later was one of Napoleon's victims, for he caught
pneumonia on the precipitous return to Paris from Lithuania after Napoleon's debacle.

During the years that Barlow was living in Europe (1788 to 1805), he plunged into political
controversy. His tract *Advice to the Privileged Orders* was one of the important answers to
Burke's *Reflections on the Revolution in France,* and it was proscribed in England, along with
Paine's *The Rights of Man.* He also wrote political polemics in support of France and the
Jeffersonians during the contentious days of Adams Administration, and as a result made
himself unpopular with the conservative Federalists he had grown up with in Connecticut. Of

all that group of writers known as The Connecticut Wits, who flourished in and about Hartford after the Revolution, Barlow was the only one who became a political liberal.

—James Woodress

BARNES, Barnabe. English. Born in Yorkshire c. 1569. Educated at Brasenose College, Oxford, 1586. A volunteer in the expedition led by the Earl of Essex to Dieppe, to assist Henry IV, 1591. *Died in December 1609.*

PUBLICATIONS

Collections

   Poems, edited by Alexander B. Grosart.   1875.

Verse

   Parthenophil and Parthenophe: Sonnets, Madrigals, Elegies, and Odes.   1593; edited by
      Victor A. Doyno, 1971.
   A Divine Century of Spiritual Sonnets.   1595.

Play

   The Devil's Charter (produced 1607).   1607; edited by J. H. Farmer, 1913.

Other

   Four Books of Offices Enabling Private Persons for the Service of Princes.   1606.

Reading List: *Lyric Forms in the Sonnet Sequences of Barnes* by Philip E. Blank, Jr., 1974.

*   *   *

The unifying characteristics of Barnabe Barnes's life and work are consistent extravagance and artfulness. His earliest publication, *Parthenophil and Parthenophe* (Virgin-Lover and Virgin), was intended to be anonymous, but the sole surviving copy has an insertion which identifies the author. The volume presents a wide variety of types of poems: sonnets, elegies, odes, madrigals, and sestinas. The volume narrates a love affair; several poems, such as Sonnet 66 and Elegies 4 and 5, have a pleasing combination of a life-like tone and a clever wit. The story sequence has an unusual solution to the conventional woes of the Petrarchan lover: in the last major poem the lover casts a magical spell upon the mistress and rapes her. This extraordinary conclusion is rendered in a triple sestina which is, in part, a translation

58

and transformation of poems by Theocritus and Virgil. The volume represents the Renaissance ability to emphasize the human while absorbing and transforming earlier culture; the poems include translations from many Classical and Renaissance poets. The discriminating reader will find this major work of a minor writer to be both an example of growth of prosodic control and a significantly different treatment of a tradition, combining Petrarchan idealism and classical eroticism.

The wit and rhetorical flourish of the secular love poems are duplicated, but the object of adoration is different, in *A Divine Centurie of Spiritual Sonnets*, Barnes's collection of devotional verse. The volume offers a combination of the rhetorical method of poetic development with the meditative habit of mind. The tone of worship is effectively rendered.

Barnes's achievement also includes several non-poetic pieces. *Four Bookes of Offices* is a conduct book. The text is developed in terms of the classical virtues. It includes extensive translations or paraphrases and personal remarks, such as Barnes's complimentary thoughts about the executed rebel Essex. Barnes's final work is in yet another genre. *The Divils Charter* is a melodramatic complicated revenge play. Barnes represents, in a minor key, the variety of achievement which typifies an Elizabethan man of letters.

—Victor A. Doyno

———————

BARNES, William. English. Born at Rushay, near Sturminster Newton, Dorset, 22 February 1801. Educated at the Church School, Sturminster Newton, to age 13; St. John's College, Cambridge, B.D. 1850. Married Julia Miles in 1827 (died, 1852); four daughters, two sons. Clerk to the solicitors Mr. Dashwood, 1814–17, and Mr. George Score, 1817, in Sturminster Newton; Engrossing Clerk, Thomas Coombs and Son, Dorchester, 1818–23. Schoolmaster, Mere, Wiltshire, 1823–25, and Dorchester after 1835. Ordained a deacon, 1847; Curate of Whitcombe, Dorset, 1847–62; Rector, Winterborne Came, Dorset, 1862–86. Also an artist: engraver in metal and wood, and water colour painter. A Founder, 1845, and Honorary Secretary, 1845–58, Dorchester County Museum; Co-Founder, Institution for Adult Education, Dorchester, 1850. Granted Civil List pension, 1861. *Died 7 October 1886.*

PUBLICATIONS

Collections

    Poems, edited by Bernard Jones. 1962.
    A Selection, edited by Robert Nye. 1972.

Verse

    Poetical Pieces. 1820.
    Orra: A Lapland Tale. 1822.
    Poems of Rural Life in the Dorset Dialect. 1844; revised edition, 1847; *Hwomely Rhymes: A Second Collection,* 1859; *Third Collection,* 1862; collected edition 1879.
    Poems Partly of Rural Life in National English. 1846.

The Songs of Solomon in the Dorset Dialect. 1859.
Poems of Rural Life in Common English. 1868.
A Selection of Unpublished Poems. 1870.

Plays

The Honest Thief (produced 1831).
The Blastings of Revenge; or, Justice for the Just (produced 1831).
Ruth. 1881.

Other

Etymological Glossary. 1829.
A Catechism of Government. 1833.
The Mnemonic Manual. 1833.
A Few Words on Mathematics as a Branch of Education. 1834.
A Mathematical Investigation of the Principle of Hanging Doors. 1835.
An Arithmetical and Commercial Dictionary. 1840.
An Investigation of the Laws of Case in Language. 1840.
A Pronouncing Dictionary of Geographical Names. 1841.
The Elements of English Grammar. 1842.
The Elements of Linear Perspective. 1842.
Exercises in Practical Science. 1844.
Outlines of Geography and Ethnography. 1847.
Se Gefylsta (The Helper): An Anglo-Saxon Delectus. 1849.
Humilus Domus: Some Thoughts on the Abodes, Life, and Social Conditions of the
   Poor. 1849.
A Philological Grammar. 1854.
A Guide to Dorchester and Its Neighbourhood. 1857(?).
Notes on Ancient Britain and the Britons. 1858.
Views of Labour and Gold. 1859.
Tiw; or, A View of the Roots and Stems of English as a Teutonic Tongue. 1862.
A Grammar and Glossary of the Dorset Dialect. 1863.
Early England and the Saxon English. 1869.
An Outline of English Speech-Craft. 1878.
An Outline of Rede-Craft (Logic) with English Wording. 1880.
A Glossary of the Dorset Dialect, with a Grammar of Its Word Sharpening and
   Wording. 1886.
A Fadge of Barnes: Pieces Contributed to The Hawk 1867, edited by J. Stevens
   Cox. 1956.

Editor, *A Glossary of the Old Dialect of the English Colony in County Wexford,* by Jacob
   Poole. 1867.

Reading List: *The Life of Barnes* by Lucy Barnes Baxter, 1887; *Barnes, Linguist* by W. D.
Jacobs, 1952; *Barnes of Dorset* by Giles Dugdale, 1953; *Barnes, The Man and the Poems* by
W. T. Levy, 1960; *Barnes* by Trevor W. Hearle, 1966.

*   *   *

Probably every English county can provide a poet who wrote verses in the local dialect,
and who enjoyed a certain local reputation. William Barnes stands out from among these

minor figures in being a true and highly original poet in his own right. Nor is he to be regarded as merely a provincial poet, even though his subject matter is drawn almost exclusively from his Dorset background. He is in the main stream of poetic development, since his work was admired by and influenced the two most forward-looking poets of the late nineteenth century, Hopkins and Hardy.

Barnes was a prodigious scholar. His prose writings include studies in mathematics, astronomy, geography, ethnography, archaeology, and sociology as well as philology. Besides the classical languages, Barnes learnt Italian, and made translations from Petrarch and Metastasio. He later acquired Persian, Hindustani, Welsh, and Hebrew. Nor were his studies purely academic, since he possessed a strong social conscience. In his *Views of Labour and Gold* he stood against the economic system of his time, stressing the Church's traditional condemnation of usury.

As a philologist Barnes regarded his native Dorset dialect as a purer form of the language than what he called National or Book English. He advocated the elimination of Latin or Greek origin, and the substitution of new coinages of Anglo-Saxon provenance – e.g. "redcraft" for logic, "rimecraft" for arithmetic, "mindsight" for imagination, and even "folk wain" for omnibus. These may seem like eccentricities, but were really part of a wider movement in nineteenth-century stylistic theory, with which the scholar F. J. Furnivall was also associated, and which is reflected in the practice of such writers as Hopkins and Doughty.

Barnes' two series of poems of rural life in the Dorset dialect are, within the limits the author set himself, much more varied than one might suppose. As well as lyrical and descriptive pieces, they include, especially among the Eclogues, some lively and humorous depictions of rural manners. Metrically they are extremely skilful, Barnes sometimes employing devices, such as internal rhyming, derived from his Persian and Welsh studies. There is deep feeling in such a poem as "The Wife A-lost." This, together with "Linden Lea" (well known from its setting as a song by Vaughan Williams) are probably the most widely current of Barnes' poems, but there are many others equally fine. When writing in National English, or when persuaded to translate his Dorset poems into it, he was less successful.

—John Heath-Stubbs

BARNFIELD, Richard. English. Born in Norbury, Shropshire, baptized 13 June 1574. Educated at Brasenose College, Oxford, 1589–92, B.A. 1592. Country gentleman: settled at Darlaston, Staffordshire. *Died 6 March 1627.*

PUBLICATIONS

Collections

Poems 1594–1598, edited by Edward Arber. 1882.
Poems, edited by Montague Summers. 1936.

Verse

The Affectionate Shepherd, Containing the Complaint of Daphnis for the Love of Ganymede. 1594.

Cynthia, with Certain Sonnets and The Legend of Cassandra.   1595.
The Encomium of Lady Pecunia, The Complaint of Poetry for the Death of Liberality, The
   Combat Between Conscience and Covetousness, Poems in Divers Humours.   1598;
   revised edition, 1605.

Reading List: *Barnfield, Colin's Child* by Harry Morris, 1963.

*   *   *

Richard Barnfield demonstrated at an early age that he was capable of emulating the styles
of England's most skillful poets, but the curious variety in his three slim volumes attests to
the difficulty he encountered in developing his art. About a year after he came to London
with a B.A. from Oxford he published his first volume, *The Affectionate Shepherd*. Its most
ambitious piece is its title poem, a two-part complaint in which an aging Daphnis bemoans
the absence of his youthful Ganymede (a situation derived from Virgil's second Eclogue).
Possibly the poet hoped to exploit the popularity of Shakespeare's *Venus and Adonis* (1593) or
to invite comparison with it, for Barnfield's poem is cast in the same stanza form and imitates
its diction and imagery:

> His Ivory-white and Alabaster skin
> Is staind throughout with rare Vermillion red,
> Whose twinckling starrie lights do never blin
> To shine on lovely Venus (Beauties bed:)
>   But as the Lillie and the blushing Rose,
>   So white and red on him in order growes.

Despite Barnfield's success with Shakespeare's style, the poem is encumbered with narrative
inconsistencies, a recurring fault in Barnfield's longer poems. The remainder of the volume is
made up of diverse matter indeed: a pastoral poem celebrating the contentment of rustic life;
a sonnet which attempts to be an envoy to the first two pieces; a confusing harangue entitled
"The Complaint of Chastity"; and "Helen's Rape," an amusing piece of nonsense, sometimes
brilliant, satirizing by implication the hexameters it is written in:

> Happie Helen, Woman's most woonder, beautiful Helen.
> Oh would God (quod he) with a flattering tongue he repeated:
> Oh would God (quod he) that I might deserve to be husband
> To such a happy huswife, to such a beautiful Helen.

Although there are some happy moments in *The Affectionate Shepherd*, one senses the truth
of Harry Morris's observation: Barnfield pasted poems together to complete a first volume.

   In a preface to his second volume, *Cynthia, with Certain Sonnets and The Legend of
Cassandra*, Barnfield announces that his title poem, a paean to Elizabeth, is "the first
imitation of the verse of that excellent Poet, Maister Spenser, in his Faerie Queene." Since the
poem's situation is taken from Peele's *The Arraignment of Paris*, little room exists for
originality; nonetheless the narrative is well-structured, the verses highly accomplished.
Following "Cynthia" Ganymede returns as the object of praise in twenty sonnets, most of
which are better than competent. In the most imposing work in this volume, "The Legend of
Cassandra," Barnfield takes up the Ovidian-Mythological genre, elements of which had
informed his earlier pastoral laments, but, as in those pastorals, Barnfield's inability or lack of
concern to keep his narrative free from extraneous elements (such as several stanzas late in
the poem in praise of Cassandra's chastity when initially she is portrayed as treacherous)
mars his characterization and muddles the poem's effect.

   In his third volume Barnfield tries his hand at lightly ironic verse satire ("The Encomium
to Lady Pecunia"), a pastoral elegy for an unusual "personage" ("The Complaint of Poetry,

for the Death of Liberality"), and a debate poem ("The Combat Between Conscience and Covetessnesse"). Included in the volume are eight "Poems: in Divers Humors," two of which were printed in *The Passionate Pilgrim* and attributed to Shakespeare ("If music and sweet poetry agree"; "As it fell upon a day/In the merry month of May"). It is a workmanlike volume, the longer poems showing none of the structural deficiencies of those in his earlier volumes, but lacking their occasional brilliance. Some of the "Poems: in Divers Humors," as do the sonnets to Ganymede, suggest that the abilities of this talented young poet, whose literary career lasted only four years, were best employed upon the short forms.

—Frank Fabry

BAUGHAN, Blanche (Edith). New Zealander. Born in Putney, London, in 1870; emigrated to New Zealand, 1900. Educated at Brighton High School, Sussex; Royal Holloway College, University of London, B.A. Social worker, prominent in penal reform: Honorary Secretary, and Vice-President, 1928, Howard League for Penal Reform. *Died in August 1958.*

PUBLICATIONS

Verse

> *Verses.* 1898.
> *Reuben and Other Poems.* 1903.
> *Shingle-Short and Other Verses.* 1908.
> *Hope.* 1916(?).
> *Poems from the Port Hills.* 1923.

Other

> *The Finest Walk in the World* (on the Milford Track). 1909; revised edition, 1926.
> *Snow Kings of the Southern Alps.* 1910.
> *Uncanny Country: The Thermal Country of New Zealand.* 1911.
> *Brown Bread from a Colonial Oven, Being Sketches of Up-Country Life in New Zealand.* 1912.
> *Forest and Ice.* 1913.
> *A River of Pictures and Peace* (on Wanganui River). 1913.
> *The Summit Road: Its Scenery, Botany, and Geology,* with Leonard Cockayne and Robert Speight. 1914.
> *Studies in New Zealand Scenery.* 1916; revised edition, as *Glimpses of New Zealand Scenery,* 1922.
> *Akaroa.* 1919.
> *Arthur's Pass and Otira Gorge.* 1925.
> *Mt. Egmont.* 1929.
> *People in Prison,* with F. A. de la Mare. 1936.

* * *

Blanche Baughan's essential writing is in *Reuben and Other Poems, Shingle-Short and Other Verses*, and her by no means negligible prose sketches (rather of people, like her verse, than places) *Brown Bread from a Colonial Oven*. Her "gift" died after illness in 1910 – "I did not desert it, it deserted me." Through nearly six decades following she became a pioneer of prison reform and was involved with Indian thought. Of one anthologised poem in *Shingle-Short*, New Zealand's leading poet, an uncompromising critic, Allen Curnow, writes: "But nothing about this time compares with Blanche Baughan's 'A Bush Section,' written within a few years of her arrival in 1900. No earlier New Zealand poem exhibits such unabashed truth to its subject....It is the best New Zealand poem before Mason and how different in kind!" Here is its "burned-off" landscape:

> ... the opposite rampart of ridges
> Bristles against the sky, all the tawny, tumultuous landscape
> Is stuck, and prickled, and spiked with standing black and grey splinters....

Its child protagonist is: "Here, to this rough and raw prospect, these black-blocks of Being assign'd –" and so:

> Standing, small and alone:
> Bright Promise on Poverty's threshold!
> What art thou? Where hast thou come from?
> How far, how far! wilt thou go?

"Reuben" masters Wordsworthian blank verse and Crabbe-like realism; other poems in that book echo, say, Christina Rossetti or are increasingly colloquial ("The Old Place"); some use cantering dactyls and fourteeners reminiscent of Australiana.

With some unevenness *Shingle-Short* shows her full strength. The title character is mentally handicapped; outcasts and isolates (compare Patrick White's *The Burnt Ones*) recur; yet (as in *Brown Bread*) a dominant theme is the prevailing colonial work ethic. Her chief mode is dramatic monologue; tone, language, topics are for the most part sophisticatedly demotic; generally these pages may recall Browning, the Christina Rossetti of "Goblin Market," or numerous analogues in comparable North America, say, Lanier or James Whitcomb Riley (as *Brown Bread* may suggest Sarah Orne Jewett). "Maui's Fish" is a stunning free verse rendering of that legend. "The Paddock" is a long "cantata" in many styles and voices, a patch-work quilt most authentically colonial (her titles are revealing!) on colonial dilemmas of youth and age and place; a Maori component is, again, in rhetorical free verse; there are passages of brilliance in this unjustly neglected work.

In *Brown Bread* a "foreigner" expostulates: "Oh you live so bad, you do live so bad!" Our author comments: "Art comes at all times scantly to the back-blocks; and with what hope can Literature appeal to brains exhausted already by the exhaustion of the body?" Miss Baughan's contemporaries – Satchell in fiction, Jessie Mackay in poetry – lack either her single-minded *esthetic* commitment or ability, yet she has been "out of step" both with her own and later generations. In breadth and consistency of technical achievement, and in themes and strategies alike, Miss Baughan both far surpasses her predecessors and has no peer until the generations of R. A. K. Mason and Robin Hyde. The new ground on which she stands is precisely that where Maui's envious elders slither and fall, the ground, slippery and changing, of truth to emergent New Zealand consciousness.

—Peter Alcock

BAXTER, James K(eir).   New Zealander.   Born in Dunedin, 29 June 1926; son of the writer Archibald Baxter. Educated at Quaker schools in New Zealand and England; Otago University, Dunedin; Victoria University, Wellington, B.A. 1952. Married Jacqueline Sturm in 1948; two children. Worked as a labourer, journalist, and school-teacher. Editor, *Numbers* magazine, Wellington, 1954–60. Spent 5 months in India studying school publications, 1958; started commune in Jerusalem (a Maori community on the Wanganui River), 1969. Recipient: Unesco grant, 1958; Robert Burns Fellowship, Otago University, 1966, 1967. *Died 22 October 1972.*

PUBLICATIONS

Verse

Beyond the Palisade: Poems.   1944.
Blow, Wind of Fruitfulness.   1948.
Hart Crane.   1948.
Rapunzel: A Fantasia for Six Voices.   1948.
Charm for Hilary.   1949.
Poems Unpleasant, with Louis Johnson and Anton Vogt.   1952.
The Fallen House: Poems.   1953.
Lament for Barney Flanagan.   1954.
Traveller's Litany.   1955.
The Night Shift: Poems of Aspects of Love, with others.   1957.
The Iron Breadboard: Studies in New Zealand Writing (verse parodies).   1957.
In Fires of No Return: Poems.   1958.
Chosen Poems, 1958.   1958.
Ballad of Calvary Street.   1960.
Howrah Bridge and Other Poems.   1961.
Poems.   1964.
Pig Island Letters.   1966.
A Death Song for M. Mouldybroke.   1967.
A Small Ode on Mixed Flatting: Elicited by the Decision of the Otago University
    Authorities to Forbid This Practice among Students.   1967.
The Lion Skin: Poems.   1967.
A Bucket of Blood for a Dollar: A Conversation Between Uncle Sam and the Rt. Hon.
    Keith Holyoake, Prime Minister of New Zealand.   1968.
The Rock Woman: Selected Poems.   1969.
Ballad of the Stonegut Sugar Works.   1969.
Jerusalem Sonnets: Poems for Colin Durning.   1970.
The Junkies and the Fuzz.   1970.
Jerusalem Daybook (poetry and prose journal).   1971.
Jerusalem Blues (2).   1971.
Autumn Testament (poetry and prose journal).   1972.
Four God Songs.   1972.
Letter to Peter Olds.   1972.
Runes.   1973.
The Labyrinth: Some Uncollected Poems, 1944–1972.   1974.
The Bone Chanter: Unpublished Poems 1945–1972.   1977.
The Holy Life and Death of Concrete Grady: Various Uncollected and Unpublished
    Poems, edited by J. E. Weir.   1977.

Plays

> *Jack Winter's Dream* (broadcast 1958). In *The Wide Open Cage and Jack Winter's Dream*, 1959.
> *The Wide Open Cage* (produced 1959). In *The Wide Open Cage and Jack Winter's Dream*, 1959.
> *The Wide Open Cage and Jack Winter's Dream: Two Plays.* 1959.
> *The Spots of the Leopard* (produced 1963).
> *The Band Rotunda* (produced 1967). In *The Devil and Mr. Mulcahy and The Band Rotunda*, 1971.
> *The Sore-Footed Man*, based on *Philoctetes* by Euripides (produced 1967). In *The Sore-Footed Man and The Temptations of Oedipus*, 1971.
> *The Bureaucrat* (produced 1967).
> *The Devil and Mr. Mulcahy* (produced 1967). In *The Devil and Mr. Mulcahy and The Band Rotunda*, 1971.
> *Mr. O'Dwyer's Dancing Party* (produced 1968).
> *The Day Flanagan Died* (produced 1969).
> *The Temptations of Oedipus* (produced 1970). In *The Sore-Footed Man and The Temptations of Oedipus*, 1971.
> *The Devil and Mr Mulcahy and The Band Rotunda.* 1971.
> *The Sore-Footed Man and The Temptations of Oedipus.* 1971.

Radio Play: *Jack Winter's Dream*, 1958.

Other

> *Recent Trends in New Zealand Poetry.* 1951.
> *The Fire and the Anvil: Notes on Modern Poetry.* 1955; revised edition, 1960.
> *Oil* (primary school bulletin). 1957.
> *The Coaster* (primary school bulletin). 1959.
> *The Trawler* (primary school bulletin). 1961.
> *New Zealand in Colour*, photographs by Kenneth and Jean Bigwood. 1961.
> *The Old Earth Closet: A Tribute to Regional Poetry.* 1965.
> *Aspects of Poetry in New Zealand.* 1967.
> *The Man on the Horse* (lectures). 1967.
> *The Flowering Cross: Pastoral Articles.* 1969.
> *The Six Faces of Love: Lenten Lectures.* 1972.
> *A Walking Stick for an Old Man.* 1972.

Reading List: *The Poetry of Baxter* by J. E. Weir, 1970; *Baxter* by Charles Doyle, 1976; *Baxter* by Vincent O'Sullivan, 1976.

* * *

At his best one of the finest English-language poets of the past thirty years, James K. Baxter is the one New Zealand poet of undeniable international reputation. Although he died in his mid-forties, his literary career lasted for over thirty years. Its fruits were many volumes of poems, a number of plays, works of literary commentary or criticism, essays on religious topics, and a small amount of fiction (he was a fine exponent of the parable).

With publication of his first book, *Beyond the Palisade*, when he was eighteen, Baxter at once became a figure of note in New Zealand letters. Within a few years, he already occupied a central position in the literary scene, so that his booklet, *Recent Trends in New Zealand Poetry*, a beautifully condensed commentary, was from the first accepted as authoritative.

Alongside his literary reputation, Baxter quickly began to build one as a maverick and a bohemian. When, late in the 1940's, he moved to Wellington and began his long friendship and collaboration with Louis Johnson, they became the focus of the "romantic" element in New Zealand writing, which found its centre in Wellington for the next dozen years or so.

Throughout the 1950's Baxter produced a prolific variety of poems, plays, stories, and criticism, work which ranged from makeshift to brilliant. With Johnson and Charles Doyle (and, latterly, others) he edited the characteristically erratic periodical *Numbers*, then the only alternative to the few "establishment" periodicals such as *Landfall*.

1958 was a crucial moment in Baxter's career. Until then, his adult life had been a strange compound of Christian concern and rip-roaring bohemianism. That year he stayed for a long spell in the Trappist monastery at Kopua, Hawke's Bay, and was converted to Roman Catholicism. At the same time, his superb collection *In Fires of No Return* drew upon the work of his whole career to that point. *Howrah Bridge and Other Poems* followed in 1961 and was composed of new poems plus fine pieces ranging back to the 1940's; but Baxter's talent as a poet for a time seemed to lose focus. It was typical of Baxter that he made little or no effort to become known outside his own country; untypical as he was, he was very deeply a New Zealander, though anguished at his country's unspiritual puritanism.

After a low-energy period, Baxter's career gathered momentum again when he was awarded a Burns Fellowship at the University of Otago. Writing in the *Dominion* on 23 October 1965, Louis Johnson suggested that "the Burns scholarship may well mark a turning-point in his career" and this proved to be the case in remarkable ways. First, it produced what many consider to be Baxter's best verse collection, *Pig Island Letters*, a book in which he learned from, and transcended, the unlikely twin influences of Lawrence Durrell and Robert Lowell. Besides the critical-autobiographical pieces of *The Man on the Horse* and *Aspects of New Zealand Poetry*, those years in Dunedin witnessed the flowering of Baxter's career as a playwright. During 1967 and 1968, Patric Carey at the Globe Theatre produced seven Baxter plays, including all the most important. Although secondary to the poetry, those plays make it a reasonable claim that, besides being the country's foremost poet, Baxter is the most productive and interesting New Zealand playwright up to the present.

The Dunedin years also led him more deeply into religious and social concerns. After a period of catechetical work in the city, he went into solitude for some months at Jerusalem (Hiruharama), a tiny religious settlement on the Wanganui River. Later he founded a commune there for troubled youths and social drop-outs, and he was also the moving spirit in setting up doss-houses in both Auckland and Wellington. These ventures, pursued in a Franciscan spirit, including a vow of poverty, took much of his energy, but the commitment also carried over into his vocation as a poet and this period witnessed a further remarkable shift in the development of his writing, especially in the Jerusalem writings, *Jerusalem Sonnets*, *Jerusalem Daybook*, and *Autumn Testament*. He developed a very personal "sonnet" form, in fluid pentameter couplets, and, particularly in *Jerusalem Daybook*, made effective use of an amalgam of prose and verse. Baxter was also important in his community as a man. His best poems have a natural incandescence which partly derives from his being permeated from boyhood with the finest poetry of the British tradition, but which also comes from a human commitment based on religion. New Zealand is a relatively successful social welfare state, secular in spirit. Baxter, notably, brought to it a strong religious consciousness. A literary talent with a touch of genius was deepened and strengthened by the religious element in his character. That this did not escape the notice of his fellow-countrymen is evident from the crowds which thronged to his funeral and memorial services. Baxter's legacy to his country is a double one, a substantial amount of first-rate writing, especially poems, and the example of a man able to carry the spiritual life as far as it can go.

—Charles Doyle

BEATTIE, James. Scottish. Born in Laurencekirk, Kincardineshire, 25 October 1735. Educated at Marischal College, Aberdeen, 1749–53, M.A. 1753. Married Mary Dunn in 1767; two sons. Schoolmaster and Parish Clerk, Fardoun, near Laurencekirk, 1753–58; Master, Aberdeen Grammar School, 1758–60; Professor of Moral Philosophy and Logic, Marischal College, 1760–93, and lectured occasionally until 1797. LL.D.: Oxford University, 1770. Granted pension from the king, 1773. *Died 18 August 1803.*

PUBLICATIONS

Collections

　　Poetical Works, edited by Alexander Dyce.   1831.

Verse

　　Original Poems and Translations.   1760.
　　The Judgement of Paris.   1765.
　　Verses Occasioned by the Death of Charles Churchill.   1765.
　　Poems on Several Subjects.   1766.
　　The Minstrel; or, The Progress of Genius.   2 vols., 1771–74.
　　The Minstrel, with Some Other Poems.   1775; revised editon, 1799.
　　Poems on Several Occasions.   1776.

Other

　　An Essay on the Nature and Immutability of Truth.   1770.
　　Essays.   1776.
　　Scoticisms, Arranged in Alphabetical Order.   1779.
　　Dissertations Moral and Critical.   1783.
　　Evidences of the Christian Religion.   2 vols., 1786.
　　The Theory of Language.   1788.
　　Elements of Moral Science.   2 vols., 1790–93.
　　Some Unpublished Letters, edited by A. Mackie.   1908.
　　London Diary 1773, edited by Ralph S. Walker.   1946.
　　Day-Book 1773–98, edited by Ralph S.Walker.   1948.

　　Editor, *Poems,* by Gray.   1768.
　　Editor, *Essays and Fragments,* by James Hay Beattie.   1794.

Reading List: *An Account of the Life and Writings, Including Many Letters* by W. Forbes, 2 vols., 1806; *Beattie's Theory of Rhetoric* by V. M. Bevilacqua, 1967; *Beattie* by Everard H. King, 1978.

*　　*　　*

　　When James Beattie's name comes to mind today, it is less likely to be because of his poetry than for Dr. Johnson's remark: "We all love Beattie. Mrs. Thrale says if ever she has another husband she will have him." As a metaphysician, although hailed by the devout for his *Essay on Truth,* he failed to demolish Hume, whose scepticism his work was designed to combat. As a critic, he was taken in by the alleged genuineness of the verses of James "Ossian" Macpherson. As a Scottish man of letters, he was one of that to us now slightly absurd company who anxiously compiled and compared lists of Scoticisms which should be eradicated from their speech. However, when Christians in England excitedly hailed his attack on Hume, Beattie was offered, but refused, English clerical preferment. His lines "On the Proposed Monument to Churchill" do not spare a versifier whose antipathy to Scots and Scotland made him unloved north of the Border. An isolated Scots poem by Beattie in the epistle style — encouragement to his fellow poet in Scots, Alexander Ross, to keep writing — suggests that Beattie could have achieved work of substance in his native tongue had he been sure of his literary aims.

But he never was. For the most part, he modelled himself on his English contemporaries and produced the once-popular poem which traces the progress of the poet from a "rude age" to a period in which he could earn a loftier title. *The Minstrel*, widely hailed and much reprinted during the 18th century, purls along pleasantly, its nature painting still acceptable. Unfortunately, like most other later handlers of the Spenserian stanza, Beattie is apt to achieve an unintentional comic effect when applying the form to topics concerned with daily life.

A frequently anthologised stanza from *The Minstrel* give a flavour of Beattie's scene painting at its best:

> But who the melodies of morn can tell? —
>   The wild brook babbling down the mountain side;
> The lowing herd; the sheepfold's simple bell;
>   The pipe of early shepherd dim descried
>   In the lone valley; echoing far and wide,
> The clamorous horn along the cliffs above;
>   The hollow murmur of the ocean-tide;
> The hum of bees; the linnet's lay of love;
> And the full choir that wakes the universal grove.

—Maurice Lindsay

BEAUMONT, Sir John. English. Born, probably at Grace-Dieu, Leicestershire, in 1582; brother of the dramatist Francis Beaumont. Educated at Oxford University, 1596–98; Inner Temple, London. Married a lady of the Fortescue family; four sons. Succeeded to his father's estates, 1605; court career under the patronage of his relative, the Duke of Buckingham. Associated with Edmund Bolton in plans for a Royal Academy. Created Baronet, 1626. *Died 19 April 1627.*

PUBLICATIONS

Collections

Poems, edited by Alexander B. Grosart. 1869.
The Shorter Poems, edited by Roger D. Sell. 1974.

69

Verse

The Metamorphosis of Tobacco. 1602.
Bosworth Field, with a Taste of the Variety of Other Poems. 1629.

Play

The Theatre of Apollo (produced 1625). Edited by W. W. Greg, 1926.

Reading List: "Beaumont's 'The Crowne of Thornes': A Report" by Ruth Wallerstein in *Journal of English and Germanic Philology,* 1954.

*   *   *

Sir John Beaumont recommends, and himself illustrates, a style which Hobbes must later have admired: neither too prosaic, nor "dancing"; avoiding ostentatious roughness and Metaphysical obscurities; favouring the couplet, as involving little padding; emulating the Greeks and Romans only in

> Pure phrase, fit Epithets, a sober care
> Of Metaphors, descriptions cleare, yet rare,
> Similitudes contracted smooth and round,
> Not vext by learning, but with Nature crown'd;

and otherwise using normal contemporary English, with exactly referential statement rather than figurative elaboration. This style contributes a steady tempo and a certain matter-of-factness to, say, "Bosworth Field."

Less soberly, Beaumont can anticipate Waller. Many pieces addressed to James I, Charles I, and Buckingham are patently sycophantic and ornately artificial, recalling the imagery and paraphernalia of a court masque. And in "Bosworth Field" Henry VII, idealized as a forerunner of James I both in pedigree and as unifier of the realm, dreams a tableau-vision of his glorious descendant.

Again, whereas Ben Jonson reproved "Womens-*Poets*" who "write a verse, as smooth, as soft, as creame;/In which there is no torrent, nor scarce streame," Beaumont can envisage a milky smoothness redeemed by torrential force: "When verses like a milky torrent flow,/ they equall temper in the Poet show." His stream metaphor, and the *media via* proposed, anticipate the qualities for which Denham, in a famous passage, emulated the Thames. Hardly less than "Cooper's Hill," "Bosworth Field," where Beaumont's balanced smoothness can be seen at large, became a touchstone of Augustan literary taste, though what was then an asset has since become something of a liability.

To Beaumont's contemporaries, however, including Ben Jonson, he was primarily a Renaissance Christian Humanist. He himself stresses that poetry has a religious and ethical role; its true themes are "brave examples, sage instructions" and "celestiall things," its aim to "knit chaines of vertue in the hearers mind." His translations from Latin and Greek are of poems which recommend the ancient rural simplicities and self-examination, Stoicism and Christianity. His funeral elegies, besides expressing affectionate grief, trumpet the fame of the dead for the moral enlightenment of posterity. His Christian-Stoic didactic poems declaim an Augustinian view of man and traditional concept of right reason, with an occasional anti-Petrarchanism and a certain neo-Platonism. And, despite its sycophancy, "Bosworth Field" shares with Edmund Bolton's proposed Royal Academy the aim of presenting the great men of British history in an effort to raise the tone of the Stuart court. Writing from these interests, Beaumont sometimes achieves considerable force.

His most distinctive work is his more purely religious poetry, which is again not forward-looking. Sometimes he conceives his state in powerfully Ignatian terms, fluctuating between a black desolation conscious of Hell's gaping jaws and a joy so ecstatic as to be fearful. The best writing in "Bosworth Field," the portrayal of Richard III, is actually a study of damnation. And his "sacerdotal" writing, extensively in the unpublished "The Crowne of Thornes" and more pithily in some shorter poems, encourages his fellow-religionists to vicarious participation in biblical events with a sometimes sharply Metaphysical wit and an ability to spiritualize the physical. Despite his successful court career, Beaumont, a recusant, is the voice of the persecuted Old Religion.

Sometimes there is conflict between his new-style acquiescing conformity and his old-fashioned religious and ethical concerns. But his best work has a unique interest in its fusion of the neo-classical and Augustan stylistic impulses with the themes of an earlier age.

—Roger D. Sell

BEAUMONT, Joseph. English. Born in Hadleigh, Suffolk, 13 March 1616. Educated at Hadleigh Grammar School; Peterhouse, Cambridge, 1631–38, B.A. 1634, M.A. 1638. Married Miss Brownrigg in 1650; six children. Fellow, Peterhouse, 1636 until expelled by the Puritans, 1644; returned to his home at Hadleigh; Non-Resident Rector of Kelshall, Hertfordshire, 1643; appointed Prebend, Ely Cathedral, 1651, installed 1660; lived at his wife's home at Tatingston Place, Suffolk, 1650–60; appointed a king's chaplain, 1660; Master of Jesus College, Cambridge, 1662–63; appointed Master of Peterhouse, 1663, and Professor of Divinity, Cambridge University, 1674. *Died 25 September 1699.*

PUBLICATIONS

Collections

    Complete Poems, edited by Alexander B. Grosart.   2 vols., 1877–80.
    Minor Poems, edited by Eloise Robinson.   1914.

Verse

    Psyche; or, Love's Mystery, Displaying the Intercourse Betwixt Christ and the Soul.   1648; revised edition, edited by Charles Beaumont, 1702.
    Original Poems in English and Latin, edited by John Gee.   1749.

Other

    Some Observations upon the Apology of Henry More for His Mystery of Godliness.   1665.

Reading List: "St. Teresa in Beaumont's *Psyche,*" in *Journal of English and Germanic Philology,* 1963, and "A Portrait of Stuart Orthodoxy," in *Church Quarterly Review,* 1964, both by P. G. Stanwood.

*   *   *

Joseph Beaumont composed nearly two hundred brief lyrics, mostly devotional, in the manner of Herbert and Crashaw, but his chief distinction is to have written the longest narrative poem in the English language. His *Psyche; Or, Love's Mystery* consists of 38,670 lines in *Venus and Adonis* stanzas. Although the narrative is chiefly concerned with the attempts of Satan to seduce the young woman, Psyche, who is protected and instructed by her guardian angel, Phylax, nearly half the poem is devoted to a retelling of the life of Jesus. Psyche is tested by lust, heresy, persecution, and dereliction; with the help of Phylax she passes all these tests and, in the last lines of the poem, dies with the assurance that her heavenly yearnings will be fulfilled.

The narrative interest is very slight and Beaumont is relentlessly didactic. All his characters are allegorical except for Satan, whose energy and proud defiance remind one of Milton's fallen archangel. Both the length of the poem and the allegorical method invite comparison with *The Faerie Queene*. Beaumont had reservations about Spenser: "Right fairly dress'd were his welfeatur'd *Queen*,/Did not her Mask too much her beauties screen." Nevertheless his allegorical figures frequently resemble Spenser's, and the Palace of Ecclesia episode reminds one of the House of Alma. The other obvious comparison is with Bunyan. But Spenser and Bunyan, both committed to a narrative, use their allegorical characters in the action, while Beaumont's figures are, with few exceptions, quite inactive. The quest, which gives strength and unity to Spenser's and Bunyan's narratives, is lacking in *Psyche*.

Beaumont's verse flows smoothly but without power. He pays the highest praise to Crashaw, Herbert, Marino, and Tasso. And his allegorical figures frequently recall Virgil. But his verse is too lacking in character to suggest a pedigree. It is simply competent English verse, seldom distinguished by qualities of sound, meter, or metaphor. The following stanza, spoken by Satan, is unusually vigorous.

> I yield not yet; Defiance *Heav'n*, said He,
> And though I cannot reach thee with my fire,
> Yet my unconquer'd Brain shall able be
> To grapple with thee; nor canst thou be higher
> Than my *brave Spight*: Know, though below I dwell,
> Heav'n has no stouter Hearts than strut in Hell.

A careful poet would not have allowed such a combination as "Know, though below," and *strut* is the wrong word in Satan's mouth. But the lines do suggest energy and strength.

Beaumont's besetting vice is prolixity. To tell the reader that virtue is active, he uses eleven stanzas of analogies and thirteen stanzas of general statement − 144 lines in all. Ecclesia, described in 24 stanzas, has 22 handmaidens, described in 45 stanzas. There are fine passages in *Psyche*, but Beaumont's work is not likely to appeal to the general reader. Scholars, however, will be interested in it as an excellent example of English baroque sensibility.

—Thomas Wheeler

BEDDOES, Thomas Lovell. English. Born in Clifton, Bristol, Somerset, 20 July 1803. Educated at Bath Grammar School; Charterhouse School, London, 1817–20; Pembroke College, Oxford, 1820–25, B.A. 1825, M.A. 1828; studied medicine at the University of Göttingen, 1825–29, and University of Wurzburg, 1829–32, M.D. 1832. Physician and anatomist; visited England, 1842, 1846, but otherwise lived on the Continent; involved in various radical movements in Germany and Switzerland; settled in Zurich, 1835–40, Frankfurt, 1847. *Died* (by suicide) *26 January 1849.*

PUBLICATIONS

Collections

Letters, edited by Edmund Gosse. 1894.
Works, edited by Henry W. Donner.   1935.
Plays and Poems, edited by Henry W. Donner.   1950.
Selected Poems, edited by J. Higgins.   1976.

Verse

The Improvisatore, in Three Fyttes, with Other Poems. 1821.
Poems Posthumous and Collected.   2 vols., 1851.

Plays

The Bride's Tragedy. 1822.
Death's Jest-Book; or, The Fool's Tragedy.   1850.

Reading List: *Beddoes: The Making of a Poet* by Henry W. Donner, 1935; *Beddoes* by
Edward H. W. Meyerstein, 1940; *Beddoes: A Psychiatric Study* by Hiram K. Johnson, 1943.

*   *   *

It would be easy to see in Thomas Lovell Beddoes's work no more than a series of
particularly skilful variations on the stock Gothic themes of late Romantic poetry. As he
himself writes (in "Song: A Cypress-Bough, and a Rose-Wreath Sweet"), "Death and Hymen
both are here," and this combination of the morbid and the sexual characterized most of his
best poems, furnishing them with an imagery as lovingly detailed as it is repellent. Webster
and Tourneur are obvious models here; the Keats of "Lamia" and "Isabella" is a nearer
antecedent. And Beddoes himself may well be counted an influence on Browning, for the
complex of ambivalent attitudes which animates Beddoes's work is sometimes fused (as in
"The Ghost's Moonshine") into a coherent psychological whole which puts one in mind of
such dramatic monologues as "Porphyria's Lover."
    Although Beddoes can thus be defined as a minor contributor to a tradition which was
itself all too literary by the nineteenth century, it should be emphasised that his best work
possesses an idiosyncratic force which sometimes deserves the name of originality. His own
unhappy life gave personal meaning to the conventional pseudo-Jacobean death-obsession:
his father died when he was an infant, his beloved mother just as he entered adulthood. He
spent his later years wandering in Germany, where his wild drinking and his radicalism
made him unpopular with the authorities, and his eventual suicide was the end of a lonely
and eccentric existence. It seems likely that he was a homosexual, and his feelings of guilt on
this score, together with the anatomical knowledge he acquired studying medicine, may have
helped to endow the Gothic imagery of his poetry with its conviction and emotional force.
    Despite the *succès d'estime* enjoyed by his play *The Bride's Tragedy*, published when he
was not yet twenty, Beddoes never completed any major work, and in his belief that his was a
dramatic talent he shared a common delusion of his time. But although *Death's Jest-Book*, the
semi-dramatic work whose obsessive revision occupied the poet's later life, fails as a whole,
its incidental lyrics (of which "Old Adam, The Carrion Crow" is the best-known), together
with a number of other poems and verse-letters, constitute a body of verse which confirms
Beddoes's own deathbed self-estimate, according to which he "ought to have been a good

poet." Modern readers who take the trouble to look at Beddoes's work are likely to regret that this distinctive and compelling voice never found more ample utterance.

—James Reeves

BELLOC, (Joseph) Hilaire (Pierre).   British.   Born in St. Cloud, near Paris, France, 27 July 1870; naturalized British subject, 1902. Educated at the Oratory School, Edgbaston; Balliol College, Oxford (Brackenbury History Scholar), 1892–95, B.A. (honours) in history 1895. Served in the 10th Battery of the 8th Regiment of Artillery of the French Army, 1891. Married Elodie Agnes Hogan in 1896 (died, 1914); three sons, two daughters. Journalist: Editor, with A. H. Pollen, *Paternoster Review*, 1890–91; Literary Editor, *Morning Post*, 1906–09; Editor, with Maurice Baring, *North Street Gazette*, 1910; Editor, with others, *Eye-Witness*, 1911–12; Editor, *G. K.'s Weekly*, 1936–38; columnist ("A Wanderer's Notebook"), *Sunday Times*, 1938–53. Liberal Member of Parliament for South Salford, 1906–10. Head of the English Department, East London College. LL.D.: University of Glasgow, 1902. Knight Commander with Star, Order of St. Gregory the Great, 1934. *Died 16 July 1953.*

PUBLICATIONS

Collections

> *The Verse*, edited by W. N. Roughead.   1954; as *Complete Verse*, 1970.
> *Selected Essays*, edited by J. B. Morton.   1958.
> *Belloc: A Biographical Anthology*, edited by Herbert Van Thal and Jane Soames Nickerson.   1970.

Verse

> *Verses and Sonnets.*   1896.
> *The Bad Child's Book of Beasts.*   1896.
> *More Beasts (for Worse Children).*   1897.
> *The Modern Traveller.*   1898.
> *A Moral Alphabet.*   1899.
> *Cautionary Tales for Children: Designed for the Admonition of Children Between the Ages of Eight and Fourteen Years.*   1907.
> *Verses.*   1910.
> *More Peers.*   1911.
> *Sonnets and Verse.*   1923; revised edition, 1938; as *Collected Verse*, 1958.
> *New Cautionary Tales.*   1930.
> *The Praise of Wine: An Heroic Poem.*   1931.
> *Ladies and Gentlemen: For Adults Only and Mature at That.*   1932.
> *Cautionary Verses: The Collected Humorous Poems.*   1939.
> *Songs of the South Country.*   1951.

Play

> *The Candour of Maturity* (produced 1912).

Fiction

> *Emmanuel Burden, Merchant.*   1904.
> *Mr. Clutterbuck's Election.*   1908.
> *A Change in the Cabinet.*   1909.
> *Pongo and the Bull.*   1910.
> *The Girondin.*   1911.
> *The Green Overcoat.*   1912.
> *The Mercy of Allah.*   1922.
> *Mr. Petre.*   1925.
> *The Emerald of Catherine the Great.*   1926.
> *The Haunted House.*   1927.
> *But Soft — We Are Observed!* 1928; as *Shadowed!*,   1929.
> *Belinda: A Tale of Affection in Youth and Age.*   1928.
> *The Missing Masterpiece.*   1929.
> *The Man Who Made Gold.*   1930.
> *The Postmaster-General.*   1932.
> *The Hedge and the Horse.*   1936.

Other

> *Danton: A Study.*   1899.
> *Lambkin's Remains.*   1900.
> *Paris.*   1900.
> *Robespierre: A Study.*   1901.
> *The Path to Rome.*   1902.
> *The Aftermath: or, Gleanings from a Busy Life, Called upon the Outer Cover, for Purposes of Sale, Caliban's Guide to Letters.*   1903
> *The Great Inquiry (Only Authorised Version) Faithfully Reported.*   1903.
> *The Old Road.*   1904.
> *Avril, Being Essays on the Poetry of the French Renaissance.*   1904.
> *An Open Letter on the Decay of Faith.*   1906.
> *Esto Perpetua: Algerian Studies and Impressions.*   1906.
> *Sussex Painted by Wilfrid Ball.*   1906; revised edition, as *The County of Sussex,* 1936.
> *Hills and the Sea.*   1906.
> *The Historic Thames.*   1907.
> *The Eye-Witness* (incidents in history).   1908.
> *On Nothing and Kindred Subjects.*   1908.
> *An Examination of Socialism.*   1908; as *The Alternative,* 1947.
> *The Pyrenees.*   1909.
> *On Everything.*   1909.
> *Marie Antoinette.*   1909.
> *The Church and Socialism.*   1910.
> *The Ferrer Case.*   1910.
> *The International.*   1910.
> *On Anything.*   1910.
> *On Something.*   1910.
> *The Party System,* with Cecil Chesterton.   1911.

Socialism and the Servile State (debate with J. Ramsay Macdonald).   1911.
First and Last.   1911.
The French Revolution.   1911.
British Battles.   6 vols., 1911–13; revised edition, as *Six British Battles,* 1931.
The Four Men: A Farrago.   1912.
The River of London.   1912.
Warfare in England.   1912.
The Servile State.   1912.
This and That and the Other.   1912.
The Stane Street: A Monograph.   1913.
The Book of the Bayeux Tapestry, Presenting the Complete Work in a Series of Colour Facsimiles.   1914.
Anti-Catholic History: How It Is Written.   1914.
Three Essays.   1914.
The History of England from the First Invasion by the Romans to the Accession of King George the Fifth (volume 11 only).   1915.
A General Sketch of the European War: The First and *Second Phase.*   2 vols., 1915–16: as *The Elements of the Great War.*   2 vols., 1915–16.
A Picked Company, Being a Selection from the Writings of Hilaire Belloc, edited by E. V. Lucas.   1915.
High Lights of the French Revolution.   1915.
The Two Maps of Europe and Some Other Aspects of the Great War.   1915.
Land and Water Map of the War and How to Use It.   1915.
At the Sign of the Lion and Other Essays.   1916.
The Last Days of the French Monarchy.   1916.
The Second Year of the War.   1916.
The Free Press.   1918.
Religion and Civil Liberty.   1918.
The Catholic Church and the Principle of Private Property.   1920.
The House of Commons and Monarchy.   1920.
Europe and the Faith.   1920.
Pascal's Provincial Letters.   1921.
Catholic Social Reform Versus Socialism.   1922.
The Jews.   1922.
The Contrast.   1923.
The Road.   1923.
On (essays).   1923.
Economics for Helen.   1924; as *Economics for Young People,* 1925.
The Political Effort.   1924.
The Campaign of 1812 and the Retreat from Moscow.   1924; as *Napoleon's Campaign of 1812 and the Retreat from Moscow,* 1926.
The Cruise of the "Nona".   1925.
England and the Faith.   1925.
A History of England.   4 vols., 1925–31.
Miniatures of French History.   1925.
The Highway and Its Vehicles. edited by Geoffrey Holme.   1926.
Short Talks with the Dead and Others.   1926.
Mrs. Markham's New History of England. Being an Introduction for Young People to the Current History and Institutions of Our Times.   1926.
A Companion to Mr. Wells's "Outline of History."   1926.
Mr. Belloc Still Objects to Mr. Wells's "Outline of History."   1926.
The Catholic Church and History.   1926.
Selected Works.   9 vols., 1927.
Towns of Destiny.   1927: as *Many Cities,* 1928.

Oliver Cromwell. 1927.

James the Second. 1928.

How the Reformation Happened. 1928.

A Conversation with an Angel and Other Essays. 1928.

Joan of Arc. 1929.

Survivals and New Arrivals. 1929.

Richelieu. 1929.

Wolsey. 1930.

A Pamphlet, July 27th, 1930. 1930; as *World Conflict,* 1951.

A Conversation with a Cat and Others (essays). 1931.

Cranmer. 1931; as *Cranmer, Archbishop of Canterbury, 1533–1556.* 1931.

Essays of a Catholic Layman in England. 1931: as *Essays of a Catholic,* 1931.

How We Got the Bible. 1932.

Napoleon. 1932.

The Question and the Answer. 1932.

The Tactics and Strategy of the Great Duke of Marlborough. 1933.

William the Conqueror. 1933.

Becket. 1933.

Charles the First, King of England. 1933.

Cromwell. 1934.

A Shorter History of England. 1934.

Milton. 1935.

Hilaire Belloc (humorous writings), edited by E. V. Knox. 1935.

An Essay on the Restoration of Property. 1936: as *The Restoration of Property,* 1936.

Selected Essays, edited by John Edward Dineen. 1936.

The Battle Ground (on Syria). 1936.

Characters of the Reformation. 1936.

The Crusade: The World's Debate. 1937: as *The Crusades: The World's Debate.* 1937.

The Crisis of Our Civilization. 1937; as *The Crisis of Civilization,* 1937.

An Essay on the Nature of Contemporary England. 1937.

The Issue. 1937.

The Great Heresies. 1938.

Monarchy: A Study of Louis XIV. 1938; as *Louis XIV,* 1938.

Stories, Essays, and Poems. 1938.

The Case of Dr. Coulton. 1938.

Return to the Baltic. 1938.

Charles II: The Last Rally. 1939: as *The Last Rally: A Story of Charles II,* 1940.

The Test Is Poland. 1939.

On Sailing the Sea: A Collection of the Seagoing Writings of Belloc. edited by W. N. Roughead. 1939.

The Catholic and the War. 1940.

On the Place of G. K. Chesterton in English Letters. 1940.

The Silence of the Sea and Other Essays. 1940.

Places. 1941.

Elizabethan Commentary. 1942: as *Elizabeth: Creature of Circumstance.* 1942.

Selected Essays. 1948.

Hilaire Belloc: An Anthology of His Prose and Verse. edited by W. N. Roughead. 1951.

One Thing and Another: A Miscellany from His Uncollected Essays. edited by Patrick Cahill. 1955.

Essays. edited by Anthony Forster. 1955.

Letters from Belloc. edited by Robert Speaight. 1958.

Advice. 1960.

Editor, *Extracts from the Diaries and Letters of Hubert Howard.* 1899.
Editor, *The Footpath Way: An Anthology for Walkers.* 1911.
Editor, *Travel Notes on a Holiday Tour in France,* by James Murray Allison. 1931.

Translator. *The Romance of Tristan and Iseult.* by J. Bedier. 1903.
Translator. *The Principles of War.* by Marshal Foch. 1918.
Translator. *Precepts and Judgments.* by Marshal Foch. 1919.

Bibliography: *The English First Editions of Belloc* by Patrick Cahill, 1953.

Reading List: *Belloc* by Renée Haynes, 1953, revised edition, 1958; *Belloc, No Alienated Man: A Study in Christian Integration* by Frederick Wilhelmsen. 1954; *Belloc: A Memoir* by J. B. Morton, 1955; *The Young Belloc* by Marie Belloc Lowndes, 1956; *Testimony to Belloc* by E. and R. Jebb, 1956; *The Life of Belloc* by Robert Speaight, 1957.

*   *   *

Hilaire Belloc's career as crusading man-of-letters puts to shame by its polish, energy, and range any subsequent English propagandists for a radically Catholic point of view in politics and history. His many polemical works of historical biography, his essays and tracts, form a kind of armed column of anti-modern opinions, now passed well below the horizon of active readership, except perhaps among the Knights of Malta. He was anti-Drefusard, anti-socialist, and anti-Protestant, and the residue of feelings left us by the Second World War debars him from modern democratic sympathies. Yet the glitter and the rumour of his passage live on, perhaps most readably (among his serious works) in *The Servile State, Robespierre,. Napoleon,* and *Cromwell.* As these titles suggest, he was also a radical, a rebel, a republican, and a revolutionary, and his history, always very personal and actual, has the vividness of the memoirs of a combatant.

His years as a Liberal M.P. (1906–1910), which went into his later political novels, left him with a distaste for British political life, best represented by his epigram "On a General Election":

> The accursed power which stands on Privilege
> (And goes with Women, and Champagne and Bridge)
> Broke – and Democracy resumed her reign:
> (Which goes with Bridge, and Women and Champagne).

His great ally in journalism, radicalism, Romanism, and light verse, G. K. Chesterton, had more humour and an Englishness which made his crusading acceptable. Belloc was half-French and had been to Balliol, and his combination of clarity, wit, rhetoric, and sentiment made him a dangerously unpredictable figure to the English: he had principles and liked to win arguments. "Europe is the Faith, and the Faith is Europe" was one of his battle-cries; and by Europe he meant France, just as by England he meant Oxford. He admired Napoleon, was against the Boer War, and did not feel that "Judas was a tolerable chap."

Much of his distinct personality and charm remain in his travel books, especially *The Path to Rome,* partly autobiographical. His lucid prose was sometimes brazened in his tendentious later works, and his English set into a Gallic mannerism which now seems dated.

Belloc was fatally skilful in too many fields at a time when the press could support a versatile pen – or "a free lance" – the age of his opponents Shaw and Wells, as later of John Buchan and Ronald Knox, also Balliol man. There is a consciousness of waste in his verse –

one thinks of Milton's "that one talent which is death to hide," a phrase Belloc would have admired. He thought of himself as a poet *manqué*. His serious verse strikes sentimental attitudes with style and he is still best loved for his light verse, especially the *Cautionary Tales*. Here his gifts found a minor triumph:

> Augustus Horne was nobly born,
> He held the human race in scorn.
> He lived with all his sisters where
> His father lived, in Berkeley Square.

—M. J. Alexander

BENÉT, Stephen Vincent. American. Born in Bethlehem, Pennsylvania, 22 July 1898; brother of the poet William Rose Benét, *q.v.* Educated at Summerville Academy; Yale University, New Haven, Connecticut (Chairman, *Yale Literary Magazine*, 1919), A.B. 1919, M.A. 1920; the Sorbonne, Paris. Married Rosemary Carr in 1921; one son, two daughters. During the Depression and war years became an active lecturer and radio propagandist for the liberal cause. Editor, Yale Series of Younger Poets. Recipient: Poetry Society of America Prize, 1921; Guggenheim Fellowship, 1926; Pulitzer Prize, 1929, 1944; O. Henry Award, 1932, 1937, 1940; Shelley Memorial Award, 1933; National Institute of Arts and Letters Gold Medal, 1943. D.Litt.: Middlebury College, Vermont, 1936. Vice-President, National Institute of Arts and Letters. *Died 13 March 1943.*

PUBLICATIONS

Collections

> *Selected Poetry and Prose,* edited by Basil Davenport.   1960.
> *Selected Letters,* edited by Charles A. Fenton.   1960.

Verse

> *The Drug-Shop; or, Endymion in Edmonstoun.*   1917.
> *Young Adventure.*   1918.
> *Heavens and Earth.*   1920.
> *The Ballad of William Sycamore 1790–1880.*   1923.
> *King David.*   1923.
> *Tiger Joy.*   1925.
> *John Brown's Body.*   1928.
> *Ballads and Poems 1915–1930.*   1931.
> *A Book of Americans,* with Rosemary Benét.   1933.
> *Burning City.*   1936.
> *The Ballad of the Duke's Mercy.*   1939.
> *Nightmare at Noon.*   1940.

Listen to the People: Independence Day 1941.   1941.
Western Star.   1943.
The Last Circle: Stories and Poems.   1946.

Plays

Five Men and Pompey: A Series of Dramatic Portraits.   1915.
The Headless Horseman, music by Douglas Moore (broadcast 1937).   1937.
The Devil and Daniel Webster, music by Douglas Moore, from the story by Benét (produced 1938).   1939.
Elementals (broadcast 1940–41). In *Best Broadcasts of 1940–41,* edited by Max Wylie, 1942.
Freedom's a Hard Bought Thing (broadcast 1941).   In *The Free Company Presents,* edited by James Boyd, 1941.
Nightmare at Noon, in *The Treasury Star Parade,* edited by William A. Bacher.   1942.
A Child Is Born (broadcast 1942).   1942.
They Burned the Books (broadcast 1942).   1942.
All That Money Can Buy (screenplay), with Dan Totheroh, in *Twenty Best Film Plays,* edited by John Gassner and Dudley Nichols.   1943.
We Stand United and Other Radio Scripts (includes *A Child Is Born, The Undefended Border, Dear Adolf, Listen to the People, Thanksgiving Day – 1941, They Burned the Books, A Time to Reap, Toward the Century of Modern Man, Your Army*).   1945.

Screenplays: *Cheers for Miss Bishop,* with Adelaide Heilbron and Sheridan Gibney, 1941; *All That Money Can Buy,* with Dan Totheroh, 1941.

Radio Plays: *The Headless Horseman,* 1937; *The Undefended Border,* 1940; *We Stand United,* 1940; *Elementals,* 1940–41; *Listen to the People,* 1941; *Thanksgiving Day – 1941,* 1941; *Freedom's a Hard Bought Thing,* 1941; *Nightmare at Noon; A Child Is Born,* 1942; *Dear Adolf,* 1942; *They Burned the Books,* 1942; *A Time to Reap,* 1942; *Toward the Century of Modern Man,* 1942; *Your Army,* 1944.

Fiction

The Beginning of Wisdom.   1921.
Young People's Pride.   1922.
Jean Huguenot.   1923.
Spanish Bayonet.   1926.
The Barefoot Saint (stories).   1929.
The Litter of Rose Leaves (stories).   1930.
James Shore's Daughter.   1934.
Thirteen O'Clock: Stories of Several Worlds.   1937.
The Devil and Daniel Webster.   1937.
Johnny Pye and the Fool-Killer (stories).   1938.
Tales Before Midnight.   1939.
Short Stories: A Selection.   1942.
O'Halloran's Luck and Other Short Stories.   1944.

Other

A Summons to the Free.   1941.

Selected Works.   2 vols., 1942.

America.   1944.

Benét on Writing: A Great Writer's Letter of Advice to a Young Beginner, edited by
George Abbe.   1964.

Editor, with others, *The Yale Book of Student Verse 1910–1919.*   1919.

Bibliography: "Benét: A Bibliography" by Gladys Louise Maddocks, in *Bulletin of
Bibliography 20,* 1951–52.

Reading List: *Benét* by William Rose Benét, 1943; *Benét: The Life and Times of an American
Man of Letters* by Charles A. Fenton, 1958; *Benét* by Parry Stroud, 1962.

*   *   *

Stephen Vincent Benét occupies a curiously equivocal position in American letters. One
of America's best known and rewarded poets and storytellers, he has at the same time been
virtually ignored in academic discussions of major 20th-century writers, and seldom
anthologized. In light of the greater critical success enjoyed by his student friends at Yale –
Thornton Wilder, Archibald MacLeish, and Philip Barry, themselves often unremarked
among "major" writers – Benét's reputation seems thin indeed.

Benét's permanent place in the history of American fiction is nevertheless assured by the
fact that among his many volumes of prose and verse there are several minor classics that are
widely read and admired. His early light and ironic verse, such as "For City Spring" and
"Evening and Morning," and such frolicking ballads as "Captain Kidd," "Thomas Jefferson,"
"The Mountain Whippoorwill," and "The Ballad of William Sycamore" are highly regarded.
His long narrative poem about the Civil War, *John Brown's Body,* dramatized by Charles
Laughton in 1953 and called by Henry Steele Commager "not only the best poem about the
Civil War, and the best narrative, but also the best history," won Benét his first Pulitzer Prize.
Benét's best known short story, "The Devil and Daniel Webster," which combines the
author's flare for fantasy and old folktale traditions, shares an equally prominent place in the
tall-tale genre of American story-telling. Finally, *Western Star,* another long narrative poem
about the heroic pioneering of America, begun in 1934 and incomplete at his death, won for
Benét a second Pulitzer prize in 1944.

Among the notes for the continuation of *Western Star* found after Benét's death, the
following quatrain was saved:

> Now for my country that it still may live,
> All that I have, all that I am I'll give.
> It is not much beside the gift of the brave
> And yet accept it since tis all I have.

What Benét had – an unbounded, 19th-century faith in the promises of American
democracy, and an expansive, Whitmanesque love for what seemed the nation's special
attributes, diversity, amplitude, self-sufficiency, frankness, innocence – he poured into every
poem, story, and novel he wrote. He praised New York as the communal achievement of the
spirit of man, and America because there every man could most freely become what God
meant him to be. "Out of your fever and your moving on," he said in the "Prelude" to
Western Star, "Americans, Americans, Americans ... I make my song."

Both in sentiment and in style, Benét's work attempts to embody the very democratic
virtues it is about. Like Sandburg, Hart Crane, and Vachel Lindsay, he uses the zesty tempos,
conversational rhythms, and laconic vernacular to capture the spirit of greatness in the
strength and simplicity of the nation's common people. In his book of fifty-six verses about

famous American men and women, great and small, *A Book of Americans*, Benét says of the greatest and humblest of American native sons:

> Lincoln was a long man
> He liked out of doors.
> He liked the wind blowing
> And the talk in country stores.

Just as *John Brown's Body* projects Benét's sensitive feeling for half a dozen countrysides, racial strains, and political attitudes, so this book stands in praise of the nation's heroic ability to reconcile its opposites among that "varied lot" who "each by deed and speech/Adorned our history."

Despite the warmth, genuineness, and impish charm with which Benét celebrates the country's democratic potential, his failure to win wider critical respectability is clearly attributable to the fact that his breadth of sympathy and deep-rooted patriotism seem parochial and old-fashioned to today's audiences, and that even his best work, viewed along side the more realistic and richly inventive fiction of such contemporaries as Crane, Joyce, Proust, and Eliot, appears lacking in depth, subtlety, and originality. The pastoral rebellion of the earth against machines, against the "Age of Steam," which pervades so many of his poems, and his use of conventional verse forms and technical devices that have made him dear to school teachers, seem, in the words of one critic, "all too clear and all too facile." It is significant that Benét's writing has been praised more for its lively evocation of American history than for its aesthetic value.

—Lawrence R. Broer

BENÉT, William Rose. American. Born in New York City, 2 February 1886; brother of the poet Stephen Vincent Benét, *q.v.* Educated at Albany Academy, New York; Yale University, New Haven, Connecticut (Chairman, *Yale Courant*; Editor, *Yale Record*). Served in the United States Army Air Force in Europe, 1918: Second Lieutenant. Married 1) Teresa Frances Thompson in 1921 (died), one son, two daughters; 2) the poet Elinor Wylie, *q.v.*, in 1923 (died, 1928); 3) Lora Baxter; 4) the writer Marjorie Flack in 1943. Journalist: Reader, 1911–14, and Assistant Editor, 1914–18, *Century* magazine; Assistant Editor, *Nation's Business*, 1918–19; Associate Editor, *New York Evening Post* "Literary Review," 1920–24; Founder, with Christopher Morley, 1924, Associate Editor, 1924–29, and Contributing Editor after 1929, *Saturday Evening Post*; Editor, Brewer and Warren, publishers, 1929–30. Recipient: Pulitzer Prize, 1942. Secretary, National Institute of Arts and Letters. *Died 4 May 1950.*

PUBLICATIONS

Verse

Merchants from Cathay. 1913.
The Falconer of God and Other Poems. 1914.

The Great White Wall.   1916.
The Burglar of the Zodiac and Other Poems.   1918.
Perpetual Light: A Memorial.   1919.
Moons of Grandeur.   1920.
Man Possessed: Selected Poems.   1927.
Sagacity.   1929.
Rip Tide: A Novel in Verse.   1932.
Starry Harness.   1933.
Golden Fleece.   1935.
Harlem and Other Poems.   1935.
A Baker's Dozen of Emblems.   1935.
With Wings as Eagles: Poems and Ballads of the Air.   1940.
The Dust Which Is God: A Novel in Verse.   1941.
Adolphus; or, The Adopted Dolphin and the Pirate's Daughter (juvenile), with Marjorie
    Flack. 1941.
Day of Deliverance.   1944.
The Stairway of Surprise.   1947.
Timothy's Angels (juvenile).   1947.
Poetry Package, with Christopher Morley.   1949.
The Spirit of the Scene.   1951.

Play

Day's End, in *The Best One-Act Plays of 1939,* edited by Margaret Mayorga.   1939.

Fiction

The First Person Singular.   1922.

Other

Saturday Papers: Essays, with Henry Seidel Canby and Amy Loveman.   1921.
The Flying King of Kurio (juvenile).   1926.
Wild Goslings: A Selection of Fugitive Pieces.   1927.
Stephen Vincent Benét: My Brother Steve.   1943.

Editor, *Poems for Youth: An American Anthology.*   1925.
Editor, with John Drinkwater and Henry Seidel Canby, *Twentieth-Century
    Poetry.*   1929.
Editor, *Collected Poems, Collected Prose,* by Elinor Wylie.   2 vols., 1932–33.
Editor, *Fifty Poets: An American Auto-Anthology.*   1933.
Editor, *Guide to Daily Reading.*   1934.
Editor, *The Pocket University.*   13 vols., 1934.
Editor, with others, *Adventures in English Literature.*   1936.
Editor, *Mother Goose: A Comprehensive Collection of the Rhymes.*   1936.
Editor, *From Robert to Elizabeth Barrett Browning* (letters).   1936.
Editor, with Norman Holmes Pearson, *The Oxford Anthology of American
    Literature.*   1938.
Editor, with Adolph Gillis, *Poems for Modern Youth.*   1938.
Editor, *Supplement to Great Poems of the English Language,* edited by Wallace Alvin
    Briggs.   1941.

Editor, with Conrad Aiken, *An Anthology of Famous English and American Poetry*. 1945.
Editor, with Norman Cousins, *The Poetry of Freedom*. 1945.
Editor, *The Reader's Encyclopedia*. 1948.

Translator, with Teresa Frances, *The East I Know*, by Paul Claudel. 1914.

*   *   *

William Rose Benét has perhaps been more remarked upon in recent American literary history as the "older brother" of the writer Stephen Vincent Benét, and as husband of the poet Elinor Wylie, than as an accomplished poet in his own right. Serious attention to his verse has also been diverted by his prominence as a reviewer, critic, and anthologist, and by his numerous activities as a promoter of the arts. But despite this dispersion of energies, Benét managed to publish many volumes of verse whose value has not properly been acknowledged.

The obvious unevenness of Benét's creative output is hinted at by the fact that Rolfe Humphries rates him no better than a mere "journeyman of letters," while Marguerite Wilkinson says he was a "builder [whose] strongest rhythms have the certitude of an arch...." Certainly Benét's weakest poems are unapologetically romantic and lacking in intensity. When he announces his poetic intentions in his most celebrated work, *The Dust Which Is God*, as "I will be plain at least," he does more than alert us to what he hopes will be a poetic voice free of bombast and ornamentation; unwittingly, he indicts a good number of poems whose over-statedness results in an absence of colour or emotional vitality. "Throw wide/The gates of the heart," he counsels in his poem "Study of Man," "Taking your part/In percipient life ... Ever extend/Your boundaries, and be/Inwardly free!"

Such direct statement issues from the poet's almost passionate reverence for the freedom and dignity of man, and for the ample spirit of God and nature, which he finds so abundantly manifest in his native America, as in "Men on Strike":

> The Country of the Free! Yes, a great land.
> Thank God that I have known it East to West
> And North to South, and still I love it best
> Of all the various world the seas command.

From the point of view of the wise primitivist, Benét celebrates the democratic virtues of common men, and envisions portents of disaster in the encroachments of the machine age. In "The Stricken Average," he writes:

> Little of brilliance did they write or say.
> They bore the battle of living, and were gay.
> Little of wealth or fame they left behind.
> They were merely honorable, brave, and kind.

He yearns for that "pristine creation/Unsullied by our civilization," ("Young Girl") whose elemental harmonies are forever threatened by factories, corporations, "towers of glass and steel" ("Shadow of the Mountain Man").

Such romantic attitudes were bound to lessen the appeal of Benét's work in an age whose best literary efforts were in direct opposition to such simple and sentimental verse. Yet there are indisputable qualities in Benét's best work, perhaps most forcibly realized in *The Dust Which Is God*, which in 1942 won him a Pulitzer Prize. An autobiographical verse narrative, it demonstrates a remarkable range of interests and intellect, and admirable versatility in the use of changing forms and rhythms to capture the diverse and sprawling nature of his subject – the birth and growth of the country, which he treats as synonymous with his own life. The poetry here reveals a lively and sophisticated grasp of cultural ideas, and often achieves a rich synthesis of opposites: classical and modern, noble and banal, holy and sensual, lyrical and prosaic. At their best, these "vignette illustrations" project for us a poetic talent of greater potential stature than that of the author's more celebrated brother – more original, more sensuous, and more varied and universal in scope.

—Lawrence R. Broer

BENLOWES, Edward. English. Born at Brent Hall, Finchingfield, Essex, 12 July 1602; eldest son of a recusant family. Educated as a Protestant at St. John's College, Cambridge, 1620–22; Lincoln's Inn, London, 1622–23. Inherited Brent Hall in 1613, and lived as a country gentleman, except for a grand tour of Europe, 1627–30; abandoned Catholicism by 1630. Captain of a troop of horse in Essex Militia by 1636; took no part in the Civil War until 1648, when he was commissioned in Royalist army. After destruction of Brent Hall by fire in 1653, lived in London; sold estate, 1657, and involved in litigation, 1657–65; lived with niece at Mapledurham, Oxfordshire, 1665–67; briefly imprisoned for debt in Oxford Castle, 1667; lived in poverty in Oxford after 1667. *Died 18 December 1676.*

PUBLICATIONS

Collections

In *Minor Poets of the Caroline Period 1*, edited by George Saintsbury. 1905.

Verse

Sphinx Theologica (Latin verse and prose). 1636.
Theophila; or, Love's Sacrifice: A Divine Poem. 1652.
The Summary of Wisdom. 1657.
Oxonii Encomium (verse and prose). 1672.

Reading List: *Benlowes: Biography of a Minor Poet* by Harold Jenkins, 1952 (includes bibliography); "Benlowes' Borrowings from Herbert" by E. E. Duncan-Jones, in *Review of English Studies*, 1955.

*   *   *

Edward Benlowes is one of those unfortunate authors whose chief claim to fame consists of having been derided by a greater writer. He was pilloried for the extravagance and eccentricity of his style in Samuel Butler's "Character of a Small Poet," yet his verse is not without life and a certain quaint attractiveness.

Discussion of Benlowes may be confined to his spiritual epic, *Theophila*, since his handful of shorter English poems shows similar characteristics. The subject of *Theophila* is the spiritual warfare and victory of the soul, celebrated in thirteen cantos. Most of the poem is in English, but parts are in Latin, while some English sections, for no discernible reason, reappear in Latin later. For the most part Benlowes uses a strange stanza composed of a decasyllable, an octosyllable and an alexandrine rhyming together, but verses in other forms are inserted from time to time. The argument is as incomprehensible as the construction, for in Benlowes the witty, strong-lined style was carried to such an extreme that it is hard to gain any sense of connection between one stanza and the next. *Theophila* provides an experience more like solving a puzzle than reading a poem. This effect is increased by Benlowes' fondness for borrowing from his contemporaries: lines from Milton, Jonson, Herbert, and others, only slightly altered, are woven into his text throughout, providing all the pleasures of a literary quiz.

Benlowes' frequent coinages contribute to his obscurity and oddity. He is fond of learned or technical expressions ("ovant," "angelence," "collyrium," "Danaize") and compounds ("Sodom-storms," "dwarf-words," "woolly-curdled"). These are jumbled together with colloquialisms and abbreviations, just as the poem mixes mystical ardours with political satire and natural description. One mixed metaphor treads upon another's heels, while startling epithets, far-fetched conceits, and word-play of every kind are brought in at any opportunity. Adam "yielding to a wo[e]man, made man yeild to woe"; Theophila "fears want of fears ... depraved by vice, deprived by grace"; drunkards are warned "healths, health deprive"; blood is "luke-warm claret," men, "our wormships." Distortion of syntax and omission of connecting words produce packed lines whose difficulty is reminiscent of Hopkins, and titles for the cantos like "Prelibation" and "Disincantation" hardly make the course of the poem any clearer.

Yet that same lack of discrimination and judgement which makes *Theophila* an example of the metaphysical style at its worst also contributes to its disarming zest. Exhausting though the poem is, it is seldom boring; and the glittering heap contains real gems among the curious baubles and coloured glass. The poet who could write "th'icy mantle of a wrinkled skin/ Candies the bristles of thy chin" could also produce the strangely beautiful line "No planet seen to sail through that dead ebb of night." Benlowes' imagination is fired by genuine ardour, and though the results are usually odd and not infrequently comic, they are far from being the work of a seventeenth-century William McGonagall. *Theophila* is not bad verse; it is poetry run mad.

—Margaret Forey

BENNETT, Louise. Jamaican. Educated at primary and secondary schools in Jamaica; Royal Academy of Dramatic Art, London (British Council Scholarship). Worked with the BBC (West Indies Section) as resident artist, 1945–46, 1950–53, and with repertory companies in Coventry, Huddersfield, and Amersham. Returned to Jamaica, 1955: Drama Specialist with the Jamaica Social Welfare Commission, 1955–60; Lecturer in drama and Jamaican folklore, Extra-Mural Department, University of the West Indies, Kingston, 1959–61. Represented Jamaica at the Royal Commonwealth Arts Festival in Britain, 1965. Has lectured in the United States and the United Kingdom on Jamaican music and folklore. Recipient: Silver Musgrave Medal, Institute of Jamaica. M.B.E. (Member, Order of the British Empire). Lives in Jamaica.

PUBLICATIONS

Verse

Dialect Verses. 1940.
Jamaican Dialect Verses. 1942; expanded version, 1951.

Jamaican Humour in Dialect.   1943.
Miss Lulu Sez.   1948.
Anancy Stories and Dialect Verse, with others.   1950.
Laugh with Louise: A Potpourri of Jamaican Folklore, Stories, Songs, Verses.   1960.
Jamaica Labrish.   1966.

Reading List: Introduction by Rex Nettlefold to *Jamaica Labrish,* 1966.

*   *   *

Afters years of popularity Louise Bennett is now attracting the attention of the critic and scholarly researcher. This belated attention is partly in response to Bennett's formidable merits as a poet, but it also reflects the current interest in Afro-Caribbean folk arts (music, songs, dances, folktales) − not simply as sources for writers and folklorists, but more importantly as significant art forms in their own right. And as a poet whose art has always been based on oral performance and rooted in Jamaican folk idioms, Bennett fully exploits the potentiality of folk arts in the Caribbean. Indeed her themes repeatedly emphasize both the oral nature of her poetry and her own role as a performer. Moreover her language and the loquacious characters in her poems dramatize the political, emotional, and cultural significance of the spoken word among Jamaica's poor and unlettered classes.

Conversely her unlettered but robust folk often ridicule the literate middle-class world of the printed word, not because they reject literacy and middle-class values as such, but because Bennett questions the tendency, in some quarters, to elevate the European values inherent in standard English literacy at the expense of the experience represented by the folk idiom and its Afro-Caribbean cultural milieu. For that cultural milieu results from a complex cultural synthesis of African, European, and New World sources which is in danger of being ignored or minimized by a narrowly literate value system. Bennett's techniques (particularly her choice of language and the oral nature of her poetry) are therefore integral to her vision as an artist. These techniques enable her to immerse her audience in the experience of the folk, affirming in the process that that experience is central rather than peripheral to a Jamaican (and West Indian) consciousness.

This cultural immersion is aided by another Bennett technique: she never allows her authorial voice to obtrude upon the theme of any work, and this is a constant in her work, notwithstanding the authoritarian, even overbearing, voice which discourses on a variety of topics in her poetry. The voice we hear belongs to the persona of the moment, whether it is a politician, a trades unionist, a loyal Black colonial, or a spirited anti-colonialist. And on the whole her poetry relies upon the unfettered self-description of her characters rather than upon some comprehensive definition or overview by the author herself. Hence although Bennett the poet says nothing directly about the status and experience of women, her work represents the most thorough exploration of the woman's experience in the Caribbean. Nearly all of her poems are presented through the eyes − and energetic voices − of women, and in the process they reveal a wide variety of women's attitudes towards men, themselves, and society as a whole. In their vocal self-expressiveness Bennett's women emerge as a rather diverse lot − militant, conventional, strong, or weak. They are therefore representations of Bennett's special kind of poetic truth − a relentless realism that confronts her audience with society and its people as they are and as they express their diverse selves in their oral modes.

—Lloyd W. Brown

BEOWULF POET.

PUBLICATIONS

Verse

De Danorum Rebus Gestis Seculis III et IV Poema Danicum Dialecto Anglosaxonica,
edited by Grim. Johnson Thorkelin. 1815.
Beowulf and the Fight at Finnsburg, edited by Fr. Klaeber. 1922; revised edition, 1950.
Beowulf and the Finnsburg Fragment, edited by C. L. Wrenn. 1953; revised edition,
1958.
Beowulf: A Verse Translation, by M. J. Alexander. 1973.

Reading List: *Beowulf: The Monsters and the Critics* by J. R. R. Tolkien, 1937; *The Audience
of Beowulf* by Dorothy Whitelock, 1951; *The Art of Beowulf* by Arthur G. Brodeur, 1959;
Beowulf: An Introduction by R. W. Chambers, revised by C. L. Wrenn, 1963; *The Structure
of Beowulf* by Kenneth Sisam, 1965; *A Reading of Beowulf* by Edward B. Irving, 1968;
Beowulf and Its Analogues by G. N. Garmonsway and J. Simpson, 1968.

*   *   *

The *Beowulf* poet is anonymous, but most scholars have placed him North of the Thames,
in the Anglian kingdoms in the early or middle eighth century, and have supposed him to be
a Christian nobleman or ecclesiastic, since the poem has some Christian and aristocratic
colouring. The Northumbria of the Age of Bede (died 735) and the Mercia ruled by Offa from
757 to 796 have suggested themselves as the milieux where such a monumental court poem
might have been composed and appreciated. The language of the poem supports such a
provenance, though the Late West Saxon form in which it survives (in a unique manuscript
of about the year 1000, now in the British Library) overlies the largely Anglian language of
its composition.

We know less about the *Beowulf* poet than we do about Homer, since we lack even his (or
her) name, but it is proper to think of a *Beowulf* poet rather than of the author of *Beowulf*,
since the monster-slaying story and its associated historical material seem to have been in
circulation long before the poem achieved its literary form of 3,182 Old English verses. The
name of Beowulf the Geat does not appear elsewhere, but his king, Hygelac, is recorded by
Bishop Gregory of Tours as having died in a raid on the Franks in 521. The setting of the
poem is Southern Scandinavian, and the historical and legendary characters, such as Offa the
Angle and Hrothgar the Dane, belong to the heroic Age of Migration, before the Angles had
fully settled in Britain, a land which is not mentioned in the poem.

The *Beowulf* poet seems to have inherited not only his matter but also his medium of
composition (and his world-view) from his Germanic ancestors. The language and style of
Beowulf are shaped by the traditions of public, oral-formulaic verse composition, and
recitations are described several times in the poem. Christianity and literacy, however, also
contribute to *Beowulf*, which portrays a heroic world from a post-heroic and even elegiac
viewpoint. The poem achieves a profound synthesis between these pre-Christian and
Christian traditions, and its Anglian redactor may have been a "unifier" (a meaning of the
Greek *Homēros*) as well as a creator.

The story of Beowulf, who slew monsters in his youth and a dragon in his last fight, is set
in a world of heroic feuds between the tribes of the Baltic and North Seas. After his death his
own people will be over-run by their neighbours; the seeds of the destruction of heroic
civilisations are seen to be contained in the heroic code itself, where magnanimity and

courage are accompanied by the duty of revenge. The monster Grendel and his mother, who terrorise the Danes, are the descendants of Cain, the first murderer; Tolkien interprets them as embodiments of evil. Human heroic society is portrayed in the ceremonious and hospitable court of Hrothgar at his hall, Heorot, where a poet sings of the creation of the world; Grendel attacks Heorot at night, and devours the bodies of the sleeping Danes: "Night's table-laughter turned to morning's/lamentation."

A young Geat, Beowulf, comes to Heorot to rid it of Grendel. Beowulf is an exemplary hero, loyal, generous, brave, courteous, and gentle, though of immense bear-like strength, and above the common motive of revenge. He heeds Hrothgar's warnings against pride and complacency in his youthful successes, but falls in old age against the dragon who ravages the Geat countryside after his hoard has been robbed of a golden cup. Some recent critics have developed Christian interpretations of the poem in which the hero is doomed by the limitations of his paganism; but the emphasis of the ending is clearly admiring:

> Then the warriors rode around the barrow,
> twelve of them in all, athelings' sons.
> They recited a dirge to declare their grief,
> spoke of the man, mourned their King.
> They praised his manhood and the prowess of his hands,
> they raised his name; it is right a man
> should be lavish in honouring his lord and friend,
> should love him in his heart when the leading-forth
> from the house of flesh befalls him at last.
> This was the manner of the mourning of the men of the Geats,
> sharers in the feast, at the fall of their lord:
> they said that he was of all the world's kings
> the gentlest of men, and the most gracious,
> the kindest to his people, the keenest for fame.

Beowulf is the longest Old English poem, and easily the most considerable piece of literature in English before the reign of Richard II. It has a grave and profound understanding of life and has poetic merits of the highest sort; it is a work of art of mature complexity and balance.

—M. J. Alexander

BERRYMAN, John. American. Born in McAlester, Oklahoma, 25 October 1914. Educated at South Kent School, Connecticut; Columbia University, New York, A.B. 1936 (Phi Beta Kappa); Clare College, Cambridge (Kellett Fellow, 1936–37; Oldham Shakespeare Scholar, 1937), B.A. 1938; Princeton University, New Jersey (Creative Writing Fellow), 1943–44. Married 1) Eileen Patricia Mulligan in 1942 (divorced, 1953); 2) Ann Levine in 1956 (divorced, 1959); 3) Kathleen Donahue in 1961; three children. Instructor in English, Wayne State University, Detroit, 1939, and Princeton University, 1940–43; Briggs-Copeland Instructor in English Composition, Harvard University, Cambridge, Massachusetts, 1945–49; Lecturer in English, University of Washington, Seattle, 1950; Elliston Lecturer in Poetry, University of Cincinnati, 1951–52; Member of the English Department, rising to the rank of Professor, University of Minnesota, Minneapolis, 1954–72. Recipient: Rockefeller grant, 1944, 1946; Shelley Memorial Award, 1949; National Institute of Arts and Letters grant, 1950; Hodder Fellowship, Princeton University, 1950; Guggenheim Fellowship,

1952, 1966; Harriet Monroe Award, 1957; Brandeis University Creative Arts Award, 1959; Loines Award, 1964; Pulitzer Prize, 1965; Academy of American Poets Fellowship, 1966; National Endowment for the Arts grant, 1967; Bollingen Prize, 1968; National Book Award, 1969. D.Let.: Drake University, Des Moines, Iowa, 1971. Member, National Institute of Arts and Letters, American Academy of Arts and Sciences, and Academy of American Poets. *Died* (by suicide) *7 January 1972.*

PUBLICATIONS

Verse

Five Young American Poets, with others.   1940.
Poems.   1942.
The Dispossessed.   1948.
Homage to Mistress Bradstreet.   1956; as *Homage to Mistress Bradstreet and Other Poems*, 1959.
His Thought Made Pockets and the Plane Buckt.   1958.
77 Dream Songs.   1964.
Berryman's Sonnets.   1967.
Short Poems.   1967.
His Toy, His Dream, His Rest: 308 Dream Songs.   1968.
The Dream Songs.   1969.
Love and Fame.   1970; revised edition, 1972.
Selected Poems 1938–1968.   1972.
Delusions, Etc.   1972.
Henry's Fate and Other Poems, edited by John Haffenden.   1977.

Fiction

Recovery.   1973.

Other

Stephen Crane (biography).   1950.
The Freedom of the Poet (miscellany).   1976.

Editor, with Ralph Ross and Allen Tate, *The Arts of Reading* (anthology).   1960.
Editor, *The Unfortunate Traveller; or, The Life of Jack Wilton,* by Thomas Nashe.   1960.

Bibliography: *Berryman: A Descriptive Bibliography* by Ernest C. Stefanik, Jr., 1974; *Berryman: A Reference Guide* by Gary Q. Arpin, 1976.

Reading List: *Berryman* by William J. Martz, 1969; *Berryman* by James M. Linebarger, 1974; *The Poetry of Berryman* by Gary Q. Arpin, 1977; *Berryman: An Introduction to the Poetry* by Joel Conarroe, 1977.

*   *   *

John Berryman spent his childhood on a farm in Oklahoma under the sombre and difficult aegis of a father whose improvidence finally led to his suicide, an event which haunted and disturbed the poet for the rest of his life. From these dark beginnings, he leapt into the brighter world of his education, first at a private school in Connecticut, and then at Columbia University, where his immense energies and brilliance were manifested. A scholarship to Cambridge University led to his studies in Shakespeare and the English Renaissance, the stylistic exuberance of which was to influence his own discordant, richly embellished mode of verse. At Princeton University, he began a frenzied pace of writing that led to his first full-length collection of short poems, *The Dispossessed*. He had also completed much of the cycle of poems later published as *Berryman's Sonnets*. In both volumes Berryman is a mature craftsman of traditional forms and meters, which he renewed with his energetic speech.

Berryman's major work begins with *Homage to Mistress Bradstreet*, which includes poems from *The Dispossessed*. The title poem, a sequence of 57 eight-line stanzas, evokes the life and hardships of this American poet through an original strategy of merging the narrator's voice with his subject's, in which all the details of her sickness, frailty, and harsh family life are rendered with powerful immediacy. The poet's speech slips into the Colonial tongue and out again into a flinty modern colloquialism with masterful control. Berryman etches the character of Bradstreet and holds her up as an instance of the artist's eternal struggle against adversity:

> Headstones stagger under great draughts of time
> after heads pass out, and their world must reel
> speechless, blind in the end
> about its chilling star: thrift tuft,
> whin cushion − nothing. Already with the wounded flying
> dark air fills, I am a closet of secrets dying,
> races murder, foxholes hold men,
> reactor piles wage slow upon the wet brain rime.

Included in *Homage* is the series "The Nervous Songs," where he again inhabits other strained minds and articulates their emotions. They are important, however, chiefly for their form; each poem is cast in three six-line stanzas, the form employed throughout his greatest work, *The Dream Songs*.

The persona of the *Dream Songs* is variously referred to as Henry, Pussy-Cat, and Mr. Bones, and the poems evoke his daily inner life as he struggles through the routines of teaching, drying-out from chronic alcoholism, and writing ambitious books of poems. His deepest dilemma is with his own identity, which fits him in the middle of every extreme of life: he is middle-aged, of the middle-class, and of middling talent. Against all these middlings he struggles to find an edge, by occasionally daubing burnt cork on his face, by heavy drinking, and by hard working, but each time falls back into the slough of his middleness depressed and exhausted:

> He lay in the middle of the world, and twicht.
> More Sparine for Pelides,
> human (half) & down here as he is,
> with probably insulting mail to open
> and certainly unworthy words to hear
> and his unforgivable memory.

Or again, "Henry felt baffled, in the middle of the thing," which is a refrain of his efforts and sufferings.

The desire to transcend his undefined existence wears down into defeat in later sections of this sequence, until "Henry hates the world. What the world to Henry/did will not bear thought." The despair deepens into rejection: "This world is gradually becoming a place/

where I do not care to be any more." He broods upon death in all its forms and nightmare possibilities, including the frequent lamentations for other poets who have died recently, and who seem to share his dark view of the world:

> I'm cross with God who has wrecked this generation.
> First he seized Ted [Roethke], then Richard [Blackmur], Randall [Jarrell], and now
> Delmore [Schwartz].
> In between he gorged on Sylvia Plath.
> That was a first rate haul. He left alive
> fools I could number like a kitchen knife
> but Lowell he did not touch.

In a later, grimmer juncture of the *Songs*, Henry remarks bitterly, "The world grows more disgusting dawn by dawn." The poems then take up a plot of sorts with a residence in Ireland, followed by a return to the United States and the long attempt to recover from alcoholism, a turn that also involves Henry in religious conversion.

The whole work, including the posthumous additions, *Henry's Fate*, amounts to a vast mosaic of pieces of Henry's life and character, without transforming such pieces into a unified vision. The work is discordant throughout, in its language and in its jagged progression of themes and motifs. It is essentially a long and despairing examination of a poet's alienation from the post-war world, in which his brilliance and cultural inheritance appear to have no place or value. The grave, devoted artist founders and ultimately destroys himself, lamenting throughout the cursed and crooked fate of his fellow poets. This tragedy is lifted above self-pity and sentimentality by the essential good character of Henry, whose complicated interiors give us a Hamlet for this age.

Berryman's later works, *Love and Fame*, *Delusions, Etc.*, and the novel *Recovery*, turn away from the *Dream Songs* to treat more directly of the poet's life. *Love and Fame* is unabashed autobiography of the poet's education and rise to prominence, delivered in a flat, narrative style unlike his earlier verse. In *Delusions, Etc.* his religious turning is expressed in a section of liturgical poems where Berryman is again the effortless master of sonorous lyrics. *Recovery*, unfinished at the poet's death, exposes the torment of the alcoholic and eloquently pleads for understanding of this disease from which the poet suffered much of his life.

—Paul Christensen

BETHELL, Mary Ursula. New Zealander. Born in Surrey, England, 6 October 1874. Educated in England and New Zealand; studied music and painting. Social worker in London and Scotland, 1898–1902; returned to New Zealand permanently in 1919, and settled in Canterbury. *Died 15 January 1945.*

PUBLICATIONS

Verse

From a Garden in the Antipodes. 1929.
The Glad Returning and Other Poems. 1932.
The Haunted Gallery and Other Poems. 1932.

Time and Place.   1936.
Day and Night: Poems 1924–1934.   1939.
Collected Poems.   1950.

Reading List: *Bethell* by M. M. Holcroft, 1975.

*   *   *

Almost all of Mary Ursula Bethell's verse was written (though not published) during a single period of sustained creative activity from 1924 to 1934, between her fiftieth and sixtieth years. Her late flowering began when, after a lifetime spent moving back and forth between England (where she was born) and New Zealand (where she had spent her childhood), she finally settled permanently in New Zealand. With her beloved companion Effie Pollen she moved into a house on the Cashmere Hills overlooking the city of Christchurch, with the Pacific coast of the South Island curving away to the north and east and the Canterbury plains stretching away to the mountains of the Southern Alps in the north and west, as described in "Southerly Sunday":

> The great south wind has covered with cloud the whole of the river-plain,
> soft white ocean of foaming mist, blotting out, billowing
>
> fast to the east, where Pacific main surges on vaster bed.
> But here, on the hills, south wind unvapoured encounters the sunshine,
> lacing and interlocking, the invisible effervescence
> you almost hear, and the laughter of light and air at play overhead.
>
> Seabirds fly free; see the sharp flash of their underwings!
> and high lifted up to the north, the mountains, the mighty, the white ones
> rising sheer from the cloudy sea, light-crowned, established.

Her productive phase ended when Miss Pollen died in 1934 and the house and garden on the hills was vacated. Little was added to her work in the last decade of her life beyond a sequence of annual anniversary poems, written to commemorate the friend whom she considered the "only begetter" of her verse.

Her first book, *From a Garden in the Antipodes*, consists of brief, unpretentious, apparently mundane but deceptively simple poems recording the trivia of a gardener's chores and observations through the seasonal cycle from one autumn to another. Digging, planting, weeding, planning, watching shrubs and plants sprout and bloom, reporting changes in the weather and the view – such is the substance of these modest, prosaic but delightful verses. Beyond the simple surface, however, are wider implications, as suggested by the phrase "garden of exile, garden of my pilgrimage" from an unpublished poem. Ursula Bethell felt herself to be a transplanted Englishwoman for whom her garden (and her poetry which she tends to identify with it) was both a reminder of her exile and a compensation for it. To some degree she stands for all New Zealanders, colonists all, gardening the antipodes. The garden is also her pilgrimage, her way to God. She was a deeply religious woman, and her garden poems were her means of localising the transcendent truths of her religion, though the religious meaning is seldom pointed directly as it is almost invariably in her later volumes.

In *Time and Place* and *Day and Night* the symbolism is more explicit and the message more manifestly Christian. The final stanza of "Southerly Sunday," for example, points the religious meaning of the preceding landscape description (quoted above):

> This sparkling day is the Lord's day. Let us be glad and rejoice in it;
> for he cometh, he cometh to judge and redeem his beautiful universe,
> and holds in his hands all worlds, all men, the quick and the dead.

Time and Place is organised according to the sequence of the seasons, *Day and Night* according to the diurnal cycle, thereby underlining the theme of death and resurrection which is central to her work. The religious poems tend on the whole to be less spontaneous than the garden poems, and are occasionally overwrought both emotionally and technically. When the natural occasion, however, is sufficiently realised to sustain the supernatural meanings attributed to it, Ursula Bethell achieves poems of considerable beauty and force.

—Peter Simpson

BETJEMAN, Sir John. English. Born in Highgate, London, in 1906. Educated at Marlborough; Magdalen College, Oxford. Served as Press Attaché, Dublin, 1941–42; in the Admiralty, London, 1943. Married the author Penelope Valentine Hester in 1933; one son and one daughter. Book Reviewer, *Daily Herald*, London; radio and television broadcaster. Columnist ("City and Suburban"), *Spectator*, London, 1954–58. Founder, Victorian Society; Member, Royal Fine Art Commission; Governor, Pusey House (Church of England). Recipient: Heinemann Award, 1949; Foyle Poetry Prize, 1955, 1959; Loines Award, 1956; Duff Cooper Memorial Prize, 1958; Queen's Gold Medal for Poetry, 1960. LL.D.: Aberdeen University; D.Litt.: Oxford, Reading, and Birmingham universities. Honorary Fellow, Keble College, Oxford, 1972. Companion of Literature, Royal Society of Literature, 1968. Honorary Associate, Royal Institute of British Architects; Honorary Member, American Academy of Arts and Letters, 1973. C.B.E. (Commander, Order of the British Empire), 1960; knighted, 1969. Poet Laureate since 1972. Lives in London.

PUBLICATIONS

Verse

> *Mount Zion; or, In Touch with the Infinite.* 1931.
> *Continual Dew: A Little Book of Bourgeois Verse.* 1937.
> *Sir John Piers.* 1938.
> *Old Lights for New Chancels: Verses Topographical and Amatory.* 1940.
> *New Bats in Old Belfries.* 1945.
> *Slick But Not Streamlined: Poems and Short Pieces,* edited by W. H. Auden. 1947.
> *Selected Poems,* edited by John Sparrow. 1948.
> *A Few Late Chrysanthemums.* 1954.
> *Poems in the Porch.* 1954.
> *Collected Poems,* edited by the Earl of Birkenhead. 1958; revised edition, 1962, 1972.
> *(Poems).* 1958.
> *Summoned by Bells* (verse autobiography). 1960.
> *A Ring of Bells,* edited by Irene Slade. 1962.
> *High and Low.* 1966.
> *Six Betjeman Songs,* music by Mervyn Horder. 1967.
> *A Nip in the Air.* 1974.
> *Betjeman in Miniature: A Selection of Short Poems.* 1976.
> *Metro-land: Selected Verses from His Commentary for the Film.* 1977.

Plays

Television Documentaries: *The Stained Glass at Fairford*, 1955; *Pity about the Abbey*, with Stewart Farver, 1965; *Metro-land*, 1973; *A Passion for Churches*, 1974; *Vicar of This Parish* (on Francis Kilvert), 1976.

Other

Ghastly Good Taste; or, A Depressing Story of the Rise and Fall of English Architecture. 1933; revised edititon, 1970.
Devon. 1936.
An Oxford University Chest: Comprising a Description of the Present State of the Town and University of Oxford, with an Itinerary Arranged Alphabetically. 1938.
Vintage London. 1942.
English Cities and Small Towns. 1943.
John Piper. 1944.
Murray's Buckinghamshire Architectural Guide, with John Piper. 1948.
Murray's Berkshire Architectural Guide, with John Piper. 1949.
Murray's Shropshire Architectural Guide, with John Piper. 1951.
First and Last Loves (essay on architecture). 1952.
Collins Guide to English Parish Churches, Including the Isle of Man. 1958; as *An American's Guide to English Parish Churches*, 1959; revised edition, as *Collins Pocket Guide to English Parish Churches*, 2 vols., 1968.
Ground Plan to Skyline. 1960.
English Churches, with Basil Clarke. 1964.
Cornwall. 1964.
The City of London Churches. 1965.
London's Historic Railway Stations. 1972.
A Pictorial History of English Architecture. 1972.
West Country Churches. 1973.
A Plea for Holy Trinity Church. 1974.
Archie and the Strict Baptists (juvenile). 1977.

Editor, *Cornwall Illustrated: In a Series of Views of Castles, Seats of the Nobility, Mines, Picturesque Scenery, Towns, Public Buildings, Churches, Antiquities, Etc.* 1934.
Editor, *A Pickwick Portrait Gallery, from the Pens of Divers Admirers.* 1936.
Editor, *Selected Poems*, by Sir Henry Newbolt. 1940.
Editor, with Geoffrey Taylor, *English, Scottish, and Welsh Landscape, 1700–ca. 1860* (verse anthology). 1944.
Editor, with Geoffrey Taylor, *English Love Poems.* 1957.
Editor, *Altar and Pew: Church of England Verses.* 1959.
Editor, with Sir Charles Tennyson, *A Hundred Sonnets*, by Charles Tennyson Turner. 1960.
Editor, with Winifred Hindley, *A Wealth of Poetry.* 1963.
Editor, *Victorian and Edwardian London from Old Photographs.* 1968.
Editor, with J. S. Gray, *Victorian and Edwardian Brighton from Old Photographs.* 1972.
Editor, with A. L. Rowse, *Victorian and Edwardian Cornwall from Old Photographs.* 1974.
Editor, *A Selection of Poems*, by John Masefield. 1978.

Bibliography: *Betjeman: A Bibliography of Writings by and about Him* by Margaret L. Stapleton, 1974.

Reading List: *Betjeman: A Study* by Derek Stanford, 1961; *Ronald Firbank and Betjeman* by Jocelyn Brooke, 1962; *Betjeman* by John Press, 1974.

*   *   *

Had anybody prophesied in 1936 that John Betjeman would become an immensely popular figure on television, the most financially successful living poet, a Knight, and the successor to Cecil Day Lewis as Poet Laureate, his forecast would have seemed ludicrously far-fetched. For Betjeman was known in the mid 1930's only as the author of a volume of poems, *Mount Zion*, published in 1931 by a friend who owned a small printing firm, and of a book on architecture with the somewhat frivolous title, *Ghastly Good Taste*. Betjeman describes *Mount Zion* in the dedication as a "precious hyper-sophisticated book," and its subtitle, *In Touch with the Infinite*, taken in conjunction with some of the poems, bears out the promise or the threat of the dedication. "Competition," one of the nine poems from *Mount Zion* omitted from Betjeman's *Collected Poems*, contains some lines that exude what casual readers still regard as the quintessence of Betjeman's poetry, a half-mocking, half-affectionate celebration of Victorian piety and Victorian architecture:

> The Gothic is bursting over the way
>   With Evangelical Song,
> For the pinnacled Wesley Memorial Church
>   Is over a hundred strong.

Betjeman has continued over the years to write about architecture and to delight mass audiences on TV with his guided tours of city and suburban buildings in Britain and Australia. Anybody who takes the trouble to read his architectural writings, from *Ghastly Good Taste* onwards, will discover that he is no mere antiquary bent on preserving anything that is quaint or amusing but, on the contrary, a serious historian of English architecture.

W. H. Auden, who dedicated *The Age of Anxiety* to Betjeman, wrote a preface to his choice of Betjeman's verse and prose, *Slick But Not Streamlined*. He stressed the importance of *topophilia* in Betjeman's poetry, taking up a remark made by Betjeman in his preface to *Old Lights for New Chancels*: "I see no harm in trying to describe overbuilt Surrey in verse. But when I do so I am not being satirical but topographical." He has continued to write such poems throughout his career, but they are only one of the several kinds of verse that he has made peculiarly his own. His satirical poems are among his weakest, and what has been called his *New Statesman* competition verse is even less rewarding. Yet anthologists continue to reprint "Slough," "In Westminster Abbey," and "How to Get On in Society," even though Betjeman himself has remarked that "they now seem to me merely comic verse and competent magazine writing, topical and tiresome."

His exploration of "Betjeman country" in poems such as "Pot Pourri from a Surrey Garden" (a title cribbed from a late Victorian book by a high-born lady) is a more original and more serious achievement. Through those landscapes with figures there stalk such formidable Amazons as Pam, that "great big mountainous sports girl," and a young woman apostrophised in "The Olympic Girl" as "Fair tigress of the tennis courts." Yet his topographical poems are most moving when precise observation is fused with irony tempered by compassion. "Middlesex" begins by portraying "Fair Elaine the bobby-soxer,/ Fresh-complexioned with Innoxa," but it broadens into a lament for the enormous hayfields of the Middlesex countryside obliterated by Elaine's suburban world, and concludes with an evocation of the Carrara-covered cemeteries where the Victorian dead repose, "Long in Kensal Green and Highgate silent under soot and stone."

In the late 1940's a new theme — the sea, linked with memories of childhood — entered Betjeman's poetry, at much the same time as he embarked on his first attempts at blank verse, "Sunday Afternoon Service in St. Enodoc Church, Cornwall" and "North Coast Recollections." He handles blank verse with considerable skill in those poems, in his long autobiographical poem, *Summoned by Bells*, and in a few other pieces, notably in the valediction, "On Leaving Wantage 1972," from *A Nip in the Air*.

Betjeman, however, is one of those poets who enjoy the challenge presented by rhyming schemes and metrical patterns. He tells us that, with him, a poem begins when some recollection "hammers inside the head," that "a line or a phrase suggests itself," and that the next step is "the selection of a metre. I am a traditionalist in metres and have made few experiments. The rhythms of Tennyson, Crabbe, Hawker, Dowson, Hardy, James Elroy Flecker, Moore and Hymns A & M are generally buzzing about in my brain and I choose one from these which seems to me to suit the theme." To that list we may add the names of Frederick Locker-Lampson, Father Prout, Dibdin, William Allingham, Longfellow, and Newbolt. The chances are that the more intricate the pattern the more accomplished the poem. Examples that come to mind are "Pot Pourri from a Surrey Garden," "Henley-on-Thames," "Middlesex," "Ireland with Emily," and "I. M. Walter Ramsden."

Some of Betjeman's most powerful and memorable poems are inspired by the contemplation of death, recollections of childhood, memories of lust, the spectacle of change and decay, the longing for eternal peace in the presence of God. When two or more of those elements are commingled in a poem they yield a potent brew. "Late-Flowering Lust" dwells on the image of two skeletons:

> Dark sockets look on emptiness
> Which once was loving-eyed,
> The mouth that opens for a kiss
> Has got no tongue inside.

"N.W.5 & N.6" evokes Betjeman's childhood fears awakened by a nursery-maid's talk of damnation as church bells rang out in the evening sky, infecting the child with

> her fear
> And guilt at endlessness. I caught them too,
> Hating to think of sphere succeeding sphere
> Into eternity and God's dread will.
> I caught her terror then. I have it still.

In "Felixstowe *or* The Last of Her Order" the only survivor of an order founded in 1854 avows her faith: "Safe from the surging of the lonely sea/My heart finds rest, my heart finds rest in Thee." Many of Betjeman's finest poems derive their energy from the tension between faith and despair.

—John Press

BINYON, (Robert) Laurence. English. Born in Lancaster, 10 August 1869. Educated at St. Paul's School, London; Trinity College, Oxford (Newdigate Prize, 1890). Married Cicely Margaret Pryor Powell, 1904; three daughters. Entered the Department of Printed Books, British Museum, London, 1893; transferred to the Department of Prints and Drawings, 1895; Assistant Keeper, 1909; Deputy Keeper in charge of the sub-department of Oriental Prints and Drawings, 1913–32; Keeper of Prints and Drawings, 1932–33. Lectured in the U.S.A., 1912; Lowell Lecturer, U.S.A., 1914, 1926; lectured in Japan, 1929; Charles Eliot Norton Professor of Poetry, Harvard University, Cambridge, Massachusetts, 1933–34;

Byron Professor, University of Athens, 1940. President, English Association, 1933–34, and English Verse-Speaking Association, 1934–35. Officier de l'Instruction Publique; Chevalier of the Legion of Honour; Fellow, Royal Society of Literature; Honorary Fellow, Trinity College, Oxford, 1933. Companion of Honour, 1932. *Died 10 March 1943.*

PUBLICATIONS

Verse

> *Persephone.* 1890.
> *Lyric Poems.* 1894.
> *Poems.* 1895.
> *London Visions.* 2 vols., 1896–99; revised edition, 1908.
> *The Praise of Life.* 1896.
> *Porphyrion and Other Poems.* 1898.
> *Odes.* 1901; revised edition, 1913.
> *The Dream of Adam and Other Poems.* 1903.
> *Dream Come True.* 1905.
> *Penthesilia.* 1905.
> *England and Other Poems.* 1909.
> *Auguries.* 1913.
> *The Winnowing-Fan: Poems on the Great War.* 1914.
> *The Anvil and Other Poems.* 1916.
> *The Cause: Poems of the War.* 1917.
> *For the Fallen and Other Poems.* 1917.
> *The New World.* 1918.
> *The Four Years: War Poems.* 1919.
> *Six Poems on Bruges.* 1919.
> *The Secret: Sixty Poems.* 1920.
> *The Sirens: An Ode.* 1924.
> *Little Poems from the Japanese.* 1925.
> *A Binyon Anthology.* 1927.
> *The Idols: An Ode.* 1928.
> *Collected Poems.* 2 vols., 1931.
> *Koya San: Four Poems from Japan.* 1932.
> *Three Poems.* 1934.
> *The North Star and Other Poems.* 1941.
> *The Burning of the Leaves and Other Poems,* edited by Cicely Margaret Binyon. 1944.
> *The Madness of Merlin,* edited by Gordon Bottomley. 1947.

Plays

> *The Supper: A Lyrical Scene.* 1897.
> *Paris and Oenone* (produced 1906). 1906.
> *Attila* (produced 1907). 1907.
> *Bombastes in the Shades.* 1915.
> *Sakuntala,* from a play by Kalidasa (produced 1919). 1920.
> *Arthur* (produced 1923). 1923.
> *Ayuli.* 1923.
> *The Young King* (produced 1924). 1934.

Boadicea.   1927.
Sophro the Wise (juvenile).   1927.
Love in the Desert.   1928.
Three Short Plays: Godstow Nunnery, Love in the Desert, Memnon.   1930.
Brief Candles.   1938.
British Museum Diversion: A Play for Puppets, in *Horizon.*   1944.

Other

Dutch Etchers of the Seventeenth Century.   1895.
John Crome and John Sell Cotman.   1897.
Western Flanders: A Medley of Things Seen, Considered, and Imagined.   1899.
Thomas Girton: His Life and Works.   1900.
Japanese Art.   1907.
Painting in the Far East.   1908; revised edition, 1913, 1923, 1934.
The Flight of the Dragon: An Essay in the Theory and Practice of Art in China and Japan.   1911.
The Art of Botticelli.   1913.
Mr. Yuan's Landscape Roll in the Freer Collection.   1916.
For Dauntless France.   1918.
Poetry and Modern Life.   1918.
The Court Painters of the Grand Moguls.   1921.
Japanese Colour Prints, with J. J. O. Sexton.   1923; edited by Basil Gray, 1960.
Asiatic Art in the British Museum: Sculpture and Painting.   1925.
The Followers of Blake: Edward Calvert, Samuel Palmer, George Richmond, and Their Circle.   1925.
The Engraved Designs of Blake.   1926.
Tradition and Reaction in Modern Poetry.   1926.
The Poems of Nizami Described.   1928.
Landscape in English Art and Poetry.   1930.
Akbar.   1932.
English Water-Colours.   1933.
The Case of Christopher Smart.   1934.
The Spirit of Man in Asian Art (lectures).   1935.

Editor, *Index of Artists in the Department of Prints and Drawings in the British Museum,* revised edition.   1893.
Editor, *Pictures by Japanese Artists.*   1908.
Editor, *Masterpieces of Etching.*   2 vols., 1914.
Editor, *Poetical Works,* by Keats.   1916.
Editor, *The Golden Treasury of Modern Lyrics.*   1924.
Editor, *The Letters of Maurice Hewlett.*   1926.
Editor, *Songs of Love and Death,* by Manomohana Ghosha.   1926.
Editor, *The Golden Treasury of Songs and Lyrics, Nineteenth Century,* supplement to Palgrave.   1926.
Editor, *Poems of Blake.*   1931.

Translator (verse only), with Eric R. D. Maclagan, *The Book of the Duke of True Lovers,* by Christine de Pisan.   1907.
Translator, with P. Tonapetean, *The Meeting of the Kings,* by Mekertich Khrimean.   1915.
Translator, *Episodes from the Divine Comedy,* by Dante.   1928.
Translator, *The Inferno, Purgatorio, and Paradiso of Dante.*   3 vols., 1933–43.

Reading List: in *Sowing the Field* by J. G. Southworth, 1940.

*   *   *

Laurence Binyon was a man of rare achievement in several different fields. He wrote on English and on Far Eastern art; he was a poet and playwright; and he translated Dante's *Divine Comedy* into English triple rhyme. The work on English watercolours might have been expected from "the very learned British Museum assistant" whom Ezra Pound mentions in "Pagani's, November 8." But, as Pound's poem suggests, Binyon had surprising depths; as a poet, Pound himself learned much from *The Flight of the Dragon*. And Binyon's other pioneering works of appreciation of Chinese and Japanese art made fruitful use of his reading in literary sources.

Binyon is a minor though highly accomplished poet, not much read today, though his poem "For the Fallen" (of the Great War) is very well known through its use in Remembrance Day ceremonies. It is a dignified and moving public tribute. His more personal poem on the Second World War, "The Burning of the Leaves," has been widely anthologised. He is a perfectionist in verse and diction, but too correct and literary for modern taste, though markedly less academic than, say, Robert Bridges.

His scholarly and artistic talents found their ideal vehicle in his version of Dante, by far the finest English verse translation, since all others lack gravity and consistency of style. His reproduction of *terza rima* in English is remarkable in itself, but the combination of terseness and decorum was an even more indispensable element in the success of this apparently impossible exercise. The publication of the *Paradiso* in 1943 completed his most lasting achievement. The skills of versification and the profound culture that produced Binyon's poetic language are not likely to be found again in any of his successors in this task of unique importance for English literature.

—M. J. Alexander

BIRNEY, Earle. Canadian. Born in Calgary, Alberta, 13 May 1904. Educated at the University of British Columbia, Vancouver, B.A. 1926; University of Toronto, M.A. 1927, Ph.D. 1936; University of California, Berkeley, 1927–30; Queen Mary College, London, 1934–35. Served in the Canadian Army, in the reserves, 1940–41, and on active duty, 1942–45; Major-in-Charge, Personnel Selection, Belgium and Holland, 1944–45. Married Esther Bull in 1940; one child. Instructor in English, University of Utah, Salt Lake City, 1930–34; Lecturer, later Assistant Professor of English, University of Toronto, 1936–42; Supervisor, European Foreign Language Broadcasts, Radio Canada, Montreal, 1945–46; Professor of Medieval English Literature, 1946–63, and Professor and Chairman of the Department of Creative Writing, 1963–65, University of British Columbia; Writer-in-Residence, University of Toronto, 1965–67, and University of Waterloo, Ontario, 1967–68; Regents Professor in Creative Writing, University of California at Irvine, 1968. Since 1968, free-lance writer and lecturer. Literary Editor, *Canadian Forum*, Toronto, 1936–40; Editor, *Canadian Poetry Magazine*, Edmonton, 1946–48; Editor, *Prism International*, Vancouver, 1964–65; Advisory Editor, *New: American and Canadian Poetry*, Trumansburg, New York, 1966–70. Recipient: Governor-General's Award, 1943, 1946; Stephen Leacock Medal, 1950; Borestone Mountain Poetry Award, 1951; Canadian Government Overseas Fellowship, 1953, Service Medal, 1970; Lorne Pierce Medal, 1953; President's Medal,

University of Western Ontario, 1954; Nuffield Fellowship, 1958; Canada Council Senior
Arts Grant, 1962, 1974, Medal, 1968, Special Fellowship, 1968, and Travel Grant, 1971,
1974. LL.D.: University of Alberta, Edmonton, 1965. Fellow, Royal Society of Canada,
1954. Lives in Toronto.

PUBLICATIONS

Verse

    David and Other Poems.   1942.
    Now Is the Time.   1945.
    Strait of Anian: Selected Poems.   1948.
    Trial of a City and Other Verse.   1952.
    Ice Cod Bell or Stone.   1962.
    Near False Creek Mouth.   1964.
    Selected Poems 1940–1966.   1966.
    Memory No Servant.   1968.
    Poems.   1969.
    Pnomes, Jukollages and Other Stunzas.   1969.
    Rag and Bone Shop.   1971.
    Five Modern Canadian Poets, with others, edited by Eli Mandel.   1970.
    Four Parts Sand: Concrete Poems, with others.   1972.
    Bear on the Delhi Road.   1973.
    What's So Big about Green?   1973.
    Collected Poems.   2 vols., 1974.

Play

    The Damnation of Vancouver: A Comedy in Seven Episodes (broadcast, 1952).   *In Trial
    of a City,* 1952; revised version (produced 1957), in *Selected Poems,* 1966.

    Radio Play: *The Damnation of Vancouver,* 1952.

Fiction

    Turvey: A Military Picaresque.   1949.
    Down the Long Table.   1955.

Other

    The Creative Writer.   1966.
    The Cow Jumped over the Moon: The Writing and Reading of Poetry.   1972.

    Editor, *Twentieth Century Canadian Poetry.*   1953.
    Editor, *Record of Service in the Second World War.*   1955.
    Editor, with others, *New Voices.*   1956.
    Editor, with Margerie Lowry, *Selected Poems of Malcoim Lowry.*   1962.
    Editor, with Margerie Lowry, *Lunar Caustic,* by Malcolm Lowry.   1963.

Bibliography: in *West Coast Review*, October 1970.

Reading List: *Birney* by Richard Robillard, 1971; *Birney* by Frank Davey, 1971; *Birney* edited by Bruce Nesbitt, 1974.

*   *   *

Earle Birney is almost certainly the most distinguished of living Canadian poets. Even in his earliest verse we can see his essential poetic qualifications, a gift for cut and graven detail, a flowing empathy, and a natural rhythm in which the breathing meets the sense to produce an evolving, living line. Impressive miniatures of these powers are "Slug in Woods" and "Aluroid."

Landscape is a traditional theme in Canadian poetry, a fact which is hardly surprising in a country so physically overwhelming and so variously beautiful as Canada, where even today life is intimately harnessed to the rhythms of the climate and the seasons. Some of the most notable members of Birney's Canadian scene are "Atlantic Door," "Maritime Faces," "Dusk on the Bay," "Hands," "North of Superior," "Ellesmere Land, I," "North Star West," "The Ebb Begins from Dream," "Winter Saturday," "Holiday in the Foothills," "Bushed," "Images in Place of Logging." "David," an energetic narrative poem about climbing, and reminiscent of those "action" poems of the 1930's in England, is less successfully realised, perhaps spoilt by moralising, as is another well-known poem, "November Walk by False Creek Mouth." But the successful poems of this kind compose a poetic geography of Canada, defining its bone, frame, moods, and treacheries. Birney evokes in each of these poems of landscape the natural world in process: the verbs are continuous, there is a sense of stirring molecular activity implicit in the stoniest, harshest landscape, the mountains are weathering, the rooms lighting, the dampness steams. At the same time, something enduring in the country matches something stubborn in the poet. Birney's sensibility has, indeed, a hard and cobbled quality, a strength which does not forbid sensitivity and delicate registration but which sustains and toughens them. It is a note which we find in that slim, perfectly articulated poem, "Ellesmere Land, I."

What is clear from these poems and many others is a central fact of human existence for Birney: that man exists in a state of stoic detachment from the supporting earth, from his neighbours, from everything. In the candid and occasionally tetchy preface to his *Selected Poems 1940–1966* he explains that the poems are not so much efforts to bridge the gap as recognitions of the fact:

> That I go on so stubbornly to publish my incantations,
> in a world which may not last long enough to read them,
> and has shown little need for them so far, might be
> construed as mere vanity, or again as proof that the
> outer me is as abnormally compulsive as the inner. I
> prefer to believe, rather, that my poems are the best
> proof I can print of my humanness, signals out of the
> loneliness into which all of us are born and in which
> we die, affirmations of kinship with the other wayfarers....

Just so: and man is joined to man not by his effort, and its necessary failure, to cross over to his neighbour or his lover, but by the acknowledgment of a common predicament.

Buoyant and balanced: this phrase aptly describes his work at large. About its buoyancy one can say that the poet's natural sense of rhythm, itself the development of a profound human instinct, has been educated over fifty years of severe professional practice to such a pitch of intuitive taste, as to be utterly responsive to the needs of the poetry, and completely clean of any involuntarily deposited sludge or accidental silt. The medium has become an instrument. The same is true of the self. By unremitting application, by the most disinterested discipline, Birney's nature has been scraped and scrubbed free of affectation, presupposition, prejudice, so that it appears in the poetry of these last years in its authentically individual, true, worn state.

Buoyancy, not bounce, the product of discipline and a certain ease and confidence of character, itself the hard-won consequence of a life spent in the service of poetry and the mind, enables Birney in his poems, particularly in those of travel, to see a situation squarely with no distorting squint of preconception, without the patronage of self-indulgent pity or defensive guiltiness. He deals with it solely out of his own resources and purely on its own merits. There is, then, a balance or proportion between subject and object, a wholeness and unity in the former recognising the fullness and complexity of the latter. A Birney poem is never just the evocation of a scene. It always has an intellectual and moral structure. In all his poems of place, place itself aspires to support, or even to be, an event.

—William Walsh

BISHOP, Elizabeth. American. Born in Worcester, Massachusetts, 8 February 1911. Educated at Vassar College, Poughkeepsie, New York, A.B. 1934. Lived in Brazil for 16 years. Consultant in Poetry, Library of Congress, Washington, D.C., 1949–50. Poet-in-Residence, University of Washington, Seattle, 1966, 1973. Since 1970, Lecturer in English, Harvard University, Cambridge, Massachusetts. Recipient: Guggenheim Fellowship, 1947; National Institute of Arts and Letters grant, 1951; Shelley Memorial Award, 1953; Pulitzer Prize, 1956; Amy Lowell Traveling Fellowship, 1957; Chapelbrook Fellowship, 1962; Academy of American Poets Fellowship, 1964; Rockefeller Fellowship, 1967; Ingram Merrill Foundation grant, 1969; National Book Award, 1970; Harriet Monroe Prize, 1974. LL.D.: Smith College, Northampton, Massachusetts, 1968; Rutgers University, New Brunswick, New Jersey, 1972; Brown University, Providence, Rhode Island, 1972. Chancellor, Academy of American Poets, 1966; Member, American Academy of Arts and Letters, 1976. Order of Rio Branco (Brazil), 1971.

PUBLICATIONS

Verse

North and South.   1946.
Poems: North and South — A Cold Spring.   1955.
Poems.   1956.
Questions of Travel.   1965.
Selected Poems.   1967.
The Ballad of the Burglar of Babylon (juvenile).   1968.
The Complete Poems.   1969.
Geography III.   1977.

Other

Brazil, with the Editors of Life.   1962.

Editor and Translator, *Anthology of Contemporary Brazilian Poetry,* vol. 1.   1972.

Translator, *The Diary of Helena Morley.*   1957.

Reading List: *Bishop* by Anne Stevenson, 1966.

*   *   *

Elizabeth Bishop's autobiographical "In the Village," a story which moves towards poetry and was included at the center of *Questions of Travel,* shows how the sounds and sights and textures of a Nova Scotia village enable a child to come to terms with the sound of the scream which signified her mother's madness and, ultimately, with human isolation, loss, mortality; the child's capacity for meticulous attention serves not merely as a method of escaping from intolerable pain, but also as an opening from the prison of the self and its wounds to a rejoicing in both human creativity and the things and events of an ordinary day. The story, with its nod of homage to Chekhov, provides an accurate anticipation of the peculiar virtues of Elizabeth Bishop's poetry: her fantastic powers of observation, her impeccable ear, and her precise and often haunting sense of tone.

Her first volume, *North and South,* was a rigorous selection from earlier work. Although some of its poems are set in New York or Paris or New England or have no localized geographical setting, a number of the best ones are firmly placed in Nova Scotia or Florida. *A Cold Spring* continued the emphasis on place: a farm in Maryland, Nova Scotia again, Washington, D.C., Key West and New York, and, with "Arrival at Santos," Brazil, which was to be her home for a number of years. The poems in *Questions of Travel* are divided into two groups: "Brazil" and "Elsewhere." (Another result of her residence in Brazil was her beautiful translation of *The Diary of Helena Morley.*) *The Complete Poems* included new original poems set in Brazil as well as translation from Carlos Drummond de Andrade and João Cabral de Melo Neto.

The title and some of the directions of *Geography III* were anticipated in the final line of "The Map," the first poem in her first volume: "More delicate than the historian's are the map-maker's colors." The map-maker (not the tourist) who comes truly to know differing peoples and their places for himself can see with fresh and multiple perspectives, and his discriminations may well be finer than the historian's if his powers of observation are intense, his sympathies wide, his moral judgments delicate, and his imagination that of a poet.

Miss Bishop's geography is also of the imagination and the soul. Her poems treat their readers with unusual consideration. With the beginning of each poem we know that we *are* somewhere interesting (whether in a real or a surreal or a dream world), and we hear immediately a recognizable human voice: the poems make absorbing sense on a simple or naturalistic level. She is interested in, and asks our respectful attention for, everything that she puts into her poems; ultimate and "large" significances come only (and naturally) out of our experience of the whole.

The consideration is real, and one of its chief instruments is an unusual purity of diction. On a number of occasions one may be surprised to discover an image or detail or even a quoted phrase from the poetry of George Herbert. She found Herbert's example thoroughly congruent with one of the things she admired most about modernist poetry of the early twentieth century: the rejection of familiar public rhetoric and the consciously poetic for a language closer to that of a conversation between literate friends. Miss Bishop has consistently sustained her own high version of that standard: no inversions and no inflations, no Ciceronian periods, no elevated "poetic diction." Her indebtedness to Marianne Moore's imaginative precision is handsomely acknowledged in "Invitation to Miss Marianne Moore" (the poem also owes something to Pablo Neruda). Her uses of other writers are markedly individual: her few epigrams are from Bunyan, Hopkins, and Sir Kenneth Clark; the poignant "Crusoe in England" owes as much to Charles Darwin as to Defoe.

Also like Herbert, Miss Bishop seems to have sought a unique form for almost every poem. Her range extends from prose poems such as "Rainy Season; Sub-Tropics" and "12 O'Clock News" through relatively "free" and blank verse and unrhymed Horatian forms to strict quatrains and elaborately "counter-pointed" stanzas, a double sonnet ("The Prodigal," one of her best poems), sestinas and a villanelle, including along the way the lengthening triplets of "Roosters," derived from Crashaw's "Wishes to his (supposed) Mistress," "Visits to St. Elizabeths," modelled on "The House that Jack Built," a true ballad, "The Burglar of Babylon," and the songs that she wrote for Billie Holiday. Whatever the forms, they provide opportunities rather than limitations, and their art is self-effacing: the lines of "Sestina" end with the words *house, grandmother, child, stove, almanac,* and *tears.* Her use of assonance and slant-rhymes and variable line-lengths and rhyme patterns promises a useful freedom. Her example suggested to Robert Lowell the "way of breaking through the shell of my old manner" indicated by "Skunk Hour."

Miss Bishop has remained remarkably independent of schools or movements, religious, political, or literary. One modern practice that has proved fruitful for her is that of the collage, in which the artist discovers his subject and his form in ordinary or unexpected materials and objects. ("Objects and Apparitions," Bishop's translation of Octavio Paz's poem for Joseph Cornell, suggests the relation between collage and all art – as do her poems on the pictures of her great-uncle George.) Although the fictional speakers of her poems are often moving or witty (the Trollope of the Journals, a Brazilian friend in "Manuelzinho," Crusoe, a giant snail, a very small alien who reports on the writer's desk as a foreign landscape – all remarkable observers), in most of the poems the poet speaks in a voice recognizably her own. That the poems remain deeply personal rather than confessional may owe something to how firmly they are rooted in the "found": "Trouvée" in the flattened white hen on West 4th Street, "The Man-Moth" in a newspaper misprint for *mammoth,* "The Burglar of Babylon" in the fact that on the hills of Rio the rich and poor live their melodramas and lives within sight and sound of each other, "The Moose" in the Nova Scotia busride, "In the Waiting Room" in the events of late afternoon, "the fifth/of February, 1918." Almost every poem of Elizabeth Bishop's represents a human discovery both of the world and of an angle of vision. It is only superficially paradoxical that such creative novelty returns us, like "The Prodigal," to a familiar place and life: "But it took him a long time/finally to make his mind up to go home."

—Joseph H. Summers

BISHOP, John Peale. American. Born in Charles Town, West Virginia, 21 May 1892. Educated at high school in Hagerstown, Maryland; Mercersburg Academy, Pennsylvania; Princeton University, New Jersey, 1913–17 (Managing Editor, *Nassau Literary Magazine*), Litt.B. 1917 (Phi Beta Kappa). Served in the United States Army Infantry, 1917–19: First Lieutenant; Director of the Publications Program, 1941–42, and Special Consultant, 1943, Office of the Coordinator of Inter-American Affairs, Washington, D.C. Married Margaret Grosvenor Hutchins in 1922; three sons. Managing Editor, *Vanity Fair,* New York, 1920–22; free-lance writer from 1922; lived in Paris and Sorrento, 1922–24, New York, 1924–26, France, 1927–33, Louisiana and Connecticut, 1933–37, and in South Chatham, Massachusetts, 1937–44. *Died 4 April 1944.*

PUBLICATIONS

Collections

> *Collected Poems,* edited by Allen Tate.   1948; *Selected Poems,* 1960.
> *Collected Essays,* edited by Edmund Wilson.   1948.

Verse

> *Green Fruit.*   1917.
> *The Undertaker's Garland* (poems and stories), with Edmund Wilson.   1922.
> *Now with His Love.*   1933.
> *Minute Particulars.*   1935.
> *Selected Poems.*   1941.

Fiction

> *Many Thousands Gone* (stories).   1931.
> *Act of Darkness.*   1935.

Other

> Editor, with Allen Tate, *American Harvest: Twenty Years of Creative Writing in the United States.*   1942.

Bibliography: "Bishop: A Checklist" by J. Max Patrick and Robert W. Stallman, in *Princeton University Library Chronicle 7,* 1946.

Reading List: *A Southern Vanguard: The Bishop Memorial Volume* edited by Allen Tate, 1947; "The Achievement of Bishop" by Joseph Frank, in *The Widening Gyre,* 1963; *Bishop* by Robert L. White, 1966; "Bishop and the Other Thirties" by Leslie Fiedler, in *Commentary 43,* 1967; "Bishop" by Allen Tate, in *Essays of Four Decades,* 1968.

*   *   *

John Peale Bishop seems to owe his posthumous reputation to Allen Tate and Edmund Wilson, whose editing of the *Collected Poems* and *Collected Essays* in 1948 brought his most important work to the attention of a small audience. These books have long been out of print, but he continues to attract critics as different as Joseph Frank and Leslie Fiedler, and no account of American literary life between the two World Wars is complete without his name. He was at Princeton with Wilson and F. Scott Fitzgerald and consequently has associations with the milieu popularized by Fitzgerald's early novels; indeed he is the original for a character in *This Side of Paradise.* During the 1930's, especially after his return to America, he was thought of as a Southerner, partly because of his friendship with Tate. His two works of prose fiction are set in the "lost" part of West Virginia where he spent his boyhood and certainly have something in common with the Southern tradition of Faulkner, Caroline Gordon, and the others.

Bishop, however, must be thought of mainly as a poet, and it is the verse of his last decade that is most impressive. His regional allegiances count for very little here, though his residence on Cape Cod after 1938 was surely responsible for such late poems as "A Subject of Sea Change" and the group called "The Statues." These meditations on the sea and the destiny of civilizations carry forward the strongly pictorial qualities of such earlier poems as "The Return." Eventually one should see Bishop as an American poet who is descended from a great tradition of European humanism, and his criticism of the American scene is conducted from this point of view. One of his finest poems, "The Burning Wheel," sets the American pioneers beside the figure of Aeneas:

> They, too, the stalwart conquerors of space,
> Each on his shoulders wore a wise delirium
> Of memory and age: ghostly embrace
> Of fathers slanted toward a western tomb.
>
> A hundred and a hundred years they stayed
> Aloft, until they were as light as autumn
> Shells of locusts. Where then were they laid?
> And in what wilderness oblivion?

This refined yet deeply felt humanism is perhaps not characteristic of American writers, and Bishop was a writer on a small scale, but his best work in poetry and criticism survives very well.

—Ashley Brown

BLACKMORE, Sir Richard.   English.   Born in Corsham, Wiltshire, in 1653. Educated at Westminster School, London; St. Edmund Hall, Oxford, B.A. 1674, M.A. 1676; University of Padua, M.D.; Fellow of the Royal College of Physicians, 1687. Married Mary Blackmore. Schoolmaster after leaving Oxford; then travelled and studied on the Continent; appointed Physician to William III, 1697, and later to Queen Anne. Censor, 1716, and Elect, 1716–22, Royal College of Physicians. Knighted, 1697. *Died 9 October 1729.*

PUBLICATIONS

Verse

   Prince Arthur.   1695.
   King Arthur.   1697.
   A Satire Against Wit.   1700; edited by F. H. Ellis, in *Poems on Affairs of State 6,* 1971.
   A Paraphrase on the Book of Job.   1700.
   Discommendatory Verses.   1700; edited by R. C. Boys, in *Blackmore and the Wits,*
      1949.
   A Hymn to the Light of the World.   1703.
   Eliza.   1705.
   Advice to the Poets.   1706.
   The Kit-cats.   1708.

Instructions to Vander Bank: A Sequel to the Advice to the Poets. 1709.
The Nature of Man. 1711.
Creation: A Philosophical Poem. 1712.
A Collection of Poems on Various Subjects. 1718.
A New Version of the Psalms of David. 1721.
Redemption: A Divine Poem. 1722.
Alfred. 1723.

Other

A Short History of the Last Parliament. 1699.
*The Report of the Physicians and Surgeons Dissecting the Body of His Late Majesty
   (William III),* with Thomas Millington and Edward Hannes. 1702.
The Lay-Monastery, Consisting of Essays, Discourses, etc., with John Hughes. 1714.
Essays upon Several Subjects. 2 vols., 1716–17.
Just Prejudices Against the Arian Hypothesis. 1721.
Modern Arians Unmasked. 1721.
A Discourse upon the Plague. 1721.
A True and Impartial History of the Conspiracy Against King William in 1695. 1723.
A Treatise upon the Small-Pox. 1723.
A Treatise of Consumptions and Other Distempers. 1724.
A Critical Dissertation upon Spleen. 1725.
A Treatise of the Spleen and Vapours. 1725.
Discourses on the Gout, Rheumatism, and the King's Evil. 1726.
Dissertations on a Dropsy, a Tympany, the Jaundice, the Stone, and a Diabetes. 1727.
Natural Theology; or, Moral Duties Considered Apart from Positive. 1728.
The Accomplished Preacher; or, An Essay on Divine Eloquence, edited by J.
   White. 1731.

Reading List: *Blackmore and the Wits* by R. C. Boys, 1949; *Blackmore* by Albert Rosenberg,
1953.

*   *   *

In the preface to *Prince Arthur* Richard Blackmore confesses, "Poetry has been so far from
being my business ... that it has employed but a small part of my time ... as the entertainment
of my idle hours...." No English writer better illustrates the sad fact that integrity, loyalty,
diligence, and information do not in themselves make a poet. Blackmore has all these, yet his
neglect by all save scholars picking over the debris of Augustan literary battlefields is
perfectly understandable.

Even among his contemporaries his reputation was unsure. He was unfortunate in his
choice of enemies, antagonising Dryden, Swift, and Pope, as well as lesser men like Garth
who had more wit if not vastly more talent than himself. Hence he comes to us as pure
buffoon; a figure from a Molière satire, scribbling in his coach as he goes from one
consultation to another; or pontificating in Will's coffee-house amidst his heavy, Whiggish,
city friends.

Blackmore's great defect is the unexciting quality of his language: he was said to be equally
cautious in his medical practice (sound enough, however, to be Royal Physician to William
and to Anne). He often preaches rather than teaches, and is entirely bound by those rules
which the great writers of epic understand but often break or extend. His work is
undramatic: never once does he create a character like Milton's Adam, let alone his Satan.
Exactly where he should rise – in the set-piece descriptions of battle, journey, and debate –
Blackmore falls. The following (from *Eliza*) is typical of the physician-poet:

He raised his reeking sword with slaughter red,
And aimed his blow between the breast and head,
Which did the pipe, that breath conveys, divide,
And cut the Jugulars from side to side.
And had it met the juncture of the bone
The Spaniard's head had from his shoulders flown.

His epic similes too often slide into this dismal world of eighteenth-century McGonagall-ism. The *Essays* are equally heavy-handed and ungracious: dissent at its most gawky. Yet his claim that "I have impartially pursued the interests of truth and virtue, without a design of pleasing or provoking any" is honestly meant. But it remains Blackmore's misfortune that he cannot "sing," and that his sense of "wonder" remains uncommunicated through his inert language.

Yet his first epic, *Prince Arthur*, was not ill received, and Johnson and Addison both praised *Creation*, his lengthy rhymed answer to the Aristotelian and Lucretian origins of the universe. As a document in the history of ideas, *Creation* does have interest, and its total sincerity can be engaging:

I would th'Eternal from his works assert,
And sing the wonders of creating art.

—T. Bareham

BLAIR, Robert. Scottish. Born in Edinburgh in 1699. Educated at the University of Edinburgh: also studied in Holland, took a degree there. Married Isabella Law in 1738; five sons, one daughter. Lived in Edinburgh, on an independent income, 1718–30; licensed to preach, 1729; ordained, Presbyterian Church, 1731; Minister of Athelstaneford, Haddingtonshire, 1731 until his death. *Died 4 February 1746*.

PUBLICATIONS

Collections

Poetical Works, with Beattie and Falconer, edited by George Gilfillan. 1854.

Verse

A Poem Dedicated to the Memory of William Law. 1728.
The Grave. 1743; revised edition, 1747.

Reading List: *The Background of Gray's Elegy: A Study in the Taste for Melancholy Poetry 1700–1760* by A. L. Read, 1953.

*   *   *

Robert Blair, though a minister of the episcopal Church of Scotland, has strong Evangelical, and even somewhat Calvinistic, leanings. His published verse consists only of the unremarkable *A Poem Dedicated to the Memory of William Law* and his famous blank-verse meditation *The Grave*, which was contemporaneous with Edward Young's *Night Thoughts*, and has commonly been associated with Parnell's *A Night-Piece on Death* and with Gray's *Elegy*, as a production of "the Graveyard School." Blair's avowed purpose is to recall men to an awareness of their own sinfulness by fixing their attention upon the facts of death and judgement; but his self-indulgent relish in describing cadaverous horrors goes well beyond the requirements of mere didacticism; so the poem becomes largely a succession of picturesque descriptions of such objects as mouldy damps, ropy slime and high-fed worms lazily coiled as they feed upon damask cheeks. The free movement of Blair's lines, as well as his occasional dry humour and macabre images, owes more to Jacobean dramatists and early seventeenth-century mortuary verse than they do to the eighteenth-century tradition of writing in blank verse. Most modern readers will find Blair grotesque, and perhaps even silly, where he seeks to be sublime; but in the heyday of the early nineteenth-century Evangelical Movement *The Grave* was immensely popular. One incidental consequence of this popularity was that Blake's magnificent designs to illustrate an edition of Blair's poem in 1808 were, in Blake's lifetime, his best-known work. Now *The Grave* is remembered more in connection with Blake than with Blair.

—A. J. Sambrook

BLAKE, William. English. Born in London, 28 November 1757. Studied at Pars' Drawing School, Strand, London, 1767; apprentice to the engraver James Basire, 1772–79; subsequently studied at the Royal Academy of Arts, London. Married Catharine Boucher in 1782. Worked as an illustrator and graphic designer, and gave drawing lessons, London, after 1778; moved to Felpham, Sussex, under the patronage of William Hayley, 1800; returned to London, 1803; after unsuccessful one-man show of his works in 1809 retreated into obscurity; in the 1820's attracted a group of young painters. *Died 12 August 1827.*

PUBLICATIONS

Collections

> *Writings*, edited by Geoffrey Keynes.   3 vols., 1925; revised edition, as *Poetry and Prose*, 1927, 1939; as *Complete Writings*, 1957, 1966.
> *Letters*, edited by Geoffrey Keynes.   1956; revised edition, 1968.
> *Poetry and Prose*, edited by David Erdman.   1965.
> *Complete Poems*, edited by W. H. Stevenson.   1973.
> *The Illuminated Blake*, edited by David Erdman.   1974.
> *Complete Poems*, edited by A. Ostriker.   1977.
> *Writings*, edited by G. E. Bentley, Jr.   2 vols., 1978.

Verse

> *Poetical Sketches*.   1783.
> *The Book of Thel*.   1789.

Songs of Innocence.   1789; expanded edition, as *Songs of Innocence and of Experience,*
   Shewing the Two Contrary States of the Human Soul, 1794.
The French Revolution.   1791.
The Marriage of Heaven and Hell.   1793.
For Children: The Gates of Paradise.   1793; revised edition, as *For the Sexes,* 1818(?).
Visions of the Daughters of Albion.   1793.
America: A Prophecy.   1793.
Europe: A Prophecy.   1794.
The First Book of Urizen.   1794.
The Book of Ahania.   1795.
The Book of Los.   1795.
The Song of Los.   1795.
Milton.   1804–09(?).
Jerusalem: The Emanation of the Giant Albion.   1804–20(?).
The Ghost of Abel: A Revelation in the Visions of Jehovah Seen by William Blake.   1822.
Tiriel.   1874; edited by G. E. Bentley, Jr., 1967.
Vala, edited by H. M. Margoliouth.   1956; as *The Four Zoas,* edited by G. E. Bentley,
   Jr., 1963.

Other

Notebook, edited by Geoffrey Keynes.   1935; edited by David Erdman, 1973.
Engravings, edited by Geoffrey Keynes.   1950.
The Blake-Varley Sketchbook of 1819, edited by Martin Butlin.   1969.
The Complete Graphic Works, edited by David Bindman.   1977.

Bibliography: *A Blake Bibliography: Annotated Lists of Works, Studies, and Blakeana* by G.
E. Bentley, Jr., and M. K. Nurmi, 1964, revised by Bentley, as *Blake Books,* 1977.

Reading List: *The Life of Blake* by Mona Wilson, 1927, revised editon, 1948, edited by
Geoffrey Keynes, 1971; *Fearful Symmetry* by Northrop Frye, 1947; *Infinity on the Anvil: A
Critical Study of Blake's Poetry,* 1954, and *Blake,* 1968, both by Stanley Gardner; *Blake,
Prophet Against Empire* by David Erdman, 1954, revised edition, 1969; *The Everlasting
Gospel: A Study in the Sources of Blake* by Arthur L. Morton, 1958; *The Valley of Vision:
Blake as Prophet and Revolutionary* by Peter F. Fisher, edited by Northrop Frye, 1961;
Blake's Apocalypse: A Study in Poetic Argument by Harold Bloom, 1963; *Innocence and
Experience: An Introduction to Blake* by E. D. Hirsch, Jr., 1964; *Blake's Humanism,*1968,
and *Blake's Visionary Universe,* 1969, both by John B. Beer; *Blake: The Lyric Poetry* by John
Holloway, 1968; *Blake and Tradition* by Kathleen Raine, 2 vols., 1969; *A Blake Dictionary:
The Ideas and Symbols of Blake* by S. Foster Damon, 1973; *Blake: The Critical Heritage*
edited by G. E. Bentley, Jr., 1976.

                                    *   *   *

   It is hardly too much to say that William Blake achieved greatness in several different
fields. He was not merely one of the best lyrical poets of the last five hundred years. His
engravings for *Job,* and the unfinished series for Dante's *Divine Comedy,* are generally
recognised as one of the peaks of English art. As a painter his quality is still a matter of
controversy: he was in violent reaction against the fashionable portraits by Sir Joshua
Reynolds, his own visionary pictures being regarded as crazy. In his old age, however, he
acquired several disciples, including Richmond and Palmer. He was, finally, a prophet,
convinced that he had rediscovered the truth of Christianity, which had become perverted by
the Churches.

Blake was a radical who supported the French Revolution before the Reign of Terror. He was horrified by the results of the Industrial Revolution and he was almost alone in his outright condemnation of the age, in which he saw "A pretence of Art to destroy art; a pretence of liberty/To destroy liberty; a pretence of religion to destroy religion." He believed that "the arts of life had been changed into the arts of death"; that a world had been created "In which Man is by his nature the enemy of man," a world in which the poor were mercilessly exploited. But although Blake was a passionate critic of social evils, he was also a mystic. This can be illustrated by the experience related in a letter to Thomas Butts (22 November 1802) or by the opening quatrain of "Auguries of Innocence":

> To see a World in a Grain of Sand,
>   And heaven in a Wild Flower,
> To hold Infinity in the palm of your hand,
>   And Eternity in an hour.

Blake had many brilliant insights which he expressed in marginalia, in note-books, in letters, and most incisively in *The Marriage of Heaven and Hell*, but he also picked up a number of eccentric ideas. He believed, for example, that the English were the lost Ten Tribes, and he had curious notions about Druids. But the silliness is often transformed by the poetry. Not many who sing his most famous verses really believe that Jesus visited Britain, but they rightly accept that the building of Jerusalem in "England's green and pleasant land" is a powerful symbol of their social aspirations.

For two reasons it is impossible to consider Blake's poetry in isolation from his work as an artist and from his social and political ideas. First, because nearly all his verse was printed by himself from engraved copper plates, with hand-coloured illustrations, and these often give a necessary clue to the meaning; and, secondly, because even some of his simple songs embody his religious and political views.

Blake's first book, *Poetical Sketches*, written in his nonage, shows him imitating the precursors of romanticism – Gray, Collins, Ossian – and, inspired by Percy's *Reliques*, producing songs in the Elizabethan style. But the finest poem in the book, and arguably the best poem of the second half of the eighteenth century, is an address "To the Muses," lamenting their departure from England, and unconsciously proving their return. It might serve as a model of pure classical style.

Songs of Innocence, Blake's first illustrated poems, are simple without being naive, childlike without being childish, innocent without being insipid. Their subject is childhood as a symbolic representation of the Kingdom of Heaven; but, as we can see from the illustrations to "Infant Joy" and "The Blossom," several of the poems are concerned with sex and procreation. *Songs of Experience*, published five years later, are written in deliberate contrast. There love is treated as a crime; religion is mere hypocrisy; society is in the grip of a tyrannical class system; instead of the Divine Image of Mercy, Pity, Peace, and Love, we have Cruelty, Jealousy, Terror, and Secrecy; instead of sexual freedom there is enforced virginity; instead of the Lamb there is the Tyger.

Blake published no more lyrical verse, although he continued to write it for another ten years. A few of these later poems are as lucid as the *Songs*, but "The Mental Traveller" is as difficult as any of the prophetic books, and "The Everlasting Gospel," in which Blake gives his plainest statement of his disagreements with the Churches, was left unfinished. He probably came to feel that the propagation of his gospel could best be accomplished by means of the prophetic books.

It is characteristic of Blake's dialectical method that after the contrast in the *Songs* between the two contrary states of the human soul – good and bad – he should declare in *The Marriage of Heaven and Hell* that without contraries there is no progression. The marriage is that of energy and reason. Satan symbolises energy, and Blake's famous epigram that Milton "was a true Poet and of the Devil's party without knowing it" means in its context almost what Wordsworth meant when he said that poetry was "the spontaneous overflow of powerful feelings." The book, apart from prefatory and concluding poems in free verse, is written in witty and humorous prose: it is the most entertaining of Blake's writings. It was followed soon afterwards by *Visions of the Daughters of Albion*, a plea for the sexual emancipation of women, written in vigorous and eloquent verse. Blake rejected the use of blank verse, "derived from the modern bondage of rhyming," and he claimed later that in *Jerusalem* "Every word and every letter is studied and put into its fit place; the terrific numbers are reserved for the terrific parts, the mild & gentle for the mild & gentle parts, and the prosaic for inferior parts." This seems to conflict with his other statement that the poem was dictated to him, he being merely the secretary. Some critics have suspected that the verse of the prophetic books is really prose cut up into length. This may be true of the prosaic parts: Blake's chief model was the King James Bible. But it is important to recognize that there are many passages where rhythm, alliteration, and assonance bear out Blake's claims.

A more serious obstacle to enjoyment is the mythology, invented by Blake to avoid the misleading associations of classical mythology. (Keats, it will be remembered, found some discrepancy between the story of Hyperion and the meaning he wished to convey in his poem.) Blake's names, such as Urizen, Oothoon, Theotormon, Bromion, need a key; and the need is increased by the fact that the significance of the characters varies from poem to poem. Yet the difficulties can easily be exaggerated. Years ago, a recital of the last part of *Jerusalem* in Masefield's private theatre was enthusiastically received by an audience who did not know the difference between Enitharmon and Palamabron.

Although their strictly poetical qualities have usually been undervalued, the greatness of *Milton* and *Jerusalem* depends largely on their prophetic message. *Milton* originated in Blake's difficulties with Hayley and in his wish to correct the "errors" of *Paradise Lost*. On these foundations Blake constructed a metaphysical drama of great profundity, in which the religion, the art, the morality, and the literature of his time were tried and found wanting. The climax of his attack comes in the splendid speech beginning "Obey thou the words of the Inspired Man" (Plate 40), in which he goes on to protest at "the aspersion of Madness/Cast on the Inspired" by the poetasters of the day.

In *Jerusalem* Blake introduces Scofield, the soldier who had accused him of sedition, but he is mainly concerned with the necessity of mutual forgiveness and of self-annihilation, which to him were the essentials of Christ's teaching, and the conditions for the establishment of the Kingdom of Heaven on earth, and specifically in England. In *Milton* Bacon, Locke, and Newton were treated as symbols of barren rationalism, but towards the end of *Jerusalem*, no longer enemies of the imagination, they are welcomed alongside Chaucer, Shakespeare, and Milton as part of the English tradition.

Bronowski argued in *The Man Without a Mask* that Blake turned from political to religious subjects because he was afraid of prosecution, and that he adopted the obscure style of the prophetic books for the same reason. But, despite the repressive age in which he lived, Blake did not become obscure for this reason. He continued to advertise two of his most radical works (*America* and *Europe*); some of his earlier prophecies are much more obscure than *Milton*; and his move away from politics was more likely due to his disappointment with the course of the French Revolution. We should remember, too, that Blake's politics and religion are inseparable: art, poetry, and politics are all part of his religion. It is significant that in *America* he uses the resurrection as a symbol of political emancipation, and in *Jerusalem* he asks: "Are not Religion & Politics the same Thing? Brotherhood is Religion." Jesus in the same poem declares that Man cannot "exist but by Brotherhood."

Blake's message fell on deaf ears. The one coloured copy of *Jerusalem* – artistically his most beautiful book – was unsold at his death; and it was not until the present century that critics and readers began to understand him.

—Kenneth Muir

BLOOMFIELD, Robert. English. Born in Honington, near Bury St. Edmunds, Suffolk, 3 December 1766. No formal education other than from his mother; apprenticed to a shoemaker in London. Married; four children. Worked as a shoemaker, London; given the post of undersealer in the Seal Office, then an allowance, by the Duke of Grafton, 1802; thereafter worked at making Aeolian harps, and as a bookseller, but went bankrupt; visited Wales, 1811; settled in Shefford, Bedfordshire, 1812, and died there in poverty. *Died 19 August 1823.*

PUBLICATIONS

Collections

> *Works.* 1883.
> *A Selection from the Poems,* edited by J. L. Carr. 1966.

Verse

> *The Farmer's Boy: A Rural Poem,* edited by Capel Lofft. 1800.
> *Rural Tales, Ballads, and Songs.* 1802.
> *Good Tidings; or, News from the Farm.* 1804.
> *Wild Flowers; or, Pastoral and Local Poetry.* 1806.
> *The Poems.* 2 vols., 1809.
> *The Banks of Wye.* 1811.
> *The History of Little Davy's New Hat* (juvenile). 1815; edited by Walter Bloomfield, 1878.
> *Collected Poems.* 2 vols., 1817.
> *May Day with the Muses.* 1822.

Play

> *Hazelwood Hall: A Village Drama.* 1823.

Other

> *Selections from the Correspondence,* edited by W. H. Hart. 1870.

> Editor, *Nature's Music, Consisting of Extracts from Several Authors in Honour of the Harp of Aeolus.* 1808.

Reading List: *The Farmer's Boy, Robert Bloomfield: His Life and Poems* by William Wickett and Nicholas Duval, 1971.

* * *

Robert Bloomfield achieved overnight fame with the publication of *The Farmer's Boy* in 1800; while this volume thoroughly deserves to be remembered, the neglect of his other work is a loss to the lover of simple but accomplished poetry.

The Farmer's Boy follows the tradition of Thomson's *The Seasons,* of "L'Allegro" and "Il

Penseroso," and the English georgics such as Somerville's *The Chase*. It is also redolent of the atmosphere which informs *The Compleat Angler* or *The Natural History of Selbourne*, offering an uncomplicated description of a farm labourer's daily round through each season of the year. The poem gains a freshness from Bloomfield's personal experience as jack-of-all-trades on a Suffolk farm.

Bloomfield's lines are frequently utilitarian though seldom banal. The heroic couplet is a medium rather than an ornament to him, and the charm of his poem lies in the freshness of his descriptions rather than in the exercise of a lush or individualised lyrical power, though moments like "Stopped in her song, perchance the starting thrush/Shook a white shower from the blackthorn bush ..." show that he was not deficient in delicacy of apprehension. He describes the dairy "with pails bright scoured and delicately sweet" and the shepherd who "idling lies,/And sees tomorrow in the marbling skies," and even his humblest tasks are dignified by the powers of observation with which they are described.

He has moments of "romantic" awareness, as in his Turner-esque appreciation of colour and movement in the gathering stormclouds:

> Now eve o'erhangs the western cloud's thick brow:
> The far-stretch'd curtain of retiring light,
> With fiery treasures fraught; that on the sight
> Flash from its bulging sides, where darkness lowers,
> In Fancy's eye, a chain of mouldering towers;
> Or craggy coasts just rising into view,
> Midst javelins dire, and darts of streaming blue.

Occasionally he shows a nice critical apprehension of the dangers inherent in employing georgic language to realistic descriptions, as when the ploughman trudges along his furrows "till dirt usurp the empire of his shoes."

Throughout *The Farmer's Boy* Bloomfield maintains a steady balance of common sense and delicacy of feeling. If his sociological comments are unoriginal they are still interesting. He feels that Nature has a double rapport with man: there is a mystic, poetic communion, but this is not prejudiced by a shrewd delight in commerce and in the time-honoured daily round of labour. At times his feelings for the land remind one of Cobbett's *Rural Rides*.

Bloomfield's later volumes – especially *Rural Tales* and *Wild Flowers* – have an honourable place among those poems which sought to link country stories and ballad measures to a higher purpose, an aspiration realised in Wordsworth's *Lyrical Ballads*. Purely as ballads, pieces like "The Broken Crutch" or "The Horkey" hold their own very well, managing rustic dialogue with a skill which avoids archness or stereotype. Bloomfield has more power to please than is consistent with the neglect into which he has fallen, and he offers a healthy corrective to those sociologists who regard the agricultural labourer's lot as one of unmitigated misery at the turn of the century. Bloomfield's stories of village revels and agricultural pursuits sometimes depend too much on squirarchal benevolence for their happy endings, but at his best he can achieve a comic dignity which looks forward to the Hardy of *Under the Greenwood Tree*.

—T. Bareham

BLUNDEN, Edmund (Charles). English. Born in London, 1 November 1896. Educated at Cleave's Grammar School, Yalding, Kent; Christ's Hospital; Queen's College, Oxford, M.A. Served with The Southdowns, Royal Sussex Regiment, in France and Belgium,

1916–19: Military Cross; Staff Member, Oxford University Senior Training Corps, 1940–44. Married Claire Margaret Poynting in 1945; four daughters. Professor of English Literature, University of Tokyo, 1924–27; Fellow and Tutor in English Literature, Merton College, Oxford, 1931–43; Member, U.K. Liaison Mission, Tokyo, 1948–50; Professor of English Literature, 1953–64, and Emeritus Professor, 1964–74, University of Hong Kong. Clark Lecturer, Cambridge University, 1932; Professor of Poetry, Oxford University, 1966–68. Recipient: Hawthornden Prize, 1922; Royal Society of Literature Benson Medal, 1932; Queen's Gold Medal for Poetry, 1956; Corporation of London Midsummer Prize, 1970. Litt.D.: Leeds and Leicester universities. Companion of Literature, Royal Society of Literature: Member, Japan Academy. C.B.E. (Commander, Order of the British Empire), 1951; Order of the Rising Sun, 3rd class (Japan), 1963. *Died 20 January 1974.*

PUBLICATIONS

Collections

Verse

> *Poems, 1913 and 1914.* 1914.
> *Poems, Translated from the French, July 1913-January 1914.* 1914.
> *The Barn, with Certain Other Poems.* 1916.
> *Three Poems.* 1916.
> *The Harbingers.* 1916.
> *Pastorals: A Book of Verses.* 1916.
> *The Waggoner and Other Poems.* 1920.
> *The Shepherd and Other Poems of Peace and War.* 1922.
> *Dead Letters: Poems.* 1922.
> *To Nature: New Poems.* 1923.
> *Masks of Time: A New Collection of Poems, Principally Meditative.* 1925.
> *English Poems.* 1925.
> *Retreat.* 1928.
> *Japanese Garland.* 1928.
> *Near and Far: New Poems* 1929.
> *The Poems 1914–1930.* 1930.
> *A Summer's Fancy.* 1930.
> *To Themis: Poems on Famous Trials, and Other Pieces.* 1931.
> *Halfway House: A Miscellany of New Poems.* 1932.
> *Choice or Chance: New Poems.* 1934.
> *An Elegy and Other Poems.* 1937.
> *On Several Occasions, by a Fellow of Merton College.* 1938.
> *Poems 1930–1940.* 1940.
> *Shells by a Stream: New Poems.* 1944.
> *After the Bombing and Other Short Poems.* 1949.
> *Eastward: A Selection of Verses Original and Translated.* 1949.
> *Records of Friendship: Occasional and Epistolary Poems,* edited by T. Nakayama. 1950.
> *Poems of Many Years.* 1957.
> *A Hong Kong House: Poems 1951–1961.* 1962.
> *Eleven Poems.* 1965.

Poems on Japan, Hitherto Uncollected and Mostly Unprinted, edited by T. Saito.   1967.
The Midnight Skaters: Poems for Young Readers, edited by C. Day Lewis.   1968.

Play

The Dede of Pittie: Dramatic Scenes Reflecting the History of Christ's Hospital and Offered in Celebration of the Quatercentenary (produced 1953).   1953.

Fiction

We'll Shift Our Ground; or, Two on a Tour, with Sylvia Norman.   1933.

Other

The Appreciation of Literary Prose.   1921.
The Bonadventure: A Random Journal of an Atlantic Holiday.   1922.
Christ's Hospital: A Retrospect.   1923.
More Footnotes to Literary History: Essays on Keats and Clare.   1926.
On the Poems of Henry Vaughan: Characteristics and Imitations, with His Principal Latin Poems Carefully Translated into English Verse.   1927.
Lectures in English Literature.   1927; revised edition, 1952.
Undertones of War.   1928.
Leigh Hunt's "Examiner" Examined.   1928.
Leigh Hunt: A Biography.   1930; as *Leigh Hunt and His Circle,* 1930.
De Bello Germanico: A Fragment of Trench History.   1930.
Votive Tablets: Studies Chiefly Appreciative of English Authors and Books (includes verse).   1931.
Fall In, Ghosts: An Essay on a Battalion Reunion.   1932.
The Face of England, in a Series of Occasional Sketches.   1932.
The Mind's Eye: Essays.   1934.
Keats's Publisher: A Memoir of John Taylor 1781–1864.   1936.
English Villages.   1941.
Thomas Hardy.   1941.
Cricket Country.   1944.
Shelley: A Life Story.   1946.
Shakespeare to Hardy: Short Studies of Characteristic English Authors.   1948.
Two Lectures on English Literature.   1948.
Sons of Light: A Series of Lectures on English Writers.   1949.
Addresses on General Subjects Connected with English Literature.   1949.
Poetry and Science and Other Lectures.   1949.
Favourite Studies in English Literature.   1950.
Blunden: A Selection of His Poetry and Prose, edited by Kenneth Hopkins.   1950.
Influential Books.   1950.
Reprinted Papers, Partly Concerning Some English Romantic Poets.   1950.
Chaucer to "B.V.," with an Additional Paper on Herman Melville.   1950.
Hamlet and Other Studies.   1950.
A Wanderer in Japan: Sketches and Reflections in Prose and Verse (bilingual edition).   1950.
John Keats.   1950; revised edition, 1954, 1966.
Sketches and Reflections.   1951.
Essayists in the Romantic Period, edited by I. Nishizaki.   1952.

Charles Lamb.   1954; revised edition, 1964.
War Poets 1914–1918.   1958; revised edition, 1964.
Three Young Poets: Critical Sketches of Byron, Shelley, and Keats.   1959.
A Wessex Worthy: Thomas Russell.   1960.
A Corscambe Inhabitant.   1963.
William Crowe 1745–1829.   1963.
Guest of Thomas Hardy.   1964.
A Brief Guide to the Great Church of the Holy Trinity, Long Melford.   1965.
John Clare: Beginner's Luck.   1972.
A Tribute to Walter de la Mare, with Leonard Clark.   1974.

Editor, with Alan Porter, *Poems Chiefly from Manuscript,* by John Clare.   1920.
Editor, *Madrigals and Chronicles, Being Newly Found Poems,* by John Clare.   1924.
Editor, *A Song to David and Other Poems,* by Christopher Smart.   1924.
Editor, *Shelley and Keats as They Struck Their Contemporaries.*   1925.
Editor, with B. Brady, *Selected Poems,* by Bret Harte.   1926.
Editor, *A Hundred English Poems from the Elizabethan Age to the Victorian.*   1927.
Editor, *The Autobiography of Leigh Hunt.*   1928.
Editor, *Last Essays of Elia,* by Charles Lamb,   1929.
Editor, *The Poems of William Collins.*   1929.
Editor, with others, *The War 1914–1918: A Booklist.*   1930.
Editor, *Great Short Stories of the War.*   1930.
Editor, *Sketches in the Life of John Clare Written by Himself.*   1931.
Editor, *The Poems of Wilfrid Owen.*   1931.
Editor, with E. L. Griggs, *Coleridge: Studies by Several Hands on the Hundredth Anniversary of His Death.*   1934.
Editor, *Charles Lamb: His Life Recorded by His Contemporaries.*   1934.
Editor, *Return to Husbandry: An Annotated List of Books Dealing with the History, Philosophy, and Craftsmanship of Rural England.*   1943.
Editor, *Hymns for the Amusement of Children,* by Christopher Smart.   1947.
Editor, *Shelley's Defence of Poetry.*   1948.
Editor, with others, *The Christ's Hospital Book.*   1953.
Editor, *Poems, Principally Selected from Unpublished Manuscripts,* by Ivor Gurney.   1954.
Editor, *Selected Poems of Shelley.*   1954.
Editor, *Selected Poems of Keats.*   1955.
Editor, *Selected Poems of Tennyson.*   1960.
Editor, with Bernard Mellor, *Wayside Poems of the Early Seventeenth Century.*   1963; *Early Eighteenth Century,* 1964; *Wayside Sonnets 1750–1850,* 1970.

Translator, *Lee Lan Flies the Dragon Kite,* by R. Herrmanns.   1962.

Bibliography: *A Bibliography of Blunden* by B. J. Kirkpatrick, 1978.

Reading List: "The Poetry of Blunden" by Margaret Willy, in *English 11,* 1957; *Blunden* by A. M. Hardie, 1958; *Heroes' Twilight: A Study of the Literature of the Great War* by Bernard Bergonzi, 1965; *The Poetry of Blunden* by Michael Thorpe, 1971.

*   *   *

One of the most eloquent and versatile writers of this century, and – because of his generosity to other writers, to scholars, and to students – one of the most influential, Edmund Blunden has nevertheless been too often condemned by literary historians and anthologists to an unenviably restricted fame as a First World War poet who happened to survive for a half-a-century after the war of which he wrote, and as a Georgian who had the misfortune to outlive both the utility and the respectability of the movement to which he is said to have belonged.

Blunden was in truth a poet of the countryside and a poet of war; it is the conjunction of these two attributes which gives his poetry and his prose-work *Undertones of War* their especial quality, and sets his work above the range of conventional ruralist writing. He was nineteen when he went to the Western Front. His countryman's delight in the fecundity of his own Sussex informed his sorrow as he watched the destruction of Flanders:

> I have seen a green country, useful to the race,
> Knocked silly with guns and mines, its villages vanished,
> Even the last rat and kestrel banished –
> God bless us all, this was peculiar grace.

For him the guns were never silenced; over fifty years the bombardment of mind and spirit continued. Destruction, waste, futility: these caused him pain but above the discords he found beauty and beyond the grief he discovered optimism.

"Haunted ever by war's agony" he remained for the rest of his days within the fraternity of soldiers. It was just one of the communities to which he gave his loyalty and his literary service. There were others, in Japan and Hong Kong, where he taught and is revered and perhaps above all, his old school, Christ's Hospital. No author in the whole history of English letters has paid such generous attention to the place of his education as did Blunden to Christ's Hospital. Not only did he write a full-length history and several poems and essays about the school, but he also produced sensitive books on Lamb and Leigh Hunt, two of his predecessors as Christ's Hospital authors, and was at work on a biography of Coleridge, "the greatest of our Bluecoat clan," when the last illness ended his life. His sturdy support for that fine poet of the Second War, Keith Douglas, was by his own account inspired in part by responsibility for one of his pupils at Merton College, Oxford, in part by respect for Douglas's gifts as poet and as soldier, but not least because Douglas was yet another Christ's Hospital product.

Wide-ranging and prolific exercise as a literary journalist, the most literate of all books about cricket, *Cricket Country*, editions of Clare, a biography of Shelley, innumerable introductions contributed to other men's books, a range of correspondence such as is rare in our times (and all of it in an exquisite calligraphy) – and still there is more to say about Blunden, for it was he who first presented the poems of Wilfred Owen to the public. But the evidence exists that what would have pleased him most in his long, varied and distinguished career is that two of the finest and most sensitive books about the Second World War, Keith Douglas's *Alamein to Zem Zem* and Douglas Grant's *The Fuel of the Fire*, were by authors who had served their literary apprenticeship under the author of *Undertones of War*.

—J. E. Morpurgo

BLUNT, Wilfrid Scawen.   English.   Born in Petworth, Sussex, 17 August 1840. Educated at a private school in Pyrford, Hampshire, 1847–51; Stonyhurst Jesuit School, Lancashire, 1853; Oscott School, Surrey, 1853–57. Married Lady Anne Noel, granddaughter of Lord Byron, 1869 (died, 1917); two children. Entered the Diplomatic Service as an unpaid attaché, 1858: served in Athens, 1859–60, Frankfurt, 1860–62, 1865–67, Madrid, 1862–63, Paris,

1863–65, Lisbon, 1865, Buenos Aires, 1868–69, Berne, 1869; retired, 1869. Founded, with his wife, Crabbet Arabian Stud, Sussex, 1878. Travelled in the Near and Middle East, Egypt, Ceylon, India; involved in the cause of Arabi Pasha and Egyptian nationalism, 1882; stood for Parliament; imprisoned in Ireland in 1886 for activity in Irish Land League; associated with the magazine *Egypt*, 1911–13. *Died 12 September 1922.*

PUBLICATIONS

Collections

Poems, edited by Floyd Dell. 1923.

Verse

Sonnets and Songs by Proteus. 1875.
The Love Sonnets of Proteus. 1881.
The Wind and the Whirlwind. 1883.
In Vinculis. 1889.
A New Pilgrimage and Other Poems, 1889.
The Celebrated Romance of the Stealing of the Mare, from a translation by Anne Blunt of a work by Abu Zaid. 1892.
Esther, Love Lyrics, and Natalia's Resurrection. 1892.
The Love Lyrics and Songs of Proteus. 1892.
Griselda: A Society Novel in Rhymed Verse. 1893.
The Poetry of Blunt, edited by W. E. Henley and George Wyndham. 1898.
Love Poems, edited by F. Chapman. 1902.
Mu'allaakat: The Seven Golden Odes, from a translation by Anne Blunt. 1903.
Poetical Works, 2 vols., 1914.

Plays

The Bride of the Nile (produced 1893). 1907.
Satan Absolved: A Victorian Mystery. 1899.
Fand of the Fair Cheek (produced 1907). 1904.
The Little Left Hand, in *Poetical Works.* 1914.

Other

Proteus and Amadeus: A Correspondence, with Wilfrid Meynell, edited by Aubrey De Vere. 1878.
The Future of Islam. 1882.
Ideas about India. 1885.
The Shame of the Nineteenth Century. 1900.
Atrocities of Justice under British Rule in Egypt. 1906.
Secret History of the English Occupation of Egypt and India, Being a Personal Narrative of Events. 2 vols., 1907.
Francis Thompson. 1907.
India under Ripon: A Private Diary. 1909.

The New Situation in Egypt. 1910.
The Fiasco in Egypt. 1910.
Gordon at Khartouwm. 1911.
The Italian Horror and How to End It. 1911.
The Land War in Ireland. 1912.
History of the Crabbet Estate in Sussex. 1917.
The Crabbet Arabian Stud. 1917.
My Diaries 1888–1914 (The Scramble for Africa, The Coalition Against Germany). 2 vols., 1919–20.

Editor, *Bedouin Tribes of the Euphrates,* by Anne Blunt. 2 vols., 1879.
Editor, *A Pilgrimage to Nejd,* by Anne Blunt. 2 vols., 1881.

Reading List: *Blunt* by Edith Finch, 1938; *The Writings of Blunt: An Introduction and a Study* by Mary J. Reinehr, 1941; *Blunt: A Memoir* by the Earl of Lytton, 1961; *The Cousins* (on Blunt and George Wyndham) by Max Egremont, 1977; *Blunt: A Biography* by Elizabeth Longford, 1978.

* * *

The Byronic stereotype of the romantic poet has many examples in Continental literature but few in English apart from Wilfrid Scawen Blunt. The image which he projects in his life and in his work is that of the poet as aristocrat, man of action, champion of oppressed peoples, and philanderer. His verse has vigour and panache, but, as with that of Byron himself, it is often marred by careless or over-rhetorical diction and a degree of egotistical posturing. The irony and satirical power (for which we nowadays most highly value Byron) is, however, largely lacking in Blunt.

Blunt's *Esther* is a series of sonnets making up an actual narrative or short novel in verse. It tells the story of the sexual initiation of a young Englishman by a French actress. It is a remarkably effective piece of work. The fiftieth sonnet ("He who has once been happy is for aye/Out of destruction's reach") is well known but gains immeasurably when read in its proper context. Blunt's mastery of the sonnet had already been shown in *The Love Sonnets of Proteus*, which celebrate a whole gallery of his conquests.

The Wind and the Whirlwind is a lengthy piece of rhetorical invective, written in protest against Britain's bombardment of Alexandria in 1882 and the crushing of Ahmed Ibn Arabi's Egyptian Nationalist revolt. Blunt's involvement in the cause of Irish Home Rule, and his consequent imprisonment for a brief spell, produced another sonnet sequence, *In Vinculis*. These prison poems, though somewhat marred by self-pity, really do express the affront to human dignity which imprisonment involves.

Blunt's loathing of British Imperialism also informs his drama *Satan Absolved*, written in alexandrines. Satan is absolved before the bar of Heaven because, however great his crimes, they cannot compare with those of the British Empire. "The Wisdom of Merlyn" summarises Blunt's romantic philosophy of action: "where doubt is, do." Of his shorter poems, "The Old Squire" is perhaps the best known.

Blunt's translations from the Arabic, done in collaboration with his wife, are a remarkable achievement. They are among the few translations from Classical Arabic poetry which can be read as English poems, admittedly in a somewhat Swinburnian style. *The Stealing of the Mare* is a rendering of an episode from the Egyptian Arabic epic of Antar. Like other popular Egyptian works of this type, it is in prose with verse passages interspersed.

—John Heath-Stubbs

BLY, Robert (Elwood). American. Born in Madison, Minnesota, 23 December 1926. Educated at St. Olaf College, Northfield, Minnesota, 1946–47; Harvard University, Cambridge, Massachusetts, B.A. (magna cum laude) 1950; University of Iowa, Iowa City, M.A. 1956. Served in the United States Navy, 1944–46. Married Carolyn McLean in 1955; four children. Since 1958, Founding-Editor, *The Fifties* magazine (later *The Sixties* and *The Seventies*) and The Fifties Press (later The Sixties and The Seventies Press), Madison, Minnesota. Recipient: Fulbright Fellowship, 1956; Amy Lowell Traveling Fellowship, 1964; Guggenheim Fellowship, 1964, 1972; National Institute of Arts and Letters grant, 1965; Rockefeller Fellowship, 1967; National Book Award, 1968. Lives in Madison, Minnesota.

PUBLICATIONS

Verse

> *Silence in the Snowy Fields.* 1962.
> *The Lion's Tail and Eyes: Poems Written Out of Laziness and Silence,* with James Wright and William Duffy. 1962.
> *The Light Around the Body.* 1967.
> *Chrysanthemums.* 1967.
> *Ducks.* 1968.
> *The Morning Glory: Another Thing That Will Never Be My Friend: Twelve Prose Poems.* 1969; revised edition, 1970.
> *The Teeth-Mother Naked at Last.* 1970.
> *Poems for Tennessee,* with William Stafford and William Matthews. 1971.
> *Jumping Out of Bed.* 1973.
> *Sleepers Joining Hands.* 1973.
> *Point Reyes Poems.* 1974.
> *The Hockey Poem.* 1974.
> *Old Man Rubbing His Eyes.* 1975.
> *This Body Is Made of Camphor and Gopherwood.* 1977.

Other

> Editor, with David Ray, *A Poetry Reading Against the Vietnam War.* 1966.
> Editor, *The Sea and the Honeycomb: A Book of Tiny Poems.* 1966.
> Editor, *Forty Poems Touching on Recent American History.* 1970.
> Editor, *Selected Poems,* by David Ignatow. 1975.
> Editor, *Leaping Poetry: An Idea with Poems and Translations.* 1975.

> Translator, *Reptiles and Amphibians of the World,* by Hans Hvass. 1960.
> Translator, with James Wright, *Twenty Poems of Georg Trakl.* 1961.
> Translator, *The Story of Gösta Berling,* by Selma Lagerlöf. 1962.
> Translator, with James Wright and John Knoepfle, *Twenty Poems of César Vallejo.* 1962.
> Translator, with Eric Sellin and Thomas Buckman, *Three Poems,* by Thomas Tranströmer. 1966.
> Translator, *Hunger,* by Knut Hamsun. 1967.
> Translator, with Christina Paulston, *I Do Best Alone at Night,* by Gunnar Ekelöf. 1967.
> Translator, with Christina Paulston, *Late Arrival on Earth: Selected Poems of Gunnar Ekelöf.* 1967.

Translator, with others, *Selected Poems* by Yvan Goll. 1968.
Translator, with James Wright, *Twenty Poems of Pablo Neruda.* 1968.
Translator, *Forty Poems of Juan Ramón Jiménez.* 1969.
Translator, *Ten Poems,* by Issa Kobayashi. 1969.
Translator, with James Wright and John Knoepfle, *Neruda and Vallejo: Selected Poems.* 1971.
Translator, *Twenty Poems of Tomas Tranströmer.* 1971.
Translator, *The Fish in the Sea Is Not Thirsty: Versions of Kabir.* 1971.
Translator, *Night Vision,* by Tomas Tranströmer. 1971.
Translator, *Lorca and Jiménez: Selected Poems.* 1973.
Translator, *Basho.* 1974.
Translator, *Ten Sonnets to Orpheus,* by Rilke. 1974.
Translator, *Friends, You Drank Some Darkness: Three Swedish Poets, Henry Martinson, Gunnar Ekelöf, Tomas Tranströmer.* 1975.
Translator, *Try to Live to See This: Versions of Kabir.* 1976.
Translator, *The Kabir Book.* 1977.
Translator, *The Voices,* by Rilke. 1977.

Bibliography: "Bly Checklist" by Sandy Dorbin, in *Schist 1,* Fall 1973.

Reading List: *Alone with America* by Richard Howard, 1969; "Bly Alive in Darkness" by Anthony Libby, in *Iowa Review,* Summer 1972.

*   *   *

The spirited presence of Robert Bly is felt throughout the realms of modern poetry and literary criticism; he emerged from the early 1960's as one of the more stubbornly independent and critical poets of his generation, bold to state his positions against war and commercial monopoly, spread of federal government, and crassness in literature wherever a forum was open to him. He was a dominating spokesman for the anti-war circles during the course of the Vietnam War, staging readings around the United States and compiling (with David Ray) the extraordinary poetic protests in the anthology, *A Poetry Reading Against the Vietnam War.* Throughout his career, he has been a cranky but refreshing influence on American thought and culture for the very grandeur of his positions and the force he has given to his artistic individuality.

Although his output of poetry has been relatively small in an era of prolific poets, his books follow a distinctive course of deepening conviction and widening of conceptions. *Silence in the Snowy Fields,* his first book, is a slender collection of smooth, mildly surreal evocations of his life in Minnesota and of the landscape, with its harsh winters and huddled townships. Bly's brief poems animate natural settings with a secret, wilful life-force, as in this final stanza from "Snowfall in the Afternoon":

> The barn is full of corn, and moving toward us now,
> Like a hulk blown toward us in a storm at sea:
> All the sailors on deck have been blind for many years.

Silence in the Snowy Fields has an immediacy of the poet's personal life that reflects the inward shift of poetry during the late 1950's and early 1960's, a direction that Bly then actively retreated from, claiming poetry deserved a larger frame of experience than the poet's own circumstances and private dilemmas.

The Light Around the Body moves into the political and social arena, with poems against corporate power and profiteering, presidential politics, and the Vietnam War. Here the poems are charged with greater flight of imagination and a more intensely surreal mode of discourse. The poems wildly juxtapose the familiar with the bizarre, in "A Dream of Suffocation" – "Accountants hover over the earth like helicopters,/Dropping bits of paper engraved with Hegel's name" – and "War and Silence" –

> Filaments of death grow out.
> The sheriff cuts off his black legs
> And nails them to a tree

To explain his poetic and to give it context, Bly edited a volume of poems entitled *Leaping Poetry* in which he argued that consciousness had now expanded to a new faculty of the brain where spiritual and supralogical awareness is stored. His commentary is wonderfully speculative and vivid, but bluffly assertive of its premise. Building on this provocative thesis, he commented in an essay, "I Came Out of the Mother Naked," part of his volume *Sleepers Joining Hands*, that society is now returning to a matriarchal order, where sensuousness of thought and synthetic reason are replacing the patriarchal emphasis on rationality and analytic thinking. *The Kabir Book*, Bly's translations of the 15th-century Indian poet, are an effort to present the work of a figure who both "leaps" in his poetry and illustrates the kind of thinking Bly has argued for recently.

Bly continues to read poetry on the university circuit and to translate Scandinavian literature as his livelihood, but even in these facets of his life he has rooted his new convictions. His readings are now made dramatic with masks, singing, and extemporaneous lectures on the new mind he feels is emerging throughout the West.

—Paul Christensen

BOGAN, Louise. American. Born in Livermore Falls, Maine, 11 August 1897. Educated at Mount St. Mary's Academy, Manchester, New Hampshire, 1907–09; Girls' Latin School, Boston, 1910–15; Boston University, 1915–16. Married 1) Curt Alexander, 1916 (died, 1920), one daughter; 2) Raymond Holden in 1925 (divorced, 1937). Poetry Editor of *The New Yorker*, 1931–70. Visiting Professor, University of Washington, Seattle, 1948; University of Chicago, 1949; University of Arkansas, 1952; Salzburg Seminar in American Studies, 1958; Brandeis University, Waltham, Massachusetts, 1964–65. Recipient: Guggenheim Fellowship, 1933, 1937; Harriet Monroe Poetry Award, 1948; National Institute of Arts and Letters grant, 1951; Bollingen Prize, 1955; Academy of American Poets Fellowship, 1959; Brandeis University Creative Arts Award, 1961; National Endowment for the Arts grant, 1967. Library of Congress Chair in Poetry, 1945–46. L.H.D.: Western College for Women, Oxford, Ohio, 1956; Litt.D.: Colby College, Waterville, Maine, 1960. Member, American Academy of Arts and Letters. *Died 4 February 1970.*

PUBLICATIONS

Collections

What the Woman Lived: Selected Letters 1920–1970, edited by Ruth Limmer.   1973.

Verse

> *Body of This Death.*   1923.
> *Dark Summer.*   1929.
> *The Sleeping Fury.*   1937.
> *Poems and New Poems.*   1941.
> *Collected Poems 1923–1953.*   1954.
> *The Blue Estuaries: Poems 1923–1968.*   1968.

Other

> *Works in the Humanities Published in Great Britain 1939–1946: A Select List.*   1950.
> *Achievement in American Poetry 1900–1950.*   1951.
> *Selected Criticism: Prose, Poetry.*   1955.
> *A Poet's Alphabet: Reflections on the Literary Art and Vocation,* edited by Robert Phelps
> and Ruth Limmer.   1970.

> Editor, with William Jay Smith, *The Golden Journey: Poems for Young People.*   1965.

> Translator, with W. H. Auden and Elizabeth Mayer, *The Sorrows of Young Werther,*
> *and Novella,* by Goethe.   1971.

Reading List: "Bogan and Léonie Adams" by Elder Olson, in *Chicago Review 8,* Fall 1954.

*   *   *

Louise Bogan's collected poems, *The Blue Estuaries,* make up a slender volume that brings together work published from 1923 to 1968. She rarely wrote poems longer than a page, and all her earlier published books are brief and cut to the bone. She was a relentless reviser of her work and a slow, cautious craftsman who refused publishers' urgings to increase her output.

Although she was keenly aware of the revolutions in poetic technique throughout her life, her poems adhered to rhyme and set meter and treated the themes of love, regret, death, memory, landscape meditation in subtly alliterative language. Her style shows the influence of Emily Dickinson and perhaps the wit of Metaphysical poetry, but the essential charm of her best work is the quiet, feminine perception she expresses in her strict, tightly framed forms, as in "Second Song," an early poem:

> I said out of sleeping:
> Passion, farewell.
> Take from my keeping
> Bauble and shell.
>
> Black salt, black provender.
> Tender your store
> To a new pensioner,
> To me no more.

Although she relaxes into a certain lyric frankness of feeling in her later work, her style of spare restraint remains consistent throughout her work. In several of her poems a more strident feminine consciousness flares, as in "Women," with its sardonic portrayal of woman caught in her stereotype of the put-upon mate:

125

Their love is an eager meaninglessness
Too tense, or too lax.

They hear in every whisper that speaks to them
A shout and a cry.
As like as not, when they take life over their door-sills
They should let it go by.

Bogan regarded the poem as a deliberate and highly worked distillation of thought, and was perhaps too strict with her own imagination. The fire and wit of her mind are muted in most of her poetry but luxuriously displayed in her brilliant correspondence, collected in *What the Woman Lived*, where her sarcasm and acute critical nature are shared with a circle of notable literary figures of her time, including Edmund Wilson, Morton Dauwen Zabel, Rolfe Humphries, and Theodore Roethke.

Like her poetry, her critical writing eschewed partisanship and fashion in favor of a classical standard of moderation, balance, and form. As the poetry critic for *The New Yorker*, she was well known for her honest and abrasive judgments of the work of even her close friends, and her essays of these years, published in *A Poet's Alphabet*, endure in their accuracy and acumen. A brief treatise on modern poetry, *Achievement in American Poetry 1900–1950*, though merely a sketch of the main trends of these years, argues a provocative thesis that female poets of the late 19th century were chiefly responsible for revitalizing poetry with their sensuous, daring imaginations.

—Paul Christensen

BOWLES, William Lisle. English. Born in King's Sutton, Northamptonshire, 24 September 1762. Educated at Winchester College, (scholar), 1775–81; Trinity College, Oxford (Chancellor's Prize for Latin Verse, 1783; Cobden Exhibitioner, 1785–89), B.A. 1786, M.A. 1792. Married Madgaden Wake in 1797 (died, 1844). Ordained deacon, 1788: Curate, Knoyle, now Bishop's Knoyle, Wiltshire, 1788; Rector, Chicklade, 1795–97, Dumbleton, 1797, and Bremhill, Wiltshire, 1804–45; Prebendary, 1804, and Canon Residentiary, 1828, Salisbury. *Died 7 April 1850.*

PUBLICATIONS

Collections

Poetical Works, with Lamb and Hartley Coleridge, edited by William Tirebuck.   1887.
A Wiltshire Parson and His Friends: Correspondence, edited by Garland Greever.   1926.

Verse

Fourteen Sonnets, Elegiac and Descriptive.   1789; revised edition, as Sonnets Written Chiefly on Picturesque Spots, 1789; as Sonnets, with Other Poems, 1794, 1796.

Verses to John Howard. 1789.
The Grave of Howard. 1790.
Verses on the Benevolent Institution of the Philanthropic Society. 1790.
A Poetical Address to Edmund Burke. 1791.
Elegy Written at the Hot-Wells, Bristol. 1791.
Monody, Written at Matlock. 1791.
Elegiac Stanzas, Written During Sickness at Bath. 1796.
Hope: An Allegorical Sketch. 1796.
St. Michael's Mount. 1798.
Coombe Ellen. 1798.
Song of the Battle of the Nile. 1799.
Poems. 1801.
The Sorrows of Switzerland. 1801.
The Picture: Verses Suggested by a Landscape of Rubens. 1803.
The Spirit of Discovery; or, The Conquest of Ocean. 1804.
Bowden Hill. 1806.
Poems, Written Chiefly at Bremhill. 1809.
The Missionary. 1813; revised edition, 1815; as *The Ancient Missionary of Chile*, 1835.
The Grave of the Last Saxon; or, The Legend of the Curfew. 1822.
Ellen Gray; or, The Dead Maiden's Curse. 1823.
Charity. 1823.
Days Departed; or, Banwell Hill: A Lay of the Severn Sea. 1828.
St. John in Patmos. 1832.
The Little Villager's Verse Book. 1837.

Play

The Ark: A Dramatic Oratorio. 1824(?).

Other

A Few Plain Words for the Bible. N.d.
Sermons. 1815.
Thoughts on the Increase of Crimes, The Education of the Poor, and the National Schools. 1818.
Vindiciae Wykehamicae; or, A Vindication of Winchester College. 1818.
The Invariable Principles of Poetry in a Letter to Thomas Campbell. 1819.
A Reply to the Reviewer. 1820.
A Vindication of the Editor of Pope's Works. 1821.
Two Letters to Lord Byron. 1821.
A Voice from St. Peter's and St. Paul's. 1823.
A Final Appeal Relative to Pope. 1825.
Lessons in Criticism to William Roscoe. 1826.
Paulus Parochialis (sermons). 1826.
Hermes Britannicus. 1828.
The Parochial History of Bremhill. 1828.
The Life of Thomas Ken. 2 vols., 1830.
A Word on Cathedral-Oratorios and Clergy-Magistrates. 1830.
A Few Words on the Cathedral Clergy. 1831.
A Last and Summary Answer to the Question "Of What Use Have Been, and Are, the English Cathedral Establishments" with a Vindication of Anthems and Cathedral Services. 1833.

Annals and Antiquities of Lacock Abbey.   1835.
Scenes and Shadows of Days Departed (includes verse).   1835.
The Patronage of the English Bishops.   1836.
The Cartoons of Raphael (sermons).   1838.
A Final Defence of the Rights of Patronage in Deans and Chapters.   1838.

Editor, *The Works of Pope.*   10 vols., 1806.

Bibliography: "Some Uncollected Authors XVIII: Bowles" by Cecil Woolf, in *Book Collector* 7, 1958.

Reading List: *Bowles, Byron, and the Pope-Controversy* by J. J. van Rennes, 1927; *Bowles: A Lecture* by A. J. A. Waldock, 1928; *Bowles* by Oskar Rietmann, 1940.

*   *   *

Coleridge acknowledged a debt to the *Fourteen Sonnets* of William Lisle Bowles, speaking of "their mild and manliest melancholy" as giving impetus to his own youthful feelings. Looking back from his mid-Victorian vantage point, Gilfillan, perhaps influenced by Coleridge's praise, hailed Bowles as "the father of modern poetry." Both accolades now seem surprising. Bowles is the epitome of the second rank of writing which prevailed below the "Romantic" surface between 1780 and 1830, and his place, historically, is fixed by this representative quality. It is difficult to discern much individuality in him.

The *Fourteen Sonnets*, first published in 1789, proved very popular and certainly had the merit of restoring dignity to a verse form which had been neglected by the two previous generations. In them Bowles seems the natural successor to the refined, almost debilitated, sensitivity of Gray or Shenstone. In "A Garden-Seat at Home," he speaks of himself as

> ... scarce wishing to emerge
> Into the troubled ocean of that life,
> Where all is turbulence, and toil, and strife.
> Calm roll the seasons o'er my shaded niche;
> I dip the brush or touch the tuneful string....

His work is full of such aspirations for rural retirement, but he lacks the slow, dignified reflection which allowed Cowper to make major statements from within such isolation. Nor was Bowles' life as a busy cleric and magistrate consistent with his adopted poetic persona. There is not enough human passion in his writing to persuade the reader that his claim to have been spiritually wounded by an early unhappy love affair is necessary to an understanding of his work.

He never sinks below a mellifluous and careful competence, but seldom rises to anything fresh or startling. In reading a public poem like *The Battle of the Nile* one could forget that there had been any prosody in the previous hundred years other than that written by imitators of Dryden. Though in the preface to *The Grave of the Last Saxon* he speaks of "that which alone can give dignity to poetry – the cause of moral and religious truth," there is no urgent sense of an impassioned moral crusade in his work. *St. John in Patmos* describes the visionary experience of the disciple from outside rather than probing for an empathy with it.

It is the more surprising that such a poet could have been a vigorous and racy controversialist, yet there is no lack of energy about his war with Byron and the *Quarterly Review* over the merits of Alexander Pope. In 1806 Bowles published an edition of Pope in which he claimed that Pope was the leader only of a second rank of poets since he directed his attention to "artificial" life rather than to nature. This began a war of words in which Bowles maintained his standpoint, against powerful opposition, and with vigour and wit. The literature of this controversy is still of interest.

Bowles is a poet for dipping into. His minute care for detail, his eye for landscape, and his evocations of a mild nostalgia can be pleasing. He sometimes demonstrates a technical competence in handling narrative which makes, for instance, *The Grave of the Last Saxon* still readable, and even a poem like *The Spirit of Discovery* can convey a sense of the dignity with which the second flight of poets in the Regency period gave utterance to their personal accounts of common emotions.

—T. Bareham

BRADSTREET, Anne (née Dudley). American. Born probably at Northampton, England, on 1612. Educated privately. Married Simon Bradstreet, afterwards Governor of Massachusetts, in 1628 (died, 1697); eight children. Emigrated to America, with the Winthrops, 1630, and lived in Ipswich, 1635–45, and North Andover, 1645–72, both in Massachusetts. *Died 16 September 1672.*

PUBLICATIONS

Collections

> *Works,* edited by Jeannine Hensley.   1967
> *Poems,* edited by Robert Hutchinson.   1969.

Verse

> *The Tenth Muse Lately Sprung Up in America.*   1650; revised edition, as *Several Poems Compiled with Great Variety of Wit and Learning,* 1678.

Bibliography: "A List of Editions of the Poems of Bradstreet" by Oscar Wegelin, in *American Book Collector 4,* 1933; "Bradstreet: An Annotated Checklist" by Ann Stanford, in *Bulletin of Bibliography 27,* 1970.

Reading List: *Bradstreet and Her Time* by Helen S. Campbell, 1891; *Bradstreet* by Josephine K. Piercy, 1965; *Bradstreet, The Tenth Muse* by Elizabeth Wade White, 1971; *Bradstreet, The Worldly Puritan* by Ann Stanford, 1974.

*   *   *

Anne Bradstreet has long been recognized as the first genuine poet to develop in the English-speaking New World. A recent biographer, Elizabeth Wade White, maintains further that she "was also the first significant woman poet of England." The one volume that appeared during her lifetime as *The Tenth Muse Lately Sprung up in America* – published in

129

England without her knowledge and with a title she did not supply – was the first collection of poetry to come out of the New England colonies, to which Mrs. Bradstreet had emigrated as a young wife in 1630.

Paradoxically, Mrs. Bradstreet continues to attract an appreciative audience not for the poetry in *The Tenth Muse* but for a considerable number of poems that were first published in 1678, six years after her death. Of the thirteen poems in *The Tenth Muse*, only one, the 48-line "Prologue," appeals to the modern reader; the others are lengthy and tedious exercises in imitation of various poets – chiefly du Bartas (as rendered into English by Joshua Sylvester), Spenser, and Sidney. Their works, together with Ralegh's *History of the World*, she first read as a precocious child in the library of her indulgent father, Thomas Dudley, for many years steward to the Earl of Lincoln. Mrs. Bradstreet's obvious indebtedness to these authors suggests that she carried her favorite books aboard the *Arbella* and into the New England wilderness in 1630.

Life in that wilderness, however – rather than her father's books – prompted the poetry that has won for her a modest but permanent place in English-American literature. Her *Several Poems* contained – in addition to the pieces in *The Tenth Muse* – almost a score of poems that show her abandoning her old models and striking out with nuances, texture, and techniques that are her own. One of these is "The Author to Her Book," a well-controlled sustained metaphor that dramatizes her chagrin on first seeing the poorly printed *The Tenth Muse*. "Contemplations," often regarded as her best poem, anticipates the romantic view of nature and hints at her discomfort lest her physical reactions be at odds with her spiritual convictions. A number of love poems written for her devoted husband, Simon Bradstreet – a busy colonial official often away from home – reveal a healthy sensuality and suggest that, although she was a Puritan, she was not puritanical. In other poems to and about her children and about the fortunes and misfortunes of her family, she avoids sentimentality and brings to her work the same quiet strength that helped her to survive for forty-two years in remote Massachusetts.

—Thomas F. O'Donnell

BRATHWAITE, Edward. Barbadian. Born in Bridgetown, Barbados, 11 May 1930. Educated at Harrison College, Barbados; Pembroke College, Cambridge (Barbados Scholar), 1950–54, B.A. (honours) in history 1953, Cert. Ed. 1954; University of Sussex, Brighton, 1965–68, D.Phil. 1968. Married Doris Monica Welcome in 1960; one son. Education Officer, Ministry of Education, Ghana, 1955–62; Tutor, University of the West Indies Extra Mural Department, St. Lucia, 1962–63. Lecturer, 1963–72, and since 1972 Senior Lecturer in History, University of the West Indies, Kingston. Plebiscite Officer in the Trans-Volta Togoland, United Nations, 1956–57. Founding Secretary, Caribbean Artists Movement, 1966. Since 1970, Editor, *Savacou* magazine, Mona. Recipient: Arts Council of Great Britain bursary, 1967; Camden Arts Festival prize, London, 1967; Cholmondeley Award, 1970; Guggenheim Fellowship, 1972; City of Nairobi Fellowship, 1972; Bussa Award, 1973. Lives in Kingston, Jamaica.

PUBLICATIONS

Verse

> *Rights of Passage.* 1967; *Masks,* 1968; *Islands,* 1969; combined version, as *The Arrivants,* 1973.
> *Other Exiles.* 1975.
> *Mother Poem.* 1977.

Plays

> *Four Plays for Primary Schools* (produced 1961–62). 1964.
> *Odale's Choice* (produced 1962). 1967.

Other

> *The People Who Came, 1–3* (textbooks). 3 vols., 1968–72.
> *Folk Culture of the Slaves in Jamaica.* 1970.
> *The Development of Creole Society in Jamaica.* 1971.
> *Caribbean Man in Space and Time.* 1974.
> *Contradictory Omens: Cultural Diversity and Integration in the Caribbean.* 1974.

> Editor, *Iouanaloa: Recent Writing from St. Lucia.* 1963.

Bibliography: in *Savacou Bibliographical Series 2,* 1973.

*   *   *

Edward Brathwaite has emerged as one of the major writers in contemporary West Indian literature. His trilogy *Rights of Passage, Masks,* and *Islands* (reprinted as *The Arrivants*) is an epic of sorts on Black West Indian history and culture. Much of his present reputation rests on that trilogy, although he has published other poetry, and his scholarly writing has established him as a West Indian historian. Paradoxically, however, Brathwaite's reputation as a poet-historian of the "Black diaspora" sometimes has the effect of minimizing rather than illuminating his full achievements as a poet. The point is not, of course, that the themes of Black ethnicity are themselves insignificant. Indeed the opposite is the truth, a truth that needs to be repeatedly emphasized in light of the fact that ethnic and national consciousness has historically been an underdeveloped aspect of West Indian life. And, accordingly, writers like Brathwaite have had a significant impact on their Caribbean readership because their ethnic themes appeal to a cultural consciousness that has only assumed mass proportions since the achievement of nationhood. Brathwaite's appeal as an ethnic poet is in itself an interesting reflection on the belated nature of the ethnic awakening.

Indeed, the intensity with which Brathwaite has been received in some quarters has tended to limit perception and analysis of his less obtrusive but crucial emphasis on the complex texture of West Indian history and identity. That texture reflects the distinctive intermingling of African, European, and American elements that is characteristic of West Indian society. For like the equally distinguished Derek Walcott (St. Lucia) with whom he is more often contrasted than compared, Brathwaite really perceives and describes the West Indies as a synthesis of diverse cultural traditions. *Islands,* for example, reflects the contributions of Western religion and literature, just as much as the symbols of Akan culture pervade the language and vision of *Masks*. And on the whole the techniques and themes of the trilogy are an example as well as explication of this Afro-Caribbean diversity.

There is also a danger of approaching Brathwaite, in strictly thematic terms, as a compiler of historical statements about the West Indian experience rather than as a complex artist whose crucial cultural themes are interwoven with a sophisticated awareness of the nature of his own art as poet. In fact his poetry is not only socially descriptive but also introspective in that it explores the function of the poetic imagination itself and by extension the implications of the artist's identity. The quest themes of the trilogy are illustrative here. In one sense they reinforce a sense of cultural and historical continuities, or movements, as we move with Brathwaite's composite cultural archetypes from the Caribbean to North America and back (*Rights of Passage*), to West Africa (*Masks*) and back to the Caribbean (*Islands*). But in another sense this cultural quest is an allegory, dramatizing the nature and function of the artist's imagination: art is a journey through time and space, analogous to and at the same time inseparable from memory itself – the memory of the poet as individual artist, the imaginative memory of all artists like himself (the Black musician, for example) and the collective memory of the poet's people as it is manifested in their songs, dances, and other folk art forms. Moreover, as an act of memory the artistic imagination imitates the cycles of time itself, imitating and exemplifying the manner in which the mind simultaneously anticipates the future and recreates the past in the present: the Akan sounds of welcome in *Masks*, for example, greet the West Indian visitor returning to West African roots but they simultaneously evoke the earlier, unsuspecting offer of hospitality to the seventeenth-century slavetrader. Brathwaite is therefore a poet-historian both on the basis of his vision of cultural history and in light of the manner in which his poetic imagination imitates perceived patterns of time and history.

—Lloyd W. Brown

BRENNAN, Christopher (John). Australian. Born in Sydney, New South Wales, 1 November 1870. Educated at Riverview School, Sydney; University of Sydney, M.A. 1892; studied philosophy and classics at the University of Berlin (travelling scholarship), 1892–94. Married Anna Elizabeth Werth in 1897 (divorced, 1925); two sons. Assistant Librarian, rising to Chief Cataloguer, Sydney Public Library, 1897–1908; joined the Modern Languages Department, University of Sydney, 1908; Lecturer in French and German, 1908–1920; Associate Professor of German and Comparative Literature, 1920–25; schoolteacher, 1926–32. Recipient: Commonwealth Literary Fund pension. *Died 7 October 1932.*

PUBLICATIONS

Collections

The Verse, The Prose, edited by A. R. Chisholm and J. J. Quinn.   2 vols., 1960–62.

Verse

XVIII Poems, Being the First Collection of Verse and Prose.   1897.
XXI Poems (1893–1897): Towards the Source.   1897.

132

Poems 1913. 1914.
A Chant of Doom and Other Verses. 1918.
Twenty-Three Poems. 1928.

Play

A Mask, with John Le Gay Brereton, Jr. (produced 1913). 1913.

Other

Editor, with G. G. Nicholson, *Passages for Translation into French and German.* 1914.

Bibliography: *Brennan: A Comprehensive Bibliography* by Walter Stone and Hugh Anderson, 1959.

Reading List: *Brennan* by H. M. Green, 1939; *Brennan: The Man and His Poetry,* 1946, and *A Study of Brennan's "A Forest of Night,"* 1970, both by A. R. Chisholm; *New Perspectives on Brennan's Poetry* by G. A. Wilkes, 1952; *Brennan* by James McAuley, 1973.

*   *   *

Christopher Brennan, a legend still in Australian literature, belonged, like Herman Melville in *Clarel* and Walter Pater in *Marius the Epicurean* to that numerous company of 19th-century writers who, finding belief too difficult, found unbelief even more difficult, and so embarked on an impossible quest for certainties. Writing of the doctrine of correspondences, Brennan said in an essay on Nineteenth Century Literature (1904): "What spiritual fact needs is corroboration, and of corroboration it can never have enough." His verse traces the inner history of an unremitting search, as elusive as the alchemists' dream, for corroboration, for intellectual confirmation of faith.

Brennan was a devout Catholic, of Irish parentage, who as a young university student abandoned his intention to become a priest and became estranged from the practice of his faith. This loss of commitment is likely to have affected him more deeply than he admitted, and it is possible he tried to internalize his vocation, first as a philosopher, then as a poet, seeking a religion without a personal god. Keats's *Endymion* seems to have initiated him into the poet's perennial quest, and it is possible that he came into contact with esoteric ideas before he left Sydney, perhaps by reading Maitland's novels, or by associating with Spiritualists, or through hints in Pater. When he arrived in Berlin and became aware of the French Symbolist movement, he found Mallarmé's theory and practice of poetry immensely congenial to him, though the cast of his mind and his style in prose and verse belong much more to the German tradition than to the French. As a technician Brennan is indeed a mosaic of the Victorians, and, through the Victorians, an inheritor of Miltonic eloquence. His chief affinities, he said later in life, were Mallarmé and Coventry Patmore! More important, Brennan was above all a scholar-poet; he was indeed one of Australia's most brilliant classical scholars, whose theories about the manuscripts of Aeschylus attracted the attention of Jowett, and have since been vindicated. On this foundation and on that of a wide knowledge of German, Italian and French, he pursued his studies in German theosophy, Jewish mysticism, and Eastern gnosticism, while his personal and professional life began to crumble around him, and in the end he returned, with enriched understanding of the common human predicament, to the simple pieties of his youth, "*naturaliter Christiana.*" In an essay on Mallarmé he spoke of throwing the mystics overboard and returning to the visible world: "Our daily bread, if we are satisfied with it, will prove richer than we thought."

Brennan's reputation rests principally on *Poems 1913*, though "Fifteen Poems," circulated in typescript and published after his death as "The Burden of Tyre," is of great interest in foreshadowing the complexities of his Eden symbol, to be fully explored in the main work.

Brennan is the one Australian poet who practised what Arnold would have recognised as "the grand style," and, though it was going out of fashion when he wrote and is quite obsolete now, it could be argued that no other would have served his theme quite so well, even though it lays him open to charges of using archaic poetic diction, occasional Victorian lushness or Pre-Raphaelite sweetness, and syntactically convoluted paragraphs.

It is divided into five sections or "movements," for if, as has been claimed, *Poems 1913* is a *livre composé*, it is so in a musical rather than a purely literary sense. "Towards the Source" is the first step on the journey towards the innermost self, through the agency of love and marriage. Though, as in the poems as a whole, the autobiographical element is strong, it would be unwise to ignore esoteric interpretations of "nuptial exchanges," especially in view of the alchemical references scattered throughout. "The Forest of Night" is the most sustained and powerful attempt to penetrate to the depths of the unconscious, and the brooding and majestic figure of Lilith, "mournful until we find her fair," is one of the most compelling symbols in modern English verse of the mysterious, terrible, yet fascinating womb of becoming, of the Void in which all possibilities wait for being, where "gods and stars and songs and souls of men/are the sparse jewels in her scattered hair." The third movement, "The Wanderer," returns us to the conscious world with its ever-present conflict between social and individual man, between the longing for security and the urge to explore, symbolised in contrasting images of window and hearth, of winds and sea. Questing is accepted as an end in itself, necessary to continuing life, and courage is its moral imperative. The two final sections, "Pauca Mea" and "Epilogues," in turn agonised and defiant, culminate not in capitulation, but in the quiet wisdom of "1908," which offers staff and scrip for the journey. In spite of Brennan's deep involvement with the French symbolists and the legacy of Hegel and Novalis, it is conceivable that he drew his theories of poetry from earlier sources, from Augustine's "Rhetoric of Silence," for example, with its vision of the world as a divine poem which man had to learn, while in the flesh, to read, in the expectation of encountering its meaning in the spirit, face to face. The notion of the "grand man" may also have come to him, not from Swedenborg, but more directly from Origen.

As a poet, Brennan is still, as he was in his lifetime, isolated from the main tradition of Australian poetry. His is the work of a man struggling with a great internal solitude, and in it he accuses not only himself, but his society and his civilisation of a "total dereliction from the human path, the human dream" and sees mankind, perhaps, as a fellow-poet saw him: "a star in exile, unconstellated at the south," alienated from his true self as the image of God.

—Dorothy Green

BRETON, Nicholas.   English.   Born in London c. 1545; stepson of George Gascoigne, *q.v.* Possibly educated at Oriel College, Oxford. Married Ann Sutton in 1592; two sons, one daughter. Mary, Countess of Pembroke, was an early patron – little else is known of his life. *Died c. 1626.*

PUBLICATIONS

Collections

The Works in Verse and Prose, edited by Alexander B. Grosart.   2 vols., 1879.

A Mad World My Masters and Other Prose Works, edited by Ursula Kentish-Wright.   2 vols., 1929.

Verse

A Small Handful of Fragrant Flowers.   1575.
A Flourish upon Fancy.   1577; revised edition, 1582.
Breton's Bower of Delights.   1591; edited by Hyder E. Rollins, 1933.
The Pilgrimage to Paradise.   1592.
Mary Magdalen's Love, A Solemn Passion.   1595.
The Passions of the Spirit.   1599.
Pasquil's Mad-Cap and Mad-Cap's Message.   1600.
The Second Part of Pasquil's Mad-Cap, The Fool's-Cap.   1600.
Pasquil's Mistress.   1600.
Pasquil's Pass and Passeth Not.   1600.
Melancholic Humours.   1600; edited by G. B. Harrison, 1929.
No Whipping nor Ripping, But a Kind Friendly Snipping.   1601; edited by A. Davenport, 1951.
A Divine Poem: The Ravished Soul and the Blessed Weeper.   1601.
An Excellent Poem upon the Longing of a Blessed Heart to Be with Christ.   1601.
The Soul's Heavenly Exercise.   1601.
Mary Magdalen's Lamentations.   1601.
The Mother's Blessing.   1602; revised edition, 1621.
A True Description of Unthankfulness.   1602.
Old Mad-Cap's New Gallimaufry.   1602.
The Passion of a Discontented Mind.   1602.
The Soul's Harmony.   1602.
The Passionate Shepherd.   1604.
Honest Counsel.   1605.
The Soul's Immortal Crown.   1605.
The Honour of Valour.   1605.
I Would and Would Not.   1614.
The Hate of Treason.   1616.
Machiavel's Dog.   1617.
Poems Not Hitherto Reprinted, edited by Jean Robertson.   1952.

Fiction

The Miseries of Mavillia.   1597.
The Strange Fortunes of Two Excellent Princes.   1600.
Grimello's Fortunes.   1604; edited by E. G. Morice, in *Two Pamphlets,* 1936.

Other

The Works of a Young Wit.   1577.
A Discourse in Commendation of Francis Drake.   1581.
The History of Don Federigo de Terra Nuova.   1590.
The Will of Wit, Wit's Will or Will's Wit.   1597.
Auspicante Jehova.   1597.
Wit's Trenchmour.   1597.
A Post with a Mad Packet of Letters.   1602; revised edition, 1603; part 2, 1605; revised edition, 1607, 1609.

Wonders Worth the Hearing. 1602.
A Dialogue Full of Pith and Pleasure Between Three Philosophers. 1603.
A Merry Dialogue Betwixt the Taker and the Mistaker. 1603; as *A Mad World My Masters*, 1635.
A Piece of Friar Bacon's Brazen-Head's Prophecy. 1604.
An Old Man's Lesson and a Young Man's Love. 1605; edited by E. G. Morice, in *Two Pamphlets*, 1936.
I Pray You Be Not Angry. 1605.
Choice, Chance, and Change; or, Conceits in Their Colours. 1606.
A Murmurer. 1607.
Wit's Private Wealth. 1607.
The Uncasing of Machiavel's Instructions to His Son. 1613; as *Machiavel's Advice*, 1681.
Characters upon Essays Moral and Divine. 1615.
The Good and the Bad; or, Descriptions of the Worthies and Unworthies of This Age. 1616; abridged edition, as *England's Selected Characters*, 1643.
Crossing of Proverbs: Cross-Answers and Cross-Humours. 2 vols, 1616; revised edition, 1676(?).
The Court and the Country. 1618; edited by S. Pargellis and W. H. Dunham, Jr., in *Complaint and Reform in England 1436–1714*, 1938.
Conceited Letters Newly Laid Open. 1618.
Strange News Out of Divers Countries. 1622.
Soothing of Proverbs. 1626.
Fantastics, Serving for a Perpetual Prognostication. 1626; selection edited by Brian Rhys, as *The Twelve Moneths*, 1927.
The Figure of Four; or, A Handful of Sweet Flowers. 2 vols., 1626–31.

Bibliography: *Breton: A Concise Bibliography* by S. A. and D. R. Tannenbaum, 1947; *Breton* by T. R. Howlett, 1975.

Reading List: *Breton und Seine Prosaschriften* by T. F. C. Kuskop, 1902; *Breton as a Pamphleteer* by Nellie E. Monroe, 1929.

*   *   *

Except for a period of eight years when he may have been on the Continent (1582–1590), Nicholas Breton steadily published poetry and prose in nearly equal quantity for almost 50 years. The variety in his extensive canon gives proof of one who was obliged to write for a living. We find love lyrics and "pastorals"; meditative, moral, and religious poems; satires in prose and verse; pamphlets, letters, dialogues, character sketches, and essays. Although Grosart, the first editor of Breton's collected works, praised the prose for its economy of expression and attention to specific detail (and in his enthusiasm recommended its style to his contemporaries as a corrective to their rhetorical excesses), Breton's prose is of little literary worth nor was it influential in his own time, though some was popular. While his prose is interesting as an index of popular taste, its study belongs more to the realm of sociology than to literature.

Breton's poetry is somewhat more significant: he published just before and throughout England's most important period of poetic development, and early in his career he is recognized by Puttenham to be among that "crew of courtly makers, noblemen and gentlemen ... who have written exceedingly well" (*The Arte of English Poesie*, 1589). His early poems show the influence of his stepfather, George Gascoigne, in their metrical heaviness and their dependence upon alliteration (characteristics which, except in his few pastoral poems, his later poetry never entirely lost). They place the poet squarely in the native tradition of versifying, separating him from the later English Petrarchans like Watson, Sidney, and Drayton – even when his subject is love, as "The Toyes of an Idle Head":

> If I had skill to frame a cunning Vearse
> Wherein I mought my loathsome life lament,
> Or able were in rimes for to rehearse
> The gryping griefes, that now my haeart have hent:
>   Such privie panges of love I could descrie,
>   As never any lover felt but I.

Yet, despite his provincialism he would later learn from the new poets to handle gracefully the content of the imported pastoral, as in this simple but charming trochaic passage reminiscent of Campion from *The Passionate Shepherd*:

> Pretty twinckling starry eyes,
> How did nature first devise,
> Such a sparkling in your sight,
> As to give love such delight,
> As to make him like a flye,
> Play with looks untill he die?

Although his pastoral lyrics comprise a very small fraction of his poems, Breton's name remained alive to posterity through those which first appeared in *Britton's Bowre of Delights* and, subsequently, in *England's Helicon*, an anthology still admired in the nineteenth century when it was reissued.

More characteristic of the bulk of Breton's work are those long poems in six-line or rhyme royal stanzas affirming the received values of his time – in successive poems he is against "unthankfulness," for honor, against treason, for constancy, humility, patience, and wisdom. An extension of this moralizing attitude is found in the satires of his "Pasquil" series, four lengthy verse tracts all published in 1600, attacking in catalogue fashion the general abuses of his (or any) time or decrying such unwholesome types as the proud courtier, the lady quean, and the wealthy beggar. These poems bear the stamp of a poet in search of a patron and a market, variously dedicated as they are to members of the nobility and the wealthy middle-class alike and attempting overtly to appeal to the widest possible readership.

At the end of his career Breton was apparently reduced to doing hack-work for booksellers; nonetheless his name will endure because of those well wrought pastoral lyrics which found their way into *England's Helicon*, where they are displayed to advantage among lyrics by Sidney, Lodge, Drayton, Marlowe, Ralegh, and Shakespeare.

—Frank Fabry

BRIDGES, Robert (Seymour). English. Born in Walmer, Kent, 23 October 1844. Educated at Eton College; Corpus Christi College, Oxford, 1863–67; studied medicine at St. Bartholomew's Hospital, London, M.B.; Fellow of the Royal College of Physicians. Married Monica Waterhouse in 1884; one son, two daughters. Casualty Physician, St. Bartholomew's Hospital, and Assistant Physician, Children's Hospital, Great Ormond Street, London; retired, 1881. Settled in Yattendon, Berkshire, in the 1880's; from 1907 lived at Boar's Hill, Oxford. Co-Founder, Society for Pure English, 1913. D.Litt.: Oxford University; LL.D.: University of St. Andrews; University of Michigan, Ann Arbor; Harvard University, Cambridge, Massachusetts. Honorary Fellow, Corpus Christi College, Oxford, 1895. Poet Laureate, 1913 until his death. Order of Merit, 1929. *Died 21 April 1930.*

Collections

Poetry and Prose, edited by John Sparrow.   1955.
Selected Poems, edited by Donald E. Stanford.   1974.

Verse

Poems.   1873.
Carmen Elegiacum.   1876; revised edition, 1877.
The Growth of Love.   1876; revised edition, 1889.
Poems, Second Series.   1879.
Poems, Third Series.   1880.
Eros and Psyche.   1885; revised edition, 1894.
Shorter Poems.   2 vols., 1890; revised edition, 1894, 1896, 1931.
Ode for the Bicentenary Commemoration of Henry Purcell with Other Poems.   1896.
Poetical Works.   6 vols., 1898–1905; revised edition, 1912, 1936, 1953.
Now in Wintry Delights.   1903.
Poems Written in the Year MCMXIII.   1914.
Ibant Obscuri.   1916.
October and Other Poems.   1920.
The Tapestry.   1925.
New Verse.   1925; revised edition, 1926.
The Testament of Beauty.   5 vols., 1927–29; revised edition, 1929, 1930.
Verses Written for Mrs. Daniel.   1932.
On Receiving Trivia from the Author.   1932.
Four Collects.   1947.

Plays

Prometheus the Firegiver.   1883; revised edition, 1884.
Nero.   2 vols., 1885–94.
The Feast of Bacchus.   1889; revised edition, 1894.
Palicio.   1890.
The Return of Ulysses.   1890.
The Christian Captive.   1890.
Achilles in Scyros (produced 1912).   1890.
Eden: An Oratorio, music by Charles Stanford (produced 1891).   1891.
The Humours of the Court and Other Poems.   1893.
Demeter: A Mask.   1905.

Other

Milton's Prosody.   1893; revised edition, 1901, 1921.
John Keats: A Critical Essay.   1895.
A Practical Discourse on Hymn-Singing.   1901.
Henry Bradley: A Memoir.   1926.
Collected Essays, Papers ..., edited by M. M. Bridges.   30 vols., 1927–36.

Three Friends: Memoirs of D. M. Dolben, R. W. Dixon, Henry Bradley, edited by M. M.
   Bridges.   1932.
Correspondence of Bridges and Henry Bradley 1900–23.   1940.
XXI Letters: Correspondence Between Bridges and R. C. Trevelyan.   1955.
The Correspondence of Bridges and W. B. Yeats, edited by Richard J. Finneran.   1977.

Editor, *Yattendon Hymnal* (and hymns, selections, and four-part chants).   7 vols.,
   1895–99.
Editor, *Songs and Odes,* by R. W. Dixon.   1896.
Editor, *The Small Hymn-Book.*   1899.
Editor, *Last Poems of R. W. Dixon.*   1905.
Editor, *Poems: A Selection,* by R. W. Dixon.   1909.
Editor, *The Poems of D. M. Dolben.*   1911; revised edition, 1915.
Editor and Contributor, *Tracts for the Society of Pure English.*   31 vols., 1913-29.
Editor, *The Spirit of Man* (anthology).   1916.
Editor, *Poems of G. M. Hopkins.*   1918.
Editor, *The Chilswell Book of English Poetry.*   1924.
Editor, *Selections from the Letters of Walter Raleigh.*   1928.
Editor, *The Collected Papers of Henry Bradley.*   1928.

Bibliography: *A Bibliography of Bridges* by George L. MacKay, 1933.

Reading List: *Bridges: A Study of Traditionalism in Poetry* by Albert Guerard, 1942; *Bridges*
by Edward J. Thompson, 1944; *Metaphor and Sound and Meaning in Bridges' "The
Testament of Beauty"* by E. C. Wright, 1951; *Bridges and Hopkins 1863–89: A Literary
Friendship* by J. G. Ritz, 1960; *Bridges* by John Sparrow, 1962; *The Prosodic Structure of
Bridges' Neo-Miltonic Syllabics* by Mary G. Berg, 1962.

                                    *   *   *

   The publication of his *Shorter Poems* in 1890 won for Robert Bridges immediate
recognition as a master of the lyric. Throughout his career the technical accomplishment of
his poems never faltered, and he was a great experimenter, especially with the use of metres
derived from the prosody of Greek and Latin verse. His reputation has declined during the
past forty years. Many readers, while granting that he is a master of his craft, have detected in
his verse a coldness and aloofness that outweigh his gifts and virtues as a poet; nor have they
much relish for his employment of classical metres, which culminated in the composition of
his long philosophical poem, *The Testament of Beauty.*
   The partial eclipse of his reputation has been accompanied, and probably caused, by the
recognition of Gerard Manley Hopkins as a major poet. Bridges delayed publication of his
friend's poems until 1918, although including a few of them in his anthology *The Spirit of
Man* (1916). His cautious reservations about certain aspects of Hopkins's art incurred some
odium in the 1930's, especially as the publication of the correspondence between the two
poets displayed Bridges in the light of a rather timid, conservative, academic poet who was
apparently blind to the genius of Hopkins.
   During the past few years there has been a growing awareness that Bridges is a fine poet
from whom we can derive pleasure and illumination. Granted that his diction is often stilted
and frigid, he remains a master of phrasing and of subtle rhythm. Even though *The
Testament of Beauty* has some dull patches, it is still one of the few long poems of the 20th
century that command attention. And among his shorter poems, both early and late, there are
a score of lyrics whose mingled delicacy and strength assure them of a place in the canon of
English poetry. His emotional and technical range are wider than many critics imagine,
encompassing the passionate joy of "Awake, my heart, to be loved, awake, awake!," the

quiet perfection and gentle rhythms of "London Snow," the grim warning note of "Low Barometer," with its fierce, taut quatrains, and the serene affirmation of "Johannes Milton, Senex," in which Bridges assumes the mask of the poet with whom he has the closest affinity.

—John Press

BRONTË, Emily (Jane).   English.   Born in Thornton, Yorkshire, 30 July 1818; sister of the writers Anne and Charlotte Brontë; moved with her family to Haworth, Yorkshire, 1820, and lived there for the rest of her life. Educated at home, at a school for clergymen's daughters, Cowan Bridge, Yorkshire, 1824–25, Miss Wooler's School, Roe Head, Yorkshire, 1835; Pensionnat Heger, Brussels, 1842. Taught in a school at Law Hill, Halifax, 1837–38. *Died 19 December 1848.*

Publications

Collections

> *Complete Works,* edited by C. K. Shorter and W. R. Nicoll.   2 vols., 1910–11.
> *The Shakespeare Head Brontë,* edited T. J. Wise and J. A. Symington.   19 vols., 1932–38.
> *Complete Poems,* edited by C. W. Hatfield.   1941.
> *Poems,* edited by Rosemary Hartill.   1973.

Verse

> *Poems,* with Anne and Charlotte Brontë.   1846.
> *Two Poems,* edited by Fannie E. Ratchford.   1934.
> *Gondal Poems,* edited by Helen Brown and Joan Mott.   1938.
> *Gondal's Queen: A Novel in Verse,* edited by Fannie E. Ratchford.   1955.

Fiction

> *Wuthering Heights,* with *Agnes Grey,* by Anne Brontë.   1847.

Other

> *Five Essays Written in French,* translated by Lorine White Nagel, edited by Fannie E. Rathcford.   1948.

Bibliography: *A Bibliography of the Writings in Prose and Verse of the Brontë Family* by T. J. Wise, 1917.

Reading List: *Brontë: Her Life and Work* by Muriel Spark and Derek Stanford, 1953; *Brontë* by Winifred Gérin, 1971; *Brontë: A Critical Anthology* edited by Jean-Pierre Petit, 1973; *The Mind of Brontë* by Herbert Dingle, 1974.

*   *   *

Emily Brontë's reputation might appear at first sight disproportionate to her meagre output: one novel and 193 poems. Their quality, however, is unique, so visionary and powerful as to rank her indisputedly among the writers of genius.

Few influences on her writing can be traced. She was a very private person, rejecting such contacts with the world as were offered her through her sister Charlotte, notably, and her London publishers. Though her work has many affinities with the English Metaphysical poets, Traherne and Vaughan in particular, there is no evidence that she ever read them. Her reading was, on her own showing, very limited, very desultory, and without method. She reproached herself repeatedly in her diary papers for the want of "regularity" in her studies. She knew the romantic poets, Wordsworth especially, and Shakespeare, whom she often quotes. She had little schooling, falling ill whenever sent from home. All the source of her health and happiness, and the inspiration of her writing, were the moors that stretch twenty miles round about her home, Haworth, her father's Yorkshire curacy, where she spent her whole life. Her intimate knowledge of the moors at all seasons of the year, and of the wild-life inhabiting them, gave her all the stimulus she needed to enrich her imagination and inspire her writing.

The nature of her poetry and of her one novel – *Wuthering Heights* – is profoundly metaphysical, nourished by the visions that she undoubtedly experienced and was able to describe with all the clarity of facts perceived. The following lines are drawn from a poem about a young captive who awaits her liberator. As with much of her poetic imagery, the awaited visitant is not a corporeal but a spiritual presence.

> He comes with the western winds, with evening's wandering airs,
> With that clear dusk of heaven that brings the thickest stars;
> Winds take a pensive tone, and stars a tender fire,
> And visions rise and change which kill me with desire....
>
> But first a hush of peace, a soundless calm descends;
> The struggle of distress and fierce impatience ends;
> Mute music soothes my breast – unuttered harmony
> That I could never dream till earth was lost to me.
>
> Then dawns the Invisible, the Unseen itself reveals;
> My outward sense is gone, my inward essence feels –
> Its wings are almost free, its home, its harbour found;
> Measuring the gulf it stoops and dares the final bound!
>
> Oh, dreadful is the check – intense the agony
> When the ear begins to hear and the eye begins to see;
> When the pulse begins to throb, the brain to think again,
> The soul to feel the flesh and the flesh to feel the chain!

The religious terminology of much of Emily Brontë's poetry does not obscure the fact that hers was no conventional religion (despite her father's calling). So far as her intensely personal beliefs can be defined, she was a Pantheist, seeing all Life as One – the Visible and the Invisible, the human, the elemental, the animal and vegetable all imbued with the same spiritual forces.

She made a marked distinction between her personal and her Gondal poetry by transcribing them in two separate and clearly marked notebooks. Through the Gondal poems runs a dramatic Saga relating to the royal houses of Angora and Almedore, who contended for the thrones of the island kingdoms of Gondal and Gaaldine, the location of the drama; the principal theme is the love-hate relationship binding the Queen of Angora, Augusta Geraldine Almeda, to her various lovers, primarily Julius Brenzaida. Under cover of this scenario, begun in childhood, Emily Brontë found the substitute identities and the adventurous actions lacking in her life, the freedom that her spirit craved. Freedom was, for her, a pre-condition of life. As she wrote in one of her personal poems:

> And if I pray, the only prayer
> That moves my lips for me
> Is – "Leave me the heart that now I bear
> And give me liberty.
>
> Yes, as my swift days near their goal
> 'Tis all that I implore –
> Through life and death, a chainless soul
> With courage to endure."

The situations of which she wrote in the Gondal poems, often describing passionate love relations, led her early readers to suppose them autobiographical, revealing a real-life love affair. Their true context in the Gondal Saga, however, has dispelled this notion for good (the known circumstances of her life leave no room for such a relationship), though the "love-poems," like the famous lament "Cold in the earth," when placed in their right context, are seen to resemble the subject of *Wuthering Heights* so closely as to show the overall unity of her creative work.

For years before the writing of *Wuthering Heights*, the Gondal poems dealt with an orphan boy, "black of mien, savage in disposition," passionately involved with a fair girl, his superior in social standing, the very situation of Heathcliff and Catherine Earnshaw in the novel. Emily Brontë's belief in the indissoluble nature of earthly love, first treated in the poems, found its complete expression in the novel, where even the separation of death is shown as powerless to sever a spiritual connection. Catherine Earnshaw gives utterance to this Credo early in the novel when Heathcliff runs away and she is urged to forget him and make a suitable marriage with Edgar Linton: "... my great thought in living is [Heathcliff]. If all else perished, and *he* remained, I should still continue to be; and if all else remained, and he were annihilated, the universe would turn to a mighty stranger; I should not seem a part of it.... My love for Heathcliff resembles the eternal rocks beneath.... Nelly, I *am* Heathcliff!" Catherine's faith is shown as justified in the novel's end where Heathcliff even desecrates her grave, so as to be buried with her; and their ghosts are ultimately seen, wandering freely together upon the hill-side. The death of Heathcliff, self-induced by his longing for Catherine, is one of the most powerful and daring climaxes in English fiction.

The boldness of the conception that man is the master of his own fate is matched by her last poem, "No coward soul is mine." Addressed to the "God within my breast," she makes her declaration of faith in the universal nature of the soul inhabiting each individual:

> Though Earth and moon were gone
> And suns and universes ceased to be
> And thou wert left alone
> Every Existence would exist in thee
>
> There is not room for Death
> Nor atom that his might could render void
> Since thou art Being and Breath
> And what thou art may never be destroyed.

That is the metaphysical message of *Wuthering Heights*: the indestructability of the spirit. Such a subject was so far removed from the general run of Victorian fiction – it belonged, if anywhere, to the Gothic tradition, still being followed by Mary Shelley with her *Valperga* (1823) in Emily Brontë's childhood – that it explains the novel's failure when first published. Only two critics, Sydney Dobell and Swinburne, praised it (in 1850 and 1883 respectively), too late to bring recognition to the author in her lifetime.

The book's curious and lasting appeal rests upon a number of qualities: the unflagging excitement of the plot; the wild moorland setting and the splendour of the descriptions; the originality of the characters; the unearthly, not to say ghostly atmosphere created by the interplay of the elements in the affairs of men; the homely background of the old house, The Heights, in which the decaying fortunes of the Earnshaw family are – literally – played out, gambled away, by the last of the line. The author's close familiarity with the local rustic types, the fiercely independent hill-farmers living about the moors, enabled her to create the old curmudgeon Joseph, the general factotum to the family, with both humour and fidelity: his permanent ill-humour and girding condemnation of his associates as all destined for Hell fire, faithfully portrays the primitive attitudes left in the wake of the Methodist Revival in Yorkshire; and acts as a counter-balance to the gothic atmosphere of much of the plot and the high Romanticism of the larger-than-life hero and heroine, Heathcliff and Catherine. In creating such a character as Joseph, Emily Brontë showed that, undoubted visionary as she was, she also had her feet firmly planted on earth.

—Winifred Gérin

BROOKE, Rupert (Chawner). English. Born in Rugby, Warwickshire, 3 August 1887. Educated at Hillbrow School; Rugby School, 1901–06; King's College, Cambridge, 1906. Served in the Artists' Rifles and the Royal Naval Division, 1914–15: Sub-Lieutenant. Wrote travel letters from the U.S.A. and the South Seas for the *Westminster Gazette*, London, 1913. *Died 23 April 1915.*

PUBLICATIONS

Collections

    Poetical Works, edited by Geoffrey Keynes. 1946.
    The Prose, edited by Christopher Hassall. 1956.
    The Letters, edited by Geoffrey Keynes. 1968.
    A Reappraisal and Selection, edited by Timothy Rogers. 1971.

Verse

    Poems. 1911.
    1914 and Other Poems. 1915.
    Collected Poems. 1915; revised edition, 1918, 1928; as *Complete Poems,* 1932.
    Selected Poems. 1917.

Play

Lithuania (produced 1915).   1915.

Other

John Webster and the Elizabethan Drama.   1916.
Letters from America.   1916.
Fragments Now First Collected, edited by R. M. G. Potter.   1925.
Democracy and the Arts.   1946.

Bibliography: *A Bibliography of the Works of Brooke* by Geoffrey Keynes, 1954, revised edition, 1964.

Reading List: *Brooke: A Biography* by Christopher Hassall, 1964; *The Handsomest Young Man in England: Rupert Brooke: A Biographical Essay* by Michael Hastings, 1967.

*   *   *

When Rupert Brooke died in 1915, he was twenty-seven years old and at the height of his fame and popularity. Henry James wrote of his death: "If there was a stupid and hideous disfigurement of life or outrage to beauty left for our awful conditions to perpetrate, these things have now been supremely achieved and no other brutal blow in the private sphere can better them for making one just stare through one's tears"; and D. H. Lawrence commented: "Bright Phoebus smote him down. It was all in the saga." His apotheosis was achieved then and rests now on the legend of his physical beauty and the passionate and patriotic sonnets which he wrote on the outbreak of war. These poems of 1914 proclaim the value of sacrifice and suffering over the "little emptiness" and selfishness of everyday life. Their appeal and the appeal of such arguments have been diminished by the slaughter which Brooke never saw, and which informs the now better-known poetry of Sassoon, Owen, and Rosenberg.

The contemporary enthusiasm for and equally excessive later reaction against the war sonnets have tended to obscure the considerable achievement of Brooke's other work in poetry and prose. The graceful and ironic earlier love sonnets, like "Oh! Death will find me, long before I tire/Of watching you," deserve to be better known, as do Brooke's more realistic experiments. The twin sonnets "Menelaus and Helen," for example, picture their dramatic reunion as Troy burns, and then the unsung "Long, connubial years." He grows deaf and she becomes a scold: "So Menelaus nagged; and Helen cried;/And Paris slept on by Scamander side." "The Old Vicarage, Grantchester" − Brooke's best-known poem, apart from "The Soldier" − indicates the elegance and wit of which he was capable:

> And in that garden, black and white,
> Creep whispers through the grass all night;
> And spectral dance, before the dawn,
> A hundred Vicars down the lawn;
> Curates, long dust, will come and go
> On lissom, clerical, printless toe;
> And off between the boughs is seen
> The sly shade of a Rural Dean...

This witty facility with poetic diction and the rhyming couplet is seen to good advantage elsewhere in Brooke's verse, as in "Heaven," where the fish hope for an aquatic Paradise and the poet smiles at the shapes taken by such faith:

But somewhere, beyond Space and Time,
Is wetter water, slimier slime!
And there (they trust) there swimmeth One
Who swam ere rivers were begun,
Immense, of fishy form and mind,
Squamous, omnipotent, and kind;
And under that Almighty Fin,
The littlest fish may enter in.

He succeeds easily in this whimsically witty and very English vein, but there are signs of a wider range of interest and a less silvery style, which render suspect the too common deployment of Brooke as a gilded foil to later and grimmer war poets.

—M. J. Alexander

BROOKS, Gwendolyn. American. Born in Topeka, Kansas, 17 June 1917. Educated at Wilson Junior College, Chicago, graduated 1936. Married Henry L. Blakely in 1939; one son, one daughter. Publicity Director, National Association for the Advancement of Colored People Youth Council, Chicago, in the 1930's. Taught at Northeastern Illinois State College, Chicago, Columbia College, Chicago, Elmhurst College, Illinois, and the University of Wisconsin, Madison; Distinguished Professor of the Arts, City College of the City University of New York, 1971. Editor, *The Black Position* magazine; Member, Illinois Arts Council. Recipient: Guggenheim Fellowship, 1946, 1947; National Institute of Arts and Letters grant, 1946; Pulitzer Prize, 1950; Friends of Literature Award, 1964; Monsen Award, 1964; Anisfield-Wolf Award, 1968; Black Academy Award, 1971; Shelley Memorial Award, 1976. L.H.D.: Columbia College, 1964; D. Litt.: Lake Forest College, Illinois, 1965; Brown University, Providence, Rhode Island, 1974. Poet Laureate of Illinois, 1969. Member, National Institute of Arts and Letters, 1976. Lives in Chicago.

PUBLICATIONS

Verse

A Street in Bronzeville. 1945.
Annie Allen. 1949.
Bronzeville Boys and Girls. 1956.
The Bean Eaters (verse for children). 1960.
Selected Poems. 1963.
In the Time of Detachment, In the Time of Cold. 1965.
In the Mecca. 1968.
For Illinois 1968: A Sesquicentennial Poem. 1968.
Riot. 1969.
Family Pictures. 1970.
Aloneness. 1971.
Beckonings. 1975.

Fiction

Maud Martha. 1953.

Other

A Portion of That Field, with others. 1967.
The World of Gwendolyn Brooks (miscellany). 1971.
Report from Part One: An Autobiography. 1972.
The Tiger Who Wore White Gloves; or, You Are What You Are (juvenile). 1974.

Editor, *A Broadside Treasury.* 1971.
Editor, *Jump Bad: A New Chicago Anthology.* 1971.

*   *   *

Gwendolyn Brooks solves the critical question of whether to judge black poetry in America by standards different from those applied to white poetry: she simply writes so powerfully and universally out of the black American milieu that the question does not arise. Her poems may sometimes be bitter, angry, or threatening, but always they are poems and never mere propaganda. She may personally feel caught between racial allegiance and the need for social action on the one hand and purer and higher art on the other, but in her work the distinction dissolves.

Indeed, *In the Mecca,* published in 1968, and especially the poems published since, reflect the conversion from deep racial pride to a harsher militancy that she experienced under the tutelage of a group of young blacks at a meeting at Fisk University in 1967. Thus she speaks in "Young Africans" (from *Family Pictures*) of "our black revival, our black vinegar,/our hands and our hot blood," and warns in the acerbic *Riot,* "Cabot! John! You are a desperate man,/and the desperate die expensively today." But nearly always she finds the tight poetic structure, the *things* in which to embody the idea, so that the reader comes away with that sense of surprise and delight at the insight – in addition to any other emotion – that means that the work was a poem, and that the poem was a fine one.

Gwendolyn Brooks has devoted much of her time since the late 1960's to helping young black Americans, and especially writers. But she speaks out of the American consciousness and to the American conscience, and it is the color-blind America that has rightly given her a Pulitzer Prize, the Poet Laureateship of the State of Illinois, and other testaments to her great lyrical voice.

—Alan R. Shucard

BROWN, Sterling (Allen). American. Born in Washington, D.C., 1 May 1901. Educated at public schools in Washington, D.C.; Williams College, Williamstown, Massachusetts, A.B. 1925 (Phi Beta Kappa); Harvard University, Cambridge, Massachusetts, A.M. 1930. Married Daisy Turnbull in 1919. Teacher, Virginia Seminary and College, Lynchburg, 1923–26, Lincoln University, Jefferson City, Missouri, 1926–28, and Fisk University, Nashville, Tennessee, 1929. Since 1929, Professor of English, Howard University, Washington, D.C. Visiting Professor, New York University, New School for Social Research, New York, Sarah Lawrence College, Bronxville, New York, and Vassar College, Poughkeepsie, New York. Literary Editor, *Opportunity* magazine, in the 1930's; Editor of *Negro Affairs* for the Federal Writers' Project, 1936–39. Recipient: Guggenheim Fellowship, 1937. Lives in Washington, D.C.

PUBLICATIONS

Verse

Southern Road.   1932.
The Last Ride of Wild Bill and Eleven Narrative Poems.   1975.

Other

Outline for the Study of the Poetry of American Negroes (study guide for James Weldon
   Johnson's *The Book of American Negro Poetry*).   1931.
The Negro in American Fiction.   1937.
Negro Poetry and Drama.   1937.

Editor, with Arthur P. Davis and Ulysses Lee, *The Negro Caravan.*   1941.

*   *   *

Essentially a traditional song-maker and story teller, Sterling Brown has witnessed cross-currents of American literature, and chooses in his poetry to depict blacks and the clash of their roles with those of whites in the variegated society of the American South, particularly in the time caught between two world wars.

His poetry has been collected in anthologies as early as James Weldon Johnson's *The Book of American Negro Poetry* (1922), and, like Johnson himself and Langston Hughes, he set about disrupting the patently false and banal image of the docile American Negro with his charming *patois*, artificially stylized and mimicked by the whites in the minstrel shows still popular in the 1920's and 1930's. Johnson says in his preface of Hughes and Brown that they "*do* use a dialect, but it is not the dialect of the comic minstrel tradition or the sentimental plantation tradition; it is the common, racy, living, authentic speech of the Negro in certain phases of real life."

Brown uses original Afro-American ballads such as "Casey Jones," "John Henry," and "Staggolee" as counterpoint for his modern ones, but the portent of his ironic wit should not be underestimated, for it is actually a tool to shape an ironic, infernal vision of American life as Hades: "The Place was Dixie I took for Hell," says Slim in "Slim in Hell." The American Negro is heralded not as Black Orpheus but as modern tragic hero Mose, a leader of *all* people while futilely attempting to save his own: "A soft song, filled with a misery/Older than Mose will be." In "Sharecropper" he is broken as Christ was broken; his landlord "shot him in the side" to put him out of his misery; he is lost and wild as Odysseus in "Odyssey of a Big Boy"; and found again:

> Man wanta live
> Man want find himself
> Man gotta learn
> How to go it alone.

Though minimal in quantity, Brown's poetry is epic in conception; his ballad, blues, and jazz forms are the vehicles for creative insight into themes of American life.

—Carol Lee Saffioti

BROWNE, William.   English.   Born in Tavistock, Devon, in 1591. Educated at Tavistock Grammar School; Exeter College, Oxford, M.A. 1625; Inner Temple, London, 1611. Married the daughter of Sir Thomas Eversfield; two sons. Tutor at Oxford to Robert Dormer, Earl of Carnarvon, 1624; subsequently in the service of the Earls of Pembroke at Wilton. *Died in 1643.*

PUBLICATIONS

Collections

>   *Whole Works,* edited by W. C. Hazlitt.   2 vols., 1868.
>   *Poems,* edited by Gordon Goodwin.   2 vols., 1894.

Verse

>   *Two Elegies,* with Fulke Greville.   1613.
>   *Britannia's Pastorals.*   2 vols., 1613–16; book 3 edited by T. C. Croker, 1852.
>   *The Shepherd's Pipe,* with George Wither.   1614.
>   *Original Poems,* edited by Egerton Brydges.   1816.

Play

>   *The Inner Temple Masque* (produced 1614; as *Ulysses and Circe,* produced
>   1615).   Edited by Thomas Davies, in *Works,* 1772; edited by R. F. Hill, in *A Book of
>   Masques in Honour of Allardyce Nicoll,* 1967.

Other

>   Translator, *The History of Polexander,* by Marin Le Roy.   1647.

Reading List: *Browne* by F. W. Moorman, 1897; "Browne as Satirist" by J. McLennan, in *Papers of the Michigan Academy 33,* 1949.

*   *   *

Little is known of William Browne's early life. His circle of friends included Michael Drayton, George Wither and John Davies of Hereford. Browne, Drayton, and Wither, especially, shared a close literary association, inspired by a common allegiance to the poetry of Spenser. All three were professional poets, conscious of a vocation, and they firmly resisted the literary developments after 1600 – an antipathy largely directed at the metaphysical school, but also towards the progress of the drama.

Browne was, first and foremost, a pastoralist. In *Britannia's Pastorals* the poet superimposes classical borrowings on an English landscape drawn largely from Spenser. The stories are typical pastoral accounts of love-lorn swains, suicidal nymphs, lustful satyrs, and Ovidian metamorphoses. Fletcher, Tasso, and Guarini as well as Spenser are plundered for stories. For a great undertaking, the rewards are rare. There are passages and lyrical interludes where poetic skill is evident, but a rambling narrative and a great deal of allegory, satire, and didacticism too often produce dullness and prolixity.

In *The Shepheards Pipe*, a series of seven eclogues, something of the closeness of the Browne-Wither-Drayton group can be seen. In the first eclogue, Willie (Browne) tries to cheer up Roget (Wither), who has suffered from ill reports of his piping. Then in the second eclogue their insular, pastoral world is invaded by a troublesome swineherd. A sullen, hostile mood such as this often surfaces in Browne's work. We find it again in the third book of *Britannia's Pastorals* and in his odes and sonnets. The poet, however, is not simply disgruntled at a dearth of artistic integrity, but he relates this to a wider decline in morality, politics, and religion which he sees as having set in at the end of the Elizabethan Golden Age.

The inability of Browne, Drayton, and Wither to heed changes in literary taste meant that neglect inevitably fell upon their work. Browne, therefore, largely uses the shepherd persona to air personal grievances about what he regards as a malaise in society and to celebrate the poetic commitment of himself and his associates – when reasons for celebration are often conspicuously absent. The result of this self-centred stance is frequently an unhealthy one: Browne's tedious longwindedness is the direct result of his determination to play the role of the poet as saviour, usually to the detriment of the poetry.

Though Browne's work is thus sometimes marred by self-indulgence, yet he remains one of the few successful imitators of Spenser. The influence of Spenser as a model is of course strongly felt in the multitude of poets who dragged the tradition into the middle of the seventeenth century. In most, however, the matter is merely borrowed with slavish emulation, and is not developed or individualised. Browne, Wither, and Drayton, on the other hand, responded to specific elements in *The Shepheardes Calender*, such as the role of the shepherd persona, the archaic language and the realistic landscape, and made them their own.

In Browne it is primarily the closely detailed and affectionate treatment of nature and the countryside that we can value today. In typically native manner, he tells us in *Britannia's Pastorals* of his intention to eschew the artifice and unreality of the Arcadian landscape: "My Muse for lofty pitches shall not rome/But homely pipen of her native home." And, despite moments of rather stilted rhetoric, he provides us with some agreeably down-to-earth vignettes of, for example, the local blacksmith who "spits in his Buckthorne fist,/And bids his Man bring out the five-fold twist,/His shackles, shacklocks, hampers, gyves and chains,/His linked bolts." It is the influence of Shakespeare, perhaps, rather than Spenser that is present in his description of winter "when hardly fed the flocks/And Isicles hung dangling on the Rocks.... When every Barne rung with the threshing Flailes,/And Shepherds Boyes for cold gan blow their nailes."

In *Britannia's Pastorals*, the background is one of homely English activities, farming, hunting, fishing; buxom milkmaids replace the elegant shepherdesses of Arcadia, and conventional Classical myth frequently gives way to native fairy lore. Of course this semi-realistic backdrop often clashes incongruously with the Ovidian narrative material, and it would be futile to pretend that the pastorals of Browne of Tavistock can lay any claim to being considered as coherent works of art. Neither, however, do they merit the almost total oblivion they enjoy at present – a far cry from the days when, according to George Eliot (in *Daniel Deronda*), "the welfare of our Indian Empire [might] be somehow connected with a quotable knowledge of Browne's Pastorals."

—B. W. Lyle

BROWNING, Elizabeth Barrett.   English.   Born at Coxhoe Hall, in Kelloe, near Durham, 6 March 1806; spent her childhood on her father's estate near Ledbury, Hertfordshire. Educated privately. Married Robert Browning, *q.v.*, in 1846; one son. Injured her spine,

1821, and thereafter lived as a semi-invalid; her family settled in Sidmouth, 1826–28, then in London, 1828; her delicate condition was exacerbated from shock at the drowning of her brother at Torquay, and she was thereafter confined to her sick-room in London, writing verse, contributing literary articles to the *Athenaeum*, and helping friends with editorial projects; after her marriage she lived with Browning in Pisa, 1846, and Florence, 1847 until her death. *Died 30 June 1861.*

PUBLICATIONS

Collections

    Complete Works, edited by Charlotte Porter and Helen A. Clarke. 6 vols., 1900.

Verse

    The Battle of Marathon. 1820.
    An Essay on Mind with Other Poems. 1826.
    Promentheus, Translated from the Greek of Aeschylus, and Miscellaneous Poems. 1833.
    The Seraphim and Other Poems. 1838.
    Poems. 2 vols., 1844; as *A Drama of Exile and Other Poems*, 1844; revised edition, as *Poems*, 1850; as *Poetical Works*, 5 vols., 1866; *Sonnets from the Portuguese* edited by Fannie E. Ratchford and D. Fulton, 1950.
    Casa Guidi Windows. 1851.
    Two Poems, with Robert Browning. 1854.
    Aurora Leigh. 1857; revised edition, 1859.
    Poems Before Congress. 1860; as *Napoleon in Italy and Other Poems*, 1860.
    Last Poems, edited by Robert Browning. 1862.
    Psyche Apocalypte: A Lyrical Drama, with R. H. Horne. 1876.
    Epistle to a Canary, edited by Edmund Gosse. 1913.
    The Enchantress and Other Poems, edited by T. J. Wise. 1913.
    Leila: A Tale, edited by T. J. Wise. 1913.
    New Poems, with Robert Browning, edited by F. G. Kenyon. 1914.
    The Poet's Enchiridion, edited by H. Buxton Forman. 1914.
    Hitherto Unpublished Poems and Stories, edited by H. Buxton Forman. 2 vols., 1914.

Other

    A New Spirit of the Age (essays), with R. H. Horne. 2 vols., 1844.
    The Greek Christian Poets, and The English Poets. 1863.
    Letters, edited by F. G. Kenyon. 2 vols., 1897.
    Letters of Robert and Elizabeth Barrett Browning 1845–46, edited by R. B. Browning. 2 vols., 1899; edited by Elvan Kintner, 2 vols., 1969.
    Browning in Her Letters, edited by Percy Lubbock. 1906.
    The Art of Scansion: Letters to Uvedale Price, edited by Alice Meynell. 1916.
    Letters, edited by T. J. Wise. 1916.
    Letters to Her Sister 1846–59, edited by Leonard Huxley. 1929.
    Twenty-Two Unpublished Letters of Elizabeth Barrett and Robert Browning, edited by William Rose Benét. 1935.
    Letters to Benjamin Robert Haydon, edited by Martha Hale Shackford. 1939; edited by W. B. Pope, as *Invisible Friends*, 1972.

Elizabeth Barrett to Miss Mitford: Unpublished Letters, edited by Betty Miller. 1954.

Elizabeth Barrett to Mr. Boyd: Unpublished Letters, edited by Barbara P. McCarthy. 1955.

Letters of the Brownings to George Barrett, edited by Paul Landis and Ronald E. Freeman. 1958.

Diary by E. B. B.: The Unpublished Diary of 1831–1832, edited by Philip Kelley and Ronald Hudson. 1969.

Letters to Mrs. David Ogilvy 1849–61, edited by Peter N. Heydon and Philip Kelley. 1974.

The Barretts at Hope End: The Early Diary of Browning, edited by Elizabeth Berridge. 1974.

Bibliography: *A Bibliography of Browning* by Warren Barnes, 1967.

Reading List: *Browning* by D. Hewlett, 1953; *Life of Browning* by Gardner B. Taplin, 1957; *Browning: A Poet's Work and Its Setting*, 1962, and *Browning*, 1965, both by Alethea Hayter.

*   *   *

Mrs. Browning was a prolific poet and reviewer, as well as the partner of Robert Browning in one of the most famous romances of the nineteenth century. Despite her invalidism – brought on initially by an accident with a horse when she was fifteen – Elizabeth was already well-known as a poet when Robert came to meet her in 1846. Her Byronic *The Seraphim* attracted attention, and "The Cry of the Children" was one of the humanitarian poems, in the manner of Hood's "Song of a Shirt," which paralleled Dickens's efforts in his early novels to draw sympathetic attention to the sufferings of the poor, and especially the children:

> They look up with their pale and sunken faces
>   And their look is dread to see,
> For they mind you of their angels in high places,
>   With eyes turned on Deity.

Unfortunately the style remains conventional, and there is little of Dickens's strange particularizing power.

This is in fact true of much of Mrs. Browning's poetry, which shows little of the innovating energies of her husband's best work. She seems to have felt that the significant subject matter of her poems would of itself give them the requisite force, with the result that the modern reader often finds them too full of romantic echoes and conventional phraseology. The *Sonnets from the Portuguese* – not in fact translations, but a celebrating of her love for Robert – probably succeeds best in transcending her limitations, as the sonnet form imposes its own discipline. The sequence bears comparison with others of the period like Christina Rossetti's "Monna Innominata" and D. G. Rossetti's more elaborate *House of Life*, but lacks the energy of Meredith's *Modern Love* – though fortunately also its sense of failure and suffering:

> – I love thee with the breath,
> Smiles, tears, all of my life! – and, if God choose,
> I shall but love thee better after death.

Mrs. Browning goes some way towards achieving the difficult task of celebrating conjugal happiness, though her appeal was far greater to a reading public less cynical than today's.

Mrs. Browning's most ambitious poem, *Aurora Leigh*, has recently been republished as an important feminist document. It is a long narrative poem, in the form used more succinctly by Tennyson for his "English Idyls"; that is to say, it tells a contemporary story such as might have found expression in one of the social-problem novels of the period. Its nine books of blank verse deal with a world in which women are under various pressures from a male-dominated society, but it ends optimistically with the coming together of Aurora and a more humbled Romney in a true and equal love, sanctified by religion. But the fact that *The Tablet* found it necessary to condemn the author as "a brazen-faced woman" suggests that the poem made its impact: the declaration of the seduced Marian Erle – "Here's a hand shall keep for ever clean without a wedding ring" – struck a deliberately unconventional note. We can only regret that the poem lacks the dramatic vigour that would make its lines consistently interesting.

The later poetry expresses Mrs. Browning's liberal political concerns in relation to Italy, but neither *Casa Guidi Windows* nor *Poems before Congress* manages to raise these concerns to an artistically memorable level. She is buried in Florence, and a tablet on the walls of Casa Guidi expresses the city's gratitude for her advocacy of Italian freedom. There can be no doubt that her principles deserve respect, but despite that fact that she had at least as high a reputation as her husband in her life-time, the modern reader finds most of her poetry turgid. She is probably more alive to us now in the pages of her letters, or in Virginia Woolf's fanciful tale, written from the point of view of her dog, *Flush*. Nevertheless, her writings remind us of a very honourable tradition of Victorian liberalism.

—Peter Faulkner

BROWNING, Robert. English. Born in Camberwell, London, 7 May 1812. Educated at the school of the Rev. Thomas Ready, Peckham, London, also tutored at home; attended the Greek class at the University of London, 1829–30. Married Elizabeth Barrett, i.e., Elizabeth Barrett Browning, *q.v.*, in 1846 (died, 1861); one son. Visited Russia, 1833, Italy, 1834; moved with his family to Hatcham, 1835, and devoted himself to his studies and poetry, also worked at writing for the theatre, encouraged by the actor W. C. Macready, 1836–46; visited Italy, 1838, 1844; after his marriage lived in Pisa, 1846, and in Florence, 1847–61; settled in London after his wife's death; revisited Italy, 1878, and often thereafter. Life Governor, University College, London, 1871; Foreign Correspondent to the Royal Academy, 1886. M.A.: Oxford University, 1868; LL.D.: University of Edinburgh, 1884. Honorary Fellow, Balliol College, Oxford, 1868. *Died 16 December 1889.*

PUBLICATIONS

Collections

 Works, edited by F. G. Kenyon.   10 vols., 1912.
 Poems and Plays, edited by S. Commins.   1934.
 Complete Works, edited by Roma A. King.   1969–
 Poetical Works 1833–1864, edited by Ian Jack.   1970.

Verse

Pauline: A Fragment of a Confession.   1833; edited by John Berkey, in *Complete Works 1,* 1969.

Paracelsus.   1835; edited by Morse Peckham, in *Complete Works 1,* 1969.
Sordello.   1840.
Dramatic Lyrics.   1842; edited by John Hulsman, in *Complete Works 3,* 1971.
Dramatic Romances and Lyrics.   1845; edited by Raymond Fitch, in *Complete Works 4,* 1973.
Poems.   2 vols., 1849; as *Poetical Works,* 3 vols., 1863; revised edition, 1865, 1868, 1889.
Christmas Eve and Easter Day.   1850.
Two Poems, with Elizabeth Barrett Browning.   1854.
Men and Women.   2 vols., 1855; edited by F. B. Pinion, 1963.
Dramatis Personae.   1864.
The Ring and the Book.   4 vols., 1868–69; edited by Richard D. Altick, 1971.
Balaustion's Adventure, Including a Transcript from Euripides.   1871.
Prince Hohenstiel-Schwangau, Saviour of Society.   1871.
Fifine at the Fair.   1872.
Red Cotton Night-Cap Country; or, Turf and Towers.   1873.
Aristophanes' Apology, Including a Transcript from Euripides, Being the Last Adventures of Balaustion.   1875.
The Inn Album.   1875.
Pacchiarotto and How He Worked in Distemper, with Other Poems.   1876.
La Saisiaz, and The Two Poets of Croisic.   1878.
Dramatic Idyls.   2 vols., 1879–80.
Jocoseria.   1883.
Ferishtah's Fancies.   1884.
Parleyings with Certain People of Importance in Their Day.   1887.
Asolando: Fancies and Facts.   1889.
New Poems, edited by F. G. Kenyon.   1913.

Plays

Strafford (produced 1837).   1837.
Pippa Passes.   1841; edited by Morse Peckham, in *Complete Works 3,* 1971.
King Victor and King Charles.   1842; edited by Park Honan, in *Complete Works 3,* 1971.
The Return of the Druses.   1843; edited by Morse Pickham, in *Complete Works 3,* 1971.
A Blot in the 'Scutcheon (produced 1843).   1843; revised version, 1843; edited by Thomas F. Wilson, in *Complete Works 4,* 1973.
Colombe's Birthday (produced 1853).   1844; edited by Park Honan, in *Complete Works 4,* 1973.
Luria, and A Soul's Tragedy.   1846; *Luria* edited by Morse Peckham in *Complete Works 4,* 1973.
The Agamemnon of Aeschylus.   1877.

Other

Shelley, edited by F. J. Furnivall.   1881.
Letters of Robert and Elizabeth Barrett Browning 1845–46, edited by R. B. Browning.   2 vols., 1899; edited by Elvan Kintner, 2 vols., 1969.
Browning and Alfred Domett (letters), edited by F. G. Kenyon.   1906.
Letters Collected by T. J. Wise, edited by T. L. Hood.   1933.
Twenty-Two Unpublished Letters of Robert and Elizabeth Barrett Browning, edited by William Rose Benét.   1935.

From Robert to Elizabeth Barrett Browning, edited by William Rose Benét. 1936.
Browning and Julia Wedgwood (letters), edited by Richard Curle. 1937.
Essay on Chatterton, edited by Donald Smalley. 1948.
New Letters of Browning, edited by W. C. DeVane and K. L. Knickerbocker. 1950.
Dearest Isa: Letters to Isabella Blagden, edited by E. C. McAleer. 1951.
Letters of the Brownings to George Barrett, edited by Paul Landis and Ronald E. Freeman. 1958.
Browning to His American Friends: Letters Between the Brownings, the Storys, and James Russell Lowell 1841–90, edited by G. R. Hudson. 1965.
Learned Lady: Letters to Mrs. Thomas Fitzgerald, edited by E. C. McAleer. 1966.

Editor, *Last Poems*, by Elizabeth Barrett Browning. 1862.
Editor, with Una Hawthorne, *Septimus: A Romance*, by Nathaniel Hawthorne. 1872; as *Septimus Felton; or, The Elixir of Life*, 1872.

Bibliography: *Browning: A Bibliography 1830–1950* by L. N. Broughton, C. S. Northup, and Robert B. Pearsall, 1953; supplement 1951–1970 by William S. Peterson, 1974.

Reading List: *A Browning Handbook* by W. C. DeVane, 1935, revised edition, 1955; *Browning: A Portrait* by Betty Miller, 1952; *The Bow and the Lyre: The Art of Browning* by Roma A. King, 1957; *Browning's Characters: A Study in Poetic Technique* by Park Honan, 1961; *The Triple Soul: Browning's Theory of Knowledge* by N. B. Crowell, 1963; *The Faith of Browning* by Hugh Martin, 1963; *Browning: A Study of His Poetry* by Thomas Blackburn, 1967; *Browning and His World* by Maisie Ward, 2 vols., 1967–69; *Browning's Major Poetry* by Ian Jack, 1973; *The Book, The Ring, and the Poet: A Biography* by William Irvine and Park Honan, 1974; *Browning's Later Poetry 1871–1889* by Clyde de L. Ryals, 1975; *Browning and the Modern Tradition* by B. Flowers, 1976; *Browning's Youth* by John Maynard, 1977.

*   *   *

"A tremendous and incomparable modern," was Henry James's verdict on the achievement of Robert Browning; and Pater, too, saw him as "the most modern, to modern people the most important of poets." Less perceptive critics, however, conditioned to Tennysonian diction, metres and attitudes, were bitterly antagonized by what one of them condemned as a "reckless and sometimes vulgar colloquialism." Yet that vigorous and inventive handling of colloquial idiom and flexible speech-rhythms was the source, in his brilliant development of the dramatic monologue, of Browning's most original contribution to English poetry.

This form was peculiarly suited to Browning's natural talents for depicting action in character, as he put it, rather than character in action. After his early failure as a dramatist, he turned with increasing ambition and assurance to presentation of single individuals progressively revealing their predicaments. His portrait gallery encompasses an immense range of character and circumstance: from those of the ordinary and obscure "any wife" and "any husband" to historical figures like the Italian painters Andrea del Sarto and Fra Lippo Lippi, or such creatures of his invention as the Greek philosopher Cleon and the Arab physician Karshish.

So intense and intimate is Browning's involvement in the lives and feelings of his people that some critics have contended that they are no more than projections of his own personality and preoccupations. Yet his participation is essentially dramatic; and it is often the opposition between his speakers' pronouncements and his own implied viewpoint which constitutes one of the most effective elements in Browning's dramatic monologues – his use of irony. The doubt-tinged adulation of the students in "A Grammarian's Funeral" unequivocally communicates their creator's attitude towards the spectacle of a wasted life. Both Cleon and Karshish make plainly perceptible Browning's opinion about the obtuseness of their failure to recognize the Christian revelation, which could liberate them from the limitations of inherited religions each finds ultimately unsatisfying. The shrewd, casuistical churchman with epicurean tastes, in "Bishop Blougram's Apology," is endowed with dispassionate insights into his own and his adversary's nature which lend conscious irony to most of his monologue. The ironical subtlety of "Andrea del Sarto," on the other hand, springs from its unwitting self-disclosure by a man whose self-knowledge is only partial and intermittent. In the shorter "Up at a Villa – Down in the City" the discontented "Italian person of quality," yearning for city distractions, is clearly afflicted by parsimony rather than the poverty he pleads.

All these exemplify Browning's gift for creating *personae* in no way resembling himself and his own beliefs. The style of each monologue unfailingly reflects both speaker and situation, skilfully echoing every shade of mood and shift of thought. The elegiac melancholy of Andrea's autumnal twilight-piece makes a striking contrast to the racy vigour, with its exuberant exclamations and syntactical dislocations, of the briskly extrovert Fra Lippo Lippi. In the more emotionally charged passages in their monologues, Blougram's argumentative austerity and Cleon's cool rationalism warm and quicken into the eloquence of personal conviction or regret. The speaker's man-to-man tone with the old composer in "A Toccata of Galuppi's" establishes the imaginative sympathy between them as surely as the long, flowing lines and crowding images evoke the sound of the music. This idiomatic appropriateness and metrical versatility work equally well in the shorter monologues: where, for example, a telling use of the very short line communicates the controlled grief in "A Woman's Last Word" and the numbed bleakness of the deserted girl of "In a Year." Detail and setting, too – the thistledown imagery of "Two in the Campagna," the desolate landscape of "Childe Roland," which so effectively externalizes the hero's spiritual barrenness – intensify the mood and meaning of each poem with vivid sensuous precision. Like the speaker of "Transcendentalism," translating into song the "dry words" of "stark-naked thought," or the poet of "How It Strikes a Contemporary," "scenting the world, looking it full in face," Browning even at his most disputatious prefers to embody his perceptions in pictures and analogies rather than convey them through abstract philosophizing.

Three major subjects dominate Browning's poetry: the worlds of love and of art, and the problems of religious faith and doubt. His subtle and sensitive delineation of the varied moods of love owes much to personal experience. His life had, he affirmed, flower and fruit in his marriage; and his debt to Elizabeth is acknowledged in "By the Fireside" and "One Word More." In "Love among the Ruins" and "The Last Ride Together," worldly success and artistic achievement dwindle to insignificance beside the immediate joy of love. "A Lovers' Quarrel" and "A Serenade at the Villa" discover the surrounding world meaningless, even actively hostile, when love is withdrawn. Browning's poems, like Donne's, strive for a fusion of the lovers' inmost essences; but whereas in Donne that unity is achieved, in Browning it remains perpetually elusive. Frustrated longing for total identification with the beloved echoes through the tantalizing pursuit of "Love in a Life" and "Life in a Love"; the calculated submission of a "A Woman's Last Word" and the aspirations of "In a Balcony"; above all "Two in the Campagna," so poignantly crystallizing this awareness of "Infinite passion and the pain/Of finite hearts that yearn." Browning's unerringly acute insight into feminine sensibility is universalized in his ironic comment on man's fidelity, compared with woman's, in "Any Wife to Any Husband."

An informed and sympathetic response to music emerges from "A Toccata of Galuppi's," "Master Hughes of Saxe-Gotha," and "Saul"; and to the painter's problems and purposes in the two great "artist" monologues, and lesser-known poems like "The Guardian Angel" and "Old Pictures in Florence." Yet for all his keen appreciation of life's enrichment by art, Browning's final allegiance is to the source. In his reality as a man, the young poet of "Transcendentalism" is worth more than his poem; while Norbert of "In a Balcony" affirms the power of life within him more vital than that of any painted masterpiece. "The Last Ride

Together," like "Cleon," shows the artist's activity of re-creating life fall far short of the intensity of living it.

Through the ruminative regret of Andrea del Sarto, his most searching exploration of the artist's psychology and creative processes, Browning presents an important aspect of his own philosophy: "Ah, but a man's reach should exceed his grasp,/Or what's a Heaven for?" Blougram voices a similiar aspiration on behalf of his opponent: "the trying shall suffice:/ The aim, if reached or not, makes great the life." "The Last Ride Together," "A Grammarian's Funeral," and "Saul" variously embody the idea that, as Rabbi Ben Ezra recognizes, life may "succeed in that it seems to fail." The paradoxical triumph of the unsuccessful quest is most fully realized in the strange, dark parable of "Childe Roland." That final horn-blast, symbolizing the stoical courage which can confront apparent failure and still affirm its own invincibility, is typical of the Browning character thwarted of fulfilment. Far from that blind and bouncing optimism of which he is often accused, Browning's is in fact a hard-won faith based on his perception of the uses of adversity. He sees the world as a testing-ground — Keats's "vale of soul-making" — whose hazards and hostilities are necessary conditions for the achievement of maturity. "I count life such a stuff," declares Norbert, "To try the soul's strength on, educe the man"; while Cleon demands, "Why stay we on the earth unless to grow?" Despite its manifold disappointments, existence is a privilege supremely to be prized, contends Lippo, exulting in

> The beauty and the wonder and the power,
> The shapes of things, their colours, lights and shades,
> Changes, surprises ...
> > This world's no blot for us,
> Nor blank — it means intensely, and means good:
> To find its meaning is my meat and drink.

His creed is echoed by David in "Saul" — one of Browning's most explicitly Christian poems — as the harpist's song soars from praise of creation to that of the power and love of its Author. Browning is, however, acutely conscious of the obstacles to unquestioning religious acceptance. More often he prefers, as in "Bishop Blougram's Apology," "Cleon," and the epistle of Karshish, to anatomize the struggle between faith and doubt or the aspirations of unsatisfied spiritual desire.

The influence of Browning's spirited, enquiring men and women has continued to be felt in twentieth-century poetry and drama. Their informal, frequently contentious self-justifications, as they defend some debatable position or philosophy, anticipate the special pleading of Shaw's characters, the casuistry of the Knights in *Murder in the Cathedral*. Much of Eliot's work, indeed, is foreshadowed in Browning's ironic use of the *persona*: Prufrock, and Pound's Hugh Selwyn Mauberley, are direct descendants of Blougram, Andrea del Sarto, and their company. So Browning remains the most invigoratingly modern of the Victorian poets; and in the sheer diversity, psychological complexity, and universality of his characters and situations, perhaps unsurpassed by any poet since Shakespeare.

—Margaret Willy

BRYANT, William Cullen. American. Born in Cummington, Massachusetts, 3 November 1794. Educated privately, and at Williams College, Williamstown, Massachusetts, 1810–11; studied law under Mr. Howe, Worthington, Massachusetts, 1811–14, and in the office of William Baylies, Bridgewater, Massachusetts, 1814–15; admitted to the Massachusetts Bar, 1815. Married Frances Fairchild in 1821 (died, 1865); two children.

Practised law in Great Barrington, Massachusetts, 1816–25; Editor, with Henry J. Anderson, *New York Review and Athenaeum Magazine*, 1825; Assistant Editor, 1826–29, and Editor, and part owner, 1829–78, *Evening Post*, New York. President, American Free Trade League, 1865–69. *Died 12 June 1878.*

PUBLICATIONS

Collections

> *Poetical Works, Prose Writings,* edited by Parke Godwin.   4 vols., 1883–84.
> *Poetical Works,* edited by Henry C. Sturges and Richard Henry Stoddard.   1903.
> *Selections,* edited by Samuel Sillen.   1945.
> *Letters,* edited by William Cullen Bryant II and Thomas G. Voss.   1975–

Verse

> *The Embargo; or, Sketches of the Times: A Satire.*   1808.
> *The Embargo and Other Poems.*   1809.
> *Poems.*   1821.
> *Poems.*   1832; revised edition, 1834, 1836, 1850.
> *The Fountain and Other Poems.*   1842.
> *The White-Footed Deer and Other Poems.*   1844.
> *Poems.*   2 vols., 1855.
> *Thirty Poems.*   1864.
> *Hymns.*   1864; revised edition, 1869.
> *Poems.*   1871.
> *Poems.*   3 vols., 1875.
> *Poems.*   1876.

Other

> *Letters of a Traveller; or, Notes of Things Seen in Europe and America.*   1850; as *The Picturesque Souvenir,* 1851.
> *Reminiscences of The Evening Post.*   1851.
> *Letters of a Traveller, Second Series.*   1859.
> *A Discourse on the Life, Character, and Genius of Washington Irving.*   1860.
> *Letters from the East.*   1869.
> *Orations and Addresses.*   1873.
> *Bryant and Isaac Henderson: 21 Letters,* edited by Theodore Hornberger.   1950.

> Editor, *Tales of Glauber-Spa.*   2 vols., 1832.
> Editor, *Selections from the American Poets.*   1840.
> Editor, *The Berkshire Jubilee.*   1845.
> Editor, *A Library of Poetry and Song.*   1871; revised edition, as *A New Library,* 1876(?).
> Editor, with Oliver B. Bunce, *Picturesque America; or, The Land We Live In.*   2 vols., 1872–74.
> Editor, *A Popular History of the United States,* vols. 1–2, by Sydney Howard Gay.   1876–78.

Editor, with Evert A. Duyckinck, *Complete Works of Shakespeare.*   25 vols., 1888.

Translator, *The Iliad and the Odyssey of Homer.*   4 vols., 1870–72.

Bibliography: in *Bibliography of American Literature* by Jacob Blanck, 1955; *A Bibliography of Bryant and His Critics 1909–1972* by Judith T. Phair, 1975.

Reading List: *A Biography of Bryant* (includes letters) by Parke Godwin, 2 vols., 1883; *Gotham Yankee: A Biography of Bryant* by Harry Houston Peckham, 1950; *Politics and a Belly-Full: The Journalistic Career of Bryant* by Curtiss S. Johnson, 1962; *Bryant* by Albert F. McLean, Jr., 1964; *Bryant* by Charles H. Brown, 1971.

*   *   *

When in his poem "The Poet" William Cullen Bryant urges a writer to eschew the "empty gust/Of passion" but to express "feelings of calm power and mighty sweep,/Like currents journeying through the windless deep," he is making an apt comment on his own best work. For though in "A Fable for Critics" James Russell Lowell goes too far in joking at Bryant for his coldness, his lack of enthusiasm, his "supreme *ice*olation," Bryant's strong points are indeed not passion, not delicacy, not soaring imagination, but dignity and power. Even through his lighter poems sounds a strong didactic note that reminds one that his literary forbears were New England Puritans, his work also has overtones of the sober eighteenth-century neoclassicism of Gray and Collins. He is at his best when with stately force he depicts the grand sweeping cycle of life which carries all away with its resistless current.

Thus his first major poem, "Thanatopsis," written in the tradition of the British Graveyard Poets in grave, resounding lines, pictures man, even new American man, living on the tombs of countless races. When we too join the caravan to the inevitable tomb, Bryant says, may we face our fate with stoic dignity. "The Journey of Life," "The Ages," "The Past," and "The Flood of Years," though with a more specifically Christian hope of immortality, similarly emphasize with stately resonance and images the cyclical patterns of human existence. The same theme is effectively voiced in such poems as "The Prairies," "Monument Mountain," and "An Indian at the Burial Place of His Fathers," which delineate the successive destruction of America's aboriginal races and remind the white man that he too may disappear. Because of such epic grandeur in his own themes it is not surprising that Bryant was a highly successful translator of Homer.

But the classic dignity of much of Bryant's best work is nicely balanced by his Romantic sense of the soothing power and divinity of nature. Bryant was America's first major Romantic poet. Poems like "A Forest Hymn," "Green River," and "Inscription for the Entrance to a Wood" earnestly inculcate the creed that nature can give solace to the weary heart. Some of these poems verge on pantheism and foreshadow Emerson's doctrine that the divine creation has never ceased. Throughout even the simple nature poems, such as "The Yellow Violet" and "To a Fringed Gentian," Bryant preaches, sometimes somberly, sometimes wittily; his favorite lyric form is a series of descriptive stanzas followed by one or two of moral. Though he is playful in "A Meditation on Rhode Island Coal" and "Robert of Lincoln," he rarely writes for fun. Yet in such a poem as "To a Waterfowl" he can so superbly blend his moralism with telling imagery and restrained emotion that it becomes an integral part of a powerful work of art, indeed one of America's finest lyrics.

Though Bryant was intensely concerned with mutability and nature, he was also acutely awake to American life around him. His first published volume, *The Embargo*, was a satire against the Jeffersonians. Not only was he for many years the writer of powerful liberal editorials in the New York *Evening Post*, of which for many years he was editor, but he also wrote many effective and graceful occasional poems such as his elegy on Lincoln. Like the Hudson River School painters with whom he was closely associated (see "To Cole, The

Painter, Departing for Europe"), he patriotically celebrated American landscape, American nature, and American history and legend. He even edited a collection of essays and engravings entitled *Picturesque America*. He wrote on popular causes such as slavery ("The African Chief") and Greek independence ("The Massacre at Scio"). Sometimes, as in "The Death of the Flowers," he verged toward the mawkish sentimentalism that was the bane of America's "Feminine Fifties," but his lack of pretentiousness, quiet integrity, and basic good sense, seen also in his anthologies of American poetry and especially in his first-rate critical essays on poets and poetry, ordinarily saved him from banality. Like so many American authors of his time he also wrote hymns.

With some justice Bryant's poetry has been derogated as bloodless, undramatic, too orotund, too much concerned with death and mutability, out of touch with vivid life, even morbid. To read his verse, Marius Bewley says, is "a little like listening to a harmonium with the pedal stuck," and his poetry gives the impression of "a best parlor filled with marmoreal statuary." But such comment is unfair. Bryant is a significant pioneer in American literature. His best work is also still worthy to be read for what Lowell calls "the grace, strength, and dignity" of his art and for the quiet depth and earnestness of his vision of the ever-flowing stream of nature and human life. His was surely the most powerful poetic voice in America between Edward Taylor and Poe.

—Curtis Dahl

BUNTING, Basil. English. Born in Scotswood on Tyne, Northumberland, 1 March 1900. Educated at Ackworth School; Leighton Park School; London School of Economics. Jailed as a conscientious objector during World War 1. Married 1) Marian Culver in 1930; 2) Sima Alladadian in 1948; two children. Assistant Editor, *Transatlantic Review*, Paris, in the 1920's; Music Critic, *The Outlook*, London; lived in Italy and the United States in the 1930's; Persian Correspondent for *The Times*, London, after World War II; Sub-Editor, Newcastle *Morning Chronicle*, for 12 years. Taught at the University of California, Santa Barbara; Poetry Fellow, universities of Durham and Newcastle, 1968–70; taught at the universities of British Columbia, Vancouver; Binghamton, New York; and Victoria, British Columbia. Since 1972, President, the Poetry Society, London; since 1973, President, Northern Arts. Recipient: Arts Council bursary, 1966. D. Litt.: University of Newcastle, 1971. Lives in Northumberland.

PUBLICATION

Verse

Redimiculum Matellarum.   1930.
Poems 1950.   1950.
Loquitur.   1965.
The Spoils.   1965.
Ode II/2.   1965.
First Book of Odes.   1966.
Briggflatts.   1966.

Two Poems.   1967.
What the Chairman Told Tom.   1967.
Collected Poems.   1968.
Descant on Rawley's Madrigal (Conversations with Jonathan Williams).   1968.
Collected Poems.   1978.

Other

Editor, *Selected Poems,* by Joseph Skipsey.   1976.

Bibliography: *Bunting: A Bibliography of Works and Criticism* by Roger Guedalla, 1973.

Reading List: "Bunting Issue" of *Agenda 4,* 1966.

*   *   *

Until the mid-1960's Basil Bunting was almost completely neglected in England, although he had established an enthusiastic and discriminating group of admirers in America, including some of the leading Beat and Black Mountain poets. This was partly because most of his literary connections were with American poets, notably Ezra Pound and Louis Zukofsky. The critical euphoria at the time of his "re-discovery" in the later 1960's, which presented him as an overlooked genius almost comparable to Hopkins, has now given way to a more balanced view of him as a distinguished but minor poet; Bunting himself has always insisted on his minor status.

In the 1920's and 1930's Bunting came into contact with many of the leading literary figures of the time, including Yeats, Eliot, Lawrence, Ford Madox Ford, Tzara, Williams, and Hemingway, as well as Pound and Zukofsky, both of whom exerted a powerful influence on his earlier work, although he maintains that a fellow-northerner, Wordsworth, is the most important literary force behind his poetry. Of the English poets who emerged during the inter-war years, Bunting is probably the one most in tune with American modernism, and his work exhibits many characteristics of early Pound and Eliot, such as musical free verse, a wealth of literary and mythological allusions, and the satiric use of parody and irony. During the 1930's Bunting eschewed the political and propagandist poetry of many of his English contemporaries, although, as someone who had been imprisoned during World War I as a conscientious objector, he could not be accused of being an aesthete without any social commitment or political views. Eliot eventually decided against publishing Bunting among the Faber poets in 1951 because he was "too Poundian." Poundian as his poems of the 1920's and 1930's are, they reveal some of the best qualities of Pound: meticulous craftsmanship, an acute ear for the music of words, and a freedom from the stultifying conventions of much English, as opposed to American, poetry of the time. And poems like "Villon," "Chomei at Toyama," and many of the odes are not simply derivative. Bunting's own voice can be heard clearly not only in his well-known dialect ballad "The Complaint of the Morpethshire Farmer," but also in such delicate and well-wrought lyrics as "Southwind, tell her what" and "A thrush in the syringa sings."

Bunting was a music critic in the 1920's and he has always adhered to the Symbolist view that poetry should aspire to the condition of music, and insists on its aural nature. For him, a poem on the page is incomplete; it exists fully only when read aloud: to experience poetry is to hear it. He has collected all but one of his longer poems under the heading "Sonatas" and his work contains numerous references to music. But it is in his masterpiece, *Briggflatts*, a spiritual and Symbolist "autobiography" written after a long period of silence, that he brings his preoccupation with the music of poetry to full flower. Its rich assonantal and alliterative textures and its concentrated pithiness of expression, recalling Anglo-Saxon poetry as well as

Hopkins, are the culmination of his efforts to produce pure poetry, but the structure of the entire work is itself musical, in the way that Eliot's *Four Quartets* are. Like each of the *Quartets*, to which it is indebted, *Briggflatts* is in five sections or "movements," as Bunting calls them, although it also contains a short coda, and the analogy to musical form is pursued throughout. One reason for the success and individuality of *Briggflatts* is that Bunting draws more heavily than in any other poem on his own north-country heritage, which he greatly values. He is intent on defining himself in terms of his cultural origins, and the poem relates the present to a tradition descending from the ancient kingdom of Northumbria. Compared with his two poetic masters, Wordsworth and Pound, Bunting appears as a poet decidedly limited in range and scope, but, within the fairly narrow confines within which he has chosen to work, his poetry is exquisitely written, and *Briggflatts* is likely to remain one of the outstanding English poems from the second half of this century.

—Peter Lewis

BURNS, Robert.   Scottish.   Born at Alloway, near Ayr, 25 January 1759. Educated at a school in Alloway Mill, and at home. Married Jean Armour in 1788; nine children, and three other illegitimate children. Farmer at Mossgiel, near Mauchline, 1784; commissioned as excise officer (i.e., tax inspector), 1788, and settled at Ellisland, near Dumfries, combining official duties with farming; when farm failed moved with his family to the town of Dumfries. Honorary Member, Royal Company of Archers, 1792. *Died 21 July 1796.*

PUBLICATIONS

Collections

> *Works.*   4 vols., 1800–04.
> *Letters*, edited by J. Delancey Ferguson.   2 vols., 1931; *Selected Letters*, 1953.
> *Poems and Songs*, edited by James Kinsley,   3 vols., 1968

Verse

> *Poems, Chiefly in the Scottish Dialect.*   1786; revised edition, 1787; 2 vols., 1793; 1794; 1801.
> *The Scots Musical Museum*, with others, edited by James Johnson.   6 vols., 1787–1803.
> *A Select Collection of Original Scottish Airs*, with others, edited by G. Thomson.   4 vols., 1793–99.
> *Merry Muses of Caledonia.*   1800(?).

Other

> *Notes on Scottish Song*, edited by James C. Dick.   1908.
> *Journal of a Tour in the Highlands Made in 1787*, edited by J. C. Ewing.   1927; edited by Raymond Lamont Brown, 2 vols., 1972–73.

161

Journal of the Border Tour, edited by J. Delancey Ferguson, in *Burns, His Associates and Contemporaries,* edited by Robert T. Fitzhugh. 1943.

Bibliography: *A Bibliography of Burns* by J. W. Egerer, 1964; *Burns* by G. R. Roy, 1966.

Reading List: *Burns* by David Daiches, 1950, revised edition, 1966; *The Burns Encyclopedia* by Maurice Lindsay, 1959, revised edition, 1970; *Burns Today and Tomorrow* by Hugh MacDiarmid, 1959; *Burns: His Life and Tradition in Words and Sounds* by Ian A. Nimmo, 1965; *Burns in His Time* by Alan H. Dent, 1966; *Burns, The Man and the Poet: A Round, Unvarnished Account* by Robert T. Fitzhugh, 1970; *Burns: The Critical Heritage* edited by Donald A. Low, 1974; *Burns: A Life* by Hugh Douglas, 1976.

*   *   *

Like many artists whose achievement is regarded as the crowning glory of a particular school or movement, Robert Burns was not an innovator. He took existing stanza forms and the Scots tongue as shaped for the purposes of colloquial poetry by his predecessors, notably Allan Ramsay and Robert Fergusson, and applied them with sharpened awareness to his own situations.

The fact that, unlike Ramsay and Fergusson, Burns was born a farmer, ensured that his upbringing would bring him into contact with rural Scotland where, before the triumph of the Industrial Revolution, agriculture was still the mainstay of the Scottish economy. The rural way of life, like the speech of the countryside, had changed comparatively little since mediaeval times. Yet changes which were stirring during Burns's lifetime had, by the end of the 18th century, transformed the very basis of Scottish life, and begun to alter the physical appearance of the environment, particularly of the countryside around Glasgow. Burns caught and fixed in poetry the essential quality of that old agrarian way of life just before it finally gave place to the new industrial emphasis.

He did so by making use of the images and particular situations he found around him in the rural life of Ayrshire, projecting the universal from the merely local. Thus "Holy Willie's Prayer," using for its prototype a petty, arid and dishonest old elder of the Church of Scotland, William Fisher, becomes what is probably the most effective denunciation of the sin of hypocrisy to be found in European literature. The picture of oozing unctuousness, of deadly self-revelation, unfolds as Holy Willie, on his knees, before his God, rationalises his catalogue of sins:

> O L ——d! yestreen, Thou kens, wi' Meg –
> Thy pardon I sincerely beg,
> O! may't ne'er be a livin' plague
>   To my dishonour,
> An' I'll ne'er lift a lawless leg
>   Again upon her ...
>
> Maybe Thou lets this fleshly thorn
> Buffet Thy servant e'en and morn,
> Lest he owre proud and high shou'd turn,
>   That he's sae gifted:
> If sae, Thy han' maun e'en be borne,
>   Until Thou lift it.

The main target of the young Burns's satirical anger was the Church of Scotland, which in his day still endeavoured to exercise a depressing and restrictive influence over even the most private aspects of everyday life. It was especially vigorous in its unmasking of sexual offences.

As Burns was highly sexed, and already the father of an illegitimate daughter by one of his father's servants before he attained his majority, the poet and the Church came into vigorous conflict. Hypocrisy, usually rife in narrow sectarian forms of religious worship, was also flayed in the "Address to the Unco Guid," in which Burns's glancing ironic contrasts have a lasting deadliness:

> Ye high, exalted, virtuous dames
>   Tied up in godly laces,
> Before ye gie poor Frailty names,
>   Suppose a change o' cases;
> A dear-lov'd lad, convenience snug,
>   A treach'rous inclination;
> But, let me whisper i' your lug,
>   Ye're aiblins* nae temptation.   * perhaps

Moving into English for his serious conclusion, Burns pronounces proverb-like wisdom in language which has proved memorable even to the less literate:

> Then gently scan your brother man,
>   Still gentler sister woman:
> Tho' they may gang a kennin wrang,
>   To step aside is human,
> One point must still be greatly dark,
>   The moving *Why* they do it;
> An just as lamely can ye mark,
>   How far perhaps they rue it.

Whether he is celebrating family religious observance in the old style, as in "The Cottar's Saturday Night," or, as in "The Twa Dogs," using the old Scots animal tradition in poetry (best exemplified by the "Fables" of Henryson) to set the burden of the poor against the wasteful ease of the rich, Burns is throughout the spokesman for ordinary men and women. This radical quality was immediately recognised when *Poems, Chiefly in the Scottish Dialect*, was first published in Kilmarnock in 1786.

The most important poem left out of that collection, probably for political reasons, was his unbuttoned celebration of common humanity, "The Jolly Beggars," a "cantata," the songs of which were written to specified Scots airs. In the overheated atmosphere of a Mauchline tavern, a crowd of drop-outs meet together to celebrate the kind of total freedom which rejects any social organisation, though paradoxically such "freedom" can only flourish as a protected minority in a socially adjusted society. They sing:

> Life is all a variorum
>   We regard not how it goes;
> Let them cant about decorum,
>   Who have character to lose.
>
> A fig for those by law protected!
>   Liberty's a glorious feast!
> Courts for cowards were erected,
>   Churches built to please the priest.

This concept of liberty echoes through Burns's poems, songs, and letters, just as it concerned him practically, and sometimes indiscretely, throughout his life. It is one of many ways in which he anticipated early 19th-century European Romanticism, when poets and composers, notably Schiller and Beethoven, hymned Freedom as an end in itself.

Up to 1786, Burns's achievement was mainly that of a social satirist, using the "Standard Habbie" stanzas. This, a variation of *rime couée*, was so-called because it seems to have been first employed before the beginning of the 18th-century Scots revival by Robert Sempill in a poem "The Life and Death of Habbie Simson, the Piper of Kilbarchan" (about 1640), although it had also been used colloquially by Sir David Lyndsay a hundred years earlier in *The Thrie Estatis*, and stems from an early form employed by the French troubadours and in some mediaeval English miracle plays. It is the stanza of "Holy Willie" and many other Burns poems. He was no less successful with more elaborate stanza forms derived from the Scots Makars (or Scottish Chaucerians as they are sometimes rather unfairly described). During the remaining years of his short life he added to his already considerable corpus of songs, and composed his solitary narrative poem, "Tam o' Shanter," with its modulations of pace, subtlety of movement, and sustained dramatic implication, an effortless masterpiece.

Burns's song output began with a love song addressed to a girl with whom he shared the task of harvesting. Almost his last love song was addressed to the woman who was helping his wife nurse him in his final illness. In between came songs celebrating every aspect of the relationship between man and woman, from the first bashful stirrings of "I'm owre young to marry yet" through the rich satisfaction of "Corn Riggs" to the calm content near the end of married life in "John Anderson, My Jo." His best songs differ from those of all other Scottish and English poets of the period in that they infer physical realities and are infused with the same directness and sincerity that in his young manhood fired the flames of his social satire.

Burns's main strengths lay in his firm commitment to the Scots tongue at a time when the higher social classes were abandoning it in favour of English, and to his radical alignment with the common-sense interests of the ordinary man at a time when the justification of privilege was being questioned increasingly throughout Europe. (It is not without significance that Burns's Kilmarnock *Poems* and Mozart's *The Marriage of Figaro* appeared in the same year.) His weakness lay in the fact that he had to try to come to terms with a linguistic dichotomy first brought about by the haste of the Reformers of 1560, who introduced the vernacular Bible in English rather than in Scots, and furthered by the political effects of the Unions of 1603 and 1707. If a late 18th-century man wanted to succeed in the power-world of England, he had to eradicate all traces of Scoticisms from his speech, as Boswell, Hume, Beattie, and others so ridiculously strove to do. The traditional culture of the old Scotland thus fell under siege from within.

In an attempt to achieve the best of both worlds, besides writing in Scots Burns also copied the "bosom-melting throes" of Shenstone, Gray, and others. But their Augustan habit sat poorly on him, and encouraged him to adopt poetic postures, both in verse and in his letters, otherwise usually couched in a clear and balanced prose. The man whose warm sincerity has endeared him for more than two centuries even to those of his countrymen who never otherwise read poetry, could on occasion be guilty of achieving fatuities like "though something like moisture conglobes in my eye" when describing a tear.

Whenever he attempted the "high style," the 18th-century equivalent of the aureate manner of Dunbar and the other Scots Makars, Burns used English, and was at his least successful. The tone of the whole of the 18th-century Scots revival was colloquial, a reflection of fast-moving daily Scots speech. Burns excelled all other Scots poets in harnessing this aspect of this age to worthy poetic purpose. He achieved his wider fame through the warmth and emotional universality of his songs.

He is Scotland's "National Bard," celebrated by suppers every 25th January, on his birthday, wherever Scots are gathered together, for yet another reason. He shares with Sir Walter Scott the distinction of rescuing the Scottish sense of nationhood from the oblivion which under gathering English pressure threatened it. Scott, through the best six or so of the Waverley Novels, made the Scots more aware of the significant moments of historic confrontation in their past (and, incidentally, confirmed the interest of Romantic Europe, aroused by Macpherson's "Ossian," in Scotland). Burns, through his poems and songs, similarly established and consolidated lasting awareness of nothing less than the sense of being Scots, of Scottishness. This may perhaps seem an unimportant non-literary factor to readers outside Scotland, yet it explains the unique position of popular reverence and celebration that Burns, alone among world poets, enjoys from his own countrymen.

—Maurice Lindsay

BUTLER, (Frederick) Guy.   South African.   Born in Cradock, Cape Province, 21 January 1918. Educated at a local high school; Rhodes University, Grahamstown, M.A. 1939; Brasenose College, Oxford, M.A. 1947. Served during World War II in the Middle East, Italy, and the United Kingdom. Married Jean Murray Satchwell in 1940; three sons, one daughter. Lecturer in English, University of the Witwatersrand, Johannesburg, 1948–50. Since 1952, Professor of English, Rhodes University, Grahamstown. Editor, with Ruth Harnett, *New Coin* poetry quarterly, Grahamstown. D.Litt.: University of Natal, Durban, 1968. Lives in Grahamstown.

PUBLICATIONS

Verse

> *Stranger to Europe.*   1952; augmented edition, 1960.
> *South of the Zambezi: Poems from South Africa.*   1966.
> *On First Seeing Florence.*   1968.
> *Selected Poems.*   1975.
> *Ballads and Songs.*   1977.

Plays

> *The Dam* (produced 1953).   1953.
> *The Dove Returns* (produced 1956).   1956.
> *Take Root or Die* (produced 1966).   1970.
> *Cape Charade* (produced 1968).   1968.

Other

> *An Aspect of Tragedy.*   1953.
> *The Republic of the Arts.*   1964.

> Editor, *A Book of South African Verse.*   1959.
> Editor, *When Boys Were Men.*   1969.
> Editor, *The 1820 Settlers.*   1974.

*   *   *

When Guy Butler was serving as a soldier in Italy he carried his paintings with him in a shell-case, hoping to return to his native South Africa with a pictorial record of his European experiences. His poems and plays reflect a life-long attempt to contrast what Europe and Africa mean to him. In "Cape Coloured Batman" Butler finds himself on the "terraced groves of Tuscany," contemplating the pathetic fusion of Europe and Africa in the shape of the despised half-caste. But in "Servant Girl" he is aware of his distance from true African culture:

> [She is] singing a song which seems more integral
> With rain-rinsed sky and sandstone hill
> Than any cadence wrung
> From my taut tongue.

Butler's descriptive talent enables him to present sympathetically the African ritualistic killing of an ox, or, in "Isibongo of Matiwane," a legendary warrior:

> Matiwane, royal, wearing the blood-red feathers of the lourie,
> his eyes red, red his lips from drinking the blood of strong men,
> moves over the earth with the speed of a startled gnu.

Sometimes, as in "The Underdogs," Butler is sharply satirical about White South Africa:

> "Lord, save the shining Christian culture
> Of White South Africa!" Then squat
> Heroically behind clean Vickers guns
> Jabbering death in our innocent hands.

But a more characterisitc attitude is the positive desire, as expressed in the long poem, "Home Thoughts," to "civilize my semi-barbarous land" by the meeting and mating of European clarity (Apollo) and African primitive instinct (Black Dionysus).

Guy Butler's range is wide. He can recount family anecdotes in a simple, but moving, manner; recall poignantly the ironies of war; or paint for us his Cradock Mountains in lines both detailed and lyrical. Varied though his style is, it is always verbally inventive (a train whistle "drove a long spear through/The unexpecting stillness") and rich with a painter's vision. It can adapt itself to many poetic strands – social satire, elegy, narrative, or religious meditation. His stylistic flexibility succeeds outstandingly in the long poem *On First Seeing Florence*, a masterly evocation of personal experiences leading to profound metaphysical intuitions.

His major plays, *The Dam* and *The Dove Returns*, are verse dramas on South African themes. *The Dam* is an anguished, but not despairing, symbolic play about personal destinies within a multi-racial society, written in a verse which modulates remarkably from colloquial idiom to impassioned utterance.

Guy Butler's achievement, in poems and plays, has been to look profoundly and honestly at South African life today, and to write about it with sensitive clarity in an original style which avoids eccentricities.

—Dennis Davison

BUTLER, Samuel. English. Born in Stevensham, Worcestershire, baptized 14 February 1613. Educated at King's School, Worcester; possibly at Oxford or Cambridge university; may have been a member of Gray's Inn, London. Married. As a young man, in the service of the Countess of Kent; thereafter held posts as clerk/secretary to Leonard Jeffrey, justice of the peace of Earls-Croome, Worcestershire, or his son Thomas, and as steward to Richard

Vaughan, Earl of Carbery; by 1670 in the service of the Duke of Buckingham. Granted an annual pension of £100 from King Charles II for *Hudibras*. After initial success, ignored by the court, and thereafter lived and died in poverty. *Died 25 September 1680.*

PUBLICATIONS

Collections

   Complete Works, edited by A. R. Waller and René Lamar.   3 vols., 1905–28.

Verse

   Mola Asinaria.   1659.
   The Lord Roos His Answer to the Marquess of Dorchester's Letter.   1660.
   Hudibras, part 1.   1662; part 2, 1663; revised edition, 1678; part 3, 1678; complete
      edition, 1684; edited by John Wilders, 1967.
   To the Memory of the Most Renowned Du-Vall; A Pindaric Ode.   1671.

Other

   Two Letters.   1672.
   Mercurius Menippeus: The Loyal Satirist; or, Hudibras in Prose.   1682.
   The Plagiary Exposed.   1691.
   Posthumous Works in Prose and Verse.   3 vols., 1715–17; revised edition, 1732.
   Genuine Remains, edited by R. Thyer.   2 vols., 1759; revised edition (vol. 1 only),
      1822.
   Characters, edited by Charles W. Daves.   1970.

Bibliography: In *Complete Works 3,* 1928.

Reading List: *Hudibras in the Burlesque Tradition* by E. A. Richards, 1937; *Augustan Satire* by Ian Jack, 1952; "The Last of the Epics: The Rejection of the Heroic in *Paradise Lost* and *Hudibras*" by Michael Wilding, in *Restoration Literature: Critical Approaches* edited by Harold Love, 1972; *The Restoration Mode from Milton to Dryden* by Earl Miner, 1974.

*   *   *

Hudibras seems to have been composed in three stages: ca. 1658–60, 1660–63, and 1663–74. Its popularity is beyond question. Charles II memorized long portions and, in Zachary Grey's lavish two-volume edition in 1774, Butler received a seriously executed edition before his greater contemporaries, Milton and Dryden. So popular was *The First Part* that it ran through nine editions in its first year, four of them pirated, and a spurious second part also appeared in 1663. The bang-about tetrameter couplets with odd rhymes and other jocularities have been known thereafter as hudibrastics, and their inventor was sometimes called Hudibras, which would have angered him the more. Contrary to most modern tastes, the third part was better liked than the second. The only other important poem published by Butler was the mock heroic pindaric to Du-Vall, a lady-killer highwayman hanged at Tyburn on 21 January 1670. He left behind numerous manuscripts in verse and prose, including nearly 190 prose characters, random notes of caustic character, satires, parodies, and a couple of positive pieces.

Hudibras swallows up the importance of the other writings. It is the worst great poem in the language, a degraded mockery of *Don Quixote*. Each of the three parts has three cantos. Much is promised and nothing happens in I.i., except maddening argument between the Presbyterian anti-hero and Ralpho, his Independent Sancho Panza. In I. ii Hudibras routs bearbaiters by falling on their animal with all his gross bulk. In I. iii he is defeated in combat by a woman, Trulla (that is, trull, whore) who, unlike him, fights fairly. Put in the stocks with Ralpho, Hudibras is eventually let out by the Lady, a widow, whose property he seeks. Laughing over his plight, she rejects his suit unless he meets her condition:

> That never shall be done (Quoth she)
> To one that wants a *Tayl*, by me:
> For *Tayls* by Nature sure were meant
> As well as *Beards*, for ornament:
> And though the *Vulgar* count them homely,
> In *man* or *beast* they are so comely,
> So *Gentee*, *Allamode*, and handsom
> I'l never marry *man* that wants one.

She releases him from the stocks on promise that he will whip himself.

The two men next (II. ii) argue over who should whip himself until they are interrupted by a Skimmington, a folk procession mocking a henpecked husband and his shrewish wife. Hudibras's sally is beaten off. Having decided not to whip himself, Hudibras betakes himself and Ralpho to an Astrologer, Sidrophel, whom Hudibras attacks and knocks down senseless. (II. iii). Meanwhile, Ralpho has gone off to acquaint the Lady with Hudibras's deceit. When he arrives (III. i) she tortures him in the dark with "devils" to make him confess his misdeeds. In III. ii the plot merges with history, as the Interregnum ends. In the last canto (iii), Hudibras consults a lawyer about his suit.

Two other elements extend the stupid plot. Throughout there is argument, or harangue, on matters religious, political, and logical. And there are three "heroical epistles" nailed on: one from Hudibras to Sidrophel at the end of II. iii; one from Hudibras to the Lady at the end of III. iii; and one as her reply. A "heroical epistle" was properly a woman's address to her faithless lover. Butler spoils that of course, and has the Lady declare that women really hold power in the world. In the poem's last lines, she rejects Hudibras and male supremacy: just let them dare: "Let men usurp Th'unjust Dominion,/As if they were *the Better Women*."

All this is excuse and means for learned nonsense and unremitting degradation of truly awesome power. The poem does have some design in treating three days of action and three decades:

Parts – Cantos	Day	Decade
I. i-II. i	first	1640's
II. ii-III. i	second	1650's
(III. ii	transition	transition)
III. iii	third	1660's

Days correspond to decades but are of little importance otherwise; neither days nor decades correspond to Parts. The most important fact is that the satire moves into the 1660's, including the strange metamorphosis of Sidrophel from an Interregnum astrologer into a Royal Society virtuoso.

Given the topics of debate, the decades covered, and Butler's Tory Anglicanism, it is strange but crucial that he does not mention God, the Church, or the King. His refusal to allow decency into the poem is clearer still from the perverted misogyny represented by female victories (Trulla, the Skimmington shrew, the Lady). Nothing of redeeming value is allowed. The poem delivers us into noise, degradation, and nonsense. The humor grows ever more cruel and less funny; the joke is on the characters, the reader, and the poetry, which is steadily spoilt. Butler so skillfully evokes our worst passions and strongest fears of insanity and irrelevance as to make *Hudibras* one of the most powerfully moving and objectionable poems in English.

—Earl Miner

BYROM, John. English. Born in Broughton, near Manchester, 29 February 1692. Educated at Merchant Taylors' School, London; Trinity College, Cambridge, 1708–15 (Scholar, 1709), B.A. 1712, M.A. 1715; studied medicine briefly at Montpellier, 1716. Married a cousin in 1721. Fellow of Trinity College, 1714; after his travels on the Continent returned to England, 1718; copyrighted and taught his new system of shorthand in Manchester, London, and Cambridge; succeeded to the family estate, 1740. Fellow of the Royal Society, 1724. *Died 26 September 1763.*

PUBLICATIONS

Collections

   Poems, edited by A. W. Ward.   3 vols., 1894–95.

Verse

   An Epistle to a Gentleman of the Temple.   1749.
   Enthusiasm: A Poetical Essay.   1751.
   Miscellaneous Poems.   2 vols., 1773.
   *Seasonably Alarming and Humiliating Truths in a Metrical Version of Some Passages
      from the Works of William Law,* edited by F. Okely.   1774.

Other

   A Review of the Proceedings Against Dr. Bentley.   1719.
   Letter to Mr. Comberbach in Defence of Rhyme.   1755.
   The Universal English Short-Hand.   1767.
   Private Journal and Literary Remains, edited by Richard Parkington.   4 vols., 1854–57.
   Selections from His Journals and Papers, edited by Henri Talon.   1950.

Reading List: *Byrom and the Wesleys* by Elijah Hoole, 1864; *William Law and Eighteenth-Century Quakerism* by Stephen H. Hobhouse, 1927; *The Story of Christians Awake,* 1948, and *Previously Unpublished Bryomiana,* 1954, both by W. H. Thomson; *The Edges of Augustanism: The Aesthetics of Spirituality in Thomas Ken, Byrom, and William Law* by John Hoyles, 1972.

*   *   *

Those who sing the Christmas hymn "Christians, awake, salute the happy morn" may not realise its authorship. It appears among John Byrom's poems, the greater part of which are, however, devoted to the versification of the views of the non-juring mystic, William Law.

With Law Byrom rejects the Augustan regard for external evidence and ratiocinative method in matters religious. For him reason confirms the facts of experience, but does no more, while literal adherence to Scripture as objective record and submission to the Church as outward authority are equally valueless. Byrom looks rather to the direct enlightenment of the Holy Spirit. Not surprisingly therefore and in a very non-eighteenth-century fashion Bryom extols "enthusiasm." Indeed, he has a poem with that title, in the course of which he renders Law's idea that "in will, imagination and desire consists the life or fiery driving of every intelligent creature. And so every intelligent creature is its own *self-mover.*" This view of imagination takes us forward from Hobbes, Dryden, and even Addison, reflecting Young and foreshadowing Blake and Coleridge.

Byrom, following Law, interpreted grace as love from God, exciting love for God, and this Abelardian cast resulted in their rejection of Calvinistic Evangelical soteriologies of penal satisfaction, associated chiefly with Whitefield. Their soteriology, however, tended to by-pass justification in making a short cut towards sanctification.

There is little to be said about Byrom's verse as such. It is a plain, workmanlike versifying of his master's ideas.

—Arthur Pollard

BYRON, Lord; George Noel Gordon, 6th Baron Byron, of Rochdale.   English.   Born in London, 22 January 1788; lame at birth. Educated at Aberdeen Grammar School, 1794–98; Harrow School, 1801–05; Trinity College, Cambridge, 1805–08, M.A. Married Annabella Milbanke, 1815; had one daughter, Augusta Ada; had affair with Mary Godwin Shelley's step-sister Claire Clairmont, 1816–17, who bore him daughter Allegra; settled with Teresa Guiccioli, 1819. With his friend, John Cam Hobhouse, toured Portugal, Spain, Malta and Greece, 1809–11; returned to London and took his seat in the House of Lords and was briefly active on the extreme liberal wing of the Whig Party. Ostracized by English society for his supposed incestuous affair with his half-sister, Augusta Leigh, he left England permanently, 1816; lived with Shelley, his wife Mary Godwin, and Claire Clairmont, Geneva, 1816; moved to Venice, 1817; joined Shelley at Pisa, 1818, and remained there as part of the "Pisan Circle" until 1822; organized an expedition to assist in Greek war of independence from the Turks, 1823, and died in Missolonghi. *Died 19 April 1824.*

PUBLICATIONS

Collections

The Works, edited by E. H. Coleridge and Rowland E. Prothero.   13 vols., 1898–1904.
Poems, edited by G. Pocock.   3 vols., 1948; revised by V. de Sola Pinto, 1963.
Letters and Journals, edited by Leslie Marchand.   1973–

Verse

Fugitive Pieces. 1806.

Poems on Various Occasions. 1807.

Hours of Idleness: A Series of Poems, Original and Translated. 1807; revised edition, 1808.

English Bards and Scotch Reviewers: A Satire. 1809; revised edition, 1809, 1816.

Childe Harold's Pilgrimage, cantos 1–2, 1812; *Canto the Third,* 1816; *Canto the Fourth,* 1818; complete edition, 2 vols., 1819.

The Curse of Minerva. 1812.

Waltz: An Apostrophic Hymn. 1813.

The Giaour: A Fragment of a Turkish Tale. 1813; 4 revised editions, 1813.

The Bride of Abydos: A Turkish Tale. 1813.

The Corsair: A Tale. 1814.

Ode to Napoleon Buonaparte. 1814.

Lara: A Tale. 1814.

Hebrew Melodies Ancient and Modern. 2 vols., 1815.

The Siege of Corinth; Parisina. 1816.

Poems. 1816.

The Prisoner of Chillon and Other Poems. 1816.

Monody on the Death of Sheridan. 1816.

The Lament of Tasso. 1817.

Beppo: A Venetian Story. 1818; revised edition, 1818.

Mazeppa. 1819.

Don Juan, cantos 1–2. 1819; cantos 3–5, 1821; cantos 6–14, 3 vols., 1823; cantos 15–16, 1824; complete edition, 2 vols., 1826; *Dedication,* 1833; edited by Truman Guy Steffan and Willis W. Pratt, 4 vols., 1957.

The Irish Avatar. 1821.

The Vision of Judgment. 1822.

The Age of Bronze; or, Carmen Seculare et Annus Haud Mirabilis. 1823.

The Island; or, Christian and His Comrades. 1823.

A Political Ode. 1880.

A Version of Ossian's Address to the Sun. 1898.

Plays

Manfred (produced 1834). 1817.

Marino Faliero, Doge of Venice (produced 1821). With *The Prophecy of Dante: A Poem,* 1821.

Sardanapalus; The Two Foscari; Cain: A Mystery. 1821.

The Two Foscari (produced 1837). In *Sardanapalus ...,* 1821.

Heaven and Earth: A Mystery. 1823.

Werner (produced 1830). 1823.

The Deformed Transformed. 1824.

Other

A Letter to John Murray on Bowles' Strictures on the Life and Writings of Pope. 1821.

The Parliamentary Speeches. 1824.

Correspondence of Byron with a Friend, edited by R. C. Dallas. 1824.

Letters and Journals of Byron, with Notices of His Life by Thomas Moore. 2 vols., 1830.

Astarte, edited by Mary, Countess of Lovelace. 1921.

Correspondence, edited by John Murray.   2 vols., 1922.
Byron in His Letters, edited by V. H. Collins.   1927.
The Ravenna Journal, 1821, edited by Rowland E. Prothero.   1928.
The Self Portrait: Letters and Diaries 1798 to 1824, edited by Peter Quennell.   2 vols., 1950.
His Very Self and Voice: Collected Conversations, Medwin's Conversations with Byron, and *Lady Blessington's Conversations of Byron*, edited by Ernest J. Lovell.   3 vols., 1954–69.

Bibliography: in *The Works*, 1898–1904; *A Bibliography of the Writings of Byron* by T. J. Wise, 2 vols., 1932–33; *Byron: A Comprehensive Bibliography of Secondary Materials in English* by O. J. Santucho, 1977.

Reading List: *Byron: The Years of Fame*, 1935, and *Byron in Italy*, 1940, both volumes revised in 1967, both by Peter Quennell; *Byron: Christian Virtues* by G. Wilson Knight, 1953; *Byron: A Biography*, 3 vols., 1957, *Byron's Poetry: A Critical Introduction*, 1965, and *Byron: A Portrait*, 1971, all by Leslie Marchand; *Byron and the Spoiler's Art* by Paul West, 1960; *The Style of Don Juan* by G. M. Ridenour, 1960; *The Late Lord Byron* by Doris L. Moore, 1961; *The Structure of Byron's Major Poems* by W. H. Marshall, 1962; *The Byronic Hero: Types and Prototypes* by P. L. Thorslev, 1962; *Byron: A Critical Study* by A. Rutherford, 1962; *Byron the Poet* by M. K. Joseph, 1964; *Byron and the Ruins of Paradise* by R. Gleckner, 1967; *Fiery Dust* by J. J. McGann, 1968; *Byron and Shelley* by J. Buxton, 1968; *Byron* by B. Blackstone, 3 vols., 1970–71; *Byron* by J. D. Jump, 1972.

*   *   *

The vast reputation Byron enjoyed as a poet during his life suffered some diminution during the high Victorian era as a consequence of Matthew Arnold's rating of Wordsworth as the supreme poet of the Romantic Movement, and the gradual promotion of other poets of that Movement to high critical esteem. During the twenties and thirties of this century, a new poetic practice – in which irony, reticence, ambiguity were aims, in sharpest contrast to those of Byron – accelerated the decline of a reputation which was once pre-eminent. Rightly, I think, the initial great reputation of Byron is now being restored, though with some redistribution of emphases. Meanwhile, the discovery by a wide readership of Byron's letters and journals has forced a recognition of virtues – for example, an engaging, rakish frankness and generous humour – scarcely found in such radiant abundance in other writers.

In contrast to the irony, reticence and cautious verse of the middle of this century, Byron's is wonderfully robust, charged with vigour and colour, and it has a bold rhythmic movement. This description may be incomplete where *Beppo* or his comic masterpiece *Don Juan* are concerned, but it applies to the bulk of his early work. The early poetry is declamatory and deserves to be declaimed. If this is to concede that it is rhetorical, this is no denigration: Byron was the last English poet who, with an assured audience in mind – a large audience of cultured men and women, informed in matters of public interest – spoke out boldly to that audience, and held that audience spellbound. If this poetry lacks subtlety in syntax, nuance of rhythm, complexity of thought, these are the necessary defects of the virtues of a poetic voice and style demanding a strong and immediate effect at a first hearing. Byron does not mince matters; he knows what he wants to say; he says it bravely and magnificently; and the simple but grand surge of the rhythm matches the strength of his convictions and is its appropriate organ. Whereas the subtle rhythms and tones of a Keats resist translation, Byron can be largely rendered into other languages successfully, and this helps to account for a fame and influence on the continent scarcely less than in England during his life and; after his death, in Greece.

Much recent criticism has been concerned with dividing the poet Byron from the man

Byron who lived a poetic – if at times wickedly glamourous – life. Such a dissociation is not easy, and perhaps should not be attempted. For, eminently, Byron is the poet who lived his poetry. Prime evidence for this oneness of the man and his writing is the image of the chief figure, the hero, who appears again and again in the poems. This Byronic hero, it has been alleged, is less of a projection of Byron as he actually was than a projection of the figure he liked to consider himself to be, and wished others to accept as his true self. It is a saturnine figure, "pathetic, statuesque, posturing," conscious of his suffering, remorseful for some obscure sin with which he is tainted, yet proud, whether as "an outlaw of his own dark mind" or as wrongfully ostracized by others. He is mysterious, attractive to women, yet self-sufficient, lonely. He is capable of brave acts. No doubt such a figure, especially if he is handsome, and old enough to have had, as the saying is, a "past," can engage the romantic speculations of women and an envious, if undeclared, rivalry of those women's men. Childe Harold, the Giaour, Manfred, and the others, are recognizably akin: fascinating, yet repelling of pity, disdainful even of a larger sympathy. So it must not be thought therefore that this real or phantasied self-projection made, or makes, his poems less attractive on account of their author's self-absorption. At the time of their publication they had an immense appeal. Many like Captain Benwick, in Jane Austen's novel *Persuasion*, would indulge and magnify their own sorrow by identifying with the Byronic hero, appropriating to themselves "all the impassioned descriptions of hopeless agony." Moreover, a hero, like Childe Harold, was conveyed through a variety of scenes in a Europe, contemplating actual events or historic occasions, that were the concern of all educated men and women. If these heroes have a fascination today, it may well be that they have a strange resemblance to some modern terrorist leaders or others who, however viciously destructive their acts, may sincerely picture themselves, though wrongly and romantically, as heroes, hated and outlawed became of their noble ideals.

All of Byron is worth reading, but the first production which brought him overnight fame continues as a massive testament of his poetic vitality. Yet *Childe Harold* was published by instalments from 1812 to 1818. The management of the Spenserian stanza is, at first, occasionally awkward and the archaisms annoy, but gradually, as the thought becomes more sombre, the authentic Byronic assurance, weight, and impetus are established. But excellencies glow even in Cantos I and II, narrating the Childe's travels in Portugal, Spain, Greece, and Albania. The stanzas on the bull-fight in Cadiz are superb in the concrete vividness of the realization of the *corrida*, its sights, sounds, movements of those in the arena and of the spectators. Superb too is the honesty of the report of the reactions of the Childe – he is stirred by the ritual but he deplores the cruel sufferings of the animals. However, it is in the closing stanzas of Canto IV, by which time the mask of Harold has been dropped and the poet is speaking in his own person, that one of the most assured and sonorous voices in English poetry is heard.

With the oriental tales, some of them in octosyllabic metres, we are reminded of the poet's narrative skills, and especially of one he was to use to such effect later: he was a master in the skill of creating diversions with the intent of increasing suspense in the issue of the main story.

Yet the Byron who has received the most acclaim in the last two decades is not the Romantic poet of *Childe Harold* or the oriental tales, but the satirical and comic poet of *The Vision of Judgment, Beppo,* and *Don Juan*. His early *English Bards and Scotch Reviewers,* a biting attack on those who had upbraided his juvenilia, had revealed his gift for invective, the existence of another aspect of Byron's personality – more in tune with Pope and the Augustans than with what is commonly regarded as Romantic, even though Byron can also, and rightly, be regarded as *the* type of the Romantic poet. But it is this anti-romantic side which emerged to dominance in *The Vision of Judgment, Beppo,* and, above all, in *Don Juan*.

Auden has said that *Don Juan* is the only long poem which is nowhere boring. It is the only great comic poem in English. Don Juan is, of course, Byron, who can now see himself with detachment as a frequently ludicrous and exploited figure. On the back of the MS of Canto I are some poignant lines in which Byron cries "for God's sake – hock and soda water." This mixture alleviated the effects of the excesses of the night before, a hangover. It is with a "morning after" sanity that the poem was conceived. With its writing came the discovery that the Italian *ottava rima* form, used by early Italian poets for solemn purposes, was, especially when employing di- or tri-syllabic rhymes, ideally suited for comic effects in English. But the lines "If that I laugh at any mortal thing/'Tis that I may not weep" warn us of the seriousness of the comedy of *Don Juan*. If the long, though unfinished, mock-epic is conceived in a mainly comic spirit, that comedy embraces good-natured burlesque, banter, angry invective, the fiercest indignation, light-hearted gaiety. Byron chooses mainly to laugh at mortal things that he may not weep. There are many different kinds of laughter.

It has been right to have concentrated on *Childe Harold*, representative of one mode, and on *Don Juan*, representative of the other mode, but mention should be made of Byron's lyrics. Unlike those of most other Romantic poets, but like those of his friend, Thomas Moore, these (for instance, "She walks in beauty like the night" or "So we'll go no more a-roving") appear not to be the utterances of a singular individual – though they are that – but the utterances of sociable Regency mankind. They are turned for rendering in song in an Assembly room. The private anguish and the class interest in their themes are combined.

The poet's immense production includes the plays which, though ostensibly not for production, make profound searchings into political and family themes. And his prose, as already observed, affords almost matchless interest and entertainment.

—Francis Berry

CALVERLEY, Charles Stuart. English. Born Charles Stuart Blayds in Martley, Worcestershire, 22 December 1831; family name of Calverley resumed, 1852. Educated at Marlborough; Harrow School, 1846–50; Balliol College, Oxford, 1850–52 (Chancellor's Prize, 1851); Christ's College, Cambridge, 1852–58 (Craven Scholarship, 1854; Camden Medal, 1853, 1855; Browne Medal, 1855; Members' Prize, 1856), B.A. 1856, M.A. 1859; called to the Bar, Inner Temple, London, 1865. Married his cousin Ellen Calverley in 1865. Fellow, Christ's College, Cambridge, 1858–65; joined northern circuit to practice law, 1865, but fall on ice during the winter of 1866–67 ended his career; spent his last years as an invalid. *Died 17 February 1884.*

PUBLICATIONS

Collections

>   *Complete Works,* edited by Walter J. Sendall.   1901.
>   *The English Poems,* edited by Hilda D. Spear.   1974.

Verse

>   *Verses and Translations.*   1862; revised edition, 1865, 1871.
>   *Translations into English and Latin.*   1866; revised edition, 1885.
>   *Theocritus Translated into English Verse.*   1869; revised edition, 1883.
>   *Fly Leaves.*   1872; as *Verses and Fly Leaves,* 1885.
>   *The Idylls of Theocritus* (translation).   1908.
>   *The Eclogues of Virgil, Translated into English Verse,* edited by Moses Hadas.   1960.

Other

>   *The Literary Remains,* edited by Walter J. Sendall.   1885.

Bibliography: "Catalogue of the Calverley Material in the Toronto University Library" by H. D. King, in *Notes and Queries,* October–December 1954.

Reading List: *Browning and Calverley; or, Poem and Parody: An Elucidation* by Percy L. Babington, 1925; *Calverley and Some Cambridge Wits of the Nineteenth Century* by Richard B. Ince, 1929.

                              *   *   *

Charles Stuart Calverley was one of the group of "Cambridge Wits" writing in the second half of the nineteenth century. He was a poet who found his true voice in mockery and humour, and became a master in this vein.

A brilliant classical scholar, Calverley wrote poetry with facility in Latin and Greek as well as in English. As a translator he was accurate and conscientious; his edition of the *Idylls of Theocritus* is still well thought of, but with the decline of classical learning in Britain his translations from and into Latin and Greek have gone out of print. His Latin *jeu d'esprit,* "Carmen Saeculare" ("A Hymn for the Age"), should not be completely forgotten, though, for it is a witty pastiche of lines from Horace, Virgil, and other writers, fitted together with consummate skill and great verve to make a comic winter's tale for Calverley's own time.

His most memorable work, however, is to be found in the parodies and light verse published in the two slim volumes *Verses and Translations* and *Fly Leaves*. His poems evoke the atmosphere of upper-middle-class Victorian England, the comfortable, leisured, protected milieu in which Calverley himself lived, the world of tutors and preparatory schools, "coming-out" balls and romantic dreams. Calverley does for the second half of the century what Praed did for the first half, yet his social comments are merely incidental, for his poems are chiefly literary in flavour. Poem after poem is enlivened by references to familiar literature, an apt quotation, a fitting allusion, a joke perfected by the *mot juste* borrowed from another author; for instance, "Visions" has references to, or direct quotations from, Wordsworth, Scott, Gray, T. H. Bayly, Bunyan, and "Annie Laurie"; "Voices of the Night," the title itself taken from Longfellow, borrows as well from Tennyson, Pope, Bayly, Thackeray, and Scott. Most of the poems in his first book are of this kind and for sheer sparkling gaiety they are not equalled in the later volume.

Calverley's finest poems, however, are undoubtedly the critical parodies published in *Fly Leaves*. Two of them, "Lovers, and a Reflection" and "The Cock and the Bull," rank among the best parodies ever written in English. The first parodies the whole volume of Jean Ingelow's *Poems* (1863). By imitating her style, her facile rhyming, meaningless parentheses, and effete vocabulary, Calverley makes an uncompromising criticism of a volume which, despite its sentimentality and banality, was given by the contemporary reviewers praise out of all proportion to its worth. "The Cock and the Bull" is a skilful pastiche and parody of Browning's *The Ring and the Book* (1868). By employing Browning's own idiosyncratic language and eccentricities of style Calverley makes implicit criticisms of Browning's unconventionalities, and he makes explicit criticism by specific comment on method:

> You see this pebble-stone? It's a thing I bought
> Of a bit of a chit of a boy i' th mid o' the day –
> I like to dock the smaller parts-o'-speech,
> As we curtail the already cur-tailed cur
> (You catch the paronomasia, play 'po' words?)
> Did, rather, i' the pre-Landseerian days.

Calverley was a writer whose ambition never outran his ability, and his modest literary achievements are perfect of their kind.

—Hilda D. Spear

CAMPBELL, Alistair (Te Ariki). New Zealander. Born in Rarotonga, Cook Islands, 25 June 1925; emigrated to New Zealand in 1933. Educated at Otago Boys' High School, Dunedin; Victoria University of Wellington, B.A. in Latin and English. Married 1) the poet Fleur Adcock (divorced), two sons; 2) Meg Anderson in 1958, three children. Editor, Department of Education School Publications Branch, Wellington, 1955–72. Since 1972, Senior Editor, New Zealand Council for Educational Research, Wellington. Lives in Wellington.

PUBLICATIONS

Verse

Mine Eyes Dazzle: Poems 1947–49.   1950; revised edition, 1951, 1956.
Sanctuary of Spirits.   1963.
Wild Honey.   1964.
Blue Rain.   1967.
Drinking Horn.   1971.
Walk the Black Path.   1971.
Kapiti: Selected Poems, 1947–71.   1972.
Dreams, Yellow Lions.   1975.

Plays

When the Bough Breaks (produced 1970).   1970.

Radio Plays: The Homecoming; The Proprietor; The Suicide; The Wairau Incident.

Television Documentaries: Island of Spirits, 1973; Like You I'm Trapped, 1975.

Other

The Fruit Farm (juvenile).   1953.
The Happy Summer (juvenile).   1961.
New Zealand: A Book for Children.   1967.
Maori Legends.   1969.

Reading List: essay by James Bertram, in Comment, January–February 1965; "Campbell's Mine Eyes Dazzle: An Anatomy of Success" by David Gunby, in Landfall, March 1969; "Campbell's Sanctuary of Spirits: The Historical and Cultural Context" by F. M. McKay, in Landfall, June 1978.

*   *   *

Alistair Campbell's first book, Mine Eyes Dazzle, laid out as his territory the natural world. The descriptions of nature are notable for an animism which gives them a primitive strength and which is perhaps to be accounted for by Campbell's part-Polynesian background. The volume announced him as a Romantic poet who had learnt much from Yeats, though Campbell's concern has always been to explore feeling rather than ideas. His Romanticism is deepened by an empathy with Maori culture in which the spoken arts are highly poetical and a good deal of imagery is drawn from nature. One of the best of these early poems is "The Elegy," in memory of a fellow-student killed while climbing in the Southern Alps. As James K. Baxter wrote, in this poem "mountain, gorge, tree, and river become protagonists in the drama." The mysterious poem "The Return," peopled by strange figures on a beach, "Plant gods, tree gods, gods of the middle world," for some readers expresses a kind of race memory of the early Polynesian migrations.

The vividness of Campbell's evocation of the landscape is matched by the strong physicality of his love poetry, with its truly pagan delight in youth and beauty. Campbell's poetry is rooted in this world and he is the least metaphysical of New Zealand poets.

Sanctuary of Spirits is a lyrical sequence based on the history of the great pre-colonial

Maori fighting-chief Te Rauparaha. To his theme Campbell brought a realism made possible by his capacity to enter into the actualities of an oral culture and to acclimatise the style of Maori oratory into English verse. The allusive method of the sequence allowed Campbell to compress into a brief compass the rich and complex history of the chief who has been called the Maori Napoleon. Success with Maori themes has evaded most previous New Zealand poets; by showing how they might be handled Campbell has reclaimed a valuable territory for New Zealand poetry.

Campbell's early poems were written in tight forms inherited from Yeats. More recently he has loosened his style. This has allowed him to develop the talent for creating moods he demonstrated in earlier poems like "At a Fishing Settlement" and "Hut Near Desolated Pines," where every detail establishes that feeling of sadness and loneliness which Campbell's verse often conveys. He is not a prolific poet, but he has established himself as one of the best lyric writers New Zealand has produced.

—F. M. McKay

CAMPBELL, (Ignatius) Roy (Dunnachie). South African. Born in Durban, 2 October 1901. Educated at Durban High School; Oxford University. Served with the British Army in Africa, 1942–44. Married Mary Margaret Garman in 1922; two daughters. Spent most of his adult life in Provence, Spain, and Portugal. Editor, with William Plomer, *Voorslag*, 1926–27; Member, Literary Advisory Board, BBC, London, 1945–49. Recipient: Foyle Prize, 1952. Fellow, Royal Society of Literature, 1947; Member, Society of Provençal Poets, 1954. *Died 22 April 1957.*

PUBLICATIONS

Collections

Selected Poetry, edited by J. M. Lalley. 1968.

Verse

The Flaming Terrapin. 1924.
The Wayzgoose: A South African Satire. 1928.
Adamastor: Poems. 1930.
Poems. 1930.
The Georgiad: A Satirical Fantasy in Verse. 1931.
Pomegranates. 1932.
Flowering Reeds. 1933.
Mithraic Emblems. 1936.
Flowering Rifle: A Poem from the Battlefield of Spain. 1939.
Sons of the Mistral. 1941.
Talking Bronco. 1946.
Collected Poems. 3 vols., 1949–60.

Other

The History of a Rejected Address, with Satire and Fiction by Wyndham Lewis.   1930.
Burns.   1932.
Taurine Provence: The Philosophy, Technique, and Religion of the Bullfighter.   1932.
Wyndham Lewis: An Essay.   1932.
Broken Record: Reminiscences.   1934.
Light on a Dark Horse: An Autobiography 1901–1935.   1951.
Lorca: An Appreciation of His Poetry.   1952.
The Mamba's Precipice (juvenile).   1953.
Portugal.   1957.

Translator, Three Plays, by Helge Krog.   1934.
Translator, The Poems of St. John of the Cross.   1951.
Translator, Poems of Baudelaire.   1952.
Translator, Cousin Bazilio, by Eça de Queiroz.   1953.
Translator, The City and the Mountains, by Eça de Queiroz.   1955.
Translator, The Trickster of Seville and His Guest of Stone, by Tirso de Molina, Life Is a
    Dream, by Calderón, The Siege of Numantia, by Cervantes, and Fuente Ovejuna, by
    Lope de Vega, in The Classic Theatre, edited by Eric Bentley.   1959.
Translator, Nostalgia: A Collection of Poems, by J. Paco d'Arcos.   1960.
Translator, The Surgeon of His Honour, by Calderón.   1960.

Reading List: Campbell by David Wright, 1961, revised edition, 1971; Lyric and Polemic:
The Literary Personality of Campbell by Rowland Smith, 1972; "Campbell: Outsider on the
Right" by Bernard Bergonzi, in The Turn of a Century, 1973.

                    *   *   *

Roy Campbell was in every sense an outsider. He grew up in South Africa, in an idyllic
pre-industrial world, and was familiar from his early childhood with boats and horses. As a
very young man he came to England and began to establish himself as a poet, but he had little
in common with the English literary world which he later lampooned in his long satirical
poem The Georgiad. He returned to South Africa for some years in the 1920's and found
himself equally at odds with the literary life of his own country, which he duly satirized in
The Wayzgoose. Eventually Campbell came back to Europe, and spent the rest of his life –
apart from the years during and just after the Second World War – in Provence, Spain, and
Portugal. He reached his maximum alienation from other writers during the Spanish Civil
War, when, a convert to Catholicism, he became an ardent supporter of General Franco's
cause – the only poet of any stature in the English-speaking world to do so. He expressed his
convictions, and his hatred for conventional left-wing attitudes, in a third long satirical poem,
Flowering Rifle. During the Second World War Campbell somewhat rehabilitated himself
with liberal opinion by serving in the British Army. Throughout his life Campbell saw
himself as a man of action rather than an intellectual, and during the thirties he lived among
cattlemen and fishermen in Provence and Spain and despised the sedentary life of men of
letters. But for all his anti-intellectual, "plain man" pose, Campbell was in fact a cultured man
of wide reading in several languages: the third volume of his Collected Poems is made up of
translations from French, Spanish, Portuguese, and Latin.
    As a poet Campbell was not in any clear English tradition. He wrote exclusively formal
verse, in stanzas and couplets, and was immensely fluent, so that many of his poems, whether
lyrics or satires, are diffuse and repetitive. His literary antecedents were in some ways un-
English: he admired and imitated French poets, like Baudelaire, Rimbaud, and Valéry, and
from those sources he acquired a characteristically rhetorical lyricism that is assertive rather
then subtle. Yet in some of his lyrical poems, such as "The Zulu Girl," "Mass at Dawn,"

"Horses on the Camargue," "Autumn," and "Choosing a Mast," Campbell could write with delicacy as well as force. The *tour de force* of his earliest poetry is *The Flaming Terrapin*, a long poem in couplets which celebrates in exuberant and colourful verse a mythical beast, a giant tortoise that towed Noah's Ark during the flood. This poem shows a capacity for mythopoeic inventiveness that did not often recur in Campbell's later work, though we find it in a more severe and chastened form in the sequence called "Mithraic Frieze," published in 1936. Another early poem, "Tristan da Cunha," provides an instance of Campbell's image of himself as a lonely and misunderstood figure. He once saw the isolated island in the South Atlantic when sailing from South Africa, and in the poem he uses it as a symbol for himself as an aloof, Byronic figure, contemptuous of modern mass society. The present-day reader may have difficulty in responding to the more assertively rhetorical side of Campbell's poetry, though his lyrical quality is unmistakable. The satire has inevitably dated, though passages of *The Georgiad* are still vigorously comic and enjoyable. *Flowering Rifle*, though, is now best regarded as an over-extended footnote to the history of the Spanish Civil War rather than a living poem. "Mithraic Frieze" reflects Campbell's interest in the ancient Roman Mithraic religion, which he tried to interpret in a Catholic fashion. These poems are unlike most of Campbell's other work in that they are elliptical and compressed and allusive rather than extended and assertive; they present a group of enigmatic emblems and are poetically very effective in a symbolist way. They may prove in the long run to be the most enduring poetry that Campbell wrote.

After the outbreak of the Spanish Civil War Campbell declined in power as a poet; he became increasingly repetitive and crude in his invective. But in his verse translations he revealed himself as still capable of expressing a wide range of feeling, and some of them have a remarkable sensitivity, notably those from the mystical poetry of St. John of the Cross. Campbell remains an outsider in modern English literature: too idiosyncratic to be easily assimilated, and too gifted and rewarding to be ignored.

—Bernard Bergonzi

CAMPBELL, Thomas. Scottish. Born in Glasgow, 27 July 1777. Educated at Glasgow Grammar School, 1785–91; University of Glasgow, 1791–96; studied law in Edinburgh, 1797. Married Matilda Sinclair in 1803 (died, 1828); two sons. Tutor at Downie, near Lochgilphead, 1796–97; worked for the publishers Mundell and Company, and as a private tutor, Edinburgh, 1797–1800; toured Germany and Denmark, 1800–01; lived in London and Edinburgh, 1801–03, and settled in London, 1803, having refused a chair at Wilna, to pursue a literary career: lectured at the Royal Institution, 1810, and the Surrey Institution, 1820; Editor, *The New Monthly Magazine*, London, 1820–30, and *The Metropolitan*, London, 1831–32. Advocate and planner of a university for London, 1825; Founder, Polish Association, 1832. Lord Rector, University of Glasgow (elected three times), 1826–29. Granted Crown pension, 1805. *Died 15 June 1844.*

PUBLICATIONS

Collections

Poetical Works, edited by J. Logie Robertson. 1907.

Verse

The Wounded Hussar.   1799.
The Pleasures of Hope with Other Poems.   1799; revised edition, 1800, 1803.
Poems.   1803.
Gertrude of Wyoming: A Pennsylvanian Tale, and Other Poems.   1809.
Miscellaneous Poems.   1824.
Theodoric: A Domestic Tale, and Other Poems.   1824.
Poland; Lines on the View from St. Leonard's.   1831.
The Pilgrim of Glencoe and Other Poems.   1842.

Other

Life of Mrs. Siddons.   2 vols., 1834.
Letters from the South.   2 vols., 1837; as The Journal of a Residence in Algiers, 1842.
Memoir of Dugald Stewart.   1838.
Life of Petrarch.   2 vols., 1841.

Editor, Specimens of the British Poets.   7 vols., 1819.
Editor, The Dramatic Works of Shakespeare.   1838.
Editor, The Scenic Annual for 1838.   1838.

Reading List: Life and Letters of Campbell by William Beattie, 3 vols., 1849; Campbell by
James C. Hadden, 1899; Campbell: An Oration by W. Macneille Dixon, 1928.

*   *   *

Like his contemporary, the Irish poet Thomas Moore, Thomas Campbell gives the
impression of having worked from the outside. He did not, therefore, achieve the highest
flights of his art. Like Moore, Campbell specialised in cantering metres. Like Moore too, he
scored outstanding success in one, though not the same, department of poetry. Campbell's
gusto found perfect expression in "Ye Mariners of England," generally regarded with the
"Marseillaise" and "Scots wha hae" as one of the three greatest war songs ever written.
"Hohenlinden" and "The Battle of the Baltic" are other striking examples of his ability to
achieve memorability in action poetry. He scored another success, too, in the field of the
lighter lyric. Everyone knows the poem beginning "How delicious is the winning/Of a kiss at
Love's beginning," though the less familiar "Florine," set to music by the Scottish composer
Francis George Scott, is finer still.

For the rest, Campbell is a poet of remembered words and phrases, mostly from his
youthful poem in heroic couplets, modelled on Milton and on Thomson's Seasons, "The
Pleasures of Hope." To that poem, which quickly ran through four editions, we are indebted
for: "Tis distance lends enchantment to the view," "like angels' visits, few and far between,"
and "what millions died — that Caesar might be great." Scott thought that Campbell's
achievement so scantily lived up to its promise because Campbell "feared the shadow his
own fame cast before him." W. Macneille Dixon, on the other hand, believed the poet "had a
fear of the world's best," adding "and there can be no more wholesome type of alarm."

"Lord Ullin's Daughter" is as good as anything Scott himself achieved in the Scots ballad
vein, while in its different way "Lochiel" is very little inferior. "Gertrude of Wyoming," a
tale of the destruction of Pennsylvanian settlers, lacks narrative force, difficult in any case to
keep moving in the Spenserian stanza. It also perpetrates numerous scientific errors and
anachronisms, such as locating tigers on the shores of Lake Erie, and panthers in Ohio.

As an editor and critic, Campbell was cool towards the Lake Poets, especially Coleridge,
but warm in his defence and attempted restitution of Pope. This led Byron to record in his

journal: "[Campbell's] defence of Pope is glorious; to be sure it is his *own cause* too – but no matter, it is very good, and does him much credit."

While Campbell was editor of *The Metropolitan*, the novelist Captain Marryat submitted a contribution on the merits of flogging to maintain naval discipline. Campbell printed it, followed by his own lines:

> Ingenious author of this article,
> I believe in your doctrine not one particle,
>   But if e'er the power be mine
> To flog contributors, my boy,
> Your back shall be the first to enjoy
>   The benefit of the Nine.

It is impossible not to warm to that.

—Maurice Lindsay

CAMPION, Thomas. English. Born in Witham, Essex, 12 February 1567. Educated at Peterhouse, Cambridge (gentleman pensioner), 1581–84; admitted to Gray's Inn, London, 1586; studied medicine, probably at the University of Caen, qualified c. 1605. A volunteer in the expedition led by the Earl of Essex to Dieppe, to assist Henry IV, 1591. Composer and physician: practised as a physician, 1606 until his death. *Died 1 March 1620.*

PUBLICATIONS

Collections

> *Works*, edited by P. S. Vivian. 1909.
> *Works: Complete Songs, Masques, and Treatises*, edited by Walter R. Davis. 1967.
> *Selected Poems*, edited by Joan Hart. 1976.

Verse

> *Poemata: Ad Thamesin, Fragmentum Umbrae, Liber Elegiarum, Liber Epigrammatum.* 1595.
> *A Book of Airs to Be Sung to the Lute, Orpherian, and Bass Viol*, by P. Rosseter (part 1 by Campion). 1601.
> *The First Book of Airs.* 1613(?).
> *Two Books of Airs.* 1613(?).
> *Songs of Mourning Bewailing the Death of Prince Henry.* 1613.
> *The Third and Fourth Book of Airs.* 1617(?).
> *Epigrammatum Libri II, Umbra, Elegiarum Liber Unus.* 1619.
> *A Friend's Advice in a Ditty Concerning the Variable Changes in the World.* 1625(?).

Plays

> The Description of a Mask at Whitehall in Honour of the Lord Hayes and His Bride;
> Other Small Poems (produced 1607).   1607.
> The Description of a Mask at the Marriage of the Earl of Somerset and Frances Howard
> (produced 1613).   1614.
> A Relation of the Late Royal Entertainment Given by Lord Knowles on the Marriage Night
> of the Count Palatine and the Lady Elizabeth (produced 1613).   1613.
> The Lords' Masque (produced 1613).   With A Relation ..., 1613.

Other

> Observations in the Art of English Poesie.   1602.
> A New Way of Making Four Parts in Counterpoint.   1613.

Reading List: England's Musical Poet, Campion by Miles M. Kastendieck, 1938; Campion, Poet, Composer, Physician by Edward Lowbury, Timothy Slater, and Alison Young, 1970; Campion: His Poetry and Music 1567–1620 by Muriel T. Eldridge, 1971.

*   *   *

Thomas Campion's artistic reputation was much enhanced by the vogue for Elizabethan music and poetry which began in the 1920's. E. H. Fellowes's editorial work prompted a younger generation of critics to counter misconceptions surviving from the days of earlier "revivals." A typical view, adopted by such enthusiasts as Cecil Gray and Peter Warlock, was that Campion, though an interesting song-writer, was a better poet than musician. "He may be conceded to possess a fertile vein of pleasant, but rather undistinguished melody," wrote Gray (History of Music, 1928), "and that is about all." Warlock also finds the music less engaging than "the superlative excellence of the poems" (The English Ayre, 1926). To Bruce Pattison Campion was "the finest lyric poet of his age" (Music and Poetry of the English Renaissance, 1948).

The somewhat derogatory attitude towards Campion the musician may have been due to an unconscious preference for Dowland, whose idiom largely rules out the possibility of those "complacent four-square songs of the conventional hymn-tune pattern to be found in Campion's song-books ..." (Warlock). Few, however, would now deny that at his best Campion is a composer of real genius. The term "lyric" has several connotations, and in Campion's work more than one of these apply. In his shorter pieces he evolved word-patterns which fall naturally into acceptable melodic shapes; yet when considered independently of their music, these poems evoke emotional situations which are of interest for their own sake. Thus in "Breake now my heart and dye" (Third Book of Ayres) we have a miniature essay in self-questioning which avoids the customary clichés of amatory experience; sung to a melodic line supported by adventurous modulations, it achieves a striking poignancy. Many similar examples could be given; but in the light of this sort of accomplishment we can appreciate why Campion stressed the "epigrammatic" nature of the solo song as he conceived it.

Campion's ingenuity in this field, indeed, is such that we must revise our notions of him as an "amateur." His penchant for experimenting with classical metres was seldom an excuse for elegant trifling since he believed that the Greek and Latin poets were the "first inventers of Ayres." Yet, paradoxically, although the much-quoted "Rose-cheekt Lawra, come" (Chapter 8 of Campion's Observations) is a successful application of quantitative measure to English poetry, the musical setting of "Come, let us sound with melody" (a paraphrase of Psalm 19 in Sapphics from A Book of Ayres) is less than congenial. In fact, Campion's plea for a reversion to older metrical forms was something he could not fully live up to, and his objections to rhyme are, as Daniel's *Defence* suggests, slightly misplaced. In his masques he uses rhyme extensively, interspersing it with lyrical stanzas and racy prose dialogue. The masque form, in fact, suited Campion's versatility admirably. As a song-writer he was rivalled by John Danyel, Robert Jones, and others; yet in some respects he was slightly in advance of his time. His *New Way of Making Fowre Parts in Counter-point* advocates a system of musical composition in which the bass rather than the tenor is the starting-point for the harmonic structure. In both poetry and music, however, Campion's attitude to his art reveals a searching mind and creative powers of uncommon inventiveness.

—E. D. Mackerness

CAREW, Thomas. English. Born in West Wickham, Kent, c. 1595. Educated at Merton College, Oxford, 1608–11, B.A. 1611; Middle Temple, London, 1612. Secretary to the English Ambassador to Venice, Sir Dudley Carleton, c. 1612–16; accompanied Lord Herbert of Cherbury to France, 1619; Gentleman of Charles I's Privy Chamber, 1630, and Sewer in Ordinary, c. 1630. With the King's forces in First Bishops' War, 1639. *Died 21 March 1640.*

PUBLICATIONS

Collections

   Poems, with His Masque Coelum Britannicum, edited by Rhodes Dunlap. 1949.
   Cavalier Poets, edited by Thomas Clayton. 1978.

Verse

   Poems. 1640; revised edition, 1642, 1651.

Play

   Coelum Britannicum: A Masque at Whitehall (produced 1634). 1634.

Reading List: *The Flourishing Wreath: A Study of Carew's Poetry* by E. I. Selig, 1958.

*   *   *

The slapdash Suckling, in "A Sessions of the Poets," good-naturedly chides his friend Tom Carew for being so slow and painstaking a writer. Such a reproach could hardly have disturbed Carew, whose poetic address "To Ben Jonson" emphasises the high value he set on the Jonsonian (and Horatian) ideal of hard-won perfection:

   Repine not at the Taper's thrifty waste
   That sleeks thy terser Poems; nor is haste
   Praise, but excuse.

The result of Carew's careful writing was a set of lyrics – probably the finest poetry produced at the court of Charles I – which seem almost effortless.

Most of his work circulated only in manuscript; unlike Jonson, whose "itch of praise" he deplored, he troubled himself little about any wider audience or more lasting fame than might be found in his own select world. He read widely, though, and his poems contain images and ideas borrowed from French and Italian writers such as Ronsard and Marino. His longest poem, "A Rapture," was apparently one of the first by which he attracted serious attention; its eighty-three pentameter couplets, which summon his mistress Celia to a paradise of love, achieve a powerful intensity which derives not merely from an accumulation of boldly sensuous images but from the precision with which these images take form within a framework of logically expounded libertinism. Carew's shorter lyrics, mostly stanzaic, achieve similar control through a strong pattern of thought which guides and reinforces the flow of feeling. Skilfully versified, many of these lyrics were set to music by Henry Lawes and other contemporary composers.

His single masque, *Coelum Britannicum*, was written to order for performance by the King and his gentlemen at Whitehall, and it carries the Jonsonian pattern of the masque to an elaborate extreme, with no less than eight anti-masques. The central idea derives from philosophic dialogues by Giordano Bruno, and perhaps in response to this source some of the speeches achieve a striking degree of grave eloquence. But whereas it had been the object of Bruno's speakers to decide what virtues are worthy of a place among the stars, Carew solves the question more simply by elevating his King and Queen to that symbolic eminence.

He contributed perceptive commendatory poems to the publications of his friends, and wrote the best of the Elegies which accompanied the posthumous publication of Donne's poems in 1633. Here, in an extended analysis of Donne's distinctive achievement, he shows critical insights which go far beyond his own poetical practice, which only occasionally allowed itself a touch of the metaphysical. In another poem, prefixed to George Sandys' translated *Psalms* in 1638, he professes a desire to turn from earthly beauties to the love of God. But his own translated Psalms seem to have been youthful exercises rather than the product of any important spiritual urge, early or late.

—Rhodes Dunlap

CARMAN, (William) Bliss. Canadian. Born in Fredericton, New Brunswick, 15 April 1861. Educated at Fredericton Collegiate School, 1872–78; University of New Brunswick, Fredericton, 1878–81, B.A. 1881, M.A. 1884; University of Edinburgh, 1882–83; Harvard University, Cambridge, Massachusetts, 1886–87. Became associated with Mary Perry King in 1897; lived with the King family in Haines Falls, New York, and New Canaan, Connecticut, 1897–1929. Taught at Fredericton Collegiate School, 1883–84; studied law with the firm of James Douglas Hazen, Fredericton, 1884–86; private tutor, 1885; Literary Editor, New York *Independent*, 1890–92; Staff Member, *Current Literature*, New York, 1892, and *Cosmopolitan*, New York, 1894; Editor, *The Chapbook*, Cambridge, Massachusetts, 1894; Staff Member, *Atlantic Monthly*, Boston, 1895; Columnist, Boston *Transcript*,1895–1900; Reader, Small Maynard and Company, publishers, Boston, 1897–1903; Editor, *The Literary World*, 1905; Staff Member, *Gentleman's Journal*, 1909; part-time advertising writer, 1909–19; made lecture tours of Canada in the 1920's. Recipient: Lorne Pierce Gold Medal, 1929; Poetry Society of America Award. LL.D.: University of New Brunswick, 1906; Litt.D.: Trinity College, Hartford, Connecticut. Corresponding Member, Royal Society of Canada, 1925. *Died 8 June 1929.*

Collections

Selected Poems, edited by Lorne Pierce.   1954.

Verse

Low Tide on Grand-Pré.   1889(?).
Low Tide on Grand-Pré: A Book of Lyrics.   1893; revised edition, 1894.
Saint Kavin: A Ballad.   1894.
Songs from Vagabondia, with Richard Hovey.   1894; *More Songs*, 1896; *Last Songs*, 1901.
Behind the Arras: A Book of the Unseen.   1895.
A Seamark: A Threnody for Robert Louis Stevenson.   1895.
Ballads of Lost Haven: A Book of the Sea.   1897.
By the Aurelian Wall and Other Elegies.   1898.
The Green Book of the Bards.   1898.
A Winter Holiday.   1899.
The Vengeance of Noel Brassard: A Tale of the Acadian Expulsion.   1899.
Christmas Eve at S. Kavin's.   1901.
Ballads and Lyrics.   1902.
Coronation Ode.   1902; revised edition, 1902.
Pipes of Pan Number One, From the Book of Myths.   1902; revised edition, 1904; *Number Two, From the Green Book of the Bards*, 1903; *Number Three: Songs of the Sea Children*, 1904; *Number Four: Songs from a Northern Garden*, 1904; *Number Five, From the Book of Valentines*, 1905; complete version, 1906.
Sappho: Lyrics.   1902.
The Word at St. Kavin's.   1903.
A Vision of Sappho.   1903.
Sappho: One Hundred Lyrics.   1904.
Poems.   2 vols., 1904.
The Princess of the Tower, The Wise Men from the East, and To the Winged Victory.   1906.
The Gate of Peace.   1907.
The Rough Rider and Other Poems.   1909.
A Painter's Holiday and Other Poems.   1911.
Echoes from Vagabondia.   1912.
Album of Six Songs, by Henri Duparc, music by Debussy.   1914.
April Airs: A Book of New England Lyrics.   1916.
Four Sonnets.   1916.
The Man of the Marne and Other Poems, with Mary Perry King.   1918.
Later Poems.   1921.
Ballads and Lyrics.   1923.
Far Horizons.   1925.
Wild Garden.   1929.
Sanctuary: Sunshine House Sonnets.   1929.
The Music of Earth.   1931.
Poems.   1931.
Youth in the Air.   1932.
To a Chickadee (Sierra Madre Mountains, California).   1933.
A Little Child's Prayer.   1939.

Plays

> *The Daughters of Dawn: A Lyrical Pageant or Series of Historical Scenes*, with Mary
>   Perry King.   1913.
> *Earth Deities and Other Rhythmic Masques* (includes *Children of the Year, Dance
>   Diurnal, Pas de Trois*), with Mary Perry King.   1914.

Other

> *The Kinship of Nature*.   1903.
> *The Friendship of Art*.   1904.
> *The Poetry of Life*.   1905.
> *The Making of Personality*, with Mary Perry King.   1908.
> *James Whitcomb Riley: An Essay*.   1918.
> *Talks on Poetry and Life* (lectures), edited by Blanche Hume.   1926.
> *Bliss Carman's Scrap-Book*, edited by Lorne Pierce.   1931.

> Editor, *The World's Best Poetry*.   10 vols., 1904.
> Editor, with Lorne Pierce, *Our Canadian Literature: Representative Verse*.   1922.
> Editor, *The Oxford Book of American Verse*.   1927.

Reading List: *Carman* by Julian Hawthorne, 1929; *Carman and the Literary Currents and
Influences of His Times* by James Cappon, 1930; *Carman: A Portrait* by Muriel Miller, 1935;
Carman: Bibliography, Letters, Fugitive Pieces and Other Data by William Inglis Morse,
1941; *Carman* by Donald G. Stevens, 1966.

*   *   *

There was a time, two or three decades ago, when Bliss Carman was the best-known of
Canadian poets, with a reputation that extended throughout the English-reading world. Yet it
is evident, now his vogue has declined, that Carman was the least interesting of the company
of poets in which literary history places him. He began to write and publish as one of the
small group that emerged in the early 1880's in Fredericton under the leadership of his cousin
Charles G. D. Roberts. Later his fame became national, even for a brief period international.
He is remembered now as one of the Confederation poets, the men born in the same decade
as the dominion of Canada and whose work came to maturity in the final years of the
nineteenth century.

Carman began with the kind of sensitive evocation of Canadian landscape and rural life
that all the members of his group attempted, but there are few among the poems he produced
so prolifically in the 1890's and the early years of this century that show either the precise
observation of nature and of human occupations that characterized the rural poems of
Charles G. D. Roberts or the taut and craftsmanly adaptation of romantic styles to Canadian
themes shown by Archibald Lampman, another Confederation poet. The dreamy resonance
of even Carman's best poems, like the famous *Low Tide on Grand Pré*, tends to be marred by
thinness of feeling, by a weakening vagueness of imagery and statement:

> And that we took into our hands
>   Spirit of life or subtler thing –
> Breathed on us there and loosed the bands
> Of death, and taught us, whispering,
>   The secret of some wonder-thing.

Carman soon fell under the influence of Whitman and W. E. Henley, and in books like

Songs from Vagabondia he tried to develop a poetry of the manly life and the open road, but lost himself in a kind of meretricious heartiness, as in poems like "Lord of My Heart's Elation."

> Bear out, bear out, bear onward
> This mortal soul alone,
> To selfhood or oblivion
> Incredibly thine own....

Yet Carman's influence was by no means wholly negative, for, like the other Confederation poets, he helped to teach Canadian writers that the substance of poetry lay in giving expression to their own life and their own world and not in attempting, as the versifiers of the pioneer past had done, to recreate the poetry of England in an alien land.

—George Woodcock

CHANNING, William Ellery. American. Born in Boston, Massachusetts, 29 November 1818; nephew of the writer William Ellery Channing; raised by a great-aunt in Milton, Massachusetts. Educated at Round Hill School, Northampton, Massachusetts, and Boston Latin School; attended Harvard University, Cambridge, Massachusetts, 1834. Married Ellen Fuller in 1842. Farmed in Woodstock, Illinois, 1839–40; tutor and newspaper writer, Cincinnati, 1840–41; settled in Concord, Massachusetts, to be near Emerson, 1842, and remained there for the rest of his life; associated with other members of the Concord community, especially Thoreau; lived in New York, writing for the *Tribune*, 1844; visited France and Italy, 1845; Editor, *New Bedford Mercury*, Massachusetts, 1855–58. *Died 23 December 1901.*

PUBLICATIONS

Collections

    Poems of Sixty-Five Years, edited by F. B. Sanborn. 1902.

Verse

    Poems. 1843; second series, 1847.
    Conversations in Rome: Between an Artist, A Catholic, and a Critic. 1847.
    The Woodman and Other Poems. 1849.
    Near Home. 1858.
    The Wanderer: A Colloquial Poem. 1871.
    The Burial of John Brown. 1878.
    Eliot. 1885.
    John Brown and the Heroes of Harper's Ferry. 1886.

Other

Thoreau, The Poet-Naturalist. 1873; revised edition, 1902.

Editor, with Sophia Thoreau, *The Maine Woods,* by Henry David Thoreau. 1864.
Editor, with Sophia Thoreau, *Cape Cod,* by Henry David Thoreau. 1865.
Editor, with Sophia Thoreau, *A Yankee in Canada, with Anti-Slavery and Reform Papers,* by Henry David Thoreau. 1866.

*   *   *

When Emerson helped found *The Dial* in 1840, it was just such a poet as William Ellery Channing for whom he intended the new magazine. Channing was a young man with a talent but with no readily available place for his verses. Under Emerson's sponsorship, Channing went on to publish not only poems in *The Dial,* but two books of lyrics and four book-length poems later in his life. These early lyrics are in many ways most characteristic of him. His themes were beauty, self-reliance, and nature. He was hostile to the development of urban America, and in such poems as "Reverence" and "Walden Spring" he gave voice to his fears and to his longings for a pastoral life which was quickly vanishing in the 1840's. What he wanted was the union of nature and self such as he imaged in "Wachusett":

> It went within my inmost heart,
> The overhanging Arch to see,
> The liquid stream, became a part
> Of my internal Harmony.

Typical of his time and place, he insisted on a union of art and life. To write well was to live well; to *be* a poet was itself a creation of supreme importance.

His increasing awareness of his own loneliness and his isolation was most apparent in two of his book-length poems, *Near Home* and *The Wanderer.* The first of these is a charming hymn to New England as a place of healing power.

> Perpetual newness and the health in things.
> This, is the startling theme, the lovely birth
> Each morn of a new day, so wholly new,
> So absolutely penetrated by itself,
> The fresh, the fair, the ever-living grace....

In *The Wanderer,* Channing completed his journey from the simplicity of his lyrics to a more complex recognition of the tensions between man's love of nature and the forces working against the fulfillment of his pastoral idealism. The poem counterpoises a reverence for the land with a stark awareness of the destructive forces of death and technology. A poetic career beginning in enthusiasm ends in a mature perception of frustration.

Beyond the achievement of his poetry, Channing's career included the first biography of Thoreau, who had been the poet's close friend from 1841. *Thoreau, The Poet-Naturalist* is a narrative built on extensive quotations from Thoreau's journal, which was then unpublished. The book had the virtue of thus putting before the public quite a bit of Thoreau's little-known writing, and it also offered a cogent commentary by Channing who rightly emphasized the ethical strictness and the aesthetic craftsmanship in Thoreau's writing. Appearing at a time when Thoreau was all but unknown, the biography had the virtue of keeping his name alive and making his work more readily accessible.

Finally, it is as a friend that Channing may be best remembered. He was the only close friend of Thoreau; he was a constant companion of Emerson for forty years; he was a frequent visitor in the homes of Alcott and Hawthorne; he was Margaret Fuller's brother-in-law. Ellery Channing was a brilliant talker, full of wit and spontaneity. The universal report from his contemporaries was that he spoke better than he wrote. Emerson was convinced that "In walking with Ellery you shall always see what was never before shown to the eye of man." For his part, Hawthorne wrote in *Mosses from an Old Manse*, "Could he have drawn out that virgin gold [of his conversation] and stamped it with the mint mark that alone gives currency, the world might have had the profit, and he the fame." In a narrow society such as New England was, the vitality of Channing's conversation was not to be ignored. He showed his gifted friends how they might see better; he was a receptive audience, a sympathetic and shrewd critic, one who made it possible for men such as Emerson and Thoreau to act on their talent.

—Robert N. Hudspeth

CHAPMAN, George. English. Born near Hitchin, Hertfordshire, c. 1560. Educated possibly at Cambridge University and Oxford University. Lived on the Continent, 1585–91, and served with the forces of Sir Francis Vere in the Low Countries; returned to London and wrote for Philip Henslowe until 1599, then for the Children of St. Paul's Chapel (later known as the Children of the Queen's Revels) until 1608, and thereafter devoted himself mainly to his translations; Sewer-in-Ordinary to Prince Henry, 1603–12; imprisoned in the Tower of London for satirical references to James I, 1605; in later life enjoyed patronage of the Earl of Somerset. *Died 12 May 1634.*

PUBLICATIONS

Collections

   Tragedies, Comedies, edited by T. M. Parrott.   2 vols., 1910–14.
   Poems, edited by Phyllis Brooks Bartlett.   1941.
   Plays: The Comedies. edited by Allan Holaday.   1970.

Verse

   The Shadow of Night, Containing Two Poetical Hymns.   1594.
   Ovid's Banquet of Sense, A Coronet for His Mistress Philosophy, and His Amorous Zodiac.   1595; edited by Elizabeth Story Donno, in *Elizabethan Minor Epics,* 1963.
   Seven Books of the Iliad of Homer.   1598; *Achilles' Shield,* 1598; *Twelve Books,* 1609(?); complete work, 1611.
   Hero and Leander, Begun by Marlowe, Finished by Chapman.   1598; edited by Louis L. Martz, 1972.
   Euthymiae Raptus; or, The Tears of Peace, with Interlocutions.   1609.
   An Epicede or Funeral Song on the Death of Henry Prince of Wales.   1612.
   Petrarch's Seven Penitential Psalms, Paraphrastically Translated with Other Philosophical Poems and a Hymn to Christ upon the Cross.   1612.
   Andromeda Liberata; or, The Nuptials of Perseus and Andromeda.   1614.

Eugenia; or, True Nobility's Trance for the Death of William Lord Russell. 1614.
Homer's Odyssey, 12 books. 1614(?); complete work, 1615(?).
The Divine Poem of Musaeus. 1616; edited by Elizabeth Story Donno, in *Elizabethan Minor Epics,* 1963.
The Georgics of Hesiod. 1618.
Pro Vere Autumni Lachrymae, Inscribed to the Memory of Sir Horatio Vere. 1622.
The Crown of All Homer's Works, Batrachomyomachia, or, The Battle of Frogs and Mice, His Hymns and Epigrams. 1624(?).
A Justification of a Strange Action of Nero, Being the Fifth Satire of Juvenal Translated. 1629.
Chapman's Homer: The Iliad, The Odyssey, and the Lesser Homerica, edited by Allardyce Nicoll. 2 vols., 1956.

Plays

Fedele and Fortunio: The Deceits in Love, with Munday and Stephen Gosson (produced 1584?). 1585; edited by P. Simpson, 1909.
The Blind Beggar of Alexandria (produced 1596). 1598; edited by Lloyd E. Berry, in *Plays,* 1970.
An Humorous Day's Mirth (produced 1597). 1599; edited by Allan Holaday, in *Plays,* 1970.
The Gentleman Usher (produced 1602?). 1606; edited by Robert Ornstein, in *Plays,* 1970.
All Fools (produced 1604). 1605; edited by G. Blakemore Evans, in *Plays,* 1970.
Monsieur D'Olive (produced 1604). 1606; edited by Allan Holaday, in *Plays,* 1970.
Bussy D'Ambois (produced 1604). 1607; edited by M. Evans, 1965.
Eastward Ho, with Jonson and Marston (produced 1605). 1605; edited by C. G. Petter, 1973.
Sir Giles Goosecap, Knight (produced?). 1606; edited by W. Bang and R. Brotanek, 1909.
The Conspiracy and Tragedy of Charles, Duke of Byron, Marshal of France (produced 1608). 1608; edited by W. L. Phelps, 1895.
May Day (produced 1609). 1611; edited by Robert F. Welsh, in *Plays,* 1970.
The Widow's Tears (produced before 1609). 1612; edited by Robert Ornstein, in *Plays,* 1970.
The Revenge of Bussy D'Ambois (produced 1610?). 1613; edited by F. S. Boas, 1905.
The Memorable Masque of the Middle Temple and Lincoln's Inn (produced 1613). 1613; edited by G. Blakemore Evans, in *Plays,* 1970.
The Wars of Caesar and Pompey (produced 1613?). 1631.
Chabot, Admiral of France (produced 1613?). Version revised by Shirley, published 1639; edited by Ezra Lehman, 1906.

Other

A Free and Offenceless Justification of Andromeda Liberata. 1614.

Bibliography: *Chapman: A Concise Bibliography* by S. A. Tannenbaum, 1938; supplement, 1946.

Reading List: *Chapman: The Effect of Stoicism upon His Tragedies* by John W. Weiler, 1949; *Chapman: Sa Vie, Sa Poésie, Son Théâtre, Sa Pensée* by Jean Jacquot, 1951; *The Tragedies of*

Chapman: Renaissance Ethics in Action by Ennis Rees, 1954; *Homeric Renaissance: The Odyssey of Chapman* by George de F. Lord, 1956; *Chapman: A Critical Study* by Millar MacLure, 1966; *Chapman* by C. Spivak, 1967; *An Index to the Figurative Language of Chapman's Tragedies* by L. C. Stagg, 1970; *The Mind's Empire: Myth and Form in Chapman's Narrative Poems* by Raymond B. Waddington, 1974; *Chapman: Action and Contemplation in His Tragedies* by Peter Bement, 1974.

*   *   *

Chapman's activities as poet, dramatist, and translator place him second only to his friend and sometimes collaborator Ben Jonson as a man of letters. While the two men shared a devotion to learning and a sense of vocation as professional writers, in other respects the differences are large. To the clarity which is Jonson's stylistic ideal, Chapman retorts that oratorically plain poetry "were the plaine way to barbarisme." His own style is so notoriously difficult that – mistakenly – he has been associated with the Metaphysicals. Instead, Chapman wrote as a Platonic mystagogue, using meaningful obscurity to conceal his truth from the many and reveal it to the worthy few. He should be seen as one in the line of visionary poets extending from Spenser through Milton and Blake.

Chapman was influenced heavily by Marsilio Ficino; and Chapman's Platonism supplies the key to his thought and poetics, as his various theoretical statements make clear. Poetry is an epiphany of Truth, always associated with wisdom and learning, attained through divine inspiration. The vatic poet accommodates this Truth to human understanding through symbolic images, fables, and myths. Although few men will undertake the intellectual and spiritual discipline necessary to comprehend such poetry, for the "understanders" it will "turne blood to soule" and "heighten [man's] transition into God." Central to Chapman's poetics is his conception of *form*: this includes conventional literary form (genre) by which the poet announces his general intentions; the inner form of the myth, fable, or story (understood via the traditions of allegorical commentary); and the indwelling form or "soul" of the Truth, a notion deriving from the Platonic Idea.

Chapman's most important poems were those published at the beginning of his career. *The Shadow of Night* consists of two hymns addressed to Night and to Cynthia, both revealed by the Orphic poet as religious mysteries, which anatomize man's condition and prescribe remedies. In the second, around the triune identity of the goddess as Cynthia-Diana-Hecate, Chapman interweaves a complex, three-level allegory – philosophical, political, and poetic. *Ovids Banquet of Sence*, an oblique riposte to the fashion of Ovidian erotic narratives, ironically presents Ovid as seducer, glibly misusing Platonic doctrine to achieve his end; deliberately ambiguous, the entire poem – as the title-page emblem suggests – is a *trompe l'oeil*, warning us not to trust our senses. Chapman's continuation of *Hero and Leander* "corrects" Marlowe's incomplete narrative (as does his editing of the Marlowe), restoring the moral balance and high seriousness in an Ovidian epic, written from the perspective of the allegorical commentaries upon *The Metamorphoses*. Of the Jacobean poems, two deserve mention: *The Teares of Peace*, oddly combining medieval dream-vision and Hermetic revelation, is Chapman's most sustained defense of learning; and *Andromeda Liberata* projects political allegory through mythological narrative in a manner reflecting the influence of court masques.

By 1598 Francis Meres could list Chapman among "the best Poets" for both comedy and tragedy; and theatrical writing in several dramatic genres dominated his activities for the next decade. M. C. Bradbrook credits *An Humorous Day's Mirth* with initiating the comedy of humours; and Jackson Cope has demonstrated that *The Gentleman Usher* and *The Widow's Tears* – tragi-comic romance and satiric comedy, respectively – are philosophic dramas, using mythic frameworks to explore positive and negative versions of the Platonic quest for absolute knowledge. In the tragedies Chapman obsessively rewrites the script of a flawed Titan, greater by far than the surrounding society, yet contaminated and eventually destroyed by his compromises with that society and by his own hubris. It is conventional to mark the shift from the Achillean active heroes, Bussy and Byron, to the passive, Stoic virtue of Clermont, Cato, and Chabot. But, just as Platonism always informs his poetics, so Stoicism is the foundation of his ethics throughout, a personal and eclectic Stoicism that is flexible enough to encompass both Achilles's justified wrath and the encomium of Clermont as "this Senecal man." *Bussy D'Ambois* "inwardly" measures its hero's greatness and failure against the myths of Hercules, Prometheus, and Christ; "outwardly" it is heroic tragedy and sensational melodrama. This combination of dimensions has earned its modern status as the single "anthology piece" among the tragedies. An age as receptive as ours to the drama of ideas, however, might well give more attention to the interiorized tragedies of *Byron* and *The Revenge of Bussy D'Ambois*. Although only *The Memorable Maske* survives as evidence of Chapman's skill at this new form, we have Jonson's testimony "That next himself only Fletcher and Chapman could make a Mask."

Chapman launched his Homer translation with *Seaven Bookes of the Iliades* and *Achilles Shield* (1598); *The Teares of Peace* (1609) announces his visionary inspiration by Homer and his renewed dedication to the task. *The Iliads* was finished in 1611, the complete *Odyssey* in 1615, the two published together as *The Whole Works* the next year, and the lesser Homerica followed later. Despite his unfulfilled promise to present "my Poeme of the mysteries/ Reveal'd in Homer," Chapman does not encumber the epics with Platonic exegesis; rather, he sees "naked *Vlysses* clad in eternall Fiction" as totally mythic. Disdaining "word-for-word traductions," he regarded his job as *translation*, making the universal values of Homer comprehensible and therefore relevant to his own time and culture. His English systematically renders explicit the ethical and philosophical attitudes which he perceived as implicit in the text. Chapman's famous statement that the "Proposition" of each epic is contracted in the first word (*wrath* and *man*) itself epitomizes his approach to translation: "in one, the Bodie's fervour and fashion of outward Fortitude to all possible height of Heroicall Action; in the other, the Mind's inward, constant and unconquered Empire...." The adequacy of Chapman's Greek and the degree of fidelity to the original are much mooted questions which can distract attention from his very considerable achievement. Despite the hiatus in composition, Chapman's *Iliads* is generally viewed as more successful than his *Odyssey* in its consonance to the meaning of the Homer and in its unity. Certainly Chapman's *Iliads* is a splendid poem. His other literary accomplishments notwithstanding, his description of the Homer translations as "The Worke that I was borne to doe" is one to which most readers give assent.

—Raymond B. Waddington

CHATTERTON, Thomas. English. Born in Bristol, 20 November 1752. Educated at Colston's Bluecoat School, Bristol, 1760–67; apprenticed to John Lambert, an attorney, Bristol, 1767–70. Produced Rowleie (Rowley) manuscript, 1768–69, and was encouraged by Horace Walpole, until he became convinced the Rowleyan works were modern. Went to London in 1770 and produced a great variety of work. *Died* (perhaps a suicide, but more probably the victim of an overdose of drugs) *25 August 1770.*

PUBLICATIONS

Collections

    Complete Works, edited by Donald S. Taylor and Benjamin B. Hoover.   2 vols., 1971.

Verse

> *The Execution of Sir Charles Badwin.* 1772.
> *Poems, Supposed to Have Been Written at Bristol by Thomas Rowley and Others in the Fifteenth Century,* edited by Thomas Tyrwhitt. 1777.

Other

> *Miscellanies in Prose and Verse,* edited by John Broughton. 1778; *Supplement,* 1784.

Reading List: *A Life of Chatterton* by E. H. W. Meyerstein, 1930; *Chatterton* by Basil Cottle, 1963; *The Marvelous Boy: The Life and Myth of Chatterton* by Linda Kelly, 1971; *Chatterton's Art: Experiments in Imagined History* by Donald S. Taylor, 1978.

*   *   *

Thomas Chatterton was an instinctive imitator of and innovator with forms and modes, and so his two-hundred-odd extant works are at first bewildering in their variety. His literary creditors range from Chaucer, Shakespeare, and the historian William Camden, through major 17th- and 18th-century writers – Dryden, Pope, Swift, Gay, Collins, Churchill – to contemporary periodicals with their evanescent spectrum of sub-literary genres. A clearer picture emerges if we view his works in four chronological groups – the hymns and verse fables of his tenth and eleventh years, the supposedly medieval Rowleyan works of his seventeenth year, the verse satires and journalistic prose of his last (eighteenth) year, and a miscellaneous group of four modes worked through both of his last two years – descriptive lyrics, pastorals, satiric epistles, and Ossianic prose poems. Nothing is extant from his twelfth through sixteenth years, though there is evidence that he then wrote a good deal of insipid, conventional amatory verse, some of it to order.

The early hymns are formally and prosodically precocious but conventional. The early fables, however, show – in diction, character portrayal, and prosody – skillful adaptation of the quietly ironic manner of John Gay. The best of these – "Apostate Will" and "The Churchwarden and the Apparition" – are succinct moral anatomies of Bristolians who mask consuming greed with complacent religious respectability. The prose "Letter from Fullford, The Grave-digger," probably Chatterton's, pursues the same theme with Swiftian ironies in the mock-pastoral mode.

In the Rowleyan year (summer 1768 through spring 1769), stimulated by heraldry, old books, architectural remains, and Bristol place names, Chatterton invented a rich history of his native city from pre-Roman origins through the late fifteenth century. He presented this history in an invented fifteenth-century English which is never *pure* invention. All but a few of its words can be traced to glossaries, dictionaries, and old books, all of which he took as equally reliable evidence for an English whose essence was grammatic and spelling lawlessness. His basic Rowleyan vocabulary of about 1800 words was enlarged by applying this posited lawlessness to current English. The sequence of the Rowleyan works can be fairly accurately fixed by calculating the percentages of Rowleyan words, for the language constantly grew as Chatterton used it. Efforts to translate the Rowley poems into modern English – those of Walter Skeat, for example – seem invariably to strip them of their expressive power.

The Rowleyan works consist of "documents" and drawings which "prove" the existence of Chatterton's historical Bristol and the literary works proper. Of the scores of documents, the elaborate "Discorse on Brystowe" gives the clearest sense of how Chatterton's imagination worked. His model for Rowley as historian is William Camden, especially Edmund Gibson's 1695 translated and emended *Camden's Britannia.* The Rowleyan literary works grow from a search for heroes and heroic modes that could express what Chatterton felt about his invented history, his poet-priest-connoisseur-historian Rowley, and that poet's generous, witty, warm-hearted patron, the merchant prince and builder of Redcliff Church William Canynge. Chatterton's own father died before the poet was born, and both Bertrand Bronson and Phyllis Greenacre have convincingly suggested that searches for patrons, beneficent paternal figures, catalyze much of the Rowleyan effort and much also of Chatterton's later satire, though here the filial stance emerges through acts of rebellion against authority figures in church and state. Pope is his major *poetic* father: Rowley is regularly shown as bringing a Popean correctness and polish to a coarse fifteenth-century poetry (this too invented in detail). Rowley regularly borrows and reworks imagery, ideas, and stances from Pope's translations and satires, and Rowley, Canynge, and their cozy circle of wits are seen as a fifteenth-century Scriblerus Club whose Pope is Rowley.

The strong Rowley poems begin with "Bristowe Tragedie," an English epic influenced by Percy's *Reliques* but gaining its major power from visual, almost cinematographic contrasts. The heroic odes "Songe of Sayncte Baldwyn" and "Songe toe Ella" are perfect in their kind – constructionally and prosodically brilliant. The major work is the "discoorseynge tragedie" *AElla*, an operatic Anglo-Saxon reworking of *Othello*. Though AElla's concluding suicide is unmotivated, the action is urgent and compelling, its characters are vividly evoked, and the striking and flexible rhetoric and prosody are nicely contrasted to fine intermittent pastoral songs which quietly reinforce the theme of thwarted love. Another heroic ode – "On Richard I" – effectively drew Horace Walpole's interest and, almost, his patronage. In "Englysh Metamorphosis" Chatterton builds an effective Ovidian narrative, with brilliant empathic strokes, from the Trojan Brutus tradition. "The Gouler's Requiem" is a flawless sympathetic-comic return to Chatterton's early interest in consuming greed; this and the intimately comic "Acconte of W. Canynges Feast" are attributed to Canynge. The best of Rowley's poems conclude with three eclogues which rework Collins' *Persian Eclogues* in medieval English tones and "An Excelente Balade of Charitie," the Good Samaritan parable in expressive medieval dress.

Two Popean satiric epistles effectively introduce *AElla*. Thence, in Chatterton's last year, various satiric modes develop, with help both poetical and in his religious and political radicalism from Charles Churchill. "Intrest" [*sic*], "Conversation," the freethinking "Epistle to Catcott," Chatterton's teasing "Will," a sexual mock-epic "The Exhibition," and his burletta "The Revenge" are the most artistically interesting and expressive of the longer satires. "To Miss Lydia Cotton" and "A New Song" bring freethinking vigor to tired amatory conventions. With the exception of "Kew Gardens," in which a central metaphor of an enforced state religion almost metaphysically organizes lengthy, slashing political and religious satire, most of the Churchillean political satires, the Junius-aping political letters, and the journalistic fiction of his last year demonstrate more a drive for Grub Street survival than for literary expression.

But Chatterton's final year was not entirely given over to Grub Street. After the Rowleyan pastorals, he writes both effective mock pastoral ("Hobbinol and Thyrsis") and the brilliantly colored African eclogues, which begin in the mode of Collins but move toward supposed ritualistic and mythic roots of the pastoral impulse. Chatterton's interestingly allusive and elaborate Ossianic writings are an attempt to imagine for pre-Norman Britain a pre-Rowleyan heroic mode. In Rowley, in these two modes, and in his better descriptive poetry (influenced most strongly by Gray and Collins) Chatterton partially justifies the Romantic legend which made him the proto-martyr of the new poetic faith. What the Romantics and the Victorians failed to see was that, to the end, the roots of his best poetry cling to eighteenth-century soil: Chatterton embodies in the writing of his last two years the course of English poetry from Pope through Keats. It is probable, however, that he will continue to be read primarily for the intensity, color, prosodic strength, and verbal richness by which his Rowleyan works bring his imagined medieval Bristol to life.

—Donald S. Taylor

CHAUCER, Geoffrey.   English.   Born in London, c. 1343. Possibly educated at Oxford or Cambridge. Served in the King's forces in France, 1359; captured and ransomed, 1360. Married Philippa de Roet c. 1366; probably had two sons, one daughter. Entered the household of Lionel of Antwerp, son of King Edward III, as a page, 1357; on return from France entered the royal service under the patronage of John of Gaunt, 1360; promoted to Valet to Edward III, 1367, and Esquire, 1368; sent to Italy to assist in arranging a trade agreement with the Genoese, 1372, on diplomatic mission in France, 1377; Controller of the Customs and Subsidies on Wool, Port of London, 1374–86; Justice of the Peace, and Knight of the Shire (Member of Parliament) for the County of Kent, 1385–86; Clerk of the King's Works, 1389–91. Granted a pension, 1394. *Died 25 October 1400.*

PUBLICATIONS

Collections

  Complete Works, edited by F. N. Robinson.   1933; revised edition, 1957.

Verse

  The Parliament of Fowls, edited by W. Caxton.   1477; edited by D. S. Brewer, 1960.
  Minor Poems, edited by W. Caxton.   2 vols., 1477.
  The Canterbury Tales, edited by W. Caxton.   1478; edited by John M. Manly and
     Edith Rickert, 8 vols., 1940; edited by Nevill Coghill, 1972.
  Troilus and Criseyde, edited by W. Caxton.   1484; edited by R. K. Root, 1926; Corpus
     Christi College, Cambridge, Manuscript, 1977.
  The House of Fame, edited by W. Caxton.   1484.
  The Book of the Duchess, in *Works.*   1526.
  The Legend of Good Women, in *Works.*   1526.
  The Romaunt of the Rose, in *Works.*   1532; edited by R. Sutherland, 1967.

Other

  The Book of the Astrolabe, in *Works.*   1526; edited by R. T. Gunther, 1930.

  Translator, *The Consolation of Philosophy,* by Boethius, edited by W. Caxton.   1478.

Bibliography: *A Bibliography of Chaucer* by A. S. Cook, 1886; *Five Hundred Years of Chaucer Criticism and Allusion* by C. F. E. Spurgeon, 3 vols., 1925; *Bibliography of Chaucer 1908–53* by D. D. Griffith, 1955, supplement by W. R. Crawford, 1967.

Reading List: *Chaucer and His Poetry* by George Lyman Kittredge, 1916; *The Poet Chaucer* by Nevill Coghill, 1947; *The Mind and Art of Chaucer* by J. S. P. Tatlock, 1950; *Chaucer* by D. S. Brewer, 1953, revised edition, 1973; *Of Sondry Folk: The Dramatic Principle in the Canterbury Tales* by R. M. Lumiansky, 1955; *A Reader's Guide to Chaucer* by Muriel Bowden, 1965; *Chaucer Life Records* edited by M. M. Crow and C. C. Olson, 1966; *Chaucer* by John Lawlor, 1968; *Chaucer: An Introduction* by S. S. Hussey, 1971; *Chaucer and the English Tradition* by Ian Robinson, 1961; *Chaucer and the Making of English Poetry* by P. K. Kean, 2 vols., 1972; *Chaucer's Dream Poems* by James Winny, 1973; *Chaucer* by John

Norton-Smith, 1974; *Chaucer: The Critical Heritage* edited by D. S. Brewer, 2 vols., 1976; *The Life and Times of Chaucer*, 1977, and *The Poetry of Chaucer*, 1977, both by John Gardner.

*   *   *

The appreciation of Geoffrey Chaucer has suffered a good deal in the past from his reputation as the "Father of English poetry." It has been easy to think of him as a "naif," the possessor of a charming simplicity of outlook which tends to convey itself, for a modern reader, through language considered "picturesque" or simply childish, alternately "quaint" or redolent of innocence for readers who think of themselves as more sophisticated and more psychologically complex.

All this is a long way from the truth about Chaucer, whose work is not so much the beginning as the fruit of a long development of civilization, and whose personality, as reflected in that work, is subtle, penetrating, and very deliberately elusive. His early poems show him engaged in exploring the possibilities of the English language as an instrument for sophisticated literary creation. The earliest poem of any length, *The Book of the Duchess* (1370), was almost certainly written as a eulogy for the recently dead Blanche, Duchess of Lancaster, in the form of a consolation addressed to her husband, John of Gaunt. Adapting the conventions of a love-vision to the purposes of an elegy it handles its theme with the exquisite tact which the delicate subject-matter must have required, and contrives in the process to reflect seriously, but without pretentious solemnity, on the natural grief to which bereavement gives rise, and on the need to temper that grief with a realistic acceptance of the humanly inevitable.

A second poem, *The House of Fame*, which must have been written some years later, was left conspicuously unfinished, as though Chaucer, having reached the moment of climax towards which he was moving, felt dissatisfied with the nature of his effort and impelled to make a fresh beginning. Before breaking off, he contrives to present himself in a typically self-depreciatory way and, in the process of reflecting on the nature and uncertainty of literary fame, to direct a good deal of unemphatic satire at the expense of his more serious poetic predecessors, including very notably Dante. Finally, in *The Parliament of Fowls* (c. 1380), Chaucer marries a dream-vision, based in part on Macrobius's version of Cicero's *Dream of Scipio*, to a vivid debate conducted by very human birds who have assembled before the goddess of Nature to choose their mates on St. Valentine's Day. The poem, which is perhaps the most finished of Chaucer's lesser writings, is marked by an exquisite blend of humour and seriousness; and, as in the other poems, much of its effect is obtained through the gently ironic presence of the narrator-poet, simultaneously involved in his creation and inviting on the part of the reader a saving detachment in its regard.

These early works led eventually, in *Troilus and Criseyde* (c. 1379–1383), to the first of Chaucer's two mature masterpieces: a long poem which clearly invites comparison, by its scope and universality, with the great Italian models – Dante, Petrarch, Boccaccio – which had by now in part replaced or supplemented the original French sources of his inspiration, and which he clearly thought of as capable of standing with the great poets of classical antiquity – "Virgil, Ovide, Omer, Lucan and Stace," as he lists them in bringing his poem to a conclusion – and of being incorporated as a work in the vernacular into the great tradition to which he asserted his right of entry.

Troilus and Criseyde is the first great poem to be written in what we can call "modern" English. Based principally on Boccaccio's treatment of the story in his *Filostrato*, Chaucer's poem shows him notably expanding his subject matter and, in the process, giving it an entirely new dimension. Boccaccio's is the story of two young lovers who conduct their relationship on lines laid down by the literary convention of courtly love and who are frustrated by the adverse external reality represented by the Trojan war. The tone is sophisticated, and on occasion cynical, and the author is evidently remembering, as he writes, his own vain attachment to the Napolitan lady Maria d'Aquino. Chaucer, by comparison, notably "medievalizes" his source and invites us, through his typically ambivalent narrator, both to participate in the unhappy story of love ending in betrayal and to see the events described in the light of a "philosophic" vision which sees disappointment and betrayal as the inevitable alternative face of "romantic" love. His pair of lovers, whom he treats with a marvellously sustained blend of detachment and sympathy, differs from those of Boccaccio in being notably young, inexperienced, and insecure, while the figure of the go-between, Pandarus, who plays a relatively minor role in the Italian story, is developed with a humour and psychological depth so far unparalleled in English literature. The result is a poem of superb and balanced humanity which, taking for a background the always relevant reality of the Trojan war, concentrates on the interlocking fortunes of three central personages, giving at each turn a new sense of depth to old conventions and inserting them into a narrative progress geared at each moment to the larger processes of a destinally conceived universe and conducted to its necessary conclusion through deceptively fluent, forward-moving verse.

If it can be argued that *Troilus and Criseyde* is Chaucer's most "artistic" and his most deliberately contrived poem, *The Canterbury Tales*, the writing of which occupied the last fifteen years of his life and remained unfinished at his death, constitutes unquestionably his greatest work. Aiming at the portrayal of a society, a "fellowship," on its various levels, it imparts to each of the individuals taking part in a journey, a pilgrimage to the shrine of St. Thomas Becket at Canterbury, a significance that emerges as more than merely personal (though it always remains certainly, and splendidly, all that is implied by *that*), to produce finally the effect of something like an allegory, a figural reflection of human life in time. As William Blake put it, over four hundred years later: "Of Chaucer's characters, as described in his Canterbury Tales, some of the names are altered by Time, but the Characters themselves for ever remain unaltered and consequently they are the Physiognomies or lineaments of Universal Human Life beyond which Nature never steps."

The Canterbury Tales is a series of stories told by an interacting group of characters in the course of a journey which is seen, in accordance with a common medieval conception, as an image of human life in time. The pilgrims travel from the Tabard Inn in Southwark to Canterbury, where they will recognize their sins and hear Mass at the shrine of "the holy blisful martir": but their journey is, beyond this, a "figure" for that of each and every man from birth to death, and in his quest for fulfilment in the "heavenly Jerusalem," outside and beyond the temporal process, which is his final and necessary goal. In the course of the journey the tales told by the pilgrims illuminate their respective natures and respond to significant facets of human life; and, as they move onwards, they are shown reacting to one another, more especially in the vivid interludes which constitute one of Chaucer's most significant contributions to his theme. Some of the interventions – more especially those of the Knight, the Wife of Bath, and the Pardoner – are so developed as to constitute nodal points around which it seems that the matter of the pilgrimage is largely concentrated; and beyond this, beyond the tales in their rich variety, we are aware throughout of a subtle distinction between the pilgrim-narrator, participating in the journey and responding with apparent naivety to much of what he sees, and the poet shaping his material from outside and lending to it his own detached, humorous, and barely definable irony. The final impression, as the journey draws to its close, is one of the necessity, and the limitation, of tale-telling in its relation to whatever "truth" men may be able to discern in the course of their common journey through life. The poet has given imaginative life to all his creatures – to the Miller not less than to the Knight whom he sets out to "quite," to the Pardoner not less than to the Parson, to the Wife of Bath not less than to the Clerk who tells the story of the "patient" Griselda. By so doing, and by refusing to reduce the complexity of life to an arid or impoverishing moralizing scheme, he has been true to the nature of his vocation as he has come to understand it in the course of a life-time devoted to the working out of its full implications. The same regard for "truth," however, impels him to recognize at the last that imaginative creation has its limits, and that what is, on its own terms, complete, valid, and satisfying is necessarily the *shadow*, the incomplete and partial reflection of a greater reality to which it points but which it cannot, in its time-conditioned and transient humanity, expect to compass.

Towards the end of *The Franklin's Tale*, Chaucer puts into the mouth of his central character the phrase "Trouthe is the hyeste thyng that man may kepe." The word "trouthe," indeed, in its medieval acceptance, which is considerably more ample than that generally associated with our modern "truth," seems to come closer than any other to conveying Chaucer's distinctive sense of human life. "Trouthe" is, in the first instance, the reality of things, which men at their peril ignore or seek to distort in the interest of their desire to live comfortably in the pursuit of illusion. As such it needs to be accepted in a spirit of "patience," by which Chaucer means not an attitude of supine or unnatural resignation, but rather a realistic acceptance of what is not subject to change or manipulation. But "trouthe" is also that "trust" by which men realize their *human* "truth": the trust which is based on an understanding of the "bond" by which they are drawn together and in recognition of which they fulfil their essential humanity. Finally, "trouthe" is also related to the word "betroth" and so with "marriage," in which the free and mutual gift of self becomes, for man, the central manifestation of the universal "bond" by recognizing which men and women incorporate themselves into the order of a universe conceived as a manifestation of creative, overflowing "love." In this cluster of related and mutually illuminating meanings concentrated on the rich connotations of a single word, we touch perhaps most closely the essential source of Chaucer's inspiration.

—Derek A. Traversi

CHIVERS, Thomas Holley. American. Born in Washington, Georgia, 18 October 1809. Educated at a preparatory school in Georgia, and at Transylvania University, Lexington, Kentucky, M.D. (honors) 1830. Married twice; married second wife, Harriet Hunt, in 1834; two sons, two daughters. Gave up medicine soon after graduation, and thereafter devoted himself to literature, contributing to numerous periodicals throughout his life; settled near Decatur, Georgia, c. 1840; contributed to Poe's *Graham's Magazine*, met Poe, 1845, and was later involved in a controversy about plagiarism of Poe's work. *Died 18 December 1858.*

PUBLICATIONS

Collections

    Chivers: A Selection, edited by Lewis Chase. 1929.
    Correspondence 1838–1858, edited by Emma Lester Chase and Lois Ferry Parks. 1957.

Verse

    The Path of Sorrow; or, The Lament of Youth. 1832.
    Nacoochee; or, The Beautiful Star. 1834.
    The Pleiad and Other Poems. 1845.

Search after Truth; or, A New Revelation of the Psycho-Physiological Nature of Man.   1848.
Eonchs of Ruby: A Gift of Love.   1851; revised edition, as *Memoralia; or, Phials of Amber Full of the Tears of Love,* 1853.
Virginalia; or, Songs of My Summer Nights: A Gift of Love for the Beautiful.   1853.
Atlanta; or, The True Blessed Island of Poesy: A Paul Epic in Three Lustra.   1853.
Birth-Day Song of Liberty: A Paean of Glory for the Heroes of Freedom.   1856.

Plays

Conrad and Eudora; or, The Death of Alonzo.   1834.
The Sons of Usna: A Tragi-Apotheosis.   1858.

Other

Life of Poe, edited by Richard Beale Davis.   1952.

Bibliography: in *Bibliography of American Literature* by Jacob Blanck, 1957.

Reading List: *Chivers* (with selections) by S. Foster Damon, 1930; *Chivers: His Literary Career and Poetry* by Charles H. Watts, 1956; "Chivers, Mystic" by Edd W. Parks, in *Ante-Bellum Southern Criticism,* 1962.

*   *   *

Unlike many of his American and Southern contemporaries, Thomas Holley Chivers was free to devote himself to poetry since he had independent means, and, though he could hardly be called a professional man of letters, he took literature seriously and developed a theory of poetry and an aesthetic. Over a period of twenty-five years he published, usually at his own expense, a great deal of verse and a smattering of prose in periodicals in Washington and Decatur, Georgia, as well as occasionally in the *Knickerbocker* and *Graham's,* and in book form in Macon, Georgia, and Franklin, Tennessee, as well as in New York and Philadelphia.

Chivers's theory of poetry as expressed in his prefaces to his collections of poems, especially *Nacoochee, Memoralia,* and *Atlanta,* and in his unpublished and incomplete articles and lectures is, according to Edd W. Parks, that true poetry is "divinely inspired" and the poet is "at once the mediator and the revelator of God." "Poets," Chivers says in "The Beauties of Poetry," "are the apostles of divine thought, who are clothed with an authority from the Most High, to work miracles in the minds of men." The poet sees all things with "*internal,* or spiritual eyes," though, admittedly, celestial beauty can only be partially glimpsed on earth. Still, the inspired writer can recognize transcendental truth and can "convey the idea of a heavenly truth by an earthly one."

In his own practice Chivers tried the usual forms – drama, ode, sonnet, narrative – but he gradually became fascinated with rhythm, diction, and sound, and his experimentation with ballad-like forms, refrains, and language in his last three collections led him to a special vocabulary and declamatory style that manifest themselves, among others, in "Lily Adair," "Avalon," "Apollo," and "Rosalie Lee."

The first and last of these poems, to be sure, suggest the work of Poe, and, despite a certain amount of critical attention in the past twenty years, Chivers's work is still largely of interest because of its relationship to Poe's. The thorny problems of precedence and influence have not yet been fully resolved, despite recent efforts by scholars interested in each poet. Even if it is established that Chivers provided Poe with hints concerning rhythm, meter, and refrain, the disinterested critic can only conclude with Jay B. Hubbell in *The South in American Literature* that Poe's supposed "borrowings" are "all assimilated and transformed into something original and Poesque." This, of course, is to say nothing of Chivers's borrowings from Poe, nor to mention that nothing was said of plagiarism until Poe was dead.

Whatever one may say, however, of the Poe-Chivers matter, one must also conclude that Chivers's work, erratic and uneven as it may be, is fascinating in its own right and deserves more critical consideration than it has hitherto received.

—Rayburn S. Moore

CHURCHILL, Charles. English. Born in Westminster, London, February 1732. Educated at Westminster School, 1741–48; St. John's College, Cambridge, 1748. Married Martha Scott in 1749 (separated, c. 1760); one daughter, two sons. Ordained deacon, 1754: Curate of South Cadbury and Sparkford, Somerset, 1754–56, and of Rainham, Essex (to his father), 1756–58; Curate (and lectureship), St. John's, Westminster, 1758–63. Tutor at Mrs. Dennis's School for Girls, London, 1758. Bankrupt, c. 1760. Resigned Orders in the Church, 1763. Associated with John Wilkes and the *North Briton*, 1762–63; with Wilkes, member of the "Hell-Fire Club." *Died 4 November 1764.*

PUBLICATIONS

Collections

> *Poetical Works*, edited by Douglas Grant.   1956.
> *Poems*, edited by James Laver.   1970.

Verse

> *The Rosciad.*   1761; revised edition, 1763.
> *The Apology.*   1761.
> *Night: An Epistle to Robert Lloyd.*   1761.
> *The Ghost.*   3 vols., 1761–63.
> *The Conference.*   1763.
> *The Author.*   1763.
> *An Epistle to William Hogarth.*   1763.
> *The Prophecy of Famine: A Scots Pastoral.*   1763.
> *Poems.*   2 vols., 1763–65.
> *The Duellist.*   1764.
> *The Candidate.*   1764.
> *Gotham.*   3 vols., 1764.

Independence. 1764.
The Times. 1764.
The Farewell. 1764.
The Journey: A Fragment. 1765.

Other

The North Briton, with John Wilkes and others. 3 vols., 1763.
Sermons. 1765.
Correspondence of Wilkes and Churchill, edited by E. H. Weatherley. 1954.

Bibliography: in *Seven 18th-Century Bibliographies* by Iolo A. Williams, 1924.

Reading List: *The North Briton* by G. Nobbe, 1939; *Churchill, Poet, Rake, and Rebel* by Wallace Cable Brown, 1953; *Portraits in Satire* by Kenneth Hopkins, 1958; *Forms of Discovery* by Yvor Winters, 1967.

*   *   *

Charles Churchill, in Byron's phrase, "blazed the comet of a season." His poetic career in fact lasted for about three years, and his admirers hailed him as "the British Juvenal." Subsequently his verse has been largely neglected, though not wholly with desert. It is true that the subjects of his satire are to a considerable degree ephemeral, and that he failed to give them that universality which would have made them enduring. His first poem, *The Rosciad,* gained him much acclaim, and is still of interest to those concerned with eighteenth-century theatrical history. *The Ghost,* in octosyllabic couplets, dealing with the episode of the "Cock Lane Ghost," is remembered for its unsympathetic portrait of Samuel Johnson as "pomposo, insolent and loud." Most of Churchill's other satires were written in the hurly-burly of party politics – clearly hastily – and are unequal in quality. But they possess remarkable energy and, at times, power.

The tradition of classical Augustan satire in Dryden, Swift, Pope, Johnson, and Goldsmith is a Tory one. The writer is able to criticise society as a moralist, from the point of view of a set of traditional values which are assumed to be universal and permanent. With Churchill, associated as he was with the Radicalism of Wilkes, the stance is necessarily somewhat different, and his work ought perhaps to be judged by rather different criteria. He abandoned the polished epigrammatic couplet, as it had been perfected by Pope, for a style marked by some of the original vigour of Dryden. Like Dryden, he tends to make the paragraph rather than the couplet the unit of his thought; but wanting Dryden's supreme technical mastery, he arrives too often at an effect of breathlessness. His language is strong and masculine, but he lacks alike the harmony and the memorability of Dryden. Cowper, who admired Churchill's work, learnt from him a certain conversational and colloquial ease (less rigid than the Popean model), though modulating it from the Juvenalian to the Horatian manner.

We have already mentioned Byron in connection with Churchill. When Byron visited the earlier poet's grave at Boulogne, he saw in him in some sense a forerunner. There are confessional passages in parts of Churchill's work, for example in *The Candidate,* which do partly make him the harbinger of Romanticism. The final line of his last poem *The Journey* – "I on my journey all alone proceed" – has this kind of resonance.

—John Heath-Stubbs

CHURCHYARD, Thomas. English. Born in Shrewsbury, Shropshire, in 1520. Married. Served as a page to the Earl of Surrey; lived a wandering life, partly as a soldier and partly as a hanger-on of the court and nobility, hoping, unsuccessfully, for preferment: served under Sir William Drury in Scotland, and thereafter in Ireland, the Low Countries, and France; served under Lord Grey for eight years. Granted a pension by Queen Elizabeth I, 1592. *Died 4 April 1604.*

PUBLICATIONS

Verse

A Mirror for Man. 1552; revised edition, 1594.
The Contention Betwixt Churchyard and Camell upon David Dycer's Dream (flyting pamphlets). 1560.
Shore's Wife, in *A Mirror for Magistrates.* 1563; *Thomas Wolsey,* in 1587 edition; edited by Lily B. Campbell, 1938.
A Farewell Called Churchyard's Round. 1566.
A Greater Thanks for Churchyard's Welcome Home. 1566.
Churchyard's Lamentation of Friendship. 1566.
Churchyard's Farewell. 1566.
The Epitaph of the Earl of Pembroke. 1570.
The First Three Books of Ovid's De Tristibus Translated. 1572.
Churchyard's Chips, part 1. 1575.
A Pleasant Labyrinth Called Churchyard's Chance. 1580.
The Epitaph of Sir Philip Sidney. 1587.
A Light Bundle of Lively Discourses Called Churchyard's Charge. 1580; edited by John Payne Collier, 1870.
A Reviving of the Dead. 1591.
A Handful of Gladsome Verses Given to the Queen's Majesty at Woodstock. 1592.
A Feast Full of Sad Cheer. 1592.
Churchyard's Challenge. 1593.
The Mirror of Man, and Manners of Men. 1594; edited by A. Boswell, in *Frondes Caducae,* 1816.
The Honour of the Law. 1596.
A Sad Funeral of Sir F. Knowles. 1596; edited by A. Boswell, in *Frondes Caducae,* 1816.
A Pleasant Discourse of Court and Wars Called His Cherishing. 1596; edited by A. Boswell, in *Frondes Caducae,* 1816.
The Fortunate Farewell to the Earl of Essex. 1599; edited by J. Nichols, in *Progresses of Queen Elizabeth,* 1788–1823.
The Wonders of the Air, The Trembling of the Earth. 1602.
Sorrowful Verses on the Death of Queen Elizabeth. 1604; edited by Hyder E. Rollins and H. Baker, in *The Renaissance in England,* 1954.
Churchyard's Good Will: An Epitaph for the Archbishop of Canterbury. 1604; edited by H. Huth, in *Fugitive Tracts 2,* 1875.

Plays

The Whole Order How Queen Elizabeth Was Received into the City of Bristol (produced 1574). 1575.

A Discourse of the Queen's Majesty's Entertainment in Suffolk and Norfolk, A Welcome Home to M. Frobisher, A Commendation of Sir H. Gilbert's Venturous Journey. 1578.

A Pleasant Conceit Presented to the Queen's Majesty. 1593; edited by J. Nichols, in Progresses of Queen Elizabeth, 1788–1823.

A Musical Consort Called Churchyard's Charity; A Praise of Poetry Out of Sir Philip Sidney. 1595; edited by A. Boswell, in Frondes Caducae, 1816.

Other

Come Bring in May with Me: A Discourse of Rebellion   1570.

A Praise and Report of Master Martin Frobisher's Voyage to Meta Incognita.   1578.

A Lamentable and Pitiful Description of the Woeful Wars in Flanders.   1578.

The Misery of Flanders, Calamity of France, Misfortune of Portugal.   1579.

The Most True Report of James Fitz Morrice' Death.   1579(?).

A Warning for the Wise of the Late Earthquake.   1580.

A Plain Report of the Taking of Macklin.   1580.

A Scourge for Rebels.   1584.

The Worthiness of Wales.   1587; edited by C. E. Simms, 1876.

A Spark of Friendship and Warm Good Will; A Description of a Paper-Mill Built by M. Spilman.   1588; edited by J. Nichols, in Progresses of Queen Elizabeth, 1788–1823.

A Wished Reformation of Wicked Rebellion.   1598.

Editor, The Censure of a Loyal Subject, by George Whetstone.   1587.

Editor, Giacomo di Grassi His True Art of Defence Englished by I. G.   1594.

Translator, with R. Robinson, A True Discourse of the Succeeding Governors in the Netherlands and the Civil Wars There, by E. van Meteren.   1602.

Reading List: Churchyard by H. W. Adnitt, 1880 (includes bibliography).

*   *   *

Thomas Churchyard wrote a score of narrative and descriptive poems, most of them black-letter broadsides, with alliterative titles like Churchyard's Chips and Churchyard's Challenge. He began his poetic career in the early 1550's with a collection of wooden, didactic verses, A Mirror for Man, and was still writing in the same drab, early Tudor style into the reign of James I. His longevity is alluded to by Spenser in Colin Clout, wherein Churchyard is "Old Palaemon" who "sung so long until quite hoarse he grew." Most of his poems are descriptive or narrative, and reflect his experiences as a minor courtier and professional soldier. His Woeful Wars in Flanders is rich in autobiographical reminiscences, and The Worthiness of Wales is still worth reading for its occasional descriptive power. Churchyard wrote numerous elegies on Elizabethan worthies such as his early patron, the Earl of Surrey, and contributed poems to the first edition of Tottel's Miscellany. His best poem is "Shore's Wife," the narrative he contributed to the second edition of William Baldwin's A Mirror for Magistrates. Churchyard's concluding observation on the sad fate of Jane Shore, Edward IV's much-abused mistress ("And bent the wand that might have grown full straight") was picked up by Marlowe to form his famous epilogue to *Doctor Faustus:* "Cut is the branch that might have grown full straight."

—James E. Ruoff

CLARE, John.   English.   Born in Helpston, Northamptonshire, 13 July 1793. Educated at a local dame school, and at schools in Glinton, Northamptonshire, to age 16. Married Martha Turner in 1820; seven children. Farm labourer; worked for Francis Gregory, 1809–10, and as gardener at Burghley House, 1810–11; attracted brief celebrity as "peasant-poet" on publication of his first volume, 1820; ill after 1830: committed to High Beech asylum for the insane, Epping, Essex, 1837–41, and to St. Andrew's Asylum, near Northampton, 1841–64. *Died 20 May 1864.*

PUBLICATIONS

Collections

> *Poems,* edited by J. W. Tibble.   2 vols., 1935.
> *Poems of Clare's Madness,* edited by Geoffrey Grigson.   1949.
> *Prose, Letters,* edited by J. W. and Anne Tibble.   2 vols., 1951.
> *Later Poems,* edited by Eric Robinson and Geoffrey Summerfield.   1964.
> *Selected Poems and Prose,* edited by Eric Robinson and Geoffrey Summerfield.   1966

Verse

> *Poems Descriptive of Rural Life and Scenery.*   1820.
> *The Village Minstrel and Other Poems.*   2 vols., 1821.
> *The Shepherd's Calendar, with Village Stories and Other Poems.*   1827; edited by Eric
>   Robinson and Geoffrey Summerfield, 1964.
> *The Rural Muse.*   1835.
> *Poems Chiefly from Manuscript,* edited by Edmund Blunden and Alan Porter.   1920.
> *Madrigals and Chronicles, Being Newly Found Poems,* edited by Edmund
>   Blunden.   1924.
> *The Midsummer Cushion,* edited by Anne Tibble.   1978.

Other

> *Sketches in the Life of Clare by Himself,* edited by Edmund Blunden.   1931.

Reading List: *Clare: A Life,* 1932, revised edition, 1972, and *Clare: His Life and Poetry,* 1956, both by J. W. and Anne Tibble; *The Idea of Landscape and the Sense of Place 1730–1840: An Approach to the Poetry of Clare* by John Barrell, 1972; *Clare: The Critical Heritage* edited by Mark Storey, 1973, and *The Poetry of Clare* by Storey, 1974.

*   *   *

John Clare was born in the village of Helpston (then Helpstone) in Northamptonshire. In that rural setting, except for a move three miles to the fen village of Northborough in 1832, he remained until he was incarcerated in first one asylum and then a second where he spent 27 years of his life. Clare's father was a flail-thresher who, Clare said, could recite over a hundred ballads and songs. His mother, a shepherd's daughter, also sang ballads and told traditional stories.

Contemporary with Blake, Keats, Shelley, and Byron, Clare is still not recognized as a poet of the first standing; yet he is the foremost English poet of the countryside. His poetry divides into two kinds. Most was descriptive, often repetitive, verse concerning an England changing, after 500 years of stability under a system of "common fields," to a system of "enclosure." Bigger "enclosed" farms were already beginning to use the mechanical methods that have resulted in today's "factory" farming with less of the hard labour in which leisure was an important part of work. Beside the major part of his poetry on country life and on nature, Clare wrote a small but important amount of reflective, visionary poetry.

His first poems were attempts at "imitations of my father's songs," but he burnt them during the many years of the long apprenticeship he set himself. In 1820 Clare's first book of poems was published by the London publisher of Keats, Lamb, and Hood – John Taylor. This, with the clumsy title of *Poems Descriptive of Rural Life and Scenery*, caught the end of a temporary vogue in country verse, went into four editions within a year, and was an undoubted success. Clare visited London, was "lionized," and returned to inevitable isolation at Helpston. His other books, *The Village Minstrel, The Shepherd's Calendar*, and *The Rural Muse*, did not, however, sell. An important manuscript, *The Midsummer Cushion*, having lain unprinted for a century and a half, was published in 1978.

By 1837 the strain of writing, poverty, and the needs of his parents and growing family began to tell on Clare. He developed illusions – that he was Lord Byron (the *successful* poet), a wrestler Tom Spring, a boxer Jack Randall; that his childhood love, Mary Joyce, was his first wife, while Patty, mother of his children, was but his second. With the help of his publisher Clare was sent to High Beech, a private asylum in Essex – he was there for four years. In the summer of 1841 he escaped "those jailors called warders" and walked the 80 miles home to Northborough. For five months he was at home, finishing two long poems with Byronic titles, "Don Juan" and "Child Harold." His physical health improved but his delusions were as strong as ever. In December 1841 Clare was certified insane by two doctors and confined to St. Andrew's asylum near Northampton. He was allowed freedom to walk into the town and encouraged to continue to write. Here he wrote over a thousand verses, some traditional jingle, but a few important to his achievement.

Edmund Blunden introduced Clare to the present century with *Poems Chiefly from Manuscript* of 1920. Clare's half-dozen or so reflective lyrics of his St. Andrew's period contain "Love Lies Beyond the Tomb," "An Invite to Eternity," "I Am," "A Vision," "Hesperus," "Love's Story," "I Hid My Love," and "Love's Pains." A few more mystical, reflective poems lie scattered among the bulk of his country, descriptive work. This handful of lyrics, rhythmically new, Edmund Blunden writes, places Clare where "William Blake and only he can be said to resemble him." Geoffrey Grigson believes that they push Clare into "greatness, however circumscribed that greatness." They are concerned with the confusion into which, during man's civilized development, sexual love has fallen, from its original innocence.

From "An Invite to Eternity":

> Wilt thou go with me, sweet maid,
> Say, maiden, wilt thou go with me
> Through the valley-depths of shade,
> Of night and dark obscurity;
> Where the path has lost its way,
> Where the sun forgets the day,
> Where there's no life nor light to see,
> Sweet maiden, wilt thou go with me?...

The land of shadows wilt thou trace,
And look – nor know each other's face;
The present mixed with reason gone,
And past and present all as one?
Say, maiden, can thy life be led
To join the living with the dead?
Then trace thy footsteps on with me;
We're wed to one eternity.

Clare's major work, his country verse, with, as De Quincey wrote, scarcely one "commonplace image," remains: sonnets on the blackcap, the reed-bird, the redcap, in fact hundreds on animals, flowers, birds, in what he saw as an "Eternity of Nature." He was a non-scientific but excellent naturalist:

Within a thick and spreading hawthorn bush
    That overhung a mole-hill large and round,
I heard from morn to morn a merry thrush
    Sing hymns to sunrise, while I drank the sound
With joy; and often an intruding guest,
    I watched her secret toils from day to day –
How true she warped the moss to form a nest,
    And modelled it within with wood and clay;
And by and by, like heath-bells gilt with dew,
    There lay her shining eggs, as bright as flowers,
Ink-spotted over shells of greeny blue;
    And there I witnessed, in the sunny hours,
A brood of nature's minstrels chirp and fly,
Glad as that sunshine and the laughing sky.

Clare's mental disorder was cyclothymic. He endured this form of insanity in common with Hölderlin, Smart, Cowper, Newton, Goethe, and Samuel Johnson. It is a sickness to which men of broad general powers coupled with a sensitive imagination are naturally exposed.

—Anne Tibble

CLARK, John Pepper. Nigerian. Born in Kiagbolo, 6 April 1935. Educated at Warri Government College, Ughelli, 1948–54; University of Ibadan, 1955–60, B. A. (honours) in English 1960; Princeton University, New Jersey (Parvin Fellowship), 1962–63; University of Ibadan (Institute of African Studies Research Fellowship, 1961–64). Married; has one daughter. Nigerian Government Information Officer, 1960–61; Head of Features and Editorial Writer, *Daily Express*, Lagos, 1961–62. Founding Editor, *The Horn* magazine, Ibadan. Since 1964, Member of the English Department, and currently Professor of English, University of Lagos. Founding Member, Society of Nigerian Authors. Lives in Lagos.

Verse

>Poems.   1962.
>*A Reed in the Tide: A Selecton of Poems.*   1965.
>*Casualties: Poems 1966–1968.*   1970.

Plays

>*Song of a Goat* (produced 1961).   1961.
>*Three Plays: Song of a Goat, The Raft, The Masquerade.*   1964.
>*The Masquerade* (produced 1965).   In *Three Plays,* 1964.
>*The Raft* (broadcast 1966).   In *Three Plays,* 1964.
>*Ozidi.*   1966.

>Screenplays (documentaries): *The Ozidi of Atazi; The Ghost Town.*

>Radio Play: *The Raft,* 1966.

Other

>*America, Their America*   1964.
>*Example of Shakespeare: Critical Essays on African Literature.*   1970.

*   *   *

John Pepper Clark says about himself in the introduction to *A Reed in the Tide* that he is "a cultural mulatto." In this way he draws attention to the fact that his outlook is the result of a synthesis of two different cultures, the traditional Nigerian and the modern Western. This is reflected in his authorship which deals with traditional Ijaw myths as well as the modern American way of life which he criticizes from the point of view of an outsider, bringing an African sensibility to bear on the excesses of modern society. On the other hand his choice of the English language is deliberate, born of the desire to reach as many people as possible.

Clark is playwright, poet and prose writer. *Three Plays* contains *Song of a Goat, The Masquerade,* and *The Raft.* The first two plays deal with the tragic events that befall a family in the Niger river delta as a result of an initial crime against the gods. The plays move with a relentless inevitability towards final death and destruction, and the prevailing atmosphere of doom as well as a dramatic use of a chorus show Clark's debt to classical Greek drama. The subject matter, however, is firmly rooted in traditional tales from the Niger delta. *The Raft* is about a group of fishermen set adrift on a raft on the Niger drawing towards their final destruction in the whirlpools at the mouth of the river. The play explores the psychology of the fishermen, but it is also capable of an allegorical interpretation dealing with the Biafran war and Nigerian unity. In *Ozidi* Clark returns to the traditional Ijaw myth. *Ozidi* is based on an Ijaw saga, which took seven days to tell and was accompanied by music and mime. In all the plays the language is very poetic and imaginative, rich in metaphors which are often surprisingly fresh and which show Clark's ability as a poet.

A Reed in the Tide is a collection of occasional poems, varied in aspect and theme (visual images, moral reflections, myths), written in free verse, often deliberately echoing Dylan Thomas or W. H. Auden. The poem "Night Rain," describing a heavy tropical downpour in the wet and swampy Niger delta stands out as an excellent example of successful nature poetry about exotic places.

Casualties deals with the Biafran war. Clark was very close to the events and had an inside knowledge which is denied the ordinary reader, and the collection is therefore heavily glossed and cannot be read without an intimate knowledge of the movements of the war.

As a prose writer Clark has chosen "straight reporting" as his medium for his criticism of America in *America, Their America*. The criticism is flamboyant and often idiosyncratic.

From his writings Clark emerges as a person with strong beliefs, tempered with a compassion and tenderness which appear mainly in his poetry.

—Kirsten Holst Petersen

CLARKE, Austin. Irish. Born in Dublin, 9 May 1896. Educated at Belvedere College, Dublin; University College, Dublin, M.A. Married Nora Walker; three sons. Lecturer in English, University College, Dublin, 1917–21; book reviewer in London, 1923–37, also Assistant Editor, *Argosy*, London, 1929; returned to Ireland as free-lance reviewer and broadcaster, 1937. Founding Member, 1932, and President, 1952–54, Irish Academy of Letters; President, Irish P.E.N., 1939–42, 1946–49. Chairman, Dublin Verse Speaking Society, and Lyric Theatre Company; Literary Adviser, Radio Eireann. Recipient: Tailteann Games National Award, 1932; Denis Devlin Memorial Award, 1964; Arts Council Special Poetry Prize, 1964; Irish Academy of Letters Gregory Medal, 1968. D. Litt.: Trinity College, Dublin, 1966. *Died 19 March 1974.*

PUBLICATIONS

Collections

   Collected Poems, edited by Liam Miller.   1974.
   Selected Poems, edited by Thomas Kinsella.   1976.

Verse

   The Vengeance of Fionn.   1917.
   The Fires of Baäl.   1921.
   The Sword of the West.   1921.
   The Cattledrive in Connaught and Other Poems.   1925.
   Pilgrimage and Other Poems.   1929.
   The Collected Poems.   1936.
   Night and Morning.   1938.
   The Straying Student.   1944.
   Ancient Lights: Poems and Satires.   1955.
   Too Great a Vine: Poems and Satires.   1957.
   The Horse-Eaters: Poems and Satires.   1960.

Collected Later Poems.   1961.
Forget-Me-Not.   1962.
Flight to Africa and Other Poems.   1963.
Poems: A Selection, with Tony Connor and Charles Tomlinson.   1964.
Mnemosyne Lay in Dust.   1966.
Old-Fashioned Pilgrimage and Other Poems.   1967.
The Echo at Coole and Other Poems.   1968.
A Sermon on Swift and Other Poems.   1968.
Orphide.   1970.
Tiresias: A Poem.   1971.

Plays

The Son of Learning (produced 1927).   1927.
The Flame (produced 1932).   1930.
Sister Eucharia (produced 1941).   1939.
Black Fast (produced 1941).   1941.
As the Crow Flies (broadcast 1942).   1943.
The Kiss, from a play by Théodore de Banville (produced 1942).   In *The Viscount of Blarney and Other Plot,* 1944.
The Plot Is Ready (produced 1943).   In *The Viscount of Blarney and Other Plays,* 1944.
The Viscount of Blarney (produced 1944).   In *The Viscount of Blarney and Other Plays,* 1944.
The Viscount of Blarney and Other Plays.   1944.
The Second Kiss (produced 1946).   1946.
The Plot Succeeds (produced 1950).   1950.
The Moment Next to Nothing (produced 1958).   1953.
Collected Plays.   1963.
The Student from Salamanca (produced 1966).   In *Two Interludes,* 1968.
Two Interludes Adapted from Cervantes: The Student from Salamanca, and The Silent Lover.   1968.
The Impuritans.   1973.
The Third Kiss.   1976.

Other plays: *Liberty Lane; St Patrick's Purgatory.*

Fiction

The Bright Temptations: A Romance.   1932.
The Singing-Men at Cashel.   1936.
The Sun Dances at Easter: A Romance.   1952.

Other

First Visit to England and Other Memories.   1945.
Poetry in Modern Ireland.   1951; revised edition, 1962.
Twice round the Black Church: Early Memories of Ireland and England.   1962.
A Penny in the Clouds: More Memories of Ireland and England.   1968.
The Celtic Twilight and the Nineties.   1969.

Editor, *The Poems of Joseph Campbell.*   1963.

210

Reading List: *A Tribute to Clarke on His Seventieth Birthday* edited by John Montague and Liam Miller, 1966 (includes bibliography by Miller); *Clarke: His Life and Works* by Susan Halpern, 1974.

*   *   *

Austin Clarke began his literary career in the manner of a Celtic Revival poet, with a number of epic narratives drawn from Irish material. In this he was affected by the work of W. B. Yeats, Standish O'Grady, Samuel Ferguson, and many others poets and scholars who had responded before him to the Irish heritage of myth and saga. He soon developed a more individual response: where Yeats presented a dichotomy between the pagan, aristocratic world of Cuchulain and the democratic present, Clarke dramatised a contrast between the medieval, Christian past and the dogmatic, Catholic present. For him the religious question was central and in his poems, plays, and prose romances the problem of the individual Catholic conscience became part of Irish literature. The conflict is between repressive Church teachings and natural instincts. Clarke's response to the Gaelic past also included the adaptation of various forms of Gaelic prosody to poetry in English; his experiments in prosody, and in the uses of rhyme and assonance, are an important aspect of his poetry.

Clarke's setting for his three prose romances, for many of his verse plays, and for much of the poetry of his middle period is the Celtic-Romanesque period in Ireland that lasted from the introduction of Christianity in the fifth century to the coming of monastic reform at the end of the twelfth. It was a time in which Irish art flourished in the illumination of manuscripts, the making of ornaments, and the building of the round towers and celtic crosses, a time when the country was largely independent of the Roman church and experienced much literary activity. Clarke's work celebrates this period, and he also uses it as a framework of reference through which to comment on his own time. In his work after 1955, he had a renewal of power, producing several books of poetry in which he is both satirical observer of the contemporary scene, warm recorder of his own life, and, finally, the cheerful sensualist in a number of narrative poems based on Irish and classical myth.

Like Joyce, whom he resembles in many ways, Clarke drew strength from his acceptance of things as he found them. Drawn initially to the remote past in the manner of the early Yeats, he later faced up to his personal problems, making poems out of his anguish of conscience, and accepted then the realities of Irish life in the modern period. This ability to appropriate the minutiae of Irish life is based on his characteristic ability to write with precision about sensuous details. Through his long career he has revitalized many aspects of the Irish past, with the result that he is a central figure in Irish poetry.

—Maurice Harmon

CLEVELAND, John.   English.   Born in Loughborough, Leicestershire, baptized 20 June 1613. Educated by Reverend Richard Vynes in Hinckley, Leicestershire; Christ's College, Cambridge, 1627–34, B.A. 1631, M.A. 1635; Rhetoric Reader, 1636, and possibly M.A., 1637, Oxford University. Joined the King at Oxford, 1643; Fellow, St. John's College, Cambridge, 1643–45; served as Judge-Advocate at the garrison at Newark, 1645–46; after defeat of Royalists, subsequent activities unknown until he arrived in Norwich to take up position as tutor, arrested by the Puritan forces, imprisoned at Yarmouth, 1655; released by Cromwell, and lived in various places, probably finally at Gray's Inn, London. *Died 29 April 1658.*

PUBLICATIONS

Collections

Poems, edited by Brian Morris and Eleanor Withington.   1967.

Verse

The Character of a London Diurnal, with Several Select Poems (includes prose).   1645;
   revised edition, as *Poems*, 1651; revised edition, as *Poems, Characters, and Letters*,
   1658.
The Scots' Apostacy.   1646.
The Character of a Moderate Intelligencer, with Some Select Poems (includes
   prose).   1647.
The King's Disguise.   1647.
The Hue and Cry after Sir John Presbyter.   1649.
Cleveland Revived.   1659.
On the Most Renowned Prince Rupert.   N.d.

Other

Majestas Intemerata; or, The Immortality of the King.   1649.
Character of a Country Committee-Man.   1649.
Character of a Diurnal-Maker.   1653.
The Idol of the Clowns; or, The Insurrection of Wat the Tyler.   1654; as *The Rustic
   Rampant*, 1658; as *The Rebellion of the Rude Multitude*, 1658.
Petition to the Lord Protector.   1657.
Clevelandi Vindiciae; or, Cleveland's Genuine Poems, Orations, Epistles, etc.   1677.

Bibliography: *Cleveland: A Bibliography of His Poems* by Brian Morris,   1967.

Reading List: *Cleveland* by Lee A. Jacobus, 1975.

*   *   *

   With John Cleveland the metaphysical mode of John Donne and his school becomes an
academic style in which inventiveness and ingenuity are the sole concerns. A coterie poet
with many admirers in his day who, like the editors of *Clevelandi Vindiciae*, extolled the
intellectual brilliance of his wit, he yet found a detractor in John Dryden, who dubbed
catachresis (the compressed conceit) a wretched "Clevelandism"; and the detractors have
since, by and large, won the day.
   His most frequently attacked poem is the elegy on Edward King (the subject of Milton's
Lycidas), whose beginning illustrates catachresis:

> I like not tears in tune; nor will I prise
> His artificiall grief, that scannes his eyes....
> I am no Poet here: my penne's the spout
> Where the rain-water of my eyes runs out.

The elegy is little more than a series of loosely related ingenious conceits, each of which achieves point and closure, like an epigram, and hence does little more than make a witty "clench" which is then left for another one. Yet, there is a kind of decorum to this elegy, for its disjointed manner illustrates well the mind of the poet disjointed by grief which its opening stresses; Lee A. Jacobus further suggests that his academic audience would see that "in the extremes of his invention are embedded the extremes of his grief." "Fuscara; or, The Bee Errant" and "Upon Phillis Walking in a Morning Before Sun-Rising" are more successful poems; while they lack sequential development, they do have thematic unity that pulls all the conceits together — Fuscara is sweeter than anything, Phillis is like the sun — and the hyperbolic conceits become purposeful in the service of a playful tone. In them, we see the metaphysical poem becoming a display of wit, deflating all assumptions of seriousness by over-inflation; the deliberate seeking of conceits that pull together as unlikely images as possible becomes a comic gambit. His most successful poem is "The Hecatomb to His Mistresse," in which the reader's attention is deliberately drawn to the playful poet's ability to outdo others' praise of their mistresses (even Donne's, line 4) in one hundred lines of extreme conceits, in so doing demonstrating how his mistress excels all thought; as he proceeds through a series of "shifts in gear" (to use a modern catechresis), he takes her first beyond all previous love poetry, then beyond all sensation, finally beyond all imagining.

It is no surprise that Cleveland excels as a satirist, for in satire deliberate hyperbole appears as grotesque humor. In "The Rebell Scot," for instance, deliberate disparity carries the theme of the overturn of natural order by the Scots, and the poet's self-display (as in "The Hecatomb") serves the action of the poem, which is incantation, rhyming the Scots out of existence. Cleveland at his worst is full of tactless self-display; at his best he uses poetry as a kind of incantation, and harnesses the deliberate ingenuity of fancy and far-fetched conceits to the purposes of playful poetic ritual.

—Walter R. Davis

CLOUGH, Arthur Hugh. English. Born in Liverpool, 1 January 1819; lived in Charleston, South Carolina, 1822–28. Educated at a preparatory school in Chester, 1828–29; Rugby School, 1829–37; Balliol College, Oxford, 1837–42. Married Blanche Smith in 1854; two sons, two daughters. Fellow, Oriel College, Oxford, 1842–48 (resigned because unable to subscribe to doctrines of Church of England); Principal, University Hall, a hostel of University College, London, 1849–52; held chair of English Language and Literature, University College, 1851–52; lived in Cambridge, Massachusetts, 1852; Examiner, Education Office, London, 1853–61. *Died 13 November 1861.*

PUBLICATIONS

Collections

Poems, edited by H. F. Lowry, A. L. P. Norrington, and Frederick L. Mulhauser. 1951; revised edition, edited by Mulhauser, 1974.
Correspondence, edited by Frederick L. Mulhauser. 2 vols., 1957.
Selected Prose Works, edited by B. B. Trawick. 1964

Verse

> *The Close of the Eighteenth Century.*   1835.
> *The Longest Day.*   1836.
> *The Bothie of Toper-na-Fuosich.*   1848.
> *Ambarvalia,* with Thomas Burbidge.   1849.
> *Poems.*   1862; revised edition, 1863.

Other

> *Letters and Remains,* edited by Mrs. Clough.   1865.
> *Poems and Prose Remains,* edited by Mrs. Clough.   1869.
> *Emerson-Clough Letters,* edited by H. F. Lowry and R. L. Rusk.   1934.

> Editor, *Plutarch's Lives.*   5 vols., 1859; selections as *Greek History from Themistocles to Alexander,* 1860.

Bibliography: *Clough: A Descriptive Catalogue* by Richard M. Gollin, Walter E. Houghton, and Michael Timko, 1967.

Reading List: *Clough* by Goldie Levy, 1938; *Clough: The Uncommitted Mind* by Katharine Chorley, 1962; *Clough* by Isobel Armstrong, 1962; *The Poetry of Clough: An Essay in Revaluation* by Walter E. Houghton, 1963; *Clough* by Paul Veyriras, 1964; *Innocent Victorian: The Satiric Poetry of Clough* by Michael Timko, 1966; *Clough: The Growth of a Poet's Mind* by Evelyn B. Greenberger, 1970; *Clough: Towards a Reconsideration* by Robindra K. Biswas, 1972; *Clough: The Critical Heritage* edited by Michael Thorpe, 1972.

*   *   *

Troubled by religious doubts, Arthur Hugh Clough – the friend of Matthew Arnold and the subject of his elegy "Thyrsis" – could yet see the comical side of his own and others' vacillations. But since religious doubt could disable the doubter for effective political, or even social action, Clough may justly be styled a serio-comic poet. For his two novels in verse, the poet devised an accentual, not a quantitative, hexameter metre, which admirably suits a range of colloquial tones, by turns witty, ironic, rueful, amused.

The earlier of the two, *The Bothie of Tober-na-Vuolich* (first entitled *The Bothie of Toper-na-Fuosich,* which – though Clough was innocent of the Gaelic meaning – was extremely indecent), relates the events of an Oxford long vacation's reading party in the Highlands of Scotland. There is much that is light-hearted, but the serious and the comic combine in the situation where the undergraduate, Philip Hewson, falls in love with a Scots lassie, Elspie. Is this a *mésalliance?* Hewson has radical political views, is a Chartist, but he is well-connected (his "uncle and cousins,/Sister, and brother, and brother's wife" are of the gentry) and well-educated, while Elspie is the unschooled daughter of a peasant. Besides, earlier in this vacation, Hewson was ready to forswear his socialist views when he was attracted by Lady Maria, the daughter of a Scottish peer. Hewson, after gaining his First at Oxford, does marry Elspeth, but their disparity in social class and background can be easily accepted only in the colonies. They emigrate to New Zealand, where Hewson "hewed, and dug; subdued the earth and his spirit." But Clough is modern enough to be sceptical about idealising love: "Rachel we dream of at night: in the morning, behold, it is Leah."

"Amours de Voyage" is, as one of its epigraphs, "il doutait de tout, même de l'amour," suggests, is wider in its range. It is also more serious but also more deliciously comical: the solemnities of doubt are absurd. The form is epistolary: three of an English party in Rome are writing to their friends at home, and the distinct intonations of voice and cast of mind of the three correspondents are conveyed in a verse of great mimetic virtue.

Claude, over-fastidious, writes to his friend Eustace. Lonely, and with poor Italian, he is dependent for company on an English middle-class family, "not wholly/ Pure of the taint of the shop," whose taste and conversation, as an Oxford Fellow, he cannot refrain from disdaining, despite his attraction towards one of the daughters.

The routine of the English abroad in their *pension* is interrupted by the sudden attack against the Roman Republic. The glamorous, colourful, if operatic, gallantry of the Republic's defenders, among them Garibaldi, issues from a passionate, though unquestioned, simplicity of mind and heart which Eustace, the over-civilized, cannot share. And if the French or Neapolitan soldier should attack Claude's countrywomen, "Am I prepared to lay down my life for the British female? .../Somehow, Eustace, alas! I have not felt the vocation." In doubting everything, Eustace is without the motives for action. The interest he had in Mary Trevellyn fades to Mary's regret. But the question is asked of the tale whether it is "not evil and good"; the poem, on behalf of its poet, replies,

> "I am flitting about many years from brain unto brain of
> Feeble and restless youths born to inglorious days:
> But," so finish the word, "I was written in a Roman chamber
> When from Janiculan heights thundered the Cannon of France."

The doubt as to the worth of significant individual, social, and political action, implicit in "Amours de Voyage," had its foundation and origin in Clough's religious doubts and struggle to believe. His lines, which Churchill made famous during the war, when he applied them to England's military struggle to survive, "Say not the struggle nought availeth," were, in fact, written by Clough to express his intellectual and spiritual struggle with the articles of faith of Christianity. As to the application of those articles, as it was practised in his England, Clough could take a bitterly sardonic view in "The Latest Decalogue" ("Thou shalt not steal; an empty feat,/When it's so lucrative to cheat .../Thou shalt not covet; but tradition/Approves all forms of competition"), while the harsh intensity of "Easter Day: Naples 1849" and of much of "Dipsychus" reveals an anguish surprising to those who had previously only been acquainted with *The Bothie* and "Amours de Voyage" in which the accents of a suave sophistication and amused self-mockery are carried with such graceful assurance.

—Francis Berry

COLERIDGE, Samuel Taylor.   English.   Born in Ottery St. Mary, Devon, 21 October 1772. Educated at the Blue Coat School, Christ's Hospital, London, 1782–90; Jesus College, Cambridge (Christ's Hospital Exhibitioner; Greek Verse Medal), 1791–94; attended classes at the University of Göttingen, 1798. Married Sara Fricker, sister-in-law of the poet Robert Southey, in 1794. Involved with Southey in an abortive scheme for a "pantisocracy" in America, 1794; lived in Bristol, 1794–97; settled at Nether Stowey, Somerset, near the Wordsworths at Alfoxden, 1797; spent winter in Germany with the Wordsworths, 1798; given an annuity by the Wedgwood family, 1798; moved to Greta Hall, Keswick, near Southey, and the Wordsworths at Grasmere, 1800; became addicted to opium and lived in Malta in an effort to restore his health, 1804–06: Secretary to the Governor, Sir Alexander Bell, 1804–05; quarrelled with Wordsworth, 1810; final residence at Highgate, near London, under the care of Dr. James Gillman, 1816 until his death; reconciled with Wordsworth and toured the Rhineland with him, 1828. Lecturer and journalist: Editor, *The Watchman*, 1796; wrote for the *Morning Post*, 1799; lectured extensively in London, 1808–19; Editor, *The Friend*, 1809–10; Assistant Editor, *The Courier*, 1810–11. Associate of the Royal Society of Literature (with pension), 1824. *Died 25 July 1834.*

<small>PUBLICATIONS</small>

Collections

> *Complete Works*, edited by W. G. T. Shield.   7 vols., 1853.
> *Complete Poetical Works*, edited by W. H. Coleridge.   2 vols., 1912.
> *Collected Letters*, edited by E. L. Griggs.   6 vols., 1956–68.
> *Collected Works*, edited by Kathleen Coburn.   1969 –

Verse

> *Ode on the Departing Year.*   1796.
> *Poems on Various Subjects.*   1796; revised edition, as *Poems*, with Charles Lamb and Charles Lloyd, 1797; revised edition, by Coleridge alone, 1803.
> *Fears in Solitude, France: An Ode, and Frost at Midnight.*   1798.
> *Lyrical Ballads, with a Few Other Poems*, with William Wordsworth.   1798; revised edition, 2 vols., 1800; edited by W. J. B. Owen, 1967.
> *Christabel, Kubla Khan: A Vision, The Pains of Sleep.*   1816.
> *Sybilline Leaves: A Collection of Poems.*   1817.
> *Poetical Works.*   3 vols., 1828.
> *The Devil's Walk*, with Robert Southey, edited by H. W. Montagu.   1830.

Plays

> *The Fall of Robespierre*, with Robert Southey.   1794.
> *Wallenstein*, from the play by Schiller.   1800.
> *Remorse*, music by Michael Kelly (produced 1813).   1813; earlier version, *Osorio*, edited by R. H. Shepherd, 1873.
> *Zapolyta: A Christmas Tale* (revised version by T. J. Dibdin produced 1818).   1817.
> *Dramatic Works*, edited by Derwent Coleridge.   1852.
> *The Triumph of Loyalty*, in *Complete Poetical Works*.   1912.

Other

> *Omniana; or, Horae Otiosiores*, with Robert Southey.   2 vols., 1812; edited by Robert Gittings, 1969.
> *The Friend.*   1812; revised edition, 3 vols., 1818; edited by Barbara E. Rooke, in *Collected Works*, 2 vols., 1969.
> *Biographia Literaria; or, Biographical Sketches of My Literary Life and Opinions.*   2 vols., 1817; edited by George Watson, 1956.
> *On Method.*   1818; as *Mental Science*, 1855; edited by A. D. Snyder, 1934.
> *Aids to Reflection in the Formation of a Manly Character.*   1825; edited by H. N. Coleridge, 1839.

On the Constitution of the Church and State According to the Idea of Each. 1830; edited
   by John Colmer, in *Collected Works,* 1975.
Specimens of the Table-Talk, edited by H. N. Coleridge. 2 vols., 1835.
Literary Remains, edited by H. N. Coleridge. 4 vols., 1836–39; reprinted in part as
   Notes on English Divines, 2 vols., 1853.
Letters, Conversations, and Recollections of Coleridge, by T. Allsop. 2 vols., 1836.
Confessions of an Inquiring Spirit, edited by H. N. Coleridge. 1840.
Hints Toward the Formation of a More Comprehensive Theory of Life, edited by S. B.
   Watson. 1848.
*Notes and Lectures upon Shakespeare and Some of the Old Poets and Dramatists, with
   Other Literary Remains,* edited by Mrs. H. N. Coleridge. 2 vols., 1849; as *Essays
   and Lectures* ..., 1907.
Essays on His Own Time, edited by Sara Coleridge. 3 vols., 1850; edited by David V.
   Erdman, with additional material, in *Collected Works,* 3 vols., 1975.
Notes Theological, Political, and Miscellaneous, edited by Derwent Coleridge. 2 vols.,
   1853.
Anima Poetae, from the Unpublished Notebooks, edited by E. H. Coleridge. 1895.
Biographia Epistolaris, Being the Biographical Supplement of Biographia Literaria,
   edited by A. Turnbull. 2 vols., 1911.
Coleridge on Logic and Learning, with Selections from the Unpublished Manuscripts,
   edited by A. D. Snyder. 1929.
Shakespearean Criticism, edited by T. M. Raysor. 2 vols., 1930.
Miscellaneous Criticism, edited by T. M. Raysor. 1936.
The Philosophical Lectures, edited by Kathleen Coburn. 1949.
Coleridge on the Seventeenth Century, edited by Roberta Florence Brinkley. 1955.
Notebooks, edited by Kathleen Coburn. 1957–

Bibliography: *A Bibliography of the Writings in Prose and Verse of Coleridge,* by T. J. Wise,
1913, supplement, 1919; *An Annotated Bibliography of Criticism and Scholarship,* vol. 1,
1793–1899 by Josephine and Richard Haven and Maurianne Adams, 1976.

Reading List: *The Road to Xanadu* by John Livingston Lowes, 1927, revised edition, 1930;
Coleridge by Humphrey House, 1953; *Coleridge* by Kathleen Raine, 1953; *Coleridge the
Visionary* by J. B. Beer, 1959; *Coleridge, Critic of Society* by John Colmer, 1959; *The Idea of
Coleridge's Criticism* by R. H. Fogle, 1962; *Coleridge: A Collection of Critical Essays* edited
by Kathleen Coburn, 1967; *The Waking Dream* by Patricia M. Adair, 1967; *Coleridge: The
Work and the Relevance* by William Walsh, 1967; *Coleridge and the Pantheist Tradition* by
Thomas McFarland, 1969; *Coleridge: The Critical Heritage* edited by J. R. de J. Jackson,
1970; *Coleridge* by John Cornwell, 1973; *Coleridge's Meditative Art* by Reeve Parker, 1975;
Coleridge and the Idea of Love by Anthony John Harding, 1977.

*   *   *

Samuel Taylor Coleridge, in *Biographia Literaria,* describes in an oft-quoted passage what
was to be his part in the *Lyrical Ballads,* the book of verses which he and Wordsworth
planned together: "my endeavours should be directed to persons and characters supernatural,
or at least romantic." Wordsworth on the other hand was to "propose to himself as his object,
to give the charm of novelty to things of everyday, and to excite a feeling analogous to the
supernatural, by awakening the mind's attention from the lethargy of custom, and directing it
to the loveliness and the wonders of the world before us." When the volume appeared in
1798 this intention of Coleridge's was realised in one poem, "The Rime of the Ancient
Mariner" (in its original form).
   If Coleridge had written nothing else, this poem would be enough to establish his greatness

as a Romantic poet. Essentially it is an imitation of the traditional ballads, a tale of adventures and of the supernatural, and can be read simply as such. But it is full of wider overtones, and we can see it as both a presentation of the Romantic archetype of Man as wanderer, and as a record of Coleridge's own spiritual pilgrimage. The Mariner's shooting of the albatross is an affront to the spirit of Nature, who pursues the Mariner and his companions with its vengeance. The thirst which torments them may be taken as a symbol of spiritual as well as physical drought, and the Life-in-Death to which the Mariner is given over is a state which Coleridge himself experienced continually and tragically. The redemption of the Mariner begins when he spontaneously blesses the water-snakes – a gratuitous act which complements the previous gratuitous slaying of the bird. But the redemption is not finally complete. The Mariner is still compelled to wander, and compulsively to relive his experience in recounting it. These and a great many other complexities of meaning are to be discovered in the poem, whether Coleridge intended them consciously or no. But the whole is given a sense of reality, especially by the use Coleridge makes of his wide reading in books of voyages and travelling.

Two other poems of the *annus mirabilis* 1797 have the same kind of imaginative power, but both of them, as with so much of Coleridge's work, are unfinished. Coleridge's account of the composition of "Kubla Khan," which he tells us was presented to him in a vision induced by laudanum and which he was unable to complete owing to the interruption of the person from Porlock, may be open to question. But the poem, represented by Coleridge as a "psychological experiment," is the forerunner of that imaginative exploitation of the subconscious which was to issue in later Symbolist and Surrealist poetry. Like "The Ancient Mariner," "Kubla Khan" can be made to reveal many levels of meaning. Its genesis is from the contemporary genre of Oriental romance. Its controlling images of a Dome associated with the permanence of Art, and moving waters suggestive of the world of shifting phenomena, point backwards to Chaucer's *Hous of Fame* and forward to Yeats' "Byzantium."

In "Christabel" we are superficially in the world of Gothic romance, though Coleridge's metrical originality in reviving the stressed or sprung rhythms of earlier English poetry is noteworthy. But the real subject of the poem is the mystery of iniquity – the pure and innocent Christabel obsessed by the vampire Geraldine, another figure of Life-in-Death. Coleridge's inability to find an answer to this may account for the poem's unfinished state. It is true that many years later he gave an account of how it was to be finished: Geraldine, after all, was to turn out to be a good spirit, sent by Christabel's dead mother – but this, though in line with Coleridge's later thinking that all things work together for good, is difficult to square with the text of the poem as it stands.

Nothing in the rest of Coleridge's poetical works quite lives up to the promise of these three relatively early poems. A number of reasons have been adduced to account for this, and all perhaps contributed. There is the debilitating effect of his use of opium, the temptation to abstraction which his study of philosophy brought, the breakdown of his marriage to Sara Fricker, and the quarrel with Wordsworth. Coleridge himself suffered deeply from the sense that he had not fulfilled his potentiality, in particular in not creating that synthesis of philosophy, theology, and poetry at which he aimed. If anyone in the nineteenth century could have brought about such a synthesis it might well have been Coleridge – but the sense that a unified vision of all knowledge is within one's grasp may itself be part of the false riches which narcotic addiction offers. Nevertheless, one should not underestimate what he actually did achieve. Shelley called Coleridge "a mighty poet/And a subtle-souled psychologist." Indeed he was in many ways the originator of psychology as a science, and this enters into his poetry continually. The poem entitled "Love," which begins

> All thoughts, all passions, all delights,
> Whatever stirs this mortal frame,
> All are but ministers of Love,
>   And feed his sacred flame.

218

in fact enunciates a principle later to be formulated by Freud. What on a cursory reading appears to be a rather facile sentimental narrative is in fact a study in psychology, where the poet in the poem through his poetry elicits from the lady feelings she has not been previously aware of.

Very characteristic of Coleridge are his blank verse conversational poems, in which the form of thought, moving on from association to association, itself creates the form of the poem. Fine examples are "Frost at Midnight," "The Nightingale," and "This Lime-Tree Bower My Prison." These poems are full of natural observation, which relates them to yet also differentiates them from the poems of Wordsworth. Coleridge's sensibility to Nature is in some ways more subtle and delicate than that of his friend. He is particularly aware of atmospheric effects of light and of clouds, in which indeed he evinced a scientific interest. "Fears in Solitude" also belongs among the conversational poems, though it takes on a more oratorical and public tone. It was written at a time when a French invasion was widely expected, and Coleridge's analysis of the state of England may well present the modern reader with present day analogies.

In its opening lines "Dejection" begins as if it also were to be a conversational poem. But it is worked out in terms of the free pseudo- or Pindaric ode. Coleridge had already attempted the ode form in such early political poems as the *Ode to the Departing Year* and "France." But these are on the whole unsuccessful, being over-rhetorical and full of vague abstractions. It is the deep personal crisis which makes of "Dejection" a far greater poem. Originally addressed to Wordsworth, it was intended as a reply to the latter's "Ode on Intimations of Immortality." In both poems the poet is aware of the drying up of the sources of his earlier inspiration. Wordsworth feels that he has somehow moved away from the reality of living Nature, whereas for Coleridge the cause is subjective and psychological:

> we receive but what we give,
> And in our life alone does Nature live:
> Ours is her wedding garment, ours her shroud!
>   And would we aught behold, of higher worth,
> Than that inanimate cold world allowed
> To the poor loveless ever-anxious crowd,
>   Ah! from the soul itself must issue forth
> A light, a glory, a fair luminous cloud
>   Enveloping the Earth—

As Jacob Bronowski has pointed out in his book *The Poet's Defence,* what Coleridge is saying here is really the exact opposite of what Wordsworth believed, and the poem marks the parting of the ways between the two poets. As with Wordsworth's "Ode" the decline of Coleridge as a poet can largely be dated from "Dejection."

Yet, as with Wordsworth, the later years were not wholly barren. Nor were Coleridge's philosophic studies quite unproductive of poetry. We might cite the difficult but very beautiful little allegory of "Time, Real and Imaginary." The extremely obscure fragments "Ne Plus Ultra" and "Limbo" deserve more attention than they receive. They show the influence of Coleridge's reading in Dante and Donne and reach forward to a neo-metaphysical poetry such as was to be characteristic of the twentieth century. There is a surprise of another kind in the late "The Garden of Boccaccio" which exhibits a genial acceptance of sensuality which is otherwise rare in the often rather prudish Coleridge:

> O all-enjoying and all-blending sage,
> Long be it mine to con thy mazy page,
> Where, half-conceal'd, the eye of fancy views
> Fauns, nymphs, and winged saints, all gracious to thy muse!

219

> Still in thy garden let me watch their pranks,
> And see in Dian's vest between the ranks
> Of the trim vines, some maid that half believes
> The vestal fires, of which her lover grieves,
> With that sly satyr peeping through the leaves!

As with his verse, Coleridge's prose writings are frequently fragmentary and unsystematic. They are full of profound insights, but these are often obscurely or imperfectly expressed. His most important critical work, *Biographia Literaria*, is notable for his definition of the imagination. Coleridge sees the poetic or secondary Imagination as an echo of the primary Imagination, "the prime Agent of all human Perception, and as a repetition in the finite mind of the eternal act of creation in the infinite I AM." His *Lectures on Shakespeare* shift from a preoccupation of earlier critics with the so-called Rules to those matters of psychology and characterisation which were to dominate the nineteenth-century approach. As a metaphysician Coleridge has often been thought of as merely the first interpreter of German Idealistic thought in England, and has even been accused of plagiarism in this respect. But he was deeply grounded in an indigenous British tradition, represented by the Cambridge Platonists and by Berkeley, as well as Hartley's theory of the association of ideas. There is much in Coleridge that anticipates later thinking, as in the evolutionary point of view of *A Theory of Life*.

In religion Coleridge returned by way of Unitarianism and naturalistic pantheism to the Anglican orthodoxy in which he had been brought up. In his *Constitution of Church and State* he puts forward a view of church and state as representing respectively the religious and secular aspects of the nation, organically conceived. This is in the line of conservative and Anglican thinking which stems from Hooker and Burke.

—John Heath-Stubbs

COLLINS, William.   English.   Born in Chichester, Sussex, 25 December 1721. Educated at Winchester College, 1733–40; Queen's College, Oxford, 1740–41, and Magdalen College, Oxford, 1741–43, B.A. 1743. Lived in London, attempting to support himself by his writing; befriended by Samuel Johnson; in ill-health after c. 1754, chronic fits of depression leading, finally, to insanity. *Died 12 June 1759.*

PUBLICATIONS

Collections

> *Poems*, edited by C. Stone and R. L. Poole.   1914.
> *Poems*, with Gray and Goldsmith, edited by R. H. Lonsdale.   1969.

Verse

> *Persian Eclogues.*   1742; as *Oriental Eclogues*, 1757.
> *Verses Humbly Addressed to Sir Thomas Hanmer on His Edition of Shakespeare's
>   Works.*   1743; as *An Epistle*, 1744.
> *Odes on Several Descriptive and Allegoric Subjects.*   1747.

Ode Occasioned by the Death of Mr. Thomson.   1749.
The Passions: An Ode.   1750.
Poetical Works, edited by John Langhorne.   1765.
Drafts and Fragments of Verse, edited by J. S. Cunningham.   1956.

Bibliography: in *Seven 18th-Century Bibliographies* by Iolo A. Williams, 1924.

Reading List: "The Romanticism of Collins" by Alan D. McKillop, in *Studies in Philology 20,* 1923; *Collins* by H. W. Garrod, 1928; *Poor Collins: His Life, His Art, and His Influence* by Edward G. Ainsworth, 1937; *Collins* by Oswald Doughty, 1964; *Collins* by Oliver F. Sigworth, 1965; "The Poetry of Collins Reconsidered" by A. S. P. Woodhouse, in *From Sensibility to Romanticism,* 1965; *The Poetry of Vision: Five Eighteenth Century Poets* by P. M. Spacks, 1967; *The Life of a Poet: A Biographical Sketch of Collins* by P. L. Carver, 1967; *Precious Bane: Collins and the Miltonic Legacy* by Paul S. Sherwin, 1977.

*   *   *

William Collins and Thomas Gray are often linked, not only because the corpus of each is small and can be usefully published in a joint volume, but because both display a tendency for nervous depression (a melancholia popularly associated with the "romantic" artist), controlled by a strong classical tradition in verse. This finds its ideal poetic realization in the Pindaric Ode and the short lyric where there is freedom within formal structure, while the aesthetic tension common to both poets is expressed through dramatic personification that distances emotion, making the subjective experience an objective reality.

Collins' lyrical facility marks him as an important contributor to the English tradition of verse. There is a simplicity of diction and rhythm in his "Young Damon of the Vale Is Dead" which prefigures the *Lyrical Ballads,* for instance. In contrast, his poetry can plumb the depths of the dark and irrational mind. The "Ode to Fear," as an example, breaks down into intense "psychomachia" where emotion becomes oppressively and obsessively present:

> Ah *Fear!* Ah frantic *Fear!*
> I see, I see Thee near.
> I know they hurried Step, thy haggard Eye!
> Like Thee I start, like Thee disorder'd fly,
> For lo what *Monsters* in thy Train appear!

The literary influences are Shakespeare, Spenser, and, of course, Milton whose "Gothic classicism" was akin to that of Collins.

The pastoral is Collins' natural forte, lending its classical mantle to natural imagery or Oriental and exotic subject-matter as in the *Persian Eclogues.* He moves towards the emotive and the sublime in description, while remaining within the pale of classical convention. The *Odes* also display an emotional range and dramatic realization beneath allegorical pictorialism (reminiscent of the painting of Thornhill or La Guerre). The odes to Pity, Fear, and Simplicity, for example, illustrate the poet's vacillating moods, always invoking a quiet, Horatian solitude, while aware of the "Gobblins" haunting his imagination and the "Fear" which tells him that true art can only be born out of divine fury, those "shad'wy Tribes of *Mind*" found in the "Ode on the Poetical Character."

Such sensitivity finds its most tranquil expression in the "Ode to Evening" with its impressionistic evocation of darkening day "where the Beetle winds/His small but sullen Horn." This midsummer night's dream (and there are clear echoes of Shakespeare) is marred only by a clumsy retreat into personification at the close. This must be set against the terrible Teutonic vision of Fiends in the "Ode to Fear" who "O'er Nature's Wounds, and Wrecks preside." Nature, for his tortured imagination, had a keen and double edge.

221

New ground is broken in Collins' "Ode on the Popular Superstitions of the Highlands," leaving conventional, celebratory verse like the "Ode to Liberty" to embrace a northern culture poles apart from classical norms. Here he follows the "Old RUNIC bards" to accept "Fancy" as his guide over landscapes haunted by supernatural shadows. In this poem, Collins' desire to pursue the "grandeur of wildness, and the novelty of extravagance" (Dr. Johnson) finds its fulfilment, creating a precedent for the Ossianic fantasies and Gothic terror of the later decades of the century.

Collins takes his place as a so-called pre-romantic poet alongside Gray, the Wartons, and Thomson, bridging the early neo-classic world and that of romantic revolution, very much as, in his own mind, he struggled to reconcile the rational, formal experience with the disorder and derangement of his inner life.

—B. C. Oliver-Morden

COLUM, Padraic. Irish. Born in Longford, 8 December 1881. Educated at the National School, Sandycove, County Dublin. Married the writer Mary Maguire. Worked as a clerk in a railway office, Dublin, until 1904; associated with Lady Gregory and Yeats at the beginning of the Irish Theatre movement, 1902; Founder, 1911, with James Stephens, *q.v.*, and Thomas MacDonagh, *Irish Review*, Dublin; Editor, 1912–13. Settled in the United States, living in New York and Connecticut after 1939. President, James Joyce Society, New York. Recipient: Academy of American Poets Fellowship, 1952; Irish Academy of Letters Gregory Medal, 1953; Catholic Library Association Regina Medal, 1961. Member, Irish Academy of Letters, and National Institute of Arts and Letters (U.S.). *Died 11 January 1972.*

PUBLICATIONS

Verse

Heather Ale. 1907.
Wild Earth. 1907; revised edition, as *Wild Earth and Other Poems*, 1916.
Dramatic Legends and Other Poems. 1922.
The Way of the Cross: Devotions on the Progress of Our Lord Jesus Christ from the Judgement Hall to Calvary. 1926.
Creatures. 1927.
Old Pastures. 1930.
Poems. 1932; revised edition, as *Collected Poems*, 1953.
The Story of Lowry Maen. 1937.
Flower Pieces: New Poems. 1938.
The Jackdaw. 1939.
Ten Poems. 1952.
The Vegetable Kingdom. 1954.
Irish Elegies. 1958; revised edition, 1961.
The Poet's Circuits: Collected Poems of Ireland. 1960.
Images of Departure. 1969.

Plays

The Children of Lir, and *Brian Boru*, in *Irish Independent*, 1902.
The Kingdom of the Young (produced 1902).   In *United Irishman*, 1903.
The Foleys, and *Eoghan's Wife*, in *United Irishman*, 1903.
The Saxon Shillin' (produced 1903).   Edited by Robert G. Hogan and J. F. Kilroy, in
    Lost Plays of the Irish, 1970.
The Fiddler's House (as *Broken Soil*, produced 1903; revised version, as *The Fiddler's
    House*, produced 1907).   1907.
The Land (produced 1905).   1905.
The Miracle of the Corn: A Miracle Play (produced 1908).   In *Studies*, 1907.
Thomas Muskerry (produced 1910).   1910.
The Destruction of the Hostel (juvenile; produced 1910).
The Desert.   1912; as *Mogu the Wanderer; or, The Desert: A Fantastic Comedy*, 1917;
    as *Mogu of the Desert* (produced 1931).
The Betrayal (produced 1913).   N.d.
The Grasshopper, with F. E. Washburn-Freund, from a play by Count Keyserling
    (produced 1917).
Balloon (produced ?).   1929.
The Show-Booth, from a play by Alexander Blok (produced 1948).
Moytura: A Play for Dancers.   1963.
The Challengers: Monasterboice, Glendalough, Cloughoughter (produced 1966).
The Road round Ireland, with Basil Burwell, from works by Colum (produced 1967; as
    Carricknabauna, produced 1967).

Fiction

Castle Conquer.   1923.
Three Men.   1930.
The Flying Swans.   1957.

Other

Studies (miscellany).   1907.
My Irish Year.   1912.
A Boy in Eirinn (juvenile).   1913.
The Irish Rebellion of 1916 and Its Martyrs: Erin's Tragic Easter, with other, edited by
    Maurice Joy.   1916.
The King of Ireland's Son (juvenile).   1916.
The Boy Who Knew What the Birds Said (juvenile).   1918.
The Adventures of Odysseus and the Tale of Troy (juvenile).   1918; as *The Children's
    Homer*, 1946.
The Girl Who Sat by the Ashes (juvenile).   1919.
The Children of Odin: A Book of Northern Myths (juvenile).   1920.
The Boy Apprenticed to an Enchanter (juvenile).   1920.
The Golden Fleece and the Heroes Who Lived Before Achilles (juvenile).   1921.
The Children Who Followed the Piper (juvenile).   1922.
The Six Who Were Left in a Shoe (juvenile).   1923.
Tales and Legends of Hawaii: At the Gateways of the Day and *The Bright Islands*
    (juvenile).   2 vols., 1924–25; as *Legends of Hawaii*, 1937.
*The Island of the Mighty, Being the Hero Stories of Celtic Britain Retold from the
    Mabinogion* (juvenile).   1924.

The Peep-Show Man (juvenile).   1924.
The Voyagers, Being Legends and Romances of Atlantic Discovery (juvenile).   1925.
The Forge in the Forest (juvenile).   1925.
The Road round Ireland.   1926.
The Fountain of Youth: Stories to Be Told (juvenile).   1927.
Orpheus: Myths of the World (juvenile).   1930; as *Myths of the Old World*, n.d.
Cross Roads in Ireland.   1930.
Ella Young: An Appreciation.   1931.
A Half-Day's Ride; or, Estates in Corsica.   1932.
The Big Tree of Bunlahy: Stories of My Own Countryside (juvenile).   1933.
The White Sparrow (juvenile).   1935; as *Sparrow Alone*, 1975.
The Legend of Saint Columba.   1935.
Where the Winds Never Blew and the Cocks Never Crew (juvenile).   1940.
The Frenzied Prince, Being Heroic Stories of Ancient Ireland (juvenile).   1943.
Our Friend James Joyce, with Mary Colum.   1958.
Arthur Griffith.   1959; as *Ourselves Alone! The Story of Arthur Griffith and the Irish Free State*, 1959.
Story Telling Old and New.   1961.
The Stone of Victory and Other Tales (juvenile).   1966.

Editor, *Oliver Goldsmith.*   1913.
Editor, *Broad-Sheet Ballads, Being a Collection of Irish Popular Songs.*   1913.
Editor, with Joseph Harrington O'Brien, *Poems of the Irish Revolutionary Brotherhood.*   1916; revised edition, 1916.
Editor, *Gulliver's Travels* (juvenile edition), by Swift.   1917.
Editor, *An Anthology of Irish Verse.*   1922; revised edition, 1948.
Editor, *The Arabian Nights, Tales of Wonder and Magnificence* (juvenile).   1953.
Editor, *A Treasury of Irish Folklore: The Stories, Traditions, Legends, Humor, Wisdom, Ballads, and Songs of the Irish People.*   1954; revised edition, 1962, 1967.
Editor, with Margaret Freeman Cabell, *Between Friends: Letter of James Branch Cabell and Others.*   1962.
Editor, *The Poems of Samuel Ferguson.*   1963.
Editor, *Roofs of Gold: Poems to Read Aloud.*   1964.

Reading List: "Colum: The Peasant Nation" by Richard J. Loftus, in *Nationalism in Modern Anglo-Irish Poetry*, 1964; *Colum: A Biographical-Critical Introduction* by Zack R. Bowen, 1970.

*   *   *

Padraic Colum's poetry which, in a long career of writing fiction, drama, biography, and children's literature, is his chief claim to remembrance, is rooted in a realistic sense of Irish rural life. It is this direct knowledge of the rural scene which distinguishes his work from much of the poetry of the Irish literary revival with which his name was first associated. Of a younger generation than W. B. Yeats, Lady Gregory and George Russell, his background and upbringing were Catholic rather than Protestant. This he felt allowed his poetry a more truly national flavour than could be achieved by poets with their roots in the Irish Protestant Ascendancy. His poetic philosophy is most clearly expressed in his poem "The Poet":

> But close to the ground are reared
> The wings that have widest sway,
> And the birds that sing best in the wood ...
> Were reared with breasts to the clay.

His best work, much of it contained in his volume *Wild Earth*, is a simple, lyrical celebration of the properties and personages of the Irish rural scene mediated in a verse redolent of national and religious pieties. The Gaelic folk-poem, the broadsheet ballad are the poetic modes to which Colum's poems pay their respects, and his most compelling work combines traditional simplicity of metaphor with a dramatic objectivity of tone. The colours, movements, and textures of Irish life are caught in this volume, as in his later collection *The Poet's Circuits: Collected Poems of Ireland*, with a realism that is only occasionally marred by sentimental provincialism and quaint pastoral feeling. At his best, as in his justly famed ballad (based on traditional materials) "She moved through the fair," Colum's work merits praise for its moments of lyric universality. In L. A. G. Strong's words "the work of Padraic Colum, which presents us with poetic experience in its most innocent, naked form, embarrasses criticism. Often there are no allusions, no symbols, only the simplest images, nothing but the singing tone and the thing itself."

—Terence Brown

COMBE, William.   English.   Born in London, 25 March 1742. Educated at Eton College, 1752–56; Inner Temple, London, 1760–63. Married 1) Maria Foster in 1777; 2) Charlotte Hadfield in 1795. Journalist, editor, ghost-writer, political pamphleteer, in London, from 1775: Editor and writer for John Walter, book and newspaper publisher, 1786–92; Editor, *The Pic Nic*, later *The Cabinet*, newspaper, 1803; Editor, *The Times*, 1803–08. Jailed for debt, King's Bench Prison, London, 1785–86, 1799–1823, with limited freedom from 1800. *Died 19 June 1823.*

PUBLICATIONS

Verse

Clifton: A Poem in Imitation of Spenser.   1775.
The Diaboliad, Dedicated to the Worst Man in His Majesty's Dominions.   2 vols.,
    1777–78; vol. 1 revised, 1777; Additions, 1777.
The First of April; or, The Triumphs of Folly.   1777.
An Heroic Epistle to the Noble Author of The Duchess of Devonshire's Cow.   1777.
The Justification.   1777.
A Poetical Epistle to Sir Joshua Reynolds.   1777.
The Auction: A Town Eclogue.   1778.
An Heroic Epistle to Sir James Wright.   1779.
The World As It Goes.   1779.
The Fast-Day: A Lambeth Eclogue.   1780.
The Traitor: A Poetical Rhapsody.   1781.
The Royal Dream; or, The P[rince] in a Panic: An Eclogue.   1785.
The Tour of Doctor Syntax, in Search of the Picturesque, illustrated by Thomas
    Rowlandson.   1812; Second Tour, in Search of Consolation, 1820; Third Tour, in
    Search of a Wife, 1821; Three Tours, 3 vols., 1826; edited by J. C. Hotten, 1868.
Six Poems Illustrative of the Engravings by the Princess Elizabeth.   1813.

The English Dance of Death, illustrated by Thomas Rowlandson.   2 vols., 1815–16.
The Dance of Life, illustrated by Thomas Rowlandson.   1817.
The History of Johnny Quae Genus, The Little Foundling of the Late Doctor Syntax, illustrated by Thomas Rowlandson.   1822.
Forget Me Not: A Christmas and New Year's Present for 1823.   1823.

Play

The Flattering Milliner; or, A Modern Half Hour (produced 1775).

Fiction

The Philosopher in Bristol.   1775.
Letters Between Two Lovers and Their Friends.   1781.
Letters of an Italian Nun and an English Gentleman.   1781.
Original Love-Letters Between a Lady of Quality and a Person of Inferior Station.   1784.
The Devil upon Two Sticks in England.   6 vols., 1790–91.
Letters Between Amelia in London and Her Mother in the Country.   1824.

Other

Letters to His Friends on Various Occasions, by Laurence Sterne.   1775 (six letters by Combe).
A Dialogue in the Shades.   1777.
A Letter to the Duchess of Devonshire.   1777; *Second Letter*, 1777; *Interesting Letter*, 1778.
The R[oya]l Register.   9 vols., 1778–84.
Letters Supposed to Have Been Written by Yorick and Eliza.   2 vols., 1779.
Letters of the Late Lord Lyttelton.   2 vols., 1780–82.
Original Letters of Laurence Sterne.   1788.
An History of the Late Important Period.   1789.
A Letter from a Country Gentleman to a Member of Parliament.   1789.
The Royal Interview: A Fragment.   1789.
Observations on the Present State of the Royal Academy.   1790.
Considerations on the Approaching Dissolution of Parliament.   1790.
A Word in Season to the Traders and Manufacturers of Great Britain.   1792.
An History of the River Thames.   2 vols., 1794.
Two Words of Counsel and One of Comfort, to the Prince of Wales.   1795.
Letter to a Retired Officer.   1796.
Plain Thoughts of a Plain Man.   1797.
Brief Observations on a Letter to Pitt by W. Boyd.   1801.
The Letters of Valerius.   1804.
The Thames; or, Graphic Illustrations.   2 vols., 1811; revised edition, as *Views on the Thames*, 1822.
Microcosm of London, vol. 3.   1811.
The History of the Abbey Church of St. Peter's Westminster.   2 vols., 1812.
Antiquities of York.   1813.
A History of the University of Oxford.   2 vols., 1814.
A History of the University of Cambridge.   2 vols., 1815.
The History of the Colleges.   1816.
Swiss Scenery.   1820.

A History of Madeira. 1821.
Letters to Marianne. 1823.

Editor and Contributor, *The Pic Nic.* 2 vols., 1803.

Translator, *History of the Campaigns of Count Alexander Suworow Rymniski,* by Friedrich Anthing. 2 vols., 1799.
Translator, *Memoir of the Operations of the Army of the Danube,* by Count Jean-Baptiste Jourdan. 1799.
Translator, *Report to the First Consul Bonaparte on the Antiquities of Egypt,* by Louis-Medeleine Ripault. 1800.
Translator, *Travels in Upper and Lower Egypt,* by C. N. S. Sonnini de Manoncourt. 1800.

Ghost-Writer or editor of the following: *A Description of Patagonia* by Thomas Falkner, 1774; *The Oeconomy of Health* by the School of Salerno, 1776; *A Practical Treatise on the Diseases of the Teeth* by John Hunter, 1778; *An Historical and Chronological Deduction of the Origin of Commerce* by Adam Anderson, 4 vols., 1787–89; *Voyages Made in the Years 1788 and 1789 from China to the North West Coast of America* by John Meares, 1790; *Alf von Deulman; or, The History of the Emperor Philip and His Daughters* by C. B. E. Naubert, translated by A. E. Booth, 2 vols., 1794; *A Letter to Uvedale Price,* 1794, and *Sketches and Hints on Landscape Gardening,* n.d., both by Humphry Repton; *A Narrative of the British Embassy to China 1792–94,* 1795, and *A Journal of the Forces Which Sailed in 1800,* 1802, both by Aeneas Anderson; *Voyage to the South Atlantic and round Cape Horn into the Pacific Ocean* by James Colnett, 1798; *Official Correspondence Containing the Whole of the State Papers from 1797 to 1799, of the Congress of Rastadt,* 1800; *The History of Mauritius* by Charles Grant, Viscount de Vaux, 1801; *The Life, Adventures, and Opinions of Col. George Hanger, Written by Himself,* 2 vols., 1801; *Voyages from Montreal Through the Continent of North America* by Alexander Mackenzie, 1802; *Fashionable Follies,* vol. 3, by Thomas Vaughan, 1810; *The Life of Arthur Murphy* by Jesse Foot, 1811; *Pompeii* by T. L. Donaldson, 1827.

Reading List: "Combe and the Original Letters of Sterne," in *Publications of the Modern Language Association,* 1967, and *Doctor Syntax: A Silhouette of Combe* (includes bibliography), 1969, both by Harlan W. Hamilton.

*   *   *

By his lifelong insistence upon anonymity William Combe avoided contemporary recognition and almost succeeded in excluding himself from literary history. He was, to be sure, a hack-writer, but hack-writers are part of literary history, and Combe was a very good one. In several respects his work has lasting literary importance.

He achieved sensational success in 1777 with a verse satire, *The Diaboliad,* a highly personal and scathing attack upon scandalous figures in London Society. Going into many editions and prompting a host of imitations, it attracted much attention and was remembered for many years. By April 1778 the *Monthly Review* was calling the author a "distinguished master of the poetical tomahawk and scalping knife." Though uneven in execution and concerned with long-forgotten personalities, Combe's satires are often imaginative and witty, his couplets neatly turned and sharply edged. He also wrote prose satires of which the longest and best are *The R[oya]l Register,* filled with scandals concerning 300 thinly veiled personalities, and *The Devil upon Two Sticks in England,* a bitter comment on London life at the turn of the century and, being more generalized, still a readable work.

Combe's friendship with Laurence Sterne gave rise to his equivocal "imitations" of

Sterne's letters. These have muddied the waters of Sterne scholarship because they are not wholly devoid of authentic material; a few of them may be substantially Sterne's. This mixture of the fabricated and the authentic, now exasperating, was common at that time. Combe himself had published the highly successful but fabricated *Letters of the Late Lord Lyttelton.*

From 1788 to 1806 Combe was employed as propagandist for the Pitt Ministry and produced pamphlets on the controversies of those tortured years. Students of the period will find him an able polemicist writing in yet another of his many manners. As virtual editor of *The Times* from 1803 to 1808 he assisted John Walter II in establishing the independence of that newspaper.

Throughout his career Combe was busily producing journeyman work to order: editing, ghost-writing, translating, or simply filling blank space. It was for the last of these talents that he was employed by Rudolph Ackermann who wished him to provide letterpress to accompany those prints which were Ackermann's stock in trade. It was thus that he came to write the octosyllabic couplets describing the travels of Doctor Syntax. These achieved book form in 1812 as the *Tour of Doctor Syntax in Search of the Picturesque,* followed by second and third tours. These three *Tours,* reprinted again and again for nearly a century, were family favorites in Britain and America. They are, perhaps unjustly, the only work of Combe's still known. Doubtless the famous Rowlandson caricatures were a major reason for this popularity, but the *Tours* continued to sell even after the quality of the prints deteriorated, and there were editions with no illustrations at all. From his first appearance the good Doctor Syntax found a warm place in the hearts of thousands. He was a nostalgic, old-fashioned figure, an amalgam of Parson Adams, Parson Primrose, and Parson Yorick. The verses are often genuinely comic and are by no means to be held in contempt by the hypercritical.

—Harlan W. Hamilton

CONSTABLE, Henry. English. Born in Newark in 1562. Educated at St. John's College, Cambridge, B.A. 1580. After conversion to Roman Catholicism, settled in Paris; possibly a spy for the English government, 1584–85, afterwards served the French government: employed in confidential missions to England; Papal Envoy to Edinburgh, 1599–1603; received a pension from the French king, 1603, and returned to London, 1604; imprisoned, released, and probably returned to the Continent: nothing is known of his later life. *Died 9 October 1613.*

PUBLICATIONS

Collections

Poems, edited by Joan Grundy.   1960.

Verse

Diana, The Praises of His Mistress.   1592; revised edition, 1594.

Other

Examen Pacifique de la Doctrine des Huguenots.   1589.

Reading List: in *Biographical Studies* vol. 2, by George A. Wickes, 1954.

*   *   *

Henry Constable was known to his contemporaries and later readers as the author of the sonnet sequence *Diana*. We know him also from the much larger collection of secular sonnets left in manuscript, as well as from the seventeen *Spiritual Sonnets*, also existing only in manuscript.

By his contemporaries, including fellow poets such as Drayton and Jonson, he was highly esteemed, and, although we may not altogether endorse their estimate, we can understand it. His love sonnets (some of them, like Sidney's, addressed to Penelope Rich) came at the very start of the great Petrarchan explosion of the 1590's, and provided a strikingly pure example of the form. The "sweet conceits" from which they were fashioned were the stock-in-trade of the Petrarchan tradition: his lady is an object of adoration, far above him – a queen, a sun, a goddess; her beauty is the source of beauty in Nature; her hair is a golden net which entraps the lover like a bird; her hand wounds him with its "ivory arrows," and so on. Yet, though typical, the conceits are not hackneyed, for Constable handles them freshly, giving to the thought a graceful turn which makes it legitimately his own. Since the essence of Petrarchan discipleship was the production of variations on a theme, this makes him an almost model examplar. A modern reader misses the richness of texture, the sensuous warmth, and the elegiac note he finds in other practitioners, such as Shakespeare or Daniel, to say nothing of the "true voice of feeling," which, whenever it occurs in such sequences, is to be regarded as a bonus. The virtues of these sonnets are, rather, their neatness, elegance, order, delicacy, and control. Their very artificiality is their charm. Seldom producing a memorable phrase, they are to be enjoyed like a song or an Elizabethan air, as, on the whole, trifles, but agreeable ones. Nor perhaps was personal feeling entirely lacking in them: distanced very far, Constable's "busyness" (he was described on one occasion as "a busie yong man"), his ambition, and his anxiety, may have found both an outlet and a sedative in them.

Not all his secular sonnets were love sonnets. Some were poems of compliment, addressed to various influential people, including Queen Elizabeth I and King James. The interest of these sonnets is slight.

Much more rewarding are the Spiritual Sonnets, written after Constable's conversion to Roman Catholicism. These, addressed to "God and His Saints," have a fervour, and with it a poetic density, both intellectual and emotional, lacking in the secular sonnets. They are among the finest religious sonnets produced in English before Donne. Their style approaches the Metaphysical: it has a certain intellectual toughness and energy, and thought and emotion are fused in a compelling way which makes the conceits more than merely decorative. The completeness of Constable's conversion is clear: most of the saints addressed are women, and, as in much Counter-Reformation literature, the feeling expressed turns the poems into sacred love-poems, considerably more passionate than the love-sonnets themselves.

—Joan Grundy

COOKE, Ebenezer.   American.   Born, probably in London, England, c. 1671; emigrated to Maryland after 1711 when he inherited a family estate in Dorchester County. Deputy

Receiver-General, Cecil County, Maryland, 1721–23; admitted to the Prince George's
County Bar, 1728. *Died in 1732.*

PUBLICATIONS

Verse

> *The Sot-Weed Factor; or, A Voyage to Maryland.*   1708; edited by Brantz Mayer, 1865.
> *Sotweed Redivivus; or, The Planter's Looking-Glass.*   1730.
> *The Maryland Muse* (includes *The Sot-Weed Factor* and *The History of Colonel*
> *Nathaniel Bacon's Rebellion in Virginia*).   1731.

Reading List: *Cooke: The Sot-Weed Canon* by Edward H. Cohen, 1975; "Cooke: Satire in
the Colonial South" by Robert D. Arner, in *Southern Literary Journal 8,* 1975.

*   *   *

Known as the self-proclaimed "Poet Laureate" of colonial Maryland, Ebenezer Cooke was
among the first American poets to write satire about the colonies from the point of view of a
disgruntled colonist. He is also recognized as the most popular and successful of America's
early Southern poets.

While little is known for certain about Cooke's early life, he is thought to have been born
in England, to have spent a brief period of time in Maryland in 1694, and to have migrated
there sometime after 1711. His first visit to the "Western Shoars" is thought to have inspired
his most famous work, *The Sot-Weed Factor*, published in London in 1708 but believed to
have been written much earlier. About the experiences of a British merchant who comes to
America to trade with the colonists and is cheated and insulted during the course of his visit,
The Sot-Weed Factor is a biting satire on the manners and mores of the people who lived in
the colony of Maryland at the beginning of the eighteenth century. Written in hudibrastic
couplets, the poem burlesques the escapades of drunken lawyers, inept physicians, illiterate
and oftentimes dishonest planters, crude and debased women, and even degenerate Indians,
all of whom are said to typify the culture in which they lived. Omitted in the American
edition of 1731, the final lines of the poem are a "Curse," delivered by the narrator as he
departs from America for England, on the "Inhospitable Shoar," which he has just visited,
"Where no Man's Faithful, nor a Woman Chast."

A sequel to *The Sot-Weed Factor*, once attributed to an imitator but now correctly
attributed to Cooke, was published in Maryland in 1730 by the famous colonial printer
William Parks under the title *Sotweed Redivivus*. By the time of the poem's publication,
Cooke had permanently established himself in Maryland, where he had become a respected
member of the community. As a result, *Sotweed Redivivus* is less a satire of colonial manners
than an attempt to write serious didactic poetry on the necessity of remedying the economic
woes of Maryland through legislative reform. According to Cooke, the standard of living in
Maryland would be greatly improved if its people would endorse legislation to control
inflation, limit the production of tobacco for which there was no market, and halt the
indiscriminate waste of natural resources, particularly the wanton destruction of forests.

Other poems in the Cooke canon which merit critical analysis are "The History of Colonel
Nathaniel Bacon's Rebellion in Virginia," published along with *The Sot-Weed Factor* in a
volume entitled *The Maryland Muse* (1731), and a series of elegies on the deaths of public
figures with whom Cooke was associated. A mock-heroic epic of the type then popular in
England, "The History of Colonel Nathaniel Bacon's Rebellion" reflects Cooke's

conservative thinking on the subject of revolution and colonial self-government. Far from praising Nathaniel Bacon, the popular American hero who in 1676 had led the people of frontier Virginia to revolt against the tyrannical administration of Governor William Berkeley, Cooke's stated aim in writing a history of the rebellion was to "Cooke *this* Bacon," whose "dire ... Wars" he considered a threat to civilization and an act of extreme folly. While they lack the clever wit and polished charm of his other poems, Cooke's elegies are among the finest surviving examples of colonial American elegiac verse. Particularly noteworthy is "An Elegy on the Death of the Honourable William Lock" (1732), in which Cooke uses the death of a local dignitary as the occasion for poetic commentary on the inevitability and universality of death.

After 1732 Cooke stopped writing poetry, and because nothing is known about his subsequent activities, scholars have assumed that he died at this time. In recent years, Cooke has attracted the attention of John Barth, whose novel *The Sot-Weed Factor* (1960) has earned Cooke a lasting reputation in tha annals of American literary history.

—James A. Levernier

CORBETT, Richard.   English.   Born in Ewell, Surrey, in 1582. Educated at Westminster School, London; Broadgates Hall, now Pembroke College, Oxford, 1598; Christ Church, Oxford, 1599–1612, B.A. 1602, M.A. 1605, B.D. 1617; Proctor, 1612; took holy orders, 1613. Married Alice Hutten (died, 1628). Vicar of Cassington, near Oxford; Chaplain to James I; Dean of Christ Church, Oxford, 1620–28; Prebendary of Salisbury, 1620–31; Vicar of Stewkley, Berkshire, 1620–35; Bishop of Oxford, 1628–32; Bishop of Norwich, 1632–35. *Died 28 July 1635.*

PUBLICATIONS

Collections

  Poems, edited by J. A. W. Bennett and H. R. Trevor-Roper.   1955.

Verse

  Certain Elegant Poems.   1647.
  Poetica Stromata; or, A Collection of Sundry Pieces.   1648.
  The Times' Whistle; or, A New Dance of Seven Satires and Other Poems, edited by J. M. Cowper.   1871.

*   *   *

Poetry had for Richard Corbett essentially a social function. It was therefore naturally incorporated in his place-seeking activities, which account for several tasteless pieces whose forced wit contrasts with the simplicity and restraint (enhanced by the use of octosyllabics) found in poems on his father, mother, and son. These give the impression of genuine feeling and achieve a dignity unusual in Corbett.

But most of Corbett's better pieces are the result of his conviviality and the literary interchange of Caroline Oxford. His longest poem "Iter Boreale," a lively account in his favourite decasyllabic couplet of a tour made with friends, was popular and influential in its day. It remains the best example of Corbett's characteristic virtues: pace, gusto, humour (generally in the form of ludicrous exaggeration), and delighted awareness of the teeming life of inns and market-places, kitchens and conventicles. He transports us to the world of Dogberry and Bottom the weaver; we savour the authentic life of Jacobean England in the energy of his colloquial speech larded with proverbs and allusions, and in the people with whom his poems are crammed: waiters at a banquet purloining tarts and pies, an "old Popish-Lady" fasting on gingerbread, tapsters fiddling accounts, a Puritan distracted from prayer by the sight of girls dancing round a maypole. Humour touches everything, from the broken crosses now making "stools for horsemen that have feeble knees" to the chucker-out who hurls Corbett repeatedly for an hour, while onlookers measure the record throw. Corbett's solid world bustles with activity; in a Vice-Chancellor's preparations before a royal visit ("Both morn and even he cleansed the way,/The streets he gravelled thrice a day"), in the nation's excitement over a new comet ("The mason's rule, the tailor's yard alike/Take altitudes"), or in the anguish of dons biting their finger-nails as they struggle to compose verses for their aristocratic pupils to publish as their own, we sense vigorous involvement which is partly Corbett's own, partly that of the society he portrays.

Mentally, Corbett's world looks back, not forwards. His enjoyment of popular culture (shown particularly in his love of ballads, which he both sang and wrote) enables him to recreate for us an intellectual climate in which Puck and Bevis of Hampton are realities, men still talk of the days of the abbeys and the old religion, sing of Arthur or Chevy Chase, and dance at Whitsun Ales. Had Corbett sensed how much his Merrie England was threatened by his constant butts, the Puritans, his mockery of them might have been less good-humoured. Appropriately, he is best remembered today by "Farewell, Rewards and Faeries," the charming lament for the passing of the old order which he wrote to be sung as a ballad by learned and unlearned alike.

Extroverted and morally insensitive, Corbett lived exuberantly on the surface of his age. His humorous delight in the everyday, the unsophisticated, and the traditional aspects of his society is what chiefly endures in his verse.

—Margaret Forey

COTTON, Charles. English. Born at Beresford Hall, Staffordshire, 28 April 1630. Educated privately; travelled on the Continent as a boy. Married 1) Isabella Hutchinson in 1656 (died, 1669), three sons, five daughters; 2) Mary Russell, Dowager Countess of Ardglass in 1675. Landowner; Revenue Commissioner for Derbyshire and Staffordshire, 1660; Magistrate, 1665; commissioned Captain in Lord Chesterfield's regiment, 1667. *Died in February 1687.*

PUBLICATIONS

Collections

   Poems, edited by John Buxton.   1958.
   Selected Poems, edited by Geoffrey Grigson.   1975.

Verse

A Panegyric to the King's Most Excellent Majesty.   1660.
Scarronides; or, Virgil Travestie: A Mock Poem on the First and Fourth Books of Virgil's
  Aeneis.   2 vols., 1664–65; revised edition, 1667.
Burlesque upon Burlesque; or, The Scoffer Scoft, Being Some of Lucian's Dialogues
  Newly Put into English Fustian.   1675.
The Wonders of the Peak.   1681.
Poems on Several Occasions.   1689.

Plays

Horace, from the play by Corneille.   1671.
The Fair One of Tunis, from a French play.   1674.

Other

The Nicker Nickt; or, The Cheats of Being Discovered.   1669.
The Complete Gamester.   1674; as How to Play at Billiards, Trucks, Bowls, and Chess,
  1687; revised edition, 1709.
The Planter's Manual.   1675.
The Compleat Angler, part 2.   1676; edited by R. B. Marston, with Walton's Compleat
  Angler, 1888.

Translator, The Moral Philosophy of the Stoics, by G. du Vair.   1664.
Translator, The History of the Life of the Duke of Espernon.   1670.
Translator, The Commentaries of Blaize de Montluc.   1674.
Translator, Essays of Montaigne.   3 vols., 1685–86; edited by W. C. Hazlitt, 1877.
Translator, Memoirs of de Pontis.   1694.

Reading List: The Life and Poetry of Cotton by Charles J. Sembower, 1911; Cotton and His
River by Gerald G. P. Heywood, 1928; The Cavalier Mode from Jonson to Cotton by Earl
Miner, 1971.

                              *   *   *

    Few facts have survived about the life of Charles Cotton the younger, poet, translator,
ardent royalist, and bon vivant, capacities hidden from readers who identify him solely as
author of a second part of The Compleat Angler. He was born at Beresford in Staffordshire,
which he never left without becoming homesick. He was tutored there; tradition, rather than
certain knowledge, holds that he went to Cambridge. From some quarter, including
continental travel in 1655, he learned French and Italian as well as Greek and Latin. He was
born to a good estate, but he was generous to others as well as himself and often writes of his
creditors.
    Cotton's first known published work appeared with Dryden's in the collection of elegies,
Lachrymae Musarum (1649), mourning the Lord Hastings. His most popular poems during
his lifetime were burlesques: of Virgil in Scarronides and of Lucian in Burlesque upon
Burlesque.
    The Wonders of the Peake was also popular. It is a redoing of Hobbes' De Mirabilibus
Pecci, reversing the order of sites visited in the Peak district of Derbyshire. The poems
contributed to the nascent interest in the sublime. This poem, the burlesques, and The

Planter's Manual were published in *The Genuine Works* (1715, often reprinted), but Cotton's finest poetry appeared in *Poems on Several Occasions*.

Among his descriptive poems, the quatrain poetry of "Winter" ("Morning," "Noon," and "Evening") ring the freshest note of nature poetry heard in the seventeenth century, as the Romantics understood. Coleridge discovered "every excellence of thought, images, and passions" in natural language. Another group of excellent poems includes those addressed to Izaak Walton, including "Contention" and "The Retirement" as well as others with Walton's name in their main title. A poem "To the Countess of Chesterfield" must be included among his best occasional poems, as "Day Break" and "To Chloris. Stanzes Irreguliers" represent his best love poems, and "On Christmas-day" his best religious. His most extraordinary poem is the "Epitaph on M. H.," a prostitute of beauty and charm long remembered "With such a superstitious Lust/That I could fumble with her dust." With that we must poise lines from "The Retirement": "Good God! how sweet are all things here!/ How beautiful the Fields appear!" along with praise of his "beloved Nymph! fair Dove,/ Princess of Rivers" and even the rocky hills of the area.

The same sensibility is reflected in Cotton's addition to *The Compleat Angler* and *The Planter's Manual*. His clear, lively prose will also be found in his translations, whose addresses to the reader sparkle with humor. The greatest of his translations, *Essays of Montaigne* appeared in three volumes (1685–86). Other works have been attributed to Cotton, of which the most important is *The Compleat Gamester*. His translations also include one play, the *Horace* of Pierre Corneille and dozens of poems in *Poems on Several Occasions*, which closes with his one narrative, "The Battail of Yvry" (963 ll.).

—Earl Miner

COWLEY, Abraham.   English.   Born in London, 24 July 1618. Educated at Westminster School, London (King's Scholar), 1628–35; Trinity College, Cambridge (Scholar), 1637–42, B.A. 1639, M.A. 1642; Oxford University, 1656–57, M.D. 1657. Fellow, Trinity College, Cambridge, 1640–44 (ejected by Parliament because of Royalist sympathies); lived at St. John's College, Oxford, 1644–45; Secretary to Lord Jermyn (Queen's Chamberlain), from 1645, and lived in the exiled court in France, 1646–56; employed in various diplomatic missions, also a cipher secretary to Queen Henrietta Maria; returned to London, possibly as a spy, imprisoned briefly by mistake, and released on bail, 1656; returned to France, 1658; restored to fellowship at Trinity College, 1661; associated with Davenant's Duke Theatre from 1661. Retired to Chertsey, Surrey. *Died 28 July 1667.*

PUBLICATIONS

Collections

> *Prose Works,* edited by J. R. Lumby, 1887; revised by Arthur Tilley, 1923.
> *English Writings,* edited by A. R. Waller.   2 vols., 1905–06.
> *Poetry and Prose,* edited by L. C. Martin.   1949.

Verse

> *Poetical Blossoms.*   1633; revised edition, 1636.
> *A Satire: The Puritan and the Papist.*   1643.
> *The Mistress; or, Several Copies of Love-Verses.*   1647.
> *Poems.*   1656.
> *Ode upon the Blessed Restoration and Return of His Sacred Majesty Charles the Second.*   1660.
> *Plantarum Libri Duo.*   1662; revised edition, edited by Thomas Sprat, as *Angli Poemata Latina,* 1668.
> *Verses Lately Written upon Several Occasions.*   1663.
> *A Poem on the Late Civil War.*   1679; edited by Allan Pritchard, as *The Civil War,* 1973.

Plays

> *Love's Riddle* (produced ?).   1638.
> *Naufragium Joculare* (in Latin) (produced 1638).   1638.
> *The Guardian* (produced 1641).   1650; revised version, as *Cutter of Coleman Street* (produced 1661), 1663.

Other

> *A Proposition for the Advancement of Experimental Philosophy.*   1661.
> *Visions and Prophecies.*   1661; as *Definition of a Tyrant,* 1668.
> *Works.*   3 vols., 1668–89.

Bibliography: *Cowley: A Bibliography* by M. R. Perkin, 1977.

Reading List: *Cowley, The Muse's Hannibal* by Arthur H. Nethercot, 1931; *Cowley's World of Order* by Robert B. Hinman, 1960; *Cowley* by James G. Taaffe, 1972.

*   *   *

Often described as the last of the seventeenth-century metaphysical poets, Abraham Cowley actually wrote in a variety of styles, and his intellect and temperament incline as much toward the Age of Enlightenment as to the Renaissance. His *Poetical Blossoms,* written at fifteen while still at Cambridge, reflects the influences of Spenser and the Latin pastoralists, and his comedy of manners *The Guardian,* also done at Cambridge, shows him to be an admirer of Jonson's London comedies. The metaphysical strains in his work are not sounded until *The Mistress; or, Several Copies of Love Verses,* a conscious imitation of Donne's *Songs and Sonnets.* Of the nearly one hundred poems in *The Mistress,* some are philosophical reflections and eulogies of rural life; others are loosely connected to suggest the story of Cowley's unrequited passion for a beautiful woman of superior social position. *The Mistress* is in a medley of styles, combining echoes of Donne and the cavalier "sons of Ben," coupling archly obscure metaphysical conceits and lucid, polished rhetoric; but the affinities to Donne are most salient. Several poems, such as "The Exstasie," Cowley composed expressly to contrast with Donne's. Like Donne, he often begins a love lyric with a dramatic exclamation reminiscent of "For God's sake, hold your tongue and let me love," and many of Donne's images, only slightly modified, reappear in *The Mistress;* "Resolve to Be Beloved," for example, offers a magnetic needle to do somewhat the same work as Donne's two twin compasses. Most of the poems reverberate with what Ben Jonson called "strong lines" – elegantly complex metaphors designed to wring the last drop of intellectual speculation out of cunningly constructed paradoxes. In reaction to these calculated incongruities, Samuel Johnson in his famous life of Cowley (1779) described him as a writer of *discordia concors* perversely enamored of obscure paradoxes, forced wit, and absurd quibbles. Johnson's essay remains the most perceptive analysis ever written of Cowley's poetry, but Johnson, in his effort to discredit the "metaphysicals," may have exaggerated Cowley's similarities to Donne. In reality, Cowley is an imitator of Donne's poetic devices; totally lacking in Donne's intellectual passion, he copies the form but not the substance. He depends upon rhetorical precision rather than complexity of metaphors, and his versification is as smoothly regular as Jonson's.

The Mistress provides only a glimpse of Cowley's variegated style, which is more apparent in his *Poems*, containing his Pindaric odes, elegies, Anacreonics, and the incomplete Biblical epic "Davideis." The fifteen Pindaric odes, or "pseudo-Pindaric" odes, as they were called, were widely imitated in the eighteenth century. Only two follow Pindar closely; the rest are constructed in a dozen or more stanzas of very irregular, rhymed free verse of ingenious prosody and on a variety of philosophical and religious subjects. One ode is a stately tribute to Thomas Hobbes. A somewhat similar tribute, but in elegiac form, is his lengthy poem commemorating his Cambridge friend William Hervey, a magnificent elegy which, if Milton had not composed *Lycidas*, might well stand as the best of the century. Of equally high quality are Cowley's witty and joyous imitations of Anacreon which exhibit a classical compression comparable to Pope's. Taken as a whole, Cowley's poetry suggests poetic instincts that were essentially classical; occasional conceits notwithstanding, his verse is characterized by economy, lucidity, and precision. His "Davideis" was a project he wisely abandoned as alien to his temperament. Written in monotonous decasyllabic couplets, it may have inspired Milton's invectives against rhyme in his preface to *Paradise Lost*. By the time he came to write "Davideis," Cowley's heart was more stirred by the literary beauties of Virgil than the spiritual revelations of the Old Testament. Johnson condemned the poem for its plethora of conceits, but its real flaw is simply absence of inspiration. Exhausted by the religious turbulence of his times, and looking toward the cool rationalism of Bacon and Hobbes and the new science as guides, Cowley could summon only token enthusiasm for angels, miracles, and prophecies.

His retirement to Chertsey after the Restoration enabled him to continue his botanical studies, write tracts for the Royal Society (e.g., *The Advancement of Experimental Philosophy*), and compose his collection of brilliant personal essays. Like Bacon's, Cowley's essays are on abstract subjects such as ambition, solitude, and procrastination, but Cowley avoids Bacon's aloofness of tone and tautness of style. Instead, he writes in the flowing, digressive, and intimate style of his other master, Montaigne. One of his finest essays, the autobiographical "Of My Life," sets a landmark in that genre for its freshness and candor. The most "modern " prose stylist before Dryden, Cowley writes in the lucid, concrete, and direct manner advocated by Bacon and the founders of the Royal Society. Thus, at the conclusion of his life the precocious imitator of the fiery and visionary Donne found his emotional and intellectual resting place in the Age of Reason.

—James E. Ruoff

COWPER, William.   English.   Born in Great Berkhamsted, Hertfordshire, 15 November 1731. Educated at Dr. Pittman's School, Markyate Street, Hertfordshire, 1738–40, and at Mrs. Disney's (oculist), London, 1740–42; Westminster School, London, 1742–49; articled to Mr. Chapman, a London solicitor, 1750–52; took chambers in the Middle Temple, London, 1752; called to the Bar, 1754. A commissioner of bankrupts, 1759–64; Clerk of the Journals, House of Lords, 1763. Abandoned career after an attack of madness, 1763;

periodically insane for the remainder of his life. Lived with the Evangelical clergyman Morley Unwin from 1765, and after Unwin's death in 1767 with Unwin's wife Mary until her death, 1796: lived in Olney, Buckinghamshire, 1767–95, and in East Dereham, Norfolk, 1795–1800. *Died 25 April 1800.*

PUBLICATIONS

Collections

Works: Poems, Correspondence and Translations, edited by Robert Southey.   15 vols., 1835–37.
Correspondence, edited by Thomas Wright.   4 vols., 1904.
Complete Poetical Works, edited by H. S. Milford, 1905; revised edition, edited by Norma Russell, 1967.
Selected Poems and Letters, edited by A. Norman Jeffares.   1963.
Poetry and Prose, edited by Brian Spiller.   1968.

Verse

Olney Hymns, with John Newton.   1779.
Anti-Thelyphthora: A Tale in Verse.   1781.
Poems.   1782; revised edition, 1794–95, 1797, 1800, 1806, 1808.
The Task, vol. 2 of *Poems.*   1785.
The History of John Gilpin.   1785.
Poems: On the Receipt of My Mother's Picture, The Dog and the Water-Lily.   1798.
Adelphi, edited by John Newton.   1802.
Posthumous Poetry, edited by John Johnson.   1815.
Poems Now First Published, edited by James Croft.   1825.
Unpublished and Uncollected Poems, edited by Thomas Wright.   1900.
New Poems, edited by Falconer Madan.   1931.

Other

Memoir of the Early Life of Cowper Written by Himself.   1816; as *Autobiography,* 1835; edited by Maurice Quinlan, in *Proceedings of the American Philosophical Society 97,* 1953.
Unpublished and Uncollected Letters, edited by Thomas Wright.   1925.

Editor, *The Force of Truth,* by T. Scott.   1779 (or 1789 edition?).
Editor, *Original Poems by a Lady* [Maria F. C. Cowper].   1792.
Editor, *Sir Thomas More,* by James Hurdis.   1792.

Translator, with others, *Works,* by Horace.   2 vols., 1757–59.
Translator, with others, *The Henriade,* by Voltaire.   1762.
Translator, *The Iliad and Odyssey,* by Homer.   2 vols., 1791.
Translator, *The Power of Grace,* by H. R. Van Lier.   1792.
Translator, *Poems,* by Jeanne Marie Guyon, edited by W. Bull.   1801.
Translator, *Latin and Italian Poems of Milton,* edited by William Hayley.   1808; revised edition, as *Cowper's Milton,* 1810.

Bibliography: *Cowper: The Continuing Revaluation: Bibliography of Cowperian Studies from 1895 to 1960* by Lodwick Hartley, 1960; *A Bibliography of Cowper to 1837* by Norma Russell, 1963.

Reading List: *The Stricken Deer; or, The Life of Cowper* by David Cecil, 1929; *Cowper* by Norman Nicholson, 1951; *Cowper: A Critical Life* by Maurice Quinlan, 1953; *Cowper, Nature Poet* byRoderick Huang, 1957; *Cowper of the Inner Temple, Esq.: A Study of His Life and Work to 1768* by Charles Ryskamp, 1959; *In Search of Stability: The Poetry of Cowper* by Morris Golden, 1960; *The Life of Cowper* by John S. Memes, 1972.

*   *   *

William Cowper's early volume, the *Poems* of 1782, contained Augustan poetry with a dash of Evangelicism. But Cowper was not successful as a general satirist of society; in these poems – apart from a few passages on country life and some particular pieces of satire, notably on bores, the press, and Lord Chesterfield – he had not found his own voice. His friendship with Lady Austen helped him to find it. She suggested less abstract subjects which were part of his actual life – notably the sofa of *The Task*, where blank verse allowed him to be discursive, to indulge himself in what Coleridge called his "divine chit-chat." And Lady Austen told him the story of an actual London draper one evening in 1782 when he was in a depressed mood. The result of his night's work was "The Diverting History of John Gilpin." In writing to his friend the Rev. William Unwin about it Cowper revealed his aim, of laughing himself and making two or three others laugh too. And while he enjoyed hearing the world laugh, he remarked that he was reduced to trifling "by necessity – a melancholy, that nothing else so effectually disposes, engages me sometimes in the arduous task of being merry by force.... To say truth, it would be but a shocking vagary, should the mariners on board a ship buffeted by a terrible storm, employ themselves in fiddling and dancing; yet sometimes much such a part act I...."

The underlying melancholia of the poet is there in *The Task*. In Book III he describes himself as a stricken deer that left the herd; and the whole poem is itself part of his cure, a quiet life in the countryside. To this he brought sharp, close, detailed observation, as in Book VI, "The Winter Walk at Noon," or else witty application of Augustan elegance of diction as in his mock heroic description of the ways of cultivating the cucumber, with the "stercoraceous heap" yielded by the stable, of dispersing the "gross fog Boeotian" from the drenched conservatory, or again of comfortable contemplation, in Book IV's "The Winter Evening," with its memorable description of the arrival of the post and its reception:

> Now stir the fire, and close the shutters fast
> Let fall the curtains, wheel the sofa round,
> And, while the bubbling and loud-hissing urn
> Throws up a steamy column, and the cups,
> That cheer but not inebriate, wait on each,
> So let us welcome peaceful evening in.

There were less cheerful poems, the despairing "Lines Written During a Period of Insanity" for example, with their disturbed rhythm, "The Shrubbery," and, a poignant poem, "The Castaway" with the sea imagery Cowper used to such effect. More general reflections were captured in the poem "On the Loss of the Royal George," which matches the obviousness – and the truth – of Gray's Elegy.

The Olney Hymns, written mostly during 1771 and 1772, drew upon Biblical imagery; they paraphrase Biblical texts, and they catch some of the ecstasy that Evangelicism gave Cowper briefly. They are honest hymns which record his own occasional delight and doubt, and yet express universal religious experience. "Light Shining Out of Darkness," written before Cowper's attack of madness in 1773, is perhaps the best known, its simplicity highly effective:

> God moves in a mysterious way,
> His wonders to perform;
> He plants his footsteps in the sea,
> And rides upon the storm

"Walking with God" and "Lively Hope and Gracious Fear" also capture general attitudes, but "Lovest Thou Me" and "Temptation" are filled with Cowper's own intense contemplation of existence.

Mrs. Unwin's friendship with Cowper was recorded in a notable sonnet of 1793, a year in which he also wrote "To Mary" to her. His directness of utterance (he thought the poetry of his own time artificial: "over-refined and delicate to exception") suited his recording of domestic drama: "The Retired Cat" lost in a drawer, "The Dog and the Water-Lily," and the magnificent "Epitaph on a Hare." Cowper, in short, was a master of the familiar style. He could express easily profound reflections upon life's progress in "Yardley Oak"; he could also translate Homer's "majestic plainess" effectively, and his two volume translation of Homer was a commercial success. And his translations of Milton's Latin and Italian poems are still immensely readable.

Cowper, one of the twelve most quoted writers in the *Oxford Dictionary of Quotations*, is attractive because of his blending of public speech and private emotion, his profound seriousness illuminated by his urbane wit, his religious enthusiasm matched by classical restraint, his melancholia mellowed by his "constant enjoyment of country air and retirement." And the *Letters* show us the kind of conversation we might have had with him; a man of moods – of demonic dreams at the horror of hell balanced by carefully ordered days creating peace and ease – sensitive, ruminative, ironic, and unfailingly courteous.

—A. Norman Jeffares

CRABBE, George. English. Born in Aldeburgh, Suffolk, 24 December 1754. Educated at schools in Bungay and Stowmarket, Suffolk; apprenticed to a village doctor at Wickham Brook, near Bury St. Edmunds, Suffolk, 1768–71, and to Mr. Page, a surgeon, at Woodbridge, Suffolk, 1771–75. Married Sarah Elmy in 1783 (died, 1813); two sons. Practised medicine in Aldeburgh, 1775–80, but found it difficult to make a living; settled in London, 1780, and attracted the patronage of Edmund Burke, who persuaded him to enter the church: ordained deacon, 1781, priest, 1782: Curate in Aldeburgh, 1781–82; Chaplain to the Duke of Rutland at Belvoir, 1782–85; Curate of Stathern, Leicestershire, 1785–89; Rector of Muston, Leicestershire, 1789; Curate of Sweffling and Great Glemham, 1792; returned to Muston, 1805; Vicar of Trowbridge, Wiltshire, 1814–32. *Died 3 February 1832.*

PUBLICATIONS

Collections

   Tales, 1812, and Other Selected Poems, edited by Howard Mills.   1967.
   Poems, edited by Norma Russell and Arthur Pollard.   1973.

Verse

Inebriety.   1775.
The Candidate.   1780.
The Library.   1781.
The Village.   1783.
The News-Paper.   1785.
Poems.   1807.
The Borough: A Poem in Twenty-Four Letters.   1810.
Tales in Verse.   1812.
Poetical Works.   4 vols., 1816; revised edition, 7 vols., 1820; 8 vols., 1834.
Tales of the Hall.   2 vols., 1819.
New Poems, edited by Arthur Pollard.   1960.

Other

Posthumous Sermons, edited by John D. Hastings.   1850.

Bibliography: A Bibliography of Crabbe by T. Bareham and S. Gattrell, 1978.

Reading List: The Life of Crabbe by his son, 1834; Crabbe by Alfred Ainger, 1903; The Poetry of Crabbe by Lilian Haddakin, 1955; Crabbe by Raymond L. Brett, 1956; Nature's Sternest Painter: Five Essays on the Poetry of Crabbe by Oliver F. Sigworth, 1965; Crabbe by Robert L. Chamberlain, 1965; Crabbe: The Critical Heritage edited by Arthur Pollard, 1972; Crabbe's Poetry by Peter New, 1976; Crabbe's Arabesque: Social Drama in the Poetry of Crabbe by Ronald B. Hatch, 1977; Crabbe: A Critical Study by T. Bareham, 1977.

*   *   *

George Crabbe is usually remembered as the author of The Village (written early in his career) or of "Peter Grimes," which is better known in the much altered operatic version. Neither work is really characteristic of his enormous and protean output. His creative life was long – from magazine poems in 1772 to the posthumous tales of 1834. This lengthy career, from the age of Johnson to the age of Byron, is divided into three parts.

His early works – The Library, The Village, and The News-Paper – seem content not only with the heroic couplet which he had inherited from the Augustans, but with the subject matter and moral attitudes of an earlier generation. These early poems seek general topics upon which Crabbe can weave moral comments and social aphorisms. He is never completely at home in this genre. Though The Library has patches of sombre brooding power, and The Village is shot through with a savage indignation at the unpleasantness of rustic life, there is no steady guiding principle in these works, no sustained intellectual thesis which will carry the sometimes lame couplets to a memorable conclusion. It is not even clear what is being attacked in The Village – for all that it is quoted ad nauseam by social historians of the period. The descriptions of rural hardship are strongly written, and the denunciation of pastoral poetry which glosses over them is warmly felt. Yet the blame for rustic ills is never squarely laid at any social or political door and the poem is void of any proper suggestions for the amelioration of the suffering it describes.

This phase of his work was followed by a twenty-two year silence, until the publication of Poems in 1807. The new volume showed a fresh side of Crabbe. His trenchant eye for detail, and his interest in human character made themselves manifest in poems like "The Parish Register," "Sir Eustace Grey" and "The Hall of Justice." Though many of his poems are character studies of his parishioners, observed in their daily lives by the parson, Crabbe also reveals a strong curiosity about the workings of aberrant minds – madness, thwarted love, disappointed ambition. In these dual concerns for humble life and for deranged states of mind he is as much a member of the Romantic avant-garde as, in his pontifical generalities, he can seem the last upholder of the post-Augustan order. His contemporaries found him difficult to "place," though he had the admiration of both liberal and conservative critics, and commanded an enormous readership. The tendency of his poetry to insist upon the graphic details of painful reality sometimes offended. Yet to people as divergent as Scott, Byron, Wordsworth, and Jane Austen he provided a unique fusion of the painful, the original, and the moral views of the world around him.

In *The Borough* his interest in shaping his material towards complete narratives is developed. It commences as a genre poem, describing the topography and life of an east coast seaport, gradually becoming a series of narratives linked only loosely to the central theme. Some of the twenty-four letters which comprise the poem are satiric descriptions of phenomena such as the borough election, lawyers and other professions, and the Church. These frequently have a vigour and saltiness which were absent from his earlier work, but they still require a capacity for compendious generalisation and methodical summation which was never Crabbe's forte. The best of the letters are those where he analyses individual characters – "The Parish Clerk," "Peter Grimes," "Abel Keene," and the loathsome scapegrace "Blaney." In this vein Crabbe is a totally original poet, reminding the reader of Chaucer in his handling of material, while often managing a manly concentration in his couplets, which he acknowledged he owed to a lifelong love for Dryden.

The last two volumes published in his lifetime – *Tales in Verse* and *Tales of the Hall* – carry his progress in narrative method to its conclusion. Character analysis is now avowedly the object of his art, and he develops a capacity for correlating the people in his tales with the objects, furniture, and backgrounds with which they choose to live. Dickens and Hardy admired him for this quality and learned much from him. *Tales in Verse* does not provide a linking narrative. Each story is complete in itself, a compressed account of the crisis in a man's life encompassed in about 750 terse, graphic lines. *Tales of the Hall* provides a somewhat sentimental frame-narrative, and for some critics this detracts from the power of the individual tales. Old age had possibly mellowed Crabbe's picture of the world. Certainly this is his most benign volume, though in tales like "Ellen" and "Smuggler and Poachers" he can still touch the genuine heights of tragedy.

Crabbe must not be seen as exclusively or even predominantly a gloomy writer, however. His humour, evident on many occasions, is quiet, wry, and trenchant, and his pity for men's follies and self-delusions always tempers his judgement. Pieces like "The Lovers' Journey," "The Dumb Orators," and "The Frank Courtship" are richly humorous, both verbally and situationally. Perhaps because of the length at which he wrote, Crabbe's technical skill has been undervalued. He can be prosaic to the point of banality, and his verbal wit is often arch; yet both these qualities are usually dramatic factors in controlling overall tone in a poem. He learned a great deal about control of atmosphere from Shakespeare, whom he had read in great depth. Shakespeare also provided the sanction for Crabbe's interest in the disturbed psyche. Crabbe is a moral poet, and there is a close link between his primary role as a dedicated teacher of practical morality, his poetic integrity, and his function as an Anglican priest. The degree to which he enlivens and gives permanent life to this fusion is what makes him a memorable and valuable contributor to the English poetical heritage.

—T. Bareham

CRANE, (Harold) Hart. American. Born in Garrettsville, Ohio, 21 July 1899; spent his childhood in Cleveland. Educated in local schools. Assistant Editor, *The Pagan*, 1918; worked in a shipyard in Cleveland, and as a reporter in New York, 1918; Advertising

Solicitor, *The Little Review*, 1919; worked for his father in a drug store in Akron, Ohio, 1919–20, and in a Cleveland warehouse, 1920; worked in Washington, D. C. briefly, 1920, and in Cleveland, 1920–21; Copywriter, Cleveland advertising agencies, 1922–23; moved to New York, 1923: clerk, then copywriter, in an advertising agency, 1923; clerk in a publishing firm, 1924–25; patronized by Otto Kahn, 1925; travelled in Europe, 1928, Mexico, 1931–32. Recipient: Guggenheim Fellowship, 1931. Drowned himself on the voyage back from Mexico. *Died 27 April 1932.*

PUBLICATIONS

Collections

> *Letters 1916–1932*, edited by Brom Weber.   1952.
> *Complete Poems and Selected Letters and Prose*, edited by Brom Weber.   1966.

Verse

> *White Buildings: Poems.*   1926.
> *The Bridge.*   1930.
> *Ten Unpublished Poems.*   1972.

Other

> *Twenty-One Letters to George Bryan*, edited by Joseph Katz and others.   1968.
> *Letters of Crane and His Family*, edited by Thomas S. W. Lewis.   1974.
> *Crane and Yvor Winters: Their Literary Correspondence*, edited by Thomas Parkinson.   1978.

Bibliography: *Crane: A Descriptive Bibliography* by Joseph Schwartz and Robert C. Schweik, 1972.

Reading List: *Crane: A Biographical and Critical Study* by Brom Weber, 1948; *Crane: An Introduction and Interpretation*, 1963, and *Smithereened Apart: A Critique of Crane*, 1977, both by Samuel Hazo; *Crane* by Vincent Quinn, 1963; *Crane* by Monroe K. Spears, 1965; *The Poetry of Crane* by R. W. B. Lewis, 1967; *The Crane Voyages* by Hunce Voelcker, 1967; *Crane: An Introduction to the Poetry* by Herbert A. Leibowitz, 1968; *Voyager: A Life of Crane* by John Unterecker, 1969; *Crane: The Patterns of His Poetry* by M. D. Uroff, 1974; *Crane's The Bridge: A Description of Its Life* by Richard P. Sugg, 1977.

*   *   *

As with some other American writers, it is difficult to give a final and objective estimate of Hart Crane's place as a poet. He is important, on more than one count, for what he set out to do, but critics have differed widely as to his actual achievement. Furthermore, there is the legend, as we may call it, of his life. We are presented with the picture of a man driven by compulsive and self-destructive urges, both alcoholic and sexual, culminating in a spectacular suicide. Hart Crane himself identified with such doomed and outcast figures as Christopher Marlowe and Arthur Rimbaud, and it is easy to make him into the romantic scapegoat of

American civilisation. On the other hand, a critic like Ivor Winters can too readily move from a moral disapproval of the undisciplined life to a total dismissal of the work.

The Bridge is Crane's longest and clearly his most important poem. In form it is modelled on Eliot's The Waste Land, and it is generally agreed that Crane intended his own poem as a kind of riposte, giving a positive rather than a negative view of the modern metropolitan city. In The Waste Land, and in Joyce's Ulysses, the protaganist moves about the city – London or Dublin – which becomes a symbolic landscape, crowded with mythical and heroic archetypes. Past splendours contrast with modern squalor. The Bridge follows the same plan. The setting is New York. The protagonist wakes in the morning, passes over Brooklyn Bridge, wanders about the city and returns in the evening by the subway under the River Hudson. Hart Crane tries to create a mythology for America out of scraps of literature, history, and tradition. Columbus, Rip Van Winkle and the Wright brothers appear, as well as Whitman, Poe, Emily Dickinson, and Isadora Duncan. In the section entitled "Powhatan's Daughter" Pocahontas represents the American earth itself and its Red Indian past: "Lie to us. Dance us back our tribal dawn." In "The Tunnel," through the suffocating atmosphere of a rush hour subway, Crane encounters the ghost of Edgar Allan Poe:

> And why do I often meet your visage here,
> Your eyes like agate lanterns – on and on
> Below the toothpaste and the dandruff ads?
> – And did their riding eyes right through your side,
> And did their eyes like unwashed platters ride?
> And Death, aloft, – gigantically down
> Probing through you – toward me, O evermore!

In this remarkable passage, Crane shows that he is aware that the American dream of materialistic, technological progress has its reverse side of neurotic nightmare, and that Poe represents this nightmare. But it is Brooklyn Bridge itself which is the unifying symbol of the poem. The bridge unites the two halves of the city, and by the railroad that it carries unites the city with the country and thus its present with its past. As a feat of engineering it denotes human achievement, and in its clean functional beauty the union of aesthetics and technics.

We may thus consider Crane, as does Harold Bloom, as standing in the succession of Romantic, myth making, and visionary poets. He is one of the explorers of what Charles Williams called "the Image of the City." But as an urban poet he differs sharply from his British and American successors of the 1930's in that his poetry is almost devoid of social and political comment. He has indeed been reproached by left-wing critics for his unreflecting celebration of the American capitalist system. Indeed, the sudden collapse of that system in the Slump was one of the factors contributing to his despair and his suicide.

Crane may also be considered, at least in part, as the most notable representative in the English speaking world of the Futurist movement of the 1920's. The term "Futurism" was coined by the Italian Marinetti, a figure more notable for self-publicity than literary genius. But his claim that art should celebrate the achievements and imitate the rhythms of a machine civilisation influenced poets better than himself. These included Apollinaire in France and Mayakovsky in Russia. The latter, like Crane, found his new faith inadequate to sustain him and ended in suicide. But Crane, as we have seen, did not regard the traditions of the past as irrelevant. He suffered, however, from a certain paucity in his own cultural background: it really does seem that he thought the phrase "Panus angelicus" which he quotes in the "Cape Hatteras" section of The Bridge meant "angelic Pan" and could be applied to Walt Whitman. And some may feel that the only religious tradition he seems to have been acquainted with, his mother's Christian Science, lacked a richness compared with the theological currents which fertilised the work of Eliot and Joyce.

Although Whitman's popularist rhetoric represents one of Crane's stances, his free verse is not in the least Whitmanesque. Like that of Eliot, it is based on an extension of principles already found in the blank verse of Shakespeare's contemporaries. But while Eliot's is founded upon that of Webster and his generation, that of Crane is to be related to the practice of Marlowe, with its strongly stressed iambic rhythm and its terminal pause. As in Marlowe there is an element of bombast in Crane, and a certain degree of rhythmical monotony. At his best he sweeps us along by the sheer energy of his writing, in spite of the frequent difficulty of grasping the exact sense of what he is saying. Crane is undeniably often very obscure. But his much quoted letter to Harriet Monroe, defending his poem "At Melville's Tomb," shows that he was very much intellectually in control. The poem consists in fact of a series of compressed conceits, rather different from the extended metaphysical conceits of Donne and his school. At times it is difficult to translate these into completely logical terms. These lines (from "Voyages") are difficult – "In all the argosy of your bright hair, I dreamed/Nothing so flagless as this piracy" – yet their haunting quality is manifest. As a visual poet Crane is remote from Pound and the Imagists; instead of a clear pictorial impression of a scene or object we get a kind of kaleidoscope of sense impressions. His style might best be described as manneristic, and in this respect his affinities are less with his contemporaries and immediate predecessors than with certain poets who came into prominence a decade later, such as George Barker and Dylan Thomas. Crane has indeed been claimed as an influence on the latter poet, but this is difficult to determine.

When Crane moved from the early short poems of *White Buildings* to the elaborately planned *The Bridge* he was attempting to encompass something in the nature of an epic style. What he in fact achieved might more properly be described as quasi-Pindaric or dithyrambic lyric. This dithyrambic quality is even more marked in "For the Marriage of Faustus and Helen." This sequence of three poems continues some of the themes of *The Bridge*. Faustus's evocation of the shade of Helen is, of course, one of the most memorable moments in Marlowe's *Doctor Faustus*; and Marlowe, as we have seen, was one of Crane's heroes. The marriage of Faust and Helen, in the second part of Goethe's *Faust*, was a symbol of the union of the modern and the antique spirits. Crane may have taken his cue from this, since the theme of these three poems is the union of American technological civilization with the traditional idea of beauty. Crane here forces language almost to the breaking point as he strives to evoke Helen first from a vision of the metropolitan city, second (it would seem) from a scene of jazz revelry at the summit of a skyscraper, and third from the airman's conquest of distance:

> Capped arbiter of beauty in this street
> That narrows darkly into motor dawn, –
> You, here beside me, delicate ambassador
> Of intricate slain numbers that arise
> In whispers, naked of steel;
>   religious gunman!
> Who faithfully, yourself, will fall too soon,
> And in other ways than as the wind settles
> On the sixteen thrifty bridges of the city:
> Let us unbind our throats of fear and pity.

In contrast to this, the series of poems entitled "Voyages" represent Crane's return to a purer and more personal lyricism. These may in the end constitute his most enduring, though not his most ambitious achievement. In these poems Crane imagines himself united with one of his lovers, a merchant seaman, as he voyages through imaginary seascapes. The verse of these poems has a new kind of music, and they are less rhetorically accentuated. Hart Crane now uses enjambment with effect, especially a characteristic trick of ending a line with a grammatically unimportant word as in the second line of the following quotation:

> O minstrel galleons of Carib fire,
> Bequeath us to no earthly shore until
> Is answered in the vortex of our grave
> The seal's wide spindrift gaze toward paradise.

Crane's final days were spent in Mexico. He had gone there on a grant from the Guggenheim Foundation, with a project to compose a long poem on the Spanish Conquest of Mexico. This historical theme, almost too highly charged with imaginative potential, has more than once proved a trap for poets. What Hart Crane might have made of it we can only conjecture. In fact his Mexican days were a disaster, and, before he committed suicide by drowning on his return voyage to the U.S.A., he knew that he had no work on the project to show and in the light of the changed economic situation it was unlikely his grant would be renewed. Nevertheless, some of the last poems, such as "The Idiot" and "Bacardi Spreads the Eagle's Wings," give a compassionate view of the poor and outcast which hints at a grasp of reality previously somewhat wanting in Hart Crane's poetry.

—John Heath-Stubbs

CRASHAW, Richard. English. Born in London c. 1613. Educated at Charterhouse, London; Pembroke Hall, Cambridge (exhibitioner), 1631–37, B.A. 1634. Fellow, Peterhouse, Cambridge, 1635–43 (deprived of Fellowship because of his religious beliefs); Curate, Little St. Mary's, Cambridge, 1639; went to Paris, and by 1645 had embraced Roman Catholicism; through intervention of Cowley was introduced to Queen Henrietta Maria who recommended him to Cardinal Palotto: given a post in Palotto's entourage, 1647; appointed a sub-canon at the Cathedral of Santa Casa, Loreto, 1649. *Died 21 August 1649.*

PUBLICATIONS

Collections

> *Complete Works,* edited by Alexander B. Grosart. 2 vols., 1872–73; *Supplement,* 1887–88.
> *Poems English, Latin, and Greek,* edited by L. C. Martin. 1927; revised edition, 1957.
> *Complete Poetry,* edited by George Walton Williams. 1970.

Verse

> *Epigrammatum Sacrorum Liber.* 1634; as *Poemata et Epigrammata,* 1670.
> *Steps to the Temple: Sacred Poems, with Other Delights of the Muses.* 1646; revised edition, 1648, 1670.
> *Carmen Deo Nostro, Te Decet Hymnus, Sacred Poems,* edited by Miles Pinckney. 1652.

Other

> Translator, *The Suspicion of Herod,* by Giovanni Battista Marini. 1834.

Reading List: *Crashaw: A Study in Style and Poetic Development* by Ruth Wallerstein, 1935; *Crashaw: A Study in Baroque Sensibility* by Austin Warren, 1939; *Crashaw* by Mario Praz,

1945; *Three Metaphysical Poets: Crashaw, Traherne, Vaughan* by Margaret Willy, 1961; *Rhyme and Meaning in Crashaw* by Mary E. Rickey, 1961; *Image and Symbol in the Sacred Poetry of Crashaw* by George Walton Williams, 1963; *The Art of Ecstasy: St. Teresa, Bernini, and Crashaw* by Robert T. Petersson, 1970.

*   *   *

Richard Crashaw is the odd man out among 17th-century English devotional poets, and it is difficult for a 20th-century reader to do justice to his poetry without a well-developed historical imagination. Some knowledge of the Counter-Reformation and of the consequent upsurge of religious fervour in Catholic countries, especially in Spain, enables us to put Crashaw's ardent devotion to the saints, the blessed sacrament, and the holy name of Jesus into perspective. Some familiarity with Baroque architecture, sculpture, and painting helps to illuminate Crashaw's poetic techniques. "Un-English" is an epithet frequently applied to him. He is accused of sensationalism, affectation, errors of taste. Whereas Palladian restraint appealed to English connoisseurs, the Baroque never became acclimatised. Yet the Rome which Milton visited before the Civil War, and to which Crashaw migrated after his conversion, was a city which embodied a new vision of splendour. Baroque is essentially an assertive style, rhetorical, often theatrical. It arouses amazement and impresses by sheer sumptuousness. As a term of literary criticism, Baroque is often misused, but it does apply to Richard Crashaw.

Possibly the current vogue for Baroque music may herald a new appreciation of Crashaw's flamboyant poems. He described his version of the "Stabat Mater" as "A Patheticall Descant upon the devout plainsong"; and "The Weeper" might be viewed as the verbal equivalent of virtuoso variations on a theme. Nevertheless, words and phrases are capable of conveying such mundane associations that poetical and musical compositions produce very different impressions and reactions. One of Crashaw's dominant topics was religious ecstasy. The vocabulary he used to describe it was of course not peculiar to himself. Many writers in the western mystical tradition, notably St. John of the Cross and St. Teresa, employ the metaphors of sexual love and of eating and drinking to express the closeness of the union between the soul and God. Unfortunately it is all too easy for post-Freudian readers to interpret such language as the utterance of sexual frustration. There are indeed morbidities in some of Crashaw's image-clusters which are hard to explain in any other way, no matter how much account is taken of the prevalence of bleeding hearts, milky or panting breasts, and fiery darts in the devotional manuals and emblem-books with which the poet was familiar. Nowadays, too, when the Church of Rome itself is abandoning the cult of the saints, it is more than ever difficult to respond to Crashaw's passionate devotion to swooning and weeping holy women. Yet he is a poet of great enterprise and accomplishment, whose strength of feeling is allied with considerable intellectual force.

In the preface to his *Steps to the Temple*, published after he had quitted England, Crashaw is described as "Herbert's second but equal." In tenderness of tone and sometimes in purity of diction, Crashaw does resemble his predecessor; but he differs from him radically in a total absence of self-analysis. The texture of his verse is less sinewy, his wit less compact. He has strong poetic affinities with Cowley. They were friends at Cambridge, and engaged in a famous poetic dialogue on Hope. Milton, too, four years Crashaw's senior, overlapped with him at Cambridge. There are a good many stylistic and thematic parallels between Milton's 1645 *Poems* and Crashaw's *Steps to the Temple*, printed in 1646. Unlike Herbert, Crashaw produced some good secular verse. Like both Herbert and Milton, he was a precocious scholar and an exceptionally fine Latinist. He resembles Milton in being a literary poet, drawing his inspiration from books, pictures, and music rather than from the life of his fellow-men. Like him, he was an extremely careful craftsman, tireless in revision. He experimented with odes of a Pindaric type, and was master of many lyric and narrative measures. Crashaw's verse is rhythmically varied and never discordant. There is more intellectual vigour in his poems than their sensuous imagery and mellifluous fluency might at first suggest. A fine example of ardour controlled by brainwork is his "Hymn to the Name of Jesus."

If Crashaw's poems are considered in the context of Caroline culture, they do not appear particularly exotic. The King's taste in art and entertainment was refined and cosmopolitan. His piety was profound, and he was as anxious as Archbishop Laud to emphasise the Catholic heritage of the Anglican church. Dignity of ritual and beauty of ornament were not lacking in the places of worship frequented by Crashaw at Cambridge. The chapels of Pembroke College and Peterhouse had recently been embellished, as had Little St. Mary's, of which Crashaw became a curate. The Master of Peterhouse was Dr. John Cosin, an eminent liturgical scholar, interested in church music, whose *Collections of Private Devotions in the Practice of the Ancient Church* may well have been "the little volume but large book" which Crashaw sent to "Mrs M. R." The community at Little Gidding, visited in time of tribulation by King Charles himself, was very dear to Crashaw, who shared in the devotional life and became an intimate friend of the Ferrar family – another link, incidentally, with Herbert. The young cleric was famed for the ravishing eloquence of his sermons and the intensity of his prayer-life. He was in no sense a misfit in Cambridge during the 1630's.

Many of his ardently devout poems were composed while he was still a member of the Church of England. Those published posthumously, in *Carmen Deo Nostro*, are on the whole rather more subdued in tone, more disciplined in feeling, than the earlier pieces. They include his variants on some of the great Latin hymns. These celebrate, perhaps, his sense of home-coming. For it cannot be denied that Crashaw's was an *anima naturaliter cattolica*, as Mario Praz observed. The zeal of Parliament and its Commissioners against Laudian Anglicanism eventually drove Crashaw into exile, and into the arms of Mother Church. The Rome of St. Filippo Neri, the Rome of Bernini, offered him marvels beyond the scope of Cambridge; and in the fulness of Catholic doctrine, ritual, and piety his spirit found unbounded satisfaction. The elegy by his friend Cowley opens with the lines: "Poet and Saint! to thee alone are given/The two most sacred names of earth and heaven." A very different poet from "holy Mr. Herbert," who was esteemed "little less than sainted"; but one who in his most exalted moments far outsoared him.

—Margaret Bottrall

CRAWFORD, Isabella Valancy. Canadian. Born in Dublin, Ireland, 25 December 1850; emigrated to Canada, 1858. Lived in Paisley, Lakefield, Peterborough, Ontario, and in Toronto, after c. 1876. *Died 12 February 1887.*

PUBLICATIONS

Collections

Collected Poems, edited by J. W. Garvin. 1905.
Selected Stories, edited by Penny Petrone. 1975.

Verse

Old Spookses' Pass, Malcolm's Katie, and Other Poems.   1884.
Hugh and Ion, edited by Glenn Clever.   1977.

Reading List: *Crawford* by Amelia B. Garvin, 1923; "Crawford" by James Reaney, in *Our Living Tradition,* edited by R. G. McDougall, 1959; "The Hunters Twain" by Dorothy Livesay, in *Canadian Literature 55,* Winter 1973.

*   *   *

The life of Isabella Valancy Crawford is the most obscure of all the 19th-century Canadian writers of prose or poetry. How she came to write in such a wide variety of styles and on such a range of subject matter when she was relatively isolated from the literary life of the period is a matter of wonderment. After the death of her doctor father in Peterborough, Ontario, the writer must have persuaded her mother that Toronto, the publishing centre of English Canada, was the place where she could best eke out a living.

In Toronto, she wrote a quantity of occasional verse for the local papers, a number of serialized novels and novellas for Frank Leslie's New York publications, and articles for *The Fireside Weekly* and, probably, Dickens's journal *All the Year Round.* In 1886, she became the first local writer to have a novel, *The Little Bacchante; or, Some Black Sheep,* serialized in the Toronto *Evening Globe.* It was called "vastly superior to the ordinary run of newspaper fiction," but for the most part Crawford's prose followed the fashion of the *feuilletons* of the day. It was formula fiction, romantic-gothic, flowery, melodramatic. Yet there are indications that the young woman possessed an ability to write realistically concerning pioneer life in Canada.

Crawford published one book of poetry at her own expense, *Old Spookses' Pass, Malcolm's Katie, and Other Poems.* For this she received scant recognition in her life-time, but increasing respect and delight from twentieth-century critics. She was one of those Victorian poets for whom Tennyson was the guide and idol. But in her long poems "Malcolm's Katie" and "Old Spookses' Pass" she displayed a remarkable flair for narrative, and for combining plot, theme, and characterization with an exuberant and arresting use of wilderness imagery. She lived at the beginning of our time in Canada, and saw, with remarkable vision, what paths we might take.

—Dorothy Livesay

CREELEY, Robert (White).   American.   Born in Arlington, Massachusetts, 21 May 1926. Educated at Holderness School, Plymouth, New Hampshire; Harvard University, Cambridge, Massachusetts, 1943–46; Black Mountain College, North Carolina, B.A. 1955; University of New Mexico, M.A. 1960. Served with the American Field Service in India and Burma, 1944–45. Married 1) Ann McKinnon in 1946 (divorced, 1955), two sons, one daughter; 2) Bobbie Louise Hall in 1957, three daughters. Taught on a finca in Guatemala for two years; Instructor, Black Mountain College, Spring 1954, Fall 1955; Visiting Lecturer, 1961–62, and Lecturer, 1963–66, 1968–69, University of New Mexico; Lecturer, University of British Columbia, Vancouver, 1962–63. Visiting Professor, 1966–67, and since 1967 Professor of English, State University of New York at Buffalo. Visiting Professor of Creative Writing, San Francisco State College, 1970–71. Operated the Divers Press, Palma, Majorca,

1953–55; Editor, *Black Mountain Review*, North Carolina, 1954–57, and associated with *Wake, Golden Goose, Origin, Fragmente, Vou, Contact, CIV/n*, and *Merlin* magazines in the early 1950's, and other magazines subsequently. Recipient: D. H. Lawrence Fellowship, 1960; Guggenheim Fellowship, 1964, 1971; Rockefeller Fellowship, 1965. Lives in Bolinas, California.

PUBLICATIONS

Verse

Le Fou. 1952.
The Kind of Act of. 1953.
The Immoral Proposition. 1953.
A Snarling Garland of Xmas Verses. 1954.
All That Is Lovely in Men. 1955.
Ferrini and Others, with others. 1955.
If You. 1956.
The Whip. 1957.
A Form of Women. 1959.
For Love: Poems 1950–1960. 1962.
Words. 1965.
About Women. 1966.
Poems 1950–1965. 1966.
A Sight. 1967.
Words. 1967.
Robert Creeley Reads (with recording). 1967.
The Finger. 1968.
5 Numbers. 1968.
The Charm: Early and Uncollected Poems. 1968.
Numbers. 1968.
Divisions and Other Early Poems. 1968.
Pieces. 1968.
Hero. 1969.
A Wall. 1969.
Mary's Fancy. 1970.
In London. 1970.
The Finger: Poems 1966–1969. 1970.
As Now It Would Be Snow. 1970.
America. 1970.
Christmas: May 10, 1970. 1970.
St. Martin's. 1971.
Sea. 1971.
1.2.3.4.5.6.7.8.9.0. 1971.
A Day Book (includes prose). 1972.
For My Mother. 1973.
Kitchen. 1973.
Sitting Here. 1974.
Thirty Things. 1974.
Selected Poems. 1976.
Away. 1976.
Hello – A Journal February 23-May 3, 1976. 1978.

Play

  Listen (produced 1972).   1972.

Fiction

  The Gold Diggers.   1954.
  The Island.   1963.
  Mister Blue.   1964.
  The Gold Diggers and Other Stories.   1965.
  Mabel.   1976.
  Presences.   1976.

Other

  An American Sense (essay).   1965(?).
  Contexts of Poetry.   1968.
  A Quick Graph: Collected Notes and Essays.   1970.
  A Day Book.   1970.
  A Sense of Measure (essays).   1973.
  Contexts of Poetry: Interviews 1961–1971, edited by Donald Allen.   1973.

  Editor, *Mayan Letters,* by Charles Olson.   1953.
  Editor, with Donald Allen, *New American Story.*   1965.
  Editor, *Selected Writings,* by Charles Olson.   1966.
  Editor, with Donald Allen, *The New Writing in the U.S.A.*   1967.
  Editor, *Whitman.*   1973.

Bibliography: *Creeley: An Inventory 1945–1970* by Mary Novik,   1974.

Reading List: *Three Essays on Creeley* by Warren Tallman, 1973; *Measures: Creeley's Poetry* by Ann Mandel, 1974; *Creeley's Poetry: A Critical Introduction* by Cynthia Edelberg, 1978.

*   *   *

In his 1967 Berlin lecture, "I'm Given to Write Poems," Robert Creeley acknowledged his indebtedness to William Carlos Williams for teaching him the use of an American speech in poetry and for the emotional perception he has achieved, as well as his debt to Charles Olson for "the *freedom* I have as a poet." This freedom lies not in the lyric itself, which is tightly restrained from committing verbal excess, but in the flow of the thought which ranges freely over a complex psychological interior. Creeley's best poems contain remarkable articulation of shades and hues of mood, often achieved by the subtle word play of the discourse. The poems, brief seizures of attention, are a chronicle of his two marriages, in which the self undergoes remorseless scrutiny and analysis. The larger canon of these miniature self-portraits reveals a life of emotional isolation as a man attempts both to possess and submit to women who are repelled by his profound vulnerability.

The early poems, collected in *For Love: Poems 1950–1960*, are intensely formal in their compactness and closure. Many tend toward epigram in their brevity and pithy advice. A typical instance is "The Warning":

> For Love − I would
> split open your head and put
> a candle in
> behind the eyes.
>
> Love is dead in us
> if we forget
> the virtue of an amulet
> and quick surprise.

But the best of the short poems define the self from an oblique but penetrating angle of insight, as in the three couplets of "The End":

> When I know what people think of me
> I am plunged into my loneliness. The grey
>
> hat bought earlier sickens.
> I have no purpose no longer distinguishable.
>
> A feeling like being choked
> enters my throat.

Creeley's marital theme is expressed in the majority of poems in *For Love*, but "The Whip," "A Form of Women," "The Way," "A Marriage," and "Ballad of the Despairing Husband" capture its dilemmas with deep poignance. Other poems in this large collection depict the female as not only a sexual partner, but as a force or element to sustain male consciousness. "The Door," among the longest and most ambitious of these poems, explores the female in her divine and archetypal aspect.

In recent years, Creeley has dissolved the formalism of his verse in order to create verse fields in book-length serial compositions, in the manner of Charles Olson and Robert Duncan. He has abandoned the structural neatness of his earlier verse, but the more fluid compositions of *Words, Pieces,* and *A Day Book* tend to be lax and to include much trivial detail of his daily life.

His prose work follows the themes of his verse. The novel *The Island* deals with his marriage to his first wife. Creeley's prose is unique in modern fiction: his use of detail is extraordinarily delicate and precise, producing an uncanny perceptiveness in his narrators. Self-absorption in *The Island* is all the more compelling as the narrator dismantles his own thinking process to inspect the deterioration jealousy causes in him. Although a highly provocative writer of prose, his poetry has had a more pervasive influence.

In his criticism *A Quick Graph*, and in interviews, collected in *Contexts of Poetry*, he has proved an astute chronicler of modern poetry, particularly on the work and influence of Charles Olson, with whom he launched the movement now known as Black Mountain poetry.

—Paul Christensen

CULLEN, Countée. American. Born Countée L. Porter in New York City, 30 May 1903; adopted by Reverend and Mrs. Cullen, 1918. Educated at De Witt Clinton High School, New York; New York University, B.A. 1925 (Phi Beta Kappa); Harvard University,

Cambridge, Massachusetts, M.A. in English 1926. Married 1) Yolande Du Bois in 1928 (divorced, 1930); 2) Ida Mae Roberson in 1940. Assistant Editor, *Opportunity*, magazine of the National Urban League, 1927; French teacher, Frederick Douglass Junior High School, New York, 1934–46. Recipient: Guggenheim Fellowship, 1929. *Died 9 January 1946.*

PUBLICATIONS

Collections

On These I Stand: An Anthology of the Best Poems of Cullen.   1947.

Verse

Color.   1925.
Copper Sun.   1927.
The Ballad of the Brown Girl: An Old Ballad Retold.   1927.
The Black Christ and Other Poems.   1929.
The Medea and Some Poems.   1935.
The Lost Zoo (A Rhyme for the Young, But Not Too Young).   1940.

Plays

St. Louis Woman, with Arna Bontemps (produced 1946).
The Third Fourth of July, with Owen Dodson, in *Theatre Arts,* August 1946.

Fiction

One Way to Heaven.   1932.
My Lives and How I Lost Them (juvenile).   1942.

Other

Editor, *Caroling Dusk: An Anthology of Verse by Negro Poets.*   1927.

Bibliography: *Cullen: A Bio-Bibliography of Cullen* by Margaret Perry,   1971.

Reading List: *Roots of Negro Racial Consciousness: Three Harlem Renaissance Authors* by Stephen H. Bronz, 1964; *Cullen and the Negro Renaissance* by Blanche E. Ferguson, 1966; *In a Minor Chord* (on Cullen, Hurston, and Toomer) by Darwin T. Turner, 1971; *A Many-Colored Coat of Dreams: The Poetry of Cullen* by Houston A. Baker, Jr., 1974.

*   *   *

Countée Cullen, a Negro American, was a lyricist who found his inspiration among the 19th-century Romantic poets, especially John Keats. As Cullen himself said in 1928, "good poetry is a lofty thought beautifully expressed" (*St. Louis Argus,* 3 February 1928). Even though Cullen wrote poetry that was racially inspired, he was, first of all, a poet consciously in search of beauty.

Cullen was described frequently as being the least race-conscious among the early modern Negro poets who achieved fame in the 1920's during the period labelled "The Harlem Renaissance." Cullen suffered in his efforts to pay homage to Beauty and his race, and critics were divided about the effect of this conflict of universal vs. black experience (few then, including Cullen, speculated on aesthetic value from a strictly black point of view). When Cullen's first book, *Color*, appeared, one reviewer wrote, "Countée Cullen is a supreme master of Beauty" (*International Book Review*, March 1926). What a reader of Cullen's poetry must understand, however, is that Cullen was trying to place all of his poetry on the same level of achievement, rather than have his "racial" poetry (e.g., "Heritage," "Shroud of Color") judged by one set of standards and his "non-racial" poetry (e.g., "Wisdom Cometh with the Years," "To John Keats, Poet. At Spring Time") judged upon another, more universal, academic set.

As a black man, Cullen was not insensitive to the genre of music and sound indigenous to black Africa. The influence on Cullen's poetry, in most cases, is extremely subtle. Indeed, there is an interesting combination of black sensuousness and Romantic language in such lines as "Her walk is like the replica/Of some barbaric dance/Wherein the soul of Africa/Is winged with arrogance" ("A Song of Praise"). In his poetry, Cullen was consistently absorbed by the themes of love (both its joy and sorrow), beauty, and the evanescence of life as well as racial sorrow and racial problems; and he also revealed a romantic evocation of the African heritage he shared with his fellow poets in Harlem.

In his one novel, *One Way to Heaven*, Cullen displayed a deft skill at characterization and symbolism. His novel was, in Cullen's words, a "two-toned picture" of the upper and lower classes of blacks in Harlem during the 1920's.

Countée Cullen never achieved the heights many felt he was destined to reach when the reading public was exposed to his famous poem "Heritage" in March 1925. But he may have been restrained by the poignant last lines of this particular poem – "Yet do I marvel at this curious thing/To make a poet black and bid him sing!"

—Margaret Perry

CUMMINGS, E(dward) E(stlin). American. Born in Cambridge, Massachusetts, 14 October 1894. Educated at a private school in Cambridge; Cambridge High and Latin School; Harvard University, Cambridge, 1911–16 (Co-Founder, Harvard Poetry Society, 1915), B.A. (magna cum laude), 1915, M.A. 1916. Served in the Norton Harjes Ambulance Corps, 1917; prisoner of war, 1917–18. Married 1) Marion Morehouse; 2) Anne Barton. Worked at P. F. Collier and Company, mail order books, New York, 1916–17; lived in Paris, 1921–23; writer for *Vanity Fair*, New York, 1925–27. Artist: paintings included several times in group shows at the Society of Independent Artists, Paris; one-man shows include Painters and Sculptors Gallery, New York, 1932; American British Art Center, New York, 1944, 1949; Rochester Memorial Art Gallery, New York, 1945, 1950, 1954, 1957. Charles Eliot Norton Professor of Poetry, Harvard University, 1952–53. Recipient: Guggenheim Fellowship, 1933; Shelley Memorial Award, 1945; Academy of American Poets Fellowship, 1950; Harriet Monroe Poetry Award, 1950; National Book Award, 1955; Bollingen Prize, 1958. *Died 3 September 1962.*

Publications

Collections

> *Three Plays and a Ballet,* edited by George Firmage.   1967.
> *Complete Poems.*   1968.
> *Poems 1905–1962,* edited by George Firmage.   1973.

Verse

> *Tulips and Chimneys.*   1923; complete edition, 1937; edited by George Firmage, 1976.
> *Puella Mea.*   1923.
> *XLI.*   1925.
> *&.*   1925.
> *Is 5.*   1926.
> *Christmas Tree.*   1928.
> *(No Title).*   1930.
> *VV (Viva: Seventy New Poems).*   1931.
> *No Thanks.*   1935; edited by George Firmage, 1978.
> *1/20 (One Over Twenty).*   1936.
> *Collected Poems.*   1938.
> *Fifty Poems.*   1940.
> *1 × 1.*   1944.
> *Xaipe.*   1950.
> *Poems 1923–1954.*   1954.
> *95 Poems.*   1958.
> *100 Selected Poems.*   1959.
> *Selected Poems 1923–1958.*   1960.
> *73 Poems.*   1963.

Plays

> *Him.*   1927.
> *Tom: A Ballet.*   1935.
> *Anthropos; or, The Future of Art.*   1945.
> *Santa Claus: A Morality.*   1946.

Fiction

> *The Enormous Room.*   1922; edited by George Firmage, 1978.

Other

> *CIOPW* (drawings and paintings).   1931.
> *Eimi* (travel).   1933.
> *i: Six Nonlectures.*   1953.
> *Cummings: A Miscellany,* edited by George Firmage.   1958; revised edition, 1965.
> *Adventures in Verse,* photographs by Marion Morehouse.   1962.
> *Fairy Tales* (juvenile).   1965.

Selected Letters, edited by F. W. Dupee and George Stade.   1969.

Translator, *The Red Front*, by Louis Aragon.   1933.

Bibliography: *Cummings: A Bibliography* by George Firmage, 1960.

Reading List: *The Magic-Maker: Cummings* by Charles Norman, 1958, revised edition, 1964; *Cummings: The Art of His Poetry*, 1960, and *Cummings: The Growth of a Writer*, 1964, both by Norman Friedman; *Cummings and the Critics* edited by Stanley V. Baum, 1962; *Cummings* by Barry Marks, 1964; *The Poetry and Prose of Cummings* by Robert E. Wegner, 1965; *Cummings* by Eve Triem, 1969; *Cummings: A Collection of Critical Essays* edited by Norman Friedman, 1972; *Cummings: A Remembrance of Miracles* by Bethany K. Dumas, 1973.

*   *   *

Edward Estlin Cummings, better known in lower case as e. e. cummings, is a major poet of the modern period, who grew up in a comfortable, liberal household in Cambridge, Massachusetts, where ingenuity was energetically cultivated. The neighborhood of the Irving Street home was populated by Harvard faculty; his father had taught at Harvard before becoming a Unitarian minister of considerable renown in Boston. Cummings's parents had been introduced to each other by the distinguished psychologist William James, also a neighbor. Summers were spent on the family farm in New Hampshire, where the young Cummings spent his hours musing in a study his father had built him; another was situated in a tree behind their Cambridge house. Both father and mother encouraged the gifted youth to paint and write, and, by their excessive indulgence, perhaps nurtured his diffident character. At Harvard, Cummings distinguished himself and graduated with honors in Greek and English studies, and delivered a commencement address entitled "The New Art," his survey of Cubism, new music, the writings of Gertrude Stein and Amy Lowell, all of which he defended with insight and daring before his proper Bostonian audience. It was an early declaration of Cummings's bold taste and artistic direction.

At Harvard, Cummings wrote and published poems in the undergraduate reviews, but most of them were conventional and uninspired, except for a brief collection of poems issued in a privately printed anthology, *Eight Harvard Poets* (1917). After a brief stint of work in a mail-order publishing house, the first and only regular employment in his career, Cummings quit and volunteered for service in the Norton Harjes Ambulance Corps in France. Soon after he and a friend, William Slater Brown, were interrogated by security police regarding Brown's correspondence with a German professor at Columbia University, and both were incarcerated in a French concentration camp. Cummings was freed after three months, but only after his father had written to President Wilson requesting special attention to his son's internment. From that experience, Cummings wrote *The Enormous Room*, a World War I classic, at the insistence of his father who viewed the incident as a sinister act of an ally. The long autobiographical account sparkles with reportorial details, insight, and comic invention, and asserts a theme of anti-authoritarianism throughout.

Cummings submitted his first book of poems to the publisher of *The Enormous Room*, Boni, but was refused there and at other houses. The large manuscript, entitled *Tulips and Chimneys*, contained 152 poems ranging from a long, rambling epithalamion and other derivative exercises to short, pithy works of explosive energy and significant innovation. As a last resort, Cummings's old classmate John Dos Passos found a publisher for a shortened version of 60 poems in 1923. Two years later 41 more poems were issued as *XLI*, and Cummings printed the remaining poems with some additions in *&*. In 1937, the original manuscript was issued in its entirety under its first title and now stands as one of the great classics of Modernist poetry.

255

For lyric energy, imagination, and verve, few books of poems compare with it. Even Cummings's later books do not have the vigor of this first work. Among the poems in the collection are "All in green went my love riding," "In Just," "O sweet spontaneous," "Buffalo Bill's/defunct." The work is astounding for its variety of voice, tone, technique, and theme, and the content ranges widely from outrageous satire to jazzy lyrics, from naive rhymes to sexually explicit portraits. Cummings caught the irreverent, slapdash tonality of the jazz age in his sprawling, sensuous lyrics. The old decorums were exploded and replaced by a humor Cummings had absorbed from vaudeville shows, burlesque houses, and music halls of the day.

But there is more to these experiments than we might suspect. The young Cummings was fascinated with the asyntactic language of Stein and the grotesque, paralogical imagery of Amy Lowell, and in the dismantled shapes of Cubist paintings, all of which seemed to liberate the artist from traditional logic. The new art made spontaneous perception the basis of expression. This was equally the force of jazz itself: the soloist departed from the melodic pattern to perform his own spontaneous variations according to his mood. Cummings attacked the conventional lyric with the lesson of these other arts. He took the formal lyric apart and redistributed each of its components: punctuation becomes a series of arbitrary signals he sometimes uses even as words. The function of nouns, pronouns, adverbs, and adjectives could all be interchanged in verbal flights. The barrel shape of the standard lyric could simply be blown open, as though the staves had all been unhooped. Language drips, spills, dribbles, runs over the frame in one of Cummings's Cubist-style poems. The genius in the experiment is that Cummings caught upon a series of innovations that seemed to Americanize the European-born lyric poem: in his irreverent care, the poem had become a display of verbal energy and exuberance, a vehicle of melting-pot humor and extravagance, a youthfully arrogant jazz variation of an old standard form. The modern lyric has continued to sprawl whimsically down the page ever since Cummings first scattered it in *Tulips and Chimneys*.

Cummings's innovations in other forms and media are less sure and significant, but he is nonetheless a refreshing influence. In the play form, he was drawn to over-subtle psychological comedy, as in *Him*, but he was far ahead of his time in his absurdist dialogue and surreal sets and costumes. Cummings was also a prolific graphic artist who worked in most media. Some of this work was published in *CIOPW*. Cummings strained the immediacy of prose with his massive account of a visit to Russia entitled *Eimi*, in which he assails the Marxist state and the regimented condition of Soviet citizens. The book offended the American left at home, which dominated the publishing field during the first years of the depression, and for several years Cummings published little work. A volume entitled *No Thanks*, the title directed at publishers who had rejected the manuscript, appeared in 1935, followed three years later by his first *Collected Poems*.

The many books of poems that succeeded *Tulips and Chimneys* sustained the nervous energy of his first experiments, but Cummings did not advance in new techniques so much as refine and consolidate his discoveries from the first book. As Norman Friedman points out, Cummings experimented with different aspects of his style in the years after 1923. In the 1930's, in *VV* (*ViVa*) and *No Thanks*, Cummings sought the limits of typographical experiment, extending to the curious strategy known as *tmesis*, or, the breaking up and mingling of words to achieve intense immediacy. The dismantled language of his poems focused attention on the individual word and its component letters, and often gave expressiveness to the word through its spatial arrangement. A famous poem of his later years, "l(a," is an arrangement of letters that plummet abruptly down the page, emblematic of a falling leaf and of autumn.

Over the span of his career, Cummings moved slowly away from the simple delight in love, in the seasons, in nature and simplicity, to more urgent and didactic poems that finally came to preach the virtues of naive existence, as in *Xaipe* and *95 Poems*. His argument against science, with he sometimes equated with "death," may have turned him too much against the modern world and toward pastoral themes. As a result, he is a poet of a large canon of work that is marked by much repetition of theme and perspective, but his status as a major poet is secure; one has only to "look" at an anthology of new poems to see his pervasive influence.

—Paul Christensen

CUNNINGHAM, John. Scottish. Born in Dublin, Ireland in 1729. Educated at Drogheda. Appeared on the stage in Dublin, 1747, and thereafter travelled throughout the British Isles as a strolling actor. *Died 18 September 1773.*

PUBLICATIONS

Verse

A Poetical Essay in Manner of Elegy on the Death of His Majesty. 1760.
An Elegy on a Pile of Ruins. 1761.
Day and Other Pastorals. 1761.
The Contemplatist: A Night Piece. 1762.
Fortune: An Apologue. 1765.
Poems, Chiefly Pastoral. 1766; revised edition, 1771.
Poetical Works. 1781.

Play

Love in a Mist (produced 1747). 1747.

Reading List: *Poets of Ireland* by D. J. O'Donoghue, 1912; "Cunningham" by E. J. Morley, in *Essays by Divers Hands,* 1942.

*   *   *

After the early success of his farce *Love in a Mist,* acted in Dublin in 1747, Cunningham lived the precarious life of a strolling player and occasional poet. He was favoured in youth with a letter or two from Shenstone, who advised him to "proceed in the pastoral manner." This Cunningham duly did in the short pieces eventually collected into *Poems, Chiefly Pastoral.* His conventional pastoral dialogues between Damon, Phillis, Phoebe, etc., his pastoral love-songs to Phillis, Delia, etc., and his pastoral elegy on Corydon (i.e., Shenstone), are all conventional exercises in an exhausted tradition. There is little originality either in his jog-trot pastoral ballads about contented millers, pretty country lasses, and general rural contentment, though his songs "Kate of Aberdeen" and "Kitty Fell" have some simple charm. Best, and best known, is the little series of well-observed landscape vignettes which make up his "Day: A Pastoral" in three parts – "Morning," "Noon," and "Evening."

His longest poem, *An Elegy on a Pile of Ruins* is an avowed imitation of Gray's *Elegy,* but has more extravagant and stagey Gothick romantic effects than Gray's. The manner may be adequately illustrated by one stanza:

Where the mild sun, through saint-encyphered glass,
Illum'd with mellow light yon dusky aisle,
Many rapt hours might Meditation pass,
Slow moving 'twixt the pillars of the pile.

Cunningham wrote two other moral, reflective pieces – *The Contemplatist: A Night Piece* and *Fortune: An Apologue* – and wrote prologues, epilogues, fables, anacreontics, and occasional lyrics, but nearly all his work is derivative and factitious. There is, perhaps, most vigour and originality in his song in praise of Newcastle Beer, a "liquor so lively, so potent and clear."

—A. J. Sambrook

CURNOW, Allen. New Zealander. Born in Timaru, 17 June 1911. Educated at Christchurch Boys High School, 1924–28; University of New Zealand, Canterbury, 1929–30, and Auckland, 1931–38, B.A. 1938; St. John's College (Anglican theological), Auckland, 1931–33. Married 1) Elizabeth J. LeCren in 1936; 2) Jenifer Mary Tole in 1965; three children. Cadet Journalist, *Sun*, Christchurch, 1929–30; Reporter and Sub-Editor, 1935–48, and Drama Critic, 1945–47, *The Press*, Christchurch; Member of the News and Sub-Editorial Staff, *News Chronicle*, London, 1949. Lecturer, 1951–53, Senior Lecturer, 1954–66, and since 1967 Associate Professor of English, University of Auckland. Recipient: New Zealand State Literary Fund travel award, 1949; Carnegie grant, 1950; New Zealand University Research Committee grant, 1957, 1966; Jessie Mackay Memorial Prize, 1957, 1962; Institute of Contemporary Arts Fellowship, Washington, D.C., 1961; Whittall Fund award, Library of Congress, 1966; New Zealand Poetry Award, 1975. Litt.D.: University of New Zealand, Auckland, 1966; University of Canterbury, Christchurch, 1975. Lives in Auckland.

PUBLICATIONS

Verse

Valley of Decision. 1933.
Another Argo, with Denis Glover and A. R. D. Fairburn. 1935.
Three Poems. 1935.
Enemies: Poems 1934–1936. 1937.
Not in Narrow Seas. 1939.
Recent Poems, with others. 1941.
Island and Time. 1941.
Verses, 1941–1942. 1942.
Sailing or Drowning. 1943.
Jack Without Magic. 1946.
At Dead Low Water, and Sonnets. 1949.
Poems 1947–1957. 1957.
A Small Room with Large Windows: Selected Poems. 1962.
Whim Wham Land. 1967.

Trees, Effigies, Moving Objects: A Sequence of 18 Poems.   1972.
An Abominable Temper and Other Poems.   1973.
Collected Poems 1933–1973.   1974.

Plays

The Axe: A Verse Tragedy (produced 1948).   1949.
Moon Section (produced 1959).
The Overseas Expert (broadcast 1961).   In *Four Plays,* 1972.
Doctor Pom (produced 1964).
The Duke's Miracle (broadcast 1967).   In *Four Plays,* 1972.
Resident of Nowhere (broadcast 1969).   In *Four Plays,* 1972.
Four Plays (includes *The Axe, The Overseas Expert, The Duke's Miracle, Resident of Nowhere*).   1972.

Radio Plays: *The Overseas Expert,* 1961; *The Duke's Miracle,* 1967; *Resident of Nowhere,* 1969.

Other

Editor, *A Book of New Zealand Verse, 1923–1945.*   1945; revised edition, 1951.
Editor, *The Penguin Book of New Zealand Verse.*   1960.

Reading List: "Curnow's Poetry (Notes Towards a Criticism)" by C. K. Stead, in *Landfall,* March 1963; "Curnow's *The Axe*" by A. Krishna Sarma, in *The Achievement of Christopher Fry and Other Essays,* 1970.

*   *   *

Allen Curnow is the New Zealand poet who has been most closely associated with the pursuit, common to all emergent societies, of a national identity. His sense of the complex possibilities of language as personality, individual and national, made him one of the outstanding poets of his time and place.

Self-scrutiny and a sense of identity are urgent, perhaps primary, objectives in any small and isolated community where Allen Tate's sense of the word regionalism may be applied. Curnow's major subject has been what he called the imaginative discovery of New Zealand, and his most "major" poetry came in the years when he led the search. His later poetry, technically even more accomplished, is characterised by a search for what Kendrick Smithyman (in an essay in *Essays on New Zealand Literature,* edited by Wystan Curnow, 1962) called the "true voice of feeling."

Smithyman's own favoured definition for poetry, a way of saying, is perhaps too limiting a term for Curnow. Consistently doctrinaire, though courteously argumentative rather than abrasive, he is always conscious of the isolation not only of his country but of the poet himself in the community generally indifferent or even hostile to the linguistic and moral aspects of aesthetics which the poet is the first to record. His life and his poetry show him consistently rejecting the ivory tower and the easy assumption that poets write only for other poets. For many years in fact, he wrote a weekly verse column for an Auckland newspaper, commenting on current events, and he has written verse broadsheets attacking local philistinism. Curnow's efforts to activate his ideas in the community appear on a different level in his plays, but it is perhaps best to consider them as complex, well-articulated presentations of themes accessible in his poems.

Island and Time, *At Dead Low Water*, and *A Small Room with Large Windows* are his best collections of verse. They include highly wrought meditative poems, mostly short, in a voice that sounds mannered without being idiosyncratic or exhibitionistic. No single poem can be taken as representative of a poetic career as long as Curnow's or of an *oeuvre* in which every poem is a carefully achieved entity, but the verbal precision and concentration are well demonstrated by the opening lines of "The Eye Is More or Less Satisfied with Seeing" (from *Poems 1949–57*):

> Wholehearted he can't move
> From where he is, nor love
>
> Wholehearted that place,
> Indigene janus-face,
>
> Half mocking half,
> Neither caring to laugh.
>
> Does true or false sun rise?
> Do both half eyes tell lies?

Curnow's voice is uniquely his own. Stylistic and other debts do show up in his poetry, but he never seems imitative. Such influences as do show themselves indicate a firmly eclectic collector's instinct. He has Eliot's concern for tradition and for a literate Europeanism. More conspicuously though, in view of his efforts towards an imaginative discovery of his region's identity, his work does show graftings from American poetry of the 1930's and 1940's, especially the poets of the American South.

C. K. Stead has made the point that the perspectives in Curnow's poems are simultaneously physical, local realities and moral, intellectual, and emotional landscapes. Imaginative self-discovery integrates the two. That kind of concern uses poetic devices as it absorbs influences, without attitudinising, without falling into a single idiom as many poets more ready with words than Curnow have done. His grappling with words and realities alike is slow, earnest, and scrupulous. Curnow is one of the three or four life-size – to use his own term – writers New Zealand has produced.

—Andrew Gurr

CYNEWULF.   Anglo-Saxon; late 8th or 9th century.

PUBLICATIONS

Collections

The Poems, translated into English prose by Charles W. Kennedy.   1910.

Verse

Andreas und Elene, edited by J. Grimm. 1840; *Elene* edited by P. O. E. Gradon, 1958.
The Fates of the Apostles, in Appendix B to *Cooper's Report on Rymer's Foedera*, by B.
   Thorpe. 1869; *Andreas and The Fates of the Apostles* edited by Kenneth R. Brooks,
   1961.
Christ, edited by I. Gollancz. 1892; *Christ: A Poem in Three Parts: The Advent, The
   Ascension, and The Last Judgment*, edited by Albert S. Cook, 1900.
Juliana, edited by W. Strunk. 1904; edited by Rosemary E. Woolf, 1955, revised
   edition, 1966.

Reading List: "Cynewulf and His Poetry" by Kenneth Sisam, in *Proceedings of the British
Academy 18*, 1932; *Cynewulf and the Cynewulf Canon* by S. K. Das, 1942; *Critical Studies in
the Cynewulf Group* by C. Schaar, 1949; "The Diction of the Signed Poems of Cynewulf" by
R. E. Diamond, in *Philological Quarterly 38*, 1959.

                                    *   *   *

Cynewulf is the author of four extant Old English poems, *Elene, The Fates of the Apostles,
Juliana*, and the second of three poems which collectively are called *Christ*. The first two are
found in the *Vercelli Book* and the others in the *Exeter Book*, both of around 1000 A.D.,
though the language of the poems suggests that they were composed in the ninth century
somewhere in the Anglian area (i.e., north of the Thames). Cynewulf's authorship is known
because he included in each of these poems autobiographical epilogues, in the texts of which
he contrived to interweave his name in runic letters.
    Juliana is a conventional saint's life, recounting the heroine's determined resistance to
marriage with a powerful pagan nobleman. She suffers indescribable torture and dies a
martyr's death. Cynewulf's lack of interest in straightforward narrative is shown by the long
section in which the devil is made to confess to Juliana the evil deeds he has contrived since
the world began. There are two large gaps, the result of missing leaves in the manuscript, but
the lost passages can be reconstructed by reference to a Latin prose source.
    The first part of *Christ B* is a dramatic treatment of the Ascension, and in the second and
rather longer part Cynewulf adds his own comments, drawing upon a variety of sources
ranging from patristic writings to vernacular gnomic verse. *Christ B* is separated in the
manuscript from the other *Christ* poems, but there are no great differences in style and all of
them could conceivably be the work of Cynewulf, although *B* alone contains his signature.
The three events dealt with in the complete poem — Nativity, Ascension and Last Judgement
— were often treated together in early Christian art.
    In *The Fates of the Apostles* Cynewulf enumerates briefly the deeds and deaths of the
twelve Apostles in a style reminiscent of the secular heroic poem *Widsith*. He mourns the
passing of former glory in a reflective, elegiac mood which is found in other of his poems.
    Elene is Cynewulf's masterpiece. It tells the story of the discovery and veneration of
Christ's Cross by Saint Helena, mother of Constantine the Great. Beginning with an account
of Constantine's conversion, it goes on to relate the mission of Helena and the refusal of the
Jews to help. The Jewish spokesman, Judas, is made to suffer imprisonment and torture, and
is eventually converted and leads the searchers to where the cross is buried, proving its
authenticity by performing with it a miraculous cure. He assumes the new name of Cyriac,
becomes a bishop, and later, with the aid of a miraculous light, discovers the Crucifixion
nails. The poem ends with a reference to the Feast of the Elevation of the Cross, which was
perhaps the occasion for which it was written. Cynewulf's source was a version of the Latin
Life of Saint Cyriac, but he developed this in his own way, concentrating on the main events,
using secular poetic diction for descriptions of battles, speeches, journeys, etc., and
externalising emotional events (e.g., Judas's altercation with the devil at the time of his

conversion). The passages describing the Cross have unmistakable parallels in the better-known poem *The Dream of the Rood.*

Most Old English poems are anonymous, the only other exceptions being Caedmon's *Hymn* and Bede's *Death Song.* Many others have at some time in the past been attributed to Cynewulf, but such theories do not find much support in the present day.

—G. A. Lester

DANIEL, Samuel. English. Born near Taunton, Somerset, c. 1562. Educated at Magdalen Hall, Oxford, 1581–84. Served with the English Ambassador to Paris, Lord Stafford, 1586; with Sir Edward Dymoke, the Queen's Champion, in Italy, c. 1590–91, at Lincoln, 1592; with the Countess of Pembroke, c. 1592–94; with Lord Mountjoy, c. 1595; Tutor to the Countess of Cumberland's daughter, Lady Anne Clifford, c. 1599; Licenser to the Children of the Queen's Revels, 1604–05; served with the Earl of Hertford, c. 1605–08; Groom of the Queen's Privy Chamber, 1607–12, and Gentleman Extraordinary of the Queen's Privy Chamber, 1613–19; also Manager of the Youths of Her Majesty's Royal Chamber of Bristol, 1615–18. Lived in Beckington, Somerset, after 1611. *Buried 14 October 1619.*

PUBLICATIONS

Collections

> *Complete Works in Verse and Prose,* edited by Alexander B. Grosart.   5 vols., 1885–96.
> *Poems, and A Defence of Rhyme,* edited by Arthur Colby Sprague.   1930.

Verse

> *Delia, An Ode, The Complaint of Rosamond.*   1592; revised edition, 1592; as *Delia and Rosamond Augmented, Cleopatra,* 1594; revised edition of *Delia,* in Works, 1601; *Delia* edited by A. Esdaile, with *Idea* by Michael Drayton, 1908; *The Complaint of Rosamond* edited by N. Alexander, in *Elizabethan Narrative Verse,* 1967.
> *The Civil Wars,* books 1–5.   1595; books 1–6, in *Works,* 1601; books 1–8, 1609; edited by Laurence Michel, 1958.
> *Poetical Essays.*   1599; *Musophilus* edited by Raymond Himelick, 1965.
> *Works.*   1601.
> *A Panegyric Congratulatory to the King's Majesty, Certain Epistles.*   1603.
> *Certain Small Poems, Philotas.*   1605; revised edition, as *Certain Small Works,* 1607, 1611.
> *A Funeral Poem upon the Earl of Devonshire.*   1606.
> *The Whole Works in Poetry.*   1623.

Plays

> *Cleopatra* (produced 1593?).   In *Delia and Rosamond Augmented, Cleopatra,* 1594; edited by Geoffrey Bullough, in *Narrative and Dramatic Sources of Shakespeare 5,* 1964.
> *The True Description of a Royal Masque* (produced 1604).   1604; as *The Vision of the 12 Goddesses,* 1604; edited by Joan Rees, in *A Book of Masques in Honour of Allardyce Nicoll,* 1967.
> *Philotas* (produced 1604).   In *Certain Small Poems, Philotas,* 1605; edited by Laurence Michel, 1949.
> *The Queen's Arcadia* (produced 1605).   1606.
> *Tethys' Festival* (produced 1610).   In *The Creation of Prince Henry, Prince of Wales,* 1610; edited by J. Nichols, in *Progresses of James I,* 1828.
> *Hymen's Triumph* (produced 1614).   1615.

Other

A Defence of Rhyme, in A Panegyric Congratulatory to the King's Majesty. 1603; edited by G. B. Harrison, with Observations in the Art of English Poesie by Thomas Campion, 1925.
The First Part of the History of England.   1612; revised edition, as The Collection of the History of England, 1618.

Translator, The Worthy Tract of Paulus Jovius Containing a Discourse of Imprese.   1585.

Bibliography: Daniel: A Concise Bibliography by S. A. Tannenbaum, 1942; supplement by G. R. Guffey, 1967.

Reading List: Daniel: A Critical and Biographical Study by Joan Rees, 1964; Daniel by Cecil Seronsy, 1967; Daniel: Sa Vie, Son Oeuvre by Pierre Spriet, 1968.

*   *   *

Samuel Daniel's literary career is of a kind and quality which have always brought him the attention and admiration of the discriminating. The range of his work includes lyric, Ovidian narrative, plays (both closet drama and works intended for performance), masques, an historical poem of epic character, and a prose history. He also wrote a critical essay of unusual breadth and penetration, verse epistles of distinction, and an admirable verse treatise embodying a "general defence of all learning." His sonnet sequence, Delia, one of the earliest and best of the time, using, predominantly, the English or Shakespearian form, lacks the drama and variety found in some others but compensates for this by its skilful patterns of imagery and subtle use of assonance, alliteration, and balance. The lyric impulse is fortified by an intelligence which controls the verse patterns and penetrates to some depth the situation of the frustrated lover.

As Daniel grew older, a vein of mature reflectiveness became one of his most striking characteristics. Beautiful and powerful passages may occur anywhere in his work but the distinctive tone is one of sober, thoughtful eloquence. He is among the most humane of the Elizabethans and his commentaries on people and events, in all the modes which he employed, are marked by a firm sense of moral values coupled with a sympathetic and imaginative understanding of human predicaments. This is as true when he deals with the life of Cleopatra in a play as when he writes a fine funeral elegy for his friend and patron, Charles Blount, Duke of Devonshire. He was keenly aware of the many-sidedness of experience and may have learnt to treat this with special insight and feeling because of the degree of conflict in his own personality, between his lyric gifts on the one hand and his critical and scholarly intelligence on the other. The duality sometimes weakens his work but often enriches it, for the range and intelligence of his sensitivity and responsiveness constitute a large part of his attractiveness as a writer. Those readers who allow his quiet voice to speak to them understand why his contemporaries (including Shakespeare) found him worth imitating and why Wordsworth and Coleridge, among many others, singled him out for praise.

—Joan Rees

DARLEY, George. Irish. Born in Dublin in 1795. Educated at Trinity College, Dublin, 1815–20, B.A. 1820. Moved to London in 1822: wrote, mainly on the drama, for *London Magazine* and the *Athenaeum*. Also a mathematician. *Died 23 November 1846.*

PUBLICATIONS

Collections

Complete Poetical Works, edited by Ramsay Colles.   1908.

Verse

The Errors of Esctasy: A Dramatic Poem, with Other Pieces.   1822.
Nepenthe.   1835.
Poems.   1889.

Plays

Sylvia; or, The May Queen.   1827.
Thomas à Becket.   1840.
Ethelstan; or, The Battle of Brunanburg.   1841.

Other

The Labours of Idleness; or, Seven Nights' Entertainments.   1826.
A System of Popular Geometry, Algebra, Trigonometry.   3 vols., 1826–27.
The Geometrical Companion.   1828.
The New Sketch Book.   2 vols., 1829.
Familiar Astronomy.   1830.

Editor, The Works of Beaumont and Fletcher.   2 vols., 1840.

Bibliography: "Some Uncollected Authors 28: Darley" by Cecil Woolf, in *Book Collector 10,* 1961.

Reading List: *Life and Letters of Darley, Poet and Critic* by Claude Colleer Abbott, 1928; *Darley* by Abraham J. Leventhal, 1950; Introduction by James Reeves to *Five Late Romantic Poets,* 1974.

*   *   *

George Darley published a good deal of creative work, including prose tales and sketches (*Labours of Idleness*) and plays (among which was *Thomas à Becket*, which Henry Crabb Robinson thought "a work of genius"); and he was also an incisive dramatic critic, writing for the *London Magazine* under the pseudonym of John Lacy, as well as an amateur of painting, a mathematician, and a literary scholar. If he is known today, however, it is for his lyrics, the best of which are to be found in the collection entitled *Nepenthe*.

Although he had firm opinions about the poetry of his time, deprecating in particular the dominant influence of Byron, Darley was never able to realize in his own work the ideals to which he aspired. He spoke in an article called "The Enchanted Lyre" of his "unsystematised" and "heterogeneous" nature, and his verse acquires much of its consistency only insofar as it is derivative, for he sought escape from the impasse of contemporary poetry by turning back to the work of earlier writers – to the middle ages, to the Elizabethans, and to the cavalier lyrists. "It Is Not Beauty I Demand" is a pastiche of seventeenth-century lyric sufficiently accomplished to have been included in early editions of Palgrave's *Golden Treasury* as an anonymous Cavalier piece; "O May, Thou Art a Merry Time" is an effective exercise in the Elizabethan manner; and in such pieces as "The Demon's Cave" we find a quasi-Jacobean fascination with the macabre. There is also an obvious debt to Shelley and Keats, and Darley's best lyric, "O Blest Unfabled Incense-Tree," a vivid fantasy on the self-regeneration of the phoenix, puts one in mind of Coleridge, although Darley here achieves a distinctive idiom and movement of his own.

It must, however, be conceded that his inspiration is almost entirely literary, and, as Ian Jack points out in his *English Literature, 1815–1832*, his diction is enfeebled by its lack of contact with the spoken English of the time. These qualities of his verse reflect the hesitancy and diffidence of his character, and bespeak Darley's withdrawal from life into the less harsh world of books. Darley's work can accordingly be praised only within narrow limits, for it must always evoke an atmosphere of the study; but within these limits we can recognize and take pleasure in the technical artistry and delicacy of perception which are features of his best work.

—James Reeves

DARWIN, Erasmus. English. Born in Elston, Nottinghamshire, 12 December 1731. Educated at Chesterfield School, 1741–50; St. John's College, Cambridge (Exeter Scholar), B.A. 1754, M.B. 1755; studied medicine in Edinburgh, 1754–55. Married 1) Mary Howard in 1757 (died, 1770), three sons; 2) Mrs. Chandos Pole in 1781, four sons, three daughters. Physician: settled in Lichfield, 1756, Derby, 1781, and afterwards at Breadsall Priory. Founder, Philosophical Society, Derby, 1784; Founder, Lichfield Dispensary, 1784; formed a botanical garden near Lichfield, 1778. *Died 18 April 1802.*

PUBLICATIONS

Collections

Essential Writings, edited by Desmond King-Hele.   1968.

Verse

The Loves of the Plants.   1789.
The Botanic Garden.   2 vols., 1791.
The Golden Age: A Poetical Epistle to T. Beddoes.   1794.
The Temple of Nature; or, The Origin of Society.   1803.
Poetical Works.   3 vols., 1806.

Other

Zoonomia; or, The Laws of Organic Life.   2 vols., 1794–96.
A Plan for the Conduct of Female Education in Boarding School.   1797.
Phytologia; or, The Philosophy of Agriculture and Gardening.   1800.

Editor, *Experiments Establishing a Criterion,* by Charles Darwin.   1780.

Translator, *The Families of Plants,* by Carolus Linnaeus.   1787.

Reading List: *Doctor Darwin* by Hesketh Pearson, 1930; *The Poetry and Aesthetics of Darwin* by James V. Logan, 1936; *Darwin,* 1963, and *Doctor of Revolution: The Life and Genius of Darwin,* 1977, both by Desmond King-Hele; *The Comedian as the Letter D: Darwin's Comic Materialism* by Donald M. Hassler, 1973.

*   *   *

Erasmus Darwin was a renowned medical doctor and the grandfather of Charles Darwin. His own early theories of biological evolution and other daring scientific speculations have been overshadowed by the work of his grandson, but his imaginative expressions of these speculations in ornate and comic Popean couplets and vigorous prose notes remain an interesting example of the late 18th-century Age of Sensibility. The literary effects in his verse, in particular, are deliberately contrived both to raise and to evade the notion of limitless fecundity in nature. Darwin was closely associated with other materialists, natural philosophers, and inventors such as Joseph Priestley, Josiah Wedgwood, and James Watt, with whom he founded the famous Lunar Society of Birmingham. His influence on the British romantic poets was considerable, and Coleridge coined the word "Darwinizing" to refer to his imaginative and wide-ranging speculations.

His long poems and prose treatises, world famous in his time but now available only in facsimile, were originally published by the radical London bookseller Joseph Johnson. Most notable among them are the poems *The Botanic Garden* and *The Temple of Nature* and the medical treatise containing evolutionary theory *Zoonomia.* Darwin's influences as a speculator and enthusiast of causes ranging from the French Revolution to the anti-slavery movement also extended to the circle of radicals such as William Godwin; and Godwin's daughter, Mary Shelley, mentions Darwin in her account of the intellectual origins of *Frankenstein.* William Blake illustrated some of Darwin's poems and delighted in his wide-ranging speculations, although he abominated the compressed and rational poetic form. Finally, Darwin should be remembered for his energy, his inventiveness, and his subtle expression of many ideas of the Enlightenment.

—Donald M. Hassler

DAVIDSON, Donald (Grady).   American.   Born in Campbellsville, Tennessee, 18 August 1893. Educated at Branham and Hughes School, 1905–09; Vanderbilt University, Nashville, B.A. 1917, M.A. 1922. Served in the 324th Infantry, 81st Division, of the United States Army, in France, 1917–19: First Lieutenant. Married Theresa Sherrer in 1918; one daughter. Teacher in schools in Cedar Hill and Mooresville, Tennessee, 1910–14, and Pulaski, Tennessee, 1916–17, and at Kentucky Wesleyan College, Winchester, 1919–20; Instructor in English, 1920, Professor, 1927–64, and Professor Emeritus, 1964–68, Vanderbilt University;

also, Member of the Faculty, Bread Loaf School of English, Middlebuty College, Vermont, Summers 1931–68. Co-Founder, *Fugitive* magazine, Nashville, 1922; Literary Editor and Columnist ("Spyglass"), *Nashville Tennessean*, 1924–30. Member, Advisory Board, *Modern Age* and *The Intercollegiate Review*. Chairman, Tennessee Federation for Constitutional Government, 1955–59. Litt.D.: Cumberland University, 1946; Washington and Lee University, Lexington, Virginia, 1948; L.H.D.: Middlebury College, 1965. *Died 25 April 1968.*

PUBLICATIONS

Verse

Avalon, with *Armageddon* by John Crowe Ransom and *A Fragment* by William Alexander Percy. 1923.
An Outland Piper. 1924.
The Tall Men. 1927.
Lee in the Mountains and Other Poems. 1938.
The Long Street. 1961.
Poems 1922–1961. 1966.

Play

Singin' Billy, music by Charles Faulkner Bryan (produced 1952).

Other

The Attack on Leviathan: Regionalism and Nationalism in the United States. 1938.
American Composition and Rhetoric. 1939; revised edition, with Ivar Lou Myhr, 1947, 1959.
The Tennessee. 2 vols., 1946–48.
Twenty Lessons in Reading and Writing Prose. 1955.
Still Rebels, Still Yankees, and Other Essays. 1957.
Southern Writers in the Modern World. 1958.
Concise American Composition and Rhetoric. 1964.
The Spyglass: Views and Reviews 1924–1930, edited by John T. Fain. 1963.
It Happened to Them: Character Studies of New Testament Men and Women. 1965.
The Literary Correspondence of Davidson and Allen Tate, edited by John T. Fain and T. D. Young. 1974.

Editor, *British Poetry of the Eighteen-Nineties.* 1937.
Editor, with Sidney E. Glenn, *Readings for Composition.* 1942; revised edition, 1957.
Editor, *Selected Essays and Other Writings of John Donald Wade.* 1966.

Reading List: *The Fugitive Group,* 1957, and *The Southern Critics,* 1971, both by Louise Cowan; *The Fugitive Poets* edited by William Pratt, 1965; *Davidson: An Essay and a Bibliography* by T. D. Young and M. Thomas Inge, 1965; *Davidson* by T. D. Young, 1971.

*   *   *

An original member of the group of poets who published *The Fugitive*, Davidson published some of his first poems in that journal. From 1924 to 1930 he was literary editor of the *Nashville Tennessean* and produced what one critic has called the "best literary page ever published in the South." He contributed to both agrarian symposia, *I'll Take My Stand* (1930) and *Who Owns America?* (1938), and is widely known and respected as poet, essayist, editor, historian, and critic.

As poet Davidson's reputation must stand on *The Tall Men*, "Lee in the Mountains" (1934), and a half dozen poems from *The Long Street*. *The Tall Men*, a book-length narrative, is organized around a young man's search for a meaningful tradition, a heritage of heroism and humanism. The exploration of Davidson's protagonist, a modern southern American, is not a vague, nostalgic meandering into a far distant past. Instead, his excruciating self-analysis is an attempt "to name and set apart from time/One sudden face" and to understand his present situation by discovering how he is related to the history and history makers of his own section of the country. He finally becomes aware not only of his traditional heritage but of the forces that would destroy it. "Lee in the Mountains," Davidson's most widely anthologized poem, presents Davidson's art at its best. In its epic dignity, its purity of form, its dramatic presentation of theme, it demonstrates as no other poem of his does the totality of his vision and the range of his imagination. The force and clarity of his presentation in this and many other of his poems give him a place almost unique among the poets of his generation. For Davidson, however, prose was the dominant means of expression throughout his career. As literary critic and social and political philosopher he offered cogent and convincing arguments in a prose that was lucid, smooth, and supple. As a prose stylist Davidson has few peers in contemporary American literature.

—T. D. Young

DAVIDSON, John. Scottish. Born in Barrhead, Renfrewshire, 11 April 1857. Educated at the Highlander's Academy, Greenock, to 1870; University of Edinburgh, 1876. Married Margaret Cameron MacArthur in 1884; two sons. Worked in Walker's Chemical Laboratory; Assistant to the Public Analyst, 1871–72; Teacher, Alexander's Endowed School, Glasgow, 1877–78, Perth Academy, 1878–81, Kelvinside Academy, Glasgow, 1881–82, and Hutchinson Charity School, Paisley, 1883–84; Clerk in a Glasgow thread factory, 1884; Teacher, Morrison's Academy, Crieff, 1885–88, and in a public school in Greenock, 1888–89; lived in London, 1890–1907, Penzance, 1907–09: regular contributor, *The Speaker*, London, 1890–99, and the *Star* and *Yellow Book*, London; reader for Grant Richards, publishers, London, 1907–09. Granted Civil List pension, 1906. *Died* (by suicide) *23 March 1909.*

Publications

Collections

> *A Selection of His Poems*, edited by Maurice Lindsay.   1961.
> *Poems*, edited by Andrew Turnbull.   2 vols., 1973.

Verse

In a Music-Hall and Other Poems. 1891.
Fleet Street Eclogues. 1893; *Second Series*, 1895.
Ballads and Songs. 1894.
New Ballads. 1896.
The Last Ballad and Other Poems. 1898.
The Testament of a Vivisector, a Man Forbid, an Empire-Builder, a Prime Minister, John Davidson. 5 vols., 1901–08.
Selected Poems. 1905.
Holiday and Other Poems, with a Note on Poetry. 1906.
Fleet Street and Other Poems. 1909.

Plays

Diabolus Amans. 1885.
Bruce. 1886.
Smith. 1888.
Plays (includes *An Unhistorical Pastoral, A Romantic Farce, Scaramouch in Naxos*). 1889.
For the Crown, from a play by François Coppée (produced 1896). 1896; revised version, as *The Cross and the Crescent*, music by Colin McAlpine (produced 1903).
The Children of the King, from a translation by Carl Armbruster of a play by Ernst Rosmer (produced 1897); revised version, as *Children of Kings* (produced 1902).
Godfrida. 1898.
Self's the Man. 1901.
A Rosary. 1903.
The Knight of the Maypole. 1903.
A Queen's Romance, from a play by Hugo (produced 1904). 1904.
Bohemos, from a play by M. Zamacois (produced 1904).
The Theatrocrat: A Tragic Play of Church and State. 1905.
God and Mammon (*The Triumph of Mammon, Mammon and His Message*). 2 vols., 1907–08.
Where the Heather Grows (produced 1913).

Fiction

The North Wall. 1885.
Perfervid: The Career of Ninian Jamieson. 1890.
The Great Men and a Practical Novelist (stories). 1891.
Laura Ruthven's Widowhood, with Charles J. Wills. 1892.
Baptist Lake. 1894.
A Full and True Account of the Wonderful Mission of Earl Lavender. 1895.
Miss Armstrong's and Other Circumstances (stories). 1896.

Other

Sentences and Paragraphs. 1893.
A Random Itinerary. 1894.
A Rosary (miscellany). 1903.
The Man Forbid and Other Essays. 1910.

Editor, *Pictures of Rustic Landscape,* by Birkett Foster. 1895.

Translator, *Persian Letters,* by Montesquieu. 1892.

Bibliography: *Davidson: A Grub Street Bibliography* by J. S. Lester, Jr., 1958.

Reading List: *Davidson: A Study in Personality* by Robert D. Macleod, 1957; *Davidson, Poet of Armageddon* by J. Benjamin Townsend, 1961.

*   *   *

John Davidson represents the reverse side of the Calvinist coin. The son of a minister belonging to an extreme sect, and from a family in which there was a history of mental unbalance – Davidson's brother tried to kill his mother with a carving knife – over-reaction against his Calvinistic upbringing took the form of the assertion of a passionate atheism allied to the philosophy of Schopenhauer and Nietzsche, the evolutionary theories of Darwin, and the popular scientific discoveries of his own day.

Of his early verse-plays, written before he had become a *Yellow Book* contributor in London, *Scaramouch in Naxos,* the best, seems today an odd blend of misdirected energy, once-fashionable cliché, and flashes of poetic talent embedded in a contrivance of sheer unreadability. Shortly before his suicide, he completed two parts of a trilogy of verse dramas, *God and Mammon,* achieving a certain forceful grandeur to buttress his rhetoric:

> We ourselves are fate;
> We are the universe; we are all that is;
> Outside of us nothing that is not us
> Can be at all....
> We are ether, we are the universe,
> We are eternity: not sense, not spirit,
> But matter; but the whole become self-conscious.
> Whatever Heaven there is, whatever Hell,
> Here now we have it....

His many volumes of lyrical poetry contain much that is flawed by contemporary mannerisms of diction, insufficient revision, and, as he grew older, simply shrillness. Yet his handful of good things, like "The Runable Stag," "In Romney Marsh," and the epitaph from *The Testament of John Davidson* show an emotional honesty and a directness of expression uncommon in their day. With James ("B. V.") Thomson, another inverted anti-Calvinist and poet of despair, and, like Davidson, also from industrial Clydeside, he thus helped lay the foundation of the 20th century Scottish Renaissance movement. Indeed, his poem "Thirty Bob a Week," with its workaday Cockney clerk's language, was to influence not only Hugh MacDiarmid but T. S. Eliot. (See the selection edited by Maurice Lindsay, with an Introduction by T. S. Eliot and an essay by Hugh MacDiarmid.)

Davidson's novels suffer from the same fault of under-revision as his poetry: he was constantly striving to make ends meet through creative work, despising the prop of journalism, and so always poverty-striken. Yet the novels are not without interest; such realism as is represented by the character of Mrs. Tiplady in *Baptist Lake* and the motives behind the quest of that prophet of Evolution, J. Smith, in *A Full and True Account of the Wonderful Mission of Earl Lavender* are both healthier and more forward-looking than the then fashionable and much more popular Kailyard novels of Davidson's contemporaries Ian Maclaren and J. M. Barrie.

—Maurice Lindsay

DAVIE, Donald (Alfred).   English.   Born in Barnsley, Yorkshire, 17 July, 1922. Educated at Barnsley Holgate Grammar School; St. Catharine's College, Cambridge, B.A. 1947, M.A. 1949, Ph.D. 1951. Served in the Royal Navy, 1941–46. Married Doreen John in 1945; two sons, one daughter. Lecturer in English, 1950–57, and Fellow of Trinity College, 1954–57, University of Dublin; Visiting Professor, University of California at Santa Barbara, 1957–58; Lecturer in English, 1958–64, and Fellow of Gonville and Caius College, 1959–64, Cambridge University; Professor of English, 1964–68, Dean of Comparative Studies, 1964, and Pro-Vice-Chancellor, 1965–68, University of Essex, Wivenhoe, Colchester; Visiting Professor, Grinnell College, Iowa, 1965; Leo S. Bing Professor of English and American Literature, University of Southern California, Los Angeles, 1968–69. Since 1969, Professor of English, and since 1974 Olive H. Palmer Professor of the Humanities, Stanford University, California. British Council Lecturer, Budapest, 1961; Elliston Lecturer, University of Cincinnati, 1963. Recipient: Guggenheim Fellowship, 1973. Honarary Fellow, St. Catharine's College, Cambridge, 1973; Fellow, American Academy of Arts and Sciences, 1973. Lives in Stanford, California.

PUBLICATIONS

Verse

> *(Poems).*   1954.
> *Brides of Reason.*   1955.
> *A Winter Talent and Other Poems.*   1957.
> *The Forests of Lithuania,* from a poem by Adam Mickiewicz.   1959.
> *A Sequence for Francis Parkman.*   1961.
> *New and Selected Poems.*   1961.
> *Events and Wisdoms: Poems 1957–1963.*   1964.
> *Poems.*   1969.
> *Essex Poems 1963–1967.*   1969.
> *Six Epistles to Eva Hesse.*   1970.
> *Collected Poems, 1950–1970.*   1972.
> *The Shires: Poems.*   1974.
> *In the Stopping Train.*   1977.

Other

> *Purity of Diction in English Verse.*   1952.
> *Articulate Energy: An Enquiry into the Syntax of English Poetry.*   1955.
> *The Heyday of Sir Walter Scott.*   1961.
> *The Language of Science and the Language of Literature, 1700–1740.*   1963.
> *Ezra Pound: Poet as Sculptor.*   1964.
> *Thomas Hardy and British Poetry.*   1972.
> *Poetry in Translation.*   1975.
> *Ezra Pound.*   1976.
> *The Poet in the Imaginary Museum: Essays of Two Decades,* edited by Barry Alpert.   1976.

> Editor, *The Victims of Whiggery,* by George Loveless.   1946.
> Editor, *The Late Augustans: Longer Poems of the Later Eighteenth Century.*   1958.
> Editor, *Poems: Poetry Supplement.*   1960.

Editor, *Poetics Poetyka.* 1961.
Editor, *Selected Poems of Wordsworth.* 1962.
Editor, *Russian Literature and Modern English Fiction: A Collection of Critical Essays.* 1965.
Editor, with Angela Livingstone, *Pasternak.* 1969.
Editor, *Augustan Lyric.* 1974.
Editor, *The Collected Poems of Elizabeth Daryush.* 1975.

Translator, *The Poems of Dr. Zhivago*, by Pasternak. 1965.

Reading List: essay by Calvin Bedient, in *Iowa Review*, 1971; "A Breakthrough into Spaciousness" by Donald Greene, in *Queen's Quarterly*, 1973.

*   *   *

In one of his early poems, "Homage to William Cowper," Donald Davie describes himself as "A pasticheur of late-Augustan styles"; and many of the poems in his early collections *Brides of Reason* and *A Winter Talent* display certain qualities associated with English poets of the mid-18th century – decorum, elegance, and wit. Moreover, his critical work *Purity of Diction in English Verse* can be read not merely as a study of the principles of purity in diction but also as an apology for the young poets of the 1950's whose verse appeared in Robert Conquest's anthology *New Lines* (1956).

Yet some of the poems in *A Winter Talent* suggest that Davie had already moved away from the confines of the late-Augustan tradition. In "Dream Forest," for example, he names as types of ideal virtue Brutus, Pushkin, and Strindberg: "Classic, romantic, realist,/These I have set up." His admiration for Ezra Pound and his discovery of Pasternak have been partly responsible for the increasing richness and complexity of his later poems. His departure for Stanford University, where he succeeded to the chair formerly held by Yvor Winters (much revered by Davie as a poet and a critic), added still more complexity. Yet he has never forgotten his native roots: *The Shires* is made up entirely of descriptions of and reflections on the English counties; and his recent volume *In the Stopping Train* ends with a poem about going back to the Yorkshire town of Barnsley where he was born.

Davie is probably the finest critic of his generation, his most important critical works, apart from *Purity of Diction*, being *Articulate Energy, Ezra Pound: Poet as Sculptor*, and *Thomas Hardy and British Poetry*. The title of his collected essays in literary criticism, *The Poet in the Imaginary Museum*, indicates his attitude towards poetry. He is an extremely learned man: it is right, he believes, that poets should be learned, since poetry is a product of the intellect and of the imagination fused into unity by the poetic faculty.

His poetry has always been noteworthy for its technical inventiveness, and he has consistently sought to enlarge the range of his sensibility. His finest poems are those in which his emotional and lyrical powers are allowed to attain their full strength unimpeded by cautious reservations and self-questionings. Davie is an impressive, immensely gifted writer whose creative powers show no signs of slackening.

—John Press

DAVIES, Sir John. English. Born in Tisbury, Wiltshire, baptized 16 April 1569. Educated at Winchester School; Queen's College, Oxford, 1586–90, B.A. 1590; Middle Temple, London, 1588–94; called to the Bar, 1595; disbarred, 1597; reinstated, 1601.

Married Eleanor Touchet in 1609; two children. Member of Parliament for Corfe Castle, 1601, and for Newcastle under Lyme, 1615, 1621; also, Member of the Irish Parliament: Solicitor-General for Ireland, 1603–06, Attorney-General for Ireland, 1606–19, and Speaker of the Irish Parliament, 1613; King's Sergeant after 1609; named Lord Chief Justice of the King's Bench, 1626. A Founder, Society of Antiquaries, c. 1615. Knighted, 1609. *Died 8 December 1626.*

PUBLICATIONS

Collections

Works in Verse and Prose, edited by Alexander B. Grosart.   2 vols., 1869–76.
Poems, edited by Clare Howard.   1941.

Verse

Epigrams and Elegies of Ovid, with Christopher Marlowe.   1595(?); as *Epigrams,* with
   All Ovid's Elegies: 3 Books, 1598(?).
Orchestra; or, A Poem of Dancing.   1596; revised edition, 1622; edited by E. M. W.
   Tillyard, 1945.
Hymns of Astraea in Acrostic Verse.   1599.
*Nosce Teipsum: This Oracle Expounded in Two Elegies: Of Humane Knowledge, Of the
   Soul of Man and the Immortality Thereof.*   1599.
A Poetical Rhapsody, edited by F. Davidson.   1602.
Gulling Sonnets, edited by Alexander B. Grosart.   1873.

Other

*A Discovery of the True Causes Why Ireland Was Never Entirely Subdued until His
   Majesty's Reign.*   1612; as *A Discovery of the State of Ireland,* 1613; edited byHenry
   Morley, in *Ireland under Elizabeth and James I,* 1890.
Le Primer Report des Cases Resolves en les Courts del Roy en Ireland.   1615.
*The Question Concerning Impositions, Tonnage, Poundage, Prizage, Customs,
   etc.*   1656.

Editor, *A Perfect Abridgement of the Eleven Books of Reports,* by Sir Edward
   Coke.   1651.

Reading List: *Philosophy in Poetry: A Study of Nosce Teipsum* by E. N. Sneath, 1903; *The Poet as Philosopher: A Study of Nosce Teipsum* by Mabel D. Holmes, 1921; *Five Poems* by E. M. W. Tillyard, 1948.

*   *   *

Written primarily during the 1590's, when expulsion from the Middle Temple threatened the great public career as a jurist he ultimately achieved, Sir John Davies's poetry, with the notable exception of *Orchestra,* stays gracefully within the technical and intellectual range of the gifted amateur and divides neatly into either serious or comic verse.

Nosce Teipsum, his best known and, until recently, most admired work, enjoins man to "Use all thy powers that blessed power to praise/Which gives thee power to *be*, and *use the same*." The optimistic tone derives not only from Davies's manipulation of his sources in classical and Christian thought but also from the order and balance of the over 1900 lines, however apparently somber their theme:

> The wits that div'd most deepe, and soar'd most hie;
> Seeking Mans powers, have found his weaknes such:
> "Skill comes so slow, and life so fast doth flie,
> We learne so litle, and forget so much."

The mood of this representative stanza prefigures much 18th-century elegiac verse and explains Davies's popularity and influence in that period. The positive reactions of a wider range of readers from James I to T. S. Eliot presumably derive from Davies's embodying of complex philosophical ideas in concrete images.

But this apparent clarity is merely a soothing over-simplification with little emotional coloration, an effect making the poem's reputation puzzling. Further, Davies's explications of Renaissance psychology sometimes sink to a monosyllabic textbook style which flattens even his attempts at paradox: "Though *will* do oft, when *wit* false formes doth show,/Take *ill* for *good*, and *good* for *ill* refuse." Yet his technique is often subtle, and his analogy between the soul and a river demonstrates that elegant clarity the style can attain:

> Yet *nature* so her streames doth leade and carry,
> As that her course doth make no finall stay,
> Till she her selfe unto the *Ocean* marry,
> Within whose watery bosome first she lay.

The same technical skill informs *Hymnes of Astraea*, 26 16-line acrostics with initial letters spelling ELISABETHA REGINA. Hymnes XXI, XXII, and XXIV are especially felicitous. His *Epigrammes* earned him much contemporary praise as a comic writer (Guilpin's epithet of "English Martiall") and some condemnation (ecclesiastical authorities ordered the public burning of the volume containing the *Epigrammes* and Marlowe's *Elegies* in 1599). Like his serious verse, Davies's *Epigrammes* are competent, and he was apparently serious enough about his role as innovator to define for his audience the function of the epigram: "Which taxeth under a particular name,/A generall vice that merits publique blame" ("Ad Musam 1"). Davies is, however, often repetitive and unsubtle, as he condescendingly mocks the pretentions and excesses, primarily sexual, of his contemporaries. Perhaps familiarity with the actual victims would give needed substance to the humor, which only rarely, as in the climax to the satiric catalogue of tobacco's virtues, wittily illuminates the reality threatening Elizabethan fashionable life: "I would but say, that it the pox wil cure:/This were inough, without discoursing more,/All our brave gallants in the towne t'alure" ("Of Tobacco 36").

Davies's other major comic venture, the *Gullinge Sonnets* (composed 1594?), displays similar competence as he mocks excesses of Elizabethan imagery and implies the contrasting ideal of a utilitarian style like that of *Nosce Teipsum*. Perhaps the best is Sonnet 8, which celebrates a passion for Zepheria in an elaborate metaphor built from legal jargon like "distrein'de," "impounds," "highe Shreife," "esloynde," and "withername," imagery that threatens with ridicule even Shakespeare's powerful "sessions of sweet silent thought."

Davies wrote many occasional verses, including some recently accepted into his canon, but none approaches the brilliant fusion of philosophy and parody that characterizes *Orchestra Or a Poeme of Dauncing*, a gloss on the *Odyssey* in which a very un-Homeric Antinous uses all the charms of "courtly love" to persuade Penelope to dance, an activity combining cosmic significance with sexual innuendo. His speech of persuasion lovingly traces the concept of the universe as a dance to its genesis:

Dauncing (bright lady) then began to be,
When the first seedes whereof the world did spring,
The Fire, Ayre, Earth and Water did agree,
By Loves perswasion, Natures mighty King,
To leave their first disordred combating;
And in a daunce such measure to observe,
As all the world their motion should preserve.

This sempiternal equation of dancing and order pervades all levels of cosmic and earthly activity, from planetary motions to military exercises. Although most of *Orchestra* focuses on Antinous's exposition of this argument (like Sidney's painstaking amplification of the antiquity and power of poetry in the *Defense*), Penelope's interruptions illuminate the delicate situation within which he discourses. Antinous carries his translation of even sexual myth into the dance metaphor so far that the process tends ironically to reverse itself, undercutting the professed motive of his invitation to the dance. Like a moralizer of Ovid obsessed by dance, he retells the stories of Mars and Venus, Caenus, and Tiresias as dance allegories; the puns in the portrait of Tiresias show that play of wit for its own sake overshadows the serious theme: "He took more pleasure in a womans part."

That Davies revised the ending of the 1622 version of *Orchestra* and added the phrase "not finished" raises further questions about the poem's tone. He may have wished to remove all reference to the original dedicatee, Richard Martin, with whom he had quarrelled, or to sharpen the satiric thrust of the poem with the added stanzas on Elizabeth. Antinous's gift of a magic mirror with a vision of Elizabeth and her court dancing seems about to cause Penelope's capitulation, a curious effect for one Elizabethan archetype of chastity to have on another, when the poem abruptly ends. Though Penelope's fascination with the mirror seems to satirize the effect of similar admonitory gifts in the popular Elizabethan complaint genre, and other elements mock the equally popular Ovidian mythological poetry, *Orchestra* has no consistent satiric pattern.

Irony and parody everywhere flank straightforward, though exuberant, exposition of the dance metaphor. Davies seems secure enough in his view of the universe to be playful with one of its key images, and to glance wittily at a number of Elizabethan excesses. His most distinctive poem, a dazzling catchall of Renaissance wit and cosmology, occasionally fuses, sometimes confuses the serious and comic elements that inform his other verse.

—Burton Kendle

DAVIES, W(illiam) H(enry). Welsh. Born in Newport, Monmouthshire, 3 July 1871. Educated at local schools; worked for an ironmonger; apprenticed to a picture framer and gilder, 1886–91. Married Helen Payne in 1923. Travelled across America, tramping, 1893–99 (lost a leg jumping from a freight train in Ontario, 1899); lived in London, 1899–1906, Sevenoaks, Kent, 1906–14, London, 1914–22, and East Grinstead, Sussex, 1922; in Gloucestershire after 1931. Recipient: Royal Literary Fund grant, 1911. D.Litt.: University of Wales, 1926. Granted Civil List pension, 1919. *Died 26 September 1940.*

PUBLICATIONS

Collections

> *The Essential Davies,* edited by Brian Waters.   1951.
> *Complete Poems,* edited by Daniel George.   1963.

Verse

The Soul's Destroyer and Other Poems.   1905.
New Poems.   1906; revised edition, 1922.
Nature Poems and Others.   1908.
Farewell to Poesy and Other Pieces.   1910.
Songs of Joy and Others.   1911.
Foliage: Various Poems.   1913; revised edition, 1922.
The Bird of Paradise and Other Poems.   1914.
Child Lovers and Other Poems.   1916.
Collected Poems.   1916; *Second Series,* 1923; revised edition, 1928.
Forty New Poems.   1918.
Raptures: A Book of Poems.   1918.
The Song of Life and Other Poems.   1920.
The Captive Lion and Other Poems.   1921.
The Hour of Magic and Other Poems.   1922.
Selected Poems.   1923.
Secrets.   1924.
A Poet's Alphabet.   1925.
The Song of Love.   1926.
A Poet's Calendar.   1927.
Forty-Nine Poems, edited by Jacynth Parsons.   1928.
Selected Poems, edited by Edward Garnett.   1928.
Ambition and Other Poems.   1929.
Poems 1930–31.   1932.
The Lovers' Song-Book.   1933.
The Poems: A Complete Collection.   1934; revised edition, 1940, 1943.
Love Poems.   1935.
The Birth of Song: Poems 1935–36.   1936.
The Loneliest Mountain and Other Poems.   1939.
Common Joys and Other Poems.   1941.

Play

True Travellers: A Tramp's Opera.   1923.

Fiction

A Weak Woman.   1911.
Dancing Mad.   1927.

Other

The Autobiography of a Super-Tramp.   1908.
Beggars.   1909.
The True Traveller.   1912.
Nature.   1914.
A Poet's Pilgrimage.   1918.
Later Days.   1925.
The Adventures of Johnny Walker, Tramp.   1926.
My Birds.   1933.
My Garden.   1933.

Editor, *Shorter Lyrics of the Twentieth Century 1900–1922.*   1922.
Editor, *Poetical Works,* by Burns.   1925.
Editor, *Jewels of Song: An Anthology of Short Poems.*   1930.

Reading List: *Davies* by Thomas Moult, 1934; *Davies: A Critical Biography* by Richard J. Stonesifer, 1963; *Davies* by Lawrence W. Hockey, 1971.

*   *   *

W. H. Davies is still thought of by many people as a poet who composed verses about kingfishers, cuckoos, and rainbows, and when critical taste turned against the rural verses of the Georgians Davies was often dismissed as a sentimental poet who took refuge from the world in an idealized countryside. He was, in fact, a tough little Welshman who had experienced at first hand urban squalor, dosshouses, slums, and rural poverty. It is true that he wrote lyrics about the birds and beasts that inhabited a countryside more beautiful and less spoiled than it is now, and some of these poems retain their charm because they are notable for exact observation as well as for lyrical grace. But Davies was also a poet who drew upon his knowledge of what it was like to be a vagabond, and who got into his poems something of the harshness and realism that characterized his prose reminiscences, *The Autobiography of a Super-Tramp.*

Arthur Waugh (the father of Evelyn Waugh), who regarded the Georgians as rather unpleasant, clever young men who wrote coarse poems, described Davies's "The Bird of Paradise" as a piece of "sheer ugliness." It is one of Davies's best poems, an unsentimental description of a prostitute's deathbed. "The Inquest," a poem put into the mouth of a juryman, describes the inquest into the death of a four-month-old illegitimate child. It is a grim little piece, presenting us with a horribly accurate picture of the corpse:

> One eye, that had a yellow lid,
> Was shut — so was the mouth, that smiled;
> The left eye open, shining bright —
> It seemed a knowing little child.

In poems such as this Davies attained a memorable strength and truthfulness that will keep his best work alive for a long while.

—John Press

DAY LEWIS, C(ecil).   British.   Born in Ballintubber, Ireland, 27 April 1904. Educated at Sherborne School, Dorset; Wadham College, Oxford, M.A. Served as an Editor in the Ministry of Information, London, 1941–46. Married 1) Constance Mary King in 1928 (divorced, 1951), two sons; 2) Jill Balcon in 1951, one son, one daughter. Assistant Master, Summerfields School, Oxford, 1927–28; Teacher, Larchfield, Helensburgh, 1928–30, and Cheltenham College, 1930–35; Professor of Poetry, Oxford University, 1951–56; Norton Professor of Poetry, Harvard University, Cambridge, Massachusetts, 1964–65. Clark Lecturer, 1946, and Sidgwick Lecturer, 1956, Cambridge University; Warton Lecturer, British Academy, London, 1951; Byron Lecturer, University of Nottingham, 1952; Chancellor Dunning Lecturer, Queen's University, Kingston, Ontario, 1954; Compton

Lecturer, University of Hull, Yorkshire, 1968. Director, Chatto and Windus Ltd., publishers, London, 1954–72. Member, Arts Council of Great Britain, 1962–67. D.Litt.: University of Exeter, 1965; University of Hull, 1969; Litt.D.: Trinity College, Dublin, 1968. Honorary Fellow, Wadham College, Oxford, 1968. Fellow, 1944, Vice-President, 1958, and Companion of Literature, 1964, Royal Society of Literature; Honorary Member, American Academy of Arts and Letters, 1966; Member, Irish Academy of Letters, 1968. C.B.E. (Commander, Order of the British Empire), 1950. Poet Laureate, 1968 until his death. *Died 22 May 1972.*

<small>PUBLICATIONS</small>

Collections

The Poems, 1925–1972, edited by Ian Parsons.   1977.

Verse

Beechen Vigil and Other Poems.   1925.
Country Comets.   1928.
Transitional Poem.   1929.
From Feathers to Iron.   1931.
The Magnetic Mountain.   1933.
Collected Poems, 1929–1933.   1935; with *A Hope for Poetry,* 1935.
A Time to Dance and Other Poems.   1935.
Noah and the Waters.   1936.
A Time to Dance, Noah and the Waters and Other Poems, with an Essay, Revolution in Writing.   1936.
Overtures to Death and Other Poems.   1938.
Poems in Wartime.   1940.
Selected Poems.   1940.
Word over All.   1943.
(Poems).   1943.
Short Is the Time: Poems, 1936–43 (includes *Overtures to Death and Word over All).*   1945.
Poems, 1943–1947.   1948.
Collected Poems, 1929–1936.   1948.
Selected Poems.   1951; revised edition, 1957, 1969, 1974.
An Italian Visit.   1953.
Collected Poems.   1954.
The Newborn: D.M.B., 29th April, 1957.   1957.
Pegasus and Other Poems.   1957.
The Gate and Other Poems.   1962.
Requiem for the Living.   1964.
On Not Saying Anything.   1964.
A Marriage Song for Albert and Barbara.   1965.
The Room and Other Poems.   1965.
Day Lewis: Selections from His Poetry, edited by Patric Dickinson.   1967.
Selected Poems.   1967.
The Abbey That Refused to Die: A Poem.   1967.
The Whispering Roots.   1970; as *The Whispering Roots and Other Poems,*   1970.

Fiction

The Friendly Tree. 1936.
Starting Point. 1937.
Child of Misfortune. 1939.

Fiction (as Nicholas Blake)

A Question of Proof. 1935.
Thou Shell of Death. 1936; as *Shell of Death,* 1936.
There's Trouble Brewing. 1937.
The Beast Must Die. 1938.
The Smiler with the Knife. 1939.
Malice in Wonderland. 1940; as *Summer Camp Mystery,* 1940.
The Case of the Abominable Snowman. 1941; as *Corpse in the Snowman,* 1941.
Minute for Murder. 1947.
Head of a Traveller. 1949.
The Dreadful Hollow. 1953.
The Whisper in the Gloom. 1954.
A Tangled Web. 1956; as *Death and Daisy Bland,* 1960.
End of Chapter. 1957.
A Penknife in My Heart. 1958.
The Widow's Cruise. 1959.
The Worm of Death. 1961.
The Deadly Joker. 1963.
The Sad Variety. 1964.
The Morning after Death. 1966.
The Private Wound. 1968.

Other

Dick Willoughby (juvenile). 1933.
A Hope for Poetry. 1934.
Revolution in Writing. 1935.
Imagination and Thinking, with L. Susan Stebbing. 1936.
*We're Not Going to Do Nothing: A Reply to Mr. Aldous Huxley's Pamphlet "What Are
    You Going to Do about It?"* 1936.
Poetry for You: A Book for Boys and Girls on the Enjoyment of Poetry. 1944.
The Poetic Image. 1947.
Enjoying Poetry: A Reader's Guide. 1947.
The Colloquial Element in English Poetry. 1947.
The Otterbury Incident (juvenile). 1948.
The Poet's Task. 1951.
The Grand Manner. 1962.
The Lyrical Poetry of Thomas Hardy. 1953.
Notable Images of Virtue: Emily Brontë, George Meredith, W. B. Yeats. 1954.
The Poet's Way of Knowledge. 1957.
The Buried Day (autobiography). 1960.
The Lyric Impulse. 1965.
Thomas Hardy, with R. A. Scott-James. 1965.
A Need for Poetry? 1968.

Editor, with W. H. Auden, *Oxford Poetry 1927.* 1927.
Editor, with John Lehmann and T. A. Jackson, *A Writer in Arms,* by Ralph Fox. 1937.
Editor, *The Mind in Chains: Socialism and the Cultural Revolution.* 1937.
Editor, *The Echoing Green: An Anthology of Verse.* 3 vols., 1937.
Editor, with Charles Fenby, *Anatomy of Oxford: An Anthology.* 1938.
Editor, with L. A. G. Strong, *A New Anthology of Modern Verse, 1920–1940.* 1941.
Editor, with others, *Orion: A Miscellany 2–3.* 2 vols., 1945–46.
Editor, *The Golden Treasury of the Best Songs and Lyrical Poems in the English Language,* by Francis Turner Palgrave. 1954.
Editor, with John Lehmann, *The Chatto Book of Modern Poetry, 1915–1955.* 1956.
Editor, with Kathleen Nott and Thomas Blackburn, *New Poems 1957.* 1957.
Editor, *A Book of English Lyrics.* 1961; as *English Lyric Poems, 1500–1900,* 1961.
Editor, *The Collected Poems of Wilfred Owen.* 1963; revised edition, 1964.
Editor, *The Midnight Skaters: Poems for Young Readers,* by Edmund Blunden. 1968.
Editor, *The Poems of Robert Browning.* 1969.
Editor, *A Choice of Keats's Verse.* 1971.
Editor, *Crabbe.* 1973.

Translator, *The Georgics of Virgil.* 1940.
Translator, *The Graveyard by the Sea,* by Paul Valéry. 1947.
Translator, *The Aeneid of Virgil.* 1952.
Translator, *The Eclogues of Virgil.* 1963; with *The Georgics,* 1964.
Translator, with Mátyás Sárközi, *The Tomtit in the Rain: Traditional Hungarian Rhymes,* by Erzsi Gazdas. 1971.

Bibliography: *Day Lewis, The Poet Laureate: A Bibliography* by Geoffrey Handley-Taylor and Timothy d'Arch Smith, 1968.

Reading List: *Day Lewis* by Clifford Dyment, 1955, revised edition, 1963; *Spender, MacNeice, Day Lewis: A Critical Essay,* by Derek Stanford, 1969; *Day Lewis* by Joseph N. Riddel, 1971; *"The Angry Young Men" of the Thirties* by Elton E. Smith, 1975.

*   *   *

C. Day Lewis, radical Marxist in his youth, yet the successor of John Masefield as Poet Laureate in 1968, died in the home of his friend Kingsley Amis, one of the Angry Young Men of the 1950's. He had been schoolmaster, writer of detective fiction under the pseudonym Nicholas Blake, and lecturer on poetry at Cambridge, Oxford, and Harvard. His charmed decade was the proletarian 1930's when, along with Auden, Spender, and MacNeice, he made a poetic diagnosis of what was wrong with England. Exploring the roots of disease in the past, he rode a light-engine backwards amid rusting iron-works and worked-out mines (*Transitional Poem*). Four years later he played the role of a Socialist Christ, calling Britons to leave all that moribund past, join hands in brotherhood, and make pilgrimage together to the economic heaven of *The Magnetic Mountain*. Four years later still, he was insisting that liberal individualism had lost its chance (*Starting Point*); the encrusted conditions of the life of modern man required radical breakthrough (*Overtures to Death*).

A constitutional dualist, he was always torn between absolute and particular beauty (*Beechen Vigil*), idea and actuality. Although he wrote less about politics than Spender or Auden, he was convinced that a poet in the 1930's must be a propagandist for a new and better world (*A Hope for Poetry*). But he had to keep convincing himself that socialism was the only ideology that offered any hope (*A Time to Dance*). Even in his prayer for his unborn child, he recognizes the two options of complete, unquestioning conformity and total rebellion which needs no props from public opinion (*From Feathers to Iron*).

After having begun with a stirring call to revolution, and holding out the vision of a new and nobler race of men, the capitalistic confrontation of World War II made him reluctantly aware that it was too late to warn, too early to hope (*Word over All*).

Increasingly he turned back to a neo-Georgian verse and the practical expediencies of detective fiction, remuneratively received by the reading public, and to academic lectureships in England and the United States. Undoubtedly the clearest singing voice of the Auden Group, he managed to unite traditional prosody to radical thought. When the radical element lost its strident message, the lyric voice continued as the special gift of the rebel who became Laureate.

—Elton E. Smith

---

de la MARE, Walter. English. Born in Charlton, Kent, 25 April 1873. Educated at St. Paul's Cathedral Choristers' School, London (Founder, *The Choristers Journal*, 1889). Married Constance Elfrida Ingpen in 1899 (died, 1943); two sons, two daughters. Clerk, Anglo-American Oil Company, 1890–1908. Reviewer for *The Times* and *The Westminster Gazette*, London. Recipient: Polignac Prize, 1911; Black Memorial Prize, for fiction, 1922; Library Association Carnegie Medal, for children's book, 1948; Foyle Poetry Prize, 1954. D.Litt.: Oxford, Cambridge, Bristol, and London universities; LL.D.: University of St. Andrews. Honorary Fellow, Keble College, Oxford. Granted Civil List pension, 1908; Companion of Honour, 1948; Order of Merit, 1953. *Died 22 June 1956.*

PUBLICATIONS

Collections

    de la Mare: A Selection from His Writings, edited by Kenneth Hopkins. 1956.
    The Complete Poems, edited by Leonard Clark and others. 1969.

Verse

    Poems. 1906.
    The Listeners and Other Poems. 1912.
    The Old Men. 1913.
    The Sunken Garden and Other Poems. 1917.
    Motley and Other Poems. 1918.
    Flora. 1919.
    Poems 1901 to 1918. 2 vols., 1920.
    The Veil and Other Poems. 1921.
    Thus Her Tale: A Poem. 1923.
    A Ballad of Christmas. 1924.
    The Hostage. 1925.

St. Andrews, with Rudyard Kipling.   1926.
Selected Poems.   1927.
Stuff and Nonsense and So On.   1927; revised edition, 1946.
The Captive and Other Poems.   1928.
The Sunken Garden and Other Verses.   1931.
Two Poems.   1931.
The Fleeting and Other Poems.   1933.
Poems 1919 to 1934.   1935.
Poems.   1937.
Memory and Other Poems.   1938.
Two Poems, with Arthur Rogers.   1938.
Collected Poems.   1941.
Time Passes and Other Poems, edited by Anne Ridler.   1942.
The Burning-Glass and Other Poems, Including The Traveller.   1945.
The Burning-Glass and Other Poems.   1945.
The Traveller.   1946.
Two Poems: Pride, The Truth of Things.   1946.
Inward Companion: Poems.   1950.
Winged Chariot.   1951.
Winged Chariot and Other Poems.   1951.
O Lovely England and Other Poems.   1953.
Selected Poems, edited by R. N. Green-Armytage.   1954.
The Morrow.   1955.
Envoi.   1965.

Play

Crossings: A Fairy Play (juvenile), music by C. Armstrong Gibbs (produced 1919).   1921.

Fiction

Henry Brocken: His Travels and Adventures in the Rich, Strange, Scarce-Imaginable Regions of Romance.   1904.
The Return.   1910; revised edition, 1922.
Memoirs of a Midget.   1921.
Lispet, Lispett, and Vaine.   1923.
The Riddle and Other Stories.   1923; as The Riddle and Other Tales, 1923.
Ding Dong Bell.   1924.
Two Tales: The Green-Room, The Connoisseur.   1925.
The Connoisseur and Other Stories.   1926.
At First Sight.   1928.
On the Edge: Short Stories.   1930.
Seven Short Stories.   1931.
A Froward Child.   1934.
The Nap and Other Stories.   1936.
The Wind Blows Over.   1936.
The Picnic and Other Stories.   1941.
Best Stories.   1942.
The Collected Tales, edited by Edward Wagenknecht.   1950.
A Beginning and Other Stories.   1955.
Ghost Stories.   1956.

Other

Songs of Childhood (juvenile).   1902.
M. E. Coleridge: An Appreciation.   1907.
The Three Mulla-Mulgars (juvenile).   1910; as *The Three Royal Monkeys; or The Three Mulla-Mulgars,*   1935.
A Child's Day: A Book of Rhymes (juvenile).   1912.
Peacock Pie: A Book of Rhymes (juvenile).   1913.
Story and Rhyme: A Selection (juvenile).   1921.
Down-Adown-Derry: A Book of Fairy Poems (juvenile).   1922.
Broomsticks and Other Tales (juvenile).   1925.
Miss Jemima (juvenile).   1925.
Old Joe (juvenile).   1927.
Told Again: Traditional Tales (juvenile).   1927; as *Tales Told Again,* 1959.
Some Women Novelists of the 'Seventies.   1929.
Stories from the Bible (juvenile).   1929.
Desert Islands and Robinson Crusoe.   1930; revised edition, 1932.
Poems for Children.   1930.
The Dutch Cheese and the Lovely Myfanwy (juvenile).   1931.
The Early Novels of Wilkie Collins.   1932.
Lewis Carroll.   1932.
The Lord Fish and Other Tales (juvenile).   1933.
Early One Morning in the Spring: Chapters on Children and on Childhood as It Is Revealed in Particular in Early Memories and Early Writings.   1935.
This Year, Next Year (juvenile).   1937.
Arthur Thompson: A Memoir.   1938.
An Introduction to Everyman.   1938.
Stories, Essays, and Poems, edited by M. M. Bozman.   1938.
Animal Stories, Chosen, Arranged, and in Some Part Re-Written (juvenile).   1939.
Pleasures and Speculations.   1940.
Bells and Grass: A Book of Rhymes (juvenile).   1941.
The Old Lion and Other Stories (juvenile).   1942.
The Magic Jacket and Other Stories (juvenile).   1943.
Collected Rhymes and Verses (juvenile).   1944; as *Rhymes and Verses: Collected Poems for Children,* 1947.
The Scarecrow and Other Stories (juvenile).   1945.
The Dutch Cheese and Other Stories (juvenile).   1946.
Collected Stories for Children.   1947.
Selected Stories and Verses (juvenile), edited by Eleanor Graham.   1952.
Private View (essays).   1953.
A Penny a Day (juvenile).   1960.
Poems (juvenile), edited by Eleanor Graham.   1962.

Editor, *Come Hither: A Collection of Rhymes and Poems for the Young of All Ages.*   1923.
Editor, with Thomas Quayle, *Readings: Traditional Tales Told by the Author* (juvenile).   5 vols., 1926–28.
Editor, *Poems,* by Christina Rossetti.   1930.
Editor, *The Eighteen-Eighties: Essays by Fellows of the Royal Society of Literature.*   1930.
Editor, *Tom Tiddler's Ground: A Book of Poetry for the Junior and Middle Schools.*   3 vols., 1931.
Editor, *Old Rhymes and New, Chosen for Use in Schools.*   2 vols., 1932.
Editor, *Behold, This Dreamer! Of Reverie, Night, Sleep, Dream, Love-Dreams,*

Nightmare, Death, The Unconscious, The Imagination, Divination, The Artist, and Kindred Subjects (anthology). 1939.

Editor, *Love*. 1943.

Reading List: *de la Mare: An Exploration* by John Atkins, 1947; *de la Mare: A Study of His Poetry* by H. C. Duffin, 1949; *de la Mare* by Kenneth Hopkins, 1953; *de la Mare* by Leonard Clark, 1960; *de la Mare* by D. R. McCrosson, 1966; *L'Oeuvre de de la Mare: Une Aventure Spirituelle* by Luce Bonnerot, 1969 (includes bibliography).

*   *   *

"The lovely in life is the familiar," declared Walter de la Mare, "and only the lovelier for continuing strange." Those lines crystallize the poet's renewing sense of wonder in the most apparently ordinary sights and sounds of every day. Through his perception of the miracle shining out from the accepted commonplace, tiny and transient things may mirror, and often illuminate, the nature of the tremendous and timeless: "noonday's immensity ... in a bead of dew," the answer to "a lifetime's mysteries" discovered in a flower or fragment of moss.

The prevalence of the word "strange," with its evocative associates "ghost," "phantom," "haunt," infuse de la Mare's work with its unique, pervasive quality of "otherness." For much of the time his imagination inhabits a twilit borderland between dream and waking. His ubiquitous, enigmatic Strangers, Wanderers, Travellers seem to personify an irresistible compulsion to explore the shadowy regions of fantasy – "the spell of far Arabia" – beckoning just across the frontiers of the visible, known world.

De la Mare's fiction, with its recurring theme of an exile's return, contains like his poems elusive presences by no means always benign. The stories *The Return*, "Seaton's Aunt," and *Memoirs of a Midget* and such sinister poems as "The Feckless Dinner Party," "Good Company," and "Fear" vividly communicate de la Mare's sense of macabre and malignant influences at work. And yet, he affirms, "There is a radiant core of rapture/None but the fearful know"; and his conviction of the potency of evil is equalled by a firm faith in its antithesis. His reverence for innocence is memorably embodied in his portraits of the children in "Pollie," "A Child Asleep," "Tom's Angel," and many other poems; above all, perhaps, in the stubbornly persistent questioner of "Reserved," posing such a disconcerting challenge to adult materialism.

Like Vaughan, Traherne, Blake, and Wordsworth, de la Mare believes that man in his early years is closer than at any other time to understanding the truth of things; and that never again can he recapture the world-without-end contentment of the small boy by the river in "A Sunday." Yet in his own immediacy of response, he himself retains a child's-eye freshness of vision, and brings to it the wisdom and enrichment, rather than the disillusion or cynicism, of maturity. Proof of his rare sympathy with the very young is the perennial popularity of the rhymes and verses in *Peacock Pie*, *Stuff and Nonsense*, and *Bells and Grass*, with their individual blend of fantasy and fun so spellbinding to the imagination of childhood.

The concluding lines of "All That's Past" enshrine two very characteristic de la Mare themes: "Silence and sleep like fields/Of amaranth lie." Listening intently with the ear of spirit rather than sense, in such poems as "Music Unheard," "Unheard Melodies," and "The Sunken Garden," de la Mare finds that echo-haunted "music men call silence here" more pregnant than the most seductive sound. Sleep, for him, holds a similar enchantment, and appears in a variety of guises: from the mother discovered by the wondering child in "The Sleeper" to the shepherd Nod and his "blind old sheepdog, Slumber-Soon." De la Mare has devoted an anthology, *Behold, This Dreamer!*, to "All the enchanted realm of dream/That burgeons out of night"; and the recurrence of the words "dream" and "dreamer" throughout his poems epitomizes his preoccupation with the imagination's adventures once it has slipped free of the curbing reins of consciousness.

Time, in many of de la Mare's poems, is the "quiet enemy" relentless in pursuit and destruction. With a "poppied hand" it steals youth's simplicity and innocence, robs women of their beauty ("beauty vanishes; beauty passes,/However rare, rare it be"), and takes away into death those most deeply loved. Such losses are inconsolably mourned in the poignant lament of "Alone," with its refrain "Alas, my loved one is gone,/I am alone:/It is winter"; the two poems entitled "The Ghost"; and "Autumn," which ends on a dying fall of grief, "Silence where hope was." The plangency of the word "forlorn," in that poem, echoes through many more to express not only regret for time's thefts and human transience, but a sense of man's exile from Eden. He alone among created things is burdened by doubt and inner division, vain subtleties of thought and questioning of the "riddle of life .../An endless war twixt contrarieties." In such moods, the joys of earth are no more than echoes, and shadows, of that lost imperishable delight: "Betrayed and fugitive, I still must roam/A world where sin, and beauty, whisper of home."

As de la Mare grew older, he became increasingly preoccupied, in poems like "The Last Chapter," "Anatomy," "The Death-Dream," and "Even in the Grave," with the ultimate mystery as the subject of endless speculation and surmise. Here the most frequent note is the sadness, revealed at the end of his fine and moving "A Portrait," of "A foolish, fond old man, his bedtime nigh," who "scarce can bear it when the sun goes in." "A Farewell" ("When I lie where shades of darkness") also expresses his reluctance to leave the world it so memorably celebrates − "whose wonder," he confesses, "Was the very proof of me." Yet that poem is also a positive and triumphant affirmation that his love of earth, as that of others before him has done, will intensify and perpetuate its beauty for future generations.

—Margaret Willy

DENHAM, Sir John. English. Born in Dublin, Ireland, in 1615. Educated at Trinity College, Oxford, 1631–34; Lincoln's Inn, London, 1634; called to the Bar, 1639. Married 1) Anne Cotton in 1634 (died, 1647), two sons, two daughters; 2) Margaret Brooke in 1665 (died, 1667). Succeeded to the family estate at Egham, Surrey, 1638; Sheriff for Surrey, 1642; a royalist: during Civil War defended Farnham Castle unsuccessfully, and imprisoned briefly in London; in Oxford, 1643, and France, 1646, possibly serving the Queen; exiled after 1648, in Charles II's entourage, though returned to England for various periods during the 1650's; after Restoration: Surveyor-General of Works, 1660–69, and Member of Parliament for Old Sarum, 1661–69. Founding Member, Royal Society. Knight, Order of the Bath, 1661. Became ill in 1666; confined to a mental asylum, 1666–67. *Died 19 March 1669.*

PUBLICATIONS

Collections

Poetical Works, edited by Theodore Howard Banks, Jr.   1928.

Verse

Cooper's Hill.   1642; revised edition, 1655; edited by Brendan O Hehir, in *Expans'd Hieroglyphicks,* 1969.

Mr. Hampden's Speech.   1643.
The Destruction of Troy, from the *Aeneid* of Virgil.   1656.
Panegyric on General Monck.   1659.
A Relation of a Quaker That Attempted to Bugger a Mare near Colchester.   1659.
The Second Advice to the Painter, in Imitation of Waller.   1667.
Poems and Translations.   1668.
A Version of the Psalms of David.   1714.

Plays

The Sophy (produced 1641).   1642.
Horace, by Katherine Phillips, completed by Denham, from a play by Corneille
   (produced 1668).   1678.

Other

The Anatomy of Play.   1651.

Translator, *Cato Major, Of Old Age,* by Cicero.   1669.

Bibliography: in *Poetical Works,* 1928.

Reading List: *The Subtler Language* by Earl R. Wassermann, 1959; *Harmony from Discords:
A Life of Denham* by Brendan O Hehir, 1968.

                                    *   *   *

In asserting that John Denham was the originator of "*local poetry,* of which the
fundamental subject is some particular landscape," Dr. Johnson might seem to have
overlooked or discounted some earlier seventeenth- or even sixteenth-century examples, but
if Johnson had in mind the contemplation and celebration of a distant view or prospect of a
place, then *Cooper's Hill* indeed initiated a "new species of composition," and one which was
to be emulated, imitated, or burlesqued for more than a hundred years.
    From the crown of the Hill, Denham surveys the Thames in its valley below, and
exclaims:

> O could I flow like thee, and make thy stream
> My great example, as it is my theme!
> Though deep, yet clear, though gentle, yet not dull,
> Strong without rage, without o'erflowing full.

His verse should flow like the river which is the subject of his verse. This is the aspiration,
and in these lines it could be said that the prescription is nearly met: the verse, if not
profound, has, like the Thames contained within its banks, perspicuity, ease, strength. In
general, here is the prescribed formula or model of the closed rhymed couplet which was to
rule for several generations. Again Johnson, quoting Matthew Prior, recognizes this:
"Denham and Waller improved our versification, and Dryden perfected it." Apart from the
versification, *Cooper's Hill* set the pattern that a poetic contemplation of a landscape should
provide, besides the description, a series of moralizing reflections on the events associated
with the place.
    The celebrity of *Cooper's Hill* has overshadowed the remainder of Denham's output

which, though not large, is in several kinds. His blank-verse play, *The Sophy*, performed at Court in 1641 and "admired by all ingenious men," was daring inasmuch as the high-handed actions of Charles I, shortly to precipitate the civil war, appear to be clearly indicated by the behaviour of the Persian despot in the drama. When the war did break out, however, Denham – though, like Waller, "zealous against Ship-money" – was on the side of the Royalists.

A precursor of and an example in his poetic style for Dryden, Denham was eminently the poetic commentator on the current political events and personalities of his time. Unlike Dryden's verse though, Denham's rarely has the ring and magnificence to fire the modern reader who, unless he is an historian, may have slight interest in mid-seventeenth-century figures and controversies. Still, his lines "On the Earl of Strafford's Tryal and Death," representative of this main category of his writing, can be admired for their wit and incisiveness.

Of his verse translations from French, Latin, and Greek, "composing more than half the body of his work" as his editor T. H. Banks observes, the most interesting is his rendering of part of *The Aeneid*, Bk II, "The Passion of Dido for Aeneas." Conveying little or nothing of Virgil's emotive richness, the couplets have an elegance and neat rapidity of movement. The relation between these and Waller's and Dryden's renderings of Virgil is of interest. The latter certainly admired Denham's version.

From our present perspective, *Cooper's Hill* remains as Denham's one triumphant success as a poet.

—Francis Berry

---

de TABLEY, Lord; John Byrne Leicester Warren, 3rd Baron de Tabley; succeeded to the title, 1887. Born at Tabley House, Cheshire, 26 April 1835; brought up in Italy and Germany. Educated at Eton College; Christ Church, Oxford, B.A. 1859, M.A. 1860; Lincoln's Inn, London; called to the Bar, 1860. Served in the British Embassy at Constantinople, 1859–60. Officer in the Cheshire yeomanry; Liberal candidate for Parliament for Mid-Cheshire, 1868; lived in London from 1871. *Died 22 November 1895.*

PUBLICATIONS

Collections

    Collected Poems. 1903.
    Select Poems, edited by John Drinkwater. 1924.

Verse

    Poems, with G. Fortescue. 1859.
    Ballads and Metrical Sketches. 1860.
    The Threshold of Atrides. 1861.
    Glimpses of Antiquity. 1862.

Praeterita. 1863.
Eclogues and Monodramas. 1864.
Studies in Verse. 1865.
Rehearsals. 1870.
Searching the Net. 1873.
Poems, Dramatic and Lyrical. 2 vols., 1893–95.
Orpheus in Thrace and Other Poems, edited by Eleanor Leighton-Warren. 1901.

Plays

Philoctetes. 1866.
Orestes. 1867.
The Soldier of Fortune. 1876.

Fiction

A Screw Loose. 1868.
Ropes of Sand. 1869.
Hence These Tears. 1872.
Salvia Richmond. 1878.

Other

An Essay on Greek Federal Coinage. 1863.
On Some Coins of Lycia. 1863.
A Guide to the Study of Book Plates. 1880; edited by Eleanor Leighton-Warren, 1900.
The Flora of Cheshire, edited by Spencer Moore. 1899.

Reading List: *The Life, Works, and Literary Reputation of Lord de Tabley* by G. B. Taplin, 1946; "de Tabley: Poet of Frustration" by G. Pitts, in *West Virginia University Philological Papers 14,* 1963.

*   *   *

If Lord de Tabley may be said to belong to any poetical tradition at all, it must be that of the Decadent 1890's, though he had little or no contact with the better known figures of the movement other than Richard Le Gallienne who, as a reader for the Bodley Head press, recommended that de Tabley's *Poems Dramatic and Lyrical* be published.

Although de Tabley published a number of monographs on a wide variety of subjects – numismatics, the flora of Cheshire, a *Guide to Book Plates* – he is best remembered as a poet. He began writing verse at an early age, his first volume of poetry being published in 1859 under the pseudonym of G. F. Preston. Other volumes, under different pseudonyms, appeared during the next two decades, including two verse tragedies *Philoctetes* and *Orestes.* However, his work passed unnoticed until the Bodley Head took him up, and published a sampling of his poetry in handsomely bound volumes embellished with designs by Charles Ricketts. The prevailing note of both these volumes is studied melancholy which, according to contemporary records, seems to have been a genuine reflection of the poet's temperament. In spite of such poems as "John Anderson's Answer," in which the effect of Time on human love is treated with a light, ironic touch – "Time goes, old girl, time goes" – more typical is "An Ode," a somewhat heavy-footed exercise on the same theme:

289

Gone? all shall go, the fable and the truth;
Ambrosial glimpses of an antique day,
Lost, as the love dream of a withered youth
In wintry eyes where charmed laughter lay.

Much of de Tabley's gloomy lyricism recalls Tennyson, a poet whom de Tabley openly admired, while another influence is clearly that of the Pre-Raphaelites, notably Swinburne, whose classical drama *Atalanta in Calydon* has much in common with *Philoctetes*. Unlike Swinburne, however, whose descriptions of natural phenomena tend to be generalised reminiscences, de Tabley presents us with precisely observed images, such as the "ripening slips and tangles of cork-woods, in the bulrush pits where oxen lie soaking chin-deep," and the mulberry orchard with its "milky kexes and marrowy hemlocks, among the floating silken under-darnels." In spite of such sharply perceived images, however, de Tabley seems not to have been a keen lover of Nature in the Wordsworthian sense. On the contrary, Nature is merely the backdrop for the poet's morbid reveries, its transient forms reinforcing his melancholy awareness of human mortality.

—John M. Munro

DE VERE, Aubrey (Thomas). Irish. Born in Adare, County Limerick, 20 January 1814; son of Sir Aubrey De Vere, Baronet. Educated privately at his family's home, Curragh Chase, Adare; Trinity College, Dublin, 1832–38, B.A. 1837. Visited Oxford and met Newman, 1838; visited Cambridge and met Tennyson, 1838; met Wordsworth, 1841, and stayed with him at Rydal, 1843; travelled in Europe, 1843–44; lived in London, 1845; returned to Ireland and lived at Curragh from 1846; went to Rome and was received into the Roman Catholic church, 1851; appointed by Newman to the honarary post of Professor of Political and Social Science in the new Catholic University, Dublin, 1854–58. *Died 21 January 1902.*

PUBLICATIONS

Collections

Poems (selection), edited by Margaret Domvile. 1904.

Verse

The Waldenses; or, The Fall of Rora: A Lyrical Sketch with Other Poems. 1842.
The Search after Proserpine, Recollections of Greece, and Other Poems. 1843.
Poems. 1855.
May Carols. 1857.
The Sisters, Inisfail, and Other Poems. 1861.
Inisfail: A Lyrical Chronicle of Ireland. 1863.
The Infant Bridal and Other Poems. 1864.

The Legends of St. Patrick. 1872.
Alexander the Great: A Dramatic Poem. 1874.
St. Thomas of Canterbury: A Dramatic Poem. 1876.
Antar and Zara: An Eastern Romance, Inisfail and Other Poems, Meditative Lyrics. 1877.
The Fall of Zara, The Search after Proserpine, and Other Poems. 1877.
Legends of the Saxon Saints. 1879.
The Foray of Queen Maeve and Other Legends of Ireland's Heroic Age. 1882.
Poetical Works. 6 vols., 1884–98.
Legends and Records of the Church and Empire. 1887.
Saint Peter's Chains; or, Rome and the Italian Revolution: A Series of Sonnets. 1888.
Poems: A Selection, edited by John Dennis. 1890.
Medieval Records and Sonnets. 1893.
Selections from the Poems, edited by George Edward Woodberry. 1894.

Other

English Misrule and Irish Misdeeds: Four Letters. 1848.
Picturesque Sketches of Greece and Turkey. 2 vols., 1850.
Heroines of Charity. 1854.
The Church Settlement in Ireland; or, Hibernia Pacanda. 1866.
Ireland's Church Property and the Right to Use It. 1867.
Pleas for Secularization. 1867; *Postscript,* 1868.
Ireland and Proportional Representation. 1885.
Essays, Chiefly on Poetry. 2 vols., 1887.
Essays, Chiefly Literary and Ethical. 1889.
Religious Problems of the Nineteenth Century, edited by J. G. Wenham. 1893.
Recollections. 1897.

Editor, *Select Specimens of the English Poets.* 1858.
Editor, *The Church Establishment in Ireland.* 1867.
Editor, *Proteus* [Wilfrid Blunt] *and Amadeus* [Wilfrid Meynell]: *A Correspondence.* 1878.
Editor, *The Household Poetry Book: An Anthology.* 1893.

Reading List: *De Vere: A Memoir* by Wilfrid Ward, 1904; *De Vere as a Man of Letters* by T. A. Pijpers, 1941; *De Vere: Victorian Observer* by Mary P. Reilly, 1953.

*   *   *

Aubrey De Vere is remembered today chiefly as a Victorian man of letters and as a thoughtful if unadventurous critic. As well as four volumes of essays, two travel books, a volume of recollections and many articles and reviews, he did in fact publish two dramatic poems and several volumes of verse. These latter works reveal a prolific if undirected talent, a poet capable of verses in the manner of Wordsworth, Landor, and Shelley. Indeed, it was Swinburne's view that De Vere's "Song" ("When I was young I said to sorrow") was "one lyrical poem ... not written by Shelley yet possible and even likely to be taken for Shelley's." A sense comes from De Vere's poetry of broad literary and human sympathies without any sense of real imaginative amplitude. At his best (e.g., in a poem like "Ione") he can manage a tone of unforced, fluent simplicity or a justly measured, sweet-tempered gravity (which served him as a hymn-writer) but he is often insipid and dull. His inspirations dissipate in charm, or in sentimental religiosity.

In 1862 Gavin Duffy, who had published the collection of revolutionary ballads *The Spirit of the Nation*, published in Dublin De Vere's volume *Inisfail: A Lyrical Chronicle of Ireland*. This book is an extended poetic treatment of Irish history between the Norman Conquest and the end of the eighteenth century in which Irish national feeling and a developed sense of Ireland as a Catholic nation are combined in a collection of poems of which its author wrote, "Its aim is to embody the *essence* of a nation's history – a theme, I believe, original in poetry." At moments in the book this noble aspiration seems to have charged the author's imagination with something more arresting than is usual in his felicitous verses. There are the rhetorical dirges on historical disasters, the heightened religiosity of "Religio Novissima" (in which the Irish race is imagined as a suffering religious order), and the notes of genuine anguish in the poem on the famine, "The Year of Sorrow." Perhaps most interesting are those moments which seem to anticipate the Celtic twilight melancholy of early Yeats –

> I heard a woman's voice that wailed
> Between the sandhills and the sea.
> The famished sea-bird past me sailed
> Into dim infinity

– and the poem "Song" which, conceiving of Ireland as the little black rose of the Gaelic tradition, achieves an atmosphere of mystical veneration:

> The little black rose shall be red at last.
>   What made it black but the east wind dry?
> And the tear of the widow that fell on it fast?
>   It shall redden the hills when June is nigh!
>
> The silk of the kine shall rest at last!
>   What drave her forth but the dragon-fly?
> In the golden vale she shall feed full fast
>   With her mild gold horn, and her slow dark eye.

—Terence Brown

DIAPER, William.   English.   Born in Bridgewater, Somerset, in 1685. Educated at Balliol College, Oxford, B.A. 1710. Ordained deacon at Wells Cathedral, 1709; Curate, Brent, Somerset, c. 1711, and probably at Crick, Northamptonshire, and Dean, Northamptonshire, 1713–14. Associated for a time with Swift and the Tory Wits. *Died in 1717.*

PUBLICATIONS

Collections

Complete Works, edited by Dorothy Broughton.   1952.

Verse

    Nereides; or, Sea-Eclogues.   1712.
    Dryades; or, The Nymph's Prophecy.   1713.
    An Imitation of the Seventeenth Epistle of the First Book of Horace, Addressed to Dr.
      Swift.   1714.

Other

    Translator, with others, *Callipaedia,* by Claudius Quillet.   1712.
    Translator, with others, *Oppian's Halieuticks of the Nature of Fishes and Fishing of the*
      Ancients.   1722.

Reading List: "Faery Lore and The Rape of the Lock" by Pat Rogers, in *Review of English Studies,* 1974.

*   *   *

William Diaper reached the summit of his brief career in 1712, when he was taken up for a time by Swift and the Tory wits. His trajectory as a poet bears a close similarity to that of John Philips. Both came from the West of England; studied at Oxford (where Philips lingered sufficiently to allow Diaper to join him as a contemporary), attracted the attention of Henry St. John, later Lord Bolingbroke, and died at the age of thirty-two. Each constructed variations on the existing pastoral forms, and each extended the compass of descriptive writing to include a wider range of philosophic and political themes.

Diaper's topographic poem "Brent" (probably written c. 1711) is an amusing complaint regarding his exile in the damp alluvial countryside of coastal Somerset, where he was briefly a curate. Viewing himself as a second Ovid, cast away to the Scythian shores, he manages some pleasant turns of wit in the manner which Prior had evolved from seventeenth-century models. It has been much debated, he asserts, at what time of year the earth was created, but the scenery near bleak Brent Knoll "and all the marshes round," termed "a sort of chaos, and unfinish'd ground," leaves no room for doubt – the places round about "Were made in winter, one may safely swear,/For winter is the only season there." The imitation of Horace, addressed to Swift and published in 1714, is less assured in tone, but it handles the octosyllabic couplet with reasonable fluency, and achieves a certain bite in places: as when Diaper slyly pictures "the well-bred Dean" going about town "Drest up as spruce, as th'Author looks/When plac'd by *Gucht* before his Books." The two extended translations, from Oppian and Quillet, display a talent for leisurely paraphrase along with tactful amplification of the original.

Diaper's major achievement appears in the poems he produced in 1712, *Nereides* and *Dryades.* The former sticks closely to the traditional Theocritan eclogue-structures, but adds a vein of fantasy and bizarre occultism in transferring the setting to mysterious submarine regions: "Happy are those who know the secret Cause/Of strange Effects, and Nature's hidden Laws." Diaper's picturesque imagination is even more evident in *Dryades,* a kind of displaced Georgic where practical instruction is supplanted by detailed observation of nature (insects, particularly) and half-whimsical applications of native faery lore to patriotic and political ends. Its delicate imagery and minute observation produce some sensitive verbal effects which may well have influenced Pope in his revisions of *The Rape of the Lock.* There is a slightly archaic note in the phrasing here and there, as though Dryden were still a live and indeed contemporary force. But the closeness to natural phenomena and the freshness of the writing give *Dryades* a lasting charm which lifts it above the ruck of topographico-political poetry:

293

Men Nature in her secret Work behold,
Untwist her Fibres, and her Coats unfold;
With Pleasure trace the Threds of stringy Roots,
The various Textures of the ripening Fruits;
And Animals, that careless live at ease,
To whom the Leaves are Worlds, the Drops are Seas.

—Pat Rogers

DICKEY, James (Lafayette). American. Born in Atlanta, Georgia, 2 February 1923. Educated at Clemson College, South Carolina, 1942; Vanderbilt University, Nashville, Tennessee, B.A. (magna cum laude) 1949 (Phi Beta Kappa), M.A. 1950. Served in the United States Army Air Force during World War II, and in the Air Force during the Korean War. Married 1) Maxine Syerson in 1948 (died, 1976), two sons; 2) Deborah Dobson in 1976. Taught at Rice University, Houston, 1950, 1952–54, and University of Florida, Gainesville, 1955–56; Poet-in-Residence, Reed College, Portland, Oregon, 1963–64, San Fernando Valley State College, Northridge, California, 1964–66, and the University of Wisconsin, Madison, 1966. Consultant in Poetry, Library of Congress, Washington, D.C., 1966–68. Since 1969, Professor of English and Writer-in-Residence, University of South Carolina. Recipient: Vachel Lindsay Prize, 1959; Longview Foundation Award, 1960; Guggenheim Fellowship, 1961; Melville Cane Award, 1966; National Book Award, 1966; National Institute of Arts and Letters grant, 1966. Lives in South Carolina.

PUBLICATIONS

Verse

Into the Stone and Other Poems. 1960.
Drowning with Others. 1962.
Helmets. 1964.
Two Poems of the Air. 1964.
Buckdancer's Choice. 1965.
Poems 1957–1967. 1967.
The Achievement of James Dickey: A Comprehensive Selection of His Poems, edited by Laurence Lieberman. 1968.
The Eye-Beaters, Blood, Victory, Madness, Buckhead, and Mercy. 1970.
The Zodiac. 1976.

Plays

Screenplay: *Deliverance,* 1972.

Television Play: *The Call of the Wild,* from the novel by Jack London, 1976.

294

Fiction

Deliverance.   1970.

Other

The Suspect in Poetry.   1964.
A Private Brinksmanship.   1965.
Spinning the Crystal Ball: Some Guesses at the Future of American Poetry.   1967.
Babel to Byzantium: Poets and Poetry Now.   1968.
Self-Interviews, edited by Barbara and James Reiss.   1970.
Sorties (essays).   1971.
Exchanges ...., Being in the Form of a Dialogue with Joseph Trumbull Stickney.   1971.
Jericho: The South Beheld.   1974.
God's Images: The Bible – A New Vision.   1977.
Tucky the Hunter (juvenile).   1978.

Translator, *Stolen Apples,* by Evgenii Evtushenko.   1971.

Bibliography: *Dickey, The Critic as Poet: An Annotated Bibliography* by Eileen Glancy, 1971;
Dickey: A Checklist by Franklin Ashley, 1972.

Reading List: *Dickey: The Expansive Imagination* edited by Richard J. Calhoun, 1973.

*   *   *

James Dickey emerged as an important American poet and as a still underrated literary critic through an astonishing period of creative productivity from 1957 to 1967. He was regarded so much as a poet without imitators and without specific social or political concerns that his important contributions to post-modernism, both as poet and critic, were not adequately recognized. But Dickey should be seen as a post-modernist romantic – because of his desire to make imaginative contact with natural forces which have been lost to modern man, because of his romantic faith in the power of his imagination, and because of the expansive, affirmative character of most of his poems.

Dickey has always violated the modernist practice of impersonality in poetry, for there has always been a close correspondence between the chronology of his poems and his life. In his earliest poems he drew from such autobiographical data as the death (before Dickey was born) of his brother Eugene and his experiences as a fighter pilot in two destructive wars, as well as from his love for hunting, archery, and the southern landscape. Many of these poems feature encounters leading to vividly imagined exchanges of identity between the living and the dead, between men and "unthinking" nature, for the purpose of understanding through the imagination what reason alone cannot comprehend.

Dickey early declared himself as an affirmative poet, with an acknowledged affinity for the poetry of his friend and mentor, Theodore Roethke; but his affirmations were from the knowing perspective of a grateful survivor of two wars. His poems have always portrayed those who were *not* survivors and affirmed the risk inherent in an exchange of identity. In his later poems, especially in *The Eye-Beaters*, Dickey's persona is a middle-aged survivor of the destructive forces of nature. In addition, Dickey has exhibited a fascination with fantasy, with what he has called his "country surrealism," blurring distinctions between reality and dreams, or even hallucinations. His intention has been to produce a poetry that releases the unconscious and the irrational, with results that are both life affirmative and life threatening.

Two poems that might serve as transitions from his earlier to his later themes are "Power and Light" and "Falling," both from *Poems 1957–1967*. There is a shift of emphasis from a celebration of "more life" through the imaginative comprehension of nature to the necessity of confronting destructive forces and of finding spiritual resources for that confrontation. Dickey's formal interests have likewise shifted from regular towards more irregular forms, from the directness of "the simple declarative sentence" to the intimations of open and "big forms," and to such devices a split space punctuation within lines – effective in a tour de force like "Falling," but less effective in more recent poems.

Dickey is by birth and residence a southern poet, with academic credentials from the stronghold of agrarianism, Vanderbilt University. Yet he makes it clear that he is no "latter-day Agrarian." Still, like John Crowe Ransom, who feared the loss of "the world's body," and Allen Tate, who feared the loss of "complete knowledge" of man and his universe in an era dominated by science, Dickey has his own version of agrarian fears of technology and urbanization. He is "much more interested in a man's relationship to the God-made world, or the universe made, than to the man-made.... The relationship of the human being to the great natural cycles of birth and death, the seasons, the growing up of seasons out of dead leaves, the generations of animals and of men, all on the heraldic wheel of existence is very beautiful to me" (*Self-Interviews*).

In the 1970's Dickey's production of poetry has lessened with a developing interest in the novel, television and movie scripts, and a form of literary criticism, the self-interview. His successful novel, *Deliverance*, shares with his poetry a concern with the cycle of entry into "unthinking nature," followed by a return to the world, perhaps having become while in nature "another thing." The return to the human realm is just as important as the entry into the natural. He has most recently been engaged in writing prose-poem celebrations of the southern landscape (*Jericho*), and poetic "imitations" of the poems of a drunken, Dutch sailor-poet of the 1940's (*The Zodiac*) and of the King James version of the Bible (*God's Images*).

—Richard J. Calhoun

DICKINSON, Emily (Elizabeth). American. Born in Amherst, Massachusetts, 10 December 1830. Educated at Amherst Academy; Mount Holyoke Female Seminary, South Hadley, Massachusetts, 1847. Lived a secluded life in Amherst except for brief visits to Washington, Philadelphia, and Boston; semi-invalid, 1884–86. *Died 15 May 1886.*

PUBLICATIONS

Collections

The Poems, edited by Thomas H. Johnson. 3 vols., 1955.
Letters, edited by Thomas H. Johnson and Theodora Ward. 3 vols., 1958; *Selected Letters*, 1971.
Complete Poems (single version of all poems), edited by Thomas H. Johnson. 1960; *Final Harvest* (selections), 1961.

Verse

Poems, edited by Mabel Loomis Todd and T. W. Higginson. 1890; Second Series,
    1891; Third Series, edited by Todd, 1896.
The Single Hound: Poems of a Lifetime, edited by Martha Dickinson Bianchi. 1914.
The Complete Poems, edited by Martha Dickinson Bianchi. 1924.
Further Poems, edited by Martha Dickinson Bianchi and Alfred Leete Hampson. 1929.
Unpublished Poems, edited by Martha Dickinson Bianchi and Alfred Leete
    Hampson. 1936.
Bolts of Melody: New Poems, edited by Mabel Loomis Todd and Millicent Todd
    Bingham. 1945.

Other

Letters (includes some poems), edited by Mabel Loomis Todd.   2 vols., 1894.

Bibliography: Dickinson: An Annotated Bibliography: Writings, Scholarship, Criticism, and
Ana 1850–1968 by Willis J. Buckingham, 1970.

Reading List: The Life and Letters of Dickinson by Martha Dickinson Bianchi, 1924;
Dickinson by Richard Chase, 1951; Dickinson: An Interpretative Biography by Thomas H.
Johnson, 1955; The Years and Hours of Dickinson edited by Jay Leyda, 2 vols., 1960;
Dickinson's Poetry: Stairway of Surprise by Charles R. Anderson, 1960; Dickinson: A
Collection of Critical Essays edited by Richard B. Sewall, 1963; The Recognition of Dickinson:
Selected Criticism since 1890 edited by Caesar R. Blake and Carlton F. Wells, 1964;
Dickinson: An Introduction and Interpretation by John B. Pickard, 1967; The Poetry of
Dickinson by Ruth Miller, 1968; Dickinson by Denis Donoghue, 1969; After Great Pain: The
Inner Life of Dickinson by John J. Cody, 1971; The Life of Dickinson by Richard B. Sewall, 2
vols., 1974.

*   *   *

Emily Dickinson's importance as a poet is not in any doubt. Her cause may have been
damaged by injudicious partisanship during the 1930's, but a longer retrospect sets her firmly
among the major poets who have written in English. She never prepared her poems for
publication, and had she done so must in all probability have rejected many of those which
are now in print. It follows from this that the general reader is likely to read no more than a
selection of her work; and yet nothing that she wrote is without interest, and even the
"failures" take their place in an oeuvre which is marked by a distinctive union of style and
sensibility. In this respect, then, she satisfies T. S. Eliot's criterion (see his "What Is Minor
Poetry?," On Poetry and Poets) by which all the work of a major poet should be read. Nor can
we deny that her work possesses "significant unity," another of Eliot's desiderata; and if we
accept his third point, that a poet's majority does not depend on his having written lengthy
works, then Emily Dickinson's status cannot be in doubt.
    Even the most enthusiastic appreciations of her work have tended, however, to contain a
note of reservation. She has been reproached for faults of technique, and her idiosyncratic
sensibility has been criticised on account of the alleged whimsicality of its perceptions. The
technical objections fall, insofar as they are not merely general, into three categories. First
there is the question of her "bad grammar" (Yvor Winters wrote, in his Maule's Curse, of her
"habitual carelessness"). The chief issue here is that of her very frequent use of a sort of
subjunctive mood, of which the following lines provide an instance:

> Time is a test of trouble
> But not a remedy.
> If such it prove, it prove too
> There was no malady.

The usage here is surely justified, at least in the case of the first "prove," insofar as the subjunctive mood expresses an awareness that the statement is provisional: time may or may not "prove" a remedy. And the second "prove" contains a similar elliptical suggestion: "may prove" or "will prove" are implied. At all events, this feature of Emily Dickinson's poetry occurs far too often to be ascribed to "carelessness," and is better seen as a (largely successful) attempt to express linguistically the poet's tentative and scrupulous searching for the truth, which she could never see as straightforward or self-evident. Nor should we forget that there are, especially during the period of Emily Dickinson's greatest creative power in the early 1860's, many poems of confident assertion, strongly indicative in mood, like "Because I could not stop for Death."

Other critics speak of failings in metre and in rhyme. It is certainly difficult to find any consistent explanation for the irregularities of Emily Dickinson's verse, any principle on which they can be said deliberately to occur. This does not, however, oblige us to consider such irregularities as weaknesses. Emily Dickinson composed by instinct (which is not to say automatically), adapting the basic rhythms of the hymns she had heard from childhood; and her instinct told her that mechanical regularity would make for monotony. Her poems are a great deal more varied than their appearance on the page might suggest. Generalisation is inappropriate in this connection, for her rhythms, considered as personal variations on a rigid pattern, are to be acclaimed or found wanting according to the shapes and sounds of particular poems. To the ear of this author, at least, her rhythmic sense is seldom absolutely deficient, and often inspired.

In the matter of rhyme, it is probably equally misconceived to search for a uniform pattern, although some have tried to show that her use of assonance in place of full rhyme is always deliberate artistry. It would be truer to say that full rhyme usually, though not invariably, accompanies moods of confidence, while assonance implies uncertainty. But there are significant exceptions to this rule. All we can safely assert is that she felt no compulsion to find exact rhymes, and that the use of assonance also helped her to get away from the mechanical jingle of hymn-forms.

Those who object to the quality of Emily Dickinson's sensibility cannot, of course, be answered "in good set terms." This is inevitably a subjective matter; moreover, the idiosyncratic vision of which we are speaking is not evident only intermittently, in this image or that turn of phrase, but informs every line, so that despite their differences Emily Dickinson's poems are always unmistakably hers. One can do no more here than offer a brief sketch of her sensibility, hoping to counter the charge of whimsicality or childishness – as opposed to what might be called child*like*ness, which certainly is present in her work, and helps to account for the immediacy as well as the strangeness of such an image as "Great streets of silence led away/To neighbourhoods of pause." Immediacy of perception; a predominantly spatial (rather than temporal) apprehension; a direct and yet uncanny confrontation with natural phenomena – these qualities, epitomised in poems such as "A narrow fellow in the grass" or "I started early, took my dog" go to make up the distinctive atmosphere of her work. But, although these qualities might in themselves be called childlike or naif, those epithets would quite fail to characterize Emily Dickinson's poetry as a whole. In the following, for instance, we find indeed a physical image, but this is no more than the beginning of the poem, the vivid introduction to the metaphor whose meaning the lines develop:

> It dropped so low in my regard
> I heard it hit the ground
> And go to pieces on the stones
> At bottom of my mind;

> Yet blamed the fate that fractured less
> Than I reviled myself
> For entertaining plated wares
> Upon my silver shelf.

This is scarcely the observation of a child. The poem, moreover, is typical in this respect of its author's work. The clarity of physical image serves above all to enforce what we must call the poem's abstract meaning, which in this case is moral and psychological. Similarly, the poem "Presentiment is that long shadow on the lawn" does not describe any particular lawn at dusk so much as it invokes, with wonderful economy, the essential nature of all presentiment and all nightfalls. The same, finally, is true of many of those poems whose theme is death. If we think of the graphic spareness of "There's been a death in the opposite house," of the more exuberant images of "As far from pity as complaint," or of the triumphantly bold conceit which ends "Ample make this bed" ("Let no sunrise' yellow noise/Interrupt this ground"), we recognize that the poet has not only made alive for us an unfamiliar world of the senses, but in doing so has created a new awareness of the experience underlying the phenomena which she has described.

The underlying common quality which especially characterizes Emily Dickinson's poetry is best denoted by her own term "awe." Awe is fear divested of its physical attributes and raised to the status of a mental attitude. It is the spiritual form of fear, or the corporeal form of reverence, and defines the nature of the childlike sensibility's response to the wonder and ecstasy of simple existence. This sense of awe is clearly present in a poem like "I know some lonely houses off the road," but it is also a general presence, found to some degree even in so brief and seemingly impersonal a poem as this:

> How still the bells in steeples stand
> Till swollen with the sky,
> They leap upon their silver feet
> In frantic melody.

The sensibility which perceived bells in this way was not, it goes without saying, "normal" – any more than were the sensibilities of John Clare or Vincent van Gogh. But the intensity of the vision defies the charge of eccentricity, and the perception, although so wholly personal, is at the same time universal. The analogy with van Gogh can be pursued, for in the case of the poet as of the painter an initial sense of strangeness gives way to a recognition that we too have known just such experiences as are being depicted, but could never acknowledge them as ours until they were articulated for us by another's art.

In order further to apprehend, if not to understand, the success of this articulation, we have to consider Emily Dickinson's language. To examine her use of words in constructing the world in which she lived out her poems is a long and rewarding study which cannot be undertaken here. One might usefully begin with a consideration of her undoubted sensitivity to the quality which makes English unique among European languages as a poetic medium, its contrasting and complementary Saxon and Romance elements. Not all poets have recognized the exceptional resources of this vocabulary, but the greatest, of whom Chaucer and Shakespeare are the pre-eminent examples, have undoubtedly done so. Emily Dickinson, as a close reading of her poems will confirm, is to be counted among their number.

—James Reeves

DIXON, Richard Watson. English. Born in Islington, London, 5 May 1833. Educated privately; Methodist College, Richmond, Surrey, 1847; King Edward's School, Birmingham, 1847–52; Pembroke College, Oxford, 1852–58 (Arnold Historical Essay Prize, 1858), B.A. 1856. Married Maria Thomson in 1861 (died, 1876); three stepchildren. Ordained deacon, 1858; Curate, St. Mary the Less, Lambeth, London, 1858–61, and St. Mary's, Newington Butts, London, 1861; Assistant Master, Highgate School, London, 1861–62; Second Master, Carlisle High School, 1862–68; Minor Canon and Honorary Librarian, Carlisle Cathedral, 1868–75; Honorary Canon of Carlisle, 1874; Vicar of Hayton, 1875–83, and of Warkworth, 1883–1900. D.D.: Oxford University, 1899. Honorary Fellow, Pembroke College, Oxford, 1899. *Died 23 January 1900.*

PUBLICATIONS

Collections

    Poems: A Selection, edited by Robert Bridges.   1909.

Verse

    The Sicilian Vespers.   1852.
    Christ's Company and Other Poems.   1861.
    St. John in Patmos.   1863.
    Historical Odes and Other Poems.   1864.
    Mano.   1883.
    Odes and Eclogues.   1884.
    Lyrical Poems.   1887.
    The Story of Eudocia and Her Brothers.   1888.
    In Obitum Edwini Natch.   1892.
    Songs and Odes, edited by Robert Bridges.   1896.
    The Last Poems, edited by Robert Bridges.   1905.

Other

    The Close of the Tenth Century of the Christian Era.   1858.
    The Life of James Dixon, D.D., Wesleyan Minister.   1874.
    Essay on the Maintenance of the Church of England as an Established Church.   1874.
    History of the Church of England from the Abolition of the Roman Jurisdiction.   6 vols., 1878–1902.
    The Correspondence of G. M. Hopkins and Dixon, edited by Claude Colleer Abbott.   1935; revised edition, 1955.

    Editor, *The Bible Birthday Book.*   1887.
    Editor, *Seven Sermons.*   1888.

Reading List: *Three Friends: Memoirs of Dolben, Dixon, and Bradley* by Robert Bridges, 1932; *A Poet Hidden: The Life of Dixon* by A. J. Sambrook, 1962.

                      *   *   *

Much of the verse in Richard Watson Dixon's first collection, *Christ's Company*, represents a Christianizing of Dante Gabriel Rossetti's distinctive romanticism, and reflects the ritualizing "aesthetic" afterglow of the Tractarian Movement. His long *terza-rima* narrative poem on a medieval subject, *Mano*, has an imaginative coherence and depth which comes from the combination of scholarship and religious insight. In *Odes and Eclogues* and *Lyrical Poems* there are plaintive, introspective odes on "Conflicting Claims" and "Advancing Age," and other poems, notably "The Spirit Wooed," "The Fall of the Leaf," and a handful of songs, which look at external nature in a distinctively innocent, fresh, and unselfconscious way.

Dixon corresponded with Hopkins, who was then completely unknown to the public as a poet, and gave him comfort and encouragement which might well be regarded as a significant indirect contribution to English poetry. Dixon was the only contemporary who came close to a full understanding of Hopkins's verse, because he had himself experienced the kind of spiritual struggles which underlay it. The high praise which Dixon earned from Hopkins and Bridges is a tribute to the saintliness of the man and the truth of his vision rather than to the skill of the artist, for he never fully mastered the techniques of versification – a failure that is all the more glaring when he is set beside his friends, Rossetti, Swinburne, Hopkins, and Bridges.

—A. J. Sambrook

DOBELL, S(ydney) T(hompson).   English.   Born in Cranbrook, Kent, 5 April 1824; moved to Cheltenham, 1836. Educated privately. Married Miss Fordham in 1844. Associated with his father as a wine merchant in Cheltenham, and lived in or near Cheltenham for most of his adult life; lived in Scotland, 1854–57, and lectured at the Philosophical Institution in Edinburgh, 1857; after 1862, because of delicate health, spent each winter abroad; injured by a fall in 1866, and thereafter an invalid. *Died 22 August 1874.*

PUBLICATIONS

Collections

 Poetical Works, edited by J. Nichol.   1875.
 Home in War Time: Poems Selected, edited by W. H. Hutchinson.   1900.

Verse

 The Roman: A Dramatic Poem.   1850.
 Balder, part 1.   1853.
 Sonnets on the War, with Alexander Smith.   1855.
 England in Time of War.   1856.
 Poems.   1860.
 Love, To a Little Girl.   1863.

Other

Of Parliamentary Reform: A Letter to a Politician. 1865.
Thoughts on Art, Philosophy, and Religion, edited by J. Nichol. 1876.

Reading List: *Life and Letters of Dobell* by E. Jolly, 2 vols., 1878; "Dobell and the Victorian Epic" by R. Preyer, in *University of Toronto Quarterly,* 1961.

*   *   *

S. T. Dobell is a solid Victorian figure: one of those obscure poets who by their lives and "examples" are unequalled as short studies of the age. Dobell is finest at revealing the conception of the Victorian artist at work: one imagines him at his study window, observing nature, meditating, and working on his epic poem. His letters reflect a man open, generous, conscientious, very attached to his parents' large family and to his wife. He was particularly conscious of his duty to younger poets for whom he was always ready to edit, criticize, or find a publisher. His youth was very solitary: it seems to have had an effect on him rather like fermentation. When he was married at 20, his intensity was at its peak. After that he seems to have effervesced, contributing the greater part of his richness to his two dramatic poems, *The Roman* and *Balder,* while keeping a very level and perceptive head for essays and literary criticism.

The Roman was a great success and is actually very fine, though to present readers it will seem older than its date of 1850 would suggest. It is the sort of writing that needs to be waded into and rolled about on the tongue until the rhythm catches one. At the time, the subject – the liberation of the Italian peninsula – gave the work a special, prophetic, contemporary flavor; at present it reads as a more individualistic and artistic work. *Balder,* a longer dramatic poem that he worked on for three years, takes for its subject the artist's relation to his work and society. At the same time *Balder* is a piece of moralizing against the negative aspect of the grandiose, egotistical "Artist." Dobell had rather a comprehensive view of the role of the artist, but was quite against such extremism as his hero Balder reflects. He wrote to his father that "the name Balder ... is the abstraction of the natural good, temporarily overcome by circumstances; but the legend goes on to say, that in after ages, Balder shall return transfigured and glorified to restore and bless the world." Dobell planned but did not complete the second part where he hoped to present the "idea of the Christian Balder." He continues: "the full length name of my hero – Balder Sorvigin, signifies Balder in the strife of Sorrow." *Balder,* as published, unfortunately does not signify as much as Dobell hoped; its moral was misunderstood when it was published. But it remains an engrossing, heightened piece of writing which is extremely rare in English poetry.

Dobell's ideas of the artist's role are thought-provoking and lasting. His few articles of literary criticism, especially that on the Brontë sisters, are sensitive and forward-looking. His collected essays are idiosyncratic, as are those of all good Victorians: like them he kept his youthful views intact over the years. His poetry maintains a nice balance between large-minded Christianity and art for art's sake. His essays in contrast are careful in judgment and closely thought, though they also reflect a warm generosity and impulsiveness characteristic of him.

—Brady Nordland

DOBSON, (Henry) Austin. English. Born in Plymouth, Devon, 18 January 1840; grand-father of the poet Rosemary Dobson, *q.v.* Educated at Beaumaris Grammar School; Coventry private school; Gymnase, Strasbourg; trained as a civil engineer. Married Frances Mary Beardmore; five sons, five daughters. Entered the Board of Trade, London, as a clerk, 1856: First Clerk, 1874–84; Principal, 1884–1901. Member of the Council, Society of Authors, and the Royal Literary Fund. LL.D.: University of Edinburgh, 1902. Granted a Civil List pension. *Died 2 September 1921.*

PUBLICATIONS

Collections

Complete Poetical Works, edited by Alban Dobson.   1923.

Verse

Vignettes in Rhyme and Vers de Société.   1873; revised edition, 1874.
Proverbs in Porcelain.   1877; revised edition, 1878, 1893.
Vignettes in Rhyme and Other Verses.   1880; revised edition, as *Old World Idylls,* 1883.
At the Sign of the Lyre.   1885; revised edition, 1889.
Poems on Several Occasions.   2 vols., 1889; revised edition, 1895.
Selected Poems.   1892.
The Ballad of Beau Brocade and Other Poems of the XVIIIth Century.   1892.
The Story of Rosina and Other Verses.   1895.
Collected Poems.   1897; revised edition, 1902, 1909, 1913.
A Whitehall Eclogue.   1899.
Carmina Votiva and Other Occasional Verses.   1901.
Poems (selection).   1905.
Three Unpublished Poems.   1930.

Other

The Civil Service Handbook of English Literature.   1874; revised edition, 1880.
Hogarth.   1879.
Fielding.   1883.
Thomas Bewick and His Pupils.   1884.
Richard Steele.   1886.
Life of Oliver Goldsmith.   1887.
Four Frenchwomen.   1890.
Horace Walpole.   1890.
William Hogarth.   1891; revised edition, 1898, 1907.
Eighteenth Century Vignettes.   3 vols., 1892–96.
Miscellanies.   2 vols., 1898–1901; vol. 1 revised as *A Paladin of Philanthropy,* 1899.
Samuel Richardson.   1902.
Side-Walk Studies.   1902.
Fanny Burney.   1903.
De Libris (includes verse).   1908; revised edition, 1911.
Old Kensington Palace and Other Papers.   1910.
At Prior Park and Other Papers.   1912.

Rosalba's Journal and Other Papers. 1915.
A Bookman's Budget. 1917.
Later Essays 1917–20. 1921.
Dobson: An Anthology, edited by Alban Dobson. 1922.
Letter Book, edited by Alban Dobson. 1935.

Editor, *The Civil Service History of England,* by Frederick A. White, revised
    edition. 1870.
Editor, *Eighteenth Century Essays.* 1882.
Editor, *Selections from the Poetry of Herrick.* 1883.
Editor, *Ballades and Verses Vain,* by Andrew Lang. 1884.
Editor, *Steele: Selections from the Tatler, Spectator, and Guardian.* 1885.
Editor, *Selected Poems,* by Goldsmith. 1887.
Editor, *London Lyrics,* by Frederick Locker-Lampson. 1904.

Bibliography: *A Bibliography of the First Editions of Dobson,* 1925, and *Catalogue of the Collection of the Works of Dobson, London University Library,* 1960, both by Alban Dobson.

Reading List: *Dobson: Some Notes* by Alban Dobson, 1928; *Das 18th Jahrhundert in Dobsons Dichtung* by E. Hasenclever, 1939.

*   *   *

Known primarily as a writer of *vers de société,* Austin Dobson was also a perceptive critic and versatile man of letters in the best Victorian sense. Although he wrote on Fielding, Goldsmith, Johnson, Prior, Pope, Fanny Burney, and a host of other eighteenth-century littérateurs, his reputation rests chiefly on his poetry. It is noteworthy for an intimate knowledge of the eighteenth century, a familiarity that distinguishes Dobson's graceful, mannered verse. His other major contribution is prosodic: the utilization of older French forms in English poetry.

Dobson is facile; occasionally, euphony outweighs content, and his work seems vapid – inoffensive but vacuous. Furthermore, there are too many instances of sentiment predominating over theme. But in his best dramatic monologues (and dialogues) he is a discriminating analyst of character. In "To 'Lydia Languish,' " not only do the attraction, petulance, and vanity of the subject shine through, but the discretion and the sensitivity of the speaker also emerge. If "A Virtuoso" is less subtle than Browning's "My Last Duchess," it better embodies the articulate but narrow rationality of the nineteenth century, much as Clough's "The Latest Decalogue" does.

Poems as diverse as "The Ballad of 'Beau Brocade,' " a genteel tale of a highway man, and "A Dialogue: To the Memory of Mr. Alexander Pope," a balanced appraisal of the intellect and rancor of this warped genius, manifest Dobson's encyclopedic knowledge of the preceding century. But his other distinction, mastery of small, closed forms, could only appear in shorter works whose technique redeems then from banality. As J. K. Robinson ("Dobson and the Rondeliers," *Modern Language Quarterly,* March 1953) has pointed out, a poet who could rhyme with the facility of Dobson was in jeopardy of becoming a mere versifier, and he needed the discipline of demanding structures; such forms as the rondeau, roundel, triolet, villanelle, ballade, and chant royal satisfied this requirement. Dobson mastered these forms, more so than perhaps greater poets. A comparison of a Henley or Swinburne rondeau with one by Dobson amply demonstrates the point.

Dobson aided the development of the Aesthetic movement in Britain. The role of the eighteenth century in this Victorian emphasis on pure beauty (see L. C. Dowling, "The Aesthetes and the Eighteenth Century," *Victorian Studies,* Summer 1977) is being increasingly recognized. Like Andrew Lang, Dobson chose titles that stress the Aesthetic interest in objects d'art, e.g., *Proverbs in Porcelain* and "On a Nankin Plate."

Perhaps cognizant of John Henry Newman's paradigm of a gentleman, Dobson never inflicted pain through his poetry. Graceful and erudite, he tried to preserve the amenities of the Augustan period in a century less secure in its values.

—Daniel Rutenberg

DOBSON, Rosemary (de Brissac).   Australian.   Born in Sydney, New South Wales, 18 June 1920; grand-daughter of the poet Austin Dobson, *q.v.* Educated at Frensham, Mittagong, New South Wales; University of Sydney; studied art. Married A. T. Bolton in 1951; one daughter, two sons. Recipient: Myer Award, 1966. Lives in Canberra.

PUBLICATIONS

Verse

> *In a Convex Mirror.*   1944.
> *The Ship of Ice and Other Poems.*   1948.
> *Child with a Cockatoo and Other Poems.*   1955.
> *(Poems).*   1963.
> *Cock Crow: Poems.*   1965.
> *Rosemary Dobson Reads from Her Own Work* (with recording).   1970.
> *Collected Poems.*   1973.
> *Greek Coins.*   1977.

Other

> *Focus on Ray Crooke.*   1971.
>
> Editor, *Australia, Land of Colour, Through the Eyes of Australian Painters.*   1962.
> Editor, *Songs for All Seasons: 100 Poems for Young People.*   1967.

Reading List: "Dobson: A Portrait in a Mirror" by A. D. Hope, in *Quadrant*, July–August 1972; "The Poetry of Dobson" by James McAuley, in *Australian Literary Studies*, May 1973.

*   *   *

A detachment in Rosemary Dobson's poetry, a high-bred reserve, as well as a reticence in publishing it, has tended to cause her work to be overlooked by the general public. Its fine craftsmanship, its formal elegance, its lack of obvious emotional appeal are not to the taste of this technicolour age. It is true that in the early poems in *In a Convex Mirror* one can perhaps detect here and there a genuine inhibitedness, a fear of feeling, in "Foreshore," "The Dove,"

305

or "The Rider." The very title of the book suggests remoteness and detachment: a convex mirror causes objects to look smaller and farther away than they are, though it sharpens their outlines and gives them a curious, brilliant patina. This sheen is characteristic of the work as a whole, and lends a certain distinction to the poems independent of their general success. The poems written in the 1940's, like so many Australian poems of that period, were concerned with the metaphysics of time but it is not certain that the author was merely following a fashion. She is the granddaughter of the Victorian poet and essayist Austin Dobson, and it may have been his poem "The Paradox of Time" which first interested her in the notion of time standing still while humanity moves on. This idea attracts her to great pictures, for example, about which she has written so often and so acutely: their power to hold a given moment forever, as well as their power to lift the commonplace to an other-worldly dimension. Her fullest treatment of the time theme is the long dramatic poem "The Ship of Ice," the title-poem in a book which also contains the masterly sequence "The Devil and the Angel," a series of sharp, dramatic, Browningesque sketches in which lyricism, wit, and humour combine to convey a metaphysical idea. In these poems, the Devil and the Archangel Michael meet various figures who are about to die to invite them to make a final decision on which direction they wish to take – to Heaven or to Hell. The poems point up not only the difference between the two angels, but the subtle similarities between them, especially in the last poems where we find them subject to flattery from a poet. One of the most interesting is the encounter with a scarecrow in a summer field, who refuses to choose at all. He prefers life as an inanimate object in a world of natural objects to eternal, spiritual life – ironic praise of the visible world.

Child with a Cockatoo contains many poems about paintings, including the beautiful "The Bystander" and "Detail from an Annunciation by Crivelli." More traditional in form than Auden's they are, like his "Musée des Beaux Arts," points of departure for individual meditations. More of the poems in this volume, however, are concerned with personal experience, especially the experience of motherhood. One, "Cock Crow," conveys poignantly the difficulties of being at once daughter, mother, and poet. Some pieces are influenced by medieval ballads and have an eerie, legendary, magical quality entirely their own, for example, the haunting "The Stepdaughter":

> She went to the well for water,
> More beautiful than morning,
> Than sweet, clear running water
> And humble as the day.
> She fetched for her sister
> And carried for her mother,
> And the flame on the hearth-stone
> Spoke to her "Stay."

This book contains a few poems which herald Rosemary Dobson's interest in Greek themes. *Greek Coins*, which she has also illustrated, is inspired by J. G. Frazer's and Peter Levi's translations of Pausanias's *Guide to Greece*. These four-line "coin-sized" poems are as exquisitely evocative as epigrams from the *Greek Anthology* itself.

—Dorothy Green

DOMETT, Alfred. English. Born in Camberwell Grove, Surrey, 20 May 1811. Educated at St. John's College, Cambridge, 1829–33; Middle Temple, London, 1835–41; called to the Bar, 1841. Married Mrs. Mary George in 1856. A friend of Robert Browning from c. 1840;

emigrated to New Zealand, 1842; Editor of the *Nelson Examiner*, 1844–46; Member of the New Zealand Legislative Council, 1846; Colonial Secretary for New Munster, 1848; Civil Secretary for the colony of New Zealand, 1851; Commissioner of Crown Lands and Magistrate of Hawke's Bay, 1853–56; Member of the New Zealand Parliament for Nelson, 1855–63; Commissioner of Crown Lands, Nelson, 1856; Member, Provincial Council for Nelson, 1857–63; Prime Minister of New Zealand, 1862–63; Secretary for Crown Lands, Legislative Councillor, and Commissioner of Old Lands Claims, 1864; Registrar-General of Land, 1865; Administrator of Confiscated Lands, 1870; retired from New Zealand politics and returned to England, 1871. C.M.G. (Companion, Order of St. Michael and St. George), 1880. *Died 2 November 1887.*

PUBLICATIONS

Verse

    Poems.   1833.
    Venice.   1839.
    Ranolf and Amohia: A South-Sea Day Dream.   1872; revised edition, 2 vols., 1883.
    Flotsam and Jetsam: Rhymes Old and New.   1877.
    It Was the Calm and Silent Night: A Christmas Hymn.   1884.

Other

    Narrative of the Wairoan Massacre.   1843.
    Petition to the House of Commons for the Recall of Governor Fitzroy.   1845.
    Diary 1872–85, edited by E. A. Horsman.   1953.
    Canadian Journal, edited by E. A. Horsman and Lillian Rea Benson.   1955.

Reading List: *Robert Browning and Domett* by Frederic G. Kenyon, 1906.

*   *   *

Alfred Domett is more notable as a New Zealand statesman and friend of Robert Browning, who immortalized him in "Waring" (1842) and "The Guardian Angel" (1855), than as a poet in his own right. Prior to his emigration, Domett's major publication was *Poems* (1833). Largely experimental, the contents consist of translations, occasional verse, unfinished poems, untitled poems, and comic verse, written mainly in quatrians, though some are in couplets and two are Petrarchan sonnets. They display a certain limited competence, but are lacking in versatility and originality. Two (Untitled, pp. 73–75 and "Long Ago," pp. 78–85) are distinctly derived from Wordsworth's "Ode: Intimations of Immortality." Domett later contributed a few poems to *Blackwood's Magazine*, one of which, "A Christmas Hymn (Old Style, 1837)," has been frequently reprinted and is included in *The Oxford Book of Victorian Verse* (1913). Written in ten-line stanzas – two quatrains and a refrain – it is an imaginative projection to the time of Christ's birth, capturing the unsuspecting and quiet moment preceding a miraculous event which is to change the way of life forever.

During Domett's nearly thirty years in New Zealand, he published little other than official, legal, and political exposition; but doubtless he had nearly completed his long narrative poem *Ranolf and Amohia* which appeared the year after his return. It is a philosophical romance with the usual colonial overtones of the period – the white man's burden of bringing light and wisdom to the untutored savage – but, unlike Kipling, Domett finds a ground for the figurative East and West to meet in the common belief in an eternal spirit, an intelligent First Cause. The union is symbolized by the ultimate marriage, via difficulties and doubt, of Ranolf, a sailor-adventurer, and Amohia, daughter of a Maori king. The essentially British view is gradually meliorated by the wild natural setting and native legend and song until, through an act of faith alone, the union is consummated. A tribute to Browning as "Subtlest Assertor of the Soul in Song! –" is interjected. Domett in his *Diary* says that Tennyson afforded *Ranolf and Amohia* faint praise, but the work was revised in 1883.

In 1877, Domett published a random collection of poems, *Flotsam and Jetsam*, written before and after his New Zealand tenure and dedicated to Robert Browning, "A mighty poet and a subtle-souled psychologist." Much more versatile in verse form and meter than his 1833 *Poems*, the first part contains many works inspired by his travels in the United States, Canada, and Europe. Nature, however, is not used as a central theme, but rather as a simile suggesting some fleeting emotion or human characteristic. Also notable is his witty defense in "Lines Sent to Robert Browning, 1841, on a Certain Critique on *Pippa Passes*." Among the poems in the second part, written in his later years, are an elegy on Livingstone; a previously unpublished proem to *Ranolf and Amohia*; a tribute to Milton entitled "Cripple-gate"; "A Christmas Hymn (New Style, 1875)," which takes cognizance of the growth of science, but expresses the faith that it will one day show the spirit-realm; and, finally, a remarkable poem on St. Paul's which marvellously captures the soul-expanding spirit of the cathedral.

Domett was not a great poet, but he was good enough to recognize that his major talents lay elsewhere.

—Wesley D. Sweetser

DONNE, John. English. Born in London, January/June 1572; grandson of the writer John Heywood, great-grandson of the writer John Rastell. Educated at Hart Hall, Oxford, 1584–87; Cambridge University; Thavies Inn, London, 1591; Lincoln's Inn, 1592 (Master of the Revels, 1593–95). Married (secretly) Ann More in 1601 (died, 1617); six daughters, four sons. Took part in the Earl of Essex's expeditions to Cadiz, 1596, and to the Azores, 1597. Entered the service of the Lord Keeper, Sir Thomas Egerton, as Private Secretary, London, 1598; also, Member of Parliament for Brackley, 1601; discovery of his secret marriage to the Lord Keeper's niece caused him to be dismissed from his post and briefly imprisoned, and destroyed his hopes of political advancement. Lived in Pyrford, Surrey, 1602–06, and Mitcham, Surrey, 1606–11; travelled to the Continent, with Sir Walter Chute, 1605–06, with Sir Robert Drury, 1611–12. Born a Roman Catholic: at the instigation of King James, ordained in the Anglican Church, 1615; as royal chaplain attended James at Cambridge; Rector, Keyston, Hampshire, 1616–21, and Sevenoaks, Kent, 1616; Divine Reader (Preacher), Lincoln's Inn, 1616–21; Chaplain, Viscount Doncaster's embassy to Germany, 1619; Dean of St. Paul's, London, 1621; Rector, Blunham, Bedfordshire, 1622; Prebendary of Chiswick, 1622; Vicar, St. Dunstan's-in-the-West, London, 1624; Prolocutor of Convocation, 1626. Honorary Member of the Council, Virginia Company, 1622; Governor of the Charterhouse, London, 1626; Justice of the Peace, Kent and Bedfordshire, 1622, and Bedfordshire, 1626; served on the Court of Delegates, 1622–31. M.A.: Oxford University, 1610; D.D.: Cambridge University, 1615. *Died 31 March 1631.*

Publications

Collections

Poems, edited by H. J. C. Grierson.   2 vols., 1912.
Complete Poems and Selected Prose, edited by John Hayward.   1929; revised edition, 1936.
Complete Poetry, edited by John T. Shawcross.   1967.
Complete English Poems, edited by A. J. Smith.   1971.

Verse

The Anatomy of the World.   1611; *The Second Anniversary: Of the Progress of the Soul,* 1612; edited by Frank Manley, as *The Anniversaries,* 1963.
Poems.   1633.
Divine Poems, edited by Helen Gardner.   1952; revised edition, 1978.
Elegies, and Songs and Sonnets, edited by Helen Gardner.   1965.
Satires, Epigrams, and Verse Letters, edited by W. Milgate.   1967.
The Anniversaries, Epithalamions, and Epicedes, edited by W. Milgate.   1978.

Other

Pseudo-Martyr.   1610.
Conclave Ignati.   1611; as *Ignatius His Conclave,* 1611; edited by T. S. Healy, 1969.
Three Sermons.   1623.
Devotions upon Emergent Occasions.   1624; edited by Elizabeth Savage, 2 vols., 1975.
Four Sermons.   1625.
Five Sermons.   1626.
Juvenilia; or, Certain Paradoxes and Problems.   1633; edited by R. E. Bennett, 1936.
Six Sermons.   1634.
Two Sermons.   1634.
LXXX Sermons.   1640.
Biathanatos.   1646.
Catalogus Librorum Aulicorum, in *Poems.*   1650; edited by Evelyn M. Simpson, as *The Courtier's Library,* 1930.
Essays in Divinity, Interwoven with Meditations and Prayers.   1651; edited by Evelyn M. Simpson, 1952.
Letters to Several Persons of Honour.   1651; edited by E. E. Merrill, Jr., 1910.
Paradoxes, Problems, Characters, with Ignatius His Conclave.   1652.
Prayers, edited by Herbert H. Umbach.   1951.
The Sermons, edited by G. R. Potter and Evelyn M. Simpson.   10 vols., 1953–62.
Prebend Sermons, edited by Janel Mueller.   1971.

Bibliography: *A Bibliography of Donne* by Geoffrey Keynes, 1914, revised edition 1973; *Donne: An Annotated Bibliography of Modern Criticism 1912–1967* by John R. Roberts, 1973.

Reading List: *Life and Letters of Donne* by Edmund Gosse, 2 vols., 1899; *A Study of the Prose Works* by Evelyn M. Simpson, 1924, revised edition, 1948; *The Monarch of Wit* by J. B. Leishman, 1951; *Donne: A Collection of Critical Essays* edited by Helen Gardner, 1962; *Discussions of Donne* edited by Frank Kermode, 1963; *Five Metaphysical Poets* by Joan

Bennett, 1963; *A Preface to Donne* by James Winny, 1970; *Donne: A Life* by R. C. Bald, 1970; *The Soul of Wit: A Study of Donne* by Murray Rosten, 1974; *Donne: The Critical Heritage* edited by A. J. Smith, 1975; *Essential Articles for the Study of Donne's Poetry* edited by John R. Roberts, 1976.

*   *   *

Perhaps at no period has a poet more strikingly embodied the characteristics of his age than John Donne, leader of the Metaphysical school. A time of transition like our own − which largely accounts for the modern revival of interest in the poets who reflected it − the seventeenth century was energized by a spirit of wide-ranging enquiry, both scientific and geographical. In *The Anniversaries* (*An Anatomie of the World* and *Of the Progresse of the Soule*) Donne powerfully indicates the currents of bewilderment and doubt in his contemporaries' response to the speculations of the "new" scientists and philosophers, so swiftly displacing the accustomed shape of the medieval world-picture. The late Elizabethan voyages of discovery had further expanded the frontiers of human consciousness; and here too Donne explores the events and ideas which were quickening public interest and imagination. "The Good-Morrow" charts the adventure of love through images of sea-discoverers, maps, new worlds, latitude and longitude; while its metaphor of the lovers' eyes as hemispheres, each reflecting the face of the other, recurs in "A Valediction: of Weeping." The souls of parted lovers in "A Valediction: Forbidding Mourning" are likened to the action of a pair of compasses. "The Sunne Rising" draws an analogy between the earth's riches − the spices of the East Indies and the gold mines of the West − and those the lover enjoys in his mistress. Even death, in "Hymne to God My God, in My Sicknesse," is envisaged as an exploration: the poet's physicians as cosmographers, his body as their map, and the evocative names of distant territories employed to interpret the spirit's final voyage of discovery. The art of alchemy, a strong attraction for the seventeenth-century mind, also furnishes Donne with metaphors as telling as others drawn from various aspects of belief inherited from medieval scholasticism (see especially "Aire and Angels" and the conclusion of "The Good-Morrow"). "The Canonization" ends with an image of the distillation of essences; while the refining of metals yields the magnificent simile, in "A Valediction: Forbidding Mourning," of two souls not divided by absence but expanded, "Like gold to ayery thinnesse beate." The alchemist's refining fire burns through the lovers' experience in "The Exstasie," as, in "A Nocturnall upon S. Lucies Day," it consumes and transmutes the bereaved spirit into an absolute of annihilation.

As a love poet Donne displays a range of mood more varied and a concept of passion more complex and profound than any of his predecessors. In reaction against the Petrarchan tradition favoured by Elizabethan sonneteers − the faithful lover for ever pining, prostrate and spurned, at the feet of a disdainful mistress − Donne's love poems often strike a defiantly disenchanted note. Conventional sentiment and diction are displaced by a testy aggressiveness in openings like "So, so, breake off this last lamenting kisse," or the still more irascible "For Godsake hold your tongue, and let me love." Prosaic adjectives and verbs − "spongy" for a weeping woman's eyes in "The Indifferent," "snorted" of the lovers in "The Good-Morrow" − are paralleled by the audacious conceit of the flea which, in uniting the blood of lover and mistress, becomes their "mariage bed, and mariage temple." "The Sunne Rising" disrespectfully apostrophizes its august subject as a "Busie old foole, unruly" and a "Sawcy pedantique wretch."

Such impudent colloquialism distressed the conservative Dryden, who lamented Donne's lack of "dignity of expression," as well as his tendency to "perplex the minds of the fair sex with nice speculations of philosophy, when he should engage their hearts, and entertain them with the softnesses of love." Certainly the subtle, close-knit, and often paradoxical argument, complicated syntax, and erudite allusions of the *Songs and Sonnets* make considerable demands upon Donne's readers; while their metrical flexibility drove Ben Jonson to declare that "for not keeping of accent" their author "deserved hanging." Yet in his greatest love poems, intellectual content and verbal ingenuity are charged with deep feeling. Describing himself, in "The Blossome," as the owner of a "naked thinking heart ... which lov'st to be/ Subtile to plague thy selfe," Donne crystallizes his unique blend of reason with passionate imagination. As T. S. Eliot said, "A thought, to Donne, was an experience; it modified his sensibility."

The metaphysical vision, which consistently seeks to establish the underlying unity of existence, is admirably summed up by Joan Bennett's observation (in *Five Metaphysical Poets*) that "The same flame that lights the intellect warms the heart; mathematics and love obey one principle ... one law is at work in all experience." Dr. Johnson attacked the Metaphysicals' habit of "ransacking" nature and art "for illustrations, comparisons, and allusions," their "heterogeneous ideas ... yoked by violence together." Yet Donne's most daring analogies and juxtapositions are invariably felicitous. Human love is enlarged, intensified, and dignified by its cosmic context, as it echoes and is echoed by the activity of sun and moon, seas and floods, tempest and earthquake, the very air itself.

The supremacy of a full relationship between man and woman is one of Donne's most constant themes. Love bestows safety upon the couple in "The Anniversarie"; encompasses and concentrates human experience, in "The Sunne Rising," "The Good-Morrow," and "The Canonization," to make "one little roome, an every where." Its ultimate aim is that fusion of two separate identities into a perfect whole explored with such metaphysical subtlety in "The Exstasie." Here, too, Donne expresses his most urgent and explicit recognition of the interdependence of body and soul in love. Passion, however rarefied, cannot exist indefinitely in abstraction; as he says in "Aire and Angels," "Love must ... take a body too."

But love, in Donne, is seldom unshadowed by mortality. He was, as Eliot said of Webster, "much possessed by death,/And saw the skull beneath the skin." In poems like "The Apparition," "The Legacie," or "The Dampe," the treatment is lighter and more ironic; but many others probe the mysteries of love and death at a profounder level. Both "The Canonization" and "The Relique" (with its unforgettable image of "A bracelet of bright haire about the bone") contemplate from beyond the grave the perfection of a past relationship. "The Anniversarie" triumphantly proclaims love's sole invincibility over corruption and dissolution; but the sombre finality of the St. Lucy's Day "Nocturnall" evokes a winter darkness of the soul from which there can be no rebirth. That poem provides the unassailable answer to Johnson's contention that the Metaphysicals' "courtship was void of fondness and their lamentation of sorrow."

In many of these poems Donne suggests affinities between earthly and divine love. The sardonic opening stanzas of "The Relique" develop into a searching investigation of the nature of miracles which makes human and heavenly implicitly synonymous. The concept of dead lovers worshipped as saints recurs in "The Canonization," with an insistence on love's other-worldliness which is echoed in the reference to the rest of mankind as "the layetie" in "A Valediction: Forbidding Mourning." This idea of love as divine revelation is perhaps strongest in "The Exstasie," whose lovers are liberated from their bodies into a mystical state of clarified perception unhampered by senses or reason.

The death of Donne's wife, two years after his ordination in 1615, strengthened the wholeness of his own surrender to religion. Yet in the Holy Sonnet "Batter my heart, three person'd God," he entreats the Almighty to storm his defences and penetrate the citadel of his spirit with an ardour as personal and passionate as for any of his human loves. In the audacity of the culminating erotic metaphor ("Nor ever chast, except you ravish mee") the experience is envisaged as an essentially similar invasion and possession of the self.

Donne does not hesitate to communicate this conviction through every poetic device at his command, even, in "A Hymne to God the Father," a boldly sustained punning on his own name. The metaphysical conceit is for him no mere frivolous decoration, but intrinsic to a poem's intensity and meaning. The geometrical "binding of a circle and the union of lovers," as Joan Bennett observes, "are equivalent symbols of eternity and perfection"; erudite abstract dialectic expresses the total desolation of loss experienced by the lover in the "Nocturnall"; and wit is equally compatible with the solemnity of sin, salvation, and the love of God.

From the tensions imposed by his vocation upon a turbulent and sensual nature flowed the power and passion of Donne's *Divine Poems*. Confessing in "A Hymne to God the Father" his fear of the finality of physical death, Donne invokes the light of God's Son to shine upon him at the last. The entreaty is answered in "Hymne to God My God, in My Sicknesse," where all doubts are submerged in certain hope of resurrection. Donne's supreme affirmation of faith triumphant over what, in a sermon, he called "the last and in that respect the worst enemy," is the conclusion of his Holy Sonnet "Death be not proud":

> One short sleepe past, wee wake eternally,
> And death shall be no more, Death thou shalt die.

—Margaret Willy

DOOLITTLE, Hilda ("H. D."). American. Born in Bethlehem, Pennsylvania, 10 September 1886. Educated at Gordon School, and Friends' Central School, 1902–04, both in Philadelphia; Bryn Mawr College, Pennsylvania, 1904–06. Married the writer Richard Aldington in 1913 (divorced, 1937); one daughter. Lived in Europe after 1911. Closely associated with the Imagist movement after 1913: took over editorship of *Egoist* magazine from her husband, 1916–17. Recipient: Brandeis University Creative Arts Award, 1959; American Academy of Arts and Letters Award of Merit Medal, 1960. *Died 28 September 1961.*

PUBLICATIONS

Verse

Sea Garden. 1916.
Choruses from the Iphigenia in Aulis by Euripides. 1916.
The Tribute, and Circe. 1917.
Choruses from the Iphigenia in Aulis and the Hippolytus by Euripides. 1919.
Hymen. 1921.
Helidora and Other Poems. 1924.
Collected Poems. 1925.
The Usual Star. 1928.
Red Roses for Bronze. 1929; revised edition, 1931.
What Do I Love. 1943(?).
The Walls Do Not Fall. 1944.
Tribute to the Angels. 1945.
The Flowering of the Rod. 1946.
By Avon River. 1949.
Selected Poems. 1957.
Helen in Egypt. 1961.
Hermetic Definition. 1972.

Plays

    Hippolytus Temporizes.   1927.
    Ion, by Euripides.   1937.

Fiction

    Palimpsest.   1926, revised edition, 1968.
    Hedylus.   1928.
    Kora and Ka.   1930.
    Nights.   1935.
    The Hedgehog (juvenile).   1936.
    Bid Me to Live: A Madrigal.   1960.

Other

    Tribute to Freud, with Unpublished Letters by Freud to the Author.   1956, revised
    edition, 1974.

Reading List: *The Classical World of H. D.* by Thomas Burnett Swann, 1962; *Doolittle – H. D.* by Vincent Quinn, 1967; "Doolittle Issue" of *Contemporary Literature 10,* 1969.

*   *   *

Hilda Doolittle, whose works were published under the initials H. D., was an American poet of considerable significance. Her work itself is precise, careful, sharp, and compressed; it gives one the sense that the poet is excluding much more than she expresses. Natural objects (e.g., "Oread," "Pear Tree") are presented in lines that are free of conventional poetic rhythms and that are yet as carefully shaped as a piece of Greek statuary. So the immediate pleasure of much of H. D.'s work is a response to an object that is created by a few carefully chosen phrases: phrases that exist in the presence of easy and facile language that has been excluded. As painters say, the "negative space" – the area around a represented object – is as important as the object itself.

Miss Doolittle's work has an air of being isolated, of being simply her considered and purified record of what has stirred her senses and her emotions: the natural world with, for human context, the ancient Greek world as Miss Doolittle remembers it. Birds fly through air that is radiantly Greek, love intensifies its expression in the presence of Helen and Lais, and the mysteries of life and death bring into view satyrs and not Christian saints.

But Miss Doolittle's work did not actually proceed in isolation; she was closely associated with the Imagist movement from 1913 onwards. Ezra Pound, John Gould Fletcher, Amy Lowell, and others thought of their poetic effort as a realization of Walt Whitman's demand for new words that would bring poetry closer to the object it was "rendering" and free poetic expression from the abstractions and the overt moral purposes which had made much nineteenth-century poetry vague and imprecise. Poetry – and this was a main drive of Imagist theory – was a medium in which could appear the poet's direct apprehension of physical entities and the poet's immediate reaction to those entities. In pursuit of object and emotion, the poet should be free to discard both conventional rhythms and shop-worn poetic diction. Much of Miss Doolittle's poetry achieves these aims. Thus, the emotion in many a poem is coerced, to be recreated in the mind of the reader, by the carefully selected physical details – details which pass before the reader following a syntax that is simple and uninvolved and expressed in words that are familiar and unmysterious. But the poems, in the long run, are not free of general impressions or even abstractions although they state very few. The impressions and abstractions must vary from reader to reader, but they concern the beneficence that reaches the human mind through the senses; it is a beneficence unsullied by ancient dogma and more recent social purpose. Poets like Shelley and Tennyson did not hesitate to offer "gospels." If there is some sort of message in much of Miss Doolittle's work, it is very nearly fused with the external world she duplicates.

A modification of these effects appears in a late work like *The Walls Do Not Fall*. This work, using the techniques of the writer's previous verse, moves beyond the innocent and "natural" invocations of Greek health – health which is also of the physical world. But the destructions of World War II make the Greek health an insufficient corrective to modern chaos. *The Walls Do Not Fall* becomes quite specific about the sources of human health. Those sources find expression not only in halcyon flight and the play of light on the Aegean Sea. They can be traced in the essence of all great religions, and it is particularly the work of Egyptian gods that allows us to see the physical world achieving completion in myths and rituals. In such a body of faith as the Egyptian are myth and "Vision" coming into a focus of great human relevance. H. D. sees the Egyptian Amen and the later "Christos" as identical. They and other august entities are the symbols if not the ultimate élan of the eternal cycles of excellence and health which modern insanity – in its pursuit of power and inferior sorts of knowledge – has ignored.

This concluding attitude in the work of H. D. may strike some readers as going beyond the confines of the early Imagism. The attitude can also be regarded as an effort to defend and exploit the initial stance of Imagist simplicity and directness. These are opposing judgments. At any rate, in her late work Miss Doolittle's implications intensify and complicate themselves. But the modes of expression do not change. Perhaps their persistence indicates an essential continuity in the entire body of Miss Doolittle's poetry.

—Harold H. Watts

DORSET, Earl of; Charles Sackville, 6th Earl of Dorset and Earl of Middlesex. English. Born in England, 24 January 1638. Privately educated. Married 1) Mary Berkeley (died); 2) Mary Compton in 1685 (died, 1691); 3) Anne Roche in 1704; one son. Known for excesses in his youth, in company with Sir Charles Sedley and others; a courtier of Charles II; elected to the first Parliament after the Restoration as Member for East Grinstead, Sussex, 1660; indicted for murder, 1662, but released; involved in the naval battle with the Dutch, 1665; sent on a diplomatic mission to France, 1668; withdrew from court during the reign of James II; returned to serve King William as Lord Chamberlain of the Household, 1689–97, and served as one of the regents during the king's absences. Inherited considerable estates on accession as Earl of Middlesex, 1675, and Earl of Dorset, 1677; known for his patronage of writers and artists, particularly Dryden. Knight of the Garter, 1691. *Died 29 January 1706.*

PUBLICATIONS

Collections

The Works of the Earls of Rochester, Roscommon, Dorset, etc.   2 vols., 1714.

Play

  Pompey the Great, with others, from a play by Corneille (produced 1664).   1664.

Reading List: *Charles Sackville, Patron and Poet* by Brice Harris, 1940; *The Restoration Court Poets* by V. de Sola Pinto, 1965.

* * *

"... your lyric poems ... are the delight and wonder of this age, and will be the envy of the next.... There is more of salt in all your verses than I have seen in any.... Donne alone, of all our countrymen, had your talent ... this age and the last ... have excelled the Ancients in both [tragedy and satire] ... Shakespeare of the former ... your Lordship in the latter sort." The Earl of Dorset is the recipient of this extravagant praise from Dryden (in "A Discourse Concerning Satire," 1693). Early in Dryden's career, he had designated Dorset an elegant and gentlemanly defender of the Moderns, naming him Eugenius ("well-born") in the *Essay of Dramatick Poesie* (1668). And, because he displayed many of the cavalier features of the gentleman and courtier that Dryden extolled (wit; easy, natural language), Dorset was highly-regarded by his peers and by several succeeding generations. Addison found him one "who had the greatest Wit tempered with the greatest Candour, and ... one of the finest Criticks as well as the best Poets of his Age" (*Spectator 85*). At court, he held high office under three monarchs, and was a generous patron of authors (including Dryden). For such reasons, unlike the dissolute Rochester, he is remembered as a polished aristocrat, an exemplar of an ideal that the Restoration too seldom attained.

  Yet, for all that, as concerns the praise for his poetry, we must remain with Dr. Johnson, incredulous. For the truth is that Dorset published nothing under his own name during his lifetime; a few poems crept into the numerous poetical miscellanies of the period, but that was all.

  Doubtless his most well-known Song is the eleven-stanza poem that Johnson alluded to in his *Life*, "To all you ladies now at land":

Then, if we write not by each post,
 Think not we are unkind;
Nor yet conclude our ships are lost
 By Dutchmen, or by wind:
Our tears we'll send a speedier way,
The tide shall bring 'em twice a day.

A number of his songs are love lyrics, with a certain virility and facility in their expression, to numbers of Phillises and Chlorises; they are marked by relaxed and easy delivery:

My love is full of noble pride,
 Nor can it e'er submit,
To let that fop, discretion, ride
 In triumph over it.

  Dorset could be, upon occasion, satiric – though many would find such poems mere scurrilous *ad hominem* lampoons ("To Mr. Edward Howard, On His Plays" and "On Mr. Edward Howard upon his *British Princes*"). Dorset was doubtless at his best in writing little biting, acerbic "songs," such as "Dorinda's sparkling wit, and eyes." Here, the flashy beauty overwhelms her would-be suitors: "Her Cupid is a black-guard boy,/That runs his link full in your face."

  James Sutherland has aptly summed up Dorset's performance: "the satirical song is his special contribution to English poetry," and his shaped argumentation in verse "gives to the Restoration lyric its characteristic form: what is said, no matter how trivial or specious, is said with grace and control and finality" (*English Literature of the Late Seventeenth Century*). For a minor poet, that is a fairly impressive achievement.

—John R. Clark

DOUGLAS, Gavin.   Scottish.   Born at Tantallon Castle, 1474 or 1475; son of the third Earl of Angus. Educated at the University of St. Andrews, 1490–94; studied for the priesthood. Rector of Monymusk, 1496, of Glenquhom, 1498; Parson of East Linton and Rector of Prestonkirk, 1499; Provost of St. Giles, Edinburgh, 1501–14; Bishop of Kunkeld, 1515–20. *Died in September 1522.*

PUBLICATIONS

Collections

   Poetical Works, edited by J. Small.   4 vols., 1874.
   Douglas: A Selection from His Poetry, edited by Sydney Goodsir Smith.   1959.
   Shorter Poems, edited by Priscilla Bawcutt.   1967.

Verse

   The Palace of Honour.   1553(?).
   The XII Books of Virgil's Aeneid Translated into Scottish Metre.   1553; edited by David
      F. C. Coldwell, 4 vols., 1957–64.

Reading List: *Douglas: A Critical Study* by Priscilla Bawcutt, 1976.

*   *   *

Of the only two significant works attributed with certainty to Gavin Douglas, *The Palice of Honour* and the great translation of Virgil, the first is of small value as literary art. *The Palice of Honour* is a long allegorical poem, traditionally medieval, about man's quest for honor, with elaborate mythological machinery and the typical fusion of Christian ideas with classical lore. The poem reveals immense scholarly learning, but is mediocre in style, often boring, with little to suggest the poetic power that was to emerge a dozen years later.

   Douglas's fame, then, rests solidly upon his *Eneados*, a vigorous rendering in Middle Scots of the *Aeneid* of Virgil (12 books), together with the fifteenth-century sequel (Book XIII) by

Mapheus Vegius, prefaced by thirteen original "prologues" by Douglas himself. Considered simply as a verse translation of Virgil this remains today, after nearly five centuries, among the finest in British literature. Indeed, Ezra Pound (in *How to Read*) goes so far as to argue that Douglas's version is poetically superior to Virgil's work itself! At any rate, it is a magnificent translation, based on sound principles. In the fascinating Prologue to Book I, Douglas explicitly states his aims: to produce a version that adheres faithfully to Virgil's text, while at the same time capturing something of the spirit and feeling of the original. The result is a fairly "free" translation; Douglas always renders Virgil's meaning with reasonable accuracy, but does not hesitate to add images of his own for greater clarity and vigor. Thus, on occasion, he will expand a single line of Virgil into two or even three.

In this task Douglas faced a formidable language problem, as he himself explains. He was, incidentally, the first to call his language "Scottis," as distinguished from "Inglys" or "sudron," and he recognized that his mother tongue was often inadequate for purposes of classical translation. Accordingly, like earlier Scots poets, he felt free to coin or to Scotticize scores of Latinate words to suit his special needs. In this way he achieved a rich and flexible amalgam, combining the dignity and precision of Latinate terms with the colloquial strength of his Scots.

Douglas's "prologues" are in themselves a remarkable creative achievement, ranging through a wide gamut of subject matters and styles – from literary criticism (Prol. I) to religious and moral preachments (Prols. IV, VIII, XI) to powerful nature poetry (Prols. VII, XII, XIII), from the high style to the earthy. In these wholly original prefaces, Douglas shows extraordinary poetic talent, especially in the great "nature" prologues in which he presents amazingly detailed and compelling pictures of the various seasons in Scotland.

Altogether, the *Eneados*, with its entrancing new prologues and its splendidly strong and colorful rendering of old Virgil, is one of the major performances in Scots poetry.

—Allan H. MacLaine

DOUGLAS, Keith (Castellain). English. Born in Tunbridge Wells, Kent, 24 January 1920. Educated at Edgeborough School, Guildford, Surrey, 1926–31; Christ's Hospital, Sussex, 1931–38; Merton College, Oxford, 1938–40. Served in the 2nd Derbyshire Yeomanry, British Army, in the Middle East, 1940–44; killed in action in the Normandy invasion. *Died 9 June 1944.*

PUBLICATIONS

Collections

The Collected Poems, edited by John Waller and G. S. Fraser.   1951; revised edition, 1966.
Selected Poems, edited by Ted Hughes.   1964.
Complete Poems, edited by Desmond Graham.   1978.

Verse

Selected Poems, with John Hall and Norman Nicholson.   1943.

Other

Alamein to Zem Zem.   1946; edited by John Waller, G. S. Fraser, and John Hall, 1966.

Editor, with A. M. Hardie, *Augury: An Oxford Miscellany of Verse and Prose.*   1940.

Reading List: "Douglas: A Poet of the Second World War" by G. S. Fraser, in *Proceedings of the British Academy 42,* 1956; *Douglas: A Biography* by Desmond Graham, 1974.

*   *   *

Although his work was admired on its first (posthumous) publication, it was only in the 1960's that Keith Douglas was widely and variously hailed as the finest war poet of his time, the best poet of his generation, the most talented British poet since Auden. His new champions were poets – Hughes, Hill, Silkin, Tomlinson, Hamburger – who saw in his work an object lesson for the poetry of their own time.

The centre of Douglas's art lies in what Geoffrey Hill, linking Douglas with Isaac Rosenberg, has called "a fearlessness of the imagination ... the willingness to lay the mind completely open to experience" (*Stand,* 1964–65). Most intense in his poems and ink sketches of the desert war, this quality of mind was present from the start of a remarkably precocious writing life. Technically accomplished from the age of fourteen, published in *New Verse* while a school-boy, widely published at Oxford and in the Middle East, but fitting neither the coteries nor the fashions of his period, Douglas rapidly assimilated Auden, Yeats and Eliot, Shakespeare and Donne, translated Rimbaud and Horace, read Rilke in German. In a trenchant letter of August 1943 (in *Complete Poems*) he described his progress in terms of a conflict between lyric and cynic. The one early established a fluency of metaphor and sureness of cadence; the other tested his harmonies with the scepticism of intelligence and the abrasiveness of speech. Before experience of battle his style had already clarified into a more metaphysical manner, and his war poems sharpen this focus, looking through appearances and expressing what he finds, in a verse which "combines a colloquial prose readiness with poetic breadth" (Ted Hughes), as in "How to Kill":

> Now in my dial of glass appears
> the soldier who is going to die.
> He smiles, and moves about in ways
> his mother knows, habits of his.
> The wires touch his face: I cry
> NOW. Death, like a familiar, hears
>
> and look, has made a man of dust
> of a man of flesh. This sorcery
> I do. Being damned, I am amused
> to see the centre of love diffused
> and the waves of love travel into vacancy.
> How easy it is to make a ghost.

For Douglas the desert battlefield is "an altered planet" of which the dead are the "true inheritors," a "looking-glass world" where "a man with no head/has a packet of chocolate and a souvenir of Tripoli." It surprises his curiosity, showing fools to be truly heroes, pity to be useless, killing to be pleasing, cynicism to give way to love. He observes honestly, seeking meanings, patterns, employing detachment as a means of contact, a way in which passionate care for consequences can function undeterred. At once assured and unnerving, Douglas looks into war just as, at six, terrified of an injection, he had fixed his gaze on the needle, stared as it entered his arm.

—Desmond Graham

DOWSON, Ernest (Christopher). English. Born in Lee, Kent, 2 August 1867. Educated, sporadically, in France, while travelling with his family; Queen's College, Oxford, 1886–88. Worked at his father's dry dock, London, intermittently 1888–93; associated with the Rhymers Club, London, 1890–94; moved to France, 1894, and lived by doing translations for the English publisher Leonard Smithers, 1895–90; returned to London, 1890. *Died 23 February 1900.*

PUBLICATIONS

Collections

   Poems and Prose. 1932.
   Stories, edited by Mark Longaker. 1962.
   Poems, edited by Mark Longaker. 1962.
   Letters, edited by Desmond Flower and Henry Maas. 1967.

Verse

   Verses. 1896.
   Decorations: In Verse and Prose. 1899.
   Poems. 1905.

Play

   The Pierrot of the Minute (produced 1892). 1897.

Fiction

   A Comedy of Masks, with Arthur Moore. 1893.
   Dilemmas: Stories and Studies in Sentiment. 1895.
   Adrian Rome, with Arthur Moore. 1899.

Other

Translator, with A. Teixeira de Mattos, *Majesty*, by Louis Couperus.   1894.
Translator, *La Terre*, by Zola.   1894.
Translator, with G. A. Greene and A. C. Hillier, *History of Modern Painting*, by Richard
   Muther.   3 vols., 1895–96.
Translator, *La Fille aux Yeux d'Or*, by Balzac.   1896.
Translator, *Les Liaisons Dangereuses*, by Laclos.   1898.
Translator, *Memoirs of Cardinal Dubois*, by Paul La Croix.   1899.
Translator, *La Pucelle d'Orléans*, by Voltaire.   1899.
Translator, *The Confidantes of a King: The Mistresses of Louis XV*, by Edmonde de
   Goncourt.   1907.
Translator, *The Story of Beauty and the Beast.*   1907.

Bibliography: in *Bibliographies of Modern Authors 2* by C. A. and H. W. Stonehill, 1925.

Reading List: *Dowson: Reminiscences, Unpublished Letters, and Marginalia* by Victor Plarr,
1914; *Dowson* by Mark Longaker, 1945, revised edition, 1967; *Dowson* by Thomas B.
Swann, 1964.

*   *   *

Ernest Dowson is one of the most typical of the poets of the 1890's, of the group that
constituted the Rhymers Club. If we exclude the figure of W. B. Yeats, with his extraordinary
later development, Dowson may also be considered the best of this group. His range is very
limited, but within that range he had an impeccable ear. Poe's line "the viol, the violet and the
vine" constituted his ideal. His style can mainly be regarded as a muted version, self-
consciously minor, of that of Swinburne and the Pre-Raphaelites. But Winchester had given
him a thorough grounding in the Greek and Roman Classics which made for a high degree of
polish and concision. He was also influenced by Verlaine and his four translations from that
poet are probably the best that we have, though their slightly affected diction does not do
justice to the directness of the originals. Dowson also translated part of Voltaire's mock-
heroic poem *La Pucelle*. It is slightly improper, and shows Dowson to be not wholly destitute
of a sense of humour.

Of Dowson's original lyrics by far the best known is "*Non sum qualis eram bonae sub
regno Cynarae.*" Like the Ode of Horace from which it takes its title, it deals with an obsessive
and haunting passion. It may come as something of a shock to learn that the real Cynara was
a Polish girl-waitress in a Soho restaurant (though this identification has been questioned).
This poem has more substance than most of Dowson's. In general, "*Vitae summa brevis spem
nos vetat inchoare longam*" might be considered typical:

> They are not long, the weeping and the laughter,
>   Love and desire and hate:
> I think, they have no portion in us after
>   We pass the gate.
>
> They are not long, the days of wine and roses:
>   Out of a misty dream
> Our path emerges for a while, then closes
>   Within a dream.

Even the poems springing from Dowson's conversion to Roman Catholicism, such as
"Extreme Unction" and "Nuns of the Perpetual Adoration" breathe a spirit of world-

weariness and renunciation, rather than an affirmation of faith. He finds a stronger and more public voice in his fine poem on the death of Tennyson, and in his satire "Against My Lady Burton." The latter was elicited by the story that Sir Richard Burton's widow had destroyed some of her husband's translations of Oriental erotica.

Dowson's only work of any length is his one-act verse play *The Pierrot of the Minute*. It illustrates the contemporaneous fashion for the rococo and the Watteauesque. It can hardly be said that its fragile charm stands the test of time.

—John Heath-Stubbs

DRAKE, Joseph Rodman. American. Born in New York City, 7 August 1795. Studied medicine at a school in Barclay Street, New York, and qualified 1816. Married Sarah Eckford in 1816. Toured Europe, 1816–19; Partner, with William Langstaff, in a drug store in New York, 1819–20. *Died 21 September 1820.*

PUBLICATIONS

Collections

Life and Works: A Memoir and Complete Text of His Poems and Prose, by Frank Lester Pleadwell. 1935.

Verse

Poems, with Fitz-Greene Halleck. 1819; revised edition, as *The Croakers,* 1860.
The Culprit Fay and Other Poems. 1835.

Bibliography: in *Bibliography of American Literature* by Jacob Blanck, 1957.

*   *   *

Joseph Rodman Drake is an American member of the brotherhood of poets whose small measure of lasting fame depends on one or two popular successes. His fanciful 639-line poem "The Culprit Fay" – written in 1816 but not published until long after his death – continues to please many readers. "The American Flag," written and published pseudonymously in 1819, was widely admired in America and set to music by numerous composers (including Dvorak). His memory also survives because of the monody "On the Death of Joseph Rodman Drake," written by his friend Fitz-Greene Halleck, that opens with the well-known quatrain:

> Green be the turf above thee,
>   Friend of my better days!
> None knew thee but to love thee,
>   Nor named thee but to praise.

Otherwise, Drake is remembered only by some historical critics who – following the example set by Edgar Allan Poe in the 1830's – are still outraged by the vogue that Drake's work enjoyed in America after his death.

Except for one excursion abroad, Drake lived out his short life in New York City. Trained as a physician, he never aspired to literary fame; he published little during his lifetime, and he reportedly requested on his deathbed that his poetry manuscripts be burned as "valueless." The request was ignored, however, and when his verse appeared in 1835 he was revealed as one of the authors (the other was his friend Halleck) of the "Croaker" poems that had titillated readers of New York newspapers during the summer of 1819. This revelation, together with the appearance of Drake's only long poem, "The Culprit Fay," prompted extravagant praise that Poe deplored (*Southern Literary Messenger*, April 1836), as did later critics. More recently, a biographer of Poe (Vincent Buranelli, *Edgar Allan Poe*, 1961) labeled Drake "a third-rate versifier."

Despite such judgments, Drake's poetry reflects a promising if aborted talent. A number of his "Croaker" poems – "To Ennui," "The National Painting," "To John Minshull, Esquire," to name only a few – poke healthy fun at an America that was already beginning to take itself too seriously. In "The Culprit Fay" – reportedly written in three days – Drake anticipated both Washington Irving and James Kirke Paulding in experimenting with fantasy; the poem tells the story of a Hudson River fairy who, for having fallen in love with "an earthly maid," is sentenced by his "lily-king" to perform herculean tasks in miniature. Derivative as it is, "The Culprit Fay" reflects not only Drake's perceptive reading of great masters – ranging from Shakespeare and Michael Drayton to his own contemporaries Coleridge and Keats – but an exciting young imagination that was too soon stilled by death.

—Thomas F. O'Donnell

———————

DRAYTON, Michael. English. Born in Hartshill, Atherstone, Warwickshire, in 1563. Educated (possibly) at a school in Coventry. Probably in the service of Henry, later Sir Henry, Goodere of Polesworth, and his brother Thomas, from age 10, and of Lucy Harrington, Lady Bedford, after 1595; possibly employed by Queen Elizabeth in a diplomatic mission to Scotland; writer for the Admiral's Players, London, 1597–1602; a friend of Jonson and Shakespeare; an esquire of Sir Walter Aston, 1603; associated with the Children of the King's Revels, at the Whitefriars Theatre, London, c. 1607. *Died in 1631.*

PUBLICATIONS

Collections

> *Complete Works*, edited by J. W. Hebel, Kathleen Tillotson, and Bernard H.
> Newdigate. 5 vols., 1931–41.
> *Poems*, edited by John Buxton. 2 vols., 1953.
> *Poems* (selection), edited by Vivien Thomas. 1977.

Verse

> The Harmony of the Church: Spiritual Songs and Holy Hymns.   1591; as A Heavenly
> Harmony, 1610.
> Idea: The Shepherds' Garland in Nine Eclogues.   1593.
> Piers Gaveston.   1593; revised edition, as The Legend of Piers Gaveston, with Robert,
> Duke of Normandy and Matilda, 1596.
> Idea's Mirror: Amours in Quaterzains.   1594; revised edition, as Idea, with England's
> Heroical Epistles, 1600.
> Matilda, The Daughter of Lord Fitzwater.   1594; revised edition, as The Legend of
> Matilda, with Robert, Duke of Normandy, and Piers Gaveston, 1596.
> Endymion and Phoebe: Idea's Latmus.   1594; edited by Elizabeth Story Donno, in
> Elizabethan Minor Epics, 1963.
> Mortimeriados: The Civil Wars of Edward the Second and the Barons.   1596; revised
> edition, as The Barons' Wars, 1603.
> The Tragical Legend of Robert, Duke of Normandy; The Legend of Matilda; The Legend
> of Piers Gaveston.   1596.
> England's Heroical Epistles.   1597; revised edition, 1598, 1600.
> Moses in a Map of His Miracles.   1604; revised edition, as Moses His Birth and
> Miracles, in The Muses' Elysium, 1630.
> The Owl.   1604.
> Poems.   1605.
> Poems Lyric and Pastoral.   1606(?); The Ballad of Agincourt edited by B. Juel-Jensen,
> 1951.
> The Legend of Great Cromwell.   1607.
> Polyolbion.   2 vols., 1612–22.
> The Battle of Agincourt, The Miseries of Queen Margarite, Nimphidia, The Quest of
> Cinthia,   The   Shepherd's   Sirena,   The   Moon-Calf,   Elegies   upon   Sundry
> Occasions.   1627; Nimphidia reprinted as The History of Queen Mab, 1751.
> The Muses' Elysium: Ten Nymphals, Noah's Flood, Moses His Birth and Miracles, David
> and Golia.   1630.

Plays

> Sir John Oldcastle, part 1, with others (produced 1599).   1600; edited by Peter
> Simpson, 1908.
> A Paean Triumphal for the Society of Goldsmiths Congratulating His Highness Entering
> the City.   1604.

Bibliography: Drayton: A Concise Bibliography by S. A. Tannenbaum, 1941; supplement by
G. R. Guffey, 1967.

Reading List: Drayton's Secondary Modes by G. P. Haskell, 1936; Drayton and His Circle by
Bernard H. Newdigate, 1941; Drayton by Paul G. Buchloh, 1964; Drayton by Joseph A.
Berthelot, 1967; The Spenserian Poets by Joan Grundy, 1969; Drayton and the Passing of
Elizabethan England by Richard F. Hardin, 1973; The Evolution of Drayton's Idea by Louise
H. Westling, 1974.

*   *   *

When he was "scarse ten years of age," Michael Drayton asked his tutor to make him a
poet, and his long literary life was spent achieving that end. While the doctrine of inspiration

had a certain cachet in the Renaissance, the art of poetry was acknowledged as an acquired skill, the means spelled out in numerous treatises, most generally, if succinctly, by Sir Philip Sidney: art (rules), imitation (of the best models), and exercise (practice). In adhering to these precepts and in following poetic fashion, Drayton might well be called the representative Elizabethan poet except that he was also an innovator, introducing the ode into English and inventing, with a nudge from Ovid, the historical epistle. Stylistically ranging from the initial (unsatisfactory) imitation of Spenser (*Idea: The Shepherds' Garland*) to a special amalgam of the finer tones heard in many different poets – Sidney, Marlowe, Shakespeare, Donne – he seems quintessentially Elizabethan, but there are also notes anticipating the Cavaliers or even the Augustans.

Drayton opted for the pastoral mode early and late: the most effective passages, for example, in his epyllion *Endymion and Phoebe* (later, surprisingly, revised as a satire) have to do with pastoral description, while late examples – "The Shepherd's Sirena" and "The Muses' Elizium" – blend together the fanciful with realistic touches of country life. The early Spenserian imitations were also revised for 17th-century publication.

He responded too to the vogue for historical poetry, first by that popular derivative of the *Mirror for Magistrates*, the tragical complaint – *Piers Gaveston, Matilda*, and *Robert of Normandy* – and then by the *Mortimeriados*. In the latter, history is allied with epic and the hero projected in a romantic context. Again indicative of concern for his craft is the revision of that long poem, nearly 3,000 lines in rime royal, into the even longer *Barons' Wars* in ottava rima. In stressing its political and historical aspects, Drayton reduced the epical and romantic elements with a consequent sobering of tone and treatment. The most novel as well as popular example of his writing in this vein, however, was *England's Heroical Epistles*; here pairs of historical (rather than legendary) lovers exchange letters at a critical juncture in their relationship, creating a dramatic interaction that allows the poet to set forth shifting emotional states. The couplet is used with enormous skill, retaining in Drayton's hands a degree of openness and flexibility while anticipating something of the formality of the Augustans.

He was personally most concerned with his "Herculean toil," the composition of *Polyolbion*, a mammoth chorographical tribute to Great Britain, but his most assured achievement is the often revised collection of sonnets entitled *Idea*. Attacks on sonneteering by satirists induced him to inject an astringent cynical tone in describing his "oft-varying fate" as a lover or in counter-attacking his critics (hailing one as "crooked mimic," another as "leaden brain"). The lively colloquial tone of these sonnets is offset by an enchanting lyricism or by the immediacy of dramatic exchange. Furthermore, unlike most other examples, the sequence is structured: despite the astonishing variety of moods and motifs, according with the literary libertinism he openly adopts, the final sonnet brings it full circle. Having alternately extolled and abused his beloved, he challenges her:

> I send defiance, since if overthrown,
> Thou vanquishing, the conquest is mine own.

—Elizabeth Story Donno

DRUMMOND, William; Laird of Hawthornden.   Scottish.   Born in Hawthornden, near Edinburgh, 13 December 1585. Educated at Edinburgh High School; University of Edinburgh, M.A. 1605; also studied law at Bourges, and in Paris, 1607–08. Married Elizabeth Logan in 1632; five sons, four daughters. Succeeded to the estate of Hawthornden, 1610; a friend of Ben Jonson and Michael Drayton; also an inventor: patented various military and scientific instruments, 1627; a political moderate: worked for peace during the

Scottish political turmoil, 1638, protested against the national league and convenant, 1643, and wrote in favor of negotiating with Charles I, 1646. *Died 4 December 1649.*

PUBLICATIONS

Collections

> *Works*, edited by John Sage and Thomas Ruddiman.   1711.
> *Poetical Works, with A Cypresse Grove*, edited by L. E. Kastner.   2 vols., 1913.
> *Poems and Prose*, edited by Robert H. MacDonald.   1976.

Verse

> *Tears on the Death of Moeliades.*   1613.
> *Poems.*   1614(?); revised edition, 1616.
> *In Memory of Euphemia Kyninghame.*   1616.
> *Forth Feasting: A Panegyric to the King's Most Excellent Majesty.*   1617.
> *Flowers of Sion.*   1623.
> *To the Exequies of the Honourable Sr. Antonye Alexander, Knight: A Pastoral Elegy.*   1638.
> *Polemo-Medinia inter Vitarvam et Nebernam.*   1645(?); as *Accedit Jacobi ...*, 1691.
> *Poems.*   1656.
> *Muckomachy; or, The Midden-Fecht.*   1846.

Play

> *The Entertainment of the High and Mighty Monarch Charles King of Great Britain* (produced 1633).   1633.

Other

> *Auctarium Bibliothecae Edinburgenae.*   1627.
> *A Midnight's Trance.*   1619; as *A Cypress Grove, with Flowers of Sion*, 1630; edited by Robert Ellrodt, 1951.
> *The Drunkard's Character.*   1646.
> *The History of Scotland 1423–1542.*   1655.
> *The Drunkard Forewarned.*   1680.
> *Conversations of Jonson with Drummond*, edited by D. Laing.   1842; edited by C. H. Herford and P. Simpson, in *Collected Works of Jonson 1*, 1925.
> *The Diary.*   1942.

Reading List: *Drummond* by A. Joly, 1935; *A Critical Study of Drummond* by French R. Fogle, 1952.

*   *   *

William Drummond of Hawthornden is generally thought of, and indeed thought of himself as the successor of Sidney, Daniel, and Drayton, carrying on the fashion for

Petrarchan sonneteering into the age of Donne. But we should recognise his special position as the first important representative of Renaissance poetry in Scotland. Scottish poets, such as Drummond's friend Sir William Alexander (later Viscount Stirling), had only just begun to write in Southern English and to use the Italianate forms which had been established in England since the days of Wyatt and Surrey. Drummond not only modelled himself on his English predecessors, but also made a close study of the Italians, especially Petrarch, Tasso, Guarini, Sannazaro, and Marino, as well as Ronsard and other French poets of the sixteenth century. The influence of these foreign models, and the fact that Southern English would not have been Drummond's natural spoken tongue, make him imbue the language with special qualities. He gives it much of the smoothness and melody of Italian, while at the same time somewhat distancing it from actual speech. In this Drummond may be considered to anticipate Milton, with whom his characteristic Christian-Platonist humanism also gives him an affinity.

Drummond's earliest published poem was *Tears on the Death of Moeliades*, an elegy for Prince Henry, eldest son of James I. Its tone is heroic rather than pastoral and in his use of the couplet, Drummond almost anticipates the Augustans. Indeed the whole poem strongly suggests the vein of heroic panegyric later exploited by Waller and Dryden.

It is, however, for his sonnets that Drummond is chiefly remembered. The early death of his father enabled Drummond to retire to his family estate at Hawthornden, and to conform to the Renaissance ideal of rustic retreat and study adumbrated by Petrarch at Vaucluse. Drummond's betrothal, to Miss Cunningham of Barns, and her untimely death on the eve of their wedding, were the occasion for what is perhaps the most truly Petrarchan sonnet sequence in the English language. Petrarch's *Rime* are divided into two sections, the first telling of his wooing of Laura, the second mourning her death and treating of the poet's turning away from earthly joys to the contemplation of things heavenly. Drummond follows an exactly similar scheme. Furthermore, Petrarch interspersed his sonnets with lyrical forms – the ballata, the canzone, and the sestina. Drummond's equivalents for these are the madrigal, the song, and the sestain. The first two of these are written, not in the set Italian forms but in a very effective rhymed free verse; his sestains are also rhymed, but the rhyme words are repeated in each stanza and shift places according to the same formula as do the end-words in the Italian sestina. In his sonnets Drummond usually follows the general Elizabethan practice of concluding each poem with a couplet, rather than a strict Petrarchan form.

Drummond's later work, such as "Urania" and *Flowers of Sion*, is mainly religious in character. *Flowers of Sion* form an interesting parallel to the earlier sonnet sequence. It is likewise a sequence in which the sonnets are interspersed with lyrical forms, and narrate, instead of the courtship, death, and apotheosis of the beloved, the events of the Incarnation and earthly ministry of Christ culminating in His Passion, Resurrection, and Ascension. The sonnet on John the Baptist is the best known of these poems, and has power and simplicity. But equally fine in its own way is the extended lyric on the Ascension, in which Christ's ascent through the celestial spheres is imagined. The traditional scheme of the nine spheres and their harmony seems always to have fired Drummond's imagination. The final poem of this sequence, "The First Fair," written in couplets, is, together with his prose meditation *A Cypress Grove*, the fullest exposition of Drummond's Christian Platonism.

Other poems include *Forth Feasting*, written for King James's visit to Edinburgh in 1618, and *The Entertainment*, written for Charles I's visit to the same city in 1633. A macaronic satire on the Presbyterians *Polemo-Medinia*, was first printed as Drummond's work in 1691, but according to Daniel Defoe its author was Samuel Colvil. Various translations of mediaeval Latin hymns have also been attributed to Drummond but are doubtfully his. W. C. Ward also doubts the authenticity of "The Five Senses" among Drummond's posthumous poems, for no very cogent reasons. It is an outspoken but not distasteful satire alluding to King James's homosexuality.

—John Heath-Stubbs

DRYDEN, John. English. Born in Aldwinckle All Saints, Northamptonshire, 19 August 1631. Educated at Westminster School, London (King's Scholar), 1646–50; Trinity College, Cambridge (pensioner), 1650–54, B.A. 1654. Married Lady Elizabeth Howard in 1663. Remained in Cambridge, 1654–57; settled in London, 1657, and possibly held a minor post in Cromwell's government; thereafter supported himself mainly by writing plays. Appointed Poet Laureate, 1668, and Historiographer Royal, 1669; converted to Roman Catholicism, c. 1685, and lost his royal offices at the accession of William and Mary, 1689. Member, Royal Society, 1660. *Died 1 May 1700.*

PUBLICATIONS

Collections

The Works, edited by Sir Walter Scott. 18 vols., 1808; revised edition edited by George Saintsbury, 1882–92.
Dramatic Works, edited by Montague Summers. 6 vols., 1931–32.
Letters, edited by Charles E. Ward. 1942.
Works, edited by Edward N. Hooker and G. T. Swedenberg, Jr. 1956–
Poems, edited by James Kinsley. 4 vols., 1958.
Four Comedies, Four Tragedies (includes *Secret Love, Sir Martin Mar-All, An Evening's Love, Marriage A-la-Mode, The Indian Emperor, Aureng-Zebe, All for Love, Don Sebastian*), edited by L. A. Beaurline and Fredson Bowers. 2 vols., 1967.
A Selection, edited by John Conaghan. 1978.

Verse

Heroic Stanzas to the Memory of Oliver, Late Lord Protector, in *Three Poems upon the Death of His Late Highness Oliver, Lord Protector*, with Waller and Sprat. 1659.
Astraea Redux: A Poem on the Happy Restoration and Return of His Sacred Majesty Charles the Second. 1660.
To His Sacred Majesty: A Panegyric on His Coronation. 1661.
To My Lord Chancellor, Presented on New Year's Day. 1662.
Annus Mirabilis, The Year of Wonders 1666: An Historical Poem. 1667.
Ovid's Epistles, with others. 1680.
Absalom and Achitophel. 1681; *Second Part*, with Nahum Tate, 1682; edited by James and Helen Kinsley, 1961.
The Medal: A Satire Against Sedition. 1682.
Mac Flecknoe; or, A Satire upon the True-Blue-Protestant Poet T[homas] S[hadwell]. 1682.
Religio Laici; or, A Layman's Faith. 1682.
Miscellany Poems. 1684; *Sylvae; or, The Second Part*, 1685; *Examen Poeticum, Being the Third Part*, 1693; *The Annual Miscellany, Being the Fourth Part*, 1694; *Fifth Part*, 1704; *Sixth Part*, 1709.
Threnodia Augustalis: A Funeral-Pindaric Poem Sacred to the Happy Memory of King Charles II. 1685.
The Hind and the Panther. 1687.
A Song for St. Cecilia's Day 1687. 1687.
Britannia Rediviva: A Poem on the Birth of the Prince. 1688.
Eleonora: A Panegyrical Poem Dedicated to the Memory of the Late Countess of Abingdon. 1692.

The Satires of Juvenal, with others, *Together with the Satires of Persius*.   1693.
An Ode on the Death of Henry Purcell.   1696.
The Works of Virgil, Containing His Pastorals, Georgics, and Aeneis.   1697; edited by
   James Kinsley, 1961.
*Alexander's Feast; or, The Power of Music: An Ode in Honour of St. Cecilia's
   Day*.   1697.
Fables Ancient and Modern.   1700.
Ovid's Art of Love, Book 1, translated.   1709.
Hymns Attributed to Dryden, edited by George Rapall and George Reuben
   Potter.   1937.
Prologues and Epilogues, edited by William B. Gardner.   1951.

Plays

The Wild Gallant (produced 1663).   1669; in *Works 8*, 1962.
The Indian Queen, with Sir Robert Howard (produced 1664).   In *Four New Plays*, by
   Howard, 1665.
The Rival Ladies (produced 1664).   1664; in *Works 8*, 1962.
*The Indian Emperor; or, The Conquest of Mexico by the Spaniards, Being the Sequel of
   The Indian Queen* (produced 1665).   1667; in *Works 9*, 1966.
Secret Love; or, The Maiden Queen (produced 1667).   1668; in *Works 9*, 1966.
Sir Martin Mar-All; or, The Feigned Innocence, from a translation by William
   Cavendish of a play by Molière (produced 1667).   1668; in *Works 9*, 1966.
The Tempest; or, The Enchanted Island, with William Davenant, from the play by
   Shakespeare (produced 1667).   1670; edited by Vivian Summers, 1974.
An Evening's Love; or, The Mock Astrologer (produced 1668).   1671; in *Works 10*,
   1970.
Tyrannic Love; or, The Royal Martyr (produced 1669).   1670; in *Works 10*, 1970.
The Conquest of Granada by the Spaniards, 2 parts (produced 1670, 1671).   1672; in
   Works 2, 1978.
Marriage A-la-Mode (produced 1672).   1673; in *Works 2*, 1978.
The Assignation; or, Love in a Nunnery (produced 1672).   1673; in *Works 2*, 1978.
Amboyna (produced 1673).   1673.
Aureng-Zebe (produced 1675).   1676; edited by Frederick M. Link, 1971.
The State of Innocence and Fall of Man.   1677.
All for Love; or, The World Well Lost, from the play *Antony and Cleopatra* by
   Shakespeare (produced 1677).   1678; edited by David M. Vieth, 1974.
The Kind Keeper; or, Mr. Limberham (produced 1678).   1680; edited by A. Norman
   Jeffares, in *Restoration Comedy*, 1974.
Oedipus, with Nathaniel Lee (produced 1678).   1679.
Troilus and Cressida; or, Truth Found Too Late, from the play by Shakespeare
   (produced 1679).   1679.
The Spanish Friar; or, The Double Discovery (produced 1680).   1681.
The Duke of Guise, with Nathaniel Lee (produced 1682).   1683.
Albion and Albanius, music by Lewis Grabu (produced 1685).   1685.
Don Sebastian, King of Portugal (produced 1689).   1690; in *Four Tragedies*, 1967.
Amphitryon; or, The Two Socias (produced 1690).   1690.
King Arthur; or, The British Worthy, music by Henry Purcell (produced 1691).   1691.
Cleomenes, The Spartan Hero (produced 1692).   1692.
Love Triumphant; or, Nature Will Prevail (produced 1694).   1694.
The Secular Masque, in *The Pilgrim*, by Vanbrugh (produced 1700).   1700.
Comedies, Tragedies, and Operas.   2 vols., 1701.

Other

> *Of Dramatic Poesy: An Essay.*   1668; revised edition, 1684; edited by George Watson,
>   in *Of Dramatic Poesy and Other Critical Essays,* 1962.
> *Notes and Observations on The Express of Morocco,* with John Crowne and Thomas
>   Shadwell.   1674.
> *His Majesty's Declaration Defended.*   1681.
> *The Vindication.*   1683.
> *A Defence of An Essay of Dramatic Poesy.*   1688.
> *Works.*   4 vols., 1695.
> *Critical and Miscellaneous Prose Works,* edited by Edmond Malone.   4 vols., 1800.
> *Essays,* edited by W. P. Ker.   2 vols., 1900.
> *Literary Criticism,* edited by A. C. Kirsch.   1966.

> Editor, *The Art of Poetry,* by Nicolas Boileau, translated by William Soames, revised
>   edition.   1683.

> Translator, *The History of the League,* by Louis Maimbourg.   1684.
> Translator, *The Life of St. Francis Xavier,* by Dominique Bouhours.   1688.
> Translator, with Knightly Chetwood, *Miscellaneous Essays,* by St. Evremond,   1692.
> Translator, with others, *The Annals and History of Tacitus.*   3 vols., 1698.

Bibliography: *Dryden: A Bibliography of Early Editions and of Drydeniana* by Hugh
Macdonald, 1939; *Dryden: A Survey and Bibliography of Critical Studies 1895–1974* by
David J. Latt and Samuel J. Monk, 1976.

Reading List: *The Poetry of Dryden* by Mark van Doren, 1920, revised edition, 1931; *Dryden:
Some Biographical Facts and Problems* by J. M. Osborn, 1940, revised edition, 1965; *Dryden
and the Conservative Myth* by B. N. Schilling, 1961; *Life of Dryden* by Charles E. Ward,
1961; *Dryden's Imagery* by Arthur W. Hoffman, 1962; *Essential Articles for the Study of
Dryden* edited by H. T. Swedenberg, Jr., 1966; *Dryden's Major Plays* by Bruce King, 1966;
Dryden's Poetry by Earl Miner, 1967; *Contexts of Dryden's Thought* by Philip Harth, 1968;
Dryden: The Critical Heritage edited by James and Helen Kinsley, 1971; *Dryden* by William
Myers, 1973; *Dryden and the Development of Panegyric* by James Dale Garrison, 1975;
Dryden, The Public Writer 1660–1685 by George McFadden, 1978.

                              *   *   *

John Dryden's life is largely obscure until he commences as author. He was born on 19
August 1631 at Aldwinckle All Saints in Northamptonshire, and about 1646 he entered, as a
King's Scholar, Westminster School under the famous master Richard Busby. Much later he
recalled that about 1648 he had translated Persius's third satire as a Thursday night exercise
for the school. His first published poem, "Upon the Lord Hastings," appeared in 1649; on 18
May of the following year he was admitted as pensioner to Trinity College, Cambridge,
proceeding B.A. in 1654. The next years are yet more obscure. Some color is given to the
tradition he served the Protectorate by the publication in 1659 of the *Heroique Stanza's* on
Cromwell's death.

His career may be said to begin, however, with the Restoration, and its first period to run
from 1660–1680. Early in these years he published poems on the new order, bringing
together historical, political, religious, and heroic elements. Although such a poem as *Astraea
Redux* is inferior to the poem on Cromwell, it is more ambitious. Somewhat of the new effort
succeeds in *Annus Mirabilis,* whose year of wonders (1666) included the second naval war
with Holland and the Great Fire of London. Dryden seeks too hard to connect these diverse

events, and his execution is uneven. But it has bounding energy and is his sole fully narrative poem till far later. His talents were being recognized – in 1668 he succeeded Davenant as poet laureate, and in 1669 Howell as historiographer royal. By the end of this period he had completed but not published his first poetic masterpiece, *Mac Flecknoe*. If Elkanah Settle was its first dunce hero, Thomas Shadwell finally gained the honor. The poem assesses good and bad art, using a mock coronation skit. Father Flecknoe abdicates for his son (Shadwell). Art, politics, and religious matters combine with paternal love to assess both the dunces and true drama. Flecknoe is "King by Office" and "Priest by Trade." He passes to his son *Love's Kingdom*, his own dull play, as "Sceptre." From "this righteous Lore" comes Shadwell's soul, his opera *Psyche*. Humor and allusion combine to establish the true canons of drama and to fix Shadwell immemorially.

Mac Flecknoe shows that Dryden's chief interest in these decades is the stage. After a first comedy, he turned to the rhymed heroic play, rising to the high astounding terms of the two-part *Conquest of Granada*. He approached earth thereafter. *Marriage A-la-mode* consists of a mingling of serious and comic plots especially congenial to him, and a favorite still. In the Prologue to his heroic play *Aureng-Zebe*, he professes himself "weary" of rhyme, and in *All for Love* he wrote a blank verse tragedy on Antony and Cleopatra, thought by many his finest play. His collaboration with Nathaniel Lee for *Oedipus* altered his smooth earlier blank verse style to a harsher, more various medium that appears again in his adaptation of *Troilus and Cressida*. After his enormously popular *Spanish Fryar* (1680), he wrote no plays single-handedly till 1689.

The next period, 1680–1685, is dominated by engagement with the tumultuous times. In the state of near revolution over the Popish Plot and efforts to seize power from Charles II, Dryden published *Absalom and Achitophel*, his poem most admired today. Using the biblical parallel of the plot against David (Charles), Dryden creates an epic-historic-satiric blend for the machinations of Achitophel (Earl of Shaftesbury) and his dupe Absalom (Duke of Monmouth). The Chaucer-like portraits of individuals and the personal statement on government (ll. 751–810) show Dryden in full command of a public poetry.

1682 brought Dryden further attention. *Mac Flecknoe* now first appeared in print, pirated. When Shaftesbury was released from prison by a Whig jury in November 1681, a triumphant medal was struck. Next March Dryden's one bitter poem, *The Medall*, appeared. Perhaps his anger was feigned. His usual composure is evident in *Religio Laici*, his first religious poem, which curiously begins with rich imagery and progresses to a direct, non-metaphorical style unique in his poetry. In 1684 he published one of his poems most popular today, "To the Memory of Mr. Oldham," on a young poet recently dead. In that year and the next he joined the bookseller Jacob Tonson in putting out the first two of a series of "Dryden miscellanies," collections of poetry by various hands. Charles II died, and James acceded, in 1685. Dryden celebrated these events in *Threnodia Augustalis*, his first pindaric ode after one of his finest poems, the translation of Horace, *Odes*, III, xxix.

The next period, 1685–1688, coincides with the brief rule by James II. Probably about the summer of 1685 Dryden became a Roman Catholic, and in 1687 published his second religious poem, *The Hind and the Panther*, whose 2592 lines make it his longest poem apart from translations. Its style is as complex as that of *Religio Laici* had been simple. Using sacred zoögraphy (the Hind represents Catholicism, the Panther Anglicanism, etc.), fables, myth, allusion, allegory, and the slightest of plots, Dryden sets forth a timeless version of the times, including the recent and distant past (Part I), present contentions (II), and the ecclesiastical as well as national future (III). Each part has a moving personal passage and those who have most opposed Dryden's doctrine or his fable have often called the style of this poem his finest. The poetic and personal confidence thereby implied finds expression in the ode, so praised by Dr. Johnson, on Anne Killigrew, whose small poetic abilities nonetheless may represent the artist's high vocation. Music is an equally confidently used metaphor in *A Song for Cecilia's Day*, which enacts history from Creation to Judgment.

When James fled late in 1688, and when William and Mary were invited as sovereigns by Parliament, Dryden entered into the most difficult period of his career, 1688–1694. Stripped of offices and denied full engagement with his times, he turned again to "the ungrateful stage." Two plays that now seem his greatest resulted: *Don Sebastian*, concerned with tragic fate, and *Amphitryon*, a very bleak comedy. Both deal with human identity in a hostile world. In 1691 he enjoyed a fortunate collaboration with Henry Purcell on *King Arthur*, an opera. In 1694, his last play, *Love Triumphant*, featured a happy ending engineered by an unconvincing change of heart. Such doubts and sputters in these years had fullest exercise in the *Satires* of 1693 (translating Juvenal and Persius) and the Preface to *Examen Poeticum*, the third miscellany.

In the last period, 1694–1700, Dryden worked through his problems. If he could not address all his contemporaries, he could focus on individuals. In 1694 two of his finest poetic addresses appear: "To my Dear Friend Mr. Congreve" and "To Sir Godfrey Kneller." Gloom remains in both, but the gloomier "Kneller" shows chastened faith even in "these Inferiour Times." The "Congreve" bears uncanny resemblance in motif to *Mac Flecknoe*. Drama is again the topic, with comparisons again settling values. Now Dryden must abdicate and Congreve have legitimate succession, even if a usurper should sneak in for a time. The "son" merits, however, and the "father" loves.

Addresses lacked the capaciousness to adjust new strains to old hopes. Such scale was achieved in the 1697 *Virgil*. Although it and his comedies most require re-assessment, it does seem that he darkens the second half of his *Aeneis* (as if the military and the public worlds do not quite merge), and that he renders the *Georgics* even more heroically and sympathetically than Virgil to show the terms on which hope remained. His real epic was to come in cento, *Fables Ancient and Modern* (1700). It combines seventeen poems made over from Ovid, Boccaccio, Chaucer, and Homer with four solely Dryden's: those two handsome ones to the Duchess of Ormonde and to John Dryden of Chesterton toward the beginning, as also *Alexander's Feast* and "The Monument of a Fair Maiden Lady" toward the end. In redoing the *Metamorphoses* as Milton had redone the *Aeneid* in *Paradise Lost*, Dryden relates his poems by links, themes, motifs, and central subject – the human search for the good life. A serene wisdom shows that such a life can finally be gained only on Christian terms. Yet the vain and sinful race continues to endear itself to the old poet. *Fables* is once again becoming a favorite of readers as it had been for the Romantics and Dryden's own contemporaries. He died on May Day 1700 of degenerative diseases, yet calm of mind to the end.

The limitations of such periodizing are represented by its failure to allow for his constant writing in "the other harmony of prose" (Preface to *Fables*). He was by no means the modern stylist some claim. He writes in numerous styles and sometimes shows no more knowledge than Milton of modern paragraph and sentence writing. In his styles, however, he established English criticism, struggling like others before him to create the critical essay. As early as *The Rival Ladies* (1664) he found his way in use of the preface, employing a method inquisitive, devoted to current issues, and yet enough assured to deal with general principles. *Of Dramatick Poesy. An Essay* is really a dialogue, his most elaborate criticism, a semi-fiction, offering heroic debate on the proper character of drama. In the "Parallel Betwixt Poetry and Painting" (a preface to *De Arte Graphica* in 1695) we see most clearly his attempt to unite neo-Aristotelian mimesis with neo-Horatian affectivism. Once more he asserted the poet's right to heighten – to take a better or worse "likeness" and remain true, or to deal with the best "nature," unlike the scientist. In a way prescient for his career, the "Account" prefixed to *Annus Mirabilis* (1667) had placed historical poetry and panegyric (by implication satire also) under the aegis of epic. These prefaces, the *Dramatick Poesy*, and his poems as well dealt with the concept of hope for human progress, which was relatively new in England, and also introduced critical and historical principles. The element most neglected by historians of criticism was his historical understanding, which permitted him to compare and differentiate and evolve a historical relativism that would later undermine mimetic presumptions. To him we owe the concept of a historical age or period possessing its own temper or Zeitgeist, with all that such assumptions have meant to subsequent thought about literature.

Such diversity – there are over thirty plays, operas, and cantatas alone – yields to no easy summary. We can observe what joins him to, or differentiates him from, his great contemporaries – or the next century. Like Marvell, Dryden was a gifted lyric poet, although in odes rather than ruminative lyrics. Like Butler, he was a learned satirist, but where Butler degrades Dryden exalts. Like Milton, he excelled in varieties of narrative and drama, just as both also overcame crises toward the end of their lives. Dryden had what Milton lacked – wit, humor, and generosity. But his extraordinary intellectual power to liken and assimilate was incapable of Milton's higher fusion of all into a single intense reality. And where Milton, like Spenser, created an artistic language spoken by no one, Dryden like Donne and Jonson created a more natural language founded on actual speech. Born early enough to remember the outbreak of civil war (1642) and to live through four different national constitutions, Dryden wrote of subjects that poets no longer treat directly – the most momentous events of their times. For all that, his powers took on greatness only in the second half of his life, developing to the end. He practiced every literary kind except the novel, never repeating himself except in songs for plays. He is a rare example of a writer whose finest work comes at the end of a lifetime, of a century, and of a distinct period of literature. The next equivalent of *Fables* is not heroic poetry but the novel.

—Earl Miner

DUCK, Stephen. English. Born in Charlton, Wiltshire, in 1705. Agricultural labourer after age 14. Married in 1724 (first wife died in 1730), three children; 2) Sarah Big, the Queen's housekeeper, in 1733. His literary efforts were encouraged by Queen Caroline, who gave him money and made him a Yeoman of the Guard, 1733, and Keeper of the Queen's Library at Richmond. Ordained in 1746: preacher at Kew Chapel, 1751; Rector of Byfleet, Surrey after 1752. *Died* (by suicide) *21 March 1756.*

PUBLICATIONS

Verse

Royal Benevolence; A Poem on Providence. 1730.
Poems on Several Subjects. 1730.
To the Duke of Cumberland on His Birthday. 1732.
A Poem on the Marriage of the Prince of Orange; Verses to the Author by a Divine, with the Author's Answer; and His Poem on Truth and Falsehood. 1734.
Poems on Several Occasions. 1736; as *The Beautiful Works of Duck,* 1753.
The Vision: A Poem on the Death of Queen Caroline. 1737.
The Year of Wonders. 1737.
Curious Poems on Several Occasions (revised versions of *On Poverty, The Thresher's Labour, The Shunammite*). 1738.
Alrick and Isabel; or, The Unhappy Marriage. 1740.
Every Man in His Own Way: An Epistle to a Friend. 1743.
An Ode to the Battle of Dettingen. 1743.
Caesar's Camp; or, St. George's Hill. 1755.

Reading List: *Duck, The Thresher-Poet* by Rose M. Davis, 1926; "Duck, The Wiltshire Phenomenon" by R. G. Furnival, in *Cambridge Journal,* May 1953; "Duck, The Thresher Poet" by A. Warner, in *Review of English Literature 8,* 1967.

*   *   *

The Thresher's Labour is among the first of those poems describing rural activities and written from first-hand experience by untutored peasant-poets which gained some currency in the later eighteenth century. Stephen Duck had virtually no formal education; he taught himself to write verses by reading Milton with the aid of a dictionary, and formed his style and taste according to the precepts of Addison, whose *Spectator* papers he read avidly. He was eventually taken up and patronised by Queen Caroline (a little to the chagrin of Pope and the other literary giants of the day), was made Royal Librarian, and took holy orders. Duck's sad death – he drowned himself in a fit of depression – may reflect the pressures that this unnatural existence had brought to bear upon him.

Those pressures are equally apparent in his verse. He is rarely able to escape from the straitjacket of the Augustan couplet, and he lacks the wit or the crispness of phrase to make that measure rise above the pedestrian. Yet *The Thresher's Labour* has moments of charm and authenticity. Its rueful account of harvest-time toils, of the unavailing attempts to find some mitigation or relief, still strike true:

> When sooty pease we thresh, you scarce can know
> Our native colour, as from work we go:
> The sweat and dust, and suffocating smoke,
> Make us so much like Etheopians look,
> We scare our wives when evening brings us home;
> And frightened infants think the Bugbear come.
> Week after week we this dull task pursue,
> Unless when winnowing days produce a new:
> A new, indeed, but frequently a worse!
> The threshal yields but to the master's curse.
> He counts the bushels, counts how much a day:
> Then swears we've idled half our time away ...

In this vein Duck is attractive and readable. All too often he allows himself to fall prey to the temptation of writing society verse, panegyric, and compliment. He has neither the poise nor the authority to make anything of such forms. Some of his verse tales are unjustly neglected, though. In "Felix and Constance" and in "Avaro and Amanda" he shows an ability to conduct narrative and the heavy diction adds a period charm to his tales. And in *The Shunammite* (a redaction of the Biblical story from 2 Kings iv) his simple faith lends a credibility and directness to the story and makes it very readable. Hence, while it may be fair to say that Duck's real importance is as a historical curiosity – the peasant poet in an age of great erudition – there is enough of his work which rises above mere curiosity value and makes him worthy of inclusion among the English poets.

—T. Bareham

DUGGAN, Eileen (May).   New Zealander.   Born in Tua Marina, 21 May 1894. Educated at Marlborough Girls' High School; Victoria University College, M.A. (honours) in history 1918. Teacher, Dannevirke High School, St. Patrick's College; Lecturer in History, Victoria

University College. Recipient: Royal Society of Literature Honarary Fellowship, 1943.
O.B.E. (Officer, Order of the British Empire). *Died in 1972*.

PUBLICATIONS

Verse

Poems. 1921.
New Zealand Bird Songs. 1929.
Poems. 1937.
New Zealand Poems. 1940.
More Poems. 1951.

Other

Editor, *Letters from the North Solomons,* by Emmet McHardy.   1935.

Reading List: *Duggan* by F. M. McKay, 1977.

*   *   *

Eileen Duggan was the first New Zealand poet to establish an international reputation. Her background – the daughter of Irish immigrants and a childhood coloured by tales of famine, rack rents, and evictions – gives her verse its direction. She came to see that the restlessness of exile, experienced through identification with the dispossessed Irish, could be resolved only in New Zealand. This realisation is the basis of her search for a national identity, later a preoccupation of the poets of the 1930's. Her nationalism is apparent in her themes, imagery, and turns of expression. The landscape, in particular that of the Marlborough province, is closely observed and memorably expressed in many lines. In a poem such as "The Tides Run up the Wairau" personal emotion is firmly located in New Zealand. Duggan's interest in Maori themes is part of her nationalism, and she is a pioneer in marrying Maori words and phrases to the natural movement of English verse.

The sense of disinheritance experienced in New Zealand by Katherine Mansfield, Robin Hyde, and others of Duggan's generation took in her case a second and a deeper channel in a ceaseless and growing aspiration for the divine. Her religious faith is grounded in our humanity; "the mystic is no refuge if it forsake the human." "Contrast" presents through the images of the shepherds and the magi the rational and the intuitive approach to belief. In the many poems that explore the dark ways of providence, Duggan's faith is that of the shepherds who instinctively abandon themselves to the incomprehensible mystery of divine love.

The best of her early poems have the qualities of good Georgian verse, simplicity, warmth, and moral innocence. They have, too, clarity, technical skill, and appreciation of the countryside, the unnoticed, and the ordinary. Notable among her early verse is folk-poetry such as the ballad "The Bushfeller" and a striking evocation of childhood, "Twilight." Her later work goes beyond her Georgian origins to find an individual expression in an alert, imaginative, and deeply thoughtful poetry. In her final volume her verse has a greater reach and concentration. Her imagination is possessed by a cosmic vision forced on her by the events of World War II, which like many others she saw as threatening the collapse of civilisation. The didactic nature of many of these poems comes from her diagnosis that

334

bewilderment was the real danger of the time, and that when mankind is bewildered it can be "baffled or hectored to its spiritual ruin." In a time of disillusionment, even despair, she wrote optimistic poetry whose characteristic utterance is affirmation.

—F. M. McKay

———————

DUNBAR, Paul Laurence. American. Born in Dayton, Ohio, 27 June 1872; son of a former slave. Educated at Dayton High School, graduated 1891. Married Alice Ruth Moore in 1898. Elevator operator, Dayton, 1891–93; employed at the Haiti Building, World's Columbian Exposition, Chicago, 1894; encouraged in his writing by prominent Dayton men, and by William Dean Howells, at whose instigation he joined the Pond Lecture Bureau, 1896; attained great popularity throughout the United States as a reader of his own works, and visited England, 1897; Assistant in the Library of Congress, Washington, D.C., 1897–98. Suffered from tuberculosis. *Died 9 February 1906.*

PUBLICATIONS

Collections

    Complete Poems. 1913.
    The Dunbar Reader, edited by Jay Martin and Gossie H. Hudson. 1975.

Verse

    Oak and Ivy. 1893.
    Majors and Minors. 1895.
    Lyrics of Lowly Life. 1896.
    Lyrics of the Hearthside. 1899.
    Poems of Cabin and Field. 1899.
    Candle-Lightin' Time. 1901.
    Lyrics of Love and Laughter. 1903.
    When Malindy Sings. 1903.
    Li'l' Gal. 1904.
    Chris'mus Is A-Comin' and Other Poems. 1905.
    Howdy, Honey, Howdy. 1905.
    Lyrics of Sunshine and Shadow. 1905.
    Joggin' Erlong. 1906.
    Speakin' o' Christmas and Other Christmas and Special Poems. 1914.

Plays

    The Gambler's Wife, in *Dayton Tattler,* Ohio, 13, 20, and 27 December 1890.
    African Romances, music by Samuel Coleridge Taylor. 1897.

Clorindy; or, The Origin of the Cakewalk, music by Will Marion Cook.   1898.
Dream Lovers, music by Samuel Coleridge Taylor.   1898.
Jes Lak White Fo'ks (lyrics only, with others), music by Will Marion Cook.   1900.
Uncle Eph's Christmas, music by Will Marion Cook.   1900.
Plantation Melodies Old and New (lyrics only, with others), music by H. T.
   Burleigh.   1901.
In Dahomey (lyrics only, with others), music by Will Marion Cook.   1903.
My Lady (lyrics only, with others), music by Will Marion Cook.   1914.

Fiction

The Uncalled.   1898.
Folks from Dixie (stories).   1898.
The Love of Landry.   1900.
The Strength of Gideon and Other Stories.   1900.
The Fanatics.   1901.
The Sport of the Gods.   1902; as *The Jest of Fate,* 1902.
In Old Plantation Days (stories).   1903.
The Heart of Happy Hollow (stories).   1904.

Bibliography: *Dunbar: A Bibliography* by E. W. Metcalf, Jr., 1975.

Reading List: *The Life and Works of Dunbar,* biography by Lida Keck Wiggins, 1907;
Dunbar and His Song by Virginia Cunningham, 1947; *Oak and Ivy: A Biography of Dunbar*
by Addison Gayle, Jr., 1971; *A Singer in the Dawn: Reinterpretations of Dunbar* edited by Jay
Martin, 1975.

*   *   *

There were, in truth, two Paul Laurence Dunbars. One was the writer supported by the
interest of white Americans because some of his work was sufficiently faithful to black
stereotypical images designed and demanded by white Americans. The other, in a sense the
more "real" Paul Laurence Dunbar, was the writer of genuine literary talent and dramatic
sensibility, whose true literary worth could not be widely assessed until a wide range of his
work was gathered and published as late as 1975 in *The Paul Laurence Dunbar Reader.*
   In his first manifestation, that of dialect poet, Dunbar was not so much pandering to the
demands of white editors and a white reading public as indulging his own natural affinity for
the rhythms of common speech and often for comedy; dialect in literature was, after all, very
much *à la mode* with the interest in local color in late nineteenth-century America. That he
had a gift as a dialect poet is undeniable, but it is rather too bad that his white audience could
not accept him as anything more.
   Much more he was, as William Dean Howells recognized early. As a writer of fiction and
essays, he used the stuff of black lore to greater effect than any black writer had previously,
and at least as well as such whites as Joel Chandler Harris had done. Particularly noteworthy
in his work is the reflection of religion in black-American life and of the implications of the
black migration to American cities. As a poet, Dunbar often superbly starched his ready
lyricism with a keen sense of drama. It is a truism to say that while his material was mainly
black, his insights were universal.
   Dunbar did not choose to be the examplar of the white view of black America in his time,
during the adult years of his 33-year life, but he was, and he made a sturdy pivot. He
managed to entertain and enlighten whites while helping to imbue fellow blacks with a sense
of history and importance that make him a close spiritual ancestor of Countée Cullen,

Langston Hughes, James Baldwin, and the host of other powerful twentieth-century black-American voices for pride.

—Alan R. Shucard

DUNBAR, William. Scottish. Born in East Lothian, c. 1460. Educated at the University of St. Andrews, 1475–79, B.A. 1477, M.A. 1479. Joined the Franciscan order, and for a time was a begging friar, later left the order; subsequently served James IV as both court poet and diplomatic envoy until 1513; granted court pension, 1500–13. *Died c. 1522.*

PUBLICATIONS

Collections

> *Poems,* edited by D. Laing. 2 vols., 1834; supplement, 1865.
> *Poems,* edited by J. Small. 3 vols., 1884–93.
> *Poems,* edited by W. Mackay Mackenzie. 1932; revised edition, 1960.
> *Selected Poems,* edited by Hugh MacDiarmid. 1955.
> *Poems,* edited by James Kinsley. 1958.

Reading List: *Dunbar: The Poet and His Period* by R. A. Taylor, 1932; *Dunbar: A Biographical Study* by John W. Baxter, 1952; *Dunbar: A Critical Exposition of the Poems* by Thomas M. Scott, 1966; *Two Scots Chaucerians* (Dunbar and Henryson) by H. Harvey Wood, 1967.

*   *   *

William Dunbar, the greatest of the Scottish Makars (or Scottish Chaucerians, as they are sometimes referred to by the English), and one of Scotland's three finest poets (the others being Burns and MacDiarmid), was not only a man of moods, of extreme exultations and dejections which are reflected in his work, but a virtuoso deploying his brilliant technique upon several styles, all of them – whether the aureate, the vernacular, the secular, or the religious – shot through with contrasted lights, and characterised by energetic brush-strokes. For these reasons, even Dunbar's use of the mediaeval literary man's stock-in-trade phrases, like *A per se, fyre on flint, hair like golden wire* stand out more sharply than in the gentler context of Henryson's poetry.

We know a certain amount about Dunbar's life from official sources, but much more about his nature and manner of living from his personal poems. The dampness and draughtiness and the long, dark hours of a Scottish winter depressed him, as he tells us in "On His Heid-Ache":

> Whone that the nicht dois lengthen hours,
> With wind, with hail and heavy schours,
>   My dule spreit does lurk for schoir,
>   My hairt for langour does forloir.

337

> For laik of simmer with his flours.
> I walk, I turn, sleep may I nocht,
> I vexit am with heavy thocht ...

Yet he was well aware of the subjective nature of his depression, and made an effort to master it, concluding "Ane His Awin Enemy" with an exhortation:

> Now all this time lat us be mirry,
> And set nocht by this warld a chirry,
> Now, whill thair is gude wine to sell,
> He that does on dry bread wirry,
> I gif him to the Devil of hell.

Although he held minor orders in the church, the Christian affirmation in his roll-call of dead poets in "Lament for the Makaris," with its liturgical use of the tolling refrain *Timor mortis conturbat me*, is scarcely enthusiastic:

> Sen for the deid remeid is none,
> Best is that we for dede dispone,
> Eftir our deid that lif may we:
> *Timor mortis conturbat me.*

As a fluent exponent of the Scots tradition of "flyting" − hurling versified abuse at your opponent without regard either to good manners or accuracy − he achieved resounding effect in "The Flyting of Dunbar and Kennedy." His sharp, satirical muse found comic exercise in unfrocking the pretensions of John Damien to fly, using birds' wings, in "The Fenyeit Freir of Tungland." "The Treatis of the Twa Maryit Wemen and the Wedo," in which the three ladies discuss what interests them most, their sex lives, shows Dunbar as a master of comedy, a role in which he appears more delightfully in "The Ballad of Kynd Kittock." (Although no manuscript of this associates it with Dunbar directly, there could scarcely have been another undiscovered master-poet capable of writing it in Dunbar's style alive at the same time.)

In full aureate flight, Dunbar's great Christmas and Easter hymns ring out like solemnly triumphant organ-music. Here is the sonorous opening of " Of the Resurrection of Christ":

> Done is a battle on the dragon black,
> Our campioun Christ confoundet hes his force;
> The yetts* of Hell are broken with a crack,   *gates
> The sign triumphal rasit is of the croce,
> The divillis trymmillis with hiddous voce,
> The sauls are borrowit and to the bliss can go,
> Christ with his blud our ransonis dois indoce:
> *Surrexit Dominus de sepulchro.*

He could turn off a set of begging verses, seeking a benefice for himself from the King, with a skill which made them outlive the occasion that called them forth. He produced a mellifluous flourish for Margaret Tudor when she arrived in Scotland for her marriage to James IV in 1503:

> Now fair, fairest, of every fair,
> Princess most pleasant and preclare,*   *famous
> The lustiest* one alive that been,   *most beautiful
>   Welcome of Scotland to be Queen!

Indeed, he seems to have remained a favourite with the Queen, travelling to Aberdeen with her in 1511, and saluting that city with an aureate splendour he matched in another poem on London.

"The Dance of the Seven Deidly Sins," characterised by rhyming exuberance and remarkable verbal energy, the anti-Highland "Epetaffe for Donald Owre," its sharp short lines stabbing home the poet's angry contempt, and his splendid love-allegory "The Golden Targe," full of the colours of leaves and flowers, and birdsong newly refreshed by sunshine after rain, further reveal the breadth of Dunbar's forceful genius. MacDiarmid, in his best work, outdid him in intellectual range as Burns outdid both of them in his warmth of human concern. But out of the mediaeval shadows, Dunbar, cavorting in the Queen's chamber, celebrating the main religious festivals of his church or setting down aspects of his daily life, displays a commanding personality, a skill with vocabulary and a competent mastery of stanza-forms nowhere surpassed in Scottish literature.

—Maurice Lindsay

DUNCAN, Robert (Edward).   American.   Born in Oakland, California, 7 January 1919. Educated at the University of California, Berkeley, 1936–38, 1948–50. Editor, *The Experimental Review*, Berkeley, 1938–40, and *The Berkeley Miscellany*, 1948–49. Lived in Majorca, 1955–56; taught at Black Mountain College, North Carolina, 1956; Assistant Director of the Poetry Center (Ford grant), 1956–57, and Lecturer in the Poetry Workshop, 1965, San Francisco State College. Recipient: Guggenheim Fellowship, 1963; National Endowment for the Arts grant, 1966 (two grants). Lives in San Fransisco.

PUBLICATIONS

Verse

    Heavenly City, Earthly City.   1947.
    Poems 1948–1949.   1950.
    Medieval Scenes.   1950.
    Caesar's Gate: Poems 1949–1950.   1955; revised edition, 1972.
    Letters.   1958.
    Selected Poems.   1959.
    The Opening of the Field.   1960.
    Roots and Branches: Poems.   1964.
    Writing, Writing: A Composition Book of Madison 1953, Stein Imitations.   1964.
    A Book of Resemblances: Poems 1950–1953.   1966.
    Of the War: Passages 22–27.   1966.
    The Years As Catches: First Poems 1939–1946.   1966.
    Fragments of a Disordered Devotion.   1966.
    Epilogos.   1967.
    Bending the Bow.   1968.
    Names of People.   1968.
    The First Decade: Selected Poems 1940–1950.   1968.
    Derivations: Selected Poems 1950–1956.   1968.

Play Time, Pseudo Stein, 1942: A Story, and A Fairy Play. 1969.
Achilles' Song. 1969.
Poetic Disturbances. 1970.
Tribunals: Passages 31–35. 1970.
Ground Work No. 1. 1971.
In Memoriam Wallace Stevens. 1972.
Poems from the Margins of Thom Gunn's "Moly." 1972.
A Seventeenth Century Suite in Homage to the Metaphysical Genius in English Poetry 1590–1690. 1973.
An Ode and Arcadia, with Jack Spicer. 1974.
Dante. 1974.

Plays

Faust Foutu (produced 1955). 1958; complete edition, as *Faust Foutu: An Entertainment in Four Parts,* 1960.
Medea at Kolchis: The Maiden Head (produced 1956). 1965.

Other

The Artist's View. 1952.
On Poetry (radio interview with Eugene Vance). 1964.
As Testimony: The Poem and the Scene. 1964.
The Sweetness and Greatness of Dante's "Divine Comedy," 1265–1965. 1965.
Six Prose Pieces. 1966.
The Cat and the Blackbird (juvenile). 1967.
The Truth and Life of Myth: An Essay in Essential Autobiography. 1968.
65 Drawings: A Selection of 65 Drawings from One Drawing-Book: 1952–1956. 1970.
An Interview with George Bowering and Robert Hogg, April 19, 1969. 1971.

Reading List: Robert Duncan Issue of *Origin,* June 1963, of *Audit 4,* 1967, and of *Maps 6,* 1974; *Godawful Streets of Man* by Warren Tallman, 1976.

*   *   *

The poet, Robert Duncan has said, is akin to the paranoiac: everything seems to belong to the plot. Raised in a Theosophist environment, in much of his work Duncan seeks, like the paranoiac but without his fear, for something that does *not* belong to the coherent cosmic plot. Duncan, therefore (as he expounds it most clearly in the sections of the incomplete "The H. D. Book"), lives in a world in which "things strive to speak," where the poet seeks to read "the language of things," where "the poet must attend not to what he means to say but to what what he says means" (*Caterpillar 7*). The poet is, then, subject not to "inspiration" so much as he is to "possession," where he may be had by an idea, and poetry is – in Duncan's language – an Office: the text the poet writes is part of a larger text: the Poem, and the office of poet is subsumed in the larger Office, of Poet.

It is thus perhaps to be expected that Duncan, of all poets associated with Black Mountain College and with post-Modernism, should be the American writer most closely associated with the great tradition of English poetry and of mystical poetry, while at the same time he is the one who seems most consistently and perversely to be at odds with the traditions and conventions of English poetry. Such apparent perversity arises in part from Duncan's insistence, drawn from Heraclitus that "an unapparent connexion is stronger than an apparent": it derives also, in part, from "the strongest drive of my life, that things have not come to the conclusions I saw around me, and this involved the conclusions that I saw shaping in my own thought and actions" (*Caterpillar 8/9*). Thus "A Poem Beginning with a Line by Pindar" (1958) is a combination of traditional devices, forms, and sources with the unexpected and unconventional. The synecdoche of "the light foot *hears*," quoted from Pindar's First Pythian Ode, involves the breaking of things "normal" in the language; this in turn suggests a range of possible meanings for "*light* foot." The poem, an extended meditation and discovery on – among other things – the notion of Adulthood, proposes a world in which the Real is found, not in a landscape, but "in an obscurity" – hidden, that is to say, from normal, familiar, conventional (or mortal) sight. In two essays central to his work, "Ideas of the Meaning of Form" (*Kulchur 4*) and "Man's Fulfillment in Order and Strife" (*Caterpillar 8/9*), Duncan insists that "to the conventional mind" form is "what can be imposed," and, in all of his writing, conventional syntax and language are a part of conventional form, and man is a creature of language. In section Two of the "Pindar" poem the language, individual words and syllables, breaks down, loses its articulation, becomes almost nonsense. The breakdown is triggered by the word "stroke" which – initially of a brush, painting, or of a pen, writing – becomes a medical stroke (Eisenhower's?), and the poem, which at that point seems to be struggling to a halt, moves into a firm political rhetoric which reveals adulthood as a condition of nations as well as of individuals, and the condition itself as a process. Reading the poem, we witness the testimony of the poet discovering the world as it reveals itself to him through language. Meaning, in such poems as this, is to be found in the play of possible meanings, rather than in the conventionally ordered exposition of rational or reasonable thought. Duncan's insistence "not to reach a conclusion but to keep our exposure to what we do not know" has led to *Passages*, a series of rhetorical poems which, resting on the Julian motto "The even is bounded, but the uneven is without bounds," explores all possible voices as its testimony to What Is.

—Peter Quartermain

DUTTON, Geoffrey (Piers Henry).   Australian.   Born in Anlaby, South Australia, 2 August 1922. Educated at Geelong Grammar School, Victoria, 1932–39; University of Adelaide, 1940–41; Magdalen College, Oxford, 1946–49, B.A. 1949. Served in the Royal Australian Air Force, 1941–45: Flight Lieutenant. Married Ninette Trott in 1944; three sons, one daughter. Senior Lecturer in English, University of Adelaide, 1954–62; Visiting Lecturer in Australian Literature, University of Leeds (Commonwealth Fellow), 1960; Visiting Professor of English, Kansas State University, Manhattan, 1962. Editor, Penguin Australia, Melbourne, 1961–65. Since 1965, Editorial Director, Sun Books, Melbourne. Co-Founder, *Australian Letters*, Adelaide, 1957, and *Australian Book Review*, Kensington Park, 1962. Member, Australian Council for the Arts, 1968–70, and Commonwealth Literary Fund Advisory Board, 1972–73; Member, Australian Literature Board, 1972–74. Lives in South Australia.

PUBLICATIONS

Verse

Nightflight and Sunrise.   1945.
Antipodes in Shoes.   1955.

Flowers and Fury. 1963.
On My Island: Poems for Children. 1967.
Poems Soft and Loud. 1968.
Findings and Keepings: Selected Poems 1940–70. 1970.
New Poems to 1972. 1972.

Fiction

The Mortal and the Marble. 1950.
Andy. 1968.
Tamara. 1970.
Queen Emma of the South Seas. 1976.

Other

A Long Way South (travel). 1953.
Africa in Black and White. 1956.
States of the Union (travel). 1958.
Founder of a City: The Life of William Light. 1960.
Patrick White. 1961.
Walt Whitman. 1961.
Paintings of S. T. Gill. 1962.
Russell Drysdale (art criticism). 1962.
Tisi and the Yabby (juvenile). 1965.
Seal Bay (juvenile). 1966.
*The Hero as Murderer: The Life of Edward John Eyre, Australian Explorer and Governor
     of Jamaica, 1815–1901.* 1967.
Tisi and the Pageant (juvenile). 1968.
Australia's Censorship Crisis. 1970.
Australia's Last Explorer: Ernest Giles. 1970.
Australia since the Camera: 1901–14. 1971.
From Federation to War. 1972.
White on Black: The Australian Aborigine Portrayed in Art. 1974.

Editor, *The Literature of Australia.* 1964; revised edition, 1976.
Editor, *Australia and the Monarchy.* 1966.
Editor, *Modern Australian Writing.* 1966.
Editor, with Max Harris, *The Vital Decade: 10 Years of Australian Art and
     Letters.* 1968.
Editor, with Max Harris, *Sir Henry Bjelke, Don Baby, and Friends.* 1971.

Translator, with Igor Mezhakoff-Koriakin, *Bratsk Station,* by Yevgeny
     Yevtushenko. 1966.
Translator, with Igor Mazhakoff-Koriakin, *Fever,* by Bella Akhmadulina. 1968.
Translator, with Eleanor Jackman, *Kazan University and Other New Poems,* by Yevgeny
     Yevtushenko. 1973.

*   *   *

Wartime air-force experience has had a seminal effect on Geoffrey Dutton's poetry – not so
much in subject matter as in its lasting synthesis into a perspective of aerial vision: the lone
pilot among the clouds pondering the meaning of existence, the freshness and intensity of his

perceptions of the world below enriched by a grateful return to base. Thus we find in Dutton's work a rare marriage of delicate observation and abstract discourse. Expectations of breath-taking vistas, or what he wryly calls "high octane/illusions of freedom," are thwarted by the apocalyptic vision of his early work: "the end uncertain and the past dissolved," "the future groping and the memory slain." Many of his poems give the impression of being specifically addressed, for in the face of this uncertainty, hope lies in the discovery of a meaningful realationship.

The threat of solitude haunts his poetry. "Abandoned Airstrip" poses the attractions of a dingo's freedom against innate fears of isolation: "Lacking lions and wars, our country bred/ In us a fear of loneliness instead." Love and affection, an obvious counterforce, are accordingly given considerable attention, and the wide range of treatments testifies to the variety found in his work. In "Night Fishing" the elaboration of a conceit in a manner reminiscent of the Metaphysicals climaxes with the duality of analogy fused into images of profound tranquillity, the lovers

> Exposed in their ghostly nakedness ...
> Welcome or terrible as they share
> In and around her in his arms the sea.

At the other extreme, the sustained treatment of love manifest in the day-to-day occurrences of a living relationship recalls Williams, particularly in the reverence towards flowers and the disarming fidelity of "Let's risk being obvious in happiness" – complexity is not an end in itself.

Dutton's talent for evocation is well seen in the travel poetry: an English landscape sheltering from industrialization; the "dark centre" of the Danube; a derelict aerodrome in France, when a skylark mockingly alights on a rotting disembowelled aircraft whose "shattered instruments measure the speed of rust"; and the outstanding poem sequence "A Russian Journey" which subtly exposes the blurred vision of conditioning meeting reality – austerity is not compensated by "Remembering the blood that tyranny wrings."

A study of Whitman inspired in the 1960's what Dutton has called "a more complex human response to my own country." Though there is evidence of Whitman's dramatic soliloquizing and a new sense of responsibility brought about by the re-orientation ("Land, that I love, lying all open to me ... I will protect you, I have promised that"), the catalogue is for the most part avoided – there are other ways of conveying vastness. By stressing the elemental in all his descriptions, Dutton can be both comprehensive and express a sense of unity in the imposing massiveness of his subject: "And the winter sun is filling all the ranges/With the blue smoke of the flameless fires of light."

Yet travel has given his Whitmanesque bravura a Jamesian awareness of cultural ambiguity, a "torrent of comparative values" that is also explored in greater detail in the novels (increasingly occupying his attention). Critical of the British legacy, he nevertheless concedes "No style grows out of nothingness"; and, while resenting the "shrivelled sacred umbilical cord" from Mother England, he links it to the bestially mature "hairy bellies" of the uncivilised colonists. Dutton sees Australia's innocent potentiality in the young; their ignorance leads him to treasure "the gift of suffering" and those insights peculiar to the travelling sensibility of a cultural and continental aviator, a heightened awareness with which to seek out contentment in the poetry.

—Garth Clucas

DWIGHT, Timothy. American. Born in Northampton, Massachusetts, 14 May 1752. Educated at Yale University, New Haven, Connecticut, 1766–69, 1771–72, B.A. 1769, M.A. 1772. Served as a Chaplain in General Parson's Connecticut Brigade during the Revolutionary War, 1777–79. Married Mary Woolsey in 1777. Headmaster, Hopkins Grammar School, New Haven, Connecticut, 1769–71; Tutor at Yale University, 1771–77; licensed to preach, 1777; Member, Massachusetts Legislature, 1781–82; ordained to the ministry of the Congregational Church, 1783; Pastor, Greenfield Hill Congregational Church, Connecticut, 1783–95; Professor of Divinity, and President, Yale University, 1795–1817 (founder of the medical department). A projector of the Andover Theological Seminary and Missionary Society of Connecticut; Member, American Board of Commissioners for Foreign Missions. LL.D.: Harvard University, Cambridge, Massachusetts, 1810. *Died 11 January 1817.*

PUBLICATIONS

Verse

America; or, A Poem on the Settlement of the British Colonies. 1780(?).
The Conquest of Canaan. 1785.
The Triumph of Infidelity. 1788.
Greenfield Hill. 1794.
The Psalms of David, by Watts, altered by Dwight. 1801.

Other

The Nature, and Danger, of Infidel Philosophy. 1798.
Remarks on the Review of Inchiquin's Letters. 1815.
Theology Explained and Defended in a Series of Sermons. 5 vols., 1818–19; abridged
    edition, as *Beauties of Dwight,* 4 vols., 1823.
Travels in New England and New York. 4 vols., 1821–22; edited by Barbara Miller
    Solomon, 4 vols., 1969.
An Essay on the Stage. 1824.
Sermons. 2 vols., 1828.

Bibliography: in *Bibliography of American Literature* by Jacob Blanck, 1957.

Reading List: *A Sketch of the Life and Character of Dwight* by Benjamin Silliman, 1817; *Dwight: A Biography* by Charles E. Cunningham, 1942; *Dwight* by Kenneth Silverman, 1969.

*   *   *

In his own time Timothy Dwight was a figure of towering significance, president of Yale University, foremost among the Hartford Wits, educator, and theologian. Today, however, he is in the main remembered as a staunch advocate of Federalist and Calvinist orthodoxies in a world of change, and as a poet who made modest if seminal contributions to the growth of an indigenous American literature.

Dwight's reputation for obstinance originates mostly in his crabbed and dogmatic prose works. In 1798, for instance, with Deism and Thomas Jefferson on the rise, he announced in his sermon "The Duty of Americans, at the Present Crisis" that a return to Calvin and to Federalism was mandatory. In *The Nature, and Danger, of Infidel Philosophy*, published that same year, he castigated the liberal politics of John Locke, David Hume, and Thomas Paine. As for his own hero he would go on record two years later with a laudatory *Discourse on The Character of George Washington*. And his *Theology Explained and Defended*, a five-volume collection of sermons which he had delivered to his students at Yale, was an apologia for the theocracy which he sought to maintain.

Dwight's orthodoxy also informed some of his verse. For example, *The Conquest of Canaan*, an epic in eleven books reminiscent of Milton, was a veiled allegory of the American War for Independence, with Joshua in the role of Washington. And his most venomous verse, *The Triumph of Infidelity*, recounted in heroic couplets the sins of Voltaire, Hume, and other expositors of liberalism. Still other of his poems, however, revealed another, softer, side of Dwight. In his most famous poem, *Greenfield Hill*, for instance, he spoke in seven different sections – now as narrator, now as rural mother or clergyman or farmer – of the virtues of pastoral life in the new nation in ways which are actually Jeffersonian in intonation.

It was also in *Greenfield Hill*, and to a lesser degree in *The Conquest of Canaan*, that Dwight made an important contribution to the growth of an indigenous literature by employing landscapes and personalities of an indubitably American nature. Unfortunately, the more reactionary of Dwight's writings, together with the prevailing view that the setting of poetry should be other than American, conspired to hide Dwight's attempts at a native literature. In another generation, however, the authors of the American Renaissance would build a successfully native literature upon the earlier efforts of poets such as Timothy Dwight.

—Bruce A. Lohof

DYER, John.   Welsh.   Born in Llanfynydd, Caermarthenshire, 13 August 1699. Educated at Westminster School, London; studied painting with Jonathan Richardson. Married Miss Ensor; one son and three daughters. After a brief period in his father's solicitor's office in Aberglasney, traveled in Italy and studied painting: practiced as an itinerant painter in South Wales. Ordained: vicar of Calthorpe, Leicestershire, 1741–51; held livings of Belchford, 1751–55, Coningsby, 1752, and Kirkby-on-Bane, 1755, all in Lincolnshire. LL.B.: Cambridge University, 1751. *Died in 1758.*

PUBLICATIONS

Collections

    Poems, edited by Edward Thomas.   1903.
    Minor Poets of the Eighteenth Century, edited by Hugh I'A. Fausset.   1930.

Verse

    A New Miscellany, Being a Collection of Pieces of Poetry from Bath, Tunbridge, Oxford, Epsom, and Other Places in 1725.   1726; *Grongar Hill* edited by Richard C. Boys, 1941.

345

The Ruins of Rome.   1740.
The Fleece.   1757.
Poems.   1761.

Reading List: *Poet, Painter, and Parson: The Life of Dyer* by R. M. Williams, 1956.

*   *   *

Before he was a poet John Dyer was a painter, studying with Jonathan Richardson, and visiting Italy, and especially Rome, in 1724–25. His first considerable poem, *Grongar Hill* (most familiar in the final octosyllabic version which appeared in D. Lewis's *Miscellaneous Poems by Several Hands*, 1726), shows a painterly and sympathetic response to the scenery of the vale of Towy, and draws on the contemplative tradition of Milton's *Il Penseroso*. The poet narrates in his own person, relishing the various beauty of the opening landscape and meditating and moralising upon it. To a modern reader it may seem that the poem's sententious morality is at least as notable as its appreciation of a visualised natural scene, but it was as a picturesque nature-poem that *Grongar Hill* was chiefly appreciated in the eighteenth century, and by such romantics as Wordsworth and Southey.

Dyer's later, and longer, poems, *The Ruins of Rome* and *The Fleece*, have been less well known. *The Ruins of Rome* describes the decaying remains of ancient Rome as an English traveller, such as Dyer himself, might have seen them in his time. In this melancholy scene Dyer gives an account of the loss of Roman virtue and liberty in the luxury of empire, and infers a warning lesson for Britain. Written on the model of Virgil's *Georgics, The Fleece* is a didactic poem about the British wool trade, describing the progress of the wool from the sheep on the hillside to the sale of the cloth. Most English georgic poems of the eighteenth century tread an uneasy path on the frontiers of burlesque, but *The Fleece* is entirely serious, written on a subject capable of bearing some at least of the Miltonic grandeur with which Dyer loads it. Wool was the commercial basis of British empire, and *The Fleece* is, especially in its climactic fourth book, a remarkable work in an English tradition of patriotic poetry.

—Marcus Walsh

EBERHART, Richard (Ghormley). Born in Austin, Minnesota, 5 April 1904. Educated at the University of Minnesota, Minneapolis, 1922–23; Dartmouth College, Hanover, New Hampshire, B.A. 1926; St. John's College, Cambridge, B.A. 1929, M.A. 1933; Harvard University, Cambridge, Massachusetts, 1932–33. Served in the United States Naval Reserve, 1942–46: Lieutenant Commander. Married Helen Butcher in 1941; has two children. Worked as floorwalker, and as deckboy on tramp ships; tutor to the son of King Prajadhipok of Siam, 1930–31; English Teacher, St. Mark's School, Southboro, Massachusetts, 1933–41, and Cambridge School, Kendal Green, Massachusetts, 1941–42; Assistant Manager to the Vice-President, Butcher Polish Company, Boston, 1946–52 (Honorary Vice-President, 1952, and Member of the Board of Directors, 1958); Visiting Professor, University of Washington, Seattle, 1952–53, 1967, 1972; Professor of English, University of Connecticut, Storrs, 1953–54; Visiting Professor, Wheaton College, Norton, Massachusetts, 1954–55; Resident Fellow and Gauss Lecturer, Princeton University, New Jersey, 1955–56; Distinguished Visiting Professor, University of Florida, Gainesville, Winters 1974, 1977, 1978. Professor of English and Poet-in-Residence, 1956–68, Class of 1925 Professor, 1968–70 and since 1970 Professor Emeritus, Dartmouth College. Elliston Lecturer, University of Cincinnati, 1961. Founder, 1950, and First President, Poets' Theatre, Cambridge, Massachusetts; Member, 1955, and since 1964, Director, Yaddo Corporation; Member, Advisory Committee on the Arts, John F. Kennedy Memorial Theatre, Washington, D.C. Consultant in Poetry, 1959–61, and Honorary Consultant in American Letters, 1963–69, Library of Congress, Washington, D.C. Recipient: New England Poetry Club Golden Rose, 1950; Shelley Memorial Award, 1952; Harriet Monroe Poetry Award, 1955; National Institute of Arts and Letters grant, 1955; Bollingen Prize, 1962; Pulitzer Prize, 1966; Academy of American Poets Fellowship, 1969; National Book Award, 1977. D.Litt.: Dartmouth College, 1954; Skidmore College, Saratoga, New York, 1966; College of Wooster, Ohio, 1969; Colgate University, Hamilton, New York, 1974. Since 1972, Honorary President, Poetry Society of America. Member, National Institute of Arts and Letters, 1960, and American Academy of Arts and Sciences, 1967. Lives in New Hampshire.

PUBLICATIONS

Verse

A Bravery of Earth. 1930.
Reading the Spirit. 1936.
Song and Idea. 1940.
Poems, New and Selected. 1944.
Burr Oaks. 1947.
Brotherhood of Men. 1949.
An Herb Basket. 1950.
Selected Poems. 1951.
Undercliff: Poems 1946–1953. 1953.
Great Praises. 1957.
The Oak: A Poem. 1957.
Collected Poems 1930–1960, Including 51 New Poems. 1960.
The Quarry: New Poems. 1964.
The Vastness and Indifference of the World. 1965.
Fishing for Snakes. 1965.
Selected Poems 1930–1965. 1965.
Thirty One Sonnets. 1967.
Shifts of Being: Poems. 1968.

347

The Achievement of Richard Eberhart: A Comprehensive Selection of His Poems, edited
   by Bernard F. Engle. 1968.
Three Poems. 1968.
Fields of Grace. 1972.
Two Poems. 1975.
Collected Poems 1930–1976. 1976.
Selected Poems. 1978.

Plays

The Apparition (produced 1951). In *Collected Verse Plays,* 1962.
The Visionary Farms (produced 1952). In *Collected Verse Plays,* 1962.
Triptych (produced 1955). In *Collected Verse Plays,* 1962.
The Mad Musician, and Devils and Angels (produced 1962). In *Collected Verse Plays,*
   1962.
Collected Verse Plays (includes *Preamble I* and *II*). 1962.
The Bride from Mantua, from a play by Lope de Vega (produced 1964).

Other

Editor, with Selden Rodman, *War and the Poet: An Anthology of Poetry Expressing
   Man's Attitude to War from Ancient Times to the Present.* 1945.
Editor, *Dartmouth Poems.* 12 vols., 1958–71.

Reading List: *Eberhart* by Ralph J. Mills, Jr., 1966; *Eberhart: The Progress of an American
Poet* by Joel H. Roache, 1971; *Eberhart* by Bernard F. Engle, 1972.

*   *   *

Even Richard Eberhart's most ardent admirers admit the striking unevenness of his work
– stirring and exquisite poems published with others marred by sentimentality, pedantic
diction, and banal abstractions. That his work might indeed be so uneven derives from
Eberhart's vision of what poetry is, as well as his method of composition: "Poetry is
dynamic, Protean," he writes. "In the rigors of composition ... the poet's mind is a filament,
informed with the irrational vitality of energy as it was discovered in our time in quantum
mechanics. The quanta may shoot off any way." Eberhart rewrites little. His is an
inspirational poetry; through it, he discovers life's significances. "You breathe in maybe
God," and at those moments, "the poet writes with a whole clarity."
   Unlike many of his contemporaries during the 1930's Eberhart never worked for the hard,
spare line; he created no personae. He wrote a personal poetry, much in the vein of the
Romantics, especially Blake, Wordsworth, and Whitman, a poetry concerned with
understanding and transcending concrete experience. Regardless of the inevitable problems
such an aesthetic might invite, there remains a large body of inspired and original verse
wherein Eberhart is able to "aggravate" perception into life. Eberhart's best work results
from his success in transforming keenly felt sense perceptions, through the language of the
experience itself, into meaning – moral, metaphysical, mystical, even religious. His most
significant work retains the urgency and radiance of the felt experience, as it simultaneously
transforms it into the significant; Eberhart is epiphanic much like Gerard Manley Hopkins.
"The poet," he states, "makes the world anew; something grows out of the old, which he
locks in words."

In Eberhart's first volume, *A Bravery of Earth*, he writes about the three types of "awareness" one must accomplish in order to gain maturity − mortality, mentality, and men's actions. These goals have been reflected throughout Eberhart's career. However, particular subjects have also persisted − the poet's sheer wonder in nature, the fierce exhilaration inspired by "lyric" and "lovely" nature, within which is "God" "incarnate," as in "This Fevers Me":

> This fevers me, this sun on green,
> On grass glowing, this young spring.
> The secret hallowing is come,
> Regenerate sudden incarnation,
> Mystery made visible
> In growth, yet subtly veiled in all,
> Ununderstandable in grass,
> In flowers, and in the human heart,
> This lyric mortal loveliness,
> The earth breathing, and the sun.

Such an intimate involvement with physical nature, nevertheless, involves the poet in its cycles of growth and decay, and Eberhart, always aware of his own mortality, searches for intimations of immortality. Some of his poems address death as a creative force, in its recurrent cycles:

> When I can hold a stone within my hand
> And feel time make it sand and soil, and see
> The roots of living things grow in this land,
> Pushing between my fingers flower and tree,
> Then I shall be as wise as death,
> For death has done this and he will
> Do this to me, and blow this breath
> To fire my clay, when I am still.

Eberhart's compassion extends toward all living things which share a common fate. In a poem like "For a Lamb," after describing the lamb as "putrid," "on the slant hill," and "propped with daisies," the poet speaks of the fundamental continuity of life in nature:

> Where's the lamb? whose tender plaint
> Said all for the mute breezes.
> Say he's in the wind somewhere,
> Say, there's a lamb in the daisies.

"The Groundhog," one of Eberhart's best known poems, evokes another sort of wild, extravagant transcendence in the face of physical decay. The poet now experiences an exhilaration not through an awareness of nature's eternal, recurrent cycles, but rather through his creative articulation of the fact of decay. Returning year after year to the dead groundhog, he wishes for its absorption within nature's processes, but instead he witnesses its transformation from simple decay − "I saw a groundhog lying dead./Dead lay he" − to something artistically beautiful, its few bones "bleaching in the sunlight/Beautiful as architecture." He moves from a sense of "naked frailty" to "strange love," "a fever," a "passion of the blood." Elsewhere Eberhart has said: "Poetry is a spell against death," and he concludes "The Groundhog" with:

I stood there in the whirling summer,
My hand capped a withered heart,
And thought of China and of Greece,
Of Alexander in his tent;
Of Montaigne and his tower,
Of Saint Theresa in her wild lament.

Eberhart comes to identify with the mighty figures of the past who transcended the ravages of time through the very energy of their creative living, and through the legacy of historical memory and art. The poet has transcended through the creation of his poem.

Eberhart writes about a variety of experiences associated with death. In "Imagining How It Would Be to Be Dead" and "When Golden Flies upon My Carcass Come," he tries to apprehend his own death. Death may also be the moment of revelation and transcendence, of "worldless Ecstasy/Of mystery." But death may also be "merely death" — "This is a very ordinary experience./A name may be glorious but death is death" ("I Walked over the Grave of Henry James"). In "The Cancer Cells," he expresses an aesthetic glee in the artistic design of malignant cells: "They looked like art itself .../I think Leonardo would have in his disinterest/enjoyed them precisely with a sharp pencil."

Poems like "If I Could Only Live at the Pitch That Is Near Madness" represent another theme through Eberhart's poetry — his desire to retain the intensity of childhood, "the incomparable light," "when everything is as it was in my childhood/Violent, vivid, and of infinite possibility." But Eberhart accepts, indeed embraces, the "moral answer," that awareness that one cannot leave the world of men and maturity; and, as he returns "into a realm of complexity," there is a sense of new wonder and exaltation, as of joyful paternity, in his acceptance of the responsibilities of adulthood. One must not just feel experience; one must understand and articulate it.

Also recurrent are the variety of images of man's fallen state, his cruelty to his fellow man, the varieties of human suffering that grow out of social, political, and family strife. One is under obligation, implies Eberhart in his famous "Am I My Neighbor's Keeper?," to care for his fellow man. Perhaps best known among this group is his "The Fury of Aerial Bombardment," one of his many poems concerned with the inhumanity of war, where the poet ultimately wonders what sort of God would permit the barbarism of war: "You would feel that after so many centuries/God would give man to relent."

Throughout his fifty years of writing, Eberhart has emphasized the importance of man's creating a credo, a transcending vision, through personal and concrete experience. As intensely aware of man's existential condition as many of his contemporaries, Eberhart focuses on life and its creative possibilities. (In his acceptance speech of the National Book Award 1977, he lamented the suicides of some of his contemporaries and said, "Poets should not die for poetry but live for it.") Eberhart has focused upon concrete and everyday experience as the avenue toward transcendence, even if just momentary. For him, words, poetry itself, leads to "joy" and "ecstasy": "The only triumph is some elegance of style."

But each man is a poet, in a sense, for each man is, in his everyday life, the creator of any meaning his life will have. Each man must "make ... [his] own myth." Nature remains benignly indifferent. As James Cotter expressed it, in reviewing Eberhart's *Collected Poems 1930–1976* (*America*, 18 September 1976), the owl's cry tells man nothing unless one goes "somewhere beyond realism," and learns to "listen to the tune of the spiritual. Nature does not love or heed us. We are the lovers of nature."

—Lois Gordon

ELIOT, T(homas) S(tearns). English. Born in St. Louis, Missouri, U.S.A., 26 September 1888; naturalized, 1927. Educated at Smith Academy, St. Louis, 1898–1905; Milton Academy, Massachusetts, 1905–06; Harvard University, Cambridge, Massachusetts (Editor, *Harvard Advocate*, 1909–10; Sheldon Fellowship, for study in Munich, 1914), 1906–10, 1911–14, B.A. 1909, M.A. 1910; the Sorbonne, Paris, 1910–11; Merton College, Oxford, 1914–15. Married 1) Vivienne Haigh-Wood in 1915 (died, 1947); 2) Esmé Valerie Fletcher, 1957. Teacher, High Wycombe Grammar School, Buckinghamshire, and Highgate School, London, 1915–17; Clerk, Lloyds Bank, London, 1917–25; Editor, later Director, Faber and Gwyer, later Faber and Faber, publishers, London, 1926–65. Assistant Editor, *The Egoist*, London, 1917–19; Founding Editor, *The Criterion*, London, 1922–39. Clark Lecturer, Trinity College, Cambridge, 1926; Charles Eliot Norton Professor of Poetry, Harvard University, 1932–33; Page-Barbour Lecturer, University of Virginia, Charlottesville, 1933; Theodore Spencer Memorial Lecturer, Harvard University, 1950. President, Classical Association, 1941, Virgil Society, 1943, and Books Across the Sea, 1943–46. Resident, Institute for Advanced Study, Princeton University, New Jersey, 1950; Honorary Fellow, Merton College, Oxford, and Magdalene College, Cambridge. Recipient: Nobel Prize for Literature, 1948; New York Drama Critics Circle Award, 1950; Hanseatic Goethe Prize, 1954; Dante Gold Medal, Florence, 1959; Order of Merit, Bonn, 1959; American Academy of Arts and Sciences Emerson-Thoreau Medal, 1960. Litt.D.: Columbia University, New York, 1933; Cambridge University, 1938; University of Bristol, 1938; University of Leeds, 1939; Harvard University, 1947; Princeton University, 1947; Yale University, New Haven, Connecticut, 1947; Washington University, St. Louis, 1953; University of Rome, 1958; University of Sheffield, 1959; LL.D.: University of Edinburgh, 1937; University of St. Andrews, 1953; D.Litt.: Oxford University, 1948; D.Lit.: University of London, 1950; Docteur-ès-Lettres, University of Aix-Marseille, 1959; University of Rennes, 1959; D.Phil.: University of Munich, 1959. Officer, Legion of Honor; Honorary Member, American Academy of Arts and Letters; Foreign Member, Accademia dei Lincei, Rome, and Akademie der Schönen Künste. Order of Merit, 1948. *Died 4 January 1965.*

PUBLICATIONS

Collections

    Selected Prose, edited by Frank Kermode. 1975.

Verse

    Prufrock and Other Observations. 1917.
    Poems. 1919.
    Ara Vos Prec. 1920; as *Poems,* 1920.
    The Waste Land. 1922; *A Facsimile and Transcripts of the Original Drafts Including the Annotations of Ezra Pound,* edited by Valerie Eliot, 1971.
    Poems 1909–1925. 1925.
    Ash-Wednesday. 1930.
    Sweeney Agonistes: Fragments of an Aristophanic Melodrama. 1932.
    Collected Poems 1909–1935. 1936.
    Old Possum's Book of Practical Cats. 1939.
    The Waste Land and Other Poems. 1940.
    East Coker. 1940.
    Later Poems 1925–1935. 1941.

The Dry Salvages. 1941.
Little Gidding. 1942.
Four Quartets. 1943.
A Practical Possum. 1947.
Selected Poems. 1948.
The Undergraduate Poems of T. S. Eliot. 1949.
Poems Written in Early Youth, edited by John Hayward. 1950.
Collected Poems 1909–1962. 1963.

Plays

The Rock: A Pageant Play (produced 1934). 1934.
Murder in the Cathedral (produced 1935). 1935; revised version, as *The Film of Murder in the Cathedral,* 1952.
The Family Reunion (produced 1939). 1939.
The Cocktail Party (produced 1949). 1950; revised edition, 1950.
The Confidential Clerk (produced 1953). 1954.
The Elder Statesman (produced 1958). 1959.
Collected Plays: Murder in the Cathedral, The Family Reunion, The Cocktail Party, The Confidential Clerk, The Elder Statesman. 1962; as *The Complete Plays,* 1969.

Other

Ezra Pound: His Metric and Poetry. 1917.
The Sacred Wood: Essays on Poetry and Criticism. 1920.
Homage to John Dryden: Three Essays on Poetry in the Seventeenth Century. 1924.
For Lancelot Andrewes: Essays on Style and Order. 1928.
Dante. 1929.
Thoughts after Lambeth. 1931.
Selected Essays 1917–1932. 1932; revised edition, 1950.
John Dryden: The Poet, The Dramatist, The Critic. 1932.
The Use of Poetry and the Use of Criticism: Studies in the Relation of Criticism to Poetry in England. 1933.
After Strange Gods: A Primer of Modern Heresy. 1934.
Elizabethan Essays. 1934; as *Elizabethan Dramatists,* 1963.
Essays Ancient and Modern. 1936.
The Idea of a Christian Society. 1939.
Points of View, edited by John Hayward. 1941.
Reunion by Destruction: Reflections on a Scheme for Church Unity in South India Addressed to the Laity. 1943.
Notes Towards the Definition of Culture. 1948.
The Complete Poems and Plays. 1952.
Selected Prose, edited by John Hayward. 1953.
On Poetry and Poets. 1957.
George Herbert. 1962.
Knowledge and Experience in the Philosophy of F. H. Bradley (doctoral dissertation). 1964.
To Criticize the Critic and Other Writings. 1965.
The Literary Criticism of Eliot: New Essays, edited by David Newton de-Molina. 1977.

Editor, *Selected Poems,* by Ezra Pound. 1928; revised edition, 1949.
Editor, *A Choice of Kipling's Verse.* 1941.

Editor, *Introducing James Joyce.* 1942.
Editor, *Literary Essays of Ezra Pound.* 1954.
Editor, *The Criterion 1922–1939.* 18 vols., 1967.

Translator, *Anabasis: A Poem* by St.-John Perse. 1930; revised edition, 1938, 1949, 1959.

Bibliography: *Eliot: A Bibliography* by Donald Gallup, 1952, revised edition, 1969; *The Merrill Checklist of Eliot* by B. Gunter, 1970.

Reading List: *The Achievement of Eliot: An Essay on the Nature of Poetry* by F. O. Matthiessen, 1935, revised edition, 1947, with additional material by C. L. Barber, 1958; *Four Quartets Rehearsed* by R. Preston, 1946; *Eliot: The Design of His Poetry* by Elizabeth Drew, 1949; *The Art of Eliot* by Helen Gardner, 1949; *The Poetry of Eliot* by D. E. S. Maxwell, 1952; *Eliot's Poetry and Plays: A Study in Sources and Meaning* by Grover Smith, 1956, revised edition, 1975; *The Invisible Poet: Eliot* by Hugh Kenner 1959; *Eliot: A Collection of Critical Essays* edited by Hugh Kenner, 1962; *Eliot's Dramatic Theory and Practice* by Carol H. Smith, 1963; *Eliot* by Northrop Frye, 1963; *Eliot: Movements and Patterns* by Leonard Unger, 1966; *Eliot* by Bernard Bergonzi, 1972; *Eliot in His Time: Essays on the Occasion of the Fiftieth Anniversary of The Waste Land* edited by A. Walton Litz, 1973; *Eliot: The Longer Poems* by Derek Traversi, 1976.

*   *   *

T. S. Eliot's influence was predominant in English poetry in the period between the two World Wars. His first small volume of poems, *Prufrock and Other Observations* appeared in 1917. The title is significant. Eliot's earliest verse is composed of *observations*, detached, ironic, and alternately disillusioned and nostalgic in tone. The prevailing influence is that of French poetry, and in particular of Jules Laforgue; the mood is one of reaction against the comfortable certainties of "Georgian" poetry, the projection of a world which presented itself to the poet and his generation as disconcerting, uncertain, and very possibly heading for destruction.

The longest poem in the volume, "The Love Song of J. Alfred Prufrock," shows these qualities, but goes beyond them. The speaker is a kind of modern Hamlet, a man who after a life passed in devotion to the trivial has awakened to a sense of his own futility and to that of the world around him. He feels that some decisive act of commitment is needed to break the meaningless flow of events which his life offers. The question, however, is whether he really dares to reverse the entire course of his existence by a decision the nature of which eludes him:

> And indeed there will be time
> To wonder, "Do I dare?" and, "Do I dare?"
> Time to turn back and descend the stair,
> With a bald spot in the middle of my hair ...
> Do I dare
> Disturb the universe?

The answer, for Prufrock, is negative. Dominated by his fear of life, misunderstood when he tries to express his sense of a possible revelation, Prufrock concludes "No! I am not Prince Hamlet, nor was meant to be," refuses to accept the role which life for a moment seemed to have thrust upon him, and returns to the stagnation which his vision of reality imposes.

After a second small volume, published in 1919, which shows, more especially in its most impressive poem, "Gerontion," a notable deepening into tragedy, the publication in 1922 of

The Waste Land burst upon its readers with the effect of a literary revolution. Many of its first readers found the poem arid and incomprehensible, though it was in fact neither. The poet tells us that he is working through "a heap of broken images." He does this because it is a world of dissociated fragments that he is describing; but his aim, like that of any artist, is not merely an evocation of chaos. The poem is built on the interweaving of two great themes: the broken pieces of the present, as it presents itself to a disillusioned contemporary understanding, and the significant continuity of tradition. These two strains begin apart, like two separate themes in a musical composition, but the poem is animated by the hope, the *method*, that at the end they will converge into some kind of unity. Some critics, reading it in the light of Eliot's later development, have tried to find in the poem a specifically "religious" content, which however is not there. At best, there is a suggestion at the close that such a content, were it available, might provide a way out of the "waste land" situation, that the life-giving rain *may* be on the point of relieving the intolerable drought; but the poet cannot honestly propose such a resolution and the step which might have affirmed it is never rendered actual.

For some years after 1922, Eliot wrote little poetry and the greater part of his effort went into critical prose, much of it published in *The Criterion*, the literary quarterly which he edited until 1939. Eliot's criticism, which profoundly affected the literary taste of his generation, contributed to the revaluation of certain writers – the lesser Elizabethan dramatists, Donne, Marvell, Dryden – and, more controversially, to the depreciation of others, such as Milton (concerning whom, however, Eliot later modified his views) and some of the Romantic poets. It was the work of a poet whose interest in other writers was largely conditioned by the search for solutions to the problems raised by his own art; and, as such, it was marked by the idiosyncrasies which constitute at once its strength and its limitation.

In 1928, in his preface to the collection of essays *For Lancelot Andrewes*, Eliot declared himself Anglo-Catholic in religion, royalist in politics, classicist in literature: a typically enigmatic statement which indicated the direction he was to give to the work of his later years. 1930 saw the publication of *Ash-Wednesday*, his first considerable poem of explicitly Christian inspiration: a work at once religious in content and modern in inspiration, personal yet without concession to sentiment. The main theme is an acceptance of conversion as a necessary and irretrievable act. The answer to the question posed by Prufrock – "Do I dare/ Disturb the universe?" – is seen, in the translation of the first line of the Italian poet Guido Cavalcanti's ballad, "Because I do not hope to turn again," as an embarkation, dangerous but decisive, upon the adventure of faith.

The consequences of this development were explored in the last and in some respects the most ambitious of Eliot's poetic efforts: the sequence of poems initiated in 1935 and finally published, in 1943, under the title of *Four Quartets*. The series opens, in *Burnt Norton*, with an exploration of the *possible* significance of certain moments which seem to penetrate, briefly and elusively, a reality beyond that of normal temporal experience. "To be conscious," the poem suggests, "is not to be in time": only to balance that possibility with the counter-assertion that "Only through time time is conquered." The first step towards an understanding of the problems raised in the *Quartets* is a recognition that time, though inseparable from our human experience, is not the whole of it. If we consider time as an ultimate reality, our spiritual intuitions are turned into an illusion: whereas if we seek to deny the reality of time, our experience becomes impossible. The two elements – the temporal and the timeless – need to be woven together in an embracing pattern of experience which is, in fact, the end to which the entire sequence points.

The later "quartets" build upon this provisional foundation in the light of the poet's experience as artist and human being. The impulse to create in words reflects another, still more fundamental, impulse which prompts men to seek *form*, coherence, and meaning in the broken intuitions which their experience offers them. The nature of the search is such that it can never be complete in time. The true value of our actions only begins to emerge when we abstract ourselves from the temporal sequence – "time before and time after" – in which they were realized; and the final sense of our experience only reveals itself when the pattern is completed, at the moment of death. This moment, indeed, is not properly speaking a single final point, but a reality which covers the whole course of our existence.

These reflections lead the poet, in the last two poems of the series, *The Dry Salvages* and *Little Gidding*, to acceptance and even to a certain optimism. The end of the journey becomes the key to its beginning, and this in turn an invitation to confidence: "Not fare well,/But fare forward, voyagers." The doctrine of detachment explored in the second poem, *East Coker*, becomes an "expanding" one of "love beyond desire." The conclusion stresses the continuity between the "birth" and "death" which are simultaneously present in each moment, in each individual life, and in the history of the human race. It is true, as the closing section of *Little Gidding* puts it, that "we die with the dying"; but it is equally true, as they also go on to say, that "we are born with the dead." We die, in other words, as part of the tragedy which the fact of our humanity implies, but we are born again when, having understood the temporal process in its true light, we are ready to accept our present position within a still-living and continually unfolding tradition.

Eliot's poetic output was relatively small and intensely concentrated: a fact which at once confirms its value and constitutes, in some sense, a limiting factor. It should be mentioned that in his later years he devoted himself to the writing of verse plays, in an attempt to create a contemporary mode of poetic drama. The earlier plays, *Murder in the Cathedral* and *The Family Reunion*, which are also the best, take up the themes which were being explored at the same time in his poetry and develop them in ways that are often interesting. *The Cocktail Party*, though still a skilful work, shows some decline in conception and execution, and the later plays – *The Confidential Clerk* and *The Elder Statesman* – can safely be said to add little to Eliot's achievement.

—Derek A. Traversi

ELLIOTT, Ebenezer.   English.   Born in Masborough, Rotherham, Yorkshire, 17 March 1781. Attended Hollis School briefly; largely self-educated. Married; had 13 children. Worked in his father's iron-foundry, Rotherham, 1797–1804, and maintained a share in the business until it went bankrupt; bar-iron merchant, Sheffield, 1821–42; retired to Great Houghton, near Barnsley. Active in the Chartist Movement: delegate from Sheffield at the public meeting in Palace Yard, Westminster, 1838; withdrew from the movement when the Chartists refused to support repeal of the corn laws. *Died 1 December 1849*.

PUBLICATIONS

Collections

  Poetical Works, edited by Edwin Elliott.   2 vols., 1876.

Verse

  The Vernal Walk.   1801.
  The Soldier and Other Poems.   1810.

355

Night: A Descriptive Poem. 1818.
Peter Faultless to His Brother Simon, Tales of Night, in Rhyme, and Other Poems. 1820.
Love: A Poem, The Giaour: A Satirical Poem. 1823.
Scotch Nationality: A Vision. 1824.
The Village Patriarch. 1829.
Corn Law Rhymes: The Ranter. 1830; revised edition, 1831.
The Splendid Village: Corn Law Rhymes and Other Poems. 1833.
Poetical Works. 3 vols., 1834–35.
Poems, edited by R. W. Griswold. 1844.
More Verse and Prose of the Cornlaw Rhymer. 2 vols., 1850.

Bibliography: *Elliott, The Corn Law Rhymer: A Bibliography and List of Letters* by Simon Brown, 1971.

Reading List: *The Life, Poetry and Letters of Elliott* by J. Watkins, 1850; *Two Sheffield Poets: James Montgomery and Elliott* by William Odom, 1929; *Fiction for the Working Man* by Louis James, 1963.

*   *   *

Towards the end of his life it was customary for Ebenezer Elliott to append to his name the initials, C.L.R., standing for Corn Law Rhymer. During the 1830's and 1840's his poems (in particular the *Corn Law Rhymes*) had been quoted from hundreds of political platforms and he himself was an active member of the movement to repeal the Corn Laws. The American poet John Greenleaf Whittier wrote in 1850: "Ebenezer Elliott was to the artisans of England what Burns was to the peasantry of Scotland. His *Corn Law Rhymes* contributed not a little to that overwhelming tide of popular opinion and feeling which resulted in the repeal of the tax on bread." The breadth of his popular appeal may be gauged from the fact that while at one time his work was quoted from Chartist platforms, his poem, "The People's Anthem," slightly altered to remove some prickles of class antagonism, found its way into *Songs of Praise,* the Anglican hymnbook.

Elliott came from the radical autodidactic tradition. He claimed at one time to have most of the Bible and *Paradise Lost* by heart. As an iron-dealer in Sheffield, he kept a bust of Shakespeare amidst the stacked iron in his warehouse, and in his day-book quotations mingled with calculations. His earliest poetry was Romantic and pastoral, but the influence of Crabbe and a first-hand knowledge of working-class life in Sheffield changed the focus of his verse. Like other poets of the time he observed the encroachment of the town on the countryside but saw the problem of pollution in its political perspective: "Cursed with evils infinitely worse than a sooty atmosphere we are bread-taxed."

Corn Law Rhymes was first printed in pamphlet form by order of the Sheffield Mechanics Anti-tax Society. Many of the poems, like Thomas Hood's "The Song of the Shirt," are an attempt to voice directly the complaints of the oppressed. In doing so they both feed from and back into the common stock of industrial and urban folk-song. Their language is in general unliterary and has a rigour and energy coming partly from their urgency of purpose and partly from a presentation of facts and conditions as much as of rhetoric and opinion. In general the lachrymose plaint is avoided in favour of abrasive social satire, as in these lines from "Drone v. Worker":

> How God speeds the tax-bribed plough,
>   Fen and moor declare, man;
> Where once fed the poor man's cow,
>   ACRES drives his share, man.

But he did not *steal* the fen,
   Did not *steal* the moor, man;
If he feeds on starving men,
   Still he loves the poor, man.
Hush! he bullies, State and Throne,
   Quids them in his jaw, man;
Thine and mine he calls *his* own;
   Acres' lie is law, man.
Acres eats his tax on bread,
   Acres loves the plough, man;
Acres' dogs are better fed,
   Beggar's slave! than thou, man.

George Saintsbury in a short piece on Elliott in the *Cambridge History of English Literature* spoke of "the rubbish of partisan abuse which feeds his furnace." It was for helping keep alive a vigorous partisan tradition in English poetry that Elliott can be valued long after the repeal of the Corn Laws. He belongs to the tradition of Burns, Hood, Robert Buchanan, and John Davidson whose eloquence lies in their concrete presentation of the real lives of the majority of the population.

—Bridget O'Toole

EMERSON, Ralph Waldo. American. Born in Boston, Massachusetts, 25 May 1803. Educated at Harvard University, Cambridge, Massachusetts, graduated 1821; studied for the ministry. Married 1) Ellen Louisa Tucker in 1829 (died, 1831); 2) Lydia Jackson in 1835 (died, 1892), one son. Worked for a time as a schoolmaster; Pastor, Old Second Church of Boston (Unitarian), 1829 until he retired from the ministry, 1832; visited Europe, 1832–33; moved to Concord, Massachusetts, 1834: one of the leaders of the Transcendental Club, and contributor to the club's periodical *The Dial*, from 1840; lectured in England, 1847–48. LL.D.: Harvard University, 1866. *Died 27 April 1882.*

PUBLICATIONS

Collections

   Complete Works. 12 vols., 1883–93; edited by Edward Waldo Emerson, 12 vols., 1903–04.
   Letters, edited by Ralph L. Rusk. 6 vols., 1939.
   The Portable Emerson, edited by Mark Van Doren. 1946.
   Collected Works, edited by Alfred R. Ferguson. 1971–

Verse

   Poems. 1847.
   Selected Poems. 1876.

Other

Nature.   1836; edited by Kenneth W. Cameron, 1940.

Essays.   1841; revised edition, as *Essays: First Series,* 1847; *Second Series,* 1844; revised edition, 1850.

The Young American.   1844.

Nature: An Essay, and Lectures of the Times.   1844.

Orations, Lectures, and Addresses.   1844.

Nature: Addresses and Lectures.   1849.

Representative Men: Seven Lectures.   1850.

English Traits.   1856; edited by Howard Mumford Jones, 1966.

The Conduct of Life.   1860.

Complete Works.   2 vols., 1866.

May-Day and Other Pieces.   1867.

Prose Works.   3 vols., 1868–78(?).

Society and Solitude.   1870.

Letters and Social Aims.   1876.

The Preacher.   1880.

The Correspondence of Carlyle and Emerson 1834–1872, edited by Charles Eliot Norton.   2 vols., 1883; supplement, 1886; edited by Joseph Slater, 1964.

The Senses and the Soul, and Moral Sentiment in Religion: Two Essays.   1884.

Two Unpublished Essays: The Character of Socrates, The Present State of Ethical Philosophy.   1896.

Journals 1820–76, edited by Edward Waldo Emerson and Waldo Emerson Forbes.   10 vols., 1909–14.

Uncollected Writings, edited by Charles C. Bigelow.   1912.

Uncollected Lectures, edited by Clarence Gohdea.   1932.

Young Emerson Speaks: Unpublished Discourses on Many Subjects, edited by Arthur Cushman McGiffert, Jr.   1938.

The Early Lectures, edited by Stephen E. Whicher, Robert E. Spiller, and Wallace E. Williams.   3 vols., 1959–72.

The Journals and Miscellaneous Notebooks, edited by William H. Gilman.   14 vols. (of 16), 1960–78.

Editor, *Essays and Poems,* by Jones Very.   1839.

Editor, with James Freeman Clarke and W. H. Channing, *Memoirs of Margaret Fuller Ossoli.*   2 vols., 1852.

Editor, *Excursions,* by Henry David Thoreau.   1863.

Editor, *Letters to Various Persons,* by Henry David Thoreau.   1865.

Editor, *Parnassus* (verse anthology).   1875.

Translator, *Vita Nuova,* by Dante, edited by J. Chesley Mathews.   1960.

Bibliography: *A Bibliography of Emerson* by George Willis Cooke, 1908; in *Bibliography of American Literature* by Jacob Blanck, 1959.

Reading List: *The Life of Emerson* by Ralph L. Rusk, 1949; *Spires of Form: A Study of Emerson's Aesthetic Theory* by Vivian C. Hopkins, 1951; *Emerson's Angle of Vision: Man and Nature in American Experience* by Sherman Paul, 1952; *Emerson Handbook* by Frederic I. Carpenter, 1953; *Freedom and Fate: An Inner Life of Emerson* by Stephen E. Whicher, 1953; *Emerson: A Collection of Critical Essays,* edited by Milton R. Konvitz and Stephen E. Whicher, 1962; *Emerson: A Portrait* edited by Carl Bode, 1968; *The Recognition of Emerson: Selected Criticism since 1837* edited by Milton R. Konvitz, 1972; *Emerson: Portrait of a*

Balanced Soul by Edward Wagenknecht, 1973; *Emerson as Poet* by Hyatt H. Waggoner, 1974; *Emerson: Prophecy, Metamorphosis, and Influence* edited by David Levin, 1975; *The Slender Human Word: Emerson's Artistry in Prose* by William J. Scheick, 1978.

*   *   *

Ralph Waldo Emerson was the most distinguished of the New England Transcendentalists and one of the most brilliant American poets and thinkers of the nineteenth century. Although Transcendentalism as a mode of Romantic thought has been largely discredited by modern scientific theory, Emerson's essays and poems remain remarkably provocative – and much more tough-minded than they have frequently been given credit for being.

Emerson was not a highly systematic philosopher. His thought was an amalgam from a wide variety of sources: (1) New England religious thought and related English writings of the seventeenth and eighteenth centuries; (2) Scottish realism, which he absorbed principally while at Harvard college; (3) French and English skepticism, the lasting effects of which should not be underestimated; (4) Neo-Platonism, the dominant element in his thought, especially as it was interpreted by the English Romantic poets and the German and French Idealists; (5) Oriental mystical writings, even though he never accepted their fatalism or their concept of transmigration; (6) Yankee pragmatism, which was latent in almost all of his work and which muted his Romantic Idealism, especially in his essays on political and economic affairs. In Coleridge's explanation of Platonic dualism Emerson found the ordering principle for these disparate strands of thought. The discovery of Coleridge's distinction between the Reason and the Understanding brought such a surge of confidence in him that it is hardly an exaggeration to say that it transformed Emerson's life. Certainly it transformed his thinking.

Within one great Unity, he came to believe, there are two levels of reality, the supernatural and the natural. The supernatural is essence, spirit, or Oversoul as Emerson most frequently called it. It is an impersonal force that is eternal, moral, harmonious, and beneficent in tendency. The individual soul is a part of the Oversoul, and man has access to it through his intuition (which like Coleridge Emerson called the Reason, thereby confusing his readers then and now). One of the tendencies of the Oversoul is to express itself in form, hence the world of nature as an emanation of the world of spirit. The individual has access to this secondary level of reality through the senses and the understanding (the rational faculty). To explain the relation between the spiritual and physical levels of being Emerson used such oppositions as One and Many, cause and effect, unity and diversity, object and symbol, reality and appearance, truth and hypothesis, being and becoming. Since laws of correspondence relate the two levels of being, the study of physical laws can generate intuitions of spiritual truths. What especially delighted Emerson about this dualism was that it allowed him to entertain both faith and doubt: to accept the promptings of the intuition without question and yet to view the hypotheses of the understanding as only tentative and hence constantly open to question.

In his earlier essays, Emerson particularly stressed the unlimited potential of the individual. The most notable of these, *Nature* (1836), argues that, although nature serves as commodity, beauty, language, and discipline, its most important function is to excite the intuition so that the individual through a mystical experience becomes aware of the power of the Oversoul residing within him. "Nature always speaks of Spirit. It suggests the absolute." "The American Scholar" (1837) warns that books and scholarship can divert one from seeking the spiritual power within, and the "Divinity School Address" (1838) suggests that historical Christianity can do the same. "Self Reliance" (1844), in metaphor after metaphor, challenges the reader to seek the truths of the Reason: "Trust thyself; every heart vibrates to that iron string." In many respects "Self Reliance" is the capstone of American Romanticism. Later essays are more guarded in announcing the individual's limitless potential. In "Experience" (1844), for example, he admits that such this-world elements as health, temperament, and illusion can prevent one from exploiting all of the vast possibilities asserted in *Nature*. The enormous confidence of his earlier essays dwindles to "Patience and Patience, we shall win at last."

On subjects of public interest, Emerson's philosophical liberalism had to contend with his pragmatism. At most he was a cautious liberal. The Democrats, he thought, had the better causes, the Whigs the better men. Following Adam Smith, he believed that "affairs themselves show the best way they should be handled." So he was for *laissez-faire* and free trade, though he was more of an agrarian than Smith. Of the followers of Smith he rejected the utilitarians and the pessimists, and approved of only the optimists, particularly such members of the American school as Daniel Raymond, A. H. Everett, and Henry C. Carey. Emerson had nothing against wealth *per se*, but was against rule by the wealthy because the wealthy were too likely to be nothing more than materialists, persons without intuitive insight. Rule by an upper class, however, was agreeable to him so long as the upper class consisted of persons who are wise, temperate, and cultivated, persons who have the insight and courage necessary to protect the poor and weak against the predatory. Clearly his thinking did not drift far in the direction of Marxism. Nor was he willing to admit that the socialistic experiments of Owen and Fourier, though he admired their objectives, had the magic key to Utopia. Even the Transcendental experiments at Fruitlands and Brook Farm he believed impractical. Bereft of their romance, he said, they were projects that well might make their participants less intuitive and self-reliant rather than more so. Of the other major reforms of his day, Emerson lectured only in favor of child labor legislation, a public land policy, and the abolition of slaves. The passage of the Fugitive Slave Bill in 1850 made him as angry as he probably ever became on a public issue. More practical than most abolitionists, however, he argued that slavery was basically an economic matter, and that if the Northern church people really wanted to emancipate the slaves they should sell their church silver, buy up the slaves, and themselves set them free. He saw the Civil War not only as necessary for liberating the slave but "a hope for the liberation of American culture."

Emerson's aesthetic theory, to the extent that he had one, is a direct outgrowth of his Idealistic philosophy. As he conceived of it, the great work of art is not an imitation of nature but a symbolization of Truth realized intuitively. It is the result of resigning oneself to the "divine *aura* which breathes through forms." In his most quoted statement on the subject he put it this way: "It is not metres, but a metre-making argument that makes a poem − a thought so passionate and alive that like the spirit of a plant or animal it has an architecture of its own, and adorns nature with a new thing." Thus the poet (or any great artist) must first of all be the Seer, intuitively experiencing the absolutes of the Oversoul, and secondly the Sayer, communicating those absolutes so compellingly that readers are stimulated to have intuitions of their own. Emerson was realistic enough to realize that such a process is not easy. Intuitions fade quickly. And words, being but symbols of symbols, are inadequate even at best to convey them. The most that a writer can do is to suggest his intuitions by a series of half-truths. The greatest writing, therefore, must be provocative, not descriptive or explanatory. Such a conviction lies behind Emerson's epigrammatic prose style and the liberties he takes with poetic conventions.

There is a good reason for considering Emerson as primarily a poet even though one must go to his journals and essays to realize the fullness of his thought. His concentration on the concrete image, the simplicity of his symbols and words, and his willingness within limits to let form follow function were practices that profoundly influenced such widely divergent followers as Whitman and Dickinson and through them much of modern poetry. Many of Emerson's best-known poems, such as "Concord Hymn" and "The Snow Storm," celebrate local events. But his more notable ones give expression to elements of his philosophy. Through the voice of the cosmic force, "Brahma" suggests the enclosure of all diversity in the one great Unity; so does "Each and All" in which the beauty and meaning of "each" is seen to be dependent upon its context, or the "all." "The Problem" contrasts the unlimited freedom of the poet's imagination with the stultifying routine of the "cowled churchman." Perhaps Emerson's most poignant poem is "Threnody," written in two periods after the death of his young son Waldo. The first part, composed immediately after Waldo's death, describes the poet's disillusionment with nature, indeed with the cosmic scheme, which he had spent so many years celebrating. The second part, written several years later, asserts his resurgent confidence. Nathaniel Hawthorne probably spoke for some modern readers when he said that he "admired Emerson as a poet of deep beauty and austere tenderness, but sought nothing from him as a philosopher." Yet his philosophy cannot be dismissed so summarily. It resulted in a freedom of spirit, a respect for the individual human being, a sense of awe and wonder before the inexplicable that many modern readers still find stirring and reassuring.

—John C. Gerber

EMPSON, William English. Born in Yokefleet, East Yorkshire, 27 September 1906. Educated at Winchester College; Magdalene College, Cambridge, B.A. in mathematics 1929, M.A. 1935. Married Hester Henrietta Crouse in 1941; two children. Held Chair of English Literature, Bunrika Daigaku University, Tokyo, 1931–34; Professor of English Literature, 1937–39, and Professor, Western Languages Department, 1947–53, Peking National University; Professor of English, University of Sheffield, 1953–71, now Emeritus. Worked in the Monitoring Department, 1940–41, and as Chinese Editor, Far Eastern Department, 1941–46, BBC, London. Visiting Fellow, Kenyon College, Gambier, Ohio, Summers 1948, 1950, 1954; Visiting Professor, University of Toronto, 1973–74, and Pennsylvania State University, University Park, 1974–75. Litt.D.: University of East Anglia, Norwich, 1968; University of Bristol, 1971; University of Sheffield, 1974. Lives in London.

PUBLICATIONS

Verse

Letter IV. 1929.
Poems. 1935.
The Gathering Storm. 1940.
Collected Poems. 1949; revised edition, 1961.

Other

Seven Types of Ambiguity: A Study of Its Effects on English Verse. 1930; revised edition, 1947, 1953, 1955, 1963.
Some Versions of Pastoral. 1935; as English Pastoral Poetry, 1938.
Shakespeare Survey, with George Garrett. 1937.
The Structure of Complex Words. 1951.
Milton's God. 1961; revised edition, 1965.

Editor, The Outlook of Science, by J. B. S. Haldane. 1935.
Editor, Science and Well-Being, by J. B. S. Haldane. 1935.
Editor, Shakespeare's Poems. 1969.
Editor, with David Pirie, Coleridge's Verse: A Selection. 1972.

361

Reading List: *Empson* by J. H. Wills, Jr., 1969; *Modern Heroism: Essays on D. H. Lawrence, Empson, and Tolkien,* by Roger Sale, 1973; *Empson: The Man and His Work* edited by Roma Gill, 1974 (includes bibliography by Moira Megaw); *Empson and the Philosophy of Literary Criticism* by Christopher Norris, 1978.

*   *   *

"How extravagantly romantic he is, and how he has to cover it up!" This remark, in a private letter by the American poetess and critic Anne Stevenson, suggests the peculiar fascination of William Empson's poems, and why a whole group of young English poets, fleeing from the romanticism of Dylan Thomas, imitated from about 1953 onwards the verse forms (villanelle and terza rima with a last hanging line) of his second volume, *The Gathering Storm*, and were ready to accept the label "Empsonians." The difference was, as Edwin Muir shrewdly pointed out, that Empson's bluff, dry, and off-hand manner was a way of controlling and half-concealing, half-revealing an inner agony, whereas there was not such evidence that his young admirers and imitators had suffered much, or would ever be capable of suffering. Of his two volumes, the first, *Poems*, is the more difficult in its manner (making a great deal of use, like Donne, of references to the science of his time), but the simpler in its themes, broadly the non-responsiveness of love and the absence of God. The second, *The Gathering Storm*, dealt with the social and political situation, and the emotions it aroused, just before the Second World War.

Empson is probably, in *Seven Types of Ambiguity*, *Some Versions of Pastoral*, *The Structure of Complex Words*, and *Milton's God*, very much more widely influential in his work as a theoretical critic than as a poet. The theory of ambiguity is that double meanings in poetry are not muddles but represent a true doubt in the poet's mind. The pastoral form, in Empson's usage, is not a poem about shepherds but any literary mode of representing a complex social situation in terms of a simpler mode of life. A complex word is a word like "native" or "honest" whose positive meaning is good or neutral but which we use only about our inferiors. The book on Milton is a vivid diatribe against the Christian idea of God as represented by Milton (of course, by no means orthodoxly, since he seems to be a tritheist rather than a trinitarian, and the Son appears to be of like rather than one substance with the Father). The best answer to it is that Milton, by incliniation or instinct, is no more a Christian than Empson. The general influence of these critical books, though silent, has been pervasive. They are part of the furniture of any good English or American critic's mind.

—G. S. Fraser

FAIRBURN, A(rthur) R(ex) D(ugard). New Zealander. Born in Auckland, 2 February 1904. Educated at Parnell Primary School, Auckland; Auckland Grammar School, 1918–20. Served in the New Zealand Army, 1943. Married Jocelyn Mays in 1931; one son, three daughters. Clerk, New Zealand Insurance Company, Auckland, 1920–26; Labourer, freelance writer, and part-time teacher, 1926–30; came to London, 1930, and lived in Wiltshire, 1931–32; Spokesman for the radical writers of the Phoenix group, Auckland, 1932–33; held various relief jobs in New Zealand, 1932–34; Assistant Secretary, and Editor of *Farming First* magazine, Auckland Farmer's Union, 1934–42; radio scriptwriter, Auckland, 1943–46; produced and designed fabrics, 1946–47; Tutor in English, 1947–54, and Lecturer, Elam School of Fine Arts, 1954–57, Auckland University College. *Died 25 March 1957.*

PUBLICATIONS

Collections

> *Collected Poems,* edited by Denis Glover. 1966.
> *The Woman Problem and Other Prose,* edited by Denis Glover and Geoffrey Fairburn. 1967.

Verse

> *He Shall Not Rise.* 1930.
> *The County.* 1931.
> *Another Argo,* with Allen Curnow and Denis Glover. 1935.
> *Dominion.* 1938.
> *Recent Poems,* with others, 1941.
> *Poems 1929–1941.* 1943.
> *The Rakehelly Man and Other Verses.* 1946.
> *Three Poems.* 1952.
> *Strange Rendezvous: Poems 1929–1941, with Additions.* 1953.
> *The Disadvantages of Being Dead and Other Sharp Verses,* edited by Denis Glover. 1958.
> *Poetry Harbinger,* with Denis Glover. 1958.

Fiction

> *The Sky Is a Limpet (A Pollytickle Parrotty), also Four (4) Stories, or Moral Feebles.* 1939.

Other

> *A Discussion on Communism Between Fairburn and S. W. Scott.* 1936.
> *Who Said Red Ruin?* 1938.
> *Hands Off the Tom Tom.* 1944.
> *We New Zealanders: An Informal Essay.* 1944.
> *How to Ride a Bicycle in Seventeen Lovely Colours.* 1947.
> *Crisis in the Wine Industry.* 1948.
> *R. M. S. Rangitoto.* 1949.

Bibliography: *Fairburn: A Bibliography* by Olive Johnson, 1958.

Reading List: *Fairburn* by W. S. Broughton, 1968.

                              *   *   *

A. R. D. Fairburn's poetic development may be seen as a paradigm for the New Zealand writers of his generation. Allen Curnow has described their "common line of development" in these terms: "A mostly personal lyric impulse in the first place changed early to more or less direct lyric argument in which assertions about New Zealand itself ... became a dominant theme." Later these poets returned to "more personal and universal themes, lest their discovery of New Zealand should end in isolation." After a ritual pilgrimage "Home" to England exposed him to the reality of English life in 1930, Fairburn repudiated his limply derivative early verse. His first book, *He Shall Not Rise*, ended with a poem (from which the title was taken) that, in effect, disowned its own contents. Georgianism, he wrote after returning to New Zealand, was "another string which tripped up the feet of New Zealand poets." Instead they must embrace "the anarchy of life in a new country." Fairburn attempted this in *Dominion*, an ambitious portrait of New Zealand in the depression years, a poem which, in the words of one contemporary, decided "the struggle for poetry in New Zealand – rata blossoms v. reality, spooju v. style." Ranging from intemperate Poundian tirades to Wordsworthian celebrations of Nature, *Dominion* is an uneven but vigorous survey of the history and institutions, the land and the people of New Zealand. Fairburn is most effective and original when the lyrical and satirical modes merge, as in "Conversation in the Bush":

> "Observe the young and tender frond
> Of this punga: shaped and curved
> like the scroll of a fiddle: fit instrument
> to play archaic tunes."
> > "I see
> the shape of a coiled spring."

Here accurate natural description is made to serve wider purposes; from the speakers' difference of opinion over the shape of a fern leaf can be inferred contrasting aesthetic and political attitudes to the national crisis of the time.

After the thirties Fairburn turned away from national issues. His longer poems became more personal in emphasis (*Three Poems*), his satire more occasional, more amusing, but unfortunately, much slighter. *The Rakehelly Man* contains the best of his comic verse, immensely enjoyable if seldom of permanent interest. Much more of his creative energy went into lyric poetry, the best of which was collected in *Strange Rendezvous*. In his first book Fairburn had written of "the peace/and the forgetting/of the instant of love;/and the flat calm of death," and these traditional themes remain his central preoccupations; but his style matured into a flexible and distinctive idiom, combining a lovely relaxed movement with vividly particular sensations, as in "The Cave":

> We climbed down, and crossed over the sand,
> and there were islands floating in the wind-whipped blue,
> and clouds and islands trembling in your eyes.

Out of the conflict between sexual love on the one hand and time and death on the other Fairburn wrote several lyrics of great intensity ("The Cave," "Tapu," "A Farewell"), but perhaps his most distinctive poem, one of the few in which he achieved total integration of his complex nature, was "Full Fathom Five," both an Arnoldian exploration of the conflict of imagination and reality and an oblique self portrait:

And eventually and tragically finding he could not drown
he submitted himself to the judgment of the desert
and was devoured by man-eating ants
with a rainbow of silence branching from his lips.

—Peter Simpson

FALCONER, William. Scottish. Born in Edinburgh, 11 February 1732. Self-taught. Married Miss Hicks in 1763. Merchant seaman: served as a second mate on a ship that was wrecked on a voyage from Alexandria to Venice; entered the Royal Navy, 1762: midshipman on the *Royal George*, 1762–63; purser on the frigate *Glory*, 1763–67, and of the *Swiftsure*, 1767–68; purser on the *Aurora*, 1769, which went down with all hands near Capetown. *Died in December 1769.*

PUBLICATIONS

Collections

Poetical Works, with Blair and Beattie, edited by George Gilfillan. 1854.

Verse

A Poem on the Death of Frederick Prince of Wales. 1751.
The Shipwreck. 1762; revised edition, 1764, 1769.
Ode on the Duke of York's Departure. 1763.
The Demagogue. 1766.

Other

An Universal Dictionary of the Marine. 1769; abridged by Claude S. Gill, as *The Old Wooden Walls*, 1930.

Reading List: *Falconer: The Shipwreck* by J. Friedrich, 1901; "Falconer" by M. K. Joseph, in *Studies in Philology*, 1950.

*   *   *

A self-educated writer, William Falconer spent most of his short life at sea as a merchant-seaman and later as a half-pay purser, and was mysteriously lost at sea. Leaving aside some magazine-verse of little merit, his reputation rests on two main works, the *Universal Dictionary of the Marine* and the poem *The Shipwreck*.

The *Dictionary*, a distinguished product of its encyclopaedic age, is of great authority in its own field, thorough, well-organised, and written in plain, vigorous prose.

The Shipwreck is the story, presumably autobiographical, of a trading-ship, the *Britannia*, which sails from Crete about 1750, is caught in a violent storm, and driven on to the rocks of Cape Sounion (near Athens) where nearly the whole crew perish. In three successive editions Falconer carefully reworked the poem, doubling its length. The many nineteenth-century editions are all based on a conflated text; for anyone who wishes to read the original, the third is Falconer's considered and final version, but a reader might prefer what one early reviewer called the "copious simplicity" of the first.

Falconer's revisions turned this originally simple narrative, rather heavily loaded with nautical technicalities, into a short neo-classical epic with fictitious characters and set episodes, modelled on Virgil, Milton, Dryden, and Pope. Whether or not he consciously intended it, the revised poem contains a judicious mixture of elements which appealed to contemporary taste. The "social horrors" of the stormy sea are right in the tradition of the sublime, while the hard fates of the sailors and their interspersed stories, "the tides of social woe," appeal to "sensibility" and humanitarianism. There is an element of the descriptive picturesque, and a long survey passage (in Canto III) is a landmark in the growing appreciation of Grecian antiquities.

But what makes it an original work is its combination of the heroic couplet and other standard elements of late Augustan poetry with first-hand, matter-of-fact detail. Its basic reality is the *Britannia* itself, every part of which Falconer knows and can use, even though in revision he smoothes out the use of the technical vocabulary, the "terms of art." The prevailing emotion reflects his own experience of "the faithless sea." And the poem is animated by his ambition, which is also the force behind the *Dictionary*, to instruct his fellow-seamen, in this case through a didactic poem (a kind of graphic treatise on how to handle a ship in a storm), then to dignify their craft by a narrative with distinct epic overtones, and further to arouse in the British public a proper sympathy for the brave and dangerous lives of their "faithful sailors." It won the admiration of the nineteenth-century public and of poets as different as Blake and Byron, and (like the *Dictionary*) maintained its reputation until the end of the great sailing-ships.

—M. K. Joseph

FEARING, Kenneth (Flexner). American. Born in Oak Park, Illinois, 28 July 1902. Educated at public schools in Oak Park; University of Wisconsin, Madison, B.A. 1924. Married 1) Rachel Meltzer in 1933, one son; 2) Nan Lurie in 1945 (divorced, 1958). Free-lance writer in New York City from 1924: contributor to various poetry magazines. Recipient: Guggenheim Fellowship, 1936, 1939; National Institute of Arts and Letters award, 1945. *Died 26 June 1961.*

PUBLICATIONS

Verse

Angel Arms. 1929.
Poems. 1935.

Dead Reckoning.   1938.
Collected Poems.   1940.
Afternoon of a Pawnbroker and Other Poems.   1943.
Stranger at Coney Island and Other Poems.   1948.
New and Selected Poems.   1956.

Fiction

The Hospital.   1939.
Dagger of the Mind.   1941.
Clark Gifford's Body.   1942.
The Big Clock.   1946.
Loneliest Girl in the World.   1951.
The Generous Heart.   1954.
The Crozart Story.   1960.

Reading List: "The Meaning of Fearing's Poetry" by M. L. Rosenthal, in *Poetry*, July 1944.

*   *   *

Poet, novelist, and editor, Kenneth Fearing is associated with the literature of disillusionment which was written in America during the 1930's and 1940's when technological achievements and social institutions appeared incapable of remedying the profound evils of economic depression. Severely affected by the suffering which he encountered in his environment, Fearing became disillusioned with capitalistic systems of government and industry, espousing instead a Marxist belief in the inherent goodness of the common man, whom he hoped would unite with one another and lead the world into a new era of utopian humanism.

Into this crusade for social justice, Fearing enlisted his talents as a writer. His poetry earned him the admiration of his contemporaries and a lasting position of respect in modern literature. The deft ironic tone which characterizes much of Fearing's poetry and which undercuts the optimism of the Whitmanesque lines in which he wrote is admirably suited to capturing his anger and bitterness at the disregard of institutions for the liberties of the individual, and his sympathy and pity for those people who were trapped by social circumstance in sterile urban environments where they were forced by industrial and political taskmasters to lead mechanical lives of quiet desperation.

But if the economic and social conditions of the 1930's provided Fearing with the subject matter for his poetry, they also limited the scope of his poetic growth. In many respects, Fearing's hatreds and fears shackle his imagination to themes and obsessions which do not sustain repeated or extended treatment. As a result, the reader who indulges in more than one volume of Fearing's poems receives the impression that while the setting and characters of his poems may vary from volume to volume the ideas which they embody remain the same. In his best poems, however, Fearing captures the anxieties, hopes, and frustrations of his generation in a manner which reflects both sensitivity and talent, and *Dead Reckoning* and *Afternoon of a Pawnbroker and Other Poems* are deserving of serious critical analysis.

As a novelist, Fearing specialized in pulp thrillers into which he interjected social commentary. His first novel, *The Hospital*, is replete with scandals and intrigues which expose the machinations behind the workings of the medical profession. Equally shocking and equally involved are *Clark Gifford's Body*, a murder mystery which explores the possibility of revolution in America, and *The Generous Heart*, a novel which depicts the graft and greed involved in the misappropriation of funds by a charitable organization. Another novel, *The Big Clock*, proved so popular that it became the subject of a film. Ostensibly about a murder, *The Big Clock* also analyzes the ruthlessness of journalistic rivalry and muckraking.

—James A. Levernier

FERGUSON, Sir Samuel. Irish. Born in Belfast, 10 March 1810. Educated at the Belfast Academical Institution; Trinity College, Dublin, B.A. 1826, M.A. 1832; called to the Irish Bar, 1838. Married Mary Catharine Guinness in 1848. Practised law on the north-east circuit of Ireland, 1838–67; Queen's Counsel, 1859; gave up legal practise on appointment as Deputy Keeper of the Irish Records, Dublin, 1867: reorganized the Irish Records Office. President, Royal Irish Academy, 1882. LL.D.: Trinity College, Dublin, 1864. Knighted, 1878. *Died 9 August 1886.*

PUBLICATIONS

Collections

> *Poems,* edited by Alfred Percival Graves.   1918.
> *Poems,* edited by Padraic Colum.   1963.

Verse

> *The Cromlech on Howth.*   1861.
> *Lay of the Western Gael and Other Poems.*   1865.
> *Congal.*   1872.
> *Deirdre.*   1880.
> *Poems.*   1880.
> *The Forging of the Anchor.*   1883.
> *Hibernian Nights' Entertainments.*   3 vols., 1887.
> *Remains of St. Patrick: The Confessio and Epistle to Coroticus.*   1888.
> *Lays of the Red Branch.*   1897.

Other

> *Ogham Inscriptions in Ireland, Wales, and Scotland.*   1887.

Reading List: *Ferguson in the Ireland of His Day* by Mary Ferguson, 2 vols., 1896; *Ferguson, Poet and Antiquarian* by Arthur Deering, 1931; *Ferguson* by Malcolm Brown, 1973; *Northern Voices* by Terence Brown, 1975.

*   *   *

Like W. B. Yeats, Sir Samuel Ferguson was an Irish Protestant and proud of it. For him the Protestants were "an interest acknowledged on all hands to be the depository of Ireland's fate for good or evil." They were to be the cultural leaders of Victorian Ireland because they had the independence of spirit to bring the Irish nation out of its spiritual and material improverishment to become "a truly integral portion of the empire." Ferguson was a Unionist and a conservative, but he in no way believed that Ireland should obliterate her cultural identity. It was vital for her future as part of the empire that she retain as many links as possible with her native past. This conviction determined all that Ferguson wrote in the way of poetry, history, historical romance, and indeed archaeology.

Ferguson's purpose was to recover the "facts" (as he called them) of the acts, opinions, and conditions of the dead generations of Irishmen, so that "the people of Ireland will be able to *live back* in the land they *live in*." Only by such a connexion between past and present could the Irish retain their individuality in the modern world.

As a poet, then, Ferguson was drawn to Gaelic literature for his material, for in that literature could be found the essentials of native Irish "sentiment," by which he meant those features of racial consciousness that persist throughout history, the "facts" of a people's emotional life. Wishing in no way to corrupt the purity of native sentiment he made one of the best translators of Gaelic folk-song ever. His versions have a clarity and receptivity to the vivid strangenesses of their originals, and a rhythmic and vocalic subtlety that are entirely new in nineteenth-century Irish poetry. He was drawn to these songs for their savage sincerity. Similar qualities, which he read as national characteristics, attracted him in the early saga material, and it is for his re-handling of this that he is best known.

The world he creates in these retellings of Gaelic sagas is an energetic and external one, done in broad strokes without much attention to the niceties of characterization. His heroes have what Ferguson saw as the Irish capacity for devoted service and loyalty, an innate heroism and nobility. The style he adopts for these poems is one that frequently attempts a re-enactment of the styles of the sagas themselves. This meets with only limited success. Sometimes the effect is curiously startling, creating an impression of urgency and energy, but more often than not it is simply awkward. By invoking the savage strength of those days, qualified by Protestant judgement and seriousness, Ferguson hoped to invigorate the imaginative life of Victorian Ireland. It was a vain hope. For the second half of his life Ferguson was almost entirely without an audience.

—Robert Welch

FERGUSSON, Robert. Scottish. Born in Edinburgh, 5 September 1750. Educated at Edinburgh High School; Dundee High School; University of St. Andrews, 1765–68. Lawyer's Clerk, Edinburgh, 1769–73; Contributor, Ruddiman's *Weekly Magazine*, Edinburgh, 1771–73. Died insane from effects of a fall down stairs. *Died 16 October 1774.*

PUBLICATIONS

Collections

Poetical Works, edited by Matthew P. McDiarmid.   2 vols., 1954–56.
Poems of Allan Ramsay and Fergusson, edited by Alexander M. Kinghorn and
     Alexander Law.   1974.

Verse

Auld Reikie. 1773.
A Poem to the Memory of John Cunningham. 1773.
Poems. 1773; revised edition, as *Poems on Various Subjects,* 1779.

Bibliography: *Bibliography of Fergusson* by John A. Fairley, 1915.

Reading List: *Fergusson: Essays by Various Hands* edited by Sydney Goodsir Smith, 1952; *Fergusson* by Allan H. MacLaine, 1965; *Fergusson and the Edinburgh of His Time* by Alexander Law, 1974.

*   *   *

Robert Fergusson is, above all, the poet of Edinburgh. The bulk of his significant work consists of brilliant satiric portraits of his beloved city in the 1770's, of the teeming, dramatic life of the streets and taverns. In depicting this world of the Old Town more vividly perhaps than any other writer has done, he uses traditional Scots poetic forms such as the 6-line *Habbie Simson* stanza (or "Burns stanza"), the stanza of "Christis Kirk on the Green," and tetrameter couplets; but he adapts these metres to new and modern purposes, thereby setting vital technical precedents for the work of Burns a few years later.

Fergusson's most characteristic genre is the poem of humorous social description, usually good-natured in tone, but occasionally marked by sharp satiric thrusts at sham or corruption. Among his more genial treatments of Edinburgh life are such pieces as "The Daft-Days," "The King's Birth-Day in Edinburgh," "Mutual Complaint of Plainstanes and Causey," "Caller Oysters," "Hallow-fair," and "Leith Races." In "The King's Birth-Day," for example, he makes fun of the custom of stilted, ceremonial "birthday odes," and opens with a hilarious burlesque invocation to the Muse (addressed as though she were a barmaid being warmed up with whisky for the task at hand); he then goes on to depict the livelier social aspects of the annual celebration. "Plainstanes and Causey" is a highly original fantasy, a kind of "flyting eclogue" between the sidewalk and roadway of the High Street which, by a clever twist, turns into a light-hearted social satire on Edinburgh street life. Similarly, in "Caller Oysters" the sea food serves only as a springboard for a humorous commentary on Edinburgh drinking habits.

In others of his town poems Fergusson cuts a little deeper. "Braid Claith," a small gem of a poem, is pure satire on a universal theme – pride in dress, symbolizing a whole social attitude. Here Fergusson clinches his theme with remarkable economy of expression:

> Braid Claith lends fock an unco heese,*   *Lift
> Makes mony kail-worms butter-flies,
> Gies mony a doctor his degrees
>   For little skaith:
> In short, you may be what you please
>   Wi' gude Braid Claith.

Again, in "The Election" and especially in "The Ghaists" he introduces pointed attacks on political corruption. The latter is informed by a strong spirit of Scottish nationalism, deploring the Union with England, a theme which Fergusson voiced repeatedly in such poems as "Hame Content" and "A Drink Eclogue."

The most ambitious of Fergusson's Edinburgh sketches, however, is *Auld Reikie,* a panoramic poem with morning, afternoon, and evening scenes, in which he attempts to capture the essence of the whole city. His method here is one of dramatic contrast, and it works extremely well. Fergusson perceives that the unique atmosphere of old Edinburgh lies in the startling contrasts, both physical and social, which the city presents. Thus, he juxtaposes images of beauty and squalor – a picture of the fleeting loveliness of sunrise over the ancient spire of St. Giles followed by a passage on the foul morning smell of sewage, a scene of drunkenness and bestiality followed by one of wholesome merriment and friendship. The total effect is cumulative and powerfully evocative, one of the finest treatments of city life in British poetry.

Apart from the Edinburgh poems, Fergusson achieved notable work in other directions. He wrote well in special traditional Scottish genres such as the verse epistle and the comic elegy, for example. In the latter form his "Elegy on John Hogg" has been judged the most brilliant specimen in Scots poetry. Even more important, however, was his development of Scottish pastoralism. In this realm, especially in the piece entitled "An Eclogue," he far surpassed his predecessor Allan Ramsay in the direction of convincing realism. More ambitious is the remarkable poem in modified Spenserian stanzas called "The Farmer's Ingle," which became the obvious model for Burns's more pretentious "Cotter's Saturday Night." Here Fergusson, in his most important serious poem, gives us a slightly idealized picture of Scottish rural life built upon the cumulative impression of simple, homely details. The effect, in its modest, well-wrought fashion, is strangely moving and impressive.

Because of his catalytic impact upon Burns, Fergusson has too often been considered a mere "forerunner," a lucky poet who is important only because he happened to have influenced Burns, rather than as a creative artist in his own right. Yet Fergusson's work has a perennial freshness, an enduring appeal. Though he seldom goes deeply below the surface of life, he has a bold yet sensitive imagination, a finished artistry of style, and a genial, insinuative humor. His significant career was pitifully brief (about two years); consequently his work is small in bulk and relatively narrow in scope; but within its special range it is unquestionably the finest body of Scots poetry of the eighteenth century before Burns.

—Allan H. MacLaine

FIELD, Eugene. American. Born in St. Louis, Missouri, 3 September 1850; moved to Amherst, Massachusetts, 1856. Educated at Williams College, Williamstown, Massachusetts, 1868–69; Knox College, Galesburg, Illinois, 1869–70; University of Missouri, Columbia, 1870–71. Married Julia Sutherland Comstock in 1873; eight children. Travelled in Europe, 1872; worked as a reporter for the St. Joseph, Missouri, *Gazette*, St. Louus *Journal*, Kansas City, Missouri, *Times*, and the Denver *Tribune*, 1873–83; Columnist ("Sharps and Flats"), Chicago *Morning News*, later called the Chicago *Record*, 1883–1895. *Died 4 November 1895.*

PUBLICATIONS

Collections

   Writings in Prose and Verse.   10 vols., 1896.
   Hoosier Lyrics, edited by Charles Walter Brown.   1905.
   Poems, Complete Edition.   1910.

Verse

A Little Book of Western Verse. 1889.
Echoes from the Sabine Farm, Being Certain Horatian Lyrics, with Roswell M.
    Field. 1891; revised edition, 1893.
Second Book of Verse. 1892.
Love-Songs of Childhood. 1894.
Songs and Other Verse. 1896.
A Little Book of Tribune Verse: A Collection of Hitherto Uncollected Poems, Grave and
    Gay, edited by Joseph G. Brown. 1901.

Fiction

A Little Book of Profitable Tales. 1889.
The Holy-Cross and Other Tales. 1893.
The House: An Episode in the Life of Reuben Baker, Astronomer, and of His Wife
    Alice. 1896.
Second Book of Tales. 1896.
The Stars: A Slumber Story, edited by Will M. Clemens. 1901.

Other

Tribune Primer. 1881.
The Model Primer. 1882.
Culture's Garland, Being Memoranda of the Gradual Rise of Literature, Art, Music, and
    Society in Chicago and Other Western Ganglia. 1887.
With Trumpet and Drum. 1892.
The Love Affairs of a Bibliomaniac. 1896.
Field to Francis Wilson: Some Attentions. 1896.
The Eugene Field Book: Verses, Stories, and Letters, edited by Mary E. Burt and Mary
    B. Cable. 1898.
Sharps and Flats, edited by Slason Thompson. 2 vols., 1900.
Clippings from Denver Tribune 1881–1883, edited by Willard S. Morse. 1909.
Verse and Prose from the George H. Yenowine Collection, edited by Henry H. Harper.
    1917.
Some Love Letters. 1927.

Reading List: Field's Creative Years by Charles H. Dennis, 1924; Life of Field, The Poet of
Childhood by Slason Thompson, 1927; The Gay Poet: The Story of Field by Jeannette C.
Nolan, 1940; Field Days: The Life, Times, and Reputation of Field by Robert Conrow, 1974.

*   *   *

Eugene Field's was a motley genius, for he was a modern jester, the man and his works
being a puzzling combination of perverse contrasts. Field is generally remembered as a
children's writer of charming if dated bits of verse like "Little Boy Blue" and "Wynken,
Blynken, and Nod," yet he still enjoys a sub rosa reputation for off-color lines, his "Little
Willie" perhaps the best known of these naughty verses. Field openly professed a dislike for
children – other than his own – and his Tribune Primer, written in sardonic imitation of
grade-school readers, encourages young folks to cultivate the aquaintanceship of wasps and
gluepots. While capable of turning out in apparent sincerity the most pious of verses like

"The Divine Lullaby," Field was the libidinous originator of pornographic exercises which, like "Bangin' on the Rhine," enjoyed a long underground life even before seeing formal (if surreptitious) print.

Commencing his career as a newspaper columnist of the humorous one-liner breed, Field, despite his New England birth and education, was fond of identifying himself with the West, hence with the vital western tradition of journalism that produced Mark Twain, Ambrose Bierce, and (closer in generation and region to Field) James Whitcomb Riley. It is a tradition that accommodates Field's many sides, his love of hoaxes, his use of public print to roast friends and enemies alike, his fierce (in all senses) loyalties, his displays of saccharine sentimentality, and his airing of public dislikes and private passions. Most of what he wrote did not outlive him, and he died relatively young, at the height of his career and powers. Though he was a skillfull and witty occasional poet, that alone doomed his work to ephemerality. The best of his writing is the early dialect verse which in its masculine vitality and mining-camp settings anticipates Robert Service and parallels in chronology and spirit Kipling's barracks-room voice.

Field possessed a genuinely comic sense, which from his inveterate love of practical jokes to his humorous verse and prose, was thoroughly of his times and did not transcend them. He was a classic instance of Victorian madness, in which dilettantism took on a thoroughly middle-class, cigar-smoking, feet-on-desk pose, and self-conscious archaicism gained a popular audience. Born in 1850, he was absolutely in synchronization with his half-century, and died, most timely, five years before it ran out.

—Catherine Seelye

———————

FitzGERALD, Edward. English. Born Edward Purcell at Bredfield House, near Woodbridge, Suffolk, 31 March 1809; name changed to that of his mother's family, 1818. Educated at King Edward VI Grammar School, Bury St. Edmunds, Suffolk, 1821–26; Trinity College, Cambridge, 1826–30, B.A. 1830. Married Lucy Barton in 1856 (separated). Scholar of comfortable means: lived a secluded life in various parts of Suffolk, Wherstead Lodge, near Ipswich, 1825–35, Boulge Hall, near Woodbridge, 1835–53, Farlingby Hall, near Woodbridge, 1853–60, and in Woodbridge, 1860–83. *Died 14 June 1883.*

PUBLICATIONS

Collections

> *The Variorum and Definitive Edition of the Poetical and Prose Writings,* edited by George
>   Bentham.   7 vols., 1902–03.
> *Letters and Literary Remains,* edited by W. Aldis Wright.   7 vols., 1902–03.
> *Letters,* edited by J. M. Cohen.   1960
> *Selected Works,* edited by Joanna Richardson.   1962.

Verse

> *Sálámán and Absál: An Allegory Translated from the Persian of Jámi.*   1856; revised
>   edition, 1871; with *Rubáiyát,* 1879; edited by A. J. Arberry, 1956.

Rubáiyát of Omar Khayyám, The Astronomer-Poet of Persia. 1859; revised edition, 1868, 1872; with *Sáláman and Absál,* 1879; edited by C. J. Weber, 1959.
Occasional Verses. 1891.

Other

Euphranor: A Dialogue on Youth. 1851; revised edition, 1855, 1882.
Polonius: A Collection of Wise Saws and Modern Instances. 1852; edited by S. S. Allen, 1905.
Some New Letters of FitzGerald to Bernard Barton, edited by F. R. Barton. 1923.
Dictionary of Madame de Sevigné, edited by Mary Eleanor FitzGerald. 2 vols., 1914.
Letters to Bernard Quaritch 1853–83, edited by C. Quaritch Wrentmore. 1926.
A FitzGerald Friendship: Letters to William Bodham Donne, edited by N. C. Hannay. 1932.
FitzGerald to His Friends (letters), edited by Alethea Hayter. 1977.

Editor, *Readings in Crabbe's Tales of the Hall.* 1879.

Translator, *Six Dramas of Calderón.* 1853; edited by H. Oelsner, 1903.
Translator, *The Mighty Magician, and Such Stuff as Dreams Are Made of,* by Calderón. 1865.
Translator, *Agamemnon,* by Aeschylus. 1869.
Translator, *The Downfall and Death of King Oedipus,* by Sophocles. 2 vols., 1880–81.

Bibliography: in *Variorum Edition,* 1903; *A Bibliography of the Rubaiyat* by A. G. Potter, 1929.

Reading List: *The Life of FitzGerald* by A. McKinley Terhune, 1947; *The Rubáiyát of Omar Khayyám,* 1949, and *Omar Khayyám,* 1952, both by A. J. Arberry; *FitzGerald* by Joanna Richardson, 1960.

*   *   *

Born in the same year as Tennyson, Edward FitzGerald, like that poet, was oppressed by religious doubts, but his poetic reaction to those doubts manifested itself in an utterly different way. In his *Rubáiyát of Omar Khayyám,* we have a black and blasphemous rejection of God presented in a poem of surpassing grace, elegance, and sweetness. This is achieved by a ruse. The protestant Christian God of Victorian England is presented in the disguise of the Allah of eleventh-century Islamic Persia. The rejection reaches a climax in quatrain LVIII in the first edition of 1859:

> Oh, Thou, who man of baser Earth didst make,
> And who with Eden didst devise the Snake;
>   For all the Sin wherewith the Face of Man
> Is blacken'd, Man's Forgiveness give – and take!

At this point, it is right to remark that Omar Ali-Shah, who claims a remote but direct descent from the eleventh-century Persian, declared in 1967 that FitzGerald had shamefully travestied his illustrious ancestor. He affirms that the "Wine" that FitzGerald's Omar bibs, as the sole recompense for the punishment inflicted on man for his transgression, is not alcoholic liquor but the mystical contemplation of Allah. The Persian Omar Khayyám was a Sufi, a saintly ascetic, who could assume that the informed would instantly recognize that the

Wine was the spiritual refreshment which was the reward for devout contemplation.

Omar Ali-Shah may well be right and FitzGerald consequently utterly deluded in his literal understanding of "Wine." However, Robert Graves's rendering, in accordance with Ali-Shah's understanding of his ancestor's intentions, cannot begin to compete with FitzGerald's exquisite poem. "Drink and be merry, for to-morrow we die" is an ugly and crass prescript for life. Grant this, and the wonder is that FitzGerald made a work of such exquisite musical grace that the shallow hedonism is dissolved and subsumed in the lyrical patterning.

The manuscripts show that the eleventh-century Persian poet composed a large number of independent complete quatrains, a bundle of little poems. FitzGerald patterned these, created a "tesselation." The dawn begins and Omar, drinking, lives through the day, his indignation against the injustices of God growing ever more savage as that day moves towards its closing. Yet at no time is the musical grace and control surrendered.

The bitterness of FitzGerald against the Victorian Protestant God was spurred not only by a Victorian doubt of His existence. FitzGerald started to work on his translation after the cruellest of personal blows. The long-delayed but eventual acclaim – indeed, enormous popularity of his *Rubáiyát* – may have been a partial salve for this wound. A late dedicatory poem by Tennyson well expresses "Old Fitz's" merits.

The other works, mostly translations from Spanish, Persian, Greek, are subordinate to his masterpiece which appeared in four editions. A prose essay is related to the central calamity of his life. He had a gift for friendship, and his letters are enchanting.

—Francis Berry

FitzGERALD, Robert D(avid). Australian. Born in Hunters Hill, New South Wales, 22 February 1902. Educated at Sydney Grammar School; Sydney University, 1920–21; Fellow, Institute of Surveyors. Married Marjorie-Claire Harris in 1931; four children. Surveyor, FitzGerald and Blair, 1926–30; Native Lands Commission Surveyor, Fiji, 1931–36; Municipal Surveyor, 1936–39; Surveyor, Australian Department of the Interior, 1939–65, now retired. Visiting Lecturer, University of Texas, Austin, 1963. Recipient: Australian Sesqui-Centenary Poetry Prize, 1938; Australian Literature Society Gold Medal, 1938; Grace Leven Prize, 1952, 1959, 1962; Fulbright grant, 1963; Encyclopedia Britannica Award, 1965. O.B.E. (Officer, Order of the British Empire), 1951. Lives in Hunters Hill, New South Wales.

PUBLICATIONS

Verse

> *The Greater Apollo.* 1927.
> *To Meet the Sun.* 1929.
> *Moonlight Acre.* 1938.
> *Heemskerck Shoals.* 1949.
> *Between Two Tides.* 1952.
> *This Night's Orbit.* 1953.
> *The Wind at Your Door.* 1959.

Southmost Twelve. 1962.
Of Some Country: 27 Poems. 1963.
(Poems). 1963.
Forty Years' Poems. 1965.
Product. 1978.

Other

The Elements of Poetry. 1963.
Of Places and Poetry. 1976.

Editor, *Australian Poetry 1942.* 1942.
Editor, *(Poems),* By Mary Gilmore. 1963.
Editor, *The Letters of Hugh McCrae.* 1970.

Reading List: *Six Australian Poets* by T. Inglis Moore, 1942; *FitzGerald* by A. Grove Day, 1973.

                                        *   *   *

Robert D. FitzGerald is the only Australian poet of any real importance whose work can be described as deliberately and consistently philosophical (as distinct from mystical or theosophical), one of the few whose verse generates a continual intellectual excitement, sensuously expressed. In his first two books, *The Greater Apollo* and *To Meet the Sun,* FitzGerald, using metaphor as a scientist uses hypothesis, is already tossing up philosophical ideas: determinism, as in "Meeting"; freewill, as in "Calm"; and concepts of change, endurance, and eternality, as in the sequence "The Greater Apollo." His interest in the last three questions places him in the tradition of Brennan and the 19th-century Romantics of Germany and France, an interest which his family connections may have fostered. A more direct impulse towards exploring these ideas was the reading of A. N. Whitehead's *Science and the Modern World,* with its base of Bergsonian thought, though it would be wrong to assume that FitzGerald is mere versified Whitehead. The analysis of the nature of continuity itself is, indeed, FitzGerald's permanent theme, and the phrase "diamond waterfalls" an early metaphor for it.

Moonlight Acre shows an increasing confidence and craftsmanship, a more idiosyncratic style, probably based on Browning. There is a growing preoccupation with concepts of freedom and a willingness to challenge accepted conventions, as in "Exile," a poem which should be compared with "Law-breakers," written during the Vietnam war thirty years later. The cragginess of the diction and the occasionally tortuous syntax in the longer poems in this book are evidence not of an absence of a lyrical sense, but of the inherent difficulty of the subject matter. FitzGerald can be simple and sensuous if he wants to, as the love-poems and the verses about some of his Fijian encounters indicate.

With "The Hidden Bole," a long elegy on the death of Pavlova, however, FitzGerald reaches his full stature, displaying both intellectual toughness and a lyric sweetness far less characteristic of him. The poem explores the nature of beauty, with its inseparable element of transience; the use of Pavlova's dancing as an image of its perfection parallels Whitehead's statement that "the only endurances are structures of activity." The fusion of the ballet image, with Pavlova as its centre, and the image of the sacred banyan tree with its "hidden bole," the symbol of life, is not accomplished without some strain, but the vigour and excitement of the poem are enough to carry us over the rough place; the last two stanzas, which bring the focus of attention back to Pavlova herself, are an exquisite evocation of the dancer:

Eyes, were you drunk or blind
not knowing her steps, although you watched their thief,
the wind's toe-pointing leaf,
not seeing her chase the pebbled river?
She is the prisoned sunshine that became
delicate contour of escaping fire;
she is the snowflake blown upon the flame—
song and the melting wraith of song's desire.

The use of images as hypotheses to be successively eliminated in analysing concepts is employed also in "Essay on Memory." It is an impressive, if not wholly successful poem, and certainly the most interesting of the attempts to provide the country with "a usable past." "Heemskerck Shoals and "Face of the Waters" and "Fifth Day" (from the volume *This Night's Orbit*) are far more accomplished pieces, the first expressing the paradox that the practical man is often the truest dreamer, the second on the agony of "striving to be" and of "not-being," the third on the impossibility of writing history, using the trial of Warren Hastings as an instance: "history hooks/the observer into the foreground as he looks...."

FitzGerald's most ambitious poem is *Between Two Tides*, though his most disturbing one, morally, is perhaps *The Wind at Your Door*, on a convict theme. *Between Two Tides* has for its subject the struggle for power between two Tongan chiefs, a vehicle for the argument that events present "straws" for man's choosing, that it is his duty to choose, and that by choosing he is able to determine the nature of the "straws" themselves. Human life is the indefinable moment between two tides when man is able to assert his "thusness" through his choosing. The poem is slow-moving but compellingly structured as a series of dissolving views: Finau's tale, filtered through several intermediaries to the poet, who becomes the omniscient narrator interpreting for the reader. In this poem FitzGerald makes use of the early experience of his life in Fiji, which had been working in him for many years below the surface. Unfamiliar setting and exotic characters provide the distancing necessary to an economical working out of the theme, and the result is the first really powerful narrative poem in Australian literature. The interconnections between what men are and the institutions they create are developed perhaps with greater human sympathy and humility in *The Wind at Your Door*. History, the past within us becoming the present and shaping the future, is one of FitzGerald's life-long preoccupations; in it he seems to discern, in spite of relapses into savagery, some secret "force towards order," though he is no facile optimist. His profession, surveying, has been a discernible influence on his work, and so has the Irish component in his ancestry, while his long sojourn in the Fijian Islands gives a mysterious dimension to his work, a perspective that marks him off from his contemporaries, some of whom seem culture-bound in comparison.

Besides his books of verse, FitzGerald has edited a selection of Mary Gilmore's poems, and a selection of the letters of Hugh McCrae. He has also published a book of criticism, *The Elements of Poetry*, robust, sensitive and individual. *Of Places and Poetry* is a collection of family reminiscences, portraits, literary explorations, and essays on the theory and practice of verse. Some of his sketches of literary personalities are illuminating and reasonably objective; his poetic theory is his own and strongly held, if not particularly stimulating, but there is a curious naivety about his prose style which is absent from his verse. Poetry is his native element.

—Dorothy Green

FLECKER, James Elroy.   English.   Born Herman Elroy Flecker in Lewisham, London, 5 November 1884; grew up in Cheltenham, Gloucestershire. Educated at Cheltenham Ladies College Kindergarten; preparatory school, Cheltenham; Dean Close School, Cheltenham,

1893–1900; Uppingham School, 1901–06; Trinity College, Oxford, 1902–06, B.A. 1906; studied Oriental languages at Caius College, Cambridge, 1908–10. Married Helle Skiadaressi in 1911. Teacher, Hampstead, London, 1907; entered the British diplomatic service, 1910: served in Constantinople, 1910–11; Vice-Consul, Beirut, 1911–13. Tubercular: retired from the diplomatic service and lived in Switzerland, 1913–15. *Died 3 January 1915.*

PUBLICATIONS

Collections

> *Collected Poems,* edited by J. C. Squire.   1916; revised edition, 1946.
> *Collected Prose.*   1920.

Verse

> *The Bridge of Fire.*   1907.
> *Thirty-Six Poems.*   1910; augmented edition, as *Forty-Two Poems,* 1911.
> *The Golden Journey to Samarkand.*   1913.
> *The Burial in England.*   1915.
> *The Old Ships.*   1915.
> *God Save the King.*   1915.
> *Selected Poems.*   1918.
> *Unpublished Poems and Drafts,* edited by Martin Booth.   1971.

Plays

> *Hassan,* revised by Basil Dean (produced 1923).   1922.
> *Don Juan* (produced 1926).   1925.
> *Joseph and Mary,* in *With Pipe and Tabor,* by R. Moorhouse.   1928.

Fiction

> *The Last Generation: A Story of the Future.*   1908.
> *The King of Alsander.*   1914.

Other

> *The Best Man: Eights' Week 1906.*   1906.
> *The Grecians: A Dialogue on Education.*   1910.
> *The Scholar's Italian Book: An Introduction to the Study of the Latin Origins of Italian.*   1911.
> *The Letters to Frank Savery,* edited by Helle Flecker.   1926.
> *Some Letters from Abroad.*   1930.

Reading List: *Flecker: From School to Samarkand* by Thomas S. Mercer, 1952 (includes bibliography); *No Golden Journey* (biography) by John Sherwood, 1973; *Flecker* by John M. Munro, 1976.

*   *   *

Although James Elroy Flecker wrote a number of short prose pieces, fiction, and plays (*Hassan* was magnificently staged by Basil Dean in 1923), he is perhaps best remembered as a poet. Such frequently anthologised poems as "A Ship, An Isle, A Sickle Moon," "The Old Ships," "Tenebris Interlucentem," and "The Golden Journey to Samarkand," later incorporated into *Hassan*, all testify to his skill as a literary craftsman. Therefore, although he is frequently lumped together with the Georgians, Flecker is perhaps best appreciated as a late survival of the European Parnassian tradition, his verses being an expression of the belief that good poetry finds its beauty in perfection of form and clarity of outline. In his more introspective moments, however, Flecker considers the relationship between Art and Life, and speculates whether Art may not be an escape from life rather than an affirmation of it, an idea which he tentatively expresses in "The Old Ships."

Attracted by the exoticism of the East, and finding inspiration in Arabian legend and the local color of the Levant, he nonetheless remained temperamentally attached to his native country, and a number of his poems, for example "Brumana," reflect his nostalgia for the English countryside. While much of his verse owes its origins to literary sources rather than to life, after being struck by tuberculosis in 1910 he wrote poetry of a more somber tone, as for example "In Hospital," which clearly reflects the poet's awareness of the transience of human existence.

While it is easy to dismiss *Hassan* as an oriental extravaganza in the tradition of *Chu Chin Chow*, Flecker's play is far from being a hollow spectacle. Rather, as Priscilla Thouless has noted in *Modern Poetic Drama* (1935), it reflects an artistic dilemma that is central to a proper understanding of Flecker. As she expresses it: "[Flecker] clung to the Parnassian path because he feared self-expression; he feared that if he did not strictly confine himself he would turn to gross egoism, like that of Victor Hugo, or to didacticism like that of Wordsworth. He feared moreover that his 'healthy manliness' might fade away, and that his divided soul might be revealed. In *Hassan* it is revealed, for in *Hassan* we find the hand of the Parnassian and of the Romantic...."

Flecker is admittedly a minor figure, and, although he was writing at a time when poets such as T. S. Eliot and Ezra Pound were shaping the modern aesthetic, his work shows no trace of the forces which were to exert such a profound influence on the development of modern poetry. Essentially he must be regarded as a late practicioner of the doctrine of Art for Art's sake, writing poetry which was devoid of "dullness, weakness, bad workmanship, vulgar thought and shoddy sentiment," as he expressed it in his essay "The Public as Art Critic." For these artistic vices, he believed, were ultimately "slanders on mankind."

—John M. Munro

FLETCHER, Giles, The Elder. English. Born in Watford, Hertfordshire, in 1546. Educated at Eton College; King's College, Cambridge, 1565–68, B.A. 1569, M.A. 1573, LL.D. 1581. Married Joan Sheafe in 1580; one daughter, three sons, including Phineas Fletcher, *q.v.*, and Giles Fletcher the Younger, *q.v.* Fellow, King's College, Cambridge, 1568; Deputy Orator of Cambridge University, 1577; Commissary to the Chancellor of Ely, 1580; Member of Parliament for Winchelsea, 1585; undertook various diplomatic missions for the court to Scotland, Germany, Holland, and Russia, 1586–89; Remembrancer of the City of London, 1586–1605; Treasurer of St. Paul's Cathedral, London, 1597; granted lease of rectory at Ringwood, Hampshire, 1600. *Died in 1611.*

PUBLICATIONS

Collections

> *English Works,* edited by Lloyd E. Berry.   1964.

Verse

> *Licia; or, Poems of Love, The Rising to the Crown of Richard the Third.*   1593(?).
> *De Literis Antiquae Britanniae* (in Latin), edited by Phineas FLetcher.   1633.

Other

> *Of the Russe Commonwealth.*   1591; edited by Lloyd E. Berry and R. O. Crummey, in
>   *Rude and Barbarous Kingdom,* 1969.
> *Israel Redux,* with S. Lee.   1677.

Bibliography: "Fletcher: A Bibliography" by Lloyd E. Berry, in *Transactions of the Cambridge Bibliographical Society,* 1961.

Reading List: Introduction by R. Pipes to *Of the Russe Commonwealth,* 1966.

*   *   *

Giles Fletcher's poetic voice is quiet, but often unmistakably personal. At first sight the sonnets in *Licia* seem to be constructed out of the common properties of the Petrarchan hoard – "Roses and Lillies strive" in the loved one's face (Sonnet XXXV), but her heart is "Tyger-like," and she cannot love (VIII). The setting is appropriately pastoral, where "sweetest flowers enameld have the ground" (XXVI), and "Chrystal streames" join their murmurs to the lover's woe (XXVII). Yet a sudden genuine (as opposed to literary) perception breaks in from time to time; as when Cupid beats a hasty retreat from the lady, "as the foote, that treads the stinging snake, Hastes to be gone, for feare what may ensewe" (II). Occasionally, Fletcher seems to anticipate Donne, as in Sonnet XXIX where, with a conversational opening – "Why dy'd I not when as I last did sleepe" – he recounts a dream in which his mistress came to him. Commenting on her breasts and thighs, he passes with an Ovidian delicacy over "those sportes, in secret that are best" and longs for full consummation, either in dream or "indeede."

Fletcher, like so many of his contemporaries, plunders the writings of his continental counterparts: but he rarely attempts to pass off direct translation as his own work, and his borrowings are well assimilated into his English poems. His technique, more often than not, is to begin with a couple of lines translated from his source, and then develop the idea to a personal conclusion.

Included in *Licia* is a long poem somewhat in the manner of *The Mirror for Magistrates*, in which the speaker is Richard III. He recounts his triumphs with some pleasure, explaining that his entire family shared one dominant trait: "Sparkes of ambition did possesse us all" (line 62); given such a driving force, and the longing for a kingdom, Richard moved through blood ("For crownes with blood the brighter will they shine," line 70) until he achieved the throne. At the end of the poem he shows, unlike the *exempla* in *The Mirror for Magistrates*, no remorse for his deeds:

> Nor speake I now, as if I did repent,
> Unlesse for this a crowne I bought so cheap.
> For meaner things men wittes and lives have spent,
> Which blood have sowne, and crowns could never reap.
>   Live *Richard* long, the honour of thy name,
>   And scorne all such, as doe thy fortune blame.

In 1591 Fletcher published a prose work, *The Russe Commonwealth*, which proved to be the most important book on Russia by any sixteenth-century Englishman. He describes the geography of the country, and its hierarchy of government, deploring the servile condition of the common people who were so oppressed by their overlords that they "have no more courage in following their trades: for that the more they have, the more daunger they are in, not onely of their goods, but of their lives also." The Russian Orthodox Church – or rather, its ministers – shocked him: "As for preaching the worde of God, or any teaching, or exhorting such as are under them, they neyther use it, nor have any skill of it: the whole Cleargie beyng utterlie unlearned bothe for other knowledge, and in the word of God." Although parts of *The Russe Commonwealth* are derivative, there are occasional observations from personal experience; Fletcher spent at least a year in Russia, as ambassador specially commissioned to treat of trade matters. His letters tell how the Russians behaved "as if they had divised meanes of very purpose to shew their utter disliking both of the trade of the Marchant, and of the whole English nation."

—Roma Gill

FLETCHER, Giles, The Younger. English. Born in London c. 1585; son of Giles Fletcher the Elder, *q.v.*; younger brother of Phineas Fletcher, *q.v.* Educated at Westminster School, London; Trinity College, Cambridge, B.A. 1606. Married Anne, c. 1619. Fellow of Trinity College, Cambridge, 1608; Reader in Greek Grammar, 1615–18, and Reader in Greek Language, 1618–19, Cambridge University; Rector, Helmingham, Suffolk, 1617–18, and Alderton, Suffolk, 1619–23. *Died in 1623.*

PUBLICATIONS

Collections

Poetical Works of Giles and Phineas Fletcher, edited by F. S. Boas. 2 vols., 1908–09.
Complete Poems, edited by D. C. Sheldon. 1938.

Verse

Christ's Victory and Triumph in Heaven and Earth, over and after Death. 1610; edited by N. Alexander, in *Elizabethan Narrative Verse,* 1967.

Other

The Reward of the Faithful. 1623.

Editor, *The Young Divine's Apology for His Continuance in the University, with Certain Meditations,* by Nathaniel Pownoll. 1612.

Reading List: *Spenser, The School of the Fletchers, and Milton* by Herbert E. Cory, 1912; "Fletcher and the Puritans," in *Journal of English and Germanic Philology,* 1955, and "Fletcher and the Catholics," in *Studies in Honor of T. W. Baldwin,* edited by D. C. Allen, 1958, both by A. Holaday; *The Spenserian Poets* by Joan Grundy, 1969.

*   *   *

Giles Fletcher the Younger is virtually the poet of a single poem. That poem, however, *Christ's Victory and Triumph,* itself consists of four poems that are at once separated and united, namely "Christ's Victory in Heaven," "Christ's Victory on Earth," "Christ's Triumph over Death," "Christ's Triumph after Death." Each has more independence than a book or canto, yet together they form a sequence sufficiently unified to give them the character of a "brief epic."

Beginning with a debate between Justice and Mercy in Heaven, they depict, dramatize, and celebrate (rather than simply narrate) the main events in the life of Christ, including the Temptation, Passion, Resurrection, and Ascension. Their treatment of these topics is at times allegorical and imitative of Spenser. This applies especially to the second poem, dealing with the Temptation. The stanza Fletcher adopts is itself a modified Spenserian stanza, having eight lines instead of nine but ending with an alexandrine. In style and temper, however, the poem's closest affinities are with the religious poetry of the counter-Reformation. Although Fletcher's Protestantism is never in doubt, his artistic sympathies with Catholic Italy are considerable. His writing is sensuous, often florid, passionate, fervent, and ecstatic. He employs the figures of rhetoric constantly, both in order to keep up the emotional temperature and to impress upon the reader, through paradox and antithesis especially, the wonder and mystery of his subject. The work as a whole is structured (through the juxtaposing of the four poems) in such a way as to illustrate or "enact" the central mystery of the Incarnation:

> And how the Infinite far greater grew
> By growing less, and how the rising Morn,
> That shot from heaven, did back to heaven return.

Fletcher's lyricism and genuine religious devotion make him at his best a fine and moving poet. His finest passages come in the celebration of the joys of heaven in the last poem, which achieves a sustained and exhilarating eloquence. But there is pathos too in his account of the Crucifixion, and tenderness in some of his lines on the Nativity. Milton knew Fletcher's poem and echoed it occasionally. His evident admiration of it was fully deserved.

Fletcher also wrote two short elegies, on the deaths of Queen Elizabeth and of Prince Henry, but the interest of these is slight. His prose work, *The Reward of the Faithful,* is a piece of devotional writing in which he again creates an ecstatic vision of the joys of heaven. Both here and in his major poem he appears essentially as a rapt, unworldly, rather Shelleyan spirit, pouring his full heart in strains of a highly conscious yet incantatory art.

—Joan Grundy

FLETCHER, John Gould. American. Born in Little Rock, Arkansas, 3 January 1886. Educated at high school in Little Rock, 1899–1902; Phillips Academy, Andover, Massachusetts, 1902–03; Harvard University, Cambridge, Massachusetts, 1903–07. Married 1) Florence Emily Arbuthnot in 1916; 2) Charlie May Simon in 1936. Lived in England, 1908–14, 1916–33: one of the founders of the Imagist group of poets; returned to the United States and settled in Arkansas, 1933: associated with the Agrarian group of writers. Recipient: Pulitzer Prize, 1939. LL.D.: University of Arkansas, Fayetteville, 1933. Member, National Institute of Arts and Letters. *Died 10 May 1950.*

PUBLICATIONS

Verse

The Book of Nature 1910–1912. 1913.
The Dominant City. 1913.
Fire and Wine. 1913.
Fool's Gold. 1913.
Visions of the Evening. 1913.
Irradiations: Sand and Spray. 1915.
Goblins and Pagodas. 1916.
Japanese Prints. 1918.
The Tree of Life. 1918.
Breakers and Granite. 1921.
Preludes and Symphonies. 1922.
Parables. 1925.
Branches of Adam. 1926.
The Black Rock. 1928.
XXIV Elegies. 1935.
The Epic of Arkansas. 1936.
Selected Poems. 1938.
South Star. 1941.
The Burning Mountain. 1946.

Other

La Poésie d'André Fontainas. 1919.
Some Contemporary American Poets. 1920.
Paul Gauguin: His Life and Art. 1921.
John Smith – Also Pocahontas. 1928.
The Crisis of the Film. 1929.
The Two Frontiers: A Study in Historical Psychology (on Russia and America). 1930; as *Europe's Two Frontiers,* 1930.

Life Is My Song (autobiography). 1937.
Arkansas. 1947.

Editor, *Edgar Allan Poe.* 1926.

Translator, *The Dance over Fire and Water,* by Elie Favre. 1926.
Translator, *The Reveries of a Solitary,* by Rousseau. 1927.

Reading List: *Fletcher* by Edna B. Stephens, 1967 (includes bibliography); *Fletcher and Imagism* by Edmund S. de Chasca, 1978.

*   *   *

Although most often linked with the Imagist movement because of his early association with Amy Lowell, John Gould Fletcher belongs to no one "school" of poetry; his work covers a wide range of styles and themes. But in all of his work an emphasis upon the visual is a reflection not only of his interest in art but of his early experience with Imagist philosophy. In 1908, at the age of twenty-two, Fletcher left America for Europe, and spent the next twenty-five years moving between the two continents. In 1913, having published, at his own expense, five volumes of poetry, he went to Paris where he came under the influence of Impressionist art, new music, and Ezra Pound. But it was with Amy Lowell that he aligned himself, joining her Imagist circle in 1914; Lowell included some of Fletcher's poems in her anthologies, he dedicated some of his work to her, and together they formulated a poetic style of "polyphonic prose."

Of Fletcher's many works, the most famous are his "symphonies"; these are expressions of mood symbolized by a distinct color, one for each symphony. They are all divided into movements (the poems of *Sand and Spray* are even given tempo markings), each reflecting another aspect of the color stressed in the imagery of the poem. The result is an effective synaesthetic blend of verbal, visual, and musical elements. In "White Symphony," for instance, mood is reflected in white peonies "like rockets in the twilight," the "white snow-water of my dreams," and a "white-laden" snowy landscape. Fletcher retains the idea of symphonic form in later poems as well. Orientalism, so influential upon the Imagists, also had a profound effect upon Fletcher; Chinese philosophy and Japanese poetry (especially *haiku*) were important to the writing of the symphonies, and Fletcher's viewing of Oriental art exhibited in America in 1914 and 1915 is reflected in *Goblins and Pagodas* and *Japanese Prints.* The subjects of the latter volume are not necessarily Japanese, as Fletcher notes in his preface, "but all illustrate something of the charm I have found in Japanese poetry and art." Here he seeks "to universalize our emotions," to show "that the universe is just as much in the shape of a hand as it is in armies, politicians, astronomy, or the exhortations of gospel-mongers; that style and technique rest on the thing conveyed and not the means of conveyance." This emphasis upon the concrete remains constant throughout all of Fletcher's poetry, which, in general, is fairly traditional in form.

In the 1920's, traveling through the American South, Fletcher met the writers of the agrarian "Fugitive" movement, in whom he had been interested for several years. Although he did not embrace the Fugitives' belief in purely intellectual poetry, he did share their concept of Southern agrarian culture as a bastion against modern industrialism. His contribution to the 1929 Fugitive symposium was a discussion of "Education, Past and Present" (published in 1930 in *I'll Take My Stand*), in which he stressed the importance of encouraging folk education to help the South maintain its distinct culture. In 1933, Fletcher returned to his native Little Rock, and from that point he can be considered a Southern regional writer.

—Jane S. Gabin

FLETCHER, Phineas.   English.   Born in Cranbrook, Kent, baptized 8 April 1582; son of Giles Fletcher the Elder, *q.v.*; elder brother of Giles Fletcher the Younger, *q.v.* Educated at Eton College; King's College, Cambridge, 1600–04, B.A. 1604, M.A. 1608, B.D. Married Elizabeth Vincent in 1615; four daughters, four sons. Fellow, King's College, Cambridge, 1611–16; ordained, 1611; Chaplain to Sir Henry Willoughby, Risley, Derbyshire, 1615–21; Rector, Hilgay, Norfolk, 1621–50. *Died in December 1650.*

Publications

Collections

> *Poetical Works*, with Giles Fletcher the Younger, edited by F. S. Boas.   2 vols., 1908–09.
> *Venus and Anchises – Britain's Ida – and Other Poems*, edited by Ethel Seaton.   1926.

Verse

> *Locustae: Vel Pietas Jesuitica* (Latin and English versions).   2 vols., 1627; English version edited by William B. Hunter, as *The Locusts, or Apollyonists*, in *The English Spenserians*, 1977.
> *Britain's Ida.*   1628.
> *Joy in Tribulation; or, Consolations for Afflicted Spirits.*   1632.
> *The Purple Island; or, The Isle of Man, Together with Piscatory Eclogues and Other Poetical Miscellanies.*   2 vols., 1633.
> *Sylva Poetica*, in *De Literis Antiquae Britanniae*, by Giles Fletcher the Elder.   1633.

Play

> *Sicelides.*   1631.

Other

> *The Way to Blessedness; or, A Treatise on the First Psalm.*   1632.
> *A Father's Testament.*   1670.

> Editor, *De Literis Antiquae Britanniae*, by Giles Fletcher the Elder.   1633.

Reading List: *Spenser, The School of the Fletchers, and Milton* by Herbert E. Cory, 1912; *Fletcher, Man of Letters, Science, and Divinity* by Abram B. Langdale, 1937; "Fletcher: His Modern Readers and His Renaissance Ideals" by R. G. Baldwin, in *Philological Quarterly*, 1961; *The Spenserian Poets* by Joan Grundy, 1969.

*   *   *

Phineas Fletcher is remembered principally as the author of *The Purple Island; or, The Isle of Man*, an allegorical poem in twelve cantos enlarging – to the point of absurdity, most readers will feel – upon the idea that man is a microcosm or little world. The Island (man's body – it is dew from its rivers – i.e., the blood-stream – that gives it its colour) is described in elaborate geographical detail, the anatomical meaning of which is explained in lengthy and learned marginal glosses. The poem's action concerns the battle fought between the Virtues and Vices for possession of the King and Queen of the Island, Intellect and Will, who are besieged in their castle by the Vices, and culminates in the triumphant overthrow of the Dragon of the Apocalypse by a knight who is Christ himself. Much of the poem consists of character-sketches of the various personifications, some florid, some satirical. The poem's most attractive feature is its pastoral framework, in which the shepherd Thirsil is presented, entertaining his friends with this story. As a whole, however, the poem is unappealing: its allegory is at once over-ingenious and over-explicit, and lacks imaginative life.

The *Piscatory Eclogues* use the image of the fisherman's life (instead of the more usual shepherd's) to represent in pastoral form the various concerns of the poet – his poetry, his love-affairs real or invented, his pursuit of preferment. The poems, whose setting is the river (Cam, Medway, or Trent), not the sea, have a certain charm, if only for their novelty: it is amusing to watch Fletcher devising "fishy" equivalents for the usual pastoral symbols. His play *Sicelides*, also a "piscatory," is a very dull affair.

Fletcher's narrative poem *Venus and Anchises* was published as Spenser's in 1628, under the title of *Britain's Ida*. It is an ornate, heavily sensuous poem, centred on a love-encounter of the type popularized by Marlowe's *Hero and Leander* and Shakespeare's *Venus and Adonis*. Its sensuousness is surpassed in Fletcher's poetry only by the rapturous *Epithalamium* of the Sion College manuscript.

The *Apollyonists*, an English paraphrase of his Latin poem *Locustae*, is a "brief epic" on the subject of the Gunpowder Plot, depicted as the work of the Jesuits who are portrayed as the locusts of *Revelation*. The poem is effective, though harsh and repellent in tone. Fletcher's representation of Satan may have been remembered by Milton in the Satan of *Paradise Lost*.

Fletcher's most attractive poems are the elegy "Elisa," the lyrics in *Poetical Miscellanies*, and the verses in his prose work *A Father's Testament*, itself an eloquent and quietly convincing devotional meditation. The personal themes of home, family, and friendship seem to have been near his heart, and he writes of them with a genuine tenderness and urgency. The religious "Verses and Translations" touch greatness in their intense spirituality and glowing moral fervour. The true poet in Fletcher, often obscured elsewhere by common-place subject-matter, platitudinous treatment, and an imitative manner, here asserts himself unmistakably.

—Joan Grundy

FOSTER, Stephen Collins. American. Born in Pittsburgh, Pennsylvania, 4 July 1826. Studied privately, Allegheny, Pennsylvania; at Towanda Academy, Pennsylvania, 1841; Athens Academy, Tioga Point, Pennsylvania, 1840–41; Jefferson College, Canonsburg, Pennsylvania, 1841. Married Jane McDowell in 1850; one daughter. Worked as a bookkeeper for his brother, Cincinnati, 1847; thereafter made song writing his life's work: contracted to Firth Pond and Company from 1849. *Died 13 January 1864.*

PUBLICATIONS

Collections

The Melodies. 1909.

Foster's Forgotten Songs, edited by Hamilton A. Gordon. 1941.
A Treasury of Foster. 1946.

Bibliography: *A Pictorial Bibliography of the First Editions* by James J. Fuld, 1957.

Reading List: *Foster, America's Troubadour,* 1935, and *The Literature of Foster,* 1944, both by John T. Howard; *Foster, Boy Minstrel* by Helen B. Higgins, 1944; *The Songs of Foster* by William W. Austin, 1975.

*   *   *

While Stephen Collins Foster's literary output is inextricably linked to the music to which he set it, he must nevertheless be considered as a poet, and more influential in his writing of words than of music. The abstract art of his music surrounds and complements his lyrics in an inimitable Bellinian "simplicity of genius," but his carefully crafted words ultimately reflect and refine the mores of American society in the pre-Civil War period: optimistic, sentimental, patriotic, and proudly unsophisticated.

Foster has been criticised as too sentimental, as having embodied the patronising racism of his time, and of having been not a poet at all but a musician who wrote some of his own lyrics. About a third of Foster's 180-odd songs were, it is true, written to the texts of others, but only two or three of these have survived among the forty and more Foster songs with which most Americans are familiar. As a musician, he responded best to himself as poet.

Of Foster's own lyrics, most, and the most important, form two groups: the sentimental ballad and the Negro dialect song. His few political, patriotic, and non-dialect comic lyrics are neither greatly distinguished in themselves nor sources of memorable musical accompaniments. The sentimental ballads, such as "Beautiful Dreamer," "Come Where My Love Lies Dreaming," and "Jeannie with the Light Brown Hair" are comparable in intensity of emotion to, and less pretentious stylistically than, the sentimental poetry of such contemporaries as Poe and Lanier. At the same time, his lyrics are more metrically and verbally sophisticated than those of his contemporaries who wrote not as poets but only as lyricists.

The Negro-dialect lyrics, or "Etheopian Songs" as they were popularly known, demonstrate Foster's keen ear for the rhythms and patterns of black speech. In his earliest efforts, such as "Oh Susanna" and "Old Folks at Home," some crudities and a tendency to see the black, slave or free, as a happy buffoon, can be traced. But the poet's close observation of blacks for both poetic and musical veracity resulted in a gradual and progressive move away from stereotype to the image of the black person as dignified, sensitive, and empathetic rather than simple and ridiculous. He jettisoned objectionable words commonly descriptive of blacks, leading to later lyrics such as "Old Black Joe" in which dialect disappears entirely, though by then his grasp of it, in "Nelly Bly," "My Old Kentucky Home," and "Massa's in de Cold Ground" demonstrate a command equal to Sidney Lanier's of the contemporary white southerner.

The Civil War, which abolished black servitude and replaced sentimentality with expansionism and urbanism, cut off the possibility of Foster's being an influence on the poetry which followed his death, and froze him into the posture of a spokesman for a vanished age. The strong American sense of nostalgia has thus deified him, and the mythic figure thus created has so far repelled any serious study of his considerable talents as a poet.

—William J. Collins

FRENEAU, Philip (Morin). American. Born in New York City, 2 January 1752. Educated privately, and at the College of New Jersey, now Princeton University, 1768–71. Enlisted in the militia and commanded a privateer in the Revolutionary War: captured by the British, 1780. Married Eleanor Forman in 1789. Teacher on Long Island, and at Somerset Academy, Back Creek, Maryland, 1772; Planter's Secretary, Santa Cruz, West Indies, 1776–79; worked in the Philadelphia Post Office, and helped to edit Jefferson's *Freeman's Journal*, Philadelphia, 1781–84; master of a brig bound for Jamaica, 1784, and lived in the West Indies, serving as an officer on ships in the Caribbean and Atlantic coast trade, 1784–89; Editor, *Daily Advertiser*, New York, 1790–91; Translating Clerk, United States Department of State, and Editor of the *National Gazette*, Philadelphia, 1791–93; Editor of the *Jersey Chronicle*, 1795–96, and of *The Time-Piece*, New York, 1797–98; retired from journalism, and for the rest of his life alternated between the sea and his New Jersey farm. *Died 19 December 1832.*

PUBLICATIONS

Collections

> *Poems*, edited by Fred Lewis Pattee. 3 vols., 1902–07.
> *Poems*, edited by Harry Hayden Clark. 1929.
> *Prose*, edited by Philip M. Marsh. 1955.
> *A Freneau Sampler*, edited by Philip M. Marsh. 1963.

Verse

> *A Poem on the Rising Glory of America*, with H. H. Brackenridge. 1772.
> *The American Village.* 1772.
> *American Liberty.* 1775.
> *A Voyage to Boston.* 1775.
> *General Gage's Confession.* 1775.
> *The British Prison-Ship.* 1781.
> *Poems.* 1786; as *Poems on Various Occasions*, 1861.
> *A Journey from Philadelphia to New York.* 1787; as *A Laughable Poem*, 1809.
> *The Village Merchant.* 1794.
> *Poems Written Between the Years 1768 and 1794.* 1795.
> *Poems.* 2 vols., 1809.
> *A Collection of Poems on American Affairs.* 2 vols., 1815.
> *Some Account of the Capture of the Ship Aurora*, edited by Jay Miller. 1899.
> *Last Poems*, edited by Lewis Leary. 1946.

Other

> *Miscellaneous Works.* 1788.
> *Letters on Various Interesting and Important Subjects.* 1799.
> *Unpublished Freneauiana*, edited by Charles F. Heartman. 1918.
> *The Writings of Hezekiah Salem*, edited by Lewis Leary. 1975.

> Editor, *An Historical Sketch of the Life of Silas Talbot.* 1803.

> Translator, *New Travels Through North America*, by Abbé Claude Robin. 1783.

Bibliography: *A Bibliography of the Separate and Collected Works of Freneau* by Victor Hugo Paltsits, 1903; in *Bibliography of American Literature* by Jacob Blanck, 1959; *Freneau's Published Prose: A Bibliography* by Philip M. Marsh, 1970.

Reading List: *That Rascal Freneau: A Study in Literary Failure* by Lewis Leary, 1941; *Freneau and the Cosmic Enigma* by Nelson F. Adkins, 1949; *Freneau, Champion of Democracy* by Jacob Axelrod, 1967; *Freneau, Poet and Journalist*, 1967, and *The Works of Freneau: A Critical Study*, 1968, both Philip M. Marsh.

*   *   *

Philip Freneau's poetry and prose reflect his life and times: he gloried in matching the image of the Enlightened gentleman-scholar, one who could be as content administering his estate as intriguing in the latest political uproar, as happy translating the classics as being the master of a ship safely brought into port. Current politics, the latest scientific discovery, the newest philosophy, the recent misfortune of a neighbor, the chance observation of a terrapin: Freneau thought all fit subjects for his pen.

Many of his poems were propaganda, either for political party or for the United States during the two wars against Great Britain. In his poems of the Revolution, he moved from personal attacks on the British ("Cain, Nimrod, Nero – fiends in human guise,/Herod, Domitian – these in judgment rise,/And, envious of his deeds, I hear them say/None but a George could be more vile than they") to calls for greater exertion by the patriots ("Rouse from your sleep, and crush the thievish band,/Defeat, destroy, and sweep them from the land"). But his War of 1812 verse is more urbane: both sides are pictured with wit and humor. Freneau's pen was also lent to other causes: for the Revolution in France, against the American lack of support for poetry ("An age employed in edging steel/Can no poetic raptures feel"), against the dislocation of the Indians, against debtors' prisons. Much of this occasional verse, written in the heat of the moment, deserves to be forgotten, but occasionally, as in "Stanzas to an Alien" or "Stanzas on the Decease of Thomas Paine," he achieves lasting feeling.

The best known of Freneau's prose is that of his essay series. In the early series, the major characters, "The Pilgrim" and "The Philosopher of the Forest," tend to be preachy and fuzzily drawn. The Indian "Tomo-Cheeki" of another series voices the expected noble-savage statements in elegant prose: he is but a device for social criticism through the contrast of cultures. Used somewhat similarly is "Hezekiah Salem," the chief character of a light series that appeared in New York. As a New Englander, Salem is an early progenitor of American humor based on regional differences. But Freneau's greatest prose creation was Robert Slender, spokesman of an electioneering series. Robert Slender is the common man: he speaks as one, he feels as one, his fears are those of one. He views government from the point of view of everyday life, as here where he talks to himself on the way to a tavern:

> Had I, said I, (talking to myself all the while) the disposal of but half the income of the United States, I could at least so order matters, that a man might walk to his next neighbour's without splashing his stockings, or being in danger of breaking his legs in ruts, holes, gutts, and gullies. I do not know, says I to myself, as I moralized on my splash'd stocking, but money might with more profit be laid out in repairing the roads, than in marine establishments, supporting a standing army, useless embassies, exhorbitant salaries, given to many flashy fellows that are no honour to us, or to themselves, and chartering whole ships to carry a single man to another nation.

Freneau's best prose pieces are those in which he speaks in this colloquial, common style.

But the works of Freneau which are read today are not the occasional verse which made him famous, nor his prose, but poems which capture the melancholy so admired by the pre-

Romantics. Best known of this type is "The Wild Honeysuckle," which presents the inevitable decay of the flower's beauty: "Smit with those charms, that must decay,/I grieve to see your future doom." The emotion is restrained, is never permitted to become more than a pleasing melancholy:

> From morning suns and evening dews
> At first thy little being came
> If nothing once, you nothing lose,
> For when you die you are the same;
> The space between, is but an hour,
> The frail duration of a flower.

As Freneau revised the last couplet several times, so he revised his best poems frequently, polishing them as a craftsman. One of his best is "Ode to Fancy," a late revision of his very early "The Power of Fancy." The poem begins with Fancy's origin and nature: "Wakeful, vagrant, restless thing,/Ever wandering on the wing,/Who thy wondrous source can find,/Fancy, regent of the mind." The poet then presents the analogy between the creations of man's fancy and the elements of the universe, "Ideas of the Almighty mind!" After a description of Fancy's power, the poem ends with this plea: "Come, O come – perceiv'd by none,/You and I will walk alone." The whole is a unified, satisfying poem. As, later in life, Freneau became a better poet, he also became a more philosophical one, often presenting in verse his views on nature and the universe, still clinging to that most cherished virtue of the Enlightenment – moderation. In one of his last poems, "Winter," he again emphasizes this virtue:

> Happy with wine we may indulge an hour;
> The noblest beverage of the mildest power.
> Happy, with Love, to solace every care,
> Happy with sense and wit an hour to share;
> These to the mind a thousand pleasures bring
> And give to winter's frosts the smiles of spring.

These virtues appear also in Freneau's works: they show wit and sense, and feeling.

—Mary Weatherspoon Bowden

FRERE, John Hookham. English. Born in London, 21 May 1769. Educated at Eton College, where he met his life-long friend, George Canning, 1785–89 (Founder/Editor, with Canning and others, *The Microcosm*, 1786–87); Caius College, Cambridge, 1789–92 (Members Prize for Latin Essay, 1792), B.A. 1792, M.A. 1795. Married Elizabeth Jemima Blake, widow of the Earl of Errol, 1816 (died, 1831). Fellow, Caius College, Cambridge, 1793–1816; entered the British Foreign Office as a Clerk, 1795; Member of Parliament for West Looe, Cornwall, 1796–1802, and Under-Secretary of State in the Foreign Office, 1799; contributor, with Canning and others, to *The Anti-Jacobin; or, The Weekly Observer*, 1797–98; British Envoy to Portugal, 1800–02; Ambassador to Spain, 1802–04; Privy Councillor, 1805; Minister to the Junta in Spain, during the invasion of Napoleon, 1808–09. Succeeded to the family estates, 1807. Retired to Malta, 1818. *Died 7 January 1846.*

Collections

Works in Verse and Prose.   2 vols., 1872; edited by W. E. Frere, 3 vols., 1874.

Verse

The Anti-Jacobin (verse selections), with others, edited by W. Gifford.   2 vols., 1799;
   The Poetry of the Anti-Jacobin, edited by L. Rice-Oxley, 1924.
Prospectus and Specimen of an Intended National Work Relating to King Arthur.   2
   vols., 1817–18; as *The Monks and the Giants,* 1818; edited by R. D. Waller, 1926.
Fables for Five-Year-Olds.   1830.
Psalms.   1839(?).
Parodies and Other Burlesque Pieces, with George Canning and George Ellis, edited by
   H. Morley.   1890.

Other

The Microcosm, with others.   1788.
Theognis Restitutus: The Personal History of the Poet, with a Translated Section.   1842;
   as *The Works of Theognis,* 1856.

Translator, *The Frogs,* by Aristophanes.   1839.
Translator, *The Acharnians, The Knights, and the Birds,* by Aristophanes.   1840.

Reading List: *Frere and His Friends* by Gabrielle Festing, 1899; *Frere: Sein Leben und Seine
Werke, Sein Einfluss auf Byron* by A. von Eichler, 1905.

*   *   *

John Hookham Frere came of a Norfolk landowning family which contributed a number
of able men to public life. His own career in politics and diplomacy was distinguished, though
it came to a rather sudden end in 1809. Writing was a pastime, but one in which he showed
outstanding talent. It was at Eton, in close friendship with George Canning, that he began to
display his gifts as a humorous writer, in *The Microcosm,* a remarkably sophisticated weekly
periodical. Canning's contributions at this stage were more brilliant than Frere's, just as he
was later to outshine him in the world of affairs.
   The two joined forces again in 1797 when Canning, by that time Under-Secretary of State
at the Foreign Office, initiated *The Anti-Jacobin; or, The Weekly Examiner.* This directed its
attack against what the Tory wits saw as dangerous absurdities in both political thinking and
contemporary literary practice. It is now remembered chiefly for its verse, which has been
collected and republished more than once. "The Friend of Humanity and the Needy Knife-
grinder" ridicules simultaneously the politico-moral indignation and the halting Sapphics of
Southey. Godwin was repeatedly pilloried as Mr. Higgins of St. Mary Axe, a philanthropist
who hoped by didactic poems to spread his belief in universal benevolence and the
sovereignty of Reason. "The Progress of Man" and "The Loves of the Triangles," with their
pedestrian critical apparatus, are hilarious parodies of Godwin's ideas and Erasmus Darwin's
verse. Contemporary German drama is also caricatured in "The Rovers," a fragment in
which Frere's vein of high-spirited nonsense is reminiscent of Sheridan's in *The Critic.*

Twenty years later, when Frere's early retirement left him plenty of leisure for literary pursuits, he published *The Monks and the Giants*. He was an excellent linguist, and made some lively translations of Aristophanes; but this *ottava rima* poem sprang from his enjoyment of Pulci's racy *Morgante Maggiore*. Reading the Renaissance Florentine poet, Frere conceived the idea of treating an Arthurian theme in a deliberately homespun and comic way. The narrative purports to be the work of the brothers Whistlecraft, harness-makers of Stowmarket. It is a splendid piece of learned foolery, mildly satirical, in which off-hand colloquial diction is effortlessly combined with an elaborate stanza form. Byron was so delighted by the first two cantos, that he at once set about writing *Beppo*, "in or after the excellent manner of Mr. Whistlecraft (whom I take to be Frere)" as he wrote to John Murray, Frere's publisher as well as his own. Frere could hardly believe that the anonymous *Beppo* (1818) could be by the Romantic author of *Childe Harold*. When convinced by Murray, he commented "Lord Byron has paid me a compliment indeed." It is not too much to say that *Don Juan* also is considerably indebted to the Whistlecraft model. The resourcefulness of Frere's rhyming, his easy handling of dialogue, above all his confidential, button-holing manner, helped to set Byron on the road to his most brilliant achievements in comic narrative and satire.

—Margaret Bottrall

FROST, Robert (Lee).   American.   Born in San Francisco, California, 26 March 1874. Educated at Lawrence, Massachusetts, High School, graduated 1892; Dartmouth College, Hanover, New Hampshire, 1892; Harvard University, Cambridge, Massachusetts, 1897–99. Married Elinor Miriam White in 1895; one son, three daughters. Mill worker and teacher, Lawrence, 1892–97; farmer, Derry, New Hampshire, 1900–12; English Teacher, Pinkerton Academy, Derry, 1905–11; conducted course in psychology, State Normal School, Plymouth, New Hampshire, 1911–12; sold the farm, and lived in England, 1912–15; returned to America and settled on a farm near Franconia, New Hampshire, 1915; Poet-in-Residence, Amherst College, Massachusetts, 1916–20; subsequently Visiting Lecturer at Wesleyan University, Middletown, Connecticut; University of Michigan, Ann Arbor, 1921–23, 1925–26; Dartmouth College; Yale University, New Haven, Connecticut; and Harvard University. A Founder, Bread Loaf School, Middlebury College, Vermont, 1920. Poetry Consultant to the Library of Congress, Washington, D.C., 1958. Recipient: Pulitzer Prize, 1924, 1931, 1937, 1943; New England Poetry Club Golden Rose, 1928; Loines Award, 1931; American Academy of Arts and Letters Gold Medal, 1939; Academy of American Poets Fellowship, 1953; Sarah Josepha Hale Award, 1956; Emerson-Thoreau Medal, 1959; U.S. Senate Citation of Honor, 1960; Poetry Society of America Gold Medal, 1962; MacDowell Medal, 1962; Bollingen Prize, 1963. Litt.D.: Cambridge University, 1957; D.Litt.: Oxford University, 1957. Member, American Academy of Arts and Letters. *Died 29 January 1963.*

PUBLICATIONS

Collections

   The Poetry, edited by Edward Connery Lathem.   1969.
   Selected Letters, edited by Lawrance Thompson.   1964.
   Selected Prose, edited by Hyde Cox and Edward Connery Lathem.   1966.

Verse

Twilight. 1894.
A Boy's Will. 1913.
North of Boston. 1914.
Mountain Interval. 1916.
Selected Poems. 1923.
New Hampshire: A Poem with Notes and Grace Notes. 1923.
West-Running Brook. 1928.
The Lovely Shall Be Choosers. 1929.
Collected Poems. 1930; revised edition, 1939.
The Lone Striker. 1933.
Three Poems. 1935.
The Gold Hesperides. 1935.
From Snow to Snow. 1936.
A Further Range. 1936.
Selected Poems. 1936.
A Considerable Speck. 1939.
A Witness Tree. 1942.
Come In and Other Poems, edited by Louis Untermeyer.   1943; revised edition, as *The Road Not Taken,* 1951.
A Masque of Reason. 1945.
The Courage to Be New. 1946.
Poems. 1946.
Steeple Bush. 1947.
A Masque of Mercy. 1947.
Complete Poems. 1949.
Hard Not to Be King. 1951.
Aforesaid. 1954.
Selected Poems. 1955.
Dedication: The Gift Outright. 1961.
In the Clearing. 1962.
One Favored Acorn. 1969.

Plays

A Way Out (produced 1919?). 1929.
The Cow's in the Corn. 1929.

Other

Two Letters. 1931.
Frost and John Bartlett: The Record of a Friendship, edited by Margaret Bartlett Anderson. 1963.
Letters to Louis Untermeyer. 1963.
Frost: Farm-Poultryman, edited by Edward Connery Lathem and Lawrance Thompson. 1963.
Frost: Life and Talks-Walking, edited by Louis Mertins. 1965.
Frost and the Lawrence, Massachusetts "High School Bulletin": The Beginning of a Literary Career, edited by Edward Connery Lathem and Lawrance Thompson. 1966.
Interviews with Frost, edited by Edward Connery Lathem. 1967.

Family Letters of Robert and Elinor Frost, edited by Arnold Grade.   1972.
Frost on Writing, edited by Elaine Barry.   1973.
A Time to Talk, edited by Robert Francis.   1973.

Bibliography: A Descriptive Catalogue of Books and Manuscripts in the Clifton Waller Barrett Library, University of Virginia by Joan St. C. Crane, 1974; The Critical Reception of Frost: An Annotated Bibliography of Secondary Comment by Peter VanEgmond, 1974.

Reading List: Frost: A Collection of Critical Essays edited by James M. Cox, 1962; An Introduction to Frost by Elizabeth Isaacs, 1962; The Major Themes of Frost by Radcliffe Squires, 1963; The Poetry of Frost: Constellations of Intention by Reuben Brower, 1963; Frost by Elizabeth Jennings, 1964; Frost by James Doyle, 1965; Frost by Philip L. Gerber, 1966; Frost: The Early Years, 1966, The Years of Triumph, 1970, and The Later Years, 1977, by Lawrance Thompson and R. H. Winnick; Frost by Elaine Barry, 1973; Frost: The Work of Knowing by Richard Poirier, 1977.

*   *   *

In 1959, at a dinner celebrating Robert Frost's eighty-fifth birthday, Lionel Trilling gave an after-dinner address that was later incorporated in "A Speech on Robert Frost: A Cultural Episode." Trilling announced his antipathy for those poems by Frost which expressed a "distaste for the life of the city" and for "the demand that is made upon intellect to deal with whatever are the causes of complexity, uncertainty, anxiety." Then Trilling specified poems he did admire, poems that led him to define Frost as a "terrifying poet" who depicted a "terrifying universe." The speech confused Frost (who was not sure whether he had been attacked or praised), outraged many of his friends, and caused quite a furor.

It would seem ludicrous that as late as at the time of Frost's eighty-fifth birthday there could be so much confusion concerning what constituted Frost's basic point of view. Yet several factors make this situation plausible. For one thing, although such critics as John Crowe Ransom and Randall Jarrell praised Frost's poetry, his work gained comparatively little critical attention in the decades when the practitioners of the New Criticism reigned supreme. Further complications were caused by many of the critics who did laud his work. These admirers touted precisely the glib, sentimental, shallow poems by Frost that Trilling disliked. The main source of the confusion, however, was Robert Frost himself. Because Frost hungered so insatiably for popularity and esteem, he meticulously created a "folksy" public image of himself that his audiences would be entranced by. He never read any of his somber poems in public. He saw to it that his unattractive traits – his obsessive need to win at everything, his violent temper, his delight in back-biting, his race prejudices – remained totally unknown to the public. With equal skill, he hid his family misfortunes – his sister's insanity, his severe marital problems, his son's suicide, a daughter's insanity.

It is no wonder, then, that although Frost began writing in the late 1800's, we are still only beginning to formulate an intelligent evaluation of his poetry. Yet, despite all the obfuscations, such an evaluation is well worth pursuing, for Frost's best poems – and there are many of them – are of a very high quality. Frost was a consummate craftsman. He mastered a variety of forms; he wrote excellent sonnets, heroic couplets, and blank verse poems. His rime patterns are deftly wrought. He was even more adroit in matters of meter and rhythm. He proved repeatedly that there is no reason to believe that traditional rhythmical patterns inevitably lead to monotony.

What ultimately makes Frost's best poems valuable, however, is their dynamic view of our daily life. Frost believed that we live in a God-directed universe, but despite all his religious meditations Frost found God's ways absolutely inscrutable. At his most grim, as represented in "Design," Frost not only acknowledges the presence of the appalling in physical reality, but wonders if there is any cosmic design at all. It is certain in any case, as "Nothing Gold

Can Stay" states, that no purity can abide in physical reality. What is pure is almost immediately contaminated. Nature is lovely at times, yet its very loveliness can prove fatally alluring, as the speaker in "Stopping by Woods on a Snowy Evening" testifies. Nor can we imitate the animal world and rely on our instincts; "The White-Tailed Hornet" reports that nature's creatures, acting on pure instinct, often blunder ridiculously.

Man experiences no clarifying visions. "The Fear" insists that we live surrounded by a literal and metaphorical darkness which harbors the hostile and the terrifyingly ambiguous. Weariness and loneliness define the archetypal human being who narrates "Acquainted with the Night." Isolation and poverty can crush a person physically, mentally, and spiritually, as they do characters in "A Servant to Servants" and "The Hill Wife." Moreover, man is badgered by his suppressed desires – the point of "The Sound of the Trees." Yet "The Flood" states that man cannot always control his destructive urges.

Frost also makes it clear that people cannot easily offer each other solace. The difficulty of understanding another human being is sometimes insurmountable. In "Home Burial," a husband and wife attempt to cope with the death of their child in two different ways. Neither can understand the other's attitude or behavior; neither can in any way help the other.

In his recent essay " 'The Death of the Hired Man': Modernism and Transcendence," Warren French pinpoints why Frost's poetry is especially valuable today. French remarks that, aware of modern man's grim situation, Frost – unlike the pre-Modernists – did not proclaim the need for every individual to retreat at all costs to the safety of society; nor did Frost adopt or advocate the lifestyle lauded by Modernist writers – the deliberate withdrawal on the part of the individual from society. Instead, Frost concentrated on what marks him – in French's term – as a "post-Modernist." He struggled to discover what positive course is possible for a man who wants to maintain his individuality without exiling himself from society.

The affirmative albeit starkly limited goal Frost strove for and suggested to others is best indicated by his statement that his poems offer "a momentary stay against confusion." A series of momentary stays, created by the individual, is all man can hope for. As Lawrance Thompson wrote in his introduction to Frost's *Selected Letters*, Frost "bluntly rejected all the conventional stays which dogmatists call permanent"; they are too inflexible to contend successfully with physical reality's ever-shifting conditions. Frost was equally uninterested in trying to transcend the physical – material – world. He thought that the label "materialist" was used too quickly as a pejorative term. He said that it was "wrong to call anybody a materialist simply because he tried to say spirit in terms of matter, as if that were a sin." Nor did Frost fall back on the Romantic belief that man is basically good. He spurned the view that because man and nature are God's creations, they can do no wrong.

According to Frost, in order to achieve a momentary stay against confusion the first thing man needs is courage. A character in *A Masque of Mercy* says, "The saddest thing in life/Is that the best thing in it should be courage." Man must also try to maintain his equilibrium. Again and again, as in "The Vantage Point," "Goodbye and Keep Cold," and "To Earthward," Frost underscores the need to have the right perspective on all things, including oneself. Men should focus on the facts – and not daydream. In "Mowing," he declares that "The fact is the sweetest dream that labor knows." "Labor" is another key word. In "Two Tramps in Mud Time," he states that we should work and that our work should be motivated simultaneously by "love" and "need."

In some ways, nature can be supportive. "The Onset" and "The Need of Being Versed in Country Things" remind us that many things on earth are cyclical; this means that although evil comes to us, it will not last. So, too, nature is a revitalizing force, and sometimes awesomely beautiful, as described in "Iris by Night." It can also startle us out of a black mood created by too much self-centeredness – the development recorded in "Dust of Snow." It should also be remembered, as "Our Hold on the Planet" points out, that nature is at least "one fraction of one per cent" in "favor of man" – otherwise we would never have been able to thrive on earth.

Finally, Frost specifically advises us to preserve our individual integrity, but to link ourselves to society. Frost's emphasis on the value of society (often symbolized by the home) is coupled with his emphasis on the value of love. Love can be tenderly lyrical, as described in "Meeting and Passing." "Putting In the Seed" proclaims that love can be dynamically fertile. Love can alter reality – the point in "Never Again Would Birds' Song Be the Same." Love, breeding forgiveness and acceptance, provides a home against adversity. This is what Mary, in "The Death of the Hired Man," knows to be so, and what her husband Warren comes to realize. They decide to nurse Silas, their old hired man, but also to allow him his self-respect. Perhaps the finest example of Frost's stress on the importance of a viable balance between the individual and society is "The Silken Tent." Here, the woman described is a vibrant individual, yet held – willingly – by "countless ties of love and thought/To everything on earth."

—Robert K. Johnson

FULLER, Roy (Broadbent).   English.   Born in Failsworth, Lancashire, 11 February 1912. Educated at Blackpool High School; qualified as a solicitor, 1933. Served in the Royal Navy as a radar mechanic in East Africa, 1941–43, and as a Lieutenant with the Royal Naval Volunteer Reserve at the Admiralty, London, 1944–46. Married Kathleen Smith in 1936; one son, the poet John Fuller. Assistant Solicitor, 1938–58, Solicitor, 1958–69, and since 1969 Director, Woolwich Equitable Building Society, London. Chairman of the Legal Advisory Panel, 1958–69, and since 1969 Vice-President, Building Societies Association. Chairman, Poetry Book Society, 1960–68; Professor of Poetry, Oxford University, 1968–73; Chairman, Arts Council, 1976–77. Since 1972, Governor of the BBC. Recipient: Arts Council Poetry Award, 1959; Duff Cooper Memorial Prize, 1968; Queen's Gold Medal for Poetry, 1970. Fellow, Royal Society of Literature, 1958. C.B.E. (Commander, Order of the British Empire), 1970. Lives in London.

PUBLICATIONS

Verse

   Poems.   1939.
   The Middle of a War.   1942.
   A Lost Season.   1944.
   Epitaphs and Occasions.   1949.
   Counterparts.   1954.
   Brutus's Orchard.   1957.
   Collected Poems, 1936–1961.   1962.
   Buff.   1965.
   New Poems.   1968.
   Off Course.   1969.
   Tiny Tears.   1973.
   An Old War.   1974.
   Waiting for the Barbarians.   1974.
   From the Joke Shop.   1975.
   The Joke Shop Annexe.   1975.
   An Ill-Governed Coast.   1976.

Fiction

> *The Second Curtain.*   1953.
> *Fantasy and Fugue.*   1954.
> *Image of a Society.*   1956.
> *The Ruined Boys.*   1959; as *That Distant Afternoon,* 1959.
> *The Father's Comedy.*   1961.
> *The Perfect Fool.*   1963.
> *My Child, My Sister.*   1965.
> *The Carnal Island.*   1970.

Other

> *Savage Gold* (juvenile).   1946.
> *With My Little Eye* (juvenile).   1948.
> Catspaw (juvenile).   1966
> *Owls and Artificers: Oxford Lectures on Poetry.*   1971.
> *Seen Grandpa Lately?* (juvenile).   1972.
> *Professors and Gods: Last Oxford Lectures on Poetry.*   1973.
> *Poor Roy* (juvenile).   1977.

> Editor, *Byron for Today.*   1948.
> Editor, with Clifford Dyment and Montagu Slater, *New Poems 1952.*   1952.
> Editor, *Supplement of New Poetry.*   1964.

Reading List: "The Novels of Fuller" by F. McGuinness, in *London Magazine 3,* 1963; "Private Images of Public Ills: The Poetry of Fuller" by George Woodcock, in *Wascana Review 4,* 1969.

*   *   *

Roy Fuller has consistently striven in his poetry to be intelligent, skilful, and disciplined, which, he persistently maintains in his criticism, many popularly acclaimed artists in contemporary culture are not. He has often been categorised, in consequence, as an opponent of innovation and a supporter of the literary "status quo." His political sympathies, however, have always been with the need for social change. The desire to re-order society is to be seen most clearly in his earliest verse, though even in these poems he does not deal with specific political events or issues. His concern in all his poetry is with the pains and anxieties of the human condition. The war poems, for instance, concentrate not on the global disasters or on individual death and pain, but on the fears, loneliness, and boredom of the ordinary man, isolated by war from loved ones. As the end of the war approaches these individual anxieties re-assert their importance in life – "the permanent and real/Furies are settling in upstairs" ("During a Bombardment by V-Weapons"). Nevertheless, a constant theme in his poetry has been forebodings of the imminent collapse of civilisation, frequently seen as analogous to the fall of the Roman Empire and the ensuing "dark ages," and closely linked with autumnal images and references to the frailty of the human body. Another major preoccupation is the purpose of art and its relation to reality. The poet must continually endeavour to speak relevantly of the times he lives in and to represent reality faithfully, so that "the crude/World and my words marry like a joint" ("Dialogue of the Poet and His Talent"). He is constantly aware, however, of how words fail "to make/a world parallel to blind creation/and replace that with its order" ("Homage to Balthus"). Art, particularly by seductive and sensuous images, distorts and falsifies reality.

The sensuous phrase is not frequent in Fuller's poetry; as he himself says, his verse is "a muted, sparse accompaniment" ("Dedicatory Epistle") to our times. The tone of the poems is meditative and serious, sometimes ironical and self-deprecating ("Chinoiserie"). They often begin with a carefully detailed observation of an object, which provides the starting-point for the poet's thoughts, and in recent years he has frequently interwoven several strands of thought, allowing the separate ideas to resonate and sometimes coalesce, as in "Reading *The Bostonians*." This poem is also the earliest example of his use of syllabic verse, which, he feels, has allowed him to write with greater freedom. The poems since the mid-1950's have become more direct and forceful in style, and have shed much of the early influence of Auden, but his characteristic manner has remained essentially restrained and thoughtful.

This is equally true of Fuller's novels. After two "novels of pursuit" he explored, in *Image of a Society*, the inter-relationship of the social and the personal. While not abandoning this theme entirely, later novels, notably his finest achievement, *My Child, My Sister*, have focussed more directly on the individual consciousness.

—David Astle

GARTH, Sir Samuel. English. Born in Bowland Forest, Yorkshire, in 1661. Educated at Peterhouse, Cambridge, B.A. 1679, M.A. 1684, M.D. 1691; also studied medicine in Leyden, 1687; Fellow of the Royal College of Physicians, 1693. Married Martha Beaufoy (died, 1717); one daughter. Practised as a physician in London from 1693 until the end of his life: delivered the Gulstonian lecture, 1694, Harveian oration, 1697, and the funeral oration for Dryden, 1700, at the Royal College of Physicians, London; member of the Kit-Cat Club, London, 1702; knighted and appointed Physician-in-Ordinary to King George I and Physician-General to the Army, 1714. *Died 18 January 1719.*

PUBLICATIONS

Collections

   Works, edited by A. Chalmers.   1810.

Verse

   The Dispensary.   1699; revised edition, 1700, 1706; edited by F. H. Ellis, in *Poems on Affairs of State 6,* 1971.
   A Poem to the Earl of Godolphin.   1710.
   Claremont.   1715.

Other

   Translator, with others, *Ovid's Metamorphoses.*   1717.

Reading List: *Garth und Seine Stellung zum Komischen Epos* by T. Schenk, 1900.

*   *   *

The Dispensary is the only poem of Sir Samuel Garth's we now remember. This mock-heroic account of the squabble between the College of Physicians and the apothecaries over the charitable dispensing of medicines to the poor of London was written by Garth (a member of the College) "to rally some of our disaffected members into a sense of their duty." The poem influenced Pope's *Rape of the Lock,* but it is wrong to remember *The Dispensary* only for this.

   Garth has dexterity with words and a robust wit: he lacks the exquisite tact with which Pope can juxtapose the trivial and the serious, or the sustained grandiloquence with which Dryden annihilates his adversaries. Garth's Whiggish insistence on flattery of William III can also be tedious, and his personal involvement in the quarrel makes the dispassionate rallying tone difficult to sustain; nevertheless, his rumbustious fun deserves to be better known, offering an English counterpart to Boileau's *Le Lutrin,* with which *The Dispensary* has affinities. Lee, the warden of Apothecaries Hall, is thus described:

> In trifling show his tinsel talent lies;
> And form the want of intellect supplies....
> Hourly his learn'd impertinence affords
> A barren superfluity of words;
> The patient's ears remorseless he assails,
> Murders with jargon where his medicine fails.

Garth's own lazy colleagues are epigramatised: "Each faculty in blandishment they lull/ Aspiring to be venerably dull." The action of the poem includes mock-heroic debates, visions, a battle, a descent to the underworld – all garnished with solemn epic similes. Garth was probably the first Englishman to employ all of these devices in one satirical-comic poem. Here he describes the rumpus at its height:

> Whole heaps of warriors welter on the ground,
> With gally-pots and broken phials crowned;
> Whilst empty jars the dire defeat resound.
> Thus when some storm its crystal quarry rends,
> And Jove in rattling showers of ice descends;
> Mount Athos shakes the forests on his brow,
> Whilst down his wounded sides fresh torrents flow,
> And leaves and limbs of trees o'erspread the vale below.

This is predictable, if nicely contrived. Less expected is Garth's sense of wonderment at Nature:

> Eternal Spring with smiling verdure here
> Warms the mild air, and crowns the youthful year.
> The vine undress'd her swelling clusters bears,
> The labouring hind the mellow olive cheers;
> Blossoms and fruit at once the citron shews,
> And, as she pays, discovers still she owes.
> The orange to her sun her pride displays,
> And gilds her fragrant apples with his rays.

A similar view runs through *Claremont*, Garth's pastoral panygyric based on Denham's *Cooper's Hill*, where it is accompanied by some shrewd social commentary. This poem never gained the popularity which *The Dispensary* rightly achieved in Garth's lifetime. It is a loss to modern readers that the responses required in the reading of mock-heroic are no longer readily accessible.

—T. Bareham

GASCOIGNE, George.   English.   Born in Cardington, Bedfordshire, in 1539. Educated at Trinity College, Cambridge, left without a degree; Middle Temple, London; Gray's Inn, London. Married Elizabeth Breton c. 1566; stepson, the poet Nicholas Breton, *q.v.* Soldier and courtier: Member of Parliament for Bedford, 1557–59; travelled in England and France, 1563–64; imprisoned for debt, 1571; elected Member of Parliament for Midhurst, 1572, but protests of his creditors caused him to flee to the Continent: served as Captain under William, Prince of Orange, in the Low Countries, 1572–75; returned to London and settled at Walthamstow; visited Kenilworth with Queen Elizabeth and Leicester, 1575. *Died 7 October 1577.*

PUBLICATIONS

Collections

Complete Works, edited by J. W. Cunliffe. 2 vols., 1907–10.

Verse

A Hundred Sundry Flowers, Bound Up in One Small Posie. 1573; as *The Posies*, 1575; edited by Charles T. Prouty, 1942.
A Delicate Diet for Daintymouthed Drunkards. 1576.
The Drum of Doomsday. 1576.
The Steel Glass: A Satire. 1576; edited by William L. Wallace, 1975.

Plays

Supposes, from a play by Ariosto (produced 1566). In *A Hundred Sundry Flowers*, 1573; edited by F. S. Boas, in *Five Pre-Shakespearean Comedies*, 1934.
Jocasta, with Francis Kinwelmershe (produced 1566). In *A Hundred Sundry Flowers*, 1573; edited by J. W. Cunliffe, 1906.
A Device of a Masque for Viscount Montacute (produced 1572). In *A Hundred Sundry Flowers*, 1573.
The Glass of Government (produced 1575?). 1575; edited by J. S. Farmer, 1914.
The Princely Pleasures at the Court at Kenilworth (produced 1575). 1821.
The Pleasant Tale of Hemetes the Hermit (produced 1575). In *A Paradox Proving Baldness Better Than Bushy Hair*, by Synecius, 1579.

Fiction

A Pleasant Discourse of the Adventures of Master F. J., in *A Hundred Sundry Flowers*. 1573; edited by E. M. Moseley, in *Elizabethan Prose Fiction*, 1968.

Other

The Spoil of Antwerp. 1576(?).
The Whole Art of Venery or Hunting. 1611.

Editor, *A Discourse for a Discovery of a New Passage to Cataia*, by Humphrey Gilbert. 1576.

Reading List: *Gascoigne, Elizabethan Courtier, Soldier, and Poet* by Charles T. Prouty, 1942; *Gascoigne* by Ronald C. Johnson, 1972.

*   *   *

The main problem facing the modern reader of George Gascoigne is how to reconcile the lighthearted, erotic, courtly verse of "the Green Knight" (as he called himself in youth) with the grimly moralistic sermonising of the older man. The differences in themes, style, and attitude between his early productions and the works that he published in 1576 are so marked that at first it is hard to believe that they all emanate from the same pen.

The *Posies* contains most of Gascoigne's lyrical poetry. The first set (subtitled "Flowers") is composed largely of occasional amatory verse ("The Passions of a lover," "The lamentations of a lover," etc.), written in conventional mid-century manner after the style of Surrey and Vaux: "Amid my Bale I bath in blisse,/I swim in heaven, I sinke in hell." Sometimes a more satirical note is heard: in "*Sat cito, si sat bene*" he casts a critical eye on the beguiling lures of the "glistring Courte" and openly admits the fascination it has exercised upon his youthful mind, concluding, however, that in the long run "the gaines doth seldome quitte the charge." Also noteworthy is the plain, down-to-earth, proverbial style of "*Magnum vectigal parcimonia*." But on the whole it is difficult to justify Gascoigne's defence of his "Flowers" as exhibiting "rare invention and Methode before not commonly used" (Introductory Epistle to the Yong Gentlemen). The "Hearbes" follow much the same lines, though a trifle more moralistic in tone, while the "Weedes" consist of a series of complaints against fortune who smiled on him in his youth but now seems totally to have deserted him, leaving him "in prison pent,/ My gaines possessed by my foes, my friends against me bent." (Gascoigne was imprisoned for debt in 1571). Notable is "The Greene Knights farewell to Fansie" wherein he surveys his days amid the "glosse of gorgeous courtes," recollecting how he "liked sometimes well" to "lie along in Ladies lappes, to lispe and make it nice," but determining now, since it has proved to be all vanity, to bid a firm farewell to the fancies of the soldier and the courtier and seek instead the "comfort of Philosophie." It's an appealing poem − direct, frank, and unaffected. Indeed the most attractive quality of many of these early poems is their fresh, spontaneous tone: in "The Arraignment of a Lover," for example, Gascoigne manages successfully to combine a law-court allegory with a nicely balanced strain of self-directed irony.

It is a far cry from this to the morbid predictions of *The Droome of Doomes day* (with its woodcuts depicting the tortures of the damned in hell) or the thundering denunciations of *A delicate Diet, for daintiemouthde Droonkardes*. If we can safely ignore such obsessive ranting, there remains one later work well worthy our attention. This is Gascoigne's blank-verse satire *The Steele Glas*. The glass in question is not a crystal one that will reflect only the more pleasing side of life, but a mirror of steel to illuminate faults and vices − a satirical instrument to reaffirm the moral value of poetry in the face of its prevalent degeneration to mere courtly amusement. After a rueful glance in the mirror at his *own* failings, Gascoigne turns to survey the corruptions of the world. Desire for "glittring gold" lies at the root of the problem; and we are presented with a cogent and realistic picture of the decay of the countryside as all who can flock to town and court in pursuit of riches, the means to enjoy "A loytring life, and like an Epicure." All sectors of society are affected: soldiers, the defenders of the realm, have become drunken, lecherous boasters, despoilers, idlers, who set a dangerously bad example to honest craftsmen and ploughmen. Merchants and lawyers are no better.

The conclusion of the work is a tour de force: Gascoigne summons up a vision of the truly virtuous priests of the Church Militant whom he sets praying for all institutions and ranks of the realm, culminating with a celebration of the common people in the person of their representative, Peerce Plowman, the epitome of honest labour: "Behold him (priests) & though he stink of sweat/Disdaine him not: for shal I tel you what?/Such clime to heaven, before the shaven crownes." The poem ends with a Utopian vision of all trades engaged in virtuous toil and all things "ordred as they ought." Only then can the priest make holiday and the satirist lay down his pen.

Why do we find in Gascoigne this dramatic change from lyricist to moralist? It is tempting to say, as Gascoigne himself does, that age brings wisdom and with it the desire to "make amendes for the lost time which I misbetowed in wryting so wantonlie." But this is not enough to account for the obsessive quality of much of Gascoigne's later writing with its stress on the filthiness of the body, the futility of worldly ambitions, and the horrendous torments that await the sinner. These discourses are clearly allied to the Puritan tracts of men like Gosson and Stubbes, and it would not be amiss to see in the creative career of George

Gascoigne a microcosm of the poetic problems of his age: there is a genuine erotic-lyrical impulse trying to find expression only to be stifled by the stern, anti-hedonistic weight of Puritan repression. Of the later works, only *The Steele Glas* successfully united the fervour of the moralist with the aesthetic claims of the poet; and of the earlier Gascoigne we are satisfied to discern in a few poems the seeds of the much greater lyrical achievement of later celebrated soldier-courtier-poets such as Sidney and Ralegh.

—A. W. Lyle

GASCOYNE, David (Emery).   English.   Born in Harrow, Middlesex, 10 October 1916. Educated at Salisbury Cathedral Choir School; Regent Street Polytechnic, London. Lived in France, 1937–39, 1954–65. Recipient: Rockefeller-Atlantic Award, 1949. Fellow, Royal Society of Literature, 1951. Lives on the Isle of Wight.

PUBLICATIONS

Verse

   Roman Balcony and Other Poems.   1932.
   Man's Life Is This Meat.   1936.
   Hölderlin's Madness.   1938.
   Poems 1937–1942.   1943.
   A Vagrant and Other Poems.   1950.
   Night Thoughts.   1956.
   Collected Poems, edited by Robin Skelton.   1965.
   The Sun at Midnight: Notes on the Story of Civilisation Seen as the History of the Great Experimental Work of the Supreme Scientist.   1970.
   Collected Verse Translations, edited by Robin Skelton and Alan Clodd.   1970.
   Three Poems.   1976.

Play

   The Hole in the Fourth Wall; or, Talk, Talk, Talk (produced 1950).

Fiction*

   Opening Day.   1933.

403

Other

A Short Survey of Surrealism.   1935.
Thomas Carlyle.   1952.

Editor, *Outlaw of the Lowest Planet,* by Kenneth Patchen.   1946.

Translator, *Conquest of the Irrational,* by Salvador Dali.   1935.
Translator, with Humphrey Jennings, *A Bunch of Carrots: Twenty Poems,* by Benjamin
   Péret.   1936; revised edition, as *Remove Your Hat,* 1936.
Translator, *What Is Surrealism?,* by André Breton.   1936.

Bibliography: "Gascoyne: A Checklist" by A. Atkinson, in *Twentieth-Century Literature*
6, 1961.

Reading List: "A Voice in the Darkness" by Gavin Ewart, in *London Magazine,* November
1965; "Gascoyne and the Prophetic Role" by Kathleen Raine, in *Defending Ancient Springs,*
1967.

*   *   *

   While still in his teens, David Gascoyne published two books of poems, a novel, and a
critical work, *A Short Survey of Surrealism.* His own surrealist poems are, with some of
Dylan Thomas's early verse, almost the only good examples of their kind, but it was not until
the publication in 1943 of *Poems 1937–1942* that Gascoyne's remarkable talents came to
fruition. That volume, with illustrations designed by Graham Sutherland, explores themes of
guilt, anguish, and longing for spiritual certainty with unashamed eloquence. He moves
continually in a world filled with mysterious presences and mythical figures, nowhere more
effectively than in "Eve," whom he evokes in the closing lines of the poem:

> Insurgent, wounded and avenging one,
> In whose black sex
> Our ancient culpability like a pearl is set.

In that poem and in poems such as "Winter Garden," "The Fault," and the sequence
"Miserere," Gascoyne achieves an intensity and purity of utterance that he has never
surpassed and seldom equalled. In his next collection, *A Vagrant,* the eloquence trembles on
the verge of grandiloquence, the images are too often reminiscent of 19th-century
romanticism at its least happy; *Night Thoughts,* commissioned for radio, lapses into crude
rhetoric and over-emphasis.
   Gascoyne has always insisted on the sacred, prophetic nature of poetry, and has admired
those who strive to create what Carlyle called "an inspired Poesy and Faith for Man," a
quotation that Gascoyne makes use of in his essay on Carlyle. His *Collected Poems* contains
enough good poems to ensure that he will continue to be read with admiration by all who
respond to the visionary element in poetry, and one can only regret that he has remained
relatively silent since then.

—John Press

GAWAIN POET.

PUBLICATIONS

Collections

> *Manuscript* edited by I. Gollancz. 1923.
> *Complete Works of the Gawain Poet in a Modern English Version* by John Gardner. 1965.
> *Works,* edited by Charles Moorman. 1976.
> *Pearl, Patience, Cleanness, and Sir Gawain and the Green Knight,* edited by A. C. Cawley and J. J. Anderson. 1976.

Verse

> *Sir Gawain and the Green Knight,* edited by J. R. R. Tolkien and E. V. Gordon. 1925; revised by Norman Davis, 1967; edited by R. A. Waldron, 1970.
> *Pearl,* edited by E. V. Gordon. 1953.
> *Patience,* edited J. J. Anderson. 1969.
> *Cleanness,* edited by J. J. Anderson. 1977.

Reading List: *Sir Gawain and Pearl: Critical Essays* edited by Robert J. Blanch, 1966; *The Pearl-Poet* by Charles Moorman, 1968; *The Gawain-Poet: A Critical Study* by A. C. Spearing, 1970; *The Gawain-Poet* by Edward Wilson, 1977; *The Art of the Gawain-Poet* by W. A. Davenport, 1978.

*　　*　　*

The Gawain-Poet is the name usually given to the unknown author of *Sir Gawain and the Green Knight* and, by implication, of the three other poems, *Pearl, Patience* and *Cleanness* (sometimes called *Purity*), which appear with *Gawain* in the unique manuscript, British Library MS Cotton Nero A.X. The attribution of all four poems to the same poet (also called the Pearl-poet, *Pearl* being the first poem in the manuscript) is now generally accepted, if only for the sake of convenience. The strongest arguments for common authority are the striking parallels of theme, imagery, and style between the four poems. *St. Erkenwald,* which survives in a different manuscript, has often been attached to the group as a fifth poem from the same pen, but the evidence is not strong.

The four poems of Cotton Nero A.X. are the crowning achievement of the "Alliterative Revival" of the fourteenth century. This resurgence of writing in the traditional unrhymed alliterative measure has never been satisfactorily explained as a historical phenomenon, but it can certainly be associated primarily with the west and north-west of England, and perhaps with the noble households of that region. The language of the *Gawain*-poems has been localised in the region where Lancashire, Cheshire, and Derbyshire meet, and the composition of the poems has been ascribed to the last quarter of the fourteenth century. *Patience* and *Cleanness* are in the traditional form of the alliterative long line, while in *Gawain* the lines are grouped into "stanzas" of variable length (101 in all) by the insertion of five short rhymed lines ("the bob and wheel") at the end of groups of unrhymed long lines. *Pearl* is not written in the alliterative long line, but in complex 12-line stanzas (again 101 in all) based on a line of more conventional metrical (i.e. syllabic) form with heavy and regular alliteration.

Patience and *Cleanness* are cast in the form of homily based on biblical story: both recommend a virtue by portraying how God treats its opposite. In the former, the story of Jonah, through which the poet displays God's imperturbable patience contrasted with man's childish petulance and bad temper, offers full play to the poet's brilliant dramatic gifts. The human comedy of Jonah's evasions is exploited without prejudice to any of the story's moral and typological significance, while the language of dramatic realisation combines an unforgettable quality of visual imagination with an unrelaxing didactic purpose. No-one can forget the image of Jonah entering the whale's jaws "as mote in at a minster-door," but the image serves as a reminder too that Jonah's three-day sojourn in the whale's belly was a figure of Christ's entombment and therefore of the potentiality of resurrection. *Cleanness* is a longer, more loosely constructed poem, and illustrates God's punishment of three kinds of uncleanness – sexual promiscuity, sodomy, and sacrilege – in the stories of the Flood, the destruction of Sodom, and the fall of Belshazzar. Other biblical stories provide insets to these main narratives. The portrayal of God's anger often releases a fierce and terrifying power of imagination, but the remorseless moral certainty of the poem is fascinatingly combined with a cool and quizzical humanity which will for instance see the victims of God's wrath in touchingly human contexts ("Love looks to love, and his leave takes," as the Flood advances) or detect even a note of wryness in God's voice.

Pearl takes the form of a vision, in which the dreamer, lamenting the loss of his "pearl" (an infant daughter), is transported to a heavenly landscape where, across the river of death, he sees his daughter. She, now a Bride of Christ in the Heavenly City, instructs him in the ethics of grief and salvation. The dreamer's grief and bewilderment at his loss are treated with some poignancy, but the poet's main purpose is to show the nothingness of worldly concerns in the light of a transcendental understanding. To do this, he first draws us into the dreamer's grief and makes us emotionally aware of the need for solace, and then proceeds to show how every worldly attachment of the dreamer, every "natural" human expectation, must be transformed if true understanding is to be attained. The transformation is effected through delicate play with the fiction of a "dramatic" relationship between the dreamer and the Pearl-maiden (rather as with Dante and Beatrice), and perhaps most brilliantly through the metamorphosis of the pearl-image itself, from mutable object to very symbol of bridehood and communion with the Lamb. Every word and image in the poem, every speech and passage of description, is part of a consummate design to bring a transcendental and ultimately incommunicable truth within reach of the imagination.

Sir Gawain and the Green Knight differs from the other three poems in that it is not overtly didactic. It is a romance, and, on one level, quite simply the best romance that was ever written. It has a brave and noble hero, a fierce and mysterious other-worldly antagonist, a seductive temptress, and throughout an incomparable rendering of the splendour and gaiety of courtly life. Gawain braves all dangers, resists all temptations, and in the end returns to Arthur's court, the challenge of the Green Knight met and overcome. Yet a kind of ironic comedy flickers about the whole story, and the plot – in which Gawain fulfils the first public challenge, that of the beheading game, only to discover that his performance is to be assessed on the basis of another challenge, that of the bedroom temptations, which he thought was private – is a marvellous structure for reducing the paragon of romance-heroes to an almost comically bewildered state of self-justification and self-accusation. He has done all that a man could be expected to do, but he knows he should have done more. What is a romance-hero for, if not to attain the unattainable? In these scenes, the poet seems to be writing a sophisticated critique of romance, and to be questioning the possibility of a high secular idealism which combines chivalric with Christian values. Yet he does so, as always, without contempt, generous in a measured way towards man in his predicament and rich in his response to the vigour and beauty of life.

—Derek Pearsall

GAY, John.   English.   Born in Barnstaple, Devon, baptized 16 September 1685. Educated at the free grammar school in Barnstaple; apprenticed to a silk mercer in London. Secretary to the household of the Duchess of Monmouth, 1712–14; Secretary to the Earl of Clarendon on his diplomatic mission to Hanover, 1714; accompanied William Pulteney, later Earl of Bath, to Aix, 1717; lived at Lord Harcourt's estate in Oxfordshire, 1718; earned considerable income from publication of his collected poems, 1720, and made and lost a fortune in South Sea funds speculation; Commissioner for the Public Lottery, 1722–31; recovered much of his fortune from the success of the *Beggar's Opera*, 1728; lived with his patrons the Duke and Duchess of Queensberry, 1728–32. *Died 4 December 1732.*

PUBLICATIONS

Collections

>   *Poetical, Dramatic, and Miscellaneous Works.*   6 vols., 1795.
>   *Plays.*   2 vols., 1923.
>   *Poetical Works,* edited by G. C. Faber.   1926.
>   *Letters,* edited by Chester F. Burgess.   1966.
>   *Poetry and Prose,* edited by Vinton A. Dearing and Charles Beckwith.   2 vols., 1974.
>   *Selected Works,* edited by Samuel Joseloff.   1976.

Verse

>   *Wine.*   1708.
>   *Rural Sports.*   1713; revised edition, 1720; edited by O. Culbertson, 1930.
>   *The Fan.*   1714.
>   *The Shepherd's Week.*   1714.
>   *A Letter to a Lady.*   1714.
>   *Two Epistles, One to the Earl of Burlington, The Other to a Lady.*   1715(?).
>   *Trivia; or, The Art of Walking the Streets of London.*   1716.
>   *Horace, epode iv, Imitated.*   1717(?).
>   *The Poor Shepherd.*   1720(?).
>   *Poems on Several Occasions.*   2 vols., 1720.
>   *A Panegyrical Epistle to Mr. Thomas Snow.*   1721.
>   *An Epistle to Her Grace Henrietta Duchess of Marlborough.*   1722.
>   *A Poem Addressed to the Quidnunc's.*   1724.
>   *Blueskin's Ballad.*   1725.
>   *To a Lady on Her Passion for Old China.*   1725.
>   *Daphnis and Cloe.*   1725(?).
>   *Molly Mog.*   1726.
>   *Fables.*   2 vols., 1727–38; edited by Vinton A. Dearing, 1967.
>   *Some Unpublished Translations from Ariosto,* edited by J. D. Bruce.   1910.

Plays

>   *The Mohocks.*   1712.
>   *The Wife of Bath* (produced 1713).   1713; revised version (produced 1730), 1730.
>   *The What D'ye Call It* (produced 1715).   1715.
>   *Three Hours after Marriage,* with Pope and Arbuthnot (produced 1717).   1717; revised

version, in *Supplement to the Works of Pope,* 1757; 1717 edition edited by Richard
Morton and William Peterson, 1961.
Acis and Galatea, music by Handel (produced 1719).   1732.
Dione, in *Poems on Several Occasions.*   1720.
The Captives (produced 1724). 1724.
The Beggar's Opera (produced 1728).   1728; edited by Peter Lewis, 1973.
Polly, Being the 2nd Part of The Beggar's Opera (version revised by Colman the Elder
produced 1777).   1729; in *Poetical Works,* 1926.
Achilles (produced 1733).   1733.
The Distressed Wife (produced 1743).   1743; as *The Modern Wife* (produced 1771).
The Rehearsal at Goatham.   1754.

Other

The Present State of Wit.   1711.
*An Argument Proving That the Present Mohocks and Hawkubites Are the Gog and Magog
Mentioned in the Revelations.*   1712.

Bibliography: in *Poetical Works,* 1926; *Gay: An Annotated Checklist of Criticism* by Julie T.
Klein, 1973.

Reading List: *Gay, Favorite of the Wits* by William H. Irving, 1940; *Gay, Social Critic* by
Sven M. Armens, 1954; *Gay* by Oliver Warner, 1964; *Gay* by Patricia M. Spacks, 1965.

*   *   *

Although John Gay was one of the most talented English writers in the first third of the
eighteenth century, he is overshadowed by his two close friends and fellow-members of the
Scriblerus Club, Swift and Pope. Comparisons with the two literary giants of the period are
therefore inevitable and usually to Gay's detriment, which is unfortunate since his gifts are
significantly different from theirs. It is unfair to think of Gay as a lesser Swift or a lesser Pope.
Gay certainly lacks the emotional intensity, intellectual power, and penetrating insight of
Swift's great satires, and rarely equals Pope in refined verbal wit, imaginative inventiveness,
and incisive irony. The all-embracing cultural survey of *Gulliver's Travels* or even the moral
breadth of Pope's *Moral Essays* and *Imitations of Horace* were beyond Gay, as were the
gloomy visionary quality and sustained mock-heroic elaboration of *The Dunciad.* Gay's
mature work does not seem to stem from a firm ideological foundation of inter-connected
philosophical ideas, political convictions and moral values in the way that Swift's and Pope's
do. Nevertheless Swift and Pope are not the measure of all Augustan writers as they are
sometimes thought to be, and Gay, although influenced by his two friends, usually followed
his own creative impulses and did not attempt to do what they were doing. As a result he
acquired a distinctive literary voice, less relentless and angry than Swift's, less acerbic and
barbed than Pope's, more genial, warm-hearted and gentle than both. His satirical and
burlesque works, for example, are less single-minded than theirs, so that his ridicule is often
tempered with sentiment, producing a bitter-sweet amalgam that is very much Gay's own
and that is particularly evident in his masterpiece, *The Beggar's Opera.* Furthermore Gay,
with his less fixed intellectual commitment, was much more chameleon-like than his friends,
which helps to explain the extraordinary diversity of his output.

In addition to being a versatile poet, he was a fairly prolific playwright in both verse and
prose, and the only member of the Scriblerus Club to devote himself to drama. Indeed it is as
the author of *The Beggar's Opera* that he is best remembered today. As a dramatist he did not
restrict himself to the "regular" and neoclassically respectable genres of tragedy and comedy

but attempted most of the theatrical forms of the period; and with *The Beggar's Opera* he actually invented the ballad opera, which became very popular in the eighteenth century and is the precursor of English comic opera and of the modern musical, as well as being an important influence on Brecht. Gay began his dramatic career with a short farce, *The Mohocks*, and followed this with an undistinguished comedy based on Chaucer, *The Wife of Bath*, before turning his hand to two very different satirical plays. The popular *The What D'Ye Call It* is a fine burlesque of contemporary tragedy, especially "pathetic" plays, that succeeds in transcending burlesque, while the controversial *Three Hours after Marriage*, written as a Scriblerian enterprise with Pope and Arbuthnot, is a lively and frequently farcical dramatic satire attacking a number of well-known contemporary intellectuals and artists. Not long after this he provided Handel with a libretto for his pastoral opera *Acis and Galatea* and then made two not particularly successful attempts at tragedy, *Dione*, written in couplets and in a pastoral and sentimental vein, and *The Captives*, a blank-verse tragedy in a more heroic manner that ends happily with virtue rewarded and poetic justice established. Next came by far his greatest theatrical success, *The Beggar's Opera*, a truly original work of genius and one of the very few eighteenth-century plays to hold the stage until the present day. By using a mixture of speech and song and by providing his own words for well-known tunes, Gay created a new kind of music theatre, the ballad opera, while simultaneously burlesquing Italian opera, which was enjoying a vogue in England. In addition *The Beggar's Opera*, set in the London underworld, is a most unusual love-story, both romantic and anti-romantic, as well as a pungently ironic social and political satire. Amazingly enough, Gay was able to weld these diverse elements together into a unified work of art that manages to be both highly topical and universal. After the unprecedented commercial success of *The Beggar's Opera*, Gay wrote an inferior sequel, *Polly*, which was banned from the stage by the Government, offended by the scathing political ridicule of its predecessor. None of his three posthumous plays, *Achilles*, a farcical treatment of a classical legend in ballad-opera form, and the two satirical comedies, *The Distress'd Wife* and *The Rehearsal at Goatham*, adds much to his dramatic achievement.

The range and variety of his dramatic work is matched by that of his poetry, although the quality is again decidedly uneven. He wrote mock-heroic poetry, notably *The Fan*, which is indebted to *The Rape of the Lock*, an extended georgic in the manner of Virgil, *Rural Sports*, a group of pastoral poems, *The Shepherd's Week*, which burlesque Ambrose Philips's *Pastorals* yet are much more than burlesque; a long mock-georgic about London life, laced with acute social observations, guide-book advice and moral precepts, *Trivia; or, The Art of Walking the Streets of London*; a number of urbane verse *Epistles* to friends on various topics; a set of ironic *Eclogues*, mainly Town Eclogues about fashionable women and love; two series of *Fables* in the manner of Aesop and La Fontaine; various narrative poems, including bawdy tales inspired by Chaucer's *fabliaux*; a few meditative poems such as "A Contemplation on Night" (1714); some lyrics and ballads including the well-known "Sweet William's Farewell to Black-ey'd Susan" (1720); and translations of Ovid and Ariosto. Although much of his poetry is written in decasyllabic couplets, the standard form of the time, Gay is again more varied than many of his contemporaries since he uses the lighter and racier octosyllabic couplets for the *Fables* and some of the tales, blank verse for his early mock-heroic *Wine*, *ottava rima* for one of his best Epistles, "Mr. Pope's Welcome from Greece," and a variety of stanza forms for his songs and ballads. His finest poetic achievement is the first series of *Fables*, ostensibly written to entertain a young member of the Royal Family but, as in the case of earlier fable literature, having a much wider moral, social, and political significance than the apparently innocuous subject-matter suggests. Gay's *Fables* are not of the supreme quality of La Fontaine's but they remain the best examples of their kind in English since Henryson's admirable adaptations of Aesop into Middle Scots. *Trivia*, which has been claimed to be the finest poem about London in the language, is also a genuinely individual work revealing some of his best qualities: his observant eye for detail, his great sympathy for ordinary humanity, his down-to-earth good sense, his sturdy versification, and plain, unfussy diction. *The Shepherd's Week* is probably the most important Augustan contribution to the genre of pastoral. Much of Gay's work is now of interest only to the specialist, but in a few cases, notably the *Fables* and above all *The Beggar's Opera*, he transcends his own time and must therefore rank as a major Augustan writer.

—Peter Lewis

GHOSE, Manmohan. Indian. Born in Bhagalpore, 19 January 1869; lived in England from age 10. Educated at Manchester Grammar School; St. Paul's School, London; Christ Church, Oxford, 1887–90, B.A. 1890. Married Malati Bannerjee in 1898 (died, 1918), two daughters. Returned to India, 1894: taught at Patna and Dacca colleges; Professor of English, Presidency College, Calcutta, 1902–21. *Died 5 January 1924.*

PUBLICATIONS

Collections

    Selected Poems, edited by P. Lal.   1969.
    Selected Poems, edited by Lotika Ghose.   1974.

Verse

    Love-Songs and Elegies.   1898.
    Songs of Love and Death, edited by Laurence Binyon.   1926.

*   *   *

    Though Manmohan Ghose was born in India, he lived in England from the age of 10 until he was 25. English thus became his first language (Laurence Binyon says that when he returned to India in 1894 he had to relearn Bengali, his mother tongue), and the English tradition of verse became *his* tradition.

    Ghose's early poetry in the booklet *Love-Songs and Elegies,* and much of his later work as well, should be seen in the late Victorian context, and not in the Anglo-Indian tradition. Like his friends Binyon and Stephen Phillips, he wrote elegantly, and on a high technical level, of the English landscape, of London, of the melancholy and other emotions associated with the 1890's. Thus, from "London":

        Can I talk with leaves, or fall in love with breezes?
        Beautiful boughs, your shade not a human pang appeases.
        This is London. I lie, and twine in the roots of things.

or from "On His Twentieth Birthday":

        Lightly leaves he behind all the sad faces of home;
        Never again, perchance, to perceive them; lost in the tempest,
        Or on some tropic shore dying in fever and pain!

or from "April" (a late work):

> April delicious
>   Young, sunny maiden,
>   Arch, gusty, capricious,
>   With fresh flowers laden

Binyon urged him to write on Indian themes, but even after he returned to India Ghose continued to write of English Aprils rather than Indian seasons, of Greek and Christian mythology rather than Indian legends and history. He *did* write an Indian "mystery play," "Nollo and Damayanti," based on a story from the Sanskrit epic the *Mahabharata*, but his major works, unfinished and unpublished at his death, were "Perseus – The Gorgon-Slayer" and "Adam Alarmed in Paradise: A Lyric Epic."

—George Walsh

GILMORE, Mary (Jean). Australian. Born in Cotta Walla, near Goulburn, New South Wales, 16 August 1865. Pupil-teacher in Cootamundra, Albury, and Wagga. Married William Alexander Gilmore in 1897 (separated, 1911); one son. Taught in Silverton, 1888–89, and in Sydney, 1890; relief worker during maritime strike, 1890; emigrated to utopian colony "New Australia," Cosme, Paraguay, 1896: teacher, and Editor of *Cosme Evening Notes*; returned to Australia, 1902: farmer in Casterton, Victoria, 1902–11; settled in Sydney, 1911; Founding Editor of the women's page, *The Worker*, Sydney, 1908–30; Columnist, *Tribune* (communist newspaper), 1952–62. Founding Executive Member, Australian Workers Union (first woman member). D.B.E. (Dame Commander, Order of the British Empire), 1937. *Died 3 December 1962.*

PUBLICATIONS

Collections

> *(Poems)*, edited by Robert D. FitzGerald. 1963.
> *Gilmore: A Tribute*, edited by D. Cusack and others. 1965.

Verse

> *Marri'd and Other Verses.* 1910.
> *The Tale of Tiddley Winks.* 1917.
> *The Passionate Heart.* 1918.
> *The Tilted Cart: A Book of Recitations.* 1925.
> *The Wild Swan.* 1930.
> *The Rue Tree.* 1931.
> *Under the Wilgas.* 1932.
> *Battlefields.* 1939.
> *The Disinherited.* 1941.
> *Pro Patria Australia and Other Poems.* 1945.
> *Selected Verse.* 1948; revised edition, 1969.
> *All Souls.* 1954.
> *Fourteen Men.* 1954.

Other

Hound of the Road. 1922.
Old Days, Old Ways: A Book of Recollections. 1934.
More Recollections. 1935.

Bibliography: in *Gilmore: A Tribute*, 1965.

Reading List: *Gilmore* by Sylvia Lawson, 1966; *Three Radicals* by W. H. Wilde, 1969.

*   *   *

Mary Gilmore's long life spanned more than half of Australia's whole history and encompassed the most dramatic and significant events in its struggle for recognition as a nation: gold-rushes, the great strikes of the 1890's leading to the formation of the Labour Party and the consolidation of industrial unionism, Federation, the first World War and Gallipoli, the Depression, the second World War and the Pacific War, and the economic expansion of the cheap oil decades. Mary Gilmore's prose and poetry, her sixty years as a working journalist, reflect all these changes, as well as her personal response to them. This response never wavered from the religious and idealistic principles on which her moral attitudes rested: the principles of the brotherhood of man and of the Christian ethic as revealed towards the end of *Matthew* 25. In accordance with these principles, she extended the meaning of brotherhood to cover the long-forgotten convicts who helped found the country and the dispossessed Aboriginals, at a time when there were few people to see good in either. "Old Botany Bay" and "The Myall in Prison" express the tragedy of both.

Mary Gilmore was of Scottish descent, and her hearing was early attuned to the great ballads, the Bible, and the timeless hymns and psalms of her ancestors. In addition, there was in her a genuine streak of Celtic mysticism, or at least of the "feyness" common to so many Scotchwomen, added to an element of gnomic wisdom, and her work in consequence conveys a curious impression of being spoken by a tribal Wise Woman. All of it is distinguished by a warm, simple, and sincere humanity. In common with the balladists, she has a strength and vitality unusual in women poets. Like most of the balladists, she is a poet of the people and knows their struggles from the inside, not as a spectator. Her verse comes as naturally as song to a bird; she writes with the same unselfconsciousness as would attend the making of bread, and both activities are part of the unity of her personality. Like her contemporary Hugh McCrae, she thinks naturally in images, which are not, unlike McCrae's, merely the result of observation, but are bound up indissolubly with some mental state, mood, or idea:

> Nurse no long grief,
> Lest the heart flower no more;
> Grief builds no barns; its plough
> Rusts at the door.

But a simple, natural style does not always achieve such timeless perfection and Mary Gilmore's art has the defects of its qualities. A reluctance to realise the need for self-criticism, for whatever reason, sometimes results in vagueness, in the commonplace, in facile emotional self-indulgence. Nevertheless the wide range of her subjects and her sympathies, her intelligence and sensitivity, her vigour and individuality, the sense that in reading her we are listening to the voice of a race give her a place of first importance in Australian literature. She speaks in addition for women, not for Australian women alone, though she does that, but for womankind, though she was no feminist: one of the best of her poems is the early "Eve-song." Yet some of the best and the strongest come from her last book, *Fourteen Men*, published in her 90th year, in which all her gifts and her preoccupations are as vital as ever: her awareness of the natural world, her sympathy with humble people, her religious faith, her empathy with Aboriginals, her interest in world affairs, especially in peace movements, her wisdom and her passion and her sense of mystery. The risk is that she may be under-rated: it is rarely pointed out, for instance, how much is owed to her example by Judith Wright.

Mary Gilmore wrote three books of essays and recollections, besides her books of verse: *Hound of the Road*, *Old Days, Old Ways*, and *More Recollections*. These have the same qualities as her verse and bring the era in which she grew up vividly to life. Some of her best work, however, may still lie buried in *The Worker*, the women's page of which she edited for more than twenty years. Other journalistic articles wait for discovery in Argentina newspapers, to which she contributed after the New Australia experiment in Paraguay came to an end.

—Dorothy Green

GINSBERG, Allen.   American. Born in Newark, New Jersey, 3 June 1926. Educated at Paterson High School, New Jersey; Columbia University, New York, B.A. 1948. Served in the Military Sea Transport Service. Associated with the Beat movement and the San Francisco Renaissance in the 1950's. Widely travelled: has participated in many poetry readings and demonstrations. Lived in the Far East, 1962–63. Since 1971, Director, Committee on Poetry Foundation, New York; Director, Kerouac School of Poetics, Naropa Institute, Boulder, Colorado. Recipient: Guggenheim Fellowship, 1965; National Endowment for the Arts grant, 1966; National Institute of Arts and Letters grant, 1969; National Book Award, 1974. Member, National Insitute of Arts and Letters, 1973. Lives in New York City.

PUBLICATIONS

Verse

Howl and Other Poems.   1956; revised edition of *Howl*, as *Howl for Carl Solomon*, 1971.
Empty Mirror: Early Poems.   1961.
Kaddish and Other Poems, 1958–1960.   1961.
Reality Sandwiches, 1953–60.   1963.
T.V. Baby Poems.   1967.
Wales – A Visitation, July 29, 1967.   1968.
Scrap Leaves, Tasty Scribbles.   1968.
Planet News, 1961–1967.   1968.
Airplane Dreams: Compositions from Journals.   1968.
Ankor-Wat.   1969.
Iron Horse.   1972.
The Fall of America: Poems of These States 1965–1971.   1972.
The Gates of Wrath: Rhymed Poems 1948–1952.   1972.

Bixby Canyon Ocean Path Word Breeze. 1972.
New Year Blues. 1972.
Sad Dust Glories. 1975.
First Blues: Rags, Ballads, and Harmonium Songs, 1971–1974. 1975.
Mind Breaths: Poems 1972–1977. 1977.

Plays

Don't Go Away Mad, in *Pardon Me, Sir, But Is My Eye Hurting Your Elbow?,* edited by
    Bob Booker and George Foster. 1968.
Kaddish (produced 1972). 1973.

Other

The Yage Letters, with William S. Burroughs. 1963.
*Indian Journals: March 1962–May 1963: Notebooks, Diary, Blank Pages,
    Writings.* 1970.
Improvised Poetics. 1972.
Allen Verbatim: Lectures on Poetry, Politics, Consciousness, edited by Gordon
    Ball. 1974.
The Visions of the Great Remembrancer (on Jack Kerouac). 1974.
Chicago Trial Testimony. 1975.
As Ever: The Collected Correspondence of Ginsberg and Neal Cassady. 1977.
Journals: Early Fifties–Early Sixties, edited by Gordon Ball. 1977.

Bibliography: *A Bibliography of the Works of Ginsberg* by George Dowden, 1970.

Reading List: *Howl of the Censor* by J. W. Ehrlich, 1961; *Ginsberg* by Thomas F. Merrill,
1969; *Ginsberg in America* by Jane Kramer, 1969, as *Paterfamilias,* 1970; *Scenes along the
Road* edited by Ann Charters, 1971; *Ginsberg in the '60's* by Eric Mottram, 1972.

*   *   *

Like Whitman, his forebear, Allen Ginsberg is a prolific poet who writes too much: some
of his work is, like Whitman's, unfocused, emotionally scattered, and prone to large
abstractions unrelated to any concrete particularity. And, like Whitman, Ginsberg insists that
any subject is a fit one for poetry. And so, like Whitman, he has been attacked for his
vulgarity, for his failure to be "proper" or dignified; yet at the same time, like both Whitman
and Blake (from whom he has learned much), he appeals to the young, to those who do not
think that poetry and the business of daily life are essentially grave matters whose languages
have to be separated from one another. Ginsberg is a World-Poet, like Neruda and
Yevtushenko, and like Gibran, Tagore, Whitman, and Blake in previous times. And, like each
of these, he has written a quantity of slight but interesting occasional verse, of which
"Portland Coloseum" (in *Planet News*), about a Beatles concert, is representative.
    In *Improvised Poetics* Ginsberg talks about writing this poem. "I changed things," he said,
"like *Hands waving* LIKE *myriad snakes of thought* to *Hands waving myriad/snakes of
thought.* Ah ... *The million children* OF *the thousand worlds,* so I just changed *The million
children,/the thousand worlds.*" These apparently minor revisions are significant: Ginsberg
talks about his "paragraphal" mode of composition and explains, "when I'd get three or four
[phrases] that made an apposition I'd start a new paragraph." In taking out "a lot of
syntactical fat" and thus "putting two short lines together that had just images in them,"

Ginsberg prunes the lines of prepositions which express relationship and embraces the technique of juxtaposition, learned from Pound. The danger of such technique is that the poem can degenerate into a mere list (although, as Emerson remarked in *The Poet*, "bare lists of words are found suggestive to an imaginative and excited mind"). The value of such appositional language is that it can *imply* cause-and-effect relationships, but it does not state them: cause and effect are not to be assumed in or about the world of event; it is a world of immediacy. That is to say, the reader is moved into a world of event, a place *where things happen*, for (to quote Emerson again) "the quality of the imagination is to flow, and not to freeze." Ginsberg's reader can, therefore, often be overwhelmed by a rush of sensory, social, political and/or intellectual data to very good effect, as in poems like *Howl* or *Kaddish*.

The concern of the poet is for registering the precise nature of the occurrence (his thought, his feeling, the particularities from which they arise) in the here and now. So Ginsberg, like other modernists, finds crucial the accuracy of the poem as notation of the spoken voice or as notation of the processes of thought. The notation is exact: in *Airplane Dreams* the lines of the long poem "New York to San Fran" are, in Ginsberg's words, "hung out on the page a little to the right.... A little bit like diagramming a sentence, you know, the old syntactical diagrammatic method of making a little platform and you put the subject and object on it and hang adjectives and adverbial clauses down" (*Improvised Poetics*). Here is a short sequence from "Portland Coloseum":

> The million children
> the thousand worlds
> bounce in their seats, bash
> each other's sides, press
> legs together nervous
> Scream again & claphand

Like Olson's, Ginsberg's line-breaks serve an emphatic, syntactic purpose, in which the slight hesitancy at the end of the line provides for unexpected semantic conjunctions and emphases, while at the same time they direct the reader's voice into the (in this case slightly nervous) rhythm and rhetorical inflection of the verse.

Such a line, the unit of thought or the unit of speech, reinforces the air of spontaneous improvisation characteristic of much of Ginsberg's work. The publication of *Howl* in 1956, brought Ginsberg to prominence and gave wide currency to the notion that poetry might be a spontaneous art, requiring little or no skill or revision. Deceptively simple in appearance, *Howl* rests on an extensive apprenticeship in rhymed verse (some of which has been published in *The Gates of Wrath*) and in conscious craftsmanship. As Ginsberg wrote to Richard Eberhart, the "general ground plan" of the poem, "quite symmetrical, surprisingly," structures the three sections of the poem round three main devices: the fixed base of "who" and a long line; the repetition and variation of the fixed base "Moloch"; and the "fixed base/reply/fixed base/longer reply" of the final section. Such writing is not always done, of course, in a single extended burst of composition (the result of a fairly extended gestation): Ginsberg's compositions are often leisurely and deliberative, and very often, in revising a poem, Ginsberg in effect composes a completely new one. "Sunflower Sutra," for example, is a revised version of "In Back of the Real." It is fundamentally a different poem that came about as the result of "re-seeing" the same event. With its long lines, its introduction of a second person into the poem, and its focus on the *perceiver* of the flower, "Sunflower Sutra" is both less general and more immediate in its effect. At the same time it is, as is much of Ginsberg's work, more a celebration and affirmation of the individual, of the personal, and of nature than a denunciation of the world of man. Ginsberg's great strengths as poet are to be found in such visionary poems as this, with its long and carefully controlled lines juxtaposed against shorter lines, leading the poem to a crescendo which is not rhetorical only but quite literally *physical*: Ginsberg's long interest in yoga and in the breath as a measure in verse has led him to speculate on the correlations in Sanskrit poetry between prosody and human physiology, and has led him to attempt similar correlations in his own work. At the same time, the unabashed frankness of his words and the declarative nature of much of his writing have made the work accessible to the casual reader, and have thus given Ginsberg a wide following.

—Peter Quartermain

GLOVER, Denis (James Matthews). New Zealander. Born in Dunedin, 10 December 1912. Educated at Auckland Grammar School; Christ's College; Canterbury University College, A.B. Served as an officer in the Royal Navy during World War II: Distinguished Service Cross. Married 1) Mary Granville in 1936, one son; 2) Lyn Cameron in 1972. Taught English at Canterbury University, 1936–38, and typography at the Technical Correspondence Institute, Christchurch. Founder, Caxton Press, Christchurch, 1936; joined Pegasus Press, 1953, and Wingfield Press, 1955. Formerly, Journalist, *The Press*, Christchurch. Former President, New Zealand P.E.N. and Friends of the Turnbull Library, Wellington; Member of the Canterbury University Council, and of the New Zealand State Literary Fund Committee. Recipient: Jessie Mackay Award, 1960. Lives in Wellington.

PUBLICATIONS

Verse

> *Short Reflection on the Present State of Literature in This Country.* 1935.
> *Another Argo*, with Allen Curnow and A. R. D. Fairburn. 1935.
> *Thistledown.* 1935.
> *Six Easy Ways of Dodging Debt Collectors.* 1936.
> *A Caxton Miscellany*, with others. 1937.
> *The Arraignment of Paris.* 1937.
> *Thirteen Poems.* 1939.
> *Cold Tongue.* 1940.
> *Recent Poems*, with others. 1941.
> *The Wind and the Sand: Poems 1933–44.* 1945.
> *Summer Flowers.* 1945.
> *Sings Harry and Other Poems.* 1951.
> *Arawata Bill: A Sequence of Poems.* 1953.
> *Since Then.* 1957.
> *Poetry Harbinger*, with A. R. D. Fairburn. 1958.
> *Enter Without Knocking: Selected Poems.* 1964; revised edition, 1972.
> *Sharp Edge Up: Verses and Satires.* 1968.
> *Myself When Young.* 1970.
> *To a Particular Woman.* 1970.
> *Diary to a Woman.* 1971.
> *Dancing to My Tune.* 1974.
> *Wellington Harbour.* 1974.

Plays

Screenplays: *The Coaster*, 1951; *Mick Stimson*, with John Lang, 1972.

Radio Play: *They Sometimes Float at Sea*, 1970.

Fiction

3 Short Stories.   1936.

Other

Till the Star Speaks.   1939.
D. Day.   1944.
A Clutch of Authors and a Clot.   1960.
Hot Water Sailor.   1962.
Glover's Bedside Book.   1963.

Editor, with Ian Milner, *New Poems*.   1934.
Editor, *The Disadvantages of Being Dead and Other Sharp Verses*. by A. R. D. Fairburn.   1958.
Editor, *Cross Currents*, by Merrill Moore.   1961.
Editor, *Collected Poems*, by A. R. D. Fairburn.   1966.
Editor, with Geoffrey Fairburn, *The Woman Problem and Other Prose*, by A. R. D. Fairburn.   1967.

                                   *   *   *

Denis Glover, naval Commander, boxing blue, poet, publisher, printer, "looking rather like Mr. Punch in naval uniform" (John Lehmann, 1941) has been a minor kind of colonial/ Renaissance man. All which helps establish his very distinctive poetic tone, although in parenthesis one might note his admirable wartime prose in *Penguin New Writing* (notably "It Was D-Day"), and his eminently readable autobiography *Hot Water Sailor*. His poetry begins, part Georgian, part Audenesque, in the middle 1930's when that "shock of recognition" of the Depression ignited so much local creativity. He also, with developing elegance, printed and published (under the imprint Caxton Press) his own verse, along with much other significant poetry, fiction, and critical prose, through the next crucial and formative decade.

Early verse presents the dignity of labour ("The Road Builders") and lyric response to landscape ("Holiday Piece"); his very first Caxton Press book, incidentally, with that sharp, irreverent and dangerous wit he still displays, is titled *Six Easy Ways of Dodging Debt Collectors*, with the explanation "Called on the outside, because of the difficulty of selling verse, *Six Easy Ways....*" In *Recent Poems* he moves into his stride with, perhaps most notably, the memorable ballad "The Magpies" with its lyric opening, "When Tom and Elizabeth took the farm/The bracken made their bed," but lamentable conclusion:

> The farm's still there, Mortgage corporations
> Couldn't give it away.
> And *Quardle oodle ardle wardle doodle*
> The magpies say.

The same volume sustains his impudent wit ("Thoughts on Cremation"); *The Wind and the*

Sand not only promotes his St. Exupéry-like romanticism but adds themes of nostalgia and mortality and that marine sensibility he alone brings to New Zealand verse.

In my view, *Sings Harry* is his best single volume. This contains "A Note to Lili Kraus" where he articulates a representative local fear of feeling: "Lili, emotion leaves me quite dismayed:/If I'm on fire I call the fire-brigade." Alastair Campbell ("Glover and Georgianism," *Comment 21*) has shown it is through "Harry" (possibly copying Yeats) that Glover finds an emotionally liberating persona. Harry, like his subsequent fellows, 'Wata Bill and Mick Stimson, is that true colonial archetype, a rural male loner. From "Sings Harry to an Old Guitar":

> These songs will not stand –
> The wind and the sand will smother.
>
> Not I but another
> Will make songs worth the bother:
> The rimu or kauri be,
> I'm but the cabbage tree

and from "Sings Harry in the Wind-Break":

> From the cliff-top a boy
> Felt that great motion
> And pupil to the horizon's eye
> Grew wide with vision,

and from "Themes":

> What shall we sing? sings Harry.
>
> Sing all things sweet or harsh upon
> These islands in the Pacific sun,
> The mountains whitened endlessly
> And the white horses of the winter sea.

His subsequent *Arawata Bill*, though ingenious and admired, seems too contrived and rhythmically stiff to create quite the same niche for a wandering prospector. Only perhaps in "Towards Banks Peninsula: Mick Stimson" (*Since Then*) does a similar warmth, more tranquil, infuse his lines: this poem should possibly be linked with "Towards Banks Peninsula: Peraki" (*Poetry Harbinger*) as part of that poetry of the sea prominent in his later work.

—Peter Alcock

GODOLPHIN, Sidney. English. Born in Godolphin, Cornwall, baptized 15 January 1610. Educated at Exeter College, Oxford, 1624–27; entered one of the inns of court, London. Member of Parliament for Helston, Cornwall, 1628–43 (served in the Short Parliament and the Long Parliament, 1640); at outbreak of the Civil War joined Royalist forces commanded by Sir Ralph Hopton, and was killed in action in Devonshire. *Died (buried) 10 February 1643.*

PUBLICATIONS

Collections

Poems, edited by William Dighton.   1931.

Verse

The Passion of Dido for Aeneas, with Edmund Waller.   1658.

Play

Pompey the Great, with others, from a play by Corneille (produced 1664).   1664.

Reading List: "Godolphin and the Muses Fairest Light" by M. Teresa, in *Modern Language Notes*, 1946; *Private Men and Public Causes* by Irene Coltman, 1962.

*   *   *

Sidney Godolphin is an almost perfect example of a truly minor poet. He followed the poetic tastes of his time – the witty amorous lyric, the epitaph, the Psalm paraphrase, the occasional poem, the Horatian epistle, the pretty pastoral. Of the nearly 1000 lines of his original verse, not one is memorably bad; nor is there a single line that is memorably good. Though he wrote poems in tribute to both Donne and Jonson, Godolphin's verse is never fully committed to either of the two great exemplars of 17th-century English poetry. In Suckling's "A Session of the Poets" Apollo calls him "Little Cid" and advises him "not to write so strong." The term "strong" may refer to Godolphin's attempts to be witty in Donne's manner. His song, "Or love me less or love me more," ends with a witty turn reminiscent of Donne's "The Prohibition."

> Then give me more, or give me less:
>   Do not disdain a mutual sense;
> Or your unpitying beauties dress
>   In their own free indifference.
> But show not a severer eye
>   Sooner to give me liberty,
> For I shall love the very scorn
>   Which for my sake you do put on.

But Godolphin owes far more to Jonson. Ben's great legacy to his sons was the octosyllabic couplet and Godolphin is a true son of Ben. In his octosyllabics he catches the grace and poise of courtly lyric. His "Madam 'tis true, your beauties move" first appeared in Jonson's *Underwoods* (1640) as if it were Ben's own. He also has the Jonsonian preference for plain statement and courtly wit:

> Delighted by the diverse grace
> Of music and so fair a face,
> First all my soul is in mine eye;
> But then the sweet voice doth deny
> Your beauty's title and presence,
> And sows division twixt my sense.

Like many other minor poets, Godolphin never quite found his own voice. The preceding lyric sounds as much like Carew as Jonson. The short poem "Cloris, may I unhappy prove" could be by Robert Herrick. And his song "Shepherd, we do not see our looks" is in the vein of Andrew Marvell. All of Godolphin's poems illustrate the very high level of grace and sophistication which English lyric verse achieved in the 17th century.

—Thomas Wheeler

GOGARTY, Oliver (Joseph) St. John.   American.   Born in Dublin, Ireland. 17 August 1878; emigrated to the U.S. in 1939: naturalized citizen. Educated at Stonyhurst, Dublin; Clongowes Wood, Kildare; Trinity College, Dublin; Worcester College, Oxford; studied medicine in Vienna; qualified as a surgeon: Fellow of the Royal College of Surgeons of Ireland. Practiced as a nose, throat, and ear surgeon. Senator of the Irish Free State, 1922–36. *Died 22 September 1957.*

PUBLICATIONS

Collections

   The Plays.   1971.

Verse

   Cervantes: Tercentenary of Don Quixote.   1905(?).
   Hyperthuleana.   1916.
   The Ship and Other Poems.   1923.
   Wild Apples.   1928; revised edition, 1930.
   Selected Poems.   1933.
   Others to Adorn.   1938.
   Elbow Room.   1939.
   Perennial.   1944.
   The Collected Poems.   1951.
   Unselected Poems.   1954.

Plays

   Blight: The Tragedy of Dublin, with Joseph O'Connor (produced 1917).   1917.
   The Enchanted Trousers (produced 1919).   1919.
   A Serious Thing (produced 1919).   1919.

Fiction

   Mad Grandeur.   1941.
   Mr. Petunia.   1945.

420

Other

As I Was Going down Sackville Street: A Phantasy in Fact.   1937.
I Follow St. Patrick.   1938.
Tumbling in the Hay.   1939.
Going Native.   1940.
Mourning Becomes Mrs. Spendlove and Other Portraits, Grave and Gay.   1948.
Intimations.   1950.
Rolling Down the Lea.   1950.
It Isn't This Time of Year at All! An Unpremeditated Autobiography.   1954.
Start from Somewhere Else: An Exposition of Wit and Humor, Polite and Perilous.   1955.
A Week End in the Middle of the Week and Other Essays on the Bias.   1958.
William Butler Yeats: A Memoir.   1963.
Many Lives to Thee: Letters to G. K. A. Bell 1904–1907, edited by James F. Carens.   1971.

Reading List: *Gogarty* by A. Norman Jeffares, 1961; *Gogarty: A Poet and His Times* by Ulick O'Connor, 1964, as *The Times I've Seen,* 1964.

*   *   *

Oliver St. John Gogarty was a friend of James Joyce, a politician (in sympathy with the aims of Sinn Fein and a friend of its founder, Arthur Griffith; a Senator after Home Rule was achieved and the victim of an assassination attempt), and a public figure. But of his two volumes of memoirs, *As I Was Going down Sackville Street* and *Tumbling in the Hay,* it has been well said that Gogarty "eschews perspective like the Chinese" and "allowed his imagination to body forth ideas, without regard to chronology." These brisk and witty evocations of a lost Dublin, its personalities and brilliant conversations, have a vivid informality, and parts of both were transcribed directly from Gogarty's talk. The later autobiography, *It Isn't This Time of Year at All,* is more formalized and rather dull. As a critic, he is negligible, though the brief essays in *Intimations* and *A Week End in the Middle of the Week* can be read with mild pleasure.

As a poet, there was always something amateur about him. He was one of the "gentlemen who wrote with ease," and he was casual about collecting his poems. His happiest vein lay in the occasional and satirical. Attempting a severe neo-classical surface, he is lapidary or nothing (and often nothing): his lyrics tend to suffer from the expected epithet and the routine inversion, but he can offer an occasional Landorian elegance and conciseness and a sharp evocation of the natural scene.

Gogarty's three plays are vigorous and read well, but the characters are too one-dimensional to survive on the stage. The novel *Mr. Petunia,* with its American eighteenth-century background, is a virtuoso piece. Gogarty will probably be remembered first as the original of Joyce's Buck Mulligan in *Ulysses,* and second as a wit. The competing nature of his many talents prevented the full realisation of any.

—Ian Fletcher

GOLDSMITH, Oliver. Irish. Born in Pallas, near Ballymahon, Longford. 10 November 1728. Educated at the village school in Lissoy, West Meath, 1734–37; Elphin School, 1738; a school in Athlone, 1739–41, and in Edgeworthstown, Longford, 1741–44; Trinity College, Dublin (sizar), 1745–49 (Smyth exhibitioner, 1747), B.A. 1749; studied medicine at the University of Edinburgh, 1752–53; travelled on the Continent, in Switzerland, Italy and France, 1753–56, and may have obtained a medical degree. Settled in London, 1756; tried unsuccessfully to support himself as a physician in Southwark; worked as an usher in Dr. Milner's classical academy in Peckham, 1756, and as a writer for Ralph Griffiths, proprietor of the *Monthly Review*, 1757–58; Editor, *The Bee*, 1759; contributed to the *British Magazine*, 1760; Editor, *The Lady's Magazine*, 1761; also worked for the publisher Edward Newbery: worked as a proof-reader and preface writer, contributed to the *Public Ledger*, 1760, and prepared a *Compendium of Biography*, 7 volumes, 1762; after 1763 earned increasingly substantial sums from his own writing; one of the founder members of Samuel Johnson's Literary Club, 1764. *Died 4 April 1774.*

PUBLICATIONS

Collections

> *Collected Letters,* edited by Katharine C. Balderston.   1928.
> *Collected Works,* edited by Arthur Friedman.   5 vols., 1966.
> *Poems and Plays,* edited by Tom Davis.   1975.

Verse

> *The Traveller; or, A Prospect of Society.*   1764.
> *Poems for Young Ladies in Three Parts, Devotional, Moral, and Entertaining.*   1767.
> *The Deserted Village.*   1770.
> *Retaliation.*   1774.
> *The Haunch of Venison: A Poetical Epistle to Lord Clare.*   1776.

Plays

> *The Good Natured Man* (produced 1768).   1768.
> *The Grumbler,* from a translation by Charles Sedley of a work by Brueys (produced 1773).   Edited by Alice I. P. Wood, 1931.
> *She Stoops to Conquer; or, The Mistakes of a Night* (produced 1773).   1773; edited by Arthur Friedman, 1968.
> *Threnodia Augustalis, Sacred to the Memory of the Princess Dowager of Wales,* music by Mattia Vento (produced 1772).   1772.
> *The Captivity* (oratorio), in *Miscellaneous Works.*   1820.

Fiction

> *The Vicar of Wakefield.*   1766; edited by Arthur Friedman, 1974.

Other

An Enquiry into the Present State of Polite Learning in Europe. 1759.
The Bee. 1759.
The Mystery Revealed. 1762.
The Citizen of the World; or, Letters from a Chinese Philosopher Residing in London to His Friends in the East. 2 vols., 1762.
The Life of Richard Nash of Bath. 1762.
An History of England in a Series of Letters from a Nobleman to His Son. 2 vols., 1764.
An History of the Martyrs and Primitive Fathers of the Church. 1764.
Essays. 1765; revised edition, 1766.
The Present State of the British Empire in Europe, America, Africa and Asia. 1768.
The Roman History, from the Foundation of the City of Rome to the Destruction of the Western Empire. 2 vols., 1769; abridged edition, 1772.
The Life of Thomas Parnell. 1770.
The Life of Henry St. John, Lord Viscount Bolingbroke. 1770.
The History of England, from the Earliest Times to the Death of George II. 4 vols., 1771; abridged edition, 1774.
The Grecian History, from the Earliest State to the Death of Alexander the Great. 2 vols., 1774.
An History of the Earth and Animated Nature. 8 vols., 1774.
A Survey of Experimental Philosophy, Considered in Its Present State of Improvement. 2 vols., 1776.

Editor, *The Beauties of English Poesy.* 2 vols., 1767.

Translator, *The Memoirs of a Protestant,* by J. Marteilhe. 2 vols., 1758; edited by A. Dobson, 1895.
Translator, *Plutarch's Lives.* 4 vols., 1762.
Translator, *A Concise History of Philosophy and Philosophers,* by M. Formey. 1766.
Translator, *The Comic Romance of Scarron.* 2 vols., 1775.

Bibliography: *Goldsmith Bibliographically and Biographically Considered* by Temple Scott, 1928.

Reading List: *Goldsmith* by Ralph Wardle, 1957; *Goldsmith* by Clara M. Kirk, 1967; *Goldsmith: A Georgian Study* by Ricardo Quintana, 1967; *Life of Goldsmith* by Henry A. Dobson, 1972; *Goldsmith* by A. Lytton Sells, 1974; *Goldsmith: The Critical Heritage,* edited by George S. Rousseau, 1974; *The Notable Man: The Life and Times of Goldsmith* by John Ginger, 1977.

*   *   *

Oliver Goldsmith's reputation is made up of paradox. His blundering, improvident nature nevertheless won him the loyalty and friendship of figures like Dr. Johnson, Sir Joshua Reynolds, and Edmund Burke. While in society he was a buffoon, his writing testifies to personal charm and an ironic awareness of his own and others' absurdity. Critical opinion of his work similarly varies from acceptance of Goldsmith as the sensitive apologist for past values to appraisal of him as an accomplished social and literary satirist. Indeed, his work can operate on both levels, a fact perhaps recognised by the young Jane Austen in her *Juvenilia* when she took Goldsmith's abridgements of history for young persons as a model for her own exercise in irony.

Drifting into authorship after a mis-spent youth (as Macaulay notes in his disapproving

Life), Goldsmith turned to hack writing, contributing articles to the *Monthly* and *Critical Reviews* from 1757. His more ambitious *Inquiry into the Present State of Polite Learning* of 1759 won him the reputation of a man of learning and elegant expression. In this last essay he reveals his fundamental dislike of the contemporary cult of sensibility which was to generate not only his own "laughing" form of comedy in the drama but also *The Vicar of Wakefield*. Meeting Smollett, then editor of the *British Magazine*, Goldsmith was encouraged to expand his contributions to literary journalism. He produced the weekly periodical *The Bee*; many papers collected and published in 1765 and 1766 as *Essays*; and, most important, the "Chinese Letters" of 1760–61 collected as *The Citizen of the World*.

The "citizen" is, of course, an Oriental traveller, observing the fashions and foibles of the *bon ton* in London with wide-eyed innocence that carries within it implicit comment and criticism not unmixed with humour. The device was borrowed from the French, notably Montesquieu's *Lettres Persanes* (1721). In each essay the absurdities of behaviour are marked, the whole inter-woven by continuing narratives around the Man in Black, Beau Tibbs, the story of Hingo and Zelis, for instance. In many ways the ironies, improbabilities, and apparent innocence of the Chinese letters prefigure the extended prose romance of *The Vicar of Wakefield*.

This could be seen as Goldsmith's answer to Sterne's *Tristram Shandy* (1759). He had attacked Sterne's sentimental fiction as "obscene and pert" in *The Citizen*; in many ways *The Vicar* parodies Sterne's novel but with such a light hand that it has been taken on face value for many generations as the tale indeed of a family "generous, credulous, simple, and inoffensive." However, Goldsmith early establishes for the observant the manifest danger of complacency in such apparent virtues. His Yorkshire parson displays the moral duplicity of a feeling heart, for Goldsmith's approach to life and art is the opposite of Sterne's relativism and dilettante values.

Oliver Goldsmith's moral seriousness (while softened by genial good humour) dominates that other work now considered "classic," *The Deserted Village*. His earlier sortie in the genre of topographical/philosophical verse, *The Traveller*, did much to establish his reputation. It is an accomplished use of convention, where the poet climbs an eminence only to have his mind expanded into contemplation of universal questions. In *The Deserted Village*, however, the poet comes to terms with a particular social problem in a particular landscape as opposed to former abstract musings above imaginary solitudes. "Sweet Auburn" can be identified closely with the village of Nuneham Courtenay, where the local land-owner had recently moved the whole community out in order to extend and improve his landscape park. The fact becomes a catalyst for Goldsmith in a consideration of where aesthetic values and irresponsible wealth lead: a symbol taken from life and not from poetic convention.

Goldsmith's rhymed couplets have grace and ease, particularly when his verse is unlaboured, as in the prologues and epilogues to his own and others' plays. The charm and humour of these can be observed in his later poem *Retaliation*, which has a pointed raciness born out of the settling of personal scores. Always the butt of jokes in the group known as The Club, here he gets his own back with a series of comic epitaphs for the other members. Notable is that for Garrick – "On the stage he was natural, simple, affecting; Twas only that when he was off he was acting" – but he labels himself the "gooseberry fool."

As a dramatist, Goldsmith exploited both verbal dexterity and the comedy of situation, looking back to Shakespeare in the rejection of the so-called genteel comedy of Hugh Kelly or Richard Cumberland. Affected and strained in tone and action, the drama of sentiment offered to Goldsmith nothing of the "nature and humour" that he saw as the first principle of theatre. However he might despise the sentimental school, he cannot avoid using some of its conventions, the good-natured hero, of course, and the device of paired lovers, but the way these are treated is particular to himself. Together with Sheridan, Goldsmith exploits the theatrical unreality of comedy, using the stage as a separate world of experience with its own laws and therefore demanding the suspension of disbelief in order that farcical unreality might unmask farcical reality. His character Honeydew in *The Good Natured Man* has something in common with Charles Surface in *School for Scandal*, but the tone of

Goldsmith's comedy is less brittle than that of Sheridan. This mellow tone, a fundamental wholesomeness, is magnificently encapsulated in *She Stoops to Conquer*.

Oliver Goldsmith's first play met with a poor response, as being too "low" in its matter (especially the bailiffs scene), and, though *She Stoops to Conquer* was open to similar criticism, its riotous humour overcame prejudice. In short, it was good theatre and this is testified by its continuing popularity in production. Characters like Tony Lumpkin, Mrs. Hardcastle, and the old Squire have become literary personalities, while the pivot of the plot, Marlow's loss of diffidence in apparently more relaxed circumstances, holds true to human nature. The character of Kate is a liberated heroine in the Shakespearean style, contrasted as in the older comedy with a foil. One is able to relate Goldsmith's "laughing" comedy to that of Shakespeare in many ways, for the Lord of Misrule dominates both.

The range of Goldsmith's work is touched by this same humour and sensitivity, the good heart that is so easily squandered as he himself acknowledged in *The Good Natured Man*, but is just as easily extended with purpose to the reader. As Walter Scott observed, no man contrived "so well to reconcile us to human nature."

—B. C. Oliver-Morden

GOOGE, Barnabe. English. Born in Alvingham, Lincolnshire, 25 July 1540. Educated at Christ's College, Cambridge; New College, Oxford; Staple Inn, London. Married Mary Darrell c. 1563; eight children. Courtier, and member of the household of Sir William Cecil; travelled to Spain with Sir Thomas Challoner, 1561–62; appointed one of the queen's gentlemen-pensioners, 1565; sent to Ireland by Cecil to report on Essex's expedition to Ulster, 1574; performed numerous commissions in Ireland, and served as Provost Marshal of the Presidency Court of Connaught, 1582–85; returned to England and retired to his Lincolnshire estate, 1585. *Died in February 1594.*

PUBLICATIONS

Collections

    Selected Poems, edited by Alan Stephens. 1961.

Verse

    The Zodiac of Life, 3 books, from a work by Marcellus Palingenius. 1560; 6 books, 1561; 12 books, 1565.
    Eclogues, Epitaphs, and Sonnets. 1563.
    The Ship of Safeguard. 1569.

Other

    A Prophecy Predicting the Rising and Falling of the United Provinces. 1572.

    Translator, *The Popish Kingdom; or, Reign of Antichrist,* by Thomas Naogeorgus. 1570; edited in part by R. C. Hope, 1880.
    Translator, *The Overthrow of the Gout,* by C. Balista. 1577.

425

Translator, *Four Books of Husbandry*, by C. Heresbach. 1577.

Translator, *The Proverbs of Sir James Lopez de Mendoza with the Paraphrase of Peter Diaz of Toledo*. 1579.

Translator, *The Virtues of a New Terra Sigillata Lately Found Out in Germany*, by Andrew Bertholdus. 1587.

Reading List: Introduction by Rosamond Tuve to *The Zodiac of Life*, 1947; *Googe: Poet and Translator* by Brooke Peirce, unpublished dissertation, Harvard University, 1954; "Googe: A Puritan in Arcadia" by Paul E. Parnell, in *Journal of English and Germanic Philology 60*, 1961; "A Timely Anachronism: Tradition and Theme in Googe's *Cupido Conquered*"by William E. Sheidley, in *Studies in Philology*, April 1972.

*   *   *

Barnabe Googe was a respected poet and translator of the first Elizabethan generation. Educated at Christ's College, Cambridge, and Staple Inn, Googe was an ethical humanist, a strong Reformer, and an exponent of Elizabethan literary nationalism. As a distant relative of Sir William Cecil, he found opportunities to serve the Crown and the Protestant cause – at home, as courtier and member of Cecil's household; abroad, with an embassade to Spain and as intelligencer and officeholder in Ireland. But Googe best served his country with his pen, translating a series of useful and improving works, including an anti-Catholic tract, a treatise on farming, a compendium of Spanish moral proverbs, and two medical works. His version of a popular philosophical compendium, *The Zodiake of Life* by Palingenius, occupied Googe through a good part of his career. With his contemporaries, he considered it his *chef d'oeuvre*; it provided a training ground for his skills as a writer and remains useful to the modern student of Renaissance ideas.

Googe is chiefly known today, however, for his original verse in *Eglogs, Epytaphes, and Sonettes*, the first collection of poetry by a single Elizabethan author to appear in print. The eight pastoral eclogues with which the volume opens are inspired by Mantuan and contain the first English borrowings from Montemayor's *Diana*. Structurally and thematically unified into an effective analysis of and attack upon conventional amatory passion, Googe's eclogues anticipate much of what Spenser would accomplish in *The Shepheardes Calender*. Googe also mastered the visionary allegory. In "Cupido Conquered," the dreaming poet overcomes the debilitating effect on his muse of unrequited love by witnessing a psychomachy in which the army of Diana defeats the forces of Cupid. Though it cleverly exploits the ancient convention, Googe admits that his "Dreame" is "to hastely fynyshed." He took more care with the short poems that make up the rest of the collection, several of which ring with a clear and emphatic voice of personal concern that cuts through the humdrum of metrical regularity and copious elaboration typical of early Elizabethan verse. As much may not be said for Googe's longest original poem, *The Shippe of Safegarde*, which describes emblematic islands, castles, and monsters reminiscent of *The Faerie Queene*.

Critics expounding the tradition of the native plain style have praised Googe's fusion of its resources with those of the learned and rhetorical style favored in his day. In poems like "To Doctor Bale," "To the Translation of Pallingen," and the epitaph on Nicholas Grimald, Googe further channels his feelings through deftly realized particular situations, heightening their sincerity and force. In "Of Money" and elsewhere, he raises self-awareness to the level of devastating ironic wit. His best work is marked by a degree of subtlety and control unusual among the early Elizabethan writers. We may regret that Googe abandoned poetry for the "more serious" activities of translation and civil service, but his varied and innovative literary achievement continues to invite admiration.

—William E. Sheidley

GOWER, John. English. Born in London, c. 1330. Married Agnes Groundolf in 1397. Possibly travelled in France in his early life; after returning to England settled down to life as a country gentleman; also in the service of Henry of Lancaster, later Henry IV. A friend of Chaucer. Went blind c. 1400. *Died in 1408*.

PUBLICATIONS

Collections

Complete Works, edited by G. C. Macaulay. 4 vols., 1899–1902.
Major Latin Works (translated into English), edited by Eric W. Stockton. 1962.
Selections, edited by J. A. W. Bennett. 1968.

Verse

Confessio Amantis. 1483; selections edited by R. A. Peck, 1968.
Vox Clamantis (in Latin), edited by H. O. Coxe. 1850; in *Major Latin Works*, 1962.
Chronica Tripartita and Minor Poems (in Latin), edited by H. O. Coxe. 1850; in *Major Latin Works*, 1962.
Mirour de l'Omme, in *Complete Works*. 1899–1902.

Reading List: *Studien zu Gower* by M. Wickert, 1953; *Gower: Moral Philosopher and Friend of Chaucer* by John H. Fisher, 1964; *Gower: Dichter einer Ethisch-Politischen Reformation*, 1965, and *Gower: Zur Literarischen Form Seiner Dichtung*, 1966, both by Edwart Weber; *Love, The Word, and Mercury: A Reading of Gower's Confessio Amantis* by Patrick J. Gallacher, 1975.

*   *   *

Chaucer addresses John Gower as "moral Gower" in the dedication of *Troilus and Criseyde*, and probably Gower would have found the epithet neither inapt nor unappealing. His earliest poetic works were a lengthy moral treatise in Anglo-Norman (then the standard literary language of polite society) called the *Mirour de l'Omme*, and a violent diatribe in Latin on the ills of contemporary society, the *Vox Clamantis*. In the late 1380's, however, perhaps emboldened by Chaucer's example, Gower began the long poem in English on which his reputation mainly rests, the *Confessio Amantis*, and the *Confessio* is something more than a moral poem.

It begins with a long Prologue, in which Gower analyses once again, in a familiar vein, the corruption in English society. But he turns then, more lightly, to themes of love, the ubiquitous and all-consuming interest of courtly literature, and promises to write "somewhat of lust, somewhat of lore." The frame of the narrative is the Lover's Confession, in which, as in a penitential manual, the Lover (*Amans*) confesses his sins against Love to Genius, the Priest of Venus, and, after listening to strings of exemplary stories relating to each of the Seven Deadly Sins (133 in all, constituting something over half the total 33,444 lines of the poem), receives absolution. The stage seems set for the charmingly immoral morality of the "religion of love," but it soon becomes clear that Gower is using love, because of its intrinsic interest and because it is the area where man's moral being is most under challenge, as the point of reference for a scheme of traditional and rational morality. His view of love is a proper, decent and sensible one, and virtuous love is for him the control of passion, the intrinsic "goodness" of which he nowhere denies, through the exercise of reason. Thus a "sin" against love is likely to be a sin by any definition and not a paradoxical virtue.

Gower's treatment of the frame narrative is both witty and poignant, full of dry and rueful comedy in which the Lover "hops alway behind," and ending with a strangely moving epilogue in which the Lover, aged and impotent, is pensioned off from the service of Venus. There is much delightful play here with the *persona* of the Lover and his relationship to the poet. The great strength of the *Confessio*, however, is in the inset narratives, where Gower shows himself to be a narrative poet of warm human sensitivity and compassionate understanding. He takes the stories far beyond their prescriptive or exemplary function into a world where virtuous conduct is seen to spring from fineness and unconstrained decency of feeling, rather than obedience to law, and can therefore seek out a consistent universe of moral value even in stories so barbaric as those of Tereus and Medea. It is the stories of women betrayed or deceived in love that call forth his readiest imaginative sympathy, and he has a power of communicating positively the worth of the love lost as well as the sadness of its loss. Whatever role as keeper of the nation's conscience he may have cast himself for, Gower understood truly in his poetry the "civilisation of the heart."

—Derek Pearsall

GRAINGER, James.   Scottish.   Born in Duns, Berwickshire, c. 1721. Educated at a school in North Berwick; studied medicine at the University of Edinburgh, M.D. 1753; Licentiate of the Royal College of Physicians, 1758. Served as an Army Surgeon, 1745–48. Married Miss Daniel Mathew Burt in 1759; two daughters. Practised medicine in London from 1753, but was more successful as a writer than as a physician; a friend of Dr. Johnson, Bishop Percy, and Smollett; contributor to the *Monthly Review*, London, 1756–58; lived and practised medicine in St. Christopher in the West Indies, 1759–66. *Died 16 December 1766.*

PUBLICATIONS

Collections

   Poetical Works, edited by R. Anderson.   2 vols., 1836.

Verse

   A Poetical Translation of Tibullus and Sulpicia.   2 vols., 1759.
   The Sugar-Cane.   1764.

Other

   Historia Febris Anomalae Batavae.   1753.
   An Essay on the More Common West Indian Diseases.   1764.

Translator, *Cyclops,* by Euripides, in *The Greek Theatre of Father Brumoy.*   3 vols., 1759.

*   *   *

Though Johnson said that his "Ode on Solitude" (Dodsley's *Collection,* iv, 1755) was "very noble," and Percy considered his ballad "Bryan and Pereene" worth including in the first volume of the *Reliques* (1765), James Grainger's only notable poem is his 2,500 lines-long didactic blank-verse poem in four books, *The Sugar-Cane.* This poem describes with appropriate narrative and descriptive digressions the cultivation of sugar cane in the West Indies, the manufacture of sugar, and the management of negro slaves. It is avowedly an imitation of Virgil's *Georgics,* and thus claims a place alongside John Philips's *Cyder,* Somerville's *The Chace,* Smart's *The Hop-Garden* and Dyer's *The Fleece,* all of which are mentioned in Grainger's poem. *The Sugar-Cane* is more remorselessly didactic than any of those earlier eighteenth-century English georgics (for Grainger's botanical, etymological, geographical, historical, medical, zoological, and other notes to his text are as bulky as the poem itself), and deals with a novel, exotic subject which, according to Grainger's Preface, "could not fail to enrich poetry with many new and picturesque images"; but Grainger contrives only to be turgid where he tries to be sublime, and silly where he tries to be sentimental. There is a saving touch of the mock-heroic from time to time, but even here the poet is clumsy and his effects laboured. *The Sugar-Cane* fails absolutely to recapture anything approaching Virgil's perfect blend of the epical and the mundane; and so, perhaps, it is not unjust that the poem is best remembered in literary history on account of the mirth occasioned when Grainger read his manuscript to Sir Joshua Reynolds and his friends, and, after much blank-verse pomp, began a new paragraph with the words: "Now, Muse, let's sing of Rats."

—A. J. Sambrook

GRAVES, Robert (Ranke).   English.   Born in London, 24 July 1895. Educated at Charterhouse School, Surrey; St. John's College, Oxford, B.Litt. 1926. Served in France with the Royal Welch Fusiliers in World War I; was refused admittance into the armed forces in World War II. Married 1) Nancy Nicholson, one son, two daughters; 2) Beryl Pritchard, three sons, one daughter. Professor of English, Egyptian University, Cairo, 1926. Settled in Deya, Majorca; with the poet Laura Riding established the Seizen Press and *Epilogue* magazine. Left Majorca during the Spanish Civil War; settled in Glampton-Brixton, Devon during World War II; returned to Majorca after the war. Clark Lecturer, Trinity College, Cambridge, 1954; Professor of Poetry, Oxford University, 1961–66; Arthur Dehon Little Memorial Lecturer, Massachusetts Institute of Technology, Cambridge, 1963. Recipient: Bronze Medal for Poetry, Olympic Games, Paris, 1924; Hawthornden Prize, for fiction, 1935; Black Memorial Prize, for fiction, 1935; Femina Vie Heureuse-Stock Prize, 1939; Russell Loines Award, 1958; National Poetry Society of America Gold Medal, 1960; Foyle Poetry Prize, 1960; Arts Council Poetry Award, 1962; Italia Prize, for radio play, 1965; Queen's Gold Medal for Poetry, 1968; Gold Medal for Poetry, Cultural Olympics, Mexico City, 1968. M.A.: Oxford University, 1961. Honorary Fellow, St. John's College, Oxford, 1971. Honorary Member, American Academy of Arts and Sciences, 1970. Lives in Majorca.

Verse

Over the Brazier. 1916.
Goliath and David. 1916.
Fairies and Fusiliers. 1917.
Treasure Box. 1919.
Country Sentiment. 1920.
The Pier-Glass. 1921.
Whipperginny. 1923.
The Feather Bed. 1923.
Mock Beggar Hall. 1924.
Welchman's Hose. 1925.
(Poems). 1925.
The Marmosite's Miscellany. 1925.
Poems (1914–1926). 1927.
Poems (1914–1927). 1927.
Poems 1929. 1929.
Ten Poems More. 1930.
Poems 1926–1930. 1931.
To Whom Else? 1931.
Poems 1930–1933. 1933.
Collected Poems. 1938.
No More Ghosts: Selected Poems. 1940.
Work in Hand, with Alan Hodge and Norman Cameron. 1942.
(Poems). 1943.
Poems 1938–1945. 1946.
Collected Poems (1914–1947). 1948.
Poems and Satires 1951. 1951.
Poems 1953. 1953.
Collected Poems 1955. 1955.
Poems Selected by Himself. 1957; revised edition, 1961, 1966.
The Poems. 1958.
Collected Poems 1959. 1959.
More Poems 1961. 1961.
Collected Poems. 1961.
New Poems 1962. 1962.
The More Deserving Cases: Eighteen Old Poems for Reconsideration. 1962.
Man Does, Woman Is 1964. 1964.
Love Respelt. 1965.
Collected Poems 1965. 1965.
Seventeen Poems Missing from "Love Respelt". 1966.
Colophon to "Love Respelt". 1967.
(Poems), with D. H. Lawrence, edited by Leonard Clark. 1967.
Poems 1965–1968. 1968.
Poems about Love. 1969.
Love Respelt Again. 1969.
Beyond Giving: Poems. 1969.
Poems 1968–1970. 1970.
The Green-Sailed Vessel. 1971.
Poems 1970–1972. 1972.
Deyá. 1973.

Timeless Meeting: Poems.   1973.
At the Gate.   1974.
Collected Poems 1975.   1975.
New Collected Poems.   1977.

Plays

John Kemp's Wager: A Ballad Opera.   1925.
Much Ado about Nothing, from the play by Shakespeare, textual revisions by Graves
   (produced 1965).

Radio Play: *The Anger of Achilles,* 1964.

Fiction

The Shout.   1929.
No Decency Left, with Laura Riding.   1932.
The Real David Copperfield.   1933; as *David Copperfield by Charles Dickens,*
   Condensed by Robert Graves, edited by Merrill P. Paine, 1934.
I, Claudius: From the Autobiography of Tiberius Claudius, Emperor of the Romans, Born
   B.C. 10, Murdered and Deified A.D. 54.   1934.
Claudius the God and His Wife Messalina: The Troublesome Reign of Tiberius Claudius
   Caesar, Emperor of the Romans (Born B.C. 10, Died A.D. 54), As Described by
   Himself; Also His Murder at the Hands of the Notorious Agrippina (Mother of the
   Emperor Nero) and His Subsequent Deification. As Described by Others.   1934.
"Antigua, Penny, Puce."   1936; as *The Antigua Stamp,* 1937.
Count Belisarius.   1938.
Sergeant Lamb of the Ninth.   1940; as *Sergeant Lamb's America,* 1940.
Proceed, Sergeant Lamb.   1941.
The Story of Marie Powell: Wife to Mr. Milton.   1943; as *Wife to Mr. Milton: The Story*
   of Marie Powell, 1944.
The Golden Fleece.   1944; as *Hercules, My Shipmate,* 1945.
King Jesus.   1946.
Watch the North Wind Rise.   1949; as *Seven Days in New Crete,* 1949.
The Islands of Unwisdom.   1949; as *The Isles of Unwisdom,* 1950.
Homer's Daughter.   1955.
¡Catacrok! Mostly Stories, Mostly Funny.   1956.
Collected Short Stories.   1964.

Other

On English Poetry, Being an Irregular Approach to the Psychology of This Art, from
   Evidence Mainly Subjective.   1922.
The Meaning of Dreams.   1924.
Poetic Unreason and Other Studies.   1925.
My Head! My Head! Being the History of Elisha and the Shunamite Woman; With the
   History of Moses as Elisha Related It, and Her Questions to Him.   1925.
Contemporary Techniques of Poetry: A Political Analogy.   1925.
Another Future of Poetry.   1926.
Impenetrability; or, The Proper Habit of English.   1927.
The English Ballad: A Short Critical Survey.   1927.

Lars Porsena; or, The Future of Swearing and Improper Language. 1927; revised edition, as *The Future of Swearing and Improper Language,* 1936.

A Survey of Modernist Poetry, with Laura Riding. 1927.

Lawrence and the Arabs. 1927; as *Lawrence and the Arabian Adventure,* 1928.

A Pamphlet Against Anthologies, with Laura Riding. 1928; as *Against Anthologies,* 1928.

Mrs. Fisher; or, The Future of Humour. 1928.

Goodbye to All That: An Autobiography. 1929; revised edition, 1957, 1960.

But It Still Goes On: An Accumulation. 1930.

Epilogue: A Critical Summary, vols. 1, 2, and 3, with Laura Riding and others. 1935–37.

T. E. Lawrence to His Biographer Robert Graves. 1938.

The Long Week-end: A Social History of Great Britain 1918–1939, with Alan Hodge. 1940.

The Reader over Your Shoulder: A Handbook for Writers of English Prose, with Alan Hodge. 1943.

The White Goddess: A Historical Grammar of Poetic Myth. 1948; revised edition, 1958.

The Common Asphodel: Collected Essays on Poetry 1922–1949. 1949.

Occupation: Writer. 1950.

The Nazarene Gospel Restored, with Joshua Podro. 1953.

The Crowing Privilege: The Clark Lectures 1954–1955; Also Various Essays on Poetry and Sixteen New Poems. 1955; as *The Crowning Privilege: Collected Essays on Poetry,* 1956.

Adam's Rib and Other Anomalous Elements in the Hebrew Creation Myth: A New View. 1955.

The Greek Myths. 2 vols., 1955.

Jesus in Rome: A Historical Conjecture, with Joshua Podro. 1957.

They Hanged My Saintly Billy. 1957; as *They Hanged My Saintly Billy: The Life and Death of Dr. William Palmer,* 1957.

Steps: Stories, Talks, Essays, Poems, Studies in History. 1958.

Five Pens in Hand. 1958.

Food for Centaurs: Stories, Talks, Critical Studies, Poems. 1960.

The Penny Fiddle: Poems for Children. 1960.

Greek Gods and Heroes. 1960; as *Myths of Ancient Greece,* 1961.

Selected Poetry and Prose, edited by James Reeves. 1961.

The Siege and Fall of Troy (juvenile). 1962.

The Big Green Book. 1962.

Oxford Addresses on Poetry. 1962.

The Hebrew Myths: The Book of Genesis, with Raphael Patai. 1964.

Ann at Highwood Hall: Poems for Children. 1964.

Majorca Observed. 1965.

Mammon and the Black Goddess. 1965.

Two Wise Children (juvenile). 1966.

Poetic Craft and Principle: Lectures and Talks. 1967.

Spiritual Quixote. 1967.

The Poor Boy Who Followed His Star (juvenile). 1968.

The Crane Bag and Other Disputed Subjects. 1969.

On Poetry: Collected Talks and Essays. 1969.

Poems: Abridged for Dolls and Princes (juvenile). 1971.

Difficult Questions, Easy Answers. 1972.

Editor, with Alan Porter and Richard Hughes, *Oxford Poetry, 1921.* 1921.

Editor, *John Skelton (Laureate), 1460(?)–1529.* 1927.

Editor, *The Less Familiar Nursery Rhymes*. 1927.
Editor, *Old Soldiers Never Die*, by Frank Richards. 1933.
Editor, *Old Soldier Sahib*, by Frank Richards. 1936.
Editor, *The Comedies of Terence*, translated by Echard. 1962.

Translator, with Laura Riding, *Almost Forgotten Germany*, by George Schwarz. 1936.
Translator, *The Transformations of Lucius, Otherwise Known as The Golden Ass*, by Apuleius. 1950.
Translator, *The Cross and the Sword*, by Manuel de Jesus Galvan. 1954.
Translator, *The Infant with the Globe*, by Pedro Antonio de Alarcon. 1955.
Translator, *Winter in Majorca*, by George Sand. 1956.
Translator, *Pharsalia: Dramatic Episodes of the Civil Wars*, by Lucan. 1956.
Translator, *The Twelve Caesars*, by Suetonius. 1957.
Translator, *The Anger of Achilles: Homer's Iliad*. 1959.
Translator, with Omar Ali-Shah, *Rubaiyyat of Omar Khayaam*. 1967.
Translator, *The Song of Songs*. 1973.

Bibliography: *A Bibliography of the Works of Graves* by Fred H. Higginson, 1966.

Reading List: *Graves* by Martin Seymour-Smith, 1956, revised edition, 1965, 1970; *Graves* by J. M. Cohen, 1960; *Swifter than Reason: The Poetry and Criticism of Graves* by Douglas Day, 1963; *Graves* by George Stade, 1967; *Barbarous Knowledge: Myth in the Poetry of Yeats, Graves, and Muir* by Daniel Hoffman, 1967; *The Poetry of Graves* by Michael Kirkham, 1969; *The Third Book of Criticism* by Randall Jarrell, 1969.

*   *   *

Robert Graves's prolific writings in prose and verse express his own conflicting characteristics. He is at once a Romantic primitive and a classicist; a seeker of ecstasy and of formal perfection. Committed to the life of feeling and the rule of intuition, he is a compulsive systematizer and puzzle-solver. Indeed, Graves is a confirming example of what T. S. Eliot diagnosed as the characteristic modern condition: dissociation of sensibility from thought. Graves's entire career expresses his inspired, inventive, and ingenious efforts to express either side of his essential self; in his best work, both are intertwined.

Graves's childhood and adolescence were typical of his class and time. Son of A. P. Graves, a facile verse-writer and translator from the Irish who was inspector of schools in Dublin, Robert had a proper Edwardian childhood and was schooled at Charterhouse. At the outbreak of the first World War he volunteered and was commissioned in the Royal Welch Fusiliers. His choice of regiment reflects his desire to find his own Celtic roots elsewhere than in the Ireland pre-empted by his father's literary activity. The immediate result of service was his exposure to the horror of trench warfare, severe wounds, being reported dead, return to duty, subsequent hospitalization in England where he was treated for shell-shock by Dr. W. H. R. Rivers, whose patients included Siegfried Sassoon and Wilfred Owen and whose psychiatric theories influenced Graves's aesthetic in the 1920's. The war experience and its aftermath are memorably stated in his autobiography, *Goodbye to All That*, his aesthetic in *Poetic Unreason*.

By 1916 Graves had published his first book of poems, *Over the Brazier*, rather vapid stuff compared to what he would write within a decade. As a war poet Graves did not deal, as did Owen, Sassoon, and Isaac Rosenberg, with reality; his desperately self-protective imagination held fast to nursery and nature images, the pieties of Georgianism. Not until the war was over could Graves grapple with its nightmarish revelation of the madness of reality, as he does in such poems as "In Procession," "Warning to Children," "Alice," "The Cool Web," "In Broken Images," and many others. These are among the most powerful reflections of the

433

disintegration of certainty, the blasting apart of pre-war norms, the guilt of survivors, the desperation of man deprived of the traditional and institutional props of his culture.

With tenacity Graves refused, however, to surrender certain of those institutions and traditions. As a poet he resisted the modernist break-up of meter, form, and linguistic decorum. In its conventional craft his work is thus nearer to that of Hardy and Yeats than to Eliot or Pound. In theme, however, he has not essayed the range of any of these. Besides his poems of psychomachia mentioned above, his principal theme has been the recording of romantic love. In this his work shows affinities to Donne and the Cavalier poets, but Graves's view of love is unique. From the beginning he viewed love as a transcendent ecstasy immutably linked with doom, as in "Love Without Hope" (1925):

> Love without hope, as when the young bird-catcher
> Swept off his tall hat to the Squire's own daughter,
> So let the imprisoned larks escape and fly
> Singing about her head, as she rode by.

This quatrain encapsulates the convictions Graves would raise into myth in *The White Goddess*, that stupendous "historic grammar of poetic myth" which explicates what in his poem "To Juan at the Winter Solstice" he called the "one story and one story only/That will prove worth your telling." The Squire's daughter will become a queen, a goddess, while remaining the mortal woman whom the poet is fated to love; the young bird-catcher is of course the poet whose singing larks were imprisoned in his head (under his tall hat) until he gave them freedom to declare his hopeless adoration. The beloved is in fact the poet's Muse who appears to him as Mother, Lover, and Layer-out, a tripartite pattern of significance Graves traces to the once-universal matriarchal religious states that preceded the patriarchy, repressive of the life of feeling, which the Judeo-Christian tradition has foisted upon the world.

Accept this historiography (with its roots in Celtic and Classical paganism) or not; what is incontestable is that Graves has written a body of love poetry without rival in our time for its intensity, elegance, and occasional lubricity.

As novelist and essayist Graves demonstrates the erudition and intellectual ingenuity that characterize *The White Goddess*. Many of his fictions offer "answers" to conundrums historians not gifted with a poet's intuition have been unable to solve, just as Graves's discursive books often "restore" defective literary or sacred texts (e.g., the ballads, the Bible). His most admired novels, *I, Claudius* and *Claudius the God*, provide the hitherto secret memoirs of Claudius himself and give an even more intimate view than did Suetonius of the depravities of Rome's first family between the reigns of Caesar Augustus and Claudius himself. The latter, shy, stammering, introspective, and wise, has a poet's understanding of the social and personal catastrophes enacted around him. To the alert reader Graves is writing about the decline and fall of the British as well as the Roman empire, as he does overtly in *The Long Week-end*. Other novels present historical cruces from similarly unexpected points of view. *Wife to Mr. Milton* exonerates its heroine against the received calumnies of a poet Graves dislikes intensely. *Sergeant Lamb's America* treats the American Revolution as seen by a predecessor in Graves's own regiment.

Graves's measure for other poets, as for himself, is their participation in "The poetic trance derive[d] from ecstatic worship of the age-old matriarchal Greek Muse, who ruled Sky, Earth, Underworld in triad." In his Oxford lectures, *Mammon and the Black Goddess*, Graves discovers a further stage in his anatomy of love, the stations of the poet's progress. "The Black Goddess... promises a new pacific bond between men and women, corresponding to a final reality of love, in which the patriarchal marriage bond will fade away.... Faithful as Vesta, gay and adventurous as the White Goddess, she will lead man back to that sure instinct of love which he long ago forfeited by intellectual pride." Robert Graves has continued to pour forth poems on his "one story only" past his eightieth year.

—Daniel Hoffman

GRAY, Thomas. English. Born in Cornhill, London, 26 December 1716. Educated at Eton College, 1727–34; Peterhouse, Cambridge, 1734–39, 1742–43, LL.B. 1743; also studied law in London, 1741. Accompanied Horace Walpole on a grand tour of France and Italy, in 1739–41. Lived in Cambridge, as a don, at Peterhouse, 1741–56, and Pembroke Hall, 1756–71; Professor of Modern History, Cambridge University, 1768. *Died 30 July 1771.*

PUBLICATIONS

Collections

> *Works in Prose and Verse,* edited by Edmund Gosse.   4 vols., 1884.
> *Correspondence,* edited by Paget Toynbee and Leonard Whibley.   3 vols., 1935.
> *Complete Poems, English, Latin, and Greek,* edited by H. W. Starr and J. R. Hendrickson.   1966.
> *Complete English Poems,* edited by James Reeves.   1973.
> *Poetical Works,* with Collins, edited by R. H. Lonsdale.   1977.

Verse

> *Ode on a Distant Prospect of Eton College.*   1747.
> *An Elegy Wrote in a Country Church Yard.*   1751.
> *Designs by Mr. R. Bentley for Six Poems by Gray.*   1753.
> *Odes.*   1757.
> *Poems.*   1768.
> *Ode Performed in the Senate House at Cambridge.*   1769.

Other

> *Walpole's Correspondence with Gray, West, and Ashton,* edited by W. S. Lewis and others, in *Walpole's Correspondence,* vols. 13–14.   1948.

Bibliography: *A Bibliography of Gray* by Clark S. Northrup, 1917, supplement by H. W. Starr, 1953.

Reading List: *Gray as a Literary Critic* by H. W. Starr, 1941; *Gray: A Biography* by Robert R. Ketton-Cremer, 1955; *Gray* by Morris Golden, 1964; *Gray and the Bard* by A. Johnston, 1966.

*   *   *

Thomas Gray is generally and rightly regarded as a transitional figure in eighteenth-century poetry, providing a bridge between the poetic sensibility of his own generation and the Romantic revolution of the future. He combines in a unique way a classic perfection of form typical of the Augustan era with subject matters and attitudes which are clearly Romantic and anticipate later developments.

Nowhere is this fusion more obvious than in Gray's most famous poem, the "Elegy Written in a Country Churchyard." Here he works within the rigid limitations of a four-line iambic pentameter stanza, rhymed A B A B, constructing stately and memorable poetic locutions while remaining strictly conventional in his rhythms, rhymes, and diction. The very regularity of his heavy iambic beat helps to create a sense of the timeless, changeless routine of country life. In style the "Elegy" is traditional and neoclassical. But in ideas and attitudes, Gray breaks new ground. He celebrates the worth and humanity of the common man in a way that foreshadows Burns and Wordsworth; he ruminates with Romantic melancholy over "the short and simple annals of the poor." Moreover, in the later part of the poem where the focus shifts from the nameless dead to the poet himself we get a strong subjective and introspective emphasis that is startlingly new. For modern readers the poem is so familiar, so much a part of our cultural heritage, that we tend to lose the sense of its freshness for readers in 1751.

A large part of the elegy's appeal and greatness lies, of course, in its smoothly and meticulously wrought phrasing, its many unforgettable lines: "The paths of glory lead but to the grave," "Full many a flower is born to flush unseen,/And waste its sweetness on the desert air," "For from the madding crowd's ignoble strife," etc. Perhaps, after all, Dr. Johnson's is still the best distillation of the elegy's perennial power: it "abounds with images which find a mirror in every mind, and with sentiments to which every bosom returns an echo."

The same combination of classic form and emotional attitudes is observable in Gray's fine odes. The "Ode on a Distant Prospect of Eton College" evokes a nostalgic picture of the carefree life of college boys and grim forebodings of their adult futures. The poem suffers somewhat, at least for modern readers, from excessively "poetic" diction and rather wooden abstractions, but is redeemed (though to a lesser extent than the "Elegy") by some unforgettable phrasing. Lines such as the following, on schoolboys escaping on adventurous rambles, "They hear a voice in every wind,/And snatch a fearful joy," or the famous closing thought, "where ignorance is bliss,/'Tis folly to be wise," distill the special magic of Gray's style at its best. The longer ode on "The Progress of Poesy" is, on the whole, poetically superior, as Gray traces the evolution of the power of verbal harmony from Greece to Rome to England, with eloquent passages on Shakespeare, Milton, and Dryden. As in the "Elegy," the focus shifts significantly at the end to Gray himself, closing with a graceful definition of his own view of himself as poet and recluse who shall "keep his distant way/Beyond the limits of a vulgar fate." Here again Gray's gift for rich, memorable language is often evident, as in "O'er her warm cheek and rising bosom move/The bloom of young desire and purple light of love," or "The unconquerable mind, and Freedom's holy flame," or (on Milton) "He saw; but blasted with excess of light,/Closed his eyes in endless night."

The most ambitious of Gray's Pindaric odes is "The Bard," one fruit of his long and keen study of Celtic and Norse mythology and poetic antiquities. The speaker in this monologue is a Welsh bard pronouncing a terrible curse on Edward I and his invading English army, foretelling disaster for Edward's descendants. This device enables Gray to present an eloquent, impassioned summary of English history, climaxing in the ascent of a Welsh royal family (the Tudors) to usher in a golden age in the distant future. Opening with the strong lines, "Ruin seize thee, ruthless King!/Confusion on thy banners wait," the ode is Gray's most exuberant and Romantic poem, full of extravagantly emotional rhetoric, yet classic in form and impressive in its power. He followed this up with a few further experiments of the same antiquarian kind, notably two fine re-creations of Norse legends in "The Fatal Sisters" and "The Descent of Odin."

Despite the fact that Gray's work is small in bulk (Matthew Arnold called him "the scantiest" of classics), it is nevertheless remarkably varied and versatile. His achievements include poetry wholly different from the Romantic odes and elegies, such as attempts in purely neoclassical types of *vers de société* like the charming and clever "Ode on the Death of a Favourite Cat." As a letter writer, too, he is remarkable. Gray's letters are, in fact, the most humanly endearing part of his surviving writings – always interesting, full of keen observation, beautifully phrased, they give a new dimension to a personality that in the poetry often seems aloof and austere. They reveal much that is warm, witty, and sensitive in the man in the course of his daily life, as well as the fastidious elitism of his many intellectual pursuits and the obsessive enthusiasm for wild "Gothic" landscapes in his travels.

During a quiet, studious lifetime Gray immersed himself in many subjects – he was a fine scholar, historian, antiquarian, and folklorist, as well as a poet – and he achieved distinction in all of them. In poetry, however, he achieved greatness. His special power lies in the gift of precise and memorable language, the result of rigid discipline from long years of study of Greek and Roman literature combined with a soaring original imagination. Steeped as he was in the past, in his ideas and emotions Gray looked to the future.

—Allan H. MacLaine

GREEN, Matthew. English. Born in 1696. Little is known about his life, except that he held an appointment in the Customs House, London. *Died in 1737.*

PUBLICATIONS

Collections

Poetical Works, with Armstrong and Dyer, edited by George Gilfillan. 1859.
Minor Poets of the Eighteenth Century, edited by Hugh I'A. Fausset. 1930.

Verse

The Grotto. 1733.
The Spleen, edited by Richard Glover. 1737; edited by W. H. Williams, 1936.
Poems. 1796.

*   *   *

Matthew Green is one of a number of minor eighteenth-century poets who are remembered for one poem. (Dyer and Goldsmith are others who quickly spring to mind.) *The Spleen* was published posthumously in 1737, soon became popular, and was much imitated during the later years of the century. Perhaps the most absurd imitation of Green's minor masterpiece is William Thompson's *The Sickness* of 1757, while the finest poem to owe something to it is undoubtedly William Cowper's *Retirement.*

We do not know how much poetry Green wrote, but we do know that very little ever saw the light of day. *The Grotto* was privately printed, several other poems found their way into Dodsley's various collections, and a necessarily slender edition of the poems was finally published in 1796. A reader dipping into that edition would soon identify *The Grotto* as one of those charming exercises in moralised landscape which eighteenth-century poets delighted to produce. Ultimately derived from Virgil's *Georgics*, the first example in English of this kind of poem is Denham's *Cooper's Hill*, which was written as early as 1643. "The Grotto" owes much to *Cooper's Hill*, but Green's verse form, the octosyllabic couplet – it is also the form of *The Spleen* – derives from Marvell, Butler, and, perhaps, the Dyer of *Grongar Hill*. Green's poem is a charming if slight addition to a line of English poetry which is at its clearest and firmest in Pope's *Windsor Forest*. *The Grotto*, that is to say, is a derivative poem.

437

The Spleen, on the other hand, is much more original. It is also a well-nigh flawless performance: witty, unfailingly well written, and very exactly able to match the deftness of argument to smooth handling of the verse. Green appears in the poem as a spokesman for moderation: he counsels caution, self-discipline, an unforced withdrawal from the stresses of social and imaginative life, and avoidance of the follies and excesses of enthusiasm and "self-consuming spleen." Yet the poem is not a weightily moral exercise. Green knows the Augustan arguments against excess, but he does not write in didactic vein. He is less interested in homily than in adroit turns of phrase. The enthusiast's "springy soul dilates like air,/When free from weight of ambient care." "Springy soul" looks at first glance to be an unqualified compliment, but on reflection we realise that Green is inviting us to see the enthusiast's soul as a gassy compound. The compliment is subtly undermined. And "care" has just the right double-edged feel about it. On the one hand it implies those sad, massy weights of earthly cares from which we rightly seek escape; on the other, it means prudence, caution, that which we renounce at our peril. Such urbanity of tone – for the wit of the couplet I have quoted is poised, civilised, isn't at all clumsy or "butchering" – runs through *The Spleen*, and gives it its distinction.

Green's tone always seems to me to aim for and achieve such urbanity, whether he is writing with the comparative seriousness that he employs in *The Spleen*, or whether he is writing such ephemeral but delightful pieces as "The Seeker" or "The Sparrow and Diamond." In short, it may be said that Green belongs to that "line of wit" which has properly been identified as running from the Cavalier poets through to Pope and the eighteenth century.

—John Lucas

GREGORY, Horace (Victor).   American.   Born in Milwaukee, Wisconsin, 10 April 1898. Educated at the Milwaukee School of Fine Arts, Summers 1913–16; German-English Academy, Milwaukee, 1914–19; University of Wisconsin, Madison, 1919–23, B.A. 1923. Married the poet Marya Zaturenska in 1925; two children. Free-lance writer, New York and London, 1923–34; Member of the English Department, 1934–60, and since 1960, Professor Emeritus, Sarah Lawrence College, Bronxville, New York. Lecturer, New School for Social Research, New York, 1955–56. Associate Editor, *Tiger's Eye* magazine, New York. Recipient: Levinson Award, 1936; Russell Loines Award, 1942; Guggenheim Fellowship, 1951; Academy of American Poets Fellowship, 1961; Bollingen Prize, 1965; Horace Gregory Foundation Award, 1969. Member, National Institute of Arts and Letters, 1964. Lives in Rockland County, New York.

PUBLICATIONS

Verse

Chelsea Rooming House.   1930; as *Rooming House,* 1932.
No Retreat.   1933.
A Wreath for Margery.   1933.
Chorus for Survival.   1935.

438

Poems 1930–1940. 1941.
Selected Poems. 1951.
Medusa in Gramercy Park. 1961.
Alphabet for Joanna (juvenile). 1963.
Collected Poems. 1964.
Another Look. 1976.

Other

Pilgrim of the Apocalypse: A Critical Study of D. H. Lawrence. 1933; revised edition, 1957.
The Shield of Achilles: Essays on Beliefs in Poetry. 1944.
A History of American Poetry 1900–1940, with Marya Zaturenska. 1946.
Amy Lowell: Portrait of the Poet in Her Time. 1958.
The World of James McNeill Whistler. 1959.
The Dying Gladiators and Other Essays. 1961.
Dorothy Richardson: An Adventure in Self-Discovery. 1967.
The House on Jefferson Street: A Cycle of Memories. 1971.
Spirit of Time and Place: The Collected Essays. 1973.

Editor, with Eleanor Clark, *New Letters in America.* 1937.
Editor, *Critical Remarks on the Metaphysical Poets,* by Samuel Johnson. 1943.
Editor, *The Triumph of Life: Poems of Consolation for the English-Speaking World.* 1945.
Editor, *The Portable Sherwood Anderson.* 1949.
Editor, *Selected Poetry,* by Robert Browning. 1956.
Editor, with Marya Zaturenska, *The Mentor Book of Religious Verse.* 1957.
Editor, with Marya Zaturenska, *The Crystal Cabinet: An Invitation to Poetry.* 1962.
Editor, with others, *Riverside Poetry 4: An Anthology of Student Verse.* 1962.
Editor, *Evangeline and Selected Tales and Poems of Longfellow.* 1964.
Editor, *Selected Poems,* by E. E. Cummings. 1965.
Editor, with Marya Zaturenska, *The Silver Swan: Poems of Romance and Mystery.* 1966.
Editor, *Selected Poems of Lord Byron.* 1969.

Translator, *The Poems of Catullus.* 1931.
Translator, *Poems,* by Catullus. 1956.
Translator, *The Metamorphoses,* by Ovid. 1958.
Translator, *Love Poems of Ovid.* 1964.

Reading List: "Gregory Issue" of *Modern Poetry Studies,* May 1973.

*   *   *

Horace Gregory is perhaps best known as the translator of Catullus and Ovid. But he has also published critical studies on Amy Lowell, D. H. Lawrence, James McNeill Whistler and others, as well as collaborating with his wife, the poet Marya Zaturenska, on *A History of American Poetry 1900–1940.*

Elizabeth Drew has written that his "emotional range is perhaps the most comprehensive among modern poets," and Louis Untermeyer wrote that Gregory "does not share Eliot's disillusions or Crane's disorganization," a statement that is unfair to all three poets. However, poems like "Valediction to My Contemporaries" compare interestingly with Hart Crane's

"The Bridge" in their language, their idealism, their purposes; and many of Gregory's efforts to recapture in monologues the pathos and cacophony of life in the modern city remind one of Eliot. In the final analysis, however, authenticity and integrity may not be enough; subtleties of syntax, powers of condensation, originality of imagery, distinguish Eliot and Crane from those who wrote with comparable verve.

Gregory is academic, ordered, descriptive, even-paced; he might be quite properly compared with MacLeish for his intellectual ambition, rhetorical power, and sense of American history. Most of his poems are based on classical subjects in one way or another, though he often juxtaposes classical imagery with modernistic impressions; he also has many poems about paintings, European scenes, and – like MacLeish – his country's cultural history. His well-known poem on Emerson recapitulates Emerson's life in an investigation of the intellectual's role ("To know too well, to think too long") in a land where action and immortality are even more akin than rhetoric and relevance. Gregory, like MacLeish, bears a heavy weight of idealism at all times, perhaps more than his country's history can support. Because the idealism is more muted in his Chelsea rooming house poems, they are perhaps more appealing than his poems with more epic ambitions. In poems like "McAlpin Garfinkel, Poet" and "Time and Isidore Lefkowitz", Gregory seems to have absorbed the influence of Edwin Arlington Robinson and to have looked forward to the work of poets like Kenneth Fearing:

> Look at Isidore Lefkowitz,
> biting his nails, telling how
> he seduces Beautiful French Canadian
> Five and Ten Cent Store Girls,
> beautiful, by God, and how they cry
> and moan, wrapping their arms
> and legs around him
> when he leaves them....

In an age when we have come to think of poems as the swiftly captured sound of madness, Gregory's work stands as a celebration of order, with the glimpsed backstreet life crying out to have a part of that order and the consideration due to it.

> How can I unlearn
> the arts of love within a single hour:
> How can I close my eyes before a mirror,
> believe I am not wanted, that hands, lips, breast
> are merely deeper shadows behind the door
> where all is dark?

> —David Ray

GREVILLE, Sir Fulke; 1st Baron Brooke. English. Born at Beauchamp Court, Warwickshire, 3 October 1554. Educated at Shrewsbury School, Shropshire, where he met Sir Philip Sidney, 1564–68; Jesus College, Cambridge (Fellow-Commoner), from 1568. Served in the courts of both Queen Elizabeth I and James I: travelled with Sidney to Heidelberg, 1577; with Walsingham on diplomatic mission to Flanders, 1578; accompanied Sidney's friend Languet to Germany, 1579; with Sidney, Sir Edward Dyer, and Gabriel Harvey, formed the Areopagus literary society, an important center of literary influence at court; served under Henry of Navarre in Normandy, 1591; Member of Parliament for Warwickshire, 1592–93, 1597, 1601, 1620; Secretary for the Principality of Wales, 1583 until the end of his life; Treasurer of the Navy, 1598–1604; Chancellor and Under-Treasurer of the Exchequer, 1614–21, and Commissioner of the Treasury, 1618; Member, Council of

War, 1624, and Committee on Foreign Affairs, 1625. Granted Wedgnock Park by Elizabeth, 1597; and Warwick Castle, 1605, and extension of his family estates, Knowle Park, 1606, by James. Knight of the Bath, 1603; created Baron Brooke, 1621. Murdered by a discontented servant. *Died 30 September 1628.*

PUBLICATIONS

Collections

The Works in Verse and Prose, edited by Alexander B. Grosart.   4 vols., 1870.
Poems and Dramas, edited by Geoffrey Bullough.   2 vols., 1939.
Selected Poems, edited by Thom Gunn.   1968.
Selected Writings, edited by Joan Rees.   1973.

Verse

Two Elegies, with William Browne.   1613.
Caelica, in *Certain Learned and Elegant Works.*   1633; edited by Una Ellis-Fermor, 1936.
The Remains: Poems of Monarchy and Religion.   1670; edited by G. A. Wilkes, 1965.

Plays

Alaham (produced 1600?).   In *Certain Learned and Elegant Works,* 1633.
Mustapha (produced 1603–08?).   1609.

Other

Certain Learned and Elegant Works.   1633.
The Life of the Renowned Sir Philip Sidney.   1652; edited by Nowell Smith, 1907.

Reading List: *Greville tra il Mondo e Dio* by Napoleone Orsini, 1941; *Greville's Caelica: An Evaluation* by William Frost, 1942; *Die Anschauungen über Wissenschaft und Religion im Werke Grevilles* by H. W. Utz, 1948; *The Life of Greville* by Ronald A. Rebholz, 1971; *Greville: A Critical Biography* by Joan Rees, 1971; *The Fatal Mirror: Themes and Techniques in the Poetry of Greville* by Richard Waswo, 1972.

*   *   *

Sir Fulke Greville brought to the pursuit of poetry a powerful and individual mind. Stimulated by Sidney in his young manhood, he composed lyrics on the theme of love, using sometimes the devices of Petrarchan rhetoric and sometimes plainer styles. These form part of the sequence *Caelica,* a collection of 109 short poems of which 41 are sonnets. The sonnets are composed in the English form, not, like Sidney's, in the Italian, but this is only one of many differences between Greville's "love" poetry and that of his friend. It seems likely that the first 76 of the *Caelica* poems were written before Sidney's death and, at points where *Caelica* and *Astrophil and Stella* are close, Greville can be seen to be making an ironic commentary on Sidney's idealisation of sexual love. Even in these early poems, the mark of Greville's writing is a cool and sceptical intelligence and the lyrics display a shrewd and sardonic wit. A few of them adopt the neo-Platonic attitude of reverence towards the beloved but an increasingly ironic tone makes itself heard and Greville's use of religious reference and vocabulary comes to be, not a compliment to a mistress, but a means of exposing the relative worthlessness of earthly pursuits and earthly desires. The dates of the later poems of *Caelica* are unknown but Greville may have gone on composing and revising throughout his long life. Whatever the chronology, the poems in effect constitute a record of his maturing mind and temperament. In LXXXIV he says farewell to secular love, and the religious feeling, present by ironic implication earlier, reaches full expression in some subtle and splendid later poems. Greville's picture of the inner hell of man cut off from God and his sense of the saving grace offered through Christ lead to some of his most powerful and successful writing.

The later *Caelica* poems include some on political themes. In a sequence which mirrors as fully as this one does the mind of the poet, such material has a proper place. To the older Greville, a man much experienced in court and state affairs, political situations offered themselves as the perfect ground on which to observe the interplay of dominant forces in human nature: desire for power, and fear. After the early years, he treated love itself in a political context, for his temperament led him easily to a perception of sexual relations as a species of power struggle. Political choices, moreover, could be used to focus the tension between temporal advantage and eternal values, man's bondage to sin leading him always to seek the things of this world at the expense of the claims of another. Greville wrote a number of verse treatises in which the contending claims of the world and of God confront each other. Practising politician as he was, his analysis of the ways of the world is detailed and incisive but sooner or later he matches them against another conception of life in which renunciation and obedience to a higher law replace cupidity and aggression. There is much of interest in these treatises but the expression is often so sinewy and elliptical that for long passages they make tough reading.

Greville's two dramas, *Alaham* and *Mustapha*, deserve, on the other hand, to be much more read than they are. *Alaham* takes an extreme political situation and through it exposes the full capacity of human evil. *Mustapha* also treats of the worst corruptions of lust for power and makes out of its material a profound and wide-ranging drama of ultimate choices. Most men and women, as the play shows them, are selfish, or at best only partly committed to what they themselves recognise as virtue. The one truly good and innocent man is murdered and accepts death without resistance for he is really free of worldly entanglements. Such souls, Greville knows, are rare. In his so-called *Life of Sidney*, a prose work originally intended as a dedication of his poems, he is inclined to present the friend of his youth, long dead, as being among them. But for most men the conflict of God's will with the way of the world produces no sainthood but a sad awareness of the "wearisome condition of humanity/ Born under one law, to another bound," as the chorus of priests in *Mustapha* puts it.

Mustapha is a parable with religious and political meanings and it offers, besides, a keen analysis of human nature. It does on an extended scale what some of the *Caelica* poems also do; that is, it evolves a distinctive language of multiple reference which enables Greville to make his commentary on human experience at several levels simultaneously. Because of the packed meaning, and because also in non-lyrical work he rarely makes concessions to the beauty and music of language and phrasing, he is often a difficult poet to read, but there should be no doubt that he is a considerable one. His use of images bespeaks a poetic imagination, and his world view, by its coherence and force and penetration, becomes itself an imaginative creation. The two completest works that Greville wrote, *Caelica* and *Mustapha*, stand out among the rest as the most remarkable achievements of a most remarkable writer.

—Joan Rees

GRIEVE, Christopher Murray. See **MACDIARMID,** Hugh.

GUINEY, Louise Imogen. American. Born in Roxbury, Boston, Massachusetts, 7 January 1861. Educated at the Convent of the Sacred Heart, Elmhurst, Rhode Island. Worked for a time as a journalist; Postmistress, Auberndale, Massachusetts; worked in the cataloging department, Boston Public Library. Editor, with Alice Brow, *Pilgrim Scrip.* Moved to England, 1895. *Died 2 November 1920.*

PUBLICATIONS

Verse

> *Songs at the Start.* 1884.
> *The White Sail and Other Poems.* 1887.
> *A Roadside Harp.* 1893.
> *Nine Sonnets Written at Oxford.* 1895.
> *England and Yesterday: A Book of Short Poems.* 1898.
> *The Martyrs' Idyl and Shorter Poems.* 1899.
> *Happy Ending: Collected Lyrics.* 1909; revised edition, 1927.

Fiction

> *Lovers', Saint Ruth's, And Three Other Tales.* 1895.

Other

> *Goose-Quill Papers.* 1885.
> *Brownies and Bogles* (juvenile). 1888.
> *Monsieur Henri: A Foot-Note to French History.* 1892.
> *A Little English Gallery.* 1894.
> *Three Heroines in New England Romance: Their True Stories,* with Harriet Prescott Spoffard and Alice Brown. 1894.
> *Patrins, To Which Is Added an Inquirendo into the Wit and Other Good Parts of His Late Majesty King Charles the Second.* 1897.
> *Robert Emmet: A Survey of His Rebellion and of His Romance.* 1904.
> *Blessed Edmund Campion.* 1908.
> *Letters,* edited by Grace Guiney. 2 vols., 1926.
> *Colonel Guiney and the Ninth Massachusetts: A Filial Appreciation.* 1932.

> Editor, *James Clarence Mangan: His Selected Poems.* 1897.
> Editor, *Sohrab and Rustum and Other Poems,* by Matthew Arnold. 1899.
> Editor, *The Mount of Olives and Primitive Holiness,* by Henry Vaughan. 1902.
> Editor, *Selected Poems,* by Katherine Philips. 2 vols., 1904–05.
> Editor, *Hurrell Froude: Memoranda and Comments.* 1904.
> Editor, *Thomas Stanley: His Original Lyrics, Complete.* 1907.
> Editor, *Some Poems of Lionel Johnson.* 1912.

Editor, *Arthur Laurie Thomas: A Memoir,* by F. E. Thomas.   1920.
Editor, with Geoffrey Bliss, *Recusant Poets.*   1938.

Translator, *The Sermon to the Birds and the Wolf of Gubbio.*   1898.
Translator, *The Secret of Fougereuse: A Romance of the Fifteenth Century,* by Louise
    Morvan.   1898.

Bibliography: in *Bibliography of American Literature* by Jacob Blanck, 1959.

Reading List: *Guiney* by Alice Brown, 1921; *Guiney: Her Life and Works* by E. M. Tenison,
1923; *Guiney: Laureate of the Lost* by Henry C. Fairbanks, 1972.

*   *   *

Although she published more than thirty books and a hundred articles, Louise Imogen Guiney is relatively forgotten today. Her best volume of verse, *A Roadside Harp,* brings to maturity the themes and attitudes which she introduced in two previous collections, *Songs at the Start* and *The White Sail and Other Poems,* and which were to preoccupy her throughout her career: an attachment to the past, a fondness for nature, and a love for religion and learning. Technically, Guiney's poetry is conservative and genteel. Its carefully measured rhythms and conventional forms earned her the admiration of the Boston brahmin Oliver Wendell Holmes, who called her his "little golden guinea," and the disapproval of the editor and critic Horace Scudder, who found her work excessively "oblique and allusive."

For her models, Guiney looked toward the classics, in which she was extraordinarily well instructed, and the Renaissance, in which she was an acknowledged expert. Guiney was particularly fond of sonnets and elegies. *Nine Sonnets Written at Oxford* was considered by many to be one of the finest collections of sonnets published during the nineteenth century. So precise was her attention to form and so classical were her tastes that several of Guiney's poems were mistaken for translations of Greek originals. Her narrative poetry, which Guiney herself disparaged for its lack of unity, was less successful. At its best Guiney's poetry sparkles with wit and allusion; at its worst it is imitative and artificial.

Later in life, Guiney found it increasingly more difficult to write poetry, and she turned instead toward scholarship. A poorly written collection of stories, *Lovers', St. Ruth's, and Three Other Tales,* early convinced her that the essay, not fiction, was the form of prose most suited to her talents. Her most famous book of essays, *Patrins,* avoids the stylistic pitfalls of an earlier collection, *Goose-Quill Papers,* which bordered on the precious and even, at times, the euphuistic. In it she summarizes her critical theory, articulated previously in her preface to a translation of Mérimée's *Carmen* and in the introduction to her edition of the poetry of James Clarence Mangan, that literature should be emphatically humanistic and that it should express "joy" rather than what she termed "willful sadness." But Guiney's critical theories, while pronounced, were by no means intolerant. Although she disapproved of realism and naturalism, she was not beyond appreciating the artistry and talent of someone like Harold Frederic, whom she called a "country boy of genius."

Guiney's many biographical works, which include *A Little English Gallery, Robert Emmet,* and *Blessed Edmund Campion,* display a painstaking exactitude and a genuine devotion to learning, which characterize nearly everything she wrote. A knowledgeable editor, Guiney published selections from the works of Henry Vaughan, Matthew Arnold, Hurrell Froude, and Lionel Johnson, among others. Many of her essays express her lifelong commitment to Roman Catholicism, and at the time of her death, she was working on a collection, with copious biographical and bibliographical notes, of poetry written by Catholics in England from 1535 to 1735, posthumously published as *Recusant Poets.*

—James A. Levernier

GUNN, Thom(son William). English. Born in Gravesend, Kent, 29 August 1929. Educated at University College School, London; Trinity College, Cambridge, B.A. 1953, M.A. 1958; Stanford University, California, 1954–55, 1956–58. Served in the British Army, 1948–50. Moved to the United States in 1954. Member of the English Department, University of California, Berkeley, 1958–66. Poetry Reviewer, *Yale Review*, New Haven, Connecticut, 1958–64. Recipient: Maugham Award, 1959; Arts Council of Great Britain award, 1959; National Institute of Arts and Letters grant, 1964; Rockefeller award, 1966; Guggenheim Fellowship, 1971. Lives in San Francisco.

PUBLICATIONS

Verse

(Poems). 1953.
Fighting Terms. 1954; revised edition, 1958.
The Sense of Movement. 1957.
My Sad Captains and Other Poems. 1961.
Selected Poems, with Ted Hughes. 1962.
A Geography. 1966.
Positives, photographs by Ander Gunn. 1966.
Touch. 1967.
The Garden of the Gods. 1968.
The Explorers: Poems. 1969.
The Fair in the Woods. 1969.
Poems 1950–1966: A Selection. 1969.
Sunlight. 1969.
Moly. 1971.
Mandrakes. 1974.
Song Book. 1974.
To the Air. 1974.
Jack Straw's Castle. 1976.
The Missed Boat: Seven Poems. 1976.

Other

Editor, *Poetry from Cambridge 1951–52: A Selection of Verse by Members of the University.* 1952.
Editor, with Ted Hughes, *Five American Poets.* 1963.
Editor, *Selected Poems of Fulke Greville.* 1968.
Editor, *Ben Jonson.* 1974.

Reading List: *Ted Hughes and Gunn* by Alan Bold, 1976.

*   *   *

Thom Gunn's early poetry, written in the 1950's was formally fastidious, intellectually tough, and uncompromisingly rhetorical. The rhetoric led to his name being linked with that of Ted Hughes, for both poets were fascinated with violence as a welcome disruption in the quotidian malaise of social life. Yet the association was deceptive, for the preoccupations of

Gunn's poetry have always been radically different from those of Hughes's. Where the latter sought and found a glorious poise and self-sufficiency in predatory animals, Gunn was obsessed from the beginning by the traditional themes of modern western thought. In fact the whole of his career so far could be looked at as a struggle with the categories of Cartesian philosophy. To escape these categories he immersed himself first in existentialism, and then in the mysticism associated with hallucinatory drugs.

In *Fighting Terms* and *The Sense of Movement*, there are a technical expertise and an Elizabethan elegance of argument for which he became justly famous. His major theme was that of rationalist man seeking an identity in which he is not crippled by his intellectualism. The image of head-wounds recurs frequently as a metaphoric representation of a mental anguish which can only be overcome by action, and action in this early poetry often represents an undifferentiated possibility of escape from thought: "I acted, and my action made me wise" ("Incident on a Journey"). Love finds its place in this schema as a strategy or form of covert warfare, a brutalised routine of stimulus and response, as in "Carnal Knowledge":

> I prod, you react. Thus to and fro
> We turn, to see ourselves perform the same
> Comical act inside the tragic game.

In fact, the claims of humanity and companionship are viewed largely as a threat which the isolated ego must negotiate its way past. Gunn's obsessions with military uniform, motorcyclists, and petty criminals suggest a studious avoidance of communication.

"In Santa Maria Del Populo" (*My Sad Captains*) registered a shift of concern towards more sympathetic preoccupations. Life is no longer a vicious game, a mere war of identities. *Positives* in 1966 marks the transition. This volume, combining Gunn's poetry and Ander Gunn's photographs, is his opportunity to shed his previous rhetoric completely, and concern himself at length with the apparently unheroic. Daily, ordinary life from the cradle to the grave is the subject, and it is explored in a binary composition of poetic and photographic images, both concretizing images that might have remained abstract in themselves.

By the time of *Touch* in 1967, Gunn was ready to attempt his most ambitious poem. "Misanthropos" uses the poetic trope of last man/first man on earth to explore his old fixation – the relations of mind to body, and individual to society and environment. By pushing to its furthest extremity his notion of solitary, meditative, but surviving man, this poem releases Gunn into a statement of the need for generosity, for the acceptance of common failings. The poem ends:

> Turn out toward others, meeting their look at full,
> Until you have completely stared
> On all there is to see. Immeasurable,
> The dust yet to be shared.

"Misanthropos" is a poem of sustained energy and courage. His new theme was now, forcibly, the attempt to reconcile individual identity with the unperfected identities which surround it.

Later still, Gunn says of his book *Moly*: "I think of it as being about Odysseus' meeting with Hermes, his eating of that herb, and his reflections on metamorphosis in the remaining walk he has before he reaches the thick stone-built house." Just as Gunn once took the crude mythic postures of the Hell's Angels and turned them to remarkable poetic effect, so in *Moly* he approaches the chaotic dissolution through L.S.D. of San Francisco in the 1960's and uses that to equally remarkable effect. The final poem in the volume, "Sunlight," shows Gunn using his old formalistic inventiveness for the promotion of a libertarian philosophy which would have been unthinkable for him in the 1950's. A hymn to the sun, as the patron saint of all warmth, ends with this invocation:

> Enable us, altering like you, to enter
> Your passionless love, impartial but intense,
> And kindle in acceptance round your centre,
> Petals of light lost in your innocence.

Jack Straw's Castle shows Gunn at his freest, in terms of what he will allow himself to say. But this freedom has nothing to do with formal or metrical sloppiness. It has been earned by the apprenticeship of formal constraint, the meticulous study of his craft. It reinforces the notion that the poet's quest has been essentially coherent. Gunn began with an exploration of the resistance of individual identity to encroachment or possession. If his early verse was at times a celebration of this theme, it soon came to be a questioning of it. In the nature of the American contexts Gunn placed himself in, there was the possibility not only of a further questioning, but of a reversal. There is a sharp distinction, of course, between reversal and regression. In seeking to overcome the Cartesian oppositions he started out with, Gunn has not abandoned his earlier intellectual acerbity. He has sought to overcome a flaw at the centre of western philosophical thought. When the poem "The Geysers" ends:

> I am
> I am raw meat
> I am a god

it is reaching back to a source of unified energy found in Blake. The development of Gunn's poetry can be seen as an attempt to reach back to that fruitful beginning of a tradition still in its infancy.

—Alan Wall

GUSTAFSON, Ralph (Barker). Canadian. Born in Lime Ridge, Quebec, 16 August 1909. Educated at Bishop's University, Lennoxville, Quebec, B.A. 1929, M.A. 1930; Oxford University, B.A. 1933. Married Elisabeth Renninger in 1958. Music Master, Bishop's College School, 1930; Master, St. Alban's School, Brockville, Ontario, 1934; worked for the British Information Services, 1942–46. Since 1960, Music Critic, Canadian Broadcasting Corporation; since 1963, Professor of English and Poet-in-Residence, Bishop's University. Recipient: Prix David, 1935; Canada Council Senior Fellowship, 1959, Award, 1968, 1971; Governor-General's Award, 1974; A. J. M. Smith Award, 1975. M.A.: Oxford University, 1963; D.Litt.: Mount Allison University, Sackville, New Brunswick, 1973. Lives in Quebec.

PUBLICATIONS

Verse

The Golden Chalice. 1935.
Alfred the Great (verse play). 1937.
Epithalamium in Time of War. 1941.
Lyrics Unromantic. 1942.

Flight into Darkness: Poems.   1944.
Rivers among Rocks.   1960.
Rocky Mountain Poems.   1960.
Sift in an Hourglass.   1966.
Ixion's Wheel: Poems.   1969.
Theme and Variations for Sounding Brass.   1972.
Selected Poems.   1972.
Fire on Stone.   1974.

Fiction

The Brazen Tower.   1974.

Other

Poetry and Canada.   1945.

Editor, *Anthology of Canadian Poetry (English).*   1942.
Editor, *A Little Anthology of Canadian Poets.*   1943.
Editor, *Canadian Accent: A Collection of Stories and Poems by Contemporary Writers from Canada.*   1944.
Editor, *The Penguin Book of Canadian Verse.*   1958; revised edition, 1967, 1975.

Bibliography: "Ralph Gustafson: A Bibliography in Progress" by L. M. Allison and W. Keitner, in *West Coast Review,* June 1974.

Reading List: "Ralph Gustafson: A Review and Retrospect" by Robin Skelton, in *Mosaic,* 1974.

*   *   *

Ralph Gustafson is one of the most prolific, various and technically accomplished of contemporary Canadian poets. After a somewhat unpromising start with a volume of romantic lyrics and sonnets and a poetic play on the subject of King Alfred in the mid-thirties, Ralph Gustafson found an original style and an individual voice in the sardonic and tender poetry produced during and after World War II. *Flight into Darkness* assimilated, rather than shook off, influences of Hopkins and Donne and demonstrated the relevance of the metaphysical dialectic to the problem of preserving an individual integrity in the kaleidoscopic new world of the post-war breakdown.

The poet's elliptical and intensely allusive style has taken on a new subtlety and his work a wider field of interest since 1960. Travel across Canada, especially to the Rockies and the mountains of the north-west coast, and to Italy, Greece and the Scandinavian countries, has provided the stimulus for a prolific outburst of poetry in which the themes of nature, art, history, love and sex are given a highly individual treatment. As Earle Birney has written: "Ralph Gustafson has a way all his own of fusing music and passion with sophisticated feeling and graceful craft.... A stylist given to paradox and poetic wit, he is nonetheless serious, and his sensitive judgments rise from a warm heart."

—A. J. M. Smith

GUTHRIE, Ramon. American. Born in New York City, 14 January 1896. Educated at Mt. Hermon, 1912–14; University of Toulouse, Docteur en Droit, 1922; the Sorbonne, Paris, 1919, 1922–23. Served in the American Field Service, 1916–17; United States Army Air Corps, 1917–19; Office of Strategic Services, 1943–45: Silver Star. Married Marguerite Maurey in 1922. Assistant Professor of Romance Languages, University of Arizona, Tucson, 1924–26; Professor of French, 1930–63, and Professor Emeritus, 1963–73, Dartmouth College, Hanover, New Hampshire. Recipient: National Endowment for the Arts grant, 1969, 1971; Marjorie Peabody Waite Award, 1970. M.A., 1939, and D.Litt., 1971, Dartmouth College. *Died 22 November 1973.*

PUBLICATIONS

Verse

> *Trobar Clus.* 1923.
> *A World Too Old.* 1927.
> *The Legend of Ermengarde.* 1929.
> *Scherzo, From a Poem to be Entitled "The Proud City."* 1933.
> *Graffiti.* 1959.
> *Asbestos Phoenix.* 1968.
> *Maximum Security Ward, 1964–1970.* 1970.

Novels

> *Marcabrun: The Chronicle of a Foundling Who Spoke Evil of Women and of Love and Who Followed Unawed the Paths of Arrogance Until They Led to Madness, and of His Dealings with Women and of Ribald Words, the Which Brought Him Repute as a Great Rascal and as a Great Singer.* 1926.
> *Parachute.* 1928.

Other

> Editor, with George E. Diller, *French Literature and Thought since the Revolution.* 1942.
> Editor, with George E. Diller, *Prose and Poetry of Modern France.* 1964.

> Translator, *The Revolutionary Spirit in France and America,* by Bernard Faÿ. 1927.
> Translator, *The Other Kingdom,* by David Rousset. 1947.
> Translator, *The Republic of Silence,* edited by A. J. Liebling. 1947.

Reading List: *Guthrie Kaleidoscope,* 1963 (includes bibliography by Alan Cooke); "La Poésie de Guthrie" by L. Véza, in *Etudes Anglaises,* January–March 1967.

*   *   *

Ramon Guthrie's last and most important work, *Maximum Security Ward,* appeared when he was seventy-four. Indeed, although he was a contemporary of Cummings and Crane, most of his significant work belongs to the late 1950's and 1960's and is collected in *Graffiti,*

Asbestos Phoenix, and *Maximum Security Ward*. All three books contain striking poems, but the cumulative force of the last, which derives from its dramatic center, is by far Guthrie's most sustained success. The speaker, a critically ill and suffering old man, uses all the resources of his imagination, memory, intellect, and humor to overcome his bewildering isolation and disappointment in himself and his fellow human beings. The book is a particularly valuable addition to the genre of the modern lyric sequence.

The best introduction to the poet and his style comes in the first of the forty-nine poems of *Maximum Security Ward*:

> So name her Vivian. I, scarecrow Merlin —
> our Broceliande this frantic bramble of
> glass and plastic tubes and stainless steel —
> could count off such illusions as I have
> on a quarter of my thumbs.

Here are all the hallmarks of Guthrie's mature verse: the passionate immediacy of the speaking voice; the subtle internal rhymes and skilful assonance, alliteration, and colliteration (the use of related consonants); the unpretentious, humorous, colloquial tone combined with a scholarly range of reference and romantic wistfulness; and the recurrent reference to French art and literature, particularly medieval romance, as a psychological touchstone.

Guthrie was bilingual and a Francophile, and his intimate knowledge of France is reflected in his poetry. He lived, studied, and wrote in France during most of the 1920's and sporadically thereafter and knew the expatriate community of artists well. He served in France in two wars, married a Frenchwoman, and taught French literature throughout his academic career. His earliest important literary influences were French, and Proust was his philosophical mentor. But he was an eminently American poet, writing out of the traditions of American verse and at times satirizing his country's hypocrisies and cruelties — particularly her role in Vietnam — for the good of the body politic. Of course, his great subject in *Maximum Security Ward* is supranational: the meaning of the whole human enterprise — what it is to be fully human psychologically, socially, politically — and the role of any artist, whether writer, painter, musician, or sculptor, in uncovering what is essentially a sacred meaning.

A good amateur painter, Guthrie had a visual imagination that matched and reinforced his great love for the texture of language and that enhanced the exquisitely tactile sensuousness of some of his most evocative passages:

> this smooth knoll of your shoulder,
> this cwm of flank, this moss-delineated quite
> un-Platonic cave....

> Everywhere about is landscape as far as foot can feel
> lamps exude their light on flagstones
> there are quaint quiet trains in
> corridors of pure perspective

Guthrie's poems are filled with concrete, memorable phrases and imagery; he moves skilfully from tone to tone, from the most jarring to the most lyrical; wit, intelligence, and a deep sympathy and humanity inform his work. It is a pity it is not better known.

—Sally M. Gall

HABINGTON, William. English. Born in Hindlip, Worcestershire, 4 November 1605. Educated at St. Omer's, and in Paris. Married Lucy Herbert c. 1630; one son. *Died 30 November 1654.*

PUBLICATIONS

Collections

Poems, edited by Kenneth Allott. 1948.

Verse

Castara. 2 vols., 1634; revised edition, 1635, 1640.

Play

The Queen of Aragon; or, Cleodora (produced 1640). 1640; edited by W. C. Hazlitt in *Dodsley's Old Plays 13,* 1875.

Other

The History of Edward the Fourth. 1640.
Observations upon History. 1641.

*   *   *

"To write this," William Habington tells readers of his *Castara,* "love stole some hours from business, and my more serious study." But in fact he was serious and high-minded in his love-poetry as in all else. Distressed that English verse had been corrupted by licentious French models, he traces under the names Araphil (altar-lover) and Castara (chaste altar) his own exemplary courtship and marriage to the fair and virtuous Lucy Herbert – a courtship in which, he assures us, he "never felt a wanton heat."

It is evidence of Habington's independent spirit that, in an age when the love-sonnet had passed out of fashion, more than half the poems in *Castara* are "sonnets" – or at least fourteen-line poems in decasyllabic verse. But except for one sonnet, which follows the English form, all these fourteen-line poems are rhymed in couplets. It is hard to imagine what advantages Habington could have seen in such "sonnets." Perhaps, without wanting to write in a deliberately outmoded manner, he thought of the fourteen-line limitation as at least a gesture toward an older discipline. Meanwhile much of his imagery and subject-matter ("To Roses in the Bosom of Castara," "To Castara, Upon a Sigh") is the common stock of poets of his time, or at least a fastidious selection from that stock.

A Catholic and Royalist, he derived from his religion and politics strong reinforcement for his moral creed; one of his lyrics, "To Castara, Upon the Mutual Love of Their Majesties," points to Charles I and Henrietta Maria as models of married love.

His single play, a tragi-comedy called *The Queen of Aragon,* received a highly successful performance before the King and Queen at Whitehall. The lofty sentiments of the play, expressed in eloquent blank verse, could hardly have failed to appeal to the royal couple, who in their own way were as serious-minded as Habington. By all criteria it is one of the best-written of the highly artificial dramas of the period; when it was revived after the Restoration, Samuel Pepys found it "so good that I am astonished at it." Along with its nobler elements it offers mild amusement and satire in the characters of a witty lady and a foolish lord.

Besides some short *Observations upon History*, Habington wrote a *History of Edward the Fourth*, which he dedicated to King Charles. This is no less a moral work than his poems and play – so moral, indeed, that it avoids any mention of King Edward's famous mistress, Jane Shore. More importantly, it is a tract for the times, since Edward IV had succeeded in imposing a "happy calm" on his kingdom after a long period of strife. "May your Majesty long continue in peace," Habington tells King Charles in the dedicatory epistle. "But if you shall be forced to draw your sword, may your enemies submit and taste part of your mercy: if not, perish in your victories." In 1640, when this was published, neither Habington nor his King could reasonably have suspected that they were united in a losing cause.

—Rhodes Dunlap

———————

HALL, Joseph. English. Born in Ashby-de-la-Zouch, Leicestershire, 1 July 1574. Educated at a grammar school in Ashby; Emmanuel College, Cambridge, B.A. 1592, M.A. 1596, B.D. 1603, D.D. 1612. Married Elizabeth Winiffe in 1603; two daughters. Fellow, Emmanuel College, Cambridge, 1595; took holy orders c. 1600; given the living of Halstead, Suffolk, 1601, and Waltham, Essex, 1608; appointed a chaplain to James I, 1608; sent by the king as chaplain to Lord Doncaster in his embassy to France, 1616; appointed Dean of Worcester, 1616; accompanied James to Scotland in an attempt to establish the Episcopacy, 1617; Delegate to the Synod of Dort, 1618; Bishop of Exeter, 1627–41; appointed Bishop of Norwich, 1641; protested against exclusion of the bishops from Parliament, and was imprisoned in the Tower of London, 1642; released, but deprived of the bishopric, 1647; retired to a farm in Higham, Norfolk. *Died 8 September 1656.*

PUBLICATIONS

Collections

    Works, edited by P. Wynter. 20 vols., 1863.
    Devotions, Sacred Aphorisms, and Religious Table-Talk, edited by J. W. Morris. 1867.
    Collected Poems, edited by Arnold Davenport. 1949.

Verse

    Virgidemiarum: First Three Books of Toothless Satires. 1597; *Three Last Books of Biting Satires*, 1598.
    The King's Prophecy; or, Weeping Joy. 1603.
    Some Few of David's Psalms Metaphrased, for a Taste of the Rest, in Holy Observations. 1607.

Other

The Anatomy of Sin. 1603; as *Two Guides to a Good Life,* 1608.
Meditations and Vows Divine and Moral. 1605; revised edition, 1607.
Mundus Alter et Idem. 1605(?); edited by Huntington Brown, 1937.
Heaven upon Earth. 1606.
The Art of Divine Meditation. 1606; edited by Rudolf Kirk, with *Characters of Virtues and Vices,* 1948.
Holy Observations. 1607.
Characters of Virtues and Vices. 1608; edited by Rudolf Kirk, 1948.
Epistles. 4 vols., 1608–11.
Salomon's Divine Arts. 1609.
The Peace of Rome. 1609.
A Common Apology of the Church of England. 1610.
Contemplations upon the Principal Passages of the Holy Story. 8 vols., 1612–26; edited by C. Wordsworth, 1871.
Polemices Sacrae Par Prior: Roma Irreconciliabilis. 1611.
A Recollection of Such Treatises as Have Been Heretofore Severally Published and Are Now Revised. 1614; revised edition, 1621.
Quo Vadis? A Just Censure of Travel as It Is Commonly Undertaken by the Gentlemen of Our Nation. 1617.
The Honour of the Married Clergy Maintained. 1620.
Works. 1625; revised edition, 2 vols., 1628; 3 vols., 1662.
The Old Religion. 1627.
An Answer to Pope Urban, His Inurbanity. 1629.
The Reconciler. 1629.
Occasional Meditations. 1630.
A Plain and Familiar Explication of the Old and New Testament. 1632.
An Explication by Way of Paraphrase of All the Hard Texts in the Old and New Testament. 1633.
Propositiones Catholicae. 1633; translated as *Certain Catholic Propositions,* 1633.
The Residue of the Contemplation upon the New Testament, with Sermons. 1634.
Antochediasmata; vel, Meditatiunculae Subitaneae. 1635.
The Remedy of Prophaneness. 1637.
Certain Irrefragable Propositions. 1639.
An Humble Remonstrance to the High Court of Parliament. 1640.
Christian Moderation. 1640.
Episcopacy by Divine Right. 1640.
A Defense of the Humble Remonstrance. 1641.
Osculum Pacis. 1641.
A Modest Confutation. 1642.
A Modest Offer to Some Meet Considerations. 1644.
The Devout Soul. 1644.
The Peace-Maker. 1645.
The Remedy of Discontentment. 1645.
The Balm of Gilead. 1645.
Three Tractates. 1646.
Christ Mystical. 1647.
Hard Measures. 1647.
Satan's Fiery Darts Quenched; or, Temptation Repelled. 1647.
The Breathings of the Devout Soul. 1648.
Pax Terris. 1648.
Select Thoughts: One Century. 1648.
Resolutions and Decisions of Diverse Practical Cases of Conscience. 1649.

The Revelation Unrevealed. 1650.
Susurrium cum Deo. 1651.
Holy Raptures. 1652.
The Great Mystery of Godliness. 1652.
The Holy Order. 1654.
The Invisible World. 1659.
The Apostolic Institution. 1659.
The Shaking of the Olive-Tree: Remaining Works. 1659.
Diverse Treatises, vol. 3. 1662.
Psicittacorum Regis. 1669.
Contemplations upon the Remarkable Passages in the Life of Holy Jesus. 1679.
Episcopal Admonition. 1681.

Reading List: "Bishop Hall, 'Our English Seneca' " by Philip A. Smith, in *Publications of the Modern Language Association 63*, 1948; "Hall's Imitation of Juvenal" by Arnold Stein, in *Modern Language Review 43*, 1948; *The Life and Works of Hall* by Tom F. Kinloch, 1951; "Hall's *Characters of Vertues and Vices*: Notes Toward a Revaluation" by Gerard Muller-Schwefe, in *Texas Studies in Language and Literature 14*, 1972; *Hall: A Biographical and Critical Study* by Frank Livingstone Huntley, 1978.

*   *   *

To the modern reader, the most familiar passage in the works of Joseph Hall is almost certainly the long description of the Golden Age that opens the third book of his *Virgidemiarum*. But it should be noted that this celebration of the days of Saturn owes as much to Juvenal as it does to Ovid, and that Hall's main claim for his collection is that it comprises the first full-scale set of Juvenalian satires in English. The pastoral primitivism lauded in Book III, Satire I, in fact serves almost entirely as a positive prelapsarian backdrop against which Hall can vilipend with savage vehemence the follies, villainies, and abuses of degenerate modern days. This he does with a relish that combines the moral indignation of the Puritan preacher with the obsessive harshness of the original Juvenal.

All satire to some extent subscribes to a belief in progressive deterioration, and Hall is never tired of comparing the virtue of the past to the viciousness and decay of the present, when "Ech Muck-worme will be rich with lawlesse gaine" (IV, vi), when sons squander their patrimony in harlots' beds (IV, iii), when fools abandon the "home-spun *Russet*" of former days for the garish "far-fetched liuery" of France, Italy, Germany and Spain (III, i), when fops forsake the martial valour of their ancestors for effeminate rose-pulling (IV, iv). In short, all the customary targets of satire are to be found in the *Virgidemiarum*. Like Juvenal, Hall sees greed for money as the root cause of so much contemporary corruption: lawyers look only at the client's hand "lined with a larger fee" (II, iii), doctors abandon "the leane reward of Art" (II, iv), in favour of more liberal emolument from gouty peers, chaplains are treated with ignominy and paid no more than a mere serving-man (II, vi).

Of particular interest, perhaps, in terms of content is the first book. Here Hall turns his attention specifically to the failings of contemporary poetry, and, in surveying what he considers to be its decayed status, comes to the not unexpected conclusion that satire alone should be allowed to survive. Erotic poetry is now obscene ("*Cythéron* hill's become a Brothel-bed," I, ii), the high decorum of tragedy is lost "when vile *Russetings*,/ Are match't with monarchs" (I, iii), even religious poetry is polluted with secular taints (I, viii). Hall's editor, Arnold Davenport, is quite right in regarding his author as a one-sided but highly perceptive literary critic.

The style of the *Virgidemiarum* is probably something of a stumbling-block to present-day readers. At its best, it is harsh, vigorous, and crude – not at all "toothlesse" as the description on the title-page would have us believe. The usual metaphors of whipping and scourging occur regularly, and Hall himself compares satire to a porcupine "That shoots sharpe quils out in each angry line" (V, iii). His imagery is, predictably, drawn from disease and dirt – adjectives such as *rotten*, *festering*, *scabby* proliferate throughout. Sexual aberration especially seems to arouse Hall to heights of Juvenalian frenzy, as he contemplates, for example, the "close adultresse" coming "crauling from her husbands lukewarme bed,/Her carrion skin bedaub'd with odours sweete.... Besmeared all with loathsome smoke of lust" (IV, i). Unfortunately Hall is not always so direct as that, and, despite his disclaimer of "ridle-like" darkness (III, Prol.), there is much obscurity in his *Virgidemiarum* – the result both of the prevailing Renaissance tradition which prescribed a crabbed obliquity for the satiric muse and of Hall's own determination to conceal the identities of the persons he is attacking (they include Nashe, Harvey, and Greene) under the cloak of pseudonyms.

Hall lived until 1656, but none of his later work (gratulatory verse, religious verse, sermons, pamphlets, etc.) is of any literary interest. It is to the *Virgidemiarum* that we return for a fascinating array of corrupt characters, a richly-detailed survey of various moral and social abuses, and a comprehensive critique of the failing of the poets of the 1590's – all delivered with a rhetorical zest and vigour that show Hall (like all the best satirists) as much intrigued by the vices he assails as repulsed by them. Like Ben Jonson a few years later, Hall finds in the corruptions of his time a vivid source of poetic energy, and, in giving dramatic embodiment to these, becomes the first writer to naturalise in England the Juvenalian satire.

—A. W. Lyle

HALLECK, Fitz-Greene. American. Born in Guilford, Connecticut, 8 July 1790. Educated at public schools in Guilford. Worked in a store in Guilford, 1806–11; clerk in the banking house of Jacob Barker, 1812–30, New York; toured Europe, 1822; Confidential Clerk in the banking house of John Jacob Astor, 1832 until his retirement on an annuity left him by Astor, 1849; retired to Guilford. Leading member of the Knickerbocker Group, New York; Vice-President, Authors Club, New York, 1837. *Died 19 November 1867.*

PUBLICATIONS

Collections

> *Poetical Writings,* edited by James Grant Wilson.   1868.

Verse

> *Poems,* with Joseph Rodman Drake.   1819; revised edition, as *The Croakers,* 1860.
> *Fanny.*   1819; revised edition, 1821.
> *Alnwick Castle with Other Poems.*   1817.
> *The Recorder with Other Poems.*   1833.
> *Fanny with Other Poems.*   1839.
> *Poetical Works.*   1847.
> *Young America.*   1865.

Other

A Letter Written to Joel Lewis Griffing in 1814.   1921.

Editor, *The Works of Byron in Verse and Prose.*   1834.
Editor, *Selections from the British Poets.*   2 vols., 1840.

Bibliography: in *Bibliography of American Literature* by Jacob Blanck, 1959.

Reading List: *Life and Letters of Halleck* by James Grant Wilson, 1869; *Some Notices of the Life and Writings of Halleck* by William Cullen Bryant, 1869; *Halleck: An Early Knickerbocker Wit and Poet* by Nelson Frederick Adkins, 1930.

*   *   *

With the exception of William Cullen Bryant, Fitz-Greene Halleck was, among his contemporaries, the most popular of the Knickerbocker poets, and although such once-famous Knickerbockers as Samuel Woodworth, Robert Sands, and George Pope Morris have long been forgotten by virtually everyone except literary historians, Halleck is still remembered as a minor poet and satirist of New York society in the early nineteenth century.

Poetry was for Halleck, as for other Knickerbockers, an avocation, a pleasant diversion for gentlemen. His poetry is also exceedingly derivative. Campbell, Scott, and Moore are among those who most influenced him, but no poet's influence was greater then Byron's – an influence that Halleck freely acknowledged. (Indeed Halleck repaid the debt in his memoir and collected edition of Bryon's works, the first edition of this sort to be published on either side of the Atlantic.)

Although Halleck published little poetry of consequence, its range was large, including the heroic ("Marco Bozzaris"), the pastoral ("Wyoming"), the sentimental ("Alnwick Castle"), the elegiac ("On the Death of Joseph Rodman Drake"), and the satiric (*Fanny*). His reputation was established in 1819 with the publication of "The Croaker Papers," written jointly with Joseph Rodman Drake. These poems, widely read and praised in their day, satirize prominent figures in the financial, political, and social life of New York. *Fanny*, Halleck's most sustained literary effort and his best, is a pointed but delicate satire of fashionable New York society, a world which Halleck knew well. During the last four decades of his life, Halleck who died in 1867, published little of interest.

Despite his satires of fashionable New York, it was in that New York that Halleck was most at home. As personal secretary to John Jacob Astor, he was assured of access to the social realm he most admired. Here literature was a pastime, a diversion. Astor's world was the ideal setting for the accomplished but amateur poet that Halleck indisputably was.

—Edward Halsey Foster

HARDY, Thomas. English. Born in Upper Bockhampton, Dorset, 2 June 1840. Educated in local schools, 1848–54, and privately, 1854–56; articled to the ecclesiastical architect, John Hicks, in Dorchester, 1856–61; studied in evening classes at King's College, London, 1861–67. Married 1) Emma Lavinia Gifford in 1874 (died, 1912); 2) Florence Emily Dugdale in 1914. Settled in London, 1861, to practice architecture, and worked as Assistant to Sir Arthur Blomfield, 1862–67; gave up architecture to become full-time writer; lived in Max Gate, Dorchester, after 1886. Justice of the Peace for Dorset; Member of the Council of Justice to Animals. Recipient: Royal Institute of British Architects medal, for essay, 1863;

Architecture Association prize, for design, 1863; Royal Society of Literature Gold Medal, 1912. LL.D.: University of Aberdeen; University of St. Andrews; University of Bristol; Litt.D.: Cambridge University; D.Litt.: Oxford University. Honorary Fellow: Magdalene College, Cambridge; Queen's College, Oxford. Honorary Fellow of the Royal Institute of British Architects, 1920. Order of Merit, 1910. *Died 11 January 1928.*

PUBLICATIONS

Collections

New Wessex Edition of the Works. 1974–
Complete Poems, edited by James Gibson. 1976; revised *Variorum Edition,* 1978.
The Portable Hardy, edited by Julian Moynahan. 1977.
Collected Letters. edited by Richard Little Purdy and Michael Millgate. vol. 1 (of 7), 1978.

Verse

Wessex Poems and Other Verses. 1898.
Poems of the Past and the Present. 1902; revised edition, 1902.
Time's Laughingstocks and Other Verses. 1909.
Satires of Circumstance: Lyrics and Reveries, with Miscellaneous Pieces. 1914.
Selected Poems. 1916; revised edition, as *Chosen Poems.* 1929.
Moments of Vision and Miscellaneous Poems. 1917.
Collected Poems. 1919.
Late Lyrics and Earlier, with Many Other Verses. 1922.
Human Shows, Far Phantasies, Songs, and Trifles. 1925.
Winter Words in Various Moods and Metres. 1928.

Plays

Far from the Madding Crowd, with J. Comyns Carr, from the novel by Hardy (produced 1882).
The Three Wayfarers, from his own story "The Three Strangers" (produced 1893). 1893.
The Dynasts: A Drama of the Napoleonic Wars. 3 vols., 1903–08; vol. 1 revised, 1904; edited by John Wain, 1965.
The Play of Saint George. 1921.
The Famous Tragedy of the Queen of Cornwall (produced 1923). 1923; revised edition, 1924.
Tess of the d'Urbervilles, from his own novel (produced 1924). In *Tess in the Theatre,* edited by Marguerite Roberts, 1950.

Fiction

Desperate Remedies. 1871; revised edition, 1896, 1912.
Under the Greenwood Tree: A Rural Painting of the Dutch School. 1872; revised edition, 1896, 1912; edited by Anna Winchcombe, 1975.

A Pair of Blue Eyes.   1873; revised edition, 1895, 1912, 1920.

Far from the Madding Crowd.   1874; revised edition, 1875, 1902; edited by James Gibson, 1975.

The Hand of Ethelberta: A Comedy in Chapters.   1876; revised edition, 1895, 1912.

The Return of the Native.   1878; revised edition, 1895, 1912; edited by Colin Tremblett-Wood, 1975.

Fellow Townsmen.   1880.

The Trumpet-Major: A Tale.   1880; revised edition, 1895; edited by Ray Evans, 1975.

A Laodicean; or, The Castle of the De Stancys.   1881; revised edition, 1881, 1896, 1912.

Two on a Tower.   1882; revised edition, 1883, 1883, 1895, 1912.

The Romantic Adventures of a Milkmaid.   1883; revised edition, 1913.

The Mayor of Casterbridge: The Life and Death of a Man of Character.   1886; revised edition, 1895, 1920; edited by F. B. Pinion, 1975; edited by James K. Robinson, 1977.

The Woodlanders.   1887; revised edition, 1895, 1912; edited by F. B. Pinion, 1975.

Wessex Tales, Strange, Lively and Commonplace.   1888; revised edition, 1896.

A Group of Noble Dames.   1891.

Tess of the d'Urbervilles: A Pure Woman Faithfully Presented.   1891; revised edition, 1892, 1895, 1912; edited by Scott Elledge, 1965, revised 1977.

Life's Little Ironies: A Set of Tales.   1894; revised edition, 1912.

Wessex Novels.   16 vols, 1895–96.

Jude the Obscure.   1896; revised edition, 1912; edited by Norman Page, 1978.

The Well-Beloved: A Sketch of Temperament.   1897; revised edition, 1912.

A Changed Man, The Waiting Supper, and Other Tales.   1913.

An Indiscretion in the Life of an Heiress.   1934; edited by Carl J. Weber, 1935.

Our Exploits at West Poley, edited by R. L. Purdy.   1952.

Other

The Dorset Farm Labourer, Past and Present.   1884.

Works (Wessex Edition).   24 vols., 1912–31.

Works (Mellstock Edition).   37 vols., 1919–20.

Life and Art: Essays, Notes, and Letters, edited by Ernest Brennecke.   1925.

The Early Life of Hardy 1840–91, by Florence Hardy.   1928; *The Later Years of Hardy, 1892–1928*, 1930 (dictated to his wife Florence).

Letters of Hardy, edited by Carl J. Weber.   1954.

Notebooks and Some Letters from Julia Augusta Martin, edited by Evelyn Hardy.   1955.

Dearest Emmie: Letters to His First Wife, edited by Carl J. Weber.   1963.

The Architectural Notebook, edited by C. J. P. Beatty.   1966.

Personal Writings: Prefaces, Literary Opinions, Reminiscences, edited by Harold Orel.   1966.

One Rare Fair Woman (letters to Frances Henniker), edited by Evelyn Hardy and F. B. Pinion.   1972.

The Personal Notebooks, edited by Richard H. Taylor.   1978.

Editor, *Select Poems of William Barnes*.   1908.

Bibliography: *Hardy: A Bibliographical Study* by R. L. Purdy, 1954, revised edition, 1968; "Criticism of Hardy: A Selected Checklist" by M. Beebe, B. Culotta, and E. Marcus, in *Modern Fiction Studies*, 1960.

Reading List: *Hardy of Wessex* by Carl J. Weber, 1940, revised edition, 1965; *Hardy the Novelist* by David Cecil, 1943; *Hardy: The Novels and Stories* by Albert Guerard, 1949, revised edition, 1964; *The Pattern of Hardy's Poetry* by Samuel Hynes, 1961; *Hardy: A Collection of Critical Essays* edited by Albert Guerard, 1963; *Hardy* by Irving Howe, 1967; *A Hardy Companion*, 1968, revised edition, 1976, and *Hardy: Art and Thought*, 1977, both by F. B. Pinion; *Hardy: His Career as a Novelist* by Michael Millgate, 1971; *Hardy and British Poetry* by Donald Davie, 1972; *Hardy and History* by R. J. White, 1974; *Young Hardy*, 1975, and *The Older Hardy*, 1978, both by Robert Gittings; *An Essay on Hardy* by John Bayley, 1978.

*   *   *

In his early twenties Thomas Hardy aspired to be a country curate and poet, like William Barnes. Yet, after a period of intense reading in London, he rejected belief in Providence for scientific philosophy, based largely on the writings of J. S. Mill, Darwin's *The Origin of Species*, and readings in geology and astronomy. Like Mill, Hardy was impressed with Auguste Comte's emphasis on the need for altruism and a programme of reform based on education and science. Hardy never forfeited his belief in the Christian ethic; he was convinced that there was little hope for humanity without enlightened co-operation and charity. His preface to *The Woodlanders* suggests that his conscious aim in his last major novels was to further amelioration through enlisting the sympathetic awareness of his readers. Humanitarianism combines with his scientific outlook in imaginatively visualized presentations to maintain his appeal today.

Hardy's basic ideas did not change greatly and, as his London poems of 1865–67 show, they were formed early. Events are the result primarily of circumstance or chance, which is all that is immediately apparent in an evolving network of cause-effect relationships extending through space and time. In *The Woodlanders* the "web" which is for ever weaving shows, for example, a link between the death of Mrs. Charmond and the American Civil War. Chance includes heredity and character; only when reason prevails is man free to influence the course of events. Such philosophical ideas are inherent, and sometimes explicit, in Hardy's first published novel, *Desperate Remedies*. His previous novel, *The Poor Man and the Lady* (which survives only in scenes adapted to other novels and in "An Indiscretion in the Life of an Heiress"), had been loosely constructed, and too satirical, of London society and contemporary Christianity in particular, to gain acceptance.

In *Desperate Remedies* Hardy merged, for the sake of publication, a tragic situation with a thriller story and a complicated plot (in the manner of Wilkie Collins). Until the sensational dénouement takes over, the writing is enriched with poetical quotations and effects, Shelley's wintry image of adversity determining crisis settings, as in later Hardy novels. A reviewer's commendation of his rustic scenes led to *Under the Greenwood Tree*, which Hardy wrote rapidly, with notable economy, in a happy mood kindled by love of Emma Gifford, a church organist whose blue dress and vanity are the subject of light satire in a novel remarkable for its rustic humour. Though the story of *A Pair of Blue Eyes* was planned before Hardy's first Cornish visit, and its characters are almost wholly fictional, this tragic romance is based on Cornish memories. Often poetic in conception, it suffered from the pressures of serial demands. The heroine's crisis anticipates *Tess*. Writing anonymously for *The Cornhill Magazine*, Hardy was more ambitious in *Far from the Madding Crowd*, showing marked development in Wessex humour and the dramatization of passion. A suggestion that this pastoral work was written by George Eliot made Hardy put aside the story which became *The Woodlanders* for *The Hand of Ethelberta*, a comedy directed by Darwinian ideas and social satire. After a respite, during which he read a great deal, Hardy began *The Return of the Native*, but difficulties with magazine editors made him rewrite much in the first two books. Partly inspired by Arnold, more by Pater's essay on Winckelmann, his theme is hedonism (with a Greek slant) versus altruistic idealism. Life as something to be endured (and avoided by the hedonist) is represented by Egdon Heath. The insignificance of the individual in time (with reference to Egdon) is stressed in a number of scenes, the most important being Darwinian and closely associated with Mrs. Yeobright's death.

Hardy's next novels suggest that he was still searching for the direction his genius should take. After *The Trumpet-Major*, a story dependent for relief on traditional comic types and situations, against a background of threatened Napoleonic invasion, he experimented with a second novel of ideas in *A Laodicean*. Handicapped by prolonged illness, he failed to give artistic cohesion to the theme of Arnold's "imaginative reason," in resolving the conflict between modern technology and a *prédilection d'artiste* for the romantic splendours of the past. Mephistophelian villainy contributes to the counterplot, and continues on a minor scale in *Two on a Tower*, where the story, set against the immensities of stellar space, reveals Hardy's maturing emphasis on altruism. In *The Mayor of Casterbridge* he solved the problem of catering for weekly serialization without detriment to tragic grandeur, his standards being set by the great masterpieces of the past, from classical times onwards. Some of the most moving scenes are in prose of Biblical simplicity or in the vernacular of the unlettered poor. After Henchard's death, Whittle emerges more noble of heart than the shrewd Farfrae or the philosophical Elizabeth-Jane. Hardy had found where his deepest sympathies lay.

Thenceforward his tragedy is centred in the deprivation or ill-chance of the underprivileged: Marty South and Tess, Giles Winterborne and Jude. The tragedy of *The Woodlanders* hinges on false social values which induce Grace Melbury to marry a philanderer whose hypocrisy is veiled in Shelleyan idealism. Tess, as a victim of chance and the embodiment of Christian charity (which suffereth long), is a pure (but not perfect) woman. "Once victim, always victim" echoes Richardson's *Clarissa*, the most important creative influence on *Tess*. *Jude*, the most ambitious and complex of Hardy's tragedies, was not finished to his satisfaction. The Christminster-Crucifixion parallel seems forced at the critical juncture, and hereditary traits of Jude and Sue, with reference to marriage, are too exceptional and peripheral to create convincing tragedy, though the novel contains the most moving dramatic scenes Hardy ever wrote, possibly with his own domestic situation in mind.

He had reason at this time to realize more than ever his readiness to fall imaginatively in love with beautiful women, and he had made it the subject of his satirical fantasy *The Well-Beloved*. One result of this tendency is that his heroines are generally more attractive than his men, Henchard excepted.

Hardy's most characteristic natural settings are psychological rather than scenic, expressing the feelings or situations of his principal characters. His visualizing techniques serve to make his critical scenes more impressive and memorable.

Such was Hardy's sense of the relativity of things that he rarely lost his sense of humour, as may be seen in "A Few Crusted Characters," written as a relief from *Tess*. Among his short stories, there are several, ranging from anecdote to novelette, from humour to satire and tragedy, which rank high in Hardy's fiction.

Violent criticism of *Jude* made Hardy relinquish prose fiction, and return to poetry, sooner than he intended. He had time to prepare for *The Dynasts*, a work he had contemplated in various forms for many years. In this epic drama of the Napoleonic wars, with nations swayed by forces beyond the control of reason, Hardy regards the conflict philosophically through the Spirit of the Years, and tragically through the Spirit of the Pities. It is a work of immense scholarship and artistic proportion, containing some of Hardy finest prose pictures and some moving lyrics. It's main weaknesses are in the verse, however, as well as in the visual and over-mechanical presentation of the Will.

Much of Hardy's early poetry (before and after his novel-writing period) suggests that he did not write it with ease. Rigorously rejecting poetical lushness, he achieved an independence of style reflecting his own observation, thought, vision, and feeling. Integrity shines through his verse even when it is oddly laboured. Impressed by the best of Wordsworth and Browning. he disciplined himself to write lyrical poetry as little removed as possible from the idiom of spoken English; and it is this quality, combined with his personal appeal, which explains the hold he has on modern readers. Most of his poems (and most of his greatest) were composed after he had reached the age of seventy. The autobiographical element is considerable.

Fortified by Arnold's declaration that "what distinguishes the greatest poets is their powerful and profound application of ideas to life," Hardy used verse to promulgate beliefs which he hoped would help to prepare a way for the Positivist religion of humanity. He remained an "evolutionary meliorist" until, in his last years, the prospect of another European war made him place the blame for the Unfulfilled Intention in human affairs, not on abstract Immanent Will, but on the folly of mankind.

His personal poetry has deeper resonances, as may be found particularly in "Poems of 1912–13," written after the death of his first wife. Hardy wrote many narrative poems in dramatic or ballad form. Unusual events and ironies of chance attracted him as much as in his prose; but more important is the poetry which he found in everyday life. "There is enough poetry in what is left, after all the false romance has been extracted, to make a sweet pattern," he affirmed. Many of his poems were composed with song-music in mind, and in stanzas demanding high manipulative skill. So imaginatively sensitive is Hardy to experience that even readers familiar with his poetry continually find something new to admire in movement, expression, or image. His finer poems are surprisingly varied and numerous; in them and elsewhere he modulates language with exquisite art to convey a living voice. The rare distinction of being both a major poet and a major novelist belongs to Thomas Hardy.

—F. B. Pinion

HARINGTON, Sir John. English. Born in Kelston, near Bath, Somerset, 4 August 1560; godson of Queen Elizabeth I. Educated at Eton College, from 1570; King's College, Cambridge, 1576–81, B.A. 1578, M.A. 1580; Lincoln's Inn, London, 1581. Married Mary Rogers in 1583; nine children. Gave up legal career when he succeeded to the family estates at Kelston, 1582; thereafter a courtier of Queen Elizabeth; High Sheriff of Somerset, 1592; banished from the court for suspected slur against Leicester, 1596, but forgiven by the queen, 1598; accompanied Essex on expedition to Ireland, 1599; knighted by Essex, 1599; because of queen's displeasure at his attempt to justify Essex's actions, he retired to Kelston; returned to the court of James I as tutor to Prince Henry. *Died 26 November 1612.*

PUBLICATIONS

Collections

    The Letters and Epigrams, with The Praise of Private Life, edited by Norman E. McClure. 1930.

Verse

    Epigrams Both Pleasant and Serious. 1615; revised edition, as *The Most Elegant and Witty Epigrams,* 1618.

Other

A New Discourse of a Stale Subject, Called the Metamorphosis of Ajax.   1596; edited by
    Elizabeth S. Donno, 1962.
An Anatomy of the Metamorphosed Ajax.   1596.
Ulysses upon Ajax.   1596.
A Brief View of the State of the Church of England, edited by John Chetwind.   1653.
Nugae Antiquae: A Miscellaneous Collection of Original Papers, with others, edited by
    Henry Harington.   2 vols., 1769–75; edited by Thomas Park, 2 vols., 1804.
A Short View of the State of Ireland Written in 1605, edited by W. D. MacCray.   1879.
A Tract on the Succession to the Crown, edited by Clements R. Markham.   1880.

Editor, with John Harington of Kelston, The Arundel Harington Manuscript of Tudor
    Poetry, edited by Ruth Hughey.   2 vols., 1960.

Translator, Orlando Furioso in English Heroical Verse, by Ariosto.   1591; edited by
    Robert McNulty, 1972.
Translator, The Englishman's Doctor; or, The School of Salerne, by J. de
    Mediolano.   1607; edited by F. R. Packard and F. H. Garrison, 1920.

Reading List: Harington and Ariosto by Townsend Rich, 1940; The Harington Family by Ian
Grimble, 1957; Harington of Stepney, Tudor Gentleman: His Life and Works by Ruth
Hughey, 1971.

*   *   *

When Harington translated the Orlando, he demonstrated fluency in the use of the Italian
language. Ariosto's sense of high seriousness, and, paradoxically, of mockery, was congenial
to Harington, who had a fine sense of the comic, which could move quickly to the pathetic.
Both poets enjoyed introducing themselves, their families, and friends into the notes, though
Harington has been criticized for compressing and expanding his original, and for adding
details in his attacks on women. Although use of the ottava rima stanza is praiseworthy, his
translation lacks the well-structured design of the Italian. Ariosto is the better poet, but
Harington has, nevertheless, created a worthy achievement of his own. In the prefixed
Apologie, Harington's purpose is not to refute the Puritans but to defend the Orlando, its
author, and its translator. He begins by using common refutations against the critics, often
referring to Sidney.

The Metamorphosis of Ajax is in the form of a mock encomium, but it also emphasizes the
utility of the cloacal invention (a jakes, or privy). The thrust is satiric but not cynical; it is
paradoxical: if man is god-like, he is also an animal.

For Harington, "of all poems the epigram is the wittiest, and of all that write epigrams,
Martial is counted the pleasantest." Some of Sir John's epigrams are drawn from Martial, but
his most effective verses are inspired by homely incidents of his own experience, to form
oblique compliments to friends or family, especially his wife, "Sweet Mall." A satiric line
could reverse the point of the epigram. Harington also introduced merry tales which pleased
the privileged few who had access to the circulating manuscripts.

Harington was a delightful letter-writer. He tells of the exploits of his ancestors, or of the
antics of his little dog Bungay, or of the Irish campaign in 1599, or of his painful interview
with the Queen on his return. No other contemporary account reveals so penetrating an
understanding of the old Queen, still the awe-inspiring monarch, but at the same time, the
woman, deeply hurt, disillusioned, and alone.

—Ruth Hughey

HARPUR, Charles. Australian. Born in Windsor, New South Wales, 23 January 1813. Married Mary Doyle in 1850; five children. Farm worker, Hunter River, New South Wales, 1829; settled in Sydney, and worked as post office clerk and free-lance writer, 1833–39; lived in Singleton and Jerry's Plains, New South Wales, 1839–49; teacher, 1850; sheep farmer, Doyle's Creek, New South Wales, 1851–58; Assistant Gold Commissioner, Araluen, and farmer at Eurobodalla, near Nerrigundah, New South Wales, 1859–66. *Died 10 June 1868.*

PUBLICATIONS

Collections

>   *Selected Poems,* edited by Kenneth H. Gifford and Donald F. Hall.   1944.
>   *(Selected Poems),* edited by Donovan Clarke.   1963.

Verse

>   *Thoughts: A Series of Sonnets.*   1845.
>   *The Bushrangers: A Play, and Other Poems.*   1853.
>   *A Poet's Home.*   1862.
>   *The Tower of the Dream.*   1865.
>   *Poems,* edited by H. M. Martin.   1883.
>   *Rose: Love Sonnets to Mary Doyle,* edited by C. W. Salier.   1948.

Reading List: *Harpur, An Australian* by James Normington-Rawling, 1962; *Harpur* by Judith Wright, 1963.

*   *   *

The fact that Charles Harpur's parents were both convicts has occasioned surprise to some of his commentators, who remark on the moralistic emphasis of much that he wrote. But the nineteenth century, even in the colonies, was a moralistic age and, whatever his parentage, Harpur was a conforming member of the colonial intellectual community of his day. Indeed he was conventional and conformist by temperament, in spite of some peccadilloes (undefined) of his own. In his official career he was at times under a cloud for what he called "matters of minor morals and manners" and once confessed to being "somewhat lax in my sexual moralities," but in all probability the point of the criticism was mainly his fondness for the bottle. The history of colonial alcoholism has yet to be written: it will no doubt prove revealing but it will not exhibit Harpur as particularly exceptional.

Harpur first wrote for the Sydney newspapers, especially for the *Empire,* conducted by his friend Henry Parkes, who helped him to publish both prose and verse. A great deal of his writing remains uncollected. Of the poems which have reached the public (in the dubious text of *Poems,* 1883), the outstanding examples are those which, like "The Creek of the Four Graves," "A Storm in the Mountains," or "A Coast View," are most vividly and directly drawn from his experience of bush life and landscape in his early years at Windsor or from his early wanderings among the Blue Mountains. Most of his serious work is in blank verse, though a particularly charming and deservedly popular piece, "Midsummer Noon in the Australian Forest" ("Not a sound disturbs the air,/There is quiet everywhere ...") is patterned in trochaic fours. This piece in particular reflects the thoughts and mood of boyhood and has a notable colonial freshness. In poems of a more ambitiously literary cast he shows an interesting allegiance to romantic models – Milton, Wordsworth, Keats, Shelley, possibly also Tennyson – and qualifies as a true colonial Victorian, but these attempts to be literary and traditional (as in "The Tower of the Dream" or "The Witch of Hebron") do not succeed as do the simple Australian pieces, though they are interesting evidence of an awakening colonial literary sensibility.

—Brian Elliott

* * *

HARY (Blind Harry or Hary; Henry The Minstrel). Scottish. Probably a native of Lothian, born c. 1440. Nothing is known of his life except his blindness, his occupation, and that he probably served in the Scottish court of James IV, 1490–92. *Died c. 1495.*

PUBLICATIONS

Verse

Hary's Wallace, edited by Matthew P. McDiarmid. 2 vols., 1968–69.

Reading List: *The Wallace and the Bruce Restudied* by J. T. T. Brown, 1900; "On Blind Hary's *Wallace*" by George Neilson, in *Essays and Studies 1*, 1910; *Mythical Bards and the Life of William Wallace* by W. H. Schofield, 1920; "William Wallace and His 'Buke' " by W. Scheps, in *Studies in Scottish Literature 6*, 1969.

*   *   *

The nationalism that had inspired Barbour's *Bruce* is more fiercely articulate in Hary's *Wallace*, not only because fifteenth-century writing tends to be more emotive than fourteenth-century but also because the poem is polemical. It is aimed against James III's novel and dangerous policy of preferring an English to a French alliance. It implicitly supports those rebellious nobles who were soon to depose the king and accuse him of "the inbringing of Englishmen," and rebukes the "thrifty men" whose commercial interests made them willing to forget the lessons of the Wars of Independence. It is to impress these lessons that Hary presents Wallace as an example of unrelenting patriotism, a martyr sold to the enemy by selfish and disloyal fellow countrymen.

History happens to support this representation, but, unlike Barbour, Hary is more concerned to make history than to record it: lays and traditions are rehandled, episodes are imitated from the *Bruce*, a time-scale that will allow him to treat this extended matter in twelve Books is devised, and actions and scenes are invented, all in order to develop a hero whose sufferings are greater even than his achievements. Loss of father, brother, wife, friends, office (as Guardian of Scotland), life itself, and an unappreciated loyalty to king and country, are so presented as to make Wallace the tragic victim of an unnatural world (" 'Allace,' he said, 'the warld is contrar-lik!,' " XI, 210). The Wallace who so deeply affected the imaginations of "Ossian," Burns, and Wordsworth is Hary's creation, a figure larger than life who anticipates the protagonists of sixteenth-century drama in the intensity of his responses and the passion of his purpose. Pity for his, and his country's, wrongs is both modified and heightened by the shock of an unremitting, if principled, vengefulness. No historical personage had been so emotively presented, nor scenes of violent action (guerilla warfare) so effectively visualised. The poet's vision, however, so intense in parts – the episodes of the killing of Fawdon, "The Barns of Ayr," at Falkirk the betrayal of Wallace along with his winning Bruce for the cause – is felt to be finally obsessive and tiring. The driving pace of his narrative dispenses with any subtleties of versification or interpretation. One remembers Wordsworth's verdict on Walter Scott that his genius was "physical." Hary is rightly called by Friedrich Brie "a heroically minded man" (in *Die Nationale Literatur Schottlands*, 1973), and it is as a heroic poet that he wins respect, for simple lines such as this on Wallace after the defeat at Falkirk, "Amang the dede men sekand the worthiest."

—Matthew P. McDiarmid

HAWES, Stephen. English. Born, probably in Suffolk, c. 1475. Educated at Oxford University. Travelled on the Continent after leaving university; returned to England and served at court: groom of the chamber to Henry VII, from c. 1502. *Died c. 1523.*

PUBLICATIONS

Verse

> *The Pastime of Pleasure.* 1509; as *The History of the Grande Amour,* 1554; edited by W. E. Mead, 1927.
> *The Conversion of Swearers.* 1509.
> *A Joyful Meditation to All England of the Coronation of King Henry the Eighth.* 1509.
> *The Example of Virtue.* 1509(?).
> *The Comfort of Lovers.* 1515(?).
> *The Minor Poems* (all but *The Pastime of Pleasure*), edited by Florence W. Gluck and Alice B. Morgan. 1974.

Reading List: *Hawes Passetyme of Pleasure Vergleichen mit Spensers Faerie Queene* by F. Zander, 1905; "The English Chaucerians" by Derek Pearsall, in *Chaucer and Chaucerians* edited by D. S. Brewer, 1966.

*   *   *

In an age more richly endowed with poets of undisputed quality than the early sixteenth century, the verse of Stephen Hawes might appear to be merely of minor interest, yet such were the problems and uncertainties concerning metre, language, form, and content which confronted Tudor writers that the striking historical importance of his work outweighs its technical shortcomings. Hawes is a typical early English Renaissance author, still remaining conservative in literary taste and outlook, yet attempting to breathe life into outdated medieval conventions. Despite its inadequacies, his poetry retains the fascination of a transitional mode where modern topics and concerns struggle to detach themselves from earlier literary preoccupations which obscure their potential novelty and prevent their full expression. Never a conscious pioneer, if he chiefly looks back to post-Chaucerian moral allegory and chivalric romance for his models, Hawes also glances ahead to the theme and methods of *The Faerie Queene*.

His poems, the principal of which is the lengthy *Passetyme of Pleasure* dedicated to his master Henry VII, exemplify the officially sanctioned voice of early Tudor poetry, and exhibit the formal "high" style of which Hawes was an earnest and untiring exponent; the lyric grace of the song-books, the colloquial gusto of Skelton, the subtle rhythms of Wyatt, are nowhere to be found. He writes in the approved "aureate" manner of his poetic mentor John Lydgate at his most ornately periphrastic, "tellynge the tale in termes eloquent" in order to conceal the presumed crudities of the native vernacular, but his command of language is often uncertain, his epithets banal, his imagery rarely arresting. He seems to adhere to no firm metrical principles, even unorthodox ones, and his grammar and syntax can often leave a reader at a loss to discover the poet's intended meaning.

Yet from Hawes's structurally weak, conscientiously embellished, and imaginatively pedestrian verse emerges a man responsive to his literary heritage, natural and formal beauty, the chivalric ideal, and the traditional wonders and marvels of the knightly quest. *The Passetyme of Pleasure* depicts human life as an allegorical pilgrimage and devotes almost 6,000 lines to Graunde Amour's valiant efforts to win the hand of La Bell Pucell by performing feats of arms against a variety of enemies, strengthened by coaching received in the Tower of Doctrine from the Seven Liberal Arts, and assailed by the misogynistic (and somewhat wearisome) attacks of a loutish dwarf, Godfrey Gobelyve. Here Spenser is undoubtedly foreshadowed, and *The Example of Vertu*, in which Youth is guided through numerous temptations by Discretion to slay a three-headed dragon, marry Cleaness, daughter of the King of Love, and depart for a dwelling in Heaven, anticipates the adventures of both the Red Cross Knight and Sir Guyon. Hawes's tribute to Henry VIII is a standard Renaissance eulogy, and his versified sermon, *The Convercyon of Swerers*, is unlikely to appeal today, but *The Conforte of Lovers*, which describes an allegorical dream-vision culminating in an amorous encounter in a garden setting, is not without charm or merit.

—William M. Tydeman

HAWKER, Robert Stephen. English. Born in Stoke Damerel, Devon, 3 December 1803. Educated at Cheltenham School, Gloucestershire; Pembroke College, Oxford, 1823; Magdalen Hall, Oxford, 1824–28 (Newdigate Prize, 1827), B.A. 1828, M.A. 1836. Married 1) Charlotte Eliza Rawleigh in 1823 (died, 1863); 2) Pauline Anne Kuczynski in 1864, three daughters. Ordained deacon, 1829, priest, 1831; Curate in North Tamerton, Cornwall, 1831–34; Vicar of Morwenstow, Cornwall, 1834–75, with Wellcombe, Cornwall, 1851–75; embraced Roman Catholic faith just before his death. *Died 15 August 1875.*

PUBLICATIONS

Collections

Poetical Works, edited by A. Wallis. 1899.
Twenty Poems, edited by John Drinkwater. 1925.
A Selection of Hawker's Cornish Ballads, edited by F. C. Hamlyn. 1928.

Verse

> *Tendrils.* 1821.
> *Pompeii.* 1827.
> *Records of the Western Shore.* 1832.
> *Poems.* 1836.
> *Minster Church.* 1836.
> *A Welcome to the Prince Albert.* 1840.
> *Ecclesia.* 1840.
> *The Poor Man and His Parish Church.* 1843.
> *Reeds Shaken with the Wind.* 1843; *Second Cluster,* 1844.
> *Echoes from Old Cornwall.* 1846.
> *A Voice from the Place of S. Morwenna.* 1849.
> *A Letter to a Friend.* 1857.
> *The Quest of the Sangraal: Chant the First.* 1864.
> *Cornish Ballads and Other Poems.* 1869; edited by C. E. Byles, 1904.

Other

> *Rural Synods.* 1844.
> *Footprints of Former Men in Far Cornwall.* 1870; edited by J. G. Godwin, as *Prose Works,* 1893; edited by C. E. Byles, 1903.
> *Stones Broken from the Rocks: Extracts from Note-Books,* edited by E. R. Appleton and C. E. Byles. 1922.

Reading List: *Life and Letters of Hawker* by C. E. Byles, 1905; *Hawker: A Study of His Thought and Poetry* by Margaret F. Burrows, 1926; *Hawker of Morwenstow* by Piers Brendon, 1975.

*   *   *

Robert Stephen Hawker acquired fame in his lifetime as Vicar of Morwenstow and as "the Cornish poet." Both as a poet and as a lone upholder of the ideals of the Oxford Movement Hawker was known far beyond the bounds of his remote parish, to which he was inducted in 1834 and where he remained until his death forty-one years later. A. L. Rowse has described him as one of the best of the Victorian minor poets, and the constant reprinting of his work would seem to confirm this judgement. His best-known poem is the Trelawney Ballad, which he published anonymously in 1824, and which Scott and Macaulay mistook for an ancient traditional ballad. His most distinguished achievement, however, is *The Quest of the Sangraal,* a long poem in blank verse, based on the Arthurian legends and set in Cornwall. Hawker was sixty when he began the *Quest;* his health was failing, and he was mourning the death of his first wife. For these reasons he completed only the first of the three "chants" originally planned for the poem. It is, however, an impressive fragment. Byles comments, "The majesty of the sea is in this poem. The great lines follow each other with a measured roll and thunder." Longfellow considered Hawker's *Quest* "far superior" to Tennyson's *Holy Grail,* and Tennyson himself said, "Hawker has beaten me on my own ground."

In his numerous ballads Hawker celebrates old Cornish traditions and legends, and striking incidents from his own pastoral ministry. Many of these simply written poems, such as "The Figurehead of the *Caledonia,*" "The Poor Man and His Parish Church," "The Dirge," and "The Ringers of Lancells' Tower," are extremely moving, especially when read aloud; others, such as "Featherstone's Doom," strike an impressively sinister note.

Hawker's prose volume *Footprints of Former Men in Far Cornwall* has kept its popularity.

The prose of these "reprinted pieces" is sinewy and forceful, and benefits from Hawker's use of the occasional archaism, always well chosen for effect. In this book he vividly recreates bygone Cornish scenes and worthies, some famous, some obscure; drawing on the traditions current among his older parishioners, he conjures up strange episodes such as the story of "Cruel Coppinger," which Sabine Baring-Gould was later to use as the foundation for his novel *In the Roar of the Sea.*

Hawker's sermons have remained largely unpublished. A large number of them exist in manuscript in the Bodleian Library. Essentially pastoral in tone and content, their clear exposition, solid orthodoxy, and poetic use of metaphor place them in the classic tradition of the English pulpit, and qualify them for a wider public than the congregations to which they were preached.

—Brocard Sewell

HAY, John (Milton).   American.   Born in Salem, Indiana, 8 October 1838. Educated at Brown University, Providence, Rhode Island, graduated, 1858; studied law in the office of Milton Hay, Springfield, Illinois; admitted to the Illinois Bar, 1861. Served with the Union forces during the Civil War: Colonel. Married Clara Louise Stone in 1874. Secretary to Abraham Lincoln for four years; in the U.S. Diplomatic Service: Secretary of the Legation in Paris, 1865–67; Chargé d'Affaires, Vienna, 1867–68; Secretary of the Legation in Madrid, 1868–70; First Assistant Secretary of State, Washington, D.C., 1879–81; Ambassador to Great Britain, 1897–98; Secretary of State, to President McKinley, 1898–1901, and to President Theodore Roosevelt, 1901–05. Member of the staff, 1870–75, and Editor, 1881, *New York Tribune.* LL.D.: Western Reserve University, Cleveland; Princeton University, New Jersey; Dartmouth College, Hanover, New Hampshire; Yale University, New Haven, Connecticut; Harvard University, Cambridge, Massachusetts. Member, American Academy of Arts and Letters, 1904. *Died 1 July 1905.*

PUBLICATIONS

Collections

Complete Poetical Works, edited by Clarence L. Hay.   1916.

Verse

Jim Bludso of the Prairie Belle, and Little Breeches.   1871.
Pike County Ballads and Other Pieces.   1871; as *Little Breeches and Other Pieces,* 1871.
Poems.   1890.

Fiction

The Bread-Winners: A Social Study.   1884.

Other

Castilian Days.   1871; revised edition, 1890.
Abraham Lincoln: A History, with John G. Nicolay.   10 vols., 1890.
Addresses.   1906.
Letters and Extracts from Diary, edited by Henry Adams and Clara Louise Hay.   3
    vols., 1908.
A Poet in Exile: Early Letters, edited by Caroline Ticknor.   1910.
A College Friendship: A Series of Letters to Hannah Angell.   1938.
Lincoln and the Civil War in the Diaries and Letters of Hay, edited by Tyler
    Dennett.   1939.
Henry James and Hay: The Record of a Friendship, edited by George Monteiro.   1965.

Editor, with John G. Nicolay, Complete Works, by Abraham Lincoln.   2 vols., 1894.

Bibliography: in Bibliography of American Literature by Jacob Blanck, 1963.

Reading List: Life and Letters of Hay by William Roscoe Thayer, 2 vols., 1915; Hay: The
Gentleman as Diplomat by Kenton J. Clymer, 1975; Hay: The Union of Poetry and Politics by
Howard I. Kushner and Anne Hummel Sherrill, 1977; Hay by Robert L. Gale, 1978.

*   *   *

In 1904 John Hay was numbered among the first seven individuals elected to the American
Academy of Arts and Letters. He was so honored as the famous author of Castilian Days,
essays on Spain; Pike County Ballads and Other Pieces; Poems, a collected edition; and
Abraham Lincoln: A History, ten volumes written in collaboration with John G. Nicolay.
Forgotten were the essays and stories he had published in the 1860's and 1870's in Putnam's,
Harper's, and the Atlantic. It had not yet been established, moreover, that Hay was also the
author of The Bread-Winners, an anti-labor novel that so closely reflected Hay's alarm over
the growing threats to society posed by the violent strikes of 1877 and their aftermath, and
one that so obviously drew upon his own sense of himself as a beleaguered member of the
establishment that the prudent author chose to publish his novel anonymously. Its
authorship, a closely guarded secret for decades, was acknowledged only after his death. The
Bread-Winners lives today, less for its reactionary argument, than for its sharp portrait of
Maud Matchin, a self-made girl. In this pert and impertinent high-school graduate Hay
created a portrait of American girlhood to stand beside those of James's Daisy Miller and
Howells's Lydia Blood.
    Hay's short fiction antedates The Bread-Winners, some of it by more than twenty years.
Even though the stories constitute early work, they continue to warrant serious attention,
both for their intrinsic merit and for their surprisingly skilful anticipation of many of the
major technical and thematic interests of the American realists. The principal concerns of his
fiction can be described as the dangers awaiting innocent and not-so-innocent Americans
trying to make their way in Paris ("Shelby Cabell" and "Kane and Abel"), the duties of those
who would be faithful to the Union ("Red, White and Blue"), the wages of love and
miscegenation ("The Foster-Brothers") and the murderous proclivities in the heart of the
midwestern farmer ("The Blood Seedling").
    The last of these stories presents the Golyers, a family that figures as well in the Pike
County ballads, the first three of which, "Banty Tim," "Jim Bludso, of the Prairie Belle," and
"Little Breeches," catapulted Hay to immediate fame. Contemporary arguments over
whether Hay or his friend Bret Harte had been the first to exploit the dialects of the American
West served both to promote their fame and to delay the assessment of Hay's achievement. If
there was no doubt that his poems captured the rhythmic speech of the Pike County Man, the

notion that such speech did not provide fit substance for poetry would long plague Hay. It was not immediately recognized that the poems were not primarily attacks on common poetic speech, but rather sly barbs aimed at the conventional morality of his day. In Jim Bludso he presents a hard-talking bigamist who is nevertheless capable of Christian self-sacrifice. This rude practitioner of a religion of humanity, according to the poet, could hardly suffer retribution from a true Christian God. If this poetically unconventional statement did not receive unanimous approval, it did tap a vein of largely unexpressed feelings. With tears in her eyes, George Eliot frequently recited by heart "Jim Bludso," and in *Ulysses* Joyce has Leopold Bloom, on his way to the brothel, ruminate: "I did alla white man could ... Jim Bludso. Hold her nozzle again the bank."

At other times Hay wrote more conventional poems that continue to appeal, among them the political "A Triumph of Order," the skilfully devised "Una," and the witty, self-ironic "A Dream of Bric-à-Brac." But when poets are again permitted to tell stories in verse, Hay's spirited ballads will recover something of the favor they enjoyed in 1897 when, on the occasion of Hay's appointment as Ambassador to the Court of St. James's, English publishers, passing up *Castilian Days* and *Abraham Lincoln*, brought out an edition of Hay's poems, ignoring his properly understated title in 1890 for his collected *Poems* in favor of *Pike County Ballads and Other Poems*, one harking back to his first collection.

—George Monteiro

HAYDEN, Robert (Earl). American. Born in Detroit, Michigan, 4 August 1913. Educated at Wayne State University, Detroit, A.B.; University of Michigan. Ann Arbor (Hopwood Award, 1938, 1942), M.A. 1944. Married; one daughter. Teaching Fellow, University of Michigan, 1944–46; Member of the English Department, Fisk University, Nashville, Tennessee, 1946–68. Visiting Professor, 1968, and since 1969, Professor of English, University of Michigan. Bingham Professor, University of Louisville, Kentucky, Spring 1969; Visiting Poet, University of Washington, Seattle, Summer 1969, University of Connecticut, Storrs, 1971, and Denison University, Granville, Ohio, 1971; Staff Member, Breadloaf Writers Conference, Middlebury, Vermont, 1972. Member, and Poetry Editor, *World Order*, Baha'i Faith. Recipient: Rosenwald Fellowship, 1947; Ford Foundation grant, 1954; World Festival of Negro Arts Poetry Prize, Dakar, Senegal, 1966; Russell Loines Award, 1970; American Academy of Poets Fellowship, 1971. Lives in Ann Arbor, Michigan.

PUBLICATIONS

Verse

Heart-Shape in the Dust. 1940.
The Lion and the Archer, with Myron O'Higgins. 1948.
Figures of Time. 1955.
A Ballad of Remembrance. 1962.

Selected Poems.   1966.
Words in the Mourning Time.   1970.
The Night-Blooming Cereus.   1972.
Angle of Ascent: New and Selected Poems.   1975.

Other

How I Write I, with Judson Philips and Lawson Carter.   1972.
Nine Black American Doctors (juvenile), with Jacqueline Harris.   1976.

Editor, *Kaleidoscope: Poems by American Negro Poets.*   1967.
Editor, with David J. Burrows and Frederick R. Lapides, *Afro-American Literature: An Introduction.*   1971.

*   *   *

Much in the manner of Countée Cullen, the Harlem Renaissance poet, though more comfortable experimenting with free forms of verse, Robert Hayden has steadfastly claimed refusal to write racial poetry but quite consistently been at his poetic best precisely when he has used the material of the black American experience in his work. He warned in *Kaleidoscope* against placing the black writer in "a kind of literary ghetto," where he would be "not considered a writer but a species of race-relations man, the leader of a cause, the voice of protest." It must be said that even when Hayden employs racial material and themes, he usually molds them into interesting and often exquisite universal shapes that make him far more than a mere "race-relations man." If there is a criticism to be levelled at him, it would be that he is occasionally too academic (indeed, he has spent much of his life in academe), occasionally lapsing into preciousness (e.g., in "Veracruz": "Thus reality/bedizened in the warring colors/of a dream ..."").

Mostly, however, Hayden composes with notable power and beauty. For example, his evocation, in "The Ballad of Nat Turner," of the nineteenth-century leader of a slave uprising is perhaps the most succinct and spiritually true in all of imaginative literature. Such poems as "The Diver" capture the essence of the moment or act (in this case the descent of a sea diver from the sinking "through easeful azure" to the time when "somehow began the measured rise") with the felicitous marriage of sound and sense that is quintessential poetry.

—Alan R. Shucard

HAYNE, Paul Hamilton. American. Born in Charleston, South Carolina, 1 January 1830. Educated at Mr. Coates's School, Charleston; Charleston College, graduated 1850; studied law but abandoned his practice for a literary career. Served on Governor Picken's staff during the Civil War. Married Mary Middleton Michel in 1852; one son. Free-lance journalist, and member of the editorial staff of *Southern Literary Gazette*, Charleston, and the Washington *Spectator*, 1850–57; a Founder and Editor, with W. B. Carlisle, *Russell's Magazine*, Charleston, 1857–60; made homeless and bankrupt by the Civil War: moved to Groveton, near Augusta, Georgia, and subsisted on a small farm. LL.D.: Washington and Lee College, Lexington, Virginia, 1882. *Died 6 July 1886.*

PUBLICATIONS

Collections

The Southern Poets, with Lanier and Timrod, edited by J. W. Abernethy.   1904.

Verse

Poems. 1855.
Sonnets and Other Poems.   1857.
*Avolio: A Legend of the Island of Cos, with Poems Lyrical, Miscellaneous, and
   Dramatic.*   1859.
Legends and Lyrics.   1872.
The Mountain of the Lovers, with Poems of Nature and Tradition.   1875.
Poems, Complete Edition.   1882.
The Broken Battalions.   1885.

Other

Lives of Robert Young Hayne and Hugh Swinton Legaré.   1878
A Collection of Hayne Letters, edited by Daniel M. McKeithan.   1944.
The Correspondence of Bayard Taylor and Hayne, edited by Charles Duffy.   1945.

Editor, *The Poems of Henry Timrod.*   1873.

Bibliography: in *Bibliography of American Literature* by Jacob Blanck, 1963.

Reading List: *Hayne: Life and Letters* by Kate Harbes Becker, 1951; *Hayne* by Rayburn S.
Moore, 1972.

*   *   *

Paul Hamilton Hayne began publishing poems at the age of fifteen, and by 1861 his poetry
had appeared in *Graham's Magazine,* the *Atlantic Monthly,* and the *Southern Literary
Messenger* and he had collected three volumes of Romantic verse based chiefly on the
examples of Keats, Hunt, Poe, Tennyson, and Longfellow. His work attracted the critical
attention of Lowell and Whipple, but the Civil War temporarily interrupted his development.
    After the war Hayne's muse continued to develop in the mainstream of the Anglo-
American tradition. He became a versatile versifier and employed a wide range of forms,
metrical schemes, and techniques. His short poems – sonnets and nature lyrics in particular –
demonstrate his work at its best. In fact, as his career progressed, Hayne became a leading
American sonneteer, and such pieces as "Aspects of the Pines," "The Voice in the Pines,"
"To a Bee," "The First Mocking-Bird in Spring," "Hints of Spring," and "Midsummer (on the
Farm)" reflect his achievement as a lyricist on nature.
    At the same time Hayne could also write successful long poems, narratives like "The Wife
of Brittany," an interpretation of Chaucer's "Franklin's Tale" and Hayne's most ambitious
and fully realized long poem, and odes like "Muscadines," a sensuous piece whose verbal
melody derives from the "liquid magic" of the Southern grape, and "Unveiled," an irregular
ode whose tone and view of nature suggest a philosophical kinship with "Tintern Abbey."
Even late in his career Hayne continued to write long poems, frequently celebrating

occasions or commemorating events such as the centennials of the battles of King's Mountain and Yorktown in 1881 or the sesquicentennial of the founding of Georgia in 1883, among others. The ode on Georgia, it should be noted, and the production of his last four years, including three additional long poems, a fine sonnet on Robert E. Lee, and a handful of lyrics that are among the best he ever wrote on his own locale, were never collected.

After Simms's death in 1870, Hayne became the "representative" poet and literary spokesman for the South. Indeed, in the scope, versatility, and bulk of his production, he remains a substantial minor American poet of the period, even though a sizable proportion of his output is ephemeral magazine verse. Admittedly, few of his poems come near the perfection of, say, Poe's "To Helen," for he lacked Poe's sense of art and critical acumen. Moreover, he accepted without challenge the conventions of the nineteenth-century Anglo-American poetic tradition, and many of his poems embody certain aspects of its weakest features – ornate and artificial language, empty abstractions, unalloyed bookishness and monotonous metrical regularity. But these standards of time and taste cannot change the fact that Hayne's canon reflects the full scope of a striving for expression in a spectrum of poetic types and structures nor should they in any way detract from the devotion he rendered his muse despite discouraging and distressing conditions of poverty and ill health during the last part of his life. His accomplishment was modest, but his dedication to literature was exemplary.

—Rayburn S. Moore

HEANEY, Seamus (Justin).   Irish.   Born in Castledawson, County Derry, 13 April 1939. Educated at Anahorish School; St. Columb's College, Derry; Queen's University, Belfast, B.A. (honours) in English 1961. Married Marie Devlin in 1965; two sons. Teacher, St. Thomas's Secondary School, Belfast, 1962–63; Lecturer, St. Joseph's College of Education, Belfast, 1963–66; Lecturer in English, Queen's University, 1966–72; Guest Lecturer, University of California, Berkeley, 1970; moved to County Wicklow, 1972, did regular radio work and teaching at various American universities. Since 1975, Teacher at Carysfort Training College, Dublin. Recipient: Eric Gregory Award, 1966; Cholmondeley Award, 1967; Faber Memorial Prize, 1968; Maugham Award, 1968; Irish Academy of Letters Award, 1971; Denis Devlin Memorial Award, 1973; American-Irish Foundation Award, 1975; National Institute of Arts and Letters E. M. Forster Award, 1975; Duff Cooper Memorial Award, 1976; Smith Literary Award, 1976. Lives in Dublin.

PUBLICATIONS

Verse

Eleven Poems.   1965.
Death of a Naturalist.   1966.
Room to Rhyme, with Dairo Hammond and Michael Longley.   1968.
A Lough Neagh Sequence.   1969.
Door into the Dark.   1969.
Night Drive.   1970.

Boy Driving His Father to Confession.   1970.
Wintering Out.   1972.
North.   1975.
Bog Poems.   1975.
Stations.   1975.
The Watchman's Flute: New Poems.   1978.

Other

Editor, with Alan Brownjohn and Jon Stallworthy, New Poems 1970–1971.   1971.
Editor, Soundings 2.   1974.

Reading List: Heaney by Robert Buttel, 1975.

*   *   *

Seamus Heaney's poetry has been rooted in his rural background, in the activities of farm life, its crafts and skills, its relationship with the land. Many of his early poems celebrate this life and respond sensuously, in image and rhythm, commemorating the crafts of the countryside in their own respect for technical accomplishment. This response to the rural background subsequently involved the auditory imagination. In the accents of the area, in its place-names and historical antecedents, he could hear the divisions of the culture; in the vocables of place he could give intimations of history. He could also detect the divisions in his own experience between the Irish heritage and the English heritage which he had acquired through education and reading.

The dark centres of the past, of the unknown, of the self, of the mysterious region from which poems emerge, found an eloquent metaphor in the bogs of Ireland which preserve objects from the past and at times yield them up. Heaney's discovery of P. V. Glob's The Bog People confirmed his faith in this metaphor, and extended his understanding of the violence in Northern Ireland by showing that in the early Iron Age there had been similar blood-lettings. The book enriched his imaginative response to the metaphor of the bog in its moving account, together with its pictures of the Tollund Man, the Grauballe Man, and others, of how ritual sacrifices to the goddess of the earth led, through time and through the preserving and transmuting properties of the bog, to these resurrected objects of beauty. This extension has broadened the scope of his poetry even as it has deepened and confirmed the validity of his trust in his own region. Exploring the implications of the resemblances and associations between Ireland and Scandinavia (for example, in the Viking deposits recently found in Dublin), he writes now with confidence and nonchalance, making bold imaginative leaps across the landscape of northern Europe and backward through literary, linguistic, and geological periods.

—Maurice Harmon

HEMANS, Felicia (Dorothea, née Browne).   English.   Born in Liverpool, 25 September 1793; moved with her family to Abergele, North Wales, 1800. Privately educated at home. Married Captain Alfred Hemans in 1812 (separated, 1818); five sons. Lived in Wales, and devoted herself to her family and to writing; moved to Wavertree, near Liverpool, 1828; visited Scotland, and met Sir Walter Scott, and the English lakes, and met Wordsworth,

1829; moved to Dublin, 1831. Recipient: Royal Society of Literature prize, 1821. *Died 16 May 1835.*

PUBLICATIONS

Collections

> *Works,* edited by Harriet Hughes.   7 vols., 1839.
> *Poetical Works,* edited by W. M. Rossetti.   1873.

Verse

> *Poems.*   1808.
> *England and Spain; or, Valour and Patriotism.*   1808.
> *The Domestic Affections and Other Poems.*   1812.
> *The Restoration of the Works of Art to Italy.*   1816.
> *Modern Greece.*   1817.
> *Translations from Camoens and Other Poets.*   1818.
> *Wallace's Invocation to Bruce.*   1819.
> *The Sceptic.*   1820.
> *Stanzas to the Memory of the Late King.*   1820.
> *Dartmoor.*   1821.
> *Welsh Melodies.*   1822.
> *The Siege of Valencia: A Dramatic Poem, The Last Constantine, with Other Poems.*   1823.
> *The Forest Sanctuary and Other Poems.*   1825; revised edition, 1829.
> *Lays of Many Lands.*   1825.
> *The League of the Alps, The Siege of Valencia, The Vespers of Palermo, and Other Poems,* edited by A. Norton.   2 vols., 1826–27.
> *Poems.*   1827.
> *Hymns on the Works of Nature for the Use of Children.*   1827.
> *Poetical Works.*   2 vols., 1828.
> *Records of Woman with Other Poems.*   1828.
> *Songs of the Affections with Other Poems.*   1830.
> *Hymns for Childhood.*   1834.
> *National Lyrics and Songs for Music.*   1834.
> *Scenes and Hymns of Life with Other Religious Poems.*   1834.
> *Poetical Remains.*   1836.
> *Early Blossoms.*   1840.

Play

> *The Vespers of Palermo* (produced 1823).   1823.

Reading List: *Memorials of Mrs. Hemans* by Henry F. Chorley, 2 vols., 1836; *Hemans Lyrik* by W. Ledderbogen, 1913; *Une Femme Poète au Déclin du Romantisme Anglais: Hemans* by Edith Duméril, 1929 (includes bibliography).

*   *   *

Though of considerable renown as a poet in her day, both at home and abroad, Felicia Hemans is now remembered less for her writings than for her friendships – first as the recipient of the persistent attentions of the youthful Shelley, later as the visitor of Scott and guest of Wordsworth. Other prominent admirers included such diverse figures as Lord Byron, Lord Jeffrey, John Wilson, Reginald Heber, and Joanna Baillie. Such high regard cannot have been entirely misplaced, and it is an injustice to her talents to associate her only with the stately homes of England and the boy on the burning deck.

The chief attraction of Mrs. Hemans' verse is its variety: there are historical and legendary tales, Greek and Welsh melodies, patriotic effusions, devotional sonnets, nature lyrics, children's verses, hymns, songs and translations. Her collected poems, the product of over 30 years of writing, fill some 700 pages of fine print, and while there is much in them that is frankly imitative (now of Wordsworth and Coleridge, now of Bryon and Tom Moore), and much that is sweetly sentimental (chivalry, childhood, and the Church), there is nevertheless a good deal to surprise and delight, especially among her shorter pieces. Poems like "The Rock of Cader Idris," "Woman on the Field of Battle," "The Voice of Spring," "The Landing of the Pilgrim Fathers," "The Shadow of a Flower," "The Willow Song," and "I would we had not met again ..." are representative of her genuinely lyrical voice. Among the more interesting of her longer poems are "The Abencerrage" (a Spanish tale), "The Maremma" (an Italian tale, after Dante), "The Forest Sanctuary" (her own favourite), and the collection entitled *Records of Woman* (celebrating such feminine worthies as Joan of Arc, Arabella Stuart, and Properzia Rossi). The opening lines of "The Abencerrage" (1819) are a good example of the poet's exotic scene-setting:

> Lonely and still are now thy marble halls,
>   Thou fair Alhambra! there the feast is o'er;
> And with the murmur of thy fountain-falls
>   Blend the wild tones of minstrelsy no more.
>
> Hushed are the voices that in years gone by
>   Have mourned, exulted, menaced, through thy towers;
> Within thy pillared courts the grass waves high,
>   And all uncultured bloom thy fairy bowers.
>
> Unheeded there the flowering myrtle blows,
>   Through tall arcades unmarked the sunbeam smiles,
> And many a tint of softened brilliance throws
>   O'er fretted walls and shining peristyles.

C. H. Herford wrote in *The Age of Wordsworth* (1897) that: "Of all the English Romantic poets, Mrs. Hemans expresses with the richest intensity the more superficial and transient elements of Romanticism." Pathos, primitivism, and the picturesque abound in her verses, and indeed they quickly pall on the taste, but Mrs. Hemans has a rightful place in any anthology of the period.

—Greg Crossan

HENLEY, William Ernest. English. Born in Gloucester, 23 August 1849. Educated at the Crypt Grammar School, Gloucester. Married Anna Boyle in 1878; one daughter. Crippled by a tubercular disease: patient in an Edinburgh infirmary, 1873–75; member of staff of the *Encyclopaedia Britannica* in Edinburgh, 1875; Editor, *London*, 1877–78,

Magazine of Art, London, 1882–86, *Scots Observer*, Edinburgh, later the *National Observer*, London, 1889–94, and *New Review*, London, 1894–98; contributor to the *Pall Mall Magazine*, London, 1899 until his death. LL.D.: University of St. Andrews, 1893. Granted Civil List pension 1898. *Died 11 July 1903.*

PUBLICATIONS

Collections

Works.   7 vols., 1908.

Verse

A Book of Verses.   1888.
The Song of the Sword and Other Verses.   1892.
London Voluntaries and Other Verses.   1893.
Poems.   1898.
For England's Sake: Verses and Songs in Time of War.   1900.
Hawthorn and Lavender, with Other Verses.   1901.
A Song of Speed.   1903.

Plays

Deacon Brodie; or, The Double Life, with Robert Louis Stevenson (produced 1882).   1880; revised edition, 1888.
Admiral Guinea, with Robert Louis Stevenson (produced 1897).   1884.
Beau Austin, with Robert Louis Stevenson (produced 1890).   1884.
Macaire, with Robert Louis Stevenson (produced 1900).   1885.
Mephisto (produced 1886).   1887.

Other

Pictures at Play by Two Art-Critics, with Andrew Lang.   1888.
A Century of Artists, with Andrew Lang.   1889.
Views and Reviews: Essays in Appreciation.   2 vols., 1890–1902.
Some Letters, edited by V. Payen-Payne.   1933.

Editor, *Lyra Heroica: A Book of Verse for Boys.*   1892; study guide, 1900.
Editor, with Charles Whibley, *A Book of English Prose, Character, and Incident 1387–1649.*   1894.
Editor, *English Classics.*   6 vols., 1894–95.
Editor, with J. S. Farmer, *Slang and Its Analogues: A Dictionary,* vols. 2–7.   6 vols, 1894–1904.
Editor, *A London Garland.*   1895.
Editor, with T. F. Henderson, *The Centenary Burns.*   1896.
Editor, *English Lyrics, Chaucer to Poe.*   1897.
Editor, *Complete Poetical Works,* by Burns.   1897.
Editor, *Works,* by Byron, Smollett, Shakespeare, and Fielding.   4 vols., 1897–1902.

Editor, with George Wyndham, *The Poetry of Wilfrid Blunt.*   1898.
Editor, with H. F. Brown and G. Dakyns, *The Collected Poems of T. E. Brown.*   1900.

Reading List: *Henley: A Study in the "Counter-Decadence" of the 'Nineties* by Jerome H. Buckley, 1945; *Henley* by John Connell, 1949; *Henley* by Joseph M. Flora, 1970; *Henley et Son Groupe* by André Guillaume, 1973.

*   *   *

William Ernest Henley at his best wrote in the plain prosy style of the series of poems in his first volume, "In Hospital," a narrative of hospitalization presented through a series of vignettes of patients, staff, and visitors where each in turn is actor and audience in a mundane theatre. The poems exhibit a social-realism untypical of the 1870's when they were written, reinforced by vigorous onomatopoeia and a masculine syntax, and working through overt statement rather than evocation. The short poems, sometimes unrhymed, often sonnets, catch the dispirited "decent meanness" of the ward and the tedium of its routines. Though frequently polarized into description and appended response ("O, a gruesome world!"), the poems can rise, as in "Pastoral" or "Nocturn," to a refreshing romantic irony (the latter deals with a leaking cistern, the drip of which "taps upon my heart-strings" and imposes on the scansion). In "Bric-à-Brac" – a title expressive of his tone and view of the world – he returns to sharply etched sketches of people and places in a spare, angular style which delineates, in a *blason* or list, the salient features of a face or landscape. Sonnet, villanelle, and ballade are forms that offer Henley the convenient discipline of rhyme, which can prod his language into unexpected collocations and provides musical coherence to an inchoate, drifting sensibility, while repetition and refrain allow for ironic redefinition and the accumulation of resonances. Confronted by "the past's enormous disarray" and a present aimlessness, Henley often expresses a desperate carefree nihilism ("Fate's a fiddler, life's a dance"). "Of the Nothingness of Things" presents historical change as mere turmoil ("The big teetotum twirls/And epochs wax and wane/As chance subsides or swirls"); yet even when attitudinizing about "the fell clutch of circumstance" or "The bludgeoning of chance" he preserves a sententious, overwrought dignity that aches with the pain of real feeling – feeling hinted at by the characteristic physical immediacy of the vocabulary. "Echoes" contains several Hardyesque lyrics with real charm, and ballads as effective as the picture of Life as a prostitute with Death her pimp, who'll finally "stick you for her price":

> Madame Life's a piece in bloom
>   Death goes dogging everywhere:
> She's the tenant of the room,
>   He's the ruffian on the stair.

In later volumes this poise is lost: *Hawthorn and Lavender* offers "songs of the sunset" which are wordy and over-elaborate, while *For England's Sake* is an undistinguished collection of Boer War tub-thumpings. *London Voluntaries* presents the city wrapped in spurious glamour, so that even the fog is likened to "dragons of old time," though the old acerbity occasionally surfaces, as with the harlot "scouting some threepenny prey." Much better is "London Types," a sonnet sequence; but even here, despite the return to the method of "In Hospital," the poet is mannered and condescending, and the insistence on typicality, like the exclamation-marks which endlessly nudge the reader, suggests the archness of the guide-book. Nevertheless, his transcriptions of proletarian argot, and the odd urbane irony of portraits such as " 'Lady,' " "where/Brixtonian kitchens lard the late-dining air," point towards the tone and interests of his younger contemporary T. S. Eliot.

—Stan Smith

HENRYSON, Robert. Scottish. Born in Scotland c. 1425. The facts of his life are mainly conjecture: possibly educated abroad; Master of Arts; a clergyman; held a clerical appointment within Dunfermline Abbey; Headmaster of the abbey grammar school; practised as a notary from 1448. Possibly an original Member of the University of Glasgow, 1462. *Died c. 1506.*

PUBLICATIONS

Collections

   Poems, edited by G. Gregory Smith.   3 vols., 1905–09.
   Poems, edited by H. Harvey Wood.   1958.
   Poems, edited by Charles Elliott.   1963; revised edition, 1974.

Verse

   The Testament of Cresseid, in *Works,* by Geoffrey Chaucer.   1532.
   The Moral Fables of Aesop the Phrygian in Eloquent and Ornate Scottish Metre.   1570.

Reading List: *Five Poems* by E. M. W. Tillyard, 1948; *Henryson* by Marshall W. Stearns, 1949; *Henryson: A Study of the Major Narrative Poems* by John MacQueen, 1967; *Two Scots Chaucerians* by H. Harvey Wood, 1967.

*   *   *

Robert Henryson is a poet of the highest stature, the full extent of whose individuality and artistry has perhaps only been established comparatively recently. But his profound human sympathies, his keen sense of humour, his narrative skills, and his gift for characterisation have always assured him the affection and respect of readers willing to overcome the minor difficulty presented by his language. What has been recovered by the work of recent critics is something approaching the fuller medieval dimension of his work. In its turn this has enhanced our appreciation of his creative individuality, of the serious moral complexion of his work, and of his craftsmanship.

To assert Henryson's individuality is to raise a common issue with regard to medieval literature – its reliance upon commonplaces, conventions, and traditions. The old term – "Scottish Chaucerian" – applied to him and the other great Scottish poets of the period similarly implies indebtedness, lack of originality, and imitation. There can be no doubt of Chaucer's influence upon him; his use of the Chaucerian "rhyme royal" and the enlargement of Chaucer's *Troilus and Criseyde* are the most conspicuous instances. Neither is there any question of the extent to which Henryson worked consciously within the wider European context, drawing both widely and in some detail upon the full range of the literary tradition from learned scholasticism to the more popular Aesop and the beast epic of Reynard the Fox. But he shows himself equally a poet determined to stamp all with his own mark. "Quha wait if all that Chaucer wrait was true."

The Testament of Cresseid is the single poem of Henryson's which has received the greatest attention and the highest praise. In part its popularity has been due to its association with Chaucer's great narrative, to which it provides a kind of sequel, following as it does the "fatall destinie/Of fair Cresseid, that endit wretchitlie." But the conception of her tragic end appears to be entirely Henryson's own. The narrative proper begins with a laconic passage characteristic of the tragic tone of the poem:

> Quhen Diomeid had all his appetyte,
> And mair, fulfillit of this fair ladie,
> Upon ane other he set his haill delyte
> And send to hir ane Lybell of repudie,
> And hir excludit fra his companie.

Desolate, she curses the gods for having deceived her, and provokes a dream sequence in which she is summoned before the assembled gods and condemned for blasphemy. The punishment imposed upon her is leprosy. Begging with "cop and clapper," she joins the band of disfigured outcasts in the leper house, until the day that Troilus, fresh from success in battle, comes riding past on his return to Troy. This final meeting of the lovers is the more tragic and moving because they fail to recognise one another, although something in her appearance brings Cresseid into his mind, and prompts him to pour riches into her lap before riding on his way. When she discovers the identity of the knight who "hes done to us so greit humanitie" she acknowledges for the first time her own guilt and faithlessness, makes her testament, and dies repentant. "Nane but myself as now I will accuse."

In view of the harshness of her tragic fate, and the movement of Cresseid from infidelity to distress, to blasphemy, to humiliation and misery, and then to repentance, it is worth stressing the way Henryson avoids the pitfall of sententious moralising and ensures that the final effect is indeed tragic, and not something cruder. This is, of course, a matter of tone. The displacement by which punishment is exacted for blasphemy (rather than for her infidelity and the suggestion of promiscuity) helps achieve it. The moral climate she inhabits is subject to swift reversals and powerful ironies. The gods who preside are untrustworthy, like Venus, or malevolent, like Saturn. Henryson on occasion deliberately withholds moral judgement, and maintains throughout a sympathy for Cresseid which is genuine and sincere, for her fall could hardly have been more absolute. Her epitaph measures its depth:

> Lo, fair laydis, Crisseid, of Troyis toun,
> Sumtyme countit the flour of Womanheid,
> Under this stane lait Lipper lyis deid.

In terms of imaginative texture too the poem is rich. Her leprosy, for example, is linked with the attributes of astrological-mythological gods who judge her, and carries also the suggestion of venereal disease as the punishment of her lust and prostitution. As her triumphs were of the flesh, so is her terrible punishment. And this complex of images is associated with another which begins in the winter blast that opens the poem, which is woven through the poem in the references to Cresseid as flower and in the wintry portrait of Saturn, and which makes its last appearance in her epitaph.

The thirteen *Moral Fables* Henryson retails derive from the European traditions of Aesop and the Reynard cycle. They vary considerably in form and function: some are more or less developed as narratives than others; some are highly political and satirical of social abuse; others restrict themselves to allegorical interpretations of a moral or theological nature. All, however, consist of a narrative followed by a moralitas, and in all cases the moralitas (whatever else it may convey) carries a Christian allegory. The Christian allegory is the profoundest level at which the stories function, and provides an absolute standard against which the other levels of moral comment are to be related. When such comment appears to accord ill with the values implied in the narrative, or to represent some kind of tour de force of interpretation, it is safer to regard them as amplifications of the number of ways in which the stories may be read, rather than excluding one reading in favour of another. One consequence is the range of Henryson's *Fables*, stretching through religious, theological, moral, social and political dimensions. And there is very fruitful interplay between the medieval Christian view of human affairs on the one hand, and the concern with this world Henryson exhibits, whether through celebration or satire. A perspective emerges here from which both gain.

The medieval Christian commonplace prevails elsewhere in his shorter works, such as "The Abbey Walk," "The Three Deid Pollis," and "The Prais of Age." But much of the expression of Christian scorn of the world comes in the form of dissatisfaction with the way the broadly political dispensation of the world operates. This is so consistent in Henryson it can only in part be attributed to conventions of *contemptu mundi*. The tensions between Henryson's vital celebrations of natural and human and his ultimate Christianity are articulated explicitly and implicitly, in, for example, "The Reasoning Between Youth and Age" and fables like "The Preiching of the Swallow." It is in this that his attractive humanism consists.

—Brian W. M. Scobie

HERBERT OF CHERBURY, Lord; Edward Herbert, 1st Baron Herbert of Cherbury. Welsh. Born at Eyton-on-Severn, Shropshire, 3 March 1582; elder brother of George Herbert, *q.v.* Educated by tutors, 1589–96, and at University College, Oxford, 1596–99. Married his kinswoman Mary Herbert in 1598 (died, 1634); several children. Courtier and Diplomat: presented himself at court, 1600; Sheriff of Montgomeryshire, 1605; toured the Continent, 1608–09; served with the English expedition to recapture Juliers, 1610; joined the Army of the Prince of Orange, 1614, and subsequently toured Germany and Italy, and was persuaded to give help to the Savoyards but was briefly imprisoned in Lyons, 1615; returned to London: became acquainted with Ben Jonson, Donne, and Carew; Privy Councillor, and Ambassador to the French court, 1619–24; Member, Council of War, 1632–39; attended Charles I on Scottish expedition, 1639–40; briefly imprisoned for Royalist speech in the House of Lords, 1642, but otherwise neutral during the Civil War: admitted parliamentary force into Montgomery Castle to save his library, 1644; submitted to Parliament and was granted a pension, 1645; appointed Steward of the Duchy of Cornwall and Warden of the Stanneries, 1646. Knight of the Order of Bath, 1603; Irish peer, of Castle Island, County Kerry, 1624; created Baron Herbert of Cherbury, 1629. *Died 20 August 1648.*

PUBLICATIONS

Collections

> *Poems,* edited by G. C. Moore Smith. 1923.
> *Minor Poets of the Seventeenth Century,* edited by R. G. Howarth. 1931; revised edition, 1953.
> *Correspondence,* edited by W. J. Smith. 1963.

Verse

> *Occasional Verses.* 1665.

Other

> *De Veritate.*   1624; translated by M. H. Carre, 1937.
> *De Causis Errorum.*   1645.
> *De Religione Laici.*   1645; edited and translated by H. R. Hutcheson, 1944.
> *The Life and Reign of King Henry the Eighth.*   1649; edited by W. Kennett, in *Complete History of England*, 1706.
> *Expeditio in Ream Insulam, Anno 1630*, edited by T. Baldwin.   1656; as *The Expedition to the Isle of Rhé*, 1860.
> *De Religione Gentilium.*   1663; translated by W. Lewis, 1705.
> *The Life of Lord Herbert Written by Himself*, edited by Horace Walpole.   1765; edited by J. M. Shuttleworth, 1976.
> *A Dialogue Between a Tutor and His Pupil.*   1768.
> *Religio Laici*, edited by H. G. Wright, in *Modern Language Review.*   1933.

Reading List: *La Vita, le Opere, i Tempi di Herbert* by M. M. Rossi, 3 vols., 1947; "The Platonic Love Poetry of Herbert" by C. A. Hébert, in *Ball State University Forum 11*, 1970.

*   *   *

Edward Herbert was a courtier, soldier, and diplomatist, handsome, dashing, and proud of his ancestry. The self-portrait he left in his autobiography concentrates on these aspects of his life and personality. It is an extraordinarily lively picture, but it quite fails to do justice to the range of his gifts and intellectual interests. He was a considerable scholar, whose Latin philosophical treatises on Truth and Natural Religion later earned him the title Father of the English Deists. Little is said about his speculative studies in the autobiography, and nothing at all about his poetry. No doubt he took it for granted. He was the eldest son of Magdalen Herbert, and thus on familiar terms with John Donne. George Herbert was a younger brother. He knew and admired Ben Jonson, and among his more courtly literary friends were Thomas Carew and Aurelian Townshend. Naturally he wrote poetry, just as he sang, rode, danced, and duelled. But his occasional verses, collected long after his death by a nephew and dedicated to his eldest grandson, are much more interesting than we should expect if we took Lord Herbert at his own estimation. They bear the imprint of a powerfully argumentative mind. They are stylistically varied, and at their best achieve a distinctive beauty.

"Metaphysical" is an epithet truly applicable to the poetry of Edward Herbert. The relation of appearance to reality, of time to eternity, of body to spirit, were matters of major consequence to him. Even his complimentary poems move from the concrete to the abstract. His conceits have a philosophical basis, more often than not, and the framework of most of the poems is logical. Sometimes, when the topic is a trivial one, the result is a rather chilly artefact. But Herbert has lyrical as well as intellectual power. His "Elegy over a Tomb" is justly famous, and the finest of his poems, "An Ode upon a Question Moved, Whether Love Should Continue for Ever," is as beautifully cadenced as it is subtly argued. Like Donne's "The Ecstasy," it is a dramatised meditation on the nature of love, but it also has affinities with Sidney's love-dialogue "In a Grove most rich of shade." Both poems may well have provided Herbert with inspiration. To associate him solely with Donne, however, is to ignore the grace and lucidity of many of his poems. The heritage from Sidney and the links with Jonson are no less significant.

Edward Herbert was versatile in poetic invention; satires, sonnets, verse epistles, epigrams, epitaphs, songs to be sung to specific melodies, madrigals, elegies (including one on Donne), and meditative lyrics – he could produce with panache whatever the occasion called for. Yet perhaps it is understandable that, when, an elderly and disillusioned man, Lord Herbert recalled and recorded his earlier years, he made no mention of his poems. They seldom give the impression of having much emotional impetus behind them. To him, they may have been no more than pastimes; pleasurable in the execution but, because not heartfelt, of no lasting personal interest. To posterity, however, their value is beyond doubt.

—Margaret Bottrall

HERBERT, George.   Welsh.   Born at Montgomery Castle, Wales, 3 April 1593; younger brother of Lord Herbert of Cherbury, *q.v.* Educated at Westminster School, London, 1605–09; Trinity College, Cambridge, B.A. 1613, M.A. 1616. Married Jane Danvers in 1629. Minor Fellow, 1614, and Major Fellow, 1616, Trinity College, Cambridge; also, Reader in the Rhetoric School, 1618, Deputy Orator, 1618, and Public Orator, 1619–27, Cambridge University; frequently attended the court of James I, 1620–25; Member of Parliament for Montgomery, 1624–25; presented to the prebend of Layton Ecclesia, with an estate at Leighton Bromswold, Huntingdon, and ordained deacon, 1626; restored the ruined church at Leighton, with the help of Nicholas Ferrar, 1627; ordained priest, 1630; Rector, Bemerton, Salisbury, Wiltshire, 1630–33. *Died 1 March 1633.*

PUBLICATIONS

Collections

> *Works,* edited by F. E. Hutchinson.   1941; revised edition, 1945.
> *Poems,* edited by Helen Gardner.   1961.
> *The Latin Poetry: A Bilingual Edition,* edited and translated by Mark McCloskey and
>   Paul R. Murphy.   1965.
> *Selected Poems,* edited by James Reeves.   1971.
> *English Poems,* edited by C. A. Patrides.   1974.

Verse

> *The Temple: Sacred Poems and Private Ejaculations.*   1633.

Other

> *Remains* (includes *A Priest to the Temple, or, The Country Parson His Character, and A
>   Rule of Holy Life* and *Jacula Prudentum*), edited by Barnabas Oley.   1652; selections
>   from *A Priest to the Temple* edited by G. M. Forbes, as *Herbert's Country Parson,*
>   1949.

> Translator, *A Treatise of Temperance and Sobriety,* by L. Lessius.   1634; as *The
>   Temperate Man,* 1678; as *How to Live for 100 Years,* 1933.

Bibliography: *Herbert: A Concise Bibliography* by S. A. and D. R. Tannenbaum, 1946.

Reading List: *A Reading of Herbert* by Rosemond Tuve, 1952; *Herbert: His Religion and Art* by Joseph H. Summers, 1954; *Herbert* by Margaret Bottrall, 1954; *Herbert* by T. S. Eliot, 1962; *Utmost Art: Complexity in the Verse of Herbert* by Mary E. Rickey, 1966; *Herbert's Lyrics* by Arnold Stein, 1968; *Herbert: Idea and Image: A Study of The Temple* by Sister Thelka, 1974; *The Poetry of Herbert* by Helen Vendler, 1975; *A Life of Herbert* by Amy Charles, 1977.

*   *   *

The poetry of George Herbert is usually associated today with the poetry of the seventeenth-century "metaphysical poets," particularly with that of John Donne, the close friend of Herbert's mother and elder brother. As poets, however, Herbert and Sir Philip Sidney, the uncle of his patrons and distant cousins (the earls of Pembroke and Montgomery), had more in common with each other than with most of their contemporaries. Both experimented extraordinarily with varying patterns of rhymes and line-lengths, as well as with patterns of persuasion, argument, repetition, and variation. In their major collections both arranged shorter poems within a larger whole which gave a context and increased significance to the separate poems. Both conceived their major poetic works as embodying an account of a single love, and both wrote most of the poems within those works within a range of the tones of intimate address, as if they were speaking, privately or semi-privately, in their own persons. Both were convinced that an effect of sincerity was essential for such poems, and, in their practices and their attacks on the clichés of others, they showed unusual consciousness of the difficulties in achieving such an effect. Both explored the languages proper to courtesy and humility as well as to love. Although they used different kinds of diction for differing purposes, both usually employed the most direct language truly adequate to the occasion, and both showed a frequent preference for the monosyllabic line. Both poets usually created a limpid surface which invited the reader into a poem with the promise of immediate and full understanding; once within it, the reader might discover complexities of which he initially had no notion. Finally, neither Sidney nor Herbert seems to have allowed the poems in his major work to circulate in manuscript among friends – the usual manner of "publication" in an age when most gentlemen still eschewed the vulgarity of print: each seems to have felt his "love poems" in some ways too private to be generally read within his lifetime, although each carefully arranged his poems for potential readers. On his deathbed in 1633 Herbert sent the manuscript of *The Temple* to his friend Nicholas Ferrar with the instructions that Ferrar should have the poems printed if he thought they might do good to "any dejected poor soul"; otherwise, he should burn them.

In two sonnets sent from Cambridge to his mother for New Year's Day of 1610, the young poet wittily expressed his determination to devote his poetry to religious rather than secular love. Except for a few doubtful (and brief) translations, epitaphs, and dedications, Herbert seems to have abided by that determination in his English poems and in a good many of his Latin poems (particularly the epigrams of *Passio Discerpta* and the collection *Lucus*). But it may somewhat stretch the concept of religious love to consider it the primary subject of *Musae Responsoriae*, the witty collection of epigrams he may have begun at Westminster School in response to Andrew Melville's Puritanical attack on the universities and the Church of England; and it is the love of Magdalene Herbert which is primary in the fourteen Latin and five Greek poems of *Memoriae Matris Sacrum* published within a month of his mother's death in 1627. Herbert's duties as Latin Orator at Cambridge required him to provide poems as well as orations for royal and official occasions, but his poems in praise of Bacon went far beyond his official duties. Bacon acknowledged his indebtedness to Herbert (supposedly for help in translating *The Advancement of Learning* into Latin), and Bacon's influence may still be evident in the remarkably clear and effective prose of the work which Herbert almost certainly called *The Country Parson*.

The Temple, however, is Herbert's masterpiece. In his description of the source of his inspiration for its poems, Herbert begins "Jordan (II)" with his initial effort for richness

("Nothing could seem too rich to clothe the sun,/Much less those joys which trample on his head") and neatly makes the connections between over-ornamentation, vulgar display, egoism and commercialism; his conclusion may shock modern readers:

> As flames do work and winde, when they ascend,
> So did I weave my self into the sense.
> But while I bustled, I might heare a friend
> Whisper, *How wide is all this long pretence!*
> *There is in love a sweetnesse readie penn'd:*
> *Copie out onely that, and save expense.*

To "Copie out onely" the sweetness that is "readie penn'd" in love involved a wider activity than Sidney's contemplation of the beautiful image of Stella within his heart, since the work of Herbert's Love is God's work in creating and redeeming and sustaining heaven and earth, nature as well as man, that work of which man's love for God is only a reflection, made possible by God's gracious love for man. It encompasses everything that truly exists or has existed. The work of the one Love, for which all the hyperbolic praises of the Petrarchan lovers and the arguments about the mysteriously indestructible union of lovers might become simply statements of fact, is the largest subject possible.

But *The Temple* does not strike us as at all grandiose. Except in "The Sacrifice" (where Christ is the speaker) and perhaps in "The Church Militant," Herbert rarely approached the heroic mode in his English poems. He is neither epic nor thoroughly systematic in his treatment of his largest subject. Instead, he is selective, episodic, personal. It is as if he attempted to sketch only individually observed aspects or details of the vast activity of Love in the belief that any one might be suggestive of a larger whole. The altar for "The Church" is not an elaborate liturgical one, but "A broken A L T A R, .../Made of a heart, and cemented with teares," a speaking altar embodying as well as providing a place for the human sacrifice of praise and thanksgiving.

Herbert was fascinated with common speech. He made a collection of "Outlandish Proverbs," and he used proverbs in his poems – "Let losers talk" or "Most take all," for example. The Bible and proverbial speech proved as stimulating to Herbert's poetic imagination as scholastic and neoplatonic definitions and doctrines did to Donne's. (The poets shared an interest in what could be done in poetry with conversational phrases and rhythms.) At the same time, Herbert loved the intricate and the artful. Some poems ("The Fore-runners," for one) suggest that Herbert loved the English language and poetry so much that he had to put them to God's service if they were not to prove rival loves. In "A Wreath" Herbert developed one of his most elaborate forms as part of his demonstration that in spiritual matters the straight is to be preferred before the circuitous, simplicity before deception.

Herbert included at least one example of almost every known poetic species within his microcosmic ark. There are so many ingenious formal experiments and so many fine poems (sometimes the same poems, but not always) that it may seem arbitrary to discuss specific ones. *The Temple* includes an anagram, an echo poem ("Heaven"), a hidden acrostic (*"Our life is hid with Christ in God"*), poems based on the punning interpretation of initials, syllables, and a word ("Love-joy," "Jesu," and "The Sonne"), a "pruning" poem ("Paradise"), different kinds of circular poems ("Sinnes round" and "A Wreath"), different kinds of broken forms ("Denial" and "Grief"), the inner transformation of external form in "Aaron," the dissolution of form in "Church-monuments," in addition to the more startling "pattern poems," "The Altar" and "Easter-wings." Apart from his unusual sonnets (at least two of them, "Redemption" and "Prayer (I)," among his finest poems), Herbert rarely repeated a form. Concentration on the experimentation, variety, and wit, however, may prove more dazzling than illuminating. One may more readily come to understand and respond to Herbert's achievement by reading a sequence of the poems in their final order in *The Temple.*

An early manuscript collection (now in Dr. Williams's Library, London) contains slightly less than half the poems, none of which refers to Herbert's being a priest. In *The Temple*, six of those poems are omitted, and many others revised or recast or retitled. (Herbert seems to have been the first English poet who provided a significant title for every poem.) The two collections begin and end with the same groups of poems, but the remaining poems are reordered, along with many new poems, in a manner to reflect the fluctuations of mood and achievement in the spiritual life. After the introductory "The Church-porch" and "Superliminare," the opening sequence moves from "The Altar," "The Sacrifice," "Thanksgiving" and "The Reprisal" to "Josephs coat" and "The Pulley," includes two of Herbert's most moving poems concerning suffering and renewal, "The Crosse" and "The Flower," and may be thought to conclude with "The Sonne," a sonnet expressing Herbert's delight in the pun on "Sonne" and "A true Hymne," which insists that for the religious poet neither wit, ingenuity, nor craft is as important as the state of the heart: in the final line God supplies the rhyme for a poem about the poet's inability to construct a poem.

Often imagery and details within a poem anticipate its "turn" or conclusion (the fruit, the thorn, and the wine and corn in "The Collar," for example, anticipate the surprising final discovery that the hard taskmaster against whom the speaker revolts is really Love), but the syntax moves so firmly from point to point, usually temporally as well as logically, that the dramatic final "discovery" is not blunted. As we come to further understanding within the course of the poem, we are invited, not to collapse or deny the reality or importance of the initial experience or response, but to see it within a larger context – as if we viewed an event simultaneously in the lights of both time and eternity. The comforting "subtexts" no more undercut or destroy the "texts" than the Resurrection denies or casts doubt upon the reality of the Crucifixion.

Although all the poems are devoted to God, our chief impression of *The Temple* is not of monotony but of richness and variety. The volume imitates both the formal perfection and the surprising inventiveness of that provident love which hates nothing that it has made. Its workings are particularly imaged where they are usually most difficult to see: in the changes and the sufferings of an imperfect human life. Herbert's language establishes (or discovers) relationships between the most disparate human experiences and voices.

—Joseph H. Summers

HERRICK, Robert. English. Born in London, baptized 24 August 1591. Possibly educated at Westminster School, London: apprenticed to his uncle, Sir William Herrick, goldsmith and jeweller to the king, London, 1607–13; at St. John's College, Cambridge, 1613–16, and Trinity Hall, Cambridge, 1616–17, B.A. 1617, M.A. 1620. Associated with the "Sons of Ben," London, 1617–29; ordained in the Anglican Church, 1623; Chaplain to the Duke of Buckingham on the Isle of Rhé expedition, 1627; Vicar of Dean Prior, Devon, 1629 until ejected by the Puritans, 1647; lived in London, 1647–62; returned to Dean Prior, 1662–74. *Died 15 October 1674.*

PUBLICATIONS

Collections

Poetical Works, edited by L. C. Martin.   1956.
Selected Poems, edited by John Hayward.   1961.

Complete Poetry, edited by J. Max Patrick. 1963.
Cavalier Poets, edited by Thomas Clayton. 1978.

Verse

Hesperides; or, The Works Both Humane and Divine. 1648.

Bibliography: *Herrick: A Concise Bibliography* by S. A. and D. R. Tannenbaum, 1949.

Reading List: *Herrick, The Last Elizabethan* by Leon Mandel, 1927; *Herrick* by John Press, 1961; *Herrick* by Roger B. Rollin, 1966; *A Study of Herrick* by S. Ishii, 1968; *Herrick* (biography) by George Walton Scott, 1974; *Ceremony and Art: Herrick's Poetry* by Robert H. Deming, 1974; *Trust to Good Verses: Herrick Tercentenary Essays* edited by Roger B. Rollin and J. Max Patrick, 1978.

*   *   *

In his youth Robert Herrick achieved some literary renown as a follower of Ben Jonson although his poems circulated only in manuscript. Between his graduation from Trinity Hall, Cambridge, in 1617 and his appointment to the living of Dean Prior in Devonshire in 1629 we know little of his life: he took Holy Orders in 1623, went as the Duke of Buckingham's Chaplain on the expedition to the Isle of Rhé in 1627, and became acquainted with the court musicians William Lawes and Henry Lawes. He probably spent much of his time in London, where he made friends with poets and wits who frequented taverns. He resided in what he called "dull" and "loathed" Devonshire from 1629 until his death in 1674, except for the years 1647 to 1660, having been expelled for his refusal to subscribe to the Solemn League and Covenant, and returning only at the Restoration of Charles II.

Hesperides, a volume containing his profane and sacred poems, was published in 1648. In 1869 there appeared the first collection of *Hesperides* to contain poems other than those printed in the 1648 edition: we do not know whether he wrote them after 1648 (apart from the elegy on Lord Hastings written in 1649).

Herrick was endowed with an unusually powerful and discriminating sensuality. His love of jewels and of glittering surfaces may, like his fondness for ritual, have been nurtured in the years when he was apprenticed to his uncle, Sir William Herrick, a rich London goldsmith who played a prominent role in the pomp and ceremony indulged in by the great City of London Guilds. Herrick's five senses apprehend the things of this world with a quivering eagerness. He loves to contemplate, to touch, to inhale, to hear, and to savour whiteness, softness, sweetness, smoothness. He is attracted by variety and contrast, a theme often discussed in seventeenth-century aesthetics. "The Lilly in a Christal" argues that lilies, roses, grapes, cherries, cream, and strawberries are more alluring if partially shaded. Women also can arouse men's desires more fiercely if they half conceal their soft, white nakedness:

> Yet, when your Lawns & Silks shal flow;
> And that white cloud divide
> Into a doubtful Twi-light; then,
> Then will your hidden Pride
> Raise greater fires in men.

Although many of Herrick's poems are erotic, he is capable of writing gravely and delicately about the love of man and woman. One of his best-known poems, "To Anthea, who may command him anything," is a declaration of tenderness and fidelity:

487

> Bid me to live, and I will live
> Thy Protestant to be;
> Or bid me love, and I will give
> A loving heart to thee.

He admires the aristocratic ideal of early seventeenth-century England, following his mentor Ben Jonson in his praise of the great country-house whose owner cares for the well-being of his tenants. He loves the English countryside, where blossom gives way to fruition, and he celebrates the pleasures of feasting after an abundant harvest. His years of living among his Devon parishioners made him acutely aware of the relics of paganism present in every aspect of country life. "The Hag" is a poem about the darkness and terror of the rural world, the other side of the medal that depicts the elves and fairies of popular superstition.

Many of Herrick's finest poems are rooted in his sense of mortality. Even his most joyous celebrations of human gaiety and of nature's fruitfulness are overshadowed by his awareness of death: the sense of life's brevity pervades poems such as "To Daffodils," "To Blossoms," and the magnificent "Corinna's Going A-Maying," Nor does his faith as a Christian priest banish his grief and fear, although he expresses a devotion to his Saviour and prays the Holy Spirit to comfort him. His "Noble Numbers" (comprising the divine poems) are greatly inferior to the remainder of *Hesperides*.

Herrick's responsiveness to language is as acute and subtle as his responsiveness to the sensuous properties of the world. He shows a remarkable skill in handling the Anglo-Saxon and the Romance elements of the English language, and often lends variety to the verse by introducing unexpectedly a Latinism as a contrast to the monosyllabic, everyday words that make up the body of the poem: "Shew me thy feet; shew me thy legs, thy thighes;/Shew me Those *Fleshie Principalities*." He achieves weight and conciseness by incorporating into his poems reminiscences of and phrases from other writers of verse and prose. Since it is possible to date only about fifty of his poems, we cannot trace the way in which his art developed; but it seems as if his early verse draws on Catullus, Horace, and Ovid, while his later poetry owes more to Martial. The probabilities are that he picked up quotations from those writers in Florio's translation of Montaigne and in Burton's *Anatomy of Melancholy*.

When we speak of Herrick's lyrical perfection we may recall that, in the eighteenth century, when he was largely neglected, some of his poems were known in their musical settings. Indeed, certain of his sacred and profane poems had originally been designed to be sung, for Herrick writes in the tradition of the English lutanists. As for his perfection, we can tell how carefully he revised his work by comparing earlier versions of his poems with their final versions in *Hesperides*. Despite changes in taste, Herrick's place as a minor poet of consummate artistry seems secure.

—John Press

HILL, Geoffrey. British. Born in Bromsgrove, Worcestershire, 18 June 1932. Educated at Fairfield Junior School; County High School, Bromsgrove; Keble College, Oxford. Senior Lecturer in English, University of Leeds. Recipient: Gregory Award, 1961; Hawthornden Prize, 1969; Faber Memorial Prize, 1970; Whitbread Award, 1971; Alice Hunt Bartlett Award, 1971; Heinemann Award, 1972. Fellow, Royal Society of Literature, 1972. Lives in Leeds, Yorkshire.

PUBLICATIONS

Verse

(Poems).   1952.
For the Unfallen: Poems 1952–1958.   1959.
Preghiere.   1964.
King Log.   1968.
Mercian Hymns.   1971.
Somewhere Is Such a Kingdom: Poems 1952–1971.   1975.

Play

Brand, from the play by Ibsen (produced 1978).   1978.

Reading List: essay by Christopher Ricks, in London Magazine, November 1964; "The Poetry of Hill" by Jon Silkin, in British Poetry since 1960 edited by Michael Schmidt and Grevel Lindop, 1972.

*   *   *

An awareness of history is central to the modernist sensibility, though few poets writing today have made such concerted use of the spirit of the past as Geoffrey Hill. Not surprisingly, his first major collection takes the creation as a starting point, where we are confronted by the violent, menacing nature of this nascent universe:

> The second day I stood and saw
> The osprey plunge with triggered claw,
> Feathering blood along the shore,
> To lay the living sinew bare.

Death figures prominently in a world predatory from its conception, its significance magnified by his retrospective approach; the dead amass in, rather than fade away from, his vision:

> But the dead maintain their ground –
> That there's no getting round –
>
> Who in places vitally rest,
> Named, anonymous.

The manipulation of familiar phrases and the twisting paradoxical progression of thought are symptomatic of a struggle to come to terms with the suffering that surrounds him.

Hill's ventures to specific moments in history are attempts to give meaning to these perceptions – or at least a context in which they can be analysed. In what is perhaps his best work, "Funeral Music" (King Log), Hill effects a subtle interplay between the emblematic ceremonial beheading of three men and a bloody episode from the Wars of the Roses. The poem's contrapuntal movement is firmly structured within a sequence of sonnets – a form of which Hill is particularly fond, its disciplined cohesion an amenable vehicle for his complex syntax, weighted cadences, and dense verbal texture. Fifteenth-century heroic sacrifice, resolute faith, and elaborate ritual are the values to which Hill turns for explanation. His virulent scepticism towards our meaningless religious ceremonies, merely designed to alleviate anxiety, falters under the weight of the past, when the consequences of his negation become clear:

> Though I would scorn the mere instinct of faith,
> Expediency of assent, if I dared,
> What I dare not is a waste history
> Or void rule.

Mercian Hymns marks a new departure. The simultaneity often implied by the interaction of event and sensibility is made overt by Hill's mythopoeic process, where the terrain of Offa's Mercia, resonant of its medieval roots, is furnished with motorways and the shifting reflections of the poet's childhood. The pitfalls of the prose poem format chosen for the hymns are avoided; narrative and catalogue are tightly harnessed to produce a characteristic blend of objectivity and immediacy. And curiously, it is among these strange juxtapositions, when history is most abused, that a sense of chronology, of archetypal pattern, is most apparent.

There is a discernible softening of tone in his recent work, in particular the lyrical tranquillity of "The Pentecost Castle" (*Agenda*, Autumn–Winter 1972–73, and Autumn 1975), but little sign of abatement in mental anguish if we are to judge from the outstanding sonnet sequence "Lachrimae" (*Agenda*, Winter–Spring 1974–75), written with the martyrdom of Robert Southwell in mind. Endowed with the ultimate justification, suffering is embraced as a necessary, desirable prelude to salvation.

—Garth Clucas

HOCCLEVE, Thomas. English. Born, possibly in Hockcliffe, Bedfordshire, c. 1368. Appointed clerk in the Privy Seal Office, London, c. 1386, and held this position for 30 years. Granted an annuity by Henry IV, 1399. *Died c. 1430.*

PUBLICATIONS

Collections

> *Works (Regiment of Princes and Minor Poems)*, edited by F. J. Furnivall and I. Gollancz. 3 vols., 1892–1925; *Minor Poems* revised by Jerome Mitchell and A. I. Doyle, 1970.

Verse

> *Poems*, edited by G. Mason. 1796.
> *De Regimine Principum*, edited by T. Wright. 1860.

Reading List: *Six Medieval Men and Women* by H. S. Bennett, 1955; *Hoccleve: A Study in Early 15th-Century English Poetic* by Jerome Mitchell, 1968 (includes bibliography); "Conclusions: Hoccleve" by Penelope B. R. Doob, in *Nebuchadnezzar's Children: Conventions of Madness in Middle English Literature*, 1974.

*   *   *

The personal element in Thomas Hoccleve and his connection with Chaucer have engaged the attention of his readers over the years. A clear portrait of the poet emerges from his four principal "autobiographical" poems: *La Male Regle*, the Prologue to the *Regement of Princes*, the *Complaint* (in which he discusses his bout with insanity), and the *Dialogue with a Friend*. If the portrait is not flattering in all instances, it is certainly very human. Few Middle English poems contain passages of self-revelation comparable to those of Hoccleve in realism, individuality, and apparent sincerity; but even here the element of literary convention cannot be dismissed altogether.

Despite Hoccleve's assertion that he was a friend and pupil of Chaucer, it is doubtful that there was ever a close personal friendship between the two poets. The autobiographical significance of his often quoted lines in praise of Chaucer (in the *Regement of Princes*) has been exaggerated. The lines seem heartfelt because he utilized poetic conventions more convincingly than did his contemporaries in similar eulogies. The amount of his indebtedness to Chaucer for diction and phraseology has also been exaggerated. His name comes up frequently in connection with the famous portrait of Chaucer in the *Regement of Princes* (British Museum MS Harley 4866, fol. 88); this has been reproduced photographically in numerous places and is considered the finest and most authentic of all the Chaucer portraits.

Hoccleve was very much a man of his age. Literary taste in the fifteenth century is clearly reflected in his courtly poetry (e.g., the *Letter of Cupid*), his political poems (e.g., the *Address to Sir John Oldcastle*), his *De Regimine Principum*, his short begging poems, his religious verse (e.g., the *Mother of God*, formerly attributed to Chaucer), and his narrative poems (e.g., the *Tale of Jereslaus' Wife* and the *Tale of Jonathas*, translated from the Anglo-Latin *Gesta Romanorum*). He was not an innovator in his treatment of popular themes and in his handling of accepted genres; yet in small ways he often managed to give his work a distinctive character. In addition, he was a pioneer in introducing several well-known genres into English, such as the *Ars Moriendi* (i.e. his *Lerne to Dye*), the satirical panegyric of one's lady, and the manual of instruction for a prince. There is no truth in the often repeated allegation that he lacked metrical skill; his verse is *not* marred by "thwarted stress." His poetic technique is best understood and appreciated in the context of other medieval literature. Like Lydgate and other 15th-century poets, he looked on poetry as versified rhetoric, he used word pairs frequently, and he treated his sources freely. His strength as a craftsman can best be observed in passages of direct discourse, which are skillfully wrought in general and often remarkably lifelike in comparison with the French or Latin originals.

—Jerome Mitchell

HODGSON, Ralph. English. Born in Yorkshire, 9 September 1871. Journalist in London: Editor, *Fry's Magazine*; Founder, with Lovat Fraser, The Sign of the Flying Fame, 1913; Lecturer in English Studies, Imperial University, Sendai, Japan, 1924–38; settled in Minerva, Ohio. Recipient: Royal Society of Literature Polignac Prize, 1914; National

491

Institute of Arts and Letters award, 1946; Queen's Gold Medal for Poetry, 1954. Member, Order of the Rising Sun, Japan, 1938. *Died 3 November 1962.*

PUBLICATIONS

Verse

The Last Blackbird and Other Lines. 1907.
Eye and Other Poems. 1913.
The Bull. 1913.
The Song of Honour. 1913.
The Mystery and Other Poems. 1913.
Poems. 1917.
Hymn to Moloch. 1921.
Silver Wedding and Other Poems. 1941.
The Muse and the Mastiff. 1942.
The Skylark and Other Poems, edited by Colin Fenton. 1958.
Songs to Our Surnames, edited by Colin Fenton. 1960.
Collected Poems, edited by Colin Fenton. 1961.

Bibliography: *Hodgson: A Bibliography* by Wesley D. Sweetser, 1974.

Reading List: *Withdrawn in Gold: Three Commentaries on Genius* (on Hodgson, James Stephens, and Isak Dinesen) by George B. Saul, 1970.

*   *   *

Immortalized by his life-long friend T. S. Eliot in "Lines to Ralph Hodgson, Esqr.," Hodgson is chiefly remembered as a poet of the Georgian period. After World War I, the Muse seldom visited. His main productions were a collaboration on an English version of *The Manyōshū* while in residency at Imperial University and, finally, broadsheets, titled Flying Scrolls, sent to friends from Minerva, Ohio. The Scrolls, aside from the long poem *The Muse and the Mastiff,* are mostly charming, sagacious, and humorous epigrams in single lines, couplets, triplets, or quatrains ("Oaths in anguish rank with prayers"); but they contribute only slightly to his poetic canon.

The poems frequently anthologized – "Time, You Old Gipsy Man," "Eve," "The Song of Honour," "The Mystery," "Stupidity Street," and "The Bull" – are all from the 1917 *Poems.* Often marked by the pathetic fallacy and tending toward conventional metrical schemes and rapid, regular meter, they are nevertheless unique both in versatility and theme. "Eve," for example, is a remarkably compassionate view of woman's role in the Fall of Man, where Eve is tempted by an unusually seductive Satan in the form of a cobra:

> Soft as a bubble sung
> Out of a linnet's lung
> Soft and most silvery
> "Eva!" he said.

In the pubs, as "the toast goes round," her name is still accompanied by a leer, maligning all women in the name of the first, simply for having been, herself, initially betrayed. "Stupidity Street" reflects both Hodgson's ecological concern and love of birds. Here, as in many of his poems, he deplores their wanton destruction to gratify the gourmet or women's vanity and warns of danger to the balance of nature:

> I saw in vision
> The worm in the wheat
> And in the shops nothing
> For people to eat....

Nature, however, in "The Bull" is both cruel and glorious. The bloody and vanquished leader of "a thousand head," dreaming of the time when "Not a cow that said him nay," now bravely faces the last battle of all and

> Turns to meet the loathly birds
> Flocking round him in the skies
> Waiting for the flesh that dies.

Hodgson's tour de force is the mystical "The Song of Honour," his "Harmonious hymn of being" and "testament of Beautysprite/Upon a flying scroll." Entranced in wonderment at the flooding firmament and triggered by the song of a bird, the poet achieves rapport with "the universal choir." Through repeated use of synecdoche in this relatively short poem, Hodgson successfully suggests both the infinitude of the universe and, at the same time, its organic unity.

Hodgson, like Housman and FitzGerald, though limited in creative scope, produced some minor masterworks. In 1943 (in *Poets Remembered*), viewing himself in the perspective of the Georgian age, he was piercingly realistic: "New Rhythms and a New Age. A New Age that is now actually at this very moment, more than twenty-five years after, dying, discredited, and done with – no more than dead bones and a matter for the sexton."

—Wesley D. Sweetser

HOFFMAN, Charles Fenno. American. Born in New York City, 7 February 1806. Educated at Columbia University, New York, 1821–23; studied law with Harmanus Bleecker, Albany, New York; admitted to the New York bar, 1827. Practised law in New York City, 1827–30; Editor, with Charles King, New York *American*, 1830–33; Editor, *Knickerbocker* magazine, New York, 1833; toured the midwest United States, 1833–34; Editor, *American Monthly Magazine*, New York, 1835–37, and New York *Mirror*, 1837; full-time writer, 1838–39; Associate Editor, with Horace Greeley, *New Yorker*, 1840; Third Chief Clerk, 1841–43, and Deputy Surveyor, 1843–44, Office of the Surveyor of Customs of the Port of New York; full-time writer, 1844–47; Editor, *Literary World*, New York, 1847–49; became insane: confined to the Harrisburg, Pennsylvania Insane Asylum, 1849 until his death. A.M.: Columbia University, 1837. *Died 7 June 1884.*

PUBLICATIONS

Verse

The Vigil of Faith and Other Poems.   1842; revised edition, as *Songs and Other Poems*, 1846.

The Echo; or, Borrowed Notes for Home Circulation. 1844.
Love's Calendar, Lays of the Hudson, and Other Poems. 1847.
Poems, edited by Edward F. Hoffman. 1873.

Fiction

Wild Scenes in the Forest and Prairie. 1839.
Greyslaer: A Romance of the Mohawk. 1840.

Other

A Winter in the West. 1835.

Editor, *The New York Book of Poetry.* 1837; as *The Gems of American Poetry,* 1840.

Bibliography: in *Bibliography of American Literature* by Jacob Blanck, 1963.

Reading List: *Hoffman* by Homer F. Barnes, 1930.

*   *   *

During the 1830's and 1840's, Charles Fenno Hoffman was among the more influential of a group of "literati," as Edgar Allan Poe referred to them, who called themselves the "Knickerbockers," a term made famous by Washington Irving's *Knickerbocker History of New York* and by the *Knickerbocker Magazine* (1833–1865), which Hoffman helped to found. This group, which included James Fenimore Cooper, William Cullen Bryant, and Washington Irving, among others, tried to shape the literary tastes of the nation and to make New York the literary center of the day. It especially encouraged the writing of literature on American themes, and it was dedicated to improving the quality and variety of American literature, as it then existed.

Hoffman's works reflect the concerns and preoccupations of the Knickerbocker group. His best poems are those which romanticize the splendor and potentiality of the American landscape. Of these, the most memorable include "To the Hudson River," "The Morning Hymn," "Forest Musings," and "Moonlight on the Hudson." Skilled in the art of prosody, Hoffman injected a lyrical quality into his verse which made many of his poems extremely popular, especially those which were set to music. "Monterey," for example, was for many years one of the most popular ballads written in America, and it is still sung today.

Hoffman's prose, like his verse, was strongly nationalistic in its intentions and themes. His best known novel, *Greyslaer: A Romance of the Mohawk,* was a fictional adaptation of the infamous Beauchamp-Sharp murder case. Critics appreciated *Greyslaer* and for a time the novel competed successfully with the frontier romances of Cooper. The result of an excursion on horseback through Illinois, Michigan, Iowa, and Pennsylvania, *A Winter in the West* provided many Americans with their first detailed account of life on the Western frontier as it existed in the early 1830's. A skilled observer, Hoffman mastered the genre of travel literature. His discrimination and learning allowed him to select and describe incidents and characters which transcend regional particularities and which, even today, provide insight into whatever part of America he visited.

As a critic and editor, Hoffman encouraged the writing and publication of books and literature on American subjects. Hoffman believed that it was the critic's function to encourage excellence rather than to denigrate needlessly. He especially encouraged young writers who he felt might profit from some degree of public recognition, even if undeserved.

About *Typee*, Herman Melville's first novel, Hoffman wrote: "One of the most delightful and well written narratives that ever came from an American pen." He was also instrumental in helping such unknown writers as Francis Parkman, whose classic account of overland adventure, *The California and Oregon Trail*, was recommended for publication by Hoffman.

Regrettably, Hoffman's literary career was cut short by illness and financial worries. Unable to support himself by writing, he was forced to take a position in a New York customs office. For several years he had been working on a novel which he hoped would be his greatest literary success but which was accidentally destroyed by his maid, who used it as kindling. This unfortunate mishap proved too much for Hoffman. With nerves already weakened from excessive toil and worry, he began treatment for a mental disorder which eventuated in his incarceration at the state hospital in Harrisburg, Pennsylvania, where he spent the remaining thirty-five years of his life, contented but hopelessly insane.

—James A. Levernier

HOLLAND, Sir Richard. Scottish. Born in Orkney, c. 1420. Had benefices in Orkney and in Caithness, Ross, and Moray, 1441–67: Vicar of Ronaldsay, Orkney, before 1467; Precentor, Elgin Cathedral Church; Notary for the Countess of Douglas, 1455. Went into exile in England with the Earl of Douglas, 1480.

PUBLICATIONS

Verse

Buke of the Howlat, edited by Frances J. Amours, in *Scottish Alliterative Poems*, vols. 1–2. 1892–97.

Reading List: *Hollands Buke of the Howlate* by Arthur Diebler, 1893; "Holland's *Buke of the Howlat*: An Interpretation by Matthew P. McDiarmid, in *Medium Aevum 38*, 1969.

*   *   *

Sir Richard Holland's *Buke of the Howlat* is a response – none appears in English poetry of the period – to the revolutionary ferment of Europe, the strife of nobles and clerics against the centralising absolutism of princes and popes. The Douglases felt threatened by royal policy, and in Church politics were leaders of the Conciliarist ("parliamentary" Church) party in Scotland. The young poet, however, is not polemical, though he praises the Douglas tradition, and the papal arms that he describes are those of the anti-pope elected by the Council of Basle, Felix V (1440–49). It is not the strife that inspires him but the familial harmony dreamt by a reformist Europe. Nature's God-given order, in which each nation, rank, and estate is to earn its happy place by selfless service to the community, is his theme. Understanding this, Walter Scott's denial of any serious and unifying concept can at last be dismissed and appreciation can begin. The basic fable is that of the unteachable Caliban-type owl, who protests the injustice of his wretched appearance and outcast's mode of life to a

495

Council convened by the Pope and Emperor of birds, which duly submits the complaint to Dame Nature. She bids each species give one feather, and, when a second Council complains of the now splendid owl's tyrannical behaviour, explains, "My first making was unamendable." The protesting Howlat is man unfit for a Christian society, because without humility ("We cum pure, we gang pure, baith king and commoun").

Holland's lesson is enforced in a series of vivid scenes: an earthly paradise painted in the fresh colours of a May morning in Moray, where are "Mendis and medicyne for all mennis neidis"; European Councils, of which the Douglases are shown to be worthy members, where Church and laity "gang in a gait [unity]/Tendir and trew" and all is homely and festal harmony; the Howlat lonely again and self-upbraiding; the ideal lastly focussed in an image of the poet's married patrons as doves in the forest "tendir and tryde." Certainly there are moments of prolixity (the Douglas example makes a disproportionate if memorable effect), but the theme of a naturally happy society and as natural misfit is powerfully, sometimes beautifully, developed. The *Buke* shares with Chaucer's *Parlement of Foules* a debt to Alain de L'Isle's *De Planctu Naturae* but makes a more modern and meaningful use of it.

—Matthew P. McDiarmid

HOLMES, Oliver Wendell. American. Born in Cambridge, Massachusetts, 29 August 1809. Educated at Phillips Academy, Andover, Massachusetts; studied law at Harvard University, Cambridge, Massachusetts, graduated 1829; studied medicine for two years in Europe, then at Harvard Medical School, M.D. 1836. Married Amelia Lee Jackson in 1840; three children. Practised medicine in Boston; Professor of Anatomy and Physiology, Dartmouth College, Hanover, New Hampshire, 1838–40; discovered that Puerperal Fever was contagious, 1843; Professor of Anatomy, Harvard Medical School, 1847–82. Honorary degrees: Oxford, Cambridge, and Edinburgh universities, 1886. *Died 7 October 1894.*

PUBLICATIONS

Collections

> *Complete Poetical Works,* edited by Horace E. Scudder. 1895.
> *Representative Selections,* edited by S. I. Hayakawa and Howard Mumford Jones. 1939.

Verse

> *The Harbinger: A May-Gift.* 1833.
> *Poems.* 1836; revised editon, 1846, 1848, 1849.
> *Urania: A Rhymed Lesson.* 1846.
> *Astraea: The Balance of Illusions.* 1850.
> *Poetical Works.* 1852.
> *Songs and Poems of the Class of 1829,* second edition. 1859; revised edition, 1868.
> *Songs in Many Keys.* 1861.

Poems. 1862.
Humorous Poems. 1865.
Songs of Many Seasons 1862–1874. 1874.
Poetical Works. 1877.
The Iron Gate and Other Poems. 1880.
Poetical Works. 2 vols., 1881.
Illustrated Poems. 1885.
Before the Curfew and Other Poems, Chiefly Occasional. 1888.
At Dartmouth: The Phi Beta Kappa Poem 1839. 1940.

Fiction

Elsie Venner: A Romance of Destiny. 1861.
The Guardian Angel. 1867.
A Mortal Antipathy: First Opening of the New Portfolio. 1885.

Other

Boylston Prize Dissertations for 1836 and 1837. 1838.
Homoeopathy and Its Kindred Delusions (lectures). 1842.
The Autocrat of the Breakfast-Table. 1858.
The Professor at the Breakfast-Table, with the Story of Iris. 1860.
Currents and Counter-Currents in Medical Science, with Other Addresses and Essays. 1861.
Soundings from the Atlantic. 1863.
The Poet at the Breakfast-Table: His Talks with His Fellow-Boarders and the Reader. 1872.
John Lothrop Motley: A Memoir. 1878.
The School-Boy. 1879.
Poems and Prose Passages, edited by Josephine E. Hodgdon. 1881.
Medical Essays 1842–1882. 1883.
Pages from an Old Volume of Life: A Collection of Essays 1857–1881. 1883.
Ralph Waldo Emerson. 1884.
Our Hundred Days in Europe. 1887.
Over the Teacups. 1890.
Writings. 14 vols., 1891–92.
A Dissertation on Acute Pericarditis. 1937.
The Autocrat's Miscellanies (miscellany), edited by Albert Mordell. 1959.

Editor, with Jacob Bigelow, *Principles of the Theory and Practice of Medicine,* by Marshall Hall. 1839.
Editor, with Donald G. Mitchell, *The Atlantic Almanac 1868.* 1867.

Bibliography: *Bibliography of Holmes* by Thomas Franklin Currier and Eleanor M. Tilton, 1953; in *Bibliography of American Literature* by Jacob Blanck, 1963.

Reading List: *Life and Letters of Holmes* by John T. Morse, Jr., 2 vols., 1896; *Holmes of the Breakfast-Table* by Mark A. De Wolfe Howe, 1936; *Amiable Autocrat: A Biography of Holmes* by Eleanor M. Tilton, 1947; *Holmes* by Miriam R. Small, 1963.

*   *   *

The great popular reputation of Oliver Wendell Holmes in the nineteenth century receded with the eclipse of New England pre-eminence. Except for the rural Whittier, Holmes was the most provincial of the New England writers, and unlike the others he did not espouse causes. The Boston of his occasional verse and genial essays was not (according to the editors of *Representative Selections*) "the rebellious Boston, out of which came the anti-slavery societies, transcendentalism, and the feminist movement." In the opening chapter of his first novel (*Elsie Venner*) Holmes describes and provides a lasting label for cultured, mercantile Bostonians with Bulfinch houses, Beacon Street addresses, and ancestral portraits. He became the spokesman for this "Brahmin Caste of New England" when his *Autocrat of the Breakfast-Table* began to appear in the *Atlantic Monthly* in 1857. Although his public had read his occasional poems ever since he was a Harvard undergraduate, his new image as "the Autocrat" established Holmes's reputation as a major American writer.

There had been little time for writing prose between 1830 and 1857, for Holmes had become an M.D. and held professorships of anatomy at Dartmouth and Harvard. But Holmes was a brilliant and incessant talker, and when he hit upon the scheme of jotting down his own talk, he had the matter for his essay series. Literary historians agree that his personality imposed itself upon and gave unity to his writing – poetry, essays, and fiction alike. There is a consistent mental set in his writing also: he was a clear-headed rationalist who disliked even the "bullying" of science and abhorred the dogmatism of theology. His attacks on Calvinism were his closest approximation to taking up a cause, but it seems strange now that Boston thought of him as an American Voltaire. However, Holmes liked to point out the parallels between his own life and Dr. Johnson's. Johnson was born in 1709, Holmes in 1809; both were urban beings, and Holmes's devotion to Boston matched Johnson's love of London. Both were great talkers and were devoted to common sense; and, though his wit has not survived as well as Johnson's, one, at least, of Holmes's remarks is remembered: "Boston State-House is the hub of the solar system. You couldn't pry that out of a Boston man if you had the tire of all creation straightened out for a crowbar."

The *Atlantic Monthly* version of *The Autocrat of the Breakfast-Table* begins, "I was just going to say, when I was interrupted." After the twelve *Atlantic* installments had become a book in 1858, the author explains that the interruption had lasted a quarter of a century, since two articles entitled "The Autocrat of the Breakfast Table" had appeared in the *New England Magazine* in 1831 and 1832. He had matured and gained confidence in the twenty-five-year interval: along with his medical practice and professorships, he had published important medical essays – and a volume of poems. His Harvard lectures were as celebrated for their wit as for their learning, and from 1841 to 1857 he was a sought-after lyceum lecturer on literary as well as medical subjects. But Dr. Holmes was becoming even better known in Boston and Cambridge as a genial humorist and master of conversation.

His fellow-Brahmin, James Russell Lowell, accepted the editorship of the *Atlantic Monthly* on the condition that Holmes become a regular contributor. Holmes had suggested the name for the new magazine; and there were Holmes's poems, essays, articles, and reviews or installments of novels in the magazine every year until 1893. The *Atlantic* published sixty-five Holmes poems, each of his three novels, three series of *Autocrat* sequels – *The Professor at the Breakfast-Table*, *The Poet at the Breakfast-Table*, and *Over the Teacups* – and *Our Hundred Days in Europe*.

It is difficult to evaluate Holmes's writing on medical subjects, or determine how his role as a doctor and professor of anatomy related to his literary career. Scientific medicine was just beginning a phenomenal advance in Holmes's day, but it is generally agreed that his own chief claim to medical distinction was his excellence as a teacher. Most interest in recent years has focused on his three "medicated novels" (Holmes accepted the term of a "dear old lady" who refused to read them): *Elsie Venner*, *The Guardian Angel*, and *A Moral Antipathy*. None of them contributed much to the development of the novel, though they fit into a kind of American novel vacuum – Hawthorne and Melville coming before, Howells and James after. *Elsie Venner* still gets respectful attention, but the plot of *A Moral Antipathy* has been judged "so absurd that it hardly bears repetition." Psychologists and psychiatrists have found validity and importance in the neuroses pictured in these novels, some of them profoundly shocking to Holmes's readers a hundred years ago.

To the twentieth century, Oliver Wendell Holmes was a writer of verse, not poetry – which even his contemporaries might have conceded. Significantly, both "The Deacon's Masterpiece" (or "One Hoss Shay" – sometimes interpreted as an allegory of New England Calvinism) and "The Chambered Nautilus," his acknowledged masterpiece, were both "recited" by the Autocrat of the Breakfast Table.

To the generations growing up in the first half of the twentieth century, the name Oliver Wendell Holmes meant the distinguished jurist whom F. D. Roosevelt had hailed in 1933 as "the greatest living American." This son and namesake, the only member of his family to outlive Dr. Holmes, had his father's clear-headed rationalistic turn of mind – but none of his other traits. Nearly a half century after the son's death, the elder Holmes is again emerging as a distinct figure: the conservative but clear-sighted, talkative Brahmin, who liked mill-owners better than abolitionists and transcendentalists, and who lived long enough to write graceful poetic tributes to nearly all of the nineteenth-century New England worthies.

—Clarence A. Glasrud

HOOD, Thomas. English. Born in London, 23 May 1799. Educated at private schools in London; apprenticed to a merchant's counting house in the City of London, 1812–15; lived with relatives in Dundee, 1815–18; returned to London and was articled to his uncle, an engraver, 1818–20; left the profession for a literary career. Married Jane Reynolds in 1825; one son, one daughter. Sub-Editor, *London Magazine*, 1821–23; became acquainted with Lamb, Hazlitt, and De Quincey; Editor and Contributor, *The Gem*, London, 1829, and the *Comic Annual*, London, 1830–40; lived in Coblentz, 1835–37, and Ostend, 1837–40; Editor, *New Monthly Magazine*, London, 1841–43; Co-Owner, *Hood's Monthly Magazine*, 1844–45. *Died 3 May 1845.*

PUBLICATIONS

Collections

> *Works*, edited by Thomas Hood, Jr., and Frances Broderip.   10 vols., 1869–73.
> *Poems*, edited by Walter Jerrold.   1906.
> *Selected Poems*, edited by John Clubbe.   1970.
> *Letters*, edited by Peter F. Morgan.   1971.

Verse

> *Odes and Addresses to Great People*, with J. H. Reynolds.   1825.
> *Whims and Oddities in Prose and Verse.*   2 vols., 1826–27.
> *The Plea of the Midsummer Fairies, Hero and Leander, Lycus the Centaur, and Other Poems.*   1827.
> *The Epping Hunt.*   1829.

The Dream of Eugene Aram. 1831.
Whimsicalities: A Periodical Gathering (verse and prose). 2 vols., 1844; revised edition, 1870.
The Headlong Career and Woeful Ending of Precocious Piggy, edited by Frances Broderip. 1858.

Plays

Mr. Sims (produced 1829).
York and Lancaster (produced 1829).

Fiction

National Tales. 1827.
Tylney Hall. 1834.

Other

Hood's Own; or, Laughter from Year to Year. 1839; second series, edited by Thomas Hood, Jr., 1861.
Up the Rhine. 1840.
Fairy Land; or, Recreation for the Rising Generation (juvenile), with Jane Hood, edited by Frances Broderip. 1860.
Hood and Charles Lamb: The Story of a Friendship, Being the Literary Reminiscences of Hood, edited by Walter Jerrold. 1930.
Letters from the Dilke Papers in the British Museum, edited by Leslie Marchand. 1945.

Reading List: *Hood* by J. M. MacIlrath, 1935; *Hood* by Laurence Brander, 1963; *Hood* by John C. Reid, 1963; *Victorian Forerunner: The Later Career of Hood* by John Clubbe, 1968.

*   *   *

Thomas Hood began his career as a Regency man, and handled words with Romantic gusto. He shared the Romantic preference for dealing with extremes of human experience, and for stories of a supernatural world beyond those limits, taken from folk-lore and legend. The Gothic ambience of haunted houses and hag-ridden murderers had a strong appeal for him; and he couched these tales in varieties of narrative verse derived, directly or via Wordsworth and Coleridge, from ballad and romance. The fertility of his metrical and verbal invention is clear in his serious poems of this kind; but it fully emerges in his comic verse. This derives from the same sources: it is an unexpected, illuminating twist upon serious subjects, and treats of death, despair, revenant ghosts, and suicides. These tales too are often in the ballad form, drawing upon supernatural associations and the comic potential of jingling broadside metres for resonant comic contrasts.

Contrast, or incongruity, is the basic comic device in Hood's ballads. He juxtaposes the trivial and the extraordinary with such an appearance of naturalness that we are startled into a new, and comic, vision of each. His ghosts are very corporeal, concerned with the fate of their bodies as if with important luggage they are obliged to leave lying around; conversely, his pining lovers are hampered in their soaring aspirations by unromantic flesh, too fat or too tall or too old for their passionate spirits. A paternal ode on an angelic three-year-old is punctuated by the infant's hair-raising physical activities; a stag-hunt is conducted by tradesmen who cannot ride. For incongruous effects Hood utilises all the resources of the poet: verbal music, elaborate patterns of stanza and of rhyme, choruses, adaptations of "the real language of men" are all turned on their heads. But the device which Hood made especially his own and bequeathed to all his Victorian progeny of comic versifiers was the pun. Puns are the epitome of his comic style: they are an incongrous juxtaposition captured in a single word.

Hood's comic ballads achieved the accolade of authenticity coveted by Wordsworth for the *Lyrical Ballads*, becoming current in popular circulation on broadsides. He continued to use ballad styles when his rumbustious comic vein gave way abruptly, under the influence of the consciousness of the 1840's, to a mood of social protest. His "Song of the Shirt," published in *Punch* in 1843, was written as a popular song, and so passed into the consciousness of the nation. The London seamstress became the representative of the oppressed poor, and Hood's poem about her the model for an outburst of a new kind of writing, with a social purpose and message. We now find the fervour with which this and subsequent protest songs were received as strange as is the cruelty of some of his comic writing; but in both Hood reflected his times, and has much to tell us about its sensibility.

—J. S. Bratton

HOPE, A(lec) D(erwent). Australian. Born in Cooma, New South Wales, 21 July 1907. Educated at the University of Sydney, B.A. 1928; Oxford University, B.A. 1931. Married Penelope Robinson in 1938; three children. English Teacher, New South Wales Department of Education, 1933–36; Lecturer in English and Education, Sydney Teachers College, 1937–45; Senior Lecturer in English, University of Melbourne, 1945–50. Professor of English, 1951–68, Library Fellow, 1969–72, and since 1968 Professor Emeritus, School of General Studies, Australian National University, Canberra. President, Australian Society of Authors, 1965–66, and Australian Association of Teachers of English, 1966–67. Recipient: Britannica-Australia Award, 1965; Ingram Merrill Foundation Award, 1969. Litt.D.: Australian National University, 1972; University of New England, Armidale, New South Wales. Fellow, Australian Academy of the Humanities. O.B.E. (Officer, Order of the British Empire), 1972. Lives in Canberra.

PUBLICATIONS

Verse

    The Wandering Islands. 1955.
    Poems. 1960.
    (Poems), edited by Douglas Stewart. 1963.
    Collected Poems 1930–1965. 1966.
    New Poems 1965–1969. 1969.
    Dunciad Minor: An Heroick Poem. 1970.
    Collected Poems 1930–1970. 1972.
    Selected Poems. 1973.
    A Late Picking: Poems 1965–1974. 1978.

Other

Australian Literature 1950–1962. 1963.
The Cave and the Spring: Essays on Poetry. 1965.
A Midsummer Eve's Dream: Variations on a Theme by William Dunbar. 1970.
Judith Wright. 1975.

Editor, *Australian Poetry 1960.* 1960.

Bibliography: *Hope: A Bibliography,* 1968.

*   *   *

A. D. Hope is learned, passionate, sceptical – and in his work there is an insistent, almost fierce sense of a Western Latin tradition. Perhaps one is misled by the analogy of the Latin line. It may be that the creative impulse is a sense of discrepancy, an aching consciousness of the dissimilarity between the decorative density of Europe and the emptiness of the arid continent. More probably both impulses work together in the Australian sensibility, sharpening into positive existence the Latin elements – not just the linguistic ones – latent in the English language. Certainly, Hope is concerned, in a way most unusual for those currently writing in English, with order and coherence of feeling and with decorum and regularity in presentation. This preoccupation is a constant presence in the poetry, even if not always successfully realised.

Sexual love is a recurrent theme in Hope's work. Occasionally he celebrates it as the beneficent completion of life and personality. More frequently he is concerned with its turbidity and cruelty. He sees it as incestuous, murderous, carnivorous, or absurd. The sense of unalloyed delight in love, spiritual and physical, in, for example, "The Gateway," is comparatively rare in Hope's poetry. It is true that whenever he writes of love he conveys in a masterly way the pleasure of the senses and the richness and beauty of the body. But there is always something else breaking in, something sinister or ugly or mean. Monstrous and cogent memories from the Old Testament and the classics, which supply many of the fictions used in Hope's verse, intrude on the enclosed world of lovers: reminiscences of Circe surrounded by snouted beasts, of Lot and his daughters "crafty from fear, reckless with joy and greed," of Susannah and the seedy hatred of the Elders, of Pasiphae, filled with the bull's monstrous life, of Odysseus and passion punctured by the ridiculous commonplace.

"The End of a Journey" is an example of Hope's supple virtuosity in modulation, from the stately and measured to the casual and throwaway. It calls up the name of Yeats, and Hope has made no secret of his admiration for Yeats and "that noble, candid speech/In which all things worth saying may be said ...," as well as his strong preference for Yeats over Eliot. But while Yeats is clearly a vital (and absorbed) influence on Hope, his idiom is his own, being at once less gorgeous and Byzantine when full out and more flatly contemporary in the lower register.

There is something on occasion nasty, an occasional gratuitous revelling in the garbage-bin (and perhaps also the puritan self-hatred to which this is often a clue), in a few of Hope's poems, as for example in "Rawhead and Bloody Bones":

> This Belly too commits
> By a strange and self abuse,
> Chin-chopper's titbits,
> Meat of his own mint, chews.

But more often some quality in the tone, a quaver of amusement, a glint of wit, a touch of self-mockery, even a cry of innocent astonishment, shows that the macabre is being put to a

502

more complicated and controlled use. It becomes an instrument instead of a dead end, another gateway through which the poet's imagination can enter an odd, disturbed, but somehow valid world.

The grotesque depends on discrepancy, on a measured friction between manner and material or on discordant experiences crushed together. Both types of contrast contribute to the effect of "The Coasts of Cerigo" and "The Kings," as they do in another startling poem in this genre, "The Dinner." "The Dinner" is of unusual interest; we see in the poem how the imagination of a poet of the grotesque hurls itself from the given situation to one at the extreme point of difference. In this violent dialectical swing the shock of the poem comes from our realising that the second stage, in spite of its immense dissimilarity, is really a development of the first, that it was there all the time grinning under the original elegant surface. We notice, too, how Hope arrives like a poetic zoologist at the second fiercely contrasting situation by a kind of compressed evolutionary method which appears in several poems. The reductive habit of the scientist, his concern with origins and causes, becomes in Hope's hands an instrument of poetic exploration.

One of Hope's favoured metres, the rhymed couplet, is handled with remarkable naturalness, and is used as the instrument of strength rather than delicacy. Indeed the heroic couplet, employed in an easy, open way, is splendidly adapted to communicate the peculiar quality of Hope's poetry which one is aware of even in his earliest, lightest pieces. This is its powerfully − almost physically − energetic character. It is muscular, quick, and solid − with the relaxed poise of the gifted athlete who brings all his force to bear rhythmically and without strain.

Hope is the least neurotic of poets and even when he is scrutinising the stages of his own childhood, as in one of his best poems, "Ascent into Hell," his regard is gravely objective without the least touch of narcissistic droop or any suspicion of anxious self-interest. Right from the start of Hope's poetic career, the reader is aware of the formed personality beneath the finished literary character. It is positive, independent, and radical in the Australian manner − in the manner of the Australian *people*, that is; the accepted Australian literary convention lacked precisely this very virtue. It is free of the fog of middle-class pretension and gentility: sharp where that was bland, and harsh where that was cosy. At the same time Hope's poetry asserts a profound commitment to the great constitutive works of the Western − not just the British − tradition, and, not only in poetry but also in thought and morality, accepts and asserts, namely, the principles of an intellectual aristocracy, and in doing so avoids, or ignores, the clogging dangers of Australian democracy. The result is a powerful and unfashionable maturity which joins a naked freshness of original response to a richly realised conception of an ideal order.

—William Walsh

HOPKINS, Gerard Manley. English. Born in Stratford, London, 28 July 1844. Educated at Highgate School, London; Balliol College, Oxford (Classical Exhibitioner), pupil of Jowett and Pater, graduated 1867; converted to Roman Catholicism, 1866, and entered Jesuit Novitiate, sponsored by Newman, 1868; ordained Jesuit priest, 1877. Served in missions in London, Oxford, Liverpool, and Glasgow, 1877–82; Classics Teacher, Stonyhurst, 1882–84; Professor of Greek, University College, Dublin, 1884–89. *Died 8 June 1889.*

PUBLICATIONS

Collections

> *Poems*, edited by Robert Bridges. 1918; revised edition by W. H. Gardner and N. H. Mackenzie, 1967.
> *Selections*, edited by Graham Storey. 1967.

Other

> *Letters to Robert Bridges, Correspondence of Hopkins and Richard Watson Dixon*, edited by Claude Colleer Abbott. 2 vols., 1935.
> *Note-Books and Papers*, edited by Humphry House. 1937; revised edition, by House and Graham Storey, as *Journals and Papers*, 2 vols., 1959.
> *Further Letters*, edited by Claude Colleer Abbott. 1938; revised edition, 1956.
> *Sermons and Devotional Writings*, edited by Christopher Devlin. 1959.

Bibliography: *Hopkins: A Comprehensive Bibliography* by Tom Dunne, 1976.

Reading List: *Hopkins, Priest and Poet* by John Pick, 1942; *Hopkins* by W. H. Gardner, 2 vols., 1959; *Hopkins: A Study of His Ignatian Spirit* by David A. Downes, 1959; *Hopkins: The Classical Background and Critical Reception of His Work* by Todd K. Bender, 1966; *The Dragon in the Gate* by Elizabeth W. Schneider, 1968; *A Commentary on the Complete Poems of Hopkins* by P. L. Mariani, 1969; *Hopkins: Poems: A Casebook* edited by Margaret Bottrall, 1975; *Landscape and Inscape: Vision and Inspiration in Hopkins' Poetry* by Peter Milward, 1975; *Hopkins* by Bernard Bergonzi, 1976; *The Language of Hopkins* by James Milroy, 1977; *In Extremity: A Study of Hopkins* by John Robinson, 1977.

*   *   *

Gerard Manley Hopkins is one of our finest original poets, a major innovator in both language and rhythm. Almost alone among the Victorian poets, he broke down the conventional barriers between the spoken language and "the language of poetry," and used all the resources of words to the utmost. This makes him a "difficult" poet, but a highly rewarding one.

His early poems, written before he became a Catholic and a Jesuit, show little sign of this originality; the lists of unusual words and their derivations that he made as an Oxford undergraduate show much more. On becoming a Jesuit, he burnt much of his previous verse and imposed a ban on the future writing of poetry as "unprofessional"; but at the end of seven years, in the winter of 1875–76, he wrote one of the greatest religious poems in the language. "The Wreck of the Deutschland" is at once deeply personal spiritual autobiography – the history of his own struggles and conversion – and a technically triumphant ode; a vivid account of a shipwreck and an elegy for the five exiled German nuns among the drowned. The poem's excited opening – "Thou mastering me/God! giver of breath and bread" – shows a new justification for the writing of poetry: it was to the greater glory of God, Hopkins's contribution to the Jesuit ideal. All his technical innovations are here: the "chiming" of consonants he had learnt from classical Welsh poetry (he wrote the poem in St. Beuno's, North Wales); the telescoping of syntax for greater rhetorical urgency; the use of "sprung" rhythm ("scanning by accents or stresses alone, without any account of the numbers of syllables," as he explained it to his friend Canon Dixon) to "fetch out" his meaning. The result is a poem of immensely rich verbal texture, of haunting rhythms, and of brilliantly daring images: "But it rides time like riding a river" (of the Incarnation); a bursting sloe flushing us "sour or sweet,/Brim, in a flash full!" (of the acceptance of the Crucifixion).

The ten sonnets written within the next two years all share the excitement of one theme of "The Wreck": of finding God's mystery in the beauty of nature; or in natural "inscapes," the word Hopkins coined – and used frequently in his *Journal* – for the beauty of pattern which expresses a thing's inner form. Thus "The Starlight Night" evokes the order and mystery of the star-world, to reveal it as Christ's home; "Pied Beauty" conjures up all the "dappled" quality in life that Hopkins so loved ("Glory be to God for dappled things"); "Hurrahing in Harvest" brings together the strength and the grace of Christ in a remarkable image that forces the apparent paradox of the mixture on us ("And the azurous hung hills are his world-weilding shoulder/Majestic – as a stallion stalwart, very-violet-sweet!"); and the best-known of all, "The Windhover" ("the best thing I ever wrote," Hopkins told Bridges), catches and vividly communicates the very essence of the falcon in its ecstatic flight. But in each of these sonnets the feeling invoked (Hopkins called it "instress") leads to a call for action. In "Hurrahing in Harvest," when the poet suddenly sees Christ as the giver of the harvest's glory, his heart, in its joy, "hurls for him, O half hurls earth for him off under his feet." Whatever the interpretation of "The Windhover" (dedicated "To Christ our Lord") – and there have been very many – its climax is the acceptance and beauty of sacrifice:

> No wonder of it: sheer plod makes plough down sillion
> Shine, and blue-bleak embers, ah my dear,
> Fall, gall themselves, and gash gold-vermillion.

But there is already in some of these sonnets another, sadder theme: the conflict Hopkins feels between the beauty of nature and human sin or ugliness. It is a contrast that plays a major or minor role in "God's Grandeur," "The Sea and the Skylark," "Duns Scotus's Oxford" (made more poignant by Hopkins's love of the medieval philosopher Scotus), and "Ribblesdale." In some poems the feeling of loss predominates: in "Binsey Poplars" it is his lament for the felling of trees near Oxford; and in the beautiful "Spring and Fall" ("Margaret, are you grieving/Over Goldengrove unleaving?") the child's sorrow becomes the symbol of all human sorrow. Loss is the theme again of his second shipwreck-poem, "The Loss of the Eurydice" (April 1878), analogue for Hopkins of England's lapse from Rome. It lacks the personal urgency and complexity of "The Deutschland"; but its final prayer shows how much "the riving off" from Catholicism mattered to him.

In the few poems directly inspired by his work as a priest, it is the vulnerability of human beauty and innocence that moves him. But the results are uneven. To most people "The Bugler's First Communion" is sentimental; but "Felix Randal," his elegy for a blacksmith who had died in his spiritual care, brings together, with no sense of conflict, his two vocations of priest and poet.

Two other fine sonnets of this period explore and celebrate the most important "inscape" of all to Hopkins, human selfhood. "Henry Purcell" finds it at its most distinctive in Purcell's musical genius; in "As kingfishers catch fire" the "selving" of kingfishers, dragonflies, stones, and bells culminates in the highest "self" attainable: man's capacity to become – through grace – Christ Himself.

It is the loss of faith in his own selfhood as a poet, the conviction that he has lost his creative power, that contributes so much to the despair of his final great sonnets, written in Dublin between 1885 and his death. "Spelt from Sibyl's Leaves" ("the longest sonnet ever written," Hopkins called it) prophesies their mood and theme. In this menacing twilight, earth's "dapple is at an end"; selfhood has become violent, internal struggle ("self in self steeped and pashed"); mental life is now "a rack/Where, selfwrung, selfstrung, sheathe- and shelterless, thoughts against thoughts in groans grind." The eight later sonnets are utterly different to this in style: bare, austere, packed into the sonnet-form. But they share the same images of struggle and torture, and they both widen and deepen the experience by echoes (what Hopkins called "underthought") of words and images from both the Old Testament and Shakespeare's tragedies, particularly the Book of Job and *King Lear*.

"Carrion Comfort" recreates his internal struggle as a nightmare wrestling-match with God (clearly derived from Jacob's wrestling with the Angel); but, however harrowing, despair is defied: "Not, I'll not, carrion comfort, Despair, not feast on thee." Either "No worst, there is none" or "I wake and feel the fell of dark" could well be the sonnet Hopkins described to Bridges as "written in blood": both come as close to the abyss as he ever came. "To seem the stranger lies my lot" records most powerfully his agonized feeling of inability to create: a bitter lament that also ends "Thou art indeed just, Lord":

> birds build – but not I build; no, but strain,
> Time's eunuch, and not breed one work that wakes.
> Mine, O thou lord of life, send my roots rain.

Two of these sonnets end on a much more reconciled note: "Patience, hard thing!," a plea for "rare patience," and "My own heart let me more have pity on," a plea for finally, in the midst of jaded thoughts, accepting joy, "whose smile/'s not wrung, see you; unforeseen times rather – as skies/Betweenpie mountains – lights a lovely mile."

But an equally impressive achievement of these last desolate years is that in 1887 he could create the portrait of "Harry Ploughman": the beauty of physical action perfectly performed; and in the following year return to the full exuberance of his earlier sprung rhythm in "That Nature is a Heraclitean Fire and of the Comfort of the Resurrection." Nature's flux and death's blotting-out are now fully accepted; but the Resurrection restores all:

> In a flash, at a trumpet crash,
> I am all at once what Christ is, since he was what I am, and
> This Jack, joke, poor potsherd, patch, immortal diamond,
> Is immortal diamond.

Hopkins's *Journal*, kept from 1866 to 1875, shows his hypersensitive response to nature and the remarkable range of words he found – or coined – to express the inscapes he delighted in. Like his early diaries, they include many small, meticulously drawn sketches. His letters to his greatest friend Robert Bridges, and to two other poets, Canon R. W. Dixon and Coventry Patmore, reveal the attractiveness and generosity of his character as well as his powers of minute criticism. His sermons – although he was not a particularly successful preacher – show the candour and devotedness of his vocation as a priest. But more important for our understanding of Hopkins as a poet is the beginning of his commentary on the *Spiritual Exercises* of St. Ignatius, central to his inner life, as to that of every Jesuit.

—Graham Storey

HOPKINSON, Francis. American. Born in Philadelphia, Pennsylvania, 2 October 1737. Educated at the Academy of Philadelphia, now the University of Pennsylvania, A.B. 1757, A.M. 1760; admitted to the Pennsylvania Bar and New Jersey Bar, 1775. Married Ann Borden in 1768; one son. Began study of harpsichord, 1754; gave first public performance, 1757, and later set poems and psalms to music: first native American composer of secular songs, 1759; appointed Collector of Customs, Port of Salem, New Jersey, 1763, and New Castle, Delaware, 1772; practised law in Philadelphia and Bordentown, New Jersey, from 1775; Member, New Jersey Governor's Council, 1774, and New Jersey Provincial Congress,

1774–76; Member of the Continental Congress, 1776: signed the Declaration of Independence; subsequently served the new United States Government as Member of the Continental Navy Board, 1776–78, and Treasurer of the Continental Loan Office, 1778–81; Judge of Admiralty for Pennsylvania, 1779–89; Member, Pennsylvania convention to ratify the Constitution, 1787; Judge of the United States District Court for Pennsylvania, 1789–91. A Founder, American Philosophical Society; a designer of the Great Seal of New Jersey, 1776; credited with the design of the American flag, 1777; Secretary of the convention that organized the Protestant Episcopal Church, 1789. *Died 9 May 1791.*

PUBLICATIONS

Collections

The First American Composer, edited by Harold V. Milligan.   1919.

Verse

An Exercise.   1761.
Science.   1762.
A Collection of Psalm Tunes.   1762.
A Psalm of Thanksgiving.   1766.
The Psalms of David in Metre.   1767.
The Battle of the Kegs.   1779.
An Ode.   1788.
A Set of Eight Songs.   1788.
Ode from Ossian's Poems.   1794.

Fiction

A Pretty Story.   1774; as *The Old Farm and the New Farm: A Political Allegory,* 1857.

Other

Errata; or, The Art of Printing Incorrectly.   1763.
Account of the Grand Federal Procession.   1788.
Judgments in the Admiralty of Pennsylvania.   1789.
Miscellaneous Essays and Occasional Writings.   3 vols., 1792.

Reading List: *The Life and Works of Hopkinson* by George E. Hastings, 1926 (includes bibliography); "Hopkinson and Franklin" by Dixon Wecter, in *American Literature 12,* 1940.

*   *   *

Poet, politician, musician, judge, scientist, and artist, Francis Hopkinson excelled in so many activities that his contributions to American culture defy easy classification. More than any other event, the Revolutionary War shaped Hopkinson's interests, and it is with the War that he is associated today. As a member of the Second Continental Congress, Hopkinson signed the Declaration of Independence, an action which alone was enough to guarantee him historical immortality.

Not the least of his accomplishments were the many poems and essays which he wrote in support of his country's decision to separate from Great Britain. His verses, most of which satirized the British and praised the Americans, were light, humorous, and deft. While not the stuff of great poetry, they accomplished what they were intended to do. Easily set to music, they lifted the spirits of American soldiers who sang them at the front, and they helped to demoralize the British by good naturedly ridiculing their cause. Hopkinson's most famous poem, *The Battle of the Kegs*, recounts in ballad form how the British, unfamiliar with explosives, battled relentlessly with a flotilla of mines which American patriots had ingeniously floated in kegs down the Delaware River toward their camp. Other famous poems written by Hopkinson during the Revolutionary War include "A Camp Ballad," "The Toast," and "Tory Medley." Together these poems made Hopkinson one of the most popular American poets of his day.

Equally popular were the prose essays and tracts which Hopkinson directed against the British. From Arbuthnot, Swift, and Addison, Hopkinson developed a fondness for satire, particularly when it was couched in the form of allegory or a fabricated letter. Like his verse, Hopkinson's prose was extremely effective anti-British propaganda. Written in the form of a humorous allegory, *A Pretty Story* describes the events which led the Colonies to declare their independence. In "A Prophecy," also an allegory, Hopkinson uses the persona of a Biblical prophet who predicts the establishment of a new and prosperous government in North America.

Although Hopkinson frequently contributed poems and essays to such periodicals as the *American Magazine*, the *Columbian Magazine*, and the *Pennsylvania Magazine*, his writing before and after the war lacked the vigor which the conflict itself inspired in him. With the possible exception of "My Days Have Been So Wondrous Free" (1759), a work which is thought to be the oldest American song known, his early and late poetry, for the most part dull and uninteresting, is rarely read today. His letters are more profitable because he corresponded with the most important statesmen of his day, including George Washington, Benjamin Franklin, and Thomas Jefferson. *The Miscellaneous Essays and Occasional Writings of Francis Hopkinson*, collected by Hopkinson himself, contains only a small portion of his total literary output. Many of his writings, particularly those written for periodicals, have yet to be collected.

—James A. Levernier

HOUSMAN, A(lfred) E(dward). English. Born in Fockbury, Worcestershire, 26 March 1859; brother of the dramatist Laurence Housman. Educated at Bromsgrove School, Worcestershire; St. John's College, Oxford (scholar), gained first class honours in classical moderations, 1879, but failed final examinations, 1881; thereafter pursued classical studies on his own, later awarded M.A. Clerk in the Patent Office, London, 1882–92; Chair of Latin, University College, London, 1892–1911; Fellow of Trinity College, Cambridge, and Kennedy Professor of Latin, Cambridge University, 1911–36. Honorary Fellow, St. John's College, Oxford. *Died 30 April 1936.*

PUBLICATIONS

Collections

Collected Poems, edited by John Carter. 1939.
Selected Prose, edited by John Carter.   1961.

Verse

A Shropshire Lad.   1896; edited by T. B. Haber, 1966.
Last Poems.   1922.
Fragment of a Greek Tragedy.   1925.
Three Poems.   1935; edited by W. White, 1941.
More Poems, edited by Laurence Housman.   1936.
The Manuscript Poems, edited by T. B. Haber.   1955.

Other

Letters to E. H. Blakeney, edited by Blakeney.   1941.
A Morning with the Royal Family.   1941.
Thirty Letters to Witter Bynner, edited by T. B. Haber.   1957.
The Classical Papers, edited by J. Diggle and F. R. D. Goodyear.   3 vols., 1972.

Editor, *M. Manilii Astronomicon.*   1903; revised edition, 1937.
Editor, *D. Junii Juvenalis Saturae.*   1905.
Editor, *A. Mannaei Lucani Belli Civilis.*   1926.

Bibliography: *Housman: An Annotated Hand-List* by John Carter and John Sparrow, 1952.

Reading List: *Housman: A Sketch* by A. S. F. Gow, 1936; *Housman: Some Poems, Some Letters, and a Personal Memoir* by Laurence Housman, 1937; *A Buried Life* by Percy Withers, 1940; *Housman* by G. Richards, 1941; *Housman* by Ian Scott-Kilvert, 1955; *Housman: A Divided Life* by George L. Watson, 1957; *Housman, Scholar and Poet* by Norman Marlow, 1958; *The Poetic Art of Housman: Theory and Practice* by B. J. Leggett, 1978.

*   *   *

Housman's gifts as a poet seem to be much like his gifts as a classical scholar: narrow, profound, isolated, brooding, and ferocious. He brought his great powers as textual critic to bear on one of the least considered Roman writers, Manilius, and guarded him as a dragon might its cave. It was the same with his poems, most of which seem to stem from an emotional wound in his youth which he could hardly bring himself to mention except through the obliquities of his apparently stark and simple verse.

He refused to allow the intellect a place in what he took to be the basic appeal of poetry — and indeed, with Housman more than most poets, paraphrase of supposed "content" is pointless. His poems repeat again and again that love is fleeting, lovers fickle, youth decays into age, and that death is final. None of this accounts for not only his popularity (for many poets less popular have said the same things) but his considerable power. The characteristics he assigned to great poetry in his lecture "The Name and Nature of Poetry" are the characteristics of his own poetry; chiefly, that it strikes to the pit of the emotions and by-passes "thought." Though it might be hard to justify a place for Housman as a major poet – partly because the actual quantity of work is small, contained in the three slim volumes that make up the *Collected Poems*, partly because the poems themselves are on a small scale – he would seem to be a prime candidate for the title "Major Minor."

A Shropshire Lad, published by Housman at his own expense after rejection by several publishers, formed the basis of his reputation. The South African war soon afterwards helped to make popular its mixture of patriotic pride and stoical gloom, pessimism and nostalgia:

> East and west on fields forgotten
>> Bleach the bones of comrades slain,
> Lovely lads and dead and rotten;
>> None that go return again.

The "Shropshire" of the title and the poems, though apparently reinforced with names (Clun, Ludlow, Wenlock Edge), is a region of evocative emotions rather than a locality, a land of lost content. Housman was not a rural writer; instead, he based a personal mythology (of country lads betrayed in love, drinking themselves into oblivion, committing suicide, being hanged for nameless crimes) on a rediscovered pastoral tradition. As Ian Scott-Kilvert has put it, "Housman's Shropshire is a blighted Arcadia, in which the poet is constantly reminded of the limitations of mortality."

> Into my heart an air that kills
> From yon far country blows:
> What are those blue remembered hills,
> What spires, what farms are those?
>
> That is the land of lost content,
> I see it shining plain,
> The happy highways where I went
> And cannot come again.

The only other book of verse that Housman published in his lifetime is *Last Poems*, a gathering of pieces from the 1890's until the end of the First World War. It shows no real development from *A Shropshire Lad*, and almost any of its contents could be interchanged with the earlier book without strain. Its weaknesses (chiefly what might be called a hopeless emotional vulgarity – "Little is the luck I've had/And oh, 'tis comfort small/To think that many another lad/Has had no luck at all") are the same, as well as its strengths: the almost marmoreal words matched with an extraordinarily seductive rhythmical inspiration:

> In gross marl, in blowing dust,
>> In the drowned ooze of the sea,
> Where you would not, lie you must,
>> Lie you must, and not with me.

After A. E. Housman's death, his brother Laurence, as his literary executor, gathered together *More Poems* and the "Additional Poems" which form part of the *Collected Poems*. The popularity of the whole body of work has continued, though Housman's reputation has sporadically been questioned and carped at by some critics. Yet the simple intuitiveness which Housman valued both as the origin of the creative impulse and as the talisman by which he recognised poetry in others has even more often been acknowledged and praised by academics and by professional literary folk, who may find it difficult to account satisfactorily for the pleasure they get from Housman's poems but who endorse that pleasure is what they get.

—Anthony Thwaite

510

HOVEY, Richard. American. Born in Normal, Illinois, 4 May 1864. Educated at Dartmouth College, Hanover, New Hampshire, 1881–85, B.A. 1885; Episcopal Seminary, New York, 1886. Married Henriette Russell in 1894; one son. Teacher, Thomas Davidson's Summer School of Philosophy, 1888; actor, 1890; lived in England, 1894, and France, 1895–96; Teacher, Barnard College, New York, 1899–1900. *Died 24 February 1900.*

PUBLICATIONS

Verse

Poems. 1880.
The Laurel: An Ode to Mary Day Lanier. 1889.
Harmonics. 1890.
Seaward: An Elegy on the Death of Thomas William Parsons. 1893.
Songs from Vagabondia, with Bliss Carman. 1894; *More Songs*, 1896; *Last Songs*, 1901.
Along the Trail: A Book of Lyrics. 1898.
To the End of the Trail, edited by Mrs. Richard Hovey. 1907.
Dartmouth Lyrics, edited by Edwin Osgood Grover. 1924.
A Poem and Three Letters. 1935.

Plays

Launcelot and Guenevere: A Poem in Dramas (includes *The Quest of Merlin* and *The Marriage of Guenevere*). 1891; revised versions of *The Marriage of Guenevere*, 1895, and of *The Quest of Merlin*, 1898.
The Birth of Galahad. 1898.
Taliesin: A Masque. 1900.
The Holy Graal and Other Fragments, Being the Uncompleted Parts of the Arthurian Dramas, edited by Mrs. Richard Hovey. 1907.

Other

Hanover by Gaslight; or, Ways That Are Dark, Being an Exposé of the Sophomoric Career of '85. 1883(?).

Translator, *The Plays of Maurice Maeterlinck: Princess Maleine, The Intruder, The Blind, The Seven Princesses.* 1894; second series (includes *Alladine and Palomides, Pelleas and Melisande, Home, The Death of Tintagiles*), 1896.

Reading List: *Hovey, Man and Craftsman* by Allan Houston Macdonald, 1957 (includes bibliography by Edward Connery Lathem); *Hovey* by William R. Linnemann, 1976.

*   *   *

Like his contemporary Stephen Crane, Richard Hovey died tragically young, before he could fulfill the artistic promise he demonstrated, before he could make himself felt as a major force in modern poetry. But unlike Crane, Hovey did not seek to confront the turbulence and brutality of his age; yet he rebelled against it in *fin de siècle* aestheticism, in the spirit of Bohemianism, of carefree youth, cheerful pleasures, and hearty fellowship. This spirit ruled his life and his poetry.

After graduating in 1885 from Dartmouth College in New Hampshire, where he was active in campus literary life (Hovey celebrates the college in many poems, including "Men of Dartmouth," "Hanover Winter Song," and "Our Liege Lady, Dartmouth"), he studied to become an Episcopal priest, but left the seminary after one year. In 1887, he met the artist Tom Meteyard and the Canadian poet Bliss Carman, with both of whom he collaborated on the *Vagabondia* books. The dominant theme in these little volumes is that of the bold and energetic young man, "Wandering with the wandering wind,/Vagabond and unconfined!" ("The Wander-Lovers"); these short lyrics describe Hovey's world, one of adventurous, genteel Bohemianism, dedicated to comradeship and a love of Art. Hovey and Carman each wrote about half the number of poems in the books, which were popular, especially among college students, around the turn of the century.

Hovey was also a serious dramatic poet, planning (but never finishing) a series of verse plays of the Arthurian legends (a world popular with much escapist art and literature of the late nineteenth century).

A major influence acknowledged by Hovey is that of the American poet Sidney Lanier. Hovey's ode *The Laurel* (dedicated to Mrs. Lanier) and his serious lyric poetry, notably the elegy *Seaward*, reflect Lanier's rhythms and images. Hovey was also influenced by the French *symbolistes*, and translated Mallarmé and Maeterlinck. But he did not have enough time in which to develop his own lyrical talent into a unique or influential poetic voice.

—Jane S. Gabin

HUGHES, (James) Langston.   American.   Born in Joplin, Missouri, 1 February 1902. Educated at Central High School, Cleveland, 1916–20; Columbia University, New York, 1921–22; Lincoln University, Pennsylvania (Witter Bynner Award, 1926), B.A. 1929. During World War II, Member of the Music and Writers war boards. Seaman, 1923–25; busboy, Wardman Park Hotel, Washington, D.C., 1925; Madrid Correspondent, Baltimore *Afro-American*, 1937; Columnist, Chicago *Defender*, 1943–67, and New York *Post*, 1962–67. Founder of the Harlem Suitcase Theatre, New York, 1938, New Negro Theatre, Los Angeles, 1939, and Skyloft Players, Chicago, 1941. Visiting Professor in Creative Writing, Atlanta University, Gerogia, 1947; Poet-in-Residence, University of Chicago Laboratory School, 1949. Recipient: Harmon Gold Medal for Literature, 1931; Rosenwald Fellowship, 1931, 1940; Guggenheim Fellowship, 1935; National Institute of Arts and Letters grant, 1946; Anisfield-Wolfe Award, 1953; Spingarn Medal, 1960. D.Litt.: Lincoln University, 1943; Howard University, Washington, D.C., 1963; Western Reserve University, Cleveland, 1964. Member, National Institute of Arts and Letters, 1961, and American Academy of Arts and Sciences. *Died 22 May 1967.*

PUBLICATIONS

Verse

The Weary Blues.   1926.
Fine Clothes to the Jew.   1927.
Dear Lovely Death.   1931.

The Negro Mother and Other Dramatic Recitations.   1931.
The Dream-Keeper and Other Poems.   1932.
Scottsboro Limited: Four Poems and a Play in Verse.   1932.
A New Song.   1938.
Shakespeare in Harlem.   1942.
Jim Crow's Last Stand.   1943.
Lament for Dark Peoples and Other Poems, edited by H. Driessen.   1944.
Fields of Wonder.   1947.
One-Way Ticket.   1949.
Montage of a Dream Deferred.   1951.
Selected Poems.   1959.
Ask Your Mama: 12 Moods for Jazz.   1961.
The Panther and the Lash: Poems of Our Times.   1967.
Don't You Turn Back: Poems (juvenile), edited by Lee Bennett Hopkins.   1969.

Plays

The Gold Piece, in *The Brownies' Book,* July 1921.
Mulatto (produced 1935; original version produced 1939). In *Five Plays,* 1963.
Little Ham (produced 1935).   In *Five Plays,* 1963.
Troubled Island (produced 1935; revised version, music by William Grant Still, produced 1949).   1949.
When the Jack Hollers, with Arna Bontemps (produced 1936).
Joy to My Soul (produced 1937).
Soul Gone Home (produced 1937?).   In *Five Plays,* 1963.
Don't You Want to Be Free?, music by Carroll Tate (produced 1937).   In *One Act Play Magazine,* October 1938.
Front Porch (produced 1938).
The Sun Do Move (produced 1942).
Freedom's Plow (broadcast, 1943).   1943.
Pvt. Jim Crow (radio script), in *Negro Story,* May-June 1945.
Booker T. Washington at Atlanta (broadcast, 1945).   In *Radio Drama in Action,* edited by Eric Barnouw, 1945.
Street Scene (lyrics only), book by Elmer Rice, music by Kurt Weill (produced 1947).   1947.
The Barrier, music by Jan Meyerowitz (produced 1950).
Just Around the Corner (lyrics only), book by Abby Mann and Bernard Drew, music by Joe Sherman (produced 1951).
Simply Heavenly, music by David Martin (produced 1957).   1959.
Esther, music by Jan Meyerowitz (produced 1957).
Shakespeare in Harlem, with James Weldon Johnson (produced 1959).
Port Town, music by Jan Meyerowitz (produced 1960).
The Ballad of the Brown King, music by Margaret Bonds (produced 1960).
Black Nativity (produced 1961).
Gospel Glow (produced 1962).
Tambourines to Glory, music by Jobe Huntley, from the novel by Hughes (produced 1963).   In *Five Plays,* 1963.
Five Plays (includes *Mulatto, Soul Gone Home, Little Ham, Simply Heavenly, Tambourines to Glory*), edited by Webster Smalley.   1963.
Jericho-Jim Crow (produced 1963).
The Prodigal Son (produced 1965).

Screenplay: *Way Down South,* with Clarence Muse, 1939.

Radio scripts: *Jubilee*, with Arna Bontemps, 1941; *Brothers*, 1942; *Freedom's Plow*, 1943; *John Henry Hammers It Out*, with Peter Lyons, 1943; *In the Service of My Country*, 1944; *The Man Who Went to War*, 1944 (UK); *Booker T. Washington at Atlanta*, 1945; *Swing Time at the Savoy*, with Noble Sissle, 1949.

Television scripts: *The Big Sea*, 1965; *It's a Mighty World*, 1965; *Strollin' Twenties*, 1966.

Fiction

Not Without Laughter. 1930.
The Ways of White Folks (stories). 1934.
Simple Speaks His Mind. 1950.
Laughing to Keep from Crying (stories). 1952.
Simple Takes a Wife. 1953.
Simple Stakes a Claim. 1957.
Tambourines to Glory. 1958.
The Best of Simple. 1961.
Something in Common and Other Stories. 1963.
Simple's Uncle Sam. 1965.

Other

Popo and Fifina: Children of Haiti (juvenile), with Arna Bontemps. 1932.
The Big Sea: An Autobiography. 1940.
The First Book of Negroes (juvenile). 1952.
The First Book of Rhythms (juvenile). 1954.
Famous American Negroes (juvenile). 1954.
The Sweet Flypaper of Life, with Roy De Carava (on Harlem). 1955.
Famous Negro Music-Makers (juvenile). 1955.
The First Book of Jazz (juvenile). 1955; revised edition, 1962.
A Pictorial History of the Negro in America, with Milton Meltzer. 1956; revised edition, 1963.
I Wonder As I Wander: An Autobiographical Journey. 1956.
The First Book of the West Indies (juvenile). 1956; as *The First Book of the Caribbean*, 1965.
The Langston Hughes Reader. 1958.
Famous Negro Heroes of America (juvenile). 1958.
The First Book of Africa (juvenile). 1960; revised edition, 1964.
Fight for Freedom: The Story of the NAACP. 1962.
Black Magic: A Pictorial History of the Negro in American Entertainment, with Milton Meltzer. 1967.
Black Misery. 1969.
Good Morning, Revolution: Uncollected Social Protest Writings, edited by Faith Berry. 1973.

Editor, *Four Lincoln University Poets*. 1930.
Editor, with Arna Bontemps, *The Poetry of the Negro 1746–1949: An Anthology.* 1949; revised edition, 1970.
Editor, with Waring Guney and Bruce M. Wright, *Lincoln University Poets*. 1954.
Editor, with Arna Bontemps, *The Book of Negro Folklore*. 1958.
Editor, *An African Treasury: Articles, Essays, Stories, Poems by Black Africans*. 1960.

Editor, *Poems from Black Africa.*   1963.
Editor, *New Negro Poets: USA.*   1964.
Editor, *The Book of Negro Humor.*   1966.
Editor, *La Poésie Negro-Américaine* (bilingual edition).   1966.
Editor, *Anthologie Africaine et Malgache.*   1966.
Editor, *The Best Short Stories by Negro Writers: An Anthology from 1899 to the Present.*   1967.

Translator, with Mercer Cook, *Masters of the Dew,* by Jacques Roumain.   1947.
Translator, with Ben Frederic Carruthers, *Cuba Libre,* by Nicolás Guillén.   1948.
Translator, *Gypsy Ballads,* by Federico García Lorca.   1951.
Translator, *Selected Poems of Gabriela Mistral.*   1957.

Bibliography: *A Bio-Bibliography of Hughes, 1920–1967* by Donald C. Dickinson, 1967, revised edition, 1972.

Reading List: *Hughes* by James A. Emanuel, 1967; *Hughes: A Biography* by Milton Meltzer, 1968; *Hughes, Black Genius: A Critical Evaluation* edited by Therman B. O'Daniel, 1971 (includes bibliography); *Hughes: An Introduction to the Poetry* by Onwuchekwa Jemie, 1977; *Hughes: The Poet and His Critics* by Richard K. Barksdale, 1977.

*   *   *

As impressive as Langston Hughes is for his versatility and productivity, his claim to enduring literary importance rests chiefly on his poetry and his Simple sketches. In his poetry his sure lyric touch, his poignant insight into the urban black folk soul rendered with remarkable fidelity to a variety of black idioms, his negative capability of subordinating his own personality so as to convey a vivid impression of scene or incident or mood or character, and his willingness to experiment are his richest endowments, though one also often finds in his verse the comic sense (often ironic or bittersweet), the broad democratic faith, and the total understanding of character which so irradiate the Simple tales.

Although Hughes wrote some verse without specific racial reference, the three major categories of his poetry comprise poems related to black music, poems of racial protest, and poems of racial affirmation. These categories naturally overlap, but it is convenient to discuss them separately. For the entire course of his literary career, Hughes was fascinated by black music: blues, jazz in its several varieties, and gospel. The classic blues stanzaic form, consisting of a statement of a problem or situation in the first line repeated in the second (often with a slight variation) followed by a third line resolving, interpreting, or commenting on the first two, appears frequently in Hughes, as in the following from "Red Sun Blues":

> Gray skies, gray skies, won't you let the sun shine through?
> Gray skies, gray skies, won't you let that sun shine through?
> My baby's left me, I don't know what to do.

Elsewhere, as in the title poem of *The Weary Blues*, Hughes uses the blues and bluesmen as subject in a poem which may incorporate blues stanzas but has its own larger structure. His poems deriving from jazz are more complicated in their experimentation. Taken together, they provide a kind of poetic graph of developments in jazz from the Harlem cabaret life of the exuberant 1920's, through the boogie-woogie of the 1930's and the bebop of the 1940's, to the progressive jazz of the 1950's. From such early examples as "Jazzonia" and "The Cat and the Saxophone" to the ambitious later works *Montage of a Dream Deferred* and *Ask Your Mama*, Hughes used the varieties of jazz as both subject and style, designing the last-named work for musical accompaniment and often reading his poetry on tour to a jazz background. Though less prominently than blues and jazz, spirituals and gospel music figure also in Hughes's poetry (for example, the "Feet of Jesus" section in *Selected Poems*), as well as in his numerous song-plays.

As a poet of racial protest Hughes was less strident than some other well-known black writers, but not necessarily less trenchant or effective. Such poems as "I, Too" and "Let America Be America Again" express a wistful longing for racial equality. Others, such as "Brass Spittoons" and "Ballad of the Landlord" develop miniature dramas of the hardships and injustices of black life in a racist society. Some of the later poems included in the "Words on Fire" section of *The Panther and the Lash* sound notes of rising militancy. Surely among Hughes's best poems in this category are "American Heartbreak," whose laconic understatement achieves a sense of bitter finality, and "Song for a Dark Girl," a starkly tragic and strangely beautiful lyric about a girl's response to the lynching of her lover. Whether wistful, dramatic, angry, or tragic in mood, Hughes was always alive throughout his career to the oppression of his people.

He was equally sensitive to the dignity with which they endured or resisted that oppression. "Mother to Son" and "The Negro Mother" are among his many poems celebrating the black quest for freedom and social justice. Hughes was one of the first writers to use "soul" in a special racial sense, as in his very early poem "The Negro Speaks of Rivers." Color itself delights the poet in the carefully crafted "Dream Variation" and the delicious "Harlem Sweeties." And his comic vision to be developed in such loving detail in the Simple sketches is prefigured in "Sylvester's Dying Bed" and the Madam Alberta K. Johnson poems. Lowlife and working class blacks, shunned by bourgeois spokesmen of the Harlem Renaissance, often receive special tribute in Hughes's poems of racial affirmation.

Hughes's interest in fiction developed later than his instinct for poetry. The novels *Not Without Laughter* and *Tambourines to Glory* are highly readable if somewhat weak in structure. The best of his sixty-six published short stories are proficient in technique and perceptive in their treatment of a variety of human situations. The most striking achievement in fiction is the creation of Jesse B. Semple. As Richard K. Barksdale has noted, Simple "had just the right blend of qualities to be Black America's new spokesman – just enough urban humor, cynicism, and sardonic levity and just enough down-home simplicity, mother-wit, innocence, and naiveté" (*Black Writers of America*, edited by Richard Barksdale and Keneth Kinnamon). The marvelous talk elicited from this fully realized black working man by the middle-class, intellectual narrator of the sketches constitutes one of the most valuable treasures of American literary humor.

In drama Hughes is perhaps more important for the extent of his activity and the stimulus he gave to black theater than for the intrinsic artistic merit of his own plays. As translator, anthologist, historian, and biographer he played a major role in popularizing Afro-American, Afro-Caribbean, and African subjects. As devoted friend and sponsor of generations of aspiring writers he was at the center of black literary activity for more than four decades. Together with his own accomplishments as poet and humorist, these efforts constitute a total contribution to literature matched by that of few writers in this century.

—Keneth Kinnamon

HUGHES, Ted. English. Born in Mytholmroyd, Yorkshire, in 1930. Educated at Mexborough Grammar School, Yorkshire; Pembroke College, Cambridge, B.A. 1954, M.A. 1959. Served in the Royal Air Force for two years. Married 1) Sylvia Plath, *q.v.*, in 1956 (died, 1963), one son, one daughter; 2) Carol Orchard in 1970. Worked as a rose gardener and night watchman; reader for the Rank Organisation. Since 1965, Editor, with Daniel Weissbort, *Modern Poetry in Translation* magazine, London. Recipient: New York Poetry Center First Publication Award, 1957; Guinness Award, 1958; Guggenheim Fellowship, 1959; Maugham Award, 1960; Hawthornden Prize, 1961; City of Florence International Poetry Prize, 1969; Queen's Gold Medal for Poetry, 1974. O.B.E. (Officer, Order of the British Empire), 1977. Lives in England.

PUBLICATIONS

Verse

The Hawk in the Rain.   1957.
Lupercal.   1960.
Selected Poems, with Thom Gunn.   1962.
The Burning of the Brothel.   1966.
Recklings.   1966.
Scapegoats and Rabies: A Poem in Five Parts.   1967.
Animal Poems.   1967.
Five Autumn Songs for Children's Voices.   1968.
The Martyrdom of Bishop Farrer.   1970.
A Crow Hymn.   1970.
A Few Crows.   1970.
Crow: From the Life and Songs of the Crow.   1970; revised edition, 1972.
Crow Wakes: Poems.   1971.
Poems, with Ruth Fainlight and Alan Sillitoe.   1971.
Eat Crow.   1972.
Selected Poems 1957–1967.   1972.
In the Little Girl's Angel Gaze.   1972.
Cave Birds.   1975.
Earth-Moon.   1976.
Eclipse.   1976.
Gaudete.   1977.
Chiasmadon.   1977.

Plays

The Calm (produced 1961).
The Wound (broadcast, 1962).   In *Wodwo,* 1967.
Seneca's Oedipus (produced 1968).   1969.
Beauty and the Beast (televised, 1968; produced 1971).   In *The Coming of the King and Other Plays,* 1970.
The Coming of the King and Other Plays (juvenile) (includes *The Tiger's Bones; Beauty and the Beast; Sean, The Fool, The Devil and the Cats).*   1970; augmented edition, as *The Tiger's Bones and Other Plays for Children* (includes *Orpheus*), 1973.
Sean, The Fool, The Devil and the Cats (produced 1971).   In *The Coming of the King and Other Plays,* 1970.
The Coming of the King (televised, 1972).   In *The Coming of the King and Other Plays,* 1970.
Orghast (produced 1971).

517

The Iron Man (juvenile), from his own story (televised, 1972).   1973.
The Story of Vasco, music by Gordon Crosse, from a play by Georges Schehadé
(produced 1974).   1974.

Radio Plays: *The House of Aries*, 1960; *A Houseful of Women*, 1961; *The Wound*, 1962;
Difficulties of a Bridegroom, 1963; *Dogs*, 1964.

Televison Plays (juvenile): *Beauty and the Beast*, 1968; *The Coming of the King*, 1972;
The Iron Man, 1972.

Other

Meet My Folks! (juvenile).   1961.
The Earth-Owl and Other Moon-People (juvenile).   1963.
How the Whale Became and Other Stories (juvenile).   1963.
Nessie the Mannerless Monster (juvenile).   1964; as *Nessie the Monster*, 1974.
Wodwo (miscellany).   1967.
The Iron Man: A Story in Five Nights (juvenile).   1968; as *The Iron Giant*, 1968.
Poetry Is (juvenile).   1970.
Season Songs (juvenile).   1975.
Moon-Whales and Other Poems (juvenile).   1976.
Moon-Bells (juvenile).   1978.

Editor, with Patricia Beer and Vernon Scannell, *New Poems 1962*.   1962.
Editor, with Thom Gunn, *Five American Poets*.   1963.
Editor, *Here Today*.   1963.
Editor, *Selected Poems*, by Keith Douglas.   1964.
Editor, *Poetry in the Making: An Anthology of Poems and Programmes from "Listening
and Writing."*   1967.
Editor, *A Choice of Emily Dickinson's Verse*.   1971.
Editor, *A Choice of Shakespeare's Verse*.   1971; as *Poems: With Fairest Flowers While
Summer Lasts: Poems from Shakespeare*, 1971.
Editor, *Selected Poems*, by Yehuda Amichai.   1971.
Editor, *Crossing the Water*, by Sylvia Plath.   1971; as *Crossing the Water: Transitional
Poems*, 1971.

Translator, with János Csokits, *Selected Poems*, by János Pilinszky.   1976.

Reading List: *The Art of Hughes* by Keith Sagar, 1975; *Hughes and Thom Gunn* by Alan
Bold, 1976.

                              *   *   *

Few young poets can have won the instant and universal critical acclaim for a first volume
which Ted Hughes received in 1957 for *The Hawk in the Rain*. The reasons, in retrospect, are
plain to see. Hughes's poetry broke upon a dead decade in English literature; into the social-
democratic sheepishness of "The Movement" and the *New Lines* anthology, it brought "a
sudden sharp hot stink of fox" ("The Thought-Fox"), reiterating the perennial Romantic
notion of poetic inspiration as something atavistic and instinctual, a thing of the blood and
gut. This was a poetry harsh, jagged, and abrasive, which, though it often rhymed,
apparently did so as a kind of disdainful concession to order — where downbeat, unstressed,
half- or near-rhymes suggested the recalcitrance of a turbulent, energetic world reluctant to

be constrained by considerations of urbanity or the kind of formal nicety dear to "The Movement." This was clearly a poetry that had been shaped by the Cambridge English School's predilection for the muscularity, the wrenched syntax and scansion, and the extraordinary yokings of vocabulary and image in John Donne's verse. In "Wind," Hughes doesn't simply break the "rule" about not splitting adjective from noun by enjambment: he goes further and hyphenates the adjective across the line-ending, in outrageous mimesis of the action: "The wind flung a magpie away and a black-/Back gull bent like an iron bar slowly." But an equally powerful influence must have been Hughes's transfer from the English Tripos to Archaeology and Anthropology, which confirmed that taste for the primitive and the exotic, the alien, and the mythic, that finds its fullest expression in *Crow*. Finally, and a crucial component of Hughes's appeal, he brought a breath of provincial fresh air into an increasingly drab metropolitan culture. The Macmillan era needed its prophets, its avatars of an order beyond the bland superficialities of affluence and consumerism. Hughes was a grammar-school boy and shopkeeper's son from the West Riding; the burliness of his North Country physique was reproduced in the abrupt angularity of his verse; for the literary fashion-mongers of the capital, Hughes, therefore, despite his Cambridge degree, became another of those recurring discoveries of the Romantic era, the noble poetic savage, warbling his native woodnotes wild to an appreciative audience.

This is most obvious in his constant flirtation with the apocalyptic mode. In "The Horses," for example, he emerges from a world locked in "Evil air, a frost-making stillness," where "my breath left tortuous statues in the iron light" and the horses stand "megalith-still," to a vision of the sudden, cataclysmic dawn which is the objective correlative of his own anarchic feelings:

> Slowly detail leafed from the darkness. Then the sun
> Orange, red, red, erupted
>
> Silently, and splitting to its core tore and flung cloud,
> Shook the gulf open, showed blue,
>
> And the big planets hanging. ...

Though the poem then draws us back ("in the fever of a dream") to a restored stasis ("Hearing the horizons endure"), this experience is repeated throughout the early poetry. In "Famous Poet" poetry itself, "set/To blink behind bars at the zoo," still offers a glimpse of "a time when half the world still burned," and, in "Macaw and Little Miss," "The Jaguar," "Esther's Tomcat," and all those other caged or semi-domesticated carnivores in Hughes's bestiary, we are offered images of a lost world of the instincts repeatedly associated with a feudal or primordial ethos of cruelty, superstition, and a barbarous grandeur of speech and gesture. In "Pike," "An Otter," and "February" the self is drawn in fascination to this world, yet at the same time struggles to preserve the poise exemplified in "To Paint a Water Lily" ("still/As a painting, trembling hardly at all,.../Whatever horror nudge her root") or "The Retired Colonel," "Honouring his own caricature" amidst "a pimply age." One way of maintaining balance in *Lupercal*, staving off the return of the repressed, is the distancing irony which allows the poet to dissociate himself from the pretensions, for example, of "Hawk Roosting," a meritocrat whose solipsistic smugness is acutely caught in the boast with which the poem ends:

> Nothing has changed since I began.
> My eye has permitted no change.
> I am going to keep things like this.

(This humorous streak, underestimated in Hughes's work, is very apparent in his rather whimsical stories for children, and reaches the proportions of black farce in *Crow*.)

If, in his earlier books, nature was a viscous, glutinous realm seeking to engulf the mutinous spirit, by the time of *Wodwo* it has dried out. This is the poetry of an increasingly barren struggle for survival, in a landscape as bleak and relentless as that depicted in "Pibroch." In "Gog" the self wakes to its own desolation ("I ran and an absence bounded beside me"), to an unexplained guilt and self-questioning in a world where "Everywhere the dust is in power" and "The rider of iron, on the horse shod with vaginas of iron,/Gallops over the womb that makes no claim, that is of stone." That north country poem of a delusive quest through arid lands, *Sir Gawain and the Green Knight*, supplies both title and epigraph to this volume, as well as the theme of an endless warring – whether the Viking Raids of "The Warriors of the North," the Great War translated into a Beckettian charade in the radio-play "The Wound," or the twentieth-century massacres of Dresden, Buchenwald, and the Gulags, culmination of "a hundred and fifty million years of hunger" in which "Killing gratefully as breathing/Moulded the heart and mouth" ("Karma").

Crow offers a grim, sardonic vision of a world in which the worst has already happened; in the raucous, acerbic tones of Donne's satires it submits all human pretensions to Crow's cold nihilistic scrutiny. Man is "a walking/Abattoir/Of innocents," hypocritically justifying his lust for survival with a flood of words (language and its duplicity, as lie, jest, vow, curse, and prayer is a recurring motif). Crow, for whom even birth is "A Kill," who struggles into existence over the body of his mother ("Crow and Mama") cannot afford such luxuries: charity, love, compunction, remorse, forgiveness are all denied him by life itself; to come into existence is to give pain, to survive is to survive at the expense of others. Crow triumphs over Death in the "Examination at the Womb Door" in which he answers all the questions successfully, but it is only a provisional victory. *Crow* is a bitter parody of all creation myths, in which sexuality is a mutual devouring from which one emerges into the dark cycles of renewal and destruction. In "Crow's First Lesson" God tries to teach him to say "Love." But Crow's gape gives birth successively to shark, bluefly, tsetse, and mosquito, homing on "their sundry fleshpots." Another attempt retches up "Man's bodiless prodigious head" and then "woman's vulva" which "dropped over man's neck and tightened." As "God struggled to part them, cursed, wept – /Crow flew guiltily off." In such brutal parables, Hughes's considerable talent approaches "the bottom of all things" of which he writes in "How Water Began to Play"; whether it ends up, like water, "Utterly worn out," or "utterly clear," the future has yet to show.

—Stan Smith

HUME, Alexander. Scottish. Born, probably at Polwarth, Berwickshire, c. 1560; son of Baron Polwarth. Studied at the University of St. Andrews, and probably graduated B.A. in 1574; studied law for four years in Paris. Married Marione Duncanson; one son, two daughters. Unsuccessfully sought an appointment in law and subsequently at court; took holy orders, 1597; Minister of Logie, near Stirling, 1598–1609. *Died 4 December 1609.*

PUBLICATIONS

Collections

The Poems, edited by Alexander Lawson. 1902.

Verse

Hymns or Sacred Songs, Wherein the Right Use of Poesie May Be Espied. 1599.

Other

A Treatise of Conscience. 1594.
A Treatise of the Felicity of the Life to Come. 1594.
The Practice of Sanctification, edited by R. M. Fergusson. 1901.

Reading List: *Hume, An Early Poet-Pastor of Logie, and His Intimates* by R. M. Fergusson, 1899.

*   *   *

Alexander Hume's poetry is significant in two respects. In its treatment of nature, it is a link in the chain which connects the Scottish poetic tradition of Gavin Douglas with that of Thomson and ultimately Burns; and, as Alexander Lawson observes (in the introductory essay to his edition of Hume's works), it is proof, occasionally, that poetry was possible even in as rigorous and repressive a time as the late sixteenth century in Scotland. His best (and best-known) poem, "A Day Estival," has been called the best poem written in the late sixteenth century by a Scot. It is a lyric celebration of a May morning, in places evocative of Thomson's descriptive passages in *The Seasons.*

The rest of Hume's work – poetry and prose – is narrowly religious and in many ways typical of post-reformation Scottish writing. His themes are sin, damnation, gratitude to God, and earthly resignation.

—John J. Perry

JAMES I, King of Scotland.   Scottish.   Born in Dunfermline, July 1394; son of Robert III.
After capture by English, 1406, spent youth in detention; education supervised by Henry IV
and by royal tutors, 1409–13. Married Lady Jane Beaufort, daughter of the Earl of Somerset,
1424 (died, 1445); one son, six daughters. Released from prison and repatriated, 1423;
crowned King of Scotland, at Scone, 1424, and tried to restore divided and demoralized
kingdom: his reforms in curtailing the powers of the Scottish nobles eventually provoked a
conspiracy against him; he was murdered at Perth by assassins led by his kinsman Sir Robert
Graham. *Died 20 February 1437.*

PUBLICATIONS

Verse

The Kingis Quair, edited by W. W. Skeat.   2 vols., 1911; edited by J. Norton-Smith,
1971; edited by Matthew P. McDiarmid, 1973.

Reading List: *James I, King of Scots* by E. W. M. Balfour-Melville, 1936; "Tradition and the
Interpretation of The Kingis Quair" by John MacQueen, in *Review of English Studies*, 1961;
"Chaucerian Synthesis: The Art of the Kingis Quair" by W. Scheps, in *Studies in Scottish
Literature 8*, 1971; "A King's Quire" by J. A. W. Bennett, in *Poetica*, May 1976.

*   *   *

The genius of James I lies in his skill in blending Chaucerian and Lydgatian elements into a
charming and harmonious exploration of personal experience, observation of nature,
religious and philosophical insight, and dream adventure. Felicitous Chaucerian elegance of
phrasing, reminiscence, and charm of thought intertwine with Lydgate's early penchant for a
medley type of narrative construction where Chaucer's more sophisticated philosophical
tendencies are lent a relaxed, "amateurish" formal shape. An acute philosophical awareness
still informs the heart of the poem – James understands his Boethius better than many of his
modern expositors – but it is a symptom of a modern distrust of "literature" which strives to
strip the work of its marvellous variousness of appeal and genuine "gentle" charm of
expression in order to promote metaphysical dilemmas and resolutions.
    The poet's dream fascinates in its vividness, variety, and rapidity of movement. His vision
comes after a long day's anxiety and offers answers to the poet's yearnings (recalling
Chaucer's *Parlement*). It includes a lightning ascent through the spheres and almost Dantean
meetings with divine personages. It contains a description of an ideal landscape populated by
"diuerse kynd of bestes" (recalling the *Parlement*'s diverse kinds of birds). The dream is
introduced dramatically by supernatural light and voice darting in through the window
which offered the prisoner his only glimpse of the world from which he was barred – and
through that window comes later the message of his *larges*. Finally, the poet-prince
celebrates his "hertes hele," secure in an optimistic universe where Boethian perspectives
invite us to admire the harmonizing justice of the poet's passage through exile and prison to
liberation in true love. Or so it seemed in February 1424.

—J. Norton-Smith

JARRELL, Randall. American. Born in Nashville, Tennessee, 6 May 1914. Educated at Vanderbilt University, Nashville, B.S. in psychology 1936 (Phi Beta Kappa), M.A. in English 1939. Served as a celestial navigation tower operator in the United States Army Air Corps, 1942–46. Married Mary Eloise von Schrader in 1952. Instructor in English, Kenyon College, Gambier, Ohio, 1937–39, University of Texas, Austin, 1939–42, and Sarah Lawrence College, Bronxville, New York, 1946–47; Associate Professor, 1947–58, and Professor of English, 1958–65, Women's College of the University of North Carolina (later, University of North Carolina at Greensboro). Lecturer, Salzburg Seminar in American Civilization, 1948; Visiting Fellow in Creative Writing, Princeton University, New Jersey, 1951–52; Fellow, Indiana School of Letters, Bloomington, Summer 1952; Visiting Professor of English, University of Illinois, Urbana, 1953; Elliston Lecturer, University of Cincinnati, Ohio, 1958; Phi Beta Kappa Visiting Scholar, 1964–65. Acting Literary Editor, *The Nation*, New York, 1946–47; Poetry Critic, *Partisan Review*, New Brunswick, New Jersey, 1949–53, and *Yale Review*, New Haven, Connecticut, 1955–57; Member of the Editorial Board, *American Scholar*, Washington, D.C., 1957–65. Consultant in Poetry, Library of Congress, Washington, D.C., 1956–58. Recipient: Guggenheim Fellowship, 1946; National Institute of Arts and Letters grant, 1951; National Book Award, 1961; Oliver Max Gardner Award, University of North Carolina, 1962; American Association of University Women Juvenile Award, 1964; Ingram Merrill Award, 1965. D.H.L.: Bard College, Annandale-on-Hudson, New York, 1962. Member, National Institute of Arts and Letters; Chancellor, Academy of American Poets, 1956. *Died 14 October 1965.*

PUBLICATIONS

Collections

> *The Complete Poems.* 1969.
> *The Achievement of Jarrell: A Comprehensive Selection of His Poems,* edited by Frederick
>   J. Hoffman. 1970.

Verse

> *Five Young Ameri an Poets,* with others. 1940.
> *Blood for a Stra . . .* 1942.
> *Little Friend, , . .le Friend.* 1945.
> *Losses.* 1948.
> *The Seven-League Crutches.* 1951.
> *Selected Poems.* 1955.
> *Uncollected Poems.* 1958.
> *The Woman at the Washington Zoo: Poems and Translations.* 1960.
> *Selected Poems.* 1964.
> *The Lost World: New Poems.* 1965.
> *Jerome: The Biography of a Poem.* 1971.

Play

> *The Three Sisters,* from a play by Chekhov (produced 1964). 1969.

Fiction

Pictures from an Institution: A Comedy.   1954.

Other

Poetry and the Age (essays).   1953.
A Sad Heart at the Supermarket: Essays and Fables.   1962.
The Gingerbread Rabbit (juvenile).   1964.
The Bat-Poet (juvenile).   1964.
The Animal Family (juvenile).   1965.
The Third Book of Criticism (essays).   1969.
Fly by Night (juvenile).   1976.
A Bat Is Born (juvenile).   1977.
Kipling, Auden & Co.   1979.

Editor, *The Anchor Book of Stories.*   1958.
Editor, *The Best Short Stories of Kipling.*   1961; as *In the Vernacular: The English in India* and *The English in England,* 2 vols., 1963.
Editor, *Six Russian Short Novels.*   1963.

Translator, with Moses Hadas, *The Ghetto and the Jews of Rome,* by Ferdinand Gregorovius.   1948.
Translator, *The Rabbit Catcher and Other Fairy Tales of Ludwig Bechstein.*   1962.
Translator, *The Golden Bird and Other Fairy Tales,* by the Brothers Grimm.   1962.
Translator, *Snow White and the Seven Dwarfs: A Tale from the Brothers Grimm.*   1972.
Translator, *The Juniper Tree and Other Tales,* by the Brothers Grimm.   1973.
Translator, *Goethe's Faust: Part One.*   1974; *Part Two,* 1978.

Bibliography: *Jarrell: A Bibliography* by Charles M. Adams, 1958, supplement in *Analects 1,* Spring 1961; "A Checklist of Criticism on Jarrell 1941–70" by D. J. Gilliken, in *Bulletin of the New York Public Library,* April 1971.

Reading List: *Jarrell 1914–1965* edited by Robert Lowell, Peter Taylor, and Robert Penn Warren, 1967; *The Poetry of Jarrell* by Suzanne Ferguson, 1971; *Jarrell* by M. L. Rosenthal, 1972.

*   *   *

Shortly after his death, the elegant, brilliant, and quixotic Randall Jarrell was eulogized by Karl Shapiro as the greatest poet-critic since T. S. Eliot. At a memorial service at Yale, such men as Robert Lowell, Robert Penn Warren, and Richard Eberhart came to honor their dead friend as a master among men of their craft. Robert Lowell called him "the most heartbreaking English poet of his generation." Celebrated as well was Jarrell's literary criticism, for in work like *Poetry and the Age*, he had altered dominant critical trends and tastes. He had brought Walt Whitman into prominence, and had imparted new light on Frost, Stevens, Williams, and Marianne Moore, among others; he had attacked the New Critics, and he had affirmed the relevance of art to life. Not unlike Ezra Pound, Jarrell was one of those truly committed critics who, although a poet himself, had helped the writers around him to define twentieth century art.

As Walter Rideout in his essay in *Poets in Progress* (edited by Edward Hungerford, 1962) has noted, when Jarrell published his *Selected Poems* in 1955, he grouped them in such a way as to obscure the rather marked delineations in central subject matter that had distinguished volume from volume. The style of his first book, however, *Blood for a Stranger*, is noticeably derivative, and shows the influence of Allen Tate, John Crowe Ransom, and particularly W. H. Auden in its experiments with villanelles, sestinas, and unusual rhyming patterns, as well as in its intellectual brilliance and metaphysical questionings. The volume cries out against a world politically heaving itself toward catastrophe. Jarrell's tone is one of existential loneliness and despair.

Little Friend, Little Friend and *Losses* are less formal; Jarrell establishes a more direct and characteristic tone; the poet seems, in fact, personally more attracted to death. Jarrell's ambiguous view of humanity, man as murderer and victim, innocent and guilty, ultimately like the child facing the "capricious infinite" parental power, found its perfect expression in these war poems. But Jarrell's war poems treat the human condition, their central image, man as soldier/prisoner. Jarrell dramatizes man's guilt and suffering upon a stage of world-wide struggle. *Losses* treats all sorts of prisoners – children, black Americans, DP's at Haifa, Jews in concentration camps – and focuses upon how each is a victim within "the necessities that governed every act." Even the enemy contains the child, who, called upon to commit a terrible violence, is himself an innocent. Utilizing the perspective of the child, Jarrell makes the outcome of war the product of innocence:

> The other murderers troop in yawning;
> Three of them play Pitch, one sleeps, and one
> Lies counting missions, lies there sweating
> Till even his heart beats: One; One; One.
> O *murderers*! ... Still, this is how it's done.

Reality is defined as nightmare, "experience" before and after life, the dream. In "The Death of the Ball Turret Gunner," he writes: "From my mother's sleep I fell into the State/... I woke to black flak and the nightmare fighters." Jarrell supports no conventional political position, no "program for chance." Instead, the man-child is "a ticket/Someone bought and lost on, a stray animal/... Bewildered .../What have you understood, to die?" His compassion extends even to the enemy; the powerful also suffer: "Who will teach the Makers how to die?" he writes.

Jarrell's great and fertile period concluded with *The Seven-League Crutches*. The early works focused upon lost childhood and innocence, the terrible shock of awareness of adult hypocrisy and social disintegration. Jarrell now moves away from more public concerns to private life; his poems are more relaxed. Although the theme of illness remains in the poems about children, his work is more psychological, more dream-filled. One senses now, in addition, "a way out," in the face of "Necessity": "Man you must learn to live/though you want nothing but to die." Stoical, compassionate, and even at times capable of a bittersweet humor, some of Jarrell's most mature work now appears. Man may perhaps even transcend Necessity through the imaginative life, the creation and perception of art.

After this Jarrell turned to fairy tale and became preoccupied with children's stories, with German Romanticism. The fairy tale offered him the innocent's victory over the potent and evil forces of the universe. In "The Märchen" (Grimm's Tales), he wrote, for example:

> We felled our islands there, at last, with iron.
> The sunlight fell to them, according to our wish,
> And we believed, till nightfall, in that wish;
> And we believed, till nightfall, in our lives.

The title poem of *The Woman at the Washington Zoo*, a return to Jarrell's more formal style of the 1940's, crystallizes the poet's concern with aging and loneliness. The woman cries out for relief, for transformation again, from her empty life: "the world goes by my cage and never sees me." She cries: "You know what I was,/You see what I am: change me, change me!"

525

In *The Lost World*, published after a nervous breakdown, many of his recurrent themes appear: loneliness, lovelessness, age, lost youth, the world's hypocrisy, and, as Robert Lowell put it, childhood, "above all childhood!" *The Lost World* fails to exhibit the brilliance, power, elegance, and diversity that characterize his earlier work. More importantly, there is about it too much of a confessional quality; the poems are awkward and read like revelations on the analyst's couch. The speaker appears filled with a sense of guilt and helplessness. He tries to forgive, especially, his parents, but he is unsuccessful. In "The Piano Player," for example, he confesses: "I go over, hold my hands out, play I play − /If only, somehow, I had learned to live!" His childhood football hero, Daddy Lipscomb, admits: "I've been scared/Most of my life. You wouldn't think so to look at me./It gets so bad I cry myself to sleep." Many of these poems contain a female persona, a woman sometimes unfaithful to her lover, often cruel to people and animals to the point of murder, but, most frequently, unmitigatingly unkind to her child. Although one senses Jarrell's attempt to understand and forgive these people, the poet remains in despair: "I identify myself, as always/With something that there's something wrong with."

One feels a debt toward Jarrell for his enormous encouragement and advice to the poets of his time. But one must regard him as well as an important poet with a brilliant intelligence, elegance, and humor. Jarrell's uniqueness remains in his special combination of sophistication with undiminished yearnings for childhood, that bittersweet faith that through art, or dreams, or fairy tales, one could regain childhood innocence and joy and negate the inevitable processes of aging, isolation, and death.

—Lois Gordon

JEFFERS, (John) Robinson. American. Born in Pittsburgh, Pennsylvania, 10 January 1887. Tutored by his father; attended schools in Switzerland and Germany; University of Western Pennsylvania, Pittsburgh, 1902; Occidental College, Los Angeles, California, 1903–05, graduated 1905; University of Zurich; University of Southern California, Los Angeles, M.A.; School of Medicine, University of Southern California; studied forestry at the University of Washington, Seattle. Married Una Call Kuster in 1913. Turned to writing after inheriting a modest income, 1912; after 1924 lived in seclusion in a house he built on the California coast near Carmel. Recipient: Academy of American Poets Fellowship, 1958; Shelley Memorial Award, 1961. D.Litt.: Occidental College, 1937. Member, National Institute of Arts and Letters. *Died in January 1962.*

PUBLICATIONS

Collections

Selected Poems. 1965.
Selected Letters 1897–1962, edited by Ann N. Ridgeway. 1968.

Verse

Flagons and Apples. 1912.
Californians. 1916.

Tamar and Other Poems.   1924.
Roan Stallion, Tamar, and Other Poems.   1925.
The Women at Point Sur.   1927.
Poems.   1928.
An Artist.   1928.
Cawdor and Other Poems.   1928.
Dear Judas and Other Poems.   1929.
Stars.   1930.
Apology for Bad Dreams.   1930.
Descent to the Dead: Poems Written in Ireland and Great Britain.   1931.
Thurso's Landing and Other Poems.   1932.
Give Your Heart to the Hawks and Other Poems.   1933.
Solstice and Other Poems.   1935.
The Beaks of Eagles.   1936.
Such Counsels You Gave to Me and Other Poems.   1937.
The Selected Poetry.   1938.
Be Angry at the Sun.   1941.
The Double Axe and Other Poems.   1948.
Hungerfield and Other Poems.   1954.
The Beginning and the End and Other Poems.   1963.

Plays

Medea, from a play by Euripides (produced 1947).   1946.
The Cretan Women, from a play by Euripides (produced 1954?).   In *From the Modern Repertory 3,* edited by Eric Bentley, 1956.

Other

Poetry, Gongorism, and a Thousand Years.   1949.
Themes in My Poems.   1956.

Bibliography: *The Critical Reception of Jeffers: A Bibliographical Study* by Alex Vardamis, 1972.

Reading List: *The Loyalties of Jeffers* by Radcliffe Squires, 1956; *Jeffers* by Frederic I. Carpenter, 1962; *The Stone Mason of Tor House: The Life and Work of Jeffers* by Melba B. Bennett, 1966; *Jeffers: Fragments of an Older Fury* by Brother Antoninus (William Everson), 1968; *Jeffers, Poet of Inhumanism* by Arthur B. Coffin, 1971; *Jeffers* by Robert Brophy, 1973.

*   *   *

In 1925 *Roan Stallion, Tamar, and Other Poems* established Robinson Jeffers as one of the major poets of his generation. But beginning in 1927 with *The Women at Point Sur* his repeated use of forbidden themes alienated many readers, and in 1941 his opposition to American participation in World War II all but destroyed his reputation. Since his death in 1962 a better perspective has been achieved, and now he is recognized as one of the most powerful – if also most controversial – of modern poets.

Most of his volumes include one or more long narrative poems, together with many shorter lyrics. And these longer poems all deal, either implicitly or explicitly, with the materials of myth. His *Medea,* for instance, is a free adaptation of the play of Euripides, but

Solstice attempts to domesticate the violent Greek myth in a realistic California setting. His most successful narrative poems, such as "Roan Stallion" which describes a woman's passionate adoration of a horse, use mythical materials most unobtrusively. But the aura of myth and the forbidden passions which the old myths described, such as incest, parricide, and the love of man for beast, all trouble the narrative poetry of Jeffers.

Besides these myths, his poetry gives vivid expression to an extraordinary sense of place. The wild coast of the country south of Carmel, where he lived all his creative life, provides both actual setting and the conviction of immediate reality for all his poems, both narrative and lyric. But most significant of all is the symbolic nature of this actual country. Here is "Continent's End," both in fact and in idea, "the long migrations' end," where human civilization now faces "the final Pacific" and looks Westward toward its first beginnings in "mother Asia."

In his poetry this realistic sense of place combines with a consciousness of the symbolic significance of this place and a remembrance of the prehistoric origins of civilization suggested by the ancient myths. At its best this poetry realizes a vision of human history unique in its temporal scope and its imaginative power. It is small wonder if it sometimes fails to unify these disparate elements and to realize this all-inclusive vision.

The volume which first established Jeffers's reputation probably remains his best, and the three narrative poems which it includes illustrate the various combinations of narrative realism with mythical symbolism which his later poetry developed. "Roan Stallion" is most completely realistic, and perhaps for this reason has remained the favorite of traditional minded readers. "Tamar" is most extreme, both in plot and in technique, although the strange story of incest plays itself out in a California setting. "The Tower Beyond Tragedy" retells the story of the Oresteia in its original Greek setting, but with modern characterization.

The heroine of "Roan Stallion" is named "California," and both name and plot recall the Greek myth of Europa. But the god-like stallion remains simply an animal, and the woman's adoration for him remains psychological. Meanwhile the mythical dimensions of the naturalistic story are emphasized by poetic suggestion:

> The fire threw up figures
> And symbols meanwhile, racial myths formed and
> dissolved in it, the phantom rulers of humanity
> That without being are yet more real than what
> they are born of, and without shape, shape that
> which makes them.

"Tamar" is a very different poem, perhaps unique in literature. Its incestuous heroine rejects all the inhibitions of civilization, but her seemingly realistic actions are motivated by passages of dream, vision, and racial memory until the modern story seems to reenact the earliest creation myths of the incestuous union of Coelus and Terra, of gods and men. The heroine's absolute rejection of morality is paralleled only by that of the later *Women at Point Sur*. But here the repeated use of dream and vision transforms the realistic story into the realm of timeless myth.

"The Tower Beyond Tragedy" narrates the plot of the Oresteia in realistic terms, but focuses on the character of Cassandra and her predictions of doom. Midway through the poem these enlarge into an all-embracing prophecy of the ultimate destruction of future empires, ending with "a mightier to be cursed and a higher for malediction," America. The poem concludes with the refusal of Orestes to inherit Mycenae, or imperial power, and an eloquent poetic statement of his philosophy of total detachment in a "tower beyond tragedy."

This denunciation of imperial power and this celebration of human detachment is also the theme of many of Jeffers' best shorter poems, such as "Shine, Perishing Republic" and "Continent's End." Other lyrics celebrate simply the beauty of nature, such as "Night" and "Boats in a Fog." Perhaps the best of his short poems is "To the Stone Cutters," which treats the ancient theme of mutability.

After the *Roan Stallion* volume, *The Women at Point Sur* narrated a story of the total rejection of traditional morality by a renegade Christian minister. But this longest of Jeffers' poems was also most realistic, so that the mythical and instinctual incest of "Tamar" became calculated and explicit. Actually the poem recalls the story of Euripides' *Bacchae*, which Jeffers also used in his short poem "The Humanist's Tragedy," but the longer poem abandoned all reference to myth and symbol. Although most contemporary readers rejected it, Jeffers' chief modern disciple, William Everson (Brother Antoninus), has praised it highly in *Fragments of an Older Fury*.

In *Dear Judas* Jeffers retold the gospel story with new characterization, as he had retold the Oresteia in "The Tower Beyond Tragedy." The striking originality of his conception and the soaring poetry with which he clothed it make the poem memorable. But his rejection of Christian orthodoxy seemed blasphemous to many readers. "The Loving Shepherdess," a companion narrative poem, created a character of such beauty that her story seems unique among Jeffers' dark tragedies.

In the 1930's Jeffers turned to a series of more realistic long poems with contemporary California settings, without mythical overtones. "Cawdor," "Thurso's Landing," and "Give Your Heart to the Hawks" all take place in "Jeffers Country" south of Carmel, and all develop their tragic stories effectively. Only some names and passages of poetic commentary suggest larger themes. Near the end of "Thurso's Landing" the poet comments:

> The platform is like a rough plank theatre-stage
> Built on the brow of the promontory: as if our blood had labored all around the
>   earth from Asia
> To play its mystery before strict judges at last, the final ocean and sky, to prove our
>   nature
> More shining than that of the other animals. It is rather ignoble in its quiet times,
>   mean in its pleasures,
> Slavish in the mass; but at stricken moments it can shine terribly against the dark
>   magnificence of things.

After 1935 Jeffers published new volumes every few years, but only a few of the narrative poems achieved excellence. "At the Birth of an Age" develops incidents from the Niblung Saga, but the poetry overshadows the story, and the mythical and philosophic elements which it illustrates find powerful expression. The second narrative poem in *The Double Axe*, entitled "The Inhumanist," creates a hermit-hero who gives expression to Jeffers' philosophy both in speech and in action. Finally, "Hungerfield" creates a brief modern myth recalling that of Herakles.

Many readers prefer Jeffers' shorter poems to his long narratives. His "Apology for Bad Dreams" offers both illustration and explanation of the violent imagery and pessimistic philosophy which characterize all his poetry. A later poem, "The Bloody Sire," gives perfect expression to this philosophy of violence, ending: "Who would remember Helen's face/ Lacking the terrible halo of spears?"

Much of the difficulty of his poetry stems from his insistence upon the philosophy of "Inhumanism," which he attempted to define in his later writing. His opposition both to human self-importance and to the classical tradition of humanism emphasized instead the modern search for objective truth. In contrast to T. S. Eliot's traditional classicism, Jeffers celebrated the values of science and discovery.

—Frederic I. Carpenter

JOHNSON, James Weldon. American. Born in Jacksonville, Florida, 17 June 1871. Educated at Atlanta University, A.B. 1894, A.M. 1904; also studied at Columbia University, New York, for three years. Married Grace Nail in 1910. Principal, Stanton Central Grammar School for Negroes, Jacksonville; helped found *Daily American*, Jacksonville; admitted to the Florida Bar, and practised in Jacksonville, 1897–1901; moved to New York, to collaborate with his brother, the composer J. Rosamond Johnson, in writing popular songs and light opera, 1901–06; United States Consul in Puerto Cabello, Venezuela, 1906–09, and Corinto, Nicaragua, 1909–12; Executive Secretary, National Association for the Advancement of Colored People, 1916–30; Spence Professor of Creative Literature, Fisk University, Nashville, Tennessee, 1930–38; Visiting Professor of Creative Literature, New York University, 1934. Columnist, New York *Age*. Director, American Fund for Public Service; Trustee, Atlanta University. Recipient: Spingarn Medal, 1925; Du Bois Prize for Negro Literature, 1933. Litt.D.: Talladega College, Alabama, 1917; Howard University, Washington, D.C., 1923. Member, Academy of Political Science. *Died 26 June 1938.*

Publications

Verse

Fifty Years and Other Poems. 1917.
God's Trombones: Seven Negro Sermons in Verse. 1927.
Saint Peter Relates an Incident of the Resurrection Day. 1930.
Saint Peter Relates an Incident: Selected Poems. 1935.

Plays

Goyescas; or, The Rival Lovers, from a play by Fernando Periquet, music by Enrique Granados (produced 1915). 1915.
Shakespeare in Harlem, with Langston Hughes (produced 1959).

Fiction

The Autobiography of an Ex-Colored Man. 1912.

Other

The Changing Status of Negro Labor. 1918.
Africa in the World Democracy, with Horace M. Kallen. 1919.
Self-Determining Hayti. N.d.
Lynching: America's National Disgrace. 1924.
The Race Problem and Peace. 1924.
Fundamentalism Versus Spiritualism: A Layman's Viewpoint. 1925.
Native African Races and Culture. 1927.
Legal Aspects of the Negro Problem. N.d.
Black Manhattan. 1930.
The Shining Life. 1932.
Along This Way (autobiography). 1933.
Negro Americans, What Now? 1934.

Editor, *The Book of American Negro Poetry.* 1922; revised edition, 1931.
Editor, *The Book of American Negro Spirituals.* 1925; *Second Book,* 1926.

Reading List: *Roots of Negro Racial Consciousness: Three Harlem Renaissance Authors* (on Countée Cullen, Claude McKay, and Johnson) by Stephen H. Bronz, 1964; *Johnson, Black Leader, Black Voice* by Eugene D. Levy, 1973 (includes bibliography).

*   *   *

James Weldon Johnson's literary output is slight but it is a solid achievement and one that proves crucial when viewed in the perspective of an Afro-American aspiring to authorship in the United States in the early twentieth century. In *God's Trombones: Seven Negro Sermons in Verse* Johnson achieves a considerable success in melding Afro-American folk and Euro-American sophisticated modes of expression to gain the kind of artistic synthesis he hoped would assist in confirming the right to full citizenship for peoples of African descent in the United States, by virtue of a demonstrated capacity (which their detractors would argue they did not possess) to contribute significantly to the formation of a national culture. This task of recuperation becomes a theme in Johnson's influential picaresque novel now regarded as a classic, *The Autobiography of an Ex-Colored Man,* first published anonymously in 1912. The novel's "tragic mulatto" protagonist is a trained musician who earns his way as an inspired ragtime pianist. He professes, however ironically (and it is to Johnson's skillful manipulation of irony that the novel owes the greater part of its success), to bring "glory and honour to the Negro race." This he intends to achieve through compositions in the European classical tradition incorporating elements of Afro-American folk music, the projected field research for which, however, never gets done. Further insight into Johnson's recuperative aims is available in the important Prefaces to the two editions of his equally influential and classic anthology, *The Book of American Negro Poetry.* In these he compares the Afro-American poet's need to achieve a distinct mode of expression rooted in and supportive of Afro-American life ("a form that will express the racial spirit by symbols from within" rather than from without), to that recognized by the Irish poet-playwright J. M. Synge which led to the assimilation of indigenous folk material into his works.

Johnson's accidental death cut short his efforts but his poems in *God's Trombones* record a significant step in the direction he envisioned. This work has continued to serve as an inspiration and a model for Afro-American writers. Stylistically inspired by the folk preaching Johnson observed in Afro-American churches, the poems assume the form and essential rhythm of the sermons and prayers he heard. As such they score a marked stylistic departure from the prevailing Anglo-American poetic tradition of the day. Also, they constitute a corrective to the artificial and, as Johnson saw it, denigrating folk speech of the stereotype-fostering dialect mode that had been grafted onto that tradition, including its use in Johnson's own early dialect poetry. On the Euro-American side, the poems in *God's Trombones* are biblical-Whitmanesque, gaining an appeal at once sophisticated and folk oriented. Similarly, *The Autobiography of an Ex-Colored Man* delineates the artistic defusing of the various stereotypes Afro-American writers were coming to recognize as an obligatory function of their works. Toward that end, Johnson imbues his protagonist with the superficialities of the "tragic mulatto" stereotype but protrays him with psychological verisimilitude and with irony, thus enabling the stereotypical aspect to achieve a virtual self-destruction. He thus carries forward a tradition of corrective aesthetics pioneered by his predecessors, the Afro-American writers Charles W. Chesnutt and, to a lesser degree, Paul Laurence Dunbar.

—Alvin Aubert

JOHNSON, Lionel (Pigot).   English.   Born in Broadstairs, Kent, 15 March 1867; grew up in Mold, Flintshire, and Kingsmead, Windsor Forest. Educated at Durdham Down, Clifton; Winchester College (scholar), 1880–86 (Editor, *The Wykehamist*, 1884–86); New College, Oxford, 1886–90 (Winchester Scholarship, 1885; Goddard Scholarship, 1886), B.A. (honours) 1890. Settled in London, 1890, and became regular reviewer for *Academy, Anti-Jacobin, National Observer, Daily Chronicle*, and the *Pall Mall Gazette*; Member of the Rhymers Club. Became a Roman Catholic, 1891; interested in Irish nationalist politics and the Irish literary revival; visited Ireland, 1893. *Died 4 October 1902.*

PUBLICATIONS

Collections

Complete Poems, edited by Ian Fletcher.   1953.

Verse

Sir Walter Raleigh in the Tower.   1885.
Poems.   1895.
Ireland with Other Poems.   1897.

Other

Bits of Old Chelsea, with Richard Le Gallienne.   1894.
The Art of Thomas Hardy.   1894.
Poetry and Ireland: Essays, with W.B. Yeats.   1908.
Post Liminium: Essays and Critical Papers, edited by Thomas Whittemore.   1911.
Some Winchester Letters.   1919.
Reviews and Critical Papers, edited by Robert Schafer.   1921.

Reading List: *Johnson, Poète et Critique* by A.W. Patrick, 1939; "The Art of Johnson" by A.B. Feldman, in *Poet Lore 57*, 1953; "Johnson's 'The Dark Angel' " by Ian Fletcher, in *Interpretations* edited by John Wain, 1955; "Yeats and Johnson on the Limitations of Patriotic Art" by Ian C. Small, in *Studies*, Winter 1974.

*   *   *

The reputation of Lionel Johnson rests upon a surprisingly slight literary output: two volumes of verse (*Poems* and *Ireland with Other Poems*), a full critical study (*The Art of Thomas Hardy*), and a volume of critical essays collected posthumously (*Post Liminium*). Paradoxically, however, this very slightness sustains the reputation of Johnson as the typical poet of the eighteen-nineties: introspective, melancholic, isolated and self-destructive, an image due in part to W. B. Yeats's characterisation of him in his elegy "In Memory of Major Robert Gregory." But the typicality of Johnson is sustained also by the four central concerns of all his poetry: the religious tradition of Catholicism; the attractive political mythologies generated by Irish nationalism; the artistic legacies of the Aesthetic movement; and the example of classical literature. Thus in his emphasis upon the uniqueness and evanescence of experience and upon the isolation of the artist, Lionel Johnson was the heir to Aestheticism, especially to Walter Pater's celebrations of an ascetic ideal. Johnson's poems of the early 1890's offer this *persona* of the isolated, suffering poet comforted finally only by the transcendence of faith, as in "Mystic and Cavalier" –

> Go from me: I am one of those, who fall.
> What! hath no cold wind swept your heart at all,
> In my sad company? Before the end,
>   Go from me, dear my friend!

– or "The Dark Angel" –

> Do what thou wilt, thou shalt not so,
> Dark Angel! triumph over me:
> *Lonely, unto the Lone I go;*
> *Divine, to the Divinity.*

But another, perhaps contradictory, influence was that provided by Latin and Greek poetry, in which Johnson was very widely read. There is a resultant emphasis in his work on sanity, proportion, and elegance. Behind this influence there existed two important ideas: first, Johnson's reverence for authority, which found expression in his invocation of the institutional – the Church (Johnson was immensely learned in theology), Oxford, and in particular his beloved Winchester; and, second, a desire to address himself to a literary tradition conceived of as living – hence his celebration of classical authors and historical personages evocative of an ordered past.

Johnson's verse is spare, without ornament, generally devoid of metaphor, and depends for its effect fundamentally upon the impassioned reiteration of a small group of emotionally charged words, like "immemorial" or "chivalric." This technique (*anaphora*) can at times deteriorate into mere declamation and the repetition of a list of stock Aesthetic or Decadent epithets, like "wan," "stilly," or "pale"; but, at its best, by its very cumulative force, it allows the isolation of the "speaking-voice" of the poem, and the construction of the *persona* of the solitary poet.

—Ian C. Small

JOHNSON, Samuel. English. Born in Lichfield, Staffordshire, 18 September 1709. Educated at Lichfield Grammar School, and at the Stourbridge School, to age 16; Pembroke College, Oxford, 1728–29, left without taking a degree. Married Elizabeth Porter in 1735 (died, 1752). Usher in a grammar school in Market Bosworth, Leicestershire; worked for the publisher of the *Birmingham Journal*, 1732; took pupils at Edial, Staffordshire, among them David Garrick, 1736–37; travelled with Garrick to London, and settled there, 1737; supported himself by writing for Cave's *Gentleman's Magazine*, 1738–44, for which he wrote reports on debates in Parliament, 1740–43; catalogued the library of the second Earl of Oxford, 1742; worked on his *Dictionary*, 1747–55; formed the Ivy Lane Club, 1749; Author/Editor, *The Rambler*, 1750–52; contributed to *The Adventurer*, 1753–54; arrested for debt, but released on a loan from Samuel Richardson, 1756; contributed to the *Literary Magazine*, 1756–57; wrote "The Idler" for the *Universal Chronicle*, 1758–60; moved to Inner Temple Lane, now Johnson's Buildings, 1759; pensioned by the crown, 1762; founded The Literary Club, 1764; wrote pamphlets against Wilkes, 1770, a defense of government policy in the Falkland Islands, 1771, and in America, 1775; toured Scotland with James Boswell, subsequently his biographer, 1773; travelled to Wales, 1774, and Paris, 1775; formed the Essex Head Club, 1783. M.A.: Oxford University, 1775; LL.D.: Trinity College, Dublin, 1765; Oxford University, 1775. *Died 13 December 1784.*

PUBLICATIONS

Collections

> *Works.* 16 vols., 1903.
> *Letters,* edited by R. W. Chapman. 3 vols., 1952.
> *Works,* edited by A. T. Hazen and others. 1958–
> *Complete English Poems,* edited by J. D. Fleeman. 1971.
> *Selected Poetry and Prose,* edited by Frank Brady and William K. Wimsatt. 1977.

Verse

> *London: A Poem in Imitation of the Third Satire of Juvenal.* 1738.
> *The Vanity of Human Wishes: The Tenth Satire of Juvenal Imitated.* 1749.

Play

> *Irene* (produced 1749). 1749; as *Mohamet and Irene* (produced 1749).

Fiction

> *The Prince of Abyssinia: A Tale.* 1759; revised edition, 1759; as *The History of Rasselas, Prince of Abyssinia: An Asian Tale,* 1768; edited by Geoffrey Tillotson and Brian Jenkins, 1971.

Other

> *A Complete Vindication of the Licensers of the Stage.* 1739.
> *The Life of Admiral Blake.* 1740.
> *An Account of the Life of Mr. Richard Savage, Son of the Earl Rivers.* 1744; edited by Clarence Tracy, 1971.
> *An Account of the Life of John Philip Barretier.* 1744.
> *Miscellaneous Observations on the Tragedy of Macbeth.* 1745.
> *The Plan of a Dictionary of the English Language, Addressed to the Earl of Chesterfield.* 1747.
> *The Rambler.* 8 vols., 1750–52; edited by A. B. Strauss and Walter Jackson Bate, in *Works,* 1969.
> *The Adventurer,* with others. 2 vols., 1753–54; in *Works,* 1963.
> *A Dictionary of the English Language.* 2 vols., 1755; revised edition, 1773.
> *The Idler.* 2 vols., 1761; edited by Walter Jackson Bate and J. M. Bullitt, in *Works,* 1963.
> *Preface to His Edition of Shakespeare's Plays.* 1765.

The False Alarm. 1770.

Thoughts on the Late Transactions Respecting Falkland's Islands. 1771.

The Patriot, Addressed to the Electors of Great Britain. 1774.

Taxation No Tyranny: An Answer to the Resolutions and Address of the American Congress. 1775.

A Journey to the Western Islands of Scotland. 1775; edited by D. L. Murray, 1931.

Prefaces, Biographical and Critical, to the Works of the English Poets. 10 vols., 1779–81; as *The Lives of the English Poets,* 1781; revised edition, 1783; edited by G. B. Hill, 3 vols., 1905; selection edited by J. P. Hardy, 1972.

Prayers and Meditations, edited by George Strahan. 1785; revised edition, 1785, 1796; edited by D. and M. Hyde, in *Works,* 1958.

Debates in Parliament, edited by George Chalmers. 2 vols., 1787.

Letters to and from Johnson, by Hester Lynch Piozzo. 2 vols., 1788.

The Celebrated Letter to the Earl of Chesterfield, edited by James Boswell. 1790.

An Account of the Life of Johnson to His Eleventh Year, Written by Himself, edited by Richard Wright. 1805.

A Diary of a Journey into North Wales in the Year 1774, edited by R. Duppa. 1816; in *Works,* 1958.

Johnson: His Life in Letters, edited by David Littlejohn. 1965.

Literary Criticism, edited by R. D. Stock. 1974.

Editor, *The Works of Richard Savage, with an Account of the Author.* 1775.

Editor, *The Plays of Shakespeare.* 8 vols., 1765.

Translator, *A Voyage to Abyssinia,* by Father Jerome Lobo. 1735.

Translator, *A Commentary on Pope's Principles of Morality; or, An Essay on Man,* by Crousaz. 1739.

Bibliography: *A Bibliography of Johnson* by W. P. Courtney and D. N. Smith, 1915; *Johnsonian Studies 1887–1950: A Survey and Bibliography* by James L. Clifford, 1951, supplement by M. Wahba, in *Johnsonian Studies 1950–60,* 1962.

Reading List: *Life of Johnson* by James Boswell, 1791, edited by R. W. Chapman, 1953; *Passionate Intelligence: Imagination and Reason in the Work of Johnson* by Arieh Sachs, 1967; *Johnson as Critic,* 1973, and *Johnson* (biography), 1974, both by John Wain; *The Ascent of Parnassus* by Arthur Bryant, 1975; *Johnson and Poetic Style* by William Edinger, 1977; *The Stylistic Life of Johnson* by William Vesterman, 1977; *Johnson* by Walter Jackson Bate, 1978.

*   *   *

Johnson was regarded in his own time as the dominant figure of the English literary world; his achievement covers an extraordinary range: he was scholar and critic, moralist and essayist, poet and prose stylist, all in the first degree of merit.

With his verse-tragedy *Irene* in his pocket, and David Garrick as travelling companion, Johnson walked from Lichfield to London in 1737. *Irene* was not published and produced until 1749, and was no great success, but Johnson's heroic couplet satire *London,* based on Juvenal's third satire, appeared in 1738, on the same day as Pope's *Epilogue to the Satires. London* criticises the values of the city in general, and of Whig London in particular; here Johnson wears Pope's mantle of the conservative (and Tory) satirist. Johnson's first London years were spent partly in the company of such Grub Street inhabitants as Richard Savage; the *Account of the Life of Richard Savage* is a product of this friendship, and is an important early essay by Johnson in the art of biography.

Johnson turned again to verse satire in *The Vanity of Human Wishes* based on Juvenal's tenth satire. This poem, Johnson's greatest, states a favourite theme: the inevitable unhappiness of human existence whatever choice in life is made. In turn Johnson considers mankind's yearnings for the various gifts of power, learning, military fame, long life, beauty, even virtue, and gives a melancholy account, with individual examples, of the misfortunes attendant upon each. This is not, however, mere pessimism. Johnson's Christian modification of Juvenal's stoic "mens sana in corpore sano" finds in religious faith a hard-fought-for consolation: "Still raise for good the supplicating voice,/But leave to heav'n the measure and the choice."

The theme of *Rasselas*, a moral tale set in Abyssinia and Egypt which has some similarities with Voltaire's *Candide*, is again the choice of life. Johnson's princely young hero escapes, with his sister and the poet Imlac, from the secluded innocence of the Happy Valley, and makes trial of various schemes of life. One after another the delusions and inconveniences of the pastoral life and the hermit's life, the life of the stoic and the life "according to nature," the family life and the scholar's life, are exposed. Life is found to be "every where a state in which much is to be endured, and little to be enjoyed"; the moral enforced is that no choice can be happy, but a choice must be made. Johnson may perhaps be seen returning to this theme with greater hope in his moving brief elegy "On the Death of Dr. Robert Levet" (1783), whose central message is that man finds fulfilment in the steady daily application of his particular talent: "The modest wants of ev'ry day/The toil of ev'ry day supplied."

It was with the 208 issues of *The Rambler* (1750–52), periodical essays on the pattern established earlier in the century by *The Spectator* and *The Tatler*, though more serious in tone and content, that Johnson became a major literary figure in contemporary estimation. In *The Rambler*, explicitly, it was Johnson's intention "to inculcate wisdom or piety," to teach both a reasonable and a religious attitude to life, dealing with topics as fundamental to human experience as youth and old age, marriage and death, grief and sorrow. In a small number of the *Rambler* essays Johnson is a literary critic, considering notably the topics of the novel (issue 4), biography (60), prejudice and the rules in criticism (93, 156, 158), and tragedy and comedy (125). Johnson's essays in *The Adventurer* and *The Idler* are in a rather lighter vein.

In the periodical essays and *Rasselas* may already be found the characteristic Johnsonian prose style, legislative and authoritative, often imitated, though far more flexible and exact than facile imitation would suggest. Careful judgements of life are crystallised in a precisely chosen diction, and ideas are given their relations by the balanced rhythms of clause echoing clause within the sentence. To this Johnson's weighty and pointed heroic couplets in *The Vanity of Human Wishes* and *London* are a poetic equivalent.

The reputation begun by *The Rambler* was established, in a different field, by the *Dictionary*, a triumph of individual scholarship and labour. Johnson as a lexicographer is distinguished by his accurate definitions of the meanings of words, and by his use of the historical principle. Words are illustrated by passages chosen not only for their semantic aptness, but also for their literary and moral qualities. The choice of passages reveals the enormous range of Johnson's reading, and, strikingly, his admiration for and knowledge of Elizabethan literature. The *Dictionary* is more descriptive than prescriptive; though he acknowledged that "there is in constancy and stability a general and lasting advantage," Johnson was too realistic to believe (with Swift, for example), that it is possible to fix and enforce linguistic usage.

Johnson's next major project was his edition of Shakespeare, remarkable for a commentary which shows Johnson's response to have been not only informed but also sometimes intensely personal, and for the theoretically and historically important preface. In the preface Johnson judges Shakespeare in a partly conservative light, approving of his "just representations of general nature" (a neo-classical position Johnson had already enunciated in the tenth chapter of *Rasselas*), and disapproving his failure to provide a consistent and complete moral vision. Johnson shows a robust open-mindedness in defending Shakespeare against accusations that he mixes dramatic kinds and fails to observe the unities. Shakespeare's plays "are not in the rigorous and critical sense either tragedies or comedies" because they depict the mingled conditions of real life. The unities of time and place need not be observed because "the spectators are always in their senses and know ... that the stage is only a stage, and that the players are only players." Johnson rejects arbitrary prescription, steadily insisting that the primary aim of literature is a moral one, to be secured through delighting the reader: "there is always an appeal open from criticism to nature. The end of writing is to instruct; the end of poetry is to instruct by pleasing."

Johnson's literary output decreased in the late 1760's and 1770's. This is the period of gladiatorial conversation and literary dictatorship portrayed by James Boswell, whom Johnson had met in 1763. Johnson's main arena was the Club, founded at Joshua Reynolds's suggestion in 1764 and including, at its inception or in later years, many of the most eminent literary men of the time, among them Goldsmith and Garrick, Boswell and Burke, Edward Gibbon and Adam Smith.

To these years belong Johnson's most significant political writings, eloquent expressions of a personally consistent and conscientious conservatism. In *The False Alarm* Johnson defends Parliament's refusal to seat the radical John Wilkes. In *Taxation No Tyranny* he asserts the right of the British government to impose taxes upon the American colonists.

The *Journey to the Western Islands of Scotland* is a record of the tour, dangerous and adventurous for so old a man, that Johnson undertook with Boswell in 1773. If Johnson's account lacks the anecdotal vividness of Boswell's, there is here nonetheless the accustomed Johnsonian nobility of general moral reflection, in a social and physical landscape new to his experience.

Perhaps Johnson's greatest literary achievement came towards the end of his life, when he was commissioned by a group of London booksellers to provide a set of introductory essays for a collection of the works of the English poets. Each of the *Lives* consists of a detailed biography and brief character sketch, and a critical account of the poet. These critical passages are the fruition of a lifetime's reading and hard thought, providing a judicial assessment of the English poetic tradition against the twin standards of delight and truth to nature. Not surprisingly, Johnson's "great tradition" (though he has a wide range of interest and liking) is the line of satirical and ethical heroic couplet verse originating with Denham and Waller and perfected by Dryden and Pope, clear in expression and moral in intent. His aversion is poetry, whether by John Donne or Thomas Gray, which in his opinion fails to promote truth or express its meanings perspicuously. Though Johnson admired Milton's verse, and especially *Paradise Lost*, even so great a poem as *Lycidas* is attacked for what Johnson considered its harsh and unpleasing diction and metre, and its submergence of true feeling in an artificial pastoral allegory. Though the modern critical consensus does not accept all of Johnson's valuations, his criticism has the crucial virtues of exact and generally sympathetic understanding of what he reads, and the constant application of a systematic literary judgement. Johnson may seem to us sometimes too unwilling to compromise with historical relativism, or apparently insensitive to such of our favourite literary values as irony, ambiguity, imagination, and metaphor; yet his criticism is the work of a great and superbly stocked mind, always identifying the major questions, and the modern who takes issue with him needs to be armed with reasons.

—Marcus Walsh

JONES, David (Michael). English. Born in Brockley, Kent, 1 November 1895. Educated at Camberwell School of Art, London, 1910–14; Westminster School of Art, London, 1919–21. Served with the Royal Welch Fusiliers, 1915–18. Worked with Eric Gill in Wales, 1924–27. Engraver, book illustrator, painter and water colourist: exhibitions – National

Gallery, London, 1940, 1941, 1942; Paris, 1945; Brooklyn, New York, 1952–53; one-man
shows – Edinburgh and the Tate Gallery, London 1954–55; National Book League, London,
1972. Works in the collections of the Tate Gallery; Victoria and Albert Museum, London;
National Museum of Wales, Cardiff; Sydney Art Gallery; Toronto Art Gallery; Arts Council
of Great Britain, London; British Council, London. Recipient: Hawthornden Prize, 1938;
Russell Loines Award, 1954; Welsh Arts Council Award, 1960, 1969; Royal National
Eisteddfod of Wales Gold Medal for Fine Arts, 1964; Corporation of London Midsummer
Prize, 1968. D.Litt.: University of Wales, 1960. Honorary Member, Royal Society of Painters
in Water Colours; Fellow, Royal Society of Literature. C.B.E. (Commander, Order of the
British Empire), 1955; Companion of Honour, 1974. *Died 28 October 1974.*

PUBLICATIONS

Verse

> *The Anathemata: Fragments of an Attempted Writing.*   1952.
> *The Fatigue.*   1965.
> *The Tribune's Visitation.*   1969.
> *The Sleeping Lord and Other Fragments.*   1974.
> *The Kensington Mass*, edited by René Hague.   1975.

Other

> *In Parenthesis: Seinnyessit e Gledyf ym Penn Mameu.*   1937.
> *David Jones* (paintings).   1949.
> *Epoch and Artist: Selected Writings*, edited by Harman Grisewood.   1959.
> *An Introduction to The Rime of the Ancient Mariner.*   1972.
> *Use and Sign.*   1975.
> *Letters to Vernon Watkins*, edited by Ruth Pryor.   1976.
> *The Dying Gaul and Other Writings*, edited by Harman Grisewood.   1978.

Bibliography: *Jones: An Annotated Bibliography and Guide to Research* by Samuel Rees,
1977.

Reading List; *Jones: Artist and Writer* by David Blamires, 1971; *Jones: An Exploratory Study
of the Writings* by Jeremy Hooker, 1975; *Jones,* 1975, and *A Commentary on The Anathemata
of Jones,* 1977, both by René Hague.

*   *   *

Before David Jones achieved any literary recognition he was already well-known as a
watercolourist and engraver. Indeed, throughout his life he continued to draw and paint,
making some of his finest and most complex pictures in the latter part of his life. He also
fused poetry and painting in highly idiosyncratic calligraphic inscriptions, reproductions of
which adorn some of his books.

David Jones was not a typical man of letters. His reading of contemporary English
literature included Hopkins and Eliot, but little beyond that. His knowledge of the past
centred on such figures as Chaucer, Langland, Malory, Shakespeare, Milton, Coleridge,
Browning, and Quiller-Couch's *Oxford Book of English Verse*, together with whatever he

could find translated of the ancient literature of Wales. Legend, tradition, myth, and romance were of more consequence to him than realism or romanticism. His range of non-literary interests was formidable and fed directly, but with a proper metamorphosis, into his own writing. He was passionately concerned to expound the fundamental nature of man as an artist or maker (to use a favourite word of his), whether in the earliest shapes of palaeolithic art or in the abstract art of his own time, and this was inextricably linked with his understanding of man as a religious animal. He had been brought up in the Church of England by an evangelically minded Welsh father and an English mother from London, but his way of looking at the world led him in 1921 to become a Roman Catholic. Belonging to the Catholic circles in which Eric Gill moved, he met many of the radical Catholics of the day. He was deeply influenced by Thomism and the philosophy of Maritain, and his acquaintance with the theology of Maurice de la Taille, regarded with great suspicion in the 1920's, proved to be seminal in the writing of *The Anathemata*.

David Jones's first book, *In Parenthesis*, is certainly one of the most enduring works to have emerged from the First World War. Begun as late as 1927 or 1928 and not published until 1937, it is an extraordinary distillation, part prose, part poetry, of Jones's indelible experiences as a private soldier in the trenches. It is not autobiography, but rather a transmutation of typical and individual experiences centred on a man, John Ball, who belongs to a mixed company of Londoners and Welshmen. From the initial parade-ground muddles and embarkation for France the narrative moves gradually into episodes of trench life realized in acute sensory detail and with variation of mood from wry humour to stark pathos, culminating in the summer battle of the Somme. While obviously a "war book" in terms of its primary subject-matter, *In Parenthesis* relates this searing action to the continuities of Welsh and English tradition, so that telling phrases from, for example, the old Welsh elegiac poem *The Gododdin* and Malory illuminate the present day. Despite its daunting range of literary and Biblical allusion *In Parenthesis* never loses touch with concrete actuality.

The Anathemata is like no other work, though it shares the modernist, allusive poetic techniques of Joyce, Eliot, and Pound, deepened and extended from *In Parenthesis*. It was considered by David Jones as his most important work. Based on the narrative structure of the Tridentine mass, it is also a celebration of the history and essence of Britain from the earliest geological times to the pre-industrial period. The first four sections constitute an exploration, through the recurring metaphor of the voyage, of man in pre-history and history from the roots of Western culture in the ancient Near East, through Greece, Troy, and Rome to early Celtic Britain and the Anglo-Saxon settlement. The last four sections focus respectively on London as the image of the city, presided over by woman in all her guises; the tree as the keel of a ship, as mast and military engine, and as the Christian Cross; birth and incarnation; death, sacrifice and salvation. Such a bald summary does no justice to the rich mosaic of the poem, its constant references back and forwards, its emotional and spiritual reverberations. Everywhere the poet strives to bring together and interpret

> The adaptations, the fusions
> the transmogrifications
>   but always
>   the inward continuities
>   of the site
>   of place.

The Anathemata was sub-titled "fragments of an attempted writing," and *The Sleeping Lord* presents further fragments of this writing. They are more sharply focussed on the military levelling situation of the Roman Empire at the time of Christ, depicted with telling irony, with accompanying and contrasting pictures of Celtic culture from that period and somewhat later. The separate pieces have a strong political dimension which is the more universal in application as the empires of today are never explicitly brought on to the scene.

The splits in allegiance between "everything presuming difference/and all the sweet remembered demarcations" on the one hand and "the fact of empire" on the other are nowhere mere movingly expressed than in *The Tribune's Visitation*.

Although David Jones did not publish much in his lifetime, he was a prolific writer and wrote acutely and feelingly on the relationship of art and religion, the meaning of tradition, and the importance of Welsh culture for Britain. *Epoch and Artist*, a collection of broadcast talks, book reviews, essays, and letters, and a fascinating *Introduction to The Rime of the Ancient Mariner* were published in his later years. *The Dying Gaul*, a similar collection to *Epoch and Artist*, was published posthumously. So also was a brief poetic fragment, *The Kensington Mass*. It is now becoming clear that David Jones was a prolific letter-writer, and individual letters and complete sets of correspondence, shedding light on his working methods, his tireless mind, and his lovable, humble personality, have already appeared.

—David Blamires

JONES, Ebenezer.   English.   Born in Islington, London, 20 January 1820. Educated at a school in London. Married Caroline Atherstone in 1844. Worked as a clerk in the City of London in a firm connected with the tea-trade; subsequently an accountant; worked for the radical publishers Cleave and Hetherington. *Died 14 September 1860.*

PUBLICATIONS

Verse

   Studies of Sensation and Event.   1843; edited by R. H. Shepherd, 1879.

Other

   The Land Monopoly.   1849.

Reading List: *Jones, The Neglected Poet* by T. Mardy Rees, 1909; "Social Protest in Minor Poets of the Nineteenth Century" by W. G. Bebbington, in *Ariel English*, 1975.

*   *   *

"Who wrote the *Revolt of Islam*? Not Shelley! 'Tis the mighty utterance of a society whose eyes have just been opened to the glory of truth, and she made him her priest. He was but the lute; she was the God." These ecstatic words were written by Ebenezer Jones in a letter to his friend M. Considerat, and they tell us all we need to know about the source of his own poetry. Yet it is not Shelley the epic poet whom Jones follows so much as the Shelley of the *Mask of Anarchy* and of the revolutionary songs. At the end of his great *Defence of Poetry*,

Shelley spoke of poets as being trumpets who call to battle, and it is clear that Jones wished his poems to be instruments of war.

Studies of Sensation and Event was published in 1843, and is perhaps the best known of all volumes of Chartist poetry. Jones was a working-class radical, and his poems preach violence as the answer to social ills. They are literally calls to action. For example, "A Coming Cry" is feigned to be spoken by the collective voice of working-class people, and it includes the following lines:

> Will we, at earth's lords' bidding, build ourselves dishonour'd graves?
> Will we, who've made this England, endure to be its slaves?
> Thrones totter before the answer!

Even before the *Communist Manifesto* of 1848, Jones is insisting that labour is wealth, that the workers have made England, and that the future is theirs.

Jones's volume is Shelley-inspired, however, not merely because the poems are insistently those of a radical republican, but because Jones takes for granted the fact that the true poet is a prophet and is of the people. It is the *people* whom the poet sings to battle. In an untitled poem, Jones speaks of the duty of the poet, of his responsibility to confront social ills and to make others recognise them through the power and truth-telling of his art.

> Yea, at his glance, sin's palaces may fall,
> Men rise, and all their demon Gods disown;
> For knowledge of hidden resemblances is all
> Needed to link mankind in happiness round Love's throne.

Studies of Sensation and Event is therefore very much a work of those years immediately prior to 1848. Jones's verse has a crude vigour, and comes from genuine revolutionary ardour. It is propagandist verse, but it has an energy that is lacking from such middle-class imitations as Elizabeth Barrett's "Cry of the Children." As such it will always hold a small but honourable place in the history of working-class literature.

—John Lucas

JONSON, Ben(jamin).   English.   Born in Westminster, London, probably 11 June 1572. Educated at Westminster School, London, under William Camden. Fought for the Dutch against the Spanish in the Low Countries. Married Anne Lewis c. 1593; had several children. Actor, then playwright, from 1595; acted for Philip Henslowe, 1597; killed a fellow actor in a duel, 1598, but escaped the gallows by pleading benefit of clergy; enjoyed the patronage of Lord Albany and Aurelian Townshend; appointed Poet Laureate, and given royal pension, 1616, and wrote and presented masques at court, 1616–25; gained a reputation as the "literary dictator" of London and in later life attracted a circle of young writers who styled themselves the "Sons of Ben"; visited Scotland, and William Drummond of Hawthornden, 1618–19: elected a Burgess of Edinburgh, 1619; appointed City Chronologer of London, 1628. M.A.: Oxford University, 1619. *Died 6 August 1637.*

PUBLICATIONS

Collections

Works, edited by C. H. Herford and P. and E. M. Simpson.   11 vols., 1925–52.
Complete Masques, edited by S.Orgel.   1969.
Complete Poems, edited by Ian Donaldson.   1975.

Plays

The Case Is Altered (produced 1597–98?).   1609.
Every Man in His Humour (produced 1598).   1601; edited by G. B. Jackson, 1969.
Every Man Out of His Humour (produced 1599).   1600.
The Fountain of Self-Love; or, Cynthia's Revels (produced 1600).   1601.
Poetaster; or, The Arraignment (produced 1601).   1602.
Sejanus His Fall (produced 1603).   1605; edited by W. Bolton, 1966.
Entertainment of the Queen and Prince at Althorp (produced 1603).   1604.
King James His Royal and Magnificent Entertainment, with Dekker (produced
    1604).   With *Entertainment of the Queen and Prince at Althorp*, 1604.
A Private Entertainment of the King and Queen at Highgate (produced 1604).   In
    Works, 1616.
Eastward Ho, with Chapman and Marston (produced 1605).   1605; edited by C. G.
    Petter, 1973.
Volpone; or, The Fox (produced 1605).   1607; edited by J. Creaser, 1978.
The Masque of Blackness (produced 1605).   In *The Characters of Two Royal Masques*,
    1608.
Hymenaei (produced 1606).   1606.
The Entertainment of the Two Kings of Great Britain and Denmark at Theobalds
    (produced 1606).   In *Works*, 1616.
An Entertainment of King James and Queen Anne at Theobalds (produced 1607).   In
    Works, 1616.
The Masque of Beauty (produced 1608).   In *The Characters of Two Royal Masques*,
    1608.
The Hue and Cry after Cupid (produced 1608).   In *Works*, 1616.
*The Description of the Masque Celebrating the Marriage of John, Lord Ramsey Viscount
    Haddington* (produced 1608).   In *Works*, 1616.
The Masque of Queens (produced 1609).   1609.
Epicoene; or, The Silent Woman (produced 1609).   In *Works*, 1616; edited by L. A.
    Beaurline, 1966.
The Speeches at Prince Henry's Barriers (produced 1610).   In *Works*, 1616.
The Alchemist (produced 1610).   1612; edited by Alvin B. Kernan, 1974.
Oberon, The Faery Prince (produced 1611).   In *Works*, 1616.
Love Freed from Ignorance and Folly (produced 1611).   In *Works*, 1616.
Catiline His Conspiracy (produced 1611).   1611; edited by W. Bolton and J. F.
    Gardner, 1972.
Love Restored (produced 1612).   In *Works*, 1616.
The Irish Masque (produced 1613).   In *Works*, 1616.
A Challenge at Tilt (produced 1614).   In *Works*, 1616
Bartholomew Fair (produced 1614).   1631; edited by Er ward B. Partridge, 1964.
The Golden Age Restored (produced 1616).   In *Works*, 1616.
Mercury Vindicated from the Alchemists (produced 1616).   In *Works*, 1616.
The Devil Is an Ass (produced 1616).   1631; edited by M. Hussey, 1967.

Christmas His Masque (produced 1616). In *Works,* 1640.

The Vision of Delight (produced 1617). In *Works,* 1640.

Lovers Made Men (produced 1617). 1617.

Pleasure Reconciled to Virtue (produced 1618). In *Works,* 1640; revised version, as *For the Honour of Wales* (produced 1618), in *Works,* 1640.

News from the New World Discovered in the Moon (produced 1620). In *Works,* 1640.

An Entertainment at the Blackfriars (produced 1620). In *The Monthly Magazine; or, British Register,* 1816.

Pan's Anniversary; or, The Shepherd's Holiday (produced 1620). In *Works,* 1640.

The Gypsies Metamorphosed (produced 1621). In *Works,* 1640; edited by W. W. Greg, 1952.

The Masque of Augurs (produced 1622). 1622.

Time Vindicated to Himself and to His Honours (produced 1623). 1623.

Neptune's Triumph for the Return of Albion. 1624; revised version, as *The Fortunate Isles and Their Union* (produced 1625), 1625.

The Masque of Owls (produced 1624). In *Works,* 1640.

The Staple of News (produced 1625). 1631; edited by Devra Rowland Kifer, 1976.

The New Inn; or, The Light Heart (produced 1629). 1631.

Love's Triumph Through Callipolis (produced 1631). 1631.

Chloridia (produced 1631). 1631.

The Magnetic Lady; or, Humours Reconciled (produced 1632). In *Works,* 1640.

A Tale of a Tub (produced 1633). In *Works,* 1640.

The King's Entertainment at Welbeck (produced 1633). In *Works,* 1640.

Love's Welcome at Bolsover (produced 1634). In *Works,* 1640.

The Sad Shepherd; or, A Tale of Robin Hood (incomplete), in *Works.* 1640; edited and completed by Alan Porter, 1944.

Other

Works (plays and verse). 1616; revised edition, 2 vols., 1640.

Timber; or, Discoveries Made upon Men and Matter, in *Works.* 1640; edited by R. S. Walker, 1953.

The English Grammar, in *Works.* 1640; edited by S. Gibson, 1928.

Leges Convivales. 1692.

Literary Criticism, edited by J. D. Redwine. 1970.

Translator, *Horace His Art of Poetry,* in *Works.* 1640; edited by E. H. Blakeney, 1928.

Bibliography: *Jonson: A Concise Bibliography* by S. A. Tannenbaum, 1938; supplement 1947; supplement in *Elizabethan Bibliographies Supplements 3* by G. R. Guffey, 1968.

Reading List: *Jonson, Poet* by George B. Johnston, 1945; *Jonson of Westminster* (biography) by Marchette Chute, 1953; *The Accidence of Jonson's Plays, Masques, and Entertainments* by Astley C. Partridge, 1953; *Jonson and the Comic Truth* by John J. Enck, 1957; *The Broken Compass: A Study of the Major Comedies of Jonson* by Edward B. Partridge, 1958; *Jonson and the Language of Prose Comedy* by Jonas A. Barish, 1960; *Jonson's Plays: An Introduction* by Robert E. Knoll, 1965; *Jonson's Dotages: A Reconsideration of the Late Plays* by L. S. Champion, 1967; *Vision and Judgment in Jonson's Drama* by Gabriele B. Jackson, 1968; *The Aristophanic Comedies of Jonson* by Coburn Gum, 1969; *Jonson* by John B. Bamborough, 1970; *Jonson's Moral Comedy* by A. C. Dessen, 1971; *Jonson, Public Poet and Private Man* by George Parfitt, 1976.

*   *   *

The opening lines of T. S. Eliot's famous essay on Ben Jonson are now nearly sixty years old, yet they are almost as applicable today as when they were first written: "The reputation of Jonson," Eliot wrote, "has been of the most deadly kind that can be compelled upon the memory of a great poet. To be universally accepted; to be damned by the praise that quenches all desire to read the book; to be afflicted by the imputation of the virtues which excite the least pleasure; and to be read only by historians and antiquaries – this is the most perfect conspiracy of approval." Substitute "academics and students" for "antiquaries" and you have a fair summary of Jonson's current reputation. That this state of affairs is partly of Jonson's own making is certainly true but hardly sufficient justification. In his own day Jonson saw himself as the self-appointed arbiter of true critical taste, the upholder of classical standards of decorum, construction, and moral didacticism against the undiscriminating popular appetite for sensation and extravagant spectacle, and the champion of high erudition against barbarous ignorance. So successful was he in imposing this version of himself on his own age and those that followed that it was not long before the contrast was drawn by which Jonson's reputation is still largely defined – the contrast between the warm spontaneous, generous-hearted inclusiveness of the "romantic" Shakespeare and the chilly learning and cold perfection of the "classical" Jonson. Like all such sweeping contrasts, this one has enough plausibility to survive as the received truth, though it is as misleading about Shakespeare as it is about Jonson.

By way of building up a fairer picture of the nature of Jonson's achievement we may begin by recalling one of Drummond's remarks about him: "He hath consumed a whole night in lying looking to his great toe, about which he hath seen Tartars and Turks, Romans and Cartheginians, fight in his imagination." Such a detail serves to draw attention to an element in Jonson's work which meets us at every turn and which is at least as important as his undoubted learning and his emphasis on classical precept and precedent. It is a facet of his imagination at once childlike, romantic, and grotesque, and one which clearly contributed to some of his finest comic creations as well as to his tenderest lyrics and his most savage satirical epigrams.

The exuberance of Jonson's imagination is already apparent in his first great stage success, *Every Man in His Humour* first performed in 1598 by the Lord Chamberlain's Men, the most famous theatrical company of the time. (The tradition that Shakespeare himself arranged for his company to present the play is attractive, though it cannot be traced beyond the eighteenth century.) In terms of plot and setting there is nothing to distinguish Jonson's play from many others deriving from classical Roman Comedy, with its conflict of generations and the convoluted manoeuvrings of wily servants. Jonson's distinctive contribution appears in his conception of the "humorous man," a dramatic character whose personality is shaped by some leading trait (or "humour") in his temperament which was itself, according to prevailing medical notions, based on the predominance of one of the four bodily fluids, blood, choler, melancholy, and phlegm. Jonson's contemporary George Chapman had been the first to put "humorous" characters on the stage (in *A Humorous Day's Mirth* performed a year before Jonson's comedy), but the vigour and extravagance of Jonson's presentation set it apart. The sharp distinction he draws between true "humour" as an element of character and mere affectation is typical of the energy and inventiveness of Jonson's imagination:

> As when some one peculiar quality
> Doth so possess a man, that it doth draw
> All his affects, his spirits, and his powers,
> In their confluctions, all to run one way,
> This may truly said to be a Humour.
> But that a rook, in wearing a pied feather,
> The cable hat-band, or the three-piled ruff,
> A yard of shoe-tie, or the Switzer's knot
> On his French garters, should affect a Humour!
> Oh, 'tis more than most ridiculous.

Like most sequels, Jonson's attempt to capitalize on the success of his play with *Every Man Out of His Humour* was a comprehensive failure and appears to have led to the Chamberlain's Men dispensing with his services. The Children of the Queen's Chapel, one of the companies of boy actors which sprouted up towards the end of the century, were his new theatrical patrons and for them he wrote the satiric comedies which involved him in the "war of the theatres" with his contemporaries John Marston and Thomas Dekker. In spite of occasional passages of great satirical energy and some beautiful lyrics such as "Queen and huntress, chaste and fair," Jonson's contributions to this "war" are not by any means among his best plays. *Cynthia's Revels* deserves to be remembered for its portrait of Jonson himself as Crites, the impartial and well-informed judge of society and the arts; and in *The Poetaster* Jonson as Horace feeds Marston (Crispianus) an emetic that makes the latter spew great quantities of words in his typically turgid style. But Jonson's greatest achievements in drama were yet to come.

This achievement is certainly not to be found in Jonson's two classical tragedies *Sejanus His Fall* and *Catiline His Conspiracy*; though the latter especially has some magnificent speeches as well as dramatic moments of great intensity, both suffer by comparison with Shakespeare's excursions into Roman history, especially *Julius Caesar*. Jonson's enduring reputation as a dramatist rests squarely on three great comedies, *Volpone; or The Fox*, *The Alchemist*, and *Bartholomew Fair*. Each of them exemplifies Jonson's enormous capacity to dramatize the grotesque aberrations of human appetite, his zest for the variety of life, and his unfailing delight in the villain as artist. *Volpone* is scrupulously classical in its didactic import, yet what delights us is chiefly the artistry of Volpone and his henchman Mosca. *The Alchemist* is a model of the observance of the Aristotelian unities, but its dramatic appeal lies in the breakneck momentum of its plot and the almost unbearable comic tension created by it. And in *Bartholomew Fair* Jonson abandoned even the pretence of being the classical moralist in favour of the unbuttoned enjoyment of Jacobean London in all its colour and richness.

The opening years of the seventeenth century witnessed Jonson's finest dramatic productions, not only for the public stage, but in the sphere of royal entertainment, when Jonson's collaboration with the scene designer and architect Inigo Jones led to a splendid flowering of that most ephemeral of theatrical forms, the court masque. Rooted as it was in time, place, and occasion, the masque can give us little sense of its splendour through the text alone, though Jonson's scripts for such works as *Pleasure Reconciled to Virtue* and *The Gypsies Metamorphosed* are eloquent enough in the reading. It was precisely the disagreement between Jonson and Jones as to the relative importance of words versus spectacle in masque which led to the dissolution of this brilliant partnership in 1631.

Jonson's last years present a sad picture of commercial failure, declining creative powers, and increasing bodily decrepitude. Apart from the comedies already mentioned, *The Silent Woman*, *The Devil Is an Ass*, and *The Staple of News* deserve to be remembered for their occasional inventiveness and keen-eyed observation of London life and manners. But if Jonson's principal claim to fame lies in his three great comedies, his achievements as lyric and epigrammatic poet are not inconsiderable. Contemporary practitioners of verse esteemed him so highly that a group of them, which included Herrick, Suckling, and Carew styled themselves the Sons of Ben and produced a commemorative volume *Jonsonus Virbius* after his death in 1637. As a critic, too, Jonson was of the first rank, forthright, well-informed, and catholic in taste by the standards of the time. All these qualities are well illustrated in the splendid commendatory verses which he contributed to the Folio edition of Shakespeare's works published in 1623.

That Jonson was a classicist and an erudite one need not be disputed, though he was by no means the most learned classical scholar of his day (his mentor Camden and his contemporary John Selden were far better versed in the classics). But the emphasis should finally fall on the originality of his imagination, his roots in the popular idiom he affected to despise, and his enormous sense of theatre which is illustrated by the continued success on the stage of his great comedies.

—Gāmini Salgādo

545

KAVANAGH, Patrick. Irish. Born in Inniskeen, 21 October 1904. Educated at Kednaminsha National School, 1910–16. Married Katherine Moloney in 1967. Farmer and shoemaker, Inniskeen, 1920–36; lived in London and Dublin, 1936–42; Columnist ("City Commentary"), *Irish Press*, Dublin, 1942–44; Film Critic and Feature Writer, *The Standard*, Dublin, 1943–49; Editor, *Kavanagh's Weekly*, Dublin, 1952; Contributor, *Nimbus* magazine, London, 1954, *The Farmer's Journal*, Dublin, 1958–63, and *RTV-Guide*, Dublin, 1963–67; Extra-Mural Lecturer, University College, Dublin, 1956–59. Recipient: A E Memorial Award, 1940; Arts Council of Great Britain Award, 1967. *Died 30 November 1967.*

PUBLICATIONS

Collections

Complete Poems, edited by Peter Kavanagh. 1972.

Verse

Ploughman and Other Poems. 1936.
The Great Hunger. 1942.
A Soul for Sale. 1947.
Recent Poems. 1958.
Come Dance with Kitty Stobling and Other Poems. 1960.
Collected Poems. 1964.

Plays

Self Portrait (televised, 1962). 1964.
Tarry Flynn (produced 1966).

Television Feature: *Self Portrait,* 1962.

Fiction

Tarry Flynn. 1948.
By Night Unstarred, edited by Peter Kavanagh. 1977.

Other

The Green Fool (autobiography). 1938.
Collected Pruse. 1967.
Lapped Furrows: Correspondence, 1933–1967, Between Patrick and Peter Kavanagh, With Other Documents, edited by Peter Kavanagh. 1969.
November Haggard: Uncollected Prose and Verse, edited by Peter Kavanagh. 1971.
A Kavanagh Anthology, edited by Eugene Platt. 1973.

546

Bibliography: *Garden of the Golden Apples: A Bibliography of Kavanagh* by Peter Kavanagh, 1972.

Reading List: *Clay Is the Word: Kavanagh 1904–1967* by Alan Warner, 1973.

*   *   *

The early poems of Patrick Kavanagh arise like prayers from the ragged fields of his native Monaghan. As he claimed in the first poem of his *Collected Poems*, he wished to find "a star-lovely art/In a dark sod," and on occasions he succeeded.

The best of the verse in *Ploughman and Other Poems* has fibre in its unashamed paganism: he addresses the blackbird, "O pagan poet you/And I are one/In this – we lose our God/At set of sun." The Irish countryman's adherence to the elder faiths underlies his Catholicism just as vestiges of Gaelic lyricism echo behind the influence of English rural singers. Kavanagh never decisively made, however, the choice he offered himself between Venus and the Virgin: the weak verse in his first volume exhibits a cloying devotionalism and piety. Yet even in an otherwise discountable poem, tiny miracles of wings open out of clay that surprise the poet, one feels, as much as the reader. The poet never lost this gift: "My hills hoard the bright shillings of March/While the sun searches in every pocket" ("Shancoduff"); "The axle-roll of a rut-locked cart/Broke the burnt stick of noon in two" ("Spraying the Potatoes").

The "thrill/Of common things raised up to angelhood" is Kavanagh's enduring theme and pursuit, and it is not surprising that the mystical innocence he sought and that relates him to poets like Vaughan and Clare should often collapse into wilful naivety or bathos. The poet's stated distinction between the virtues of parochialism and the vices of provincialism is, though, a valid one. It permitted a sense of freedom and authority ("A road, a mile of kingdom, I am king/Of banks and stones and every blooming thing"), and even of immortality ("I cannot die/Unless I walk outside these whitethorn hedges").

Walk outside them he did, which Kavanagh lyrically describes in his autobiographical works *The Green Fool* and *Tarry Flynn*. In his long and justly famous poem, *The Great Hunger*, Kavanagh turned upon the Irish rural life he had left: not its physical beauty, but its sexual frustration and the priestly interference with the minds and bodies as well as souls of the country people. The poet later repudiated his most ambitious and varied poem, considering it to have "some kinetic vulgarity." He was in error: his portrait of a small unmarried farmer, Patrick Maguire, "whose spirit/Is a wet sack flapping about the knees of time" is an unforgettable and powerful indictment.

One half of Kavanagh's poetic character desired lyrical repose, and he believed that the poet's authority "Is bogus if the sonorous beat is broken/By disturbances in human hearts": his goal was to be "Passive, observing with a steady eye." The other, maverick half grew increasingly combative – even litigious – and prosaic, and in later poems, such as "The Paddiad" (*Come Dance with Kitty Stobling*), he abandoned poetry like that of *The Great Hunger* which required passionate engagement, and instead tried to write satire that too often sank into invective and doggerel. The satire fails because it springs from self-pity rather than social indignation, and, if on occasions self-pity is transformed into genuine poetry, it is not satire but the lyrical balladry of "If Ever You Go to Dublin Town."

Repose was hard won. In the mid-1950's he had an operation for lung cancer, in the wake of which he lost his messianic compulsion: "My purpose in life was to have no purpose." "Canal Bank Walk," "Lines Written on a Seat on the Grand Canal" and "The Hospital" are fine sonnets, in the last of which Kavanagh described as the poet's purpose what he had in fact been attempting all along in his best lyrical poems – snatching out of time "the passionate transitory." Posterity will rescue from time at least a score of Kavanagh's poems, passionate and enduring.

—John Wilson Foster

KEATS, John. English. Born in London, 31 October 1795. Educated at Reverend John Clarke's private school, Enfield, Middlesex; after death of his parents apprenticed to Thomas Hammond, surgeon and apothecary, Edmonton, London, 1810; also studied medicine at Guy's Hospital, London, 1815–16, and qualified as an apothecary 1816. Encouraged by Leigh Hunt, abandoned medicine for poetry, 1816; made walking tour of the Lake District, and Scotland and Ireland, 1818. Consumptive: went to Italy for his health, 1820, and died in Rome. *Died 23 February 1821.*

PUBLICATIONS

Collections

Poetical Works and Other Writings, edited by H. Buxton Forman.   8 vols., 1938–39.
Poetical Works, edited by H. W. Garrod.   1939; revised edition, with J. Jones, 1959.
The Letters, edited by H. E. Rollins.   2 vols., 1958.
Complete Poems, edited by John Barnard.   1973.

Verse

Poems. 1817.
Endymion: A Poetic Romance. 1818.
Lamia, Isabella, The Eve of St. Agnes, and Other Poems. 1820.
Another Version of Keats's Hyperion, edited by R. M. Milnes.   1857.

Bibliography: *Keats: A Bibliography and Reference Guide* by J. R. MacGillivray, 1949.

Reading List: *Studies in Keats* by J. Middleton Murry, 1930, revised edition as *Keats,* 1955; *The Evolution of Keats's Poetry* by Claude Finney, 2 vols., 1936; *The Stylistic Development of Keats,* 1945, and *Keats,* 1963, both by Walter Jackson Bate; *The Mask of Keats: A Study of Problems* by Robert Gittings, 1956; *Keats: A Reassessment* edited by Kenneth Muir, 1958; *Keats and the Dramatic Principle* by Bernice Slote, 1958; *Keats: The Making of a Poet* by A. Ward, 1963; *Aesthetic and Myth in the Poetry of Keats* by W. E. Evert, 1964; *Keats* by Douglas Bush, 1966; *Keats and Embarrassment* by Christopher Ricks, 1974.

*   *   *

The first works of a young poet are more frequently expressions of the intent to be a poet than exercises of a poet's powers. They are also, almost necessarily, derivative; in John Keats's case the influence of Spenser is pervasive, not the homely, English, and moral Spenser but the cultivator of the enamelled and the musical. These early poems also exhibit, often with pitiless clarity, the modes of sensibility current at the time. The character of those of Keats's time may be inferred from a remark in a letter from Haydon to Keats about *Endymion*: "I have read your delicious poem with exquisite enjoyment." The influence of Spenser is one likely to play quite happily on poetry which is "delicious" and designed to provide "exquisite enjoyment." The poems published in 1817 are generally notable for their lack of organisation: of structure they have little more than the external verse pattern and a single generalisation or introductory remark followed by a long catalogue of more or less pertinent examples. The characteristic mood is one of romantic pain, "sweet desolation" – "balmy pain"; the characteristic pose is one of indulgent relaxation. The staple of the idiom is

548

composed of such phrases as warm desires, coy muse, quaint jubilee, curious bending, luxuries bright, milky, soft and rosey, luxurious wings, pleasant smotherings. The unexpressed premise of these poems is that poetry is a drug, a more refined form of alcohol.

Undoubtedly a part of Keats's mind, the more critical and intelligent part, was in abeyance during the composition of these poems. But not wholly so. There are moments when the indolence gives way to a more energetic, a more keenly apprehensive grasp, when the fumes of indulgence are dispersed by a fresher air. At these moments the verse shows a more biting sense of reality, a firmer rhythm, a more particularised sort of imagery, and a use of language at once more strenuous and more controlled. There are other lines enlivened by an unpretentious gaiety and simplicity in the manner of Herrick. And there is that more modest, objective, and very successful poem "On the Grasshopper and the Cricket." Keats was becoming aware that a poet could not remain content to loll a prisoner of his own senses; his sensations must be filtered through a judging mind and be informed by deliberate thought.

Mawkish was the epithet Keats himself applied to *Endymion*. It is not, however, gross in any way. It is fluent, facile, sweetly insipid. There is no leading idea, unless we call Endymion's search for pleasure one, and little is remarkable in the detail. It appears to be the result of no particular pressure and engages nothing that exists at a deeper level than the decorative. Its structure is vague, its development sketchy, its length (except that Keats took length as a test of a poet's powers) pointless.

There would be no need to qualify these remarks very radically to have them apply with equal force to "Isabella; or, The Pot of Basil." This is a poetical version of an anecdote drawn from one of Keats's favourite books, *The Anatomy of Melancholy*, itself an essentially literary and academic work, the purposes of which conform closely to the ends that Keats conceived at this time as proper to poetry. "Lamia" also derives from Burton and uses a myth with a long history stretching back in English literature to the late fourteenth or early fifteenth century *Thomas of Erceldoune*. But "Lamia" differs from "Isabella" in that it is meant to present a serious idea; it is a poem written to the formula of the "vast idea." It is still plangent and melancholy but slower and fuller in movement. The poem endeavours to represent – but as in a tableau rather than a drama – the conflict between illusory beauty and the hallucination of pleasure and the life of the intellect and moral dignity. Lycius, the normal man, is caught and destroyed between the two. But there is an excessive disproportion between the important ideas formally involved and the essentially literary idiom and manner. That discrepancy is abolished in "The Eve of St. Agnes." The poem is much less pretentious than "Lamia": no vast idea rolls before the poet's eye. He remains within the limitations of a subject which gives him without pressing or manipulation natural opportunities for realising his extraordinary perception of glow, richness, and colour in the physical world. The exigencies of the narrative, slight as they are, control his delight in luxury and give it due subordination as one element in experience. Keats successfully resists the temptation merely to indulge his "sensual vision." The figure of Madeline, delicate and uncharacterised as it is, is more than an example of what Keats called the "tendency to class women in my books with roses and sweet-meats." Throughout the poem the imagery has, even in those scenes which could easily become occasions for uncritical, relaxed indulgence, a certain quality of coolness and crispness and a scope of metaphorical reference which save it from any descent into the ludicrous or into mere sensuality.

Between "The Eve of St. Agnes" and the great Odes Keats was, it is clear, astonishingly transformed, advancing from the status of a charming minor talent to that of a genius of the first order.

The fruit of Keats's maturing mind and sensibility is the set of four poems, "Ode on Melancholy," "Ode to a Nightingale," "Ode on a Grecian Urn," and "To Autumn" written in 1819, the first three during the early months of the year. (The "Ode to Psyche" was also written in 1819, but it does not belong in the same class with the others.) These poems are different in kind from their predecessors; while the earlier ones are merely decorative, these are tragic: they are enlarged, complicated by a dimension of human experience unknown in the former. Their distance from the earlier poems may be indicated by saying that while

Spenser is the dominant influence there, here it is Shakespeare; and not Shakespeare as the supplier of external literary tricks like Shelley's Shakespeare in *The Cenci*, but a Shakespeare who is grasped, subordinated to Keats's purposes, and dissolved in Keats's own idiom. To say this is not to claim for these poems, or for all of them, a complete maturity. Leavis defined the sort of inadequacy which persists in them when he said: "It is as if Keats were making major poetry out of minor – as if, that is, the genius of a major poet were working in the material of a minor poetry." And there are, without doubt, positive weaknesses in these poems, remnants of decay, touches of nostalgic softness, and moments of regression to a less disciplined past.

The unfinished *Hyperion* brings up the name of Milton, its literary ancestor. It is easy to see why Milton should have appealed as a model to a poet of Keats's character, and one engaged like Keats in an effort, intense and sustained, "to refine his sensual vision." There was a strong Miltonic current running in the eighteenth century, especially among those minor writers who were later to be thought of as writers of "true poetry," the predecessors of Romanticism. Then, with the rejection of Augustanism, Milton came to stand for all that was lofty, epic, and severe in the English tradition. He was the solitary giant, looming and self-sufficient, and the distracted second-generation Romantics were profoundly impressed by his heroic individuality, his calm assumption of the poet's public robes, and the untroubled confidence with which he undertook his enormous theme. Above all he represented a poet in his role as moral teacher and spiritual healer. But although we can see *why* Milton should have attracted Keats, we can also see *how*, in the event, Keats's choice of Milton as an exemplar was a disastrous one, as Keats himself admitted when he abandoned his project: "Life to him would be death to me." No two poets could have been so radically different, so constitutionally unsympathetic to one another, no two poetic styles could have been so naturally antagonistic. Keats's use of language which accommodated itself so easily to the influence of Shakespeare was denuded of all its proper virtue when associated with Milton's. *Hyperion* was intended to be an extension of Keats's poetic experience, an effort in a new direction, and also a stage in his spiritual progress, an exercise in moral discipline; in fact, it turned out to be a contraction of the one and a retrogressive step in the case of the other. What was meant to be as strict and ascetic as Milton proved to be as ornamental as Spenser, as relaxed as Tennyson. What was designed to be a central commentary on human life disclosed itself as merely marginal and elegiac, not a vehicle for wisdom but a symptom of weakness.

The true line of Keats's development, lost in *Hyperion* in a waste of misdirected energy, misguided submission, and frustrated purpose, is recovered in the Odes. These are the poems of a sensibility both powerful and exquisite, on the point of attaining its majority, on the point of completing its self-education. And because of this Keats is liable momentarily to be guilty of certain imperfections. But our recognition of these will only make us wonder all the more at the triumph of the spirit, the triumph of the lacerated spirit, which these poems, written at an unpropitious time and in the most tragic conditions, represent.

—William Walsh

KEBLE, John. English. Born in Fairford, Gloucestershire, 25 April 1792. Educated at home; Corpus Christi College, Oxford, 1807–10, double first 1810. Married Charlotte Clarke in 1835. Fellow, Oriel College, Oxford, 1811 (English essay prize and Latin essay prize, 1812); College Tutor, 1818–23; initiated the Oxford Movement, 1833; Professor of Poetry, Oxford University, 1832–41; Keble College, Oxford, erected as memorial, 1870. Ordained deacon, 1815; Curate, Eastleach, Gloucestershire, 1815–23; Curate, Southrop, Gloucestershire, 1823–25, Hursley, Hampshire, 1825–27, for his father at Coln St. Aldwyn, Gloucestershire, 1827–35, and Rector of Hursley, from 1835. Examiner, East India House examinations, 1830, 1832. Co-Editor, a Library of the Fathers of the Holy Catholic Church series, from 1838. *Died 29 March 1866.*

PUBLICATIONS

Collections

The Christian Year, Lyra Innocentium and Other Poems, edited by J. C. Sharp.   1914.

Verse

The Christian Year: Thoughts in Verse for Sundays and Holydays Throughout the Year.   1827.
Lyra Apostolica, with others.   1836.
The Psalter or Psalms of David in English Verse.   1839.
Lyra Innocentium: Thoughts in Verse on Christian Children.   1846.
Miscellaneous Poems, edited by G. Moberly.   1869.

Other

On Translation from Dead Languages.   1812.
Tracts for the Times.   8 vols., 1834–41.
The Case of Catholic Subscription to the Thirty-Nine Articles.   1841.
Praelectiones Poeticae.   1844; translated by E. K. Francis, as *Lectures on Poetry,* 2 vols., 1912.
Sermons, Academical and Occasional.   1847.
A Very Few Plain Thoughts on the Proposed Addition of Dissenters to the University of Oxford.   1854.
On Eucharistical Adoration.   1868.
Sermons, Occasional and Parochial.   1868.
Village Sermons on the Baptismal Service, edited by E. B. Pusey.   1868.
Letters of Spiritual Counsel and Guidance, edited by R. F. Wilson.   1870; edited by B. W. Randolph, 1904.
Sermons for the Christian Year.   11 vols., 1875–80.
Occasional Papers and Reviews, edited by E. B. Pusey.   1877.
Studia Sacra, edited by J. P. Norris.   1877.

Editor, *Works of Richard Hooker.*   3 vols., 1836.
Editor, with John Henry Newman, *Remains of R. H. Froude.*   4 vols., 1838–39.
Editor, *A Selection from the Sermons and Poetical Remains of George James Cornish.*   1850.

Reading List: *Musings over "The Christian Year" and "Lyra Innocentium"* by Charlotte Yonge, 1871; *Keble* by William E. Daniels, 1948; *Keble's Literary and Religious Contributions to the Oxford Movement* by W. J. A. M. Beek, 1959; *Keble: A Study in*

Limitations by Georgina Battiscombe, 1963; *Keble, Priest, Professor, and Poet* by Brian W. Martin, 1976.

*   *   *

John Keble's reputation does not depend primarily on his achievement as a poet. The Oxford college that bears his name commemorates the scholarly divine whose influence shaped the revival of Anglicanism that began with the Tractarians. Keble was an older contemporary of Newman and Pusey. He might have had a brilliant career as an academic, but from filial devotion he withdrew to a country parish. He did, however, hold the Oxford Professorship of Poetry from 1832–41, and delivered a series of Latin lectures which Newman considered his greatest literary work. Dedicated to Wordsworth, though entirely concerned with Greek and Latin poets, these lectures reveal Keble as a Romantic critic. Sharing Wordsworth's belief that poetry originates in the overflow of powerful feelings, he emphasises the dominant role of the imagination in assimilating and ordering impressions. Keble made much of the analogies between religion and poetry, but clearly distinguished between the two.

The lectures, not translated into English till 1912, were addressed to a restricted, highly cultivated audience. The work that brought Keble literary fame was *The Christian Year*, published in 1827. This collection of poems was intended to supplement the Book of Common Prayer, by strengthening the attachment of church-goers to Christian doctrine and practice. The book had an immense success. In later life, Keble himself sometimes spoke disparagingly of it; but it was constantly reprinted throughout the nineteenth century. Today, only a very few of Keble's poems are current, thanks to their inclusion in hymn-books; and even these are selected verses from more diffuse compositions, not integral poems.

To the Victorians, Keble seemed another George Herbert. The parallels are indeed striking. Both were exceptionally gifted men who dedicated their poetic powers to the service of God. Both were exemplary country parsons, graced by rare beauty of character. But comparable as they are in the spheres of moral virtue and religious devotion, as poets they can only be compared to Keble's detriment. He admired Herbert, and occasionally echoed him; but his piety was unaccompanied by wit, and his diction is mostly limp and undistinguished. The self-awareness and subtle modulation of temper and tone which commend Herbert's poems to readers who care little for their Christian content are not to be found in *The Christian Year*.

Keble in 1846 published *Lyra Innocentium*, a volume of poems about childhood (another indication of his admiration for Wordsworth). He also translated the Psalter into English verse, and edited a selection of the writings of Richard Hooker, the great Elizabethan divine. Keble's place in the hierarchy of English churchmen is unquestionably eminent; but it seems unlikely that his lyrics will ever regain the reputation they once enjoyed.

—Margaret Bottrall

KENDALL, Henry (Clarence). Australian. Born near Ulladulla, New South Wales, 18 April 1839. Married Charlotte Rutter in 1868. While a boy, taken by his uncle for two-year cruise in the South Sea Islands, on a whaling ship, 1855–57; shop assistant, Sydney, 1857–61; worked in a solicitor's office, Sydney, 1862–63; worked in the Lands Department of the State Survey Department, 1863, and in the Colonial Secretary's Office, 1864–68; treated for alcoholism, 1871; Clerk in the timber business of Fagan Brothers, Camden Haven, New South Wales, 1873–80; appointed Inspector of State Forests, 1881. *Died 1 August 1882.*

PUBLICATIONS

Collections

Poetical Works, edited by Thomas T. Reed.   1966.

Verse

Poems and Songs.   1862.
The Bronze Trumpet: A Satirical Poem, with others.   1866.
Leaves from Australian Forests.   1869.
Cantata for the Opening Ceremony of the Sydney International Exhibition, music by
   Paolo Giorza.   1879.
Songs from the Mountains.   1880.
Orara.   1881.
Poems.   1886.

Reading List: *Kendall* by Thomas T. Reed, 1960; *Kendall* by W. H. Wilde, 1976.

*   *   *

Henry Kendall's *Leaves from Australian Forests,* his second book of verse, represents the
first successful interweaving in Australian poetry of the two main strands in early colonial
literature: the poetry of exile, and the poetry of native, homespun material, springing directly
from the poet's own experience. What makes this verse particularly interesting is that Kendall
made symbolic use of these two contrasting strands to make a personal statement. He was a
complex man, and his verse is far more complex than appears on the surface. It makes no real
sense, for instance, to see him as a "nature-poet": his prose contains far more precise,
detailed observation of nature than his verse. It is true that he took as his region the fertile,
well-watered coastline of North-eastern and South-eastern New South Wales, and that he
does convey, impressionistically, the feel of its streams, its "glens," its gorges, and its rain-
forests. But his verse as a whole makes it plain that these for him were images of innocence,
of the fresh promise of early life, and that their resemblance in parts to the green fertile
pastures of England represented for him the remote, unsullied past of his own family. His
poems about heat, drought and the desert, on the other hand, signified for him the painful
present, the decay of his family, the death of youthful promise, the drying up of hope; while
the poems about mountains, especially the fine, dedicatory "Ode" in *Songs from the
Mountains,* express the longing for that idealised father-figure on whom he would like to
have been able to model himself.
   Kendall has been over-rated on the one hand as "the sweet singer" by those sympathetic
with Victorian romanticism, and on the other for his satirical, political, and heroic verse by
those with a special interest in the Augustan tradition. Some of the poems in the Augustan
mode are very fine, particularly "King Saul at Gilboa," but they are not his most
characteristic. A more fruitful approach to Kendall is to consider him as the first practitioner
of a deliberate, sustained symbolism in Australian poetry, and of a personal and confessional
verse which is again so much in vogue.
   Kendall is above all, as he said himself, a poet of retrospection, of nostalgia for his family's
English past. He is preoccupied with his father's fate (father, grandfather, and mother, like
himself, were all drunkards) and obsessed with a sense of obscure sin, apart from alcoholic
guilt. Over all the verse broods a sense of alienation ("alien" is a recurring adjective), of
irremediable solitariness. In many of his best poems, there is a contrast between burning heat

and coolness, and between inland Australia and England, always to Australia's disadvantage. The coolness and water are nearly always associated with purity, and the heat and dryness with sin − associations which are developed into a metaphysical opposition in poems like "Orara" and "Mooni," where the "burning outer world" is contrasted with the celestial world which is the hidden source of:

> A radiant brook, unknown to me
> Beyond its upper turn.
>
> The singing silver life I hear,
> Whose home is in the green
> Far-folded woods of fountains clear
> Where I have never been.

The poem affirms the necessity for mystery, for inaccessibility:

> Ah! haply in this sphere of change
> Where shadows spoil the beam,.
> It would not do to climb that range
> And test my radiant Dream.
>
> The slightest glimpse of yonder place,
> Untrodden and alone,
> Might wholly kill that nameless grace,
> The charm of the unknown.

Kendall's life, from the beginning almost to the end, was a series of tragic losses, of parents, lover, children, friends, position, and self-respect, though the last few years of it were calm and productive of domestic contentment, in spite of poor health. But the ineradicable sense of the poet's conviction of his own unworthiness fills the reader with unease, especially in poems like "Beyond Kerguelen" (a reminiscence of a voyage as a youth on a sailing ship) and "The Curse of Mother Flood." The curious subterranean resemblances of these two poems suggest that there is much about Kendall still to be explained.

—Dorothy Green

KEYES, Sidney (Arthur Kilworth). English. Born in Dartford, Kent, 27 May 1922. Educated at Dartford Grammar School; Queen's College, Oxford (Editor, *Cherwell*). Commissioned in the West Kent Regiment, and killed in action in Tunisia, 1943. Recipient: Hawthornden Prize, 1944. *Died 29(?) April 1943.*

PUBLICATIONS

Collections

Collected Poems, edited by Michael Meyer. 1945.
Minos of Crete: Plays and Stories, edited by Michael Meyer. 1948.

Verse

> *The Iron Laurel.*   1942.
> *The Cruel Solstice.*   1943.

Plays

> *Hosea: A Modern Morality* (produced 1941).   In *Minos of Crete: Plays and Stories,*
> 1948.
> *Minos of Crete,* in *Minos of Crete: Plays and Stories.*   1948.

Other

> Editor, with Michael Meyer, *Eight Oxford Poets.*   1941.

Reading List: *Keyes: A Biographical Inquiry* by John Guenther, 1967; *Not Without Glory: Poets of the Second World War* by Vernon Scannell, 1976.

*   *   *

Keyes's writing life consisted of his last two years at school, eighteen months at Oxford, and a year of army training. That from so little of life he completed two accomplished collections of poems (within a year gathered into a posthumous *Collected Poems* along with a useful memoir and notes), and the plays and stories of *Minos of Crete*, indicates the precocious nature of his achievement. His misfortune was to be instantly lauded as his war's successor to Owen: a claim doomed to emphasise his limitations in view of the fact that he died at the age of twenty within two weeks of reaching the Tunisian Front and not one of his poems was written from experience of battle. In consequence, today his false reputation is remembered and his work largely unread. In fact he was a promising poet with a niche in literary history as one of the Oxford poets of 1940–1942 who tried to move through romanticism away from what they regarded as "the Audenian school of poets": he was a friend of John Heath-Stubbs and contemporary of the more brilliant Drummond Allison (1921–43).

Keyes's first collection shows a surprisingly adept apprentice poet, already at eighteen able to take something of Yeats's resonance, to draw from his reading his own themes of pain and death, and to find in the seer-poets he admired echoes of his own generation's fate, as in "Poem for May the First":

> I praise this unheroic generation
> Anchored to earth and confident and hopeless
> Of bloom this May as any wry-limbed cypress.

His is a poetry of the eloquent gesture, succeeding through its assimilation of elegiac cadence. Clare, Wordsworth, Yeats, and Schiller are given tribute through monologue or elegy, and in the important sequence "The Foreign Gate" Keyes echoes Dante to extend his lament to the dead of war:

> "Remember the torn lace, the fine coats slashed
> With steel instead of velvet, Künersdorf
> Fought in the shallow sand was my relief."
> "I rode to Naseby" ...
> > "At Dunkirk I
> Rolled in the shallows, and the living trod
> Across me for a bridge ..."

Keyes more often brings specific images of this kind to bear on the poems of his second collection. Still he aspires to the grand symbolic presentation of experience, seeking, as he wrote in a letter of January 1943 (quoted in *Collected Poems*), to synthesise the discoveries of Rilke and Yeats. But it is the short poems which grow from his experience of love – "The True Heart," "Seascape," "The Kestrels" – which show his talent developing:

> When I would think of you, my mind holds only
> The small defiant kestrels – how they cut
> The raincloud with sharp wings, continually circling
> Above the storm rocked elm, with passionate cries.

—Desmond Graham

KING, Henry. English. Born in London, 16 January 1592. Educated at Westminster School, London; Christ Church, Oxford, M.A. 1614, D.D. 1625. Married Anne Berkeley in 1617 (died, 1624); six children. Prebendary of St. Paul's, London, 1616; subsequently Archdeacon of Colchester, Chaplain to the Court, and Canon of Christ Church, Oxford; Dean of Rochester, 1638; Bishop of Chichester, 1642 until deprived of his title by the Puritans; returned after the Restoration. *Died 30 September 1669.*

PUBLICATIONS

Collections

Poems, edited by Margaret Crum. 1965.

Verse

An Elegy upon Charles I. 1648.
A Groan Fetched at the Funeral of Charles the First. 1649.
The Psalms of David Turned into Meter. 1651.
Poems, Elegies, Paradoxes, and Sonnets. 1657; revised edition, 1664.

Other

Two Sermons Preached at White-Hall in Lent. 1627.
An Exposition upon the Lord's Prayer Delivered in Certain Sermons in the Cathedral Church of St. Paul. 1628.

Bibliography: *A Bibliography of King* by Geoffrey Keynes, 1977.

Reading List: *King and the Seventeenth Century* by Ronald Berman, 1964.

*   *   *

A member of a distinguished ecclesiastical family, Henry King had a professional career that is suggested by the sermons he published, his *Exposition on The Lord's Prayer*, and his metrical paraphrases of the Psalms ("To Be Sung after the Old Tunes Used in the Churches"). But, as the last item suggests, like George Herbert and many other of his contemporaries at Westminster School, he wrote verse throughout much of his life. Many of his poems were responses to public occasions common among university men: from the death of Prince Henry in 1612 until that of the Countess of Leinster in 1657, he marked public, as well as a number of private, losses with elegies. In some of his later, and most distinguished, ones, such as those on the third Earl of Essex and on Sir Charles Lucas and Sir George Lisle, King's hostility to the victorious forces of the Commonwealth led him to anticipate the pointed satire of a later age. In his elegy for Charles I he ironically congratulated the new rulers for their "preposterous Wisdoms" in both actions and propaganda:

> For as to work His Peace you rais'd this Strife,
> And often Shot at Him to Save His Life;
> As you took from Him to Encrease His wealth,
> And kept Him Pris'ner to secure His Health;
> So in revenge of your dissembled Spight,
> In this last Wrong you did Him greatest Right,
> And (cross to all You meant) by Plucking down
> Lifted Him up to His Eternal Crown.

Some of King's brief stanzaic poems (such as "The Vow-Breaker" or "The Double Rock") are more or less in the manner of Donne, and others nearer that of Jonson: "Tell mee no more how faire shee is" is one of the most graceful lyrics of the age, and King also imitated Jonson's epigrams and epistles. His characteristic vein is valedictory, whether mortuary or amatory. He is frequently "Content/... to Lament," whether particular individuals or imaginary loves or the condition of man. His characteristic couplets are frequently marked by a sort of dying fall when the major cadence occurs after the third, fourth, or fifth syllable rather than at the end of the line.

As his contemporary James Howell remarked, one finds in King's verse "not only heat and strength, but also an exact concinnity and evenness of fancy." "*Sic Vita*," for example, is a miniature masterpiece constructed of materials which served a number of other versifiers only for undistinguished exercises in commonplaces. Perhaps King's most remarkable achievement was the creation of a verse and tone proper for the most intimate personal and familial uses. "To my Sister Anne King who chid mee in verse for being angry" is a charming end to a domestic quarrel, and King's masterpiece, "An Exequy to his Matchlesse never to be forgotten Freind," written for the death of his young wife, is one of the wittiest as well as most moving personal elegies in English. King's formal and ingenious funeral rite ends with a direct and tender address to the dead loved one:

> But hark! My Pulse, like a soft Drum
> Beats my Approach, Tells Thee I come;
> And, slowe howe're my Marches bee,
> I shall at last sitt downe by Thee.
>   The thought of this bids mee goe on,
> And wait my dissolution
> With Hope and Comfort. Deare! (forgive
> The Crime) I am content to live
> Divided, with but half a Heart,
> Till wee shall Meet and Never part.

—Joseph H. Summers

KING, William. English. Born in London in 1662. Educated at Westminster School, London, 1678–81; Christ Church, Oxford, matriculated 1681, B.A. 1685, M.A. 1688, B.C.L. and D.C.L. 1692; admitted advocate at the Doctors' Commons, 1692. Secretary to Princess Anne; Judge of the Admiralty Court in Ireland, 1701–07; appointed Vicar-General of Armagh, 1703; Keeper of the Records, Birmingham Tower, Dublin Castle, 1707; returned to London, 1707, and succeeded Steele as gazetteer, 1711–12. *Died 25 December 1712.*

PUBLICATIONS

Collections

> *Original Works*, edited by John Nichols.   3 vols., 1776.
> *Poetical Works*.   2 vols., 1781.

Verse

> *The Furmetary: A Very Innocent and Harmless Poem.*   1699.
> *Mully of Mountown.*   1704.
> *The Fairy Feast.*   1704.
> *Some Remarks on the Tale of a Tub.*   1704.
> *The Art of Cookery, in Imitation of Horace's Art of Poetry.*   1708.
> *The Art of Love, in Imitation of Ovid.*   1709.

Other

> *Reflections upon Monsieur Varillas's History of Heresy,* with Edward Hannes.   1688.
> *An Answer to a Book, in Vindication of the Trinity.*   1693.
> *Animadversions on a Pretended Account of Denmark.*   1694.
> *A Journey to London in the Year 1698.*   1698; edited by K. N. Colvile, in *A Miscellany of the Wits,* 1920.
> *Dialogues of the Dead.*   1699; edited by K. N. Colvile, in *A Miscellany of the Wits,* 1920.
> *The Transactioneer, with Some of His Philosophical Fancies, in Two Dialogues.*   1700.
> *Miscellanies in Prose and Verse.*   2 vols., 1707(?).
> *Useful Transactions in Philosophy and Other Sorts of Learning.*   3 vols., 1709.
> *The Present State of Physic in the Island of Cajamai.*   1709(?).
> *A Friendly Letter from Honest Tom Bobby to Mr. G[oddar]d.*   1710; *Second Letter,* 1710.
> *A Vindication of the Rev. Dr. Henry Sacheverell,* with Charles Lambe.   1711.
> *Mr. B[isse]t's Recantation.*   1711.
> *An Answer to a Second Scandalous Book That Mr. B[isse]t Is Now Writing.*   1711.
> *An Historical Account of the Heathen Gods and Heroes.*   1711.
> *Rufinus; or, An Historical Essay on the Favourite Ministry under Theodosius the Great and His Son Arcadius.*   1712.
> *Britain's Palladium; or, My Lord Bolingbroke's Welcome from France.*   1712.
> *Useful Miscellanies.*   1712.
> *Remains,* edited by Joseph Browne.   1732; as *Posthumous Works,* 1734.

> Translator, *New Memoirs and Characters of the Two Great Brothers, the Duke of Bouillon and Mareschal Turenne,* by J. de Langlade, Baron de Saumières.   1693.

Translator, *Political Considerations upon Refined Politics,* by G. Naudé.   1711.
Translator, with others, *The Persian and Turkish Tales.*   1714.

Reading List: *King: Eine Interpretation seiner Gedichte* by Balthasar Kuebler, 1974.

*   *   *

William King is one of a very small number of English authors who, buried in undeserved obscurity, merit full resurrection. His robust originality invigorated several comic genres at the beginning of the eighteenth century. His special penchant was for burlesque, in which mode he pillories all varieties of dullness. *A Journey to London* mocks by imitation the tiresome scientific trivialities of physician and naturalist Martin Lister's record of *A Journey to Paris.* Similarly, the *Transactioneer* and *Useful Transactions in Philosophy and other Sorts of Learning* nip at the heels of Sir Hans Sloane's *Transactions of the Royal Society* in a Scriblerian vein, objecting to what King perceived as a myopic scientism. He opposed Richard Bentley's "minute" scholarship in clever *Dialogues of the Dead.* In a typical dialogue, the poetaster Richard Flecknoe contends to dramatist Thomas Dekker that his own poor epigrams would be as highly valued as the trivia Bentley perpetuates "were they sufficiently obscured by translation into Greek."

The mock-heroic method and the comic petition of Hunger to Famine in King's "very innocent and harmless poem" *The Furmetary* suggest the *Dunciad* almost as clearly as its use of gritty, concrete details anticipates Swift's "Description of the Morning." From the mock-pastoral *Mully of Mountown* to his surprisingly chaste Ovidian *Art of Love,* King reinvigorates forms that flourish later in the century. Nor is his energy undisciplined. At his best he handles the octosyllabic couplet with the delicacy of Prior and the surprise of Swift. A portion of the meal in miniature offered by the fairies in his popular tale "Orpheus and Eurydice" suggests King's grace:

> A roasted ant, that's nicely done,
> By one small atom of the sun....
> This is a dish entirely new,
> Butterflies' brains dissolved in dew;
> These lover's vows, these courtiers' hopes,
> Things to be eat by microscopes.

King draws on his adeptness in both harmonies of poetry and prose for his wittiest and most enjoyable work − *The Art of Cookery.* His old enemy Lister's outrageously pedantic edition of an obscure Latin work *Concerning the Soups and Sauces of the Ancients* elicited the facetious series of letters which precede King's Horatian treatment of that "learned, industrious, moral, upright, and warlike profession of cookery." Pretending interest only in "such parts of learning as lay remote and are fit only for the closets of the curious," King begs Lister "to communicate your remarks from the ancients concerning *dentiscalps,* vulgarly called *tooth-picks.*" In return, King promises to let the world have his treatise of forks and napkins.

Despite a constitution given to sloth, of which his friend Swift complained, King produced an amazing variety of works, and whatever he attempted was infused with a unique energy and originality which survive today. However, still one of the most consistently readable of the minor writers of his time, King anticipates and thereby suffers in comparison with the best of his contemporaries. It is one of the injustices of literary history that King has been almost totally obscured by blooms of which his works were the bud.

—Harry M. Solomon

KINSELLA, Thomas. Irish. Born in Dublin, 4 May 1928. Educated at University College, Dublin. Married Eleanor Walsh in 1955; two daughters, one son. Worked in the Irish Civil Service, 1948 until his retirement from the Department of Finance, 1965; Writer-in-Residence, 1965–67, and Professor of English, 1967–70, Southern Illinois University, Carbondale. Since 1970, Professor of English, Temple University, Philadelphia. Director, Dolmen Press, Dublin, and Cuala Press, Dublin; Founder, Peppercanister publishers, Dublin, 1972. Artistic Director, Lyric Players Theatre, Belfast. Recipient: Guinness Award, 1958; Irish Arts Council Triennial Book Award, 1961; Denis Devlin Memorial Award, 1967, 1970; Guggenheim Fellowship, 1968, 1971. Member, Irish Academy of Letters, 1965. Lives in Dublin.

PUBLICATIONS

Verse

The Starlit Eye. 1952.
Three Legendary Sonnets. 1952.
The Death of a Queen. 1956.
Poems. 1956.
Another September. 1958; revised edition, 1962.
Moralities. 1960.
Poems and Translations. 1961.
Downstream. 1962.
Six Irish Poets, with others, edited by Robin Skelton. 1962.
Wormwood. 1966.
Nightwalker. 1967.
Nightwalker and Other Poems. 1968.
Poems, with Douglas Livingstone and Anne Sexton. 1968.
Tear. 1969.
Butcher's Dozen. 1972.
A Selected Life. 1972.
Finistere. 1972.
Notes from the Land of the Dead and Other Poems. 1972.
New Poems, 1973. 1973.
Selected Poems 1956–1968. 1973.
Vertical Man: A Sequel to A Selected Life. 1973.
The Good Fight: A Poem for the Tenth Anniversary of the Death of John F. Kennedy. 1973.
One. 1974.
A Technical Supplement. 1976.

Other

Davis, Mangan, Ferguson? Tradition and the Irish Writer, with W. B. Yeats. 1970.

Editor, Selected Poems of Austin Clarke. 1976.

Translator, The Breastplate of St. Patrick, 1954; as Faeth Fiadha: The Breastplate of St. Patrick, 1957.
Translator, The Exile and Death of the Sons of Usnech, by Longes Mac n-Usnig. 1954.

Translator, *Thirty Three Triads, Translated from the XII Century Irish.* 1955.
Translator, *The Tain.* 1969.

Bibliography: by Hensley Woodbridge, in *Eire-Ireland,* 1966.

Reading List: "Kinsella Issue" of *Hollins Critic 4,* 1968; *Eight Contemporary Poets* by Calvin
Bedient, 1974; *The Poetry of Kinsella* by Maurice Harmon, 1974.

*   *   *

In *Nightwalker,* a long poem near mid-career, Thomas Kinsella aptly called himself "a
vagabond/tethered." His work is distinguished by an effort to test and extend the limits of his
own imaginative process, pitting his restless energies against a "will that gropes for/
structure." During the 1970's, Kinsella's work moved deeply and specifically into the weird
environs of the imagination, making them a primary subject of his broodings, as in "Hen
Woman" (*Notes from the Land of the Dead*):

> There is no end to that which,
> not understood, may yet be noted
> and hoarded in the imagination,
> in the yolk of one's being, so to speak,
> there to undergo its (quite animal) growth.

The act of writing became, with *Notes from the Land of the Dead,* a "fall," a journey down
into "the heart of the pit" from which to emerge "carrying my prize." In *A Technical
Supplement,* Kinsella explicitly assumes "the beginning/must be inward. Turn inward.
Divide." Turning inward, he places under scrutiny the matter of cognition and perception,
knowing he can only achieve a temporary order with it. The work is located where
anticipated connections are not always possible and therefore not always insisted upon. The
stress is internal – the impulse shaping itself – rather than external and imposed. The terms of
his inward turnings – tearings, "vital spatterings," self-surgeries, the "great private blade" –
are harsh, unlike the pleasing grace of such early poems as "Fifth Sunday after Easter"
(*Poems and Translations*):

> April's sweet hand in the margins betrayed
> Her character in late cursive daffodils;
> A gauche mark, but beautiful: a maid.

That early poetry, from *Another September* through *Wormwood,* was characterized by
traditional, formal logic and structure, narrative drive, and rich description. It was poetry of
married love, ordeal, erosion. Its language, approaching maturity in such poems as "A
Country Walk" or "Mirror in February," was packed and lush, serviceable for material
which dealt with "the swallowing and absorption of bitterness." The final effort in this
manner, "Phoenix Park," articulated certain "laws of order" such as the principle

> That life is hunger, hunger is for order,
> And hunger satisfied brings on new hunger
> Till there's nothing to come

After a pause during which Kinsella escalated his effort to finish translating the early Irish
epic, *The Tain,* his poems occupy a mythic territory of dark caves and the sea, of snakes and
"animal action." They have been characterized by an apparent formlessness, a charged
language at once compressed and wildly associative – a language of trance – and a "difficult"

561

density. For poems of the sources and processes of self and imagination, this form is direct and appropriate; the material is allowed to define its own "random/persistent coherences."

Having evolved the agitated Nightwalker and subsequent versions of him – William Skullbullet in *A Technical Supplement* or the possessed man with "the brainworm" that "will not sleep" in "The Clearing" – Kinsella discovered that only by turning finally inward, under enormous pressure and with less reliance on the old supports of persona or technique, could he find the satisfaction of capturing "in absolute hunger" the things of the mind that dominate him, as in "The Oldest Place" (*One*):

> We would need to dislodge
> the flesh itself, to dislodge that
> – shrivel back to the first drop
> and be spat back shivering into
> the dark beyond our first father

—Floyd Skloot

KIPLING, (Joseph) Rudyard.   English.   Born in Bombay, India, 30 December 1865, of English parents. Educated at the United Services College, Westward Ho!, Devon, 1878–82. Married Caroline Starr Balestier in 1892; three children. Assistant Editor, *Civil and Military Gazette*, Lahore, 1882–87; Editor and Contributor, "Week's News," *Pioneer*, Allahabad, 1887–89; returned to England, and settled in London: full-time writer from 1889; lived in Brattleboro, Vermont, 1892–96, then returned to England; settled in Burwash, Sussex, 1902. Rector, University of St. Andrews, 1922–25. Recipient: Nobel Prize for Literature, 1907; Royal Society of Literature Gold Medal, 1926. LL.D.: McGill University, Montreal, 1899; D.Litt.: University of Durham, 1907; Oxford University, 1907; Cambridge University, 1908; University of Edinburgh, 1920; The Sorbonne, Paris, 1921; University of Strasbourg, 1921; D.Phil.: University of Athens, 1924; Honorary Fellow, Magdalene College, Cambridge, 1932. Associate Member, Académie des Sciences Morales et Politiques, 1933. Refused the Poet Laureateship, 1895, and the Order of Merit. *Died 18 January 1936.*

PUBLICATIONS

Collections

> *Complete Works* (Sussex Edition).   35 vols., 1937–39; as *Collected Works* (Burwash Edition), 28 vols., 1941.
> *Verse: Definitive Edition.*   1940.
> *The Best Short Stories,* edited by Randall Jarrell.   1961; as *In the Vernacular: The English in India* and *The English in England,* 2 vols., 1963.
> *Stories and Poems,* edited by Roger Lancelyn Green.   1970.

Verse

> *Schoolboy Lyrics.*   1881.
> *Echoes,* with Alice Kipling.   1884.

Departmental Ditties and Other Verses.   1886.
Departmental Ditties, Barrack-Room Ballads, and Other Verse.   1890.
Barrack-Room Ballads and Other Verses.   1892.
Ballads and Barrack-Room Ballads.   1893.
The Seven Seas.   1896.
Recessional.   1897.
An Almanac of Twelve Sports.   1898.
Poems, edited by Wallace Rice.   1899.
Recessional and Other Poems.   1899.
The Absent-Minded Beggar.   1899.
With Number Three, Surgical and Medical, and New Poems.   1900.
Occasional Poems.   1900.
The Five Nations.   1903.
The Muse among the Motors.   1904.
Collected Verse.   1907.
A History of England (verse only), with C. R. L. Fletcher.   1911; revised edition, 1930.
Songs from Books.   1912.
Twenty Poems.   1918.
The Years Between.   1919.
Verse: Inclusive Edition, 1885–1918.   3 vols., 1919; revised edition, 1921, 1927, 1933.
A Kipling Anthology: Verse.   1922.
A Choice of Songs.   1925.
Sea and Sussex.   1926.
Songs of the Sea.   1927.
Poems 1886–1929.   3 vols., 1929.
Selected Poems.   1931.
East of Suez, Being a Selection of Eastern Verses.   1931.
The Complete Barrack-Room Ballads, edited by C. E. Carrington.   1973.

Play

The Harbour Watch (produced 1913; revised version, as *Gow's Watch,* produced 1924).

Fiction

Plain Tales from the Hills.   1888.
Soldiers Three: A Collection of Stories.   1888.
The Stories of the Gadsbys: A Tale Without a Plot.   1888.
In Black and White.   1888.
Under the Deodars.   1888; revised edition, 1890.
The Phantom 'Rickshaw and Other Tales.   1888; revised edition, 1890.
Wee Willie Winkie and Other Child Stories.   1888; revised edition, 1890.
The Light That Failed.   1890.
The Courting of Dinah Shadd and Other Stories.   1890.
Mine Own People.   1891.
The Naulahka: A Story of West and East, with Wolcott Balestier.   1892.
Many Inventions.   1893.
Soldier Tales.   1896; as *Soldier Stories,* 1896.
The Day's Work.   1898.
The Kipling Reader.   1900; as *Selected Stories,* 1925.
Traffics and Discoveries.   1904.
Actions and Reactions.   1909.

Abaft the Funnel.   1909.
A Diversity of Creatures.   1917.
Selected Stories, edited by William Lyon Phelps.   1921.
Debits and Credits.   1926.
Selected Stories.   1929.
Thy Servant a Dog, Told by Boots.   1930; revised edition, as Thy Servant a Dog and
    Other Dog Stories, 1938.
Humorous Tales.   1931.
Animal Stories.   1932.
Limits and Renewals.   1932.
All the Mowgli Stories.   1933.
Collected Dog Stories.   1934.

Other

Quartette, with others.   1885.
The City of Dreadful Night and Other Sketches.   1890.
The City of Dreadful Night and Other Places.   1891.
The Smith Administration.   1891.
Letters of Marque.   1891.
American Notes, with The Bottle Imp, by Robert Louis Stevenson.   1891.
The Jungle Book (juvenile).   1894; The Second Jungle Book, 1895.
Out of India: Things I Saw, and Failed to See, in Certain Days and Nights at Jeypore and
    Elsewhere.   1895.
"Captains Courageous": A Story of the Grand Banks (juvenile).   1897; edited by J. de
    L. Ferguson, 1959.
A Fleet in Being: Notes on Two Trips with the Channel Squadron.   1898.
Stalky & Co. (juvenile).   1899; revised edition, as The Complete Stalky & Co., 1929;
    edited by Steven Marcus, 1962.
From Sea to Sea: Letters of Travel.   1899; as From Sea to Sea and Other Sketches,
    1900.
Works (Swastika Edition).   15 vols., 1899.
Kim (juvenile).   1901.
Just So Stories for Little Children.   1902.
Puck of Pook's Hill (juvenile).   1906.
Letters to the Family (Notes on a Recent Trip to Canada).   1908.
Rewards and Fairies (juvenile).   1910.
The Kipling Reader.   1912.
The New Army in Training.   1915.
France at War.   1915.
The Fringes of the Fleet.   1915.
Tales of "The Trade."   1916.
Sea Warfare.   1916.
The War in the Mountains.   1917.
The Eyes of Asia.   1918.
The Graves of the Fallen.   1919.
Letters of Travel (1892–1913).   1920.
A Kipling Anthology: Prose.   1922.
Land and Sea Tales for Scouts and Guides.   1923.
The Irish Guards in the Great War.   2 vols., 1923.
Works (Mandalay Edition).   26 vols., 1925–26.
A Book of Words: Selections from Speeches and Addresses Delivered Between 1906 and
    1927.   1928.

The One Volume Kipling.   1928.
Souvenirs of France.   1933.
Ham and the Porcupine (juvenile).   1935.
A Kipling Pageant.   1935.
Something of Myself for My Friends Known and Unknown.   1937.
Letters from Japan, edited by Donald Richie and Yoshimori Harashima.   1962.
Kipling to Rider Haggard: The Record of a Friendship, edited by Morton Cohen.   1965.

Bibliography: *Kipling: A Bibliographical Catalogue* by J. McG. Stewart, edited by A. W. Keats, 1959; "Kipling: An Annotated Bibliography of Writings about Him" by H. E. Gerber and E. Lauterbach, in *English Fiction in Transition 3,* 1960, and *8,* 1965.

Reading List: *Kipling: His Life and Work* by C. E. Carrington, 1955; *A Reader's Guide to Kipling's Work* by Roger Lancelyn Green, 1961, and *Kipling: The Critical Heritage* edited by Green, 1971; *Kipling's Mind and Art* edited by Andrew Rutherford, 1964; *Kipling and the Critics* edited by E. L. Gilbert, 1965; *Kipling* by J. I. M. Stewart, 1966; *Kipling: Realist and Fabulist* by Bonamy Dobrée, 1967; *Kipling and His World* by Kingsley Amis, 1975; *Kipling: The Glass, The Shadow, and the Fire* by Philip Mason, 1975; *The Strange Ride of Kipling: His Life and Works* by Angus Wilson, 1977; *Kipling* by Lord Birkenhead, 1978.

*   *   *

T. S. Eliot called Rudyard Kipling "the most inscrutable of authors ... a writer impossible wholly to understand and quite impossible to belittle." On the face of it, it was an extraordinary judgement to pass on an author who was the idol of the plain, philistine, notably non-literary public, suggesting that he was as difficult, almost as hermetic to popular understanding as Eliot himself might be construed to be, and that if it was impossible to belittle him it had not been for want of many people trying. As the celebrant of British imperialism and "the white man's burden," which was one of his own phrases, in his lifetime Kipling was anathema to all good liberals both with a large and a small initial letter, and even today, forty years after his death, fairness to him is not easy.

Part of the difficulty in making a judgement lies in the complexity of his character, part in the disconcerting range of his subject-matter. It is impossible to read *Plain Tales from the Hills* generally without being forced partially to agree with the nineteenth-century critic who accused him of honouring "everywhere the brute and the bully." At the same time it is impossible not to be struck with the warmth of his sympathy both for children and for those, men and women, white and brown alike, caught up in interracial sexual relations, as in "Without Benefit of Clergy." He appears, indeed, in these stories as, to borrow Bagehot's phrase for Dickens, the "special correspondent for posterity" reporting the day-to-day life of the British Raj in the last decades of Victoria's reign. That he was an unillusioned observer of the nature of imperialism emerges clearly in what is probably the finest of his Indian stories, "The Man Born to Be King," in which two down-at-heel adventurers seize a country to the north of Afghanistan and only fail to establish a dynasty there because of the character-defects of one of them. It is an ironically grim fable on the nature of empire-building.

Though in his lifetime Kipling was seen as above all a writer about India, in fact he spent less than ten years of his adult life in the country, and it seems clear that his imagination widened and deepened after leaving it. His range is extraordinary, so much so that it is impossible to pick out any one story as typical of Kipling; instead, there are peaks of excellence, each *sui generis,* and in a narrow space all one can do is give instances. There is "Mrs. Bathurst," a study in sexual magic and, in its subtlety and indirection and mastery of the rendering of character through dialogue, possibly the most remarkable story in the language. It compels realisation that Kipling was not only a modern but at times even a modernist writer.

There are the great mythopoeic stories of Sussex life, in particular "Friendly Brook," a story very pagan in tone about what in effect is a local deity of the kind we find in Latin poetry, and "The Wish-House," a beautiful story of self-sacrifice in which something like an instance of ancient folk-lore is astonishingly invented. There are stories based in scientific invention, such as "The Eye of Allah," in which the microscope is invented – and smashed to bits – in a medieval monastery, and "Wireless," in which an early experiment in transmission by radio is magically tied up with the presence of an apothecary's assistant, whose mind in a trance is invaded by the spirit of John Keats. There are stories of morbid psychology like the chilling and in my view often misunderstood "Mary Postgate." There is the haunting story of phantom children, "They," which so influenced Eliot in the writing of "Burnt Norton."

That he was the greatest of English short-story writers can scarcely be doubted. He was never a successful novelist, though *Kim* is a case on its own, a wonderfully sympathetic evocation of Indian native life. He was, obviously, one of the great children's writers, and it was precisely in such works as *The Jungle Book, Puck of Pook's Hill* and *Stalky & Co.* that he most unambiguously dramatised his moral values, what he called the Law, which "lesser breeds" were without. Above all, perhaps, with his younger contemporaries Joyce and Lawrence, with whom one feels he would have had little sympathy, he was one of the undisputed masters of specifically modern English prose.

A definitive critical estimate of Kipling as a poet is still awaited. He stood apart from the general poetic theories and practice current in his lifetime and forged his own characteristic expression in poems like "Danny Deever" and "Mandalay" out of the music hall ballad, which he brought into literature. His most famous poem, "Recessional," is obviously one of the great hymns. He was in a very real sense that rarest of beings, a genuine popular poet, and whatever his final place in our poetry may prove to be, one thing is certain. More lines and phrases from his verse have passed into the common mind and speech than those of any other English poet of the century.

—Walter Allen

KLEIN, A(braham) M(oses).   Canadian.   Born in Montreal, Quebec, 14 February 1909. Educated at McGill University, Montreal, B.A. 1930; University of Montreal, B.C.L. 1933; called to the Bar of Quebec, 1933. Married Bessie Koslov in 1935; two sons, one daughter. Practised law in Montreal from 1933; subsequently also worked in public relations. Director of Education, Zionist Organization of Canada, 1936–37; Editor, *Canadian Zionist* and *Canadian Jewish Chronicle*. Special Lecturer in Poetry, McGill University, 1946–47; a Founder, *Preview, First Statement,* and *Northern Review* magazines, Montreal, in the 1940's. Recipient: Edward Bland Fellowship Prize, 1947; Governor-General's Award, 1949; Province of Quebec Literary Prize, 1952; Kovner Memorial Award, 1952; Lorne Pierce Gold Medal, 1957. *Died 21 August 1972.*

PUBLICATIONS

Collections

Collected Poems, edited by Miriam Waddington.   1974.

566

Verse

> Hath Not a Jew....   1940.
> Poems.   1944.
> The Hitleriad.   1944.
> Seven Poems.   1947.
> Huit Poèmes Canadiens (En Anglais).   1948.
> The Rocking Chair and Other Poems.   1948.

Play

> Hershel of Ostropol, in Canadian Jewish Chronicle 26 and 27, 1939.

Fiction

> The Second Scroll.   1951.

Other

> Translator, From Palestine to Israel, by Moishe Dickstein.   1951.
> Translator, Of Jewish Music, Ancient and Modern, by Israel Rabinovitch.   1952.

Reading List: Klein edited by Tom Marshall, 1970; Klein by Miriam Waddington, 1970.

*   *   *

The condition of being Jewish, or more positively the fierce sense of Jewish identity, is the generating feeling and the constitutive, substantial experience of all A. M. Klein's best poetry up to The Rocking Chair, where indeed it is still present if in a calmer, more implied manner. And the condition of being Jewish, as Klein felt it, is more perplexing a question than whether or not Klein lost his faith, or regained it, or didn't, as though this were a matter that could be defined in a chart or scheduled on a timetable once for all. The pattern of being Jewish revealed in Hath Not a Jew and Poems includes, it seems to me, at least three notes: first, the consciousness of the divine as totally other, as the unnameable, unqualified, and absolute ground of being; second, the enjoyment of a rich immediacy of life, and custom, habit, rite, symbol, food, of innumerable significant particulars; and third, stretching between the consciousness of the first and the living of the second, the vital sense of a continuous tradition: a tradition, it may be added, in which doubt and the questioning of reason have their place. To celebrate, to recall, to represent, and in doing so, to defend: these are the aims, not always separate one from another, which inform many of the poems, aims themselves subordinate to the larger purpose of sustaining the tradition and defining the human reality of the Jewish experience.

Klein's evocation of the Jewish sensibility is both broad and fine, joining the accuracy of the intent observer to the warmth of recovered personal experience. It includes history, the poet's own life, festivals, characters, fairy-tales, legends, psalms, the memories of a child, as well as carolling children's songs. It takes in not only sages and saints, children and elves, spidery logicians and gloomy puritans, but also Chaucerian rogues, clowns and dwarfs, unabashed hypocrites, the querulous devotee, the furious preacher, the bawling junk man, the matchmaker — "cupid in a caftan" — and the deprecating self, like the mild Moses who so spared everybody trouble "that in his tomb/He will turn dust to save some room." The rich

567

portraiture and the manifold differences of an old complex society derive from the poet's own life, and especially his childhood, and from a wide erudition fed on Jewish learning and European tradition. The tone is variously reverential and sarcastic, disillusioned and pious, indignant and resigned, witty and sad; the diction is biblical and lavish but also homely and colloquial; and the rhythms, whether solemn or nimble, organic and unforced: the whole is the product of a rarely civilised mind in possession of a marvellously humane tradition.

The world constituted in these Jewish poems has solidity and bloom and an intensely living presence, and just occasionally a taste of molasses. It is also torn and stricken by history, its existence constantly menaced and intermittently ravaged, so that one receives the paradoxical impression of something both ancient and brimming with life standing precariously on the edge of dissolution or − since this phrase may suggest the possibility of inward collapse − expecting some oceanic invasion. Working from deep within this tradition Klein's sensibility manifests the opposed attitudes corresponding to the double character of the Jewish universe: the tenderness and reverence for the humanity embodied in the tradition together with the keenest relish for its unique savour, and the hard reaction to external hostility, a stony pride of resistance.

Klein is one of the few serious Canadian writers untroubled by the problem of identity and free of its attendant, modish hysteria about alienation. His work has in it all the richness, the inclusiveness, of the Jewish character and mind, the product of an ancient, sophisticated, oppressed, and still living tradition. At the same time he is alert to the several nuances of contemporary Canadian life, and the marriage of a suffering but essential serenity with a nervous and accurate response make for a poetry which is altogether independent but also splendidly central.

The Rocking Chair, Klein's final appearance as a poet (apart from the verse in *The Second Scroll*), came out in 1948. A case could be made for its being the best single book of verse ever to be published in Canada and one of the best in English anywhere since the war. Not that it is by any means flawless. There is more than a suspicion of North American molasses in "The Sugaring," as well as rather too much unassimilated Hopkins, a degree too feverish a nostalgia in "The Sisters of the Hôtel Dieu," and more than a hint of linguistic intoxication in "Montreal," repeated readings of which leave one irritated at its contrivance and artificiality. In the achieved poems an imagination charged with history and a consciousness clarified by an ancient coherence are brought to bear on persons, places, things, processes, and conditions − saltily, stingingly, fresh, and Canadian. The past in the poet is locked with the present in the object. The effect is to produce a reality which has both roundness and depth. Each clean surface is backed by a thick supporting texture of allusion and reference from history, literature, traditional assumption, and racial memory and luminous Jewish reverence for the life of the word and the book, an unbroken order or human experience. The interior of the refrigerator deepens into a Laurentian village, "tiered and bright"; the commercial bank opens into a flowering jungle concealing silent beasts pawing the ground; bakers at their ovens appear as Levites at their altars; the dress manufacturer as he fishes becomes "at the end of his filament,/a correspondent of water and of fish"; the Quebec liquor commission store turns magically into Ali Baba's cave, offering the pleasures of "the sycophancy of glass, the palm's cool courtier,/and the feel of straw, all rough and rustical"; the break-up of the ice raises from the tomb "the pyramid fish, the unlockered ships,/and last year's blue and bloated suicides"; the social guilt implied in the pawnshop makes it "Our own gomorrah house,/the sodom that merely to look at makes one salt."

Klein's creative generosity, that is, works first to establish the being of the object, event, place, or experience at the centre of the poem, and then to enlarge its significance. The essential quality and inward shape sustain the meaning. So that, for example, in "The Rocking Chair," "Grain Elevator," "The Spinning Wheel," the thing becomes an image, the image a symbol, the symbol a style of life and feeling. Each of the major poems in *The Rocking Chair* testifies to the ease and authority with which Klein treats his Canadian theme. In this work we see detachment telescoped into identity. In none of the poems is the Jew in Klein ousted by the Canadian. Rather a sensibility fed by one of the most ancient sources of human quality shows itself superbly qualified to cope with a new hospitality to experience, and to see in the Canadian example the universal human thing. So that these poems work by combining distance and intimacy, perspective and grain, and find "the thing that makes them one" in what is common and human.

> Or find it, find it, find it commonplace
> but effective, valid, real, the unity
> In the family feature, the not unsimilar face....

The ironic truth of our strange age, enunciated by Klein in "Portrait of the Poet as Landscape," a poem notable for its wit, strength, and undespairing acceptance of a despairing part, is that the making of these creative connections, the articulation of our human experience, is the business of someone who has been dismissed from real society, the poet. He is missing but not missed, "a Mr. Smith in a hotel register − /incognito, lost...."

—William Walsh

KUNITZ, Stanley (Jasspon). American. Born in Worcester, Massachusetts, 29 July 1905. Educated at Harvard University, Cambridge, Massachusetts (Garrison Medal, 1926), A.B. (summa cum laude) 1926 (Phi Beta Kappa), A.M. 1927. Served in the United States Army, 1943–45: Staff Sergeant. Married 1) Helen Pearce in 1930 (divorced, 1937), one daughter; 2) Eleanor Evans in 1939 (divorced, 1958); 3) Elise Asher in 1958. Editor, *Wilson Library Bulletin*, New York, 1928–43; Member of the Faculty, Bennington College, Vermont, 1946–59; Professor of English, State University of New York at Potsdam, 1949–50, and Summers 1949–53; Lecturer, and Director of the Poetry Workshop, New School for Social Research, New York, 1950–57; Visiting Professor of Poetry, University of Washington, Seattle, 1955–56; Visiting Professor of English, Queens College, Flushing, New York, 1956–57, and Brandeis University, Waltham, Massachusetts, 1958–59; Director, YM-YWHA Poetry Workshop, New York, 1958–62; Danforth Visiting Lecturer, various American colleges, 1961–63; Fellow, 1969, and Visiting Professor of Poetry, 1970, Yale University, New Haven, Connecticut. Lecturer, 1963–67, and since 1967 Adjunct Professor of Writing, Graduate School of the Arts, Columbia University, New York. Since 1968, Chairman, Writing Department, Fine Arts Work Center, Provincetown, Massachusetts; since 1969, Editor, Yale Series of Younger Poets, Yale University Press. Formerly, Cultural Exchange Lecturer, U.S.S.R. and Poland. Consultant in Poetry, Library of Congress, Washington, D.C., 1974–76. Recipient: Guggenheim Fellowship, 1945; Amy Lowell Traveling Fellowship, 1953; Harriet Monroe Award, 1958; Pulitzer Prize, 1959; Ford Foundation grant, 1959; National Institute of Arts and Letters grant, 1959; Brandeis University Creative Arts Award, 1964; Academy of American Poets Fellowship, 1968; American Academy of Arts and Letters Award of Merit, 1975; Translation Center grant, 1975. Litt.D.: Clark University, Worcester, Massachusetts, 1961. Member, American Academy of Arts and Letters; Chancellor, Academy of American Poets, 1970. Lives in New York City.

Publications

Verse

   Intellectual Things.   1930.
   Passport to the War: A Selection of Poems.   1944.
   Selected Poems 1928–1958.   1958.
   The Testing-Tree.   1971.
   The Terrible Threshold: Selected Poems, 1940–1970.   1974.

Other

   A Kind of Order, A Kind of Folly: Essays and Conversations.   1975.

   Editor, *Living Authors: A Book of Biographies.*   1931.
   Editor, with Howard Haycraft and Wilbur C. Hadden, *Authors Today and Yesterday: A
      Companion Volume to "Living Authors".*   1933.
   Editor, with others, *The Junior Book of Authors.*   1934; revised edition, 1961.
   Editor, with Howard Haycraft, *British Authors of the Nineteenth Century.*   1936.
   Editor, with Howard Haycraft, *American Authors, 1600–1900: A Biographical
      Dictionary of American Literature.*   1938.
   Editor, with Howard Haycraft, *Twentieth Century Authors: A Biographical Dictionary of
      Modern Literature.*   1942; *First Supplement,* with Vineta Colby, 1955.
   Editor, with Howard Haycraft, *British Authors Before 1800: A Biographical
      Dictionary.*   1952.
   Editor, *Poems,* by John Keats.   1964.
   Editor, with Vineta Colby, *European Authors, 1000–1900: A Biographical Dictionary of
      European Literature.*   1967.
   Editor and Translator, with Max Hayward, *Poems of Akhmatova.*   1973.

   Translator, with others, *Antiworlds and the Fifth Ace,* by Andrei Voznesensky.   1967.
   Translator, with others, *Stolen Apples,* by Yevgeny Yevtushenko.   1972.
   Translator, with others, *Story under Full Sail,* by Andrei Voznesensky.   1974.

Reading List: "The Poetry of Kunitz" by James Hagstrum, in *Poets in Progress,* edited by
Edward Hungerford, 1962; *The Comtemporary Poet as Artist and Critic* edited by Anthony
Ostroff, 1964; "Man with a Leaf in His Head" by Stanley Moss, in *The Nation,* 20 September
1971.

*   *   *

   Stanley Kunitz's *Selected Poems 1928–1958* offers us a good standard of the classic forms
and modes of American poetry that largely governed poets of these three decades. Kunitz has
more often fought the form imposed on his sometimes extravagant lyrical language than
given in to it, and where this creative conflict between a restless content and a rigid,
enveloping form is sustained the result has unusual vigor and freshness. The effect is of
loosely woven statements held under intense pressure of symmetry and repeated rhythm, as
in this nervous, jaggedly expressed love lyric, "Green Ways":

Let me not say it, let me not reveal
How like a god my heart begins to climb
The trellis of the crystal
In the rose-green moon;
Let me not say it, let me leave untold
This legend, while the nights snow emerald.

Let me not say it, let me not confess
How in the leaflight of my green-celled world
In self's pre-history
The blind moulds kiss;
Let me not say it, let me but endure
This ritual like feather and like star.

Let me proclaim it – human be my lot! –
How from my pit of green horse-bones
I turn, in a wilderness of sweat,
To the moon-breasted sibylline,
And lift this garland, Danger, from her throat
To blaze it in the foundries of the night.

But "Green Ways" is the balance that Kunitz has not always been able to strike in his poetry; here passion and form give way to each other, but in some of his work the feeling has been too thoroughly subdued by order and conscious craft, creating a lyric that is too dry and rehearsed in its utterance. But even in the severest of his poems, the reader is aware of the intensity of the poet's mind, the irrepressible energy of his imagination.

Often called the poet's poet, a term he has tended to dismiss more vigorously in later years, Kunitz has himself defended the unruly side of the poetic medium. As editor of the Yale Younger Poets Series, Kunitz has been enthusiastic in his advocacy of a poetry of process and impulsive strategies. In his occasional and critical prose, he has also tended to favor the ungoverned muse: in his essay "A Kind of Order" he says: "With young writers I make a nuisance of myself talking about order, for the good reason that order is teachable; but in my bones I know that only the troubled spirits among them, those who recognize the disorder without and within, have a chance to become poets."

In the strictest balance, however, Kunitz's *Selected Poems* conveys, even it its most rigid formulations of lyric, a stubbornly individual mind that has known all the extremes of feeling and mood. "Night-Piece," "The Man Upstairs" with its Eliotic strain of irony and wit, the poems gathered under the section "The Terrible Threshold" and much else in this collection are provocative and vital.

—Paul Christensen

LAMPMAN, Archibald. Canadian. Born in Morpeth, Ontario, 17 November 1861. Educated at F. W. Barron's School, Gore's Landing, Ontario; Cobourg Collegiate Institute, Ontario (Foundation Scholar); Trinity College School, Port Hope, Ontario, 1876–79; Trinity College, University of Toronto, 1879–82, B.A. in classics 1882. Married Maud Playter in 1887; one son, one daughter. Assistant Master, Orangeville, Ontario High School, 1882; Clerk, Post Office Department, Ottawa, 1883–99. *Died 9 February 1899.*

PUBLICATIONS

Collections

 The Poems, edited by Duncan Campbell Scott.   1900.
 Selected Poems, edited by Duncan Campbell Scott.   1947.

Verse

 Among the Millet and Other Poems.   1888.
 Lyrics of Earth.   1895
 Alcyone.   1899.
 At the Long Sault and Other New Poems, edited by E. K. Brown and Duncan Campbell
   Scott.   1943.

Other

 Letters to Edward William Thomson, 1890–1898, edited by Arthur S. Bourinot.   1956.

Reading List: *The Poetry of Lampman* by Norman Guthrie, 1927; *Lampman, Canadian Poet of Nature* by Carl Connor, 1929; *Ten Canadian Poets* by Desmond Pacey, 1958; *Lampman* edited by Michael Gnarowski, 1970.

*   *   *

   Long regarded by Canadian literary historians as the country's most accomplished nineteenth-century poet writing in English, Archibald Lampman himself recognised that he was "a minor poet of a superior order." His particular excellence lies in his close and accurate description of the extremes of the Canadian environment, and in his ability to express the relationship between those extremes and human moral dilemmas. A talented technician and facile versifier, he also wasted much of his time writing lengthy and undistinguished verse dramas characteristic of what A. J. M. Smith has called "colonial romanticism." Yet by the end of his brief career, his few experiments with free verse and a variety of imagism mark him as the first Canadian poet with a twentieth-century sensibility. That these two aesthetic impulses operated simultaneously defines the quandary of the colonial poet. Nevertheless the more "realistic" of his poems strongly influenced his contemporaries until the late 1920's.
   Lampman saw only two volumes of his poetry through the presses: *Among the Millet,* published at his own expense, and *Lyrics of Earth,* issued in an edition of only 550 copies. Both were well received in the small literary community of the time (he was known as well in the United States through his contributions to periodicals in Boston and New York). He died shortly after correcting the proofs of *Alcyone,* and twelve copies were pulled from the

standing type. His friend and literary executor Duncan Campbell Scott used Lampman's manuscript books to compile the *Poems*, which went through four editions between 1900 and 1915. Scott was also responsible for a volume of selected poetry in 1925; for a new collection of work from the manuscripts, radically edited in collaboration with E. K. Brown in 1943; and for another selection in 1947. Uniquely for a nineteenth-century Canadian poet, much of Lampman's work remained in print during the half-century between the time of the "Confederation poets" who flourished in the 1890's and the publication explosion of poetry beginning in the late 1950's.

Widely anthologised as a "nature poet" (his derogatory term for critical estimates in his lifetime), Lampman also associated with a miniscule group of pale socialists in Ottawa, and occasionally wrote poetry of social protest. Most of this work remained unpublished until after he died, as nearly one-quarter of his known poetry still does. Collections of some of his prose — he indulged in literary journalism for sixteen months, and lectured infrequently — suggest that he was attracted to large humanistic and literary topics, but that his taste and judgement were at best eccentric. He has not always been well served by his editors, especially of his correspondence. Unabridged and uncensored, it reveals a tortured, confused, and insecure private personality at odds with general critical views of the publicly accessible poet.

—Bruce Nesbitt

LANDOR, Walter Savage.   English.   Born in Warwick, 30 January 1775. Educated at Rugby School, and privately; Trinity College, Oxford, 1793–94. Led a private regiment against Napoleon in Spain, 1808. Married Julia Thuillier in 1811 (separated, 1835). Writer from 1793; lived in South Wales on an income from his father from 1795, then inherited considerable wealth on his father's death, 1805; purchased Llanthony Abbey, 1809; lived in France, 1814, and in Italy, 1815–35, in Florence, 1821–35; returned to England, and lived in Bath, 1835–58; involved in an action for libel, 1858, and resided in Italy again until his death. *Died 17 September 1864.*

PUBLICATIONS

Collections

    Letters, edited by Stephen Wheeler.   1899.
    Complete Works, edited by T. Earle Welby and Stephen Wheeler.   16 vols., 1927–36.
    Poems (selection), edited by Geoffrey Grigson.   1964.
    A Biographical Anthology, edited by Herbert Van Thal.   1973.

Verse

    Poems.   1795.
    Moral Epistle Respectfully Dedicated to Earl Stanhope.   1795.
    Gebir: A Poem in Seven Books.   1798; translated by Landor, as *Gebirus Poema*, 1803; edited by Arthur Symons, with *The Hellenics,* 1907.

Poems from the Arabic and Persian.   1800.
Poetry.   1800; augmented edition, 1802.
Iambi Incerto Auctore.   1802(?).
Simonidea.   1806.
Ode ad Gustavum Regem; Ode ad Gustavum Exulem.   1810.
Idyllia Nove Quinque Heroum atque Heroidum.   1815.
Sponsalia Polyxenae.   1819.
Idyllia Heroica Decem Librum Phaleuciorum Unum.   1820.
Gebir, Count Julian, and Other Poems.   1831.
Terry Hogan: An Eclogue.   1836
A Satire on Satirists and Admonition to Detractors.   1836.
Poemata et Inscriptiones.   1847.
The Hellenics Enlarged and Completed.   1847; revised edition, 1859; edited by Arthur
    Symons, with Gebir, 1907.
The Italics.   1848.
Savagius Landor Lamartino.   1848.
Epistola ad Pium IX Pontificem.   1849.
Ad Cossuthum et Bemum.   1849.
Dry Sticks, Fagoted by Landor.   1858.
Savonarola e il Priore di San Marco.   1860.
Heroic Idyls with Additional Poems.   1863.
A Modern Greek Idyl.   1917.
To Elizabeth Barrett Browning and Other Verses.   1917.

Plays

Count Julian.   1812.
Andrea of Hungary and Giovanni of Naples.   1839.
Fra Rupert.   1840.
The Siege of Ancona, in Works.   1846.

Other

To the Burgesses of Warwick.   1797; edited by R. H. Super, 1949.
Three Letters Written in Spain to D. Francisco Riguelme.   1809.
Commentary on Memoirs of Mr. Fox.   1812; edited by Stephen Wheeler, as Charles
    James Fox: A Commentary on His Life and Character,   1907.
Letters Addressed to Lord Liverpool and the Parliament on the Preliminaries of
    Peace.   1814.
Letter from Mr. Landor to Mr. Jervis.   1814.
Imaginary Conversations of Literary Men and Statesmen.   5 vols., 1824–29; edited by
    R. H. Boothroyd, 1936.
Citation and Examiniation of William Shakespeare Before the Worshipful Sir Thomas
    Lucy Knight Touching Deer Stealing, to Which Is Added a Conference of Master
    Edmund Spenser, a Gentleman of Note, with the Earl of Essex Touching the State of
    Ireland.   1834.
Pericles and Aspasia.   2 vols., 1836; edited by G. Ravenscroft Dennis, 1903.
The Letters of a Conservative, in Which Are Shown the Only Means of Saving What Is
    Left of the English Church.   1836.
The Pentameron and Pentalogia.   1837.
To Robert Browning.   1845.
The Works.   2 vols., 1846.

Imaginary Conversation of King Carlo-Alberto and the Duchess Belgioioso on the Affairs and Prospects of Italy. 1848.
Popery, British and Foreign. 1851.
On Kossuth's Voyage to America. 1851.
Tyrannicide, Published for the Benefit of the Hungarians in America. 1851.
Imaginary Conversations of Greeks and Romans. 1853.
The Last Fruit Off an Old Tree. 1853.
Letters of an American Mainly on Russia and Revolution. 1854.
Antony and Octavius: Scenes for the Study. 1856.
Letter to Emerson. 1856.
Selections from the Writings (prose), edited by G. S. Hilliard. 1856.
Collection of Autograph Letters and Historical Documents: The Blessington Papers, edited by A. Morrison. 1895.
Letters and Other Unpublished Writings, edited by Stephen Wheeler. 1897.
Garibaldi and the President of the Sicilian Senate. 1917.
An Address to the Fellows of Trinity College Oxford on the Alarm of Invasion. 1917.
Landor: Last Days, Letters, and Conversations, edited by H. C. Minchin. 1934.

Bibliography: *The Publication of Landor's Works* by R. H. Super, 1954.

Reading List: *Landor* by M. Elwin, 1941, revised edition, as *Landor: A Replevin,* 1958; *Landor: A Biography* by R. H. Super, 1954; *Landor* by G. R. Hamilton, 1960; *L'Oeuvre de Landor* by P. Vitoux, 1964; *Landor* by E. Dilworth, 1971.

*   *   *

According to Ezra Pound in *How to Read,* "the decline of England began on the day when Walter Savage Landor packed his trunks and departed to Tuscany." And Yeats concluded his fine poem "To a Young Beauty" with the proud claim:

> There is not a fool can call me friend,
> And I may dine at journey's end
> With Landor and with Donne.

Yet Landor remains little read. We may indeed feel that what both Pound and Yeats were primarily responding to was a certain patrician high-handedness in Landor's character which found its neatest expression in his "Dying Speech of an Old Philosopher":

> I strove with none, for none was worth my strife:
> Nature I loved, and next to Nature, Art:
> I warmed both hands before the fire of life;
> It sinks; and I am ready to depart.

This has an admirable crispness and clarity, the qualities which Landor found most congenial in the Classics that he knew so well. But it may be doubted whether it shows much depth of self-knowledge in one whose whole life was spent in striving with others – usually for very good reasons. After all, Landor was rusticated from Oxford for shooting his fowling-piece at the windows of an "obnoxious Tory" who was making too much noise, and served as the original of Dickens's Boythorn in *Bleak House* who sets his estate about with notices warning "That any person or persons audaciously presuming to trespass on this property will be punished with the utmost severity of private chastisement, and prosecuted with the utmost rigour of the law."

Nevertheless, as if in proof of Yeats's belief that a writer expresses a view of life antithetical to his public behaviour, Landor sought a style in prose and verse which would embody the classical ideas of lucidity and balance. Outside the epigrams – including the well-known tribute to his loved Rose Aylmer – Landor succeeded best in prose. The early blank-verse narrative poem *Gebir* lacks the force of either narrative or characterisation to sustain it, and the same is true of his plays, which lack dramatic power and can hardly be envisaged on the stage.

It was in the *Imaginary Conversations* that Landor, perhaps encouraged by his friend Southey who was then beginning his Colloquies, found his appropriate form. In these he could bring together related or contrasting historical characters and use the juxtaposition to bring out what seem to him significant ideas about life and conduct. At first sight, the *Conversations* might seem to parallel the dramatic monologues of his later friend Browning, but in fact their aims were different. Whereas Browning was interested above all in the varieties of human character, Landor's interest lay in the presentation of ideas and attitudes. Yet there is enough variety in Landor's knowledge of history and his breadth of interests to sustain these literary dialogues, some of which have been effectively broadcast. At his best, as in "Elizabeth and Cecil," "Southey and Porson," "Washington and Franklin," "Epictetus and Seneca," and the longer *Pericles and Aspasia*, Landor shows great skill in giving expression to what is basically his own philosophy, a high-toned classical republicanism, sweetened by a sense of beauty and transience.

A neglected aspect of Landor is his excellence as a letter writer. Should the reader begin to lose interest in the formality of the *Conversations*, he will find in the letters more of the ebullient character who appealed to many close friends throughout a long life. The published *Letter to Emerson* was an expression of Landor's pleasure and interest in Emerson's recent *English Traits*. Characteristically Landor was both polite and firm in his response, going through the references to his own conversation and explaining their implications. He also clarified his own political attitude: "I was always Conservative; but I would eradicate any species of evil, political, moral or religious, as soon as it springs up, with no reference to the blockheads who cry out, '*What would you substitute in its place?*' When I pluck up a dock or a thistle, do I ask any such question?"

It is in his less formal letters that Landor's unique combination of scholarship, irascibility, and humanity finds its fullest expression.

—Peter Faulkner

LANG, Andrew.   Scottish.   Born in Selkirk, 31 March 1844. Educated at Selkirk High School; Edinburgh Academy, 1854–61; University of St. Andrews (Editor, *St. Leonard's Magazine*), 1861–63; University of Glasgow, 1863–64; Loretto School, Musselburgh, 1864; Balliol College, Oxford (Snell Exhibitioner), 1864–68, B.A. 1866. Married Leonora Blanche Alleyne in 1875. Fellow, Merton College, Oxford, 1868–75; free-lance writer after 1875: General Editor, English Worthies series, Longmans, 1885–87, and Bibliothèque de Corabas series, Nutt, 1887–96. Gifford Lecturer, University of St. Andrews, 1888; Ford Lecturer, Oxford University, 1904. LL.D.: University of St. Andrews, 1885; Oxford University, 1904. *Died 20 July 1912.*

Publications

Collections

The Poetical Works, edited by Leonora Lang.   4 vols., 1923.

Verse

Ballads and Lyrics of Old France, with Other Poems. 1872.
XXII Ballades in Blue China. 1880.
XXII and X: XXXII Ballades in Blue China 1881: revised edition. 1888.
Helen of Troy. 1882.
Rhymes à la Mode. 1884.
Ballades and Verses Vain, edited by Austin Dobson. 1884.
Lines on the Inaugural Meeting of the Shelley Society, edited by T. J. Wise 1886.
Grass of Parnassus: Rhymes Old and New. 1888; revised edition, as *Grass of Parnassus: First and Last Rhymes.* 1892.
Ban and Arrière Ban: A Rally of Fugitive Rhymes. 1894.
The Young Ruthven. 1902.
New Collected Rhymes. 1905.
Ode on a Distant Memory of "Jane Eyre," edited by Clement K. Shorter. 1912.
The New Pygmalion. 1962.
In College Gardens: Old Rhymes Written in 1871. 1972.

Play

The Black Thief (juvenile). 1882.

Fiction

Much Darker Days. 1884; revised edition, 1885.
That Very Mab, with May Kendall. 1885.
The Mark of Cain. 1886.
In the Wrong Paradise and Other Stories. 1886.
He, by the Author of It, with W. H. Pollock. 1887; as *He, A Companion to She,* 1887.
The World's Desire, with H. Rider Haggard. 1890.
A Monk of Fife: A Romance of the Days of Jeanne d'Arc. 1895.
Parson Kelly, with A. E. W. Mason. 1899.
The Disentanglers. 1901.

Other

Oxford: Brief Historical and Descriptive Notes. 1880.
The Library. 1881.
The Princess Nobody: A Tale of Fairyland (juvenile). 1884.
Custom and Myth. 1884; revised edition, 1885.
The Politics of Aristotle: Introductory Essays. 1886.
Letters to Dead Authors. 1886; revised edition, as *New and Old Letters to Dead Authors,* 1907.
Books and Bookmen. 1886.
Myth, Ritual, and Religion. 2 vols., 1887.
Pictures at Play; or, Dialogues of the Galleries by Two Art-Critics, with W. E. Henley. 1888.
The Gold of Fairnilee (juvenile). 1888.
Prince Prigio (juvenile). 1889; with *Prince Ricardo,* edited by Roger Lancelyn Green, 1961.
Letters on Literature. 1889.
Lost Leaders, edited by Pett Ridge. 1889.

Old Friends: Essays in Epistolary Parody. 1890.
Life, Letters and Diaries of Sir Stafford Northcote, First Earl of Iddesleigh. 2 vols.,
  1890.
Angling Sketches. 1891.
Essays in Little. 1891.
The Tercentenary of Izaak Walton. 1893.
Homer and the Epic. 1893.
St. Andrews. 1893; edited by G. H. Bushnell, 1951.
Prince Ricardo of Pantouflia, Being the Adventures of Prince Prigio's Son
  (juvenile). 1893; with *Prince Prigio,* edited by Roger Lancelyn Green, 1961.
Cock Lane and Common-Sense. 1894.
The Voices of Jeanne d'Arc. 1895.
The Life and Letters of John Gibson Lockhart. 2 vols., 1896.
Modern Mythology. 1897.
The Book of Dreams and Ghosts. 1897.
Pickle the Spy; or, The Incognito of Prince Charles. 1897.
The Making of Religion. 1898.
The Companions of Pickle. 1898.
Prince Charles Edward Stuart. 1900; revised edition, 1903.
A History of Scotland from the Roman Occupation. 4 vols., 1900–07.
Notes and Names in Books. 1900.
The Mystery of Mary Stuart. 1901; revised edition, 1904.
Alfred Tennyson. 1901.
Magic and Religion. 1901.
Adventures among Books. 1901.
Bibliomania. 1902.
James VI and the Gowrie Mystery. 1902.
Social Origins, with *Primal Law,* by J. J. Atkinson. 1903.
The Story of the Golden Fleece (juvenile). 1903.
The Valet's Tragedy and Other Studies in Secret History. 1903.
Historical Mysteries. 1904.
The Puzzle of Dickens's Last Plot. 1905.
The Secret of the Totem. 1905.
Adventures among Books (collection). 1905.
The Clyde Mystery: A Study in Forgeries and Folklore. 1905.
John Knox and the Reformation. 1905.
Homer and His Age. 1906.
Life of Sir Walter Scott. 1906.
Portrait and Jewels of Mary Stuart. 1906.
The Story of Joan of Arc (juvenile). 1906.
Tales of Troy and Greece (juvenile). 1907.
Tales of a Fairy Court (juvenile). 1907.
The King over the Water, with Alice Shield. 1907.
The Origins of Religion and Other Essays. 1908.
The Maid of France, Being the Story of the Life and Death of Jeanne d'Arc. 1908.
The Origin of Terms of Human Relationship. 1909.
Sir George MacKenzie, King's Advocate of Rosehaugh: His Life and Times,
  1636(?)–1691. 1909.
La "Jeanne d'Arc" de M. Anatole France. 1909.
The World of Homer. 1910.
Sir Walter Scott and the Border Minstrelsy. 1910.
Method in the Study of Totemism. 1911.
A Short History of Scotland. 1911.
Shakespeare, Bacon, and the Great Unknown. 1912.

A History of English Literature from "Beowulf" to Swinburne. 1912.
Highways and Byways in the Border, with John Lang. 1913.
Old Friends among the Fairies (juvenile). 1926.
Lang and St. Andrews: A Centenary Anthology, edited by J. B. Salmond. 1944.
The Rose Fairy Book (juvenile). 1948.
Fifty Favourite Fairy Tales, edited by Kathleen Lines. 1963: *More Favourite Fairy Tales,* edited by Lines, 1967.

Editor, *The Poems of Edgar Allan Poe.* 1881.
Editor, *Ballads of Books.* 1888.
Editor, *Euterpe, Being the Second Book of the Famous History of Herodotus,* translated by Barnaby Rich. 1888.
Editor, *Perrault's Popular Tales.* 1888.
Editor, *The Blue [Red, Green, Yellow, Pink, Grey, Violet, Crimson, Brown, Orange, Olive, Lilac] Fairy Book.* 12 vols., 1889–1910.
Editor, *The Strife of Love in a Dream,* by Francesco Colonna. 1890.
Editor, *Selected Poems,* by Robert Burns. 1891.
Editor, *The Blue Poetry Book.* 1891.
Editor, *The True Story Book.* 1893.
Editor, *The Lyrics and Ballads of Sir Walter Scott.* 1894.
Editor, *The Red True Story Book.* 1895.
Editor, *Border Ballads.* 1895.
Editor, *Poetical Works,* by Sir Walter Scott. 1895.
Editor, *The Compleat Angler,* by Izaak Walton. 1896.
Editor, *The Poems and Songs of Robert Burns.* 1896.
Editor, *The Animal Story Book.* 1896.
Editor, *A Collection of Ballads.* 1897.
Editor, *The Nursery Rhyme Book.* 1897.
Editor, *Selections from the Poets: Wordsworth, Coleridge.* 2 vols., 1897–98.
Editor, *The Arabian Nights Entertainments.* 1898.
Editor, *The Red Book of Animal Stories.* 1899.
Editor, *The Book of Romance.* 1902.
Editor, *The Gowrie Conspiracy: Confessions of George Sprot.* 1902.
Editor, *The Apology for William Maitland of Lethington, 1610.* 1904.
Editor, *The Red Romance Book.* 1905.
Editor, *Poets' Country.* 1907.
Editor, *Poems,* by Jean Ingelow. 1908.
Editor, *The Book of Princes and Princesses,* by Leonora Lang. 1908.
Editor, *The Red Book of Heroes,* by Leonora Lang. 1909.
Editor, *The All Sorts of Stories Book,* by Leonora Lang. 1911.
Editor, *Poems and Plays,* by Sir Walter Scott. 2 vols., 1911.
Editor, *The Annesley Case.* 1912.
Editor, *The Book of Saints and Heroes,* by Leonora Lang. 1912.
Editor, *The Strange Story Book,* by Leonora Lang. 1913.
Editor, *Molière's Les Precieuses Ridicules.* 1926.

Translator, *The Odyssey of Homer, Book 6.* 1877.
Translator, *Specimens of a Translation of Theocritus.* 1879.
Translator, with S. H. Butcher, *The Odyssey of Homer.* 1879.
Translator, with Walter Leaf and Ernest Myers, *The Iliad of Homer.* 1883.
Translator, *Theocritus, Bion and Moschus.* 1880.
Translator, *Johnny Nut and the Golden Goose,* by Charles Deulin. 1887.
Translator, *Aucassin and Nicolette.* 1887; as *The Song-Story of Aucassin and Nicolette,* 1902.

Translator, *The Dead Leman and Other Tales from the French*.   1889.

Translator, *The Miracles of Madame Saint Katherine of Fierbois*, by J. J. Bourassé.   1897.

Translator, *The Homeric Hymns: A New Prose Translation and Essays*.   1899.

Translator, *In Praise of Frugality*, by Pope Leo XII.   1912.

Translator, *Ode to the Opening Century*, by Pope Leo XII.   1912.

Bibliography: "Descriptions from the Darlington Collection of Lang" by Roger Lancelyn Green, in *Indiana University Bookman 7*, 1965.

Reading List: *The Poetry of Lang* by James Omerod, 1943; *Lang: A Critical Biography*, 1946, and *Lang*, 1962, both by Roger Lancelyn Green; *Concerning Lang, Being the Lang Lectures Delivered Before the University of St. Andrews, 1927–1937*, edited by A. B. Webster, 1949.

*   *   *

Andrew Lang, whom George Gordon called "the greatest bookman of his age," fits properly into no category. He came to literary London one of the best-read men of his age, notably in Greek and in Medieval French, with one book of poems, original and translated – *Ballads and Lyrics of Old France, with other Poems* – behind him, and a prose translation of *The Odyssey* (in collaboration with S. H. Butcher) ready for publication; it has remained a classic for a century. He had also a narrative poem, *Helen of Troy*, in progress, but its relative failure when it was published turned him away from serious poetry and left us the tantalisingly outstanding first attempts of a true poet who never achieved the greatness expected of him by many distinguished critics. Lang was too easily disheartened; he was to be turned away from fiction for the same reason. But his romance of the life of Odysseus and Helen after the end of *The Odyssey*, *The World's Desire*, which he wrote in collaboration with his closest friend, H. Rider Haggard, and his Jacobite romance *Parson Kelly*, written with A. E. W. Mason, are excellent.

Lang suffered also from a plurality of interests. His most important one was in folklore and anthropology, in the history of which he holds a high position; he also published outstanding books on Homer and psychical research. Later in life he turned also to historical studies, solving historical mysteries and producing a memorable life of Joan of Arc and a *History of Scotland*.

These and other scholarly works keep Lang's name alive in many academic fields. But he is most widely remembered for a side-line developed from his studies in folklore, the origin and dissemination of popular tales shown in his series of collections and retellings of this basic material for young readers. After *The Blue Fairy Book* proved to be an unexpectedly successful experiment, over 20 volumes of folk tales, and similar traditional material appeared. These collections have tended to obscure his own original ventures into Fairyland; *Prince Prigio* and its sequel *Prince Ricardo* are classics in their field.

Lang was notable for his charm of style (Quiller-Couch declared his the best of any writer's in the 1890's), and this and his charm of character come through everything that he wrote. This is even notable in his journalism; of his "literary leaders" in *The Daily News* Bernard Shaw wrote that "we counted the day empty unless an article by Lang appeared" – usually unsigned but immediately recognisable as his. But to get even closer to this charming personality we must turn back to his poems – the wistful beauty of his earlier work and also to the lightness and delicacy of his lighter verse. "My mind is gay but my soul is melancholy," Lang once said, and perhaps it is this mingling which can make him one of the best-loved of minor writers.

—Roger Lancelyn Green

LANGHORNE, John. English. Born in Winton, Westmorland, in March 1735; younger brother of the poet and translator William Langhorne. Educated at schools in Winton and Appleby. Married 1) Ann Cracroft in 1767 (died, 1768), one son; 2) Miss Thompson in 1772 (died, 1776), one daughter. Tutor to a family near Ripon, 1753; subsequently an usher in a free school in Wakefield; took deacon's orders; tutor to the sons of Robert Cracroft at Hackthorn, near Lincoln, 1759–61; matriculated at Clare Hall, Cambridge, 1760, but left without taking a degree; Curate, Dagenham, Essex, 1761–64; Curate and Lecturer at St. John's, Camberwell, London, 1764–65; Assistant Preacher at Lincoln's Inn, London, 1765; Rector, Blagdon, Somerset, from 1766; Prebendary of Wells Cathedral, 1777. *Died 1 April 1779.*

PUBLICATIONS

Collections

    Poetical Works, edited by J. T. Langhorne. 2 vols., 1804.

Verse

    The Death of Adonis, from Bion. 1759.
    Job. 1760.
    The Tears of Music: A Poem to Handel, with an Ode to the River Eden. 1760.
    Poems on Several Occasions. 1760.
    A Hymn to Hope. 1761.
    The Viceroy. 1762.
    The Visions of Fancy, in Four Elegies. 1762.
    The Enlargement of the Mind. 2 vols., 1763–65.
    Genius and Valour: A Scotch Pastoral. 1764.
    The Fatal Prophecy: A Dramatic Poem. 1766.
    Poetical Works. 2 vols., 1766.
    Precepts of Conjugal Happiness. 1767.
    Verses in Memory of a Lady Written at Sandgate Castle. 1768.
    The Fables of Flora. 1771.
    The Origin of the Veil. 1773.
    The Country Justice. 3 vols., 1774; edited by Donald Davie, in *The Late Augustans,* 1958.
    Owen of Carron. 1778.

Fiction

    Solyman and Almena: An Oriental Tale. 1762.
    The Letters Between Theodosius and Constantia, after She Had Taken the Veil. 1763; revised edition, 1765.
    Frederic and Pharamond; or, The Consolations of Human Life. 1769.

Others

    Letters on Religious Retirement, Melancholy, and Enthusiasm. 1762.

The Effusions of Friendship and Fancy, in Several Letters. 2 vols., 1763; revised
   edition, 1766.
Letters on the Eloquence of the Pulpit. 1765.
Sermons Preached Before the Society of Lincoln's-Inn. 2 vols., 1767.
Letters Supposed to Have Passed Between St. Evremond and Waller. 2 vols., 1769.
A Dialogue of the Dead Betwixt Lord Eglinton and Mungo Campbell. 1770.
Letters to Eleonora. 2 vols., 1770.

Editor, *The Poetical Works of Collins.* 1765.

Translator, with William Langhorne, *Plutarch's Lives.* 6 vols., 1770.
Translator, *A Dissertation on the Ancient Republics of Italy,* by C. G. M. Denina. 1773.
Translator, *Milton's Italian Poems.* 1776.

Reading List: "Langhorne" by H. Macdonald, in *Essays Presented to David Nichol Smith,*
1945.

*   *   *

John Langhorne is a minor poet of limited output, yet of various modes. His best poems
are *The Country Justice, Owen of Carron,* and *The Fables of Flora.* Besides his poems, he also
translated Plutarch in collaboration with his brother and contributed to *The Monthly Review.*
It is, however, as a poet that he principally matters.

Writing in the mid-eighteenth century he produced work, such as the Hymns to Plutus and
to Humanity, that is reminiscent of Collins, whose poems he edited. Langhorne's work,
however, looks backward and forward. A poem like *The Enlargement of the Mind* reminds us
by its subject of Prior's much more ambitious "Alma" and by its form and optimistic view of
human capacity and existence of Pope's *Essay on Man.*

Here Langhorne was philosophical and didactic. In *Owen of Carron,* his last work, he
produces a harrowing tale of blighted love and bloody vengeance in a mode of the four-line
stanza that he favoured increasingly in his later work. The primitive passions of this poem, set
though they are a little too neatly in the regular rhythms of the chosen verse-form, remind us
that we are in the era of Percy's *Reliques* and on the verge of that reviving medievalism that
includes Chatterton and, a little later, Scott and other Romantic poets.

The proximity of Gothic horror is the reminder behind the picture of the "bloody druid"
committing ghastly infanticide in "The Mistletoe and the Passion-Flower" (*Fables of Flora,*
XI): "Behold his crimson-streaming hand/Erect! – his dark, fix'd murderous eye!" By
contrast, there is the occasional very direct visual awareness of natural beauty, as of the
"gaily-painted Tulip" (VIII), seen and more vividly described as "crimson fading into gold/In
streaks of fairest symmetry."

This exact observation may foreshadow a Coleridge or a Clare; the moral tone, though all
too wordy, has at least some relationship with what Blake would do inimitably better in
Songs of Innocence and Experience. The link, however, is closer in "To a Redbreast":

> Little bird, with bosom red,
> Welcome to my humble shed!
> Courtly domes of high degree
> Have no room for thee and me....
>
> Daily near my table steal
> While I pick my scanty meal.
> Doubt not, little though there be,
> But I'll cast a crumb to thee

The second part of this poem is a counterpointing song of experience.

Finally, however, the resemblance is with Crabbe or Wordsworth as poet of low and rustic life. *The Country Justice*, with its vagrant, poor widow, unmarried mother, shepherd and his wife, gives us a first glimpse of types with which writers not much later make us more and better familiar. Wordsworth indeed said of this poem that, with the possible exception of Shenstone's *The School Mistress*, it was "the first poem ... that fairly brought the Muse into the company of common life." Langhorne's own achievement may be limited, but he is a quite remarkable precursor of better things.

—Arthur Pollard

LANGLAND, William. English. Born c. 1332. Educated, according to tradition, at the school of the Benedictine monastery at Great Malvern, Worcestershire. Clerk in minor orders; later moved to London. *Died c. 1400.*

PUBLICATIONS

Collections

Piers the Plowman, translated by J. F. Goodridge. 1959.
Selections (from the C-Text), edited by Elizabeth Salter and Derek Pearsall. 1967.
Piers Plowman: The B-Text: Prologue and Passus I-VII, edited by J. A. W. Bennett. 1972.

Verse

Piers Plowman:
A-Text: edited by George Kane, in *Piers Plowman: The A Version.* 1960.
B-Text: edited by George Kane and E. Talbot Donaldson, in *Piers Plowman: The B Version.* 1975.
C-Text: edited (with A-Text and B-Text) by W. W. Skeat. 1886; edited by Derek Pearsall, 1978.

Bibliography: "Piers Plowman: An Annotated Bibliography for 1900–1968" by Katherine Proppe, in *Comitatus,* 1972.

Reading List: *Piers Plowman: The C-Text and Its Poet* by E. Talbot Donaldson, 1949; *Piers Plowman and the Scheme for Salvation* by R. W. Frank, 1957; *Piers Plowman: An Introduction* by Elizabeth Salter, 1962; *Piers Plowman: An Essay in Criticism* by John Lawlor, 1962; *Piers Plowman as a Fourteenth Century Apocalypse* by M. W. Bloomfield, 1963; *Piers Plowman: The Evidence for Authorship* by George Kane, 1965; *Style and Symbolism in Piers Plowman* edited by Robert J. Blanch, 1969; *Piers Plowman: Critical Approaches* edited by S. S. Hussey, 1969; *Piers Plowman and Christian Allegory* by David Aers, 1975.

*   *   *

The poem generally called *Piers Plowman* exists in three versions, known as the A, B, and C versions, and all are now usually attributed to William Langland, of whom nothing is known but what is contained in some notes on his origin in a fifteenth-century manuscript and what can be deduced from his references to the dreamer, the "I" of his poem. From these, it appears that he was a cleric in minor orders who, his education half-completed, took up residence in London and there eked out a living saying prayers for hire and performing other odd ecclesiastical offices. The A-text, written in the 1360's, is a vision of the corruption of English society through the influence of money and self-interest, and of the attempted reform of that society through the agency of Piers Plowman, the representative of simple, honest Christian virtue and hard work. The failure of this attempt at social reformation in the first part of the poem (the *Visio*) prompts a turning inward, a search for the good life in the reformation of the will of the individual, in the second part (the *Vita de Dowel*), but this search is frustrated and incomplete. In the B-text, written in the 1370's, Langland revises the *Visio* extensively and then resumes the search of the *Vita*, making additions which altogether treble the length of the poem (to over 7,000 lines) and which bring the search, after many vagaries of will and understanding, to a triumphant conclusion in the vision of Christ as a transcendental Piers Plowman. The poem ends with a return to the disordered world of the fourteenth century and a vision of impending destruction. The C-text, probably left incomplete at Langland's death, is a piecemeal revision of all except the last two *passus* of B, with some ruthless jettisoning of what an older man saw as superfluities and some sharpening of the line of thought.

Langland chose a poetic form, the alliterative long line, which had long associations with homiletic and didactic writing, but used it in a free and informal, often prosaic manner completely different from that of the poets of the "Alliterative Revival," such as the *Gawain*-poet. He has few of their mannerisms of diction, syntax, and phraseology, and little consciousness of an alliterative *ars poetica*. His style has its own kinds of energy and particularity, but he is above all a missionary, a prophet, a voice crying in the wilderness, and niceties of language as well as versification give way to the urgency of communicating his vision.

That vision is of England and the life of the individual Christian corrupted and deformed through the influence of money. Langland sees the harmony of the estates, of a world structured in contractual obligation and mutual service, perverted to the remorseless ethic of money which dissolves all bonds of nature between man and man. He sees the Church as an institution devoted to the protection of its wealth and the extension of its privileges, its whole purpose of pastoral care, witness, and intercession blunted or forgotten. In the van he sees the friars, who have prostituted the office of confession and the sacrament of penance for the sake of profit, and who thus pervert the fundamental ministry of the Church and instead sow damnation. To combat this, Langland attempts to initiate nothing less than an immense revolution in the moral and spiritual life of society and the individual. He is part here of a larger movement which was sweeping Europe, and which responded to the growing isolation and rigidity of the Church by seeking a more personal kind of religion and a ministry closer to the original apostolic ideal.

Langland uses no set procedure for the communication of his vision. The first part of the poem, the *Visio*, is mainly an allegorical narrative of what the dreamer sees; the second part, the *Vita*, is mainly an allegorical narrative of what the dreamer experiences in his search for Dowel, the true Christian life, though he reverts to observer for the final visions of the Crucifixion, the Harrowing of Hell, and the coming of Antichrist. Within these broad structural patterns, a bewildering variety of allegorical and homiletic procedures are employed, with often only the enigmatic figure of Piers Plowman to beckon the dreamer on. Yet the poem has a profound unity, growing as it does out of a deep and prolonged search on the poet's own part for spiritual illumination and certainty. The activity of the poet's mind is embodied in the person of the dreamer who is both himself and not himself, and who engages the reader in the experience of the poem, so that its urgencies are shared, its discoveries seen and felt to be won. The representation of the progress of the dreamer to understanding is one of the poem's great sources of power, since it enforces participation rather than mere acquiescence.

Langland's other outstanding quality as a religious poet is the intense actualising power of his imagination, which annexes the world of experience and literal reality to the world of revelation and spiritual reality and makes them one. His great allegorical scenes, as of the Field Full of Folk, the Ploughing of the Half-Acre, or the Coming of Antichrist, are both intensely and memorably real, with a reality that tends to subsume all other ways of conceiving of his subject, and also receptive to a rich and wide range of allegorical significances. So too with the great moments of spiritual illumination in the dreamer's search for truth, like the Feast of Patience, or the meeting with the Good Samaritan: allegory here seems the only and perfect means through which the timeless and the temporal can be shown to intersect. This power of the concretizing imagination operates also in the detailed verbal texture of the poem where spiritual vision absorbs, sanctifies and is sanctified by a world of homely objects, most magnificently perhaps where Langland describes the origin in God's love of the Incarnation (B.I. 151–6). Here the spiritual world is made concrete, and the everyday world is spiritualised, in a vision truly made flesh.

—Derek Pearsall

LANIER, Sidney.   American.   Born in Macon, Georgia, 3 February 1842. Educated at a private academy in Macon, and at Oglethorpe University, near Milledgeville, Georgia, 1857–60, graduated 1860. Served with the Macon Volunteers in the Confederate forces during the Civil War, 1861–65: prisoner-of-war, 1864–65. Married Mary Day in 1867; four sons. Worked in his father's law office, and as a hotel clerk, and teacher, Macon, 1865–73; musician from an early age: flute player in the Peabody Orchestra, Baltimore, from 1873; Lecturer in English Literature, Johns Hopkins University, Baltimore, 1879–81. *Died 7 September 1881.*

PUBLICATIONS

Collections

   The Works (includes letters), edited by Charles R. Anderson and others.   10 vols., 1945.
   Selected Poems, edited by Stark Young.   1947.

Verse

   The Centennial Meditation of Columbia, music by Dudley Buck.   1876.
   Poems.   1877.
   Poems, edited by Mary Day Lanier.   1884; revised edition, 1891, 1916.
   Poem Outlines.   1908.

Fiction

   Tiger-Lilies.   1867.

Other

> *Florida: Its Scenery, Climate, and History.* 1875.
> *Some Highways and Byways of American Travel,* with others. 1878.
> *The Science of English Verse.* 1880.
> *The English Novel and the Principle of Its Development,* edited by William Hand Browne. 1883; edited by Mary Day Lanier, 1897.
> *Music and Poetry: Essays upon Some Aspects and Inter-Relations of the Two Arts,* edited by Henry Wysham Lanier. 1898.
> *Retrospects and Prospects: Descriptive and Historical Essays,* edited by Henry Wysham Lanier. 1899.
> *Letters of Lanier: Selections from His Correspondence 1866–1881,* edited by Henry Wysham Lanier. 1899.
> *Bob: The Story of Our Mocking-Bird,* edited by Henry Wysham Lanier. 1899.
> *Shakespeare and His Forerunners: Studies in Elizabethan Poetry and Its Development from Early English,* edited by Henry Wysham Lanier. 2 vols., 1902.

> Editor, *The Boy's Froissart, Being Sir John's Froissart's Chronicles.* 1879.
> Editor, *The Boy's King Arthur, Being Sir Thomas Malory's History of King Arthur and His Knights of the Round Table.* 1880.
> Editor, *The Boy's Mabinogion.* 1881.
> Editor, *The Boy's Percy, Being Old Ballads of War, Adventure, and Love.* 1882.

Bibliography: in *Bibliography of American Literature* by Jacob Blanck, 1969.

Reading List: *Lanier: A Biographical and Critical Study* by Aubrey H. Starke, 1933; *Lanier, Poet and Prosodist* by Richard Webb and Edwin R. Coulson, 1941; *Lanier: The Man, The Poet, The Critic* by Edd Winfield Parks, 1968; *Lanier* by Jack De Bellis, 1972.

*   *   *

The life of Sidney Lanier is an odyssey from a small Southern city to the great cultural centers of America; from a law desk in a Georgia office to a prominent place in a major professional orchestra; from an aesthetically restrictive tradition to an existence totally imbued with the arts. Throughout his career, from the time he was deciding whether to defy Southern tradition in favor of art, through the period in which he was totally devoted to art, music seems to have been in competition with poetry for his time and attention. But there was never any conflict in the negative sense, for without his musical experiences Lanier could never have arrived at the type of poetry he was finally to create.

The story of Sidney Lanier is both inspiring and pathetic. It is a series of thwarted plans, shattered hopes, incomplete projects. Lanier spent most of his life dreaming of entering artistic circles, but when he finally decided to devote himself body and spirit to attaining this end he was able to reach only slightly beyond the periphery. He was forever not quite reaching his goals. He aimed for the *Atlantic Monthly,* the country's arbiter of literary taste, but reached *Lippincott's*; he vowed to play only for Theodore Thomas' orchestra in New York, but instead worked with Asger Hamerik at the Peabody Conservatory; he craved acclaim in New York City, but had to find it in Baltimore. True, what he did accomplish was of no little consequence – *Lippincott's* was also one of the nation's leading publications, Hamerik a conductor of international reputation, and Baltimore a thriving and respected center of culture. But they were all second choices for Lanier, and represent the disappointment that underlay all his successes.

Yet considering Lanier's background, he accomplished miracles. He came from a genteel Southern tradition which scorned the arts as a profession. His education was removed from the main currents of American academic life, and he had very little formal musical training. Constantly hounded by poverty after the war, he was forced to write pot-boilers in order to support his family, wasting precious creative energy. Tuberculosis had attacked him when he was twenty-two; by the time he finally determined to pursue an artistic career, he had only seven years to live, and of this time had to spend weeks and months away from his work in desperate search of a cure.

It is remarkable that Lanier managed to do so much in so little time. He played first flute in a conservatory orchestra; delivered successful and popular lectures on Shakespeare and on the English novel; wrote numerous essays on music and about literature; wrote editions for children of legendary classics; produced a guide-book to Florida which is still popular in that state; composed numerous musical works; wrote one of the best studies of English prosody (*The Science of English Verse* is a musical analysis of poetry); and in the midst of all these activities wrote dozens of poems, some of which are the most beautifully original in American literature.

His poetic style is a unique result of an attempt to convey musical impression in verse; this stems from his lifelong interest in the unity of poetry and music. His creative technique is original, and Lanier arrived at it through music. One has only to compare the early, naive, and sentimental lyrics of his 1868 song "Little Ella" and the intricately-textured poem of 1880, "Sunrise," to see the drastic and revolutionary development of Lanier's verse. This change was brought about by music, and it is therefore music which made Lanier a poet. Without it, his verse would have remained pretty and lyrical, but simple in structure, texturally unimaginative, and tied to the limiting song-concept. But Lanier's best works, his later poems, reflect the influence of larger musical forms, the blending of voices, lines, and timbre characteristic of the symphony. Without his experience of sophisticated orchestral music, Lanier never could have developed as a poet; if he had never played Berlioz' *Symphonie Fantastique*, he might never have written his best poem, "The Marshes of Glynn." To Lanier, music and poetry were two different, but intimately related, media through which he expressed one ideal. This ideal is most notably expressed at the end of the poem "The Symphony": "Music is Love in search of a word." Lanier believed that man could come to terms with the problems of his civilization only through the redeeming powers of faith and love of art.

The most creative periods of Lanier's life – and the happiest – were those in which he was musically most active. Lanier's friends were, in the main, musical, not literary. He found enthusiastic applause for his flute-playing – which is supposed to have been astonishingly good – a compensation for the rejection-slips he received for his poetry. His writing, because it was so original, often came under harsh attack, but his performances never earned an unfavorable review.

Lanier is a unique figure – or rather a phenomenon – in American literature; and since he is one of the rare American poets who was also a professional musician, his poetry's qualities are determined by practical experience. Lanier was an innovator whose possible further accomplishments can only be wistfully speculated; but he is generally acknowledged by today's critics to be a significant figure in early modern literature.

—Jane S. Gabin

LARKIN, Philip (Arthur).   English.   Born in Coventry, Warwickshire, 9 August 1922. Educated at King Henry VIII School, Coventry; St. John's College, Oxford, B.A. 1943, M.A. 1947. Held posts in various U.K. libraries, 1943–55. Since 1955, Librarian, Brynmor Jones Library, University of Hull, Yorkshire. Jazz Feature Writer, *Daily Telegraph*, London,

1961–71; Visiting Fellow, All Souls College, Oxford, 1970–71. Recipient: Arts Council Prize, 1965; Queen's Gold Medal for Poetry, 1965; Cholmondeley Award, 1973; Russell Loines Award, 1974; Yorkshire Art Association Award, 1975; FVS Foundation of Hamburg Shakespeare Prize, 1976. D.Litt.: Queen's University of Belfast, 1969; University of Leicester, 1970; University of Warwick, 1973; University of St Andrews, 1974; University of Sussex, Brighton, 1974. Honorary Fellow, St. John's College, Oxford, 1973. Fellow, and Benson Medallist, 1975, Royal Society of Literature; Honorary Member, American Academy of Arts and Sciences, 1975. C.B.E. (Commander, Order of the British Empire), 1975. Lives in Hull, Yorkshire.

PUBLICATIONS

Verse

The North Ship.   1945; revised edition, 1966.
XX Poems.   1951.
(Poems).   1954.
The Less Deceived.   1955.
The Whitsun Weddings.   1964.
High Windows.   1974.

Fiction

Jill.   1946; revised edition, 1964.
A Girl in Winter.   1947.

Other

All What Jazz: A Record Diary 1961–68.   1970.

Editor, with Bonamy Dobrée and Louis MacNeice, New Poems 1958.   1958.
Editor, The Oxford Book of Twentieth Century Verse.   1973.

Reading List: Larkin by David Timms, 1973; An Uncommon Poet for the Common Man: A Study of Larkin's Poetry by Lolette Kuby, 1974; Larkin by Alan Brownjohn, 1975.

*   *   *

For more than twenty years Philip Larkin has been the most admired poet of his generation in England, though his reputation has not extended to other parts of the English-speaking world. American readers, for instance, seem to have difficulty in tuning into Larkin's accents or appreciating his themes. His first collection, The North Ship, attracted little attention; indeed it was scarcely known until a new edition appeared in 1966. Larkin's earliest poetry was rhetorical and Yeatsian. He soon decided that Yeats was not the right model for him, and that his true poetic master was Thomas Hardy, whom he still admires enormously. But something permanent remained from the Yeatsian phase: the capacity to produce a rich, emphatic, memorable line, and great skill in handling complex stanza forms. The North Ship was followed in the late forties by two accomplished novels, Jill and A Girl in

Winter, both studies of sensitive, lonely young people, drawing in part on autobiographical material. But Larkin seems to have made a deliberate decision not to continue with fiction and has since restricted himself to poetry. His first mature collection, *The Less Deceived*, made a considerable impact, but Larkin writes poems slowly and infrequently, and only two collections have been published since then.

Yet though Larkin's rate of production is not high his poetic craftsmanship is exemplary, and is admired even by readers who find his emotional range too narrow. He is a formally traditional poet, in the line of Hardy, Graves, Edward Thomas, and the best of the Georgians, and on the face of it he has little time for the modernism of Eliot and Pound. Nevertheless, his diction and metrics show that he has not been unaffected by poetic modernism. Even though he no longer writes fiction, Larkin brings a novelist's power of observation to the writing of poetry: he notes carefully, if without enthusiasm, the changing appearance of things in post-war English society. He writes coolly, sometimes affectionately, about provincial or suburban landscape and the frequent defeats and occasional triumphs of everyday human existence. Critics who deplore his seeming narrowness have referred to Larkin's "suburban mental ratio." He has indeed caught in his poetry something of the urbanized or suburbanized way of life of most contemporary English people, even the very tones of voice, as well as a certain familiar atmosphere of resentment and small aims and ideals. This sense of recognition certainly accounts for part of his appeal.

But he is far more than a social observer or commentator in verse, however acute and sensitive. Compared with the great poets of the recent past − the heroic generation of modernism − he is undeniably narrow; but he is also deep, in his own characteristic way. Each of his mature volumes contains one or two longish, finely wrought poems which touch on the major and perennial themes of existence: death in "Church Going" (*The Less Deceived*); love and marriage in the title poem of *The Whitsun Weddings*, and love and death in "An Arundel Tomb" in the same collection; old age in "The Old Fools" and death in "The Building" (*High Windows*). Each of his collections, too, contains a number of short lyrics, sometimes difficult, but all of marked aesthetic intensity and at times hauntingly beautiful: "Coming," "Going," "Age," "Absences," "Water," "Days," "Afternoons." Larkin's mood is, admittedly, often bleak or sad or autumnal, occasionally even despairing. But certain poems attain a note of celebration, like "The Trees" or "Show Saturday" (*High Windows*). Profoundly agnostic, Larkin still finds value and consolation in the recurring rituals that bring human beings together, like a funeral, a wedding, an annual horse-show. Reading Larkin one misses large gestures of affirmation or defiance − the kind of thing he found he could not accept in Yeats − and their absence can be a little lowering. But Larkin's poetry offers many satisfactions: like other good poets he has made positive poems out of negative feelings.

—Bernard Bergonzi

LAWRENCE, D(avid) H(erbert). English. Born in Eastwood, Nottinghamshire, 11 September 1885. Educated at Nottingham High School, 1898–1901; University College, Nottingham, now University of Nottingham, 1906–08: teacher's certificate, 1908. Eloped with Frieda Weekley in 1912, married in 1914. Worked for a firm of surgical appliance makers, Nottingham, 1901; teacher in Eastwood and Ilkeston, Nottinghamshire, 1902–06; teacher at the Davidson Road School, Croydon, Surrey, 1908–12; full-time writer from 1912; lived in Germany, 1912–14; in England, 1914–19; Editor, with Katherine Mansfield and John Middleton Murry, *The Signature* magazine, 1915; prosecuted for obscenity (*The Rainbow*), 1915; left England, 1919, and travelled in Australia, Mexico, Sicily, and Sardinia;

lived in the southwestern United States, Mexico, and Italy. Also a painter: one-man show, London, 1929 (closed by the police). Recipient: Black Memorial Prize, 1921. *Died 2 March 1930.*

PUBLICATIONS

Collections

Collected Letters, edited by Harry T. Moore.   2 vols., 1962.
Complete Poems, edited by Vivian de Sola Pinto and F. Warren Roberts.   2 vols., 1964.
Complete Plays.   1965.
A Selection, edited by R. H. Poole and P. J. Shepherd.   1970.

Verse

Love Poems and Others.   1913.
Amores.   1916.
Look! We Have Come Through!   1917.
New Poems.   1918.
Bay.   1919.
Tortoises.   1921.
Birds, Beasts, and Flowers.   1923.
Collected Poems.   2 vols., 1928.
Pansies.   1929.
Nettles.   1930.
Last Poems, edited by Richard Aldington and Giuseppe Orioli.   1932.
Fire and Other Poems.   1940.

Plays

The Widowing of Mrs. Holroyd (produced 1920).   1914.
Touch and Go.   1920.
David (produced 1927).   1926.
A Collier's Friday Night (produced 1965).   1934.
The Daughter-in-Law (produced 1967).   In *Complete Plays*, 1965.
The Fight for Barbara (produced 1967).   In *Complete Plays*, 1965.
The Married Man, and *The Merry-Go-Round*, in *Complete Plays*.   1965.

Fiction

The White Peacock.   1911; edited by Harry T. Moore, 1966.
The Trespasser.   1912.
Sons and Lovers.   1913; edited by Julian Moynahan, 1968; *A Facsimile of a Manuscript*, edited by Mark Schorer, 1978.
The Prussian Officer and Other Stories.   1914.
The Rainbow.   1915.
Women in Love.   1920.
The Lost Girl.   1920.

Aaron's Rod. 1922.

England My England and Other Stories. 1922.

The Ladybird, The Fox, The Captain's Doll. 1923; as *The Captain's Doll: Three Novelettes,* 1923.

Kangaroo. 1923.

The Boy in the Bush, with M. L. Skinner. 1924.

St. Mawr, Together with The Princess. 1925.

The Plumed Serpent (Quetzalcoatl). 1926.

Sun (story). 1926; unexpurgated edition, 1928.

Glad Ghosts (story). 1926.

Rawdon's Roof (story). 1928.

The Woman Who Rode Away and Other Stories. 1928.

Lady Chatterley's Lover. 1928; *The First Lady Chatterley* (first version), 1944; *La Tre Lady Chatterley* (three versions), in Italian, 1954; *John Thomas and Lady Jane* (second version), 1972.

The Escaped Cock. 1929; as *The Man Who Died,* 1931.

The Virgin and the Gipsy. 1930.

Love among the Haystacks and Other Pieces. 1930.

The Lovely Lady (stories). 1933.

A Modern Lover (stories). 1934.

A Prelude (story). 1949.

The Princess and Other Stories, and *The Mortal Coil and Other Stories,* edited by Keith Sagar. 2 vols., 1971.

Other

Twilight in Italy. 1916.

Movements in European History. 1921; revised edition, 1926.

Psychoanalysis and the Unconscious. 1921.

Sea and Sardinia. 1921.

Fantasia of the Unconscious. 1922.

Studies in Classic American Literature. 1923; edited by Armin Arnold, as *The Symbolic Meaning: The Uncollected Versions,* 1962.

Reflections on the Death of a Porcupine and Other Essays. 1925.

Mornings in Mexico. 1927.

The Paintings of Lawrence. 1929.

My Skirmish with Jolly Roger (introduction to *Lady Chatterley's Lover*). 1929; as *A Propos of Lady Chatterley's Lover,* 1930.

Pornography and Obscenity. 1929.

Assorted Articles. 1930.

Apocalypse. 1931.

Letters, edited by Aldous Huxley. 1932.

Etruscan Places. 1932.

We Need One Another. 1933.

Phoenix: The Posthumous Papers, edited by Edward D. McDonald. 1936.

The Paintings, edited by Mervyn Levy. 1964.

Phoenix II: Uncollected, Unpublished, and Other Prose Works, edited by F. Warren Roberts and Harry T. Moore. 1968.

Lawrence in Love: Letters to Louie Burrows, edited by James T. Boulton. 1968.

Centaur Letters, edited by Edward D. McDonald. 1970.

Letters to Martin Secker, 1911–30, edited by Martin Secker. 1970.

The Quest for Rananim: Letters to S. S. Koteliansky, 1914–30, edited by G. J. Zytaruk. 1970.

Letters to Thomas and Adele Seltzer: Letters to His American Publishers, edited by
  Gerald M. Lacy. 1976.

Translator, with S. S. Koteliansky, *All Things Are Possible,* by Leo Shestov. 1920.
Translator, *Mastro-Don Gesualdo,* by Giovanni Verga. 1923.
Translator, *Little Novels of Sicily,* by Giovanni Verga. 1925.
Translator, *Cavalleria Rusticana and Other Stories,* by Giovanni Verga. 1928.
Translator, *The Story of Doctor Manente,* by A. F. Grazzini. 1929.
Translator, with S. S. Koteliansky, *The Grand Inquisitor,* by Dostoevsky. 1930.

Bibliography: *A Bibliography of Lawrence* by F. Warren Roberts, 1963.

Reading List: *The Intelligent Heart,* 1954, revised edition, as *The Priest of Love,* 1974, and
The Life and Works of Lawrence, revised edition, 1964, both by Harry T. Moore; *Lawrence,
Novelist* by F. R. Leavis, 1955; *The Love Ethic of Lawrence* by Mark Spilka, 1955, and
Lawrence: A Collection of Critical Essays edited by Spilka, 1963; *The Dark Sun: A Study of
Lawrence* by Graham Hough, 1956; *Lawrence: A Composite Biography* edited by Edward
Nehls, 3 vols., 1957–59; *The Deed of Life: The Novels and Tales of Lawrence* by Julian
Moynahan, 1963; *Lawrence* by R. P. Draper, 1964, and *Lawrence: The Critical Heritage*
edited by Draper, 1970; *Double Measure: A Study of the Novels and Stories of Lawrence* by
George H. Ford, 1965; *The Art of Lawrence* by Keith Sagar, 1966; *Acts of Attention: The
Poems of Lawrence* by Sandra M. Gilbert, 1972; *Lawrence* by Frank Kermode, 1973.

*   *   *

D. H. Lawrence's background, which was an important influence on his work, is best
described in his own essay "Nottingham and the Mining Countryside." Life in late
nineteenth-century Eastwood, he says, "was a curious cross between industrialism and the
old agricultural England of Shakespeare and Milton and Fielding and George Eliot." His
father, a semi-literate miner who spoke the Nottinghamshire and Derbyshire dialect, was
essentially working-class in habits and outlook, but his mother, who had been a
schoolteacher, spoke "King's English" and prided herself on her superiority to the world into
which she had married. Their son owed much to both. It was his mother who encouraged
him to develop his intelligence and took pride in his educational achievements, but it was
from his father's sensuousness and the "intimate community" of the miners that he derived
his later belief in the overriding importance of non-intellectual contact between men and
women and of intuitive awareness rather than scientific knowledge.

Lawrence's first important novel, *Sons and Lovers,* is a study of working-class life seen
from within. In it he draws extensively on his own background and personal experience. Mr.
and Mrs. Morel are fictional portraits of his mother and father, and their son Paul has much
in common with Lawrence himself. Similarly, his youthful sweetheart, Jessie Chambers, is
reflected in the character of Miriam Leivers, and the farm where she lives is based on the
Haggs', near Eastwood, which helped to give Lawrence his deep understanding of, and
passion for, English country life. The theme of the novel is mother-love as a dominating and
destructive force. Lawrence himself comments that Mrs. Morel's sons, William and Paul, are
"urged into life by their reciprocal love of their mother.... But when they come to manhood,
they can't love, because their mother is the strongest power in their lives, and holds them"
(letter of 14 November 1912). But the mother is also a vital, energetic force in Paul's life.
Although her opposition to Miriam as a sweetheart for her son is in part the result of jealousy
(they compete for the same intellectual interest), it is also based on a shrewd recognition that
Miriam's soulful possessiveness is inimical to her son's fulfilment.

The sensuousness which Paul Morel inherits from his father finds expression in his purely
physical relationship with Clara. In this part of the novel, as in certain passages of natural

description which have a powerful, but indefinable, symbolic quality, Lawrence anticipates the exploration of unconscious influences on human relationships which becomes the primary theme of his two greatest novels, *The Rainbow* and *Women in Love*. Here Lawrence makes important innovations in characterization. The emphasis on analysis of motives and moral choice typical of nineteenth-century realism gives way to a sense that a subterranean life force takes over and directs the main characters at critical moments in their relations with each other. As Lawrence puts it, "You mustn't look in my novel [*The Rainbow*] for the old stable *ego* – of the character ... don't look for the development of the novel to follow the lines of certain characters: the characters fall into the form of some other rhythmic form, as when one draws a fiddle bow across a fine tray delicately sanded, the sand takes lines unknown" (letter of 5 June 1914).

In *The Rainbow* three generations of the Brangwen family struggle successively to find a balanced relationship in which their strong, instinctive sense of oneness with the natural world is harmonised with the conscious intelligence and mechanical sophistication which are increasingly the marks of modern industrialised society. A tentative resolution is achieved in the first generation when Tom and Lydia meet, like a rainbow, "to the span of the heavens" with their child Anna "free to play in the space beneath, between"; but in the succeeding generations the struggle is both intensified and less satisfactory in outcome, culminating in the complete collapse of the relationship between Ursula and Skrebensky in the third generation.

The method Lawrence employs in *The Rainbow* is highly original, and yet the result is not an obviously "experimental" novel such as Joyce's *Ulysses* or Virginia Woolf's *The Waves*. It is still, like *Sons and Lovers*, in many respects a vivid record of life in the English midlands of the late nineteenth and early twentieth century, and it has many scenes of compelling emotional realism; but it transcends these to become a symbolist exploration of human relations seen in the context of the natural rhythm of life itself, and expressed in a language which has strong biblical overtones. The result is a work which is often repetitive, sometimes obscure, and occasionally pretentious, but always bristling with a compelling immediacy of experience which demands an intensely personal response from the reader.

Women in Love (originally conceived as an integral part of *The Rainbow*) continues the experiences of Ursula into a new relationship with Rupert Birkin, which is presented as the creative counterpoint to the destructive relationship between her sister, Gudrun, and Birkin's friend, Gerald Crich. Marriage and personal fulfilment through the sexual relationship remains the theme of this novel, but a further dimension is added to it by Birkin's role as prophet of a new conception of "polarity" between man and woman, which involves both mutual commitment and a balanced independence. Birkin also believes in the need for a relationship of "blood brotherhood" between man and man to complement the marital relationship between man and woman. Altogether *Women in Love* is the most ambitious of Lawrence's novels. Criticism of social and economic conditions, a major preoccupation with Lawrence during and after the war years, mounts here to a sweeping denunciation of the devitalised materialism of contemporary England, and is skilfully interlocked with symbolic scenes which, like those of *Sons and Lovers* and *The Rainbow*, remain mysteriously evocative while being more purposefully organised in accordance with an almost epic, or mythic, design. Some of the faults of *The Rainbow* remain, and Lawrence's didacticism is at times excessive (though this is qualified by the self-criticism which is incorporated into the character of Birkin), but despite these flaws *Women in Love* is Lawrence's masterpiece and one of the undoubted classics of modern literature.

The novels which follow *Women in Love* are disappointingly inferior. The best of these is *Lady Chatterley's Lover* which has a tautness of structure and clarity of theme lacking in *Aaron's Rod* and *Kangaroo*, while its return to the treatment of the sexual relationship in warm, personal terms is a welcome contrast to the doctrinaire abstractions and the pseudo-religious revivalism of *The Plumed Serpent*. But even *Lady Chatterley* has an unsatisfactorily simplified schematic quality compared with *Sons and Lovers*, *The Rainbow*, and *Women in Love*.

There is, however, no reason to suspect a flagging of creative effort if one takes into account the tales, poems, travel books, and critical essays, and the marvellous spontaneity of the stream of letters, written without any thought of publication, which continued to flow from Lawrence's pen in the years after 1916. His special flair for the short story genre is apparent in his earliest work, in tales of the Nottingham environment such as "Odour of Chrysanthemums" and "Daughters of the Vicar," which show remarkable skill in combining atmosphere, psychological truth, and moral discrimination in terms of what makes for and against living fulfilment. These qualities are continued in the "long short stories" of his middle period, but joined with a more highly developed capacity for conveying levels of meaning which are subversive of conventionally accepted standards. In "The Ladybird" this is suggested through the dark, hypnotic influence of Count Psanek on Lady Daphne, a forerunner of the relationship between Mellors and Connie in *Lady Chatterley*, though the story is marred by the self-consciously "poetic" prose in which it is written. (A more successful attempt at the same theme is made in *The Virgin and the Gipsy*.) The colloquial freedom and syntactic naturalness of "The Fox" and "The Captain's Doll" are more characteristic of Lawrence's short story style, though in themselves they have quite separate and distinct virtues. "The Fox" is a powerful fusion of realism and symbolism, while "The Captain's Doll" is a triumph of tone and humour, looking forward to the more specifically satirical short stories such as "Things" and "The Man Who Loved Islands."

The best of Lawrence's prose work in his last years is to be found in *The Man Who Died* (first printed as *The Escaped Cock*), a re-interpretation of Christianity through the story of Jesus risen in the flesh to a new appreciation of the sensuous world and physical love. Like the travel book *Etruscan Places*, it is essentially a visionary work, offering a criticism of the modern world, but indirectly through an imaginative re-creation of a way of life enhanced by the vitality and sense of wonder which have all but disappeared from the present. In this respect it is akin to the poetry of Lawrence's *Last Poems*, which meditate on death, but in so doing heighten his keen sense of the lambent, instantaneous quality of life.

The rare achievement of Lawrence's poetry has still not been given the recognition which it deserves. When writing in traditional forms, i.e., mostly in his early verse, he often seems ill-at-ease, struggling to say something for which his medium is unsuited, but in the more fluent mode of free verse, which he used with an instinctive sense of rhythm and appropriate line length that exerted its own flexible control, he found the perfect means for communicating "direct utterance from the instant whole man" (Preface to the American edition of *New Poems*). The themes are often those of the novels and stories, but the implicit disclaimer of finality enables him to give those themes a freshness and tentativeness of expression which is a welcome relief from the assertiveness of the prose. "End of Another Home Holiday," for example, achieves a delicacy of poise between disapproval of, and sympathy for, maternal love which is perhaps finer than that of *Sons and Lovers*; and the poems of *Birds, Beasts, and Flowers*, especially "Snake" and the first part of "Fish," communicate (better than, for example, the short novel *St. Mawr* does) that sense of the inviolable otherness of the living, non-human world which acts by its very presence as a criticism of man's abuse of his own instinctual being.

His early dialect verse, like the best of his plays (*The Widowing of Mrs. Holroyd* and especially *The Daughter-in-Law*), faithfully reflects the mocking, un-stuffy, working-class voice of his Nottinghamshire background; and it is this tone of voice which gives the verse of *Pansies* and *Nettles* (labelled "satirical doggerel" by W. H. Auden) its mocking, deflationary humour. Here Lawrence, the prophet, brings himself down to earth and saves himself from his own messianic over-assertiveness. As he puts it in the poem "St. Matthew":

> So I will be lifted up, Saviour,
> But put me down again in time Master,
> Before my heart stops beating, and I become what I am not.

—R. P. Draper

LAYAMON. English. Born c. 1200. Priest of Areley Kings in Worcestershire.

PUBLICATIONS

Collections

   Selections, edited by J. Hall.   1924.
   Selections, edited by G. L. Brook.   1963.

Verse

   Layamon's Brut, edited by Sir Frederic Madden.   3 vols., 1847.
   Layamon: Brut, edited by G. L. Brook and R. F. Leslie.   2 vols., 1963–78.

Reading List: *Layamon: An Attempt at Vindication* by G. J. Visser, 1935; *The Layamon Texts: A Linguistical Investigation* by N. H. P. Bøgholm, 1944; *Layamons Brut: Eine Literarische Studie* by H. Pilch, 1960.

*   *   *

All that is known of Layamon is what he tells us is in the prologue to his sole surviving work, the *Brut* (properly *Hystoria Brutorum* – the short title is taken from later popular histories): his name (the modern form of which is a conventionally accepted misspelling), and the fact that he was parish priest at Areley Kings, in Worcestershire. His poem, probably composed about 1225, survives in two manuscripts of the third quarter of the thirteenth century, both in the Cotton collection of the British Library (Caligula A.ix and Otho C.xiii). It is a metrical composite, using indiscriminately both a form of the Old English alliterative line without rhyme and short syllabic couplets of three or four stresses, and also various combinations of the two. Layamon seems consciously to have been adapting the native verse-traditions to Anglo-Norman (French) models.

The *Brut* begins with Brutus, the eponymous founder of Britain, leaving Troy, and traces the history of Britain up to the death of Cadwallader, the last "British" king with serious claims to dominion in England. The basis for the story is Geoffrey of Monmouth's *Historia Regum Britanniae* (1130–38), one of the most influential books ever written, since it is the primary source for Arthurian legend, as well as the only source for stories of pre-Arthurian kings such as Lear and Cymbeline. Geoffrey took something from traditional legends, but invented more, his purpose being to supply Britain with the history it lacked, in the sober form of a Latin prose chronicle; to claim descent, along with Rome and other nations of Western Europe, from Troy; and to create a great national hero in Arthur. Geoffrey's work was translated into Anglo-Norman (French) verse by Wace, probably for the court of Henry II, with more dramatisation of the events of the story, more dialogue and a more "courtly" flavour. Wace was the direct source of Layamon, who seems not to have known Geoffrey.

Layamon works back from Wace towards a more heroic and martial treatment of the story. His work on the first half of the poem is not memorable, but he comes into his own with the first appearance of Arthur at line 19,252. Arthur is a focus for all Layamon's imaginative energies, a figure who provides the opportunity for an expression of all his patriotic passions and all his love of heroic battle-poetry. In the Arthurian sections of the poem, Wace is a mere springboard for Layamon, who elaborates and amplifies the narrative here with unprecedented freedom. The battles of Arthur against the Saxon invaders led by

Childric are described with immense panache, with vigorous scenes of individual combat and mêlée punctuated by vows of vengeance, cries of denunciation and execration, paeans of scorn and triumph. Layamon introduces here, and only here, the epic similes for which he is famous, of Arthur as a wolf descending upon the enemy from the woods hung with snow (20120–25), or of the fleeing Saxons drowned in the Avon as "steelen fishes," their gold-bedecked shields glinting like scales (21319–28). If battles are the essence of heroic poetry, then Layamon is our greatest epic poet, and the *Brut* the only true national epic.

—Derek Pearsall

LAYTON, Irving (Peter). Canadian. Born in Neamtz, Rumania, 12 March 1912; emigrated to Canada in 1913. Educated at Alexandra Public School, Montreal; Byron Bing High School, Montreal; MacDonald College, Sainte Anne de Bellevue, Quebec, B.Sc. in agriculture 1939; McGill University, Montreal, M.A. 1946. Served in the Canadian Army, 1942–43: Lieutenant. Married 1) Betty Frances Sutherland in 1946; one son, one daughter; 2) the writer Aviva Cantor in 1961, one son. Lecturer, Jewish Public Library, Montreal, 1943–58; high school teacher in Montreal, 1954–60; Part-time Lecturer, 1949–65, and Poet-in-Residence, 1965–66, Sir George Williams University, Montreal; Writer-in-Residence, University of Guelph, Ontario, 1968–69. Since 1969, Professor of English Literature, York University, Toronto. Co-Founding Editor, *First Statement,* later *Northern Review,* Montreal, 1941–43; former Associate Editor, *Contact* magazine, Toronto, and *Black Mountain Review,* North Carolina. Recipient: Canada Foundation Fellowship, 1957; Canada Council Award, 1959, 1967, and senior arts grant and travel grant, 1973; Governor-General's Award, 1960; President's Medal, University of Western Ontario, 1961. D.C.L.: Bishop's University, Lennoxville, Quebec, 1970. Lives in Toronto.

PUBLICATIONS

Verse

    Here and Now. 1945.
    Now Is the Place: Stories and Poems. 1948.
    The Black Huntsman. 1951.
    Cerberus, with Raymond Souster and Louis Dudek. 1952.
    Love the Conqueror Worm. 1953.
    In the Midst of My Fever. 1954.
    The Cold Green Element. 1955.
    The Blue Propeller. 1955.
    The Blue Calf and Other Poems. 1956.
    Music on a Kazoo. 1956.
    Improved Binoculars: Selected Poems. 1956.
    A Laughter in the Mind. 1958; augmented edition, 1959.
    A Red Carpet for the Sun: Collected Poems. 1959.
    The Swinging Flesh (poems and stories). 1961.
    Balls for a One-Armed Juggler. 1963.

The Laughing Rooster.   1964.
Collected Poems.   1965.
Periods of the Moon.   1967.
The Shattered Plinths.   1968.
The Whole Bloody Bird (obs, aphs, and pomes).   1969.
Selected Poems, edited by Wynne Francis.   1969.
Five Modern Canadian Poets, with others, edited by Eli Mandel.   1970.
Collected Poems.   1971.
Nail Polish.   1971.
Lovers and Lesser Men.   1973.
Selected Poems.   1974.
The Pole Vaulter.   1974.
Seventy-Five Grub Poems.   1974.
The Unwavering Eye: Selected Poems, 1969–1975.   1975.
Selected Poems.   1977.

Other

Engagements: The Prose of Layton, edited by Seymour Mayne.   1972.
Taking Sides: The Collected Social and Political Writings, edited by Howard Aster.   1977.

Editor, with Louis Dudek, *Canadian Poems 1850–1952.*   1952
Editor, *Pan-ic: A Selection of Contemporary Canadian Poems.*   1958.
Editor, *Poems for 27 Cents.*   1961.
Editor, *Love Where the Nights Are Long: Canadian Love Poems.*   1962.
Editor, *Anvil: A Selection of Workshop Poems.*   1966.
Editor, *Poems to Colour: A Selection of Workshop Poems.*   1970.
Editor, *Anvil Blood: A Selection of Workshop Poems.*   1973.

Bibliography: "Layton: A Bibliography in Progress 1931–1971" by Seymour Mayne, in *West Coast Review,* January 1973.

Reading List: "That Heaven-Sent Lively Ropewalker, Layton" by Hayden Carruth, in *Tamarack Review,* Spring 1966; *Layton* by Eli Mandel, 1969.

*   *   *

Irving Layton is undoubtedly the most prolific of Canadian poets; since his first book, *Here and Now,* appeared in 1945, hardly a year has passed without another volume or at least a brochure of his verse appearing. He has also written some short stories and a few polemical essays, the best of which were collected by his fellow poet, Seymour Mayne, in a volume entitled *Engagements.* As an editor he has been involved in a number of North American verse magazines, including *First Statement* and *Contact* in Canada, and *Black Mountain Review* in the United States. But is is essentially as a poet that Layton sees himself and makes sure that the world sees him.

Layton is a poet of various styles and equally various levels of quality; he belongs to no school and has borrowed effects from all of them. Readers are often puzzled that so much energy and so much genuine talent should be accompanied by such an evident lack of self-criticism – a lack which means that more than half of any volume Layton publishes is likely to consist of poems that should never have passed beyond the writer's desk. At the same time they are often stirred to admiration by his best poems which, as Northrop Frye has pointed out, reveal Layton as "an erudite elegiac poet, whose technique turns on an aligning of the romantic and the ironic."

Layton's work can really be considered in three phases. He first published, largely at his own expense, a series of thin volumes of verbose and flamboyant verses strong in self-advertisement and in cheap shocks for respectable minds. By the early 1950's, however, Layton was beginning to find himself; in volumes like *The Cold Green Element* his real power as a poet of compassion, in love with the splendour and sad with the transience of life, begins to emerge. It is admirably exemplified in the poem – obliquely celebrating Layton's hero Nietzsche – "The Birth of Tragedy":

> A quiet madman, never far from tears,
>   I lie like a slain thing
>   under the green air the trees
> inhabit, or rest upon a chair
>   towards which the inflammable air
> tumbles on many robins' wings;
>   noting how seasonably
>   leaf and blossom uncurl
> and living things arrange their death,
> while someone from afar off
> blows birthday candles for the world.

The period from about 1953 to 1965 can perhaps be regarded as the climax of Layton's career, when he wrote the series of vivid and moving lyrics and elegies that make his *Collected Poems* of 1965 the true core of his work, its best items rarely equalled by any of the many volumes he has published during the years since then.

It was during the 1960's that Layton moved out of small-press printing into commercial publication, while writing as prolifically as he had always done; in this decade also he became the most popular among the Canadian poets who during this period turned public entertainer, his combination of inspired rhetoric and sexual clowning making him popular with the young audience of the period's counter-culture. What has been really surprising, in view of the volume of work that Layton has continued to produce, is the lack of real change or development in his work since the middle 1960's. His poetry remains essentially didactic and constantly agitated; one encounters repeatedly – and to the degree of boredom – the familiar obsessions with sex, with the poet's ego, with the poet's detractors, with those the poet despises, the glorifications of creativity and life as against order and art, of Dionysus as against Apollo, the hatred of critics, the love for the trival and juvenile epigram, the deliberate Nietzschean waywardness. What has declined is the immediacy of the lyric urge. In recent years Layton has written no poems that really compare with the earlier series of splendidly passionate and compassionate elegies on the human and animal condition which place Layton among the best Canadian poets.

—George Woodcock

LEAR, Edward.   English.   Born in London, 12 May 1812. Studied at Sass's School of Art, London, 1835, 1849; Royal Academy, London, 1850–52; studied painting with Holman Hunt. Free-lance artist after 1827, and teacher after 1830; assistant to the artists Prideaux Selby and John Gould; illustrated the animals at the home of the Earl of Derby, 1832–37;

lived in Rome, 1837–45; gave drawing lessons to Queen Victoria, 1846; lived in Italy, 1846–49, and in San Remo, Italy, 1868–88; exhibited at the Royal Academy, London, 1850–73. *Died 29 January 1888.*

PUBLICATIONS

Collections

>The Complete Nonsense, edited by Holbrook Jackson. 1947.
>A Book of Bosh: Lyrics and Prose, edited by Brian Alderson. 1975.

Verse

>A Book of Nonsense. 1846; revised edition, 1861.
>Nonsense Songs, Stories, Botany, and Alphabets. 1870.
>More Nonsense, Pictures, Rhymes, Botany, etc. 1871.
>Laughable Lyrics: A Fourth Book of Nonsense, Poems, Songs, Botany, Music, etc. 1876.
>Queery Leary Nonsense, edited by Lady Strachey. 1911.
>Teapots and Quails and Other New Nonsenses, edited by Angus Davidson and Philip Hofer. 1953.

Other

>Illustrations of the Family of Psittacidae, or Parrots. 1832.
>Views in Rome and Its Environs. 1841.
>Gleanings from the Menagerie and Aviary at Knowsley Hall, Knowsley. 1846.
>Illustrated Excursions in Italy 2 vols. 1846.
>Journal of a Landscape Painter in Albania, etc. 1851.
>Journal of a Landscape Painter in S. Calabria, etc. 1852.
>Views in the Seven Ionian Islands. 1863.
>Journal of a Landscape Painter in Corsica. 1870.
>Tortoises, Terrapins, and Turtles, with James de Carle Sowerby. 1872.
>Letters, and Later Letters, edited by Lady Strachey. 2 vols., 1907–11.
>Lear in Sicily, May-July 1847, edited by Granville Proby. 1938.
>Journals: A Selection, edited by Herbert Van Thal. 1952.
>Indian Journal: Watercolours and Extracts from the Diary (1873–1875), edited by Ray Murphy. 1953.

Reading List: *Lear: Landscape Painter and Nonsense Poet* by Angus Davidson, 1938; *Lear* by Joanna Richardson, 1965; *Lear: The Life of a Wanderer* by Vivien Noakes, 1968; *Lear and His World* by John Lehmann, 1977; *Nonsense and Wonder: The Poems and Cartoons of Lear* by Thomas Byrom, 1977.

*   *   *

Edward Lear began writing his nonsense pieces as casual entertainment for children and as a diversion from his professional life as an artist. Ironically, his fame and influence derive from the four volumes of nonsense he published in his lifetime and not from his landscape paintings or his drawings of birds. In his collected nonsense Lear has created a self-contained, tilted world that bears little resemblance to the actual far-off places to which he was constantly travelling. His life-long wanderlust led him beyond the Ionian Isles, Egypt, and Corfu to even more exotic places, such as "the land where the Jumblies live" and "the hills of the Chankly Bore."

Lear reinforced the comic absurdity of his verse and prose by illustrating them with nonsense drawings. Thus, as in Lewis Carroll's nonsense, the reader is lured into a bizarre world through both visual and linguistic playfulness, structured by the tilted logic of nonsense. Lear's famous "The Owl and the Pussy-cat," for example, derives much of its charm from the unexpected twists of the narrative. The poem has a clear story line but its humor depends more on its absurd logic and chronology, its neologisms ("runcible spoon"), and its steady rhyme and meter. The same holds true for his other masterpieces of nonsense. "The Jumblies," for instance, provides a hauntingly melancholy refrain:

> Far and few, far and few,
> Are the lands where the Jumblies live;
> Their heads are green, and their hands are blue,
> And they went to sea in a Sieve.

"The Dong with a Luminous Nose" opens with a sonorousness worthy of Tennyson: "When awful darkness and silence reign/Over the great Gromboolian plain." The Dong's fruitless search for his long-lost "Jumbly Girl" has obvious phallic implications but, again, the charm of the work lies in the exotic language and logic:

> Since then his Jumbly Girl he seeks,
> And because by night he could not see,
> He gathered the bark of the Twangum Tree
> On the flowery plain that grows.
> And he wove him a wondrous Nose.

In all of his great nonsense, "The Pobble Who Has No Toes," "The Courtship of the Yonghy-Bonghy-Bò," "The Quangle Wangle's Hat," "Nonsense Botany," and "Nonsense Alphabet," Lear bends and twists the shapes of reality to establish bizarre new forms that resonate in our subconscious minds like childhood truths.

Although he did not invent the limerick, Lear was the unquestioned master and popularizer of the form in his day. His *Book of Nonsense* has been the inspiration for thousands of limericks to the present time. Although usually obscene and loaded with a comic punch-line, today's limerick still follows Lear's epigrammatic spirit in both meter and rhyme:

> There was an Old Person of Buda,
> Whose conduct grew ruder and ruder.
> Till at last, with a hammer, they silenced his clamour,
> By smashing that Person of Buda.

—Richard Kelly

LEE, Laurie. British. Born in Stroud, Gloucestershire, 26 June 1914. Educated at Slad Village School, Gloucestershire, and Stroud Central School. During World War II made documentary films for the General Post Office film unit, 1939–40, and the Crown Film Unit, 1941–43, and travelled as a scriptwriter to Cyprus and India; Publications Editor, Ministry of

Information, 1944–46; member of the Green Park Film Unit, 1946–47. Married Catherine Francesca Polge in 1950; one daughter. Caption Writer-in-Chief, Festival of Britain, 1950–51. Recipient: Atlantic Award, 1944; Society of Authors Traveling Award, 1951; Foyle Award, 1956; Smith Literary Award, 1960. Fellow, Royal Society of Literature. M.B.E. (Member, Order of the British Empire), 1952. Lives in Stroud, Gloucestershire.

PUBLICATIONS

Verse

The Sun My Monument. 1944.
The Bloom of Candles: Verse from a Poet's Year. 1947.
My Many-Coated Man 1955.
(Poems). 1960.

Plays

The Voyage of Magellan: A Dramatic Chronicle for Radio (broadcast, 1946). 1948.
Peasants' Priest (produced 1947). 1952.

Screenplays: *Cyprus Is an Island,* 1946; *A Tale in a Teacup,* 1947.

Radio Play: *The Voyage of Magellan* 1946.

Other

Land at War. 1945.
We Made a Film in Cyprus, with Ralph Keene. 1947.
An Obstinate Exile. 1951.
A Rose for Winter: Travels in Andalusia. 1955.
Cider with Rosie (autobiography). 1959; as *The Edge of Day: A Boyhood in the West of England,* 1960.
Man Must Move: The Story of Transport (juvenile), with David Lambert. 1960; as *The Wonderful World of Transport,* 1960.
The Firstborn (essay). 1964.
As I Walked Out One Midsummer Morning (autobiography). 1969.
I Can't Stay Long. 1975.

Editor, with Rex Warner and Christopher Hassall, *New Poems 1954.* 1954.

Translator, *The Dead Village,* by Avigdor Dagan. 1943.

*　　*　　*

To the general public Laurie Lee is known more for his magazine articles and his evocatively nostalgic prose works (high on the paperback best-seller lists) than as a poet. However, it is as a poet that he merits attention, since his lyrical, sensuous prose style, exploring the sources and stimulus of his imaginative and physical creativity, might be seen as a part of his poetic life. The biographical works like *Cider with Rosie* crystallize in a personal perspective landscapes and characters representative of an historical moment or ethnic atmosphere. The poems, by contrast, lacking the self-dramatization which characterizes the prose reminiscences, are self-contained miniatures confronting personal experience with the control and economy necessary to avoid over-sentimentality and luxuriant romanticism.

Some have seen echoes of Lorca in his verse, others recognize the English tradition of lyrical enthusiasm for love, the power of nature, and acute sense experience. Lee has the ability to contain feeling within the apposite word and passing analogy that transfer a mood, emotion and physical presence to the reader without effort, as in "Day of These Days":

> As bread and beanflowers
> the touch of their lips
> and their white teeth sweeter than cucumbers.

Always, his imagery is drawn from the earth, juxtaposing the body and nature, the senses with the other three elements. Even in his poems of pain and despair, "Black Edge," for instance, we are sustained by the positive keenness of response and the richness of his verbal dexterity.

—B. C. Oliver-Morden

LEVERTOV, Denise. American. Born in Ilford, Essex, England, 24 October 1923; emigrated to the United States, 1948; naturalized, 1955. Educated privately. Married the writer Mitchell Goodman in 1947; one son. Poetry Editor, *The Nation*, New York, 1961; taught at the YM-YWHA Poetry Center, New York, 1964; Honorary Scholar, Radcliffe Institute for Independent Study, Cambridge, Massachusetts, 1964–66; Visiting Lecturer, City College of New York, 1965, Drew University, Madison, New Jersey, 1965, Vassar College, Poughkeepsie, New York, 1966–67, and University of California, Berkeley, 1969; Visiting Professor, Massachusetts Institute of Technology, Cambridge, 1969–70; Artist-in-Residence, Kirkland College, 1970–71; Elliston Lecturer, University of Cincinnati, Spring 1973. Visiting Professor, 1973–74, 1974–75, and since 1975 Professor, Tufts University, Medford, Massachusetts. Recipient: Longview Award, 1961; Guggenheim Fellowship, 1962; National Institute of Arts and Letters grant, 1966, 1968; Lenore Marshall Prize, 1976. D.Litt.: Colby College, Waterville, Maine, 1970; University of Cincinnati, 1973. Lives in New York City.

PUBLICATIONS

Verse

> *The Double Image.* 1946.
> *Here and Now.* 1957.
> *Overland to the Islands.* 1958.
> *5 Poems.* 1958.
> *With Eyes at the Back of Our Heads.* 1959.
> *The Jacob's Ladder.* 1961.

602

O Taste and See: New Poems.   1964.
City Psalm.   1964.
Psalm Concerning the Castle.   1966.
The Sorrow Dance.   1967.
Three Poems.   1968.
A Tree Telling of Orpheus.   1968.
The Cold Spring and Other Poems.   1968.
A Marigold from North Vietnam.   1968.
Embroideries.   1969.
Relearning the Alphabet.   1970.
Summer Poems 1969.   1970.
A New Year's Garland for My Students, MIT 1969–70.   1970.
To Stay Alive.   1971.
Footprints.   1972.
The Freeing of the Dust.   1975.

Fiction

In the Night: A Story.   1968.

Other

The Poet in the World (essays).   1973.
Conversation in Moscow.   1973.

Editor, *Out of the War Shadow: An Anthology of Current Poetry.*   1967.
Editor and Translator, with Edward C. Dimock, Jr., *In Praise of Krishna: Songs from the Bengali.*   1967.

Translator, *Selected Poems of Guillevic.*   1969.

Bibliography: *A Bibliography of Levertov* by Robert A. Wilson, 1972.

Reading List: *Levertov* by Linda Wagner, 1967.

*   *   *

By her own admission, Denise Levertov began writing as a "British Romantic with almost Victorian background" and has since become one of the powerful probing voices of contemporary American poetry. Her outspoken advocacy of women's liberation, her opposition to the Vietnam War, her adherence generally to the values of the political left came about through the gradual transformations of awareness since publishing *Here and Now* in 1957.

Raised and educated in a literary household in England, she published a first book of poems, *The Double Image*, in 1946. In 1948 she emigrated to the United States with her American husband, the novelist Mitchell Goodman, whose friendship with Robert Creeley led to her association with the Black Mountain movement and the journal *Origin*, which began publishing her work. Her early poems show the influence of Williams and Olson in their diction and form, but by the middle of the 1950's, Robert Duncan encouraged her to experiment more boldly with mythic perception of her identity and circumstances. She has since explained her own poetic in the essay "Organic Form," which distinguishes between a free verse of disjointed statements and organic poetry, where "form," all facets of technique, is "a revelation of content." But her poems retain traditional verse conventions, and she has occasionally attacked the improvisatory mode of other poets.

In her first substantial work, *With Eyes at the Back of Our Heads*, her poems moved to frank self-disclosures, in an effort to grasp a personal identity underlying sexual stereotype. In "The Goddess," one of the finest poems of the volume, she dramatizes her awakening to an inner nature after her expulsion from "Lie Castle," where she has been flung

> across the room, and
> room after room (hitting the walls, re-
> bounding – to the last
> sticky wall – wrenching away from it
> pulling hair out!)
> til it lay
> outside the outer walls!
>
> There in the cold air
> lying still where her hand had thrown me,
> I tasted the mud that splattered my lips
> the seeds of a forest were in it,
> asleep and growing! I tasted
> her power!

O Taste and See pursues the implications of "The Goddess" by boldly reaching into the feminine psyche to discover its raw vitality, as in this startling image of appetite:

> In the black of desire
> we rock and grunt, grunt and
> shine

Beginning with *Relearning the Alphabet*, she has moved beyond purely personal issues to larger political concerns, war resistance, women's liberation, poverty and oppression in the Third World. The poems of *To Stay Alive* and *Footprints*, many taking a longer, serial form, follow her increasingly activist participation in various resistance movements of the last two decades.

—Paul Christensen

LEWIS, Alun.   Welsh.   Born in Aberdare, South Wales, in 1915. Educated at University College of Wales, Aberystwyth, B.A. in history; University of Manchester, M.A. Teacher at Pengam. Served in the British Army; died in the Arakan on active service, 1944. *Died in 1944.*

PUBLICATIONS

Collections

Selected Poetry and Prose, edited by Ian Hamilton.   1966.

Verse

> *Raiders' Dawn and Other Poems.*   1942.
> *Ha! Ha! among the Trumpets: Poems in Transit.*   1945.

Fiction

> *The Last Inspection* (stories).   1942.

Other

> *Letters from India.*   1946.
> *In the Green Tree* (letters; includes stories).   1948.

Reading List: "Lewis" by Gwyn Jones in *Welsh Review 3,* 1944; in *The Open Night* by John Lehmann, 1952; articles by John Stuart Williams in *Anglo-Welsh Review 14,* 1964–65; *Lewis* by Alun John, 1970.

*   *   *

Alun Lewis, Anglo-Welsh poet and short story writer, was born in a small valley near Aberdare in 1915. He grew up in a bi-lingual mining community, attended the local secondary school, and read history at the University College of Wales, Aberystwyth. After taking his Master's at Manchester, he became a teacher at Pengam. This seems to have been a temporary expedient while he waited for the war that seemed inevitable. In the meantime he wrote poems and short stories which were published in periodicals as different as *Lilliput* and *The Welsh Review.*

His reputation as an Anglo-Welsh writer remains uncertain, perhaps because the term has begun to impose its own stereotypes. While the quality of his short stories is acknowledged – he has been compared at his best with Chekhov – he has not, as a poet, received the kind of acclaim that has been given Dylan Thomas. This may be because he is in the end a different kind of poet, a poet of the relationship between man and the "complexity of the universe." He disturbs more often than he comforts. It may be worth noting that Robert Graves considered him a truer poet than Dylan Thomas. The integrity of his concern with the conflict between "self-pity and pity for the world" supports this claim.

He was already a writer of some achievement before he became a soldier – more than a third of the poems in his first collection, *Raiders' Dawn*, were written before September 1939 – but there is little doubt that his service experience in England and in India compelled an extension of sensibility upon a mind "honest with itself and humble, clear-sighted and receptive." Having rejected what he called "Virgil's imperial gaze" he achieved an economy and authority in stories like "The Orange Grove" and in poems like "The Peasants" in which "the material and the spiritual" are never separate. His death on active service in the Arakan in 1944 deprived us of a writer of unusual talent who had already achieved much and promised a great deal more.

—John Stuart Williams

LINDSAY, (Nicholas) Vachel. American. Born in Springfield, Illinois, 10 November 1879. Educated at Hiram College, Ohio, 1897–1900; studied for the ministry; studied art at the Chicago Art Institute, 1901, and New York Art School, 1905. Married Elizabeth Conner in 1925; one son, one daughter. Pen and ink designer, 1900–10; lecturer on the history of art, 1905–10; also travelled through the U.S. living by reciting his poems, 1906–12; after 1912 became known for his verses and was thereafter in demand as lecturer and reader. Taught at Gulf Park College, Mississippi, 1923–24. Litt.D.: Hiram College, 1930. Member, National Institute of Arts and Letters. *Died* (by suicide) *5 December 1931.*

<small>PUBLICATIONS</small>

Collections

   Selected Poems, edited by Mark Harris. 1963.

Verse

   The Tramp's Excuse and Other Poems. 1909.
   Rhymes to Be Traded for Bread. 1912.
   General William Booth Enters into Heaven and Other Poems. 1913.
   The Congo and Other Poems. 1914.
   The Chinese Nightingale and Other Poems. 1917.
   The Golden Whales of California and Other Rhymes in the American Language. 1920.
   The Daniel Jazz and Other Poems. 1920.
   Going-to-the-Sun. 1923.
   Collected Poems. 1923; revised edition, 1925.
   Going-to-the-Stars. 1926.
   The Candle in the Cabin: A Weaving Together of Script and Singing. 1926.
   Johnny Appleseed and Other Poems (juvenile). 1928.
   Every Soul Is a Circus. 1929.
   Selected Poems, edited by Hazelton Spencer. 1931.

Other

   The Village Magazine. 1910.
   Adventures While Preaching the Gospel of Beauty. 1914.
   The Art of the Moving Picture. 1915; revised edition, 1922.
   A Handy Guide for Beggars, Especially Those of the Poetic Fraternity. 1916.
   The Golden Book of Springfield, Being a Review of a Book That Will Appear in 2018. 1920.
   The Litany of Washington Street (miscellany). 1929.
   Letters to A. Joseph Armstrong, edited by Armstrong. 1940.

Reading List: *Lindsay: A Poet in America* by Edgar Lee Masters, 1935; *The West-Going Heart: A Life of Lindsay* by Eleanor Ruggles, 1959; *Lindsay* by Raymond Purkey, 1968; *Lindsay: Fieldworker for the American Dream* by Ann Massa, 1970.

*   *   *

Vachel Lindsay was a man out of phase with his time. He was also a writer who had the misfortune to be judged solely on the basis of his poetry, even though he produced a sizeable corpus of prose, work which he felt to be ultimately more important than his poetry. While it is true that he has recently begun to receive the critical appreciation and intepretation he deserves, it is equally true that he is still considered by many to be a writer (and reciter) of verse – a 20th-century troubadour who toured the country reciting his poems to hugely enthusiastic audiences, a propagandist for America whose exhortations were clothed in bombast, naivety, sentimentality, and theatrics, a phenomenon whose time had already come and gone. His role as social critic was unrecognized and such prose works as *Adventures While Preaching the Gospel of Beauty*, *The Art of the Moving Picture*, *A Handy Guide for Beggars*, and *The Golden Book of Springfield* were virtually ignored.

Lindsay's early books of verse, *General William Booth Enters into Heaven and Other Poems* and *The Congo and Other Poems*, established his reputation as a herald of the New Poetry. They mark a dramatic break with the genteel, derivative verse that then dominated the American literary scene, while marking a continuity with the Whitmanesque mode. His best poems ring with genuine music and vibrate with energy, and Lindsay's theatrical recitation of them established his reputation as an entertainer. But the latter reputation eclipsed the former and clung to him throughout the remainder of his life. His problem was two-fold: his superb qualities as an entertainer and the public's refusal to accept his definition of the role of the poet.

Lindsay felt poetry should serve the masses; that art for art's sake had no place on the American scene; that elitism in poetry was a negative and destructive force; and that Americans had to be awakened to the fact that they were allowing their country's true destiny to slip away. Lindsay considered his poetry to be the best means by which he could jolt the people into an awareness of what was happening; when they were made aware of it they would then fall in line behind him and join his efforts to recapture and restore to America its original promise.

But Lindsay's vision of America was not the vision of the American majority. Moreover, his pessimism and fundamentalist viewpoint (both of America's problems and of the solutions to them) were anathema to political, social, and literary arbiters of the day. And finally, since Lindsay believed poetry to be a social as opposed to artistic instrument (content should take precedence over style), he was not part of the imagist movement which influenced the course of 20th-century American poetry from his day to the present.

Lindsay never recovered from the realization that the people wanted only entertainment from him and that his crusade for "religion, equality and beauty," his "gospel," was doomed. He died by his own hand, a bitter and psychotic man, "Staking his last strength and his final fight/That cost him all, to set the old world right" ("Litany of the Heroes").

—Catherine Seelye

LIVESAY, Dorothy. Canadian. Born in Winnipeg, Manitoba, 12 October 1909. Educated at Trinity College, University of Toronto, 1927–31, B.A. 1931; the Sorbonne, Paris, diploma, 1932; London Institute of Education, 1959; University of British Columbia, Vancouver, M.Ed. 1966. Married Duncan Macnair in 1937 (died); one son and one daughter. Social worker, Englewood, New Jersey, 1935–36, and Vancouver, 1936–39, 1953–55; Correspondent, Toronto *Daily Star*, 1946–49; Documentary Scriptwriter, Canadian Broadcasting Corporation, 1950–55; Lecturer in Creative Writing, University of British Columbia, 1955–56, 1965–66; High School Teacher, Vancouver, 1956–58; UNESCO

607

English Specialist, Paris, 1958–60, and Zambia, 1960–63; Writer-in-Residence, University of New Brunswick, Fredericton, 1966–68; Associate Professor of English, University of Alberta, Edmonton, 1968–71; Visiting Lecturer, University of Victoria, British Columbia, 1974–75; Writer-in-Residence, University of Manitoba, Winnipeg, 1975–77, and University of Ottawa, 1977. Editor, *CV/II* magazine. Recipient: Governor-General's Award, 1945, 1948; Lorne Pierce Medal, 1947; President's Medal, University of Western Ontario, 1954; Canada Council grant, 1958, 1964, 1971, 1977. D.Litt.: University of Waterloo, Ontario, 1973.

PUBLICATIONS

Verse

> *Green Pitcher.*   1928.
> *Signpost.*   1932.
> *Day and Night.*   1944.
> *Poems for People.*   1947.
> *Call My People Home.*   1950.
> *New Poems.*   1955.
> *Selected Poems 1926–1956.*   1957.
> *The Colour of God's Face.*   1965.
> *The Unquiet Bed.*   1967.
> *The Documentaries: Selected Longer Poems.*   1968.
> *Plainsongs.*   1969; revised edition, 1971.
> *Disasters of the Sun.*   1971.
> *Collected Poems: The Two Seasons.*   1972.
> *Nine Poems of Farewell 1972–1973.*   1973.
> *Ice Age.*   1975.

Fiction

> *A Winnipeg Childhood* (stories).   1973.

Other

> *Right Hand, Left Hand* (memoirs).   1977.

> Editor, *The Collected Poems of Raymond Knister.*   1949.
> Editor, with Seymour Mayne, *Forty Women Poets of Canada.*   1971.

Reading List: "Livesay: The Love Poetry" by P. Stevens, in *Canadian Literature,* Winter 1971; "Livesay's Two Seasons" by Robin Skelton, in *Canadian Literature,* Autumn 1973.

*   *   *

Dorothy Livesay's efflorescence in her later years is remarkable in Canadian poetry. Her two early collections demonstrated a controlled, precise lyric verse, often praised at the time for its "feminine images" and "intense feeling." Reviewers of her overtly political work from the 1930's were reluctant to acknowledge her leftist views, although her reputation as a craftsman was well established by the time her *Selected Poems* appeared; after E. J. Pratt and Earle Birney, and with F. R. Scott, A. M. Klein, and A. J. M. Smith she was considered to be one of the country's half-dozen best poets. With seven new volumes published during the last two decades, together with her *Collected Poems* and a selection, she is now widely regarded as the most mature voice in Canadian feminist poetry. Livesay has long insisted on a "way of looking" that is distinctively from a "womans's eye," and she has edited an anthology of women poets from Canada. *Collected Poems* and *Ice Age* include all her substantial poetry.

Livesay's semi-autobiographical prose reminiscences of her youth, *A Winnipeg Childhood*, suggest the constrained literary environment reflected in her first precocious volume of verse and its sequel. Her personal preoccupations through the 1930's and later can be summed up as "love, politics, the Depression and feminism." A communist for much of that time, she was only occasionally heard in public as a revolutionary; the appearance of *Day and Night* during the Second World War revealed the strength of her commitment to the struggle against fascism and industrial capitalism. Despite the obtrusive rhetoric, her sympathies with the victims of economic and military oppression are strongly realised in the longer poetry of the 1930's and 1940's: the title poems of *Day and Night* and *Call My People Home* (a radio documentary on Japanese-Canadians interned in 1941), and "Prophet of the New World," about the nineteenth-century mystic and revolutionary Riel.

New Poems marked a substantial development. Her usual tight control, frequently emphasized by rhyme, was sharpened by a more objective tone. Later collections continue to demonstrate the dialectic structure of her work, while increasingly they embody "that pull between community and private identity that is characteristic of being a woman." In *The Unquiet Bed* Livesay had found an appropriately intimate voice, one patterned by natural speech rhythms yet preserving the sharp irony which characterizes her most acute work. The "great game" of love can involve both "an itch for the seven-inch/reach" and confidence that "aloneness is the only bliss." In her latest poetry she is secure in her stance as both observer and participant, poet and woman, listening with her "third ear" and knowing that "in the small womb/lies all the lightning."

—Bruce Nesbitt

LOCKER-LAMPSON, Frederick. English. Born Frederick Locker, in London, 29 May 1821; added his second wife's name, 1885. Educated at schools in Clapham, London, and at Yateley, Hampshire. Married 1) Lady Charlotte Bruce, daughter of the Earl of Elgin, 1850 (died, 1872); 2) Hannah J. Lampson in 1874. Junior Clerk in a colonial broker's office in London, 1837–38; Clerk at Somerset House, London, 1841, transferred to the Admiralty, London, 1842: successively Junior Clerk, Deputy Reader, and *Précis* Reader; in ill health from 1849, and left government service c. 1850; lived in Rowfant, Sussex, 1874 until his death. *Died 30 May 1895.*

PUBLICATIONS

Verse

London Lyrics. 1857; revised edition, as *London Rhymes*, 1882; edited by Austin Dobson, 1904.
A Selection from the Works. 1865.

Other

My Confidences: An Autobiographical Sketch Addressed to My Descendants, edited by
Augustine Birrell. 1896.

Editor, Lyra Elegantiarum: A Collection of Some of the Best Specimens of Vers de Société
and Vers d'Occasion in English. 1867; revised edition, with Coulson Kernaham,
1891.

Bibliography: by F. V. Livingston, in Bookman's Journal, July–September 1924.

Reading List: Locker-Lampson: A Character Sketch by Augustine Birrell, 1920.

*   *   *

William James, referring to Locker-Lampson's pleasant book of reminiscences, My
Confidences: An Autobiographical Sketch Addressed to My Descendants, published in the year
after its author's death, refers to Locker-Lampson as a typical example of the "once-born"
man, who finds life agreeable and makes it agreeable for those around him, but who does not
take it too seriously, and is therefore unlikely ever to suffer the crisis of conscience that
creates the "twice-born man," who through agony reaches the high assurance of religious
belief. Locker-Lampson's best work certainly was in his early London Lyrics, published in
1857, whose slight but charming poems have a flippant grace suggesting the eighteenth
rather than the nineteenth century, as in "Rotten Row":

> But where is now the courtly troop
> That once rode laughing by?
> I miss the curls of Cantilupe,
> The laugh of Lady Di.

Lord Cantilupe was one of the last of the dandies, and his world and Locker-Lampson's were
the same. Locker-Lampson's other important work was the anthology of which the first
edition was for some reason suppressed. But the revised edition, Lyra Elegantiarum, ranks as
a selection of light verse with Auden's excellent Oxford Book of Light Verse as one of the two
best such anthologies in English.

—G. S. Fraser

LONGFELLOW, Henry Wadsworth.   American.   Born in Portland, Maine, 17 February
1807. Educated at Bowdoin College, Brunswick, Maine, 1822. Married 1) Mary Potter in
1831 (died, 1835); 2) Frances Appleton in 1843 (died, 1861). After graduation appointed to
the new Chair of Modern Languages, Bowdoin College, on condition he study abroad for a
further three years: sent by trustees to Spain, 1826–29; Smith Professor of Modern
Languages, Harvard University, Cambridge, Massachusetts, 1836–54; visited Europe, 1842,
1868–69. Died 24 March 1882.

Collections

The Works and *Final Memorials*, edited by Samuel Longfellow.   14 vols., 1886–87.
Works.   10 vols., 1909.
The Essential Longfellow, edited by Lewis Leary.   1963.
The Letters, edited by Andrew Hilen.   4 vols., 1966–72.

Verse

Hyperion: A Romance.   2 vols., 1839.
Voices of the Night.   1839.
Ballads and Other Poems.   1842.
Poems on Slavery.   1842.
Poems.   1845.
The Belfry of Bruges and Other Poems.   1845.
Evangeline: A Tale of Acadie.   1847.
Poems, Lyrical and Dramatic.   1848.
The Seaside and the Fireside.   1849.
The Golden Legend.   1851.
The Song of Hiawatha.   1855.
Poetical Works.   1858.
The Courtship of Miles Standish and Other Poems.   1858.
Tales of a Wayside Inn.   1863.
Noël (in French).   1864.
Household Poems.   1865.
Flower-de-Luce.   1867.
The New-England Tragedies.   1868.
Poetical Works.   1868.
The Divine Tragedy.   1871.
Three Books of Song.   1872.
Christus: A Mystery (includes *The Divine Tragedy, The Golden Legend, The New-England Tragedies*).   1872.
Poetical Works.   1872; revised edition, 1875, 1880, 1883.
Aftermath.   1873.
The Hanging of the Crane.   1874.
The Masque of Pandora and Other Poems.   1875.
Kéramos and Other Poems.   1878.
The Early Poems, edited by Richard Herne Shepherd.   1878.
Ultima Thule.   1880; *In the Harbor: Ultima Thule — Part II*, 1882.
Michael Angelo.   3 vols., 1882–83.
Boyhood Poems, edited by Ray W. Pettengill.   1925.

Play

The Spanish Student (produced 1895).   1843.

Fiction

Kavanagh: A Tale.   1849.

611

Other

Syllabus de la Grammaire Italienne. 1832.
Outre-Mer: A Pilgrimage Beyond the Sea, numbers 1–2. 2 vols., 1833–34; vol. 2, 1835; revised edition, 1851.
Prose Works. 2 vols., 1857.
Complete Works, revised edition. 7 vols., 1866.

Editor, *Manuel de Proverbes Dramatiques.* 1830; revised edition, 1830, 1832.
Editor and Translator, *Elements of French Grammar,* by Lhomond. 1830.
Editor, *French Exercises.* 1830.
Editor, *Novelas Españolas.* 1830.
Editor, *Le Ministre de Wakefield,* by Oliver Goldsmith, translated by T. E. G. Hennequin. 1831.
Editor, *Saggi de' Novellieri Italiani d'Ogni Secolo.* 1832.
Editor, *The Waif: A Collection of Poems.* 1845.
Editor, *The Poets and Poetry of Europe.* 1845; revised edition, 1871.
Editor, *The Estray: A Collection of Poems.* 1846.
Editor, with George Nichols and John Owen, *The Works of Charles Sumner.* 10 vols., 1870–83.
Editor, *Poems of Places: England,* 4 vols.; *Ireland,* 1 vol.; *Scotland,* 3 vols.; *France,* 2 vols.; *Italy,* 3 vols.; *Spain,* 2 vols.; *Switzerland,* 1 vol.; *Germany,* 2 vols.; *Greece,* 1 vol.; *Russia,* 1 vol.; *Asia,* 3 vols.; *Africa,* 1 vol.; *America,* 6 vols.; *Oceanica,* 1 vol. 31 vols., 1876–79.

Translator, *Coplas de Don Jorge Manrique.* 1833.
Translator, *The Divine Comedy,* by Dante. 3 vols., 1867.

Bibliography: in *Bibliography of American Literature* by Jacob Blanck, 1969.

Reading List: *The Life of Longfellow, with Extracts from His Journals and Correspondence* by Samuel Longfellow, 2 vols., 1886; *Longfellow and Scandinavia: A Study of the Poet's Relationship with the Northern Languages and Literature* by Andrew Hilen, 1947; *Longfellow: A Full-Length Portrait,* 1955, and *Longfellow: Portrait of an American Humanist,* 1966, both by Edward Wagenknecht; *Longfellow: His Life and Work* by Newton Arvin, 1963; *Longfellow* by Cecil B. Williams, 1964; *Longfellow* by E. L. Hirsch, 1964; *Life of Longfellow* by Eric S. Robertson, 1972.

*   *   *

Some writers survive for the wrong reasons, like nostalgia or derision; some survive despite their defects, like prolixity or sentimentality; some survive – or deserve to – because of a small body of modest work culled long after the fact of popularity. Henry Wadsworth Longfellow belongs in all three categories.

No American writer was so admired, even revered, during his life; no writer has been so ridiculed subsequently. From 1839, when "A Psalm of Life" first moved his readers – as heavily influenced as the poem itself by Victorian and Puritan attitudes – to embrace its homilies ("Heart within, and God o'erhead!"), until his death in 1882, the decorous optimism of Longfellow's lyrics and the monotonous drone of his narrative poems stood him in high esteem. Oliver Wendell Holmes may have best defined Longfellow's appeal to his contemporaries: "a soft voice, a sweet and cheerful temper, a receptive rather than aggressive intelligence...." This may, however, be a more damning indictment of the limitations of popular taste than of the poet's achievement. Longfellow's sympathetic biographer, Newton

Arvin, proposed that we "agree, once for all, that he was a minor writer." Still, in the classroom at least, the myth of Longfellow's significance persists, and probably rather more than fewer students have turned away from poetry because of some educators' insistence on perpetuating the lie.

Longfellow's lack of variety and seeming inability either to escape conventional metrics or to bring any originality to them always hampered him; moreover, he did not easily judge the prosody best suited to his materials. At the age of thirteen, he had published his first poem in the *Portland Gazette*, "The Battle of Lovell Pond," hammered out in anapestic couplets with mathematical regularity. He never really advanced far in technical proficiency after that. His earliest successes − "The Skeleton in Armour," "The Wreck of the Hesperus," and the quintessential "Excelsior" suffer from this limitation. When, as in the last poem, the subject is "inspirational," he invites derision; and "higher" in its Latin comparative form is easily translated into shredded packing material − and not only by schoolboys who do not know their Latin. Longfellow was technically endowed to write light verse, had he possessed the sense of humor to do so, for he is not without extraordinary invention in manipulating syntax to suit his rhythms; and his inexhaustible command of rhyme, if employed for amusement, might not so easily undermine the content. At the zenith of his career, Longfellow beat his *Evangeline* into submission in jiggling dactyllic hexameters. This popular narrative traces the wanderings of a girl from Acadia (Nova Scotia) in search of her lost lover. Finally, after many remarkable adventures, she becomes a kind of nun in Pennsylvania in her old age, only to meet her lover on his death bed. This "first genuine ... fount which burst from the soil of America," called by one critic "one of the decisive poems of the world," sold 36,000 copies in its first ten years. *Hiawatha* did even better: 30,000 copies in six months. This pseudo-epic traces the development of an American Indian from birth to immortality: fathered by the West Wind; educated by nature and animals; loved by the beautiful Minnehaha; given mythic significance in his killing of an underwater monster, with the assistance of a helpful squirrel; sobered and matured by the deaths of Minnehaha (for whom he mourns seven days and seven nights) and his best friend (for whom he mourns seven times longer); and, finally, brought to a kind of metaphysical suicide − he simply gets in his canoe and starts paddling west − by the inevitable coming of the white race. Longfellow cramped this really promising material into 164 pages of four-trochee lines, likened by Oliver Wendell Holmes to the "normal rhythm of breathing" and by more than one high school student to tom-toms. At least *Hiawatha* didn't rhyme.

Longfellow wrote two inferior novels, *Hyperion* and *Kavanaugh*, which offer some insight into his private life and attitudes toward religion, politics, and literature. His single play, *The Spanish Student*, about a gypsy dancer named Preciosa (who turns out to be the long-lost daughter of a wealthy nobleman) and her chaste beau, suffers all the usual limitations of 19th-century melodrama. Although Longfellow had a successful career in education − he was one of the first modern language teachers, first at Bowdoin, then for 18 years at Harvard − his critical prose is distinguished by clarity rather than ingenuity or originality.

In spite of these several reservations, however, Longfellow wrote a number of valuable poems. In the sparse landscape of 19th-century American poetry, they grow sturdily. "Mezzo Camin," written in 1842 but not published until after his death, is a fine sonnet in which he laments his lack of significant poetic accomplishment. "The Cross of Snow," also unpublished during his life, and also a sonnet, is a touching tribute to his wife after her early death. Despite an insufferable circuitous dependent clause taking up all of its octet, the sonnet "Nature" ends superbly. A mother puts her child to bed: "So nature deals with us, and takes away/Our playthings one by one, and by the hand/Leads us to rest so gently, that we go/Scarce knowing if we wish to go or stay,/Being too full of sleep to understand/How far the unknown transcends the what we know." Its sustained imagery invites comparison with Whitman's "Goodbye, My Fancy," Emerson's "Terminus," and other epitaphic poems of the period. His ode to old age, "Morituri Salutamus," is especially valuable during the recent movement in America to recognize the oldest generation. "The Tide Rises, The Tide Falls" clearly anticipates Robert Frost's "Stopping by Woods on a Snowy Evening," even if less powerful a poem. Finally, his less well-known "The Jewish Cemetery at Newport" deserves attention. Its inhabitants, "Taught in the school of patience to endure/The Life of anguish and the death of fire," now abide in American soil, "not neglected; for a hand unseen,/ Scattering its bounty, like a summer rain,/Still keeps their graves and their remembrance green." Probably there are other poems as well by this mild man which reflect, not without some distinction, the age of restraint and decorum for which they were written. Further, a skeleton in armour, a village smithy, a midnight ride by Paul Revere, even an arrow shot into the air, may introduce some beginning readers to some of the pleasures in poetry.

—Bruce Kellner

LOVELACE, Richard. English. Born in Woolwich, London, in 1618. Educated at Charterhouse School, London; Gloucester Hall, Oxford, 1634–36, honorary M.A. 1636; incorporated at Cambridge, 1637. Ensign in Lord Goring's Regiment in the first Scottish expedition, 1639, and Captain in the second expedition, 1640. Inherited the family estates in Kent, 1639. Courtier and royalist: imprisoned for presenting the "Kentish Petition" to the Long Parliament, 1642, and subsequently released on bail; took up arms on behalf of the king, 1645; after defeat of the Royalists left England, served with the French Army against the Spanish, and was wounded at Dunkirk, 1646; returned to England, and was imprisoned by the Puritan government, 1648–49; depleted his estate in the king's cause and probably lived his last years in poverty in Gunpowder Alley, London. *Died in 1658.*

PUBLICATIONS

Collections

 Poems, edited by C. H. Wilkinson. 1930.
 Cavalier Poets, edited by Thomas Clayton. 1978.

Verse

 Lucasta: Epodes, Odes, Sonnets, Songs, etc., to Which Is Added Amarantha: A Pastoral. 1649.
 Lucasta: Posthume Poems, edited by Dudley Posthumus Lovelace. 1659–60.

Bibliography: *A Bibliography of Lovelace* by C. S. Ker, 1949.

Reading List: *The Cavalier Spirit and Its Influence on the Life and Work of Lovelace* by C. H. Hartmann, 1925; *Lovelace* by Manfred Weidhorn, 1970.

*   *   *

Richard Lovelace shares with the other so-called "Cavalier poets" like Thomas Carew and Sir John Suckling the traits of wit and ease, "ease" being a seventeenth-century critical term contrasted to "strength" and comprising such traits as metrical regularity, dilation of thought and image rather than compression, and care for the whole poem rather than strikingly original parts of it.

The quality that distinguishes Lovelace's verse from that of the other Cavalier poets is complexity of view, a quality that is exhibited both by his handling of his subjects and by his subtle tone. In "Gratiana dauncing and singing," for an example of the first, he sees in dancing proliferating meanings for the action of love and the operation of the universe. Similarly, in his many poems on animals and insects, Lovelace is intent on seeing the great in the small, the great usually taking the form of necessary conflict and death in a Nature seen objectively – and at a distance – as brutal (as noted by Manfred Weidhorn); one of the best of these is "The Grasse-hopper" (which alludes to the plight of the Cavaliers after the death of Charles I), in which the grass-hopper is not only praised as trusting and open but also condemned (and pitied) as heedless, and in which the Horatian conclusion advising retirement is not only serious but playful as well. "To Amarantha, That she would dishevell her hair" develops microcosmic conceits around her loosened hair so as to make it an emblem of a life as fully natural as the sunrise and as enjoyable as love; her untying the ribbon at her lover's insistence is imaged as deflowering, and with that act the lover's emotions pour forth in all their complexity – first eagerness, then acceptance of both joy and pain in the act ("I'le drink a teare out of thine eyes"), finally a realization of the limits, and even desperation, of the act of love in a fleeting world. This poem shows Lovelace's ability to keep such distance between himself and his emotions as to accept calmly disparate views of love and of reality in general, and disparate emotions toward them – enjoyment, cynicism, tenderness, brutality, grief (see Marius Bewley, "The Colloquial Mode of Byron," *Scrutiny* 16); so too does "La Bella Bona Roba," which presents the wholehearted gusto of the lover's preference for plump women against the dark background figure of a death's head, and encloses the whole within the playful yet brutal image of love as a hunt. Love and death combine with an amazing harmony in Lovelace's most famous lyric, "To Lucasta, Going to the Warres," where the serious adjustment of love with honor in facing death at the end of the lyric is achieved within a context of tender humor (treating the beloved's breast hyperbolically as a "Nunnerie," for instance) and reckless playfulness (treating war as if it were actually the sexual infidelity she thinks it is). Lovelace's is the poetry of poise – distant, judicious, open to conflict.

—Walter R. Davis

LOWELL, Amy (Lawrence).   American.   Born in Brookline, Massachusetts, 9 February 1874. Educated privately. Travelled a good deal abroad; associated with the Imagists in London, 1913, and thereafter promoted their work in America. Lecturer, Brooklyn Institute of Arts and Sciences, 1917–18. Recipient: Pulitzer Prize, 1926. Litt.D.: Baylor University, Waco, Texas, 1920. *Died 12 May 1925.*

PUBLICATIONS

Collections

The Complete Poetical Works.   1955.
A Shard of Silence: Selected Poems, edited by Glenn Richard Ruihley, 1957.

Verse

A Dome of Many-Coloured Glass.   1912.
Sword Blades and Poppy Seed.   1914.
Men, Women, and Ghosts.   1916.
Can Grande's Castle.   1918.
Pictures of the Floating World.   1919.
Legends.   1921.
Fir-Flower Tablets: Poems Translated from the Chinese by Florence Ayscough, English Versions by Lowell.   1921.
A Critical Fable.   1922.
What's O'Clock, edited by Ada Dwyer Russell.   1925.
East Wind, edited by Ada Dwyer Russell.   1926.
The Madonna of Carthagena.   1927.
Ballads for Sale, edited by Ada Dwyer Russell.   1927.

Play

Weeping Pierrot and Laughing Pierrot, music by Jean Hubert, from a work by Edmond Rostand.   1914.

Fiction

Dream Drops; or, Stories from Fairy Land, with Elizabeth Lowell and Katherine Bigelow Lowell.   1887.

Other

Six French Poets: Studies in Contemporary Literature.   1915.
Tendencies in Modern American Poetry.   1917.
John Keats.   2 vols., 1925.
Poetry and Poets: Essays, edited by Ferris Greenslet.   1930.
Florence Ayscough and Lowell: Correspondence of a Friendship, edited by Harley Farnsworth MacNair.   1946.

Reading List: Lowell: A Critical Appreciation by Bryher, 1918; Lowell: A Chronicle, with Extracts from Her Correspondence by S. Foster Damon, 1935; Lowell: Portrait of the Poet in Her Time by Horace Gregory, 1958; Lowell by Frank C. Flint, 1969; The Thorn of a Rose: Lowell Reconsidered by Glenn Richard Ruihley, 1975.

*   *   *

Even more than is commonly the case with rebel poets and personalities, Amy Lowell was subjected to heavy-handed abuse as well as uncritical admiration in her own life-time, there was little or no understanding of the nature of her work, and, following her untimely death in 1925, a shift in poetic fashions all but obliterated the memory of her unusual achievements. The reasons for that eclipse lie both in the poet and in her audience. Lowell was one of the most prolific and most uneven poets ever to appear in America. Because so much of her poetry was bad, it was easy to judge her harshly. Moreover, her best and most characteristic poetry was very puzzling to conventional readers and remains so to this day.

The language of these poems is chiefly pictorial, with the result that she was dismissed as a writer who touched only the physical surfaces of the world and so failed to illuminate any of its deeper meanings. As for the defects in her audience, the misreading of the poet was due to the ignorance and superficiality of the literary journalists of her day. After her death, the misunderstanding was perpetuated by the "new critics" who scorned writers who fell outside the pale of the poetry of wit and cultural memory promoted by T. S. Eliot and Ezra Pound. Though Lowell, at her best, is a writer of extraordinary verve, freshness, and beauty of expression, she was little better understood fifty years after her death than she was in 1912 when she published her first book of poems, *A Dome of Many-Coloured Glass*.

This book was rightly criticized for its feebleness and conventionality of expression; but it has one merit unnoticed by the interpreters of her poetry. The poems are written in a late Romantic style of direct statement and they chart with unusual thoroughness all of the facets of her idealistic and mystical thought. After 1912, as suggested above, Miss Lowell expressed herself imagistically. To a poet concerned with extrarational areas of experience, the new style was a great advance over the confines of logical statement, but it also led to the failures of communication which have persisted to the present day. Fortunately, we can study the poems published in *A Dome* and so know precisely the content of her thought and the beliefs she had adopted, as a substitute for Christianity, to explain her own insights into reality.

The most important of these concerns the existence of a transcendent power that permeates the world and accounts for the divinity that the poet sensed in all created things. In her poem "Before the Altar," a lonely and penniless worshipper offers his life and being as sacrifice to this Power, which she also celebrates in "The Poet," another early poem. Moved by the awesome splendors of creation, the poet is urged, she says, to forsake the ordinary pleasures of life to pursue the ideality symbolized by the "airy cloudland palaces" of sunset. Such a man, she says, "spurns life's human friendships to profess/Life's loneliness of dreaming ecstasy." In much of Lowell's most admirable imagistic poetry, this mystical conception of reality is rendered by means of her "numinous landscape" or scene, as in the poems "Ombre Chinoise" or "Reflections" where the physical objects concerned are presented with a kind of divine nimbus.

The realm of ideality envisioned in these four poems is sometimes perceived as a solution to the painful incompletions of life. This is the second major theme in Lowell's poetry, and the incompletion is most tragic in the case of the denial of love. Such denial is a spiritual *malaise*, in her view, because she identifies love not with sex but with inner emotional development. "Patterns," which is this author's most famous poem, dramatizes the withering of spirit resultant on the death of the heroine's lover. The poem is highly voluptuous and insists strongly on the physical beauties of lover and lady and the formal, spring-time garden where the poem is set, but the heroine's decision to live a loveless, celibate life calls attention to the deeper meaning of the relationship.

The spirituality that is implicit in romantic attachments includes recognition of an element of divinity in the beloved. The achievement of love as sacred rite is a third principal theme in Lowell's writings and it occurs in many of her most striking poems, beginning with a loose effusion in *A Dome* but ending with the sublimity of "In Excelsis" and her six sonnets written to Eleonora Duse. The loved one as sacred presence or, at the least, a part of an all-encompassing Divinity is consistent with the poet's preoccupation with a transcendent reality and completes the circle of her themes by returning her thought to its starting place. In terms of individual poems, Lowell's treatment of these themes is so varied and intermixed with nearly all the other issues of life that only a long survey can do them justice. But it is important to note that Lowell approached life *as a mystic* at a profound, intuitive level, and the imagistic mode in which she cast her poems was the one best suited to her gifts and the visionary character of her poetry. As poet her contribution is a revivification of the human sense of the beauties and mysteries of existence.

In addition to the solitary, contemplative role of poet that she adopted for herself, Lowell fulfilled another dynamic "political" role in the far-reaching effort she made to obtain public acceptance of the "new poetry" that appeared in America in 1912. The role she played was political in that the new poetry, seemingly odd and irregular in its form, challenged nearly all established social norms and ideals. Through her critical writings as well as her countless public appearances as lecturer and reader, Lowell assumed leadership of this movement and was responsible for a large measure of its success in creating a new poetic taste and awareness in America.

—Glenn Richard Ruihley

***

LOWELL, James Russell. American. Born in Cambridge, Massachusetts, 22 February 1819. Educated at Harvard College, Cambridge, 1834–38, B.A. 1838, and Harvard Law School, 1838–40, LL.B. 1840; admitted to the Massachusetts Bar, 1840. Married 1) Maria White in 1844 (died, 1853), three daughters, one son; 2) Frances Dunlap in 1857 (died, 1885). Editor, with Robert Carter, *The Pioneer: A Literary and Critical Magazine*, Boston, 1843; Editorial Writer, *Pennsylvania Freeman*, Philadelphia, 1845; Corresponding Editor, *National Anti-Slavery Standard*, 1848; lived in Europe, 1851–52; delivered Lowell lectures, Boston, 1855; Smith Professor of the French and Spanish Languages and Literatures, 1855–86, and Professor Emeritus, 1886–91, Harvard University; first Editor, *Atlantic Monthly*, Boston, 1857–61; Editor, with Charles Eliot Norton, *North American Review*, Boston, 1864–72; visited Europe, 1872–75; Delegate to the Republican National Convention, and Member of the Electoral College, 1876; American Ambassador to Spain, 1877–80, and to Great Britain, 1880–85. D.C.L.: Oxford University, 1872; LL.D.: Cambridge University, 1874; University of Edinburgh, 1884. *Died 12 August 1891.*

PUBLICATIONS

Collections

   Poetical Works, edited by Horace E. Scudder. 1896; revised edition, edited by Marjorie P. Kaufman, 1978.
   The Complete Writings, edited by Charles Eliot Norton. 16 vols., 1904.
   Essays, Poems, and Letters, edited by William Smith Clark II. 1948.

Verse

   Class Poem. 1838.
   A Year's Life and Other Poems. 1841.
   Poems. 1844.
   Poems: Second Series. 1848.
   A Fable for Critics. 1848.
   The Biglow Papers. 1848; edited by Thomas Wortham, 1977.
   The Vision of Sir Launfal. 1848.
   Poems. 2 vols., 1849.
   The Biglow Papers, Second Series. 3 vols., 1862.
   Ode Recited at the Commemoration of the Living and Dead Soldiers of Harvard University. 1865.

Under the Willows and Other Poems.   1869.
Poetical Works.   1869.
The Cathedral.   1870.
Three Memorial Poems.   1877.
Under the Old Elm and Other Poems.   1885.
Heartsease and Rue.   1888.
Last Poems, edited by Charles Eliot Norton.   1895.
Four Poems.   1906.
Uncollected Poems, edited by Thelma M. Smith.   1950.
Undergraduate Verses: Rhymed Minutes of the Hasty Pudding Club, edited by Kenneth
   Walter Cameron.   1956.

Play

Il Pesceballo: Opera Seria, with Francis J. Child.   1862; edited by Charles Eliot
   Norton, 1899.

Other

Conversations on Some of the Old Poets.   1845.
Fireside Travels.   1864.
Among My Books.   2 vols., 1870–76.
My Study Windows.   1871.
Democracy and Other Addresses.   1887.
Political Essays.   1888.
The English Poets, Lessing, Rousseau: Essays.   1888.
Books and Libraries and Other Papers.   1889.
The Writings.   10 vols., 1890; 2 additional vols. edited by Charled Eliot Norton,
   1891–92.
American Ideas for English Readers (lectures).   1892.
Letters, edited by Charles Eliot Norton.   2 vols., 1894.
Lectures on English Poets, edited by S. A. Jones.   1897.
Impressions of Spain, edited by Joseph B. Gilder.   1899.
Early Prose Writings.   1902.
The Anti-Slavery Papers, edited by William Belmont Parker.   2 vols., 1902.
The Round Table.   1913.
The Function of the Poet and Other Essays, edited by Albert Mordell.   1920.
New Letters, edited by M. A. De Wolfe Howe.   1932.
The Pioneer (magazine), edited by Sculley Bradley.   1947.
The Scholar-Friends: Letters of Francis James Child and Lowell, edited by M. A. De
   Wolfe Howe and G. W. Cottrell, Jr.   1952.
Literary Criticism, edited by Herbert F. Smith.   1969.

Editor, *The Poems of Maria Lowell.*   1855.
Editor, *The Poetical Works of Dr. John Donne.*   1855.
Editor, *The Poetical Works of Andrew Marvell.*   1857.

Bibliography: in *Bibliography of American Literature* by Jacob Blanck, 1973.

Reading List: *Lowell: A Biography* by Horace E. Scudder, 2 vols., 1901; *Lowell* by Richmond
C. Beatty, 1942; *Victorian Knight-Errant: A Study of the Early Literary Career of Lowell* by

Leon Howard, 1952; *Lowell* by Martin B. Duberman, 1966; *Lowell* by Claire McGlinchee 1967; *Lowell: Portrait of a Many-Sided Man* by Edward C. Wagenknecht, 1971.

*   *   *

Of all the schoolroom poets James Russell Lowell was easily the most talented, clearly the most versatile, and probably the one who strove hardest to achieve poetic excellence. Yet today his poetry is less critically valued and read than the verses of his contemporaries Holmes, Longfellow, and Whittier. Some explanation for the disparity between his ability and accomplishments resides in the very nature of his life and talents. Among other things he was poet, essayist, journalist, editor, critic, linguist, teacher, reformer and diplomat. In 1848, before his thirtieth birthday, he published *A Fable for Critics*, *The Biglow Papers*, and *The Vision of Sir Launfal* to secure his poetic reputation. Ten years later he assumed the first editorship of the *Atlantic Monthly* and by his critical judgment and taste made it into the finest literary journal in America. In his later years he became Minister to Spain, and from 1880–85 he served as the American Minister to England. To highlight these few achievements from so many illustrates part of Lowell's problem: his brilliance, erudition, and versatility constantly led him to new tasks and dissipated the control and self-discipline needed for artistic excellence. In addition his responsiveness to the tradition of public oratory and imitations of older writers made his serious verse declamatory and derivative. Dated by now forgotten issues and lacking a significant form, much of his longer poetry remains unreadable today.

Despite these critical problems, Lowell wrote good poetry and in selected pieces well deserves his place among American poets. His *A Fable for Critics* occupies a central place among the few critical pronouncements written by nineteenth-century American authors. Its mocking, casual humor perfectly balances shrewd critical insights, while its taut epigrams still surprise and delight. Lowell called Poe "two-fifths sheer fudge," depicted Byrant as "quiet, as cool, and as dignified,/As a smooth, silent iceberg, that never is ignified," and noted that Cooper's females were "All sappy as maples and flat as a prairie." Even his shortcomings were catalogued: "There is Lowell, who's striving Parnassus to climb/With a whole bale of *isms* tied together with rhyme." Both series of his Biglow Papers display a mastery of Down East Humor, Yankee dialect and caricature. Though their contemporary subject matter and grotesque mixture of moral aphorisms with political observations render them uneven, individual pieces like "The Courtin' " and "Sumthin' in the Pastoral Line" demonstrate Lowell's rare gift for native idiom and folk humor. His exploration of these New England materials produced his finest poem, "Fitz Adam's Story," a 632-line saga about the essential traits of a Yankee world. Though its central story concerns the attempts of a crusty Deacon Bitters to outsmart the devil, the poem's rich digressions on religion, back-country types, and rural descriptions constitute its main pleasure.

Among his longer, more serious poems, "Agassiz," *Ode Recited at the Harvard Commemoration*, *The Cathedral*, and a few others deserve continued reading and examination. In these poems Lowell's deeply felt thoughts were elaborately and skillfully presented, while the form, that of the familiar verse essay, perfectly suited his penchant for rhymed declamation and long digressions. "Agassiz," a moving tribute to the great Harvard scientist, cleverly blends the tradition of the pastoral elegy with contemporary images as the telegraph wire announces Agassiz's death. Throughout the poem Lowell balances his personal sorrow with a tenuous, yet affirmative, hope that such a nature as Agassiz's must exist somewhere "perfected and conscious." In the *Ode* Lowell uses the occasion of the Civil War to present a rhymed meditation on the complex oppositions of song and deed, war and truth, death and the ideal. The poem's conclusion and didactic tone prove acceptable because of the poem's careful development of basic images and firm structure. Perhaps Lowell's most successful longer poem is *The Cathedral*. Like Tennyson's *In Memoriam* it deals with a quest for religious certainty by a man imbued with his age's disbelief. The magnificent stone monument of Chartres Cathedral serves as the focus for the poem's imagery and structure. Its four main sections examine natural, religious, and even democratic responses to the spiritual, and build to the hesitant but honest suggestion that the commonplace of miracles is available for every age.

What Lowell achieved is best seen in a poem like *The Cathedral*. If his verse lacked the mightly choral power of Whitman and only fitfully imitated Emerson's grandeur, it deserves its own place among the American traditions of vernacular poetry, satiric verse, and rhymed public oratory. As Henry James once noted upon rereading Lowell: "He looms, in such a renewed impression, very large and ripe and sane.... He was strong without narrowness; he was wise without bitterness and bright without folly. That appears for the most part the clearest ideal of those who handle the English form, and he was altogether in the straight tradition."

—John B. Pickard

LOWELL, Robert (Traill Spence, Jr.). American. Born in Boston, Massachusetts, 1 March 1917. Educated at St. Mark's School, Southboro, Massachusetts; Harvard University, Cambridge, Massachusetts, 1935–37; Kenyon College, Gambier, Ohio, 1938–40, A.B. (summa cum laude) 1940 (Phi Beta Kappa). Conscientious objector during World War II: served prison sentence, 1943–44. Married 1) the writer Jean Stafford in 1940 (divorced, 1948); 2) the writer Elizabeth Hardwick in 1949 (divorced, 1972), one son; 3) the writer Caroline Blackwood in 1972, one son. Editorial Assistant, Sheed and Ward, publishers, New York, 1941–42; taught at the University of Iowa, Iowa City, 1949–50, 1952–53; Salzburg Seminar on American Studies, 1952; Boston University; New School for Social Research, New York; Harvard University; Professor of Literature, University of Essex, Wivenhoe, Colchester, 1970–72. Consultant in Poetry, Library of Congress, Washington, D.C., 1947–48; Visiting Fellow, All Souls College, Oxford, 1970. Recipient: Pulitzer Prize, 1947; National Institute of Arts and Letters grant, 1947; Guggenheim Fellowship, 1947, 1974; Harriet Monroe Poetry Award, 1952; Guinness Prize, 1959; National Book Award, 1960; Bollingen Poetry Translation Award, 1962; New England Poetry Club Golden Rose, 1964; Ford Foundation grant, for drama, 1964; Obie Award, for drama, 1965; Sarah Josepha Hale Award, 1966; Copernicus Award, 1974; National Medal for Literature, 1977. Member, American Academy of Arts and Letters. *Died 12 September 1977.*

PUBLICATIONS

Verse

    Land of Unlikeness. 1944.
    Lord Weary's Castle. 1946.
    Poems 1938–1949. 1950.
    The Mills of the Kavanaughs. 1951.
    Life Studies. 1959; augmented edition, 1959, 1968.
    Imitations. 1961.
    For the Union Dead. 1964.
    Selected Poems. 1965.
    The Achievement of Lowell: A Comprehensive Selection of His Poems, edited by William J. Martz. 1966.
    Near the Ocean. 1967.
    The Voyage and Other Versions of Poems by Baudelaire. 1968.

Notebook 1967–1968. 1969; augmented edition, as *Notebook,* 1970.
For Lizzie and Harriet. 1973.
History. 1973.
The Dolphin. 1973.
Poems: A Selection, edited by Jonathan Raban. 1974.
Selected Poems. 1976.
Day by Day. 1977.

Plays

Phaedra, from the play by Racine (produced 1961). In *Phaedra and Figaro,* 1961.
The Old Glory (Benito Cereno and *My Kinsman, Major Molineux)* (produced 1964). 1964; expanded version, including *Endecott and the Red Cross* (produced 1968), 1966.
Prometheus Bound, from a play by Aeschylus (produced 1967). 1969.

Other

Editor, with Peter Taylor and Robert Penn Warren, *Randall Jarrell 1914–1965.* 1967.

Reading List: *Lowell: The First Twenty Years* by Hugh B. Staples, 1962; *The Poetic Themes of Lowell* by Jerome Mazzaro, 1965; *Lowell: A Collection of Critical Essays* edited by Thomas Parkinson, 1968; *The Public Poetry of Lowell* by Patrick Cosgrave, 1970; *Lowell: A Portrait of the Artist in His Time* edited by Michael London and Robert Boyars, 1970 (includes bibliography by Jerome Mazzaro); *Lowell* by Richard J. Fein, 1970; *Critics on Lowell: Readings in Literary Criticism* edited by Jonathan Price, 1972; *The Poetic Art of Lowell* by Marjorie G. Perloff, 1973; *Pity the Monsters: The Political Vision of Lowell* by Alan Williamson, 1974; *Lowell* by John Crick, 1974.

*   *   *

Robert Lowell has been described as "a poet of restlessness without repose" (John Crick). His career is the history of violent changes in subject matter, and in manner, which often annoyed and confused his critics. Even now, after his death, there is little general agreement about his stature. But perhaps, even in this, Lowell is a *representative* figure: the last thirty years (Lowell's publishing history runs from 1944 to 1977) have witnessed a fragmentation of culture that denies us the sorts of certainty about the status that it was once possible to accord to Eliot, or to Yeats. This period will never, one suspects, be accepted as "The Age of Lowell." Individual poets seem no longer capable of this sort of centrality of significance.

But if any poet in this period has – perhaps sometimes with too earnest a deliberateness – lived through, proved upon his pulses, the central concerns, preoccupations, and pains of his time, it is Lowell. The career may, conveniently, be seen in three parts: the early poetry of Lowell's Catholicism that embraces *Land of Unlikeness, Lord Weary's Castle,* and *The Mills of the Kavanaughs*; the mid-period poetry of personal breakdown and political concern that includes *Life Studies, For the Union Dead,* and *Near the Ocean*; and the final period that saw the various attempts to create a larger, freer form through the subsequent stages of *Notebook, History, For Lizzie and Harriet,* and *The Dolphin,* a period concluding with the sustained elegiac note of *Day by Day.*

On the face of it, the three phases of the career seem to have little in common, apart from certain stylistic tics – most notably, and often irritatingly, Lowell's penchant for the triple adjective and the attention-seeking oxymoron. Some insight into an underlying continuity in

Lowell's "one life, one writing" may be provided by remarking on his exceptional insistence on revising himself in public. One of the most upsetting aspects of *Notebook*, for many of its reviewers, was the shock of coming across familiar Lowell lines either in very different contexts, or procrusteanly racked into the uniform regularity of the book's "sonnets." Lowell's apparently cavalier freedom with his own published work suggests not so much a desire to do a little better what he has done brilliantly before, but rather a deep-seated impatience with his own enormous talent and with poetry itself. In the poem "Tired Iron" in *The Dolphin*, there is an almost Beckettian dismissal of the work, even as he is engaged on it — "I can't go on with this, the measure is gone." It is possible to see in Lowell, as in some of the greatest artists of the second half of the twentieth century, a radical dissatisfaction with art itself, with its consolations, its sense of order, its morality. What gives Lowell's dissatisfaction its unique savour is his refusal of the obvious alternative of a bleak nihilism in favour of a worried, guilty commitment to a traditional New England liberalism. The oddity of Robert Lowell's sensibility is perhaps suggested in a shorthand way by pointing to the poems in *Notebook* and *History* dedicated to Eugene McCarthy and Robert Kennedy: an existential absurdist clinging precariously to sanity celebrates the pragmatic politics of liberal capitalism.

Dissatisfaction, restlessness, unease: these are the signatures of Lowell's work. The early formalist poetry nominally takes its cue from Allen Tate and the Southern Fugitives. In fact, the formal majesty of the poems is everywhere disturbed by a raucous alliterative bellowing; the Catholicism is everywhere collapsed into savage heresy and blasphemy:

> O Mother, I implore
> Your scorched, blue thunderbreasts of love to pour
> Buckets of blessings on my burning head.

If this is rhetoric, it is a rhetoric of desperation. Even in the more tender poems — "The Quaker Graveyard in Nantucket" and "Mother Marie Therese" — Lowell's sonic boom threatens his formal perfection. His dissatisfaction compels him almost to wring the neck of his magnificent rhetoric. Such dissatisfactions led to a long silence during "the tranquillized Fifties," a silence during which the dissatisfactions of his personal life involved periods in mental hospitals. The silence was broken only at the end of the decade by the publication of *Life Studies*, a book in an entirely different mode and manner; Lowell was now so dissatisfied with his earlier work that he attempted almost its polar opposite, a poetry close to Chekhovian prose. This is the one work of Lowell's about which almost all critics agree: it was *the* book of its time, following, with total assurance, a direction more hesitantly beginning to be taken by some of his contemporaries, profoundly influential in its discovery of a new sort of personal voice. It signals, in "Beyond the Alps," Lowell's break with Catholicism, and it proceeds to worry out, "confessionally," the psychic disturbances and extremities of his harrowing personal experience. This is a poetry resolutely committed to walking naked; but the voice is moving and desperate and rises to a unique and instantly recognisable "Lowellian" pathos:

> A car radio bleats,
> 'Love, O careless Love ...' I hear
> my ill-spirit sob in each blood cell,
> as if my hand were at its throat ...
> I myself am hell,
> nobody's here —.

But, unlike that of some poets who crawled in under the mantle of "confessional" poetry, Lowell's writing refuses the temptations of an easy solipsism. Christopher Ricks, in a *New Statesman* review of *For the Union Dead* (26 March 1965), maintained that "The singular strength of Robert Lowell's poetry has always been a matter of his power to enforce a sense of context." The work after *Life Studies* evidences a desire to speak, out of personal pain and catastrophe, about society and politics, and about literature, religion, and history, the sustaining "outer contexts" of our lives. Restlessly moving away from the "prose" style of *Life Studies*, Lowell wrote, in the central poems of *Near the Ocean* — especially, perhaps, in "Waking Early Sunday Morning" — the greatest elegies for a generation that suffered the Vietnam war and the threat of nuclear extinction, and he wrote them, with his casually characteristic refusal of the obvious, in a finely judged, perfectly achieved neo-classical form that recalls that other poet of the barbarities of which a "civilised" society is capable, Andrew Marvell:

> Pity the planet, all joy gone
> from this sweet volcanic cone;
> peace to our children when they fall
> in small war on the heels of small
> war — until the end of time
> to police the earth, a ghost
> orbiting forever lost
> in our monotonous sublime.

In *For the Union Dead*, the forms are again free, though the relatively uncluttered simplicity of these poems belies a carefully crafted subtlety of association, allusion, and symbolism. These haunted, nostalgic poems begin in a consideration of the joys and pains of personal relationship but extend themselves into the troubles of political life. The volume's title-poem relates private and public breakdown in a muted poetry of understatement, working by implication and suggestion. The poem's final stanza is as devastating as anything in Lowell, but the devastation comes across quietly, hesitantly, thrown off almost parenthetically compared to the aggressive climaxes of the poems in *Lord Weary's Castle*:

> The Aquarium is gone. Everywhere,
> giant finned cars nose forward like fish;
> a savage servility
> slides by on grease.

The ability to relate his own trouble to the trouble of his times is the impulse behind *Notebook*. This, and the works that grew out of it, are the most ambitious of Lowell's writing: he is attempting a large, inclusive form, a form for all occasions, in the manner of Pound's *Cantos*, of Berryman's *Dream Songs*. In the poems in the sequence — all irregular fourteen-liners — that deal with "history," there is too often the feeling of formal monotony, rhythmic inertia, a tired, mechanical repetitiveness. The lack of a real voice, and the absence of anything but the most straightforward chronology to serve as "plot," render *History* a generally wearying experience. The failure derives, perhaps, from Lowell's refusal to admit that a sonnet sequence, or its equivalent, is really capable of handling only limited types of material. The larger successes of *For Lizzie and Harriet* and *The Dolphin* are perhaps the result of their being more traditionally plotted around the themes and occasions of personal love and marriage. The idea of writing "history" as a sequence of sonnets has an almost wilful perversity about it, as though Shakespeare had decided to put the material of the history plays, as well as the story of his "two loves," into a sonnet sequence.

But such perversity, and the overall failure of a single book, are perhaps the inevitable price of an heroic refusal to repeat himself, a nervous, restless desire to define and re-define the protean self. "We are words," Lowell insists in a poem in *History* addressed to Berryman, "John, we used the language as if we made it." The claim is large; it is characteristic of Lowell's proud ambition that he should make it for himself; but in the formal variety, the technical ingenuity, and the inventiveness of his poems — and of his translations and plays — he comes, at the very least, close to justifying it.

—Neil Corcoran

LYDGATE, John. English. Born in Lydgate, near Newmarket, Suffolk, c. 1370. Admitted to the Benedictine monastery at Bury St. Edmunds, Suffolk, 1385; ordained deacon, 1393, priest, 1397; studied at Gloucester College, Oxford, before 1408. Lived most of his early life in London; a friend of Thomas Chaucer; acted as court poet, and enjoyed the patronage of the Duke of Gloucester, from 1422; also wrote pageants and occasional verse for the Corporation of London; Prior of Hatfield Broadoak, Essex, 1423–34; returned to the monastery at Bury, 1434, and remained there for the rest of his life. Granted royal pension, 1423. *Died in 1449.*

PUBLICATIONS

Collections

A Selection from the Minor Poems, edited J. O. Halliwell.   1840.
Minor Poems, edited by H. N. McCracken.   2 vols., 1911–34.
Poems, edited by J. Norton-Smith.   1966.

Verse

The Horse, The Goose, and the Sheep.   1477; in *Minor Poems*, 1934.
The Churl and the Bird.   1477(?); in *Minor Poems*, 1934.
The Temple of Glass.   1477(?); in *Poems*, 1966.
The Life of Our Lady.   1484; edited by J. A. Lauritis and others, in *Duquesne Studies, Philological Series*, 1961.
The Fall of Princes.   1494; edited by Henry Bergen, 4 vols., 1924–27.
The Siege of Thebes.   1495(?); edited by Axel Erdmann and Eilert Ekwall,   2 vols., 1911–30.
The Interpretation of the Names of Gods and Goddesses.   1498; as *The Assembly of Gods*, edited by F. J. H. Jenkinson, 1906.
The Complaint of a Lover's Life.   N.d.; in *Poems*, 1966.
The Virtue of the Mass.   N.d.; in *Minor Poems*, 1911.
The Governance of King's and Princes.   1511; edited by T. Prosiegel, 1903.
The History, Siege, and Destruction of Troy.   1513; edited by Henry Bergen, 4 vols., 1906–35.
The Testament of John Lydgate.   1515(?); in *Minor Poems*, 1911.
The Proverbs of Lydgate.   1515(?).
Flower of Courtesy, in *Works of Chaucer*, edited by T. Thynne.   1532; in *Minor Poems*, 1934.
The Life of Saint Alban and the Life of Saint Amphabel.   1534; edited by J. E. van der Westhuizen, 1974.
The Danse Macabre, in *The Fall of Princes.*   1554; edited by F. Warren and B. White, 1931.
The Serpent of Division.   1559; edited by H. N. McCracken, 1911.
The Pilgrimage of the Life of Man, edited by F. J. Furnivall.   3 vols., 1899–1904; edited by Furnivall and Katharine Locock, 1905.
Two Nightingale Poems, edited by O. Glauning.   1900.
Reason and Sensuality, edited by E. Sieper.   2 vols., 1901–03.
The Grateful Dead, edited by A. Beatty, in *A New Ploughman's Tale.*   1902.

Reading List: *Lydgate: A Study in the Culture of the 15th Century* by W. F. Schirmer, translatᵟ d by A. E. Keep, 1961; *The Poetry of Lydgate* by Alain Renoir, 1967; *Lydgate* by Derek Pearsall, 1970.

*   *   *

John Lydgate was probably born when Chaucer was in his mid-twenties. He was admitted to Bury St. Edmunds Abbey and remained attached to the foundation for the whole of his life, but for most of his life he lived outside the cloister. Lydgate had many important friends and "patrons": Henry V; Humphrey of Gloucester; Edmund Lacy, Bishop of Exeter; Isabell, Countess of Warwick; Thomas Montachute, Earl of Salisbury; Henry VI; John Whethamstede, Abbot of St. Albans. He knew nearly everybody, including Lord Mayors of London, Aldermen, and officials of the Royal Household. His special friends were the Chaucers of Ewelme, Thomas and Maud and their daughter Alice. He lived to a great age and his later works show the effect of fatigue and bad eye-sight (he complained of these). He should not be judged by the monumental hack-work he undertook as an historian and cultural cicerone (*Troy Book, Fall of Princes, Pilgrimage of the Life of Man, Life of Our Lady*).

The Bury monk's earlier poetry (before 1412) displays an interest in Chaucer's dream poems but simplifying Chaucer's poetic intelligence and urbane command of style and form. Yet *The Complaynt of a Loveres Lyfe* and *The Temple of Glas*, though emphatically didactic and matter-of-fact, are serious and interesting compositions. Autobiography enters in 1412 with the commission by the Prince of Wales of the *Troy Book*. The style cultivated by Lydgate for that work is assiduously based on Chaucer's Monk's art of versification. Later, when Lydgate undertook the *Life of Our Lady*, he assumed the learned naive style of Chaucer's *Life of St. Cecile*. This "functionalism" permits the poet a number of "styles," and those appropriated for an English Liturgical Style (aureation) and the neo-classical Latinate pressed into service for "A Defence of Holy Church" (1413–14) show Lydgate at his most inventive and eloquent. He seems never to have possessed the force of personality to cultivate this capacity for elegant, economical utterance. Lydgate's imagination was not a powerful shaping force. It is enfeebled by a too mechanical application of rhetorical discipline. His modest, shorter poems, "The Letter of Humphrey," the "Letter to Thomas Chaucer on his Departure for France," the beautiful "moral religious ballade" "As a Midsomer Rose," show his attractive, often delicate appreciation of sentiment, morality, and eloquence.

—J. Norton-Smith

LYNDSAY, Sir David. Scottish. Born in Cupar, Garmylton, near Haddington, c. 1490. Educated at the University of St. Andrews. Married Janet Douglas in 1522. Courtier of James IV: "usher" of the infant James V, 1512; employed on various missions to the Emperor Charles V, and to Denmark, France and England; Lyon King-of-Arms, 1538. Knighted, 1542. *Died in 1555.*

PUBLICATIONS

Collections

Poetical Works, edited by Douglas Hamer.   4 vols., 1931–36.
Poems, edited by Maurice Lindsay.   1948.

Verse

The Complaint and Testament of a Popinjay.   1538.
A Dialogue Betwixt Experience and a Courtier of the Miserable Estate of the
    World.   1554; augmented edition, 1558.
The Works.   1568.
The History of a Noble and Wailzeaned Squire, William Meldrum.   1594; edited by
    James Kinsley, 1959.
A Supplication in Contemplation of Side Tails and Muzzled Faces.   1690.

Play

A Satire of the Three Estates, in Commendation of Virtue and Vituperation of Vice
    (produced 1540).   1602; edited by James Kinsley, 1954.

Bibliography: in Poetical Works, 1931–36.

Reading List: Lyndesays Monarche und die Chronica Carionis by A. Lange, 1904; Lindsay by
William Murison, 1938; Dramatic Allegory: Lindsay's "Satyre of the Thrie Estaitis" by
Joanne S. Kantrowitz, 1974.

                        *   *   *

Sir David Lyndsay differs from most of the other Scottish Makars in that much of his work
had a socio-political purpose. Appropriately, this led him to indulge less frequently in the "hie
style," although "The Deploratioun of Quene Magdalene," in rime royal, shows that he could
produce aureate word-music when formal royal occasion demanded. More typical, however,
is "The Complaynt of Sir David Lyndsay," in octosyllabic rhyming couplets, which reminds
James V of the poet's services since that time when

> as ane chapman bears his pack,
> I bore thy Grace upon my back,
> And sumtynes, stridlings on my neck,
> Dansand with mony bend and beck ...

and warns of the need for reform in the church. Lyndsay was a commonsense moderate,
who urged the king to behave in a seemly manner in "The Answer to the Kingis Flyting,"
particularly in sexual matters. His most entertaining poems are The Historie of ane Nobil and
Vailzeand Squyer, William Meldrum, a racy tale in two parts, "The Testament" in the
Chaucerian heptastich, the rest in vigorous octosyllabic couplets; and, in the same metre, his
attack upon woman's fashion, Ane Supplicatioun Directed to the King's Grace in
Contemplatioun of Syde Taillis, a satire, however, which verges on becoming anti-feminist.
"The Complaint of Bagsche, An Auld Hound," in octosyllabics, rhyming ababbcbc, is a
further moral sermon, but suggests a possible prototype for Burns's "The Twa Dogs."
    Lyndsay, indeed, set the conversational tone which was to be taken up and sharpened by
the poets of the 18th-Century Revival. His masterpiece, the verse-morality play Ane Pleasant
Satyre of the Thrie Estatis, presents a wide range of good and bad characters, the good
embodying symbolically the obvious virtues desirable in Church and State, the bad, a much
more witty and appealing gallery of contemporary rogues. The purpose of the play, which in
places employs what was to become the 18th century's "Standard Habbie" stanza, was to
urge the king to reform the Catholic Church. First staged in 1540, it failed in its purpose, and
ten years later the Reformation swept the old faith aside. But the merits of the play survived

the occasion that called it forth, and, shortened and slightly modernised, it has been several times revived with outstanding success at the Edinburgh Festival. It seems improbable that *The Thrie Estates* was Lyndsay's only play, and, indeed, he lays claim to others in *The Complaynt and Testament of the Papyngo* (Parrot), but these have not survived.

The most "modern" of the Makars in the directness of his human concern, and an enshriner of proverbial wisdom in easily remembered lines, Lyndsay enjoyed wide popularity, his work being found with the Bible in many a humble Scottish household until he was displaced from popular affection by Burns.

—Maurice Lindsay

LYTTELTON, George; 1st Baron Lyttelton.   English.   Born in Hagley, Worcestershire, 17 January 1709. Educated at Eton College; Christ Church, Oxford, matriculated 1726, left without taking a degree. Married 1) Lucy Fortescue in 1742 (died, 1747), one son, two daughters; 2) Elizabeth Rich in 1749 (separated). Toured the Continent, 1728–31; Equerry, 1731–37, then Secretary, 1737–44, to the Prince of Wales; Member of Parliament for Okehampton, Devonshire, 1735–56: opposed Walpole, and with Pitt and the Grenvilles formed party known as the Cobhamites; a Lord of the Treasury, 1744–54; Member of the Privy Council, 1754; Chancellor of the Exchequer, 1755–56; created Baron Lyttelton, 1756, and thereafter sat in the House of Lords: opposed repeal of the Stamp Act, 1766. *Died 22 August 1773.*

PUBLICATIONS

Collections

> *Works*, edited by G. E. Ayscough.   1774.
> *Poetical Works.*   1785.

Verse

> *Blenheim.*   1728.
> *An Epistle to Mr. Pope, from a Young Gentleman at Rome.*   1730.
> *The Progress of Love, in Four Eclogues.*   1732.
> *Advice to a Lady.*   1733.
> *To the Memory of a Lady Lately Deceased: A Monody.*   1747.
> *The Fourth Ode of the Fourth Book of Horace.*   1749.
> *Poems.*   1773.

Other

> *Letters from a Persian in England to His Friend at Ispahan,* vol. 1.   1735.
> *Considerations upon the Present State of Our Affairs at Home and Abroad.*   1739; *Farther Considerations,* 1739.

Obersations on the Life of Cicero.   1741.

The Court Secret: A Melancholy Truth.   1742; as *The New Court Secret,* 1746.

Observations on the Conversion and Apostleship of St. Paul, in a Letter to Gilbert West.   1747.

A Modest Apology for My Own Conduct.   1748.

Dialogues of the Dead.   1760; *An Additional Dialogue,* 1760; *Four New Dialogues,* 1765.

The History of the Life of King Henry the Second and of the Age in Which He Lived.   4 vols., 1767–71.

Editor, *Works of James Thomson.*   4 vols., 1750.

Reading List: *An Eighteenth-Century Gentleman* by Sydney C. Roberts, 1930; *A Minor Augustan: The Life and Works of Lyttelton* by A. V. Rao, 1934; *The Good Lord Lyttelton* by Rose M. Davis, 1939.

*   *   *

George Lyttelton is known more for his literary patronage than as a poet. He is essentially a minor Augustan versifier, following the lead of his friend Pope, and a prose-writer in the tradition of Fénelon and Montesquieu. His poetry follows conventional forms, generally pastoral and in low key. The "Monody" written in praise of "The Conjugal and the maternal love" on the death of his wife Lucy has a particular beauty, however, as he adapts the Miltonic pastoral elegy to the expression of private grief.

Lyttelton's dexterity with the rhymed couplet never achieves the pungency of Pope, despite the attempt to exploit Augustan antitheses in a similar manner. He does reconcile the urbane and the pastoral in his realized vision of a rural retreat at his estate, Hagley Park. Here he entertained Fielding, Pope, Shenstone, and Thomson, and was celebrated by the last as the epitome of friend, patron, and host. *The Seasons* bear the unmistakable mark of editorial interference by Lyttelton in the later revisions. Thomson's idiosyncratic style is muffled by heavy general moralizing. However, Lyttelton remains as an archetype of the man of "taste."

—B. C. Oliver-Morden

MacDIARMID, Hugh. Pseudonym for Christopher Murray Grieve. Scottish. Born in Langholm, Dumfriesshire, 11 August 1892. Educated at Langholm Academy; Broughton Student Centre, Edinburgh; University of Edinburgh. Married 1) Margaret Skinner in 1918 (divorced, 1932), one son and one daughter; 2) Valda Trevlyn in 1934, one son. Journalist, 1912–15, 1920–30: Editor, *The Scottish Chapbook,* Montrose, Angus, 1922–23, *The Scottish Nation,* Montrose, Angus, 1923, *The Northern Review,* Edinburgh, 1924, and *The Voice of Scotland,* Dunfermline, Fife, 1938–39, Glasgow, 1945–49, and Edinburgh, 1955–58. A Founder, Scottish Nationalist Party; Founder, Scottish Centre of P.E.N. Recipient: Foyle Prize, 1963; Scottish Arts Council Award, 1969. LL.D.: University of Edinburgh, 1957. Professor of Literature, Royal Scottish Academy, 1974; Honorary Fellow, Modern Language Association of America. Granted Civil List pension, 1951. *Died 9 September 1978.*

PUBLICATIONS

Verse

Annals of the Five Senses. 1923.
Sangschaw. 1925.
Penny Wheep. 1926; edited by John C. Weston, 1971.
A Drunk Man Looks at the Thistle. 1926; revised edition, 1956.
The Lucky Bag. 1927.
To Circumjack Cencrastus; or, The Curly Snake. 1930.
First Hymn to Lenin and Other Poems. 1931.
Second Hymn to Lenin. 1932.
Tarras. 1932.
Scots Unbound and Other Poems. 1932.
Stony Limits and Other Poems. 1934.
Selected Poems. 1934.
Second Hymn to Lenin and Other Poems. 1935.
Direadh. 1938.
Speaking for Scotland. 1939.
Cornish Heroic Song for Valda Trevlyn. 1943.
Selected Poems, edited by R. Crombie Saunders. 1944.
Speaking for Scotland: Selected Poems. 1946.
Poems of the East-West Synthesis. 1946.
A Kist of Whistles: New Poems. 1947.
Selected Poems, edited by Oliver Brown. 1954; as *Poems,* 1955.
In Memoriam James Joyce: from A Vision of World Language. 1955.
Stony Limits and Scots Unbound and Other Poems. 1956.
Three Hymns to Lenin. 1957.
The Battle Continues. 1957.
The Kind of Poetry I Want. 1961.
Collected Poems. 1962; revised edition, edited by John C. Weston, 1967.
Bracken Hills in Autumn. 1962.
The Blaward and the Skelly. 1962.
Poems to Paintings by William Johnstone 1933. 1963.
Two Poems: The Terrible Crystal, A Vision of Scotland. 1964.
The Ministry of Water: Two Poems. 1964.
Six Vituperative Verses. 1964.
Poet at Play and Other Poems, Being a Selection of Mainly Vituperative Verses. 1965.
The Fire of the Spirit: Two Poems. 1965.
Whuculls. 1966.

On a Raised Beach.   1967.

A Lap of Honour.   1967.

Early Lyrics, Recently Discovered among Letters to His Schoolmaster and Friend, George Ogilvie, edited by J. K. Annand.   1968.

A Clyack-Sheaf.   1969.

More Collected Poems.   1970.

Selected Poems, edited by David Craig and John Manson.   1970.

The MacDiarmid Anthology: Poems in Scots and English, edited by Michael Grieve and Alexander Scott.   1972.

Song of the Seraphim.   1973.

Direadh I, II, and III.   1974.

The Complete Poems, edited by Michael Grieve and W. R. Aitken.   2 vols., 1978.

The Socialist Poems, edited by T. S. Law and Thurso Berwick.   1978.

Other

Contemporary Scottish Studies: First Series.   1926.

The Present Position of Scottish Music.   1927.

Albyn; or, Scotland and the Future.   1927.

The Present Position of Scottish Arts and Affairs.   1928.

The Scottish National Association of April Fools.   1928.

Scotland in 1980.   1929.

Warning Democracy.   1931.

Five Bits of Miller.   1934.

At the Sign of the Thistle: A Collection of Essays.   1934.

Scottish Scene; or, The Intelligent Man's Guide to Albyn, with Lewis Grassic Gibbon.   1934.

Charles Doughty and the Need for Heroic Poetry.   1936.

Scottish Eccentrics.   1936.

Scotland and the Question of a Popular Front Against Fascism and War.   1938.

The Islands of Scotland: Hebrides, Orkneys and Shetlands.   1939.

Lucky Poet: A Self-Study in Literary and Political Ideas, Being the Autobiography of MacDiarmid.   1943.

Cunninghame Graham: A Centenary Study.   1952.

The Politics and Poetry of MacDiarmid.   1952.

Francis George Scott: An Essay on the Occasion of His Seventy-Fifth Birthday, 25th January 1955.   1955.

Burns Today and Tomorrow.   1959.

The Man of (Almost) Independent Mind (on Hume).   1962.

When the Rat Race Is Over: An Essay in Honour of the Fiftieth Birthday of John Gawsworth.   1962.

MacDiarmid on Hume.   1962.

The Ugly Birds Without Wings.   1962.

The Company I've Kept (autobiography).   1966.

The Uncanny Scot: A Selection of Prose, edited by Kenneth Buthlay.   1968.

Selected Essays, edited by Duncan Glen.   1969.

An Afternoon with MacDiarmid: Interview at Brownsbank on 25th October 1968, with Duncan Glen.   1969.

On Metaphysics and Poetry, edited by Walter Perrie.   1974.

John Knox, with Campbell Maclean and Anthony Ross.   1976.

Editor, *Northern Numbers, Being Representative Selections from Certain Living Scottish Poets.*   2 vols., 1920–21.

Editor, *Robert Burns, 1759–1796.*   1926.
Editor, *Living Scottish Poets.*   1931.
Editor, *The Golden Treasury of Scottish Poetry.*   1940.
Editor, *Auntran Blads: An Outwale o Verses,* by Douglas Young.   1943.
Editor, *William Soutar: Collected Poems.*   1948.
Editor, *Poems,* by Robert Burns.   1949.
Editor, with Maurice Lindsay, *Poetry Scotland Four.*   1949.
Editor, *Scottish Arts and Letters: Fifth Miscellany.*   1950.
Editor, *Selections from the Poems of William Dunbar.*   1952.
Editor, *Selected Poems of William Dunbar.*   1955.
Editor, *Love Songs,* by Burns.   1962.
Editor, *Henryson.*   1970.

Translator, *The Handmaid of the Lord,* by Ramon Maria de Tenreiro.   1930.
Translator, *The Birlinn of Clanranald,* by Alexander MacDonald.   1935.
Translator, with Elspeth Harley Schubert, *Harry Martinson: Aniara: A Review of Man in Time and Space.*   1963.
Translator, *The Threepenny Opera,* by Brecht.   1973.

Reading List: *The Politics and Poetry of MacDiarmid* by Arthur Leslie, 1952; *MacDiarmid: A Festschrift* edited by K.D. Duval and others, 1962; *MacDiarmid and the Scottish Renaissance* by Duncan Glen, 1964; *"MacDiarmid" (C. M. Grieve)* by Kenneth Buthlay, 1964; *The Golden Lyric: An Essay on the Poetry of MacDiarmid* by Iain Crichton Smith, 1967; *MacDiarmid: A Critical Survey* edited by Duncan Glen, 1972 (includes bibliography by W. R. Aitken); *MacDiarmid: An Illustrated Biography of Christopher Murray Grieve* by Gordon Wright, 1977.

*   *   *

Hugh MacDiarmid established himself as a poet of importance when he turned from writing verse in English to writing short lyrics in his native Scots. These are the poems collected in *Sangschaw* and *Penny Wheep.* The best of the lyrics in these volumes equal anything in the whole tradition of the lyric poem in Scots – "The Watergaw," "The Eemis Stane," "Empty Vessel," "Crowdieknowe," and the four-part sequence "Au Clair de la Lune." These poems were almost immediately recognised as something quite unique in Scots poetry after the long period of imitation Burnsian verse. They not only demonstrate the usual seemingly effortless lyric cry and an equally effortless "leap into the symbol," but also show, which is more unusual at least in the Scots tradition, a seeming impersonality of stance which is yet also universally human.

If the short lyrics of *Sangschaw* and *Penny Wheep* jolted the Scottish literary scene out of its set ways, then the publication in 1926 of the 2685-line poem *A Drunk Man Looks at the Thistle* came like "the shock of a childbirth in church," as David Daiches has memorably written. *A Drunk Man* takes up the lyricism of the short poems and extends it into a long work concerned with heaven and hell and all else besides. It leaps into metaphysical speculation in verse where the real and the imaginary are as one; it contains satirical writing equal to anything in Scottish verse, including Burns's "Holy Willie's Prayer." It achieves its unquestioned unity by what may seem at first to be a disorganised flow of magnificent and varied verse. Here MacDiarmid is in full control of many verse forms, each suited to the content of the section where it is employed; the lyricism is fully at one with a speculative mind of huge imagination. This work is now being increasingly recognized as the greatest long poem in the Scots tradition.

MacDiarmid tried to repeat the success and something of the techniques of *A Drunk Man* in his next work, *To Circumjack Cencrastus,* but, despite some very fine successes including a masterly translation into English of Rilke's "Requiem – Für eine Freundin," this work lacks the unity of its predecessor, and, more important, too many passages lack poetry. But *Cencrastus* was followed by many more important poems in Scots, including some very fine short lyrics, especially "At My Father's Grave" (*First Hymn to Lenin*) and "Milk-Wort and Bog Cotton" and "The Back o' Beyond" (*Scots Unbound*). But to this period also belong poems which show a continued or even further-devoloped ability to combine lyricism with speculative thought in longer works – *Tarras*, "Water of Life," "Excelsior," "Harry Semen," and the two magnificent poems "By Wauchopeside" and "Whuchulls." Also belonging to this most creative period in the early 1930's is the beautiful long work "Water Music" in which the sounds of the Scots language are exploited as never before or since. The wonderfully conversational yet technically exact "The Seamless Garment" also belongs to this period, as do the first two Hymns to Lenin. Soon, however, MacDiarmid was turning from Scots to English and soon to an English of extended vocabulary.

To some critics MacDiarmid's finest achievement in English is to be found among the group of short poems published in *Second Hymn to Lenin*. The number of fully realised poems in this work are not numerous but the few that are make an imposing group. They certainly include: "Lo! A Child Is Born," "On the Ocean Floor," "O Ease My Spirit," and "The Two Parents." Others might see the long poem "On a Raised Beach," with its use of specialised English language, as MacDiarmid's finest poetry in English; other major long poems in English included in *Stony Limits* are the title poem, "A Point of Honour," "Lament for the Great Music," and at least parts of "Ode to All Rebels." Also in this volume are the magnificent four lines of "The Skeleton of the Future," which is perhaps the greatest, if also the shortest, expression of MacDiarmid's commitment to communism. The eight lines of "Skald's Death" are also very fine and "With the Herring Fishers" shows him still to be a master of the short lyric in Scots. *Stony Limits* also printed his most famous, or most popular, Scottish nationalist poem "The Little White Rose," but it is not one of his better poems.

By 1939 MacDiarmid had turned to the very long "poems of fact" or "world-view," the poems of his last creative period. These "world-view" poems are really one very long and unfinished, or unfinishable, work; separately published parts include *In Memoriam James Joyce* and *The Kind of Poetry I Want*, although both were perhaps largely written in the late 1930's or early 1940's and revised later. These long poems have not received the critical recognition given to other aspects of MacDiarmid's work. The temptation with these works is to pick out the passages which rise almost to lyric heights, passages such as "In the Fall" in *In Memoriam James Joyce*, but to do this is to work against their true poetry and energy. One poem of this period stands as a separate work, "The Glass of Pure Water" (*Poetry Scotland*, 1943); *Direadh I, II, and III*, first printed in MacDiarmid's autobiography *Lucky Poet*, are also excellent for leading a hesitant reader into the longer works.

This later work requires reading in mass, and the publication of *The Complete Poems* may lead to a reconsideration of it. But even without critical acclaim for this later work Hugh MacDiarmid has a body of achieved poetry which establishes him as not only the widest ranging but also as one of the greatest of Scottish poets.

—Duncan Glen

MACKENZIE, Kenneth (Ivo). Pseudonym: Seaforth Mackenzie. Australian. Born in Perth, Western Australia, in 1913. Educated at Muresk Agricultural College; studied arts and law at the University of Western Australia, Perth. Married Kate Loveday in 1934; one daughter and one son. Lived in Kurrajong from 1948. Recipient: Commonwealth Literary Fund grant, 1948, 1951, 1955. *Died in January 1955.*

PUBLICATIONS

Collections

The Poems, edited by Evan Jones and Geoffrey Little.   1972.

Verse

Our Earth.   1937.
The Moonlit Doorway.   1944.

Fiction

The Young Desire It.   1937.
Chosen People.   1938.
Dead Men Rising.   1951.
The Refuge: A Confession.   1954.

Other

Editor, *Australian Poetry, 1951–52.*   1952.

Reading List: "A Dead Man Rising: The Poetry of Mackenzie" in *Australian Quarterly 36,* 1964, and *Mackenzie,* 1969, both by Evan Jones; "Mackenzie's Novels" by Peter Cowan, in *Meanjin 24,* 1965; "Mackenzie's Fiction" by R. G. Geering, in *Southerly 26,* 1966.

                          *   *   *

   Many of Kenneth Mackenzie's poems were not published until 1972, seventeen years after his death. On the basis of his two early books *Our Earth* and *The Moonlit Doorway,* it was possible to regard him mainly as a love-poet, sensual and egoistic. The new volume, almost but not quite complete, revealed that the love-poems were far less dominant than poems about death and nothingness, and that fear of death gave way to a quiet longing for death, or "his brother sleep," submerged beneath the fear in the early verse. Mackenzie's decision to be a writer, and above all, a poet, in a country in which, in his day, it was almost impossible to exist by the pen, kept him all his short life in stark poverty, not mitigated by his alcoholism. One of the editors of his *Poems* has pointed out the remarkable parallels between his life and Dylan Thomas's, though Thomas seems to have died of too much success while Mackenzie succumbed to failure. Yet the disorders of his life were not reflected in the tone of his verse, which became more measured, serene, and controlled as outward circumstances deteriorated. His essential solitariness, with his retreat to the bush, became in the end a source of strength, and the last poems, especially those about the natural world, have a freshness, a joy, and a confidence which have no other source except in this sense of freedom from all earthly ties.
   Existential guilt and anxiety are constant notes in the verse from the beginning, as the first poem in *The Moonlit Doorway,* "Heat," indicates. It is the first of many "river" poems, which gains an ironic significance from hindsight: Mackenzie was to drown in a river at the age of forty-two. Of the thirty-five poems on the subject of death, some are associated with love, but many more with fear or anxiety. Mackenzie's adult world is on the whole a painful, candle-lit

world, full of dark presences and the need for expiation which is never quite remorse. Many of the poems lament the lost innocence of childhood, and parenthood was not for him a source of joy, as it was for Judith Wright, but an occasion for apology or a plea for forgiveness:

> What shall I say to you in my defence?
> What can I say to mate you with your stars?
> I shall say this: I got you unawares.

The sense of guilt, the anxiety, are conveyed quite often in images of murder, as in "Going Upstairs," for example, a striking if melodramatic poem, which nevertheless displays a gift for the theatrical in the proper sense of the word. It is a remarkable example of Mackenzie's gift for finding a situation to contain emotional mysteries without lapsing into frigid allegory, and the swift transition from the heroic to the sordid and the ridiculous is beautifully accomplished. A similar piece of reductionism occurs in "A Conqueror," one of the best and most neglected of Australian war-poems. The private murders and betrayals of lovers have their counterpart on the world's stage, where the lust for power, which lovers too often mistake for love, becomes destructive on a grand scale.

The poems of the final ten years are much preoccupied with physical pain, his own and other men's, in hospital. Some are pleas for oblivion, but one at least calls in question the genuineness of the death-wish, and prays for time to amend and praise. Mackenzie's poems have the faults associated with these themes. The great deliberation and the unrelenting control give an impression of slowness and monotony. It is best to read them a few at a time. He also has one of the defects of the solitary: frequent outbursts of garrulity. Lacking companionship, he conducts an eternal argument with himself, always "fighting a battle on the brink of time." He also has the narrow range of the solitary, though within that range he saw very deeply, as the references to his wife in "Two Trinities" reveal. His work is self-regarding, ego-centric, but not self-deluding – he does not romanticize his weaknesses, and with all his faults remains on the right side of the thin line between sensitivity and self-indulgence.

He wrote four novels, largely as pot-boilers. But *The Refuge*, about an extraordinary relationship between a journalist, his refugee second wife, and his son by his first wife, is as sensitive, perceptive, and compelling as the best of his verse.

—Dorothy Green

MacLEISH, Archibald.   American.   Born in Glencoe, Illinois, 7 May 1892. Educated at the Hotchkiss School, Lakeville, Connecticut; Yale University, New Haven, Connecticut, A.B. 1915; Harvard University, Cambridge, Massachusetts, LL.B. 1919. Served in the United States Army, 1917–19: Captain. Married Ada Hitchcock in 1916; three children. Lecturer in Government, Harvard University, 1919–21; Attorney, Choate Hall and Stewart, Boston, 1920–23; Editor, *Fortune* magazine, New York, 1929–38; Curator of the Niemann Foundation, Harvard University, 1938; Librarian of Congress, Washington, D.C., 1939–44; Director, United States Office of Facts and Figures, 1941–42, Assistant Director of the Office of War Information, 1942–43, and Assistant Secretary of State, 1944–45, Washington, D.C. Chairman of the United States Delegation to the UNESCO drafting conference, London, 1945, and Member of the Executive Board, UNESCO, 1946. Rede Lecturer, Cambridge University, 1942; Boylston Professor of Rhetoric and Oratory, Harvard University, 1949–62;

Simpson Lecturer, Amherst College, Massachusetts, 1964–67. Recipient: Shelley Memorial Award, 1932; Pulitzer Prize, 1933, 1953, for drama, 1959; New England Poetry Club Golden Rose, 1934; Bollingen Prize, 1952; National Book Award, 1953; Sarah Josepha Hale Award, 1958; Antoinette Perry Award, 1959; National Association of Independent Schools Award, 1959; Academy of American Poets Fellowship, 1965; Academy Award, 1966; National Medal for Literature, 1978. M.A.: Tufts University, Medford, Massachusetts, 1932; Litt.D.: Wesleyan University, Middletown, Connecticut, 1938; Colby College, Waterville, Maine, 1938; Yale University, 1939; University of Pennsylvania, Philadelphia, 1941; University of Illinois, Urbana, 1947; Rockford College, Illinois, 1952; Columbia University, New York, 1954; Harvard University, 1955; Carleton College, Northfield, Minnesota, 1956; Princeton University, New Jersey, 1965; University of Massachusetts, Amherst, 1969; York University, Toronto, 1971; LL.D.: Dartmouth College, Hanover, New Hampshire, 1940; Johns Hopkins University, Baltimore, 1941; University of California, Berkeley, 1943; Queen's University, Kingston, Ontario, 1948; University of Puerto Rico, Rio Piedras, 1953; Amherst College, Massachusetts, 1963; D.C.L.: Union College, Schenectady, New York, 1941; L.H.D.: Williams College, Williamstown, Massachusetts, 1942; University of Washington, Seattle, 1948. Commander, Legion of Honor; Commander, El Sol del Peru. President, American Academy of Arts and Letters, 1953–56. Lives in Massachusetts.

PUBLICATIONS

Verse

    Songs for a Summer's Day (A Sonnet-Cycle). 1915.
    Tower of Ivory. 1917.
    The Happy Marriage and Other Poems. 1924.
    The Pot of Earth. 1925.
    Streets in the Moon. 1926.
    The Hamlet of A. MacLeish. 1928.
    Einstein. 1929.
    New Found Land: Fourteen Poems. 1930.
    Before March. 1932.
    Conquistador. 1932.
    Frescoes for Mr. Rockefeller's City. 1933.
    Poems 1924–1933. 1933; as *Poems,* 1935.
    Public Speech: Poems. 1936.
    Land of the Free – U.S.A. 1938.
    America Was Promises. 1939.
    Actfive and Other Poems. 1948.
    Collected Poems 1917–1952. 1952.
    Songs for Eve. 1954.
    Collected Poems. 1963.
    "The Wild Old Wicked Man" and Other Poems. 1968.
    The Human Season: Selected Poems 1926–1972. 1972.
    New and Collected Poems 1917–1976. 1976.

Plays

    Nobodaddy. 1926.
    Union Pacific (ballet scenario; produced 1934). In *The Book of Ballets,* 1939.

Panic: A Play in Verse (produced 1935).   1935.

The Fall of the City: A Verse Play for Radio (broadcast, 1937).   1937.

Air Raid: A Verse Play for Radio (broadcast, 1938).   1938.

The States Talking (broadcast, 1941).   In *The Free Company Presents*, edited by James Boyd, 1941.

The American Story: Ten Radio Scripts (includes *The Admiral; The American Gods; The American Name; Not Bacon's Bones; Between the Silence and the Surf; Discovered; The Many Dead; The Names for the Rivers; Ripe Strawberries and Gooseberries and Sweet Single Roses; Socorro, When Your Sons Forget)* (broadcast, 1944).   1944.

The Trojan Horse (broadcast, 1952).   1952.

This Music Crept by Me upon the Waters (broadcast, 1953).   1953.

J.B.: A Play in Verse (produced 1958).   1958.

The Secret of Freedom (televised, 1959).   In *Three Short Plays*, 1961.

Three Short Plays: The Secret of Freedom, Air Raid, The Fall of the City.   1961.

Our Lives, Our Fortunes, and Our Sacred Honor (as *The American Bell*, music by David Amram, produced 1962).   In *Think*, July–August 1961.

Herakles: A Play in Verse (produced 1965).   1967.

An Evening's Journey to Conway, Massachusetts: An Outdoor Play (produced 1967).   1967.

Scratch, suggested by *The Devil and Daniel Webster* by Stephen Vincent Benét (produced 1971).   1971.

The Great American Fourth of July Parade (produced 1975).   1975.

Screenplays: *Grandma Moses*, 1950; *The Eleanor Roosevelt Story*, 1965.

Radio Plays: *The Fall of the City*, 1937; *King Lear*, from the play by Shakespeare, 1937; *Air Raid*, 1938; *The States Talking*, 1941; *The American Story* series, 1944; *The Son of Man*, 1947; *The Trojan Horse*, 1952; *This Music Crept by Me upon the Waters*, 1953.

Television Play: *The Secret of Freedom*, 1959.

Other

Housing America, by the Editors of *Fortune*.   1932.

Jews in America, by the Editors of *Fortune*.   1936.

Background of War, by the Editors of *Fortune*.   1937.

The Irresponsibles: A Declaration.   1940.

The Next Harvard, As Seen by MacLeish   1941.

A Time to Speak: The Selected Prose.   1941.

The American Cause.   1941.

A Time to Act: Selected Addresses.   1943.

Poetry and Opinion: The Pisan Cantos of Ezra Pound: A Dialogue on the Role of Poetry.   1950.

Freedom Is the Right to Choose: An Inquiry into the Battle for the American Future.   1951.

Poetry and Journalism.   1958.

Poetry and Experience.   1961.

The Dialogues of MacLeish and Mark Van Doren, edited by Warren V. Busch.   1964.

The Eleanor Roosevelt Story.   1965.

A Continuing Journey.   1968.

The Great American Frustration.   1968.

Riders of the Earth: Essays and Reminiscences.   1978.

Editor, *Law and Politics,* by Felix Frankfurter.   1962.

Bibliography: *A Catalogue of the First Editions of MacLeish* by Arthur Mizener, 1938; *MacLeish: A Checklist* by Edward J. Mullahy, 1973.

Reading List: *MacLeish* by Signi Lenea Falk, 1965; *MacLeish* by Grover C. Smith, 1971.

*   *   *

By 1940, Archibald MacLeish had written numerous books of poems, and was a well-known writer. He was also the target of adverse criticism. MacLeish's early work is too derivative. It abounds with the distracting influence of Eliot and Pound, among others. MacLeish writes on the same subjects as Eliot and Pound and from exactly their point of view. MacLeish's early long poems proved very weak. His most famous one is *Conquistador,* which won him the first of three Pulitzer Prizes. It is a verbose, unqualified glorification of Spain's slaughter and enslavement of Mexican Natives, and is, at best, unthinkingly adolescent. Other works in this period are marred by the confusing about-face MacLeish executes concerning the role of the poet. In his "Invocation to the Social Muse," MacLeish criticizes those who would urge the poet to concentrate on social issues. These issues, however, soon become central to his own work. MacLeish proceeds to sermonize, harangue – and produce much poor poetry, especially in *Public Speech* and his plays for radio.

Yet, despite the inferior work written in these decades, MacLeish was beginning to compile an outstanding body of lyric poetry. Some of the short poems in *Streets in the Moon* and *New Found Land* hold up very well. "L'an trentiesme de mon eage" is a superior presentation on the subject of the lost generation. Other fine peoms include "Eleven," "Immortal Autumn," and "Memorial Rain." "Ars poetic" develops the stimulating idea that "A poem should not mean/But be." Perhaps the best of all is "The End of the World," a dramatization of the belief that the universe is basically meaningless. *Poems 1924–1933* brought together such superior lyrics as "Pony Rock," "Unfinished History," and "Lines for an Interment."

What became increasingly apparent in the 1940's and thereafter is that MacLeish's primary strength as a writer resides in the lyric form. In fact, MacLeish has done most of his best work after the age of fifty.

Even some of MacLeish's later plays and long poems, two genres he never really excels at, rise above the mediocre. The full-length play *J.B.*, despite its bland poetry and tepid main character, effectively dramatizes the tragedies that engulf J.B. and offers a frequently rousing debate between Mr. Zuss (representing orthodox religion) and Nickles (representing a pragmatic outlook). MacLeish's one-act play *This Music Crept by Me upon the Waters* is also successful. The main characters, Peter and Elizabeth, are interesting; the plot builds in suspense; and the poetry and the theme (a preference for the present over the past) are powerful. *Actfive* is MacLeish's best long poem. The first section, which delineates modern man's basic predicament, is quite absorbing.

Still, it is MacLeish's lyric poetry that will be remembered the longest. Starting with the poems collected in 1948, the number of excellent lyrics mounts steadily. For this reason, the critical neglect MacLeish has suffered in recent years is unjust. These later lyrics center on three sometimes overlapping subjects. One presents MacLeish's increasing awareness of the mystery that permeates human experience. Earlier in his life, he wrote several poems that spoke confidently, if not cockily about setting out on explorations; now he writes "Voyage West," a sensitive expression of the uncertainty involved in a journey. Significantly, "Poet's Laughter" and "Crossing" are full of questions, while "The Old Man to the Lizard" and "Hotel Breakfast" end with questions, not answers. MacLeish sums up his sense of the mysterious in "Autobiography" when he says, "What do I know of the mystery of the universe?/Only the mystery."

MacLeish has also written several tender eulogies and epitaphs. Two such poems about his mother are "The Burial" and "For the Anniversary of My Mother's Death." A pair of even finer poems, "Poet" and "Hemingway," have Ernest Hemingway for their subject. Other outstanding poems in this vein include "Edwin Muir," "Cummings," and "The Danger in the Air."

Finally, MacLeish has written a host of fine poems about old age. The difficulty of creativity when one is no longer young is described in "They Come No More, Those Words, Those Finches." Tiredness is poignantly depicted in "Walking" and "Dozing on the Lawn." "Ship's Log" records the narrowing awareness of the old. Here, MacLeish states: "Mostly I have relinquished and forgotten/Or grown accustomed, which is a way of forgetting." Yet " 'The Wild Old Wicked Man' " presents an old person's wisdom and passion. In the two poems concerning "The Old Gray Couple," he offers the reader a moving portrait of the final, deepest stage of human love. Lastly, using Odysseus as narrator, MacLeish chooses human love (symbolized by his aging wife) and mortal life over love for the abstract (symbolized by the goddess Calypso) and the metaphysical in his lovely poem "Calypso's Island." This poem declares, "I long for the cold, salt,/Restless, contending sea and for the island/Where the grass dies and the seasons alter."

—Robert K. Johnson

MacNEICE, (Frederick) Louis. English. Born in Belfast, Northern Ireland, 12 September 1907. Educated at Sherborne School; Marlborough; Merton College, Oxford, 1926–30, B.A. (honours) in classics and philosophy 1930. Married 1) Mary Ezra in 1930 (divorced, 1937), one son; 2) the singer Hedli Anderson in 1942, one daughter. Lecturer in Classics, University of Birmingham, 1930–36; Lecturer in Greek, Bedford College, University of London, 1936–40; Visiting Lecturer in English, Cornell University, Ithaca, New York, 1940; Feature Writer and Producer, BBC, London, 1941–49; Director, British Council Institute, Athens, 1950–51; Visiting Lecturer in Poetry and Drama, Sarah Lawrence College, Bronxville, New York, 1954–55. Clark Lecturer, Cambridge University, 1963. Recipient: Premio d'Italia, for radio play, 1959. D.Litt.: Queen's University of Belfast, 1957. C.B.E. (Commander, Order of the British Empire), 1958. *Died 3 September 1963.*

PUBLICATIONS

Collections

The Collected Poems, edited by E. R. Dodds.   1966.

Verse

Blind Fireworks.   1929.
Poems.   1935.
Letters from Iceland, with W. H. Auden.   1937.
The Earth Compels.   1938.
Autumn Journal: A Poem.   1939.
The Last Ditch.   1940.
Selected Poems.   1940.

Poems 1925–1940.   1940.
Plant and Phantom.   1941.
Springboard: Poems 1941–1944.   1944.
Holes in the Sky: Poems 1944–1947.   1948.
Collected Poems 1925–1948.   1949.
Ten Burnt Offerings.   1952.
Autumn Sequel: A Rhetorical Poem in XXVI Cantos.   1954.
Visitations.   1957.
Eighty-Five Poems, Selected by the Author.   1959.
Solstices.   1961.
The Burning Perch.   1963.
The Revenant: A Song-Cycle for Hedli Anderson.   1975.

Plays

The Station Bell (produced 1935).
The Agamemnon, from the play by Aeschylus (produced 1936).   1936.
Out of the Picture (produced 1937).   1937.
Christopher Columbus (broadcast 1942).   1944.
The Dark Tower and Other Radio Scripts (includes Sunbeams in His Hat and The March
   Hare Saga).   1947.
Faust, parts 1 and 2 (abridged version), from the play by Goethe (broadcast
   1949).   1951.
Traitors in Our Way (produced 1957).
The Mad Island and The Administrator: Two Radio Plays.   1964.
One for the Grave: A Modern Morality Play (produced 1966).   1968.
Persons from Porlock and Other Plays for Radio (includes Enter Caesar, East of the Sun
   and West of the Moon, They Met on Good Friday).   1969.

Screenplay: The Conquest of Everest, 1953.

Radio Plays and Features: Word from America, 1941; Cook's Tour of the London
Subways, 1941; The March of the 10,000, 1941; The Stones Cry Out (series), 1941;
Freedom's Ferry, 1941; Dr. Chekhov, 1941; The Glory That Is Greece, 1941; Rogue's
Gallery, 1941; Salute to the New Year, 1941; Vienna, 1942; Salutation to Greece, 1942;
Calling All Fools, 1942; Salute to the U.S.S.R., 1942; Alexander Nevsky, 1942; The
Debate Continues, 1942; Black Gallery (series), 1942; The Undefeated of Yugoslavia,
1942; Britain to America, 1942; The United Nations: A Tribute, 1942; Halfway House,
1942; Salute to the U.S. Army, 1942; Christopher Columbus, 1942; Salute to Greece,
1942; Salute to the United Nations, 1943; Two Men and America, 1943; The Four
Freedoms (series), 1943; Long Live Greece, 1943; Zero Hour, 1943; The Death of Byron,
1943; Sicily and Freedom, 1943; The Death of Marlowe, 1943; Independence Day, 1943;
Four Years at War, 1943; Lauro de Bosis: The Story of My Death, 1943; The Spirit of
Russia, 1943; The Fifth Freedom, 1943; Ring in the New, 1943; The Sacred Band, 1944;
Sunbeams in His Hat, 1944; The Nosebag, 1944; This Breed of Men, 1944; D Day, 1944;
He Had a Date, 1944; Why Be a Poet?, 1944; The Golden Ass, 1944; Cupid and Psyche,
1944; The Year in Review, 1944; A Roman Holiday, 1945; The March Hare Resigns,
1945; London Victorious, 1945; A Voice from Norway, 1945; The Dark Tower, 1946;
Salute to All Fools', 1946; Poetry Promenade (series), 1946; Enter Caesar, 1946; The
Careerist, 1946; Agamemnon, 1946; Book of Verse (series), 1946; Aristophanes: Enemy
of Cant, 1946; The Heartless Giant, 1946; The Death of Gunnar, 1947; The Burning of
Njal, 1947; Portrait of Rome, 1947; "Autumn Journal": A Selection, 1947; India at First
Sight, 1948; Portrait of Delhi, 1948; The Road to Independence, 1948; Pakistan, 1948;

The Two Wicked Sisters, 1948; *No Other Road*, 1948; *Trimalchio's Feast*, 1948; *The Queen of Air and Darkness*, 1949; *Louis MacNeice Reads His Poetry*, 1949; *Faust* (six parts), 1949; *Portrait of Athens*, 1951; *Burnt Offerings*, 1951; *In Search of Anoyia*, 1951; *Delphi: The Centre of the World*, 1952; *One Eye Wild*, 1952; *The Twelve Days of Christmas*, 1953; *Time Hath Brought Me Hither*, 1953; *Return to Atlantis*, 1953; *Where No Wounds Were*, 1954; *Prisoner's Progress*, 1954; *Autumn Sequel* (series), 1954; *Return to a School*, 1954; *The Waves*, from the novel by Virginia Woolf, 1955; *The Fullness of the Nile*, 1955; *The Star We Follow*, with Ritchie Calder, 1955; *Also among the Prophets*, 1956; *Bow Bells*, 1956; *Spires and Gantries*, 1956; *Carpe Diem*, 1956; *From Bard to Busker*, 1956; *Nuts in May*, 1957; *An Oxford Anthology*, 1957; *The Stones of Oxford*, 1957; *Border Ballads*, 1958; *All Fools' at Home*, 1958; *Health in Their Hands*, 1958; *New Poetry*, 1959; *Scrums and Dreams*, 1959; *Poems by Tennyson*, 1959; *They Met on Good Friday*, 1959; *Mosaic of Youth*, 1959; *East of the Sun and West of the Moon*, 1959; *The Odyssey* (series), with others, 1960; *The Administrator*, 1961; *Poems of Salvatore Quasimodo*, 1961; *Let's Go Yellow*, 1961; *The Mad Islands*, 1962; *Latin Poetry*, 1963; *New Poetry*, 1963; *Mediaeval Latin Poetry*, 1963; *Persons from Porlock*, 1963; *Ireland, My Ireland*, 1976.

Fiction

Roundabout Way.   1932.

Other

I Crossed the Minch (travel and verse).   1938.
Modern Poetry: A Personal Essay.   1938.
Zoo.   1938.
The Poetry of W. B. Yeats.   1941.
Meet the U.S. Army.   1943.
The Penny That Rolled Away (juvenile).   1954; as *The Sixpence That Rolled Away*, 1956.
Astrology, edited by Douglas Hill.   1964.
Varieties of Parable (lectures).   1965.
The Strings Are False: An Unfinished Autobiography, edited by Elton R. Dodds.   1965.

Editor, with Stephen Spender, *Oxford Poetry 1929*.   1929.
Editor, with Bonamy Dobrée and Philip Larkin, *New Poems 1958: A P.E.N. Anthology*.   1958.

Bibliography: *A Bibliography of the Works of MacNeice* by C. M. Armitage and Neil Clark, 1973.

Reading List: *MacNeice* by John Press, 1965; *Spender, Day Lewis, MacNeice* by Derek Stanford, 1969; *MacNeice* by Elton E. Smith, 1970; *Apollo's Blended Dream: A Study of the Poetry of MacNeice* by William T. McKinnon, 1971; *The Poetry of MacNeice* by D. B. Moore, 1972; *Time Was Away: The World of MacNeice* edited by Terence Brown and Alec Reid, 1974; *MacNeice: Sceptical Vision* by Terence Brown, 1975.

*   *   *

Even if Louis MacNeice had never written a line of original poetry he would still be remembered as a versatile and prolific man of letters. Despite the technical skill and the arduous labour that MacNeice lavished on it, his translation of Goethe's *Faust* was only a partial success, but his version of the *Agamemnon* of Aeschylus has been justly praised as a remarkable achievement by classical scholars and by readers of poetry who have no Greek. His essay *Modern Poetry* remains the best guide to what the most intelligent young poets of the 1930's were trying to achieve; *The Poetry of W. B. Yeats*, written before the flood of Yeatsian exegesis had gathered strength, conveys MacNeice's admiration for a major poet, but makes some pertinent criticisms of Yeats's metaphysical and political attitudes; *Varieties of Parable*, published two years after MacNeice's death and unrevised by him, contains illuminating reflections on writers as dissimilar as Spenser, George Herbert, and Beckett, for whom he felt an intuitive sympathy. He was also what he called a "radio practitioner," the author of over 150 radio scripts, only a few of which have been published. And his unfinished autobiography, *The Strings Are False*, is unusually perceptive and honest.

Yet it is as a poet the MacNeice will be deservedly remembered. Although he was, at the time, classified as "a poet of the thirties," part of the pantomime monster that Roy Campbell dubbed MacSpaunday, he was a highly individual poet whose temperament, convictions, and poetic achievement differentiated him sharply from Auden, Spender, and Day Lewis, with whom he was so often ranked.

MacNeice loved the brilliance of the visible world, the surfaces of things, the life-quickening moments that suddenly awaken the lucky man who is blessed by those visitants. He rejected the Platonic belief in "a transcendental radiance" that, as MacNeice put it, imposed "a white-out on everything." An early poem, "Snow," makes explicit those implicit assumptions that colour his lyrics of the 1930's:

> World is crazier and more of it than we think,
> Incorrigibly plural. I peel and portion
> A tangerine and spit the pips and feel
> The drunkenness of things being various.

One of his best known poems of the period, "The Sunlight on the Garden," still retains its vividness, partly because it moves to a tune that continues to delight us with its ingenious elegance.

> The sunlight on the garden
> Hardens and grows cold,
> We cannot cage the minute
> Within its nets of gold,
> When all is told
> We cannot beg for pardon

There is in his early verse an underlying sadness that springs from the recognition of transience. The dazzle on the sea, the momentary sunlight, even that brief awareness of timelessness in the presence of the beloved – "Time was away and somewhere else" – would, he knew, be obliterated by the turbulence of the universal flux.

His longer poems of the 1930's that wrestle with this problem are less satisfying than the short lyrics. *Autumn Journal* is, however, a highly successful poem because, as the title implies, it is not an attempt to express a systematic philosophy but a series of observations on a variety of themes, of reactions to the events of the day in the private and public worlds. The metres of the poem are irregular, the rhyme-schemes are flexible, and the poem's themes are as diverse in range as those in Byron's *Don Juan*: civil war, political satire, autobiographical digressions, memories of a broken marriage, philosophical argument, and an evocation of ancient Greece that displays MacNeice's gifts at their most brilliant.

During the war years and the late 1940's, MacNeice's poetry becomes darker and more reflective, less given to recording the surfaces of things, less gay in its music:

> Because the velvet image,
> Because the lilting measure
> No more convey my meaning.

The ravages of war, the burning of London by enemy planes, the apparent triumph of a principle that is radically hostile to life – those are the themes that run through his poems of the decade, poems whose titles and imagery remind us that MacNeice, the son of a Bishop, was haunted always by the symbols and the morality of a Christianity that he had reluctantly but firmly rejected. No poem of his is more impressive or more universal than "Prayer Before Birth":

> I am not yet born; O hear me,
> Let not the man who is beast or who thinks he is God come near me.

Between 1948 and 1957 MacNeice published three long poems: his translation of *Faust* which, although only two-thirds of the length of the original, still ran to 8000 lines; *Ten Burnt Offerings*, ten medium-length poems described by the author as "experiments in dialectical structure"; and *Autumn Sequel*, "a rhetorical poem" in twenty-six cantos. All three of the poems were broadcast by the BBC before publication, and all have been generally considered among the least satisfactory of his works. *Autumn Journal* had been successful because of its formal variety and flexibility; *Autumn Sequel*, which MacNeice described as an attempt to marry myth to "actuality," is written in *terza rima*, a medium that has proved as dangerous to English writers of long poems as Shakespearean blank verse to aspiring poetic dramatists.

Happily MacNeice was revisited by the lyrical impulse – his first collection of short poems since *Holes in the Sky* was appropriately entitled *Visitations*. In the spring and early summer of 1960, says MacNeice, "I underwent one of those rare bursts of creativity when the poet is first astonished and then rather alarmed by the way the mill goes on grinding." The resulting volume, *Solstices*, was followed by a posthumous collection, *The Burning Perch*. The variety of moods and the mastery of tone are impressive in these poems. One section of "Notes for a Biography" is a bitter virtuoso parody of "Bonny Dundee"; "Beni Hasan" contemplates with serene gravity the prospect of death that came to the poet on the Nile; in "The Habits" MacNeice faces the truth about his own nature. Not surprisingly, he was "taken aback" when assembling the poems for *The Burning Perch* "by the high proportion of sombre pieces, ranging from bleak observation to thumbnail nightmares." One poem in particular, "The Taxis," is a kind of ghost story suffused with sardonic mirth:

> In the third taxi he was alone tra-la
> But the tip-up seats were down and there was an extra
> Charge of one-and-sixpence and an odd
> Scent that reminded him of a trip to Cannes.

Auden and MacNeice were the finest poets of their generation: it is by no means certain that Auden was the more distinguished of the two.

—John Press

MACPHERSON, James. Scottish. Born in Ruthven, Inverness-shire, 27 October 1736. Educated at the University of Aberdeen and the University of Edinburgh, but did not take a degree; studied for the ministry, but did not take holy orders. Had 4 illegitimate children. Taught in the village school in Ruthven; tutor at Moffat, 1759; at the instigation of John

Home, and later Lord Bute, published his "translations" of ancient Highland poetry, 1760, and of the two epic poems of "Ossian," 1762–63, all of which were generally believed by literary men, particularly Samuel Johnson, to be his own inventions; Secretary to the Governor of Florida, 1764–66; settled in London and worked for the government as a political writer; employed by Lord North's ministry to defend its American policy and to supervise ministerial newspapers, 1776–80; Member of Parliament for Camelford, Cornwall, 1780–96; Agent in London to the Nabob of Arcot, from 1781. *Died 17 February 1796.*

PUBLICATIONS

Collections

The Poems of Ossian and Macpherson, edited by Malcolm Laing. 2 vols., 1805.

Verse

The Highlander: An Heroic Poem in Six Cantos. 1758.
Fragments of Ancient Poetry Collected in the Highlands of Scotland. 1760; edited by J. J. Dunn, 1966.
Fingal: An Ancient Epic Poem, with Several Other Poems Translated from the Gaelic Language. 1762.
Temora: An Ancient Epic Poem, with Several Other Poems Translated from the Gaelic Language. 1763.
The Works of Ossian, translated by James Macpherson. 2 vols., 1765; as *Ossian*, edited by O. L. Jiriczek, 3 vols., 1940.

Other

An Introduction to the History of Great Britain and Ireland. 1771; revised edition, 1772.
The History of Great Britain from the Restoration to the Accession of the House of Hanover. 2 vols., 1775.
Original Papers, Containing the Secret History of Great Britain. 2 vols., 1775.
The Rights of Great Britain Asserted Against the Claims of America. 1776.
A Short History of the Opposition During the Last Session of Parliament. 1779.
The History and Management of the East India Company. 1779.

Translator, *The Iliad Translated into Prose*, by Homer. 2 vols., 1773.

Reading List: *A Critical Dissertation on the Poems of Ossian* by H. Blair, 1763; *The Gaelic Sources of Macpherson's Ossian* by Derick S. Thomson, 1952.

*   *   *

The *Ossian* controversy dominated the literary world from the 1760's until in 1805 a committee of enquiry proved beyond doubt that the supposed translations were in large part the original work of James Macpherson. The nationalistic tone of the poems appealed to the Scottish *literati* of the time (Fingal the Scottish hero is constantly represented as being superior to the Irish and to the Romans) who defended their provenance against such sceptics as Dr. Johnson. The appeal of *Fingal* and *Temora* was widespread, creating a European phenomenon that helped set the tone for a "romantic" movement.

Macpherson's major work describing wild, northern landscapes and heroes lost in a Celtic twilight embodies that form of stylistic "sublimity" which Burke had advocated in 1757, appealing to the emotions rather than the reason. Rather than harmony and number in poetry, Macpherson exploits the "fragmented" nature of the supposed translations, allowing gaps in comprehension to work for him in the creation of atmosphere. The bardic tone is borrowed from Miltonic and Biblical sources; applied to ancient northern mythology it created in its time a cult for the remote past, the mysterious, and the irrational.

—B. C. Oliver-Morden

MAIR, Charles. Canadian. Born in Lanark, Ontario, 21 September 1838. Educated at Queen's University, Kingston, Ontario. Married Elizabeth Louise MacKenny in 1868 (died, 1906). Entered government service, Ottawa, 1868; involved in the "Canada First" movement, 1868, and was imprisoned at Fort Garry by the rebels in the Riel Rebellion, 1869; escaped to Ontario, and became a fur trader at Portage La Prairie; Quartermaster, Governor-General's Body Guard, 2nd Riel Rebellion, 1885; thereafter served on government expeditions to British Columbia, and worked in the Canadian Immigration Department until 1921. LL.D.: Queen's University, 1926. Fellow, Royal Society of Canada, 1889. *Died 7 July 1927.*

PUBLICATIONS

Verse

 Dreamland and Other Poems. 1868.
 Tecumseh: A Drama, and Canadian Poems. 1901; revised edition, 1926.

Play

 Tecumseh (as *The Red Revolutionary*, produced 1972). 1886.

Other

 Through the Mackenzie Basin: A Narrative of the Athabasca and Peace River Treaty Expedition of 1899. 1908.

Reading List: *Mair* by Norman Shrive, 1965.

*   *   *

Charles Mair holds a place in Canadian literary history for his politics more than for his poetry. In the later 1860's he became a member of that early nationalist movement known as Canada First, and his desire to spread Canadian influence into the yet unsettled prairies led him to take a provocative role at the Red River during the rebellion of 1869. He strongly supported the Canadian party which stood in opposition to Louis Riel and the insurgent Métis. After Riel established his Provisional Government at Fort Garry, Mair became involved in an abortive attempt at armed resistance. He was captured by Riel's militia, and threatened with execution by Riel himself, but escaped to Ontario. In later years he wandered over the west, as a trader, as a land speculator, and in his final years as an immigration agent, a post he continued to hold until the age of 83.

Little of this adventurous life, or of the political fire which it at times projected, is anticipated in Mair's first book of poems, *Dreamland and Other Poems*, which appeared a year before his Red River adventure. It is a volume of somewhat Tennysonian lyrics that are mostly sentimental in tone, and it is mainly redeemed by occasional quite vivid renderings of natural scenes where the Upper Canadian countryside is portrayed with an observation almost pre-Raphaelite in its sharpness and directness.

Mair's nationalism emerges much more emphatically in the verse drama, *Tecumseh*, which deals with the War of 1812 and the role of the Indian leader Tecumseh, whom Mair presents as a symbol of Canadian defiance of American domination. It is a cumbersome work, unviable dramatically, but here and there the experiences of Mair's years in the west shine through in splendid passages describing the prairies before the settlers and the railway came:

> At length we heard a deep and solemn sound –
> Erupted moanings of the troubled earth
> Trembling beneath innumerable feet.
> A growing uproar blending in our ears,
> With noise tumultuous as ocean's surge,
> Of bellowings, fierce breath and battle shock,
> And ardour of unconquerable herds ...
> And, lo! before us lay the tameless stock,
> Slow wending to the northward like a cloud!
> A multitude in motion, dark and dense –
> Far as the eye could reach, and farther still,
> In countless myriads stretched for many a league.

As this passage on the great and vanished bison herds suggests, Mair is principally important in a historical way, not for the quality of his verse, but because he was one of the first poets to see Canada as a man who belonged to the land, a native in feeling as well as by birth, rather than, like most of his contemporaries, as a colonial attempting to recreate the literary culture of the motherland.

—George Woodcock

MALLET, David. Scottish. Born David Malloch in Crieff, Perthshire, c. 1705; changed name to Mallet, 1726. Educated in the parish school in Crieff, and at the University of Edinburgh, 1721–22, 1722–23; St. Mary Hall, Oxford, 1731–34, B.A. and M.A. 1734. Married 1) Susanna c. 1734 (died, 1741), one son, one daughter; 2) Lucy Elstob in 1742, two daughters. Janitor in the high school of Edinburgh, 1717; resident tutor to the sons of Mr. Home of Dreghorn, 1720–23; tutor to the sons of the Duke of Montrose, in London and at Shawford, near Winchester, 1723–31; tutor to the stepson of John Knight, whom he accompanied to Oxford, 1731–34; appointed Under-Secretary to the Prince of Wales, 1742, and received a pension from him until 1748; also enjoyed the patronage of Bolingbroke through whose influence he was appointed Inspector of the Exchequer-Book in the Outports of London, 1763 until his death. *Died 21 April 1765.*

PUBLICATIONS

Collections

Works of the English Poets 14, edited by A. Chalmers.   1810.

Verse

William and Margaret: An Old Ballad.   1723.
A Poem in Imitation of Donaides.   1725.
The Excursion.   1728.
Of Verbal Criticism: An Epistle to Mr. Pope.   1733.
Verses Presented to the Prince of Orange on His Visiting Oxford, with Walter Harte.   1734.
Poems on Several Occasions.   1743.
Amyntor and Theodora; or, The Hermit.   1747.
Edwin and Emma.   1760; edited by F. T. Dinsdale, 1849.
Verses on the Death of Lady Anson.   1760.
Poems on Several Occasions.   1762.
Ballads and Songs, edited by F. T. Dinsdale.   1857.

Plays

Eurydice (produced 1731).   1731.
Mustapha (produced 1739).   1739.
Alfred: A Masque, with James Thomson, music by Thomas Arne (produced 1740).   1740; revised version (produced 1751), 1751; as *Alfred the Great,* 1753.
Britannia: A Masque, music by Thomas Arne (produced 1755).   1755.
Elvira (produced 1763).   1763.

Other

The Life of Francis Bacon.   1740.
Works.   4 vols., 1743; revised edition, 3 vols., 1759.
A Congratulatory Letter to Selim on the Three Letters to the Whigs.   1748.
Observations on the Twelfth Article of War.   1757.

Editor, *Letters on the Spirit of Patriotism, On the Idea of a Patriot King,* by Lord Bolingbroke.   1749.
Editor, *Works of Lord Bolingbroke.*   5 vols., 1754.

647

Reading List: "The Early History of *Alfred*" by Alan D. McKillop, in *Philological Quarterly* *41*, 1962.

*   *   *

David Mallet's earliest work was his most famous and best. His *William and Margaret*, which is so free an adaptation of the authentic traditional ballad of Fair Margaret and Sweet William (F. J. Child's Ballad number 74) as to rank as an original work, was often printed in periodicals and miscellanies in the 1720's, then reprinted, often with revisions by the author, in many other collections, including Percy's *Reliques* (1765), until it came to be regarded as one of the most significant contributions to the eighteenth-century ballad revival, and so, in its small way, a contribution to the romantic revival. Another ballad, *Edwin and Emma*, wholly of Mallet's conception and composition, was published in 1760, but deservedly failed to match the success of *William and Margaret*.

The Excursion, in Miltonic blank verse, was influenced by his friend Thomson's *Winter* and *Summer*. In it Mallet makes "a short excursive survey of the Earth and Heavens," aiming at a sublime effect with his somewhat turgid descriptions of earthquakes, volcanos, thunderstorms, the vast spaces of the stellar universe, and other such natural wonders. One of the poem's more interesting romantic features is the address to the imagination as a creative principle. Mallet showed his virtuosity by then imitating his patron, Pope, in *Of Verbal Criticism*, a satire in heroic couplets, against Pope's enemies Bentley and Theobald; but in his longest poem, *Amyntor and Theodora*, Mallet returns to his romantic vein. This sentimental love story is set in an idealized primitive setting upon the remote Hebridean island of St. Kilda, and takes a hermit for its central character.

Mallet wrote part of *Alfred; A Masque*, though its one memorable song, "Rule Britannia," was the work of his co-author, Thomson. A revised version of *Alfred*, containing more work by Mallet, was acted in 1751; and Mallet was sole author of another patriotic masque, *Britannia*. His three heroic tragedies, *Eurydice*, *Mustapha*, and *Elvira*, are as vapid and stiff as Thomson's tragedies, after which they were to some extent modelled.

—A. J. Sambrook

MANGAN, James Clarence. Irish. Born in Dublin, 1 May 1803. Educated at a school in Saul's Court, Dublin, by Father Graham. Worker in a scrivener's office for 7 years and as a lawyer's clerk for 3 years; later worked briefly as an assistant in the library of Trinity College, Dublin, and in the office of the Irish ordnance survey. Member of the Comet Club, Dublin, 1831, and contributor to the club's journal and to the *Dublin University Magazine*; later wrote for the *Nation*, 1845–48, and the *United Irishman*, 1848, but was prevented from keeping any regular employment by his addiction to alcohol. *Died 20 June 1849.*

PUBLICATIONS

Collections

Poems, edited by D. J. O'Donoghue.   1903.
Prose Writings, edited by D. J. O'Donoghue.   1904.
Selected Poems, edited by Michael Smith.   1974.

Other

Autobiography, edited by James Kilroy.   1968.

Translator, *Anthologia Germanica.*   2 vols., 1845.
Translator, *The Poets and Poetry of Munster,* edited by John O'Daly.   1850.
Translator, *The Tribes of Ireland: A Satire,* by Aenghus O'Daly.   1852.

Bibliography: *A Bibliography of Mangan* by Patrick O'Hegarty, 1941; *Mangan: A Check-List of Printed and Other Sources* by Rudolf P. Holzapfel, 1969.

Reading List: *Mangan and the Poe-Mangan Question* by H. Cain, 1929; *Mangan* by John Sheridan, 1937; *Mangan* by James Kilroy, 1970; *Mangan* by Henry T. Donaghy, 1974; "Mangan ... and a Few Others: The Poet and the Scholars" by Jacques Chuto, in *Irish University Review 6,* 1976; " 'In Wreathed Swell': Mangan, Translator from the Irish" by Robert Welch, in *Eire-Ireland 11,* 1976.

*   *   *

James Clarence Mangan's literary career was a varied yet a confined one. In his own lifetime he did not publish outside Ireland, and appears never to have travelled further from Dublin than the Wicklow hills. And yet in imagination he was a frequenter of all sorts of exotic places, from Iceland to the burning deserts of Arabia. His poetic mode was translation, which for him became a means of devouring an author's experience, appropriating it to himself, then creating an eloquence based on the structure and mood of the original. Not all his translations take his author over to the same extent, but his best versions are those in which the original is subsumed in the re-creation. It is as if the process of translation were a mask which allowed him freer expression.

He translated (or pretended to translate) from an astonishing range of languages, among them German, Turkish, Arabic, Sanskrit, Spanish, and Irish. His versions of German and of Gaelic poetry had most impact on the literary life of the time. He made versions of Goethe and Schiller but he seems less comfortable with them than with the lesser German poets. He delighted in the intense emotionalism of Klopstock, the yearning of Rückert, the wildness of Freiligarth. German poetry offered an example of a living tradition of verse radically different in mood and texture from English poetry of the time, an important consideration for Mangan, who, a nationalist, was attempting to forge a style in English that would not owe everything to England.

It is in his translations from the Irish that Mangan achieved his most complete expression as a poet. Through his work on the Ordnance Survey he came into contact with the leading Gaelic scholars of the time and from them he learned about Irish bardic tradition and the images of ancient Irish life that were to be potent forces in Irish literature and politics. Fired by these he worked on literal versions of Gaelic poems, transforming them into great rhetorical gestures, full of patriotic zeal, sadness for the life that has passed away in Ireland, and anger against England that sometimes mounts into frenzy. It is a passionate poetry that has behind it the political tensions and catastrophic events of the 1840's in Ireland.

Through his versions from the Gaelic Mangan found a way of responding to contemporary events. A handful of original poems also, more than any other poems of the time, convey the horror of English mismanagement and Irish famine. Among these are "Siberia" and "A Vision of Connaught."

—Robert Welch

MARKHAM, Edwin. American. Born Charles Edward Anson Markham in Oregon City, Oregon, 23 April 1852. Educated at San Jose Normal School, California; Christian College, Santa Rosa, California. Married 1) Annie Cox in 1875 (divorced, 1884); 2) Carolvn E. Bailey in 1887; 3) Anna Catherine Murphy in 1898; one son. Schoolteacher: Headmaster, University Observation School, Oakland, California, for 10 years. Lived in New York and New Jersey from c. 1900: lecturer and editor. Recipient: Academy of American Poets Prize. Honorary Degrees: Baylor University, Waco, Texas; Syracuse University, New York; New York University. Honorary President, Poetry Society of America. Member, American Institute of Arts and Letters, 1930. *Died 7 March 1940.*

PUBLICATIONS

Collections

Poems, edited by Charles L. Wallis. 1950.

Verse

The Man with the Hoe and Other Poems. 1899.
Lincoln and Other Poems. 1901.
The Shoes of Happiness and Other Poems. 1915.
Gates of Paradise and Other Poems. 1920.
Funeral of Adam Willis Wagnalls. 1924.
New Poems: Eighty Songs at Eighty. 1932.
The Star of Araby. 1937.

Other

Modern Poets and Christian Teaching, with Richard Watson Gilder and E. R. Sill. 1906.
The Burt-Markham Primer: The Nature Method, with Mary Burt. 1907.
Children in Bondage: A Presentation of the Anxious Problem of Child Labor, with Benjamin B. Lindsey and George Creel. 1914.
California the Wonderful. 1914.
Archibald Henderson: An Appreciation of the Man. 1918.
Campbell Meeker. 1925.

Editor, *The Real America in Romance.* 15 vols., 1909–27.
Editor, *Foundation Stones of Success.* 10 vols., 1917.
Editor, *The Book of Poetry.* 3 vols., 1926.
Editor, *Songs and Stories of California.* 1931.
Editor, *The Book of English Poetry.* 1934.
Editor, *Poetry of Youth.* 1935.

Reading List: *Markham* by William L. Stidger, 1933; *The Unknown Markham: His Mystery and Its Significance* by Louis Filler, 1966.

*   *   *

Edwin Markham, best known for a single poem, "The Man with the Hoe," produced five published collections of verse in his lifetime, as well as a few other poetic attempts, and in addition a series of articles on the injustices of child labour and on various other Progressive/ Reform causes. As a poet he was an unsophisticated traditionalist (hence, a mainstream writer, as Dickinson, Whitman, Wallace Stevens, E. E. Cummings, and W. C. Williams could never be). He strove, generally with the aid of regular rhythms and conventional rhymes, to promote brotherhood, love, and all the other standard virtues. A strong sense of Christian "awareness" runs throughout his work, which reflects not only his sensitive conscience in the face of man's inhumanity to man, but his spiritual commitment: an ongoing manifesto of the need for *good works* and the security of *faith*.

A series of unlikely circumstances combined to make "The Man with the Hoe" (based on the painting by the Barbizon artist Jean-François Millet) one of America's most famous poems of all time: deeper and more suggestive than its subject, in almost a subliminal, inexpressible way. Millet's painting of course must be kept in mind here; then the opening lines of the poem: "Bowed by the weight of centuries he leans/Upon his hoe and gazes on the ground,/The emptiness of ages in his face,/And on his back the burden of the world." That the above poem and no other quite like it could profoundly affect an entire nation, was proven by the general neglect accorded Markham's comparable poem (likewise predicated on a Millet painting of a poor peasant), "The Sower" (in *Lincoln and Other Poems*): "He is the stone rejected, yet the stone/Whereon is built metropolis and throne."

Markham's "Lincoln, The Man of the People" was well received, with its image of the fallen President suggesting the fall of "a lordly cedar," leaving "a lonesome place against the sky." A good deal of comment and speculation were provoked by his poem "Virgilia" (in *The Shoes of Happiness and Other Poems*). With its companion-piece, "The Crowning Hour," it spoke of a mysterious lost love and the poet's determination to undertake a cosmic quest in order to find her; here again one can sense, despite all the changes in fashion and style since the poem was written, the basis for strong reader identification: "Our ways go wide and I know not whither,/But my song will search through the worlds for you,/Till the Seven Seas waste and the Seven Stars wither/And the dream of the heart comes true."

Staid, ultra-conventional though Markham's poems were, he himself was a deeply passionate man and a much more complicated person than generally regarded. School superintendent and principal, writer of popular poems and verses, public lecturer and anthologist of popular verse – these job designations do not begin to explain him, any more than do the facts of his unhappy childhood and his tormented relationship with his neurotic mother, or his being a product of the Oregon-California coastal region. A restless, driven man, he lived an inner life quite at variance with his outward appearance of majestic, assured, bearded dignity; this is borne out, for example, by the nightmare poem "The Ballad of the Gallows Bird" (printed originally in 1926).

—Samuel Irving Bellman

MARLOWE, Christopher. English. Born in Canterbury, Kent, 6 February 1564. Educated at King's School, Canterbury, 1579; Benet College, now Corpus Christi College, Cambridge, matriculated 1581, B.A. 1584, M.A. 1587. Settled in London c. 1587: wrote plays for the Lord Admiral's Company and Lord Strange's Company; charged with heresy, 1593: stabbed to death in a tavern brawl before the case was considered. *Died 30 May 1593.*

Publications

Collections

Works, edited by R. H. Case and others.   6 vols., 1930–33.
Poems, edited by Millar Maclure.   1968.
Plays, edited by Roma Gill.   1971.
*Complete Works,*edited by Fredson Bowers.   2 vols., 1973
Complete Plays and Poems, edited by E.D. Pendry.   1976.

Verse

Epigrams and Elegies of Ovid, with John Davies.   1595(?); as *All Ovid's Elegies: 3
    Books, with Epigrams by John Davies,* 1598(?).
Hero and Leander, Begun by Marlowe, Completed by Chapman.   1598; edited by Louis
    L. Martz, 1972.
Lucan's First Book Tanslated Line for Line.   1600.

Plays

Tamburlaine the Great, Divided into Two Tragical Discourses (produced 1587).   1590;
    edited by Irving Ribner, 1974.
Doctor Faustus (produced 1588 or 1592?).   1604; alternative text, 1616; both texts
    edited by W. W. Greg, 1950; edited by Keith Walker, 1973.
The Rich Jew of Malta (produced 1589?).   1633; edited by N. W. Bawcutt, 1977.
Edward the Second (produced 1592?).   1594; edited by Irving Ribner, 1970.
Dido, Queen of Carthage (produced 1593?).   1594.
The Massacre at Paris (produced 1593?).   1594(?).

Bibliography: *Marlowe: A Concise Bibliography by* S. A. Tannenbaum, 1937, supplement,
1947; supplement by R. C. Johnson, 1967.

Reading List: *Marlowe* by M. Poirier, 1951; *The Overreacher: A Study of Marlowe* by Harry
Levin, 1952; *Marlowe and the Early Shakespeare* by F. P. Wilson, 1953; *Suffering and Evil
in the Plays of Marlowe* by D. Cole, 1962; *Marlowe: A Collection of Critical Essays* edited by
Clifford Leech, 1964; *Marlowe: A Critical Study* by J. B. Steane, 1964; *In Search of Marlowe:
A Pictorial Biography* by A. D. Wraight and V. F. Stern, 1965; *Marlowe* by R. E. Knoll,
1968; *Critics on Marlowe* edited by J. O'Neill, 1969; *Marlowe's Agonists* by C. C. Fanta,
1970; *Marlowe, Merlin's Prophet* by Judith Weil, 1977.

*   *   *

A "Coblers eldest son" (as Robert Greene jealously scorned him), Christopher Marlowe
earned for himself the education of a gentleman at the University of Cambridge, and almost
immediately after graduating as Master of Arts startled London with *Tamburlaine.* The play's
"high astounding terms" (Prologue to Part 1) conquered the new world of the theatre with
the same *éclat* as its eponymous hero overcame the Turks and Persians; for many years after
its presumed first production, no dramatist could shake himself free of its cadences.

The echoes of *Tamburlaine* in other sixteenth-century plays whose dates are more certain
is almost the only objective means of establishing a date for the play; the same is true of all

Marlowe's works. Subjective evidence, from its style, suggests that *Dido, Queen of Carthage* was his earliest dramatic production, and that it belongs with the translations of Lucan and Ovid, perhaps accomplished while he was still at Cambridge. Translating the Latin taught him to handle his native language, and a steady progression can be observed in the facility with which he treats the classical authors. Book 1 of his version of Lucan's *Pharsalia* is a line-for-line rendering of the original; the *Elegies* convert Ovid's verse form (hexameter followed by pentameter) into racy, sometimes witty, English heroic couplets. *Dido* takes the whole of the first part of Virgil's *Aeneid* as its provenance; the plot centres on Book 4, but details of character and episode are snatched up with easy deliberation from Books 1 to 6.

The titlepage presents *Dido* as having been performed by the Children of the Chapel Royal, and it ought to be judged by the criteria obtaining for children's plays written by such authors as Lyly and Marston. Its distinction is unmistakable. Marlowe exploits the delight in costume and effect, making his characters draw attention to what they are wearing or to the efforts of the stage technicians. Children's plays aspired to verisimilitude only in the accidentals of a performance; by no stretch of the imagination could boys with unbroken voices imitate to the life the great heroes of classical mythology who were the protagonists of these plays. But if they could not act, they could recite; they had been chosen for their voices, and they were highly trained in all the Renaissance arts of elocution. In Aeneas's account of the fall of Troy Marlowe writes a stirring "aria" which augurs well for his subsequent career as a dramatist writing for the public theatres.

The Prologue to the first part of *Tamburlaine*, written perhaps in 1585, disdains the "jigging veins of rhyming mother-wits," preferring language more appropriate to its tale of the Scythian shepherd whose personal magnetism and force of arms raised him to imperial status and won the love of his captive Egyptian princess, Zenocrate. The success of Part 1 "made our poet pen his second part" (Prologue to Part 2), and the two parts together show the complete revolution of Fortune's Wheel. Tamburlaine is not vanquished by any human power; mortality itself brings about his overthrow: he falls sick, and dies, lamenting that he must "die, and this unconquered." The play is a tragedy only in the Elizabethan sense; the hero suffers no Aristotelian flaw, and the dramatist does not presume to criticize any of his callous slaughters as errors. The pride with which Tamburlaine identifies himself as "the scourge of God" is no hubris but a factual description of the English drama's first superman, larger than life in every sense. In comparison with Tamburlaine, the rest of the *dramatis personae* are two-dimensional, of interest merely as they enhance their conqueror's achievement in Part 1, and show in their deaths the waning of his power in Part 2.

In *Tamburlaine* the famous "mighty line" praised by Ben Jonson (in a poem prefixed to the First Folio of Shakespeare's works) is appropriate to the "aspiring mind" of its great hero. In Marlowe's next play, *The Jew of Malta*, rhetoric is inflated for comic purposes. In this story of a Jew's battle against Christians, neither of the opposing factions is worthy of respect; admiration is compelled only for the skill of unscrupulous dealings, and sentiment is dismissed by cruel laughter. The Jew's daughter is murdered by her father, but calls upon two friars to witness that she dies a Christian; any pathos arising from this situation is dispelled by the friar's response: "Ay, and a virgin too; that grieves me most." The audience's sympathy is with the Jew, Barabas – not because he is virtuous but because he makes no secret of his double-dealings, confiding in elaborate asides his schemes to outwit the no-less villainous, but hypocritical, Christians. Barabas of course overreaches himself and meets an appropriate end in the boiling cauldron that he had prepared for his chief enemy – but not until he has engineered the deaths of his daughter and her two suitors, an entire convent of nuns, the two friars, the army of Turkish soldiers, a prostitute, her pimp, and one of her clients (who happens to be Barabas's blackmailing slave). Like Tamburlaine, Barabas is larger than life; the rest of the characters, in this play too, are insignificant in comparison with the protagonist, and chiefly remarkable as objects or agents of his malevolence.

Marlowe probably wrote *The Massacre at Paris*, which survives only in a mangled, reported text, at much the same time as he wrote *The Jew of Malta*. Both have the same black comedy, in which murder is committed with a jest – and the laugh is the murderer's. *The*

Massacre at Paris is a political play, dealing with recent events in the struggle between Catholics and Protestants in France in the late 1580's. The central figure is the Duke of Guise, a professed villain like Barabas but more menacing than him because the crimes are not imagined but historical. In a reported text, which relies on the memory of actors, poetry suffers more damage than plot, but one can still detect in the Guise the note of true Marlovian aspiration:

> What glory is there in a common good,
> That hangs for every peasant to achieve?
> That like I best that flies beyond my reach.

In *The Jew of Malta* and *The Massacre at Paris* Marlowe makes great play with the popular concept of the machiavellian "politician" who parodied the Florentine statesman by putting self before state. In *Edward II* he treats Machiavelli's ideas more seriously, showing in the character of Young Mortimer a hot-headed patriot who, for the first half of the play, is genuinely distressed by the king's weakness and profligacy. But as the play progresses, covering twenty-three years of chronicled history, Mortimer loses principle as he gains power until, when Edward is imprisoned in the dungeon sewers of Kenilworth Castle and he himself is, as he believes, secure as Protector over the prince and lover of the queen, he manifests all the characteristics of the Italianate villain who so appealed to the Elizabethan imagination: "Fear'd am I more than lov'd; let me be fear'd,/And when I frown, make all the court look pale." Mortimer contrasts with Edward, passively homosexual and ambitious for nothing more than "some nook or corner" in which to "frolic with [his] dearest Gaveston."

Marlowe manipulates the sympathies of the audience, turning them away from Edward and his recklessness to support Mortimer and the barons in their care for the realm. But this care is not flawless: pride and ambition vitiate it from the start. Mortimer's regime is hateful, and the treatment meted out to Edward is brutal and obscene. There is no "mighty line" in this play, but the quick cut and thrust of conversations between conspirators and enemies. Isabella, Edward's queen, is allowed a languid romanticism as the despised wife, but when she comes under Mortimer's domination her speeches are at first hollow and hypocritical, and later subdued by fear. In some ways *Edward II* is Marlowe's best play: its structure is shapely, with Mortimer's fortunes rising as Edward's decline; its characterisation is diversified, and for the first time the protagonist has a worthy antagonist and a supporting cast who are characters and not merely names; its verse, though businesslike to the point of drabness, is nevertheless suited to the unheroic action. *Dr. Faustus*, the play that followed *Edward II* and which was Marlowe's last play (though some scholars think it was earlier), has none of these qualities. But while *Edward II* is a good play, *Dr Faustus* is a great one.

Two texts of *Dr Faustus* survive, but neither represents the play as Marlowe intended it. The earlier was published in 1604 and seems to be the work of actors who repeated their lines inaccurately, were sometimes vague about meaning, and often confused about which speech came next. The 1616 text is longer and more coherent, being based probably upon some theatrical document such as a prompt-book. But this too is unreliable. An "editor" has been at work, simplifying, censoring, and adding the extra material for which Henslowe, the actor-manager, paid Bird and Rowley four pounds in 1602. A twentieth-century text can only be eclectic in its attempts to approach the play that Marlowe wrote.

The plot of *Dr. Faustus* is simple: a brilliant scholar, frustrated by the limitations imposed on human learning, sells his soul to the devil for four and twenty years of knowledge, power, and voluptuousness. At the end of the play only one hour is left, after which "The devil will come, and Faustus must be damn'd." The play is remarkable for its first two and last acts. In the first, Faustus reviews the whole scope of learning available to Renaissance man in a speech where the names of Aristotle, Galen, and Justinian glitter for a while until they are extinguished by the logic which sees death as the inevitable climax of all human endeavour, and by the perverse will that presents necromancy as the only means of escaping human bondage. An interview with Mephostophilis, one of the "Unhappy spirits that fell with Lucifer," does nothing to shake Faustus's resolution even though the troubled spirit begs him to "leave these frivolous demands/Which strikes a terror to my fainting soul." The play disintegrates in the middle acts, where clownage distracts Faustus's mind from contemplation of his deed. The 1616 text's comic scenes are fully developed, but the rudiments are present in the 1604 text, forcing the conclusion that although Marlowe may not have written them himself, he nevertheless acquiesced to their presence in his play. Parts of 1616's Act V, however, are not to be found anywhere in 1604; among them is the interchange between Faustus and Mephostophilis where Faustus blames the devil for his damnation and Mephostophilis proudly claims responsibility. Eleven lines (V, ii, 80–91) are crucial to an interpretation of the play. If they are included as part of Marlowe's design, then Dr. Faustus is no more than a puppet, manipulated by external forces of good and evil, and in no way responsible for his fate; the play is in that case a Morality Play which lacks the traditional happy ending in which God's mercy prevails over His justice. But if the lines are discarded (as I think they should be), Faustus appears as an independent being who, of his own free will, although with imperfect knowledge, chooses damnation; and the play is a true tragedy.

Plague raged in London during the last year of Marlowe's life. The theatres were closed, to avoid the spread of infection; and there was consequently no demand for new plays. Like Shakespeare, Marlowe spent some of the time writing a long narrative poem. His subject, the love between Hero and Leander, is a tragic one, but the poem stops with the consummation of the love; it is not clear whether Marlowe intended to proceed to the catastrophe. The eight hundred lines that he wrote reveal a marvellously rich invention that combines tenderness with sardonic wit in a form that is, in the best sense, artificial. Describing his two protagonists, Marlowe counterpoises the elaborateness of Hero's garments with the sensuous simplicity of Leander's naked body. Of "Venus' nun" he tells us:

> Buskins of shells all silver'd used she
> And branch'd with blushing coral to the knee,
> Where sparrows perch'd, of hollow pearl and gold,
> Such as the world would wonder to behold.

Sight and sound predominate in the description of Hero, but Marlowe refers to touch and taste when he speaks of Leander:

> Even as delicious meat is to the taste,
> So was his neck in touching, and surpass'd
> The white of Pelops' shoulder. I could tell ye
> How smooth his breast was, and how white his belly.

The ease with which he moves through the polished couplets is assurance enough that Marlowe, when he died in the spring of 1593, had by no means exhausted his genius.

—Roma Gill

MARSTON, John. English. Born in Wardington, Oxfordshire, baptized 7 October 1576. Educated at Brasenose College, Oxford, 1592–94, B.A. 1594; Middle Temple, London, 1595–1606. Married Mary Wilkes c. 1605; one son. Wrote for Paul's boys company after 1599, and shareholder in the Queen's Revels company after 1604; imprisoned (for unknown reasons), 1608; ordained deacon, then priest, 1609, and ceased writing for the theatre after taking orders; Rector of Christchurch, Hampshire, 1616 until his resignation, 1631. *Died 25 June 1634.*

PUBLICATIONS

Collections

> *Works*, edited by A. H. Bullen.   3 vols., 1887.
> *Plays*, edited by H. H. Wood.   3 vols., 1934–39.
> *Poems*, edited by Arnold Davenport.   1961.

Verse

> *The Metamorphosis of Pygmalion's Image; and Certain Satires.*   1598; edited by
>   Elizabeth Story Donno, in *Elizabethan Minor Epics*, 1968.
> *The Scourge of Villainy: Three Books of Satires.*   1598; revised edition, 1599.

Plays

> *Antonio and Mellida*, part 1 (produced 1599).   1602; edited by G. K. Hunter, 1965.
> *Antonio's Revenge* (part 2 of *Antonio and Mellida*) (produced 1599).   1602; edited by
>   Reavley Gair, 1977.
> *Histriomastix; or, The Player Whipped*, from an anonymous play (produced
>   1599).   1610.
> *Jack Drum's Entertainment; or, The Comedy of Pasquill and Katherine* (produced
>   1600).   1601.
> *What You Will* (produced 1601?).   1607.
> *The Dutch Courtesan* (produced 1603–04?).   1605; edited by Peter Davison, 1968.
> *The Malcontent* (produced 1604).   1604; edited by Bernard Harris, 1967.
> *Parasitaster; or, The Fawn* (produced 1604–05?).   1606; edited by David A. Blostein,
>   1978.
> *Eastward Ho*, with Chapman and Jonson (produced 1605).   1605; edited by C. G.
>   Petter, 1973.
> *The Wonder of Women; or, The Tragedy of Sophonisba* (produced 1606).   1606.
> *The Argument of the Spectacle Presented to the Sacred Majesties of Great Britain and
>   Denmark as They Passed Through London* (produced 1606).   In *Poems*, edited by
>   Arnold Davenport, 1961.
> *The Honorable Lord and Lady of Huntingdon's Entertainment at Ashby* (produced
>   1607).   In *Works*, 1887; in *Poems*, 1961.
> *The Insatiate Countess*, completed by William Barksted (produced 1610?).   1613.
> *Works* (tragedies and comedies).   1633.

Bibliography: *Marston: A Concise Bibliography* by S. A. Tannenbaum, 1940; supplement in *Elizabethan Bibliographies Supplements 4* by C. A. Pennel and W. P. Williams, 1968.

Reading List: *Marston: Satirist* by A. Caputi, 1961; *The Satire of Marston* by M. S. Allen, 1965; *Jacobean City Comedy: A Study of Satiric Plays by Jonson, Marston, and Middleton* by B. Gibbons, 1968; *Marston of the Middle Temple: An Elizabethan Dramatist in His Social Setting* by P. J. Finkelpearl, 1969.

*   *   *

John Marston's crabbed and bitter satire quickly established his literary reputation. In the

"Parnassus Plays" of 1598–1601 at Cambridge University, Marston's satiric style was parodied in the Character of "W. Kinsayder": "What, Monsieur Kinsayder, lifting up your leg and pissing against the world? Put up, man, put up for shame. Methinks he is a ruffian in his style." His literary quarrels with Ben Jonson and Joseph Hall created a furor at the time; Drummond of Hawthornden notes that Jonson "had many quarrels with Marston, beat him and took his pistol from him, wrote his Poetaster on him." Jonson also attacked him in *Every Man Out of His Humour* and *Cynthia's Revels*, since Marston had "represented him on the stage." This so-called *Poetomachia* was not enduring, though, and the two eventually became friends.

Marston's tendency to stumble in and out of quarrels, jails and royal favour has marked him for centuries of literary criticism as a railing and often incoherently self-defeating malcontent. This is not entirely justified, however, as in all his works, from the most violent to the most flippant, there is an underlying moral concern. Many details of Marston's life are anomalous, but it is not altogether surprising that at the age of thirty-two he set aside his writing and, like his fellow satirists John Donne and Joseph Hall, took Holy Orders.

Marston's literary career begins with two collections of verse satires: the semi-erotic *Metamorphosis of Pygmalion's Image* and the snarling and snapping *Scourge of Villainy*, in which Marston ridicules the poses and pretenses of the young gallants of the Inns of Court and London. In both volumes, the satire shifts uneasily from a range of effete social pastimes to vulgar depravities; both were considered immoral, and burned in 1599. The harsh and contentious style of the verse satires is carried over to Marston's first play, *Histriomastix*, a pageant-like allegory performed at the Inns of Court, which deals with the function of law in a crumbling society. *Jack Drum's Entertainment* and *What You Will* reflect the lighter side of the verse satires, again attacking the foppish young gallants, though love themes and Shakespearean echoes complement the satire in these romantic comedies.

Antonio and Mellida and *Antonio's Revenge* introduce the dark qualities of Marston's satiric vision. In spite of its tentative comic reconciliation, the first play is largely influenced by evil and unjust characters, and the moral climate of the Venetian court is oppressive and sordid. The second play, however, lurches into perhaps the most violent and painful revenge tragedy in Elizabethan drama. As the protagonist degenerates both psychologically and morally, his "barbarism and blood lust" confirm the play's assertion that men are "vermin bred of putrifacted slime."

The Malcontent is generally considered Marston's greatest play. His tragi-comic satire of the court and of a morally degenerating world is successfully accomplished, while at the same time the play is well-structured and temperate in plot, character, and language. Through the character of Malevole, Marston probes the moral complexities of the human condition by dramatically juxtaposing neo-stoicism with worldly epicurianism. The play's Induction reveals that the King's Men stole it from the Children of Blackfriars in response to their theft of *The First Part of Jeronimo*. While *The Malcontent* was clearly influenced by Shakespeare's *Measure for Measure*, and particularly by *Hamlet*, it was also performed at the Globe, and the title role of Malevole was played by Shakespeare's Hamlet, Richard Burbage.

After *The Malcontent*, *The Dutch Courtesan* is perhaps Marston's next best work. It is a very entertaining comedy dealing again with complex moral values, in particular the relationship of love and lust, set against a colourful city background of prostitutes, rakes, and mountebanks. The satire in *Parasitaster; or, The Fawn* is to a large degree directed against James I and his Court: flattering and deluded courtiers, corrupting and corrupted governors. The Fawn's speeches expose the moral vacuum in this society, but the play ends on a reconciliatory note with a masque that acknowledges both the "Ship of Fools" and the "Parliament of Cupid." These two comedies are more epicurian than Marston's earlier works.

Marston's part in the collaborative *Eastward Ho!* with Ben Jonson and George Chapman is generally accepted as the entirety of the first act, as well as various parts throughout the play, though it is difficult to determine his specific authorship beyond this point. The play is a delightful parody of the "citizen comedy" tradition that was so popular on the London stage in the first decade of the seventeenth century. Several references to the Scots proved objectionable enough to James to result in the imprisonment of Chapman and Jonson, though Marston apparently escaped.

In his preface to *The Fawn*, Marston observes that comedies are "writ to be spoken, not read" because they consist solely in action. He wrote *The Wonder of Women; or, The Tragedy of Sophonisba*, however, as a tragedy that "shall boldly abide the most curious perusal." While sensation and spectacle abound, the highminded rhetoric in such an austere Roman tragedy demands our close reading, or "curious perusal." The play is often quite moving, and the moral dichotomy in this classical world is presented in great earnest, though there is little memorable action. Contrasted with the Stoic integrity of Sophonisba is the pathological lust of the heroine in Marston's unfinished play, *The Insatiate Countess*. Marston presumably left the various plots and characters in the play unresolved when he was sent to prison in 1608, though his hand is traceable in the 1613 edition completed by William Barksted.

Recent criticism has begun to acknowledge the considerable range and variety of Marston's dramatic works. His bold experimentation and unique characterization, particularly in the *Antonio* plays and *The Malcontent*, were completely new to Elizabethan audiences. Studies of the individual plays reveal a dramatic craftsmanship and originality that liberate him from his contemporary reputation as Kinsayder, "pissing against the world." There are many aspects of Marston's life and writings that deserve further critical analysis. His greater defects are very apparent, but T. S. Eliot's observation is still true: "for both scholars and critics he remains a territory of unexplored riches and risks."

—Raymond C. Shady

MARSTON, John Westland. English. Born in Boston, Lincolnshire, 30 January 1819. Married Eleanor Jane Potts in 1840 (died, 1870); two daughters and one son. Settled in London; articled to a solicitor, 1834–39, but gave up the law for literature; became a friend of Dickens and his circle; edited *The Psyche*, 1839; Editor, with John Saunders, *The National Magazine*, 1857–64; regular contributor of criticism to the *Athenaeum* from 1863. LL.D.: University of Glasgow, 1863. *Died 5 January 1890.*

PUBLICATIONS

Verse

    Poetry as an Universal Nature; The Poet: An Ode. 1838.
    Gerald: A Dramatic Poem, and Other Poems. 1842.
    The Death-Ride: A Tale of the Light Brigade. 1855.

Plays

    The Patrician's Daughter (produced 1842). 1841; revised version, 1842, 1843.
    Borough Politics (produced 1846). N.d.
    The Heart and the World (produced 1846). 1847.

Strathmore, from the novel *Old Mortality* by Scott (produced 1849).   1849.
Trevanion; or, The False Position, with W. B. Bernard (produced 1849).   1849.
Philip of France and Marie de Meranie (produced 1850).   1850.
Anne Blake (produced 1852).   1852.
A Life's Ransom (produced 1857).   1857.
A Hard Struggle (produced 1858).   N.d.
The Wife's Portrait: A Household Picture under Two Lights (produced 1862).   N.d.
Pure Gold (produced 1863).   N.d.
Donna Diana (produced 1864).
The Favourite of Fortune (produced 1866).   1866.
A Mere Child (produced 1866).
A Hero of Romance (produced 1868).
Life for Life (produced 1869).   1869.
Lamed for Life (produced 1871).
Broken Spells, with W. G. Wills (produced 1872).
Put to the Test (produced 1873).
Under Fire (produced 1885).   N.d.

Fiction

A Lady in Her Own Right.   1860.
The Family Credit and Other Tales.   1862.
The Wife's Portrait and Other Tales.   1870.

Other

Poetic Culture: An Appeal to Those Interested in Humany Destiny.   1839.
Dramatic and Poetical Works.   2 vols., 1876.
Our Recent Actors.   2 vols., 1888.

                              *   *   *

John Westland Marston was one of several young, would-be writers of the early Victorian period who found in P. J. Bailey's *Festus* a style, a subject, and an approach to poetry that could easily be imitated. Marston, indeed, was a friend of Bailey's. He was also a dabbler in mysticism, editor of a mystical magazine called *Psyche,* and the author of the dramatic poem *Gerald,* a work which brought him some fame, and more ridicule.

The subject of *Gerald,* in Marston's own words, is "the struggles and experiences of *Genius,*" and these are revealed, not through a conventional plot, but in "the illumination of *certain points* in Gerald's mental history – to show the *crises* of his developments, not their *progress.*" The debt to *Festus* is clear, both in subject and style. *Gerald* is a "Spasmodic" work. The eponymous hero is a great man, set apart from the rest of mankind: a poet, a seer, a life-giver:

> The truly great are fashioned so, and shed
> Their affluent beauty round – as planets shine,
> Birds sing, and rivers roll from laws within,
> From native influence, elemental life!
> Their origin, their motive – is above;
> And naught below compels them – or restrains.

Shelley is behind a good deal of this insistence on the poet's unopposable power and authority, but Marston, like his fellow Spasmodics, is hopelessly vague in all that he asserts on behalf of genius. Again and again in his work, whether it be *Gerald* or the smaller-scale poems, one comes across the grand gesture that refuses to define itself.

"Poetry/Lives but by truth. Truth is its heart. Bards write/The life of soul – the only life." Those lines from *Gerald* sum up as well as any Marston's claims for poetry and poets. R. H. Horne, a contemporary of Marston's, who was himself the author of the famous "farthing epic" *Orion*, put his finger on the essential weakness of Marston's position, when, in his *New Spirit of the Age*, he remarked that "Gerald leaves his home feeling a strong impulse to do *something* great in the world. Here at once we see the old sad error – a vague aspiration or ambition mistaken for an object or a power." Quite so. *Gerald* is more interesting as a symptom and indication of then fashionable ways of thinking about poetry and poets than for anything it achieves as a work of art in its own right. Yet as symptom I would say that it still has claims on our attention. This is not true of the rest of Marston's output. The two volumes of his collected poems show him to be a largely derivative poet, lacking in inventiveness, wit and grace.

—John Lucas

MARVELL, Andrew.   English.   Born at Winestead in Holderness, Yorkshire, 31 March 1621. Educated at Hull, Yorkshire Grammar School; Trinity College, Cambridge, 1633–41 (scholar, 1638), B.A. 1638. Evidently never married, though Mary Marvell claimed to be his widow. Travelled in Holland, France, Italy, and Spain, 1642–46; Tutor to Mary, daughter of Lord Fairfax, Lord-General of the Parliamentary Forces, 1650–52; resided at Eton College, as tutor to Cromwell's ward, William Dutton, 1653–57; Assistant to the poet John Milton, *q.v.*, then Latin Secretary for the Commonwealth, 1657–58 (intervened on Milton's behalf after the Restoration); Member of Parliament for Hull, 1659–78; Secretary to Lord Carlisle's embassy to Russia, Sweden, and Denmark, 1663–65. *Died 16 August 1678.*

PUBLICATIONS

Collections

> *Complete Works in Verse and Prose*, edited by Alexander B. Grosart.   4 vols., 1872–75.
> *Poems and Letters*, edited by H. M. Margoliouth.   2 vols., 1927; revised by Pierre Legouis and E. E. Duncan-Jones, 1971.
> *Complete Poems*, edited by Elizabeth Story Donno.   1972; as *Complete English Poems*, 1974.

Verse

> *The First Anniversary of the Government under His Highness the Lord Protector.*   1655.
> *The Character of Holland.*   1665.
> *Advice to a Painter.*   1679(?).
> *Miscellaneous Poems*, edited by Mary Marvell.   1681.

Other

> *The Rehearsal Transprosed.*   2 vols., 1672–73; edited by D. I. B. Smith, 1971.
> *Mr. Smirke; or, The Divine in Mode.*   1676.
> *An Account of the Growth of Popery.*   1677.
> *Remarks upon a Late Disingenuous Discourse by T.D.*   1678.
> *A Short Historical Essay.*   1680.

> Translator, *The History of the Twelve Caesars,* by Suetonius.   1672.

Bibliography: in *Poems and Letters,* 1971.

Reading List: *Marvell, Poète, Puritain, Patriote* by Pierre Legouis, 1928, revised and translated, as *Marvell, Poet, Puritan, Patriot,* 1965; *Marvell's Poems* by Dennis Davison, 1964; *The Art of Marvell's Poetry* by J. B. Leishman, 1966; *Marvell: Modern Judgements,* edited by M. Wilding, 1969; *"My Ecchoing Song": Marvell's Poetry of Criticism* by Rosalie Colie, 1970; *Marvell's Pastoral Art* by Donald M. Friedman, 1970; *Marvell's Allegorical Poetry* by Bruce King, 1977; *Marvell: His Life and Writings* by John Dixon Hunt, 1978; *Marvell: The Critical Heritage,* edited by Elizabeth Story Donno, 1978.

*   *   *

When Andrew Marvell died, none of his best poetry had been published; and the volume published posthumously in 1681 disappointed the admirers of his satires in prose and verse, since the contents had been written years before in a style that had come to seem old-fashioned. During the next century Marvell was chiefly famous as the friend of Milton, as the champion of toleration, and as the incorruptible member of parliament. Lamb admired his "witty delicacy" and Tennyson persuaded Palgrave to include some of the lyrics in the *Golden Treasury.* Although Marvell shared in the revival of the metaphysicals, Eliot blunted his praise by preferring the poetry of King. Now, perhaps, his reputation as a lyric poet is in danger of overshadowing his splendid prose satires, which Swift acknowledged as his model, and the verse satires, incomparably the best before Dryden's. Like Dryden he had a basic seriousness beneath the wit and banter. Everyone knows the couplet from the satire written during the first Dutch war: "Glad then, as miners that have found the ore,/They with mad labour fish'd the land to shore." Not so well-known are the lines describing Charles II in *Last Instructions to a Painter,* when he attempts to embrace a female apparition:

> But soon shrunk back, chill'd with her touch so cold,
> And th'airy Picture vanisht from his hold.
> In his deep thoughts the wonder did increase,
> And he divin'd 'twas England or the Peace.

The episode neatly combines an attack on Charles's sexual morals with criticism of his policies.

Nevertheless it is mainly on his non-satirical verse that Marvell's reputation now rests. He was not a prolific poet, but the 1681 volume is the most precious collection of lyrics between Milton's 1645 volume and the advent of the great Romantics.

Marvell began as a royalist, and his early work would not be out of place in anthologies of Cavalièr poets. He has many echoes of Lovelace, Cowley, Cleveland, and Waller – allusions which gave the thrill of recognition to his contemporaries.

The turning point in Marvell's career came with the execution of Charles I. In 1650, at the age of 29, he wrote the first of his undoubted masterpieces, the Horatian Ode in which, echoing Lucan, he compares Cromwell to Julius Caesar; and from the title we may suspect he was thinking of the way Horace was won over to support Augustus. It is characteristic of Marvell's disinterestedness that in a poem written in celebration of Cromwell the most famous lines are a tribute to Charles's deportment on the scaffold.

Soon afterwards Marvell became tutor to Mary Fairfax, the daughter of the Parliamentary General who had refused to take part in the trial of the King or to fight against the Scots. It was probably on the Fairfax estate in Yorkshire that most of Marvell's best poems were written – "The Garden," the four Mower poems, "The Nymph Complaining," and "Upon Appleton House." The last of these has been seriously undervalued by critics who have failed to appreciate the poet's strategy. It begins as a topographical poem, mingling description with incident, and full of witty absurdities, out-doing Cleveland. It moves from the house to the garden, from the garden to the meadows, and from the meadows to the solitude of the woods. As the poem progresses, Marvell purifies his style, becoming less extravagant in his conceits: he is leading his readers, one might say, from the world of Cleveland to the world of Lovelace, and then to the world of nature untamed by man, a nature right outside the boundaries of fashionable pastoral. Here he can describe birds and trees with loving accuracy, and almost identify with the natural world. The reader has been led by easy stages from the poetic world to which he was accustomed into Marvell's own. Those parts of the poem to which nearly all critics have taken exception are cunningly arranged stepping-stones from the world of fancy to the world of imagination. Marvell was the first real nature poet, and still one of the best.

The quintessence of his nature mysticism is to be found in "The Garden." It is a concentrated and complex poem, with different levels of experience juxtaposed. On one level it is about the sublimation of sex in the creation of art. On another level it is about the fortunate fall, with references to Eden and the fatal apple. But the central stanzas, absent from the Latin "Hortus" which Marvell wrote first, describe the transformation of sensual satisfaction into spiritual ecstasy:

> The Mind, that Ocean where each kind
> Does streight its own resemblance find;
> Yet it creates, transcending these,
> Far other Worlds, and other Seas;
> Annihilating all that's made
> To a green Thought in a green Shade.

In this poem Marvell celebrates solitude – Eden without Eve, "Two Paradises 'twere in one"; but in all the Nun Appleton poems he gives the impression that he knows perfectly well that the retreat from active life is only temporary, and (despite the praise of solitude) he wrote one of the best love poems in the language, "To His Coy Mistress."

Hundreds of poems have been written on this theme. What distinguishes Marvell's are the beautifully articulated argument, the delightful hyperboles of the opening paragraph, the thrilling change of tone when he describes the threat of Time and the "deserts of vast eternity," the continued use of wit when he is most serious – as in the lines "Then Worms shall try/That long preserv'd Virginity:/And your quaint Honour turn to dust" – the ability, which he shared with Shakespeare, to use desperately simple words – "The Grave's a fine and private place,/But none I think do there embrace" – and, above all, his being able to express with absolute precision an emotion he has experienced with singular clarity and intensity.

"The Nymph Complaining for the Death of her Fawn" – despite some weak couplets which remind us that Marvell never prepared his poems for publication – is a good example of his use of multiple levels of meaning. On one level it is a pastoral, based on the episode in the *Aeneid* where Silvia's fawn is killed by Ascanius (a source made obvious by the name of the Nymph's faithless lover, Sylvio). By the reference to "wanton Troopers" it is made to seem an incident of the English civil war. On another level the poem is concerned with a deserted maiden, and her reciprocated love for the fawn. On a third level, the death of an innocent victim, dying "as calmly as a saint," clearly has religious overtones.

The poem serves as a bridge between two other groups of poems, those concerned with young love, and those concerned with religion. In the former group may be mentioned the allusions to Mary Fairfax in the Nun Appleton poem, as when she is said to be sweeter than the flowers and, near the end, the dozen stanzas in which she is paid a whole series of extravagant compliments. Mary was then fourteen; "Young Love" is a charming tribute to a much younger child; and best of all in its unsentimental tenderness is "The Picture of little T.C. in a Prospect of Flowers." In all three Marvell writes of the future conquests of the girls and of their present innocence, and he avoids both the Lolita temptation and the anti-sexual feelings of Lewis Carroll. As with all Marvell's best poetry there is a splendid rightness of tone.

Marvell was described in 1656 as "a notable English Italo-Machiavellian." He was certainly not that, but his religious poems tell us little specific about his basic beliefs. "Bermudas" – one of the most beautiful – shows sympathy with the Puritan emigrants, but is unpuritanical in its celebration of an earthly paradise. "A Dialogue Between the Resolved Soul and Created Pleasure" (which reads like a libretto) is puritanical in spirit; but in the other "Dialogue Between the Soul and Body" Body is given the last word (Leishman thought some lines were missing). "On a Drop of Dew," ingeniously compared with the Soul, is only vaguely Christian. The most impressive of Marvell's religious poems, "The Coronet," has "an intricate and lovely form" which the poet calls his "curious frame." The theme is the difficulty of using his poetic talents, previously devoted to pastoral and erotic poetry, for devotional purposes. Marvell discovers that the Serpent has spoilt his garland of flowers "With wreaths of Fame and Interest." In other words, Marvell realised, however careless he was of fame, that his religious poetry had a mixture of motives, including aesthetic satisfaction.

Nothing has been said here about Marvell's early poems, although "Daphnis and Chloe," "Mourning," and "The Definition of Love" are masterly examples of his early manner. He has a wider range than readers of the half-dozen anthology pieces might suspect. He has been called an amateur, whose poems are nearly all flawed by careless workmanship. It is true that the parts are sometimes better than the whole; but, as we have seen, his longest poem, "Upon Appleton House," should not have its construction misunderstood by the selection of a few stanzas approved by the taste of the anthologist.

—Kenneth Muir

MASEFIELD, John (Edward).   English.   Born in Ledbury, Herefordshire, 1 June 1878. Educated at King's School, Warwick. Served in the Red Cross in France and Gallipoli during World War I. Married Constance de la Cherois-Crommelin in 1903 (died, 1960); one son and one daughter. Indentured on the merchant training ship *Conway*, 1891–93; apprenticed on a windjammer, 1894; Sixth Officer, White Star liner *Adriatic*; worked at various odd jobs in New York City, and Yonkers, New York, 1896–97; Literary Editor, *Speaker* magazine, after 1900; Feature Writer for the *Manchester Guardian*. President, Incorporated Society of Authors, Playwrights, and Composers, 1937–67; Member, Book and Periodicals Committee, British Council, London, and lectured for the British Council in various European countries. Recipient: Polignac Prize, 1912; Shakespeare Prize, University of Hamburg, 1938; Foyle Prize, 1962; National Book League Award, 1964. D.Litt.: Oxford University, 1922; LL.D.: University of Aberdeen, 1922. Poet Laureate, 1930 until his death. Order of Merit, 1935; Companion of Literature, Royal Society of Literature, 1961. *Died 12 May 1967.*

Collections

A Selection of Poems, edited by John Betjeman. 1978.

Verse

Salt-Water Ballads. 1902.
Ballads. 1903; revised edition, as *Ballads and Poems,* 1910.
The Everlasting Mercy. 1911.
The Story of a Round-House and Other Poems. 1912; revised edition, 1913.
The Widow in the Bye Street. 1912.
The Daffodil Fields. 1913.
Dauber. 1913.
Philip the King and Other Poems. 1914.
Good Friday and Other Poems. 1916.
Sonnets. 1916.
Poems. 1916; revised edition, 1923, 1929; as *Collected Poems,* 1935.
Sonnets and Poems. 1916.
Lollingdon Downs and Other Poems. 1917.
Cold Cotswolds. 1917.
Rosas. 1918.
Reynard the Fox; or, The Ghost Heath Run. 1919.
Animula. 1920.
Enslaved. 1920.
Enslaved and Other Poems. 1920.
Right Royal. 1920.
King Cole. 1921.
The Dream. 1922.
Selected Poems. 1922; revised edition, 1938.
King Cole and Other Poems. 1923.
The Dream and Other Poems. 1923.
The Collected Poems. 1923; revised edition, 1932, 1935, 1938, 2 vols., 1948.
Sonnets of Good Cheer to the Lena Ashwell Players. 1926.
Midsummer Night and Other Tales in Verse. 1928.
South and East. 1929.
The Wanderer of Liverpool (verse and prose). 1930.
Poems of the Wanderer: The Ending. 1930.
Minnie Maylow's Story and Other Tales and Scenes. 1931.
A Tale of Troy. 1932.
A Letter from Pontus and Other Verse. 1936.
The Country Scene in Poems and Pictures. 1937.
Tribute to Ballet in Poems and Pictures. 1938.
Some Verses to Some Germans. 1939.
Shopping in Oxford. 1941.
Gautama the Enlightened and Other Verse. 1941.
Natalie Maisie and Pavilastukay: Two Tales in Verse. 1942.
A Generation Risen. 1942.
Land Workers. 1942.
Wonderings: Between One and Six Years. 1943.
On the Hill. 1949.

In Praise of Nurses.   1950.
The Bluebells and Other Verse.   1961.
Old Raiger and Other Verse.   1964.
In Glad Thanksgiving.   1967.

Plays

The Campden Wonder (produced 1907).   In *The Tragedy of Nan and Other Plays,* 1909.
The Tragedy of Nan (produced 1908).   In *The Tragedy of Nan and Other Plays,* 1909.
The Tragedy of Nan and Other Plays (includes *The Campden Wonder* and *Mrs. Harrison*).   1909.
The Tragedy of Pompey the Great (produced 1910).   1910; revised version (produced 1914), 1914.
Anne Pedersdotter, from a play by Hans Wiers-Jenssen (as *The Witch,* produced 1910).   1917.
Philip the King (produced 1914).   In *Philip the King and Other Poems,* 1914.
The Faithful (produced 1915).   1915.
Good Friday: A Play in Verse (produced 1917).   1916.
The Sweeps of Ninety-Eight (produced 1916).   With *The Locked Chest,* 1916.
The Locked Chest (produced 1920).   With *The Sweeps of Ninety-Eight,* 1916.
Melloney Holtspur (produced 1923).   1922.
Esther and *Berenice,* from plays by Racine.   2 vols., 1922.
A King's Daughter: A Tragedy in Verse (produced 1923).   1923.
Tristan and Isolt: A Play in Verse (produced 1923).   1927.
The Trial of Jesus (produced 1926).   1925.
Verse and *Prose Plays.*   2 vols., 1925.
The Coming of Christ (produced 1928).   1928.
Easter: A Play for Singers.   1929.
End and Beginning.   1933.
A Play of Saint George.   1948.

Fiction

A Mainsail Haul (stories).   1905; revised edition, 1913.
A Tarpaulin Master (stories).   1907.
Captain Margaret: A Romance.   1908.
Multitude and Solitude.   1909.
The Street of To-Day.   1911.
Sard Harker.   1924.
Odtaa.   1926.
The Hawbucks.   1929.
The Bird of Dawning: or, The Fortune of the Sea.   1933.
The Taking of the Gry.   1934.
Victorious Troy; or, "The Hurrying Angel."   1935.
Eggs and Baker; or, The Days of Trial.   1936.
The Square Peg; or, The Gun Fella.   1937.
Dead Ned: The Autobiography of a Corpse.   1938.
Live and Kicking Ned: A Continuation of the Tale of Dead Ned.   1939.
Basilissa: A Tale of the Empress Theodora.   1940.
Conquer: A Tale of the Nika Rebellion in Byzantium.   1941.
Badon Parchments.   1947.

Other

Sea Life in Nelson's Time.   1905.
On the Spanish Main; or, Some English Forays on the Isthmus of Darien.   1906.
Chronicles of the Pilgrim Fathers.   1910.
A Book of Discoveries (juvenile).   1910.
Lost Endeavour (juvenile).   1910.
Martin Hyde, The Duke's Messenger (juvenile).   1910.
Jim Davis; or, The Captive of the Smugglers (juvenile).   1911.
William Shakespeare.   1911; revised edition, 1954.
John M. Synge: A Few Personal Recollections.   1915.
Gallipoli.   1916.
The Old Front Line; or, The Beginning of the Battle of the Somme.   1917.
The War and the Future.   1918; as *St. George and the Dragon*, 1919.
The Poems and Plays.   2 vols., 1918.
The Battle of the Somme.   1919.
John Ruskin.   1920.
The Taking of Helen.   1923.
The Taking of Helen and Other Prose Selections.   1924; as *Recent Prose*, 1924; revised edition, 1932.
The Midnight Folk (juvenile).   1927.
The Conway: From Her Foundation to the Present Day.   1933; revised edition, 1953.
The Box of Delights; or, When the Wolves Were Running (juvenile).   1935.
Collected Works.   10 vols., 1935–38.
Some Memories of W. B. Yeats.   1940.
In the Mill (autobiography).   1941.
The Nine Days' Wonder: The Operation Dynamo.   1941.
The Twenty Five Days.   1941.
I Want! I Want!   1944.
New Chum (autobiography).   1944.
A Macbeth Production.   1945.
Thanks Before Going.   1946; revised edition, 1947.
A Book of Both Sorts: Selections from the Verse and Prose.   1947.
A Book of Prose Selections.   1950.
St. Katherine of Ledbury and Other Ledbury Papers.   1951.
So Long to Learn: Chapters of an Autobiography.   1952.
An Elizabethan Theatre in London.   1954.
The Story of Ossian.   1959.
Grace Before Ploughing: Fragments of Autobiography.   1966.

Editor, with Constance Masefield, *Lyrists of the Restoration.*   1905.
Editor, *The Poems of Robert Herrick.*   1906.
Editor, *Dampier's Voyages.*   2 vols., 1906.
Editor, *A Sailor's Garland.*   1906.
Editor, *The Lyrics of Ben Jonson, Beaumont, and Fletcher.*   1906.
Editor, with Constance Masefield, *Essays, Moral and Polite, 1660–1714.*   1906.
Editor, *An English Prose Miscellany.*   1907.
Editor, *Defoe* (selections).   1909.
Editor, *The Loyal Subject,* in *The Works of Beaumont and Fletcher,* edited by A. H. Bullen.   1910.
Editor, *My Favourite English Poems.*   1950.

Translator, *Polyxena's Speech from the Hecuba of Euripides.*   1928.

Bibliography: *Bibliography of Masefield* by C. H. Simmons, 1930.

Reading List: *Masefield* by L. A. G. Strong, 1952; *Masefield* by Muriel Spark, 1953; *Masefield* by Margery Fisher, 1963; *Remembering Masefield* by Corliss Lamont, 1971; *Masefield* by Sanford Sternlicht, 1977.

*   *   *

At one time an author with a very large and devoted following, John Masefield lost much of his readership and his reputation declined during the last quarter century of his life. Some explanations may be adduced for this. In the first place, much of his writing is concerned with seafaring or with country life. But the seafaring he had himself experienced was in the age of sail, and other forms of transportation have rendered that era obsolete; the heroisms of the merchant seaman confronting wind and water, isolated from all contact with land, are no longer popular. As for the stories of country life, the rural west midlands of England he wrote about have decisively changed. If it is an exaggeration to say his England is scarcely rural any longer, yet technology, political evolution, and a social revolution have almost entirely subsumed a pattern of living which had prevailed for generations. The once familiar settings of his work are now remote. And if Masefield did not keep pace in his writings with the vast and rapid changes in transport, applied politics, and urbanization, still less did he heed the changes in poetic techniques that were expressive of those changes. He was, it might seem, a conservative in all ways. Nevertheless, Masefield had some exceptional powers, and it is not improbable that, when he is no longer regarded as "old fashioned," but as a poet of his own time, and eminently of the 1920's, he will be cherished as a poet for whom the term Georgian is quite inadequate to define his breadth, vigour, and abundance, or his innovatory tendencies, once startling, almost outrageous, though now softened and blurred through subsequent, and far more radical, tendencies.

He celebrated his favourite subjects of the sea and the countryside copiously, and in almost every form of verse and prose – lyric, dramatic, narrative, autobiographical. Yet though he achieved successes in every mode of writing, it is above all as a narrative writer that he should be valued. He is a superb straightforward story-teller. But, excellent as many of the prose stories are, it is as a story-teller in verse that he must be accounted a great master, one of the few great masters in that genre since Chaucer. The prose stories can be considered as sailors yarns: *Captain Margaret* and *The Bird of Dawning* are models of a good, clear, honest style. Of the sinuosities of a Conrad, or the psychological subtleties of a Kipling, Masefield is utterly innocent. Instead, there is a candid and unclouded focus on character and event, on people and things and deeds. Nouns or pronouns and verbs, the staple of any writing, are functional therefore to an abnormal degree in Masefield's prose stories. Sentiment, if not passion, is genuine and moving.

The objectivity and solidity of his prose, and its other virtues, are present in his narrative poems, but, under the exciting condensation of metre, rhyme, or stanza, they there attain a striking intensity – an intensity only rarely found in his chief exemplar, Chaucer. Three stories in verse, set in the countryside, are to be especially commended: *The Everlasting Mercy*, *The Widow in the Bye Street*, and *Reynard the Fox*. The first of these tells of a young reprobate, converted from drunken debauchery and crime, by a non-conforming preacher. The second, truly tragic, related in the rime-royal stanza of Chaucer's *Prioress's Tale*, follows the career of a poor widow's son to his death on the scaffold for committing a murder. The third tells of a fox hunt and imaginatively appreciates both the skill and enjoyment of the hunters, and the terror of their victim. In all three the pacing of the narrative, the economy in matching episode to space, the gradations towards climax are magnificently controlled.

Traditional as are Masefield's forms, he was pioneering in his diction. *The Everlasting Mercy* surprised readers with the rude oaths of the rough peasants. Max Beerbohm wrote "A simple swearword in a rustic slum,/A simple swearword is to some,/To Masefield something more." That "something more" was the poetic shock to be gained by admitting the

667

violent and brutal slang and monosyllabic oaths into a context illustrating divine mercy.

In all his story-poems cited, bold and accurate observation and suspense play their part in a series of situations leading to powerful climax. In most of them, Masefield's imaginative compassion shows him in advance of his time. There is no doubt that the execution of the young murderer in *The Widow in the Bye Street* rouses in the reader, because it did in Masefield, pity and terror.

Many of his shorter poems, as those in the collection *Salt-Water Ballads*, are likewise narrative in structure. His best known poem, "Cargoes," is a history of freight shipping in miniature, but its popularity should not be allowed to obscure the splendour of his longer works.

—Francis Berry

MASON, R(onald) A(lison) K(ells). New Zealander. Born in Auckland, 10 January 1905. Educated at Panmore School; Auckland Grammar School, 1917–22; Auckland University College, 1926–29, 1938–39, B.A. in classics 1939. Married Dorothea Mary Mould in 1964. Part-time tutor, University Coaching College, Auckland, 1923–29; company secretary, 1933–35; Editor, *Phoenix*, 1933; public works foreman, 1936–39; Editor, *In Print*, 1941–43; Assistant Secretary, Auckland General Labourers Union, and Editor, *Challenge*, 1943–54; landscape gardener from 1956, and part-time school teacher from 1965. Founder Member and Officer, People's Theatre and New Theatre Group, Auckland, 1940–43; first President, New Zealand-China Society. Recipient: New Zealand State Literary Fund award, 1961; Robert Burns Fellowship, University of Otago, 1962. *Died in 1971.*

PUBLICATIONS

Verse

    In the Manner of Men. 1923.
    The Beggar. 1924.
    Penny Broadsheet. 1925.
    No New Thing: Poems 1924–1929. 1934.
    End of Day. 1936.
    This Dark Will Lighten: Selected Poems 1923–1941. 1941.
    Recent Poems, with others. 1941.
    Collected Poems. 1962.

Plays

    To Save Democracy, in *Tomorrow,* 27 April 1938.
    Squire Speaks: A Radio Play. 1938.
    China (produced 1943). In *China Dances,* 1962.
    Refugee (produced 1945).
    Daddy, Paddy, and Marty, in *The People's Voice,* April 1950.
    Strait Is the Gate (produced 1964).

Other

Frontier Forsaken. 1947.
Rex Fairburn. 1962.
China Dances (miscellany). 1962.

Reading List: *Mason* by Charles Doyle, 1970.

*   *   *

If any New Zealand poet before James K. Baxter has a claim to continuing international recognition, R. A. K. Mason is the prime candidate. An independent New Zealand poetry begins in 1923 with the publication of Mason's *In the Manner of Men*.

A poet by nature rather than conscious intellectual development, Mason had done most of his best work by the time he was thirty. The poems in his first important small collection *The Beggar* were almost all written before he was eighteen. Although a handful of pieces were added to his last major collection, *This Dark Will Lighten*, the bulk of his slender collected poems were written by 1929 and published, after a series of printing delays, in *No New Thing*.

During the 1930's Mason became more consciously literary and this reduced the tension of his poems. He also turned towards Marxism and developed an interest in a kind of didactic drama. Possibly for these reasons, and because of the thinness of the cultural context in which he had to work, he wrote few poems in the latter half of his life, with the scathing "Sonnet to MacArthur's Eyes" (1950) a notable exception. From 1931 to 1956 he wrote chiefly leftist political journalism, first mainly for the *People's Voice* and then *Challenge*. One small book, *Frontier Forsaken*, deals with the disastrous effects of European colonisation on the Cook Islands. Still of some interest are several of Mason's plays, such as *Squire Speaks* and *China*, the latter a manifestation of his longtime interest in revolutionary China.

Strongly influenced by the Latin classics (especially Horace and Catullus), many of Mason's best poems are rooted also in the New Testament, particularly Christ's Passion. His central theme was grief at the body's death, an unappeasable hunger for personal immortality. From these concerns came his finest poems, such as "Footnote to John, II iv," "On the Swag," "Flow at Full Moon," "Judas Iscariot" (of which Dylan Thomas asked, "Didn't that poem shock people in New Zealand?"), and other compelling pieces, such as "After Death," "The Lesser Stars," and "The Spark's Farewell to its Clay."

Although a major figure in his own country, Mason has had no followers. In style and personality he is idiosyncratic, and the religious element is important to what is best in him; he is thus an odd poet to have sprung from a secular welfare-state society. The meeting-ground is a curious species of puritanism common to the poet and the national psyche.

—Charles Doyle

MASON, William. English. Born in Hull, Yorkshire, 12 February 1724. Educated at St. John's College, Cambridge, matriculated 1743, scholar 1744, B.A. 1745, M.A. 1749. Appointed Fellow of Pembroke Hall, Cambridge, through the influence of Thomas Gray, 1749–54 (maintained friendship with Gray and became his literary executor). Ordained: Vicar of Aston, Yorkshire, 1754–97; one of the king's chaplains, 1757–73; Canon Residentiary of York, 1762; Precentor and Prebendary of Driffield, Yorkshire, 1763–97. *Died 7 April 1797.*

Collections

Works.   4 vols., 1811.

Verse

Musaeus: A Monody to the Memory of Pope, in Imitation of Lycidas.   1747.
Isis: An Elegy.   1749.
Ode Performed in the Senate House at Cambridge.   1749.
Odes.   1756.
Elegies.   1763.
Poems.   1764; revised edition, 1764; 3 vols., 1796–97.
A Supplement to Watts' Psalms and Hymns.   1769.
The English Garden.   4 vols., 1772–81.
An Heroic Epistle to Sir William Chambers.   1773.
An Heroic Postscript to the Public.   1774.
Ode to Mr. Pinchbeck upon His Newly Invented Patent Candle-Snuffers.   1776.
An Epistle to Dr. Shebbeare, An ode to Sir Fletcher Norton in Imitation of Horace Ode VIII Book IV.   1777.
Ode to the Naval Officers of Great Britain.   1779.
An Archaeological Epistle to Jeremiah Milles.   1782.
The Dean and the 'Squire: A Political Eclogue.   1782.
King Stephen's Watch: A Tale Founded on Fact.   1782.
Ode to William Pitt.   1782.
Secular Ode in Commemoration of the Glorious Revolution.   1788.
Religio Clerici.   1810.
Satiric Poems Published Anonymously, edited by Paget Toynbee.   1926.

Plays

Elfrida.   1752.
Caractacus: A Dramatic Poem.   1759; revised version (produced 1764), 1777.
Sappho and *Argentile and Curran,* in *Poems.*   1796–97.

Other

A Copious Collection of Portions of the Psalms, A Critical and Historical Essay on Cathedral Music.   1782.
Animadversions on the Present Government of the York Lunatic Asylum.   1788.
An Occasional Discourse on the Slave Trade.   1788.
Essays on English Church Music.   1795.
Anecdotes of Reynolds.   1859.
The Correspondence of Richard Hurd and Mason, edited by E. H. Pearce and Leonard Whibley.   1932.
Gray's Correspondence with Mason, edited by Paget Toynbee and Leonard Whibley, in *Gray's Correspondence.*   3 vols., 1935.
Walpole's Correspondence with Mason, edited by W. S. Lewis and others, in *Walpole's Correspondence,* vols. 28–29.   1955.

Editor, *A Catalogue of the Antiquities, Houses, Parks, Plantations, Scenes, and Situations in England and Wales.*   1773.
Editor, *The Poems of Gray* (with a memoir).   1775.

Translator, *The Art of Painting of du Fresnoy.*   1783.

Bibliography: *First Editions of Mason* by P. Gaskell, 1951.

Reading List: *Mason: A Study in Eighteenth-Century Culture* by J. W. Draper, 1924; in *Portraits in Satire* by Kenneth Hopkins, 1958.

*   *   *

William Mason is probably best remembered for his *Memoir of Thomas Gray*, which Edmund Gosse magisterially dismissed as a "timid and imperfect work." Mason had been befriended by Gray, but he has found favour with few other writers. Thomas Seccombe, in his *The Age of Johnson*, describes Mason's tragedies as "negligible," and that is a kinder remark than most. And where commentators have not been abusive they have passed over poor Mason in stony silence. There is, indeed, a very real sense in which he can be regarded as the Enoch Soames of the eighteenth century.

How fair is this assessment? Unfairly fair, one has to admit. For it does seem unfair that someone who tried so hard to be a poet and man of letters should have had so little success. But so it is. Perhaps under the influence of Gray, Mason wrote a number of odes which at best are mediocre. George Colman published some parodies of them in his *Odes to Obscurity and Oblivion*, and yet in a sense Mason had already done the job for him. Certainly there is nothing as funny in Colman's volume as Mason's own "To a Water-Nymph" ("Thy wanton waters, volatile and free,/Shall wildly warble, as they please,/Their soft loquacious harmony").

Mason seems to have tried his hand at most kinds of poetry. Quite apart from the verse tragedies and odes, there are epistles, elegies, satires, and imitations, especially of Milton. For example, "Ill Bellicoso" is meant to be a comic, sprightly poem in the manner of early Milton (and in particular of "L'Allegro" and "Il Penseroso"). In fact, it achieves little more than a leaden buffoonery. As for the monody *Musaeus: To the Memory of Mr. Pope*, with which, according to Seccombe, Mason "began his pseudo-poetical career," the best that can be said for it is that at least Pope was out of harm's way by then. The poem is clearly indebted to Milton's great elegy "Lycidas," but unfortunately *Musaeus* is too bankrupt to be able to repay the smallest part of the debt. In fact, it has to be said that the poem is an anthology of every conceivable fault and absurdity, a lesson in how not to do it.

Yet the story is not entirely one of abject failure. For we have to accept that Mason's readiness to rush into poetic forms where better and wiser poets feared to tread helped give those forms a currency without which his great successors might have had to struggle harder than in fact was necessary to break out of what Blake called "the great cage" of the Augustan heroic couplet. Mason's attempts to write in the Spenserian stanza form are not successful. But those attempts made it that much more possible for Wordsworth and Keats to invade the form like monarchs. Mason deserves our thanks for that, if for no other reason.

—John Lucas

MASTERS, Edgar Lee. American. Born in Garnett, Kansas, 23 August 1868; brought up in Lewistown, Illinois. Educated at schools in Lewistown; Knox College, Galesburg, Illinois, 1889; studied law in his father's law office; admitted to the Illinois Bar, 1891. Married 1) Helen M. Jenkins in 1898 (divorced, 1925), three children; 2) Ellen Coyne in 1926. Practised law in Chicago, 1891–1921, when he retired and moved to New York, to devote himself to writing. Recipient: Twain Medal, 1927; Academy of American Poets Fellowship, 1946. *Died 5 March 1950.*

PUBLICATIONS

Collections

Selected Poems, edited by Denys Thompson. 1972.

Verse

A Book of Verses. 1898.
The Blood of the Prophets. 1905.
Songs and Sonnets. 2 vols., 1910–12.
Spoon River Anthology. 1915; revised edition, 1916.
The Great Valley. 1916.
Songs and Satires. 1916.
Toward the Gulf. 1918.
Starved Rock. 1919.
Domesday Book 1920.
The Open Sea. 1921.
The New Spoon River. 1924.
Selected Poems. 1925.
The Fate of the Jury: An Epilogue to Domesday Book. 1929.
Lichee Nuts. 1930.
The Serpent in the Wilderness. 1933.
Invisible Landscapes. 1935.
The Golden Fleece of California. 1936.
Poems of People. 1936.
The New World. 1937.
More People. 1939.
Illinois Poems. 1941.
Along the Illinois. 1942.
Harmony of Deeper Music: Posthumous Poems, edited by Frank K. Robinson. 1976.

Plays

Maximilian. 1902.
Althea. 1907.
The Trifler. 1908.
The Leaves of the Tree. 1909.
Eileen. 1910.
The Locket. 1910.
The Bread of Idleness. 1911.

Lee: A Dramatic Poem.   1926.
Jack Kelso: A Dramatic Poem.   1928.
Gettysburg, Manila, Acoma.   1930.
Godbey: A Dramatic Poem.   1931.
Dramatic Duologues (includes *Henry VIII and Ann Boleyn, Andrew Jackson and Peggy Eaton, Aaron Burr and Madam Jumel, Rabelais and the Queen of Whims*).   1934.
Richmond: A Dramatic Poem.   1934.

Fiction

Mitch Miller.   1920.
Children of the Market Place.   1922.
Skeeters Kirby.   1923.
The Nuptial Flight.   1923.
Mirage.   1924.
Kit O'Brien.   1927.
The Tide of Time.   1937.

Other

The New Star Chamber and Other Essays.   1904.
Levy Mayer and the New Industrial Era: A Biography.   1927.
Lincoln, The Man.   1931.
The Tale of Chicago.   1933.
Vachel Lindsay: A Poet in America.   1935.
Across Spoon River: An Autobiography.   1936.
Whitman.   1937.
Mark Twain: A Portrait.   1938.
The Sangamon (on the Sangamon River).   1942.

Editor, *The Living Thoughts of Emerson.*   1940.

Bibliography: *Masters: Catalogue and Checklist* by Frank K. Robinson, 1970.

Reading List: *The Chicago Renaissance in American Letters* by Bernard Duffey, 1954; *The Vermont Background of Masters* by Kimball Flaccus, 1955; in *America's Literary Revolt* by Michael Yatron, 1959; *Spoon River Revisited* by Lois Hartley, 1963; *Masters: The Spoon River Poet and His Critics* by John T. Flanagan, 1974.

*   *   *

One of the ancient Greek poets has written: "No man knows happiness; all men/Learn misery who live beneath the sun," thereby anticipating the spirit of Edgar Lee Masters's *Spoon River Anthology.* Though the book was brilliantly successful, the road to it was a long and arduous one. Seventeen years earlier Masters's first book of poems was an ignominious failure. The next few books were also unsuccessful. By this date the poet was a well-known lawyer, a robust man about town in Chicago who had made an unsuitable marriage but never allowed matrimony to interfere with his libertine instincts. The contrast between the poems, classic in form and hackneyed in thought, and their lusty author led one literary friend of Masters, the editor of *Reedy's Mirror*, to nudge him in the direction of a more original subject-matter. In any case, at the age of forty-five, Masters had failed at poetry, the one great passion of his life, and in his personal life. His one transcendent gift, fascination with human nature and insight into its workings, had found expression only in his legal career where he had espoused the cause of lower-class victims of capitalist greed.

This was the situation in May 1914, when the poet's mother arrived to visit him. According to Masters, this lady was witty, acutely observant, and "full of divinations" into the lives of the townspeople they had known in Petersburg and Lewistown, Illinois. Mother and son reviewed these lives, reviving emotions and interests that had long been dormant in the poet's mind. The result was the sudden eruption of his latent gifts as chronicler of a whole community of inter-related lives. Between May and December, though under heavy pressure from his legal duties, Masters composed the 214 epitaphs that were published that year in *Reedy's Mirror*. Other than the memory of his neighbors, the chief sources of inspiration were the polished epigrams of the *Greek Anthology* and the stimulus of the American free verse revolt that had just burst on a startled, genteel reading public. These three sources, along with the sobering reflections on human mortality induced by his mother's visit, produced "the most read and talked of volume of poetry that has ever been written in America."

Five years after the publication of *Spoon River*, Masters retired from the law and devoted himself to the writing of thirty or more books of poetry, novels, biographies, and Illinois history and geography. Though he showed a dogged determination to succeed, he never caught fire again. His first great achievement was his last and the remaining thirty-five years of his life were an embarrassing anticlimax as his first forty-five were a despairing preparation. Masters's own life, which he includes in his book under the name Webster Ford, was one of the most curious and ironical of the tales he tells there.

The anthology, as expanded and republished in 1916, contains a short prologue, "The Hill," and 243 individual epitaphs. The verses, of a marvelous concision and vitality, relate only the most essential features of the speakers' lives. Each soul, speaking for himself from the grave, bares his innermost nature and the secrets of his life, his own self-portrait being qualified by the words of those with whom his fate was interlocked, so that nineteen separate story lines are developed. Each epitaph has its own tone and style; each speaker treats the climactic experiences or insights of his life. Depending on the character of the speaker, the language varies from mystical utterance downwards to sonorous rhetoric and racy colloquialism. The criticism that the style is prosy and flat, made by Floyd Dell and others when the book first appeared, is traceable to the lack of conventional prettiness in meter and rhyme. Though rarely "pretty," many of the poems are written in a highly imaginative metaphoric style, all are freshly conceived on the basis of a unifying rhetorical design with ample use of every form of verbal patterning, many are haunting, and some contain images of real beauty.

Without the power of its language, *Spoon River* would never have aroused its readers as it did. But its essence is in its portraiture. As few other authors have done, and no other author, perhaps, in the compass of a single book, Masters produced a "summation" and "universal depiction of life." Every variety of human nature is represented: celebrants at life's feast and neurasthenics, rowdies and lovers, pious Christians and atheists, rapists and whores, society women and laundresses, scientists and factory hands, clairvoyants, preachers, and a stable boy who sees the face of God. One of the largest groups is the philosophers. Masters was a zealous scholar and had read widely in several languages. Along with the anti-Christian and libertarian elements in his make-up, there was also the social idealist, the cosmic optimist, and the mystic that he counted as his essential self. The epitaphs of the philosophers are usually limited to one strand of thought from which one may infer their life and character, and their reflections are framed in such a way that they are as dramatic as the life histories.

Two criticisms of Masters should be considered here. The first is that the poet is preoccupied with sex, and much of the anthology is sordid and obscene. This charge, originating with Amy Lowell and others, is curious because there are only a dozen poems that are chiefly concerned with sex, none of these is salacious, and they tend to show that the wages of sin are death. The basis of the complaint lies in the candor with which Masters treats sex wherever it appears in life. Readers had been conditioned to literature in which the subject-matter was not actual life but a given writer's conception of it so that much of the earth and roots had been removed – as well as the uppermost reaches of branches that were beyond the interests of a workaday world. One of the novelties of Masters's treatment was to eliminate authorial censorship and to allow his characters, based as they were on real-life persons, to speak honestly of their lives. Though this was not his intention, the result was the first exposé of village life, which set a new pattern for literature, while the poet's views are said to have influenced subsequent writing between the two world wars.

According to the second objection, the poet falsified the American mid-western town by presenting an overly sensationalistic and pessimistic account of its life. It is true that the incidence of crime and sudden death is greater than one would normally find, but Masters was not writing a sociological report. The epitaphs taken together form a highly patterned comical tragedy that represents life as it works on the human imagination. At some moment all of these disasters actually happen to someone, but the book, as Alice Henderson remarked, is also steeped in a "flaming idealism." There are many heroes and noble souls, and the final impression that it makes is of the dignity, stoic courage, and resilience of humanity in its hapless "fool's errand" to the grave. In writing these portraits, Masters creates the bond of understanding and sympathy with a many-faced humanity that motivated his own legal work for luckless victims of circumstances.

—Glenn Richard Ruihley

McAULEY, James (Phillip). Australian. Born in Lakemba, New South Wales, 12 October 1917. Educated at Fort Street High School, Sydney; University of Sydney, M.A., Dip. Ed. Married Norma Abernethy in 1942; four sons, one daughter. Lecturer in Government, Australian School of Pacific Administration, 1946–60; Professor of English, University of Tasmania, Hobart, 1961–76. Founding Editor, *Quadrant*, Sydney, 1956–76. Recipient: Carnegie grant, 1967. Fellow, Australian Academy of the Humanities. *Died 15 October 1976.*

PUBLICATIONS

Verse

The Darkening Ecliptic, with Harold Stewart.   1944; as *Poems,* 1961.
Under Aldebaran.   1946.
A Vision of Ceremony.   1956.
The Six Days of Creation.   1963.
(Poems).   1963.
Caption Quiros: A Poem.   1964.
Surprises of the Sun.   1969.
Collected Poems 1936–1970.   1971.

Other

> *Poetry and Australian Culture,* with *Felons and Folksongs* by Russell B. Ward.   1955.
> *The End of Modernity: Essays on Literature, Art, and Culture.*   1959.
> *C. J. Brennan.*   1963.
> *Edmund Spenser and George Eliot: A Critical Excursion.*   1963.
> *A Primer of English Versification.*   1966; as *Versification: A Short Introduction,* 1966.
> *The Personal Element in Australian Poetry.*   1970.
> *Christopher Brennan.*   1973.
> *The Grammar of the Real: Selected Prose 1959–1974.*   1976.
> *A Map of Australian Verse.*   1976.

> Editor, *Generations: Poetry from Chaucer to the Present Day.*   1969.

Reading List: *McAuley: Tradition in Australian Poetry* by Leonie Kramer, 1957; *McAuley* by Vivian Smith, 1965, revised edition, 1970.

*   *   *

James McAuley's work is zestful and, after his conversion to Roman Catholicism in 1952, certain. His was a full life and a firm faith.

Even before 1952, in his first collection *Under Aldebaran* there is much that speaks his dissatisfaction with a materialist society of narrow views and short perspectives. "The True Discovery of Australia," ironic and Gulliverian, has the local reference that the later "Letter to John Dryden" extends in scope. The alignment with Swift and Dryden reminds us not only of McAuley's classicism but also of his focus upon the European inheritance. His editing of *Quadrant* and his work for the Australian Association for Cultural Freedom should be seen as part of the same context as his regard for traditional values, which has received its most closely argued expression in his two prose works, *The End of Modernity* and *The Grammar of the Real.* His most ambitious poem, *Captain Quiros,* records its hero's voyage to establish New Jerusalem in the southern seas. The voyage can easily be applied to McAuley's own spiritual experience in a world from which he felt increasingly isolated but for which he never despaired.

As a poet he applied the strictest standards to sustain the pure dialect of the tribe, working persistently in traditional measures and wanting no other. As early as 1944 with Harold Stewart he perpetrated the Ern Malley hoax, by which several ridiculous pieces were taken seriously by the *avant-garde* as the work of a newly discovered poet. Like Spenser, McAuley "celebrates" secular and divine love, and his second collection was called *A Vision of Ceremony.* For him, in his own phrases, "Beauty is order" ("Envoi") and "Only the simplest forms can hold/A vast complexity" ("An Art of Poetry").

—Arthur Pollard

McKAY, Claude.   Jamaican.   Born Festus Claudius McKay in Sunny Ville, Clarendon Parish, Jamaica, 15 September 1889. Educated at grammar school in Jamaica; Tuskegee Institute, Alabama, 1912; Kansas State College, Manhattan, 1912–14. Married Eulalie Imelda Edwards in 1914 (separated, 1914), one daughter. Policeman in Jamaica; migrated to New

York City, did various jobs and opened a restaurant, 1914; Staff Member, *Workers' Dreadnought* communist newspaper, London, 1920; Staff Member, 1921–22, and Co-Editor, with Michael Gold, 1922, *The Liberator*, New York; visited Russia, 1922–23, and lived in Europe and Tangier, 1923–34, then returned to the United States: writer for the WPA (Works Progress Administration) in the late 1930's. Recipient: Harmon Prize, 1929. *Died 22 May 1948.*

PUBLICATIONS

Collections

    Selected Poems.   1953.
    The Passion of McKay: Selected Prose and Poetry 1912–1948, edited by Wayne
       Cooper.   1973.

Verse

    Constab Ballads.   1912.
    Songs from Jamaica.   1912; with *Constab Ballads,* as *The Dialect Poetry,* 1972.
    Songs of Jamaica.   1912.
    Spring in New Hampshire and Other Poems.   1920.
    Harlem Shadows.   1922.

Fiction

    Home to Harlem.   1928.
    Banjo: A Story Without a Plot.   1929.
    Gingertown (stories).   1932.
    Banana Bottom.   1933.

Other

    Negry v Amerike (Negroes in America).   1923.
    A Long Way from Home (autobiography).   1937.
    Harlem: Negro Metropolis.   1940.

Bibliography: "McKay" by Manuel D. Lopez, in *Bulletin of Bibliography,* October–December 1972.

Reading List: *Roots of Negro Racial Consciousness: Three Harlem Renaissance Authors* by Stephen H. Bronz, 1964; *The West Indian Novel and Its Background* by Kenneth Ramchand, 1970; *McKay: The Black Poet at War* by Addison Gayle, Jr., 1972.

*   *   *

Claude McKay attempted throughout his career to resolve the complexities surrounding the black man's paradoxical situation in the West. A widely travelled man, he lived for twelve years (1922–1934) in Great Britain, Russia, Germany, France, Spain and Morocco. It is during these years that a new wave of Afro-American writing, now widely known as the Harlem Renaissance, spread across the American continent. McKay is generally credited with having inspired the Renaissance with his militant poem "If We Must Die" (1919) when the nation was gripped with the Great Red Scare and racial riots in the Northern cities. Later, however, the self-exiled McKay developed an ambivalent relationship with the New Negroes of the 1920's; he did not share the "social uplift" philosophy of Alian Locke and W. E. B. DuBois although he had affinities as writer with Jean Toomer, Langston Hughes and Zora Neale Hurston. McKay is also considered a pioneer in the development of West Indian fiction, though he never returned to the land of his birth, Jamaica, having left it at age 23. Today, many regard his fiction as his most valuable contribution, but McKay also published four collections of poems, an autobiography, many essays, and a sociological study of Harlem.

It is as a poet that McKay first won attention in both the West Indies and the United States. In 1912, before he went to Kansas as an agriculture student (hoping to become the prophet of scientific farming on his return home!), he had published two volumes of dialect verse, *Songs of Jamaica* and *Constab Ballads*, and won himself a reputation as "the Jamaican Bobby Burns." Soon, he was drawn towards the intricacies of the American colour caste and he decided to cast his lot with working-class Afro-Americans. McKay was both stimulated and angered by the American environment – "Although she feeds me bread of bitterness/... I love this cultured hell that tests my youth!" ("America"). His background in the Jamaican society where the blacks formed a majority often gave him an edge as poet-observer over black American artists whose careers were sometimes wrecked by a debilitating bitterness. In his poems of personal love and racial protest, McKay gave strong expression to joy and anger, pride and stoicism. "If We Must Die," although not his best poem, won him great popularity because it powerfully evoked, in lines charged with emotion, the militant mood of Afro-American communities over the treatment meted out to black soldiers returning from World War I. The poem achieved a kind of universality in spite of its trite diction, as was well-demonstrated when Winston Churchill related it to the Allied cause by reading it to the House of Commons during World War II.

McKay's influence on later black poetry is measured better by the power of his sentiment than by any innovations in form, style or diction. McKay empathises with the sufferings of working-class blacks in the many poems of *Harlem Shadows*, but he succeeds best when he focusses on an individual's tragedy to protest against the forces of oppression. This is evident in poems such as "The Harlem Dancer," where a young female dancer is surrounded by a crowd of "wine-flushed, bold-eyed boys" which has no inkling of her soulful pride. In "Baptism," he expresses a Victorian stoicism that asserts the individual's victory through the harshest of tests. McKay often tried his hand at the sonnet form, using irregular rhyme and metre to achieve his own poetic ends. "One Year After," dealing with inter-racial love in a two-sonnet sequence, anticipates contemporary black attitudes in attributing the failure of a black-white relationship not to society's pressures but to the lover's black pride: "Not once in all our days of poignant love/Did I a single instant give to thee/My undivided being wholly free." McKay also wrote many poems about love and sex that had little to do with racial conflict and in some of these (e.g., "Flower of Love" and "A Red Flower") – as often in his fiction, especially in *Home to Harlem* – he creates erotic effects through suggestive portrayals of sexual pleasure. And yet, McKay's link to the more recent black literature is based primarily on his protest poems and his three novels.

McKay wrote both short stories and novels. *Gingertown*, his only collection of short stories, is important mainly as a source of clues and parallels to his development as novelist-thinker. The three novels – *Home to Harlem*, *Banjo*, and *Banana Bottom* – together form a thematic trilogy exploring the Western black man's special situation against the Manichean opposition between "instinct" and "intellect." *Home to Harlem* and *Banjo*, both essentially plotless novels, raise issues relating to the black's alleged primitivism, and its possible uses in an age when the fear of standardization was obsessive. The two protagonists – Jake and Banjo respectively – are rollicking roustabouts, taking life and women as they come. Their life of instinctive simplicity is, however, not without a Hemingway-like code. If they would not scab against a fellow worker, they would not be gullible enough to join a union either. As lovers, they do not permit themselves to become pimps or demean themselves to satisfy their women's masochistic desires. In the sexual metaphor that is McKay's lens in all the three novels, sexual deviations and perversions symbolize the pernicious influence of white values on black lives. In *Banana Bottom*, there is a tentative resolution of these conflicts in the character of Bita Plant who (like McKay himself) cannot allow self-hatred to reject native traditions completely even as she continues to find uses in her life for Western thought. Bita is, in some ways, a dramatization of the tangled thought on the significance of race and heritage in modern life that McKay had filtered through the character of Ray, who appears in both *Home to Harlem* and *Banjo*.

There is no hint in either his autobiography, *A Long Way from Home*, or his sociological study, *Harlem: Negro Metropolis*, of McKay's conversion in 1944 to Roman Catholicism, an astonishing turnabout by any standards. McKay's autobiography is unusual in not giving any details of his personal life, although useful as a mirror to his independence in the midst of stimulating encounters with issues, places, and people (including Frank Harris, H. G. Wells, Isadora Duncan, Sinclair Lewis). The section on his Russian visit is particularly valuable in determining a phase of his uneasy relationship with the leftist movement, from the days of his association with Max Eastman and *The Liberator* to the anti-Communist sentiments of his final years. *Harlem: Negro Metropolis* offers a scathing view of Harlem's community life and the obsessive fight of its leaders against segregation. The reviewers criticized the book justifiably for its frequent failures in objectivity. Although McKay never became an apologist for capitalist imperialism, he did try in his last years to vindicate his conversion to Catholicism in his essay "On Becoming a Roman Catholic" and in many letters to his life-long friend, Max Eastman. One cannot, however, help feeling that a tired McKay surrendered his difficult search for the positive meanings of black life by giving in to the traditional discipline of the Roman Church. As he himself put it in a letter (16 October 1944) to Eastman: "It seems to me that to have a religion is very much like falling in love with a woman. You love her for her ... Beauty, which cannot be defined."

—Amritjit Singh

MEREDITH, George. English. Born in Portsmouth, Hampshire, 12 February 1828. Educated at Paul's Church School, Southsea, Hampshire; Moravian School, Neuwied sur Rhine, Germany, 1843–44; articled to a solicitor in London, 1845. Married 1) Mary Ellen Nicholls, daughter of the novelist Thomas Love Peacock, in 1849 (died, 1861), one son; 2) Marie Vulliamy in 1864 (died, 1885), one son and one daughter. Abandoned the law for journalism; settled in London, then in Surrey; Co-Editor, *The Monthly Observer*, London, 1848–49; contributed to *Chambers Journal*, London, 1849, and to *Fraser's Magazine*, London, 1851–52; leader writer for the *Ipswich Journal* from 1860; literary adviser to Chapman and Hall, publishers, London, 1862–94; Special Foreign Correspondent for the London *Morning Post* during the Austro-Italian War, 1866; Editor, 1867–68, and Contributor, 1867–1909, *Fortnightly Review*, London; lectured on comedy at the London Institution, 1877. Recipient: Royal Society of Literature gold medal, 1905. President, Society of Authors, 1892; Vice-President, London Library, 1902. Order of Merit, 1905. *Died 18 May 1909.*

Collections

> *Works.*   27 vols., 1909–11.
> *Letters,* edited by C. L. Cline.   3 vols., 1968.
> *Poems,* edited by Phyllis B. Bartlett.   2 vols., 1977.

Verse

> *Poems.*   1851.
> *Modern Love, and Poems of the English Roadside, with Poems and Ballads.*   1862;
>   revised edition, 1892.
> *Poems and Lyrics of the Joy of Earth.*   1883.
> *Ballads and Poems of Tragic Life.*   1887.
> *A Reading of Earth.*   1888.
> *Jump-to-Glory Jane: A Poem.*   1889.
> *Poems: The Empty Purse, with Odes to the Comic Spirit, to Youth in Memory, and
>   Verses.*   1892.
> *Selected Poems.*   1897.
> *Odes in Contribution to the Song of French History.*   1898.
> *A Reading Life.*   1901.
> *Last Poems.*   1909.
> *Poems Written in Early Youth, Poems from Modern Love, and Scattered Poems.*   1909.

Play

> *The Sentimentalists* (produced 1910).

Fiction

> *The Shaving of Shagpat: An Arabian Entertainment.*   1855; edited by F. M. Meynell,
>   1955.
> *Farina: A Legend of Cologne.*   1857.
> *The Ordeal of Richard Feverel: A History of Father and Son.*   1859; revised edition,
>   1878; edited by Norman Kelvin, 1961.
> *Evan Harrington; or, He Would Be a Gentleman.*   1861; edited by G. F. Reynolds,
>   1922.
> *Emilia in England.*   1864; as *Sandra Belloni,* 1886.
> *Rhoda Fleming.*   1865.
> *Vittoria.*   1867.
> *The Adventures of Harry Richmond.*   1871.
> *Beauchamp's Career.*   1875; edited by G. M. Young, 1950.
> *The House on the Beach.*   1877.
> *The Egoist: A Comedy in Narrative.*   1879; edited by Robert M. Adams, 1977.
> *The Tragic Comedians.*   1880; revised edition, edited by C. K. Shorter, 1891.
> *Diana of the Crossways.*   1885.
> *The Case of General Ople and Lady Camper.*   1890.
> *The Tale of Chloe.*   1890.
> *One of Our Conquerors.*   1891.

Lord Ormont and His Aminta.   1894.
The Tale of Chloe and Other Stories.   1894.
The Amazing Marriage.   1895.
(*Novels*).   39 vols., 1896–1912 (includes miscellaneous prose and bibliography).
Short Stories.   1898.
Celt and Saxon.   1910.

Other

Works.   34 vols., 1896.
An Essay on Comedy and the Uses of the Comic Spirit.   1897; edited by L. Cooper,
1956.
Up to the Midnight: A Series of Dialogues Contributed to the Graphic.   1913.
The Contributions to the Monthly Observer, edited by H. Buxton Forman.   1928.

Bibliography: *A Bibliography of the Writings in Prose and Verse by Meredith,* 1922, and
Meredithiana, 1924, both by H. Buxton Forman; supplement by H. Lewis Sawin, in *Bulletin
of Bibliography,* 1955.

Reading List: *Meredith: Les Cinquante Premières Années* by René Galland, 1923; *The Ordeal
of Meredith* by Lionel Stevenson, 1954; *Meredith: His Life and Work* by Jack Lindsay, 1956;
A Troubled Eden: Nature and Society in the Works of Meredith by Norman Kelvin, 1961;
Meredith and English Comedy by V. S. Pritchett, 1970; *Meredith: The Critical Heritage* edited
by Ioan Williams, 1971; *Meredith Now* edited by Ian Fletcher, 1971; *The Readable People of
Meredith* by Judith Wilt, 1975; *Meredith: His Life and Lost Love* by David Williams, 1977.

*   *   *

In the year before his death, George Meredith, in an interview with Constantin Photiadès,
remarked, "my name is celebrated, but no one reads my books." Never greatly popular in his
own day, Meredith's work was nonetheless singular.

His first notable achievement was *The Ordeal of Richard Feverel.* Sir Austen Feverel,
bruised by his wife's infidelity and desertion, applies the Great Shaddock Dogma, a woman-
hating doctrine, to the scientific education of his son, Richard. Designed to bring him through
the puppy-love stage, the Blossoming Season, and the Magnetic Age free from the
temptations of Eve, or "the Apple Disease," it has disastrous consequences. Richard marries
Lucy Desborough without permission, leaves her temporarily to gain his father's
approbation, engages meanwhile in rescuing fallen women – and falls himself. A tragic
dénouement points up the insufferability of imposing a rigid code or of systematizing human
beings. Yet, at the end, incorrigible Sir Austen is plotting a program for his grandson. *The
Ordeal* is stylistically unique, an amalgam of high and low comedy, of romance, and of tragi-
comedy. In addition to the interesting narrative structure, the epigrammatic and aphoristic
wit, and the comic dialogue, there are numerous memorable characters, fewer
autobiographical and more purely literary creations than in his later works. The unbalanced
ones are Sir Austen's parasites – Adrian Harley, a seedy intellectual; the purely physical
Algernon; and Uncle Hippias, a hypochondriacal dipsomaniac. Those who read earth right
are Mrs. Berry, Lucy's counsellor ("Kissing don't last. Cookery do"); the independent,
determined, and intuitive Lucy; and Austin Wentworth, Richard's spiritual guide. Finally,
the cryptic and fluid symbolism of the "ordeal," broadening as the novel progresses, lends the
masterful touch.

In the comic romance *Evan Harrington,* Meredith adopted a form – the *Bildungsroman* –
and a subject – the illusions of class distinction – which he followed to an extent in *Emilia in*

England, *The Adventures of Harry Richmond*, and *Beauchamp's Career*. Ashamed of his birth and aspiring to social status, Evan, brought ultimately to realize the distinction between a true gentleman and a sham, is able to acknowledge his lowly origins as son of a tailor. Meredith, drawing many of the characters from his family and acquaintances, suggests not merely class snobbery, but the broader scope of Carlyle's *Sartor Resartus*, as he had done in the earlier allegorical work *The Shaving of Shagpat*.

Modern Love (1862), a sequence of near-sonnets, is a psychological analysis of incompatibility in marriage. The wife has taken a lover; the husband, whose ego is battered, takes a mistress in retaliation. The study centers on the anguish and hypocrisy of physical closeness without mental communion:

> Like sculptured effigies they might be seen
> Upon their marriage-tomb, the sword between;
> Each wishing for the sword that severs all.

Love, "the crowning sun," had initially brought a oneness to intelligence and instinct; but they look backward instead of forward and love became physical: "We are betrayed by what is false within." They at last hold "honest speech," but the wife, unable to act rationally, commits suicide to free her husband for the other woman. The omniscient narrator summarizes with a probable cause of the personal tragedy:

> Then each applied to each the fatal knife,
> Deep questioning, which probes to endless dole.
> Ah, what a dusty answer gets the soul
> When hot for certainties in this our life!

Modern Love is Meredith's most perceptive psychological study, written in his most penetrating language.

Emilia in England still displays some freshness, but the thematic thrust against sentimentalism and social climbing is a common one, and, increasingly thereafter, Meredith's work is, with a few exceptions, tired writing. *Vittoria*, the sequel to *Emilia*, deals with the Italian struggle for independence, and places the central character, now an opera diva, at the mercy of revolutionary events. *Harry Richmond* casts some oblique cross-cultural light on England through Harry's love for a German princess, Ottilia. *Beauchamp's Career* is a philosophic-political novel, with Carlyle's *Heroes and Hero Worship* in mind. Young Nevil enters politics as a Liberal, paralleling Meredith's own sympathies. This work, like many others, is flawed by a contemptuous, suspense-destroying, retrogressive narrative technique.

An Essay on Comedy gives Meredith's conception of comedy as a corrective device for pointing out right action based on reason rather than on sentimentality. Unlike satire or ridicule, it is detached and Olympian, so that it calls forth no resentment, only "volleys of silvery laughter."

The Egoist is a sustained high comedy of manners, with a style as fitted to the vain and shallow egoist, Sir Willoughby Patterne, as his trousers: "*You see he has a leg.*" While seeking a worthy match, he exercises *le droit de seigneur* by trifling with Laetitia Dale. Clara Middleton, his bride elect, gradually detects his artificial sentiment, and breaks off with him. To save face, he proposes to Laetitia, who, with delightful irony, forces him to accept her on her own terms as a disillusioned critic of his faults. There is no narrative-impeding straining for the witty phrase and comic situation of his lesser works in this novel, usually considered his masterpiece.

"The Woods of Westermain," a poem of 1883, comes closest to consolidating Meredith's optimistic evolutionary theory emerging from his total canon. "Blood and brain and spirit, three .../Join for true felicity." Instincts, intellect, and spirit are interdependent and derive nourishment and grow like the roots, limbs, and leaves on a tree. Any failure to read earth right results in imbalance of character, the anti-social disease of egoism. Such a theory perhaps explains the limitations of Meredith's work: the stereotyping of characters in terms of defects and the restriction to personal limitations within the social veneer. As an explanation of evil, it lacks cosmic import and complexity.

Nevertheless, as an unconventional, anti-Victorian experimentalist, as a humanistic free thinker, as a liberal reformer who championed equality for women, democratic political institutions, and freedom for oppressed nations – despite the fact that many of his other causes are now outdated – Meredith left to the reader of today three works of great distinction – *The Ordeal of Richard Feverel, Modern Love*, and *The Egoist*.

—Wesley D. Sweetser

—————————

MERRILL, James (Ingram). American. Born in New York City, 3 March 1926. Educated at Lawrenceville School; Amherst College, Massachusetts, B.A. 1947. Served in the United States Army, 1944–45. Recipient: National Book Award, 1967; Bollingen Prize, 1973. Member, National Institute of Arts and Letters, 1971. Lives in Connecticut.

PUBLICATIONS

Verse

> *Jim's Book: A Collection of Poems and Short Stories.*   1942.
> *The Black Swan.*   1946.
> *First Poems.*   1951.
> *Short Stories.*   1954.
> *The Country of a Thousand Years of Peace and Other Poems.*   1959; revised edition, 1970.
> *Selected Poems.*   1961.
> *Water Street.*   1962.
> *The Thousand and Second Night.*   1963.
> *Violent Pastoral.*   1965.
> *Nights and Days.*   1966.
> *The Fire Screen.*   1969.
> *Two Poems.*   1972.
> *Braving the Elements.*   1972.
> *The Yellow Pages: 59 Poems.*   1974.
> *Yannina.*   1973.
> *Divine Comedies.*   1976.

Plays

> *The Bait* (produced 1953). In *Artists' Theatre: Four Plays,* edited by Herbert Machiz,   1960.
> *The Immortal Husband* (produced 1955). In *Playbook: Plays for a New Theatre,*   1956.

Fiction

The Seraglio. 1957.
The (Diblos) Notebook. 1965.

Reading List: *Alone with America* by Richard Howard, 1969; "Feux d'Artifice" by Stephen Yenser, in *Poetry*, June 1973.

*   *   *

James Merrill's books of poems are like the rings of a tree: each extends beyond the content, expression, outlook, and craft of the previous work. Merrill has patiently, even doggedly, pursued his craft, giving each poem, however short or terse or ephemeral, a certain lapidary sheen and hardness. Merrill's complete output of verse, fiction, and plays is characterized by an absorption with technique and difficulty.

But his earliest poems are overworked with rhyme scheme, metric pattern, enamelled diction. Merrill came onto the literary scene during the vogue of revived metaphysical poetry, verse wrought in a traditional manner with high polish and much verbal flourishing under formal restraint. Such is the poetry of his first major book, *The Country of a Thousand Years of Peace*, with its elegant experiences, its widely cultivated tastes, its voice of leisured travel and gracious living – the poetry, in other words, of an American aristocrat. *Water Street* continues this elegant discourse on the vicissitudes of life, love, travel, the perennially chilly rooms and beds of his daily life.

But with *The Fire Screen* a new dimension to the persona comes into view: his life in Greece, where the warm sun, the old culture, the intimacy of life release a deeper self-awareness into his poems. Instead of the isolated, inward existence of New England, here the speaker is thrust into a more primal and assertive culture where his passions and convictions are awakened. There are also poems of return to the northeastern United States, lyrics of resignation and quiet regrets. In the American edition is the too-long verse narrative "The Summer People," with its heavy-handed irony; Robert Lowell said more about the vacation culture in his one page poem "Skunk Hour." *Braving the Elements* is both freer in its verse forms and more open and intimate in its content. Instead of the choppy quality of his earlier, too tightly wrought lines, there is now a smooth, conversational rhythm in his three or four line stanza structures. "Days of 1935," "18 West 11th Street" (which laments the death of young anti-war radicals), and "Days of 1971" are open, intimate revelations of the poet's mind.

Merrill's progress is toward a compromise between rigid formalism and the open poem, where craft would continue to discipline the choice and assembly of language but where the content would be free to take its own course. That balance is reached in the long sequence "The Book of Ephraim" in *Divine Comedies*. The twenty-six alphabetically ordered parts are interwoven through a leisurely plot where the poet and his lover communicate with the spirit of Ephraim through the Ouija board, whose insight and wit make life seem a mere changing room in a vast spiritual universe. In discovering this broader realm, Merrill is dazzling as a conversational poet. Ephraim's reckless honesty about the other side enables the speaker to unravel a complex plot of lives and after-lives, including his own father's, in a humorous, novel-like progression of poems. The verse never impedes the narrative; it enhances it with its exuberance of puns, amazing condensations of ideas and observations, feats of beautiful lyric sound.

The success of this sequence makes clear Merrill's earlier difficulties with orthodox convention: his verve and spontaneity of imagination, his life as a contemporary, were too straitened by the demands of closed forms of verse. Merrill has seized upon the cut-and-paste, leaping perceptual technique of today's poets without relinquishing his skill to craft the diction of his now fluid poems.

—Paul Christensen

MERWIN, W(illiam) S(tanley).   American.   Born in New York City, 30 September 1927. Educated at Princeton University, New Jersey, A.B. in English 1947. Married Diana Whalley in 1954. Tutor to Robert Graves's son, Majorca, 1950; Playwright-in-Residence, Poet's Theatre, Cambridge, Massachusetts, 1956–57; Poetry Editor, *The Nation*, New York, 1962; Associate, Theatre de la Cité, Lyons, France, 1964–65. Recipient: National Institute of Arts and Letters grant, 1957; Arts Council of Great Britain bursary, 1957; Rabinowitz Research Fellowship, 1961; Ford Foundation grant, 1964; Chapelbrook Award, 1966; National Endowment for the Arts grant, 1968; P.E.N. Translation Prize, 1969; Rockefeller Foundation grant, 1969; Pulitzer Prize, 1971; Academy of American Poets Fellowship, 1973; Shelley Memorial Award, 1974.

PUBLICATIONS

Verse

A Mask for Janus.   1952.
The Dancing Bears.   1954.
Green with Beasts.   1956.
The Drunk in the Furnace.   1960.
The Moving Target.   1963.
The Lice.   1967.
Three Poems.   1968.
Animae.   1969.
The Carrier of Ladders.   1970.
Signs, with A. D. Moore.   1971.
Chinese Figures: Second Series.   1971.
Japanese Figures.   1971.
Asian Figures.   1972.
Writings to an Unfinished Accompaniment.   1973.
The Compass Flower.   1977.

Plays

Darkling Child, with Dido Milroy (produced 1956).
Favor Island (produced 1957).
Eufemia, from the play by Lope de Rueda, in Tulane Drama Review, December 1958.
The Cid, from a play by Corneille (produced 1960).   In The Classic Theatre, edited by
    Eric Bentley, 1961.

The Gilded West (produced 1961).

Turcaret, from the play by Alain Lesage, in *The Classic Theatre*, edited by Eric Bentley, 1961.

The False Confession, from a play by Marivaux (produced, 1963). In *The Classic Theatre*, edited by Eric Bentley, 1961.

Yerma, from the play by Garcia Lorca (produced 1966).

Iphigenia at Aulis, with George E. Dimock, Jr., from a play by Euripides. 1978.

Other

A New Right Arm (essay). N.d.
Selected Translations, 1948–1968. 1968.
The Miner's Pale Children. 1970.
Houses and Travellers: A Book of Prose. 1977.

Editor, *West Wind: Supplement of American Poetry.* 1961.
Editor, with J. Moussaieff Masson, *Classical Sanskrit Love Poetry.* 1977

Translator, *The Poem of the Cid.* 1959.
Translator, *The Satires of Perseus.* 1961.
Translator, *Some Spanish Ballads.* 1961; as *Spanish Ballads*, 1961.
Translator, *The Life of Lazarillo de Tormes: His Fortunes and Adversities.* 1962.
Translator, *The Song of Roland*, in *Medieval Epics.* 1963.
Translator, *Transparence of the World: Poems of Jean Follain.* 1969.
Translator, *Products of the Perfected Civilization: Selected Writings*, by Sebastian Chamfort. 1969.
Translator, *Voices: Selected Writings of Antonio Porchia.* 1969.
Translator, *Twenty Love Poems and a Song of Despair*, by Pablo Neruda. 1969.
Translator, with others, *Selected Poems: A Bilingual Edition*, by Pablo Neruda, edited by Nathaniel Tarn. 1969.
Translator, with Clarence Brown, *Selected Poems of Osip Mandelstam.* 1973.
Translator, *Vertical Poetry*, by Robert Juarrox. 1977.

Bibliography: in "Seven Princeton Poets," in *Princeton Library Chronicle*, Autumn 1963.

Reading List: "Merwin Issue" of *Hollins Critic*, June 1968.

*   *   *

W. S. Merwin's writing career erupted suddenly in 1952 with the publication of *A Mask for Janus*. Both it and *The Dancing Bears* are books of traditional poetry, stressing short, consciously crafted lines that move with densely worded statement. *Dancing Bears*, slightly freer in form and showing more confidence in composition, is dry and bookish, but Merwin has exercised his skill in these earliest volumes, and his intelligence and promise are evident throughout.

In *Green with Beasts* and *The Drunk in the Furnace* Merwin is in greater control of his imagination, and the experience in his lyrics is suddenly intense and compelling. The mythic content of *Green with Beasts* anticipates the bold explorations of subjectivity of later volumes. But sheer variety of tone and diction, clarity of image, leaps of thought and perception give *Green with Beasts* surges of power. *The Drunk in the Furnace* retreats slightly from the daring pursuit of the earlier volume, but the ordinary world is rediscovered here, especially in the title poem, in which the poet discovers a man living contentedly in an abandoned furnace. The landscape of these mature works is charged with magic and the fabulous, and the drunk rattling his bottle of liquor against the iron walls of his home is typical of the uncanny world in which Merwin has rooted his lyric.

By 1960, Merwin appears to have exhausted his interest in traditional English poetry, for in translating certain Spanish poets he discovered surrealist techniques that continue to affect his unique, wistfully lyrical style. The problem with *The Moving Target*, however, is the emphasis given to a disembodied voice whose lyric statements arise from unstated situations and have little or no core of argument. There is a sameness to this poetry as each poem passes into the other with its silky array of words touching briefly on the particulars of life.

In his most recent volumes, Merwin has written what appears to be the stages of a spiritual progress. Each volume is intent to mine a deeper layer of the subjective mind, to test the limits of perception where it borders on fantasy and archetypal thought, to let merge the states of dream and waking. *The Lice* is composed in the soft, remote language of surrealist lyrics and offers a distant reflection of the turbulence of the 1960's, without indictment or direct reference to actual events. A sense of political terror and unrest pervades these sombre poems. *The Carrier of Ladders* broods on absence of meaning, on death, on spiritual transcendence of the objective and alien landscape. In *Writings to an Unfinished Accompaniment*. Merwin comes to an end of the disjunctive, loosely imagistic poem. A noticeable change of attention takes over in *The Compass Flower* where the quotidian is suddenly fresh and vital, and his poems come to crisp focus on objects of immediate experience.

—Paul Christensen

MEW, Charlotte (Mary). English. Born in London, 15 November 1869. Educated privately. Death of her father, 1897, left family in greatly reduced circumstances; brother and sister confined to mental institutions; following death of remaining sister, became mentally ill and died by suicide. Granted Civil List pension, 1922. *Died 24 March 1928.*

PUBLICATIONS

Collections

  Collected Poems. 1953.

Verse

  The Farmer's Bride. 1916; revised edition, 1921; as *Saturday Market,* 1921.
  The Rambling Sailor. 1929.

Reading List: "Mew" by Harold Monro, in *Some Contemporary Poets,* 1920.

*   *   *

Charlotte Mew began writing short stories, poems, and occasional articles of criticism (e.g., a defense of Emily Brontë in *Temple Bar*, 1904) in the 1890's. Although her stories found a ready market in the *English Woman, Temple Bar*, the *Egoist*, and other journals, she was a severe self-critic and chose to publish very little of what she wrote. One of her best stories, "Passed" (*Yellow Book*, 1894), is based on her voluntary social work; it is a highly introspective account of the speaker's new insights after being led to a sordid room where a prostitute lies dead by suicide. Because of fear of hereditary insanity, Charlotte and her sister Anne had renounced marriage, and many of her stories and poems have the theme of renunciation. The mysterious "A White Night" (*Temple Bar*, 1903) involves the living burial of a woman, who accepts this fate, by a company of monks in a Spanish church.

As a poet, Charlotte Mew was "discovered" by Alida Klemantaski; her husband, Harold Monro, published a book of 17 of her poems in 1916. In "The Farmer's Bride," the title poem, the awkward farmer longs for his frightened, deranged young wife: "She sleeps up in the attic there/Alone, poor maid. 'Tis but a stair/Betwixt us. Oh! my God! the down,/The soft young down of her, the brown,/The brown of her – her eyes, her hair, her hair!" The powerful monologue "Madeleine in Church" gives a wry stoical interpretation, typical of Charlotte's attitude toward herself: "It seems too funny all we other rips/Should have immortal souls ..." and "I do not envy Him His victories, His arms are full of broken things,/ But I shall not be in them." Charlotte Mew insisted that her occasional long lines not be run-over in the printing. She usually used rhyme. Most of her poems are short, and in inventive irregular stanzas, expressive of their strong, controlled emotion.

The painful death of Anne left Charlotte deranged. Her poems "Ken" and "On the Asylum Road" had told of insane persons being taken to dreary hospitals. The room given her in a hospital had no view but a neighboring brick wall. She had once written: "Lord, when I look at lovely things which pass,/... Can I believe there is a heavenlier world than this?" She poisoned herself in 1928.

—Alice R. Bensen

MEYNELL, Alice (Christiana Gertrude, née Thompson). English. Born in Barnes, London, 22 September 1847. Educated privately by her father. Married the author and journalist Wilfrid Meynell in 1877; eight children. Lived for most of her early life in Italy; returned to London, and wrote for various periodicals, including *The Scots Observer*, Edinburgh, subsequently *The National Observer*, London; helped her husband edit *The Weekly Register* and *Merry England*; befriended and encouraged various writers, including Thompson, Patmore, and Meredith; Weekly Columnist, 1893–98, and Art Critic, 1902–05, *The Pall Mall Gazette*, London; moved to Greatham, an estate in Pulborough, Sussex, 1911. Member, Academic Committee, Royal Society of Literature, from 1914. *Died 27 November 1922.*

PUBLICATIONS

Collections

Poems. 1923; edited by Frederick Page, 1940.
Prose and Poetry, edited by Frederick Page and others. 1947.

Verse

Preludes. 1875.
Poems. 1893.
Other Poems. 1896.
The Flower and the Mind: A Choice among the Best Poems. 1897.
Later Poems. 1902; as The Shepherdess and Other Verses, 1914.
Poems. 1913.
Ten Poems, 1913–1915. 1915.
A Father of Women and Other Poems. 1917.
Last Poems. 1923.

Other

The Poor Sisters of Nazareth: An Illustrated Record of Life at Nazareth House, Hammersmith. 1889.
The Life and Work of Holman Hunt, with W. Farrar. 1893.
The Rhythm of Life and Other Essays. 1893.
The Colour of Life and Other Essays. 1896.
The Children (essays). 1896.
London Impressions, illustrated by William Hyde. 1898.
The Spirit of Place and Other Essays. 1899.
John Ruskin: A Biography. 1900.
Children of Old Masters. 1903.
Ceres' Runaway and Other Essays. 1909.
Mary, The Mother of Jesus: An Essay. 1912.
Childhood. 1913.
Essays. 1914.
Hearts of Controversy. 1917.
The Second Person Singular and Other Essays. 1921.
Selected Essays. 1926.
Essays, edited by F. Meynell. 1947.
The Wares of Autolycus: Selected Literary Essays, edited by P. M. Fraser. 1965.

Editor, The Poems of T. G. Hake. 1894.
Editor, The Poetry of Pathos and Delight, by Coventry Patmore. 1896.
Editor, A Selction from the Verses of John B. Tabb. 1906.
Editor, Poems, by William Blake. 1911.
Editor, with G. K. Chesterton, Samuel Johnson (selections). 1911.
Editor, The School of Poetry: An Anthology for Young Readers. 1923.

Translator, Lourdes Yesterday, To-day, and To-morrow, by Daniel Barbé. 1894.
Translator, The Madonna, by Adolfo Venturi. 1901.
Translator, The Nun, by René Bazin. 1908.

Reading List: Meynell and Her Literary Generation by A. K. Tuell, 1925; Alice Meynell: A Memoir by Viola Meynell, 1929; Meynell: Her Life and Works by K. Michalik, 1934; Meynell Centenary Tribute by T. L. Connolly, 1947.

*   *   *

Although Alice Meynell's reputation rests, for most people, on the few poems, notably

"The Shepherdess" and "Christ in the Universe," which have found their way into anthologies, her output of poetry, and particularly of journalism, was fairly large. Throughout the Nineties she was a regular contributor to *The Scots Observer*, *The National Observer*, and predominantly, with a weekly column, to *The Pall Mall Gazette*. These essays are on a variety of subjects, and some are memorable for, as Coventry Patmore wrote in a review of a collection, "the ability to discern self-evident things as yet undiscerned." One of the most influential and popular of these was "Rejection" (1891) in which Meynell combines the aestheticism of the period with her own religious asceticism. She suggests that the "quality of fewness" is a positive, and praises those who "fulfill the office of exclusion." Meynell's prose style is characterised by precision of language and a carefully chosen vocabulary, in which she is concerned to give value to our "Latinity" as well as our Anglo-Saxon heritage: "Tribulation, Immortality, the Multitude: what remedy of composure do these words bring for their own great disquiet!" ("Composure," 1891).

Meynell's poetry already showed, in the first volume, *Preludes*, some of her preoccupations and images. In "The Young Neophyte" (written on her reception into the Church of Rome) we can see how she collapses the process of time into a single moment:

> Who knows what days I answer for today?
> Giving the bud I give the flower. I bow
> This yet unfaded and a faded brow;
> Bending these knees and feeble knees, I pray ....

And "The Garden" uses one of her favourite images, showing the order of gardens and contrasting it with the wildness of the uncontrollable skies. A perennial theme in both poetry and prose is that of order combined with freedom, and for Meynell this is central to the spiritual life and to literature. Just as the Catholic Church was a rooted body which she joined for "its administration of morals," so in an essay called "The Foot" (1897) she suggests that only poetry, the supreme art, has rules and measures sufficient to express the deepest thoughts: "It is no wonder that every poet worthy the name has had a passion for metre, for the very verse. To him the difficult fetter is the condition of an interior range immeasurable." "The rooted liberty of flowers in breeze" (from a poem "The English Metres") aptly expresses this idea.

Meynell experienced a renascence of poetry towards the end of her life when the pressures of journalism (much of which was engaged in from financial need – she had eight children) had receded. This late poetry is her best, terse, largely religious, and much influenced by the Metaphysical poets. These poems do not express religious certainties, but, more often, the sheer earthly business of waiting and trying to understand, "Shuddering through the paradox of prayer." They do express an awareness of God, and a sense of timeless, spaceless wholeness.

—Gabriel Bergonzi

MICKLE, William (Julius). Scottish. Born in Langholm, Dumfriesshire, 28 September 1735. Educated at Langholm Grammar School and Edinburgh High School. Married Mary Tomkins in 1781. Clerk in his father's brewery in Edinburgh, 1750–56, and subsequently Chief Partner, 1756–57, and, on his father's death, Owner, 1757 until the business failed, 1763; moved to London; Corrector, Clarendon Press, Oxford, 1765–71; worked on his translation of Camoës at Forest Hill, Oxford, 1772–75; appointed Secretary to Commodore

Johnston, sailing with a squadron to Portugal, 1779–80, and on his return to London appointed joint agent for disposal of the squadron's prizes; settled at Wheatley, near Oxford, 1781. Member, Royal Academy of Portugal, 1779. *Died 28 October 1788.*

PUBLICATIONS

Collections

Poetical Works, edited by J. Sim.   1806.

Verse

Providence; or, Arandus and Emilee.   1762.
Pollio: An Elegiac Ode.   1766.
The Concubine: A Poem in the Manner of Spenser.   1767; as *Syr Martyn,* 1778.
Almada Hill: An Epistle from Lisbon.   1781.
*The Prophecy of Queen Emma by Turgotus, Prior of Durham in the Reign of William
    Rufus.*   1782.
Poems, and a Tragedy.   1794.

Play

The Siege of Marseilles, in *Poems and a Tragedy.*   1794.

Other

A Letter to Dr. Harwood.   1768.
Voltaire in the Shades.   1770.
*A Candid Examination of the Reasons for Depriving the East India Company of Its
    Charter.*   1779.

Translator, *The Lusiads; or, The Discovery of India* (in verse), by Camoës.   1776.

Reading List: *Mickle* by Mary E. Taylor, 1937 (includes bibliography).

*   *   *

William Mickle's poems include *The Concubine* (later retitled *Syr Martyn*), a romantic narrative in Spenserian stanzas and pseudo-archaic English, and the ballad "Cumnor Hall." Both may be considered as exercises in the sentimental "Gothic" style of the late eighteenth century. "Cumnor Hall" deals with the story of Amy Robsart, the unfortunate first wife of Robert Dudley, Earl of Leicester, favourite of Queen Elizabeth I. It is said to have influenced Scott's treatment of the same story in *Kenilworth*. Of much more enduring merit than these pieces is "The Mariner's Wife" ("There's nae luck about the house"). This is surely one of the best and best-loved Scottish songs outside the works of Burns. The picture of a sailor's wife awaiting the return of her husband is brought to life by some vivid touches of detail, and without undue sentimentality. (But Mickle's authorship of this poem is doubtful; it has been attributed to Jean Adam, 1710–1765.)

Mickle's most ambitious literary venture was his translation, into herioc couplets, of the *Lusiads*, by the sixteenth-century Portuguese epic poet Luis de Camoës. He accompanied this with a life of Camoës, a dissertation upon the *Lusiads* and on epic poetry, and a sketch of the Portuguese discovery of India. Mickle sometimes expands or paraphrases his original, but his version is vigorous and readable, in the same way that Pope's Homer is readable. The subject – Vasco da Gama's voyage to India via the Cape Route – doubtless appealed to readers in the period when Britain was in the process of founding her own Indian Empire.

—John Heath-Stubbs

MILLAY, Edna St. Vincent. American. Born in Rockland, Maine, 22 February 1892. Educated at schools in Rockland and Camden, Maine; Barnard College, New York; Vassar College, Poughkeepsie, New York, graduated 1917. Married Eugen Jan Boissevain in 1923. Worked as a free-lance writer in New York City; also associated with the Provincetown Players. Recipient: Pulitzer Prize, 1923. Litt.D.: Tufts University, Medford, Massachusetts; Colby College, Waterville, Maine; University of Wisconsin, Madison; L.H.D.: New York University. Member, American Academy of Arts and Letters. *Died 19 October 1950.*

PUBLICATIONS

Collections

> *Letters*, edited by Allan Ross Macdougall.   1952.
> *Collected Poems*, edited by Norma Millay.   1956.

Verse

> *Renascence and Other Poems.*   1917.
> *A Few Figs from Thistles.*   1920.
> *Second April.*   1921.
> *The Ballad of the Harp-Weaver.*   1922.
> *The Harp-Weaver and Other Poems.*   1923; as *Poems*, 1923.
> *(Poems)*, edited by Hughes Mearns.   1927.
> *The Buck in the Snow and Other Poems.*   1928.
> *Poems Selected for Young People.*   1929.
> *Fatal Interview: Sonnets.*   1931.
> *Wine from These Grapes.*   1934.
> *Conversation at Midnight.*   1937.
> *Huntsman, What Quarry?*   1939.
> *Make Bright the Arrows: 1940 Notebook.*   1940.
> *Collected Sonnets.*   1941.
> *The Murder of Lidice.*   1942.

Collected Lyrics.   1943.
Mine the Harvest: A Collection of New Poems, edited by Norma Millay.   1954.

Plays

Aria da Capo (produced 1921).   1921.
The Lamp and the Bell (produced 1921).   1921.
Two Slatterns and a King: A Moral Interlude (produced 1921).   1921.
The King's Henchman, music by Deems Taylor (produced 1927).   1927.
The Princess Marries the Page.   1932.

Other

Distressing Dialogues.   1924.
Fear.   1927(?).

Translator, with George Dillon, Flowers of Evil, by Baudelaire.   1936.

Bibliography: A Bibliography of the Works of Millay by Karl Yost, 1937.

Reading List: The Indigo Bunting: A Memoir of Millay by Vincent Sheean, 1957; Restless Spirit: The Life of Millay by Miriam Gurko, 1962; Millay by Norman A. Brittin, 1967; Millay by James Gray, 1967; The Poet and Her Book: A Biography of Millay by Jean Gould, 1969.

*   *   *

If it is true that "You cannot touch a flower without disturbing a star," then the whole firmament must have been tremulous at the birth of Edna St. Vincent Millay. A woman of pronounced and strongly held convictions, she was catapulted to fame in 1920 by her book A Few Figs from Thistles, and became the prototype of the "new, emancipated women." The unheard of freedom which this lady demanded — freedom in love, freedom of thought in matters of morality and religion, equal rank with the male, and, above all, the freedom to act out her own individuality unhampered by outworn social codes — was one that was needed to counteract the deadening effects of Victorian proprieties. The rebellion that Millay promoted opened many new paths for the adventuresome human spirit and she is not to be blamed if the new freedoms are often abused. As she noted in one of her finest sonnets, "What rider spurs him," civilization is a contest fought in the dark against tremendous obstacles and requiring a continuous forward motion to counteract the destructive and stultifying tendencies in human nature. It is curious that Millay, the proponent of new, creative designs for life, clothed her verse in traditional forms and language, while T. S. Eliot, who harked to the past and worshipped authority as the solution to the world's ills, developed a new language and style for poetry. His contribution was also a forward motion for poetry, but the great admiration for this poet among academicians served for many years to minimize the recognition of the achievements of lyrical poets such as Millay.
      More, perhaps, than any other poet in English, Millay's stance vis-à-vis the universe was one of a human being almost totally absorbed in her own human situation, whose reactions to that situation, including, of course, the condition of the whole human race, are nearly always of an immediate, personal character. She does not stand outside herself but reports all the tumults of existence as they reverberate in her own being. Since she was a personality more than life-size and was gifted with "a high sense of drama," her personalist approach

created poetry of great vitality and conviction. On the other hand, being caught in the cage of personal, individual existence becomes suffocating, and, in her case, largely excluded awareness of the strange Otherness of things, the transcendent order of reality that we call the Divine.

Such as it was, however, Millay's outlook produced a large body of lyrical works of the highest distinction and expressiveness. It is easy to understand Louis Untermeyer's hyperbolic statement in 1923 that "Renascence," written when Millay was nineteen years old, was "possibly the most astonishing performance of this generation." Sentiments of great verve and freshness are given classic expression in a style that is always concise and musical. As James Gray says, the content of her poetry is equally attractive since it consists of her own version of the ageless contest between life and death, in both the physical and spiritual senses, the raptures and failures of love, and the ever-present struggle between the processes of decay and rebirth. There are times, as suggested above, when the reader may feel oppressed by the weight of her tortured self-absorption, but this is the price that must be paid for the sharply etched and poignant account of her soul's turnings.

—Glenn Richard Ruihley

MILLER, Joaquin. Pseudonym for Cincinnatus Hiner Miller. American. Born in Liberty, Indiana, 10 March 1839; moved with his parents to Oregon, 1850. Studied law in Oregon; admitted to the Oregon Bar, 1861. Messenger in the gold mining district of Idaho, 1856–59; Manager, *Democratic Register* newspaper, Eugene, Oregon, 1863; practised law in Canon City, Oregon, 1863–66; County Court Judge, Grant County, Oregon, 1866–70; lived in London and gained notoriety as the "frontier poet," 1870–71; returned to the United States and subsequently became a fruit grower: lived on his estate in Oakland, California, 1887 until the end of his life; Correspondent in the Klondike for the New York *Journal*, 1897–98. *Died 17 February 1913.*

PUBLICATIONS

Collections

  Poetical Works, edited by Stuart P. Sherman. 1923.
  Selections (verse), edited by Juanita Joaquina Miller. 1945.
  Selected Writings, edited by Allen Rosenus. 1976.

Verse

  Specimens. 1868.
  Joaquin, et al. 1869.
  Pacific Poems. 1871.

Songs of the Sierras. (produced 1880),   1871.
Songs of the Sun-Lands.   1873.
The Ship in the Desert.   1875.
Songs of Italy.   1878.
Songs of Far-Away Lands.   1878.
Songs of the Mexican Seas.   1887.
In Classic Shades and Other Poems.   1890.
Songs of the Soul.   1896.
Complete Poetical Works.   1897; revised edition, 1902.
Chants for the Boer.   1900.
As It Was in the Beginning: A Poem Dedicated to the Mothers of Men.   1903.
Light: A Narrative Poem.   1907.
Panama: Union of the Oceans.   1912.

Plays

The Baroness of New York.   1877.
Forty-Nine: A California Drama.   1882.
First Fam'lies in the Sierras.   1875; revised version, as *The Danites in the Sierras* (produced 1880).   1882.
The Silent Man.   1883.
Tally-Ho!, music by John Philip Sousa.   1883.
An Oregon Idyll, in *Collected Works.*   1910.

Fiction

The One Fair Woman.   1876.
Shadows of Shasta.   1881.
'49: The Gold-Seeker of the Sierras.   1884.
The Destruction of Gotham.   1886.

Other

Life Amongst the Modocs: Unwritten History.   1873; as *Paquita, The Indian Heroine,* 1881; revised edition, as *My Own Story,* 1890; as *Romantic Life Amongst the Red Indians: An Autobiography,* 1890.
The Danites and Other Choice Selections, edited by A. V. D. Honeyman.   1878.
Memory and Rime.   1884.
The Building of the City Beautiful.   1893.
An Illustrated History of the State of Montana.   2 vols., 1894.
The Battle of Castle Crags.   1894.
True Bear Stories.   1900.
Japan of Sword and Love, with Yone Noguchi.   1905.
Collected Works.   6 vols., 1909–10.
Trelawney with Shelley and Byron.   1922.
California Diary, 1855–1857, edited by John S. Richards.   1936.
Overland in a Covered Wagon: An Autobiography, edited by Sidney G. Firman (based on Introduction to *Collected Works*).   1930.

Bibliography: in *Bibliography of American Literature* by Jacob Blanck, 1973.

Reading List: *Miller: Literary Frontiersman* by Martin S. Peterson, 1937; *Splendid Poseur: Miller, American Poet* by M. Marion Marberry, 1953; *Miller* by O. W. Frost, 1967.

*   *   *

Were it not for the outlandish image of himself which he deliberately cultivated, Cincinnatus Hiner Miller, better known as Joaquin Miller, after the Mexican bandit Joaquin Murietta, whose exploits he helped to popularize, would probably be forgotten today. Dressed in Western sombrero, boots, and buckskin britches, Joaquin Miller proclaimed himself the poetic spokesman for the American West, and during his lifetime he came to symbolize, both in America and abroad, the spirit of freedom, adventure, and bravado which characterized the West in the popular imagination.

Ironically, Miller rose to fame not in America but in England, where he went to find a publisher for his book, *Pacific Poems*, and to make his presence felt in more sophisticated literary circles than those which America offered him. His earlier collections of poetry, *Specimens* and *Joaquin et al.*, had received scant recognition in America, and Miller shrewdly understood that he and his works might best appeal to a foreign audience unfamiliar with the stereotypes which he projected. Although Americans simply refused to take him seriously, Miller became something of a celebrity in Britain, where his rustic dress and primitive manners endeared him with the public and brought him to the attention of the leading literary figures of the day. From Britain, Miller's fame spread to America. His most famous book, *Songs of the Sierras*, first published in London, was issued the same year in Boston.

Most of Miller's works are vaguely autobiographical. He drew his themes from his own experiences, which he embellished or exaggerated according to the effects which he wished to achieve. Nearly all of Miller's works are about the West. *Life Amongst the Modocs* and *Memorie and Rime* are prose accounts of his early adventures in the mines and among the Indians of California. *Shadows of Shasta*, Miller's most successful novel, draws attention to the injustices done to the Indians, with whom Miller greatly sympathized. When he writes about the West, Miller was generally passionate and bold. He possessed the ability to make legend seem real and the real seem legendary. As a playwright, Miller, who possessed a flare for the dramatic, was especially effective. His most popular play, *The Danites in the Sierras*, was acted before packed audiences, much to the chagrin of Bret Harte and Mark Twain, who envied Miller's dramatic talents. When he departed from Western themes, however, as he did in the novels *The One Fair Woman* and *The Destruction of Gotham*, Miller's writing becomes forced and unconvincing.

Miller's poetry, while lacking in intrinsic merit, had a profound effect on the development of Western American Literature. For forms and techniques, Miller studied the British romantics and the American fireside poets. Like Longfellow, Miller was especially fond of rhymed iambic pentameter, and his Western heroes bear a marked resemblance to those of Byron. In those poems where form matches content, Miller's verse possesses a haunting, rhythmic quality, reminiscent of Indian chants, which captures the spirit and vitality of his Western themes. Miller is especially noted for his attempts to write poetry in the American vernacular. His most famous poem, "Columbus," has become a classic in its own right and is still recited by American schoolchildren, who see in it a primitive expression of the American Dream.

—James A. Levernier

MILTON, John. English. Born in Bread Street, Cheapside, London, 9 December 1608. Educated privately, by a Scottish friend of his father's; St. Paul's School, London; Christ's College, Cambridge, 1625–32, B.A. 1629, M.A. 1632; lived at his father's country house, Horton, Buckinghamshire, devoted to further study, 1632–38; completed his education by travel in France and Italy, 1638–39. Married 1) Mary Powell in 1642 (died, 1652), three daughters; 2) Catharine Woodcock in 1656 (died in childbirth, 1657); 3) Elizabeth Minshull in 1662. Wrote in support of the Puritan cause: appointed Latin (or Foreign) Secretary to Cromwell's Council of State, 1649; went blind, 1652, but continued to serve with the assistance of friends; deprived of office at the Restoration, 1660. Imprisoned and in danger of execution: friends, possibly including the poet Andrew Marvell, intervened, and he escaped with fine and loss of most of his property; thereafter devoted himself to his writing. *Died 8 November 1674.*

PUBLICATIONS

Collections

Works, edited by F. A. Patterson and others.   18 vols., 1931–38.
Poetical Works, edited by Helen Darbishire.   2 vols., 1952–55.
Complete Prose Works, edited by D. M. Wolfe and others.   7 vols. (of 8), 1953–74.
Poems, edited by John Carey and Alastair Fowler.   2 vols., 1971.
The Cambridge Milton, edited by J. B. Broadbent and others.   1972–

Verse

Poems. 1645.
Paradise Lost.   1667; revised edition, 1678; edited by Christopher Ricks, 1968.
Paradise Regained, to Which Is Added Samson Agonistes.   1671; *Paradise Regained* edited by Christopher Ricks, with *Paradise Lost,* 1968.
Poems upon Several Occasions.   1673.

Plays

Comus: A Mask (produced 1634).   1637; edited by F. T. Prince, 1968.
Samson Agonistes, in *Paradise Regained,* 1671.   Edited by Michael Davis, 1968.

Other

Of Reformation Touching Church Discipline in England.   1641.
Of Prelatical Episcopacy.   1641.
Animadversions Against Smectymnuus.   1641.
The Reason of Church-Government Urged Against Prelaty.   1641.
The Apology Against a Pamphlet Called a Modest Confutation.   1642; edited by M. C. Jochums, 1950.
The Doctrine and Discipline of Divorce.   1643; revised edition, 1644.
Of Education.   1644; edited by Michael Davis, with *Areopagitica,* 1963.
Areopagitica: A Speech for the Liberty of Unlicenced Printing.   1644; edited by J. C. Suffolk, 1968.
Colasterion: A Reply to a Nameless Answer Against the Doctrine and Discipline of Divorce.   1645.
Tetrachordon: Expositions upon the Four Chief Places in Scripture Which Treat of Marriage, or Nullities in Marriage.   1645.

697

The Tenure of Kings and Magistrates.   1649; edited by W. T. Allison, 1911.

Observations upon the Articles of Peace with the Irish Rebels.   1649.

Eikonoklastes, in Answer to a Book Entitled Eikon Basilika, The Portraiture of His Sacred Majesty in His Solitudes and Sufferings.   1649; revised edition, 1650.

Pro Populo Anglicano Defensio.   1651; translated by Joseph Washington, 1692.

Pro Populo Anglicano Defensio Secunda.   1654; translated by R. Fellowes, 1806.

A Treatise of Civil Power in Ecclesiastical Causes.   1659.

Considerations Touching the Likeliest Means to Remove Hirelings Out of the Church.   1659.

The Ready and Easy Way to Establish a Free Commonwealth, and the Excellence Thereof Compared with the Inconveniences and Dangers of Readmitting Kingship in This Nation.   1660; edited by E. M. Clark, 1915.

Brief Notes upon a Late Sermon Titled the Dear of God and the King, by Matthew Griffith.   1660.

Accedence Commenced Grammar.   1669.

The History of Britain, That Part Especially Now Called England.   1670; edited by F. Maseres, 1818.

Artis Logicae Plenior Institutio.   1672.

Of True Religion, Heresy, Schism, Toleration, and What Best Means May Be Urged Against the Growth of Popery.   1673.

Epistolarum Familiarum Liber Unus.   1674; translated by J. Hall, 1829; section translated by Phyllis Tillyard, as *Private Correspondence and Academic Exercises,* 1932.

Litera Pseudo-Senatus Anglicani.   1676.

Character of the Long Parliament and Assembly of Divines in MDCXLI.   1676.

A Brief History of Moscovia.   1682; edited by R. R. Cawley, 1941.

Republican Letters.   1682.

Letters of State from the Year 1649 till the Year 1659.   1694; edited by H. Fernow, 1903.

Original Letters and Papers of State Addressed to Oliver Cromwell, edited by J. Nickolls.   1743.

De Doctrina Christiana Libri duo Posthumi, edited by C. R. Sumner.   1825; translated by C. R. Sumner, 1825.

Original Papers, edited by W. D. Hamilton.   1859.

A Common-Place Book, edited by A. J. Horwood.   1876; revised edition, 1877.

Translator, *The Judgement of Martin Bucer Concerning Divorce.*   1644.

Bibliography: *A Reference Guide to Milton from 1800 to the Present Day* by H. F. Fletcher, 1930; *Milton: A Bibliographical Supplement 1929–57* by C. Huckaby, 1960, revised edition, 1969.

Reading List: *The Life of Milton* by David Masson, 7 vols., 1859–94, revised edition, 1881–96; *Milton* by E. M. W. Tillyard, 1930, revised edition, 1949; *This Great Argument* by Maurice Kelly, 1941; *A Preface to Paradise Lost* by C. S. Lewis, 1942; *Paradise Lost and Its Critics* by A. J. A. Waldock, 1947; *The Muse's Method: An Introduction to Paradise Lost* by Joseph H. Summers, 1962; *Milton: A Reader's Guide to His Poetry* by Marjorie Hope Nicolson, 1963; *Milton* by Douglas Bush, 1964; *Milton: A Biography* by Riley Parker, 2 vols., 1968 (includes bibliography); *From Shadowy Types to Truth: Studies in Milton's Symbolism* by W. G. Madsen, 1968; *On Milton's Poetry* edited by Arnold Stein, 1970; *Milton: The Critical Heritage* edited by J. T. Shawcross, 1970; *Milton and the English Revolution* by Christopher Hill, 1977; *Milton Criticism: A Subject Index* by William Johnson, 1978.

*   *   *

John Milton's poetry has been attacked in the 20th century for precisely that quality most admired by the Romantics – its uncompromising idealism. "Strictly speaking, Milton may be said never to have *seen* anything," remarked one modern critic, and T. S. Eliot felt that Milton, in imitating Spenser, had "writ no language." Miltonists have reacted to this criticism by stressing how very similar Milton's poetry is to Eliot's (see C. S. Lewis). In fact Milton's poetry is totally unlike Eliot's: Eliot is the poet of things, the most anti-idealist of poets, and Milton is the greatest English poet of ideas and ideals. Modern taste has preferred "things" to "ideas."

The reader of Milton must begin by accepting his Platonism. His characterization of Plato as "almost divine" is a key to understanding his philosophy. In an early letter to his dearest friend Diodati the *Phaedrus* is invoked:

> For, lest you threaten too much, know that it is impossible for me not to love men like you. What beside God has resolved for me I do not know, but this at least: *He has instilled into me, if into anyone, a vehement love of the beautiful.* Not with so much labor, as the fables have it, is Ceres said to have sought her daughter Proserpina as it is my habit day and night to seek for this *idea of the beautiful...* through all the forms and faces of things ... and to follow it as it leads me on by some sure traces which I seem to recognize. ... You make many anxious inquiries, even as to what I am presently thinking of. Hearken, Theodotus, but let it be in your private ear, lest I blush; and allow me to use big language with you. You ask what I am thinking of? So may the good Deity help me, – of immortality! And what am I doing? *Growing my wings.* And meditating flight; but as yet our Pegasus raises himself on very tender pinions. Let us be lowly wise.

Milton's discipleship to Spenser and Chaucer follows naturally from his love of Plato. Spenser was for Milton always "Sage and Serious." In his poetry "more is meant than meets the ear." Chaucer had "left half told/The story of Cambuscan bold" (a story from Plato dealing with a tyrant undercut by philosophical wisdom). Chaucer never lacked "high seriousness" for Milton. The attack on ecclesiastical abuses in Milton's works linked him directly to the poet of the *Canterbury Tales*. Chaucer, Spenser, and Milton, later joined by Shelley, constitute the great idealist tradition in English letters, and all were social critics and religious reformers as well as poets.

Milton believed that the great poet had first to be a great man. He also stressed that great art required the hardest kind of labor. And no one ever worked harder to become the great poet. The ideal poet had to combine the learning and wisdom of Plato's "philosopher kings" with the myth-making ability and eloquence of the Homeric poet. When such a combination appeared, then the criticism of poetry in the *Republic* was transcended. The artist was the one who gave society its ideals, and, whether they wish it or not, societies are led by ideals. For Milton, as for the classical tradition in general, these ideas were largely to be found in the literature of the past. Milton's social radicalism was always a *return* to the roots, not the conventional modern rejection of the past and belief in a utopian future. Milton's radicalism is peculiarly relevant to a world that no longer believes in the beneficence of its future.

Comus, an exceptionally difficult work for moderns to read, combines a lesson in chastity, drawn not from St. Paul but from the *Symposium*, with a sensuousness drawn from Shakespeare and Ovid. Comus himself is made physically attractive and his imagery is notably phallic. His arguments are phrased in the most voluptuous imagery possible; his castle contains every luxury, exceeding even that of Keats' St. Agnes. Such a combination of rich language and austere philosophy seems impossible for modern thought. But the great idealist poets have been the most sensual. Sexual appeal lies in ideas, not in things. No poet is less sensual than Donne, for instance, however explicitly sexual his topic.

For Milton, as for the classical writers, the essential task of art was to civilize human society. Orpheus was a mythical exposition of this idea. Men would listen to the poet even against their will. Milton's writings were an attempt to communicate Biblical and classical ideals to the modern world. The poems, the prose works, and the practical duties of the Secretary for Foreign Tongues were all means to the same end. Without the resources of poetic eloquence Milton thought he was writing with only his "left hand" – but it was the hand of a Hercules. Brief as it is, his tractate *Of Education* provides the only viable alternative to the cynical practicality of the modern university. Modern educational thought would dismiss Milton's program as hopelessly utopian. But Milton's education was the one that had produced the greatest of Athenian statesmen, and no society that demanded great leaders could knowingly accept less. Macaulay stressed the great courage required for Milton to publish his writings on divorce, given his own unhappy first marriage – but one must not lose sight of their *incredible* wisdom. In them Milton combined for the first time the practical bourgeois social unit of the family with the highest Platonic ideal of love. He reasoned that the end of love had to be the end of marriage. Met by almost universal outrage at their supposed advocacy of sexual libertinism, the divorce tracts seriously endangered Milton's chances of being taken seriously in any other writings. In them he transcended his own period: they are as fresh today as when they were written.

The *Areopagitica*, in some ways a defense of his right to publish the divorce tracts, has been almost universally admired. Because it was cited in some of the early American trials concerned with the freedom of the press, it is the only work by a poet to have legal stature in American courts. If Milton lost the battle against censorship in the 17th century, he won the war in the 18th. But it is important to note that Milton was less concerned in the tract with ending censorship than with promoting truth through free discussion of ideas.

Milton's political and religious writings were considered far too radical by most of his contemporaries. Already under attack for his divorce pamphlets from both Anglicans and Presbyterians, Milton wrote powerful attacks on tyranny in both state and church which were dismissed as the ravings of a mind that had mastered Latin but not law. But today even the most consummate of Tories would not embrace the ideas that Salmasius, Milton's famous rival, asserted in his works. The Bill of Rights of the U.S. Constitution owes far more to Milton than to John Locke. Freedom of religion and freedom of the press found early expression in Milton's works, and in far more powerful form.

Stripped of all direct political involvement by the Restoration in 1660, and forced "to stand and wait" by his critics, Milton had no choice but to write *Paradise Lost*. This, his great work, can be said to begin with an ending and to end with a beginning. Milton's epic ended the classical epic tradition by making Satan the last of the conventional military heroes. War was seen by Milton not as a form of glory but as a form of death. No writer since Milton has succeeded in writing an epic glorifying war; their hero will always end as a parody of Satan. Milton's epic *makes love, not war*. Men and women in their personal relations, and not arms and the man, became the modern epic subject matter. If it ends the classical epic, *Paradise Lost* begins the modern novel. For here the subject matter of domestic relations is seen as worthy of serious treatment. The heated quarrel that succeeds the Fall is the first full-scale marriage fight in literature, and the world that faces the reconciled couple at the end of Book XII is the world we all now live in: where shall we live? how shall we earn our living? how can we educate the kids? To these questions the heroic posturings of Satan are irrelevant. It is only a slight exaggeration to say that much of later literature is a series of footnotes to Milton. All writers who consider love (Adam and Eve) or evil (Satan) must imitate Milton. If any writer should succeed in transcending him, then that writer would be the next Milton. It is worth remarking that the modern ideas of Eden and of Satan are drawn from Milton, not from the Bible. The religious imagination has been dominated by his poem.

The rejection of classical knowledge in *Paradise Regained* has troubled sensitive readers. Was Milton rejecting his own past work? Ezra Pound ascribed it to Milton's "beastly Hebraism." But the *rejection* is contained in a work that is the purest realization of the Platonic dialogue in poetry. The Christ of *Paradise Regained* is the most eloquent exponent of the ideals of the *Republic*. Satan's Thrasymachus, the eternal apologist for the tyrant, is overthrown by Christ's Socratic wisdom. If *Paradise Lost* is Milton's greatest tribute to the epic tradition of Homer, *Paradise Regained* is his greatest tribute to Plato. Christ is the fullest realization of Plato's ideal of the philosopher-king. Precisely because he understands power and its final corruptions, he does not desire power and so is immune from all of Satan's blandishments.

Samson Agonistes remains, as Goethe perceived, the only successful modern example of classical tragedy. The modern mind makes the same objection to it – it cannot be staged. The simplest answer would be that we will solve the problem of production when we come to appreciate its informing ideals. In Greek tragedy as in Milton's *Samson* the focus is not on simple human heroism displayed through action but upon divine providence that brings wisdom only through suffering. Samson, "eyeless in Gaza," like Oedipus, blind at Colonus, find light through darkness and strength through weakness. The idea was dear to Milton.

> There is, as the apostle remarked, a way to strength through weakness. Let me be the most feeble creature alive, as long as that feebleness serves to invigorate the energies of my rational and immortal spirit; as long as in that obscurity, in which I am enveloped, the light of the divine presence more clearly shines, then, in proportion as I am weak, I shall be invincibly strong; and in proportion as I am blind, I shall more clearly see. O that I may thus be perfected by feebleness, and irradiated by obscurity! And indeed, in my blindness, I enjoy in no inconsiderable degree the favor of the Deity, who regards me with more tenderness and compassion in proportion as I am able to behold nothing but himself.

In that sense Samson is Milton, but so is Oedipus. Manoa's great epitaph for his son serves beautifully for John Milton himself: "Samson hath quit himself/Like Samson, and heroically hath finished/A life heroic...."

—Myron Taylor

MONRO, Harold (Edward). English. Born in Brussels, Belgium, 14 March 1879. Educated at Radley; Caius College, Cambridge. Served in an anti-aircraft battery during World War I. Married Alida Klemantaski in 1920; one son. Founder, *Poetry Review*, London, 1912, and Poetry Bookshop, Bloomsbury, London, 1912; Editor, *Poetry and Drama*, 1913–14; Founder Editor, *The Monthly Chapbook*, London, 1919–21. *Died 16 March 1932.*

PUBLICATIONS

Collections

Collected Poems, edited by Alida Monro. 1933.

Verse

Poems. 1906.
Judas. 1907.
Before Dawn: Poems and Impressions. 1911.

Children of Love. 1914.
Trees. 1916.
Strange Meetings. 1917.
Real Property. 1922.
The Earth for Sale. 1928.

Play

One Day Awake: A Morality. 1922.

Other

Proposals for a Voluntary Nobility, with Maurice Browne. 1907.
The Evolution of the Soul. 1907.
The Chronicle of a Pilgrimage: Paris to Milan on Foot. 1909.
Some Contemporary Poets (1920). 1920.
The War Memorial in Battersea Park. 1924.

Editor, *Twentieth Century Poetry: An Anthology.* 1929.

Reading List: in *Polite Essays* by Ezra Pound, 1937; in *The Georgian Revolt* by R. H. Ross, 1965; *Monro and the Poetry Bookshop* by Joy Grant, 1967 (includes bibliography).

                                        *   *   *

Of all the Georgian poets, Harold Monro came nearest to dealing with the concerns of life around him. His central position as organiser of the Poetry Bookshop, and of readings and discussions held there as part of his attempt to popularise poetry, made him seem to relegate his own work to a secondary role. Those who like to imagine that the making of poetry is a full-time occupation sometimes sneer at Monro and his fellow Georgians as "weekending with their talents" (overlooking the fact that one of the mightiest of symphonists, Gustav Mahler, was also a week-end and summer-holiday composer). Strength is seemingly lent to this absurd argument by the fact that Monro's sonnet-sequence "Week-end" was for many years his most frequently anthologised piece.

> The train! The twelve o'clock for paradise.
>   Hurry, or it will try to creep away.
> Out in the country everyone is wise:
>   We can be wise only on Saturday.
> There you are waiting, little friendly house:
>   Those are your chimney-stacks with you between,
> Surrounded by old trees and startled cows,
>   Staring through all your windows at the green....

Week-ending has become a popular pastime throughout much of Europe, and Monro catches its sense of quasi-romantic release better than anyone.

Like Coventry Patmore, whose rhymed *vers libres* Munro emulated in his later work, he was much concerned with the small things of domestic life, but seen in their relation to practical use as well as for what they are themselves. In a strange way, quite early he left behind the mood for Georgian poetry (though not always the tone), and looked forward to the urban poetry of Eliot and his followers. Thus, eight years before the publication of *The Waste Land*, Monro, in "London Interior," was writing:

> The evening will turn grey.
> It is sad in London after two.
> All, all the afternoon,
> What can old men, old women do?
>
> It is sad in London when the gloom
> Thickens, like wool,
> In the corners of the room;
> The sky is shot with steel,
> Shot with blue.
>
> The bells ring the slow time;
> The chairs creak, the hours climb;
> The sunlight lays a streak upon the floor.

He himself, in a late poem which both he and his wife (but not this critic) regarded as his best, "Midnight Lamentation," observed: "I think too much of death;/There is a gloom/when I can't hear your breath/calm in some room." A sense of alienation, of unhappiness, pervades most of what he wrote, as alcohol eventually pervaded his later life. The tendency to both melancholy and alcoholism was perhaps an inheritance of his Lowland Scots ancestry. His achievement, though a minor one, is distinctive, and his best work should be better known than it is.

—Maurice Lindsay

MONTAGU, Lady Mary Wortley. English. Born in London, baptized 26 May 1689; eldest daughter of the Earl, later Duke, of Kingston. Educated privately. Married Edward Wortley-Montagu in 1712 (separated, 1739; died, 1761); one son and one daughter, Countess of Bute. After her marriage lived in London, a friend of Addison, Pope, and others; lived in Constantinople (while her husband was Ambassador there), 1716–18; thereafter lived in Twickenham; after leaving her husband, 1739, lived in Italy; returned to England after his death, 1761. *Died 21 August 1762.*

PUBLICATIONS

Collections

> *Complete Letters*, edited by Robert Halsband. 3 vols., 1965–67.
> *Essays, Poems, and Simplicity: A Comedy*, edited by Robert Halsband and Isobel Grundy. 1977.

Verse

Court Poems. 1716.
Verses Addressed to the Imitator of Horace. 1733.
An Elegy to a Young Lady in the Manner of Ovid, with an Answer (James Hammond
    wrote the Elegy). 1733.
The Dean's Provocation for Writing the Lady's Dressing-Room. 1734.
Six Town Eclogues, with Some Other Poems. 1747.
Poetical Works, edited by I. Reed. 1768.

Play

Simplicity, from a play by Marivaux, in Essays, Poems, and Simplicity. 1977.

Other

Letters Written During Her Travels. 3 vols., 1763.
The Nonsense of Common-Sense (periodical), edited by Robert Halsband. 1947.

Reading List: The Life of Lady Mary Wortley Montagu by Robert Halsband, 1956.

*   *   *

Lady Mary Wortley Montagu's earliest appearances in print were anonymous or
clandestine. It is believed that she wrote Spectator 573 (28 July 1714) where, under the
character of the president of a club of widows, a kind of latter-day Wife of Bath, she argues
wittily and feelingly the cause of women's rights. Her most considerable venture into
journalism was the nine issues of The Nonsense of Common-Sense (1737–38) which she
wrote to defend Walpole's ministry against an opposition journal entitled Common-Sense,
and where she returned, in passing, to the theme of feminism. A penetrating critique of
Addison's Cato, written in 1713, furnished the playwright with many hints for his revisions
and, perhaps for that reason, was "suppressed at the desire of Mr. Addison" during Lady
Mary's lifetime, but it is difficult to understand why her own play, Simplicity: A Comedy (a
lively adaptation of Le Jeu de l'Amour et du Hasard by Marivaux) remained unacted and
unprinted until the twentieth century.
    In her day she was known as a poet, though most of her verses circulated in manuscript and
what was printed appeared usually without her authority. Six burlesque-pastoral "Town
Eclogues," satirizing specific, easily recognizable members of court society, were written in
1715 with some help from Gay and Pope, and this, perhaps, is why they are more
concentrated, vigorous, and polished than any of her other verse. There is more feeling,
however, in her graver feminist poems: for instance, the "Epistle from Mrs. Y. to her
Husband, 1724" which comments on a contemporary divorce case from the viewpoint of a
wronged wife who has committed justifiable adultery (see Review of English Studies, 1972).
The rest of her facile and sometimes extempore occasional verse includes imitations,
translations, love-lyrics, comic squibs (some quite indecent) on contemporary scandals, and
lampoons (mostly against Pope with whom she quarrelled violently in the 1720's).
    Her fame now rests mainly upon her letters. Those written from Turkey (where her
husband was ambassador from 1716 to 1718) were edited by her for posthumous publication
and make up one of the outstanding travel books of the eighteenth century – for she was an
alert, sympathetic, inquisitive, articulate, and impressionable traveller. Many of her later
letters retail gossip and London scandals with the racy vigour of a witty, tough-minded

woman of the world; others describe Italian scenes with the clarity and colour of a Canaletto; while others, addressed to a Venetian lover half her age, display, in extraordinary and touching contrast, girlish infatuation and timidity.

—A. J. Sambrook

MONTAGUE, John (Patrick). Irish. Born in Brooklyn, New York, 28 February 1929. Educated at St. Patrick's College, Armagh; University College, Dublin, B.A. in English and history 1949, M.A. 1952; Yale University, New Haven, Connecticut (Fulbright Scholar), 1953–54; University of Iowa, Iowa City, M.F.A. 1955. Worked for the State Tourist Board, Dublin, 1956–61; taught at the Poetry Workshop, University of California, Berkeley, Spring 1964 and 1965, University College, Dublin, 1967–68, and the Experimental University of Vincennes, France; currently, Lecturer in Poetry, University College, Cork. Recipient: Arts Council of Northern Ireland grant, 1970. Member, Irish Academy of Letters.

PUBLICATIONS

Verse

> *Forms of Exile.* 1958.
> *The Old People.* 1960.
> *Poisoned Lands and Other Poems.* 1963.
> *All Legendary Obstacles.* 1966.
> *A Chosen Light.* 1967.
> *Patriotic Suite.* 1966; *Home Again,* 1967; *Hymn to the New Omagh Road,* 1968; *The Bread God: A Lecture, with Illustrations in Verse,* 1968; *A New Siege,* 1969; complete version, as *The Rough Field,* 1972.
> *The Planter and the Gael,* with John Hewitt. 1970.
> *Tides.* 1971.
> *A Fair House* (translations from the Irish). 1973.
> *The Cave of Night.* 1974.
> *O'Riada's Farewell.* 1975.
> *A Slow Dance.* 1975.
> *The Great Cloak.* 1978.

Play

> *The Rough Field* (produced 1973).

Fiction

> *Death of a Chieftain and Other Stories.* 1964.

705

Other

Editor, *The Dolmen Miscellany of Irish Writing.* 1962.
Editor, with Liam Miller, *A Tribute to Austin Clarke on His Seventieth Birthday.* 1966.
Editor, *The Faber Book of Irish Verse.* 1974; as *The Book of Irish Verse,* 1977.

Reading List: articles by D. S. Maxwell, in *Critical Quarterly,* Summer 1973, Derek Mahon, in *Malahat Review,* July 1973, and Thomas Dillon Redshaw, in *Studies,* Spring 1974; *Montague* by Frank Kersnowski, 1975.

*   *   *

The celebrations in *The Great Cloak* have enticed even Irish readers to understand that John Montague has found his own place, and surely enlarged the ideal, but once national, realm of Irish poetry. Yet, only gradually has Montague's precise mastery of the lyric sequence been recognized, compared to the discovery of Thomas Kinsella and Seamus Heaney at the start and close of the 1960's. Dating from 1958, Montague's collections span more than Heaney's pagan pastorals and Kinsella's nightmare-torn memoirs, for brighter, fresher influences on Montague have been the Americans William Carlos Williams and Robert Duncan. His first American pilgrimage gave Montague subjects for *Forms of Exile,* but no mature poetic. Although *Poisoned Lands* displays forms grounded in a classical Irish schooling, it draws innovation and humor from Lawrence and Auden. Only later in sequences like *All Legendary Obstacles* and in triptychs like the title poem of *A Chosen Light* do Montague's adult and perplexing, for some, traits appear: a personal reticence alluding to, not confessing, private crises; and a delight in the open forms of extensive sequences. One can feel in these both Yeats and the new American poets – Snyder, Bly, Creeley – standing near:

(next to the milk-white telephone)

A minute wind–
Mill casting its pale light
Over unhappiness, ceaselessly
Elaborating its signals

Not of help, but of neutral energy.

A Chosen Light appeared while Montague was living in Paris, lecturing at the University of Vincennes, and weaving a new cloth of poetic rites and allegiances into *The Rough Field.* Begun in 1958, this epic sequence of ten sequences, or cantos, charts by turns a vision of the moral geography of Montague's Ulster heritage and of his spiralling progress through its torn world back to its *garbh acaidh. The Rough Field* may best be read, keeping in mind its titular metaphor, as a social allegory whose moral impulse springs from illuminations of a newly ordered self, and these required Montague to unveil for his persona a myth able to span his local subjects and ambitious themes. Such a myth Montague found first in those love poems of *A Chosen Light* that retire to intimate problems of self, resolved later in the darker lyrics of *Tides,* employing an ancient Irish genre, the *aisling,* to spin autobiography into a romance of the self renewed. *Tides* includes and *The Rough Field* ends with the romantic parable of "The Wild Dog Rose":

> Briefly
> the air is strong with the smell
> of that weak flower, offering
> its crumbling yellow cup
> and pale bleeding lips
> fading to white
>   at the rim
> of each bruised and heart—
> shaped petal.

That emblem of grace renewed enables Montague's veritable persona to metamorphose into a culture hero − scapegoat or celebrant − on a pilgrimage, as mazy as the paving of Chartres, back to spiritual yet visible origins. As his controversial *Faber Book of Irish Verse* shows, Montague has again taken up the prodigal's mantle and, writing now from Cork, begun to compose other patterns in linked elegies and lyrics of love in *A Slow Dance* and *The Great Cloak*, which counterpoint *A Chosen Light* and *Tides*.

—Thomas Dillon Redshaw

MONTGOMERIE, Alexander. Scottish. Born, probably at Beith, Ayrshire, c. 1550. Possibly educated in Argyleshire. Married; one son and one daughter. Courtier in the service of the Scottish court of James VI: Chief of the King's "Castilian band" of court poets, and Court Laureate; rewarded with a royal pension. Visited France, Flanders, and Spain, 1586; convert to Roman Catholicism: involved in the Catholic Conspiracy, 1597, and died an outlaw. *Died c. 1599.*

PUBLICATIONS

Collections

  Poems, edited by James Cranstoun.   1887; supplementary volume, edited by George Stevenson, 1910.
  Montgomerie: A Selection from His Songs and Poems, edited by Helena Mennie Shire.   1960.

Verse

  The Cherry and the Slae.   1597; edited by H. Harvey Wood, 1937.
  The Mind's Melody, Containing Certain Psalms of the Kingly Prophet David, Applied to a New Pleasant Tune.   1605.
  The Flyting Betwixt Montgomerie and Polwart.   1621.

Reading List: *Alexander Scott, Montgomerie, and Drummond of Hawthornden as Lyric Poets* by Catherine M. Maclean, 1915.

*   *   *

Alexander Montgomerie, younger son of a noble Scottish house, was already known as a poet in 1568. Serving abroad as a soldier-of-fortune, he was converted to Catholicism and became a covert partisan of counter-Reform. In 1579 a Catholic diplomat from France gained sway over the young King James VI. Montgomerie was installed at court and taught the King the art of *Scottis Poesie*. He was chief of the King's "Castalian band" of court-poets and musicians, through whose work in translation and imitation and in original composition his Majesty aimed to make little Scotland matter in the European cultural scene. Montgomerie's share in the programme brought petrarchanism, the sonnet, and the new poetry of France and Spain into Scots writing.

His finest lyrics were made for music. Some matched part-songs from France or England; some were set by Scottish court musicians. He was also a master of the old-style alliterative poetry, using it in his "Flyting" or bardic contest of invective. His fifty sonnets, single-standing or in groups, form a loose-strung life-record, ranging from personal invective to compliment deftly rendered from Ronsard.

His dream-allegory *The Cherrie and the Slae* shows, "darkly," the dreamer journeying towards a choice between the available, bitter berry (of Calvinism) and the delectable inaccessible cherry (the Catholic eucharist). (An early version was interrupted or censored in 1584.) But late in his life Montgomerie, outlawed after being discovered in a Catholic conspiracy, recast the poem, tacitly accusing King James of betraying trust. He died an outlaw in 1599 – and the early truncated version was printed! The intervening years had seen him in and out of royal favour, possibly exploited as secret envoy in the King's devious policies, certainly suffering imprisonment abroad.

On his death King James lamented the loss of "the prince of poets in this land."

—Helena Mennie Shire

MOORE, Marianne (Craig). American. Born in Kirkwood, Missouri, 15 November 1887. Educated at the Metzger Institute, Carlisle, Pennsylvania; Bryn Mawr College, Pennsylvania, B.A. 1909; Carlisle Commercial College, Pennsylvania, 1910. Head of the Commercial Studies Department, United States Indian School, Carlisle, 1911–15; worked as a private tutor and secretary in New York City, 1919–21, and as a Branch Librarian for the New York Public Library system, 1921–25; Acting Editor, *The Dial*, 1926 until it ceased publication, 1929. Visiting Lecturer, Bryn Mawr College, 1953; Ewing Lecturer, University of California, Berkeley, 1956. Recipient: Hartsock Memorial Prize, 1935; Shelley Memorial Award, 1941; Harriet Monroe Poetry Award, 1944; Guggenheim Fellowship, 1945; National Institute of Arts and Letters grant, 1946, and Gold Medal, 1953; Pulitzer Prize, 1952; National Book Award, 1952; Bollingen Prize, 1953; Poetry Society of America Gold Medal, 1960, 1967; Brandeis University Creative Arts Award, 1963; Academy of American Poets Fellowship, 1965; MacDowell Medal, 1967; National Medal for Literature, 1968. Litt.D.: Wilson College, Chambersburg, Pennsylvania, 1949; Mount Holyoke College, South Hadley, Massachusetts, 1950; University of Rochester, New York, 1951; L.H.D.: Rutgers University, New Brunswick, New Jersey, 1955; Smith College, Northampton, Massachusetts, 1955; Pratt Institute, Brooklyn, New York, 1959; D.Litt.: New York University, 1967; Washington University, St. Louis, Missouri, 1967; Harvard University, Cambridge, Massachusetts, 1969. Member, American Academy of Arts and Letters, 1955. *Died 5 February 1972.*

PUBLICATIONS

Verse

Poems. 1921.
Observations. 1924.
Selected Poems. 1935.
The Pangolin and Other Verse. 1936.
What Are Years? 1941.
Nevertheless. 1944.
Collected Poems. 1951.
Like a Bulwark. 1956.
O to Be a Dragon. 1959.
Eight Poems. 1962.
The Arctic Ox. 1964.
Tell Me, Tell Me: Granite, Steel, and Other Topics. 1966.
The Complete Poems. 1967.
Unfinished Poems. 1972.

Play

The Absentee, from a story by Maria Edgeworth. 1962.

Other

Predilections. 1955.
Idiosyncracy and Technique: Two Lectures. 1958.
Letters from and to the Ford Motor Company, with David Wallace. 1958.
A Moore Reader. 1961.
Dress and Kindred Subjects. 1965.
Poetry and Criticism. 1965.

Editor, with W. H. Auden and Karl Shapiro, Riverside Poetry 1953: Poems by Students in Colleges and Universities in New York City. 1953.

Translator, with Elizabeth Mayer, Rock Crystal: A Christmas Tale, by Adalbert Stifter. 1945.
Translator, The Fables of La Fontaine. 1954; Selected Fables, 1955.
Translator, Puss in Boots, The Sleeping Beauty, and Cinderella: A Retelling of Three Classic Fairy Tales, by Charles Perrault. 1963.

Bibliography: Moore: A Descriptive Bibliography by Craig S. Abbott, 1977.

Reading List: The Achievement of Moore: A Biography, 1907–1957 by Eugene P. Sheehy and Kenneth A. Lohf, 1958; Moore by Bernard F. Engel, 1964; Moore by Jean Garrigue, 1965; Moore: An Introduction to the Poetry by George W. Nitchie, 1969; Moore by Sister M. Thérèse, 1969; Moore: A Collection of Critical Essays edited by Charles Tomlinson, 1970; Moore: The Cage and the Animal by Donald Hall, 1970; Moore: Poet of Affection by Pamela White Hadas, 1977.

*   *   *

Marianne Moore seems the best poet of her sex to have written in the United States during this century. Her poetry is richer and more inclusive than that of H. D. or of Elizabeth Bishop, to name two who resemble her in their fastidious interest in natural history – Miss Moore's predilection and habitual material. Herself of the modernist generation of Stevens, Williams, Pound, and Eliot, she knew Williams, Pound, and H. D. in her days at Bryn Mawr College; and in the 1920's she was associated with the New York magazine *The Dial*, becoming its editor from 1926 to 1929. Like Williams, she was a naturalist in her subject-matter, and would not have disagreed with Pound's programme for Imagism. Many of the American modernist poets learned to purge their beams at her empirical eye. Yet Eliot, who could not have accepted William's *dictum* "No ideas but in things," also admired Marianne Moore's poetry for the distinction of its language. In his preface to her *Selected Poems*, he judged that she was "one of those few who have done the language some service in my lifetime."

Marianne Moore appears at first an idiosyncratic writer. She chooses odd subjects and sees them from odd angles; she is miscellaneous in her subject-matter and unpredictable in her reflections; she writes in a chopped prose in lines of spectacular irregularity, but with metrical distinctness and, surprisingly often, rhyme. Yet her style, for all its asymmetry, is rapid, clear, unself-concerned, flexible, and accurate, and her work gradually discloses her exceptional sanity, intelligence, and imaginative depth. Unmistakably modern, she has no modernist formlessness; curious and precise, she is too brave in her vision to be an old maid. Some of these paradoxical qualities appear in her openings, which demand attention by their directness, as in "The Steeple-Jack":

> Dürer would have seen a reason for living
>   in a town like this, with eight stranded whales
> to look at; with the sweet sea air coming into your house
> on a fine day, from water etched
>   with waves as formal as the scales
> on a fish.

or "Silence":

> My father used to say,
> "Superior people never make long visits,
> have to be shown Longfellow's grave
> or the glass flowers at Harvard.
> Self-reliant like the cat –
> that takes its prey to privacy,
> the mouse's limp tail hanging like a shoelace from its mouth –
> they sometimes enjoy solitude..."

or "To a Snail":

> If "compression is the first grace of style,"
> you have it. Contractility is a virtue
> as modesty is a virtue.

or "Poetry":

> I, too, dislike it.
>   Reading it, however, with a perfect contempt for it, one discovers in
> it, after all, a place for the genuine.

This last is a complete poem, and unusually brief, although most of her poems are meditations of this characteristic briskness. "The Steeple-Jack" is a classic among her longer poems, as is "A Grave," which begins:

> Man looking into the sea,
> taking the view from those who have as much right to it as you have to it yourself,
> it is human nature to stand in the middle of a thing,
> but you cannot stand in the middle of this;
> the sea has nothing to give but a well excavated grave.

The resonance of that last line states openly, with "an elegance of which the source is not bravado," the essential seriousness which Marianne Moore often took pains to bury deep in her bright-eyed concern with the external world, of which she was such a connoisseur. Like La Fontaine, whose *Fables* she translated, she was fundamentally a humane moralist, however passionate and fine her observation of animals, baseball-players, and nature's remoter aspects; and she was fundamentally serious despite her turn for the smacking epigram.

Her career illuminated the American scene for an exceptionally long time, and to increasing recognition. Her powers did not diminish, but her idiosyncrasy and allusiveness intensified. Thoroughly American and modern, she demonstrated the possibility of a highly civilised and eclectic mind operating with discrimination and unsentimental enjoyment on the premise basic to so much modern American poetry, that everything that is human is material for poetry: "Whatever it is, let it be without/affectation" ("Love in America").

—M. J. Alexander

MOORE, T(homas) Sturge. English. Born in Hastings, Sussex, 4 March 1870; brother of the philosopher G. E. Moore. Educated at Dulwich College to age 14; Croydon and Lambeth art schools. Married Marie Appia in 1903; one son and one daughter. Author, art historian, and wood engraver. Member, Academic Committee, Royal Society of Literature. Granted Civil List pension, 1920. *Died 18 July 1944.*

PUBLICATIONS

Verse

Two Poems. 1893.
The Vinedresser and Other Poems. 1899.
Danaë. 1903.
The Centaur's Booty. 1903.
The Rout of the Amazons. 1903.
The Gazelles and Other Poems. 1904.
Pan's Prophecy. 1904.
To Leda and Other Odes. 1904.

Theseus, Medea, and Lyrics. 1904.
The Little School: A Posy of Rhymes. 1905; revised edition, 1917.
The Sea Is Kind. 1914.
Danaë, Aforetime, Blind Thamyris. 1920.
Judas. 1923.
Mystery and Tragedy: Two Dramatic Poems. 1930.
Nine Poems. 1930.
The Poems. 4 vols., 1931–33.
Selected Poems, edited by Marie Sturge Moore. 1934.
The Unknown and Known, and a Dozen Odd Poems. 1939.

Plays

Aphrodite Against Artemis (produced 1906). 1901.
Absalom: A Chronicle Play. 1903.
Mariamne. 1911.
A Sicilian Idyll, and Judith: A Conflict. 1911.
Judith: A Conflict (produced 1916). In *A Sicilian Idyll, and Judith,* 1911.
The Wilderness, with Gustave Ferrari (produced 1915).
Tragic Mothers: Medea, Niobe, Tyrfing. 1920.
Medea (produced 1924). In *Tragic Mothers,* 1920.
The Powers of the Air. 1920.
Roderigo of Bivar. 1925.
Bee-Bee-Bei, music by Edmund Rubbra (produced 1933).

Other

Altdorfer. 1900.
A Brief Account of the Origin of the Eragny Press, and a Note on the Relation of the Printed Book as a Work of Art to Life. 1903.
Albert Dürer. 1905.
Correggio. 1906.
Art and Life (essays). 1910.
Hark to These Three Talk about Style. 1915.
Some Soldier Poets. 1919.
(Woodcuts). 1921.
Armour for Aphrodite (aesthetics). 1929.
Yeats and Moore: Their Correspondence 1901–1937, edited by Ursula Bridge. 1953.
Contributions to the Art of the Book and Collaboration with Yeats, edited by Malcolm Easton. 1970.

Editor, *The Passionate Pilgrim and the Songs in Shakespeare's Plays.* 1896.
Editor, *The Vale Shakespeare.* 39 vols., 1900–03.
Editor, *Little Engravings.* 1902.
Editor, *Poems from Wordsworth.* 1902.
Editor, *A Selection from the Poems of Michael Field.* 1923.
Editor, with D. C. Sturge Moore, *Works and Days, from the Journal of Michael Field.* 1933.
Editor, with Cecil Lewis, *Self-Portrait, Taken from the Journals and Letters of Charles Ricketts, R.A.* 1939.

Translator, *The Centaur, The Bacchante,* by Maurice de Guérin. 1899.

Reading List: *Moore and the Life of Art* by F. L. Gwynn, 1951 (includes bibliography).

*   *   *

T. Sturge Moore was educated at Croydon Art School where he met Charles Shannon, and by Shannon was persuaded to proceed to Lambeth Art School where Shannon's associate Charles Ricketts was teaching. By 1888 Moore was part of Rickett's "Vale" circle and contributed poems, woodcuts, and wood engravings to such periodicals as Rickett's *Dial* and Shannon and Gleeson White's *Pageant*. His first and best volume of verse, *The Vinedresser and Other Poems*, appeared in 1899. Though he published prolifically both poetry and poetic drama, he never won popular acclaim, though respected by fellow practitioners. Laurence Binyon early on pointed out the limitations of Moore's style, which were never overcome: a deficiency in clean phrasing, a choke of consonants, and obscurity of syntax. His subject matter was invariably remote, ideal, literary. He was, however, skilled in the evocation of colourful and densely realised Arcadian scenes which reflect the enthusiasm of the autodidact for classical story. He was also a great reviser of earlier poets' work, an interesting mode of composition, and one which has been recently practiced by such poets as George MacBeth.

Moore, as befitted the brother of the distinguished Cambridge philosopher G. E. Moore, was something of aesthetician. His *Art and Life* elaborates a comparison between Flaubert and Blake, somewhat in Flaubert's favour; *Armour for Aphrodite* develops his theory of beauty as creative tension – like Yeats he adds the element of struggle to the Paterian aesthetic. Moore was a skilled designer of books and bookplates. His design for *Axel* is brilliantly complex in the Ricketts manner, while his series of covers for Yeats's later poems were composed in accordance with programmes suggested by the poet. The letters he exchanged with Yeats in the later 1920's and the 1930's are fascinating examples of Moore's gifts for philosophical argument besides radiating flashes of critical insight.

—Ian Fletcher

MOORE, Thomas. Irish. Born in Dublin, 28 May 1779. Educated at Whyte's School, Dublin 1786–93; Dr. Carr's Latin School, Dublin, 1794; Trinity College, Dublin, 1795–98, B.A. 1799; Middle Temple, London, 1799. Married Bessie Dyke in 1811; three daughters and two sons. Appointed Admiralty Registrar in Bermuda, 1803: after visiting the islands, and America, committed his official duties to a deputy and returned to England, 1806; became a popular and fashionable songwriter in England, and national lyricist of Ireland with publication of *Irish Melodies*, 1808–34; met Lord Byron, 1811; made liable for funds his deputy in Bermuda had embezzled, and travelled to Italy and France to avoid arrest, 1819; given memoirs by Byron in Venice; returned to England, when the Bermuda debt had been settled, 1822, and retired to Bowood, Wiltshire; destroyed Byron's memoirs, 1824, but published a life of Byron, 1830; worked on his *History of Ireland* until 1846. Granted Civil List pension, 1835. *Died 25 February 1852.*

PUBLICATIONS

Collections

Memoirs, *Journal, and Correspondence*, edited by Lord John Russell.   8 vols., 1853–56; *Journal* edited by Peter Quennell, 1964.

The Poetical Works, edited by A. D. Godley. 1910
Letters, edited by Wilfred S. Dowden. 2 vols., 1964.

Verse

Odes of Anacreon. 1800.
The Poetical Works of the Late Thomas Little, Esq. 1801.
A Candid Appeal to Public Confidence. 1803.
Songs and Glees. 1804(?).
Epistles, Odes, and Other Poems. 1806.
Corruption and Intolerance: Two Poems with Notes, Addressed to an Englishman by an Irishman. 1808.
A Selection of Irish Melodies, with Symphonies and Accompaniments, music by John Stevenson and Henry Bishop. 10 vols. and supplement, 1808–34; words alone published as Irish Melodies, 1822.
The Sceptic: A Philosophical Satire. 1809.
A Melologue upon National Music. 1811.
Parody of a Celebrated Letter. 1812.
Intercepted Letters; or, The Two-Penny Post-Bag. 1813.
Sacred Songs. 2 vols., 1816–24.
Lalla Rookh: An Oriental Romance. 1817.
The Fudge Family in Paris. 1818.
National Airs. 6 vols., 1818–27.
Melodies, Songs, Sacred Songs, and National Airs. 1818.
The Loves of the Angels. 1823; revised edition, as The Loves of the Angels: An Eastern Romance, 1823.
Fables for the Holy Alliance; Rhymes for the Road. 1823.
Evenings in Greece. 2 vols., 1826–32.
Odes upon Cash, Corn, Catholics, and Other Matters, Selected from Columns of the Times Journal. 1828.
The Summer Fête: A Poem with Songs. 1831.
The Fudges in England, Being a Sequel to The Fudge Family in Paris. 1835.
Alciphron: A Poem, with The Epicurean, illustrated by J. M. W. Turner. 1839.
The Poetical Works. 10 vols., 1840–41.

Plays

The Gipsy Prince, music by Michael Kelly (produced 1801). 1801.
M.P.; or, The Blue Stocking, music by the author (produced 1811). 1811.
Montbar; or, The Buccaneers. 1804.

Fiction

The Epicurean. 1827.

Other

A Letter to the Roman Catholics of Dublin. 1810.
Tom Crib's Memorial to Congress (includes verse). 1819.
Memoirs of Captain Rock, the Celebrated Irish Chieftain. 1824.

Memoirs of the Life of Richard Brinsley Sheridan. 1825.
Letters and Journals of Lord Byron, with Notices of His Life. 2 vols., 1830.
The Life and Death of Lord Edward Fitzgerald. 2 vols., 1831.
Travels of an Irish Gentleman in Search of a Religion. 2 vols., 1833.
The History of Ireland. 4 vols., 1835–46.
Notes from the Letters of Moore to His Music Publisher, James Power, edited by T. C. Croker. 1854.
Prose and Verse, Humorous, Satirical, and Sentimental, with Suppressed Passages from the Memoirs of Lord Byron, edited by R. H. Shepherd. 1878.

Bibliography: *A Bibliographical Hand-List of the First Editions of Moore* by M. J. MacManus, 1934.

Reading List: *The Harp that Once* (biography) by Howard Mumford Jones, 1937; *Moore* by Miriam A. De Ford, 1967; *Bolt Upright: The Life of Moore* by Judith Wilt, 2 vols., 1975; *Moore, The Irish Poet* by Terence de Vere White, 1977.

*   *   *

No poet of his age enjoyed greater contemporary popularity than Thomas Moore. His reputation was based primarily on his long oriental poem *Lalla Rookh* and on lyrics written for traditional melodies. The former is largely (and perhaps justifiably) ignored, while his mastery of the song lyric is now generally recognized.

During his lifetime ten editions (or "numbers") of his *Irish Melodies* were published from 1808 through 1834. Arrangements and "accompaniments" for the melodies were made by Sir John Stevenson and Sir Henry Bishop, two of the most successful musicians of their day. He also produced a collection of *National Airs* (consisting mostly of lyrics written for traditional continental music) and of *Sacred Songs.* George Thomson, a pioneer in the field of collecting and arranging melodies of England, Scotland, Wales, and Ireland, asked Moore to contribute verses to his massive collection of airs; but he never produced music which satisfied the meticulous lyricist. Moore and Robert Burns (who did write for Thomson) must be placed at the top of the list of those who worked in this genre.

Moore also wrote satire, some of which would have enjoyed lasting success had it not been primarily occasional in nature. Nevertheless, his wit and satiric irony can be seen in the "squibs" and "lampoons" he wrote for the *Morning Chronicle* and other London newspapers and in his verse satire in epistolary from entitled *The Fudge Family in Paris.*

Irish nationalism is a recurring theme in his work. Most of the *Irish Melodies* have as their purpose the awakening of national consciousness, and such prose works as the *Memoirs of Captain Rock* and his *Letter to the Roman Catholics of Dublin* deal with Irish patriotism and Catholic Emancipation.

Moore's biographies of Richard Brinsley Sheridan and Lord Edward Fitzgerald, which are still mined for their contemporary insights, are examples of the best of nineteenth-century biography. His life of Byron compares favorably with Lockhart's *Life of Scott* as a highly respectable and still respected memoir of a major literary figure. Add to these works his four-volume *History of Ireland,* written for Dr. Lardner's *Cabinet Encyclopedia,* and his contributions to such literary journals as the *Edinburgh Review* and we see that he produced a body of prose work almost equal to that of his poetry. He was offered the editorship of the *Edinburgh Review* and was once asked to take on the task of writing lead articles for the *Times.*

There seems little doubt that the discovery of the MS and the publication of Moore's Journal offers a new perspective on the Irish poet. The modern edition restores passages bowdlerized by the first editor, Lord John Russell, and tends to justify Terence de Vere White's tribute to him as "after Daniel O'Connell, the greatest Irishman of his day."

—Wilfred S. Dowden

MORAES, Dom(inic Frank). Indian. Born in Bombay, 19 July 1938; son of Frank Moraes, editor of the *Indian Express*. Educated at Jesus College, Oxford, 1956–59, B.A. in English 1959. Married 1) Judith St. John in 1963 (divorced), one son; 2) Leela Naidu in 1970. Formerly, scriptwriter, Granada Television; Documentary Filmmaker. Since 1971, Editor, *The Asian Magazine*, Hong Kong. Since 1973, Consultant, United Nations Fund for Population Activities. Recipient: Hawthornden Prize, 1958.

PUBLICATIONS

Verse

A Beginning. 1957.
Poems. 1960.
John Nobody. 1965.
Poems 1955–1965. 1966.
Bedlam Etcetera. 1966.

Other

Green Is the Grass (on cricket). 1951.
Gone Away: An Indian Journal. 1960.
My Son's Father: An Autobiography. 1968; as *My Son's Father: A Poet's Autobiography,* 1969.
The Tempest Within: An Account of East Pakistan. 1971.
From East and West: A Collection of Essays. 1971.
A Matter of People. 1974; as *This Burdened Planet,* 1974.

Editor, *Voices for Life: Reflections on the Human Condition.* 1975.

Translator, *The Brass Serpent,* by T. Carmi. 1964.

*   *   *

Dom Moraes, the son of the distinguished journalist and writer Frank Moraes, is in several ways an interesting literary figure. One of the best known Indian poets writing in English, there is in his poetry, paradoxically, very little of specific "Indianness." In fact, as he himself put it once: "English is the language I think in and write in; I even dream in it ... I don't speak any Indian language – neither Hindi nor my native Konkani." And he spent the most formative years of his life – from 15 to 30 – in England.

Moraes's poetic talent has been an extremely precocious one: at eighteen, he won the Hawthornden Prize for his first collection of poems, *A Beginning*; his second, *Poems*, was a Poetry Book Society choice. The most remarkable quality of his poetry is an unusual combination of romantic naivety with a deep, underlying ironic thrust. This stems from a recurring feeling of loneliness threatening, in the initial stages, to become obsessive self-indulgence: "I have grown up, I think, to live alone,/To keep my old illusions, sometimes dream/Glumly that I am unloved and forlorn ..." ("Autobiography"). This apparently "fluent sentimentality" in fact tempts one, as Harry Fainlight has put it (*Encounter*, November 1961) "to write the whole thing off as a luxury product, the lispings of an elite-poet." The naivety, however, is only apparent, for there is "deceptive strength in this kind of verse; having the courage of one's own naivety is a difficult and promising thing and certainly a much sounder basis for growth than the clever apeing of maturity ...."

This growth registers itself in his gradual awareness of contemporary reality: the loss of identity rendered acute by his dichotomous background as an Indian writing in English, the increasing eruption of violence and disorder. If the Indian landscape is dotted with "hawks," "doe-like girls, the sun, endless delay/Bullocks and Buicks, statesmen like great auks," ("John Nobody") and "the consumptive beggars" with "the thin voice of a shell" ("Gone Away"), he realizes that this is an extension of disorder all over, symbolized by such events as the trial of Milovan Djilas and the atrocities of the Nazis.

From this awareness of a searing landscape arises the insistent longing for love ("Except in you I have no rest/For always with you I am safe"), for the tranquil, almost mystical, vision. This is expressed with great subtlety in, for instance, "Bells for William Wordsworth," in which the Wordsworthian vision does not remain a mere academic exercise ("His work is carefully studied in colleges still") but becomes a significant mode for his own regaining of tranquillity: "I have seen him risen again with the crocus in Spring./I have turned my ear to the wind, I have heard him speaking." The longing for the tranquil vision, for Moraes, is innate to the poet's vocation itself, his preoccupation with words: "I have spent several years fighting with words/And they fight back with words that perplex" ("A Small Whimper"). And eventually it is art that encapsules reality in a deathless way; for, like the stranger catching a "glimpse" of "the miles-off sea" even in the midst of ruins ("kanheri caves"), art ensures resurrection.

Poetry seems to Moraes, however, aesthetically to insulate one from the rough and tumble of life. Probably this accounts for his constant roving and, like V. S. Naipaul, interspersing his creative with non-fictional writing: travelogue, reportage, film-making. *Gone Away* (a record of his travel in India) and *My Son's Father* (autobiography) are written with great subtlety and insight and seem inalienable parts of his creative writing itself.

Moraes's weakness as a poet, however, seems to be the lack of a controlling, focussing centre. In spite of his work's wide-ranging implications, arising out of the incorporation of myth, anthropology, and medieval references, there is an absence of firm roots. Hence the irritating sense of non-belonging perceptible in his poetry.

—M. Sivaramakrishna

MORRIS, William. English. Born in Walthamstow, London, 24 March 1834. Educated at preparatory school in Walthamstow, 1843–47; Marlborough College, 1848–51; privately, 1851–53; Exeter College, Oxford, 1853–55. Member, Artists Corps of Volunteers, 1859–61. Married Jane Burden in 1859; two daughters. Staff Member, G. E. Street's architectural firm, Oxford and London, 1856; associated with the *Oxford and Cambridge Magazine*, 1856;

practising painter, 1857–62; Founding Member, design firm of Morris, Marshall, Faulkner and Company, London, 1861–74, subsequently Morris and Company, 1874–96; Founder, Kelmscott Press, London, 1890–96. Founder Member, Socialist League, 1884, Editor of its journal, *Commonweal*, 1884–90, and League Delegate to the International Socialist Working Men's Congress, Paris, 1889; Founding Member, Hammersmith Socialist Society, 1890. Examiner, South Kensington, later Victoria and Albert, Museum, London, 1876–96; President, Birmingham Society of Arts, 1878; Founding Member, and Secretary, 1877, Society for the Protection of Ancient Buildings; Master, Art Works Guild, 1892. Honorary Fellow, Exeter College, 1883. *Died 3 October 1896.*

PUBLICATIONS

Collections

> *Collected Works.*   24 vols., 1910–15; supplement, edited by May Morris, 2 vols., 1936.
> *Selected Writings and Designs,* edited by Asa Briggs.   1962.

Verse

> *The Defence of Guenevere and Other Poems.*   1858; edited by Robert Steele, 1904.
> *The Life and Death of Jason.*   1867; revised edition, 1867, 1882.
> *The Earthly Paradise.*   3 vols., 1868–70; revised edition, 1890.
> *Love Is Enough: or, The Freeing of Pharamond: A Morality.*   1872.
> *The Story of Sigurd the Volsung and the Fall of the Niblungs.*   1876.
> *Chants for Socialists.*   1885.
> *The Pilgrims of Hope.*   1886.
> *A Tale of the House of the Wolfings and All the Kindreds of the Mark* (prose and verse).   1889.
> *Poems by the Way.*   1891.

Play

> *The Tables Turned; or, Nupkins Awakened: A Socialist Interlude* (produced 1887).   1887.

Fiction

> *A Dream of John Ball, and A King's Lesson.*   1888.
> *The Roots of the Mountain, Wherein Is Told Somewhat of the Lives of the Men of Burgdale.*   1890.
> *News from Nowhere; or, An Epoch of Rest, Being Some Chapters from a Utopian Romance.*   1890.
> *The Story of the Glittering Plain Which Has Been Also Called the Land of Living Men, or the Acre of the Undying.*   1891.
> *The Wood Beyond the World.*   1894.
> *Child Christopher and Goldilind the Fair.*   1895.
> *The Well at the World's End.*   1896.
> *The Water of the Wondrous Isles.*   1897.
> *The Sundering Flood.*   1897.

Other

Hopes and Fears for Art (lectures). 1882.

Lectures on Art. 1882.

A Summary of the Principles of Socialism Written for the Democratic Federation, with H. M. Hyndman. 1884.

The Manifesto of the Socialist League. 1885; revised edition, 1885.

The Socialist League: Constitution and Rules. 1885.

The Aims of Art. 1887.

Signs of Change (lectures). 1888.

Socialist Platform (collected pamphlets), with others. 1888; revised edition, 1890.

Statement of Principles of the Hammersmith Socialist Society. 1891.

The Reward of Labour: A Dialogue. 1893.

Letters on Socialism. 1894.

How I Became a Socialist. 1896.

Architecture, Industry, and Wealth: Collected Papers. 1902.

Communism. 1903.

Letters to His Family and Friends, edited by Philip Henderson. 1950.

Unpublished Letters, edited by R. P. Arnot. 1951.

Early Romances in Prose and Verse, edited by Peter Faulkner. 1973.

Political Writings, edited by A. L. Morton. 1973.

Translator, with Eiríkr Magnússon, *Grettis Saga: The Story of Grettir the Strong* 1869.

Translator, with Eiríkr Magnússon, *Völsunga Saga: The Story of the Volsungs and Niblungs with Certain Songs from the Elder Edda.* 1870; edited by H. Sparling, 1888.

Translator, with Eiríkr Magnússon, *Three Northern Love Stories and Other Tales.* 1875.

Translator, *The Aeneid of Virgil.* 1875.

Translator, *The Odyssey of Homer.* 2 vols., 1887.

Translator, with Eiríkr Magnússon, *The Saga Library.* 5 vols., 1890–95.

Translator, *The Order of Chivalry,* by Hugues de Tabarie. 1893.

Translator, *The Tale of King Florus and the Fair Jehane.* 1893.

Translator *Of the Friendship of Amis and Amile.* 1894.

Translator, *The Tale of the Emperor Constans and of Over Sea.* 1894.

Translator, with A. J. Wyatt, *The Tale of Beowulf.* 1895.

Bibliography: *A Bibliography of the Works of Morris* by Temple Scott, 1897; *Handlist of the Public Addresses of Morris* by R. C. H. Briggs, 1961.

Reading List: *The Life of Morris* by J. W. Mackail, 2 vols., 1899; *Morris: Medievalist and Revolutionary* by Margaret Grennan, 1945; *Morris: Romantic to Revolutionary,* 1955, and *Morris* (biography), 1977, both by Edward P. Thompson; *Morris and Yeats* by Peter Faulkner, 1962, and *Morris: The Critical Heritage* edited by Faulkner, 1973; *Morris: The Man and the Myth* by R. P. Arnot, 1964; *The Work of Morris* by Paul Thompson, 1967; *The Pastoral Vision of Morris: The Earthly Paradise* by Bruce Calhoun, 1974; *Morris* by Jack Lindsay, 1975; *Conversations with Morris: Critical Views and Responses* edited by Robert E. Knoll, 1977.

*   *   *

William Morris was nothing less than a lyric and narrative poet of considerable talent and

719

originality; a writer, early in his career, of Pre-Raphaelite prose romances, and, later, of visionary Socialist prose; and a literary critic whose work includes reviews of many of his contemporaries and numerous essays on the aims and nature of art; as well as a designer, publisher, printer, translator, and political essayist and speaker. His work relates closely to diverse spheres and personages of culture to which various strands in his biography attest. As a poet he shows particular knowledge of Chaucer, Keats, Tennyson, Browning, and the Norse sagas. His early criticism and prose reflect the moral emphases of Ruskin and Carlyle, *and* the aestheticism of Rossetti and the Pre-Raphaelites which also influenced his early visual art. He eventually came to be embroiled in the worlds of architectural conservation, book and industrial design, and English Socialism. He was offered the post of Oxford Professor of Poetry (1877) and sounded for the Laureateship (1892), both of which he refused. Due to his diversity perhaps, curricula and critics tend to ignore him completely, or to emphasize a single facet of his work, and to see him largely as a part of some larger movement (thus we have Morris the Pre-Raphaelite artist, Morris of Morris and Co., Morris the aesthetic poet, and Morris the Socialist). These partial views have practically obscured the considerable achievement of the man as a whole, and readers are ill advised to dismiss the poet in favour of the Socialist, artist, designer, or critic; his formidable stature emerges from the rich combination.

From his earliest work, Morris's art was social and rebellious, and it reflected his later conviction that "art [was] the one certain solace of labour" (*How I Became a Socialist*). Inspired by *The Germ*, the magazine of the first rebel Pre-Raphaelites, Morris, Burne-Jones, and others founded the *Oxford and Cambridge Magazine* in 1856, and two of Morris's contributions, the fabular prose romances "Frank's Sealed Letter" and "Svend and his Brethren," depict vision or dream as related effectively to dynamic societies. Even in the Pre-Raphaelite poems to follow, the dreams are not simply escapist but critical comments on society.

The Defence of Guenevere and Other Poems shows Morris availing himself of the dramatic monologue, romance, and lyric already explored by Browning and Tennyson, but the setting of these striking poems is largely medieval, the detail vivid and Pre-Raphaelite, the language archaic and simplified, the mood (particularly in the poems clearly indebted to Froissart, "The Haystack in the Floods," "Concerning Geffray Teste Noire," and "Sir Peter Harpdon's End"), more violent, sexual, and stark. While Browning defended the "good minute" in "The Statue and the Bust" even when it involved adultery, the setting was Renaissance Italy; but Morris wages the argument in the more sacrosanct Arthurian (and Tennysonian) province, with Guenevere voicing the defence of an ambiguous but defiant "belle dame":

> Must I give up for ever then, I thought,
> That which I deemed would ever round me move
> Glorifying all things....

Her choice clearly affects society adversely, but is also its product: "I was bought/By Arthur's great name and his little love."

The Golden Age in the earlier Morris is fraught with difficulty, weariness, and guilt as well as with nobility and beauty, but in the later work, after *The Earthly Paradise*, weariness does not dominate, and hope supplements the energy of his vision. While the Golden Age is natural and minimally mechanized, it is not usually exclusive of pain, death, or history, as can be seen in *A Dream of John Ball*. It is normally out of the present, medieval or earlier (sometimes childhood), in the future, or coexistent with the present in dream or vision. But in it Morris implies an alternative to contemporary society, and criticism of it.

Overall, in the energy of his vision of resistance to the ills of Victorian society, Morris is akin to Browning. Not for him is the austere affirmation or laboured faith of the best Tennyson, or the closed despair of Arnold. The scale and subject of *The Earthly Paradise* project – in which Morris grouped twenty-four long narrative poems of Greek and medieval tales depicting searches for paradise in a Chaucerian framework whereby the tales are told over twelve months – clearly indicate pitfalls of escapism and unevenness. But in the month poems Morris memorably expresses the locked ironies of "modern love," with a success only equalled in his time by Meredith and Hardy. He voices too his growing disenchantment with the limitations of the romantic poet, "the idle singer," and his audience, the "empty day": Matthew Arnold's high culture was disdained by Morris who later, in 1879, wrote "real art is the expression by man of his pleasure in labour" ("The Art of the People" in *Hopes and Fears for Art*). And of the Victorian poets who looked to the long narrative, Morris's development of Old Icelandic and Norse saga material, which began with "The Lovers of Gudrun" in *The Earthly Paradise* and culminated in *Sigurd the Volsung*, is notable and comparable with Arnold's "Balder Dead," Tennyson's Idylls, and Browning's *The Ring and the Book*.

In the early 1880's when Morris became a Socialist, he experimented with a new poetry in *Chants for Socialists*, and in the more literary poems of *The Pilgrims of Hope* Morris explains his change of poetic direction:

> Yea, but life is no longer as stories of yore;
> From us from henceforth no fair words shall be hiding
> The nights of the wretched, the days of the poor.

During the last ten years of his life Morris wrote two prose dream narratives in which he interpreted the significance of the present and the curve of history through an examination of the past (*A Dream of John Ball* which is set during the Peasants' Revolt of 1381) and of the future (*News from Nowhere*). Both reflect Morris's lifelong attachment to medieval "barbarism" and romantic nature, distaste for industrial civilization, eye for concrete detail, and twin concern with comeliness and utility. Without ceding the strengths of Romanticism, Morris depicted a socialist vision of interest, wit, and colour.

His work constitutes one of the happier confrontations of Romanticism with Realism, and offers a vigorous and unstinting critique of Victorian literature and society.

—Laurel Brake

MUIR, Edwin. Scottish. Born in Deerness, Orkney, 15 May 1887. Educated at Kirkwall Burgh School, Orkney. Married Willa Anderson in 1919; one child. Worked in various commercial and ship building offices in Glasgow, and as a journalist and translator: Staff Member, *New Age*, London, 1919–21; lived in Prague after 1920; fiction reviewer, *The Listener*, 1933–45; Co-Editor, *The European Quarterly*, 1934; worked for the British Council in Edinburgh during World War II, in Prague, 1945–48, and Rome, 1948–50; Warden of Newbattle Abbey College, Dalkeith, 1950–55; Charles Eliot Norton Professor of Poetry, Harvard University, Cambridge, Massachusetts, 1955–56; retired to Swaffham Prior, near Cambridge, 1957; Visiting Winston Churchill Professor, University of Bristol, 1958. Recipient: Foyle Prize, 1950; Heinemann Award, 1953; Frederick Niven Literary Award, 1953; Russell Loines Award, 1957; Saltire Society Prize, 1957. Ph.D.: Charles University, Prague, 1947; LL.D.: University of Edinburgh, 1947; Docteur-ès-Lettres: University of Rennes, 1949; Litt.D.: University of Leeds, 1955; Cambridge University, 1958. Fellow, Royal Society of Literature, 1953. C.B.E. (Commander, Order of the British Empire), 1953. *Died 3 January 1959.*

Publications

Collections

> *Selected Poems.* 1965.
> *Selected Letters,* edited by P. H. Butter. 1974.

Verse

> *First Poems.* 1925.
> *Chorus of the Newly Dead.* 1926.
> *Six Poems.* 1932.
> *Variations on a Time Theme.* 1934.
> *Journeys and Places.* 1937.
> *The Narrow Place.* 1943.
> *The Voyage and Other Poems.* 1946.
> *The Labyrinth.* 1949.
> *Collected Poems 1921–1951,* edited by J. C. Hall. 1952.
> *Collected Poems 1921–1958,* edited by Willa Muir and J. C. Hall. 1960; revised edition, 1963.
> *One Foot in Eden.* 1956.

Fiction

> *The Marionette.* 1927.
> *The Three Brothers.* 1931.
> *Poor Tom.* 1932.

Other

> *We Moderns: Enigmas and Guesses.* 1918.
> *Latitudes.* 1924.
> *Transition: Essays on Contemporary Literature.* 1926.
> *The Structure of the Novel.* 1928.
> *John Knox: Portrait of a Calvinist.* 1929.
> *Scottish Journey.* 1935.
> *Social Credit and the Labour Party: An Appeal.* 1935.
> *Scott and Scotland: The Predicament of the Scottish Writer.* 1936.
> *The Present Age, from 1914.* 1939.
> *The Story and the Fable: An Autobiography.* 1940; revised edition, as *An Autobiography,* 1954.
> *The Scots and Their Country.* 1946.
> *Essays on Literature and Society.* 1949; augmented edition, 1965.
> *The Estate of Poetry* (lectures). 1962.

> Editor, with others, *Orion: A Miscellany 1–2.* 2 vols., 1945.
> Editor, *New Poets.* 1959.

> Translator, with Willa Muir, of more than 40 books by Kafka, Hermann Broch, Gerhart Hauptmann, Lion Feuchtwanger, Shalom Asch, Heinrich Mann, and other authors, 1925–48.

Bibliography: *Bibliography of the Writings of Muir* by Elgin W. Mellown, 1964, revised edition, 1966; *A Checklist of the Writings of Muir* by Elgin W. Mellown and Peter C. Hoy, 1971.

Reading List: *Muir* by J. C. Hall, 1956; *Muir*, 1962, and *Muir: Man and Poet,*1966, both by P. H. Butter; *Barbarous Knowledge: Myth in the Poetry of Yeats, Graves, and Muir* by Daniel Hoffman, 1967; *Belonging: A Memoir* by Willa Muir, 1969; *The Poetry of Muir: The Field of Good and Ill* by Elizabeth L. Haberman, 1971; *Verging on Another World: Notes Towards an Understanding of Muir's Poetry* by Martin Booth, 1978.

*   *   *

Not until he was over thirty did Edwin Muir recover from the need to protect himself from a hostile environment and regain something of his childhood's vividness of seeing. Then he was able to look back over the intervening period of sleep-walking, and in so doing to see not his "own life merely, but all human life," beneath the story of one man the fable of Man. His early poems are already expressions of this imaginative vision, but are limited in range and in skill. The language is sometimes stiff, the rhythms lacking in flexibility. Gradually he extended his range, finding value in the journey through the labyrinth of time as well as in the goal of a re-entered Eden, combining myth and dream with a profound understanding of what was happening immediately around him. Gradually his language and his rhythms became more flexible and varied. He remained open to experience until the end, and wrote a large proportion of his best poems when over sixty.

Stories are innumerable, the fable one. So to some Muir's poems, tending towards a common centre, appear monotonous. But they approach that centre from many points – from common things such as a dying wasp, a departing swallow, from ordinary human love ("The Confirmation") as well as from stranger experiences of neurosis ("The Strange Return") and dream vision ("The Combat," "The Transfiguration," "The Brothers"). At his best we have "the ordinary day" as well as "the deepening trance" in which Angel and girl, time and the timeless, meet ("The Annunciation"). Some would like more of the ordinary day, particular girls as well as "the girl." But in days when we are so often offered nothing but raw fragments of experience, that is a minor complaint. Everything in his work is distilled, seen imaginatively, meaningful.

Neither his language nor his rhythms draw attention to themselves, and anyone looking for great linguistic inventiveness or rhythmical excitement will be disappointed; but if one looks at subtle and slight changes of rhythm and the exact placing of ordinary words so as to control their meaning, one comes to see, with T. S. Eliot, that "possessed by his vision, he found, almost unconsciously, the right, the inevitable way of saying what he wanted to say."

Next in value to his poetry is his *Autobiography*, especially the early part of it originally published as *The Story and the Fable*. Written in beautifully lucid, quietly rhythmical prose, it does not tell of sensational events, but is nevertheless exciting, being felt as both strange and familiar. However different our particular experiences we yet feel his journey as our own. At the same time the book has, more than the poetry, the grittiness of actual life. Incidents, places, people are evoked with vivid particularity, as well as being felt as strangely representative.

Muir wrote over a thousand reviews as well as several volumes of literary and social criticism; and he and his wife translated over forty books, mostly from German. His criticism is given life by the same passionate search for values as is his creative work. In the 1920's, in a series of essays on contemporary writers, he wanted to examine "the assumptions on which people live, as well as those on which they could conceivably live"; and at the end of his life he was stressing above all the value of the imagination, not only as the main thing we look for in literature, but also as that which we most need in life in order to "apprehend ... living creatures in their individuality," and to see life whole and in proper proportion. Most of the best of his criticism is in *The Structure of the Novel* and in *Essays on Literature and Society*;

but even his ephemera, such as the fortnightly reviews of new novels in *The Listener*, has an extraordinarily high level of fairness, wit, quick perception of new merit, and sharp questioning of the merely fashionable.

Willa Muir, the better linguist, bore by far the larger share of the burden of translating. (Working separately from her he could make mistakes, as in his translations from Hölderlin's *Patmos*.) But they worked together on the translations from Kafka and Broch. Reading Kafka, he felt greatness in every sentence, and he despaired of being able to translate him without injury. "The word order of Kafka is naked and infallible," not only expressing meanings but "involved as part of it." In English the word order has to be changed, and an attempt made to write prose "as natural in the English way as his was in his own way." With Broch the problem is different. The style is self-consciously difficult – and different in each book of *The Sleepwalkers* – "the writer battling with his own style" to express the almost inexpressible and to mirror the disintegration of values which is his central subject. I cannot judge of their fidelity, but these translations are works of art in their own right, the making of them part of Muir's search for meaning.

None of Muir's three novels is satisfying as a whole, though all contain fine imaginative passages – for instance, the strange dreams and visions of Hans in *The Marionette*, David's dreams in *The Three Brothers*, Mansie's experience of a May Day parade in Glasgow and his encounter with a horse in *Poor Tom*. In them Muir's own past presses too strongly on a fictional structure too slight to contain and transform it. The right forms for this material were to be found in autobiography and in poetry.

—P. H. Butter

———————————

NAIDU, Sarojini (née Chattopadhyaya). Indian. Born in Hyderabad, 13 February 1879. Educated at Madrea University, Hyderabad; King's College, London; Girton College, Cambridge. Married M. G. Naidu in 1898; two sons and two daughters. Involved with the women's movement in India, and the welfare of Indian students: lectured widely in the chief cities of India on questions of social, religious, educational, and national progress; Member of the Bombay Municipality, 1923–29; one of the leaders of the political movement for the freedom of India; travelled throughout East Africa and South Africa on behalf of Indian settlers, 1924; Chairman of the Indian National Congress, 1925; lectured in the United States and Canada, 1928–29; took part in the Round Table Conference, London, 1931; Member, Government of India Deputation to South Africa, 1932; Acting Governor of the United Provinces, 1947. Chancellor, University of Allahabad. Recipient: Kaiser-i-Hind Medal, 1908. Fellow, Royal Society of Literature, 1914. *Died 3 March 1949.*

PUBLICATIONS

Verse

> *The Golden Threshold.* 1905.
> *The Bird of Time: Songs of Life, and Death, and the Spring.* 1912.
> *The Broken Wing: Songs of Love, Death, and Destiny, 1915–1916.* 1917.
> *The Sceptred Flute: Songs of India.* 1928.
> *Select Poems,* edited by H. G. Dalway Turnbull. 1930.
> *The Feather of the Dawn.* 1961.

Other

> *Speeches and Writings.* 1904(?); revised edition, 1925.
> *The Soul of India.* 1917.

Reading List: *Naidu: A Biography* by Padmini Sengupta, 1966.

* * *

Sarojini Naidu was born into a distinguished Bengali family. Her father, Dr. Aghorenath Chattopadhyaya, took his doctorate in Science from the University of Edinburgh in 1877. He was a pioneer in the field of education and founded the Nizam College at Hyderabad. He was also a linguist familiar with French, German, Urdu, and Hindi. Mrs. Naidu reflected in her career a comparable versatility. A sensitive poet, she was also a gifted speaker and an ardent nationalist, playing, as a close associate of Gandhi, a decisive role in the Indian freedom struggle. Above all, she was a rebel: defying all caste inhibitions, she married Dr. Govindarajulu Naidu, a non-Bengali and non-Brahmin.

Mrs. Naidu's poetic career, according to her own account, began early: "One day, when I was eleven, I was sighing over a sum in algebra: it *wouldn't* come right, but instead a whole poem came to me suddenly. I wrote it down." This poetic impulse acquired certitude and definition when she went to England in 1895 for further studies. Here the impact of writers such as Edmund Gosse was decisive. In fact, it was Gosse who advised her to avoid evoking "Anglo-Saxon sentiment in an Anglo-Saxon setting" which would condemn her poetry to derivative mediocrity. Instead, she should give, he felt, "some revelation of the heart of India, some sincere penetrating analysis of native passion."

This was a valuable suggestion and gave direction to Mrs. Naidu's emerging talent; her poetry began evidencing an impressive thematic and descriptive range. Her poetry ranges from exquisite vignettes of Indian life – "The Snake Charmers," "The Bangle-Sellers," "The Weavers" or "The Bazaars of Hyderabad" – to deeply metaphysical contemplation, as in "To a Buddha Seated on a Lotus." Whatever the subject, Mrs. Naidu shows an unusual eye for the descriptive detail and achieves remarkable success in presenting, as James H. Cousins has put it, "the amazing groupings of colour and form, human and natural, that make the surface of life in India a fascinating kaleidoscope." Mrs. Naidu's basic poetic stance, however, is invariably a delicate, almost näive, sense of romantic wonder and innocence, what Arthur Symons called "a bird-like quality," "a delicately evasive way of writing." This stemmed from, in Mrs. Naidu's own words, "a very fanciful and dreamy nature." This genteel romanticism probably explains her imperviousness to the modernist trends exemplified in the work of her contemporaries Yeats and Eliot. There is in her poetry a profusion of sentiment and images which, lacking an underlying logic of emotion, remain decorative. Even when the poem is ostensibly called "An Indian Love Song," what emerges is not so much specific "Indianness" but a plethora of images: "Like the perfume in the petals of a rose/Hides thy heart within my Bosom, O my love!/Like a garland, like a jewel, like a dove."

What is, however, remarkable in Mrs. Naidu's poetry is its prosodic virtuosity. She handled almost all the English metrical patterns – including difficult ones such as the dactylic – with ease. R. Parthasarathy credits her with "perhaps the finest ear among Indian poets for the sound of English," and cites "Palanguin-bearers" for its "springy and elastic steps":

> Lightly, O lightly we bear her along,
> She sways like a flower in the wind of our song;
> She skims like a bird on the foam of a stream,
> She floats like a laugh from the lips of a dream
> Gaily, O gaily we glide and we sing,
> We bear her along like a pearl on a string.

In effect, while Mrs. Naidu's poetry is fascinating in its evocation of the Indian landscape and prosodically excellent, it seems a bit cloying in its fulsome sentimentality.

—M. Sivaramakrishna

NASH, (Frederick) Ogden. American. Born in Rye, New York, 19 August 1902. Educated at St. George's School, Newport, Rhode Island, 1917–20; Harvard University, Cambridge, Massachusetts, 1920–21. Married Frances Rider Leonard in 1931; two daughters. Taught for one year at St. George's School, Newport; worked briefly as a bond salesman on Wall Street, 1924; worked in the editorial and publicity departments of Doubleday Doran, publishers, New York, 1925, and joined John Farrar and Stanley Rinehart when they left the firm to set up their own publishing house; Member, Editorial Staff, *The New Yorker* magazine; later retired from publishing to devote himself to his own writing. Recipient: Sarah Josepha Hale Award, 1964. Member, National Institute of Arts and Letters. *Died 19 May 1971.*

PUBLICATIONS

Collections

I Wouldn't Have Missed It: Selected Poems, edited by Linell Smith and Isabel Eberstadt. 1975.

Verse

Free Wheeling. 1931.
Hard Lines. 1931.
Hard Lines and Others. 1932.
Happy Days. 1933.
Four Prominent So and So's, music by Robert Armbruster. 1934; as *Four Prominent Bastards Are We,* 1934.
The Primrose Path. 1935.
The Bad Parents' Garden of Verse. 1936.
Bon Voyage. 1936.
I'm a Stranger Here Myself. 1938.
The Face Is Familiar: Selected Verse. 1940; revised edition, 1954.
Good Intentions. 1942.
The Nash Pocket Book. 1944.
Many Long Years Ago. 1945.
Selected Verse. 1946.
Nash's Musical Zoo. 1947.
Versus. 1949.
Family Reunion. 1950.
The Private Dining Room and Other New Verses. 1953.
You Can't Get There from Here. 1957.
Verses from 1929 On. 1959; as *Collected Verse from 1929 On,* 1961.
Scrooge Rides Again. 1960.
Everyone But Thee and Me. 1962.
Marriage Lines: Notes of a Student Husband. 1964.
The Mysterious Ouphe. 1965.
A Nash Omnibook. 1967.
Santa Go Home: A Case History for Parents. 1967.
There's Always Another Windmill. 1968.
Funniest Verses, edited by Dorothy Price. 1968.
Bed Riddance: A Posy for the Indisposed. 1970.
The Old Dog Barks Backwards. 1972.

Plays

One Touch of Venus, with S. J. Perelman, music by Kurt Weill, from *The Tinted Venus* by F. Anstey (produced 1943). 1944.
Sweet Bye and Bye (lyrics only), book by S. J. Perelman and Al Hirschfield, music by Vernon Duke (produced 1946).
Two's Company (lyrics only; revue) (produced 1952).
The Littlest Revue, with others (produced 1956).
The Beauty Part, with S. J. Perelman (produced 1961). 1963.

Screenplays: *The Firefly,* with Frances Goodrich and Albert Hackett, 1937; *The Shining Hour,* with Jane Murfin, 1938; *The Feminine Touch,* with George Oppenheimer and Edmund L. Hartmann, 1941.

Other

The Cricket of Carador (juvenile), with Joseph Alger.   1925.
Born in a Beer Garden; or, She Troupes to Conquer, with Christopher Morley and Cleon Throckmorton.   1930.
Parents Keep Out: Elderly Poems for Youngerly Readers (juvenile).   1951.
The Christmas That Almost Wasn't (juvenile).   1957.
The Boy Who Laughed at Santa Claus (juvenile).   1957.
Custard the Dragon (juvenile).   1959.
A Boy Is a Boy: The Fun of Being a Boy (juvenile).   1960.
Custard the Dragon and the Wicked Knight (juvenile).   1961.
The New Nutcracker Suite and Other Innocent Verses (juvenile).   1962.
Girls Are Silly (juvenile).   1962.
The Adventures of Isabel (juvenile).   1963.
A Boy and His Room (juvenile).   1963.
The Untold Adventures of Santa Claus (juvenile).   1964.
The Animal Garden (juvenile).   1965.
The Cruise of the Aardvark (juvenile).   1967.
The Scroobious Pip (juvenile), by Edward Lear (completed by Nash).   1968.

Editor, *Nothing But Wodehouse.*   1932.
Editor, *The Moon Is Shining Bright as Day: An Anthology of Good Humored Verse.*   1953.
Editor, *I Couldn't Help Laughing: Stories* (juvenile).   1957.
Editor, *Everybody Ought to Know: Verses Selected and Introduced.*   1961.

*   *   *

Ogden Nash's career as a writer of light verse began in the 1930's when he accepted defeat as a poet. Realizing that his serious verses were tongue-tied and sentimental, he began constructing a peculiar form of doggerel which broke all rules of symmetry and harmony in poetry. Lines grew as long as subway trains, capped by rhymes as outrageous as cocktail party chatter; philosophical questions were mocked by horse-sensical conclusions: "What is life? Life is stepping down a step or sitting on a chair,/And it isn't there." Though it wasn't great poetry, it made Nash America's most popular comic poet.

With these techniques, Nash was able to express poetically the plain-spoken American's frustration with poetic complication, as well as the conviction that, really, poetry is just prose that rhymes. (Or should be, Nash hints: "One thing that literature would be greatly the better for/Would be a more restricted use of simile and metaphor.") In the Introduction to the 1975 Nash collection *I Wouldn't Have Missed It,* Archibald MacLeish gave away the secret: "Nothing ... suggests the structure of verse but the rhymes" which are used baldly to shoehorn sentences into what looked like verse. Basing his poems not on the poetic line, but on the sentence, Nash became (in his work) a "wersifier" painting men, women, and society from their poetic backsides.

Like his wersification, Nash's subjects come straight out of everyday life: summer colds and Monday mornings, leaky faucets and crashing bores. He is assailed by the mundane torments of living, perplexed by the oddities and failings of human nature, and mystified by women, just as they are by men. Yet no matter how disastrous life may be, Nash reassures us that perhaps it isn't so bad after all: "When I consider how my life is spent,/I hardly ever repent."

—Walter Bode

NEILSON, (John) Shaw. Australian. Born in Peoria, South Australia. 22 February 1872. Educated at State School, Peoria; State School, Minimay, Victoria, 1885–86. Farmer in the bush country, 1902–22; also wrote for the *Bulletin*, Sydney, 1900, *The Book Fellow*, 1907 and from 1911, and *Clarion*, 1908; Messenger, Country Roads Board, Melbourne, 1928–41. Granted Commonwealth Literary Fund pension, 1922. *Died 12 May 1942.*

PUBLICATIONS

Collections

> *The Poems,* edited by A. R. Chisholm. 1965.

Verse

> *Heart of Spring.* 1919.
> *Ballad and Lyrical Poems.* 1923.
> *New Poems.* 1927.
> *Collected Poems,* edited by R. H. Croll. 1934.
> *Beauty Imposes: Some Recent Verse.* 1938.
> *Unpublished Poems,* edited by James Devaney. 1947.
> *Witnesses of Spring: Unpublished Poems,* edited by Judith Wright. 1970.

Bibliography: *Neilson: An Annotated Bibliography and Checklist 1893–1964* by Hugh Anderson, 1964.

Reading List: *Neilson* by James Devaney, 1944; *Neilson* by Judith Wright, 1963 (biography and selected verse); *Neilson* by H. J. Oliver, 1968; *Neilson* by Hugh Anderson and L.J. Blake, 1972.

*   *   *

Shaw Neilson's work is hard to characterize. He is purely a lyrical poet, and his subjects are those of traditional lyric: the cycle of natural renewal, love, the spring, the beauty and pathos of young girls, children, the way of the animals as superior to the ways of men. Although he knew and loved the Australian back country, his poetry is not particularly tinged with local colour; his tone is not assertively tough nor is he in search of the Australian identity. In a sense, his poems could have emerged from several cultures: delicately mystical, occasionally reminiscent of Blake, or Walter de la Mare, or, in a poem like "The Long Week End" with the colloquially bitter-sweet irony of its refrain, calling to mind John Crowe Ransom:

> Sweet is the white, they say, she will ascend
> To an unstinted country where the days
> Gone without malice there she stays and stays
> Upon the long weekend.

His central poem, "The Orange Tree," is pure poetry, language at its most literary and innocent, the Tree representing the eternal life cycle. The poem is a dialogue between a young girl who hears the deep words of the tree and a sophisticated interlocutor who tries futilely to match his questions with the "mystery" of life, and who is imperatively silenced by the girl at the end of the poem, where questioning is stilled in affirmation:

> Listen! the young girl said. For all
>   Your hapless talk you fail to see
> There is a light, a step, a call
>   This evening in the Orange Tree.
>
> Is it, I said, a waste of love
>   Imperishably old in pain,
> Moving as an affrighted dove
>   Under the sunlight or the rain? ...
>
> Silence! The young girl said. Oh, why
>   Why will you talk to weary me?
> Plague me no longer now for I
>   Am listening like the Orange Tree.

—Ian Fletcher

NEMEROV, Howard. American. Born in New York City, 1 March 1920. Educated at Fieldston School, New York; Harvard University, Cambridge, Massachusetts, A.B. 1941. Served in the Royal Canadian Air Force, and the United States Air Force, 1941–45: First Lieutenant. Married Margaret Russell in 1944; three children. Instructor in English, Hamilton College, Clinton, New York, 1946–48; Member of the Literature Faculty, Bennington College, Vermont, 1948–66; Professor of English, Brandeis University, Waltham, Massachusetts, 1966–69. Since 1969, Professor of English, Washington University, St. Louis. Visiting Lecturer, University of Minnesota, Minneapolis, 1958–59; Writer-in-Residence, Hollins College, Virginia, 1962–64; Consultant in Poetry, Library of Congress, Washington, D.C., 1963–64. Associate Editor, *Furioso*, Madison, Connecticut, later Northfield, Minnesota, 1946–51. Recipient: National Institute of Arts and Letters grant, 1961; New England Poetry Club Golden Rose, 1962; Brandeis University Creative Arts Award, 1962; National Endowment for the Arts grant, 1966; Theodore Roethke Award, 1968; Guggenheim Fellowship, 1968; St. Botolph's Club Prize, 1968; Academy of American

Poets Fellowship, 1970. D.L.: Lawrence University, Appleton, Wisconsin, 1964; Tufts University, Medford, Massachusetts, 1969. Fellow, American Academy of Arts and Sciences, 1966. Member, American Academy of Arts and Letters, 1976. Lives in St. Louis.

PUBLICATIONS

Verse

> *The Image and the Law.* 1947.
> *Guide to the Ruins.* 1950.
> *The Salt Garden.* 1955.
> *Mirrors and Windows.* 1958.
> *New and Selected Poems.* 1960.
> *The Next Room of the Dream: Poems and Two Plays.* 1962.
> *Five American Poets,* with others, edited by Ted Hughes and Thom Gunn. 1963.
> *The Blue Swallows.* 1967.
> *The Winter Lightning: Selected Poems.* 1968.
> *The Painter Dreaming in the Scholar's House.* 1968.
> *Gnomes and Occasions: Poems.* 1972.
> *The Western Approaches: Poems 1973–1975.* 1975.
> *Collected Poems.* 1977.

Fiction

> *The Melodramatists.* 1949.
> *Federigo; or, The Power of Love.* 1954.
> *The Homecoming Game.* 1957.
> *A Commodity of Dreams and Other Stories.* 1959.
> *Stories, Fables, and Other Diversions.* 1971.

Other

> *Poetry and Fiction: Essays.* 1963.
> *Journal of the Fictive Life.* 1965.
> *Reflexions on Poetry and Poetics.* 1972.
> *Figures of Thought: Speculations on the Meaning of Poetry and Other Essays.* 1978.

> Editor, *Poets on Poetry.* 1965.

Reading List: *Nemerov* by Peter Meinke, 1968; *The Critical Reception of Nemerov: A Selection of Essays and a Bibliography* edited by Bowie Duncan, 1971; *The Shield of Perseus* by Julia Bartholomay, 1972.

*   *   *

Although Howard Nemerov has written a journal, two collections of short stories, three novels, and much fine criticism (including exceptionally perceptive essays on Wallace Stevens, Dylan Thomas, and Vladimir Nabokov), his primary importance is as a poet. He is a

731

superior craftsman, particularly skilled at blank verse. Moreover, the content of his poetry is penetrating. Perhaps the foremost reason for this richness in content is that Nemerov believes that a major function of the poet is to scrutinize and describe reality precisely as it is. "The Private Eye" makes it clear that the artist should strip himself of preconceptions. In "Vermeer," Nemerov praises this painter for taking "what is, and seeing it as it is."

Despite the fact that reality contains patterns, Nemerov finds that, fundamentally, reality is primitive and chaotic. "The Town Dump" and "The Quarry" stress the relentless chaotic decay occurring in our world, while raw primitiveness is emphasized in "Lobsters." "Nightmare" shows that the primitive also exists within the human being. Nor is any Dionysian oneness fusing man and nature possible. Instead, nature is apt to paralyze man's will, as it does the speaker's in "Death and the Maiden."

Man, then, is a very limited creature, a main point in both of his verse plays, *Endor* and *Cain,* as well as in "Runes." For Nemerov the other major function of the artist is to create some kind of comforting order, even though this order is only temporary. Nemerov stresses this point again and again in such poems as "Elegy for a Nature Poet" and "Lines and Circularities." The artist can also remind us that nature can be lovely and exhilarating. However, we must not think that human creations can "replace" reality – the warning given in "Projection."

Because nature is ceaselessly changing, Nemerov suggests that man, too, should be flexible. "Lot Later" dramatizes this point. Inflexibility will trap man, for even sanctified history can later be proven false, the theme in "To Clio, Muse of History." Nevertheless, man should not let himself be crippled by cynicism, as is the Minister in *Endor.*

Nemerov's poetry is valuable because it incisively presents us with a no-nonsense view of the world, a view that is stark, but not entirely negative. In "The View from an Attic Window," he declares that we live amid chaos, that our individual lives are short, and that, as a result, "life is hopeless," yet "beautiful" – and we should try to endure and to grow. "Small Moment" states that if we do fully accept reality, we will also embody vibrant love.

—Robert K. Johnson

NICHOLSON, Norman (Cornthwaite). English. Born in Millom, Cumberland, 8 January 1914. Educated at local schools. Married Yvonne Gardner in 1956. Frequent public lecturer. Recipient: Heinemann Award, 1945; Cholmondeley Award, 1967; Northern Arts Association grant, 1969; Society of Authors bursary, 1973; Queen's Gold Medal for Poetry, 1977. M.A.: University of Manchester, 1959; Open University, 1975. Fellow, Royal Society of Literature, 1945. Lives in Cumbria.

PUBLICATIONS

Verse

Selected Poems, with J. C. Hall and Keith Douglas.   1943.
Five Rivers.   1944.
Rock Face.   1948.
The Pot Geranium.   1954.

Selected Poems. 1966.
No Star on the Way Back: Ballads and Carols. 1967.
A Local Habitation. 1972.
Cloud on the Black Combe. 1975.
Stitch and Stone: A Cumbrian Landscape. 1975.

Plays

The Old Man of the Mountains (produced 1945). 1946.
Prophesy to the Wind (produced 1949). 1950.
A Match for the Devil (produced 1953). 1955.
Birth by Drowning (produced 1959). 1960.

Television Play: *No Star on the Way Back,* 1963.

Fiction

The Fire of the Lord. 1944.
The Green Shore. 1947.

Other

Man and Literature. 1943.
Cumberland and Westmorland. 1949.
H. G. Wells. 1950.
William Cowper. 1951.
The Lakers: The Adventures of the First Tourists. 1955.
Provincial Pleasures. 1959.
William Cowper (not the same as the 1951 book). 1960.
Portrait of the Lakes. 1963.
Enjoying It All (radio talks). 1964.
Greater Lakeland. 1969.
Wednesday Early Closing (autobiography). 1975.

Editor, *An Anthology of Religious Verse Designed for the Times.* 1942.
Editor, *Wordsworth: An Introduction and Selection.* 1949.
Editor, *Poems,* by William Cowper. 1951.
Editor, *A Choice of Cowper's Verse.* 1975.

Reading List: *Nicholson* by Philip Gardner, 1973.

*   *   *

Norman Nicholson is a regional poet who, living and writing in the shadow of Wordsworth on the western edge of Cumbria, has yet asserted his own distinctive and authentic voice. The Cumbria he celebrates is partly the industrialized region of mines, blast furnaces, and slag-banks surrounding his home town, Millom, but it stretches beyond these to include the neighbouring coast and the dales and fells of Lakeland. From *Five Rivers* onwards Nicholson's strength has always been his response to this landscape, a response in which imaginative perception, an acuity of vision akin to that of the painter, blends with historical awareness to give a satisfying sense that here is a poet who "deals largely with substantial things." Botany and geology, a feeling for soil and stone, and a love of local history authenticate his landscapes. He combines reflection with description, directness with reticence. In his concern for order, clarity, and control he is in the classical tradition. His mind is, however, fertile in the production of images, and he has a strong sense of colour.

He is also a religious poet. Some of the poems in *Five Rivers*, retelling biblical stories in a modern, somewhat surrealist manner, now seen over-ambitious. The shorter ones (e.g., "Shepherd's Carol") succeed better. *The Old Man of the Mountains*, Nicholson's best known verse-play, is a retelling of the story of Elijah and the raven, given a modern setting on the Cumberland fells, and quite effectively pillories modern man's materialism and greed.

Despite many appealing poems in *Five Rivers* and *Rock Face*, Nicholson's work is probably seen at its best in *The Pot Geranium* and *A Local Habitation*. In the former, depth of feeling combined with technical mastery gives a new assurance of tone. Poems like "On Duddon Marsh" recreate their subject in precise and evocative detail. Others, like "Fossils," penetrate imaginatively into the life of inanimate rocks. (The animism of his portrayal of Nature has always been a notable feature.) There also appear here poems in the personal, anecdotal style – concerned with people as well as places – that he was to develop in *A Local Habitation*: the splendid "Rising Five"; "The Buzzer," an almost Proustian realisation; and the sharply observed "Five Minutes."

"My ways are circumscribed," the poet confesses in the title-poem "The Pot Geranium." In *A Local Habitation* this has ceased to matter; his confidence in the value of that life now leads him to write of it in an engagingly relaxed, intimate, and sometimes humorous way. (The subject-matter of some of the poems is expanded in his highly readable autobiography, *Wednesday Early Closing*.) In earlier volumes Nicholson's concern to moralise his song is sometimes rather too obvious and the application forced. Here, especially in the serenely beautiful "September on the Mosses," the physical and moral visions are fused. The local habitation convincingly mirrors the universal.

—Joan Grundy

NOYES, Alfred. English. Born in Wolverhampton, 16 September 1880. Educated at Exeter College, Oxford, 1898–1901. Married 1) Garnet Daniels in 1907 (died, 1926); 2) Mary Wild-Blundell in 1927; one son and two daughters. Delivered the Lowell Lectures in the U.S., 1913; Professor of Modern English Literature, Princeton University, New Jersey, 1914–23; returned to England and lived by his writing; became a Roman Catholic, 1927. Litt.D.: Yale University, New Haven, Connecticut, 1913; LL.D: University of Glasgow, 1927; University of California, Berkeley, 1944; L.H.D.: Syracuse University, New York, 1942. C.B.E. (Commander, Order of the British Empire), 1918. *Died 28 June 1958*.

PUBLICATIONS

Collections

Collected Poems.   1947; revised edition, edited by Hugh Noyes, 1963, 1966.

Verse

> The Loom of Years. 1902.
> The Flower of Old Japan: A Dim Strange Tale for All Ages. 1903.
> Poems. 1904.
> The Forest of Wild Thyme: A Tale for Children under Ninety. 1905.
> Drake: An English Epic. 2 vols., 1906–08.
> Poems. 1906.
> Forty Singing Seamen and Other Poems. 1907.
> The Golden Hynde and Other Poems. 1908.
> The Enchanted Island and Other Poems. 1909.
> In Memory of Swinburne. 1909.
> Collected Poems. 4 vols., 1910–27; vols. 1 and 2 revised, 1928.
> The Prayer for Peace. 1911.
> The Carol of the Fir Tree. 1912.
> Tales of the Mermaid Tavern. 1913.
> Two Christmas Poems. 1913.
> The Wine-Press: A Tale of War. 1913.
> A Tale of Old Japan. 1914.
> The Searchlights. 1914.
> The Lord of Misrule and Other Poems. 1915.
> A Salute from the Fleet and Other Poems. 1915.
> Songs of the Trawlers. 1916.
> The Avenue of the Allies, and Victory. 1918.
> The New Morning. 1918.
> The Elfin Artist and Other Poems. 1920.
> Selected Verse. 1921.
> The Torch-Bearers. 3 vols., 1922–30.
> Songs of Shadow-of-a-Leaf and Other Poems. 1924.
> Princeton, May 1917; The Call of the Spring. 1925.
> Dick Turpin's Ride and Other Poems. 1927.
> Ballads and Poems. 1928.
> The Strong City. 1928.
> Poems: The Author's Own Selection for Schools. 1935.
> The Cormorant. 1936.
> Youth and Memory. 1937.
> Wizards. 1938.
> If Judgment Comes. 1941.
> Poems of the New World. 1942.
> Shadows on the Down and Other Poems. 1945.
> The Assumption: An Answer. 1950.
> A Roehampton School Song. 1950.
> Daddy Fell into the Pond and Other Poems for Children. 1952.
> A Letter to Lucian and Other Poems. 1956.

Plays

> Orpheus in the Underworld, with Frederic Norton and Herbert Beerbohm Tree (produced 1911).
> Sherwood; or, Robin Hood and the Three Kings. 1911; revised version, as Robin Hood (produced 1926), 1926.
> Rada: A Drama of War. 1914; revised version, as A Belgian Christmas Eve, 1915.

Fiction

> *Walking Shadows* (stories)   1918.
> *Beyond the Desert: A Tale of Death Valley.*   1920.
> *The Hidden Player.*   1924.
> *The Return of the Scare-Crow.*   1929; as *The Sun Cure,* 1929.
> *The Last Man.*   1940; as *No Other Man,* 1940.
> *The Devil Takes a Holiday.*   1955.

Other

> *William Morris.*   1908.
> *Mystery Ships: Trapping the "U"-Boat.*   1916.
> *What Is England Doing?*   1916.
> *Open Boats.*   1917.
> *Some Aspects of Modern Poetry.*   1924.
> *New Essays and American Impressions.*   1927.
> *The Opalescent Parrot: Essays.*   1929.
> *Tennyson.*   1932.
> *The Unknown God.*   1934.
> *Happiness and Success,* with S. Baldwin.   1936.
> *Voltaire.*   1936.
> *Orchard's Bay* (essays; includes verse).   1939; as *The Incompleat Gardener,* 1955.
> *Pageant of Letters* (essays).   1940.
> *The Edge of the Abyss* (lectures).   1942.
> *The Secret of Pooduck Island* (juvenile).   1943.
> *Portrait of Horace.*   1947.
> *Two Worlds for Memory* (autobiography).   1953.
> *The Accusing Ghost; or, Justice for Casement.*   1957.

> Editor, *The Magic Casement: An Anthology of Fairy Poetry.*   1908.
> Editor, *The Minstrelsy of the Scottish Border,* edited by Sir Walter Scott.   1908.
> Editor, *The Temple of Beauty: An Anthology.*   1910.
> Editor, *A Book of Princeton Verse.*   1916.
> Editor, *Helicon Poetry Series.*   4 vols., 1925.
> Editor, *The Golden Book of Catholic Poetry.*   1946.

Reading List: *Noyes* by Walter Jerrold, 1930; *Noyes* by D. G. Larg, 1936; "The Poetic Achievement of Noyes" by Derek Stanford, in *English 12,* 1958.

*   *   *

Alfred Noyes's verse chimed well with the increasingly strident jingoism of the Edwardian era, earning him a place in innumerable school anthologies. His two-volume epic on Drake, serialized in *Blackwood's Magazine,* set the pattern for writing which repeatedly turned for inspiration to the sea and its heroes. Yet the hortatory, hectoring rhetoric of poems such as "In Time of War" or "Nelson's Year" (which, beginning "'Hasten the Kingdom, England,'" casts the British Empire in a divine crusade to unify the "striving nations," "England's Rose of all the roses/Dawning wide and ever wider o'er the kingdom of mankind") conceals a deeper unease and anxiety. "The Phantom Fleet" reveals this as a doubt about England's capacity to resist the challenge of the newer maritime powers, summoning the ghosts of

Nelson and the Elizabethan privateers to defend a nation "resting on her past" which has neglected her "first, last line," the Fleet.

The same insecurity pervades the personal verse, where jaunty self-confidence jostles a stale world-weariness ("The heart in its muffled anguish, the sea in its mournful voice"). Frustrated, cramped, disenchanted in an age of positivism and commerce, this grocer's son from Wolverhampton sought in fantasy an escape from "the solemn sin of truth." *The Forest of Wild Thyme* leads us as children off "to hunt the fairy gleam/That flutters through the unfettered dream." But the long-sought Flower of Old Japan turns out to be no exotic growth, but "a white/English daisy," and we are brought back, in a sentimentalism of the hearth, to see that "All the fairy tales were true,/And home the heart of fairy-land." The same domestication of the exotic underlies the Imperial dream: "A Song of England" sees her dutiful sons shipped overseas, only to find in her "silent purple harmonies" the truly magical landscape, towards which they "grope in dreams." Noyes thus manages to reconcile Little Englandism with the imperial theme. The true "Empire Builders" are similarly found, in a characteristic movement, on native soil, in the lowly round of "many a country cottage-home" or the City's "roaring streets." The heavy rhythms, emphatic rhymes and rollicking fourteeners of his Kiplingesque ballads likewise suggest the robustness of the spiritual invalid, compensating for the sado-masochistic weakness of, e.g., "The Mystic" ("My soul lay stabbed by all the swords of sense") or the fin-de-siècle cadences of "In the Heart of the Woods"; and indeed, Noyes ultimately found his refuge from desolation in Catholicism.

There is much in his verse of the sensuous languors of the early Keats; much of the alliterative opulence of Poe, Swinburne and the Decadents ("dim as a dream, rich as a reverie," "perfumed with old regret and dead desire"). Even at his best, as in the unexpected imitation of Gautier, "Art," the terseness of his model —

> Yes! Beauty still rebels!
> Our Dreams like clouds disperse:
> She dwells
> In agate, marble, verse

— is marred by a prolixity that overextends a simple idea into stanza after stanza of amplification. In form and sentiment vatic, maudlin, sententious, Noyes displays the self-indulgence of his age. His work would have benefitted from the discipline recommended in the closing stanza of this poem: "Take up the sculptor's tool!"

—Stan Smith

O'HARA, Frank (Francis Russell O'Hara). American. Born in Baltimore, Maryland, 27 June 1926. Educated privately in piano and musical composition, 1933–43; at New England Conservatory of Music, Boston, 1946–50; Harvard University, Cambridge, Massachusetts, 1946–50, B.A. in English 1950; University of Michigan, Ann Arbor (Hopwood Award, 1951), M.A. in English 1951. Served in the United States Navy 1944–46. Staff Member, 1951–54, Fellowship Curator, 1955–64, Associate Curator, 1965, and Curator of the International Program, 1966, Museum of Modern Art, New York. Editorial Associate, *Art News* magazine, New York, 1954–56; Art Editor, *Kulchur Magazine*, New York, 1962–64. Collaborated in several poem-painting and poem-lithograph projects. Recipient: Ford Foundation Fellowship, for drama, 1956. *Died 25 July 1966.*

PUBL'CATIONS

Collections

> *Collected Poems*, edited by Donald Allen. 1971.
> *Selected Poems*, edited by Donald Allen. 1974.

Verse

> *A City Winter and Other Poems.* 1952.
> *Oranges.* 1953.
> *Meditations in an Emergency.* 1956.
> *Hartigan and Rivers with O'Hara: An Exhibition of Pictures, with Poems.* 1959.
> *Second Avenue.* 1960.
> *Odes.* 1960.
> *Featuring O'Hara.* 1964.
> *Lunch Poems.* 1964.
> *Love Poems: Tentative Title.* 1965.
> *Five Poems.* 1967.
> *Two Pieces.* 1969.
> *Odes.* 1969.
> *Hymns of St. Bridget,* with Bill Berkson. 1974.
> *Poems Retrieved, 1951–1966,* edited by Donald Allen. 1975.
> *Early Poems, 1946–1951,* edited by Donald Allen. 1976.

Plays

> *Try! Try!* (produced 1951; revised version, produced 1952). In *Artists' Theatre,* edited by Herbert Machiz, 1960.
> *Change Your Bedding* (produced 1952).
> *Love's Labor: An Eclogue* (produced 1959). 1964.
> *Awake in Spain* (produced 1960). 1960.
> *The General Returns from One Place to Another* (produced 1964).

Screenplay: *The Last Clean Shirt.*

Other

Jackson Pollock. 1959.
A Frank O'Hara Miscellany. 1974.
Art Chronicles 1954–1966. 1974.
Standing Still and Walking in New York, edited by Donald Allen. 1975.
Early Writings, edited by Donald Allen. 1977.

Editor, *Robert Motherwell: A Catalogue with Selections from the Artist's Writings.* 1966.

Reading List: *O'Hara, Poet among Painters* by Marjorie Perloff, 1977.

*   *   *

Frank O'Hara's status as an important poet of the post-World War II era has only recently been established. During his lifetime he was known only to a circle of friends, many of them painters in New York whom he knew from his work as an Associate Curator of the Museum of Modern Art. But his canon is large and runs to more than five hundred pages of text in Donald Allen's edition of *The Collected Poems.*

O'Hara was cavalier about his reputation as a poet and reluctant to have his poetry in print. As a result, his work largely went unnoticed in the review columns; when his name did surface, he was taken lightly. Only very recently has his work received serious critical attention; Marjorie Perloff's book vigorously argues his major status as an innovator of lyrical poetry. Perloff and others consider O'Hara to have had an influence on younger poets comparable to Charles Olson, Robert Creeley, and Allen Ginsberg.

O'Hara's poetry from 1951 to 1954 shows the influence of Pound, William Carlos Williams, and Auden. His early poems, collected in *A City Winter and Other Poems,* are lyrical and strive very deliberately for surprising effects. His friend, the poet John Ashbery, once commented that this was O'Hara's "French Zen period," which is an astute observation of the lushly surrealistic language of these poems. As he commented in an early poem, "Poetry":

> The only way to be quiet
> is to be quick, so I scare
> you clumsily, or surprise
> you with a stab. A praying
> mantis knows time more
> intimately than I and is
> more casual.

Auden once wrote to caution O'Hara against tiring the reader with an excess of surreal statements, and he appears to have heeded his counsel, for in the poetry of the later 1950's, gathered in *Meditations in an Emergency* and *Lunch Poems,* he exerted greater control over the structure of his poems and gave himself more intense freedom in brief, dazzling displays of lyrical exuberance.

In *Second Avenue* and other longer poems – "Easter," "In Memory of My Feelings," "Ode to Michael Goldberg('s Birth and Other Births)" and the late "Biotherm (for Bill Berkson)" – O'Hara, like Pushkin and Byron before him, created perhaps the essential hero of urban cultural life, a sophisticated romantic who thrives on the city's alien and exotic elements. His many shorter poems are briefer expressions of this same captivating persona.

O'Hara also succeeds in rendering consciousness and its fringe states with intense accuracy and daring in a style partly influenced by the methods and experiments of the Abstract

Expressionist painters. O'Hara wrote several plays, and essays on contemporary painting collected in *Standing Still and Walking in New York* and *Art Chronicles 1954–1966*. Although not a theorist or trained critic of painting, his eye was sensitive to technique and his instinct sharp in discerning the great works of his time.

—Paul Christensen

OKARA, Gabriel (Imomotimi Gbaingbain). Nigerian. Born in Bumodi, Ijaw District, Rivers State, Western Nigeria, 21 April 1921. Educated at the Government College, Umuahia; trained as a bookbinder; studied journalism at Northwestern University, Evanston, Illinois, 1956. Principal Information Officer, Eastern Regional Government, Enugu, until 1967; Biafran Information Officer, Nigerian Civil War, 1967–69; travelled to the United States, with Chinua Achebe and Cyprian Ekwensi, to seek help for Biafra, 1969. Since 1972, Director of the Rivers State Publishing House, Port Harcourt. Recipient: Nigerian Festival of the Arts award, 1953.

PUBLICATIONS

Verse

The Fisherman's Invocation. 1978.

Fiction

The Voice. 1964.

Reading List: *Mother Is Gold* by Adrian A. Roscoe, 1971; *Culture, Tradition, and Society in the West African Novel* by Emmanuel Obiechina, 1975.

*   *   *

Gabriel Okara has written plays, translated folk material from Ijaw into English, and prepared documentary material for broadcasting. He is known almost exclusively, however, as a poet and as the author of an experimental novel, *The Voice*.

In 1953 Okara's poem "The Call of the River Nun" won the best all-round award in the Nigerian Festival of Arts. Like much of his poetry it has undercurrents of melancholy. The poet writes, with a slightly adolescent plangency, of how the River Nun beckons him into the mainstream of life. Later poems have been more symbolic including "The Snow Flakes Sail Gently Down," invoking impressions of exile while wintering in America:

> Then I dreamed a dream
> in my dead sleep. But I dreamed
> not of earth dying and elms a vigil
> keeping. I dreamed of birds, black
> birds flying in my inside, nesting
> and hatching on oil palms, bearing suns
> for fruits and with roots denting the
> uprooters' spades.

Okara's poems are deeply felt and usually introspective, though he is as concerned for the loss of traditional life in Nigeria as he is for his own state of mind brought about by the transition.

The Voice enjoys a reputation as a *succès d'estime*, for Okara attempted a semi-poetic novel which would render into an English equivalent some of the rhythms and sense of imagery found in his own vernacular, Ijaw. The novel is referred to whenever the possibilities of an African English are discussed. It is a short, partly allegorical novel presenting a struggle between the individual and his community; it is so lucid and distilled that it is likely to survive as a classic of African writing. In many ways *The Voice* is the archetypal rural novel in West Africa, confronting old and new values in a modern setting and demonstrating the rooted idealism which many African writers in the early 1960's believed to be the salvation of Africa. Okolo, whose name means "voice," embodies the author's faith in the liberty of personal conscience.

—Alastair Niven

OKIGBO, Christopher (Ifenayichukwu). Nigerian. Born in Ojoto, Onitsha Province, East Central State, 16 August 1932. Educated at the Government College, Umuahia; University College, Ibadan, 1951–56, B.A. in classics 1956. Served as a Major in the Biafran Army: killed in action, 1967. Married Sefi, daughter of the Attah of Igberra, in 1963; one daughter. Worked for the Nigerian Tobacco Company and the United African Company; Private Secretary to the Federal Minister of Research and Information, 1956–58; Latin Teacher, Fiditi Grammar School, near Ibadan, 1959–60; Librarian, University of Nigeria, Nsukka, then Enugu, 1960–62; West Africa Representative, Cambridge University Press, 1962–66. West African Editor, *Transition* magazine, Kampala, Uganda; Editor, Mbari Press, Ibadan. Founder, with Chinua Achebe, of Citadel Books Ltd., Enugu, 1967. Recipient: Dakar Festival of Negro Arts Poetry Prize, 1966. *Died in August 1967.*

PUBLICATIONS

Verse

Heavensgate. 1962.
Limits. 1964.
Labyrinths, with Path of Thunder. 1971.

Reading List: *The Trial of Okigbo* by Ali A. Mazrui, 1971; *Okigbo: Creative Rhetoric* by Sunday O Anozie, 1972.

*   *   *

In the Introduction to *Labyrinths*, Christopher Okigbo wrote:

> Although these poems were written and published separately, they are, in fact, organically related.
> *Heavensgate* was originally conceived as an Easter sequence. It later grew into ... an offering to Idoto, the village stream of which I drank, in which I washed, as a child....
> *Limits* and *Distances* are man's outer and inner worlds projected.... Both parts of *Silences* were inspired by the Western Nigeria crisis of 1962, and the death of Patrice Lamumba....
> *Labyrinths* is thus a fable of man's perennial quest for fulfilment ... a poet-protagonist is assumed throughout ... larger than Orpheus: one with a load of destiny on his head, rather like Gilgamesh, like Aeneas ... like the Fisher King of Eliot's *Waste Land*....

The comment makes very clear the kind of poet Okigbo was. He had an urgent sense of the poetic future of a country only recently released from pre-literacy. His education in Classical and British literature combined with his life's knowledge of Ibo ethic, myth, and verbal folk poetry allowed him to see man's past as much more interwoven than has been supposed and African culture no less rich than that of the West. Okigbo's poetry does not try to merge Ibo, Nigerian, African backgrounds or poetry with British or Classical, but to show them as if from one, perhaps the same, antecedent. In *Silences* he writes, "One dips one's tongue in ocean, and begins / To cry to the mushroom of the sky."

Okigbo made no effort to solve problems which such attitudes as that of the Negritude of the 1950's posed. English was for him his own tongue, and he did not think of using any other for his poetry. In fact, there are strong echoes from other English writers – in *Limits*, for instance, of Eliot, John Wain, even de la Mare – mingled with references to Ibo myth and ritual:

> Hurry on down–
> Thro' the cinder market –
> Hurry on down
> in the wake of the dream;
>
> Hurry on down –
> To rockpoint of Cable,
>
> To pull by the rope
> the big white elephant ...
>
> *& the mortar is not yet dry*
> *& the mortar is not yet dry....*

Okigbo's double background makes for richness of substance and metaphor. Intensity of feeling carries this intellectual poet still further. He acknowledges his debt to Gerard Manley Hopkins in his " Lament of the Silent Sisters," a poem prophetic of his own death:

> "Chorus: 'We carry in our worlds that flourish
>   Our worlds that have failed ...'
>
> Crier: 'This is our swan song
>   This is the sigh of our spirits.'"

Okibo was a religious, philosophic poet of great promise.

—Anne Tibble

OLDHAM, John. English. Born in Shipton-Moyne, Gloucestershire, 9 August 1653. Educated at Tetbury Grammar School; St. Edmund Hall, Oxford, 1670–74, B.A. 1674. Usher in Archbishop Whitgift's free school at Croydon, Surrey, 1675–78; tutor to the grandsons of Sir Edward Thurland, Reigate, Surrey, 1678–81, and to the son of Sir William Hickes, London, 1681–82; may have briefly studied medicine, 1682; befriended by Lord Kingston, 1682–83. *Died 9 December 1683.*

PUBLICATIONS

Collections

Compositions in Prose and Verse, edited by E. Thompson. 3 vols., 1770.
Poetical Works, edited by R. Bell. 1854.

Verse

Upon the Marriage of the Prince of Orange. 1677.
A Satire Against Virtue. 1679.
Garnet's Ghost. 1679.
Satires upon the Jesuits and Some Other Pieces. 1681.
Some New Pieces. 1681.
Poems and Translations. 1683.
Remains in Verse and Prose. 1684.
A Second Musical Entertainment Performed on St. Cecilia's Day. 1685.

Bibliography: by H.F. Brooks, in *Oxford Bibliographical Society Proceedings 5,* 1936.

Reading List: Introduction by Bonamy Dobrée to *Poetical Works,* 1960.

*   *   *

The Civil War in England divided the country against itself and fostered a taste for political satire. During this period, and for some time thereafter, the market was choked with vituperative tracts, vitriolic pamphlets, animadversions, lampoons, and scarcely lyrical scurrilities that had considerable influence upon Restoration poetry. During the Restoration, the more refined, cavalier mode of the courtiers and their near relations (Dorset, Rochester, Sedley, Dryden, Etherege) prevailed; their tone was most often witty, classical, relaxed – although they were certainly capable of vicious and scatological invectives and *jeux d'esprit.*

John Oldham, on the other hand, was far removed from court and courtly writing. A schoolteacher and tutor most of his life in Gloucestershire, his actual writing career spans only about six years (1677–83). Unlike Samuel Butler (similarly removed from Court), however, he aspired to more austere and classical forms of satire. Oldham's most renowned and sustained work are his four *Satyrs upon the Jesuits.* Born into a nonconformist family and himself a staunch Whig, Oldham responded to the Popish Plot by harshly attacking the Catholics as conspirators seeking to infiltrate and to overthrow the Anglican monarchy; he was especially intemperate about Loyola's Society of Jesus, which he considered to be made

up of a pack of ruthless torturers and spies: "Racks, gibbets, halters, were their Arguments."
In such a climate, Oldham felt himself vengefully "driven" to write:

> 'Tis pointed *Satyr*, and the *sharps* of Wit
> For such a *prize* are th' only Weapons fit:
> Nor needs there *Art*, or *Genius* here to use,
> Where *Indignation* can create a muse....
> All this urge on my rank envenom'd spleen,
> And with keen Satyr edg my stabbing Pen....

This particular satire met with considerable success in London, and is clearly his one major
triumph. It is harsh, dense, and unrelenting, though often wanting in polish or finesse. In an
era when the indirection, lightness, and sophistication of Horace were more and more
coming into vogue, Oldham patently prefers the caustic muse of Juvenal (and, indeed, in tone
and versification, he often sounds like the Elizabethan satirist John Marston). John Oldham
did in fact freely translate two of Juvenal's satires (III, XIII) into English, and has sometimes
been designated "the English Juvenal."

His *A Satyr Against Vertue* attempts ironically to celebrate vice, but Oldham is unequal to
such subtlety, and many readers misunderstood (as they did Defoe's similar irony). Some of
his Pindaric odes are at least workmanlike and competent in that genre, and several of his
little-known imitations and translations of Horace represent some of his best work. In all,
Oldham's *métier* seems to have been the heroic couplet. He wrote a number of satires and
even some lighter lyrics (his drinking-song, "The Careless Good Fellow," is still
anthologized). Unfortunately, his life was cut short, and he died of smallpox at the age of
thirty.

His uneven, abrupt, and too often scattergun verse struck Alexander Pope as "indelicate,"
and Dryden tended to agree. Yet it was John Dryden, in one of the most moving elegies in the
language, "To the Memory of Mr. Oldham," who perhaps does an intense and would-be
satirist some justice:

> O early ripe! to thy abundant store
> What could advancing Age have added more?
> It might (what Nature never gives the young)
> Have taught the numbers of thy native Tongue.
> But Satyr needs not those, and Wit will shine
> Through the harsh cadence of a rugged line.
> A noble Error, and but seldom made,
> When Poets are by too much force betray'd.

Oldham did indeed suffer from harsh ruggedness and excessive force, but there *was* some
nobility in his poetry.

—John R. Clark

OLSON, Charles (John).   American.   Born in Worcester, Massachusetts, 27 December
1910. Educated at Wesleyan University, Middletown, Connecticut, B.A. 1932, M A. 1933;
Yale University, New Haven, Connecticut; Harvard University, Cambridge, Massachusetts.
Taught at Clark University, Worcester, and Harvard University, 1936–39; Instructor and

Rector, Black Mountain College, North Carolina, 1951–56; taught at the State University of New York at Buffalo, 1963–65, and the University of Connecticut, Storrs, 1969. Recipient: Guggenheim grant (twice); Wenner-Gren Foundation grant, to study Mayan hieroglyphics, 1952; National Endowment for the Arts grant, 1966, 1968. *Died 10 January 1970.*

PUBLICATIONS

Verse

Corrado Cagli March 31 Through April 19 1947.   1947.
Y & X.   1948.
Letter for Melville 1951.   1951.
This.   1952.
In Cold Hell, in Thicket.   1953.
The Maximus Poems 1–10.   1953.
Ferrini and Others, with others.   1955.
Anecdotes of the Late War.   1955.
The Maximus Poems 11–22.   1956.
O'Ryan 2 4 6 8 10.   1958; expanded edition, as *O'Ryan 12345678910,* 1965.
Projective Verse.   1959.
The Maximus Poems.   1960.
The Distances: Poems.   1960.
Maximus, From Dogtown I.   1961.
Signature to Petition on Ten Pound Island Asked of Me by Mr. Vincent Ferrini.   1964.
West.   1966.
Charles Olson Reading at Berkeley, edited by Zoe Brown.   1966.
Before Your Very Eyes!, with others.   1967.
The Maximus Poems, IV, V, VI.   1968.
Reading about My World.   1968.
Added to Making a Republic.   1968.
Clear Shifting Water.   1968.
That There Was a Woman in Gloucester, Massachusetts.   1968.
Wholly Absorbed into My Own Conduits.   1968.
Causal Mythology.   1969.
Archaeologist of Morning: The Collected Poems Outside the Maximus Series.   1970.
The Maximus Poems, Volume Three, edited by Charles Boer and George F. Butterick.   1975.

Plays

The Fiery Hunt and Other Plays.   1977.

Fiction

Stocking Cap: A Story.   1966.

Other

Call Me Ishmael: A Study of Melville.   1947.

745

Apollonius of Tyana: A Dance, with Some Words, for Two Actors. 1951.
Mayan Letters, edited by Robert Creeley. 1953.
A Bibliography on America for Ed Dorn. 1964.
Pleistocene Man: Letters from Olson to John Clarke during October, 1965. 1968.
Human Universe and Others Essays, edited by Donald Allen. 1965.
Proprioception. 1965.
Selected Writings, edited by Robert Creeley. 1966.
Letters for "Origin," 1950–1956, edited by Albert Glover. 1969.
The Special View of History, edited by Ann Charters. 1970.
Poetry and Truth: The Beloit Lectures and Poems, edited by George F. Butterick. 1971.
Additional Prose: A Bibliography on America, Proprioception, and Other Notes and Essays, edited by George F. Butterick. 1974.
The Post Office: A Memoir of His Father. 1975.
Olson and Ezra Pound: An Encounter at St. Elizabeth's, edited by Catherine Seelye. 1975.
Muthologos: The Collected Lectures and Interviews, edited by George F. Butterick. 1976.

Bibliography: *A Bibliography of the Works of Olson* by George F. Butterick and Albert Glover, 1967.

Reading List: *Olson/Melville: A Study in Affinity* by Ann Charters, 1968; *A Guide to the Maximus Poems of Olson* by George F. Butterick, 1978; *Olson: Call Him Ishmael* by Paul Christensen, 1978.

*   *   *

Although any final judgment regarding the work and influence of the poet Charles Olson remains controversial, he must nevertheless be regarded as a seminal force in the reshaping of American poetry written since World War II. Olson showed little inclination to be a poet until his mid-thirties. Shortly after the death of Roosevelt, however, Olson left government and committed himself to a literary career. By then he had written only the draft of a short book on Melville, *Call Me Ishmael*, and several conventional poems published in popular magazines. From these unpromising beginnings, Olson began writing in earnest in the late 1940's. With the help of Edward Dahlberg, a completely revised *Call Me Ishmael* was published in 1947; two years later, Olson composed "The Kingfishers," among the most innovative poems to have emerged since World War II. And in 1950, largely from the example of the techniques employed in "The Kingfishers," and ideas taken from a variety of sources, including William Carlos Williams, Pound, Dahlberg and his close friend Robert Creeley, Olson synthesized the provocative and highly influential manifesto, "Projective Verse."

This essay established a new set of conventions for the short poem. In place of the old rules of repetitive measure, rhyme, and fixed stanza, Olson introduced the principle that "form is an extension of content," or that form is the result of allowing content to assume its own partly accidental shape during composition. Around this main principle are certain technical corollaries: for example, the poet, rather than treating his theme in an orderly progression of ideas, should instead rush from "perception to perception" until his argument is exhausted. The poet should allow the rhythm of his breath during composition to determine the length of each line, so that he has scored it for the reading voice. And in fitting words together in the line itself, the poet should let sound, rather than sense, determine syntax. A logic of the ear should take precedence over intellect in the fashioning of language.

Olson suggested that all of these new conventions were dependent on a new stance to experience, which he called Objectism. The poet should no longer consider his mind a clearing house of data, from which to select bits of information for his poems. Rather, the poet should include the rest of his organism in the act of perception and awareness, and should feel himself rush out of his private emotion into the realms of phenomena free of self-consciousness and inhibition. Objectism called for the poet to accept himself as merely another object inhabiting the phenomenal welter making up the world. The techniques advised in the first half of the essay, then, are all the means of making experience direct and unmediated for the poet who plunges fully into the phenomena around him.

"The Kingfishers" satisfies most of the conditions of composition set forth in the "Projective Verse" essay. Its form is the result of a rush of discourse on a series of loosely related topics, of experiments in combinations of sounds, and of the arrangement of words in clusters to show the changing shape of his thinking moment by moment. This striking poem creates the feeling of having kept pace with the random and shifting content of the poet's awareness.

Olson's projective methodology and the example of "The Kingfishers" are clearly efforts to explore and even to track the behavior of the imagination. More significant is the fact that Olson's poetic brings poetry into the general current of free-forming methods then being applied to the other arts: atonal, free-form jazz composition, abstract expressionism, improvisational theater, and kinetic sculpture.

Olson went on to refine the doctrine now known as Objectism in subsequent essays and lectures, but his several collections of short poems and the long, sequential work *The Maximus Poems* are the basis of his reputation and influence as a poet. In 1953, Robert Creeley published Olson's first full-length volume of poems, *In Cold Hell, in Thicket*, which contains not only "The Kingfishers" but many of Olson's boldest shorter poems. Many, but by no means all, of these shorter poems are composed in the projective mode; others are written in a more leisurely-paced free verse style. The whole work is concerned with the burdens of tradition and influence the poet must cast off to pursue his own direction. The poet argues, often petulantly, against Ezra Pound, whom Olson identifies as his spiritual father and arch rival.

Creeley later edited Olson's *Selected Writings*, further establishing Olson's reputation as a key figure of the new poetry. A more finished and elaborate poetry emerges in *The Distances*, but there is less bold experiment in these maturer lyrical poems. Olson had moved to less defined areas of awareness; many of the poems are startling reenactments of dreams, in which the supralogical narratives are skillfully and persuasively dramatized, and there is a greater interest in myth and the content and forms of consciousness.

But the primary text for judging Olson as poet rests with his central work, the long, epical *Maximus* sequence, begun in the late 1940's and sustained to the last months of his life. The work remains unfinished, although the final volume, found among the poet's papers, has been edited and published. The work in one way is a celebration of the seacoast town of Gloucester, Massachusetts, where communal spirit among the fishermen thrived before industry was established; in another, it is close scrutiny of life in America and a search for an alternative ideology rooted in new spiritual awareness.

In the first volume, *The Maximus Poems*, Olson's persona, Maximus, named after an itinerant Phoenician mystic of the fourth century A.D., surveys contemporary Gloucester and finds its citizenry in disarray and the local culture ugly and alien. This judgment prompts a systematic inquiry into the origins of Gloucester and of America, which takes up the remainder of the volume. In the second volume, *Maximus IV,V VI*, the speaker widens his interests to include mythological lore, the history of human migration, religious literature, and the finer details of Gloucester's past, which seem to Maximus to re-enact certain of the myths and fables of the ancient world. The final volume, more somber in mood and subject, continues Maximus's intense survey of Gloucester and himself. A vision of a new cosmos is summoned in these poems, in the hope of redeeming and possibly reconstituting the communal ethos of Gloucester's past. But that hope gives way to remorse and disparagement of the reckless present and its deadening commercial enterprises.

The poem is among the more ambitious experiments in sustained narrative in the post-war period; it ranks in conception and execution with other verse epics of the modern period, including Pound's *Cantos*, Williams's *Paterson*, and Hart Crane's *The Bridge*. Although Olson is less musical in his language, and at times a dry poet given to long quotation from historic documents, the sweep of his thought and the scope of his imaginative arguments distinguish him as a major American poet of the Whitman tradition.

—Paul Christensen

OWEN, Wilfred (Edward Salter). English. Born in Oswestry, Shropshire, 18 March 1893. Educated at Birkenhead Institute, Cheshire, 1899–1907; Shrewsbury Technical School, Shropshire, 1907–11. Served in the Artists' Rifles and the Manchester Regiment, 1915–18: military cross; killed in action. Pupil and lay assistant to Herbert Wigan, Vicar of Dunsden, Oxfordshire, 1911–13; Tutor in English, Berlitz School, Bordeaux, 1913–14; private tutor in Bordeaux, 1914–15. *Died 4 November 1918.*

PUBLICATIONS

Collections

Poems, edited by Siegfried Sassoon. 1920.
Poems, edited by Edmund Blunden. 1931.
Collected Poems, edited by C. Day Lewis. 1963; revised edition, 1964.
Collected Letters, edited by Harold Owen and John Bell. 1967.
War Poems and Others, edited by Dominic Hibberd. 1973.

Bibliography: *Owen: A Bibliography* by William White, 1967.

Reading List: *Owen: A Critical Study* by D. S. R. Welland, 1960, revised edition, 1978; *Journey from Obscurity: Owen, 1893–1918* by Harold Owen, 3 vols., 1963–65; *Heroes' Twilight* by Bernard Bergonzi, 1965; *Owen* by G. M. White, 1969; *Out of Battle: Poetry of the Great War* by Jon Silkin, 1972; *Owen* by Jon Stallworthy, 1974; *Owen* by Dominic Hibberd, 1975.

*   *   *

In the unfinished draft Preface for the volume of poems that he never lived to see in print, Wilfred Owen wrote, "My subject is War, and the pity of War," and it has since been too often assumed that the War which he made his subject made him a poet. In fact, he had discovered his vocation at the age of ten or eleven and at once bound himself apprentice to the great Romantics, Coleridge, Keats, and Shelley, steeping himself in their writings, studying their lives, in a single-minded endeavour to make himself a poet.

He came, therefore, to the Great War with a developed technique and an imagination in large measure prepared to receive and record the experience of the trenches. His religious upbringing and subsequent doubts, a compassionate humanism derived from his literary masters, boyhood interests in botany and archaeology, all shaped him for his subject as for no other. He had, however, written none of the poems by which he is now known when, after four harrowing months at the Front, he was found in May 1917 to be suffering from shell-shock and invalided back to Craiglockhart War Hospital on the outskirts of Edinburgh. There he had the good fortune to meet Siegfried Sassoon, whose first fiercely realistic "war poems" had just appeared in *The Old Huntsman and Other Poems*. Under their influence and with the encouragement and expert guidance of the older man, Owen was soon producing poems purged of an adolescent, sub-Keatsian luxuriance and far superior to any he had written before. Initially, some like "The Dead-Beat" and "Dulce et Decorum Est" relied too heavily on the colloquial shock-tactics that Sassoon had perfected. Although Owen shared his friend's indignation at the war-mongering of clerics, journalists, and politicians, the incompetence of the General Staff, and the activities of war-profiteers, elegy was a mode more suited to his temperament than satire or simple exposure of the horrors of war.

Helping him with the final revisions to "Anthem for Doomed Youth," Sassoon "realized that his verse, with its sumptuous epithets and large-scale imagery, its noble naturalness and the depth of meaning, had impressive affinities with Keats, whom he took as his supreme exemplar. This new sonnet was a revelation.... It confronted me with classic and imaginative serenity." That poem was a reply to a Prefatory Note in an anthology, *Poems of Today* (1916), whose anonymous author had written that one of the youngest of the poets represented had "gone singing to lay down his life for his country's cause," and that in the arrangement of the book "there is no arbitrary isolation of one theme from another; they mingle and interpenetrate throughout, to the music of Pan's flute, and of Love's viol, and the bugle-call of Endeavour, and the passing-bell of Death." Similar responses to the pronouncements of other authors were to produce many of Owen's most powerful poems: "Apologia pro Poemate Meo" prompted by a remark of Robert Graves's, "For God's sake cheer up and write more optimistically – the war's not ended yet but a poet should have a spirit above wars"; the fragment "Cramped in that funnelled hole" prompted, perhaps unconsciously, by Tennyson's "The Charge of the Light Brigade"; and "S.I.W." subverting its epigraph from Yeats's play *The King's Threshold*.

Throughout his months at Craiglockhart Owen suffered from the horrendous nightmares that are the principal symptom of shell-shock. His experience of battle, banished from his waking mind, erupted into his dreams and thence into his poems. In "The Sentry" he remembers

> Those other wretches, how they bled and spewed,
> And one who would have drowned himself for good, –
> I try not to remember these things now.

But when he tries to forget them, there returns the memory of the blinded sentry vainly trying to see the struck match held before his eyes: "'I can't,' he sobbed. Eyeballs, huge-bulged like squids',/Watch my dreams still.... " Those tormented eyes stare also from such other poems as "Dulce et Decorum Est," "Greater Love," and "Mental Cases." Another obsessive image is of a subterranean Hell. Derived from the lurid descriptions of the wages of sin heard as a child, this appears in pre-war poems about the excavations at Uriconium and the double grave of a mother and daughter. Experience of the trenches expanded that metaphor into the symbol of mythic significance that dominates so many of the mature poems, among them "Cramped in that funnelled hole," "Miners," and "Strange Meeting."

The distinctive music of such later poems owes much of its power to Owen's mastery of alliteration, onomatopoeia, assonance, half-rhyme, and the pararhyme that he pioneered. This last, the rhyming of two words with identical or similar consonants but differing, stressed vowels (as *Flashes/Fleshes* and *hall/Hell*), of which the second is usually the lower in pitch, produces effects of dissonance, failure, and unfulfilment that subtly reinforce his themes.

In the year of life left to him after leaving Craiglockhart in November 1917, he matured

749

rapidly both as man and poet. Success as a soldier, marked by the award of the Military Cross, and as a poet, which had won him "the recognition of his peers," gave him a new confidence. He wrote more eloquently than other poets of the tragedy of boys killed in battle because, as a latent homosexual, he felt that tragedy more acutely, and in his later elegies a disciplined sensuality, a passionate intelligence find their fullest, most moving, and memorable expression.

—Jon Stallworthy

PAGE, P(atricia) K(athleen). Canadian. Born in Swanage, Dorset, England, 23 November 1916; emigrated to Canada, 1919. Educated at St. Hilda's School for Girls, Calgary, Alberta; Art Students' League, and Pratt Institute, New York; studied art privately in Brazil and New York. Married William Arthur Irwin in 1950; three step-children. Formerly, sales clerk and radio actress, St. John, New Brunswick; filing clerk and historical researcher, Montreal, and a Founding Editor, *Preview*, Montreal; Script Writer, National Film Board, Ottawa, 1946–50. Painter, as P. K. Irwin: one-man shows at Picture Loan Society, Toronto, 1960; Galeria de Arte Moderna, Mexico City, 1962, and Art Gallery of Greater Victoria, 1965; works included in the collections of the National Gallery of Canada, Ottawa; Art Gallery of Toronto; Vancouver Art Gallery. Recipient: Governor-General's Award, 1955. Member, Academia Brazileira de Letras, Rio de Janeiro. Lives in Victoria, British Columbia.

PUBLICATIONS

Verse

Unit of Five, with others.   1944.
As Ten as Twenty.   1946.
The Metal and the Flower.   1954.
Cry Ararat! Poems New and Selected.   1967.
Leviathan in a Pool.   1973.

Fiction

The Sun and the Moon.   1944.
The Sun and the Moon and Other Fictions.   1973.

Reading List: *The Bush Garden: Essays on the Canadian Imagination* by Northrop Frye, 1971; "The Poetry of Page" by A. J. M. Smith, in *Canadian Literature*, Autumn 1971.

*   *   *

P. K. Page is a poet with two careers. She played a considerable role among the Montreal poets of the early 1940's, being one of the founding editors of the historic Canadian poetry magazine *Preview*, and she continued writing verse until the early 1950's. There followed a period of travel in Latin America, Australia, and the United States, during which she wrote comparatively little, and developed a parallel talent as a painter under the name of P. K. Irwin. Returning to Canada in 1964, she began to write poetry again, and in recent years has reoccupied her leading position among active Canadian writers.

P. K. Page's early poetry tended to take on some of the flavour of English 1930's verse, concerning itself with themes of social protest and showing the formal influence of Auden and Spender. By the end of the 1940's she was moving into a more individual kind of expression, terse and ironic, and was concerning herself less with socio-political situations than with individual predicaments – the plights of solitary people or of those whom circumstances subjected to contempt; satire and compassion are unusually mingled in these middle poems.

In her later work, P. K. Page has moved towards a stark, purified poetry of great tonal attractiveness, and at the same time towards metaphysical intents, and an almost mystical concern for the view out from the mind towards images that promise integration. Her poem, "Cry Ararat!," in the volume with the same name, is typical of this trend, as the final lines eloquently demonstrate:

> The leaves that make the tree by day,
> the green twig the dove saw fit
> to lift across a world of water
> break in a wave about our feet.
> The bird in the thicket with his whistle
> the crystal lizard in the grass
> the star and shell
> tassel and bell
> of wild flowers blowing where we pass,
> this flora-fauna flotsam, pick and touch,
> requires the focus of the total I.
>
> A single leaf can block a mountainside;
> all Ararat be conjured by a leaf.

As well as her poetry and painting, P. K. Page has produced a small amount of fiction. The novel she published in 1944 under the pseudonym of Judith Cape, *The Sun and the Moon*, was a work of romantic symbolism, and the same is true of her haunting and highly ambivalent short stories.

—George Woodcock

PARNELL, Thomas. English. Born in Dublin, Ireland, in 1679. Educated at Dr. Jones's school, Dublin; Trinity College, Dublin, 1693–1700, B.A. 1697, M.A. 1700; B.D. and D.D. of Dublin University, 1712. Married Anne Minchin in 1706 (died, 1711); two sons and one daughter. Ordained deacon, 1700, priest, 1703; Minor Canon of St. Patrick's, Dublin, 1704; Archdeacon of Clogher, 1706–16; Prebend of Dunlavin, 1713; frequently visited London after 1706: on intimate terms with Swift and other members of the Tory Party by 1711; contributed to the *Spectator*, 1712–13; Member of the Scriblerus Club, 1713; appointed Vicar of Finglas, 1716. *Died (buried) 24 October 1718.*

PUBLICATIONS

Collections

Works, in Verse and Prose. 1755.
Poems, edited by L. Robinson. 1927.
Minor Poets of the Eighteenth Century, edited by Hugh I'A. Fausset. 1930.

Verse

An Essay on the Different Styles of Poetry. 1713.
Homer's Battle of the Frogs and Mice. 1717.

Poems on Several Occasions, edited by Alexander Pope.   1722.
Posthumous Works.   1758.

Reading List: *Parnell* by Alfred H. Cruickshank, 1921.

*   *   *

Thomas Parnell is a witty and graceful minor poet, who was a friend and close literary associate of Swift and especially of Pope. He was a protégé of Swift in his literary and his clerical career, and an original member of the Scriblerus Club. He helped Pope with his translation of the *Iliad*, and wrote the "Essay on the Life, Writings, and Learning of Homer" prefixed to the translation. He also translated the pseudo-Homeric *Battle of the Frogs and Mice*, published in 1717 together with some satirical apparatus designed to support Pope in the controversy surrounding his Homeric enterprise. The main collection of Parnell's work is *Poems on Several Occasions*, edited by Pope. Pope altered Parnell's text, although we do not know exactly how, since the papers he used did not survive. Some autograph versions of these poems have, however, recently been discovered, along with many new poems. Two later collections, the *Works, in Verse and Prose* and the *Posthumous Works*, can also largely be authenticated by manuscripts. Most of the manuscripts are in my custody at the University of Warwick, and a complete edition is in preparation.

The poems, published and unpublished, include a large group of religious meditations; a verse *Essay on the Different Styles of Poetry*; some rather feeble satires; political poems on the Peace of Utrecht and related matters; poems in praise of Swift, Pope, and other Scriblerians, and contributions to Scriblerian warfare, chiefly against Pope's literary enemies; translations from Greek and Latin (*The Battle of the Frogs and Mice*, "The Vigil of Venus"); some attractive lyrics ("When thy beauty appears," "My days have been so wondrous free"); and a variety of hymns, "imitations," epigrams, and other works. But perhaps his two best-known poems are "The Hermit" (a retelling of a pious fable) and "A Night-Piece on Death" (an early example of eighteenth-century "graveyard" poetry). Oliver Goldsmith wrote a life of Parnell in 1770, and Johnson included him in the *Lives of the Poets*.

—C. J. Rawson

PATCHEN, Kenneth.   American.   Born in Niles, Ohio, 13 December 1911. Educated at Warren High School, Ohio; the Experimental College, University of Wisconsin, Madison, 1928–29. Married Miriam Oikemus in 1934. Also an artist: one-man show of books, graphics, and paintings, Corcoran Gallery, Washington, D.C., 1969. Recipient: Guggenheim Fellowship, 1936; Shelley Memorial Award, 1954; National Endowment for the Arts Distinguished Service Grant, 1967. *Died 8 January 1972.*

PUBLICATIONS

Verse

Before the Brave.   1936.

First Will and Testament. 1939.
The Teeth of the Lion. 1942.
The Dark Kingdom. 1942.
Cloth of the Tempest. 1943.
An Astonished Eye Looks Out of the Air, Being Some Poems Old and New Against War
    and in Behalf of Life. 1945.
Outlaw of the Lowest Planet, edited by David Gascoyne. 1946.
Selected Poems. 1946; revised edition, 1958, 1964.
Pictures of Life and of Death. 1947.
They Keep Riding Down All the Time. 1947.
Panels for the Walls of Heaven. 1947.
Patchen: Man of Anger and Light, with A Letter to God by Kenneth Patchen, with Henry
    Miller. 1947.
CCCLXXIV Poems. 1948.
To Say If You Love Someone and Other Selected Love Poems. 1948.
Red Wine and Yellow Hair. 1949.
Fables and Other Little Tales. 1953.
The Famous Boating Party and Other Poems in Prose. 1954.
Orchards, Thrones and Caravans. 1955.
Glory Never Guesses: Being a Collection of 18 Poems with Decorations and
    Drawings. 1956.
A Surprise for the Bagpipe Player: A Collection of 18 Poems with Decorations and
    Drawings. 1956.
When We Were Here Together. 1957.
Hurrah for Anything: Poems and Drawings. 1957.
Two Poems for Christmas. 1958.
Poem-scapes. 1958.
Pomes Penyeach. 1959.
Poems of Humor and Protest. 1960.
Because It Is: Poems and Drawings. 1960.
A Poem for Christmas. 1960.
The Love Poems. 1960.
Patchen Drawing-Poem. 1962.
Picture Poems. 1962.
Doubleheader. 1966.
Hallelujah Anyway. 1966.
Where Are the Other Rowboats? 1966.
But Even So (includes drawings). 1968.
Love and War Poems, edited by Dennis Gould. 1968.
Selected Poems. 1968.
The Collected Poems. 1968.
Aflame and Afun of Walking Faces: Fables and Drawings. 1970.
There's Love All Day, edited by Dee Danner Barwick. 1970.
Wonderings. 1971.
In Quest of Candlelighters. 1972.

Plays

Now You See It (Don't Look Now) (produced 1966).
Lost Plays, edited by Richard Morgan. 1977.

Radio Play: City Wears a Slouch Hat, 1942.

Fiction

> *The Journal of Albion Moonlight.* 1941.
> *The Memoirs of a Shy Pornographer: An Amusement.* 1945.
> *Sleepers Awake.* 1946.
> *See You in the Morning.* 1948.

Other

> *Patchen: Painter of Poems* (exhibition catalogue). 1969.
> *The Argument of Innocence: A Selection from the Pictureworks,* edited by Peter Veres. 1975.

Bibliography: *Patchen: A First Bibliography* by Gail Eaton, 1948.

Reading List: *Patchen: A Collection of Essays* edited by Richard Morgan, 1977.

*   *   *

Kenneth Patchen is in the tradition of American poets that descends from Walt Whitman through William Carlos Williams to the Black Mountain poets, and beyond them to such younger writers as Galway Kinnell and Michael Waters. That is to say, Patchen is a "redskin" poet as opposed to a "paleface." His poems do not make use of European-inspired formal devices; his language is deliberately a "barbaric yawp" (Whitman's famous phrase from *Song of Myself*); and his subject-matter is drawn from his own very American experiences. He is a poet of the open air and the open road, a hunter after experience, claiming a kind of mystical connection with the animals he kills (in this he is very like Hemingway, James Dickey, and, perhaps, Robinson Jeffers); his style is free-ranging, colloquial, wise-cracking, but also unembarrassedly ready with the big word, the huge emotion. In short, he sounds very like Carl Sandburg.

Yet Patchen is a self-conscious poet. He may *play* the cracker-barrel philosopher, but as Thomas Hardy said of William Barnes, "He sings his native woodnotes wild with a great deal of art." Look, for example, at so small a poem as "In Memory of Kathleen":

> How pitiful is her sleep.
> Now her clear breath is still.
>
> There is nothing falling tonight,
> Bird or man,
> As dear as she.
>
> Nowhere that she should go
> Without me. None but my calling.
>
> O nothing but the cold cry of the snow.

It is a very finely written poem of grief, and a subtle one. The play on "pitiful" is perhaps obvious; but the way in which "falling" anticipates the cry of the snow is not so obvious, yet entirely just; as is the extraordinarily compacted "None but my calling." "None" comes from the earlier "nowhere," and it means that Patchen finds himself utterly alone: she has gone where he can't follow, there is only *his* calling, *his* voice to be heard. That, and the cry of the snow: whiteness, death, its falling reminding him that she, too, has fallen in death. Glanced

755

casually over, this little poem may seem hopelessly slight; looked at more carefully, it emerges as the work of a considerable poet.

Patchen doesn't always write with this degree of tense urgency. It is, I think, characteristic of his kind of poetry that there should be a great deal of sprawl about it; and while one may salute the energy that has led him to produce so many volumes of verse – he must be one of the most unflaggingly fertile of twentieth-century American poets – it is also possible to wish that some of his work had been more intensively worked over. There is, for instance, a wonderful idea, partly spoiled, in *First Will and Testament* which has at its core a play for voices, featuring a Mr. Kek and his brothel, to which come, in turn, a group of famous poets, Donne, Marvell, Jonson, etc.; and then jazzmen Beiderbecke, Armstrong, Allen; gangsters, sportsmen – all outsiders, all seeking warmth and love and a good time, and trying to escape "the enemy." Much of this is obviously borrowed from Auden, but it has some fizzing wit and a great deal of hard-hitting panache that are Patchen's own. The trouble is that it degenerates into Cummings-like sentimentality: all picaros are better than all lawmen; to be an artist you have to be on the outside, a society reject, a bum. In other words the play is written out of cliché, so that although it has local life it is finally soggy.

This criticism applies to a good deal of his work. Yet nothing I say here is intended to detract from the vitality of his best writing, which can crop up anywhere, and is just as likely to show itself in a late volume, like *When We Were Here Together*, as in an early one, such as *Before the Brave*.

—John Lucas

PATERSON, Andrew Barton.   Australian.   Born in Narrambla, near Orange, New South Wales, 17 February 1864. Educated at school in Binalong; preparatory school in Sydney; Sydney Grammar School; University of Sydney; entered in the Roll of Solicitors. Ambulance Driver, Australian Hospital, Boulogne, 1914–15, and served in the British Red Cross Centre in Egypt and Palestine, 1916–18: Major. Married Alice Walker in 1903; one son and one daughter. Practised law in Sydney: Managing Clerk, later Partner, W. William Street, until 1900; Contributor to the *Sydney Bulletin* after 1886; War Correspondent for *Sydney Morning Herald* and *Melbourne Argus* during the Boer War, 1899–1901; *Sydney Morning Herald* Correspondent in China, 1901, and England, 1902; Editor, *Evening News*, Sydney, 1903–06, and *Town and Country Journal*, Sydney, 1906–08; Editor, *Sydney Sportsman*, 1921–30; freelance journalist for *Smith's Weekly* in the early 1930's. C.B.E. (Commander, Order of the British Empire), 1939. *Died 5 February 1941.*

PUBLICATIONS

Collections

   The World of "Banjo" Paterson: His Stories, Travels, War Reports, and Advice to Racegoers, edited by Clement Semmler.   1967.

Verse

The Man from Snowy River and Other Verses. 1895.
Rio Grande's Last Race and Other Verses. 1902.
Saltbush Bill, J.P., and Other Verses. 1917.
Collected Verse. 1921.
The Animals Noah Forgot (juvenile). 1933.

Plays

Radio Series: *The Land of Adventure,* 1930's.

Fiction

An Outback Marriage. 1906.
Three Elephant Power and Other Stories. 1917.
The Shearer's Colt. 1936.

Other

Australia for the Australians Showing the Necessity for Land Reform. 1889.
Happy Dispatches. 1934.

Editor, *The Old Bush Songs.* 1905.

Reading List: *Paterson,* 1965, *The Banjo of the Bush,* 1966, and *Paterson,* 1967, all by Clement Semmler; *Paterson* by Lorna Ollif, 1971.

*   *   *

The status of the popular ballad in Australia (with a run from about the mid-1880's to about 1930) was unique in its day. Andrew Barton Paterson was one of its most distinguished creators. Unlike his contemporary Henry Lawson, he accented the cheerful aspects of colonial life. Whereas Lawson saw life from ground-level (he identifies with underdogs, swagmen, and job-seekers), Paterson is reputed to have looked on the world as a rider, with the advantageous elevation of horseback to lift up his mood. His verses, incidentally, are full of a variety of riding rhythms, vigorous in style and full of joy in their motion.

Paterson has a strong predilection for energy and movement, but as a rule the action becomes suffused with reflection: "In my wild erratic fancy visions come to me of Clancy/ Gone a-droving 'down the Cooper' where the Western drovers go...." It is not merely what Clancy does, but what he enjoys that is exciting: "And he sees the vision splendid of the sunlit plains extended,/And at night the wondrous glory of the everlasting stars." In "The Man from Snowy River" action and reflection form a common conclusion as Paterson's imagination pursues the spirit of heroism into myth:

> And where around the Overflow the reed-beds sweep and sway
> To the breezes, and the rolling plains are wide,
> The Man from Snowy River is a household word today,
> And the stockmen tell the story of his ride.

Clancy and the Man and sundry other heroes of Paterson's fancy have become Australian myth-figures today. His poetical compass is not wide – there are repetitions – but for all that he epitomizes, as does also Lawson in his different way, one of the major aspects of Colonial life – in Paterson's case, a cheerful if also distinctly conservative one. Much of what he writes is from the heart of an imaginative boy; he preserves a boy's delight in nature. He also preserves a very lively, perhaps essentially a boy's sense of humour, as witness that infectious Australian comic classic "The Man from Ironbark." Not the least of his achievements was in being the author of another work of comic (and equally grotesque) genius, the ballad of "Waltzing Matilda," now an Australian national song.

Paterson's prose was less distinguished than his verse, but includes some good colonial fiction, a few excellent short stories, and much lively journalism ranging from war correspondence to "advice to racegoers."

—Brian Elliott

PATMORE, Coventry (Kersey Dighton).   English.   Born in Woodford, Essex, 23 July 1823. Educated privately. Married 1) Emily Augusta Andrews in 1847 (died, 1862), three sons and three daughters; 2) Marianne Caroline Byles in 1864 (died, 1880); 3) Harriet Robson in 1881, one son. Worked as an Assistant in the Printed Books Department of the British Museum, London, 1846–64; became acquainted with Tennyson and Ruskin; associated with the Pre-Raphaelite brotherhood from 1849; converted to Roman Catholicism, 1864; settled in Sussex, 1864–91, and in Lymington, 1891–96. *Died 26 November 1896.*

PUBLICATIONS

Collections

> *Works.*   5 vols., 1897.
> *Poems,* edited by Frederick Page.   1949.

Verse

> *Poems.*   1844.
> *Tamerton Church-Tower and Other Poems.*   1853.
> *The Angel in the House (The Betrothal, The Espousals, Faithful for Ever, The Victories of Love).*   4 vols., 1854–62; revised edition, 1 vol., 1866; revised edition of *The Victories of Love,* 1888.
> *Odes.*   1868; edited by John Merrell, 1971.
> *The Unknown Eros and Other Odes.*   1877; revised edition, 1890.
> *Amelia.*   1878.
> *Florilegium Amantis,* edited by R. Garnett.   1879.
> *Poems.*   2 vols., 1886.
> *The Poetry of Pathos and Delight,* edited by Alice Meynell.   1896.
> *Seven Unpublished Poems to Alice Meynell.*   1922.

Other

How I Managed and Improved My Estate.   1886.
Hastings, Lewes, Rye, and the Sussex Marshes.   1887.
Principle in Art.   1889; revised edition, 1898.
Religio Poetae.   1893; revised edition, 1898.
The Rod, The Root, and the Flower.   1895; edited by Derek Patmore, 1950.
Courage in Politics and Other Essays, 1885–1896, edited by Frederick Page.   1921.
Essay on English Metrical Law, edited by Mary A. Roth.   1961.

Editor, The Children's Garland from the Best Poets.   1861.
Editor, Bryan Waller Procter – Barry Cornwall: An Autobiographical Fragment and
    Biographical Notes.   1877.

Translator, with Marianne Caroline Patmore, Saint Bernard on the Love of God.   1881.

Reading List: Memoirs and Correspondence of Patmore by Basil Champneys, 2 vols., 1900;
Patmore: A Study in Poetry by Frederick Page, 1933; The Life and Times of Patmore by Derek
Patmore, 1949; Patmore by E. J. Oliver, 1956; The Mind and Art of Patmore by J. C. Reid,
1957 (includes bibliography).

*   *   *

A feature of the Victorian age which continues to astonish us is its habit of awarding
popular acclaim and professional success to people who were profoundly alien to its
prevailing spirit. Disraeli and Tennyson are obvious examples; and Coventry Patmore is
another. He was known in his time, and is perhaps still mainly known, as the purveyor of a
sugary domesticity, a kind of verse equivalent of some of the slacker passages at the end of
novels by Dickens. It is true that he gave some excuse for this mistake in certain inferior
passages in poems like "Tamerton Church Tower," but this is a very early work. In reality,
Patmore was an original and an eccentric, extremely intelligent, markedly immune to the
subtle influences of fashion, a rediscoverer of ideas largely forgotten by men of his age, and a
poet, if not of the highest rank, yet contributing something uniquely personal to the corpus of
Victorian poetry.

His deviation from the ordinary Victorian domestic ideal in his treatment of the relation
between the sexes is best studied, not in the popular Angel in the House, a rather second-rate
novel in verse, but in "The Unknown Eros." Here marriage is viewed as a real image of the
love between God and the soul. Its sacramental reality, its potentiality for tragedy and loss, its
continually questing, unsatisfied character, its deep seriousness – all set it far apart from the
love of David Copperfield and Agnes, or of Rokesmith and Bella Wilfer. The relation of the
latter pairs can only be imagined as static after marriage; it is thoroughly characteristic of
Patmore to write of the chaste and ardent wife, "She's not and never can be mine." Most
Victorian writers, though perhaps too gentlemanly to agree openly with Byron ("Man's love
is of man's life a thing apart, / 'Tis woman's whole existence") would have silently concurred.
Patmore would have disagreed with the whole force of his being. Because love concerned the
soul, because it was analogous to the religious quest, it was for both sexes the only earthly
thing that mattered.

Patmore's father was an agnostic; the poet early became a Christian, and in 1864, just after
he was forty, a Catholic. Thus, as a Catholic, he was only two years senior to Gerard Manley
Hopkins, whom he admired but did not fully understand. Their correspondence is of
particular interest. The strength of the younger man's authority over the elder can be seen
from Patmore's impulsive (and perhaps later regretted) act in burning the manuscript of
Sponsa Dei, when Hopkins commented, "That's telling secrets." It was, apparently, his most

intimate study of the mystical aspects of married love. Hopkins, who had not intended any severe condemnation, or expected such an extreme reaction, had evidently not understood the extent of his own power.

Of the two letter-writers, Patmore is the more fanciful and wayward, and occasionally earns a rebuke from Hopkins for playing with profound ideas. But both are remarkably unlike their contemporaries in the breadth and originality of their critical views and the minute exactness of their care for the technique of English verse. But while nearly all Hopkins's best criticism is to be found in his letters, Patmore published a series of articles in the *St. James's Gazette*, later reprinted as *Principle in Art* and *Religio Poetae*. Here, and in *Rod, Root, and Flower*, the full extent of his originality and intellectual loneliness in his age is seen. He was one of few Victorians – though Gladstone was another – who had meditated deeply on Dante. He was well-read, too, in scholastic philosophy and medieval love poetry. His mind shows a rather rare combination of qualities. He was at the same time a brooding, slow-moving, deeply feeling mind and an uncompromising, at times violent, commentator on public events. His reaction to that really very temperate measure, the Reform Bill of 1867, was as reckless almost as Carlyle's. Except as a devout and loyal Catholic, which he clearly was, he is always hard to classify. The mystic, the deep thinker and profound critic, impatient of the prudery of his age, the competent hard-headed man of the world and the exasperated clubman complaining that the country is going to the dogs, the associate of Ruskin and the pre-Raphaelites, the exacting craftsman in verse – all these aspects of his character are genuine, many are incongruous and surprising. He is an ornament of an age of extraordinary variety, rich in originality and in the unconventional.

—A. O. J. Cockshut

---

p'BITEK, Okot. Ugandan. Born in Gulu, Acoli District, Northern Uganda, in 1931. Educated at Gulu High School; King's College, Budo, Uganda; University of Bristol, Certificate in Education; University of Wales, Aberystwyth, LL.B.; Oxford University, B.Litt. in social anthropology 1963. Lecturer in Sociology at Makerere University College, and Director of the Uganda National Theatre and Uganda National Cultural Center, all Kampala, 1964–68; Founder, Kisumu Arts Festival, Kenya, 1968; Fellow, International Writing Program, University of Iowa, Iowa City, 1969–70; Senior Research Fellow, Institute of African Studies, Nairobi, 1971. Lives in Kisumu, Kenya.

PUBLICATIONS

Verse

> *Lak tar miyo kınyero wi lobo?* (in Acoli: Are your teeth white, then laugh!).   1953.
> *The Song of Lawino* (translated from Acoli by the author).   1966.
> *Song of Ocol.*   1970.
> *The Song of a Prisoner.*   1970.
> *Two Songs: The Song of a Prisoner, The Song of Malaya.*   1971.
> *The Horn of My Love* (Acoli traditional songs, translated by the author).   1974.
> *The Hare and the Hornbill.*   1978.

*   *   *

Okot p'Bitek is a scholar as well as a poet and a novelist. *Song of Lawino* is a traditional story in verse of an Acoli wife, as if told by herself, of her husband's turning, in his desire to be "modern," to Clementine who "aspires/To look like a white woman" ("And she believes/ That this is beautiful"):

> I do not deny
> I am a little jealous.
> It is no good lying,
> We all suffer from a little jealousy....
>
> How many kids
> Has this woman sucked?
> The empty bags on her chest
> Are completely flattened, dried.
> Perhaps she has aborted many!
> Perhaps she has thrown her twins
> In the pit latrine!

The story contains a revealing character-sketch of the husband, Okol, floundering among the problems of *Uhuru* (freedom). It is a useful stroke to have made a woman the mouthpiece while there are still too few women writing in Africa. *Two Songs: Song of a Prisoner, Song of Malaya* are in similar, short-lined, graphic verse, the first song from the mouth of a man, the second from an unmarried woman. They are biting yet compassionate satires on an emergent African society torn between its own rich traditions and a seductive, materialist modernity passed on by British and American "imperialist progress"; *Song of a Prisoner* reveals, behind this "false dawn" of assassinations, corruption great and small, tyrants and blustering power, an enduring reality of life outside the "brash new towns" – the burning optimism of the people of Africa in the face of hardship and humiliation as in the known face of hunger: "Brother/How could I/So poor/Cold/Limping/Weak/Hungry like an empty tomb/A young tree/Burnt out/By the fierce wild fire/Of Uhuru/How could I/Inspire you/To such heights of brutality?"

What p'Bitek is writing is essentially a new kind of verse. Not only is he combining modern verse-form with oral form and content: he is showing how that form *is* the oral form. Yet, beside his stark concern with human essentials, the content of some modern Western verse can sound trivial, precious, oblique, too personal, materialist. Almost the only other poetry like p'Bitek's, since the 1960's, has come from South Africa, Russia, Chile, East Europe. In his own preface to *The Horn of My Love*, he explains: "Missionaries, anthropologists, musicologists and folklorists have plucked songs, stories, proverbs, riddles etc. from their social backgrounds and, after killing them by analysis, have buried them in inaccessible and learned journals, and in expensive technical books. I believe that literature, like all the other creative arts, is there, first and foremost, to be enjoyed." Writing by Africans alone, p'Bitek thinks, can secure the development of African literature.

—Anne Tibble

PHILIPS, Ambrose.   English.   Born in Shrewsbury, Shropshire, c. 1675. Educated at St. John's College, Cambridge, B.A. 1696, M.A. 1700. Fellow of St. John's College, 1699–1707; member of Addison's circle, London, in the early 1700's; Justice of the Peace for

Westminster; Commissioner for the Lottery, 1717; Founder-Editor, *The Freethinker*, 1718–19; held various posts in Ireland from 1724: Secretary to the Bishop of Armagh, 1724, and to the Lord Chancellor, 1726; Member of the Irish Parliament for Armagh, 1727; Judge of the Prerogative Court, 1733; returned to London, 1748. *Died 18 June 1749.*

PUBLICATIONS

Collections

Poems, edited by Mary G. Segar.   1937.

Verse

Pastorals.   1710; edited by R. H. Griffith, as *A Variorum Text of Four [of the Six] Pastorals,* in *Texas University Studies,* 1932.
An Epistle to Charles Lord Halifax.   1714.
An Epistle to James Craggs.   1717.
An Ode in the Manner of Pindar on the Death of William, Earl Cowper.   1723.
To the Honourable Miss Carteret.   1725.
To Miss Georgiana.   1725.
To the Lord Carteret.   1726.
Supplication for Miss Carteret in the Smallpox.   1726.
To Miss Margaret Pulteney.   1727.
Farmer Pope and His son, with *Codrus* by Edmund Curll and Elizabeth Thomas.   1728.
Pastorals, Epistles, Odes, and Other Original Poems, with Translations from Pindar, Anacreon, and Sappho.   1748.

Plays

The Distressed Mother, from a play by Racine (produced 1712).   1712.
The Briton (produced 1722).   1722.
Humfrey, Duke of Gloucester (produced 1723).   1723.

Other

The Freethinker.   3 vols., 1722.

Editor, *Life of John Williams,* by J. Hacket.   1700.
Editor, *Letters to Several Ministers of State,* by Hugh Boulter.   2 vols., 1769–70.

Translator, *Persian Tales,* by Petis de la Croix.   1709.

*   *   *

Ambrose Philips is perhaps chiefly remembered for his pastorals, and this largely because of the quarrel with Pope their publication engendered. Addison had written a series of articles in *The Guardian* in which he acclaimed Philips as the true successor of Theocritus, Virgil, and Spenser. This enraged Pope, who had recently published his own youthful pastorals, and he sent to Steele, the *Guardian's* editor, a further anonymous article in which he quoted passages from his own work beside parallel passages from Philips, ironically praising the latter. He later satirised Philips in the character sketch entitled "Umbra." Gay's pastorals *The Shepherd's Week* owe their genesis to the same quarrel. Philips had argued that simple rusticity was the main quality to be aimed at in the pastoral and, following Spenser, had given English names, such as Hobbinol and Rosalind, to his shepherds. Gay parodied this by using names like Grubbinol and Blowselind, and giving to these characters some of the real manners and much of the folk lore of genuine English peasants. Philips's goal of simplicity too often landed him in mere insipidity – and indeed "insipid" seems to be the epithet which inevitably comes up in any discussion of Philips's work. His pastorals do however contain passages of some charm.

Philips's tragedy *The Distressed Mother* was an adaptation of Racine's *Andromaque*. With some assistance from promotion by Addison in the *Spectator*, and Addison's claque in the theatre, it achieved success and held the stage for some time. Of his other two plays, *The Briton* and *Humfrey, Duke of Gloucester*, Johnson remarks, in the *Lives of the Poets* that they "are not below mediocrity, nor above it." Johnson further remarked of Philips's translations of Pindar that "he found the art of reaching all the obscurity of the Theban bard, however he may fall below his sublimity; he will be allowed, if he has less fire, to have more smoke." His translations of Sappho appeared in a *Spectator* paper for the first time introducing the Greek lyric poetess to English readers. Philips made a thoroughly rococo job of the "Ode to Aphrodite," but his version of the "Ode to Anactoria" has some of the directness, if not the intensity, of the original.

Later in his career Philips abandoned some of the stricter canons of Augustan taste. His poems to persons of quality (some of them addressed to children) are written in short trochaic couplets. These verses earned him from Henry Carey (author of *Sally in Our Alley*) the nickname of "Namby-Pamby." The *faux naif* quality of these verses seems to have earned them the esteem of such Victorian anthologists and critics as Palgrave and Edmund Gosse, but the contemporary reader may be disposed to echo Carey's view of them. To us it may seem that Philips's "Epistle to the Earl of Dorset" (from Copenhagen) is perhaps his best poem. Here he exhibits originality and descriptive force in rendering a northern winter scene.

—John Heath-Stubbs

PHILIPS, John. English. Born in Bampton, Oxfordshire, 30 December 1676. Educated at Winchester College (scholar), 1691–97; Christ Church, Oxford, matriculated 1697. Employed by Harley and St. John as a propagandist. Consumptive. *Died 15 February 1709.*

PUBLICATIONS

Collections

Poems, edited by M. G. Lloyd Thomas. 1927.

Verse

The Sylvan Dream; or, The Mourning Muses. 1701.
The Splendid Shilling: An Imitation of Milton. 1701.
Blenheim. 1705.
Cerealia: An Imitation of Milton. 1706; revised edition, 1706.
Honoratissimo Viro Henrico Saint John, Armigero: Ode. 1707.
Ode Gratulatoria Willielmo Cowper. 1707.
Cider. 1708.
Poems. 1712.

Bibliography: in *Poems,* 1927.

Reading List: *The English Georgic* by John Chalker, 1969.

*   *   *

In his own time John Philips owed a large part of his fame to a couple of earlier works. Neither *The Splendid Shilling* nor *Blenheim* compels an equivalent degree of admiration today, when their adaptation of Miltonic style is liable to seem coy and archaic. To contemporaries, *The Splendid Shilling* appeared daring in its strategy of turning Milton's verbal gestures to a low subject-matter – the work provides a picture of the distressed poet, skulking in penury as the bailiffs make their rounds. Classical epic had been much burlesqued, but this was the first extended mock-Miltonic, that is to say a poem travestying specifically *English* modes of poeticism. Humour and a whiff of first-person authenticity help to carry off the effect. *Blenheim* attempts to enlist the grand style for propagandist ends, and falls at times into awkward postures, such as a parenthesis within parentheses at lines 16–20.

Philips's most successful poetry, both for local felicities and for overall coherence, is found in *Cyder.* To all intents and purposes a formal Georgic in two books, this mixes the comic burlesque of *The Splendid Shilling* with the patriotic aims of *Blenheim.* If it had achieved nothing else, the poem would have had the merit of showing subsequent English poets how to make use of the Virgilian combination (husbandry plus politics) for their own needs: Pope's *Windsor-Forest* is directly indebted to *Cyder* at several points. Philips is particularly successful in counterpointing an innocent rural vocation against the threats of a more active life in less temperate climes. He inserts, for example, an elevated passage describing an earthquake in a lost Roman city (usually identified with Hereford, and thus prolonging a regional theme in the poem). As John Chalker, Philips's best modern critic, observes, "By temporarily going beyond his bucolic subject matter to the wider world of a lost heroic age, and by setting his 'humble' subject against that extensive background, Philips deliberately encourages the reader to consider the value of the activities which are the subject of the poem." As well as the technical accounts of arboriculture and cider-making which provide opportunities for joking inflation of humdrum reality, Philips affords us an easy modulation into scrutiny of the natural order, the connection of beauty and use in the landscape, the values of an agrarian society. The blank verse of *Cyder,* grandiloquent as it often is, has ceased to be merely a parodic instrument; it opens the way for the garrulous, loose-jointed, and histrionic idiom of Thomson and Cowper, poets who were the freer because Philips had gone over the top. He writes of

> *Sylvan* Shades, and silent Groves,
> (Haunt of the *Druids*) whence the Hearth is fed
> With copious Fuel; whence the sturdy Oak,
> A Prince's Refuge once, th'aeternal Guard
> Of *England*'s Throne, by sweating Peasants fell'd,
> Stems the vast Main, and bears tremendous War
> To distant Nations, or with Sov'ran Sway
> Aws the divided World to Peace and Love.

At such moments the false heroics of burlesque turn into something very like mythopoeic invention, and it was on this that John Philips's successors were able to build.

—Pat Rogers

PHILIPS, Katherine (née Fowler). Pseudonym: Orinda. English. Born in London, 1 January 1631. Educated at Mrs. Salmon's School, Hackney, London. Married James Philips in 1647; one son and one daughter. After marriage divided her time between her husband's estate in Cardigan and London: centre of a literary circle that included Henry Vaughan, Jeremy Taylor, and Abraham Cowley; adopted the name Orinda to which contemporaries prefixed the epithet "matchless." *Died 22 June 1664.*

PUBLICATIONS

Collections

　Selected Poems, edited by Louise Imogen Guiney.　2 vols., 1904–05.

Verse

　Poems. 1664.
　Poems, to Which Is Added Corneille's Pompey and Horace, edited by Sir Charles
　　Cotterell. 1667.

Plays

　Pompey, from the play by Corneille (produced 1663). 1663.
　Horace, completed by John Denham, from the play by Corneille (produced
　　1668). 1678.

765

Other

Familiar Letters (by Rochester, Thomas Otway, and Philips), edited by Tom Brown and
  Charles Gildon.   2 vols., 1697.
Letters from Orinda to Poliarchus.   1705.

Reading List: The Matchless Orinda by P. W. Souers, 1931.

                              *   *   *

If "the matchless Orinda" no longer inspires, as Langbaine predicted in 1691, an immortal
memory "honour'd of all Men that are Favourers of Poetry," she still merits study as more
than historically the first significant English poetess. As one of the few active poets during the
decade before the Restoration, Katherine Philips shows in her work the tension between
metaphysical elevation of ingenuity and an evolving neo-classical admiration for pellucid
thought in "easy" versification. She is also interesting as the purest English expression of the
vogue of Platonic Précieuse – an ideal of love and honor and literacy adapted from
seventeenth-century French romances in reaction to what she perceived to be the "dull and
sullen" excesses of the Interregnum. Platonic friendship is her most characteristic theme, and
her many poems to Lucasia and Rosania escape artificiality because of the same authentic
intensity which inspired admiration in friends like Henry Vaughan, Jeremy Taylor, and
Abraham Cowley.
  Adopting the cavalier vein of William Cartwright, Orinda's lyrics move in a realm of
empyrean abstraction far above the compromises and contradictions of contemporary affairs.
Yet somehow she is best when she is abstract, for the concrete seems to have stimulated the
artificial in her and only in hymning an ideal passion does she seem unpretentious. Her best
songs continue the Caroline genius for song – lyric yet resonant with the spoken word,
wittily ingenious without self-indulgent audacity. If there is too much of the affectation of the
Précieuse in "To Mrs. M. A. at Parting," which Keats admired, her "To My Excellent
Lucasia, on Our Friendship" is nearly perfect:

                    I did not live until this time
                        Crown'd my felicity,
                    When I could say without a crime,
                        I am not thine, but Thee.

  Although her songs are her enduring claim to distinction, Orinda's didactic poems or
couplet essays are worth study as innovations in a form that was to flower in Dryden and
Pope. Nor are her couplets contemptible. They draw strength from their approximation to
human speech in the second line – an idiomatic effect often achieved by forcing the syntax of
the initial line: "Silence with things transcendent nearest suits,/The greatest Emperors are
serv'd by mutes." At their best, as in "The World," her couplets are concise without
sacrificing suggestiveness: "We live by chance and slip into events;/Have all of beasts except
their innocence." In the couplets of Pompey Katherine Philips produced what her
contemporaries considered one of the literary triumphs of the age and what may still be the
best verse translation of Corneille in English. If some of the sublimity of the French is
inevitably lost, Pompey is nonetheless meticulously faithful to the spirit and phrase of the
original and is uniquely successful in translating Corneille's rhetorical devices.
  However, it is not her writings in verse that the present age is apt to find most engaging but
her letters to the courtier Sir Charles Cotterell. These, published as Letters from Orinda to
Poliarchus, give an almost Richardsonian reality to Katherine's personal and literary life and
deserve a place in the development of the epistolary novel. As a writer of letters Katherine
Philips is inferior to no seventeenth-century woman with the possible exception of her friend

Dorothy Temple. The attractive portrait that emerges from the *Letters* gives a unique vividness to the personality which Dryden and his age regarded as the paragon of female poets.

—Harry M. Solomon

PLATH, Sylvia. American. Born in Boston, Massachusetts, 27 October 1932. Educated at Smith College, Northampton, Massachusetts, B.A. (summa cum laude) in English 1955; Harvard University, Cambridge, Massachusetts, Summer 1954; Newnham College, Cambridge (Fulbright Scholar), 1955–57, M.A. 1957. Married the poet Ted Hughes, *q.v.*, in 1956; one daughter and one son. Guest Editor, *Mademoiselle* magazine, New York, Summer 1953; Instructor in English, Smith College, 1957–58; moved to England, 1959. Recipient: Yaddo Fellowship, 1959; Cheltenham Festival Award, 1961; Saxon Fellowship, 1961. *Died (by suicide) 11 February 1963.*

PUBLICATIONS

Verse

A Winter Ship. 1960.
The Colossus and Other Poems. 1960; as The Colossus, 1967.
Ariel. 1965.
Uncollected Poems. 1965.
Fiesta Melons. 1971.
Crossing the Water, edited by Ted Hughes. 1971; as Crossing the Water: Transitional Poems, 1971.
Crystal Gazer and Other Poems. 1971.
Lyonesse: Hitherto Uncollected Poems. 1971.
Winter Trees. 1971.
Pursuit. 1973.

Play

Three Women: A Monologue for Voices (broadcast 1962; produced 1973).

Radio Play: Three Women, 1962.

Fiction

The Bell Jar. 1961.

Other

> *Letters Home: Correspondence 1950–1963,* edited by Aurelia Schober Plath.   1975.
> *The Bed Book* (juvenile).   1976.
> *Plath: A Dramatic Portrait* (miscellany), edited by Barry Kyle.   1976.
> *Johnny Panic and the Bible of Dreams, and Other Prose Writings.*   1977.

> Editor, *American Poetry Now: A Selection of the Best Poems by Modern American Writers.*   1961.

Bibliography: *A Chronological Checklist of the Periodical Publications of Plath* by Eric Homberger, 1970; *Plath and Anne Sexton: A Reference Guide* by Cameron Northouse and Thomas P. Walsh, 1975.

Reading List: *The Art of Plath: A Symposium* edited by Charles Newman, 1970 (includes bibliography); *Plath* by Eileen M. Aird, 1973; *Plath: Method and Madness* by Edward Butscher, 1976, and *Plath: The Woman and Her Work* edited by Butscher, 1977; *Plath: Poetry and Existence* by David Holbrook, 1976.

*   *   *

The adolescent heroine of Sylvia Plath's only novel, *The Bell Jar*, has looked into her grave and seen a sobering and a maddening truth. Her suicidal hysteria, like that which finally took her author, is the anguish of a being who has realized her own gratuitousness, "Factitious, artificial, sham." What she has called her "self," that unique and coddled ego, is no more than a nexus of donated being, a field of battle where the conflicting forces of her environment, her familial and social experience, clash, divide, and coalesce. Plath herself wrote of the poem "Daddy" as "spoken by a girl with an Electra complex. Her father died while she thought he was God. Her case is complicated by the fact that her father was also a Nazi and her mother very possibly Jewish. In the daughter the two strains marry and paralyze each other – she has to act out the awful little allegory before she is free of it." While the details hardly correspond accurately to Plath's own biography, their symbolic function in the emotional ecology of her work is clear. The title poem of *The Colossus* acknowledges such a condition: addressed to her dead father ("I shall never get you put together entirely") it is self-consciously post-Freudian and pre-Christian: "A blue sky out of the Oresteia/Arches above us"; if her father is now no more than a "Mouthpiece of the dead," this is equally true of all selves, whose "hours are married to shadow," the marionettes of an unconscious in whose formation they had no hand. "Poem for a Birthday" is a complex dramatic monologue in which a psyche struggles towards birth, in "the city of spare parts" which is the world. Its voice is a Cinderella or Snow-White princess in nightmare exile among incomprehensible and uncomprehending powers, feeling herself "Duchess of Nothing," "housekeep[ing] in Time's gut end" and "married [to] a cupboard of rubbish." It is a representative text.

The imagery of Plath's poems undergoes endless transformations, in which the links are often suppressed or arbitrary: sudden shifts of tack and emotion lead off in unexpected directions. Her poetic narratives fork and proliferate in this way because, in unfolding the implications of a sequence of images, she uncovers the complex and contradictory possibilities condensed within them, the infantile traumas lying treacherously beneath the surface of adult experience. The same image can be charged with quite contradictory emotional valencies. The bee, for example, a recurring motif (her father was an apiculturalist), stirs rich, ambiguous feelings. It is a female, a source of honey and creativity, but it has a male sting; the hive includes drudges and drones, but also that dark leonine queen at the core; in "The Swarm" and "The Arrival of the Bee-Box", bees are the collective "black, intractable mind" of a genocidal Europe and the "swarmy," "angrily clambering" impulses of the individual unconscious. Such transitions express her own sense of the self, not as a hierarchically ordered pyramid, but as an ensemble of possibilities, in which none usurps precedence for long, and to which only a provisional coherence can be given, in the specifying of a name and image ("The Arrival of the Bee-Box," after toying with the starvation or release of the bees which threaten and fascinate, concludes, "The box is only temporary"). Self for Plath is either a rigid, false *persona* or an amorphous, uncongealed, and fluid congeries, like the bee-swarm itself, undergoing constant metamorphosis, continually dying and being reborn in the mutations of the imagery. In "Elm," the social self speaks as a tree, rooted in its context, wrenched violently by a wind that "will tolerate no bystanding." But such fixity is an illusion, for its roots reach down to the dissolute sea, its branches "break up in pieces that fly about like clubs," it is dragged by the moon (usually the image of a sterile maternal force), and it contains subversive lives which are part of itself yet frighteningly independent:

> I am inhabited by a cry.
> Nightly it flaps out
> Looking, with its hooks, for something to love.
>
> I am terrified by this dark thing
> That sleeps in me;
> All day I feel its soft, feathery turnings, its malignity.

Plath repeatedly sees relationships as predatory, exploitative, and destructive, yet desired and necessary, as in "The Rabbit-Catcher" ("And we too had a relationship,/Tight wires between us,/Pegs too deep to uproot, and a mind like a ring/Sliding shut on some quick thing,/The constriction killing me also"). In "Tulips," even the smiles of husband and children, in a photograph, "catch onto my skin, little smiling hooks," while identity itself, in "The Applicant," is seen as a collection of functions, answers to others' questions, a poultice for their wounds, apple for their eyes, "A living doll" which is the accretion of artificial limbs and artificial commitments.

This aspect of her verse has made her co-option by the women's movement inevitable. But it is also just. Plath is, in fact, a profoundly political poet, who has seen the generic nature of these private catastrophes of the self, their public origin in a civilization founded on mass-manipulation and collective trickery. Esther Greenwood, in *The Bell Jar*, links her electric shock treatment with the electrocution which is the Rosenbergs' punishment for rebellion against the American way of life: she fears most of all being consigned to the charity wards, "with hundreds of people like me, in a big cage in the basement. The more hopeless you were, the further away they hid you." In a century which has shut away millions, in hospitals, concentration camps, and graveyards, where the self can be "wiped out ... like chalk on a blackboard" by administrative *diktat*, Plath sees a deep correspondence between the paternal concern of the psychiatrist and the authority of the modern state, even in its most extreme variants: both presuppose the self as victim, passive and compliant, as *sine qua non* of any "final solution." For Plath, concerned that "personal experience shouldn't be a kind of shut box and mirror-looking narcissistic experience," but "should be generally relevant, to such things as Hiroshima and Dachau and so on," the refusal to collaborate was a profoundly positive act, the assertion not of the nihilism of which she has been accused but of a more exacting and scrupulous conscience. If, in poems such as "Daddy" and "Lady Lazarus," she veers close to disintegration, she also promises a breakthrough into a resurrection which sheds the constricting husks of the past, a vengeful return which is only justice:

So, so. Herr Doktor.
So, Herr Enemy.
I am your opus,
I am your valuable,
The pure gold baby

That melts to a shriek.
I turn and burn,
Do not think I underestimate your great concern....

Herr God, Herr Lucifer
Beware
Beware.

Out of the ash
I rise with my red hair
And I eat men like air.

—Stan Smith

POE, Edgar Allan. American. Born in Boston, Massachusetts, 19 January 1809; orphaned, and given a home by John Allan, 1812. Educated at the Dubourg sisters' boarding school, Chelsea, London, 1816–17; Manor House School, Stoke Newington, London, 1817–20; Joseph H. Clarke's School, Richmond, 1820–23; William Burke's School, Richmond, 1823–25; University of Virginia, Charlottesville, 1826; United States Military Academy, West Point, New York, 1830–31. Served in the United States Army, 1827–29: Sergeant-Major. Married his 13-year-old cousin Virginia Clemm in 1836 (died, 1847). Journalist and editor: Assistant Editor, 1835, and Editor, 1836–37, *Southern Literary Messenger*, Richmond; Assistant Editor, *Gentleman's Magazine*, Philadelphia, 1839–40; Editor, *Graham's Lady's and Gentleman's Magazine*, Philadelphia, 1841–42; Sub-Editor, *New York Evening Mirror*, 1844; Co-Editor, *Broadway Journal*, 1845–46, New York. Lecturer after 1844. *Died 7 October 1849.*

PUBLICATIONS

Collections

> *Complete Works*, edited by James A. Harrison.   17 vols., 1902.
> *The Letters*, edited by John Ward Ostrom.   1948; revised edition, 2 vols., 1966.
> *Poems*, edited by Floyd Stovall.   1965.
> *Collected Works*, edited by Thomas O. Mabbott.   1969–

Verse

> *Tamerlane and Other Poems.* 1827.
> *Al Aaraaf, Tamerlane, and Minor Poems.* 1829.
> *Poems.* 1831.
> *The Raven and Other Poems.* 1845.

Play

> *Politian: An Unfinished Tragedy,* edited by Thomas O. Mabbott. 1923.

Fiction

> *The Narrative of Arthur Gordon Pym of Nantucket.* 1838.
> *Tales of the Grotesque and Arabesque.* 1840.
> *The Murders in the Rue Morgue, and The Man That Was Used Up.* 1843.
> *Tales.* 1845.
> *The Literati.* 1850.

Other

> *The Conchologist's First Book* (revised by Poe). 1839.
> *Eureka: A Prose Poem.* 1848; edited by Richard P. Benton, 1973.
> *Literary Criticism,* edited by Robert L. Hough. 1965.

Bibliography: *Bibliography of the Writings of Poe* by John W. Robertson, 1934; *A Bibliography of First Printings of the Writings of Poe* by C. F. Heartman and J. R. Canny, 1941; *Poe: A Bibliography of Criticism 1827–1967* by J. Lesley Dameron and Irby B. Cauthen, Jr., 1974.

Reading List: *Poe: A Critical Biography* by Arthur H. Quinn, 1941; *Poe: A Critical Study* by Edward H. Davidson, 1957; *The French Face of Poe* by Patrick F. Quinn, 1957; *Poe the Poet: Essays New and Old on the Man and His Work* by Floyd Stovall, 1959; *Poe* by Vincent Buranelli, 1961; *Poe* by Geoffrey Rans, 1965; *The Recognition of Poe: Selected Criticism since 1829* edited by Eric W. Carlson, 1966; *Poe: A Collection of Critical Essays* edited by Robert Regan, 1967; *Poe, Journalist and Critic* by Robert D. Jacobs, 1969; *Poe Poe Poe Poe Poe Poe Poe* by Daniel Hoffman, 1972; *Poe's Fiction: Romantic Irony in the Gothic Tales* by G. R. Thompson, 1973; *Poe* by David Sinclair, 1977; *The Tell-Tale Heart: The Life and Works of Poe* by Julian Symons, 1978.

*   *   *

Although Edgar Allan Poe wrote that for him "poetry has been not a purpose but a passion," he wrote only some fifty poems (excluding his album verses, jingles, and acrostics). Obliged to work at drudging journalism, he never realized his dream of founding a literary magazine of his own. While grinding out scores of reviews of some of the most forgettable books of the nineteenth century he wrote the tales, poems, and essays on which his posthumous renown is based. Aiming his work "not above the popular, nor below the critical, taste," he made use, as a professional magazinist must, of the fictional conventions of his day, turning to his own obsessive needs the Gothic horror story ("Ligeia," "The Fall of the House of Usher," "Berenice") and the tale of exploration ("A Descent into the Maelstrom," *Narrative of Arthur Gordon Pym*). In "The Gold Bug," "The Murders in the Rue Morgue," and "The Purloined Letter" he virtually invented the modern detective story, and he set the mold upon science fiction with "Mesmeric Revelations," "The Facts in the Case of Monsieur Valdemar," and "The Balloon Hoax." He also wrote dozens of satirical sketches. His critical writings were the most systematic and intelligent produced in America until his time.

Despite the paucity of his productions as a poet, he proved a major influence upon Baudelaire, who translated several of his tales and wrote that if Poe had not existed, he would have had to invent him. Through Baudelaire, Poe's critical theories influenced the entire French Symbolist movement. Although Poe believed, with Tennyson, that imprecision of meaning was necessary for the creation of beauty, he also believed that the poet is a deliberate maker who devises all of his effects to contribute to the single aim of his poem. "The Philosophy of Composition," an essay purporting to demonstrate how Poe wrote "The Raven," presents the creative process as an interlocked series of conscious choices. Although this would seem the opposite of the Romantic view of the poet as inspired seer, Poe's systematic process is in fact determined by Romantic necessity and is derived from Coleridge's aesthetic. That necessity is the excitation of the soul through the contemplation of the most melancholy of subjects – the death of a beautiful woman. The complex interaction in this theory between obsessive emotional need and what Poe is his detective stories called "ratiocination" is characteristic of all of his best work.

It seems ironic and cruel that a writer whose tales of guilt and terror won him the admiration of Dostoevsky had to live a hand-to-mouth existence and, after his death, was defamed by a hostile editor and reviled by readers who took as autobiographical the characters in his tales who were opium fiends and necrophiliacs. Allen Tate (in his essay "The Angelic Imagination") identifies what it is in Poe's work that really set on edge Victorian sensibility: the lack of any God save impersonal force, a fictive world without Christian morality. Far more evocatively than in the naturalistic novels of fifty years later, Poe imagined the nightmare of a universe without the consolations of faith.

This visionary author's life was unmitigatedly wretched. His parents were itinerant actors; the alcoholic father deserted, leaving Elizabeth Arnold Poe with three infant children. A brother and sister of Edgar's were adopted by connections in Baltimore but she kept young Eddie by her as she acted the heroine in plays no more melodramatic than his life would be. Stricken by tuberculosis, she died a lingering death in Richmond, Virginia, attended by kindly local matrons, when Edgar was only three. The boy was taken into the home of John Allan, a prosperous tobacco factor who brought Edgar to England when his business took him there and sent the boy to the school so vividly remembered in "William Wilson." Allan sent Poe to the new University of Virginia where, on a niggardly allowance among the scions of wealthy families, he ran up gambling debts and was expelled. Mrs. Allan, like Poe's natural mother, died of tuberculosis, and Poe, who had no inclination for the tobacco business, quarreled with his "Pa" (he had discovered Allan's infidelities while his wife was still alive). Allan withheld love from Edgar, never adopted him, and so Poe was cast adrift penniless to make his way as an author. Not even a hitch in the army or a later enlistment in the military academy at West Point mollified Allan. Poe, deciding to leave West Point, could not persuade "Pa" to intercede for his release and had to feign illness until he was expelled. By this time he had published two volumes of poems. One is dedicated to the Corps of Cadets.

Poe's career henceforth was as assistant or principal editor on several magazines in Richmond, Philadelphia, and New York. While so engaged, he wrote nearly 90 tales and sketches, countless critical columns and reviews, two novellas, and an astrophysical treatise on the nature of the universe, entitled *Eureka*, which he described as a poem.

Poe married his first cousin Virginia Clemm when she was thirteen and lived with her and her mother (his aunt) until Virginia, too, died of tuberculosis at twenty-three. Thereafter Poe conducted frenzied courtships of several poetesses; at this time he well may have been mad with grief. He died in delirium, under unexplained circumstances, on a trip to Baltimore.

Poe's biographers agree that he idealized women, and that sexual desire seems not to have had an overt part in any of his relationships.

Poe classified his own fiction into the categories of "Tales of the Grotesque and Arabesque." Borrowing these terms from Scott, Poe meant by them to describe satirical, bizarre, jocose writings on the one hand, and on the other the fictional equivalents of poems. These were his prose efforts to excite his readers' souls by the contemplation of beauty and terror. His review of Hawthorne outlines his theory of fiction. The tale, like the poem, must be all of a piece, each detail contributing to the desired unity of effect; symbolism (Poe in the nomenclature of the day calls it allegory) must be present as a "profound undercurrent" in the tale. His fiction will work by indirection.

In Poe's work there is a mysterious interpenetrability of the soul's excitation with subterranean dread. A *frisson* of horror runs through his most impassioned tales. The clue of Poe's contradictions may be in his sketch "The Imp of the Perverse," for the fiction frequently dramatizes its theme of man's irresistible urge toward self-destruction (a man is driven to commit a terrible crime, then to reveal his guilt). This connects also with the theme of double identity ("William Wilson," "The Cask of Amontillado") and Poe's strain of hoaxing, not entirely confined to his jocular productions. Poe delighted in tricking his readers. He would make them believe that his mesmerizer had really hypnotized a dying man so that the soul lingered and answered questions for months after the death of the body; or that his balloonists had actually crossed the Atlantic in three days, arriving in South Carolina. So too with fantastic descents into the maelstrom and journeys to the end of the earth and back. "The Philosophy of Composition" is in one respect such a hoax. Like his detective genius Monsieur Dupin, Poe demonstrates his intuitive intellectual superiority.

Although only in *Pym* did he write a successful fiction of more than thirty pages, Poe's significance is multifold. He is a systematic critic and theorist predictive of the Symbolist movement. His best poems and fictions embody his aesthetic intention that every part of the literary artifact must contribute to the unifying effect of the whole. His mastery of popular genres made him the unwitting godfather of much popular literature in the present century, as well as a major influence on films. His poetic theory passed from the Symbolists back into American poetry through T. S. Eliot and its influence continues in Allen Tate and Richard Wilbur, among others. His fiction is widely translated and widely read. Poe's work indeed has reached both the popular and the critical taste.

—Daniel Hoffman

POMFRET, John. English. Born in Luton, Bedfordshire, in 1667. Educated at Bedford Grammar School; Queens' College, Cambridge, B.A. 1684, M.A. 1688. Married Elizabeth Wingate in 1692; one son. Took holy orders: Rector of Maulden, Bedfordshire, 1695–1702, and of Millbrook, Bedfordshire, 1702. *Died* (buried) *1 December 1702.*

PUBLICATIONS

Verse

An Epistle to Charles, Earl of Dorset. 1690.

The Sceptical Muse.   1699.
Poems.   1699; revised edition, 1702, 1710, 1790.
A Prospect of Death.   1700.
Reason.   1700.
The Choice or Wish.   1700.
Two Love Poems.   1701.
Quae Rara, Chara: A Poem on Panthea's Confinement.   1707.

Reading List: "Pomfret's *Choice*" in *Reconsiderations* by E. E. Kellett, 1928.

*   *   *

Students of the eighteenth century have often sought out John Pomfret's *Choice* simply because Samuel Johnson thought it possibly the most often "perused" poem of his lifetime. The search is rewarding because the poem, published at the very beginning of the century, so well sets forth the calm moderation, the distrust of extremes, which strongly appealed to the age. The political and religious controversies and violence of the seventeenth century seemed ended when William and Mary came to the throne. Pomfret remembered Monmouth's Insurrection of 1685 and wrote of it in one early poem, "Cruelty and Lust." But by the end of the century he was writing *The Choice* in an altogether different mood. The way now seemed open for man to examine his various options and to make deliberate choice of the way he wished to live. The idea was to recur throughout the century; Goldsmith's *Traveller* is a case in point, and Johnson's first title for *Rasselas* was *The Choice of Life.*

Pomfret's formulation of the good life evidently appealed strongly to cultivated readers, at least in theory. Avoiding the extremes of rustic and urban, he would live *near* some "fair town" in a house neither too little nor too large; he would wish a modest fortune for genteel, not great, life. His table would be spread with frugal plenty, healthy but not luxurious. He would have a small wine cellar but no "high drinking." He would wish three friends, two male and one female. The latter would be a modest and obliging neighbor ("for I'd have no wife") whom he would visit occasionally: "But so divine, so noble a repast/I'd seldom, and with moderation, taste." One cannot but sympathize with the bishop who is reputed to have hesitated giving Pomfret a living because of these lines, but, as Johnson says, "It had happened to Pomfret as to almost all other men who plan schemes of life; he had departed from his purpose, and was then married."

The Choice describes a quiet life devoted to studies and friends, all worries evidently excluded. The well-turned couplets illustrate the moderation which they preach, never irregular, never disappointing ear or mind, never rising to heights of imagination, wit, or intensity. Its charm today lies in its portrayal of a world remote from modern life.

Although *The Choice* is Pomfret's best poem, several of the others have a similar antiquarian interest, chiefly those concerned with love: "Love Triumphant over Reason," "The Fortunate Complaint," "Strephon's Love for Delia Justified," and especially "An Epistle to Delia." These poems, totally unromantic of course, were all written when the poet was a young man (he died in his mid-thirties) yet reveal a strangely controlled and rational view of the matter, part of the business of life and a choice to be exercised with discretion. Most detached and prudential of all is his advice "To a Friend Inclined to Marry," setting forth his requirements for a wife as to her birth, fortune, and personal qualities. Pomfret's other poems (only nineteen are published in all) run to religious themes and Pindaric affectations. There is little reason to disturb them.

—Harlan W. Hamilton

POPE, Alexander. English. Born in London, 21 May 1688; lame at birth. Attended several schools but because of ill health did not remain long at any of them; lived at his father's house at Binfield, Windsor Forest, after 1700, and completed his education by reading; also studied Italian and French, in London, 1703. Inherited a small income from his father; excluded, as a Roman Catholic, from attending university or holding public office, he lived solely and successfully as a man of letters. Associated with the Whig writers, Congreve, William Walsh, Addison and Steele, 1706–11; with the Tory wits, Swift, Dr. Arbuthnot, John Gay, Thomas Parnell, and the politicians Oxford and Bolingbroke, from 1712: with the others formed the Scriblerus Club, 1713; supported himself by working on translations of Homer and by editing Shakespeare, 1713–26; lived at Twickenham, Middlesex, after 1718. *Died 30 May 1744.*

PUBLICATIONS

Collections

    Works, edited by W. Elwin and W. J. Courthope.   10 vols., 1871–89.
    Correspondence, edited by George Sherburn.   5 vols., 1956.
    Poems, edited by John Butt and others.   10 vols., 1939–67; revised edition of vols. 1–6,
       1 vol., 1963.
    Poetical Works, edited by Herbert Davis.   1966.

Verse

    An Essay on Criticism.   1711; edited by R. M. Schmitz, 1962.
    Windsor-Forest.   1713; edited by R. M. Schmitz, 1952.
    Ode for Music.   1713.
    The Rape of the Lock.   1714; edited by J. S. Cunningham, 1966.
    The Temple of Fame: A Vision.   1715.
    To the Ingenious Mr. Moore, Author of the Celebrated Worm-Powder.   1716.
    A Roman Catholic Version of the First Psalm.   1716.
    The Court Ballad.   1717.
    Works.   2 vols., 1717–35.
    Duke upon Duke.   1720; as *An Excellent Old Ballad, Called Pride Will Have a Fall,*
       1720.
    The Discovery.   1727; as *The 'Squire Turned Ferret,* 1727.
    Miscellanies in Prose and Verse, with others.   4 vols., 1727–32; *Peri Bathos; or, The Art*
       of Sinking in Poetry, edited by E. L. Steeves, 1952.
    The Dunciad: An Heroic Poem in Three Books.   1728; revised edition, 1728 (twice);
       The Dunciad Variorum, 1729; *The New Dunciad,* 1742; *The Dunciad in Four Books,*
       1743.
    An Epistle to Richard, Earl of Burlington.   1731; as *Of Taste,* 1732; as *Of False Taste,*
       1732.
    Of the Use of Riches: An Epistle to Bathurst.   1732; edited by E. R. Wasserman, 1960.
    An Essay on Man.   4 vols., 1733–34.
    The Impertinent.   1733.
    The First Satire of the Second Book of Horace, Imitated.   1733; with the second satire,
       1734.
    An Epistle to Richard Lord Viscount Cobham.   1733.
    Sober Advice from Horace.   1734.

An Epistle to Dr. Arbuthnot. 1734; edited by John Butt, 1954.
Of the Characters of Women. 1735.
Bounce to Fop. 1736.
Horace His Ode to Venus, lib. iv, Ode i, Imitated. 1737.
The Second Book of the Epistles of Horace Imitated (two poems). 1737.
The Sixth Epistle of the First Book of Horace Imitated. 1738.
An Imitation of the Sixth Satire of the Second Book of Horace (by Swift, completed by
    Pope). 1738.
The First Epistle of the First Book of Horace Imitated. 1738.
One Thousand Seven Hundred and Thirty Eight [*Epilogue to the Satires, Dialogue
    i*]. 1738; *Dialogue ii*, 1738.
The Universal Prayer. 1738.
Poems and Imitations of Horace. 1738 (published as *Works*, vol. 2, part 2).
Epistles of Horace Imitated. 1738.
A Blast upon Bays; or, A New Lick at the Laureate. 1742.

Plays

Three Hours after Marriage, with Arbuthnot and Gay (produced 1717). 1717; revised
    version in *Supplement to the Works of Pope,* 1757; 1717 edition edited by Richard
    Marton and William Peterson, 1961.
Esther: An Oratorio, with Arbuthnot and Samuel Humphreys, music by Handel
    (produced 1732). 1732.

Other

The Critical Specimen. 1711.
The Narrative of Dr. Robert Norris. 1713.
A Key to the Lock. 1715; revised edition, 1715.
The Dignity, Use, and Abuse of Glass-Bottles. 1715.
*A Full and True Account of a Horrid and Barbarous Revenge by Poison on the Body of
    Mr. Edmund Curll, Bookseller.* 1716; *A Further Account,* 1716.
God's Revenge Against Punning. 1716.
The Plot Discovered; or, A Clue to the Comedy of the Non-Juror. 1718.
A Receipt to Make a Soup. 1727.
Letters of Mr. Pope and Several Eminent Persons. 1735; revised edition, 5 vols.,
    1735–37.
Works. 7 vols., 1736–41.
Works in Prose. 2 vols., 1737–41.
Works, with His Last Corrections, Additions, and Improvements, edited by William
    Warburton. 9 vols., 1751.
A Supplement to the Works. 1757.
Additions to the Works. 2 vols., 1776.

Editor, *Miscellaneous Poems and Translations by Several Hands.* 1714.
Editor, *Poems on Several Occasions.* 1717; as *Pope's Own Miscellany,* edited by N.
    Ault, 1735.
Editor, *Poems on Several Occasions,* by Thomas Parnell. 1722.
Editor, *The Works of John Sheffield, Duke of Buckingham.* 2 vols., 1723.
Editor, *The Works of Shakespeare.* 6 vols., 1725.

Translator, *The Iliad of Homer.* 6 vols., 1715–20.

Translator, *The Odyssey of Homer.*   5 vols., 1725–26.

Bibliography: *Pope: A Bibliography* by R. H. Griffith, 2 vols., 1922–27; *Pope: A List of Critical Studies 1895–1944* by T. E. Tobin, 1945.

Reading List: *On the Poetry of Pope* by Geoffrey Tillotson, 1938, revised edition, 1950; *Pope's Dunciad: A Study of Its Meaning* by Aubrey Williams, 1955; *The Major Satires of Pope* by Robert W. Rogers, 1955; *Pope: The Poetry of Allusion* by R. A. Brower, 1959; *Essential Articles for the Study of Pope* edited by Maynard Mack, 1964, revised edition, 1968; *The World of Pope's Satires* by Peter Dixon, 1968; *The Garden and the City* by Maynard Mack, 1969; *Pope* by Elizabeth Gurr, 1971; *Writers and Their Background: Pope* edited by Peter Dixon, 1972; *Pope: The Critical Heritage* edited by John Barnard, 1973; *The Social Milieu of Pope* by Howard Erskine-Hill, 1975; *An Introduction to Pope* by Pat Rogers, 1976.

*   *   *

Alexander Pope found his voice so early, and began to acquire friends and influence so young, that he has seemed to hostile readers a safe establishment poet. In fact, he was a member of a beleaguered minority – the papists – and further handicapped by his wretched health, a topic well handled by Marjorie Hope Nicolson and G. S. Rousseau in their book *This Long Disease, My Life* (1968). Much of Pope's later work can be viewed as the struggle to forge a rhetoric of dissent, that is a poetic idiom expressing Opposition ideology and – in a strict sense – reactionary values, as the England of George II and Robert Walpole struck off on a new course. But from the start he had shown the capacity to deliver the unexpected, at the level of phrasing or of larger poetic strategies. A tame, house-trained writer would never have needed to evolve such a resourceful, dense, or energetic style.

By the time he was thirty Pope was exceedingly famous, with a collection of impressive works all decked out to advantage in his *Works* (1717), a sort of retrospective exhibition and also a catalogue raisonné of his preoccupations up to that date. His themes had ranged from politics to pastoralism, from history to mythology, and from the low jinks of high society to the profession of an erotic faith by a religious devotee. Generally a lyrical element is present, and while this is not undercut as it was to be in *The Dunciad* Pope often finds ways of misapplying the lyricism or of bending it to unusual purposes. Only the "Pastorals" (1709) make their claim exclusively in this vein, with their mellifluous diction, their rather passive relation to tradition, and their elaborate phonetic patterning – devices that are principally used, in fact, to image the "turn" of the year and recurrent items in the natural cycle.

Elsewhere, the lyrical element has to earn its place alongside motifs that may be harsh or humdrum. In his *Essay on Criticism*, Pope is lecturing the age upon its pedantry, ill-breeding, and narrowmindedness: but, unlike many lecturers, he avoids these qualities in his own discourse. Still more remarkable, he shows himself able to set out aesthetic theory in an aesthetically pleasing manner. The separate lines and couplets are so memorable that dozens are known out of context ("A little Learning is a dang'rous Thing"; "snatch a Grace beyond the Reach of Art"; "First follow Nature"; "True Wit is Nature to Advantage drest,/What oft was Thought, but ne'er so well Exprest"; "True Ease in Writing comes from Art, not Chance"; "To Err is Humane; to Forgive, Divine"; "For Fools rush in where Angels fear to tread"; and many more). Solemn Popians tell us we ought not to squeeze these phrases out of the poem, but really they survive their conversion to proverbial uses amazingly well. Pope's task was to instruct us through wit, and the most eloquent passages have a vivid life of their own beyond the immediate needs of the argument.

Windsor-Forest exaggerates Pope's usual habit of doing three things at once. It takes on perhaps too much: using Pope's boyhood home near Windsor as a focus of pastoral retreat and also as a fount of patriotism, the work attempts to celebrate a topical event (the signing of a peace treaty by the Tory ministry) while dealing with wider currents of history and mythology. Like many of the early poems, it raises large questions about artistic vocation. Even though we no longer misread *Windsor-Forest* as a failed nineteenth-century nature poem, its studied organisation and overpacked symbolism still ensure that it has not become a general favourite, even among those attuned to Pope's style. Neither for that matter has *The Temple of Fame*, despite Wilson Knight's impassioned advocacy and its starkly eloquent contemplation of the nature of heroism. Even "Eloisa to Abelard," direct and dramatic, as far from the marmoreal face of stoical classicism as one could get, draws readers for what it says rather than the way it is said. Although Pope is registering the feelings of a distracted woman, his rhetoric goes on defining the emotions with total accuracy. There is no linguistic breakdown, no fraying of the poetic medium, no loss of expressive control to match the speaker's nervous crisis.

Unquestionably it is *The Rape of the Lock* which comes home most strongly to the present age, as it has to most generations of readers. It is concerned with events ridiculous in their triviality and their temporality, yet it creates something that can fairly be called sublime in the fulfilment of its imaginative design. A strange vein of wonder runs through the poem, which serves (more than the chance plot-similarities) to establish a deep kinship with *A Midsummer Night's Dream*. Pope's particular genius shows itself in the way he builds around the everyday happenings in a not-very-intelligent court circle the power of a supernatural fable. From a silly book that had less to do with the Rosicrucian enlightenment than with the popular taste for blending sex with the occult, he picked up the idea of the elementals who stand in for the divine "machinery" of serious epic. Everything is proportionately downgraded, just as Swift scaled physical details down in Lilliput. A distant, heroic, masculine, martial, historic world is replaced by a drearily contemporary, petty, feminine (or effeminate), card-playing, resolutely *ephemeral* setting. Only the language remains: enough of the noble diction of epic, at least, to allow Pope reminders of the world we have lost. A kind of familiarising intimacy, appropriate to the cosy boudoir atmosphere of Belinda's life, suffuses the texture of the poetry. *The Rape of the Lock* is a living classic, which along with social and psychological observation acts out a myth of sexuality: biology and upbringing are at war, while the sylphs and the gnomes contend for the heroine's soul.

After a decade spent translating Homer and editing Shakespeare, Pope returned to original composition with the first version of *The Dunciad* in 1728. This is often treated as his swan-song, and it ought to be remembered that only the fourth book (and not even the famous conclusion to *that*) is really a late work. In some respects it might be better to think of *The Dunciad* as a "middle-period" work, still fanciful in execution and somewhat veiled in its methods. Scores of individuals do come in for attack in the poem, but only very obliquely are the King and his prime minister indicted, although the essential logic of the fable requires that they occupy a central role. (It is possible that the original intention was to produce a mock-coronation ceremony for the new king.) As it is, *The Dunciad* is an uproarious and splendidly comic version of recent political and literary history. In either version it makes powerful inroads into the court defences, especially through the medium of the poet laureate, Colley Cibber, when he is elevated to the throne of Dulness. But by the standards of Pope's true "later" style — that is, the urgent mode of topicalised Horace he perfected in the 1730's — *The Dunciad* might be regarded as just a little dispersed and wayward. Its highest merit lies in masterful use of the arts of language rather than in a completely sustained portrayal of civilisation in decay.

What I have called the "later" style was evolving around 1730, when Pope began to publish fragments of what he planned as a great moral work on a monumental scale. The outlying parts that remain are *An Essay on Man* (1733–34) and the four *Moral Essays* (1731–35). The *Essay* has today a reputation for windy eloquence and optimistic Panglossian metaphysics: neither expectation is wholly borne out by the text, but there is enough to explain the common belief on these points. As to the *Moral Essays*, they represent Pope at just about his very best — or at least three of the four do. The *Epistle to Burlington* and the *Epistle to Bathurst* both illustrate Pope's capacity to draw large poetic meanings out of tiny social circumstances. As Howard Erskine-Hill's recent book shows, he makes the small change of political and economic history into fictions expressing "the deeper loyalties and antipathies of his life." Again, in the "Epistle to a Lady," we are led with consummate skill in poetic construction from trivial aspects of the feminine round to the very inmost existential state of woman.

It is perhaps the *Imitations of Horace* (1733–38) which best exemplify Pope's mature accomplishment. They are mostly couched in a conversational idiom, now jaunty, now abrupt; vigorous, off the cuff, racily contemporaneous. Pope sets out not to translate Horace literally, but to find equivalents in his own surroundings. More anxious and more subjective than the Roman satirist, Pope confronts his own destiny as a writer while identifying the ills of society at large. The famous *Epistle to Dr. Arbuthnot*, later designated as the prologue to these imitations, exemplifies the blend of public and private themes, although it has no precise Horatian antecedent. By now Pope has become more frontal in his attack on the Walpolian system of government; poet and minister had become, as Maynard Mack puts it, "mighty opposites," spokesmen for contending orders of value. It is in these later poems that Pope became, paradoxically, both a more overtly political writer and a more nakedly confessional poet. But he had not wrung the neck of his early rhetoric: he simply pared down his style, loosened it slightly (e.g., by admitting more elisions) and let out the constraints on syntax by a notch or two. His formal skills allowed him to do even more when his themes darkened, so that his later manner has no need to repudiate its origins.

—Pat Rogers

POUND, Ezra (Weston Loomis). American. Born in Hailey, Idaho, 30 October 1885. Educated at Hamilton College, Clinton, New York, Ph.B. 1905; University of Pennsylvania, Philadelphia, M.A. 1906. Married Dorothy Shakespear in 1914. Taught at Wabash College, Crawfordsville, Indiana, 1906; travelled in Spain, Italy, and France, 1906–07; lived in London, 1908–20, in Paris, 1920–24, and in Rapallo, Italy, 1924–45: one of the creators of the Imagist movement; English Editor of *Poetry*, Chicago, 1912–19; Founder, with Wyndham Lewis, of *Blast*, 1914; English Editor of *The Little Review*, Chicago, 1917–19; Paris Correspondent of *The Dial*, 1922; Founder and Editor of *The Exile*, 1927–28. Broadcast over Italian Radio to the United States after 1941, in support of fascism, and was arrested and jailed for these broadcasts by the United States Army in 1945; imprisoned near Pisa, found unfit to stand trial for treason, and committed to St. Elizabeth's Hospital, Washington, D.C.; released in 1958; returned to Italy. Recipient: Academy of American Poets Fellowship, 1963; National Endowment for the Arts grant, 1967. *Died 1 November 1972.*

PUBLICATIONS

Collections

Selected Prose 1909–1965, edited by William Cookson. 1973.
Selected Poems 1908–1959. 1975.

Verse

A Lume Spento.   1908.
A Quinzaine for This Yule.   1908.
Personae.   1909.
Exultations.   1909.
Provença: Poems Selected from Personae, Exultations, and Canzoniere.   1910.
Canzoni.   1911.
Ripostes.   1912.
Lustra.   1916.
Lustra, with Earlier Poems.   1917.
Quia Pauper Amavi.   1919.
The Fourth Canto.   1919.
Umbra: The Early Poems.   1920.
Hugh Selwyn Mauberley.   1920.
Poems, 1918–21, Including Three Portraits and Four Cantos.   1921.
A Draft of XVI Cantos.   1925.
Personae: The Collected Poems.   1926; revised edition, 1949; as *Personae: Collected Shorter Poems,* 1952; as *Collected Shorter Poems,* 1968.
Selected Poems, edited by T. S. Eliot.   1928; revised edition, 1949.
A Draft of Cantos 17–27.   1928.
A Draft of XXX Cantos.   1930.
Homage to Sextus Propertius.   1934.
Eleven New Cantos: XXXI–XLI.   1934; as *A Draft of Cantos XXXI–XLI,* 1935.
Alfred Venison's Poems, Social Credit Themes.   1935.
The Fifth Decad of Cantos.   1937.
A Selection of Poems.   1940.
Cantos LII–LXXI.   1940.
The Pisan Cantos.   1948.
The Cantos.   1948; revised edition, 1965; revised edition, as *Cantos No. 1–117, 120,* 1970.
Selected Poems.   1949; revised edition, 1957.
Section: Rock-Drill: 86–95 de los Cantares.   1955.
Thrones: 96–109 de las Cantares.   1959.
A Lume Spento and Other Early Poems.   1965.
Canto CX.   1965.
Selected Cantos.   1967.
Cantos 110–116.   1967.
Drafts and Fragments, Cantos CX–CXVII.   1968.
Collected Early Poems, edited by Michael John King.   1976.

Other

The Spirit of Romance.   1910; revised edition, 1953.
"Noh" or Accomplishment: A Study of the Classical Stage of Japan, with Ernest Fenollosa.   1916; as *The Classical Noh Theatre of Japan,* 1959.
Gaudier-Brzeska: A Memoir.   1916; revised edition, 1959.
Pavannes and Divisions.   1918.
Instigations.   1920.
Indiscretions; or Une Revue de Deux Mondes.   1923.
Antheil and The Treatise on Harmony.   1924.
Imaginary Letters.   1930.
How to Read.   1931.

ABC of Economics.   1933.
ABC of Reading.   1934.
Make It New: Essays.   1934.
Social Credit: An Impact.   1935.
Jefferson and/or Mussolini.   1935; revised edition, as *Jefferson e Mussolini,* 1944.
Polite Essays.   1937.
Guide to Kulchur.   1938; as *Culture,* 1938.
What Is Money For?   1939.
Carta da Visita.   1942; translated by John Drummond, as *A Visiting Card,* 1952.
L'America, Roosevelt, e le Cause della Guerra Presente.   1944; translated by John
   Drummond, as *America, Roosevelt, and the Causes of the Present War,* 1951.
Oro e Lavoro.   1944; translated by John Drummond, as *Gold and Labour,* 1952.
Introduzione alla Natura Economica degli S.U.A.   1944; translated by Carmine Amore,
   as *An Introduction to the Economic Nature of the United States,* 1950.
Orientamenti.   1944.
If This Be Treason.   1948.
The Letters of Pound, 1907–1941, edited by D. D. Paige.   1950.
Patria Mia.   1950; as *Patria Mia and The Treatise on Harmony,* 1962.
The Translations of Ezra Pound, edited by Hugh Kenner.   1953; revised edition, 1970.
Secondo Biglietto da Visita.   1953.
Literary Essays, edited by T. S. Eliot.   1954.
Pavannes and Divagations.   1958.
Impact: Essays on Ignorance and the Decline of American Civilization, edited by Noel
   Stock.   1960.
EP to LU: Nine Letters Written to Louis Untermeyer by Ezra Pound, edited by J. Albert
   Robbins.   1963.
Pound/Joyce: The Letters of Ezra Pound to James Joyce, edited by Forrest Read.   1967.
Redondillas: or, Something of That Sort.   1967.
The Caged Panther: Ezra Pound at St. Elizabeth's (includes 53 letters), by Harry M.
   Meachum.   1967.
DK: Some Letters of Pound, edited by Louis Dudek.   1974.
Pound and Music: The Complete Criticism, edited by R. Murray Schafer.   1977.

Editor, *Des Imagistes: An Anthology.*   1914.
Editor, *Catholic Anthology, 1914–1915.*   1915.
Editor, *Poetical Works of Lionel Johnson.*   1915.
Editor, *Passages from the Letters of John Butler Yeats.*   1917.
Editor, *Profile: An Anthology.*   1932.
Editor, *Rime,* by Guido Cavalcanti.   1932.
Editor, *Active Anthology.*   1933.
Editor, *The Chinese Written Character as a Medium for Poetry: An Ars Poetica.* by
   Ernest Fenollosa.   1936.
Editor, *De Moribus Brachmanorum, Liber Sancto Ambrosio Falso Adscriptus.*   1956.
Editor, with Marcella Spann, *Confucius to Cummings: An Anthology of Poetry.*   1964.

Translator, *The Sonnets and Ballate of Guido Cavalcanti.*   1912; as *Pound's Cavalcanti
   Poems,* 1966.
Translator, *Cathay: Translations.*   1915.
Translator, with Ernest Fenollosa, *Certain Noble Plays of Japan.*   1916.
Translator, *Dialogues of Fontenelle.*   1917.
Translator, *The Natural Philosophy of Love,* by Rémy de Gourmont.   1922.
Translator, *The Call of the Road,* by Edouard Estaunié.   1923.
Translator, *Ta Hio: The Great Learning,* by Confucius.   1928.
Translator, *Digest of the Analects,* by Confucius.   1937.

Translator, *Italy's Policy of Social Economics 1939–1940*, by Odon Por.   1941.
Translator, with Alberto Luchini, *Ta S'en Dai Gaku, Studio Integrale*, by Confucius.   1942.
Translator, *Ciung Iung, l'Asse che non Vacilla*, by Confucius.   1945.
Translator, *The Unwobbling Pivot and The Great Digest*, by Confucius.   1947.
Translator, *Confucian Analects*.   1951.
Translator, *The Classic Anthology Defined by Confucius*.   1954.
Translator, *Women of Trachis*, by Sophocles.   1956.
Translator, *Moscardino*, by Enrico Pea.   1956.
Translator, *Rimbaud* (5 poems).   1957.
Translator, with Noel Stock, *Love Poems of Ancient Egypt*.   1962.

Bibliography: *A Bibliography of Pound* by Donald Gallup, 1963, revised edition, 1969.

Reading List: *Pound: His Metric and Poetry* by T. S. Eliot, 1917; *The Poetry of Pound*, 1951, and *The Pound Era*, 1971, both by Hugh Kenner; *A Primer of Pound* by M. L. Rosenthal, 1960; *Pound* by G. S. Fraser, 1960; *Pound, Poet as Sculptor*, 1964, and *Pound*, 1976, both by Donald Davie; *The Life of Pound* by Noel Stock, 1970: *Pound: The Critical Heritage* edited by Eric Homberger, 1972; *Pound, The Last Rower: A Political Profile* by C. David Heymann, 1976; *Time in Pound's Work* by William Harmon, 1977.

*   *   *

In his preface to his little book on popular music, *All What Jazz*, the poet Philip Larkin names the jazz musician Charlie Parker, Picasso, and Ezra Pound as standing for all that he most detests in "modernism" in the arts. Larkin is probably, without being among the startlingly great, the most distinguished poet we have in England at this moment. I am not competent to speak about Parker. But Cubism, invented by Picasso and Braque, is, in spite of its comparatively short life in its pure form, the greatest revolution in painting since the first adequate exploitation of perspective, anatomy, and the golden section at the Renaissance. Similarly, for good or evil, modern poetry would not be what it is (or have been what it was) without Pound. It may be true that what Pound had personally to say through the medium of verse was either not very interesting or, as in his praise of Fascism, positively dangerous. He remains the greatest technical inventor in poetry in his century, and the history of twentieth-century poetry would be quite different without him. As an observer of life, Larkin is in many ways a more complex and subtle man than Pound. Still, if Larkin had never existed, we should lack four slim volumes of carefully undertoned verse, but the history of poetry in our century would be much what it is already.

Yet the comparison of Picasso and Pound is critically apt. Both, the one in Spain, the other in the American mid-west, started out of the main stream. When Picasso came to Paris from Spain, he left a country that had not even caught up with Impressionism. When Pound came to England in 1908, with his first volume *A Lume Spento* privately printed in Venice, he was imitating the poets of the 1890's, including Yeats in his very early phase, Swinburne, and the Pre-Raphaelites: he was about thirty years behind the times. T. E. Hulme and other members of the Poets' Club, now forgotten, were already experimenting with what was to be called Imagism, and an Englishman, F. S. Flint, was to work out its theory; it was left to Pound, when he got round to it in 1912, only to give it a name. His own Imagist poems are among the best, but not perhaps so good as the very best of his American acquaintance, Hilda Doolittle. Of his poems before *The Cantos*, the best are two translations, "The Seafarer" (his Anglo-Saxon was self-taught, and some of the lines are sonorous but meaningless) and "Cathay" (adapted from the American scholar Ernest Fenollosa's attempts to translate classical Chinese poetry through a knowledge of the Chinese ideograms), and the two-part *Hugh Selwyn Mauberley*.

A study of cultural decay in England since the Pre-Raphaelites, *Mauberley* begins with a mock-epitaph for Pound and an ironic but affectionate picture of the tradition of the Pre-Raphaelites and Decadents from which he derives; its second half deals with an imaginary character, Hugh Selwyn Mauberley, who chooses to drift hedonistically to his death. Yet the final poem created by Pound at the end of his section is a seventeenth-century pastiche, the final poem created by Mauberley; transforming hair into metal and flesh into porcelain under the electric light is very startlingly "modern." There is a sense also that the Mauberley figure, for all his drifting, feels more deeply than the satirically observant Pound figure. Like *The Waste Land*, of which it is in some sense a forerunner, *Hugh Selwyn Mauberley* has still to be satisfactorily construed. (There is likewise no agreed judgment about whether the startling mistranslations in *Homage to Sextus Propertius* are blunders or are satirical, though some intention to satirise the British Empire is obvious.)

Pound then embarked on a poem of enormous length, *The Cantos*. This is, in a certain sense, a modern epic, except that the heroic role is played now by Odysseus and now by a Renaissance adventurer like Sigismundo de Malatesta, and the sage figure now by Confucius and now by one of the American founding fathers like Jefferson or John Adams. The poem throughout assumes a knowledge in the reader of Pound's raw material and a knowledge of the economics of Major Douglas ("Can't move them with a cold thing like economics") and of exactly what Pound means by usury. There are very dull patches in the middle, but the account of Pound's imprisonment by American troops in Pisa (*The Pisan Cantos*) at the time of the Allied invasion of Italy is vivid. The later cantos are more fragmentary and harder to understand. The poem is a failure as a whole, but an amazing manual of poetic techniques.

—G. S. Fraser

PRAED, Winthrop Mackworth. English. Born in London, 26 July 1802. Educated at Langley Broom School, near Colnbrook, 1810–14; Eton College, 1814–21 (Founder-Editor, *The Etonian*, 1820); Trinity College, Cambridge, 1821–25 (Sir William Browne Medal, 1822, 1823, 1824; Chancellor's Medal for English verse, 1823), B.A. 1825; called to the Bar, Middle Temple, London, 1829. Married Helen Bogle in 1835; two daughters. Tutor to Lord Ernest Bruce, at Eton College, 1825–27; elected Fellow, Trinity College, Cambridge, 1827; practised law on the Norfolk circuit, 1829; Conservative Member of Parliament for St. Germans, 1830–31, for Great Yarmouth, 1834–37, and for Aylesbury, 1837–39; Secretary to the Board of Control (Peel's administration), 1835. Deputy High Steward of Cambridge University. *Died 15 July 1839.*

PUBLICATIONS

Collections

Poems. 2 vols., 1864; revised edition, 1885.
Selected Poems, edited by Kenneth Allott. 1953.

Verse

>Pyramides Aegyptiacae. 1822.
>Nugae Seria Ducunt in Mala. 1822.
>In Obitum T. F. Middleton. 1823.
>Lillian: A Fairy Tale. 1823.
>Australasia. 1823.
>Athens. 1824.
>Scribimus Indocti Doctique. 1824.
>The Ascent of Elijah. 1831.
>Intercepted Letters about the Infirmary Bazaar. 4 vols., n.d.
>Trash Dedicated Without Respect to J. Halse, Esq., M.P. 1833.
>Political Poems. 1835.
>Political and Occasional Poems, edited by G. Young. 1888.

Other

>Speech in Committee on the Reform Bill, on Moving an Amendment. 1832.
>Essays, edited by G. Young. 1887.
>Every-Day Characters. 1896.

Reading List: *A Poet in Parliament: The Life of Praed* by Derek Hudson, 1939.

*   *   *

Winthrop Mackworth Praed was, in his own words, a "rhymer" rather than a poet. He was a gifted versifier whose talent found its best expression in light verse, poems celebrating the life of the leisured society in which he lived.

His work falls mainly into three categories, *vers de société*, verse tales, and political poems. Of these, the latter, topical in Praed's own day, are somewhat obscure to the modern reader. Written as ephemeral pieces, they were resurrected in book form almost fifty years after their author's death. Few of them are of interest today, though Kenneth Allott included the best of them in his edition of *Selected Poems*. The verse tales indicate considerable narrative skill and are most successful when Praed is not attempting to write seriously. The most serious of these tales, "The Legend of the Drachenfels," with its high morality ("Why turns the serpent from his prey?–/The Cross hath barred his terrible way") succeeds only in being ponderous and tedious. On the other hand, such a tale as "The Legend of the Teufel-haus," with its romantic subject matter, facetious treatment and somewhat macabre ending illustrates Praed's work in this vein at its best.

His most successful work, however, is to be found in his society verses, practically all of which were written in his most productive period, the late 1820's and early 1830's when Praed was studying law and establishing his political interests. The poems treat of the life and manners of the upper-middle-class society of Praed's day and vary from the series of poems on Every-day Characters to those which deal with the conversation and interests which occupy that society. He presents his characters with warmth and wit, but without sentimentality, writing often in an anti-romantic tone in order to guard himself against a seriousness which he is unable to sustain. Chronologically belonging to the Romantic era, his best work is, in fact, Augustan in flavour, though his intentions are more frivolous and his wit less acerbic. It is in his skill as a craftsman that he most resembles the Augustans, adopting their fashion of figures of speech, alliteration and assonance, puns and paradoxes. He is particularly fond of syllepsis, the extension of a pun by which one word serves two purposes, as for instance in "The Devil's Decoy" when "The startled Priest struck both his thighs,/And the abbey clock struck one." Another of his favourite devices is the bathetic ending which he employs in poems such as "The Belle of the Ball-Room," "My Partner," or "A Letter [The Talented Man]." A brilliant classical scholar, Praed's principal debt to his classical learning is his considerable metrical proficiency and a correctness in versification which is itself Augustan.

A poet who was aware of his own limitations, Praed is to be read as a purveyor of light verse, but light verse which, at its best, attains a degree of perfection which set a standard few later versifiers have equalled.

—Hilda D. Spear

PRATT, E(dwin) J(ohn). Canadian. Born in Western Bay, Newfoundland, 4 February 1883. Draper's apprentice, St. John's, Newfoundland, 1898–1901; educated at Methodist College, St. John's, 1901–03; school teacher and student preacher, Newfoundland, 1903–07; Victoria College, University of Toronto, 1907–17, B.A. 1911, B.D. 1913, M.A. 1915, Ph.D. 1917; ordained in the Methodist Church. Demonstrator and Lecturer in Psychology, University College, 1911–17, and Associate Professor of English, 1919–33, Professor of English, 1933–53, and Emeritus Professor, 1953–64, Victoria College, University of Toronto. Editor, *Canadian Poetry* magazine, Toronto, 1936–42; Member, Editorial Board, *Saturday Night*, Toronto, 1952. Recipient: Governor-General's Award, 1937, 1949, 1952; Lorne Pierce Gold Medal, 1940; University of Alberta Gold Medal for Literature, 1951; Canada Council grant, 1958, and medal, 1961. D.Litt.: University of Manitoba, Winnipeg, 1945; McGill University, Montreal, 1949; University of Toronto, 1953; Assumption University, Windsor, Ontario, 1955; University of New Brunswick, Fredericton, 1957; University of Western Ontario, London, 1957; Memorial University of Newfoundland, St. John's, 1961; LL.D.: Queen's University, Kingston, Ontario, 1949; D.C.L.: Bishop's University, Lennoxville, Quebec, 1949. Fellow, Royal Society of Canada, 1930. C.M.G. (Companion, Order of St. Michael and St. George), 1946. *Died 26 April 1964.*

PUBLICATIONS

Collections

Selected Poems, edited by Peter Buitenhuis. 1968.

Verse

Rachel: A Story of the Sea. 1917.
Newfoundland Verse. 1923.
The Witches' Brew. 1925.
Titans. 1926.
The Iron Door: An Ode. 1927.
The Roosevelt and the Antinoe. 1930.
Verses of the Sea. 1930.

Many Moods. 1932.
The Titanic. 1935.
The Fable of the Goats and Other Poems. 1937.
Brébeuf and His Brethren. 1940.
Dunkirk. 1941.
Still Life and Other Verse. 1943.
Collected Poems. 1944; revised edition, edited by Northrop Frye, 1958.
They Are Returning. 1945.
Behind the Log. 1947.
Ten Selected Poems. 1947.
Towards the Last Spike: A Verse Panorama of the Struggle to Build the First Canadian Transcontinental. 1952.
Here the Tides Flow. 1962.

Other

Studies in Pauline Eschatology and Its Background. 1917.

Editor, *Under the Greenwood Tree,* by Thomas Hardy. 1937.
Editor, *Heroic Tales in Verse.* 1941.

Reading List: *Pratt: The Man and His Poetry* by H. W. Wells and C. F. Klinck, 1947; *The Poetry of Pratt* by John Sutherland, 1956; *Pratt* by Milton T. Wilson, 1969; *Pratt* by David G. Pitt, 1969; *Pratt: The Evolutionary Vision* by Sandra Djwa, 1974.

*   *   *

Widely regarded as Canada's pre-eminent narrative poet, E. J. Pratt embodied in his work a nineteenth-century concern for social Darwinism and an evolving "instinct for what is imaginatively central in Canadian sensibility" (Northrop Frye). An ordained Methodist minister who wrote his M.A. and Ph.D. theses on demonology and Pauline eschatology, he experienced a crisis of faith which has caused him to be viewed variously an an atheist, Christian humanist, and agnostic. Similar ambiguity has hedged judgements about his shorter lyric poems and longer comic extravaganzas. His narrative fables and epics, particularly *Brébeuf and His Brethren,* best demonstrate his pre-occupation with themes of primaeval conflict, his fascination with technical language, and his dexterity in establishing the dramatic coherency of his stories in verse.

Four collections of Pratt's shorter poems were published between 1923 and 1943 (*Newfoundland Verse, Many Moods, The Fable of the Goats,* and *Still Life*); with some of his later poems, most are included in the second edition of the *Collected Poems.* Their tone is remarkably consistent: calm and flat, covering a moment of violence and usually concluding with a rhetorical comment. Pratt was not attracted by post-Edwardian experiments in form, and very few of these poems are in free verse. He almost never wrote about love. His most frequently anthologized short works, such as "The Shark" and "Sea-Gulls," centre on Newfoundland and the sea, or on the simultaneity of the evolutionary process, as in "The Prize Cat" and "From Stone to Steel."

Pratt's early personal and stylistic difficulties in reconciling orthodox Christianity with the aftermath of the First World War, a natural world indifferent to man, are evident in his first narratives: "Clay" (1917, published in part in *Newfoundland Verse*) and *Rachel. The Witches' Brew,* a farce about the effects of alcohol on fish, pointed more clearly to the elastic line, hyperbolic language, and juxtaposition of sober detail with vaulting commentary, all of which would mark his mature long poems. The formulation of *The Iron Door* as a dream-vision did not bear out his attempt to rationalize belief in the face of his mother's death. Thereafter he would continue to construct epic battles as metaphors for the persistence and frailty of human will, the kind of battles he dramatized in "The Cachalot" and "The Great Feud." Published together as *Titans*, his first major work, both poems set out the struggle between evolutionary Titans and Olympians: in the first, a giant squid against a sperm whale, and in the second (sub-titled "A Dream of a Pleiocene Armageddon") the animals of the land led by an ape against those of the sea, with admixtures of grotesque comedy. Man kills one victor and is himself drowned in "The Cachalot"; man's solitary ancestor remains alive in "The Great Feud."

Pratt's poetic response to the political and economic dialectic of the 1930's was curiously muted. "The Fable of the Goats," omitted from the *Collected Poems*, offers peace in our time as a solution to the Spanish Civil War. His choice of the metaphor of a gigantic dinner for "The Depression Ends" appears perversely blinkered as a political statement. More characteristic of his larger attitudes are two of the three epics set at sea: *The Roosevelt and the Antinoe* and *The Titanic*, with their themes of human rescue partially thwarted and of the limits of technology in saving man. The American ship *Roosevelt* aids the sinking British *Antinoe*, but the sea can master both. The iceberg of *The Titanic* assumes a related role, a morally neutral force which seems – but only seems – to strike man down for his pride and arrogance. The Second World War provided Pratt with a properly grand stage for his complicated concept of heroism: rhetorically in the propagandistic *Dunkirk*; intimately in the North Atlantic convoy duty described in *Behind the Log*; and mythically in "The Truant," a debate between representative man and the Panjandrum who personifies the mechanistic principle of the universe, the perfect dictator. That Pratt should later describe Canada's far western mountain ranges as "seas" is appropriate, as is his concern with individual rather than collective human effort in his last narrative, *Towards the Last Spike*. Here the construction of the transcontinental railway in the 1870's and 1880's is transmuted into an ironic commentary on the triumph of will over environment, the need to establish an empire of communication over what man sees to be moral chaos, and the belief that technological progress is a metaphor for human evolution.

Brébeuf and His Brethren, Pratt's finest (and longest) narrative, is patterned on the way of the cross in its exploration of faith in seventeenth-century New France. (It is partly based on events chronicled in the Jesuit *Relations*.) The conflict of Indian and priest moves to the inevitable martyrdom of Brébeuf and Lalement. Pratt's objectivity, careful pacing, and smooth manipulation of a quarter-century's dialogue and description conclude with a contemporary Mass at the shrine of the martyrs. The final ironies of the poem characterize Pratt's own views on man's fate in a world always new to him. The value of human life lies in the persistence of individual struggle against our collective self-willed suicide.

—Bruce Nesbitt

PRIOR, Matthew. English. Born near Wimborne Minster, Dorset, 21 July 1664. Educated at Westminster School, London, under the patronage of Lord Dorset (King's Scholar, 1681); St. John's College, Cambridge, B.A. 1686, M.A. 1700. Appointed Fellow of St. John's College, 1688; tutor to one of Lord Exeter's sons, 1688; Secretary to Lord Dursley, Ambassador to the Hague, 1689–97; secretary in the negotiations for the Treaty of Ryswick, 1697; secretary to the embassy in Paris, 1698; Under-Secretary of State, England, 1699;

Member of Parliament for East Grinstead, 1701; Commissioner of Trade and Plantations, 1701–07; joined the Tory party, 1702; appointed commissioner of Customs, 1711; sent to Paris by Oxford's Tory government to negotiate for the end of the War of the Spanish Succession, 1711: helped draft the Treaty of Utrecht, popularly known as "Matt's peace," 1713; recalled from Paris on the fall of the Tory government and imprisoned in the Tower of London in the belief that he would incriminate Oxford as a traitor, 1715, released, 1717; through a gift of Lord Harley bought Down Hall, Essex, 1719, and retired there. *Died 18 September 1721.*

PUBLICATIONS

Collections

Literary Works, edited by H. B. Wright and M. K. Spears.   2 vols., 1959.

Verse

On the Coronation. 1685.
The Hind and the Panther Transversed to the Story of the Country Mouse and the City Mouse, with Charles Montagu. 1687.
An Ode in Imitation of the Second Ode of the Third Book of Horace. 1692.
For the New Year: To the Sun. 1694.
To the King: An Ode on His Majesty's Arrival in Holland. 1695.
An English Ballad in Answer to Mr. Despreaux's Pindarique Ode on the Taking of Namure. 1695.
Verses Humbly Presented to the King at His Arrival in Holland. 1696.
Carmen Saeculare for the Year 1700 (with Latin translation by Thomas Dibben). 1700.
To a Young Gentleman in Love. 1703.
A Letter to Monsieur Boileau Depreaux Occasioned by the Victory at Blenheim. 1704.
An English Padlock. 1705.
Pallas and Venus: An Epigram. 1706.
An Epistle from the Elector Bavaria to the French King. 1706.
An Ode Humbly Inscribed to the Queen. 1706.
Poems on Several Occasions. 1707; revised edition, 1709, 1718.
Horace lib. I epist ix Imitated. 1711.
To the Right Honorable Mr. Harley, Wounded by Guiscard. 1711.
Archibaldi Pitcarnii Scoti Carmen Imitated. 1712.
Walter Danniston ad Amicos Imitated. 1712(?).
Earl Robert's Mice. 1712.
Two Imitations of Chaucer. 1712.
A Fable of the Widow and Her Cat. 1712.
A Memorial Against the Mortifying of the Ports of Dunkirk and Mardike. 1715.
The Dove. 1717.
The Conversation. 1720.
Colin's Mistakes. 1721.
A Supplement to Mr. Prior's Poems. 1722.
The Turtle and the Sparrow. 1723.
Down-Hall. 1723.

Other

A New Answer to an Argument Against a Standing Army.   1697.
The History of His Own Time (miscellany), edited by J. Bancks.   1740.
Original Letters from Prior (and others), edited by R. Warner.   1817.

Reading List: *Prior: Poet and Diplomatist* by C. K. Eves, 1939; *Prior* by R. W. Ketton-Cremer, 1957.

*   *   *

Matthew Prior is best remembered for his curt, colloquial poetic tales ("Hans Carvel," "The Ladle," "Paulo Purganti and His Wife," "Protagenes and Apelles"), for his dialogues ("Henry and Emma, A Poem, Upon the Model of The Nut-brown Maid," "The Turtle and the Sparrow"), for his amorous and cynical love lyrics to Chloes, Phyllisses, and Lisettas, for caustic epigrams, and for witty verse epistles. Yet he was also a man of action, verse-man but also politician. For over twenty years he had served with signal success (until the death of Queen Anne) as a distinguished diplomat. In a sense, Prior realized the ideals of the Restoration and Neo-Classical Age: despite his lowly birth, he was a man of wit and banter and yet a sophisticated and Horatian man of the world.

In his *The Conversation: A Tale*, he can step back and ironically take a cool look at himself. In the poem, one Damon in a tavern engages a stranger in conversation; Damon boasts of knowing Matt. Prior well. Needless to say, the "stranger" in the case is Prior himself. But listen to Damon hold forth:

> But (pass His Politics and Prose)
> I never herded with his Foes;
> Nay, in his Verses, as a Friend,
> I still found Something to commend:
> Sir, I excus'd his NUT-BROWN MAID;
> Whate'er severer Critics said:
> Too far, I own, the Girl was try'd:
> The Women All were on my Side.
> For ALMA I return'd Him Thanks:
> I lik'd Her with her little Pranks:
> Indeed poor SOLOMON in Rhime
> Was much too grave to be Sublime.

Prior displays clear perception. He had hoped that the retelling of the old "Nut-Brown Maid," called "Henry and Emma," would achieve tragic strength by his heroic couplets; and had similarly assumed that "Alma: or, The Progress of the Mind" (1718) would, though told amusingly and skeptically, portray nonetheless a serious philosophy; and he aspired in his long "Solomon on The Vanity of the World" (1708) to give grandeur to the themes and tones of Ecclesiastes.

But Matt. Prior is *not* recollected for these longer pieces. Nor is he remembered for a host of panegyrical verses, pindarics, birthday odes, and poems of praise and political celebrations of contemporary figures and events (the longest of these last being the *Carmen Seculare* to William III). There is a note of something strained when Prior seeks to be elevated or grandly auspicious. He did, after all, admire Spenser all his life (and was indeed buried at his feet), but the severe and archaic epic tone was none of his equipment.

His admiration, however, for Anacreon, for Horace, for the Chaucer of the *fabliaux*, for Montaigne is more felicitous. His lightsome verse epistles, his epigrams, love songs, and burlesque moral fables more frequently succeed. He has learned much from Jonson's casual poems, from the Cavalier poets, from Charles Sackville, Earl of Dorset (Dorset was his patron); and he has learned much indeed from Samuel Butler. His most effective moments in verse stem from his lighter, octosyllabic verse in the iambic or the anapestic vein, and he is doubtless one of the most successful writers of correct yet relaxed four-foot lines. Often too, Prior could be what Dr. Johnson disapprovingly would term "amorous" or "sensual". Nevertheless, the humor and whimsicality are always tempered by a slight and wistful melancholy; he frequently speaks of Life's "Fantastick Mazes," wherein we find but "imagin'd Pleasures" "To combat against real Cares." And there is a recurrent note that we often discover in Horace's later Odes, as in *"Quid sit futurum Cras fuge quaerere"*:

> For what To-morrow shall disclose,
> May spoil what You To-night propose:
> ENGLAND may change; or Cloe stray:
> Love and Life are for To-day.

But for all of that, Matthew Prior found his proper niche: although much abroad in 1712 and 1713, he served on the outer fringe of the renowned Scriblerus Club, composed of Swift, Pope, Gay, Arbuthnot, and Parnell; Prior improved with such company and became one of England's masters of the *sermo pedestris*, or low style. He was a correct, polished, and facile maker of pleasant verses; if he was something of the epicurean and the skeptic, he always retained a knowing cheerfulness together with a spritely, almost acid wit. He had managed to become, after all, two things that the century admired – a self-made poet and a self-made man.

In despite of some of Dr. Johnson's strictures, then, Matthew Prior has been able to prevail. What William Cowper said more than fifty years after his death (in a letter of 17 January 1782) about his poetry's "charming ease" most aptly sums the poet up:

> Every man conversant with verse-writing knows, and knows by painful experience, that the familiar style is of all styles the most difficult to succeed in. To make verse speak the language of prose, without being prosaic, – to marshal the words of it in such an order as they might naturally take in falling from the lips of an extemporary speaker, yet without meanness, harmoniously, elegantly, and without seeming to displace a syllable for the sake of the rhyme, is one of the most arduous tasks a poet can undertake. He that could accomplish this task was Prior....

—John R. Clark

PURDY, Al(fred Wellington). Canadian. Born in Wooller, Ontario, 30 December 1918. Educated at Dufferin Public School, Trenton, Ontario; Albert College, Belleville, Ontario; Trenton Collegiate Institute, Ontario. Served with the Royal Canadian Air Force during World War II. Married Eurithe Parkhurst in 1941; one son. Has held numerous jobs; taught at Simon Fraser University, Burnaby, British Columbia, Spring 1970; Poet-in-Residence, Loyola College, Montreal, 1973; Artist-in-Residence, University of Manitoba, Winnipeg, 1975–76. Recipient: Canada Council Fellowship, 1960, 1965, Senior Literary Fellowship, 1968, 1971, award, 1973, and grant, 1974; President's Medal, University of Western Ontario, 1964; Governor-General's Award, 1966. Lives in Ontario.

PUBLICATIONS

Verse

> *The Enchanted Echo.* 1944.
> *Pressed on Sand.* 1955.
> *Emu, Remember!* 1956.
> *The Crafte So Longe to Lerne.* 1959.
> *Poems for All the Annettes.* 1962.
> *The Blur in Between: Poems 1960–61.* 1962.
> *The Cariboo Horses.* 1965.
> *North of Summer: Poems from Baffin Island.* 1967.
> *Poems for All the Annettes* (selected poems). 1968.
> *Wild Grape Wine.* 1968.
> *Spring Song.* 1968.
> *Love in a Burning Building.* 1970.
> *The Quest for Ouzo.* 1970.
> *Selected Poems.* 1972.
> *Hiroshima Poems.* 1972.
> *On the Bearpaw Sea.* 1973.
> *Sex and Death.* 1973.
> *In Search of Owen Roblin.* 1974.
> *Sundance at Dusk.* 1976.

Other

> Editor, *The New Romans: Candid Canadian Opinions of the United States.* 1968.
> Editor, *Fifteen Winds: A Selection of Modern Canadian Poems.* 1969.
> Editor, *I've Tasted My Blood: Poems 1956–1968,* by Milton Acorn. 1969.
> Editor, *Storm Warning: The New Canadian Poets.* 1971.

Reading List: *Purdy* by George Bowering, 1970.

*   *   *

From an unpromising beginning in the early 1940's, Al Purdy has made himself one of the liveliest, most prolific, and most respected Canadian poets. He is also one of the four or five most accomplished. From a purveyor of banalities, both in theme and technique, he has developed into a subtle and wide-ranging craftsman, ear and eye sensitively attuned to the human scene. A self-taught poet, he took a long time to work through certain habits and attitudes gathered in from the British tradition, but by the late 1950's his distinctive gifts had begun to show through. Eclectic in means, Protean in personality, his work seems to have cohered through the discovered sense of *locus* first apparent in such poems as "At Roblin Lake" (*The Crafte So Longe to Lerne*).

His work advanced greatly in the early 1960's, as is evident in *Poems for All the Annettes*, a collection full of a new energy, in which an earlier introversion has given way, importantly, to a telling exploration of individual relationships, as in "House Guest" and "Archaeology of Snow." Beyond this, Purdy shows in poems such as "The Old Woman and the Mayflowers" how a landscape may discover its myths in the character of its people.

The Cariboo Horses is in many ways Purdy's best book. In a book in which time and space, spartan time and empty – or snow-filled – space, predominate, he makes effective technical use of the continuous-present verb form. If *Poems for All the Annettes* marks the moment when Purdy's creative energies gathered decisively, *The Cariboo Horses* follows up by confirming that he is a *Canadian* poet. The book includes "The Madwoman in the Train," remarkable both as a subtle handling of the traditional sestina and as a deployment of psychological perspective.

It was Purdy who started the trend in Canada towards books of poems with a single, usually historical, thematic focus – in *North of Summer*. But his real métier is a kind of discursive lyric which he has, with mastery, made peculiarly his own. From *Wild Grape Wine* to *Sundance at Dusk* his repeated tactic has been to infuse information (geographical, historical, cultural, scientific) with emotion, as in "The Runners," "The Horses of the Agawa," and "Sundance." He handles the contemporary device of minimal punctuation well, and his best work evinces an easy and energetic handling of line and a peculiarly personal tone which is compounded of nostalgia and irony. The strong personality which gives his work its particular quality is held in balance by a high degree of professionalism.

—Charles Doyle

QUARLES, Francis. English. Born in Romford, Essex, baptized 8 May 1592. Educated at Christ's College, Cambridge, B.A. c. 1608; Lincoln's Inn, London. Married Ursula Woodgate in 1618; eighteen children. Cup-Bearer to Princess Elizabeth on her marriage to the elector palatine, 1613; abroad, 1615–17; Private Secretary to the Archbishop of Armagh, c. 1626–30; Chronologer of the City of London, 1639–44; wrote in defense of Charles I at the beginning of the Civil War. *Died 8 September 1644.*

PUBLICATIONS

Collections

Complete Works in Prose and Verse, edited by Alexander B. Grosart. 3 vols., 1880–81.

Verse

A Feast for Worms: A Poem of the History of Jonah. 1620.
Hadasa; or, The History of Queen Esther. 1621.
Job Militant. 1624.
Sion's Elegies, Wept by Jeremie the Prophet. 1624.
Sion's Sonnets, Sung by Solomon. 1625.
Argalus and Parthenia. 1629.
The History of Samson. 1631.
Divine Poems. 1630; revised edition, 1634.
Divine Fancies. 1632.
Emblems. 1635.
An Elegy upon Sir Julius Caesar. 1636.
An Elegy upon Mr. John Wheeler. 1637.
Hieroglyphics of the Life of Man. 1638.
Memorials upon the Death of Sir Robert Quarles. 1639.
Sighs at the Deaths of the Countess of Cleveland and Cicily Killigrew, with An Elegy upon the Death of Sir John Wolstenholme. 1640.
Threnodes on Lady Masham and William Cheyne. 1641.
Solomon's Recantation, Entitled Ecclesiastes, Paraphrased. 1645.
The Shepherd's Oracle. 1644; revised edition, 1646.
Hosanna; or, Divine Poems on the Passion of Christ. 1647.

Play

The Virgin Widow (produced before 1649). 1649.

Other

Enchiridion. 1640; selection, as *Observations Concerning Princes and States upon Peace and War,* 1642; as *Institutions, Essays and Maxims, Political, Moral and Divine,* 1695; as *Wisdom's Better Than Money,* 1698.
The Loyal Convert. 1644.
The Whipper Whipt. 1644.
The New Distemper. 1645.

Barnabas and Boanerges; or, Judgment and Mercy for Afflicted Souls. 2 vols., 1644–46.

Bibliography: *Quarles: A Bibliography of His Works to the Year 1800* by John Horden, 1953.

Reading List: *Der Einfluss der Bibel auf die Dichtungen des Quarles* by A. Lohnes, 1909; *Quarles in the Civil War* by Gordon S. Haight, 1939; "The Imagery of Quarles' Emblems" by E. James, in *University of Texas Studies in English*, 1943; *Quarles: A Study of His Life and Poetry* by Masodul Hasan, 1966; Introduction by John Horden to *Hosanna and Threnodes*, 1968, and to *Hieroglyphics of the Life of Man*, 1969.

*   *   *

A voluminous writer who produced Biblical paraphrases, an Arcadian romance, political pamphlets, aphorisms by the hundreds, and a single comedy, Francis Quarles is remembered chiefly for *Emblems* and *Hieroglyphics*. Perhaps "the most popular book of verse published during the century," *Emblems* later gave its author a place in the *Dunciad*. Although recent scholarly attention to emblem books has restored sympathetic attention to Quarles, there is some suspicion that his popularity may have grown from the generally undemanding way in which his poems trace the implications of symbolic and often curiously composed engravings.

The Arcadian romance *Argalus and Parthenia* remains entertaining. Initially, the heroine's ruby lips and pearly teeth seem tediously predictable, but convention is pushed to witty exaggeration in the picture of her breasts as azure-veined spheres: "Which, were they obvious but to every eye,/All liberall Arts would turn Astronomy." Quarles competently handles the suspense of dramatic incidents which retard until Book III the union of hero and heroine. There, deliberately stepping forward as author, he refuses to end the story in the glow of the wedding feast, and, if the final unhappy adventures are even more fanciful than the rest of the plot, they justify the appended poem on mortality: "Delights vanish, the morne o'ercasteth,/The frost breaks, the shower hasteth;/The tower falls, the hower spends;/The beauty fades, and man's life ends."

In the preface to *Argalus and Parthenia*, Quarles promises, "I have not affected to set thy understanding on the Rack, by the tyranny of strong lines." Although "strong lines," the metaphysical compression of metaphor, seem to have a natural affinity with emblematic drawings, Quarles chooses in *Emblems* and *Hieroglyphics* to be clear rather than strenuous. At their blandest, the poems are straightforward exegesis of details in the engravings, but Quarles varies the surface of his verse through elaborate repetition, antithesis, apostrophe, and dialogue, and he experiments with a wide range of metrical patterns. Arrangement of diverse elements creates part of the interest, for each emblem includes a picture, a Biblical motto, the poem, quotations from the Church Fathers, and a four-line epigram. *Emblems* consists of five books, each containing fifteen such units. The engravings were taken from two continental Jesuit collections; most of the pictures are concerned with the soul's struggle for salvation. For *Hieroglyphics*, a single set of fifteen emblems, Quarles obtained plates unified by the image of a candle, and he wrote poems unified partly through recurring images of light and darkness. The final seven emblems on the Ages of Man present a progressively shortened candle; against the movement from infancy to senility which is developed in the engravings and the longer poems, Quarles balances a sequence of epigrams moving in the opposite direction, from dotage to infancy. In emphasizing the brevity and precariousness of man's life, he returns to the theme of his first published work, *A Feast for Wormes*.

—Kay Stevenson

RAINE, Kathleen (Jessie).   English.   Born in London, 14 June 1908. Educated at County High School, Ilford; Girton College, Cambridge, M.A. in natural sciences 1929. Married the poet Charles Madge (divorced); one daughter and one son. Research Fellow, Girton College, Cambridge, 1955–61; Andrew Mellon Lecturer, National Gallery of Art, Washington, D.C., 1962. Recipient: Arts Council award, 1953; Chapelbrook Award; Cholmondeley Award, 1970; Smith Literary Award, 1972. D.Litt.: University of Leicester, 1974. Lives in London.

PUBLICATIONS

Verse

Stone and Flower: Poems 1935–43.   1943.
Living in Time.   1946.
The Pythoness and Other Poems.   1949.
Selected Poems.   1952.
The Year One.   1952.
The Collected Poems.   1956.
The Hollow Hill and Other Poems, 1960–1964.   1965.
Six Dreams and Other Poems.   1968.
Ninfa Revisited.   1968.
The Lost Country.   1971.
On a Deserted Shore.   1973.
The Oval Portrait and Other Poems.   1977.

Other

William Blake.   1951; revised edition, 1965, 1969.
Coleridge.   1953.
Poetry in Relation to Traditional Wisdom.   1958.
Defending Ancient Springs (essays).   1967.
Blake and Tradition.   1968.
William Blake.   1971.
Faces of Day and Night (autobiography).   1972.
Yeats, The Tarot and the Golden Dawn.   1972.
Farewell Happy Fields: Memories of Childhood.   1973.
Blake and Antiquity.   1974.
David Jones: Solitary Perfectionist.   1974; revised edition, 1975.
A Place, A State: A Suite of Drawings, drawings by Julian Trevelyan.   1974.
The Land Unknown (autobiography).   1975.
The Inner Journey of the Poet.   1976.
The Lion's Mouth (autobiography).   1977.

Editor, with Max-Pol Fouchet, Aspects de Littérature Anglaise, 1918–1945.   1947.
Editor, Letters of Samuel Taylor Coleridge.   1950.
Editor, Selected Poems and Prose of Coleridge.   1957.
Editor, with George Mills Harper, Thomas Taylor the Platonist: Selected Writings.   1969.
Editor, A Choice of Blake's Verse.   1974.
Editor, Shelley.   1974.

Translator, *Talk of the Devil,* by Dénis de Rougemont. 1945.
Translator, *Existentialism,* by Paul Foulquié. 1948.
Translator, *Cousin Bette,* by Balzac. 1948.
Translator, *Lost Illusions,* by Balzac. 1951.
Translator, with R. M. Nadal, *Life's a Dream,* by Calderón. 1968.

Reading List: *Raine* by Ralph J. Mills, Jr., 1967.

*   *   *

Kathleen Raine is very much a poet on her own in the modern world, and her contribution to literature is difficult to classify. She belongs, perhaps, to the same poetic group as T. S. Eliot, David Gascoyne, St. John Perse, and Hugo Manning. A biologist by training, influenced by the writings of Jung and Blake, she has drawn greatly on nature and philosophy for her writings. She has made a lifelong study of the sources of tradition and makes great use of symbolism. Poetry for her is only authentic if it makes use of perennial philosophy and ancient wisdom expressed in traditional language. Her early poems had a spareness and directness about them which, coupled with a natural lyrical movement and a clear eye for significant detail, soon established her as a poet of consequence. Her later work, though often couched in simple language, is not so easy to comprehend at a first reading, since much of it conceals deep private experiences. She is essentially a poet in the Platonic tradition, who has always defended the ancient springs of civilisation, especially when these are of Christian origin. She has an individual and high-minded vision, both of life and literature, and in later years has displayed a deep sense of anger and passion against contemporary ignorance, and what she believes to be false Communistic ideas.

As a scholar she has made a name for herself in the English-speaking world by her writings about William Blake and Thomas Taylor, and is accepted as one of the leading authorities on both of them. Blake, for her, is an archetype which all poets should follow, in that he laid such great emphasis upon the powers of imagination and the need for mankind to retain his primeval innocence. Her autobiographies are very personal and often harrowing, especially *The Lion's Mouth*, revealing her complete dedication to poetry, even at the expense of everything else in her life. Her protestations, and her courage to speak out against the dilution of life and literature in the contemporary world, have brought her much criticism and misunderstanding, but they have not affected her honesty or swayed her opinions. Her poetry can be tender and straightforward on the one hand, and difficult and obscure on the other, but both styles reveal a unique gift of unusual brilliance.

—Leonard Clark

RALEGH, Sir Walter. English. Born in Hayes Barton, Devon, in 1552. Educated at Oriel College, Oxford, 1566–69. Married Elizabeth Throckmorton in 1593. Courtier, diplomatist, soldier and explorer: fought for the Huguenots in France, at Jarnac and Moncontour, 1569; joined expedition of his half-brother Sir Humphrey Gilbert, 1578; fought against the rebels in Ireland, 1580; entered the Court as a protégé of Leicester, 1581, and accompanied him to the Netherlands, 1582; on his return became a great favorite of the Queen; knighted in 1584; appointed Lord Warden of the Stannaries and Vice-Admiral of Devon and Cornwall, 1585; Member of Parliament for Devon, 1585; fitted out an expedition to America, 1584, which discovered and claimed Virginia, 1584; attempted to colonize Virginia with two more expeditions, 1585–87; went to Ireland in an attempt to make his estate there habitable, 1587; returned to court, and involved in organizing resistance to the threatened invasion of the Spanish Armada, 1588, and planning an expedition to seize Spanish treasure ships, 1592; imprisoned in the tower because of the Queen's anger at his secret relationship with her maid-of-honour Throckmorton, 1592–95; explored the coasts of Trinidad, and sailed up the Orinoco, 1595; fought the Spanish at Cadiz, 1596; allowed to resume his place as Captain of the Guard, 1597; involved in the successful attack against Spain in the Azores, 1597; Governor of Jersey, 1600–03; after James's accession, arrested as "agent of Spain," sentenced to die, but reprieved and imprisoned in the Tower of London, 1603–16; involved in a disastrous expedition to Guiana, 1617; on his return imprisoned and then executed on the former charge. *Died 28 October 1618.*

PUBLICATIONS

Collections

Works. 8 vols., 1829.
Poems, edited by Agnes M. C. Latham. 1929; revised edition, 1951.
Selected Prose and Poetry, edited by Agnes M. C. Latham. 1965.
A Choice of Ralegh's Verse, edited by Robert Nye. 1972.

Verse

Poems, edited by E. Brydges. 1813.

Other

A Report of the Fight about the Isles of the Azores. 1591; edited by H. Newbolt, 1908.
The Discovery of the Large, Rich, and Beautiful Empire of Guiana. 1596; edited by W. H. D. Rouse, 1905.
The History of the World. 1614; abridgement edited by C. A. Patrides, 1971.
The Prerogative of Parliaments. 1628.
Instructions to His Son and to Posterity. 1632; edited by Louis B. Wright, 1962.
The Prince; or, Maxims of State. 1642.
Judicious and Select Essays. 1650; *Apology for His Voyage to Guiana* edited by V. T. Harlow, 1932.
Maxims of State. 1650; augmented edition, 1656.
A Discourse of the Original and Fundamental Cause of Natural War with the Mystery of Invasive War. 1650.
The Sceptic (miscellany). 1657.
Remains. 1657.
Three Discourses. 1702.
A Military Discourse. 1734.
The Interest of England with Regard to Foreign Alliances, Explained in Two Discourses. 1750.
Journal of the Second Voyage to Guiana, edited by R. H. Schomburk. 1848; edited by V. T. Marlow, 1932.

Bibliography: *A Bibliography of Raleigh* by T. N. Brushfield, 1886, revised edition, 1908.

Reading List: *Life, with Letters* by E. Edwards, 2 vols., 1868; *Ralegh, The Last of the Elizabethans* by Edward Thompson, 1935; *Ralegh: A Study in Elizabethan Skepticism* by Ernest A. Strathmann, 1951; "The Poetry of Ralegh" by Peter Ure, in *Review of English Studies*, 1960; *Ralegh, Ecrivain* by Pierre Lefranc, 1968; *Ralegh: The Renaissance Man and His Roles* by Stephen A. Greenblatt, 1973; *Ralegh as Historian* by John Racin, 1974.

*   *   *

A report by Anthony à Wood in 1691 adequately suggests Sir Walter Ralegh's numerous interests and as many personalities. "Authors are perplex'd," Wood stated, "under what topick to place him, whether of Statesman, Seaman, Souldier, Chymist, or Chronologer; for in all these he did excell" (*Athenae Oxonienses*, I, 371). Yet even this list hardly exhausts Ralegh's variegated activities. He was also historian, philosopher, theologian, and poet. Moreover, he pursued commercial enterprises which enriched his country if not himself; he was a noted patron of literature and the sciences; he designed ships; and he was a politician distinguished for his remarkably liberal tendencies. We are also assured that he was "a pioneer in naval medicine, dietetics, and hygiene" (Christopher Hill, *Intellectual Origins of the English Revolution*, 1965).

A staunch supporter of the imperial idea, Ralegh participated in the transatlantic enterprises of his half-brother Sir Humphrey Gilbert. He later sponsored the expedition which occupied the territory he named after the Queen – Virginia – while in 1595 he sailed to South America in search of Eldorado, the fabled city of gold. Active during the threatened invasion of the Spanish Armada in 1588, he rarely lost an opportunity to oppose the Spanish empire, whether at Cadiz in 1596 or off the Azores a year later. Highly favoured by the Queen – save for the period following his secret marriage to Elizabeth Throckmorton in 1593 – he was nevertheless judged much too flamboyant to have merited elevation to the Privy Council. On the Queen's death in 1603, at any rate, his fortunes declined disastrously. Maligned by his enemies who decisively influenced James I, he was arrested on the incredible charge of being an agent of Spain and sentenced to death after a trial generally regarded as "criminal procedure seen at its worst" (Sir John Macdonell, *Historical Trials*, 1927). But the sentence was not carried out. Ralegh was instead conveyed to the Tower where he remained for nearly thirteen years, to 1616. Released, he mounted a disastrous expedition to Guiana where his son Wat was killed in an engagement with Spanish forces alerted to await his arrival. On his return home he was arrested yet again and, without benefit of a trial, was beheaded on 28 October 1618.

Within two days of Ralegh's execution it was said that "his death will doe more hurte to the faction that sought it, then ever his life could have done" (John Pory, edited by W. S. Powell in *William and Mary Quarterly*, 1952, 537). It was a prophetic utterance; for given the mounting opposition to King James, Ralegh was presently canonised as the principal martyr of royal authoritarianism and injustice. Eventually, he was even transmuted into a republican, largely on the basis of the widely circulated report by John Aubrey that upon the death of Elizabeth he had planned to set up a Commonwealth. However mistaken in itself, the claim appeared to have been implicitly advanced in the work Ralegh composed during his confinement in the Tower, *The History of the World*.

Ralegh's few poems encompass the surviving "books" of *The Ocean to Cynthia* – some five hundred lines addressed to Queen Elizabeth – where a series of frequently obscure, highly metaphorical, fragmentary (and fragmented) emotions undulate through remembered joys to currently experienced despair and hysterical hope ("She is gone, she is lost! She is found, she is ever fair!"). His other poems, hardly numerous, have been reduced still further now that the authenticity of one of the finest, "The Lie," has been questioned (see Pierre Lefranc). Yet it is a respectable collection all the same, its high peaks clearly marked by the predominant sombre mood of "Nature that washt her hands in milk," "Methought I saw the grave where Laura lay" (a prefatory poem to Spenser's *Faerie Queene*), and "The Nymph's Reply to the Shepherd" (an answer to Marlowe's "The Passionate Shepherd to His Love"), as well as the exceptionally qualified mood of "The Passionate Man's Pilgrimage." Impressed, we tend to claim with Peter Ure that Ralegh "ranks even better amongst the minor poets of his time," or that his poems are indeed "extraordinary by any standards" (M. C. Bradbrook, *The School of Night*, 1936). But John Aubrey's contrary judgement has the single advantage that it obliges us to reconsider Ralegh's poetic talents. "He was," said Aubrey sourly, "sometimes a Poet, not often."

Ralegh's prose works include the rousing account of Sir Richard Greville's encounter with the Spanish fleet in *A Report of the Truth of the Fight about the Iles of Açores*, the optimistic vision which is *The Discoverie of the Large, Rich, and Bewtiful Empire of Guiana*, and the colossal *History of the World*, which is arguably his principal contribution to English literature. *The History* was on its publication suppressed by King James partly because it was said to censure princes but especially because it appeared to be a veiled denunciation of his reign. What other reason was there for Ralegh's several comparisons of the early seventeenth century with the expired glories of the Elizabethan age? A series of "parallels" compounded the offence, notably the account of the great Queen Semiramis and her incompetent successor Ninias ("esteemed no man of warre at all, but altogether feminine, and subjected to ease and delicacie," I, ii, 1). In fact, however, Ralegh's principal thrust was in another direction. It was conceivably aimed to provide a sustained view of historical events in the light of that expressly Christian view of history which asserts God's constant supervision of the created order (see the introduction to the edition of *The History* by C. A. Patrides, 1971). But it was no less conceivably aimed to deploy "a secular and critical approach" which eventually contributed "to that segregation of the spiritual from the secular which was the achievement of the seventeenth century" (Christopher Hill). Whichever theory persuades in the end, *The History* possesses an impressive unity of style which is the direct result of Ralegh's successful modulation of an infinitely varied tone. As with the polyphonic music of *Paradise Lost*, so here different subjects have different cadences, and in each case, once the cumulative effect is achieved, the measure alters in accord with the new theme. Clarity reigns supreme throughout, in express opposition to the self-conscious obscurity so often encountered in the literature of the same period. *The History of the World*, it is evident, possesses a style answerable to its great argument.

—C. A. Patrides

RAMSAY, Allan. Scottish. Born in Leadhills, Crawford, Lanarkshire, 15 October 1686. Educated at Crawford village school until 1700; apprenticed to a wigmaker in Edinburgh, 1701. Married Miss Christian Ross in 1712 (died, 1743); eight children including the painter Allan Ramsay. Started his own business, and became prosperous, as a wigmaker in Edinburgh; member of the Jacobite Easy Club, 1712–15: Club Laureate, 1715; changed his business to that of bookseller, 1718, and founded the first circulating library in Scotland, 1728; ceased to write after 1730; built and managed the first theatre in Edinburgh, 1736–37; retired from bookselling, 1755. *Died 7 January 1758.*

PUBLICATIONS

Collections

Works, edited by Burns Martin and others.   6 vols., 1951–74.
Poems of Ramsay and Robert Fergusson, edited by Alexander M. Kinghorn and
    Alexander Law.   1974.

Verse

The Battle; or, Morning Interview: A Heroi-Comical Poem.   1716.
Christ's Kirk on the Green.   1718; revised edition, 1718.
Edinburgh's Address to the Country.   1718(?).
Scots Songs.   1718; augmented edition, 1719, 1720.
Elegies on Maggy Johnston, John Cowper, and Lucky Wood.   1718.
The Scribblers Lashed.   1718.
Tartana; or, The Plaid.   1718.
Content.   1719.
Familiar Epistles Between W— H— and A— R—.   1719.
Richy and Sandy: A Pastoral on the Death of Addison.   1719(?).
An Epistle to W[illiam] H[amilton].   1720(?).
Edinburgh's Salutation to the Marquess of Carnarvon.   1720.
To Mr. Law.   1720.
An Ode with a Pastoral Recitative on the Marriage of James Earl of Wemyss and Mrs.
    Janet Charteris.   1720.
Patie and Roger: A Pastoral.   1720.
A Poem on the South Sea.   1720; as *Wealth; or, The Woody,* 1720.
The Prospect of Plenty: A Poem on the North-Sea Fishery.   1720; as *To the Royal*
    Burrows of Scotland, 1720.
The Rise and Fall of Stocks 1720, The Satire's Comic Project.   1720.
Poems.   1721; revised edition, 2 vols.,1728
Robert, Richy, and Sandy: A Pastoral on the Death of Prior.   1721.
Fables and Tales.   1722; as *Collection of Thirty Fables,* 1730.
A Tale of Three Bonnets.   1722.
The Fair Assembly.   1723.
Jenny and Meggy: A Pastoral, Being a Sequel to Patie and Roger.   1723.
Health.   1724; revised edition, 1724 (twice), 1730.
The Monk and the Miller's Wife; or, All the Parties Pleased.   1724.
Mouldy-Mowdiwart; or, The Last Speech of a Wretched Miser.   1724.
The Poetic Sermon.   1724.
On Pride: An Epistle.   1724.
On the Royal Company of Archers Marching under the Command of His Grace Duke of
    Hamilton.   1724.
On Seeing the Archers Diverting Themselves.   1724.
A Scots Ode to the British Antiquarians.   1726.
To the Right Honourable Duncan Forbes of Culloden.   1737.
The Vision.   1748.
Curiosities of a Scots Charta Chest 1600–1800 (includes letters), edited by Mrs. Atholl
    Forbes.   1897.

Plays

>The Nuptials: A Masque on the Marriage of James Duke of Hamilton and Lady Anne
>Cochran.   1723.
>The Gentle Shepherd: A Scots Pastoral Comedy (produced 1729).   1725.

Other

>Some Few Hints in Defence of Dramatic Entertainments.   1727(?).
>An Address of Thanks from the Society of Rakes.   1735.

>Editor, The Tea-Table Miscellany.   3 vols., 1723–27; vols. 1–2 issued as A New
>Miscellany of Scots Song, 1727; 4 vols., 1740.
>Editor, The Ever Green, Being a Collection of Scots Poems Before Sixteen Hundred.   2
>vols., 1724.
>Editor, A Collection of Scots Proverbs.   1737.

Bibliography: Bibliography of the Writings of Ramsay by Burns Martin, 1931.

Reading List: Ramsay by W. H. O. Smeaton, 1896; New Light on Ramsay by Andrew
Gibson, 1927; Ramsay by Burns Martin, 1931.

*   *   *

Noticing in his preface to The Ever Green that "Readers of the best and most exquisite
Discernment frequently complain of our Modern Writings, as filled with affected Delicacies
and studied Refinements, which they would gladly exchange for that natural Strength of
Thought and Simplicity of Stile our Forefathers practised," Allan Ramsay achieved a great
deal in his lifetime to gratify this preference.

He practised his literary art at a crucial point in Scotland's cultural history, when political
union seemed complete, if uneasy, and when the pressures of commerce, cultural attitude,
and political pressure seemed likely to iron out local customs, speech-values, and writing in
favour of the metropolitan, which in this case meant literary London. Ramsay, a practical
man of business in an enlightened city which felt fiercely proud of its Scottishness, if
uncertain how best to express it, researched, published, popularised Scottish writing, both the
original verse of his immensely popular Gentle Shepherd, and the rescued oral literature of
the Tea-Table Miscellany, and the late mediaeval Scots verse published in the pages of The
Ever Green. His style was uneven, and in preparing older work for the press, he often made
interpolations which pleased his contemporaries, yet jar modern scholarship. Yet he proved
himself a witty and versatile practitioner of verse in Scots and English, in long and short
poems, in pastoral and epigram as well as lyric and descriptive verse.

He proclaimed in the same preface his scorn of "one's expressing his Ignorance of his
native Language": as a man who rescued the poetry of Scotland from threatened oblivion
and helped popularise it at a time of growing national consciousness, he plainly played an
important part in the coming "golden age" of Scottish culture. Like many men of this period,
he was a keen participant in societies of literary interest, in amateur and professional
theatricals, and an amateur of the arts in general. His works have recently been given the
thorough and scholarly editing they deserve, by the Scottish Texts Society, and in the process
been revealed in their extensiveness and variety. The explosion of talent in the two following
generations plainly owes a good deal to this pioneer. In him, too, we see some of the
ambiguities of the golden age, the uncertainty over language; the attitude to the past as
something to be maintained, yet modified to the standards of the present; a curious double

standard which exults in the Scottish for Scottish readers yet maintains a curiously defensive tone for non-Scots. A man of talent born at the threshold of an exciting period, Ramsay was an accomplished writer who deserves to be remembered for more than just his one successful pastoral.

—Ian Campbell

RANSOM, John Crowe. American. Born in Pulaski, Tennessee, 30 April 1888. Educated at Vanderbilt University, Nashville, Tennessee, B.A. 1909 (Phi Beta Kappa); Christ Church, Oxford (Rhodes Scholar), 1910–13, B.A. 1913. Served in the United States Army, 1917–19. Married Robb Reavill in 1920; three children. Assistant in English, Harvard University, Cambridge, Massachusetts, 1914; Member of the Faculty, 1914–27, and Professor of English, 1927–37, Vanderbilt University; Carnegie Professor of Poetry, 1937–58, and Professor Emeritus, 1959–74, Kenyon College, Gambier, Ohio. Visiting Lecturer in English, Chattanooga University, Tennessee, 1938; Visiting Lecturer in Language and Criticism, University of Texas, Austin, 1956. Member of the Fugitive Group of Poets: Founding Editor, with Allen Tate, *The Fugitive*, Nashville, 1922–25; Editor, *Kenyon Review*, Gambier, Ohio, 1937–59. Formerly, Honorary Consultant in American Letters, Library of Congress, Washington, D.C. Recipient: Guggenheim Fellowship, 1931; Bollingen Prize, 1951; Russell Loines Award, 1951; Brandeis University Creative Arts Award, 1958; Academy of American Poets Fellowship, 1962; National Book Award, 1964; National Endowment for the Arts award, 1966; Emerson-Thoreau Medal, 1968; National Institute of Arts and Letters Gold Medal, 1973. Member, American Academy of Arts and Letters, and American Academy of Arts and Sciences. *Died 3 July 1974.*

PUBLICATIONS

Verse

> *Poems about God.* 1919.
> *Armageddon,* with *A Fragment* by William Alexander Percy and *Avalon* by Donald Davidson. 1923.
> *Chills and Fever.* 1924.
> *Grace after Meat.* 1924.
> *Two Gentlemen in Bonds.* 1927.
> *Selected Poems.* 1945; revised edition, 1963, 1969.

Other

> *God Without Thunder: An Unorthodox Defense of Orthodoxy.* 1930.
> *Shall We Complete the Trade? A Proposal for the Settlement of Foreign Debts to the United States.* 1933.
> *The World's Body.* 1938; revised edition, 1968.
> *The New Criticism.* 1941.

A College Primer of Writing. 1943.
Poems and Essays. 1955.
Beating the Bushes: Selected Essays 1941–1970. 1972.

Editor, *Topics for Freshman Writing: Twenty Topics for Writing, with Appropriate Material for Study.* 1935.
Editor, *The Kenyon Critics: Studies in Modern Literature from the "Kenyon Review."* 1951.
Editor, *Selected Poems,* by Thomas Hardy. 1961.

Bibliography: "Ransom: A Checklist, 1967–76" by T. D. Young, in *Mississippi Quarterly 30,* 1976–77.

Reading List: *Ransom* by John L. Stewart, 1962; *The Poetry of Ransom: A Study of Diction, Metaphor, and Symbol* by Karl F. Knight, 1964; *The Equilibrist: A Study of Ransom's Poems 1916–1963* by Robert Buffington, 1967; *Ransom: Critical Essays and a Bibliography* edited by T. D. Young, 1968, and *Gentleman in a Dustcoat: A Biography of Ransom* by Young, 1976; *Ransom* by Thornton H. Parsons, 1969; *Ransom: Critical Principles and Preoccupations* by James E. Morgan, 1971; *The Poetry of Ransom* by Miller Williams, 1972.

*   *   *

As poet, teacher, critic, and editor, John Crowe Ransom was one of the most influential men of his generation. Although scholars and critics have agreed that Ransom commands an eminent position, they have disagreed on the precise nature of his contribution. The priorities Ransom established for his literary career displeased some of his friends. He was, as Allen Tate once said, "one of the great elegiac poets of the English language," who produced ten or twelve almost perfect lyrics which will be read as long as poetry is regarded as a serious art. Yet the major portion of his creative energies were devoted to the writing of poetry only for a very brief period. During the remainder of a long and active literary career, much of his thought and most of his effort were expended on speculations on the nature and function of poetic discourse; on the significance of religious myth, the need for an inscrutable God; and on discussions of the proper relations that should exist between man, God, and nature.

Most of the poetry for which Ransom will be remembered was written between 1922 and 1925 and published in *Chills and Fever* and *Two Gentlemen in Bonds.* During the winter of 1922 Ransom read at one of the Fugitive meetings his poem "Necrological," which convinced Allen Tate that almost "overnight he had left behind him the style of his first book [*Poems about God*] and, without confusion, had mastered a new style." All of his best poems are written in this "new style," what critics have come to refer to as his "mature manner": the subtle irony, the nuanced ambiguities, the wit, and the cool detached tone. In these poems Ransom uses a simple little narrative as a means of presenting the "common actuals"; an innocent character is involved in a common situation and through this involvement he comes to have a fuller understanding of his own nature. Few poets of his generation have been able to represent with greater accuracy and precision the inexhaustible ambiguities, the paradoxes and tensions, the dichotomies and ironies that make up the life of modern man. His poetry reiterates a few themes: man's dual nature and the inevitable misery and disaster that accompany the failure to recognize and accept this basic truth; mortality and the fleetingness of youthful vigor and grace, the inevitable decay of feminine beauty; the disparity between the world as man would have it and as it actually is, between what people want and need emotionally and what is available for them, between what man desires and what he can get; the necessity of man's simultaneous apprehension of nature's indifference and mystery and his appreciation of her sensory beauties; the inability of modern man, in his incomplete and fragmentary state, to experience love.

Throughout his career Ransom maintained that human experience can be fully realized only through art. In many of his critical essays – some of which are collected in *The World's Body*, *The New Criticism*, and *Beating the Bushes* – Ransom tries to define the unique nature of poetic discourse, which functions to "induce the mode of thought that is imaginative rather than logical," to recover "the denser and more refractory original world which we know loosely through our perceptions and memories." That which we may learn from poetry is "ontologically distinct" because it is the "kind of knowledge by which we must know what we have arranged that we cannot know otherwise." Only through poetry, which is composed of a "loose logical structure with a good deal of local texture," can man recover the "body and solid substance of the world." The basic kind of data which science can collect reduces the "world to a scheme of abstract conveniences." Whereas science is interesting only in *knowing*, art has a double function; it wants both to *know* and to *make*.

In many of his later essays Ransom attempts to demonstrate how the critic should react in his efforts to define the nature of poetic discourse and to justify its existence in a society becoming more and more enamored of the quasi-knowledge and the false promises of science. In essay after essay he insists that the truths that poetry contains can be obtained only through a detailed analytical study of the poems themselves, and he repeats one theme: without poetry man's knowledge of himself and his world is fragmentary and incomplete.

—T. D. Young

READ, Sir Herbert (Edward). English. Born at Muscoates Grange, Kirbymoorside, Yorkshire, 4 December 1893. Educated at Crossley's School, Halifax, Yorkshire; University of Leeds. Commissioned in The Green Howards, 1915, and fought in France and Belgium, 1915–18: Captain, 1917; Military Cross, Distinguished Service Order, 1918; mentioned in despatches. Married 1) Evelyn Roff; 2) Margaret Ludwig; four sons and one daughter. Assistant Principal, The Treasury, London, 1919–22; Assistant Keeper, Victoria and Albert Museum, London, 1922–31; Watson Gordon Professor of Fine Arts, University of Edinburgh, 1931–33; Editor, *Burlington Magazine*, London, 1933–39; Sydney Jones Lecturer in Art, University of Liverpool, 1935–36; Editor, English Master Painters series, from 1940. Leon Fellow, University of London, 1940–42; Charles Eliot Norton Professor of Poetry, Harvard University, Cambridge, Massachusetts, 1953–54; A. W. Mellon Lecturer in Fine Arts, Washington, 1954; Senior Fellow, Royal College of Art, London, 1962; Fellow, Center for Advanced Studies, Wesleyan University, Middletown, Connecticut, 1964–65. Trustee, Tate Gallery, London, 1965–68. President, Society for Education Through Art, Yorkshire Philosophical Society, Institute of Contemporary Arts, and British Society of Aesthetics. Recipient: Erasmus Prize, 1966. Prof. Honorario: University of Cordoba, Argentina, 1962; Doctor of Fine Arts: State University of New York at Buffalo, 1962; Litt.D.: University of Boston, 1965; University of York, 1966. Honorary Fellow, Society of Industrial Artists; Foreign Corresponding Member, Académie Flamande des Beaux Arts, 1953; Foreign Member, Royal Academy of Fine Arts, Stockholm, 1960; Honorary Member, American Academy of Arts and Letters, 1966. Knighted, 1953. *Died 12 June 1968.*

<small>PUBLICATIONS</small>

Verse

Songs of Chaos. 1915.
Auguries of Life and Death. 1919.
Eclogues: A Book of Poems. 1919.
Naked Warriors. 1919.
Mutations of the Phoenix. 1923.
Collected Poems, 1913–1925. 1926; revised edition, 1946, 1966.
The End of a War. 1933.
Poems 1914–34. 1935.
Thirty-Five Poems. 1940.
A World Within a War. 1944.
Moon's Farm, and Poems Mostly Elegiac. 1955.

Plays

Aristotle's Mother: An Argument in Athens (broadcast 1946). In Imaginary
Conversations: Eight Radio Scripts, edited by Rayner Heppenstall, 1948.
Thieves of Mercy (broadcast 1947). In Imaginary Conversations: Eight Radio Scripts,
edited by Rayner Heppenstall, 1948.
Lord Byron at the Opera (broadcast 1953). 1963.
The Parliament of Women. 1961.

Radio Plays: Artistotle's Mother, 1946; Thieves of Mercy, 1947; Lord Byron at the
Opera, 1953.

Fiction

The Green Child: A Romance. 1935.

Other

English Pottery: Its Development from Early Times to the End of the Eighteenth Century,
with B. Rackham. 1924.
In Retreat. 1925.
English Stained Glass. 1926.
Reason and Romanticism: Essays in Literary Criticism. 1926.
English Prose Style. 1928; revised edition, 1952.
Phases of English Poetry. 1928; revised edition, 1950.
The Sense of Glory: Essays in Criticism. 1929.
Staffordshire Pottery Figures. 1929.
Wordsworth. 1930; revised edition, 1949.
Ambush. 1930.
Julien Benda and the New Humanism. 1930.
The Meaning of Art. 1931; as The Anatomy of Art, 1932; revised edition, 1936, 1949,
1951, 1968.
Form in Modern Poetry. 1932.

Art Now: An Introduction to the Theory of Modern Painting and Sculpture. 1933; revised edition, 1936, 1948, 1961.
The Innocent Eye. 1933.
Art and Industry: The Principles of Industrial Design. 1934; revised edition, 1944, 1953, 1957.
Essential Communism. 1935.
In Defence of Shelley and Other Essays. 1936.
Art and Society. 1937; revised edition, 1945.
Collected Essays in Literary Criticism. ·1938; as *The Nature of Literature,* 1956.
Poetry and Anarchism. 1938.
Annals of Innocence and Experience. 1940; revised edition, 1946; as *The Innocent Eye,* 1947.
The Philosophy of Anarchism. 1940.
To Hell with Culture: Democratic Values Are New Values. 1941.
Education Through Art. 1943.
The Politics of the Unpolitical. 1943.
The Education of Free Men. 1944.
Flicker, with Toni del Renzio and R. S. O. Poole. 1944.
A Coat of Many Colours: Occasional Essays. 1945; revised edition, 1956.
The Grass Roots of Art: Four Lectures. 1946; revised edition, 1955.
Coleridge as Critic. 1949.
Education for Peace. 1949.
Existentialism, Marxism, and Anarchism: Chains of Freedom. 1949.
Byron. 1951.
Contemporary British Art. 1951; revised edition, 1965.
The Philosophy of Modern Art: Collected Essays. 1952.
The True Voice of Feeling: Studies in English Romantic Poetry. 1953.
Anarchy and Order: Essays in Politics. 1954.
Icon and Idea: The Function of Art in the Development of Human Consciousness. 1955.
The Art of Sculpture (lectures). 1956.
The Significance of Children's Art: Art as a Symbolic Language. 1957.
The Tenth Muse: Essays in Criticism. 1957.
A Concise History of Modern Painting. 1959; revised edition, 1968.
The Forms of Things Unknown: Essays Towards an Aesthetic Philosophy. 1960.
Truth Is More Sacred: A Critical Exchange on Modern Literature, with Edward Dahlberg. 1961.
A Letter to a Young Painter (essays). 1962.
The Contrary Experience: Autobiographies. 1963.
Selected Writings. 1963.
To Hell with Culture and Other Essays on Art and Society. 1963.
Art and Education. 1964.
A Concise History of Modern Sculpture. 1964.
Henry Moore: A Study of His Life and Work. 1965.
The Origins of Form in Art. 1965.
The Redemption of the Robot: My Encounter with Education Through Art. 1966.
T.S.E.: A Memoir (on Eliot). 1966.
Art and Alienation: The Role of the Artist in Society. 1967.
Poetry and Experience. 1967.
The Cult of Sincerity. 1968.
Essays in Literary Criticism: Particular Studies. 1969.

Editor, *Speculations: Essays on Humanism and the Philosophy of Art,* by T. E. Hulme, 1923.
Editor, *Form in Gothic,* by W. R. Worringer. 1927.

Editor, *Notes on Language and Style,* by T. E. Hulme.   1929.

Editor, with Bonamy Dobrée, *The London Book of English Prose.*   1931; as *The Book of English Prose,* 1931; revised edition, 1949.

Editor, *The English Vision.*   1933.

Editor, *Unit 1: The Modern Movement in English Architecture, Painting, and Sculpture.*   1934.

Editor, with Denis Saurat, *Selected Essays and Critical Writings,* by A. R. Orage.   1935.

Editor, *Surrealism.*   1936.

Editor, *The Knapsack: A Pocket-Book of Prose and Verse.*   1939.

Editor, *Kropotkin: Selections from His Writings.*   1942.

Editor, *The Practice of Design.*   1946.

Editor, with Bonamy Dobrée, *The London Book of English Verse.*   1949; revised edition, 1952.

Editor, *Outline: An Autobiography, and Other Writings,* by Paul Nash.   1949.

Editor, with Michael Fordham and Gerhard Adler, *The Collected Works of C. J. Jung.*   17 vols., 1953–73.

Editor, *This Way Delight: A Book of Poetry for the Young.*   1956.

Editor, *Origins of Western Art.*   1965.

Translator, with M. Ludwig, *Radio,* by M. Arnheim, 1936.

Reading List: *Read: An Introduction* edited by Henry Treece, 1944; *Read* by Francis Berry, 1953, revised edition, 1961; *Read: A Memorial Symposium* edited by Robin Skelton, 1970; *A Certain Order: The Development of Read's Theory of Poetry* by Worth T. Harder, 1971; *Read: The Stream and the Source* by George Woodcock, 1972.

*   *   *

Sir Herbert Read was of the same generation as Rosenberg and Owen. But Read survived the War, the crude fact of which permitted him to write what some may think of as not only his finest "war poem," but perhaps his best poem of all, *The End of a War* (written between 1931–2, and published 1933). Like Blunden and Sassoon, as a survivor he continued to be haunted by his experience of trench combat. Unlike Sassoon, his poetry continued to express his apprehension of war's social destructiveness, and the few lessons that might be obtained from it.

In a sense, "The Happy Warrior" can serve as a model for the former. It looks backwards with adverse judgment on Wordsworth's apparently theoretical appraisal of the "Character of the Happy Warrior," and projects on to it an experienced and thus realistic understanding of how war erodes all that best restraining consciousness which is the hallmark of civilization:

> I saw him stab
> And stab again
> A well-killed Boche.

The poem is also notable for its successful handling of the theme in imagistic form, and in this it is somewhat exceptional, for the hard edge and the controlling image are not, of themselves, attributes that can best explore the discursive nature and evaluation of such experiences as the war forced upon each person. Read noted in his autobiographies *The Contrary Experience* that Imagism could not cope with war's experiences properly; yet in all his war poems, even *The End of a War,* the kind of relation between image, rhythm, syntax, and lineation is one that developed from Imagism's original tenets. What Read cannot make

Imagism do, however, is to unfold narrative, and he is therefore forced, in *The End of a War*, to have a prefacing prose note which situates the narrative facts which may then be used as the basis for philosophic and/or sensuous projection. This solution is not an integral one, for the formal means of verse are themselves supported by the external prose activity.

Of all the war poets Yeats chose only Read's long poem for his *The Oxford Book of Modern Verse* (1936), and something of Yeats's preference for the distancing of suffering reflected in such a choice may help us to arrive at evaluating a complex poem that finally asserts a tentative optimism.

—Jon Silkin

REEVES, William Pember. New Zealander. Born in Lyttleton, 10 February 1857. Educated at Christ's College Grammar School, Christchurch, 1867–74; admitted as barrister and solicitor. Married Magdalen Stuart Robison in 1885; two daughters. Worked as a Reporter for the Canterbury Law School; Editor of the Canterbury *Times* in the 1880's; Staff Member, subsequently Editor, Lyttleton *Times*, from 1889; Liberal Member of the New Zealand House of Representatives for St. Albans, 1887–90, and for Christchurch, 1890–96: Minister of Education, Labour and Justice, 1891–96; New Zealand Agent-General in London, 1896–1909, and High Commissioner, 1905–09; Director, London School of Economics, 1908–19; Chairman, National Bank of New Zealand, London, 1917–32. Member of the Senate, University of London, 1902–19; Chairman, Anglo-Hellenic League. Ph.D.: University of Athens, 1919. Knight of the Redeemer, Greece, 1914. *Died 15 May 1932.*

PUBLICATIONS

Verse

> *Colonial Couplets,* with G. P. Williams. 1889.
> *In Double Harness,* with G. P. Williams. 1891.
> *New Zealand and Other Poems.* 1898.
> *(Poems).* N.d.
> *The Passing of the Forest and Other Verse.* 1925.

Other

> *Some Historical Articles on Communism and Socialism.* 1890.
> *Reform and Experiment in New Zealand.* 1896.
> *The Fortunate Isles.* 1897.
> *The Working of Women's Suffrage in New Zealand and South Australia,* with Sir John Cockburn. 1897.
> *New Zealand.* 1898.
> *The Long White Cloud: Ao Tea Roa* (history of New Zealand). 1898.
> *State Experiments in Australia and New Zealand.* 2 vols., 1902.
> *A Council of the Empire.* 1907.
> *The New Zealand's Shipping Company's Pocket Book: An Interesting Guide for Passengers.* 1908.

New Zealand ("described"). 1908.
A Plea for a More Civilized Epirus. 1913.
Albania and Epirus. 1914.
An Appeal for the Liberation and Union of the Hellenic Race. 1918.
The Great Powers and the Eastern Christians: Christiani ad Leones! A Protest. 1922.

Editor, with Ernest Speight, The Imperial Reader: An Account of the Territories Forming the British Empire. 1906.

Reading List: Reeves: New Zealand Fabian, 1965, and Reeves, 1969, both by Keith Sinclair.

*   *   *

William Pember Reeves was the most interesting and accomplished poet in nineteenth-century New Zealand. Yet, like most of the New Zealanders who produced readable verse in the colonial period (and they were few in number and modest in achievement), Reeves was a man for whom poetry was a minor activity in a life devoted largely to other things, pre-eminently politics, though sport, journalism, and historical writing were among his other accomplishments. His poetry was merely a civilised diversion, a private recreation taken up in the interstices of a busy public life. Nonetheless, despite the limitations of the Victorian verse tradition within which he worked, something of his emotional and intellectual engagement with the land and people of New Zealand spilled over into his poetry. A handful of his poems retain an interest for later generations of New Zealanders partly because they anticipate the concerns of the more authentically indigenous writers who emerged in the 1920's and 1930's, and partly because they document (sometimes unconsciously) a significant phase in the history of the nation's consciousness.

Reeves's one significant collection was New Zealand and Other Poems, published in London shortly after he had left New Zealand to settle permanently in England. It included the best of his verses in his first two books, Colonial Couplets and In Double Harness, both written in collaboration with G. P. Williams. The Passing of the Forest and Other Verse, privately published late in life, largely reprinted the contents of the earlier book, and added only one new poem of significance, "The Colonist in His Garden." This poem begins with a letter to a colonist from a friend in England attempting to persuade him to return to civilization. He cites the familiar complaints about life in the colonies: "lonely," "empty," "without a past," "commonplace," "Where men but talk of gold and sheep/And think of sheep and gold." The colonist replies with a spirited defense of colonial life:

> "No art?" Who serve an art more great
> Than we, rough architects of State
>   With the old Earth at strife?

But what makes the poem interesting today is the revelation of attitudes beneath the surface of the conscious argument; the bold colonial assertiveness wears thin and reveals the cringing defensiveness beneath. The New World is defended on the grounds that it is a home away from Home, just like the old country only better:

> And with my flowers about her spread
> (None brighter than her shining head),
>   The lady of my close,
> My daughter, walks in girlhood fair.
> Friend, could I rear in England's air
>   A sweeter English rose?

A further unconscious irony is that this poem was written after Reeves himself had made the decision to leave New Zealand and settle in England. In its analysis of the colonial condition this poem anticipates the work of later New Zealand poets such as Ursula Bethell, A. R. D. Fairburn, and Allen Curnow.

Other poems by Reeves which prefigure the work of later generations are "The Passing of the Forest" (a once famous but incurably portentous and sentimental account of the destruction by the settlers of the native forests), "Fragments from *Tasman, a Poem*" (anticipating the interest in the history of the country of the poets of the thirties), "New Zealand" (an early instance of nationalism), and "Nox Benigna" (a descriptive poem in which truth to landscape and region asserts itself over the conventions of English Romantic poetry which vitiated most descriptive poetry in the colonial period). Reeves pointed the way to the eventual emergence of an authentic native tradition in New Zealand poetry.

—Peter Simpson

REXROTH, Kenneth. American. Born in South Bend, Indiana, 22 December 1905; moved to Chicago, 1917. Educated at the Art Institute, Chicago; New School for Social Research, New York; Art Students' League, New York. Conscientious objector during World War II. Married 1) Andree Dutcher in 1927 (died, 1940); 2) Marie Kass in 1940 (divorced, 1948); 3) Marthe Larsen in 1949 (divorced, 1961), two children; 4) Carol Tinker in 1974. Past occupations include farm worker, factory hand, and insane asylum attendant. Painter: one-man shows in Los Angeles, New York, Chicago, San Francisco, and Paris. Columnist, *San Francisco Examiner*, 1958–68. Since 1953, San Francisco Correspondent for *The Nation*, New York; since 1968, Columnist for *San Francisco Magazine* and the *San Francisco Bay Guardian*, and Lecturer, University of California at Santa Barbara. Co-Founder, San Francisco Poetry Center. Recipient: Guggenheim Fellowship, 1948; Shelley Memorial Award, 1958; Amy Lowell Fellowship, 1958; National Institute of Arts and Letters grant, 1964; Fulbright Senior Fellowship, 1974; Academy of American Poets Copernicus Award, 1975. Member, National Institute of Arts and Letters. Lives in Santa Barbara, California.

PUBLICATIONS

Verse

In What Hour. 1941.
The Phoenix and the Tortoise. 1944.
The Art of Wordly Wisdom. 1949.
The Signature of All Things: Poems, Songs, Elegies, Translations, and Epigrams. 1950.
The Dragon and the Unicorn. 1952.
In Defence of the Earth. 1956.
The Homestead Called Damascus. 1963.
Natural Numbers: New and Selected Poems. 1963.
The Complete Collected Shorter Poems. 1967.
The Collected Longer Poems. 1968.
The Heart's Garden, The Garden's Heart. 1967.
The Spark in the Tinder of Knowing. 1968.
Sky Sea Birds Trees Earth House Beasts Flowers. 1970.
New Poems. 1974.

Plays

Beyond the Mountains (includes *Phaedra, Iphigenia, Hermaios, Berenike*) (produced 1951). 1951.

Other

Bird in the Bush: Obvious Essays. 1959.
Assays (essays). 1961.
An Autobiographical Novel. 1966.
Classics Revisited. 1968.
The Alternative Society: Essays from the Other World. 1970.
With Eye and Ear (literary criticism). 1970.
American Poetry in the Twentieth Century. 1971.
The Rexroth Reader, edited by Eric Mottram. 1972.
The Elastic Retort: Essays in Literature and Ideas. 1973.
Communalism: From Its Origins to the 20th Century. 1975.

Editor, *Selected Poems,* by D. H. Lawrence. 1948.
Editor, *The New British Poets: An Anthology.* 1949.
Editor, *Four Young Women: Poems.* 1973.
Editor, *Tens: Selected Poems 1961–1971,* by David Meltzer. 1973.
Editor, *The Selected Poems of Czeslav Milosz.* 1973.
Editor, *Seasons of Sacred Lust,* by Kazuko Shiraishi. 1978.

Translator, *Fourteen Poems,* by O. V. de L.-Milosz. 1952.
Translator, *100 Poems from the Japanese.* 1955.
Translator, *100 Poems from the Chinese.* 1956.
Translator, *30 Spanish Poems of Love and Exile.* 1956.
Translator, *100 Poems from the Greek and Latin.* 1962.
Translator, *Poems from the Greek Anthology.* 1962.
Translator, *Selected Poems,* by Pierre Reverdy. 1969.
Translator, *Love and the Turning Earth: 100 More Classical Poems.* 1970.
Translator, *Love and the Turning Year: 100 More Chinese Poems.* 1970.
Translator, *100 Poems from the French.* 1970.
Translator, with Ling O. Chung, *The Orchid Boat: Women Poets of China.* 1972.
Translator, *100 More Poems from the Japanese.* 1976.

Readling List: *Rexroth* by Morgan Gibson, 1972.

*   *   *

Kenneth Rexroth is a man of letters in the tradition of Robert Graves, W. H. Auden, and Edmund Wilson, although he has chiefly been a consolidator and synthesizer of others' ideas; this is true of his verse as well as of his many polemical essays on American culture. Rexroth came to literature with an amazing intelligence, so wide and retentive of the bewildering cross currents of thought in the twentieth century that his writings capture the essence of each decade in the broad span of his works, which cover the play *Beyond the Mountains*; *An Autobiographical Novel*; translations, encompassing poems in Japanese, Chinese, French, Greek, and Spanish; criticism; and his own vast collections of poetry. Without pedantry or empty imitation, Rexroth has tapped the spirit of each of the major figures that emerged in his lifetime and illuminated it in his own boldly assertive style. An

811

early interest in Asian poetry followed from Pound, whom Rexroth praised and criticized in his critical study, *American Poetry in the Twentieth Century*.

Rexroth's longer poems resemble the casual, narrative style of Auden, although comparisons should not be taken too far. In his polemic essays, his style and approach to the basic issues of American culture, industrial economy, depersonality in the mass population, and commerciality, are reminiscent of the early essays of Edmund Wilson, Paul Goodman, and Edward Dahlberg. Rexroth's poems on nature anticipated by many years the accurate, sensitive naturalist poems of Gary Snyder, who has in turn influenced Rexroth in his most recent work.

It is therefore difficult to isolate Rexroth from the stream of literature and ideas in which he has fashioned his work. But an essential Rexroth is perceptible in his elegant love poems and landscape meditations, gathered in *The Collected Shorter Poems*. These reveries and amorous lyrics present an unguarded, visionary persona unlike any in American poetry, as in "Camargue":

> Green moon blaze
> Over violet dancers
> Shadow heads catch fire
> Forget forget
> Forget awake aware dropping in the well
> Where the nightingale sings
> In the blooming pomegranate
> You beside me
> Like a colt swimming slowly in kelp
> In the nude sea
> Where ten thousand birds
> Move like a waved scarf
> On the long surge of sleep

The shorter poetry is brief, lyrical, touching on love, travels, occasionally social comment. The strain of the didactic is strong in Rexroth's work, especially in the long travelogue poem, *The Dragon and the Unicorn*.

Rexroth's polemical criticism of American literature and idealogy is contained in a number of volumes, *With Eye and Ear*, *The Alternative Society*, *Communalism*, and *American Poetry in the Twentieth Century*, where he is intensely perceptive and iconoclastic. In the last, he argues persuasively that American poetry should be traced not from Europe but from Native Indian cultures. As a figure central to most of the major phases of American writing throughout the century, Rexroth is a watershed of literary ideas and principles, and a writer who has communicated a stubborn, wilful intellect in a century of increasing squeamishness and doubt.

—Paul Christensen

RICH, Adrienne (Cecile). American. Born in Baltimore, Maryland, 16 May 1929. Educated at Roland Park Country School, Baltimore, 1938–47; Radcliffe College, Cambridge, Massachusetts, 1947–51, A.B. (cum laude) 1951 (Phi Beta Kappa). Married Alfred Conrad in 1953 (died, 1970); three sons. Lived in the Netherlands, 1961–62; taught at the YM-YWHA Poetry Center Workshop, New York, 1966–67; Visiting Poet, Swarthmore

College, Pennsylvania, 1966–68; Adjunct Professor, Graduate Writing Division, Columbia University, New York, 1967–69; Lecturer, 1968–70, Instructor, 1970–71, and Assistant Professor of English, 1971–72, City College of New York; Fannie Hurst Visiting Professor of Creative Writing, Brandeis University, Waltham, Massachusetts, 1972–73; Lucy Martin Donnelly Fellow, Bryn Mawr College, Pennsylvania, 1975. Since 1976, Professor of English, Douglass College, Rutgers University, New Brunswick, New Jersey. Member, Advisory Board, Feminist Press, Westbury, New Jersey. Recipient: Guggenheim Fellowship, 1952, 1961; Ridgely Torrence Memorial Award, 1955; Friends of Literature Grace Thayer Bradley Award, 1956; National Institute of Arts and Letters award, 1960; Amy Lowell Traveling Scholarship, 1962; National Translation Center grant, 1968; National Endowment for the Arts grant, 1969; Shelley Memorial Award, 1971; Ingram Merrill Foundation grant, 1973; National Book Award, 1974. D.Litt.: Wheaton College, Norton, Massachusetts, 1967. Lives in New York City.

PUBLICATIONS

Verse

A Change of World. 1951.
(Poems). 1952.
The Diamond Cutters and Other Poems. 1955.
Snapshots of a Daughter-in-Law: Poems 1954–1962. 1963.
Necessities of Life: Poems 1962–1965. 1966.
Selected Poems. 1967.
Leaflets: Poems 1965–1968. 1969.
The Will to Change: Poems 1968–1970. 1971.
Diving into the Wreck: Poems 1971–1972. 1973.
Poems Selected and New 1950–1974. 1975.
The Dream of a Common Language: Poems 1974–1977. 1978.

Other

Of Woman Born: Motherhood as Experience and Institution. 1976.

Reading List: "Voice of the Survivor: The Poetry of Rich" by Willard Spiegelman, in Southwest Review, Autumn 1975; Rich's Poetry edited by Barbara Charlesworth Gelpi and Albert Gelpi, 1975.

*   *   *

Adrienne Rich's comments on her early poems offer the best insight into the shape of her career. In "When We Dead Awaken: Writing as Re-Vision" (1971) she notices that "Beneath the conscious craft are glimpses of the split I even then experienced between the girl who wrote poems, who defined herself in writing poems, and the girl who defined herself by her relationships with men." In other contexts Rich extends her use of the term "splits" to explain the structure of all contemporary problems – artistic, psychological, and social. Insofar as she defines her poetry in terms of a response to splits within and without, Rich accepts the modernist premise that the poet begins his or her work in a fragmented world.

Her early poems in A Change of World and The Diamond Cutters use their mastery of formal elements to control and order the splits. The poems in *Snapshots of a Daughter-in-Law* continue the intense examination of experience, but they no longer insist on bringing all tensions under control by the end of the poem and risk very dearly bought defenses in order to get closer to the actual dynamics of experience. With this change of stance, her poems begin to confront the tensions she finds in the world with an eye towards changing the world, or changing that part of herself which formerly had been intimidated by the tensions. Rather than protecting the self or the poet's voice from the tensions in the world, these poems begin the process of integrating the self in order to encounter the world in a full and direct attempt to overcome the limitations of experience, or of that intimidating experience of the early poems. So, while speakers in the early poems took comfort and defined success in closing shutters and other protective habits developed by experience, the speaker in "The Phenomenology of Anger" (1972) finds the simmering frustrations and tensions a source of energy, and enjoys speculating on the shape of future experiences when the force of the anger breaks out from its containment.

Having begun this intense exploration of self and world, she finds a sense of wholeness in poems such as "Planetarium" (1971) and "Diving into the Wreck" (1973) which develop images that respect the integrity of conflicts within and without and still enable a holistic view of self and world. In one of Rich's latest and longest poems, "From an Old House in America," she extends the possibilities of her sense of an integrated identity to social and political contexts. She finds not only a positive definition of self, as she had in "Diving into the Wreck," but she also finds a place in which the self can work and interact in a positive and effective fashion. The speaker in "From an Old House in America" begins with a positive and comfortable sense of self and then extends her social and political connections with other inhabitants of the house, with other American women, contemporaries and ancestors, and finally, with all women in all places. In this re-integration of poet and world Rich gets beyond the self-conscious impasse of modernist aesthetics and begins the process of changing the world with a public voice whose authority and promise grow out of its successful resolution of "splits" in the world.

—Richard C. Turner

RICKWORD, (John) Edgell. English. Born in Colchester, Essex, 22 October 1898. Educated at Colchester Grammar School; Pembroke College, Oxford. Served in the Artists' Rifles, 1916–18; invalided out of the army. Editor, *Calendar of Modern Letters,* 1925–27; Associate Editor, *Left Review,* 1934–38; Editor, *Our Time,* 1944–47; also contributed to various other London journals. Recipient: Arts Council Prize, 1966.

PUBLICATIONS

Verse

Behind the Eyes. 1921.
Invocations to Angels, and The Happy New Year. 1928.
Twittingpan and Some Others. 1931.
Collected Poems. 1947.
Fifty Poems. 1970.
Behind the Eyes: Selected Poems and Translations. 1976.

Fiction

Love One Another: Seven Tales.   1929.

Other

Rimbaud: The Boy and the Poet.   1924; revised edition, 1963.
William Wordsworth 1770–1850.   1950.
Gillray and Cruikshank: An Illustrated Life of James Gillray (1756–1815) and of George Cruikshank (1792–1878), with Michael Katanka.   1973.
Essays and Opinions 1921–1931, edited by Alan Young.   1974.

Editor, *Scrutinies of Various Writers.*   1928; vol. 2, 1931.
Editor, with Jack Lindsay, *A Handbook of Freedom: A Record of English Democracy Through Twelve Centuries.*   1939.
Editor, *Soviet Writers Reply to English Writers' Questions.*   1948.
Editor, *Further Studies in a Dying Culture,* by Christopher Caudwell.   1949.
Editor, *Radical Squibs and Loyal Ripostes: Satirical Pamphlets of the Regency Period, 1819–1821.*   1971.

Translator, with Douglas Mavin Garman, *Charles Baudelaire: A Biography,* by François Porché.   1928.
Translator, *La Princesse aux Soleils, and Harmonie,* by Ronald Firbank.   1973 (translation into English).

Reading List: "The Poetic Mind of Rickword" by David Holbrook, in *Essays in Criticism,* July 1962.

*   *   *

Edgell Rickword's experience of the war was profound and unforgettable. He was almost sixteen when it began, joined the Artists' Rifles in 1916, and was invalided out of the army after the Armistice. His first book of poetry, *Behind the Eyes,* appeared in 1921 and revealed a preoccupation with images of a nightmarish intensity, images of battle, physical suffering, bodily decay, and the transience of beauty. There is an elegant strength in Rickword's handling of these subjects, the poems never collapsing into hysteria or incoherence. The fixed, rational gaze straight into the face of modern horrors is unswerving in its honesty and resolution, as in "Trench Poets":

> I knew a man, he was my chum,
> but he grew darker day by day,
> and would not brush the flies away,
> nor blanch however fierce the hum
> of passing shells....

Invocations to Angels saw, alongside this lyrical evocation of disaster, Rickword writing in a satirical mode. Pieces like "Poet to Punk" showed him producing the kind of verse that was to become predominant by the time of *Twittingpan and Some Others.* It is a public poetry pressed into being by political needs. It found its most famous expression in a poem published in *Left Review* in 1938. "To the Wife of a Non-Interventionist Statesman" is a powerful and accurate satire, enlisted on behalf of the Spanish republican cause, but widening its polemic to include a vision of the future at home:

Euzkadi's mines supply the ore
to feed the Nazi dogs of war:
Guernika's thermite rain transpires
in doom on Oxford's dreaming spires:
in Hitler's frantic mental haze
already Hull and Cardiff blaze....

Rickword also made some excellent translations of Rimbaud and produced a critical study of the French poet which still stands as a formidable achievement. *Rimbaud: The Boy and the Poet* was described by Enid Starkie in 1954 as the finest work on Rimbaud to have appeared in any country up to that date. Rickword's critical work has, in fact, been at least as important as his poetry. In editing *The Calendar of Modern Letters* from 1925 to 1927, he not only helped to raise the standards of critical debate at the time, but made possible the founding five years later of *Scrutiny*. Whether writing for the *New Statesman*, *The Times Literary Supplement*, *The Calendar* itself, or the *Daily Herald*, Rickword maintained the same unfaltering level of critical shrewdness and intellectual acuity. When his political commitments led him in the 1930's to the Communist Party, and the editorship for a time of *Left Review*, this did not represent the collapse of his critical standards, as some of his more condescending later admirers have said. His influence on *Left Review* was a highly beneficial one, widening the scope of the journal and increasing its sensitivity to contemporary literature.

Edgell Rickword was one of the first critics in England to understand the nature of modernism, and to grasp the revolutionary nature of the achievements of Eliot and Pound. His unquestionable integrity frequently led him into difficulties, and left him, in the cold-war atmosphere after 1945, in a kind of wilderness. The re-discovery and re-examination of his work in the 1970's has been long overdue.

—Alan Wall

RIDING, Laura. American. Born Laura Reichenthal in New York City, 16 January 1901; adopted the surname Riding in 1926. Educated at Cornell University, Ithaca, New York. Married 1) Louis Gottschalk; 2) the poet and critic Schuyler B. Jackson in 1941 (died, 1968). Associated with the Fugitive group of poets; lived in Europe, 1926–39: associated with Robert Graves, in establishing the Seizen Press and *Epilogue* magazine; returned to America, 1939, renounced poetry, 1940, and has since devoted herself to the study of linguistics. Recipient: Guggenheim Fellowship, 1973. Lives in Florida.

PUBLICATIONS

Verse

The Close Chaplet. 1926.
Voltaire: A Biographical Fantasy. 1927.
Love as Love, Death as Death. 1928.
Poems: A Joking Word. 1930.

Twenty Poems Less.   1930.
Though Gently.   1930.
Laura and Francisca.   1931.
The Life of the Dead.   1933.
The First Leaf.   1933.
Poet: A Lying Word.   1933.
Americans.   1934.
The Second Leaf.   1935.
Collected Poems   1938.
Selected Poems: In Five Sets.   1970.

Fiction

Experts Are Puzzled (stories).   1930.
No Decency Left, with Robert Graves.   1932.
14A, with George Ellidge.   1934.
Progress of Stories.   1935.
Convalescent Conversations.   1936.
A Trojan Ending.   1937.
Lives of Wives (stories).   1939.

Other

A Survey of Modernist Poetry, with Robert Graves.   1927.
A Pamphlet Against Anthologies, with Robert Graves.   1928; as *Against Anthologies,*
     1928.
Contemporaries and Snobs.   1928.
Anarchism Is Not Enough.   1928.
Four Unposted Letters to Catherine.   1930.
The Telling.   1972.
It Has Taken Long (selected writings), in "Riding Issue" of *Chelsea 35.*   1976

Editor, *Everybody's Letters.*   1933.
Editor, *Epilogue 1–3.*   3 vols., 1935–37.
Editor, *The World and Ourselves: Letters about the World Situation from 65 People of
     Different Professions and Pursuits.*   1938.

Translator, *Anatole France at Home,* by Marcel Le Goff.   1926.
Translator, with Robert Graves, *Almost Forgotten Germany,* by Georg Schwarz.   1936.

Bibliography: by Alan Clark, in *Chelsea 35,* 1976.

Reading List: *Riding's Pursuit of Truth* by Joyce Piell Wexler, 1977.

                              *   *   *

   Laura Riding is, according to Kenneth Rexroth in *American Poetry in the Twentieth
Century,* "the greatest lost poet in American literature." The inaccessibility of her poetry,
both in the literal and figurative sense, partially accounts for this lack of attention. Since the
publication of her substantial *Collected Poems* in 1938, she has published no new poetry and
has allowed the re-issue of only one slender volume selected from the earlier edition. Hence

her poetry is hard to find, and, once found, hard to follow. Her brief poem, "Grace," illustrates her obscurity:

> This posture and this manner suit
> Not that I have an ease in them
> But that I have a horror
> And so stand well upright –
> Lest, should I sit and, flesh-conversing, eat,
> I choke upon a piece of my own tongue-meat.

Characteristic of other poems by Riding, this one is virtually unadorned, with the single concrete image withheld until the last two lines. The subject matter is, typically and paradoxically, an examination of an interior feeling, a topic that one does not expect to find treated with this austerity.

Riding's definition of a poem in the preface to the *Collected Poems* is "an uncovering of truth of so fundamental and general a kind that no other name besides poetry is adequate except truth." This definition, if tautological, is indicative of Riding's strong commitment to purity in the language. This strong belief impelled her eventually to abandon the writing of poetry, for she found that she could not reconcile the necessity to keep the language pure with the desirability of making the poems sensuously appealing to the readers.

Riding's undeservedly neglected fiction has received even less attention than her poetry. Her *Progress of Stories*, a collection marked by impressive variety and a somewhat flamboyant wit, is unlike her poetry in tone although it treats similar themes. The comic sketch, "Eve's Side of It," for instance, complements such feminist poems as "Divestment of Beauty" and "Auspice of Jewels." She has deliberately adopted a lighter vein for these stories, she explains in the preface, because she is tired of the accusation of obscurity and being made "a scape goat for the incapacity of people to understand what they only pretend to want to know."

Of her numerous theoretical studies, the two she wrote in collaboration with Robert Graves are best known. Compared to her other works, *A Survey of Modernist Poetry* is a model of lucidity. It suggests a method of textual scrutiny that possibly influenced William Empson's *Seven Types of Ambiguity*. While the work of E. E. Cummings most often provides examples for the book, Riding's poem "The Rugged Back of Anger" is examined. To apply Riding's critical method to her poetry is helpful in understanding this austere and significant poet.

—Nancy C. Joyner

RILEY, James Whitcomb. American. Born in Greenfield, Indiana, 7 October 1849. Educated at local schools, and at Greenfield Academy, 1870. Worked as a house- and sign-painter, 1870–71; itinerant entertainer, giving readings and lectures, 1872–75, 1876; worked in his father's law office, 1875–76; lived in Indianapolis from 1879; Journalist, *Indianapolis Journal*, 1879–88; gave annual reading tour of the United States, 1882–1903. Recipient: American Academy of Arts and Letters Gold Medal, 1911. M.A.: Yale University, New Haven, Connecticut, 1902; D.Litt.: University of Philadelphia, 1904; D.L.: Indiana University, Bloomington, 1907. Member, American Academy of Arts and Letters, 1911. *Died 22 July 1916.*

PUBLICATIONS

Collections

Letters, edited by William Lyon Phelps. 1930.

Verse

The Old Swimmin'-Hole and 'leven More Poems. 1883; revised edition, as Neghborly
Poems, 1891.
Afterwhiles. 1887.
Nye and Riley's Railway Guide, with Edgar Watson Nye. 1888; as Nye and Riley's
Wit and Humor: Poems and Yarns, 1900.
Old-Fashioned Roses. 1888.
Pipes o' Pan at Zekesbury. 1888.
Rhymes of Childhood. 1890.
The Flying Islands of the Night. 1891.
Green Fields and Running Brooks. 1892.
Poems Here at Home. 1893.
Armazindy. 1894.
The Days Gone By and Other Poems. 1895.
A Tinkle of Bells and Other Poems. 1895.
A Child-World. 1896.
Rubáiyát of Doc Sifers. 1897.
The Golden Year, edited by Clara E. Laughlin. 1898.
Riley Love-Lyrics. 1899.
Home-Folks. 1900.
The Book of Joyous Children. 1902.
His Pa's Romance. 1903.
A Defective Santa Claus. 1904.
Riley Songs o' Cheer. 1905.
While the Heart Beats Young. 1906.
Morning. 1907.
The Boys of the Old Glee Club. 1907.
The Riley Baby Book. 1913; as Baby Ballads, 1914.

Fiction

The Boss Girl, A Christmas Story, and Other Sketches. 1885; revised edition, as
Sketches in Prose and Occasional Verses, 1891.

Other

Poems and Prose Sketches. 16 vols., 1897–1914.
Complete Works, edited by Edmund Henry Eitel. 6 vols., 1913.

Bibliography: A Bibliography of Riley by Anthony J. and Dorothy R. Russo, 1944.

Reading List: Riley, Hoosier Poet by Jeannette Covert Nolan, 1941; Hoosier Boy: Riley by

Minnie B. Mitchell, 1942; *Poet of the People: An Evaluation of Riley* by Jeannette Covert Nolan, Horace Gregory, and James T. Farrell, 1951; *Those Innocent Years: The Legacy and Inheritance of a Hero of the Victorian Era, Riley* by Richard Crowder, 1957; *Riley* by Peter Revell, 1970.

*   *   *

Although James Whitcomb Riley occasionally committed prose, he was pre-eminently a poet – one of the most famous in turn-of-the-century America. Not exactly the household word he once was, Riley remains an important figure in American popular culture; school children continued to learn "Little Orphant Annie" and "The Raggedy Man" well through the 1930's and more than sixty years after his death his work stays in print. He began to write verse in the 1870's, contributing primarily to Indiana newspapers, particularly the Indianapolis *Journal*, on the staff of which he served for years. His verse was widely reprinted and, as his reputation spread, new poems began to appear in newspapers and magazines far from his Indiana base. His first book *The Old Swimmin'-Hole and 'leven More Poems* was published in 1883 and new collections of his periodical verse quickly followed. He issued book-length poems only twice – *The Flying Islands of the Night*, a verse drama so uncharacteristic that his readers rejected it, and the more acceptable *Rubáiyát of Doc Sifers*, written in the Hoosier dialect used in his most popular poems.

He occasionally tried set forms – sonnets, for instance – but he ordinarily worked in rhymed couplets or quatrains, and the subject matter dictated the length of the poems. The stanza forms sometimes vary, and the meter is sometimes irregular, but in most cases these are designed to fit the speaking voice. Riley was as much performer as poet, traveling the country to give readings, and his admirers have always known that his verse fits better in the mouth than on the page. His dialect poems are much more effective than his other verse, which too easily succumbs to conventional poetic diction, as a comparison of "Knee-deep in June" with the sonnet beginning "O queenly month of indolent repose!" will show.

Riley wrote many happy poems – evocations of nature and recollections of childhood – but popular taste has always been as lugubrious as it is sentimental, and Riley, whose own despondency found an answering chord in his audience, fills his work with broken toys and broken hearts, dead children and cheerful cripples, lost days, lost joys, "lost sunshine/Of youth." He offers the consolation of Heaven or of time which lets one taste "the sweet/Of honey in the saltest tear." It is pain not comfort, however, that gives Riley his best images, as in the old man who wants to "strip to the soul,/And dive off in my grave like the old swimmin'-hole" or the speaker in "A Summer's Day" who longs to "spread/Out like molasses on the bed,/And jest drip off the aidges in/The dreams that never comes ag'in." Riley's triumph as a popular poet is that he gave a great deal of pleasure to a great many people over a great many years, but all his readers know, as they wink back the happy tears, that

the Gobble-uns'll git you
Ef you
Don't
Watch
Out!

—Gerald Weales

ROBERTS, Sir Charles G(eorge) D(ouglas). Canadian. Born in Douglas, New Brunswick, 10 January 1860. Eduated at the Collegiate School, Fredericton, New Brunswick, 1874–76; University of New Brunswick, Fredericton (Douglas Medal in Latin and Greek; Alumni Gold Medal for Latin Essay), 1876–81, B.A. (honours) in mental and moral science and political economy 1879, M.A. 1881. Served in the British Army, 1914–15: Captain; transferred to the Canadian Army, 1916: Major; subsequently worked with Lord Beaverbrook on the Canadian War Records. Married 1) Mary Isabel Fenety in 1880 (died, 1930), three sons and one daughter; 2) Joan Montgomery in 1943. Headmaster, Chatham Grammar School, New Brunswick, 1879–81, and York Street School, Fredericton, 1881–83; Editor, *This Week*, Toronto, 1883–84; Professor of English and French, 1885–88, and Professor of English and Economics, 1888–95, King's College, Windsor, Nova Scotia; Associate Editor, *The Illustrated American*, New York, 1897–98; Co-Editor, The Nineteenth Century series, 1900–05; lived in England, 1911–25. Recipient: Lorne Pierce Medal, 1926. LL.D.: University of New Brunswick, 1906. Fellow, 1890, and President of Section II, 1933, Royal Society of Canada; Fellow, Royal Society of Literature, 1892; Member, National Institute of Arts and Letters, 1898. Knighted, 1935. *Died 26 November 1943.*

Publications

Collections

Selected Poems, edited by Desmond Pacey. 1956.

Verse

Orion and Other Poems. 1880.
Later Poems. 1881.
Later Poems. 1882.
In Divers Tones. 1886.
Autotochthon. 1889.
Songs of the Common Day, and Ave: An Ode for the Shelley Centenary. 1893.
The Book of the Native. 1896.
New York Nocturnes and Other Poems. 1898.
Poems. 1901.
The Book of the Rose. 1903.
Poems. 1907.
New Poems. 1919.
The Sweet o' the Year and Other Poems. 1925.
The Vagrant of Time. 1927; revised edition, 1927.
Be Quiet Wind: Unsaid. 1929.
The Iceberg and Other Poems. 1934.
Selected Poems. 1936.
Twilight over Shaugamauk and Three Other Poems. 1937.
Canada Speaks of Britain and Other Poems of the War. 1941.

Fiction

The Raid from Beauséjour, and How the Carter Boys Lifted the Mortgage: Two Stories of Acadie. 1894; *The Raid from Beauséjour* published as *The Young Acadian,* 1907.

Reube Dare's Shad Boat: A Tale of the Tide Country. 1895; as *The Cruise of the Yacht "Dido,"* 1906.
Around the Campfire. 1896.
The Forge in the Forest, Being the Narrative of the Acadian Ranger, Jean de Mer. 1896.
Earth's Enigmas: A Book of Animal and Nature Life. 1896; revised edition, 1903.
A Sister to Evangeline, Being the Story of Yvonne de Lamourie. 1898; as *Lovers in Acadie,* 1924.
The Heart of the Ancient Wood. 1900.
By the Marshes of Minas (stories). 1900.
Barbara Ladd. 1902.
The Kindred of the Wild: A Book of Animal Life. 1902.
The Prisoner of Mademoiselle: A Love Story. 1904.
The Watchers of the Trails: A Book of Animal Life. 1904.
Red Fox: The Story of His Adventurous Career. 1905.
The Heart That Knows. 1906.
The Haunters of the Silences: A Book of Animal Life. 1907.
In the Deep of the Snow. 1907.
The Red Oxen of Bonval (stories). 1908.
The House in the Water: A Book of Animal Life. 1908.
The Backwoodsmen. 1909.
Kings in Exile. 1909.
Neighbours Unknown. 1910.
More Kindred of the Wild. 1911.
Babes of the Wild. 1912; as *Children of the Wild,* 1913.
The Feet of the Furtive. 1912.
A Balkan Prince. 1913.
Cock Crow (stories). 1913.
Hoof and Claw. 1913.
The Secret Trails. 1916.
The Ledge on Bald Face. 1918; as *Jim: The Story of a Backwoods Police Dog,* 1919.
In the Morning of Time (stories). 1919.
Wisdom of the Wilderness. 1922.
They Who Walk in the Wild. 1924.
Eyes of the Wilderness. 1933.
Further Animal Stories. 1935.
Thirteen Bears, edited by Ethel Hume Bennett. 1947.
Forest Folk, edited by Ethel Hume Bennett. 1949.
The Last Barrier and Other Stories. 1958.
Kings of Beasts and Other Stories, edited by Joseph Gold. 1967.

Other

The Canadian Guide-Book: A Tourist's and Sportsman's Guide to Eastern Canada and Newfoundland. 1892.
The Land of Evangeline and the Gateways Thither. 1894.
A History of Canada for High Schools and Academies. 1897.
Discoveries and Explorations in the Century (nineteenth-century series). 1904.
Canada in Flanders, vol. 3. 1918.

Editor, *Poems of Wild Life.* 1888.
Editor, *Northland Lyrics,* by William Carmon Roberts, Theodore Roberts, and Elizabeth Roberts McDonald. 1899.
Editor, *Alastor and Adonais,* by Shelley. 1902.

Editor, with Arthur L. Tunnell, *A Standard Dictionary of Canadian Biography: The Canadian Who Was Who.* 2 vols., 1934–38.

Editor, with Arthur L. Tunnell, *The Canadian Who's Who,* vols. II and III. 1936–39.

Editor, *Flying Colours: An Anthology.* 1942.

Translator, *The Canadians of Old,* by Philippe Aubert de Gaspé. 1890; as *Cameron of Lochiel,* 1905.

Reading List; *Roberts* by Elsie M. Pomeroy, 1943, and *Tributes Through the Years: The Centenary of the Birth of Roberts,* edited by Pomeroy, 1959; *Roberts* by William J. Keith, 1969.

*   *   *

Charles G. D. Roberts is now most remembered as a poet, but he wrote far more prose than verse in a long life, much of which had to be supported by the proceeds of free-lance writing. He wrote a *History of Canada* and a number of historical novels about Canada's early centuries. He also wrote what today we might term environmental romances like *The Heart of the Ancient Wood* and *In the Morning of Time,* in which he somewhat implausibly portrayed men and women trying to reconcile themselves with the world of nature. Most of his energy, however, went into the writing of stories about animals, of which, in all, he published no less than twenty volumes.

As several critics have pointed out, Roberts pioneered a peculiarly Canadian type of animal story which does not attempt to anthropomorphize the characters, as English stories of the same kind do, or to turn them into symbols of destiny, as American writers from Melville onwards have been tempted to do. Roberts sees the animals with great empathy for the non-human beings they are, with whom we may identify only because they too are victims of destiny. Consequently the best of his fiction in this genre, in collections like *The Kindred of the Wild, The Watchers of the Trails* and *Neighbours Unknown,* has a kind of inward authenticity that is still appealing.

In his first volume of verse, *Orion and Other Poems,* Roberts seemed to be setting out, in poems many of which retell the myths of classical antiquity, to prove that a Canadian poet could be as capable as any English versifier of handling traditional themes and forms. His manifest success in this aim made Roberts the leader among the group of young men – including Archibald Lampman, Bliss Carman, and Duncan Campbell Scott – who later became known as the Confederation Poets, the first real school of Canadian poetry.

It was in later volumes, like *In Divers Tones,* which included the famous nostalgic landscape poem "Tantramer Revisited," and *Songs of the Common Day,* that Roberts really found his style, applying the techniques he had learnt from the English poets to a vision of the Canadian terrain and Canadian country life as they really were and not as sham English settings. Later in life, he moved forward technically, and "The Iceberg," written in the 1930's, was one of the earliest Canadian poems to use free verse with effect.

Roberts never sprang completely free of the tone and even the diction of Victorian neo-romanticism, but by his passionate exploration of the Canadian scene as a theme for poetry he did more than any other Canadian poet writing in the nineteenth century to establish a native poetic tradition.

—George Woodcock

ROBINSON, Edwin Arlington. American. Born in Head Tide, Maine, 22 December 1869; grew up in Gardiner, Maine. Educated at Gardiner High School, graduated 1888; Harvard University, Cambridge, Massachusetts, 1891–93. Free-lance writer in Gardiner, 1893–96; settled in New York City, 1896; worked as Secretary to the President of Harvard University, 1897; returned to New York, settled in Greenwich Village, and held various jobs, including subway-construction inspector, 1903–04; through patronage of Theodore Roosevelt, who admired his poetry, became Clerk in the United States Customs House, New York, 1904–10; spent summers at the MacDowell Colony, Peterborough, New Hampshire, 1911–34. Recipient: Pulitzer Prize, 1922, 1925, 1928; National Institute of Arts and Letters Gold Medal, 1929. Honorary degrees: Yale University, New Haven, Connecticut, 1922, and Bowdoin College, Brunswick, Maine. Member, American Academy of Arts and Letters. *Died 6 April 1935.*

PUBLICATIONS

Collections

Collected Poems. 1937.
Selected Letters, edited by Ridgely Torrence and others. 1940.
Tilbury Town: Selected Poems, edited by Lawrance Thompson. 1953.
Selected Early Poems and Letters, edited by Charles T. Davis. 1960.
Selected Poems, edited by Morton Dauwen Zabel. 1965.

Verse

The Torrent and the Night Before. 1896; revised edition, as *The Children of the Night,* 1897.
Captain Craig. 1902; revised edition, 1915.
The Town Down the River. 1910.
The Man Against the Sky. 1916.
Merlin. 1917.
Lancelot. 1920.
The Three Taverns. 1920.
Avon's Harvest. 1921.
Collected Poems. 1921.
Roman Bartholow. 1923.
The Man Who Died Twice. 1924.
Dionysus in Doubt. 1925.
Tristram. 1927.
Collected Poems. 5 vols., 1927.
Sonnets 1889–1927. 1928.
Fortunatus. 1928.
Three Poems. 1928.
Modred: A Fragment. 1929.
The Prodigal Son. 1929.
Cavender's House. 1929.
The Glory of the Nightingales. 1930.
Matthias at the Door. 1931.
Poems, edited by Bliss Perry. 1931.
Nicodemus. 1932.

Talifer. 1933.
Amaranth. 1934.
King Jasper. 1935.
Hannibal Brown: Posthumous Poem. 1936.

Plays

Van Zorn. 1914.
The Porcupine. 1915.

Other

Letters to Howard George Schmitt, edited by Carl J. Weber. 1940.
Untriangulated Stars: Letters to Harry de Forest Smith 1890–1905, edited by Denham
     Sutcliffe. 1947.
Letters to Edith Brower, edited by Richard Cary. 1968.

Editor, *Selections from the Letters of Thomas Sergeant Perry.* 1929.

Bibliography: *A Bibliography of the Writings and Criticisms of Robinson* by Lillian Lippincott,
1937; supplements by William White, in *Colby Library Quarterly,* 1965, 1969.

Reading List: *Robinson: A Biography* by Hermann Hagedorn, 1938; *Robinson* by Yvor
Winters, 1946, revised edition, 1971; *Robinson: The Literary Background of a Traditional
Poet* by Edwin S. Fussell, 1954; *Where the Light Falls: A Portrait of Robinson* by Chard
Powers Smith, 1965; *Robinson: A Poetry of the Act* by W. R. Robinson, 1967; *Robinson: A
Critical Introduction* by Wallace L. Anderson, 1967; *Robinson: The Life of Poetry* by Louis O.
Coxe, 1968; *Robinson* by Hoyt C. Franchere, 1968; *Appreciation of Robinson* (essays) edited
by Richard Cary, 1969; *Robinson: Centenary Essays* edited by Ellsworth Barnard, 1969.

                              *   *   *

More than any other poet of his time, Edwin Arlington Robinson made poetry his career.
He neither travelled nor taught, married nor made public appearances. Aside from a handful
of prose pieces and two unsuccessful plays, he devoted himself exclusively to the writing of
poetry, publishing many volumes of verse in a forty-year period. He suffered during the first
half of his career from neglect and near impoverishment; he suffered during his last years
from an excess of adulation. After his signal success of *Tristram,* for which he won his third
Pulitzer Prize, he was hailed as America's foremost poet. Although his reputation has
diminished since his death, he is nevertheless established as the most important poet writing
in America at the turn of the century and has a firm place as one of the major modern poets.
     He was, as Robert Frost noted in his preface to *King Jasper,* "content with the old way to
be new." The old way was his unwavering insistence on traditional forms. His poems
demonstrate his facility in an impressive variety of verse forms, from blank verse in most of
the long narratives to Petracharan sonnets and villanelles in his shorter work, but he was
positively reactionary in his dismissal of the then current *vers libre* movement. In a letter, he
once placed free verse along with prohibition and moving pictures as "a triumvirate from
hell, armed with the devil's instructions to abolish civilization."
     Robinson was new in his attitudes in and toward his poetry. He may be called an
impersonal romantic, breaking with the nineteenth-century tradition by objectifying and
dramatizing emotional reactions while at the same time emphasizing sentiment and mystical

awareness. His combination of compassion and irony has become a familiar stance in modern poetry, and his celebrated advocacy of triumphant forbearance in the face of adversity anticipates the existential movement. In a letter to *The Bookman* in 1897, responding to the charge that he was pessimistic, he wrote, "This world is not a 'prison house,' but a kind of spiritual kindergarten where millions of bewildered infants are trying to spell God with the wrong blocks." While he was reluctant to be classified as an exponent of any formal philosophical or theological stance, he was entirely willing, in and out of his poetry, to condemn materialistic attitudes. Robinson's use of humor within his serious poetry, such as in *Amaranth*, placed a new importance on the comic.

While Robinson frequently wrote poems on conventional topics, his subject matter was new in his heavy emphasis on people. Unlike other romantic poets, he generally avoided the celebration of natural phenomena, bragging to a friend about his first volume that one would not find "a single red-breasted robin in the whole collection." Many of his short poems are character sketches of individuals, anticipating Edgar Lee Masters's *Spoon River Anthology*. All of the long narratives deal with complicated human relationships. Frequently they explore psychological reactions to a prior event, such as *Avon's Harvest*, Robinson's "ghost story" about a man destroyed by his own hatred, and *Cavender's House*, a dialogue between a man and his dead wife which deals with questions of jealousy and guilt. The people inhabiting Robinson's books include imaginary individuals; characters modeled on actual acquaintances, such as Alfred H. Louis in *Captain Craig*; figures from history, such as "Ben Jonson Entertains a Gentleman from Stratford," "Rembrandt to Rembrandt," and "Ponce de Leon"; and mythic figures, notably characters from the Bible and Arthurian legend.

Edwin S. Fussell, in his book on Robinson, devotes separate chapters to the English Bible and the Greek and Roman classics as significant influences on Robinson's work. English poets of particular importance to him are Shakespeare, Wordsworth, Kipling, Tennyson, and Robert Browning, although Robinson objected to the inevitable comparison between his character analyses and those of Browning. Among American poets Robinson found Emerson to be his most significant precursor. Because of his narrative impulse, his work is also compared to the fiction of Hawthorne and Henry James.

Robinson is best known today for his earliest work, the short sketches of characters, chiefly failures, who reside in Tilbury Town, the name he uses for Gardiner, Maine. Partially because of the frequency of their being anthologized, "Richard Cory," "Miniver Cheevy," and "Mr. Flood's Party" are his most famous poems. "Eros Turannos" has been singled out by Louis O. Coxe as the most impressive Tilbury poem. Also highly regarded are a few of the poems of medium length, notably "Isaac and Archibald" and "Aunt Imogen."

Not all of Robinson's poems are narratives, and some of the symbolic lyrics have been highly praised, particularly "For a Dead Lady" and the poem about which Theodore Roosevelt wrote, "I am not sure I understand 'Luke Havergal,' but I am sure that I like it." "The Man Against the Sky," the title poem of the first volume that received pronounced critical approval, is an ironic meditation on possibilities of philosophical attitudes. It has received a great deal of critical attention from both admirers and detractors. Robinson said that the poem "comes as near as anything to representing my poetic vision."

Critics have tended to neglect Robinson's long narratives, those thirteen book-length poems that occupied most of his attention during the second half of his career. According to his earliest biographer, Hermann Hagedorn, the difficulty Robinson had with *Captain Craig*, first in getting a publisher and then in the adverse critical reaction, was a devastating experience for the young poet. Until he issued his first *Collected Poems* in 1921, Robinson alternated his long poems with volumes of shorter, more readily acceptable pieces. After he was thoroughly established, however, he concentrated on the long narratives. Though these poems sometimes lend themselves to verbosity and repetition, they nevertheless provided Robinson with his most congenial form, allowing him to combine his talents of narration, characterization, and symbolic discursiveness.

—Nancy C. Joyner

ROCHESTER, 2nd Earl of; John Wilmot.   English.   Born in Ditchley, near Woodstock, Oxfordshire, 10 April 1647; succeeded his father as earl in 1658. Educated at Burford School, Oxfordshire; Wadham College, Oxford, M.A. 1661. Associated with Elizabeth Barry, servant to Lady Shelton of Norfolk, and had a daughter by her; kidnapped Elizabeth Malet, and was imprisoned for his actions, 1665; married her, 1667; one son and three daughters. Travelled in France and Italy, 1663–64, then attended the court of Charles II: joined Sir Thomas Teddeman on board the *Royal Katherine*, and took part in an unsuccessful attack on Dutch ships at Bergen, 1665, and served in the Channel under Sir Edward Spragge, 1666; an associate of the most dissolute set at court – Villiers, Sedley, and Savile; known for his drunken exploits and his amorous and obscene lyrics; companion to Charles in the king's amorous adventures: frequently dismissed from court in disgrace, then reinstated; appointed gentleman of the king's bedchamber, 1666; summoned to the House of Lords, 1667; appointed Keeper of Woodstock Park, 1674; retired from court when his health failed, 1679; under the influence of Bishop Burnet said to have repented of the excesses of his life on his death-bed. *Died 26 July 1680.*

PUBLICATIONS

Collections

   Complete Poems, edited by D. M. Vieth.   1968.
   Satires Against Man: The Poems, edited by Dustin H. Griffin.   1973.
   The Debt to Pleasure: An Anthology, edited by John Adlard.   1976.

Verse

   Poems on Several Occasions.   1680; edited by James Thorpe, 1950.
   Corydon and Cloris: or, The Wanton Shepherdess.   1676(?).
   A Satire Against Reason and Mankind.   1679.
   A Letter from Artemisia in the Town to Chloe in the Country.   1679.
   Upon Nothing.   1679.
   A Very Heroical Epistle from My Lord All-Pride to Dol-Common.   1679.
   The Famous Pathologist: or, The Noble Mountebank, with Thomas Alcock, edited by V.
      de S. Pinto.   1961.

Plays

   Valentinian, from the play by Fletcher (produced 1684).   1685.
   Sodom: or, The Quintessence of Debauchery, edited by L. S. A. M. von Römer.   1904;
      edited by Patrick J. Kearney, 1969 (probably not by Rochester).

Other

   A Letter to Dr. Burnet.   1680.
   Familiar Letters (by Rochester, Thomas Otway, and Katherine Philips), edited by Tom
      Brown and Charles Gildon.   2 vols., 1697.
   Miscellaneous Works, with the Earl of Roscommon.   1707.
   The Rochester-Savile Letters 1671–1680, edited by J. H. Wilson.   1941.

Reading List: *Rochester* by C. Williams, 1935; *Rochester* by V. de S. Pinto, 1935, revised edition, as *Enthusiast in Wit,* 1962; *Attribution in Restoration Poetry: A Study of Rochester's Poems of 1680* by D. M. Vieth, 1963; *Rochester: The Critical Heritage* edited by David Farley-Hills, 1972; *Lord Rochester's Monkey, Being the Life of Rochester* by Graham Greene, 1974.

*   *   *

John Wilmot, Earl of Rochester, is one of that number of English poets who seem in the popular mind more important for what they did than for what they wrote. Certainly Rochester's wild, licentious, and short life – he died at the age of 33 – gave him a posthumous reputation for wickedness that even Byron might envy. But, unlike Byron, Rochester did not live to complete a single masterpiece. Instead, even his best poems are marred by poor lines, shoddy rhymes, flat phrases. All of which suggest that he took poetry no more seriously than Congreve took play-writing (Voltaire was shocked by Congreve's refusal to discuss dramatic matters and by his insistence on talking only of "gentlemanly" ones). Certainly, Rochester is no professional writer, in the sense that the term can be applied to his great contemporary Dryden. Yet it would be absurd to dismiss Rochester as a mere dilettante. For all the technicolour quality of the life, his art represents a solid achievement.

Some lapidary phrases of Dr. Johnson get to the heart of the matter. "The glare of his general character diffused itself upon his writings.... In all his works there is sprightliness and vigour, and everywhere may be found tokens of a mind, which study might have carried to excellence." Johnson perhaps slightly overstates his case, but in the main what he says carries the unmistakable ring of truth. The exception I find to be in Rochester's Songs, where I can detect very little of either sprightliness or vigour, though there is a good deal of, largely spurious, elegance. This is not to deny that the songs have a cavalier-like polish to them, reminiscent of Carew, Lovelace, or Suckling. But the point is rather that they typically exhibit a no doubt fashionable cynicism in their statements about love and the relationship between men and women which from our vantage point looks distressingly trivial and modish. If this is particularly true of the famous and much-anthologised "Love a Woman," it seems to me equally the case with the majority of the rest, not excepting the equally famous "Song of a Young Lady to her Ancient Lover," which compares poorly with Burns's "John Anderson, My Jo."

Mention of Burns has its point. Like Rochester, the great Scottish poet was renowned for his licentious life. Yet the differences are more important than the similarities. For in Burns's love poetry one finds a much more certain regard for women than one does in Rochester, who is nearer to Byron in thinking of all women as "the sex."

All women? What then of his wife, with whom we are told he was deeply in love, and to whom he would regularly return from the dissipations of court life. She is probably the woman addressed in the song "Absent from thee I languish still."

> When wearied with a world of Woe
>   To thy safe Bosom I retire,
> Where Love, and Peace, and Truth does flow,
>   May I contented there expire.

The usual view of Rochester's marriage is that his wife represented a safe harbour from the wreck of his London life, and that he was truly appreciative of the fact. It may be so, but I do not see why her point of view should not be considered. Never mind the time he spent with her – what of the time he was away? Rochester's placing his wife in retirement so that he could visit her when exhausted by the drunken lechery of his town life is surely indicative of a thoroughly selfish and sentimental view of "the best of women." And that explains, I think, not only the slightness of the songs, but the rancid disgust of his famous pornographic satires "The Imperfect Enjoyment" and "A Ramble in St. James's Park." In the last analysis

828

Rochester, I think, hated women, turned them into things of use, and then was ferociously appalled at their willingness to be so used. We are asked to see in this a fearless readiness to take Hobbesian philosophy at face value and discover the truth of man as natural force. (A century later the Marquis de Sade was supposed to be making similar fearless discoveries.) I can see in this argument no more than a piece of not very sophisticated special pleading. I do not think Rochester set out to prove how futile life was, but that he assuredly came to recognise that *his* life was futile. And it is for this reason that he matters as a poet.

"Huddled in dirt the reasoning engine lies/That was so proud, so witty, and so wise": Tennyson reportedly could never read this couplet, from Rochester's most substantial poem, *A Satire Against Mankind*, without the tears starting to his eyes. My guess is that Tennyson is misreading the lines, and converting into "Tennysonian melancholy" and pathos what is in truth hard-edged, contemptuous, and snarlingly witty. It is the word "engine" which does the trick. It suggests that man can be seen as a mechanical object, a kind of well-oiled war weapon, a tool of aggression lacking all compassion, love, fellow-feeling. And Rochester's best work, which lies in his satires, is directed towards his sure sense of the ultimate sterility and meaninglessness of the kind of life towards which he was drawn. That is why I think that his famous deathbed conversion, for all the sugary sentimentalities with which it is coated in Bishop Burnet's famous *Some Passages of the Life and Death of the Right Honourable John Earl of Rochester*, cannot be dismissed as the vagary of an ill man. For what comes over most strongly in any encounter with Rochester's poetry is the reek of disgust at a certain kind of life. The satirist in him is likely to inflate that kind of life to life in general (and the less cautious critics assume the inflation to be no more than sober truth), but of course in the end he is writing about the life he knew best: the male dominated, trivial, sexually rapacious, mean-spirited world of Charles's court. Rochester is the best, because severest, critic of that life.

—John Lucas

RODGERS, W(illiam) R(obert).   Irish.   Born in Belfast, 1 August 1909. Educated at the Queen's University of Belfast, B.A. 1931. Married 1) Mary Harden Waddell in 1936 (died, 1953), two daughters; 2) Marianne Helweg in 1953, one daughter. Ordained in the Presbyterian Church, 1935: Minister, Loughgall Presbyterian Church, County Armagh, 1935 until he resigned, 1946; BBC Producer and Scriptwriter, associated with Third Programme productions on Ireland and Irish literary characters, 1946–66; Writer-in-Residence, Pitzer College, Claremont, California, 1966–68; Lecturer at California State Polytechnic College, San Luis Obispo, 1968. Recipient: Dublin Arts Council grant, 1968; Chapelbrook Foundation grant, 1968. Member, Irish Academy of Letters, 1951. *Died 1 February 1969.*

PUBLICATIONS

Collections

Collected Poems.   1971.

Verse

> *Awake! and Other Poems.*   1941.
> *Europa and the Bull and Other Poems.*   1952.

Play

> Radio Play: *The Return Room,* 1955.

Other

> *The Ulstermen and Their Country.*   1947.
> *Ireland in Colour: A Collection of Forty Colour Photographs.*   1957.
> *Irish Literary Portraits* (radio interviews).   1972.
> *Essex Roundabout.*   1973.

Reading List: "The Poetry of Rodgers" by Robert Greacen, in *Poetry Quarterly 12,* 1950–51; *Rodgers* by Darcy O'Brien, 1970; in *Northern Voices: Poets from Ulster* by Terence Brown, 1975.

*   *   *

W. R Rodgers published two volumes of poetry which were notable for their extraordinary, baroque verbal textures. Rodgers managed his effects as a poet through exuberant use of such techniques as assonance, internal rhyming, punning, and alliteration. Critics often compared his verse to the work of Gerard Manley Hopkins but it is important to note that Rodgers began his verbal experiments and achieved his own recognisable manner before he read that poet.

Rodgers employs verbal peculiarities to express his awareness of clash, strife, creative confusion in the natural and the psychological orders. His sense of the landscape is of a proliferation of vigorously alive phenomena engaged in a vital struggle, while his sense of human psychology is compact of sexual and religious conflicts, releasing the self into moments of ebullient celebration. Linguistic, sensuous, and moral intensity are features of his work, though an impression of excess and almost irresponsible loquacity is an aspect that some readers may find oppressive. His finest achievements were a number of brief, brilliantly energetic lyric poems of which "The Lovers" in his first volume, *Awake and Other Poems,* and "Lent" in his second, *Europa and the Bull and Other Poems,* can be cited as particularly successful examples.

Rodgers published a number of short prose travel pieces and a quantity of literary journalism, but apart from his poetry his most significant work was as a radio broadcaster. He wrote a number of radio portraits of Irish writers for the BBC and his radio feature *The Return Room* is one of the most successful evocations of life in the poet's native city of Belfast.

—Terence Brown

ROETHKE, Theodore (Huebner). American. Born in Saginaw, Michigan, 25 May 1908. Educated at John Moore School, Saginaw, 1913–21; Arthur Hill High School, Saginaw, 1921–25; University of Michigan, Ann Arbor, 1925–29, B.A. 1929 (Phi Beta Kappa), M.A. 1936; Harvard University, Cambridge, Massachusetts, 1930–31. Married Beatrice O'Connell in 1953. Instructor in English, 1931–35, Director of Public Relations, 1934, and Varsity Tennis Coach, 1934–35, Lafayette College, Easton, Pennsylvania; Instructor in English, Michigan State College, East Lansing, Fall 1935; Instructor, 1936–40, Assistant Professor, 1940–43, and Associate Professor of English Composition, 1947, Pennsylvania State University, College Park; Instructor, Bennington College, Vermont, 1943–46; Associate Professor, 1947–48, Professor of English, 1948–62, and Honorary Poet-in-Residence, 1962–63, University of Washington, Seattle. Recipient: Yaddo fellowship, 1945; Guggenheim grant, 1945, 1950; National Institute of Arts and Letters grant, 1952; Fund for the Advancement of Education Fellowship, 1952; Ford Foundation grant, 1952, 1959; Pulitzer Prize, 1954; Fulbright Fellowship, 1955; Borestone Mountain Award, 1958; National Book Award, 1959, 1965; Bollingen Prize, 1959; Poetry Society of America Prize, 1962; Shelley Memorial Award, 1962. D.H.L.: University of Michigan, 1962. *Died 1 August 1963.*

PUBLICATIONS

Collections

On the Poet and His Craft: Selected Prose, edited by Ralph J. Mills, Jr. 1965.
Collected Poems. 1966.
Selected Letters, edited by Ralph J. Mills., Jr. 1968.
Selected Poems, edited by Beatrice Roethke. 1969.

Verse

Open House. 1941.
The Lost Son and Other Poems. 1948.
Praise to the End! 1951.
The Waking: Poems 1933–1953. 1953.
Words for the Wind: The Collected Verse. 1957.
The Exorcism. 1957.
Sequence, Sometimes Metaphysical, Poems. 1963.
The Far Field. 1964.
Two Poems. 1965.

Other

I Am! Says the Lamb (juvenile). 1961.
Party at the Zoo (juvenile). 1963.
Straw for the Fire: From the Notebooks of Theodore Roethke, 1943–1963, edited by David Wagoner. 1972.
Dirty Dinky and Other Creatures: Poems for Children, edited by Beatrice Roethke and Stephen Lushington. 1973.

Bibliography: *Roethke: A Bibliography* by James R. McLeod, 1973.

Reading List: *Roethke* by Ralph J. Mills, Jr., 1963; *Roethke: Essays on His Poetry* by Arnold S. Stein, 1965; *Roethke: An Introduction to His Poetry* by Karl Malkoff, 1966; *The Glass House: The Life of Roethke* by Allan Seager, 1968; *Profile of Roethke* by William Heyen, 1971; *Roethke's Dynamic Vision* by Richard Allen Blessing, 1974; *Roethke: The Garden Master* by Rosemary Sullivan, 1975; *The Echoing Wood of Roethke* by Jenijoy La Belle, 1976.

*   *   *

Theodore Roethke's posthumous collection, *The Far Field*, is a résumé and retrospect of a lifetime's preoccupations, acknowledging its debt to those poets who have confronted the mystery of personal extinction — the later Eliot and Yeats and that "Whitman, maker of catalogues" whose "terrible hunger for objects" is repeated in these writings of a man who has "moved closer to death, lived with death." Roethke always felt "the separateness of all things," the fragility of being. In "The Dream" he had written "Love is not love until love's vulnerable"; "The Abyss" adds a new, desperate urgency to the theme, poised on a dark stair that "goes nowhere," knowing the abyss is "right where you are — /A step down the stair." Yet if this last volume broods over childhood initiations into mortality, it also celebrates the spontaneous impulse towards life, light, growth in which he shares:

> Many arrivals make us live: the tree becoming
> Green, a bird tipping the topmost bough,
> A seed pushing itself beyond itself....
>
> What does what it should do needs nothing more.
> The body moves, though slowly, towards desire.
> We come to something without knowing why.

Summoned once more to the field's end, in old age Roethke returned to "the first heaven of knowing," that second-childhood of radical innocence which has always been the American visionary's home. If "Old men should be explorers," he replies to the Eliot of *Four Quartets*, I'll be an Indian./Iroquois," thus unashamedly assuming the role of the noble savage in retreat, whose "journey into the interior," into the heart of the continent, is also a "long journey out of the self," into the unconscious and preconscious, the elemental life of the planet.

There is a paradoxical resolution of stasis and motion throughout Roethke's work. "The Sententious Man" claims to "know the motion of the deepest stone"; in "The Far Field," imagery of dwindling, darkening, and decline shifts into sudden surges and spurts of life, as not only air, fire, and water but even earth takes on the fluidity which leaves no ground secure: "the shale slides dangerously," dust blows, rubble falls, the arroyo cracks, the swamp is "alive with quicksand." Amid this movement the self floats unperturbed: "I rise and fall in the slow sea of a grassy plain" (the theological punning here recurs throughout his verse); "And all flows past.... I am not moving but they are," for the soul, preparing itself for death, has finally found that longed-for "imperishable quiet at the heart of form." Throughout his verse, the *field* is a complex metaphor: it is the green field of nature, the field of perception, and, at their intersection, a heraldic field in which matter blazons forth spirit, where "All finite things reveal infinitude," disclosing, in the words of one of his earliest poems, "skies of azure/The pageantry of wings the eyes' right treasure."

Movement from closure to openness, finitude to immensity, has been the characteristic rhythm of all his poetry. The title poem of *Open House* proclaims this:

My secrets cry aloud....
My heart keeps open house,
My doors are widely swung....
I'm naked to the bone
With nakedness my shield.
Myself is what I wear.

The Lost Son pokes around in origins, under stones, in drains and subsoil, to find the answer to his most basic question: "Where do the roots go?" Roethke felt himself at home amidst the abundant verminous life of a vegetable nature which (as in "Cuttings, *later*") strains like a saint to rise anew in "This urge, wrestle, resurrection of dry sticks" – a world to which he was introduced in his florist father's greenhouses, where he learnt to "study the lives on a leaf: the little/Sleepers, numb nudgers"; and not only to study, but to find in them, as in the "Shoots [which] dangled and drooped,/Lolling obscenely" in "Root Cellar," an imagery of his own instinctual life. He was impressed by the stubborn persistence of this residual realm: "Nothing would give up life:/Even the dirt kept breathing a small breath."

His poems are rites of passage, exits and entrances where "the body, delighting in thresholds,/Rocks in and out of itself." *Praise to the End* employs the bouncy rhythms and inconsequential surrealism of nursery rhyme and baby talk, used to such effect in his poems for children, to enact the birth or rebirth of the scattered psyche (Roethke suffered from periodic mental illness) out of a tangle of instinctual impulses – eating, touching, snuffling, sucking, licking – in all of which identity is constituted as *lack* ("I Need, I Need"), a fall from innocence into disenchantment which brings us to our proper selfhood, aware of time and consequence, and able to announce "I'm somebody else now." In "Give Way, Ye Gates," one line of six verbs charts the whole pilgrimage through need, mutuality, and loss into separated being: "Touch and arouse. Suck and sob. Curse and mourn." The technique of this volume is a riddling, exclamatory questioning, like that of an insistent child who neither expects nor receives an answer, wanting only confirmation of its own puzzling existence. Yet this catechism of the "happy asker" reveals a world of correspondences where everything *is* an answer to everything else, and the creatures sing their own richness and diversity: "A house for wisdom. A field for revelation./Speak to the stones and the stars answer."

In his love poems this most physical of poets assumes a metaphysical lightness and delicacy, a clarity of syntax and almost allegoric translucence of imagery which recall Renaissance neo-platonism and the courtly love of the troubadours. His women (even the "woman lovely in her bones") are the Beatrices of a rarefied sensuality, "know[ing] the speech of light" and "cry[ing] out loud the soul's own secret joy"; but even here Roethke's playfulness is preserved in sudden unexpected carnalities of language ("pure as a bride.../ And breathing hard, as that man rode/Between those lovely tits"). "The Renewal" shows love to be the force that moves the stars, reducing to a oneness knowing and motion, the dualities of his universe, just as "Words for the Wind," which provided the title for his *Collected Verse*, sees it as both the journey and the destination of the soul:

I cherish what I have
Had of the temporal:

I am no longer young
But the wind and waters are;
What falls away will fall;
All things bring me to love.

—Stan Smith

ROGERS, Samuel. English. Born in Stoke Newington, London, 30 July 1763. Educated at private schools in Hackney and Stoke Newington. Entered his father's bank, Cornhill, London, 1779; Partner, 1784, and, on his father's death, Principal Partner, 1793 until his retirement, 1803; thereafter, with income from the bank, lived in society as an art collector and man of letters; acted as patron to various writers, and came to be regarded as arbiter of taste. Offered poet laureateship on death of Wordsworth, 1850, but declined. *Died 18 December 1855.*

PUBLICATIONS

Collections

Poetical Works. 1856; edited by E. Bell, 1859.

Verse

The Ode to Superstition with Some Other Poems. 1786.
The Pleasures of Memory. 1792.
An Epistle to a Friend with Some Other Poems. 1798.
Verses Written in Westminster Abbey after the Funeral of Charles James Fox. 1806.
The Voyage of Columbus. 1810.
Miscellaneous Poems, with E. C. Knight and others. 1812.
Poems. 1812; edited by S. Sharpe, 1860.
Jacqueline. 1814.
Human Life. 1819.
Italy. 2 vols., 1822–28.
Poetical Works. 1852.

Other

Recollections of the Table-Talk of Samuel Rogers. 1856; edited by O. Stonor, 1952.
Recollections, edited by W. Sharpe. 1859.
Reminiscences and Table-Talk, edited by G. H. Powell. 1903.
Italian Journal, edited by J. R. Hale. 1956.
Rogers and William Gilpin: Their Friendship and Correspondence, edited by C. P. Barbier. 1959.

Reading List: *The Early Life of Rogers,* 1887, and *Rogers and His Contemporaries,* 2 vols., 1889, both by P. W. Clayden; *Rogers and His Circle* by R. E. Roberts, 1910; *Rogers et Son Poème "Italie"* by Ernest Gidden, 1959; *Rogers, The Poet from Newington Green* by Adam J. Shirren, 1963.

*   *   *

Hazlitt's stricture that Samuel Rogers was "elegant but feeble" is unkind though undeniable. The luxurious repose, the almost maidenly dignity with which his life was surrounded, renders his verse nerveless and withdrawn, though the poet described himself more flatteringly, in *Italy*:

> Nature denied him much,
> But gave him at his birth what he most values;
> A passionate love for music, sculpture, painting,
> For poetry, the language of the gods,
> For all things here, or grand or beautiful,
> A setting sun, a lake among the mountains,
> The light of an ingenuous countenance,
> And what transcends them all, a noble action.

Rogers was the last true disciple of the cult sensibility: his notable collection of *objects d'art* demonstrated the infallibility of his taste; invitations to his literary breakfasts were eagerly sought; and in his unusually long life he was true friend to many poets – Crabbe, Byron, Wordsworth, and Tennyson among them. His controversial sallies passed round with those of Sydney Smith and Lutrell; his enlightened social attitudes earned the respect of men as diverse as Fox and Wellington. And his contemporaries bought over 21,000 copies of *The Pleasures of Memory*, which Byron hailed as "one of the most beautiful didactic poems in our language." Yet the raw edge of suffering, the extremes of joy and grief, are missing. He is the poet of the elegant Regency salon; a cultivated but bloodless amateur, a dilettante. A contemporary *bon mot* declared that Rogers had laboured nine months over a couplet, was now brought to bed of it, and that parent and child were as well as could be expected. Such scrupulous care, not always evident in the finished work, leached from his verse the last drops of immediacy.

It may, today, be his misfortune that his longest poems are the most readable: both *Italy* and *The Pleasures of Memory* reveal a dignified grace, reflecting the dispassionate sensibility of Gray and Goldsmith, and the conscious style of Johnson. The Horatian "Epistle to a Friend" lacks the *merum sal* of its Latin models, but makes an articulate case for the leisured and gentlemanly life.

Where deep feelings such as heroism or love are involved Rogers fails. *Columbus* and *Jacqueline* demand these emotions, but demand them in vain. The engravings which he commissioned Turner and Stothard to make for his collected works capture perfectly his passive sense of beauty, his withdrawn and static observations. Lines like the following, (from *Italy*) need the accompaniment of Turner's graphic skill to render them moving:

> It was an hour of universal joy.
> The lark was up and at the gate of heaven,
> Singing as sure to enter where he came;
> The butterfly was basking in my path,
> His radiant wings unfolded. From below
> The bell of prayer rose slowly, plaintively;
> An odours such as welcome in the day,
> Such as salute the early traveller,
> And come and go, each sweeter than the last,
> Were rising. Hill and valley breathed delight;
> And not a living thing but blessed the hour!

—T. Bareham

ROSENBERG, Isaac. English. Born in Bristol, 25 November 1890; family lived in Whitechapel, London, after 1897. Educated at Baker Street School, Stepney, London, 1899–1904; apprentice engraver, Carl Hentschel Company, London, 1904–07; attended evening classes at the London College of Printing, 1907–10; studied at the Slade School of

Art, London, 1911–14 (Jewish Educational Aid Society grant, 1912). Visited South Africa, 1914–15; served in the British Army in World War I, 1915–18; killed in action. *Died 1 April 1918.*

PUBLICATIONS

Collections

> *Collected Works: Poetry, Prose, Letters, and Some Drawings,* edited by Gordon Bottomley and Denys Harding.   1937; revised edition of poetry section, as *Collected Poems,* 1949.
> *Collected Works,* edited by Ian Parsons.   1976.

Verse

> *Night and Day.*   1912.
> *Youth.*   1915.
> *Poems,* edited by Gordon Bottomley.   1922.

Play

> *Moses.*   1916.

Reading List: in *Heroes' Twilight* by Bernard Bergonzi, 1965; *Out of Battle: The Poetry of the First World War* by Jon Silkin, 1972; *Rosenberg: The Half Used Life* by Jean Liddiard, 1975; *Journey to the Trenches* by Joseph Cohen, 1975.

*   *   *

Isaac Rosenberg was killed on the western front on 1 April 1918. His parents were immigrants from Czarist Russia who left to avoid anti-semitism and forced conscription. The family moved to the ghetto of East London in 1897 where there was already a sizable Jewish community – a community that at one time supported a Yiddish theatre and newspaper. But although Rosenberg rejected Hebrew and the concomitant way of orthodox Judaism, Jewish culture, in the widest sense, was an essential part of his upbringing. Kenneth Allott noted in *The Penguin Book of Contemporary Verse* that for him Rosenberg's poems "are spoilt ... by his appetite for the extravagant and his rebarbative diction." Allott's taste was formed round the cool clinching wit of Auden, and the fact is that Rosenberg's poetry is imaginatively vigorous, an attribute that never had much in it for Auden, or, one supposes, Allott. Rosenberg's imagination is robust whether he is structuring a re-shaping of consciousness, as he is in his playlet *Moses* or the dramatic "Amulet/Unicorn" fragments; or in the metaphor of Absalom's hair ("Chagrin"), or the re-informed lovers of the "Grecian Urn" as we find them in "Daughters of War" and the third stanza of "Dead Man's Dump." Rosenberg was afraid of his poetry being thin, especially in ideas. He need not have worried, for, as in "Dead Man's Dump," the ideas are not only substantial but often subtle:

> What fierce imaginings their dark souls lit?
> Earth! have they gone into you!
> Somewhere they must have gone,
> And flung on your hard back
> Is their soul's sack
> Emptied of God-ancestralled essences.
> Who hurled them out? Who hurled?

Rosenberg mourns not only the body and *its* death, but, surprisingly perhaps for a Jewish writer with his concern for the total being, also the death of the soul. The "soul's sack" may be the body, but it is, more subtly and crucially, as likely to be the soul's amnion, whose contents are evacuated with the death of the flesh. Thus with the soul's death also die the essences originated by God, and this religious apprehension of what is destroyed by the human activity of war achieves the status of tragic assertion.

The language in this stanza is robust and dense, and ultimately registers tenderness and pain, responses that are more intimate and singular than the compassion Wilfred Owen articulates. Even in the work that is not ostensibly about the War (like the playlet *Moses* and the "Amulet/Unicorn" fragments), there is a greater immediacy concerning the nature of destruction in Rosenberg's work than in Owen's. As Walter Benjamin said of Brecht in "The Author as Producer": "He goes back, in a new way, to the theatre's greatest and most ancient opportunity: the opportunity to expose the present." Just so; and it is also true of Rosenberg. "Dead Man's Dump," like Owen's "Strange Meeting," is indeed a poem concerned with the imminent destruction of an at least partly humane civilisation; and as the destruction occurs the value shows up. But where Owen recollects in pity, narratively, Rosenberg's apprehensions are evolved dramatically in the present, as that is *made* by man. And this exposing of the present happens elsewhere in Rosenberg. It occurs in the trick played on God in the ingenious, Donne-like "God made Blind." In *Moses*, the protagonist has just murdered the sadistic Egyptian overseer Abinoah (whose daughter Moses is in love with) only to find that he must face the Egyptian Prince Imra and his glimmering cohorts that have come to arrest him. In "The Unicorn," the women are abducted in a kind of Sabine rape. In Owen's "Strange Meeting," the resulting admonition may be as dire as it is in Rosenberg's "Dead Man's Dump." Possibly more so. But it is not as sensuously disturbing. Samuel Johnson observed that the business of the poet was to strike through to the reader's *senses*. Rosenberg's sensuous apprehensions delay the workings of valuation until the experience is complete, and there is nowhere else that the mind can go but to full judgment.

—Jon Silkin

ROSSETTI, Christina (Georgina).   English.   Born in London, 5 December 1830; sister of Dante Gabriel Rossetti, *q.v.* Educated privately. Contributed to the *Germ*, publication of the Pre-Raphaelite Brotherhood, as Ellen Alleyne, 1850; assisted her mother in teaching at a day school in Camden Town, London, and subsequently at Frome; thereafter lived a retired life at home, caring for her mother and devoting herself to church work; wrote mainly devotional literature after 1872, and for most of her later life was an invalid. *Died 29 December 1894.*

Publications

Collections

Poetical Works, edited by William Rossetti. 1904.
A Choice of Rossetti's Verse, edited by Elizabeth Jennings. 1970.
Maude: Prose and Verse, edited by Rebecca W. Crump. 1976.

Verse

Verses. 1847; edited by J. D. Symon, 1906.
Goblin Market and Other Poems. 1862; edited by Edith Fry, 1912.
The Prince's Progress and Other Poems. 1866.
Annus Domini: A Prayer for Each Day of the Year, edited by H. Burrows. 1874.
A Pageant and Other Poems. 1881.
Time Flies: A Reading Diary. 1885.
Poems. 1890.
New Poems, edited by William Rossetti. 1896.

Play

The Months: A Pageant (juvenile). 1904.

Fiction

Commonplace and Other Short Stories. 1870.
Maude: A Story for Girls. 1897.

Other

Sing-Song: A Nursery Rhyme Book. 1872; revised edition, 1893.
Speaking Likenesses (juvenile). 1874.
Seek and Find: A Double Series of Short Studies of the Benedicite. 1879.
Called to Be Saints: The Minor Festivals Devotionally Studied. 1881.
Letter and Spirit: Notes on the Commandments. 1883.
The Face of the Deep: A Devotional Commentary on the Apocalypse. 1892.
Family Letters, edited by William Rossetti. 1908.
Three Rossettis: Unpublished Letters to and from Dante Gabriel, Christina, William, edited by Janet Troxell. 1937.
Familiar Correspondence, translated by Robert Gathorne-Hardy. 1962.
The Rossetti-Macmillan Letters, edited by Lona Packer. 1963.

Bibliography: *Rossetti: A Reference Guide* by Rebecca W. Crump, 1976.

Reading List: *Rossetti* by Sara Teasdale, 1932; *Rossetti: A Portrait with Background* by Marya Zaturenska, 1949; *Rossetti: Her Life and Religion* by M. Sawtell, 1955; *Wonder and Whimsy: The Fantastic World of Rossetti* by Thomas B. Swann, 1960; *Rossetti* by Lona

Packer, 1963; *Rossetti* by Georgina Battiscombe, 1965; *The Four Rossettis* by Stanley Weintraub, 1977.

* * *

Christina Rossetti's poems, about nine hundred in all, have considerable variety of tone, and all show great metrical skill and lyrical spontaneity. Her Tractarian Anglican faith, from one point of view, furnished her with a firm basis, so that her work has a sureness of tone which contrasts with that of her brother D. G. Rossetti. But from another point of view her religion played a negative role both in her life and in her work. She rejected two suitors on grounds of religious conscience, but was unable to commit herself, as did her sister Maria, to the conventual life. This conflict is reflected in her poem "The Convent Threshold." Many of her lyrics give evidence of an emotionally rich and sensuous nature, but others, more especially those of religious inspiration, are marked by a deep melancholy and self-distrust. Many of them dwell on the theme of death, and it is noteworthy that some of the best known and most characteristic of these, such as "Remember" and the song beginning "When I am dead, my dearest," seem to look forward to death more as a dreamless sleep than to a Christian hope of resurrection. Even in poems of a more orthodox tone, such as "Uphill" and "The Three Enemies," the stress is on the difficulties and dangers of the Christian's path.

The narrative poem "Goblin Market," which originally appeared in the Pre-Raphaelite periodical *The Germ*, was the first production of any of that group to gain wide-spread popularity. Its atmosphere is that of fairy or folk tale, but it can be read as a Christian allegory of sin and redemption. Another lengthy narrative, "The Prince's Progress," in which the prince delays on his quest and arrives to find the princess already dead, also has symbolic overtones, relating to Christina's own personal frustrations. The same closeness to the folk tradition is to be found in many of her ballads and in her poems for children, *Sing-Song*. This is combined with a clean-cut sense of colour and imagery, which again contrasts with the hectic "greenery-yallery" mode which so often characterises D. G. Rossetti. Her feeling for nature is also strong, notably in her love of the smaller forms of animal life. This naturalistic emotion expresses itself in the series of lyrics called "Months."

Like all the Rossetti circle Christina was an accomplished writer of sonnets. Many of hers are in fact written to *bouts rimés*, a game in which all the family seemed to have joined. More deeply felt is the sequence "Monna Innominata." William Michael Rossetti in his biography of his sister implies that the story of unfulfilled love which they tell is a personal one. Besides her more private devotional poems Christina Rossetti wrote a number of carols for Christmas and Easter. Two of the former, "In the Bleak Midwinter" and the children's carol "How Far Is It to Bethlehem?," have gained a wide currency.

Christina Rossetti occupies a very high place among the women poets of the nineteenth century. Perhaps only Emily Dickinson and Emily Brontë in the English-speaking world may be considered her superiors. If less space has been accorded her here than to D. G. Rossetti, it is because little can be said of her poetry except to praise its perfection. She is certainly not inferior to her brother – on the contrary, many would consider hers far the more authentic talent.

—John Heath-Stubbs

ROSSETTI, Dante Gabriel (Gabriel Charles Dante Rossetti). English. Born in London, 12 May 1828; brother of Christina Rossetti, *q.v.* Educated at King's College, London, 1837–41: studied drawing under John Sell Cotman; chose art as a profession, 1842, and studied at F. S. Cary's Academy, 1842–46, and at the Antique School of the Royal Academy, London, 1846–48; studied painting with Ford Madox Brown, 1848. Married Elizabeth

Eleanor Siddal in 1860 (died, 1862). Founder Member, with Millais and Holman Hunt, Pre-Raphaelite Brotherhood group of artists and writers, London, 1848; participated in first art exhibition in 1849, and was engaged mainly in painting, 1850–60; enjoyed patronage of Ruskin from c. 1852, and met Oxford circle of Burne-Jones and William Morris during the same period; chloral addict from c. 1870–81. *Died 9 April 1882.*

PUBLICATIONS

Collections

Works, edited by William Rossetti. 1911.
Poems, edited by Oswald Doughty. 1957.
Letters, edited by Oswald Doughty and J. R. Wahl. 4 vols., 1965–67.

Verse

Sir Hugh the Heron: A Legendary Tale in Four Parts. 1843.
Hand and Soul. 1869.
Poems. 1870; revised edition, 1881; *The House of Life: A Sonnet Sequence* edited by P. F. Baum, 1928; *The Blessed Damozel* edited by P. F. Baum, 1937; *Sister Helen* edited by Janet Troxell, 1939.
Ballads and Sonnets. 1881.
Some Scraps of Prose and Verse, edited by William Rossetti. 1898.
The Kelmscott Love Sonnets, edited by J. R. Wahl. 1954.

Other

Jan Van Hunks, edited by T. Watts-Dunton. 1912; edited by J. R. Wahl, 1952.
Rossetti: An Analytical List of Manuscripts in the Duke University Library with Hitherto Unpublished Verse and Prose, edited by P. F. Baum. 1931.
The Rossetti-Leyland Letters: The Correspondence of an Artist and His Patron, edited by Francis L. Fennell, Jr. 1976.
Rossetti-Janey Morris Letters, edited by John Bryson. 1976.

Translator, *The Early Italian Poets from Ciullo to Dante, Together with Dante's Vita Nuova.* 1861; revised edition, as *Dante and His Circle,* 1874.
Translator, *Lenore: A Ballad,* by G. A. Bürger, edited by William Rossetti. 1900.
Translator, *Henry the Leper,* by Hartmann von Aue. 2 vols., 1905.

Bibliography: in *Pre-Raphaelitism: A Bibliocritical Study* by W. E. Fredeman, 1965.

Reading List: *Rossetti: His Life and Works* by Evelyn Waugh, 1928; *Rossetti: His Friends and Enemies* by Helen R. Angeli, 1949; *A Victorian Romantic* by Oswald Doughty, 1949; *Life with Rossetti* by Gale Pedrick, 1964; *Rossetti and the Pre-Raphaelite Brotherhood* by Gordon H. Fleming, 1967; *Rossetti* by Robert D. Johnston, 1969; *Lost on Both Sides: Rossetti, Critic and Poet* by Robert M. Cooper, 1970; *Catalogue Raisonné of Paintings and Drawings* by Virginia Surtees, 1971; *The Dark Glass: Vision and Technique in the Poetry of*

Rossetti by Ronnalie R. Howard, 1972; The Four Rossettis by Stanley Weintraub, 1977; Rossetti: An Alien Victorian by Brian and Judy Dobbs, 1977.

*   *   *

It is almost impossible to separate one's notion of Rossetti the poet from that of Rossetti the Pre-Raphaelite painter. *The Blessed Damozel*, which in its first version appeared as early as 1850, might be considered as having its pictorial correlative in the *Beata Beatrix*. The latter is the most often reproduced of Rossetti's paintings, as the former is the most frequently anthologised of his poems, but it may be doubted whether either of them displays to the full those qualities which the modern critic will find of abiding interest in Rossetti's work. Both the poem and the painting employ medieval imagery; but this imagery is used decoratively only as the basis of a vague symbolism, whereas in Dante or in Giotto it would have been iconographically precise. Furthermore, the clarity and the freshness of the Middle Ages or early Renaissance are replaced in both the poem and the painting by an atmosphere of languor, even of morbidity. *The Blessed Damozel* is not a vision of a soul in glory, for Rossetti, though brought up as a Roman Catholic, was an agnostic, but a reverie: careful reading of the poem will reveal that it is really a dramatic monologue, the speaker being in fact the dead girl's lover. This gives us a clue as to the real nature of Rossetti's poetry. He is at his best when he is exploring states of mind, especially states of mind which lie somewhere between consciousness and dreaming. He learned much from Browning's dramatic monologues, but he lacks Browning's extrovert robustness. He stands rather in a line of Romanticism which includes Blake, Coleridge, Shelley, and Poe. He learned from all these poets, but from another line of Romanticism he developed the characteristically Pre-Raphaelite rendering of minute pictorial detail. Here his models were Chatterton and the Keats of "The Eve of St. Mark." Much of the method is also implicit in such early poems of Tennyson as "Mariana."

From this point of view, we might see Rossetti at his best in such a poem as "The Woodspurge." Here the speaker, remembering a mood of dejection, is characterized by his accurate observation of a fact of nature: "The woodspurge has a cup of three." Something of the same quality is to be found in the best of the songs and sonnets which make up *The House of Life*. This is an ambitious attempt at a sequence in the Italian Renaissance manner, in which the course of a love affair is charted through a series of sonnets interspersed with other lyrical forms. Dante, once more, is the ostensible model. But in Dante, through a precisely worked out metaphysical theory of the nature of love, the visible world is seen as capable of making manifest the spiritual; in Rossetti the sensual and the spiritual are confused rather than interfused. Once more it is sensual reverie which is depicted rather than sensual fulfilment.

The Pre-Raphaelite school took its name because of their preference for the early Italian painters who preceded Raphael. But it would be a mistake to think of them as entirely preoccupied with mediaeval subjects. Truth to nature was an important part of their programme, and there is a vein of social realism in the movement, particularly in the work of Ford Madox Brown. This is represented in Rossetti's poetry by "Jenny," a study of a London prostitute. This considers with some honesty and courage a subject the Victorians generally fought shy of, and its incidental urban imagery is remarkably successful. Nevertheless, the modern reader may find it a basically sentimental and morally confused poem. The same charges could be levelled against *The Blessed Damozel*, and one cannot help seeing the romantic idealisation of womanhood represented by the one poem, and the notorious state of prostitution in Victorian London explored in the other, as reverse sides of the same medal.

Rather a large number of Rossetti's other poems impress one as literary exercises rather than the product of inspiration. The numerous Sonnets for Pictures are essentially parasitic, works of art constructed on works of art. There is also an element of pastiche in the poems inspired by Rossetti's love of the Border ballads. Of these perhaps the most effective is *Sister Helen*, on a theme of sorcery possibly deriving from a classical source, Theocritus, Idyll ii, although transferred to a Border setting. "Eden Bower" deals with the subject of Lilith's jealousy of Eve. One cannot help thinking that this is only an "eternal triangle" drama, rather too commonplace for the great cosmic myth in which it is set. In the three ballad-like poems written in the later part of Rossetti's life the form is extended to a greater length than it can naturally bear. "The White Ship" and "The King's Tragedy" are on historical subjects, the drowning of Henry I's heir and the murder of James I of Scotland respectively. "Rose Mary" is a grim mediaeval tale of sorcery and treachery.

Rossetti composed two prose short stories, "Hand and Soul" and the unfinished "The Orchard Pit." The latter, written in the period of his mental breakdown, with its image of a death-dealing siren, contains the most terrifying of Rossetti's dream poems:

> This in my dreams is shown me; and her hair
>   Crosses my lips and draws my burning breath;
> Her song spreads golden wings upon the air,
> Life's eyes are gleaming from her forehead fair,
>   And from her breasts the ravishing eyes of Death.

A word must be said on Rossetti as a verse translator. Ezra Pound regarded the versions of the early Italian poets as superior to any of Rossetti's original work, and there is a lot to be said for this point of view. The Italian poems had a clarity of form and intellectual structure on which he could build, and which was precisely what was lacking in his own work. Such a rendering as that of Guido Guinicelli's canzone "The Gentle Heart," with its complex stanza structure and elaborate metaphysical argument, is absolutely masterly. Rossetti's translation of Villon's "Ballad of Dead Ladies" is open to the charge that he has introduced into it an element of Pre-Raphaelite decorativeness wanting in the original. Nevertheless, its haunting music has not been matched by any other translator.

—John Heath-Stubbs

RUKEYSER, Muriel. American. Born in New York City, 15 December 1913. Educated at Fieldston School, New York, 1919–30; Vassar College, Poughkeepsie, New York; Columbia University, New York, 1930–32. Has one son. Vice-President, House of Photography, New York, 1946–60; taught at Sarah Lawrence College, Bronxville, New York, 1946, 1956–57. Since 1967, Member, Board of Directors, Teachers–Writers Collaborative, New York. President, P.E.N. American Center, 1975–76. Recipient: Harriet Monroe Award, 1941; National Institute of Arts and Letters Award, 1942; Guggenheim Fellowship, 1943; American Council of Learned Societies Fellowship, 1963; Swedish Academy translation award, 1967. D.Litt.: Rutgers University, New Brunswick, New Jersey, 1961. Member, National Institute of Arts and Letters. Lives in New York City.

PUBLICATIONS

Verse

Theory of Flight. 1935.
U.S. 1. 1938.
Mediterranean. 1938.
A Turning Wind. 1939.

The Soul and Body of John Brown.   1940.
Wake Island.   1942.
Beast in View.   1944.
The Children's Orchard.   1947.
The Green Wave.   1948.
Orpheus.   1949.
Elegies.   1949.
Selected Poems.   1951.
Body of Waking.   1958.
Waterlily Fire: Poems 1932–1962.   1962.
The Outer Banks.   1967.
The Speed of Darkness.   1968.
29 Poems.   1970.
Breaking Open.   1973.
The Gates.   1976.

Play

The Color of the Day (produced 1961).

Fiction

The Orgy.   1965.

Other

Willard Gibbs (biography).   1942.
The Life of Poetry.   1949.
Come Back Paul (juvenile).   1955.
One Life (biography of Wendell Willkie).   1957.
I Go Out (juvenile).   1961.
Bubbles (juvenile).   1967.
Poetry and Unverifiable Fact: The Clark Lectures.   1968.
The Traces of Thomas Hariot.   1971.

Translator, with others, *Selected Poems of Octavio Paz.*   1963; revised edition, 1973.
Translator, *Sun Stone,* by Octavio Paz.   1963.
Translator, with Leif Sjöberg, *Selected Poems of Gunnar Ekelöf.*   1967.
Translator, *Three Poems by Gunnar Ekelöf.*   1967.
Translator, with others, *Early Poems 1935–1955,* by Octavio Paz.   1973.

*   *   *

Much has been said about the feminine voice in poetry, usually by critics. No one seems to know exactly what the "true" feminine voice is, except that somewhere between the despair and the joy of woman's second-class existence, a kind of experience is finally being written. Sylvia Plath wrote from this sensibility and a number of new lady poets have missed the joy expressed between the lines, where Plath had made words that work together. The assumption that despair should somehow outweigh joy in serious feminine poetry results from the Dickinson (and now, Plath) tradition.

Reading the work of Muriel Rukeyser, one quickly learns that feminism is not so easily defined. Once again, the near-answer is revealed for what it is, and we are thrown back to the poem itself. Rukeyser's work can be despairing, but her responses have larger potential. Even in moments of sad recollection, as in "Effort at Speech Between Two People," Rukeyser's voice is not entirely despondent:

> When I was three, a little child read a story about a rabbit
> who died, in the story, and I crawled under a chair :
> a pink rabbit : it was my birthday, and a candle
> burnt a sore spot on my finger, and I was told to be happy.

Here, Rukeyser has successfully combined the elements of mature narrative with a verbal sense of what it was like to live through that third birthday. The poem is not cute, in any of its aspects, and in spite of succeeding lines ("I am unhappy. I am lonely. Speak to me.") never indulges in outright despondency. It is the hope for communication that has initially caused the poem which survives, echoed by lively images, and imbuing the poem ultimately with a sense of optimism.

Rukeyser's work is always tough, however, and never assumes the false authority that is so often mistaken for wisdom. She investigates nearly every aspect of life, from the desperate haircutting of a boy who needs work to "The Power of Suicide," one of her tight, excellent four-line poems:

> The potflower on the windowsill says to me
> In words that are green-edged red leaves:
> Flower   flower   flower   flower
> Today for the sake of all the dead   Burst into flower.

The simplicity of such a poem makes explication impossible: what gimmicks of "style" has the poet employed? One knows only that the poem is bound by a natural rhythm, and seems to relate a part of the poet's experience.

Some of Rukeyser's long poems, in particular "The Speed of Darkness," are among the finest we'll have to carry with us into the next century. Her vocabulary is truly of our generation, but she's writing poems of a longer endurance:

> Whoever despises the clitoris despises the penis
> Whoever despises the penis despises the cunt
> Whoever despises the cunt despises the life of the child.
>
> Resurrection music,   silence,   and surf.

In "Waterlily Fire," she curiously mixes hard consonant sounds with a softer, feminine voice:

> We pray : we dive into each other's eyes
> Whatever can come to a woman can come to me.
> This the long body : into life from the beginning....

The toughness of these poems suggests that "feminine," with all its present connotations, is not the correct adjective for Miss Rukeyser's work. The frankness of her love poems (read "What I See") combined with her muted optimism also makes for memorable poetry.

For the moment, such "optimism" seems the only valid voice that any poet, regardless of sex, can bring to his work. Anything else is a lie, or why would the poet trouble to write at all?

Muriel Rukeyser's poetry *is* feminine, but only because the poet is a lady. It is enduring because the poet has retained all of her "seventeen senses," and utilizes every one of them in her work.

—Geof Hewitt

RUSSELL, George William. Pseudonym: AE (from the word AEon)   Irish.   Born in Lurgan, County Armagh, 10 April 1867; moved to Dublin, 1877. Educated at Rathmines School, Dublin; Metropolitan School of Art, Dublin. Married in 1898; two sons. Converted to theosophy, 1888, and lived for a time with other theosophists; Clerk at Pims, Dublin, 1890; worked with the Irish Agricultural Organization Society, Dublin, from 1897; Editor, *Irish Homestead*, subsequently *Irish Statesman*, Dublin, 1905–30. Associated with the Irish literary and artistic renaissance: a Founder, Irish National Theatre Society, 1902; paintings exhibited in the New York Armory Show and the Whitechapel exhibit of Irish Art, London, 1913. Active member of the Irish Home Rule Movement: Member, Home Rule Convention, 1917; lectured in America, 1928, 1930–31, 1934–35. Member, Irish Academy of Letters, 1932. *Died 17 July 1935.*

PUBLICATIONS

Collections

   Letters from AE, edited by Alan Denson.   1961.

Verse

   Homeward: Songs by the Way.   1894; revised edition, 1895.
   The Earth Breath and Other Poems.   1897.
   The Nuts of Knowledge: Lyrical Poems, Old and New.   1903.
   The Divine Vision and Other Poems.   1904.
   By Still Waters: Lyrical Poems.   1906.
   The Renewal of Youth.   1911.
   Collected Poems.   1913; revised edition, 1919, 1926, 1935.
   Gods of War with Other Poems.   1915.
   Salutation: A Poem on the Irish Rebellion of 1916.   1917.
   Michael.   919.
   Voices of the Stones.   1925.
   Midsummer Eve.   1928.
   Dark Weeping.   1929.
   Enchantment and Other Poems.   1930.
   Vale and Other Poems.   1931.
   Verses for Friends.   1932.
   The House of the Titans and Other Poems.   1934.
   Selected Poems.   1935.

Play

   Deirdre (produced 1902).   1907.

Fiction

   The Mask of Apollo and Other Stories.   1905.

Other

The Future of Ireland and the Awakening of the Fires. 1897.
Ideals in Ireland: Priest or Hero? 1897.
Cooperative Credit. 1898.
Literary Ideals in Ireland, with Yeats and John Eglinton. 1899.
An Artist of Gaelic Ireland. 1902.
Some Irish Essays. 1906.
Ireland and Tariff Reform. 1909.
The Hero in Man. 1909.
Cooperation and Nationality: A Guide for Rural Reformers. 1912.
The Tragedy of Labour in Dublin. 1913.
Oxford University and the Cooperative Movement. 1914.
Ireland, Agriculture, and War. 1915.
Imaginations and Reveries. 1915; revised edition, 1921.
Talks with an Irish Farmer (12 leaflets). 1916.
The National Being: Some Thoughts on an Irish Polity. 1916.
Templecrone: A Record of Cooperative Effort. 1917.
Thoughts for a Convention: Memorandum on the State of Ireland. 1917.
Conscription for Ireland: A Warning to England. 1918.
The Candle of Vision. 1918.
Literary Imagination. 1919.
*A Plea for Justice, Being a Demand for a Public Enquiry into the Attacks on Co-operative
    Societies in Ireland.* 1920; revised edition, 1921.
The Economics of Ireland and the Policy of the British Government. 1920.
*Thoughts for British Co-operators, Being a Further Demand for a Public Enquiry into the
    Attacks on Co-operative Societies in Ireland.* 1921.
The Inner and the Outer Ireland. 1921.
Ireland and the Empire at the Court of Conscience. 1921.
Ireland, Past and Future. 1922.
The Interpreters. 1922.
Song and Its Fountains. 1932.
The Avatars: A Futurist Fantasy. 1933.
Some Passages from the Letters to Yeats. 1936.
Letters to Minanlabain, edited by L. Porter. 1937.
*The Living Torch: An Anthology of Prose by AE, Principally Drawn from the Irish
    Statesman,* edited by Monk Gibbon. 1937.

Editor, *New Songs.* 1904.
Editor, *Lyrics,* by J. S. Starkey. 1910.

Bibliography: *Printed Writings by George W. Russell (AE)* by Alan Denson, 1961.

Reading List: *AE* by William M. Clyde, 1935; *A Memoir of AE* by John Eglinton, 1937;
Russell-AE: A Centennial Assessment by Alan Denson, 1968; *That Myriad-Minded Man: A
Biography of Russell* by Henry Summerfield, 1976.

*   *   *

AE's writing falls into three periods: his theosophical and Irish Agricultural Organisation
Society work before 1905; his editorship of the *Irish Homestead* (1905–23); and his last years,
highlighted by his editorship of the *Irish Statesman* (1923–30).
    Two-thirds of AE's poetry was written during his first period. His early prose is found in

the *Irish Theosophist* (1892–97), the *Internationalist* (1897–98), and the pre-1905 *Homestead*. AE was a man of letters from the beginning; his criticism of literature, art, and life runs throughout the early theosophical journals. All of his stories fall into this early period; whether set in the east, Egypt, Greece, or Ireland, they reflect the same theme as his poems: the romantic cyclical strife between body and soul that constantly moves towards some reconciliation of these opposites. His one play, *Deirdre*, is mainly of historical interest, for it was the catalyst for Yeats's and Synge's Deirdre plays.

AE's *Homestead* period was almost exclusively devoted to prose. Although that journal's policy stressed economics, AE made room in its pages for most of the young Irish writers of those years, especially in the *Celtic Christmas* numbers (before 1910). Four prose volumes came out in this second period. *Imaginations and Reveries* reprinted *Deirdre* and several early stories and essays, but the revised edition also contains such tough second-period work as "Thoughts for a Convention" (1917). The other three volumes are more visionary. *The National Being* reflects AE's vision of Ireland's co-operative soul. In *Interpreters*, several condemned leaders of the 1916 rising share their vision of what they fought for. And *Candle of Vision* romantically demonstrates that "all I saw in vision was part of the life of earth."

AE's *Irish Statesman* modified the *Homestead*'s stress on economics to a more cosmopolitan balance and encouraged second-generation Irish writers like Clarke and O'Flaherty. AE's own poetry flowered during this last period, gaining greatly in clarity and strength. After the *Statesman* came to an end in 1930, AE brought out his last two prose volumes. *Song and Its Fountains* explains the circumstances out of which his lyrics were born, while *Avatars* attempts to "will another Irish literary revival by imagining it" (Patricia McFate, *Eire-Ireland*, Winter 1974).

AE's best lyrics are found in his *Selected Poems*. His major theme is the cyclical battle between light and darkness, spirit and body, that constantly moves towards the reconciliation of these opposites. Besides the poet himself, AE's typical characters are children, lovers, and heroes. AE's children do not come trailing clouds of glory; they meet spiritual beings early in life, and their choice of them, as in "Germinal," determines a Dante, Caesar, or Judas. AE's early love poems tend to sing of the sadness found in earthly love's insufficiencies, but his later love poems contain a rich joy seldom found in his early work. AE's "Dark Lady," Shakespeare's (or Yeats's?) mistress-muse, is a harlot-virgin who had once been the "only creature that by flesh and blood/Entered the court of his spirit." AE's heroes, like Blake's idea of Milton's Lucifer, are Prometheans who bring light to earth, spirit to body. AE's best lyrics, however, reflect the Irish landscape. In them, as in Wordsworth's, nature is so concentrated upon that it becomes supernatural. This can be seen most clearly through AE's handling of light. Just as AE's best paintings are those landscapes in which, as he was fond of quoting Monet, "The light is the real person in the picture," so his best nature poems glow like an impressionist's canvas. As in "A Mountain Tarn," earth and spirit are brought together by light. Light is the catalyst that gives birth to the supernatural beings and moods that transfigure his landscapes. AE believed that "Nothing came forth from that Majesty of which we may not discover some traces of its royal lineage," and he reflects this light everywhere he finds it in Ireland's people and landscapes.

—William Daniels

SACKVILLE, Charles.   See DORSET, Earl of.

SACKVILLE, Thomas; 1st Earl of Dorset; Baron Buckhurst. English. Born in Buckhurst, Withyham, Sussex, in 1536. Educated at the grammar school in Sullington, Sussex; possibly at Hart Hall, Oxford, or St. John's College, Cambridge; entered the Middle Temple, London; called to the bar. Married Cecily Baker in 1554; four sons and three daughters. Elected Member of Parliament for Westmorland, 1558, for East Grinstead, Sussex, 1559, and for Aylesbury, Buckinghamshire, 1563; toured France and Italy, 1563–66; inherited family estates and returned to England, 1566; served in the House of Lords from 1567; on diplomatic missions for the crown to France, 1568, 1571; Privy Councillor, from 1571, and served as Commissioner at State Trials; sent to the Low Countries by the Queen to survey political affairs after Leicester's return to England, incurred her displeasure, was recalled, confined to his house, then restored to favour, 1587–88; appointed Commissioner for Ecclesiastical Causes, 1588; again sent on an embassy to the Low Countries, 1589; commissioner to sign treaty with France on behalf of the Queen, 1591; with Burghley, unsuccessfully attempted to negotiate peace with France, 1598; appointed Lord Treasurer, 1599, and confirmed in the position for life by James I, 1603; Lord High Steward, presiding at the trial of the Earl of Essex, 1601; a commissioner in the successful negotiation of a new peace treaty with Spain, and pensioned for his services by the King, 1604. Grand Master of the Order of the Freemasons, 1561–67; Chancellor of Oxford University, 1591. M.A.: Cambridge University, 1571; Oxford University, 1592. Knighted, and created Baron Buckhurst, 1567; Knight of the Garter, 1589; Earl of Dorset, 1604. *Died 19 April 1608.*

PUBLICATIONS

Collections

> *Works,* edited by R. W. Sackville-West.   1859.
> *Poems,* edited by M. Hearsey.   1936.

Verse

> *Induction,* and *Complaint of Henry, Duke of Buckingham,* in *Mirror for Magistrates.*   1563; edited by Lily B. Campbell, 1938.

Play

> *The Tragedy of Gorboduc,* with Thomas Norton (produced 1561).   1565; as *The Tragedy of Ferrex and Porrex,* 1570(?); edited by Irby B. Cauthen, 1970.

Reading List: *Sackville* by Normand Berlin, 1974.

*   *   *

In the first edition of *Gorboduc,* the first three acts are attributed to Thomas Norton and the last two to Thomas Sackville, but some current opinion also ascribes the play's first scene to

Sackville and its final one to Norton. *Gorboduc*, the first English tragedy properly so called, is based on a story from the British pseudo-history written by Geoffrey of Monmouth. The authors have altered this story (of brother-princes' rivalry, leading to the death of one of them in battle and their mother's murder of the survivor, after which the nobles fall to civil war) by making it begin with the king's abdication of rule in favour of both his sons, by causing the king and queeen to be slain in a popular rebellion which is then put down by the nobles, and by introducing in the last act an ambitious nobleman who covets the vacant throne. Their play is therefore concerned both with tragic passions (which destroy a fated royal house) and with political lessons (particularly the dangers of civil war and the importance of a settled succession): it partakes both of the world of Senecan tragedy and of that of the *Mirror for Magistrates*. In form it resembles classical tragedy, though actually defective in all three unities of time, place, and (finally, when the chief characters are dead) action. It is divided into acts and scenes, with choruses between the acts; there are long speeches containing many *sententiae*; physical action, instead of being shown, is narrated by messengers. From non-classical tradition come the symbolic dumb-shows between the acts. The speeches are in blank verse, the choruses in quatrains (sometimes double) rounded off with couplets.

Sackville also contributed to the 1563 edition of the *Mirror for Magistrates*, supplying one of the tragic narratives (the "Complaint" of the Duke of Buckingham, Richard III's right-hand-man) and a long 76-stanza "induction" to the whole work. In the induction, the poet, musing in a dreary winter landscape, encounters Sorrow personified, who escorts him to the underworld, where he sees various other appropriate personifications – Remorse of Conscience, Dread, Revenge, Misery, Care, Sleep, Age, Malady, Famine, Death, War, and Debate – before crossing in Charon's boat to interview the great men whose falls are the subject of the *Mirror*. Written in rhyme-royal pentameter, this induction powerfully evokes the sombre mood of the collection of "tragedies" by drawing partly on Virgilian and partly on medieval artistic conventions; it looks forward towards Spenser in this mingling, as also in its deliberate use of archaic words for their emotional associations.

—T. W. Craik

SANDBURG, Carl. American. Born in Galesburg, Illinois, 6 January 1878. Educated at Lombard College, Galesburg, 1898–1902. Served as a Private in the 6th Illinois Volunteers during the Spanish American War, 1899. Married Lillian Steichen in 1908; three daughters, including the poet Helga Sandburg. Associate Editor, *The Lyceumite*, Chicago, 1907–08; District Organizer, Social-Democratic Party, Appleton, Wisconsin, 1908; City Hall Reporter for the *Milwaukee Journal*, 1909–10; Secretary to the Mayor of Milwaukee, 1910–12; worked for the *Milwaukee Leader* and *Chicago World*, 1912; worked for *Day Book*, Chicago, 1912–17, also Associate Editor, *System: The Magazine of Business*, Chicago, 1913; Stockholm Correspondent, 1918, and Manager of the Chicago Office, 1919, Newspaper Enterprise Association; Reporter, Editorial Writer, and Motion Picture Editor, 1917–30, and Syndicated Columnist, 1930–32, *Chicago Daily News*; Lecturer, University of Hawaii, Honolulu, 1934; Walgreen Foundation Lecturer, University of Chicago, 1940; weekly columnist, syndicated by the *Chicago Daily Times*, from 1941. Recipient: Poetry Society of America Award, 1919, 1921; Friends of Literature Award, 1934; Roosevelt Memorial Association prize, for biography, 1939; Pulitzer Prize, for history, 1940, and for poetry, 1951; American Academy of Arts and Letters Gold Medal, 1952; National Association for the Advancement of Colored People Award, 1965. Litt.D.: Lombard College, 1928; Knox College, Galesburg, Illinois, 1929; Northwestern University, Evanston, Illinois, 1931;

Harvard University, 1940; Yale University, New Haven, Connecticut, 1940; New York University, 1940; Wesleyan University, Middletown, Connecticut, 1940; Lafayette College, Easton, Pennsylvania, 1940; Syracuse University, New York, 1941; Dartmouth College, Hanover, New Hampshire, 1941; University of North Carolina, Chapel Hill, 1955; Uppsala College, New Jersey, 1959; LL.D.: Hollins College, Virginia, 1941; Augustana College, Rock Island, Illinois, 1948; University of Illinois, Urbana, 1953. Commander, Order of the North Star, Sweden, 1953. Member, American Academy of Arts and Letters, 1940. *Died 22 July 1967.*

PUBLICATIONS

Collections

   The Letters, edited by Herbert Mitgang.   1968.

Verse

   In Reckless Ecstasy.   1904.
   The Plaint of the Rose.   1904(?).
   Incidentals.   1904.
   Joseffy.   1910.
   Chicago Poems.   1916.
   Cornhuskers.   1918.
   Smoke and Steel.   1920.
   Slabs of the Sunburnt West.   1922.
   (Poems), edited by Hughes Mearns.   1926.
   Selected Poems, edited by Rebecca West.   1926.
   Good Morning, America.   1928.
   The People, Yes.   1936.
   Bronze Wood.   1941.
   Complete Poems.   1950; revised edition, 1970.
   Harvest Poems 1910–1960, edited by Mark Van Doren.   1960.
   Six New Poems and a Parable.   1961.
   Honey and Salt.   1963.
   Breathing Tokens, edited by Margaret Sandburg.   1978.

Fiction

   Remembrance Rock.   1948.

Other

   You and Your Job.   1908.
   The Chicago Race Riots, July 1919.   1919.
   Rootabaga Stories (juvenile).   1922.
   Rootabaga Pigeons (juvenile).   1923.
   Abraham Lincoln: The Prairie Years.   2 vols., 1926 (selection, for children, as *Abe Lincoln Grows Up*, 1928); *Abraham Lincoln: The War Years*, 4 vols., 1939; revised

abridgement, as *Storm over the Land,* 1942; one volume selection *The Prairie Years and War Years,* 1954.

Rootabaga Country (juvenile).   1929.

Steichen, The Photographer.   1929.

Early Moon (juvenile).   1930.

Potato Face (juvenile).   1930.

Mary Lincoln, Wife and Widow, with Paul M. Angle.   1932.

Home Front Memo.   1943.

The Photographs of Abraham Lincoln, with Frederick Hill Meserve.   1944.

Lincoln Collector: The Story of Oliver R. Barrett's Great Private Collection.   1949.

Always the Young Strangers (autobiography).   1953; selection, for children, as *Prairie-Town Boy,* 1955.

The Sandburg Range (miscellany).   1957.

Wind Song (juvenile).   1960.

Editor, *American Songbag.*   1927; *New American Songbag,* 1950.

Editor, *A Lincoln and Whitman Miscellany.*   1938.

Screen documentary: *Bomber* 1945.

Bibliography: *Sandburg: A Bibliography* by Thomas S. Shaw, 1948.

Reading List: *Sandburg: A Study in Personality and Background* by Karl W. Detzer, 1941; *Sandburg* by Harry Golden, 1961; *Sandburg* by Richard H. Crowder, 1964; *Sandburg* by Mark Van Doren, 1969 (includes bibliography); *Sandburg: Lincoln of Our Literature* by North Callahan, 1970; *Sandburg, Yes* by W. G. Rogers, 1970; *Sandburg* by Gay Wilson Allen, 1972.

*   *   *

Harriet Monroe's magazine *Poetry* in 1914 gave conspicuous position to Carl Sandburg's early poems. Readers were drawn by his Whitman-like quality, now vigorous and rugged, now gentle and compassionate. His books *Chicago Poems* and *Cornhuskers* set the pace and established him as a leading American poet. His free-verse lines were, at their best, musical and varied. His subject matter was generally quarried from the cities and countryside of the Midwest. His themes were built on concern for the common man, concomitant with his interest in Socialism. Out of the Great Depression came his book *The People, Yes,* consisting of folk sayings cemented together by optimistic prophecies to the effect that the ordinary man would eventually receive his due. Sandburg's last book of poems, *Honey and Salt,* continued to substantiate his thesis that the life of "the family of man" is not all sweet, that it is tempered by the sobering experience of everyday existence and even by tragedy. In this book the old poet, through his reliance on a proliferation of color images unusual in a writer at the end of his career, proved to be as vigorous as a tyro one-third his age.

The People, Yes had been a product of Sandburg's interest in folklore. Two collections of the songs of the people established him as something of an authority: *The American Songbag* and the expanded *New American Songbag.* In fact, for the twenty years preceding World War II Sandburg traveled widely singing these songs to large audiences, accompanying himself on the guitar.

In prose biography Sandburg showed a skillful hand. He wrote of his wife's brother in *Steichen,The Photographer* and of the wife of his life-long hero in *Mary Lincoln, Wife and Widow.* His most famous prose work remains his 6-volume biography of Lincoln. If in this monumental work (without footnotes and index) he occasionally rearranged the chronology and indeed embroidered the facts, he nevertheless produced a rich and sensitive portrait, filled with incident, pointed up with insight, and made brilliant with poetic truth. His *Always the Young Strangers* tells the story of his own growing-up with a remarkable analytical objectivity in an enchanting style as engrossing as a novel.

Remembrance Rock was something else again. Commissioned by Metro-Goldwyn-Mayer to write a "great American novel" later to be made into a scenario for a moving picture, Sandburg turned out a wooden, repetitive piece of fiction, not only very long, but very tiresome. Like *The People, Yes* the book is packed with songs, proverbs, anecdotes, folk customs. Effective in a Depression poem, this subject matter was ill suited to the novel form. In spite of the book's ineptness, however, Sandburg was continuing to show his integrity and generosity, his hatred of bigotry, his consuming love for his native country.

He was popular with children. His *Rootabaga Stories, Rootabaga Pigeons,* and *Potato Face* enjoyed wide readership. The fantasy, inventiveness, humor, and light-heartedness in these stories were similar to many of the traits in his poems, selections from which, indeed, were collected in anthologies intended for children.

Sandburg no doubt will long be remembered for his Lincoln biography and for many of his poems. The reader can recall the alternating robustiousness and pathos of "Chicago," the delicate imagism of "Fog," the loud anger of "To a Contemporary Bunkshooter," the wholesome aspiration of *The People, Yes.* Even though one cannot place him in the very top rank of American poets, it is possible to say that to have read Sandburg is to have been the companion of a deeply rooted and dedicated citizen of the United States and of a conscious craftsman skilled in communicating the basic emotions, especially as felt by the "ordinary" person. It must be emphasized that Sandburg was moved not just by the masses, what he lovingly called "the mob." True, he was sympathetic with his "people" as they struggled toward the stars (one of his early poems chanted, "I am the people, the mob"), but his many poems about individuals showed him to be actively aware of the inescapable fact that every man and woman experiences troubles and ecstasies (e.g., "The Hangman at Home," "Helga," "Ice Handler," "Mag"). Furthermore, though Sandburg is linked with Lindsay and Masters as an Illinois poet, he is seen to be, on careful study, a poet of universals. If his most frequent subjects are the little people of his home state, his themes are nonetheless the concerns of all people everywhere.

—Richard H. Crowder

SASSOON, Siegfried (Lorraine).   English.   Born in Kent, 8 September 1886. Educated at Marlborough Grammar School; Clare College, Cambridge. Served in the Army during World War I: Captain; Military Cross. Married Hester Getty in 1933; one son. Literary Editor, *Daily Herald,* London, 1919; lectured in the United States, 1920. Recipient: Hawthornden Prize, 1928; Black Memorial Prize, 1928; Queen's Gold Medal for Poetry, 1957. D.Litt.: Oxford University, 1965. Honorary Fellow, Clare College, Cambridge, 1953. C.B.E. (Commander, Order of the British Empire), 1951. *Died 1 September 1967.*

PUBLICATIONS

Verse

Poems.   1906.
Sonnets and Verses.   1909.

Sonnets.   1909.
Twelve Sonnets.   1911.
Poems.   1911.
Melodies.   1912.
An Ode for Music.   1912.
The Daffodil Murderer.   1913.
Discoveries.   1915.
Morning-Glory.   1916.
The Redeemer.   1916.
To Any Dead Officer.   1917.
The Old Huntsman and Other Poems.   1917.
Four Poems.   1918.
Counter-Attack and Other Poems.   1917.
Picture-Show.   1919.
The War Poems.   1919.
Lines Written in the Reform Club.   1921.
Recreations.   1923.
Lingual Exercises for Advanced Vocabularians.   1925.
Selected Poems.   1925.
Satirical Poems.   1926.
The Heart's Journey.   1927.
Poems.   1931.
The Road to Ruin.   1933.
Vigils.   1934.
Rhymed Ruminations.   1939.
Poems Newly Selected, 1916–1935.   1940.
(Poems).   1943.
Collected Poems.   1947.
Common Chords.   1950.
Emblems of Experience.   1951.
The Tasking.   1954.
An Adjustment.   1955.
Sequences.   1956.
Poems, edited by D. Silk.   1958.
Lenten Illuminations, Sight Sufficient.   1958.
The Path to Peace: Selected Poems.   1960.
Collected Poems. 1908–1956.   1961.
An Octave: 8 September 1966.   1966.

Plays

Orpheus in Diloeryum.   1908.
Hyacinth: An Idyll.   1912.
Amyntas: A Mystery.   1912.

Fiction

Something about Myself (story).   1966.

Other

Memoirs of a Fox-Hunting Man.   1928; *Memoirs of an Infantry Officer,* 1930;

> *Sherston's Progress*, 1936; complete version as *The Complete Memoirs of George Sherston*, 1937; selection, as *The Flower Show Match and Other Pieces*, 1941.
> *The Old Century and Seven More Years* (autobiography).   1938.
> *The Weald of Youth* (autobiography).   1942.
> *Siegfried's Journey, 1916–1920* (autobiography).   1945.
> *Meredith*.   1948.
> *Letters to a Critic*, edited by Michael Thorpe.   1976.

> Editor, *Poems*, by Wilfred Owen.   1920.

Bibliography: *A Bibliography of Sassoon* by Geoffrey Keynes, 1962, addenda by D. Farmer, in *Publications of the Bibliographical Society of America 63*, 1969.

Reading List: *Sassoon: A Critical Study* by Michael Thorpe, 1966; *Out of Battle: Poetry of the Great War* by Jon Silkin, 1972; *Sassoon: A Poet's Pilgimage* by Felicitas Corrigan, 1973.

*   *   *

Memorably courageous both as soldier and as pacifist, Siegfried Sassoon is usually associated with the First World War. He began to write before it and continued after it for almost half a century, but the war provoked his fiercest writing: verse of an adrenalin-intensity next to which his other work seems desultory and tame.

Sassoon's early poetry evokes a pastoral dream-world, stocked rather conventionally with Georgian fauna and flora – "vagrom-hearted" boys, the "daffodilly," and the "windy lea." *Memoirs of a Fox-Hunting Man* lovingly documents in prose the actual world he knew: at first, a leisured country-life existence of spacious assurances, seasonal pleasures, and decorous ritual that now seems almost equally in the realm of idyll. Then, after 1914, the narrative draws Sassoon out from the tranquillities of "Rooks ... cawing in the vicarage elms" to the "continuous rumble and grumble of bombardment." The eye that pleasurably dawdled over rural vistas becomes focussed on mechanised slaughter.

In response, his poetry completely alters. "My trench-sketches," he said, "were like rockets, sent up to illuminate the darkness." The image is appropriate: like the rockets, these war-verses are fuelled with acrid energy; like them, in a burst of heat, they shed light on the appalling. These "harsh, peremptory, and colloquial stanzas with a knock-out blow in the last line" are anti-war propaganda. They were, Sassoon explained, "deliberately written to disturb complacency," and they attempt to do this in two ways: by reporting the atrocities of the Western Front, and by indicting those responsible for them. With unflinching realism, Sassoon depicts the hideous charnel mess into which the men are trapped, the "Golgotha" where they display courage and *camaraderie* but also fear and hysteria, unglamorous symptoms of the healthy urge to keep alive. Pity predominates in this graphic reportage: bitterness, in the contemptuous vignettes of those held to blame – "scarlet Majors," "fierce-browed prelates," "Yellow-Pressmen," and the "smug-faced crowds" with their jingoistic stridency. Two civilian categories arouse particular resentment: an older generation of fathers and "arm-chair" generals, safely bellicose, and women, dupes and feeders of the martial-glory myth. Hurriedly and rather roughly shaped, these verses are not made for detailed contemplation but convey with efficient rapidity a scalding-hot indignation at the war.

Sassoon's later poetry never regained this power. Urbane, sometimes felicitously phrased occasional verse, it progresses rather unexcitingly in traditional directions. There are love-poems blurred over with a faintly melancholy reticence; some gentle satires; ambulating meditations upon past and present; versified responses to art-galleries, concerts, monuments. In the main, an elegiac note prevails. Ghosts and memories drift wanly in and out of stanzas. Wistful for past splendours and stabilities, the verses pause fondly to contemplate painted

Victorian skies where "Large clouds, like safe investments, loitered by," or an old lady's "black-lace-mittened hands" crumbling rusks to feed the peacocks. These poems are the product and a record of that genteel cultural tradition into which the First World War so shatteringly broke: obliterating, Sassoon felt, many old decencies, and inspiring, he displayed, some impressive new ones.

—Peter Kemp

SAVAGE, Richard. English. Born in England c. 1697; claimed to be the illegitimate son of the fourth Earl Rivers and Lady Macclesfield. Very little is known for certain about his early life: probably of humble parentage, and probably had little education; chose literature for a livelihood c. 1715; acted at Drury Lane, 1718, 1723; killed a gentleman in a tavern brawl, and sentenced to die, 1727, obtained royal pardon, 1728; published his accounts of his birth: given a pension by his alleged mother's nephew, Lord Tyrconnel, on condition he abstain from further attacks on her, 1728–34; applied unsuccessfully for post of Poet Laureate, 1730; given a pension by Queen Caroline, 1732–37; subsequently lived in great poverty; died in debtor's prison in Bristol. *Died 1 August 1743.*

PUBLICATIONS

Collections

Works. 2 vols., 1775.
Poetical Works, edited by Clarence Tracy. 1962.

Verse

The Convocation; or, A Battle of Pamphlets. 1717.
A Poem Sacred to the Glorious Memory of Our Late King George. 1727.
The Bastard. 1728.
Nature in Perfections; or, The Mother Unveiled. 1728.
The Wanderer: A Vision. 1729.
Verses Occasioned by the Viscountess Tyrconnel's Recovery at Bath. 1730.
An Epistle to Sir Robert Walpole. 1732.
A Collection of Pieces in Verse and Prose, on the Occasion of The Dunciad. 1732.
The Volunteer Laureat: A Poem to Her Majesty on Her Birthday. 1732 (similar verses annually until 1738).
On the Departure of the Prince and Princess of Orange. 1734.
The Progress of a Divine: A Satire. 1735.
A Poem on the Birthday of the Prince of Wales. 1735; as *Of Public Spirit in Regard to Public Works: An Epistle,* 1737.
A Poem Sacred to the Memory of Her Majesty. 1738.
London and Bristol Compared: A Satire. 1744.
Various Poems: The Wanderer, The Triumph of Mirth and Health, The Bastard. 1761.

855

Plays

>   *Love in a Veil,* from a play by Calderón (produced 1718).   1719.
>   *The Tragedy of Sir Thomas Overbury* (produced 1723).   1724.

Other

>   *An Author to Be Let.*   1729.

>   Editor, *Miscellaneous Poems and Translations by Several Hands.*   1726.

Bibliography: "Some Uncollected Authors: Savage" by Clarence Tracy, in *Book Collector,* 1963.

Reading List: *The Artificial Bastard: A Biography of Savage* by Clarence Tracy, 1953.

*   *   *

Richard Savage's earliest poems, written about 1715 but never published in his lifetime, express Jacobite sympathies; but a depressingly large proportion of his later poems consists of panegyrics upon the illustrious house of Hanover. Such works as the 1727 elegy on George I, or the series of annual "Volunteer-Laureat" addresses on Queen Caroline's birthday, or the 1732 epistle addressed to Walpole, or the *Poem on the Birth-day of the Prince of Wales* (later republished as *Of Public Spirit in Regard to Public Works*) all express in bombastic terms unimpeachably Whig principles. These, and others in similar vein, constitute Savage's appeal for patronage either from the Government or from the Prince's opposition court; and, though Savage never obtained that patronage which he thought he deserved, he was favoured with the royal pardon in 1728 when under sentence of death for murder.

The trial and pardon added to the notoriety that Savage had already gained by repeatedly pressing his claims to be the son of the Countess of Macclesfield by her adultery with the Earl Rivers − a claim which the Countess vehemently denied − and ensured the immediate popularity of *The Bastard*. This short piece, invigorated by Savage's anger, self-pity, and extravagant egotism, remains his best poem because it is the only one in which his feelings seem to be fully engaged. His longest and most ambitious work is *The Wanderer: A Vision* in five cantos where, influenced by his friend Thomson's early poems on the Seasons, but, unlike Thomson, writing in heroic couplets, he makes a great excursion through the grandest works of Nature and offers moral reflections upon them. The most interesting feature of this would-be sublime poem is Savage's romantic conception of the poet as prophetic bard. Also in 1729, but in a very different vein is the prose pamphlet *An Author to Be Lett* "by Iscariot Hackney." Savage had provided Pope with many facts and scurrilous inventions for the notes to *The Dunciad Variorum*, and this little squib is so lively a supplement to Pope's attacks on the dunces that one wishes Savage had written more prose satire.

Though Savage never found a patron − or a mother − he had the friendship of Pope and Thomson, and especially of Johnson who had walked about London with him hungry, penniless, and homeless, and whose great *Life of Savage* (1744) rather too indulgently represents its subject as a self-destructive genius.

—A. J. Sambrook

SCHWARTZ, Delmore. American. Born in Brooklyn, New York, 8 December 1913. Educated at the University of Wisconsin, Madison, 1931; New York University (Editor, *Mosaic* magazine), 1933–35, B.A. in philosophy 1935; Harvard University, Cambridge, Massachusetts, 1935–37. Married 1) Gertrude Buckman (divorced); 2) Elizabeth Pollet in 1949. Briggs-Copeland Instructor in English Composition, 1940, Instructor in English, 1941–45, and Assistant Professor of English, 1946–47, Harvard University. Fellow, Kenyon School of English, Gambier, Ohio, Summer 1950; Visiting Professor at New York University, Indiana School of Letters, Bloomington, Princeton University, New Jersey, and University of Chicago. Editor, 1943–47, and Associate Editor, 1947–55, *Partisan Review*, New Brunswick, New Jersey; associated with *Perspectives* magazine, New York, 1952–53; Literary Consultant, New Directions, publishers, New York, 1952–53; Poetry Editor and Film Critic, *New Republic* magazine, Washington, D.C., 1955–57. Recipient: Guggenheim Fellowship, 1940; National Institute of Arts and Letters grant, 1953; Bollingen Prize, 1960; Shelley Memorial Award, 1960. *Died 11 July 1966.*

PUBLICATIONS

Collections

    Selected Essays, edited by Donald A. Dike and David H. Zucker. 1970.
    What Is to Be Given: Selected Poems, edited by Douglas Dunn. 1976.

Verse

    In Dreams Begin Responsibilities (includes short story and play). 1938.
    Genesis: Book One (includes prose). 1943.
    Vaudeville for a Princess and Other Poems (includes prose). 1950.
    Summer Knowledge: New and Selected Poems 1938–1958. 1959.

Play

    Shenandoah; or, The Naming of the Child. 1941.

Fiction

    The World Is a Wedding and Other Stories. 1949.
    Successful Love and Other Stories. 1961.

Other

    Editor, *Syracuse Poems 1964.* 1965.

    Translator, *A Season in Hell* (bilingual edition), by Arthur Rimbaud. 1939.

Bibliography: in *Selected Essays,* 1970.

Reading List: *Schwartz* by Richard McDougall, 1974; *Schwartz: The Life of an American Poet* by James Atlas, 1977.

*   *   *

It is difficult, reading Delmore Schwartz, to disentangle the poetry from the legend. The darling of the group of American intellectuals associated with the *Partisan Review* in the 1930's and 1940's – to which he contributed as poet, critic, and short story writer, and eventually became co-editor – Schwartz had a career worthy of the last *poète maudit*. A precociously brilliant first book, *In Dreams Begin Responsibilities*, was followed by a tragic decline into alcohol, insanity, and an early death, alone, in a seedy Manhattan hotel. Posthumously, Schwartz has undergone a literary "canonisation" in one of the most heartbreaking sequences of John Berryman's *Dream Songs* and as the eponymous "hero" of Saul Bellow's *Humboldt's Gift*. The life is forbiddingly close to stereotyped, "romantic" conceptions of "the Poet."

And Schwartz almost certainly saw himself in something like this role. The titles alone of some of his best known poems – "Do Others Speak of Me Mockingly, Maliciously?," "All of Us Always Turning Away for Solace" – suggest his fundamental view of the poet as one isolated from his tribe, cut off, as in the marvellous "The Heavy Bear Who Goes with Me," from contact even with his own body. The characteristic Schwartzian stance is apparent in his "Sonnet: O City, City": we live

> Where the sliding auto's catastrophe
> Is a gust past the curb, where numb and high
> The office building rises to its tyranny,
> Is our anguished diminution until we die.

In the same poem, however, he longs for an alternative human sympathy, "the self articulate, affectionate and flowing." Between these terms the course of his poetry runs.

It is a poetry that rarely loses touch with political and historical realities: "The Ballad of the Children of the Czar" and the verse play *Shenandoah* poignantly express Schwartz's understanding of his family's experience as Jewish immigrants to the States. There is the larger feeling, in many poems, of human beings *imprisoned* in time, bearing the guilt of generations, and Schwartz probes at his guilts and anxieties in a way that occasionally, as in "Prothalamion," points forward to the "confessional" poetry to be written by his more famous contemporaries Berryman and Lowell. The guardian angels of these poems, figures which haunt Schwartz's imagination and are returned to with obsessive insistence, are the heroic solitaries – Faust, Socrates, "Tiger Christ," "Manic-depressive Lincoln," and, above all, Hamlet.

But there is also in Schwartz, if less insistently, an energetically vibrant language and feeling, a kind of robust dandyism, as in "Far Rockaway":

> The radiant soda of the seashore fashions
> Fun, foam, and freedom. The sea laves
> The shaven sand. And the light sways forward
> On the self-destroying waves.

Douglas Dunn, in his introduction to *What Is to Be Given*, has referred to Schwartz's "sometimes dispiriting ebullience," and it is this that many critics have objected to in the later work. A poem like "Seurat's Sunday Afternoon along the Seine" certainly needs to be read without the expectation of those judicious ironies on which most modern poetry thrives. But, *relaxed into*, the stretch and sweep, the sheer verbal intoxication of the poem, carry persuasive power.

Schwartz is a poet, and a critic, too little read and too little understood. Recent re-publications, however, suggest that his work will survive, along with the best of his generation.

—Neil Corcoran

SCOTT, Duncan Campbell. Canadian. Born in Ottawa, Ontario, 2 August 1862. Educated at Smiths Falls High School, Ontario, 1874–75; Wesleyan College, Stanstead, Quebec, 1877–79. Married 1) Belle Warner Botsford in 1894 (died, 1929), one daughter; 2) Desiree Elise Aylen in 1931. Joined Department of Indian Affairs, Ottawa, 1879: Clerk Third Class, 1879–93; Chief Clerk, 1893–96; Secretary of the Department, 1896–1909; Superintendent of Indian Education, 1909–23; Deputy Superintendent General, 1923 until his retirement, 1932. Columnist, *Toronto Globe*, 1892–93; President, Ottawa Drama League; President, Canadian Authors Association, 1931–33. Recipient: Lorne Pierce Medal, 1927. D.Litt.: University of Toronto, 1922; LL.D.: Queen's University, Kingston, Ontario, 1939. Fellow, 1899, Honorary Secretary, 1911–21, and President, 1921–22, Royal Society of Canada; Fellow, Royal Society of Literature (England). C.M.G. (Companion, Order of St. Michael and St. George), 1934. *Died 19 December 1947.*

PUBLICATIONS

Collections

> *Selected Poems.*   1951.
> *Selected Stories,* edited by Glenn Clever.   1972.

Verse

> *The Magic House and Other Poems.*   1893.
> *Labor and the Angel.*   1898.
> *New World Lyrics and Ballads.*   1905.
> *Via Borealis.*   1906.
> *Lines in Memory of Edmund Morris.*   1915.
> *Lundy's Lane and Other Poems.*   1916.
> *To the Canadian Mothers, and Three Other Poems.*   1917.
> *Beauty and Life.*   1921.
> *Byron on Wordsworth, Being Undiscovered Stanzas of Don Juan.*   1924 (?).
> *The Poems.*   1926.
> *The Green Cloister: Later Poems.*   1935.

Plays

> *Pierre* (produced 1921).   In *Canadian Plays from Hart House Theatre 1,* edited by Vincent Massey, 1926.

Prologue (produced 1923).   In *The Poems*, 1926.
Joy! Joy! Joy! (produced 1927).

Fiction (stories)

In the Village of Viger.   1896.
The Witching of Elspie.   1923.

Other

John Graves Simcoe (biography).   1905.
Notes on the Meeting Place of the First Parliament of Upper Canada and the Early Buildings at Niagara.   1913.
The Administration of Indian Affairs in Canada.   1931.
Walter J. Phillips, R.C.A. (biography).   1947.
The Circle of Affection and Other Pieces in Prose and Verse.   1947.
Some Letters, edited by Arthur S. Bourinot.   1959; *More Letters*, 1960.

Editor, *The Poems of Archibald Lampman.*   1900; selection, 1947.
Editor, with Pelham Edgar, *The Makers of Canada.*   20 vols., 1903–08.
Editor, *The People of the Plains*, by Amelia Anne Paget.   1909.
Editor, *Lyrics of Earth: Sonnets and Ballads*, by Archibald Lampman.   1925.

Reading List: *Ten Canadian Poets* by Desmond Pacey, 1958; essay by A. J. M. Smith, in *Our Living Tradition* edited by R. McDougall, 1959.

*   *   *

Duncan Campbell Scott had a long poetic career; his first book, *The Magic House*, appeared in 1893, and his last, *The Circle of Affection*, appeared in the year of his death, 1947. He also had experiences unusual among poets in his day, for in 1879 he became a clerk in the Indian Branch in Ottawa, and continued in the service until 1932. In his work Scott had to undertake long, arduous journeys into the northern wilderness where he came into close contact with Indians, Métis, loggers, and trappers; he treasured these experiences, and the tales he heard on his travels, for use in his poetry.

Scott was not only a poet. He published two volumes of short stories, *In the Village of Viger* and *The Witching of Elspie*, both of them set in the pietist and superstition-ridden rural Quebec of the late nineteenth century. Some of these stories are humorous, others are eerie, and others have a grim starkness that reminds one of some of Scott's own poems about Indian life. His play *Pierre* was also set among French Canadians.

It is as a poet, however, that Scott is most interesting. His first volume, *The Magic House*, consisted mainly of descriptive lyrics, conventional in form and sentiment. But in his second book, *Labor and the Angel*, he displayed a real distinctiveness, not only in the romantic narrative poem "The Piper of Arll," but also in the first of his poems about the northland wilderness and the harsh life of the nomad Indian hunters. His experiences in the north continued to haunt him, and almost every later volume down to *The Green Cloister* in 1935 contained Indian poems, of which "The Onondaga Madonna," "At Gull Lake, 1810," and "The Forsaken," a poignant narrative of an old woman left to die by her tribe, are among the best-known of Canadian poems.

Scott in fact wrote two very different kinds of poem. There were the conventional and rather Tennysonian lyrics, concerned often with wild nature, sonorous and mood-provoked but essentially unexperimental, and there were the poems of the northern wilderness and of Indian life in which he strived for a stark and vivid authenticity and achieved it by breaking away from Victorian conventions to use irregular verse forms, hard images, and often harsh words. In these northern poems Scott, more than any of his contemporaries, anticipated the poets of the 1930's who took Canadian poetry out of its colonial past and into modern times.

—George Woodcock

SCOTT, F(rancis) R(eginald).   Canadian.   Born in Quebec City, 1 August 1899. Educated at Quebec High School; Bishop's College, Lennoxville, Quebec, B.A. 1919; Magdalen College, Oxford (Rhodes Scholar), 1920–23, B.A. 1922, B.Litt. 1923; McGill University, Montreal, B.C.L. 1927; called to the Quebec Bar, 1927; Queen's Counsel, Quebec, 1961. Married Marian Mildred Dale in 1928; one son. Teacher, Quebec High School, 1919, Bishop's College School, Lennoxville, 1920, and Lower Canada College, Montreal, 1923; Assistant Professor of Federal and Constitutional Law, 1928–34, Professor of Civil Law, 1934–54, Macdonald Professor of Law, 1955–67, Dean of the Faculty of Law, 1961–64, and Visiting Professor in the French Canada Studies Programme, 1967–69, McGill University. Visiting Professor, University of Toronto Law School, 1953–54, Michigan State University, East Lansing, 1957, and Dalhousie University, Halifax, Nova Scotia, 1969–71. Co-Founding Editor, with A. J. M. Smith, *McGill Fortnightly Review*, Montreal, 1925–27; Editor, *Canada Mercury*, 1928, *Canada Forum*, 1936–39, *Preview*, Montreal, 1942–45, and *Northern Review*, Montreal, 1945–47. President, League for Social Reconstruction, 1935–36; Member, National Council, Penal Association of Canada, 1935–46; Member, National Executive, Canadian Institute of International Affairs, 1935–50; National Chairman, Canadian Cooperative Commonwealth Federation Party, 1942–50; U.N. Technical Assistant, Burma, 1952; Chairman, Legal Research Committee, Canadian Bar Association, 1954–56; Chairman, Canadian Writers Conference, 1955; Civil Liberties Counsel before the Supreme Court of Canada, 1956–64; Member, Royal Commission on Bilingualism and Biculturalism, 1963–71. Recipient: Guggenheim Fellowship, 1940; Royal Society of Canada Lorne Pierce Medal, 1962; Banff Springs Festival Gold Medal, 1958; Quebec Government Prize, 1964; Canada Council Molson Award, 1965, and grant, 1974. LL.D.: Dalhousie University, 1958; University of Manitoba, Winnipeg, 1961; Queen's University, Kingston, Ontario, 1964; University of British Columbia, Vancouver, 1965; University of Montreal, 1966; Osgoode Hall Law School, Downsview, Ontario, 1966; McGill University, 1967; LL.B.: University of Saskatchewan, Saskatoon, 1965. Fellow, Royal Society of Canada, 1947. Honorary Member, American Academy of Arts and Sciences, 1967. C.C. (Companion, Order of Canada), 1967. Lives in Montreal.

PUBLICATIONS

Verse

Overture.   1945.
Events and Signals.   1954.

The Eye of the Needle: Satires, Sorties, Sundries.   1957.
Signature.   1964.
Selected Poems.   1966.
Trouvailles: Poems from Prose.   1967.
The Dance Is One.   1973.

Other

Canada Today: A Study of Her National Interests and National Policy.   1938.
Make This Your Canada: A Review of C. C. F. History and Policy, with David
   Lewis.   1943.
*Canada after the War: Attitudes of Political, Social, and Economic Policies in Post-War
   Canada,* with Alexander Brady.   1944.
Cooperation for What? United States and Britain's Commonwealth.   1944.
The World's Civil Service.   1954.
Evolving Canadian Federalism.   1958.
The Canadian Constitution and Human Rights (radio talks).   1959.
Civil Liberties and Canadian Federalism.   1959.
Dialogue sur la Traduction, with Anne Hébert.   1970.
Essays on the Constitution.   1977.

Editor, with A. J. M. Smith, *New Provinces: Poems of Several Authors.*   1936.
Editor, with A. J. M. Smith, *The Blasted Pine: An Anthology of Satire, Invective and
   Disrespectful Verse, Chiefly by Canadian Writers.*   1957; revised edition, 1967.
Editor, with Michael Oliver, *Quebec States Her Case: Speeches and Articles from
   Quebec in the Years of Unrest.*   1964.

Translator, *St. Denys Garneau and Anne Hébert.*   1961.
Translator, *Poems of French Canada.*   1976.

Reading List: *Ten Canadian Poets* by Desmond Pacey, 1958; *The McGill Movement: A. J. M. Smith, Scott, and Leo Kennedy* edited by Peter Stevens, 1969; "The Road Back to Eden: The Poetry of Scott," in *Queen's Quarterly,* Autumn 1972.

*   *   *

The humanistic irony which informs F. R. Scott's finest work has characterized his multiple career since the 1930's: political theorist, academic lawyer, satirist, translator, editor and, above all, socially sensitive poet. His most mature poetry is best seen in his *Selected Poems* and its sequel, *The Dance Is One.* Scott's early verse was influenced by imagism and marked by a strong formal sense, both of which served him well in tracing the harsh environment of northern Quebec and Canada. His precise, occasionally brittle diction matched the dominant imagery of stone, water, snow, and ice. Many of his descriptions of man's place in this "inarticulate, arctic" landscape have come to be regarded as major statements in the transformation of colonial romanticism into modernism in Canadian poetry. Later his rhythms became looser and his verse more free, but his fascination with the relation of language and meaning is still reflected in the concreteness and careful rhetoric of even his most delicate lyrics.

Language as playful dance is central to Scott's aesthetic, just as satire is an essential part of his humanism. Here his political and social vision finds its best expression in verse, and his popular reputation is largely founded on his acerbic humour. His targets are usually institutional and structural dangers, follies, and quirks, rather than individual foibles, for he has been a socialist nearly as long as he has written poetry. *The Eye of the Needle* and *Trouvailles* (a collection of found poems) gather his most familiar observations on Canadian politics, history, literature, class structure, bi-culturalism, and social stupidities – the subjects of his co-edited anthology of "satire, invective and disrespectful verse."

That Scott should have received a Governor-General's Award, not for his poetry but for the retrospective collection *Essays on the Constitution*, is itself ironic, notwithstanding his substantial contributions to Canadian law, legal education, and constitutional theory. The essays incorporate forty years' writing on civil liberties, federalism (both topics of a separate book), human rights, labour relations, public policy, and sovereignty – issues with which he had been actively involved since the beginning of his career as a professor of law. Scott is well-known for his participation in two major civil rights cases in Quebec during the 1950's, and for his role in the founding of the Co-operative Commonwealth Federation (C.C.F., now N.D.P.), the first successful democratic socialist party in Canada. Less known are his pamphlets and books on law and politics, both polemical and academic. As national chairman of the C.C.F., he co-authored a lengthy statement on the history and principles of the party, *Make This Your Canada*.

Scott's strong beliefs about the bilingual nature of Canadian federation are mirrored in his translations of Québécois poetry into English. His *Dialogue sur la Traduction* records progressively his various translations of Anne Hébert's "Tombeau des Rois," and his correspondence with her. His translated *Poems of French Canada* is evidence of his conviction that "translation is not only an art in itself, it is also an essential ingredient in Canada's political entity."

—Bruce Nesbitt

SCOTT, John. English. Born in Bermondsey, London, 9 January 1730; moved with his family to Amwell, Hertfordshire, 1740, and lived there for the reest of his life. Privately educated. Married 1) Sarah Frogley in 1767 (died, 1768); 2) Mary de Horne in 1770, one daughter. Wrote verse for *The Gentleman's Magazine*, London, 1753–58; visited London occasionally from 1760: attended Mrs. Montagu's parties; met Samuel Johnson, 1766, and entertained him at Amwell. *Died 12 December 1783*.

PUBLICATIONS

Collections

   The Works of the English Poets 17, edited by Alexander Chalmers.   1810.

Verse

   Four Elegies, Descriptive and Moral.   1760.
   Elegy Written at Amwell.   1769.
   Amwell: A Descriptive Poem.   1776.
   Moral Eclogues.   1778.
   Poetical Works.   1782.

Other

> The Constitution Defended and the Pensioner Exposed, in Remarks on the False
>   Alarm. 1770.
> A Digest of the Present Act for Amendment of the Highways. 1773.
> Observations on the Present State of the Parochial and Vagrant Poor. 1773.
> Remarks on the Patriot. 1775.
> Digests of the General Highway and Turnpike Laws. 1778.
> A Letter to the Critical Reviewers. 1782.
> Critical Essays on Some of the Poems of Several English Poets. 1785.

Bibliography: "Some Uncollected Authors: Scott" by N. Russell, in Book Collector, 1965.

Reading List: Scott of Amwell by Lawrence D. Stewart, 1956.

*   *   *

John Scott's greatest impact on his time was made with his essays on social problems, politics, and literature, and with his poetry on a variety of subjects, especially nature. In his essay on the poor, Scott spoke out for the laboring classes, directing attention to the brutal harshness of the vagrancy laws and the vicious practice of farming out work houses. He blamed the misery of the village poor upon grasping landowners who had enclosed the commons. But he provided no solutions to the problems that he discussed.

Despite his friendship with Johnson and despite Quaker objections to participation in secular politics, Scott was moved to answer Johnson's False Alarm (1770), a defence of the government's harsh views of John Wilkes, in The Constitution Defended (1770). Characteristically, Scott objected to Johnson's Toryism, the doctrines of divine hereditary right and passive obedience to the will of kings. Looking back to the Revolution like a genuine Whig, Scott insisted upon limiting the prerogatives of monarchy, protecting and extending individual rights in a system of representative government with the people as the supreme authority, and regarding Wilkes as a popular champion of libertarian principles. These liberal and Whiggish ideas he had expressed a few years before in a "Sonnet, on Arbitrary Government" and verses addressed to the egalitarian Catherine Macaulay. Scott also wrote against Johnson in Remarks on the Patriot (1775).

In his poems, Scott often wrote about personal matters, although maintaining an outer conventional form that rendered an impression of classical simplicity. For example, his intensely personal distaste for war is seen in the oft-reprinted "Ode XIII (I hate that drum's discordant sound)" directed against the recruitment of soldiers. Scott also wrote about exotic places — Mexico, China, Arabia, India, enriching the substance of his poems with details drawn from travel books. However, his greatest achievement is the result of close and continued observation of nature, especially in his "Amoebaean Eclogues," in which he introduced rural imagery not usually noticed in a series of loosely structured, hence "amoebaean" verse essays. His loco-descriptive Amwell he regarded as his magnum opus. In this poem Scott celebrated in 451 blank verse lines the picturesque rural scene around Ware, "the semblance fair of Nature's forms," and explained why through personal, literary, and historical associations the rustic scenery "Gave rapture to [his] soul." Scott's poetry, like the scenery in the poem, is not characterized by the awful sublime. His poetry is in what he himself thought (in Ode XIX) was the unfashionable classic mode and style, and his models were Horace, Virgil, Akenside, and Shenstone.

In his criticism, Scott applied his "criterion of merit," that is, "classical simplicity" (letter to Beattie, 6 June 1783), to nine important seventeenth and eighteenth century poems from Denham's Cooper's Hill to Gray's Elegy. What he meant by this measure, it becomes clear, is lucidity, conciseness, neatness and elegance, and rational consistency, a consistency determined by testing figure and diction against the sentiment intended. For example, in his essay on Pope's *Windsor Forest*, which is typical of his method, he engaged in an analysis of the diction and thought, and noted evidences of mental confusion in the imagery. Though Scott sometimes brings a rash insensitivity to the organic integrity of the creative imagination, his criticism has the virtue of forcing us to read the poems afresh and to reach an understanding and perhaps an appreciation of their subtleties of image, diction, and sense. Independent in his criticism, as in his views of politics and society, Scott courageously judges for himself and often takes issue with Samuel Johnson and prevailing taste.

—Martin Kallich

SCOTT, Sir Walter. Scottish. Born in Edinburgh, 15 August 1771; spent his childhood in the Border country. Educated at Edinburgh High School, and the University of Edinburgh; studied law as a clerk in his father's law office; admitted to the Faculty of Advocates, 1792. Married Charlotte Charpentier in 1797 (died, 1826); four children. Writer from 1796; Sheriff-Depute of Selkirkshire, 1799–1832; Clerk of the Court of Session, 1806–30; joined his brother and James Ballantyne as a partner in a printing company, Edinburgh, 1804, which went bankrupt in 1826, involving him in the discharge of its debts for the rest of his life; founded the *Quarterly Review*, 1809; built and lived at Abbotsford from 1812. Created a baronet, 1820. *Died 21 September 1832.*

PUBLICATIONS

Collections

> *Poetical Works*, edited by J. G. Lockhart. 12 vols., 1833–34; edited by J. Logie Robertson, 1904.
> *Miscellaneous Prose Works*, edited by J. G. Lockhart. 28 vols., 1834–36; 2 additional vols., 1871.
> *The Letters*, edited by Herbert Grierson. 12 vols., 1932–37.
> *Short Stories.* 1934.
> *Selected Poems*, edited by Thomas Crawford. 1972.

Verse

> *The Chase, and William and Helen: Two Ballads from the German of Gottfried Augustus Bürger.* 1796.
> *The Eve of Saint John: A Border Ballad.* 1800.
> *The Lay of the Last Minstrel.* 1805.
> *Ballads and Lyrical Pieces.* 1806.
> *Marmion: A Tale of Flodden Field.* 1808.
> *The Lady of the Lake.* 1810.
> *The Vision of Don Roderick.* 1811.
> *Rokeby.* 1813.
> *The Bridal of Triermain: or, The Vale of St. John, in Three Cantos.* 1813.
> *The Lord of the Isles.* 1815.

865

The Field of Waterloo. 1815.
The Ettrick Garland, Being Two Excellent New Songs, with James Hogg. 1815.
Harold the Dauntless. 1817.
New Love-Poems, edited by Davidson Cook. 1932.

Plays

Goetz of Berlichingen, with The Iron Hand, by Goethe. 1799.
Guy Mannering; or, The Gipsy's Prophecy, with Daniel Terry, music by Henry Bishop and others, from the novel by Scott (produced 1816). 1816.
Halidon Hill: A Dramatic Sketch from Scottish History. 1822.
MacDuff's Cross, in *A Collection of Poems*, edited by Joanna Baillie. 1823.
The House of Aspen (produced 1829). In *Poetical Works*, 1830.
Auchindrane; or, The Ayrshire Tragedy (produced 1830). In *The Doom of Devorgoil; Auchindrane*, 1830.
The Doom of Devorgoil: A Melo-Drama; Auchindrane; or, The Ayrshire Tragedy. 1830.

Fiction

Waverley; or, 'Tis Sixty Years Since. 1814.
Guy Mannering; or, The Astrologer. 1815.
The Antiquary. 1816.
The Black Dwarf, Old Mortality. 1817; *Old Mortality* edited by Angus Calder, 1975.
Rob Roy. 1817.
The Heart of Mid-Lothian. 1818.
The Bride of Lammermoor: A Legend of Montrose. 1819.
Ivanhoe: A Romance. 1819.
The Monastery. 1820.
The Abbot; or, The Heir of Avenel. 1820.
Kenilworth: A Romance. 1821; edited by David Daiches, 1966.
The Pirate. 1821.
The Fortunes of Nigel. 1822.
Peveril of the Peak. 1823.
Quentin Durward. 1823; edited by M. W. and G. Thomas, 1966.
St. Ronan's Well. 1823.
Redgauntlet: A Tale of the Eighteenth Century. 1824.
Tales of the Crusaders (The Betrothed, The Talisman). 1825.
Woodstock; or, The Cavalier. 1826.
Chronicles of the Canongate: First Series: The Highland Widow, The Two Drovers, The Surgeon's Daughter. 1827; *Second Series: The Fair Maid of Perth*, 1828.
My Aunt Margaret's Mirror, The Tapestried Chamber, Death of the Laird's Jock, A Scene at Abbotsford. 1829.
Anne of Geierstein; or, The Maiden of the Mist. 1829.
Waverley Novels (Scott's final revision). 48 vols., 1829–33.
Count Robert of Paris, Castle Dangerous. 1832.

Other

Paul's Letters to His Kinsfolk. 1816.
The Visionary. 1819.

Provincial Antiquities of Scotland.   2 vols., 1826.
The Life of Napoleon Buonaparte: Emperor of the French, with a Preliminary View of the French Revolution.   9 vols., 1827.
Tales of a Grandfather, Being Stories Taken from Scottish History.   9 vols., 1827–29.
Miscellaneous Prose Works.   6 vols., 1827.
Religious Discourses by a Layman.   1828.
The History of Scotland.   2 vols., 1829–30.
Letters on Demonology and Witchcraft.   1830.
Tales of a Grandfather, Being Stories Taken from the History of France.   3 vols., 1830.
Letters Addressed to Rev. R. Polwhele, D. Gilbert, F. Douce.   1832.
Letters Between James Ellis and Scott.   1850.
Journal 1825–32, edited by D. Douglas.   2 vols., 1890; edited by W. E. K. Anderson, 1972.
Familiar Letters, edited by D. Douglas.   2 vols., 1894.
The Letters of Scott and Charles Kirkpatrick Sharpe to Robert Chambers, 1821–45.   1903.
The Private Letter-Books edited by W. Partington.   1930.
Sir Walter's Postbag: More Stories and Sidelights from the Collection in the Brotherton Library, edited by W. Partington.   1932.
Some Unpublished Letters from the Collection in the Brotherton Library, edited by J. A. Symington.   1932.
The Correspondence of Scott and Charles Robert Maturin, edited by F. E. Ratchford and W. H. McCarthy.   1937.
Private Letters of the Seventeenth Century, edited by D. Grant.   1948.

Editor, *An Apology for Tales of Terror.*   1799.
Editor, *Minstrelsy of the Scottish Border.*   2 vols., 1802; edited by Alfred Noyes, 1908.
Editor, *Sir Tristrem: A Metrical Romance*, by Thomas of Ercildoune.   1804.
Editor, *Original Memoirs Written During the Great Civil War*, by Sir H. Slingsby and Captain Hodgson.   1804.
Editor, *The Works of John Dryden.*   18 vols., 1808 (*Life of Dryden* published separately, 1808, edited by Bernard Kreissman, 1963).
Editor, *Memoirs of Captain George Carleton.*   1808.
Editor, *Queenhoo-Hall: A Romance, and Ancient Times: A Drama*, by Joseph Strutt.   4 vols., 1808.
Editor, *Memoirs of Robert Cary, Earl of Monmouth, and Fragmenta Regalia*, by Sir Robert Naunton.   1808.
Editor, *A Collection of Scarce and Valuable Tracts.*   13 vols., 1809–15.
Editor, *English Minstrelsy, Being a Collection of Fugitive Poetry.*   2 vols., 1810.
Editor, *The Poetical Works of Anna Seward.*   3 vols., 1810.
Editor, *Memoirs of Count Grammont*, by Anthony Hamilton.   2 vols., 1811.
Editor, *The Castle of Otranto*, by Horace Walpole.   1811.
Editor, *Secret History of the Court of King James the First.*   2 vols., 1811.
Editor, *The Works of Jonathan Swift.*   19 vols., 1814 (*Memoirs of Swift* published separately, 1826).
Editor, *The Letting of Humours Blood in the Head Vaine*, by S. Rowlands.   1814.
Editor, *Memorie of the Somervilles.*   2 vols., 1815.
Editor, *Trivial Poems and Triolets*, by Patrick Carey.   1820.
Editor, *Memorials of the Haliburtons.*   1820.
Editor, *Northern Memoirs Writ in the Year 1658*, by Richard Franck.   1821.
Editor, *Ballantyne's Novelist's Library.*   10 vols., 1821–24 (*Lives of the Novelists* published separately, 2 vols., 1825).
Editor, *Chronological Notes of Scottish Affairs from the Diary of Lord Fountainhall.*   1822.

Editor, *Military Memoirs of the Great Civil War*, by John Gwynne. 1822.
Editor, *Lays of the Lindsays*. 1824.
Editor, *Auld Robin Gray: A Ballad*, by Lady Anne Barnard. 1825.
Editor, with D. Laing, *The Bannatyne Miscellany*. 1827.
Editor, *Memoirs of the Marchioness de la Rochejaquelein*. 1827.
Editor, *Proceedings in the Court-Martial Held upon John, Master of Sinclair, 1708*. 1829.
Editor, *Memorials of George Bannatyne, 1545–1608*. 1829.
Editor, *Trial of Duncan Terig and Alexander Bane Macdonald, 1754*. 1831.
Editor, *Memoirs of the Insurrection in Scotland in 1715*, by John, Master of Sinclair. 1858.

Bibliography: *Bibliography of the Waverley Novels* by G. Worthington, 1930; "A Bibliography of the Poetical Works of Scott 1796–1832" by W. Ruff, in *Transactions of the Edinburgh Bibliographical Society 1*, 1938; *A Bibliography of Scott: A Classified and Annotated List of Books and Articles Relating to His Life and Works 1797–1940* by J. C. Corson, 1943.

Reading List: *Scott as a Critic of Literature* by M. Ball, 1907; *Scott: A New Life* by Herbert Grierson, 1938; *Scott* by Una Pope-Hennessy, 1948; *Scott: His Life and Personality* by H. Pearson, 1954; *Scott* by Ian Jack, 1958; *The Heyday of Scott* by Donald Davie, 1961; *Witchcraft and Demonology in Scott's Fiction* by C. O. Parsons, 1964; *Scott* by T. Crawford, 1965; *Scott's Novels* by F. R. Hart, 1966; *The Wizard of the North: The Life of Scott* by Carola Oman, 1973; *Scott* by Robin Mayhead, 1973.

*   *   *

Walter Scott was born in Edinburgh in 1771. His father, who is affectionately satirized as Saunders Fairford, the "good old-fashioned man of method" in *Redgauntlet*, was a respected solicitor. His mother, the daughter of a well-known medical professor at the University, had brains and character, and it is tempting to believe that from her Scott inherited the ability which put him for a time at the very top of the tree. He had his education at the High School of Edinburgh and at Edinburgh University. Of formative importance, however, were the months he spent at his paternal grandfather's Border farm as a small boy recuperating from the illness (probably poliomyelitis) which left him permanently lame. The tales he heard there of old, unhappy, far-off things, and the skirmishes in which his own ancestors had fought, lit in him the love of the Scottish past which was the enduring passion of his life.

As Sheriff of Selkirkshire and a Clerk of the Court of Session, Scott was obliged to divide his time between Edinburgh and his Sherifdom; and it was near Selkirk that he built Abbotsford, the "Conundrum Castle" of a house which he embellished with all manner of historical trophies and curiosities. His two official salaries combined to give him a modest competence. They were not, however, enough to let him live in the style of the wealthier Edinburgh lawyers, the *noblesse de la robe* so important to Scottish society, nor of the landowners of the Border country round Abbotsford. That, literature alone could provide.

The literary task to which he devoted his youth was the collection of the Border ballads. His taste had run that way since early youth; he loved the country through whose remoter parts he rode in the quest for those who could recite or sing to him the old songs he wanted; he had a fantastically retentive memory and above all the endearing faculty of talking to people of all kinds. *The Ministrelsy of the Scottish Border*, inspired by the example of Percy's *Reliques*, is not, by modern standards, scholarly. There are valuable discursive notes, but modern imitations are accorded a place alongside genuine ballads, and Scott was not interested in variant readings, nor above improving or adding a verse or two. Nonetheless

The Minstrelsy confirmed Scott's bent towards the historic past, and it established his reputation as a rising man.

One poem, originally intended for the *Ministrelsy*, grew under Scott's hand into his first major independent work. *The Lay of the Last Minstrel* is a narrative poem of magic and border chivalry which, although imperfect in construction and seldom rising to real poetry, exactly struck the growing taste for the mediaeval and the supernatural. The poem's successors *Marmion* and *The Lady of the Lake* were also instantly successful; *Rokeby, The Lord of the Isles*, and *Harold the Dauntless* were less so.

Although the range of Scott's poetry is narrow, it has considerable merits. It is muscular, manly verse; its galloping rhythms suit his subjects, and it passes the first test of narrative verse that it should tell the story well. The narrative poetry reaches its heights in moments of action:

> The stubborn spearmen still made good,
> Their dark, impenetrable wood,
> Each stepping where his comrade stood,
> The instant that he fell

or in the elegiac sadness:

> Of the stern strife, and carnage drear,
> Of Flodden's fatal field,
> Where shiver'd was fair Scotland's spear,
> And broken was her shield.

Scott's best-known poems, however, are the songs interspersed with the narrative in both poems and novels. Thousands who have never read Scott are familiar with Schubert's settings of "Ave Maria" and the other lyrics from *The Lady of the Lake*.

In July 1814 a three-volume novel entitled *Waverley* was published anonymously in Edinburgh. Within five weeks it had sold out, and by the following January it was into its fifth edition. If Scott's real motive had been to protect his reputation as a poet should the novel fail, he had no need to keep up the mystery; but speculation about the unknown author amused him, and he did not acknowledge his authorship of the Waverley novels, which were published at the rate of two a year, until twelve years later.

Scott's reputation has suffered from judgements based on the mass of his work rather than the best of it. At his best – in *The Antiquary, Rob Roy, Old Mortality, The Heart of Mid-Lothian, The Bride of Lammermoor*, and *Redgauntlet* (some would add *Waverley, Guy Mannering* and *The Fair Maid of Perth*) – he was writing of a country whose history and people he knew intimately. *Redgauntlet* begins in the Edinburgh of his youth; the trial of Effie Deans is set in a court-room he knew well; Scott's grandmother remembered being carried as a child to a covenanters' field-preaching, and Scott himself had talked with a man who had been "out" with the Jacobites in 1715 and 1745. The Scottish novels are Scott's real achievement. They inspired writers as diverse as Hugo, George Eliot, Tolstoy, and James Fenimore Cooper. In a sense, they created Scotland as it is known today. They introduced to the world a new form of fiction, the historical novel.

The great historical characters – James VI, Cromwell, Mary and Elizabeth, Prince Charlie, Rob Roy – are seldom central to the novels in which they appear, for Scott's technique is to follow the fortunes of an ordinary man caught up in great events, but they are striking portraits of breathing, fallible human beings. "Sir Walter not only invented the historical novel," says Trevelyan, "but he enlarged the scope and revolutionized the study of history itself." After reading the Waverley novels men could no longer content themselves with broad generalizations about the past; Scott had taught them that it was peopled by real men and women.

As a creator of character his range is enormous. He is the first novelist in English to bring the lower orders of society to life on the page, not as figures of fun but as part of humanity. Fairservice, Ochiltree, Mucklebackit, Balderstone and Davie Deans – as well as Bailie Jarvie the merchant, lawyers like Pleydell and Fairford, and small lairds like Dumbiedykes – are both of their age and for all time.

Scott's marvellous command of the Scottish dialect, his eye for the telling detail, and the humorous yet affectionate way in which he allows his characters to reveal themselves in speech, led his contemporaries to compare him with Shakespeare. "Not fit to tie his brogues," was Scott's characteristic disclaimer. In one respect, however, he is Shakespeare's superior. His common people – his servants and gardeners and beggars – are better. To Shakespeare they are seen *de haut en bas*. There is no similar condescension in Scott.

The subtleties of Jane Austen, whom he greatly admired, were not within Scott's range. As he said in his *Journal*, his was "the Big Bow-wow strain" of writing, and he prided himself on his "hurried frankness of composition." As a story-teller, he is at his best over the shorter distance of "Wandering Willie's Tale" in *Redgauntlet* or of great scenes like the trials of McIvor and Cuddie Headrigg, the appeal of Jeanie Deans to Queen Caroline, or the fight in the Clachan of Aberfoyle.

Again and again he returns to the conflict between old ways and new. By temperament and by upbringing Scott was both a romantic and a realist. In the novels he thrills to the Jacobite past; but he settles ultimately for the age of reason, for Hume and Adam Smith rather than Rob Roy and Charles Edward Stuart. The tension of opposites characteristic of eighteenth-century Scotland remains his theme in the novels set further back in time or further off in place: Cavaliers and Roundheads in *Woodstock*, Saxons and Normans in *Ivanhoe*, Royalists and Covenanters in *Old Mortality*. The truth, for Scott, habitually lies somewhere between the extremes. He is one of the sanest of great writers.

"The greatest figure he ever drew is in the *Journal*," wrote John Buchan, "and it is the man Walter Scott." In 1825, when Scott began to keep a journal, his reputation was at its height. A few months later the slump of 1826 ruined his printer and publisher and, in those days before limited liability, Scott himself. Legally he could have declared himself bankrupt, but he would not. "My own right hand shall do it," he said, and he set himself to work, mornings and evenings, week days and Sundays, term time and holidays, to pay off the joint debt of £126,000. Thanks mainly to the collected editions of his work to which he contributed notes, the debt was finally paid off, but Scott himself, hastened to an early grave by worry and overwork, did not live to see it. Carlyle's famous sentence was fully earned: "No sounder piece of British manhood was put together in that eighteenth century of Time."

—W. E. K. Anderson

SCOTT, William Bell. Scottish. Born in Edinburgh, 12 September 1811. Educated at Edinburgh High School; studied art at the Trustees' Academy, Edinburgh. Married Letitia Margery Norquoy. Worked with his father in his business as an engraver, Edinburgh; settled in London, 1837, and supported himself as a painter: exhibited at the British Institution, 1838, Norfolk Street Gallery, 1840, and the Royal Academy, 1842–69; a friend of Rossetti and Swinburne; master in the government school of design in Newcastle-upon-Tyne, 1843–64; executed numerous paintings for Wallington Hall, Northumberland, 1855, 1863; returned to London, 1864; examiner in art schools, 1864–85; divided his time between London and Ayrshire from 1870. *Died 22 November 1890.*

870

PUBLICATIONS

Verse

Hades; or, The Transit, and The Progress of Mind. 1838.
The Year of the World: A Philosophical Poem. 1846.
Poems. 1854.
Poems: Ballads, Studies from Nature, Sonnets. 1875.
A Poet's Harvest Home, Being One Hundred Short Poems. 1882; augmented edition,
    1893.

Other

Memoir of David Scott. 1850.
Half-Hour Lectures on the Fine and Ornamental Arts. 1861; revised edition, 1867.
Albert Dürer: His Life and Works. 1869.
The Little Masters (biographies). 1879.
Autobiographical Notes, edited by W. Minto. 2 vols., 1892.

Editor, *Poetical Works of Keats.* 1873.
Editor, *Poetical Works of L. E. Landon.* 1873.
Editor, *Poetical Works of Coleridge.* 1874.
Editor, *Poetical Works of Shelley.* 1874.

Reading List: *English Poetry in the Later Nineteenth Century* by B. I. Evans, 1933; *A Pre-
Raphaelite Circle* by Raleigh Trevelyan, 1978.

*   *   *

Called "the carping Duns Scotus" by D. G. Rossetti, William Bell Scott returned in kind
with posthumous *Autobiographical Notes* which are less than charitable to the eccentricities
of Dante Gabriel and others of the Pre-Raphaelite Brotherhood with whom Scott was
associated, claiming for himself the role of patriarch. As editor of Shakespeare, Coleridge,
Scott, and Keats (all echoed in his lesser verse), as writer of art history and philosophical
poetry in the Shelley style, his work is mediocre, but contact with the Pre-Raphaelites
brought out his gift for romantic medievalism and ballad form.

Rossetti struck up a literary acquaintance with Scott, after reading "like a vulture" *The
Year of the World* in 1846. Rossetti's genius contrasts strangely with the contentious and
opinionated Scott, who always in his own eyes retained the role of master, while in fact being
on the periphery of the movement which Rossetti led. Nevertheless, Scott provided stimulus
for at least one picture-poem by Rossetti, "Jenny," and for Rossetti's choosing the theme of a
fallen woman in "Rosabel" (later named "Maryanne"). On this fact of Victorian morality
Scott was allowed certain authority. Among his female acquaintance, three women are
noteworthy: Alice Boyd of Penkill, companion until Scott's death; Christina Rossetti, with
whom he was supposed to have had an unhappy love-affair; and Pauline Trevelyan of
Wallington in Northumberland (where some of his finest paintings were executed), catalyst
of the Pre-Raphaelite circle there and protector-muse to Scott and the young Swinburne.

Poems of 1854 sees stirrings of Scott's interest in medievalism and the ballad, amid
otherwise dreary poeticizing. "Woodstock" is an example of competent handling of ballad
form, and the theme of Fair Rosamund is a favourite Pre-Raphaelite subject. He searched
Northumbrian history with poems on Bede and Saints Cuthbert and Margaret, but the verse

is blank indeed. This volume was mistakenly criticised by Carlyle as poems "of a Printer" who had done better to stick to type.

Poems of 1875 shows more confidence, indeed typically pompous self-congratulation; publishing on the advice of friends, he states, "sweet is praise from the receivers of praise" in his Preface. New material is included, revisions made and the whole sumptuously bound with illustrations by the author and Alma Tadema. "Kriemhild's Tryste" is a superb example of the Victorian ballad, with a haunting refrain and a rich atmosphere. Highlights of Scott's descriptive style appear wrought out of textiles and the decorative arts, as in "The Old Scotch House," where "dragon-flies flicker across the sheen,/Where the yellow flag-leaves bend." There are surprises; in "To the Sphinx," for instance (a symbol dear to later poets of the 1890's), the tragedy of Antony and Cleopatra is imaged in a compact and evocative two lines – "The winged seeds of autumn died amidst/The whirling sand-waste." *A Poet's Harvest Home* is autumnal in tone, as befits a poet's last volume, slight poems on decay and death lightened at moments with a proto-Georgian lyricism.

William Bell Scott is a poet only for some (Ruskin expressed disbelief that he could have written verse at all, but dislike was mutual). As a literary character and man of his times, however, and as a painter of some merit, our interest is repaid.

—B. C. Oliver-Morden

SEDLEY, Sir Charles, Baronet.   English.   Born in Aylesford, Kent, c. 1639; succeeded to the baronetcy, 1656. Educated at Wadham College, Oxford, but left without taking a degree. Married Catherine Savage, daughter of Earl Rivers, 1657; one daughter. Entered the court of Charles II, and became notorious as a fashionable profligate; withdrew from court after the death of Charles. Member of Parliament for New Romney, 1668–81, 1690–95, and 1696–1701. *Died 20 August 1701.*

PUBLICATIONS

Collections

   Poetical and Dramatic Works, edited by V. de S. Pinto.   2 vols., 1928.

Verse

   The Happy Pair; or, A Poem on Matrimony.   1702; revised edition, 1705.
   The Poetical Works, and His Speeches in Parliament, edited by W. Ayloffe.   1707
      (contains some spurious material).

Plays

   Pompey the Great, with others, from a play by Corneille (produced 1664).   1664.
   The Mulberry Garden (produced 1668).   1668; edited by A. Norman Jeffares, in
      Restoration Comedy, 1974.

Antony and Cleopatra, from the play by Shakespeare (produced 1677). 1677; revised version, as *Beauty the Conqueror*, in *Miscellaneous Works*, 1702.

Bellamira; or, The Mistress, from the play *The Fatal Contract* by William Hemmings (produced 1687). 1687.

The Grumbler, from a play by D. A. de Brueys and Jean Palaprat. 1719.

The Tyrant King of Crete, from the play *Pallantus and Eudora* by Henry Killigrew, in *Works*. 1722.

Other

Reflections upon Our Late and Present Proceedings in England. 1689.
The Speech of Sedley in the House of Commons. 1691.
The Miscellaneous Works, edited by W. Ayloffe. 1702.

Bibliography: in *Poetical and Dramatic Works*, 1928.

Reading List: *Sedley* by V. de S. Pinto, 1927; *Court Wits of the Restoration* by John H. Wilson, 1948.

*   *   *

With Rochester and Dorset, Sir Charles Sedley was one of the chief court poets of Charles II's reign. He is best known today, as he was in the Restoration, for his love poems and songs, which modern critics group into two categories: the gentler strain of poems which tend to plead with the beloved, often seeking to ingratiate the lover to the beloved, and the wittily satiric poems which are filled with such wordly wisdom as, "Tis early to begin to fear/The devil at fifteen." His poetry betrays the cynicism of Charles's Restoration court, and, as a result, it has always been overshadowed by that of the more prolific Rochester and Dorset. His satirical poems and plays all treat, sardonically, middle- and upper-class manners of the period. Sedley is undoubtedly a minor poet, but one with a perceptive eye and a cutting pen. His dramatic efforts are imitative of Etherege, Shadwell, and Dryden, and his poetry often resembles Rochester's, but his wit is always sharp.

—John J. Perry

SERVICE, Robert (William). Canadian. Born in Preston, Lancashire, England, 16 January 1874; emigrated to Canada, 1894. Educated at Hill Head High School, Glasgow; University of Glasgow. Served as an ambulance driver, 1914–16, and in Canadian Army Intelligence, 1916–18. Married Germaine Bourgoin in 1913; one daughter. Worked in the Commercial Bank of Scotland; in the Canadian Bank of Commerce, Kamloops, 1904, Whitehorse, 1904–07, Dawson, 1908–10, and Victoria, 1910–12; War Correspondent, *Toronto Star*, 1912. Travelled in Russia, Africa and the South Seas; lived in France from 1912. *Died 11 September 1958.*

PUBLICATIONS

Collections

 Collected Poems. 1961.
 Later Collected Verse. 1965.

Verse

 Songs of a Sourdough. 1907.
 The Spell of the Yukon and Other Verses. 1907.
 Ballads of a Cheechako. 1909.
 Rhymes of a Rolling Stone. 1912.
 The Rhymes of a Red-Cross Man. 1916.
 Selected Poems. 1917.
 The Shooting of Dan McGrew and Other Verses. 1920.
 Ballads of a Bohemian. 1921.
 Complete Poetical Works. 1921; as *Collected Verse,* 1930.
 Complete Poems. 1933.
 Twenty Bath-Tub Ballads. 1939.
 Bar-Room Ballads. 1940.
 Complete Poems. 1940.
 Songs of a Sun-Lover. 1949.
 Rhymes of a Roughneck. 1950.
 Lyrics of a Lowbrow. 1951.
 Rhymes of a Rebel. 1952.
 Songs for My Supper. 1953.
 Carols of an Old Codger. 1954.
 More Collected Verse. 1955.
 Rhymes for My Rags. 1956.
 Songs of the High North. 1958.

Fiction

 The Trail of '98. 1910.
 The Pretender. 1914.
 The Poisoned Paradise. 1922.
 The Roughneck. 1923.
 The Master of the Microbe. 1926.
 The House of Fear. 1927.

Other

 Why Not Grow Young? or, Living for Longevity. 1928.
 Ploughman of the Moon: An Adventure in Memory. 1945.
 Harper of Heaven: A Further Adventure in Memory. 1948.

Reading List: *Service* by Carl F. Klinck, 1976.

* * *

Robert Service arrived in Alaska too late for the Gold Rush of 1898, but his successful career rested almost exclusively on two narrative poems about it: "The Shooting of Dan McGrew" and "The Cremation of Sam McGee." He wrote these and other, similar *Songs of a Sourdough* (as he titled his first collection) largely to amuse companions in the Yukon where he worked in a bank. The popularity of this early work – 1,700 copies were sold from galley sheets alone, by word of mouth among the typesetters and proof-readers, apparently – insured Service's financial security. He further chronicled that final American horizon in *The Trail of '98*, a novel purporting to be "an authentic record ... tragic and moral in its implications" but which sacrificed characterization for melodrama and substituted lyrical flights about the terrain for psychological probing of motives and actions. Service seems to have read little, declaring late in life, "The Classics! Well, most of them bore me/The Moderns I don't understand." He aspired to be "The Bret Harte of the Northland," however, and obviously he knew the work of such oddly matched influences as Rudyard Kipling and Eugene Field.

Service abandoned the Yukon for France shortly after his early success and never returned. His popular verse narratives about Claw-Fingered Kitty, Pious Pete, One-Eyed Mike, The Dago Kid, Gum-Boot Ben, and Muckluck Meg afforded him the leisure to please readers content with romanticized tragedies and comic turns decked out in neat rhymes. (Service later guessed he had written about 30,000 couplets during his career.) Other novels followed as well, all either mysterious, violent, coarse, or lurid: *The Pretender* is about the literary life in the Latin Quarter before the First World War; *The Poisoned Paradise* complicates the same subject with gambling during the 1920's; *The House of Fear*, an overwrought gothic horror story, concluded his half-dozen ventures in this genre.

Some of Service's war poems, in *The Rhymes of a Red-Cross Man*, are of interest because they capture conflicting attitudes toward patriotism and fear through the colloquial speech of enlisted men. Two volumes of autobiography, although of little historical value, offer a readable account of a comfortable man well aware of his modest talents. "For God-sake, don't call me a poet,/For I've never been guilty of that," he wrote in one of the rhymed homilies that filled some 2,000 pages of published work. Well into his eighties, he wrote to his publisher: "Alas, my belly is concave,/My locks no longer wavy;/But though I've one foot in the grave,/The other's in the gravy."

Robert Service was probably too aware of his limitations to be an entirely successful novelist: his own sense of irony too often takes over, alienating his readers from his characters. This is particularly true in *The Trail of '98*, his most valuable work of fiction. His verse narratives, however, are always likely to draw readers who enjoy romance and adventure laced with inexhaustible rhyme and wit.

—Bruce Kellner

SEWARD, Anna. Known as the "Swan of Lichfield." English. Born in Eyam, Derbyshire, 12 December 1742; moved with her family to Lichfield, Staffordshire, 1754, and remained there for the rest of her life. Educated privately; encouraged to write by Dr. Erasmus Darwin. Lived at home, caring for her father; acquainted with Dr. Johnson and his circle at Lichfield; met Boswell c. 1776 and supplied him with anecdotes about Johnson; inherited the family estate, 1790; met Scott, 1807, who became her literary executor and editor. *Died 25 March 1809.*

PUBLICATIONS

Collections

> *Poetical Works*, edited by Walter Scott.   3 vols., 1810.
> *Letters 1784–1807*, edited by A. Constable.   6 vols., 1811.

Verse

> *Elegy on Captain Cook, to Which Is Added an Ode to the Sun.*   1780; revised edition, 1784.
> *Monody on Major André.*   1781.
> *Poem to the Memory of Lady Miller.*   1782.
> *Louisa: A Poetical Novel in Four Epistles.*   1784.
> *Ode on General Elliott's Return from Gibraltar.*   1787.
> *Llangollen Vale with Other Poems.*   1796.
> *Original Sonnets on Various Subjects, and Odes Paraphrased from Horace.*   1799.
> *Blindness.*   1806.

Other

> *Variety: A Collection of Essays.*   1788.
> *Memoirs of the Life of Dr. Darwin.*   1804.
> *Memoirs of Abelard and Eloisa.*   1805.
> *Monumental Inscriptions in Ashbourn Church, Derbyshire*, with B. Boothby.   1806.
> *Miss Seward's Enigma.*   1855.

Reading List: *The Singing Swan: An Account of Seward* by Margaret Ashmun, 1931; *Seward: An Eighteenth-Century Handelian* by R. M. Myers, 1947.

*   *   *

Anna Seward was known as the Swan of Lichfield, and, as the term suggests, she did produce a considerable body of forgettable poems. Her *Poetical Works*, published after her death, came to three volumes, and her *Letters* came to six. A contemporary critic refers to all this literary work as "written almost throughout with a disgusting affectation of verbal ornament, and everywhere tinctured with personal, political, and poetical prejudices." Nevertheless, she was a brilliant woman who never achieved a major literary accomplishment; and a reason may have been that she was part of a provincial literary circle that despised the London literary world of Samuel Johnson. Further, she received too much flattery within that limited circle of her friends in the Midlands, William Hayley, Cowper, Erasmus Darwin, without ever having to confront the major literary world of London. She was a minor writer by choice, and as such she presaged the tendency in our society for minor writers deliberately to break off into regional groupings.

One major contribution that she did make to English literature, however, came through her friendship and sometime infatuation with Erasmus Darwin, who had helped teach her to make poems when she was a girl growing up in Lichfield and who also chose deliberately to be a regional and minor writer with all the self-consciousness and sense of limits that go with that choice. Her *Memoirs of the Life of Dr. Darwin* is written in a less affected and more direct manner. She makes incisive and critical statements in that book about him and about the whole literary world of the Midlands. The book, in fact, may be her most valuable contribution to our literary heritage. During her lifetime she received the most fame for her two elegiac poems *Elegy on Captain Cook* and *Monody on Major André*. She probably received help on the Captain Cook elegy from Dr. Darwin just as she helped him with the opening lines of his poem *The Botanic Garden*. The avowedly minor writers at this time often worked together establishing the sense of small community that provided some compensation for the realization that epic works were not being produced. In this sense, Anna Seward, the assertive woman and minor writer, seems very modern.

—Donald M. Hassler

SEXTON, Anne (Harvey).   Born in Newton, Massachusetts, 9 November 1928. Educated at Garland Junior College, Boston, 1947–48. Married Alfred M. Sexton in 1948 (divorced, 1974); two daughters. Fashion Model, Boston, 1950–51; Scholar, Radcliffe Institute for Independent Study, Cambridge, Massachusetts, 1961–63; Teacher, Wayland High School, Massachusetts, 1967–68; Lecturer in Creative Writing, 1970–71, and Professor of Creative Writing, 1972–74, Boston University. Crawshaw Professor of Literature, Colgate University, Hamilton, New York, 1972. Recipient: Bread Loaf Writers Conference Robert Frost Fellowship, 1959; American Academy of Arts and Letters Traveling Fellowship, 1963; Ford Foundation grant, 1964; Shelley Memorial Award, 1967; Pulitzer Prize, 1967; Guggenheim Fellowship, 1969. Litt.D.: Tufts University, Medford, Massachusetts, 1970; Regis College, Weston, Massachusetts, 1971; Fairfield University, Connecticut, 1971. Honorary Member, Phi Beta Kappa, 1968. *Died 4 October 1974.*

PUBLICATIONS

Verse

    To Bedlam and Part Way Back.   1960.
    All My Pretty Ones.   1962.
    Selected Poems.   1964.
    Live or Die.   1966.
    Poems, with Douglas Livingstone and Thomas Kinsella.   1968.
    Love Poems.   1969.
    Transformations.   1971.
    The Book of Folly.   1972.
    O Ye Tongues.   1973.
    The Death Notebooks.   1974.
    The Awful Rowing Towards God.   1975.
    45 Mercy Street, edited by Linda Gray Sexton.   1976.

Play

    Mercy Street (produced 1969).

Other

Eggs of Things (juvenile), with Maxine Kumin.   1963.
More Eggs of Things (juvenile), with Maxine Kumin.   1964.
Joey and the Birthday Present (juvenile), with Maxine Kumin.   1971.
The Wizard's Tears (juvenile), with Maxine Kumin.   1975.
Sexton: A Self-Portrait in Letters, edited by Linda Gray Sexton and Lois Ames.   1977.

Bibliography: *Sylvia Plath and Sexton: A Reference Guide* by Cameron Northouse and Thomas P. Walsh, 1975.

Reading List: *Sexton: The Artist and Her Critics* edited by J. D. McClatchy, 1978.

*   *   *

Anne Sexton is known primarily for her remarkable imagery and apparent personal honesty in poems ranging from the formally structured early work (*To Bedlam and Part Way Back*) to the quasi-humorous prose poems of *Transformations* and the evocative free form poetry of *Love Poems*. Sexton had published much of her most mature work in the years immediately preceeding her evident suicide, and her critical reputation has yet to acknowledge that last productive period.

Sexton was a model who married, reared two daughters, and came to poetry through a workshop at Boston University conducted by Robert Lowell. Influenced by Lowell and the writing of W. D. Snodgrass to break the restraint and intellectualism common to American poetry during the 1950's, Sexton wrote such moving personal poems as "The Double Image." Her consideration here of the relationship among a mother, daughter, and grandchild is important not only for the technical prowess with which she handled a possibly sentimental subject, but for the genuine insight into the women's condition. Encouraged by her friendship with Sylvia Plath, who also was a student in the Lowell workshop, Sexton mined areas of theme and image that were virtually unknown to contemporary poetry. "Those Times" re-creates her own childhood as a time of torment; "Little Girl, My String Bean, My Lovely Woman" celebrates her joy in her daughter; "Flee on Your Donkey" plumbs the depths of personal despair; "Menstruation at Forty" questions the mortality image from a feminine view – most of Sexton's poems are adventurous in that she is writing not only about unconventional subjects, but her quick progression from image to image lends an almost surreal effect to the poetry.

Rather than simply describing Sexton's work as "confessional," the over-used label that attached itself to any writing that seemed autobiographical in origin (as what poetry is, finally, not?), readers should be aware that her work manages to distill the apparently autobiographical details into an imagistic whole which convinces any reader of its authenticity. The life in Sexton's poems is the life of the imagination, regardless of whether or not she has used the facts from her own existence in the re-creation of that life. Once the poems from the late collections have been assimilated with the earlier work, her continuous interest in religious themes and images will become as noticeable as her use of feminine psychology and concerns. Sexton's importance to American poetry will not rest simply on her mental stability or instability, her suicide, or her use of personal detail in her work; her importance will rest, finally, on her ability to craft poems that moved the reader to the act of understanding.

—Linda W. Wagner

SHAKESPEARE, William. English. Born in Stratford upon Avon, Warwickshire, baptized 26 April 1564. Probably educated at the King's New School, Stratford, 1571–77. Married Anne Hathaway in 1582; two daughters and one son. Settled in London c. 1588, and was well-known as an actor and had begun to write for the stage by 1592; Shareholder in the Lord Chamberlain's Company (after James I's accession, called the King's Men) by 1594, performing at the Globe Theatre from 1599, and, after 1609, at the Blackfriars Theatre; bought New Place in Stratford, 1597, and acquired land in Stratford; retired to Stratford in 1611. *Died 23 April 1616.*

PUBLICATIONS

Collections

Comedies, Histories, and Tragedies (First Folio), edited by John Heming and Henry Condell. 1623.
Works (New Variorum Edition), edited by H. H. Furness and H. H. Furness, Jr. 27 vols., 1871 –
Works (New Cambridge Edition), edited by J. Dover Wilson and A. H. Quiller-Couch. 1921–66.
The New Arden Shakespeare, edited by Una Ellis-Fermor and others. 1951 –.
The New Penguin Shakespeare. 1967 –.

Plays

King John (produced 1589). In First Folio, 1623.
1 Henry VI (produced 1591?). In First Folio, 1623.
2 Henry VI (produced 1592?). 1594 (bad quarto).
3 Henry VI (produced 1592?). 1595 (bad quarto).
Richard III (produced 1592?). 1597.
The Comedy of Errors (produced 1593?). In First Folio, 1623.
Titus Andronicus (produced 1594). 1594.
The Taming of the Shrew (produced 1594). In First Folio, 1623.
Love's Labour's Lost (produced 1594?). 1598.
Romeo and Juliet (produced 1594–95?). 1597 (bad quarto); 1599.
Two Gentlemen of Verona (produced 1595?). In First Folio, 1623.
A Midsummer Night's Dream (produced 1595). 1600.
Richard II (produced 1595–96?). 1597.
The Merchant of Venice (produced 1596?). 1600.
Henry IV, part 1 (produced 1596–97?). 1598.
Henry IV, part 2 (produced 1597–98?). 1600.
Much Ado about Nothing (produced 1598?). 1600.
Henry V (produced 1599). 1600 (bad quarto).
Julius Caesar (produced 1599). In First Folio, 1623.
The Merry Wives of Windsor (produced 1599–1600?). 1602 (bad quarto).
As You Like It (produced 1600?). In First Folio, 1623.
Hamlet (produced 1601?). 1603 (bad quarto); 1604.
Twelfth Night; or, What You Will (produced 1601–02?). In First Folio, 1623.
Troilus and Cressida (produced 1602?). 1609.
All's Well That Ends Well (produced 1602?). In First Folio, 1623.
Measure for Measure (produced 1604?). In First Folio, 1623.

Othello (produced 1604?).   1622.
King Lear (produced 1605).   1608 (bad quarto).
Macbeth (produced 1606).   In First Folio, 1623.
Antony and Cleopatra (produced 1606?).   In First Folio, 1623.
Coriolanus (produced 1606?).   In First Folio, 1623.
Timon of Athens (produced 1607?).   In First Folio, 1623.
Pericles (produced 1608?).   1609.
Cymbeline (produced 1609?).   In First Folio, 1623.
The Winter's Tale (produced 1610?).   In First Folio, 1623.
The Tempest (produced 1611).   In First Folio, 1623.
Henry VIII, with Fletcher (?) (produced 1613).   In First Folio, 1623.
The Two Noble Kinsmen, with Fletcher (produced 1613).   1634; edited by G. R.
   Proudfoot, 1970.

Verse

Venus and Adonis.   1593.
The Rape of Lucrece.   1594.
Sonnets.   1609.
Poems.   1640.

Bibliography: *A Shakespeare Bibliography* by Walther Ebisch and Levin L. Schücking, 1931,
supplement, 1937; *A Classified Shakespeare Bibliography 1936–1958* by Gordon Ross Smith,
1963.

Reading List: *Shakespeare: A Study of the Facts and Problems* by E. K. Chambers, 2 vols.,
1930; *Narrative and Dramatic Sources of Shakespeare* edited by Geoffrey Bullough, 8 vols.,
1957–75; *The Printing and Proof-Reading of the First Folio of Shakespeare* by C. Hinman, 2
vols., 1963; *Four Centuries of Shakespeare Criticism* edited by Frank Kermode, 1965; *A
Shakespeare Encyclopaedia* edited by O. J. Campbell and E. G. Quinn, 1966; *A New and
Systematic Concordance to the Works of Shakespeare* by M. Spevack, 6 vols., 1968–70; *A
New Companion of Shakespeare Studies* edited by Kenneth Muir and Samuel Schoenbaum,
1971; *Shakespeare: The Critical Heritage* edited by Brian Vickers, 6 vols., 1973–74;
Shakespeare: A Documentary Life by Samuel Schoenbaum, 1975, compact edition, 1977.

*   *   *

Shakespeare, "of all modern, and perhaps ancient poets, had the largest and most
comprehensive soul." Dryden's tribute, the more generous for coming from an age that
prided itself on a superior standard of polish and "politeness," sums up what students of
Shakespeare have at all times sought to express. No writer of comparable greatness is more
elusive to final definition. None has exercised a more diverse appeal or shown a greater
capacity for continual and fruitful renewal in the minds of succeeding generations.

This protean genius came only gradually to full expression. Shakespeare's earliest work is
that of a man engaged in exploring, and in some measure creating, the possibilities of his art.
The earliest work attributed to him, the three plays on *Henry VI,* show him engaged in
shaping chronicle material to dramatic ends. They lead, in *Richard III,* to the creation of a
character who stands out by his passionate dedication to the achievement of power against
the world of short-sighted time-servers, ambitious politicians, and helpless moralists in which
he moves.

Side by side with these early chronicle dramas we find Shakespeare, in a series of plays
running from *The Comedy of Errors* though *The Taming of the Shrew* to *Love's Labour's*

Lost, shaping the conventions of comedy into an instrument for expressing the finished statements about life – and more especially about love and marriage as central aspects of it – that he was already concerned to make.

In the 1590's Shakespeare also wrote two narrative poems, *Venus and Adonis* and *The Rape of Lucrece*, possibly stimulated by the success of Marlow's *Hero and Leander* of 1593, and he was also at work on his sonnets, though the 1609 *Sonnets* is now generally thought to contain poems from virtually all the periods of his development. Many of the sonnets are exercises in the conventions of the period, addressed to a patron or to an imaginary mistress. But Shakespeare was able to use the thematic conventions in a fresh way, investigating – as he would do in his later plays – the relation of individual experience (in particular the heightened emotions of friendship and love) to time. At the same time Shakespeare developed a distinctively intense and immediate language to meet the strict formal limitations of the sonnet. The stress of feeling informing the language and the exploration of shifting attitudes to a particular emotion are essentially *dramatic*, and mark out linguistic and thematic areas that Shakespeare was to explore in his "problem" plays and later.

His early works led, approximately from 1595 to 1596, to a first remarkable explosion of creative energy. Within a brief period of time, Shakespeare produced his first great tragedy, *Romeo and Juliet*, a comedy of outstanding brilliance, *A Midsummer Night's Dream*, and a historical play, *Richard II*, which gives the chronicle type of drama an entirely new dimension. In *Romeo and Juliet* a pair of young lovers seek to affirm the truth of their mutual dedication in the face of an intolerably hostile world. Their attempt ends, inevitably, in separation and death; but because it is a true emotion, involving an intuition of *value*, of life and generosity, it achieves, even in the doom which overtakes it, a measure of triumph over external circumstance. *A Midsummer Night's Dream* could be regarded as a comic counterpoise to the "romantic" tragedy. Within the framework of a rational and social attitude to marriage, it transports two pairs of youthful lovers to the mysterious woods, where the irrational but potent impulses which men ignore at their peril are released and their capacity to master them tested. By the end of their misadventures, and when the central theme of the play has been presented in the infatuation of Titania, the queen of the fairies, for Bottom the weaver with his ass's head, there is a return to daylight reality and, with it, a resolution of the issues raised by the play in terms of creative paradox. Love is seen at once to be a folly and to contain within itself, absurd indeed but not the less real, a glimpse of the divine element by which human life is imaginatively transformed in terms of "wonder."

The third play of this period, *Richard II*, is the starting-point for a series, continued in *Henry IV*, Parts I and II and *Henry V*, which traces the downfall of a traditional conception of royalty and its replacement by a political force at once more competent, more truly self-aware, and more precariously built on the foundation of its own desire for power. The Lancastrian Bolingbroke, having achieved the crown by deposing and murdering his predecessor, is seen striving to impose unity upon his realm, but foiled in his efforts by the consequences of his original crime. The success which eludes him is finally attained, in *Henry V*, by his son, but in a way which underlines the cost as well as the necessity of his triumph. The presence of Shakespeare's greatest comic creation, Falstaff, and his final rejection, underline the human complexity involved in the new king's necessary choices. As King, he can hardly do otherwise than banish the companion of his youth, and it would surely be wrong to sentimentalize Falstaff in any way; but we are required, in a manner that is very essentially Shakespearean, to weigh the *cost* against the success, and perhaps to conclude that the human and the political orders – both necessary aspects of human life – are in the real world barely to be reconciled.

At about the time that he was writing this second series of history plays, Shakespeare was engaged in developing further his concept of comedy to cover other aspects of human behaviour. In *Much Ado about Nothing* he produced a highly formal comedy which works, through strict conventions and largely in prose, to illuminate facets of truth and illusion in the reality of love. In *As You Like It* the consideration of the basic realities of love and friendship is extended to cover a concept of sociability, of true civilization. The central part of the play, which displaces the action to the Forest of Arden where human relationships are taken temporarily into the state of nature (itself presented in conventional terms) and set in contrast to the corrupt sophistication which prevails at Duke Frederick's court, presents a set of variations on the theme of love. When the various amorous combinations have been sorted out, leading into the concluding "dance" of married harmonies which is a reflection of the universal order of things, the reconciliation at which comedy aims is finally consummated.

The last of these great comedies, *Twelfth Night*, deals in its "serious" part with two characters, Orsino and Olivia, whose lives are initially a blend of sentiment and artifice, and who learn, largely through their relationship with the self-reliant Viola, that the compulsive force of their passions is such as to draw them finally beyond themselves, demanding from each the acceptance of a fuller, more natural and spontaneous way of living. The "lesson" is reinforced by the comic underplot, and more particularly by the exposure of Olivia's steward Malvolio, who is – and remains to the last – "imprisoned" in a darkness which reflects his self-infatuation. Feste, too, the most individual thus far of Shakespeare's clowns, stands rather outside the prevailing mood, answering to the constant tendency of Shakespearean comedy to qualify its imaginative harmonies with a profound sense of relativity, of a final uniqueness and autonomy in human experience.

The period which produced these great comedies was followed by a turning of the dramatist's interest towards tragedy. Two plays of obscure intention and uneven execution – *Troilus and Cressida* and *Measure for Measure* – form the background to *Hamlet* in which many of the same issues were raised to the consistent level of tragedy. The play presents a central figure of unique complexity whose motives penetrate the action at every point, seeking clarification through contact with it and illuminating it in turn ·by his central presence. In pursuing his duty to avenge his father's death, Hamlet brings to light a state of disease in "Denmark" – the "world" of the play – which affects the entire field presented to his consciousness; and, in the various stages through which the ramifications of this infection are exposed, he finds himself exploring progressively the depths of his own disaffection.

In the great tragedies that followed *Hamlet*, the conflicts there presented are polarized, on an ever-increasing scale, into more clearly defined contrasts. In the earliest of them, *Othello*, the heroic figure of the Moor, tragically compounded of nobility and weakness, is exposed to the critical scepticism of Iago which operates upon his simplicity with the effect of an anarchic and sinister dissolvent. "Perplexed" to the last, betrayed by emotions which he has never really understood in their true nature, Othello makes a last attempt to return, through suicide, to his original simplicity of nature. By then, however, the critical acid supplied by Iago has undermined the structure of his greatness.

In his next tragedy, *King Lear*, Shakespeare embarked upon what is probably the most universal of his conceptions. Lear is at once father and king, head of a family and ruler of a state. As father he produces in his daughters contrasted reactions which reflect contradictions in his own nature; as king, his wilful impulses release in society destructive forces which nothing less than their utter exhaustion can contain. In the central storm scenes, the action of the elements becomes a reflection of Lear's own condition. Man and his environment are seen as organically related in the conflicts of a universe poetically conceived. Human relationships are shattered, and the state of "unaccomodated man" is seen in terms of subjection to the beast of prey in his own nature. Through these overwhelming events we are led step by step to Lear's awakening and recognition of his returned daughter Cordelia. This is the central reconciliation, the restoration of the natural "bond" between father and child, which is seen – while it lasts – as the resolution of the ruin caused by passion and egoism in the most intimate of human relationships. It is not, however, lasting. Since we are engaged in an exploration of the human condition under its tragic aspect, not elaborating the supposedly beneficial effects of suffering in promoting moral understanding, the armies of France are defeated by the "Machiavellian" realist Edmund; and though he dies in meeting the challenge of his disguised half-brother Edgar, his death cannot reverse the hanging of Cordelia by his orders. As the play ends, Lear returns with her dead body in his arms and, in a world dominated by returning darkness, the curtain falls.

The next great tragedy, *Macbeth*, deals with the overthrow of harmony not merely in an individual of tragic stature, but in an ordered realm. Macbeth murders, not only a man and a kinsman, but order, sanity, life itself. From the moment of the execution of his deed his character and that of his wife develop on lines of rigid determinism. One crime leads logically, by a dreadful and pre-determined process, to another; and the career that began by following the illusion of "freedom," mastery of circumstance, ends by an inexorable development in a complete enslavement from which defeat and death provide the only conceivable release.

Close in time to the writing of these great tragedies, a series of plays on Roman themes represents Shakespeare's final effort in this kind. The earliest, *Julius Caesar*, is one of his most effective studies of public behaviour. The central character, Brutus, the nearest approach to a truly consistent figure which the play offers, is flawed by the self-consciousness of his determination to be true to his ideals. His need to live up to an acceptable image of himself makes him the victim of those who appeal to him in the name of friendship and devotion to freedom, but who are moved in no small part by resentment and envy. The other principal agent in the tragedy, Mark Antony, combines genuine feeling with the ability to exploit mob emotion, and ends by disclaiming responsibility for the destruction and brutality he has unleashed. Finally, after Caesar's death, the world which survives him is shown separating into its component elements of selfish "realism" and disillusionment.

The next Roman play, *Antony and Cleopatra*, is among Shakespeare's greatest masterpieces. His Cleopatra is at once the Egyptian queen of history and something more: a woman experienced in the ways of a corrupt and cynical world and ready to use her fascination over men in order to survive in it. Antony's love for her is, at least in part, the fascination of a man no longer young, who has chosen to give up his public responsibilities to become the dupe of an emotion that he knows to be unworthy. Side by side with the moral judgment that is unrelentingly pressed throughout the tragedy, the implication remains that the measure of the passion which has led this pair to accept death and ruin may be correspondingly universal in its value. It is the play's achievement to convey that *both* judgments contain a measure of truth, that neither can be suppressed without distorting our sense of the complete human reality which the play offers.

After *Coriolanus*, the disconcerting study of a gauche and inflexible hero whose unnatural desire for revenge upon his city leaves him at the last disoriented and ruined in a world that he is incapable of understanding, the last stage of Shakespeare's development consists of a series of "romances," written from 1607 onwards, which represent an effort to give dramatic form to a new "symbolic" intuition. After two plays – *Pericles* and *Cymbeline* – which can be thought of as experiments, *The Winter's Tale* presents the story of two kings whose life-long friendship is broken up by the jealous conviction of one of them – Leontes – that his friend Polixenes has replaced him in the affection of his wife Hermione. By the end of an action in which the passage of time has an essential part to play, the estranged monarchs are reconciled through the spontaneous love of their children, the divisions introduced by disordered and self-consuming passion into the harmony of life have been healed, and winter has passed through spring into the summer of gracious fulfilment.

The Tempest, which some have seen, perhaps a little over-schematically, as Shakespeare's farewell to the stage, takes us to an island in which the normal laws of nature are magically suspended. Prospero can be seen as a figure of the imaginative artist, bringing together on his island stage the men who, in another world, have wronged him and whom he now subjects to a process of judgment and reconciliation. He is accompanied by his servants Ariel and Caliban, the former of whom may represent the imaginative, creative side of his nature, the latter the passionate instincts which, as a human being, he keeps uneasily under control. By the end of the play, as in *The Winter's Tale*, a measure of reconciliation has been born out of the exposure to tragic experience. Prospero's daughter Miranda marries Ferdinand, the son of his former enemy, whom she first saw in her inexperience as a vision proceeding from a "brave new world," but whom she has learned to love as a man. The "brave new world" is seen as an ennobling vision of love in the light of an enriched experience, and upon it the "gods" are invited to bestow the "crown" which raises a new-born vision of humanity into a symbol of royalty. The "crown" they bestow is a sign of the "second," the redeemed and "reasonable" life which Prospero's action has made accessible. At this point, if anywhere, and always within the limits of the imaginative action which has created a *play*, the design presented by Shakespeare's work is substantially complete.

—Derek A. Traversi

SHAPIRO, Karl (Jay). Born in Baltimore, Maryland, 10 November 1913. Educated at the University of Virginia, Charlottesville, 1932–33; Johns Hopkins University, Baltimore, 1937–39; Pratt Library School, Baltimore, 1940. Served in the United States Army, 1941–45. Married 1) Evalyn Katz in 1945 (divorced, 1967); 2) Teri Kovach in 1969; two daughters, and one son. Associate Professor of Writing, Johns Hopkins University, 1947–50; Visiting Professor, University of Wisconsin, Madison, 1948, and Loyola University, Chicago, 1951–52; Lecturer, Salzburg Seminar in American Studies, 1952; State Department Lecturer, India, 1955; Visiting Professor, University of California, Berkeley and Davis, 1955–56, and University of Indiana, Bloomington, 1956–57; Professor of English, University of Nebraska, Lincoln, 1956–66, and University of Illinois, Chicago Circle, 1966–68. Since 1968, Professor of English, University of California at Davis. Editor, *Poetry*, Chicago, 1950–56, *Newberry Library Bulletin*, Chicago, 1953–55, and *Prairie Schooner*, Lincoln, Nebraska, 1956–66. Consultant in Poetry, Library of Congress, Washington, D.C., 1946–47. Recipient: National Institute of Arts and Letters grant, 1944; Guggenheim Fellowship, 1944, 1953; Pulitzer Prize, 1945; Shelley Memorial Award, 1946; Kenyon School of Letters Fellowship, 1956, 1957; Bollingen Prize, 1969. D.H.L.: Wayne State University, Detroit, 1960; D.Litt.: Bucknell University, Lewisburg, Pennsylvania, 1972. Fellow in American Letters, Library of Congress; Member, American Academy of Arts and Sciences, and National Institute of Arts and Letters. Lives in Davis, California.

PUBLICATIONS

Verse

Poems. 1935.
Five Young American Poets, with others. 1941.
Person, Place, and Thing. 1942.
The Place of Love. 1942.
V-Letter and Other Poems. 1944.
Essay on Rime. 1945.
Trial of a Poet and Other Poems. 1947.
Poems 1940–1953. 1953.
The House. 1957.
Poems of a Jew. 1958.
The Bourgeois Poet. 1964.
Selected Poems. 1968.
White-Haired Lover. 1968.
Adult Bookstore. 1976.
Collected Poems 1940–1977. 1978.

Play

The Tenor, music by Hugo Weisgall.   1956.

Fiction

Edsel.   1970.

Other

Poets at Work: Essays Based on the Modern Poetry Collection at the Lockwood Memorial Library, University of Buffalo, with others, edited by Charles D. Abbot.   1948.
English Prosody and Modern Poetry.   1947.
A Bibliography of Modern Prosody.   1948.
Beyond Criticism.   1953; as *A Primer for Poets*, 1965.
In Defense of Ignorance (essays).   1960.
Start with the Sun: Studies in Cosmic Poetry, with James E. Miller, Jr., and Bernice Slote.   1960.
A Prosody Handbook, with Robert Beum.   1965.
Randall Jarrell.   1967.
To Abolish Children and Other Essays.   1968.
The Poetry Wreck: Selected Essays 1950–1970.   1975.

Editor, with W. H. Auden and Marianne Moore, *Riverside Poetry 1953: Poems by Students in Colleges and Universities in New York City.*   1953.
Editor, *American Poetry.*   1960.
Editor, *Prose Keys to Modern Poetry.*   1962.

Bibliography: *Shapiro: A Bibliography* by William White, 1960.

*   *   *

Karl Shapiro is a poet of great versatility who has a sophisticated command of prosody and a sharp ear for speech rhythms and verbal harmonies. He is a man of considerable erudition, though he never finished college, and a serious though good-humored social critic. Since his first volume of poems in 1935, he has published continuously. As poet and critic, he always has taken an iconoclastic stance. He attacks intellectual poetry, poseurs, stuffed shirts, and the establishment with great vigor, and as a result has been a controversial figure. As editor of *Poetry* and *The Prairie Schooner* for 16 years, he was a significant force in contemporary poetry, and as a professor he has taught two decades of aspiring writers.

When Shapiro published *Selected Poems*, he ignored his first volume, about which he writes in "Recapitulations":

> My first small book was nourished in the dark,
> Secretly written, published, and inscribed.
> Bound in wine-red, it made no brilliant mark.
> Rather impossible relatives subscribed.

His first recognition came in 1941 when he appeared in *Five Young American Poets.* His next volume, *Person, Place, and Thing*, contains excellent poems of social comment in traditional form. "The Dome of Sunday" comments in sharp, clear imagery cast in blank verse on urban

"Row houses and row-lives"; "Drug Store" observes youth culture satirically in unrhymed stanzas; "University [of Virginia]" mounts a low-keyed attack: "To hurt the Negro and avoid the Jew/Is the curriculum."

V-Letter and Other Poems contains some of the best poems to come out of World War II, some of which are "V-Letter," "Elegy for a Dead Soldier," "Troop Train," "The Gun," "Sunday: New Guinea," and "Christmas Eve: Australia." The form usually is rhymed stanzas, even *terza rima*, and here Shapiro's social comment finds a wider context. There also begin to be foreshadowings of later preoccupations: religious themes and attacks on intellectualism. "The Jew" anticipates *Poems of a Jew*, and "The Intellectual" ("I'd rather be a barber and cut hair/Than walk with you in gilt museum halls") looks toward attacks on Pound and Eliot in *In Defense of Ignorance*.

Although Shapiro does not write long poems (the exception is *Essay on Rime*, a youthful treatise on the art of poetry in which "Everything was going to be straightened out"), *Poems 1940–1953* contains an evocative, seven-part sequence telling the story of Adam and Eve. (This interest in myth reasserts itself in *Adult Bookstore* in a poignant version in 260 lines of "The Rape of Philomel.") This volume also contains "Israel," occasioned by the founding of that country: "When I see the name of Israel high in print/The fences crumble in my flesh.... " As a boy Shapiro grew up in a Russian-Jewish family not particularly religious, and after his bar mitzvah "I lost all interest in what I had learned." But *Poems of a Jew* explores his Jewishness with pride, wit, and irony, beginning with "The Alphabet" ("letters ... strict as flames," "black and clean" and bristling "like barbed wire").

As early as 1942 Shapiro had published a prose-poem, "The Dirty Word," but in 1964 he turned to this form exclusively in *The Bourgeois Poet*, dropping the kind of verses he previously had thought best, "the poem with a beginning, a middle, and an end ... that used literary allusion and rhythmic structuring and intellectual argument." He wanted a medium in which he could say anything he pleased — ridiculous, nonsensical, obscene, autobiographical, pompous. The individual pieces cover a wide variety of topics and, as earlier, they comment on persons, places, things. The longest (14 pages), "I Am an Atheist Who Says His Prayers," which reminds one of Shapiro's enthusiasm for Whitman, could have been called "Song of Myself." These prose poems (or free verse set as prose paragraphs) had a mixed reception. But Adrienne Rich noted that in his new style Shapiro was going through a "constant revising and purifying of his speech," as all poets must, and she thought parts of this volume were "a stunning success."

In *White-Haired Lover*, a cycle of middle-aged love poems, Shapiro returned to traditional forms, often the sonnet. This also is true of *Adult Bookstore*, a collection that ranges widely in subject. "The Humanities Building," "A Parliament of Poets," and the title poem show that Shapiro has not lost the wit, irony, and technique that have always characterized his work. "The Heiligenstadt Testament" is a splendid dramatic monologue of Beethoven's deathbed delirium, and among the poems occasioned by his move to California are "Garage Sale" ("This situation .../Strikes one as a cultural masterpeice") and a perfect Petrarchan sonnet on freeways and California suburbia.

The Poetry Wreck, which contains Shapiro's most important critical statements, throws light on his poetry, his sources, his beliefs. The derogatory essays on Pound and Eliot are reprinted along with admiring appraisals of W. H. Auden ("Eliot and Pound had rid the poem of emotion completely ... Auden reversed the process"), William Carlos Williams, "whose entire literary career has been dedicated to the struggle to preserve spontaneity and immediacy of experience," Whitman, Dylan Thomas, Henry Miller, and Randall Jarrell. Jarrell, whose "poetry I admired and looked up to most after William Carlos Williams," once said in a passage Shapiro quotes: "Karl Shapiro's poems are fresh and young and rash and live; their hard clear outline, their flat bold colors create a world like that of a knowing and skillful neo-primitive painting, without any of the confusion or profundity of atmosphere, or aerial perspective, but with notable visual and satiric force."

—James Woodress

SHELLEY, Percy Bysshe. English. Born at Field Place, near Horsham, Sussex, 4 August 1792. Educated at Syon House School, Isleworth, Middlesex, 1802–04; Eton College, 1804–10; University College, Oxford, 1810–11 (expelled for pamphlet *The Necessity of Atheism*). Eloped with and married Harriet Westbrook, 1811 (died, 1816), two children, left her in 1814 for Mary Wollstonecraft Godwin (i.e., Mary Shelley) daughter of William Godwin, married in 1816, one daughter and two sons. Visited Ireland, 1812; returned to London, became a friend of William Godwin, 1813; left England for Italy, 1818, and settled in Pisa, 1820; died by drowning. *Died 8 July 1822.*

PUBLICATIONS

Collections

> *Complete Poetical Works*, edited by Thomas Hutchinson.   1904; revised edition, edited by G. M. Matthews, 1970.
> *Complete Works*, edited by Roger Ingpen and W. E. Peck.   10 vols., 1926–30.
> *Shelley's Prose; or, The Trumpet of Prophecy*, edited by D. L. Clark.   1954.
> *Alastor, Prometheus Unbound, Adonais, and Other Poems*, edited by P. H. Butter.   1970.
> *Complete Poetical Works*, edited by Neville Rogers.   2 vols. (of 4), 1972–75.
> *Poetry and Prose*, edited by Donald H. Reiman and Sharon Powers.   1977.

Verse

> *Original Poetry by Victor and Cazire*, with Elizabeth Shelley.   1810.
> *Posthumous Fragments of Margaret Nicholson.*   1810.
> *Queen Mab: A Philosophical Poem, with Notes.*   1813.
> *Alastor; or, The Spirit of Solitude, and Other Poems.*   1816.
> *Laon and Cythna; or, The Revolution of the Golden City: A Vision of the Nineteenth Century in the Stanza of Spenser.*   1817; revised edition, as *The Revolt of Islam: A Poem in Twelve Cantos*, 1818.
> *Rosalind and Helen: A Modern Eclogue, with Other Poems.*   1819.
> *Epipsychidion.*   1821.
> *Adonais: An Elegy on the Death of John Keats.*   1821.
> *Posthumous Poems*, edited by Mary Shelley.   1824.
> *The Masque of Anarchy: A Poem Now First Published.*   1832.
> *The Daemon of the World: The First Part as Published in 1816 with Alastor, the Second Part Deciphered and Now Printed from His Manuscript Revision and Interpolations*, edited by H. Buxton Forman.   1876.
> *The Wandering Jew*, edited by B. Dobell.   1887.
> *The Notebook in the Harvard Library*, edited by G. E. Woodberry.   1929.
> *The Esdaile Notebook: A Volume of Early Poems*, edited by Kenneth N. Cameron.   1964; edited by Neville Rogers, as *The Esdaile Poems*, 1966.

Plays

> *The Cenci* (produced 1886).   1819.
> *Prometheus Unbound: A Lyrical Drama, with Other Poems.*   1820; the play edited by L. J. Zillman, 1959, 1968.
> *Oedipus Tyrannus; or, Swellfoot the Tyrant*, from the play by Sophocles.   1820.
> *Hellas: A Lyrical Drama.*   1822.

Fiction

Zastrozzi: A Romance.   1810; edited by Eustace Chesser, 1965.
St. Irvyne; or, The Rosicrucian: A Romance.   1811.

Other

The Necessity of Atheism, with T.J. Hogg.   1811; edited by Eustace Chesser, 1965.
An Address to the Irish People.   1812.
Proposals for an Association of Those Philanthropists Who Convinced of the Inadequacy of the Moral and Political State of Ireland to Produce Benefits Which Are Nevertheless Attainable Are Willing to Unite to Accomplish Its Regeneration.   1812.
A Letter to Lord Ellenborough.   1812.
A Vindication of Natural Diet, Being One in a Series of Notes to Queen Mab: A Philosophical Poem.   1813.
A Refutation of Deism, in a Dialogue.   1814.
A Proposal for Putting Reform to the Vote Throughout the Kingdom, by the Hermit of Marlow.   1817.
History of Six Weeks' Tour Through a Part of France, Switzerland, Germany and Holland, with Mary Shelley.   1817; abridgement edited by C. I. Elton, 1894.
The Shelley Papers.   1833.
Essays, Letters from Abroad, Translations, and Fragments, edited by Mary Shelley.   2 vols., 1840.
Shelley Memorials, from Authentic Sources, to Which Is Added An Essay on Christianity, edited by Lady Shelley and R. Garnett.   1859.
Relics of Shelley, edited by R. Garnett.   1862.
Notes on Sculptures in Rome and Florence Together with a Lucianic Fragment and a Criticism of Peacock's Poem Rhododaphne, edited by H. Buxton Forman.   1879.
A Philosophical View of Reform, edited by T. W. Rolleston.   1920.
On the Vegetable System of Diet, edited by Roger Ingpen.   1929.
Verse and Prose from the Manuscripts, edited by Sir J. C. E. Shelley-Rolls and Roger Ingpen.   1934.

Translator, *Plato's Banquet,* edited by Roger Ingpen.   1931.
Translator, *Shelley's Translations from Plato: A Critical Edition,* edited by J. A. Notopoulos, in his *Platonism of Shelley.*   1949.

Bibliography: *A Bibliography of Studies of Shelley 1823–1950* by Clement A. E. Dunbar, 1976.

Reading List: *Shelley* (biography) by Newman Ivey White, 2 vols., 1940; *Shelley's Major Poetry* by Carlos Baker, 1948; *The Young Shelley: Genesis of a Radical,* 1950, and *Shelley: The Golden Years,* 1974 both by Kenneth N. Cameron; *Shelley's Mythmaking* by Harold Bloom, 1959; *Shelley and His Circle 1773–1822* (texts) edited by Kenneth N. Cameron and D. H. Reiman, 6 vols. (of 8 or more), 1961–73; *Shelley: A Critical Reading* by Earl R. Wasserman, 1971; *Shelley: The Pursuit* by Richard Holmes, 1974; *The Dark Angel: Gothic Elements in Shelley's Works* by John V. Murphy, 1974; *Shelley: The Critical Heritage* edited by James E. Barcus, 1975; *Shelley: A Voice Not Understood* by Timothy Webb, 1978.

*   *   *

"An enthusiasm for Shelley seems to me to be an affair of adolescence," said T. S. Eliot. No harm in that in itself, of course. If his rush of images, his lyrical intensity, his "passion for reforming the world," his idealism excite the young, that will at least start their reading of poetry in the right way, from enjoyment. But can he not remain also "the companion of age"? Did he not mature as an artist? Apart from juvenilia each volume of poetry which he published consisted of a long poem, to which sometimes a few short ones were tacked on. As he presented himself he was not primarily a lyric poet pouring out personal feelings, but one trying to deal with large themes in long poems, mostly of a dramatic or narrative kind.

Take *Alastor*, for instance, the first longish poem in which he approaches maturity. Read as autobiography it would seem sentimental, self-indulgent; but clearly it should not be so read. The unnamed protagonist should not be identified with the author (who might be accused more justly of rash involvement in relationships than of "self-centred seclusion"). *Alastor* not only movingly celebrates the romantic idealist quester, it criticises him too; it combines boundless aspiration with scepticism; it displays a remarkable ability to create symbolic landscapes suggestive of the protagonist's emotional states; and it shows a more assured handling of the verse than in earlier poems. The artist in Shelley is gaining control, but has not yet fully attained it. At the end balance is lost, and the dying hero is too extravagantly praised for qualities which have not been sufficiently created in the poem.

A more mature poem, in which again idealism and scepticism are confronted, is "Julian and Maddalo," written three years later. Here one of the characters, Julian, is openly based on Shelley himself, or on part of himself. Julian is an idealist, believing that "we might be all / We dream of, happy, high, majestical," and is confronted with Maddalo, based on Byron, showing the reality of evil and suffering. Again, more skilfully and naturally than in *Alastor*, the argument is sustained by description of scenery. The bare strip of sand on which Julian and Maddalo ride suggests the potentiality which Julian wishes to believe in; the sunset over the hills and Venice suggests the realisation of that potentiality and the possible at-oneness of heaven and earth; and the black tower in which the madman is imprisoned thrusts itself questioningly into that sunset. The language is conversational, fitted skilfully and with apparent ease into couplets. The tone, except in the madman's monologue, is light, controlled, urbane. The artist Shelley is now more fully in control, giving a fair say to Maddalo as well as to Julian and tactfully distancing the weaker side of himself in the madman.

One could try to demonstrate Shelley's maturing by continuing the survey of his poems of medium length through the delightful fantasy "The Witch of Atlas" and "Adonais" up to "The Triumph of Life," which shows a greater strength and precision in language and imagery than ever before. One could show his mastery of a wide variety of styles and metrical forms appropriate to different kinds of poem. But his claim to major status must rest mainly on his greatest complete poem, *Prometheus Unbound*. This, on the whole successfully, combines at least three levels of meaning. Psychologically, the reunion of Prometheus and Asia is the reintegration of the split human personality, like the reunion of Blake's Albion and his emanation Jerusalem. Politically, the overthrow of Jupiter is a revolution leading to the establishment of a free, expansive society. Mystically, the journey of Asia and Panthea to the cave of Demogorgon is a casting aside of the veils of illusion and an approach towards a vision of ultimate reality. By using and adapting an existing myth Shelley devised a more satisfactory surface to carry the deeper meanings than Blake usually did. His myth sustains itself better; he does not need to explain himself. Much is conveyed by sound, and by recurring images which come to have complex symbolic, seldom crudely allegorical, meanings. One can still point to weaknesses, however. Having added the fourth act he could with advantage have shortened the third, which in any case continues too long after the downfall of Jupiter and loses dramatic impact. Sometimes he loses control of his long sentences, and sometimes he is content to waft us along on a stream of sound, conveying only a vague and generalised meaning. Nevertheless this is the greatest of English romantic mythological poems.

By transferring the argument to the realm of myth Shelley was able to let Julian win, but he still knew, as his next long work, *The Cenci*, shows, what Maddalo might have to say in answer. Beatrice is a failed Prometheus, who becomes what she beholds, answering her Jupiter with murder rather than pity. It was a sign of maturity to wish to write this harshly realistic work immediately after, indeed, concurrently with, *Prometheus*. But it shows also Shelley's limitations. Like most others who have tried poetic drama, he could not escape the influence of the Elizabethans, especially Shakespeare, and create a language and a style for modern drama; and he was only to a limited extent successful in creating living, believable characters.

This last is perhaps his main limitation. It is unfair to say that all his characters are himself, but they are representative of aspects of himself or of ideas, attitudes, feelings rather than flesh-and-blood people — appropriately so in some poems, less so in others. He had a passion for ideas, and an unusual capacity to embody them concretely in images. He had a genuine passion for reforming the world, expressed in sacrificial action as well as in words, but in some degree spoiled by impatience and self-absorption, which limited him both as man and poet.

The same process of maturing as in the longer poems can be seen in the shorter — from the declamatory juvenilia through the uneven "Hymn to Intellectual Beauty" (the weak "I shrieked, and clasped my hands in ecstasy" after the strong opening stanzas) to the well-controlled use of personal experience in relation to larger themes in "Ode to the West Wind." The lyrics show a considerable range — of subject, tone, and metrical form. Some are "metaphysical" poems, using science (as in "The Cloud") and philosophical ideas (as in "Ode to Heaven") with grace and urbanity. Some (as "An old mad, blind, despised and dying king") use plain language to comment on contemporary politics. Some are dramatic, intended for private theatricals in his circle in Italy — obviously the superb "Hymn of Apollo" and "Hymn of Pan," less obviously "When the lamp is shattered." As G. M. Matthews has shown (in *Review of English Literature 2*, 1961), much of the criticism of this last poem, and of others, has been misdirected because of failure to recognise the kind of poem that it is. Many of his lyrics, quite properly, are more or less direct expressions of personal feeling. Here, when he approaches certain sensitive areas, he still tends to become strident and self-pitying; but less so towards the end. The late poems to Jane Williams, written in a quiet, conversational tone, convey a stronger sense than his earlier love poems of actual place, persons, situation. Along with the still boundless aspiration is a resigned acceptance of necessary limitation.

Shelley's prose displays a powerful, if impatient, intelligence wrestling with a wide range of problems — in religion, philosophy, morals, politics, literature, diet. Yeats called "A Defence of Poetry" "the profoundest essay on the foundation of poetry in English"; but others have found it, though eloquent, lacking in complete consistency. Mainly Shelley says that the poet, inspired, puts aside "life's dark veil" to reveal the real and ideal world behind; but his scepticism does not allow him to say this quite confidently and consistently. Sometimes he seems to say that poetry itself is a "figured curtain," which reveals, it may be, nothing external, but only "the wonder of our being." It is a common uncertainty among the romantics and their successors. Other prose works worth reading are the short philosophical essays "On Love," "On Life," "On a Future State"; *A Philosophical View of Reform*, showing him dealing quite realistically with what was immediately possible in politics as well as with more distant goals; and the translations from Plato.

"Shelley," the elderly Wordsworth said, "is one of the best artists of us all: I mean in workmanship of style." This artistry and his combination of sceptical intelligence with idealism and visionary power make him a companion for age as well as for adolescence.

—P. H. Butter

SHENSTONE, William. English. Born at Leasowes, Halesowen, Worcestershire, 13 November 1714. Educated at Halesowen Grammar School; Solihull Grammar School, Warwickshire; Pembroke College, Oxford, 1732–42, left without taking a degree. Inherited the Leasowes estate, 1735, settled there, 1745, and devoted himself thereafter to laying out the grounds. *Died 11 February 1763.*

PUBLICATIONS

Collections

> *Works.* 3 vols., 1773.
> *Poetical Works,* edited by George Gilfillan. 1854.

Verse

> *Poems upon Various Occasions.* 1737.
> *The Judgment of Hercules.* 1741.
> *The School-Mistress.* 1742; revised edition, in *A Collection of Poems by Several Hands I,* edited by Robert Dodsley, 1748.

Other

> *Letters,* edited by Marjorie Williams. 1939.
> *Letters,* edited by Duncan Mallam. 1939.
> *The Correspondence of Thomas Percy and Shenstone,* edited by Cleanth Brooks. 1977.
>
> Editor, *Miscellaneous Poems, Revised and Corrected,* by Joseph Giles. 1771.
> Editor, *Shenstone's Miscellany,* edited by Ian A. Gordon. 1952.

Bibliography: in *Seven 18th-Century Bibliographies* by Iolo A. Williams, 1924.

Reading List: *A Study of Shenstone and His Critics* by Alice I. Hazeltine, 1918; *Shenstone* by Arthur R. Humphreys, 1937.

*   *   *

William Shenstone is one of the minor writers of the eighteenth century, but his influence on the direction of English poetry was out of all proportion to the intrinsic merits of his verse. He began writing poetry when Pope was at his zenith, and his *Poems upon Various Occasions* appeared in the same year (1737) as several of Pope's epistles. Shenstone firmly rejected Pope's heroic couplet and the Augustan ideal of correctness and public poetry. His first volume was made up of ballads, songs, and the earliest version of *The School-Mistress,* written in unfashionable Spenserian stanzas. Thereafter Shenstone went his own way, retreating to live in the country, to become an arbiter of the altering taste of the mid-eighteenth century.

When Robert and James Dodsley launched their influential anthology *A Collection of Poems* (1748), Shenstone's poetry appeared in company with such forward-looking poetry as odes by Gray and by Collins, Warton's *Enthusiast,* and Dyer's *Grongar Hill.* He became the adviser to the Dodsleys for the later volumes, and was responsible for the inclusion of Gray's *Elegy in a Country Churchyard,* Akenside's "Hymn to the Naiads," and many of his own best lyrics (e.g., "Pastoral Ballad," "Rural Elegance,""Slender's Ghost," "Written at an Inn"). Shenstone became a close associate of Bishop Percy and had a considerable hand in the selection and editing of the old ballads (published after his death) in Percy's *Reliques of Ancient English Poetry* (1765). His own anthology of old ballads, Elizabethan lyrics, and verse by his contemporaries remained in manuscript until it was discovered and published in our own day.

Shenstone's reputation was for a long time diminished by the slighting references in Dr. Johnson's *Lives of the Poets.* Johnson's Augustan judgment of his lyrics – "all of the light and airy kind, such as trip lightly and nimbly along, without the load of any weighty meaning" – misses Shenstone's achievement. He was an innovator both in theme and in his metrical freedom. Gray in his own day thought highly of *The School-Mistress*; and, in the next generation of poets, Shenstone found favour with Robert Burns, who quoted in the preface to his Kilmarnock volume (1768) the "divine elegies" of "that celebrated poet."

—Ian A. Gordon

SIDNEY, Sir Philip.   English.   Born in Penshurst, Kent, 30 November 1554. Educated at Shrewsbury School, Shropshire, 1564–68; Christ Church, Oxford (left without a degree). Married Frances Walsingham in 1583. Travelled in France, Germany, and Italy, as Gentleman of the Bedchamber to Charles IV, 1572–75; Member of Elizabeth's court: Ambassador to Emperor Rudolf and then to the Prince of Orange, 1577; in disfavor with the Queen, retired to his sister's estate at Wilton, 1580; Member of Parliament, 1581; knighted, 1582; Governor of Flushing, 1585; accompanied Leicester to the Netherlands to fight against Spain, and died in battle there. *Died 17 October 1586.*

PUBLICATIONS

Collections

> *Complete Works,* edited by Albert Feuillerat.   4 vols., 1912–26.
> *Poems,* edited by William A. Ringler, Jr.   1962.
> *Selected Poetry and Prose,* edited by David Kalstone.   1970.

Verse

> *Astrophel [i.e., Astrophil] and Stella* (includes sonnets by other writers), edited by
>   Thomas Nashe.   1591; revised edition, in *Arcadia,* 1598; edited by M. Putzel, 1967.
> *The Psalms of David,* with the Countess of Pembroke, edited by S. W. Singer.   1823;
>   edited by J. C. A. Rathmell, 1963.

Fiction

The Countess of Pembroke's Arcadia.   1590; revised edition, including material from
   earlier version, 1593; edited by Albert Feuillerat, in *Complete Works,* 1922; earlier
   version, edited by Albert Feuillerat, in *Complete Works* 1926; as *The Old Arcadia,*
   edited by J. Robertson, 1973; 1590 edition edited by Maurice Evans, 1977.

Other

The Defense of Poesy.   1595; as *An Apology for Poetry,* 1595; edited by Jan van Dorsten,
   1966.
The Countess of Pembroke's Arcadia (miscellany; includes *Certain Sonnets, Defense of
   Poesy, Astrophel and Stella, The Lady of May*).   1598; augmented edition, including
   A Dialogue Between Two Shepherds, 1613.
Miscellaneous Prose, edited by Katherine Duncan-Jones and Jan van Dorsten.   1973.

Bibliography: *Sidney: A Concise Bibliography* by S. A. Tannenbaum, 1941, supplement by G.
R. Guffey, 1967; *Sidney: An Annotated Bibliography of Modern Criticism, 1941–1970* by
Mary A. Washington, 1972.

Reading List: *Sidney and the English Renaissance* by J. Buxton, 1954; *Sidney* by Kenneth
Muir, 1960; *Symmetry and Sense: The Poetry of Sidney* by R. L. Montgomery, Jr., 1961;
Sidney's Poetry: Contexts and Interpretations by David Kalstone, 1965; *The Epic Voice:
Arcadia* by R. Delasanta, 1967; *Heroic Love: Studies in Sidney and Spenser* by Mark Rose,
1968; *Sidney* by Robert Kimbrough, 1970; *Young Sidney 1572–1577* by James M. Osborn,
1972; *The Poetry of Sidney: An Interpretation in the Context of His Life and Times* by John G.
Nichols, 1974; *Sidney: A Study of His Life and Work* by A. C. Hamilton, 1977; *Sidney: The
Maker's Mind* by Dorothy Connell, 1978.

*   *   *

The keynote of Sir Philip Sidney's work is self-conscious artistry in the service of
psychological exploration. In his *Defense of Poesy,* he defined poetry as an art of imitation, as
did theorists before him; but he insisted that the object of imitation exists not in nature but in
the poet's mind, so that poetry becomes the giving form or image to ideas. Thus the poet
becomes a maker of fictions, and fiction becomes the exercise of hypothesis, whereby the
poet,"freely ranging within the zodiac of his own wit," explores "the divine consideration of
what may be, or should be." The end of knowledge for Sidney is the repair of the Fall by
implanting self-knowledge and action; and poetry does that better than philosophy or history,
not only because it presents precepts of virtue in apprehensible images, but also because, by
so doing, it causes delight which moves men to "take that goodness in hand which, without
delight, they would flee as from a stranger." By casting his treatise into the form of a
delightful classical oration – with its changes of tone from the relaxed humor of the opening
to the passionate exhortation of the ending – Sidney made the defending of poetry itself an
imaginary action, whereby his persuasion to love poetry became analogous to poetry's
persuasion to embrace virtue.
   Sidney's great prose romance, *Arcadia,* exists in two different forms. The *Old Arcadia* (ca.
1579–80) is a straightforward narrative in five "books" or "acts" following the five-act
structure of Terentian comedy; the books are separated by four verse interludes or
entertainments by the Arcadian shepherds, each with its special theme which both ties
together the various actions preceding it in the narrative and contrasts the main action
tonally. The romance belongs to the pastoral tradition, with its concerns over humility,

figured as man's harmony with nature, and pride, as man's attempt to rise above nature. It centers around questions of human control over events, and these dilate into parallel actions of love, in the private, and order, in the political, realms, book-by-book. Sidney's sophisticated narrative persona views these actions with objectivity and, frequently, with wry comedy.

The comic tone disappears in the incomplete *New Arcadia*, an extensive revision of the first two and one-half books (ca. 1583–4) which elaborated characterization, ideas, style, and especially plot. Sidney added thirteen new episodes that showed events in the main plot from a variety of angles and created thematic density whereby the three books of the revised romance became small disquisitions on love, reason against passion, and the nature of marriage. By focusing on a clearly articulated ideational structure thus, Sidney forged the pastoral romance into an ethical and psychological tool, according to the aims of poetry set out in the *Defense*. The verse interludes of both *Arcadias* are marked by interesting experiments with classical meters and Romance forms. Some of them – the sapphic "If mine eyes can speak," the great double sestina "Ye goatherd gods" – are really accomplished poems.

In *Astrophil and Stella* Sidney made his most telling experiments. He made the sonnet psychologically dramatic by emphasizing conflict in the form, specifically by polarizing octave and sestet to dramatize the clash of different states of mind. In sonnet 15 the octave parodies bookish modes of composition, while the sestet reverently presents the natural emergence of poetry from love. The stylistic clash in this and other sonnets suggests the replacement of a less by a more valid perception of a situation, usually an external viewpoint by an internal one. In sonnet 31, the contrast between the sentimental octave and the satiric sestet frames a dramatic action whereby the sentimental lover gradually reaches contact with the whole moral man. The histrionics of the Sidneyan sonnet come out strikingly in sonnets like 47, which reads like a soliloquy in a play, the internal argument of Astrophil suddenly crumbling with the appearance of Stella, and 74, wherein, after Astrophil's presentation of himself as bumbling poet, he suddenly emerges as the sophisticated lover-poet who teases the simple reader.

In the 108 sonnets and 11 songs of *Astrophil and Stella* we observe an anatomy of the mind of the lover in its infinite variety. When read consecutively, the collection outlines a psychological action, in a series of lyric moments, describing the influence of love on the relation between the self and reality. The first 22 sonnets lay out themes of love and poetry in a dispersed manner; with the twenty-third sonnet, interrelations become firmer by contiguous themes and rhyme links, and the action settles into the rejection of external reality for the sake of love. Sonnets 31 to 40 explore the precise nature of this love, its difficulty in the face of a real-life husband for Stella and the desire to retreat from it in sleep and dream. With Sonnet 41, we move from the "prospective musings" internal to Astrophil outward to his experience of the reality of life in love; sonnets are now directly addressed to Stella and describe experiences with her. From Sonnet 52 through the first Song (the songs presenting public events in the love experience), sensuality enters the sequence, and for a while external action determines the progress of the affair, first in a series of linked sonnets on hope (66–67), joy (68–70), and desire (71–72), then by a stolen kiss described in the Second Song and celebrated in the ensuing sonnets (79–82). This external action is shown directly in the Fourth through Ninth Songs describing a meeting, Astrophil's open declaration, and Stella's firm rejection of him. The sequence then returns to internal experience in a group of sonnets on absence (87–92) wherein Astrophil turns inward and Stella becomes abstract to him; the final movement shows Astrophil alone, bound up in his mind once more; night characterizes his state, as do images of the self as prison.

Sidney's works offer various hypotheses about love's influence on the mind. In both prose and verse he experimented with form as a means of conveying psychological insight. Whereas in the two *Arcadias* he infused fiction with poetic and dramatic devices, in *Astrophil and Stella* he welded lyrics together into a psychological fiction. The effects of such bold experimentation were quick to be grasped by Sidney's contemporaries, especially after the publication of his works in the early 1590's, and they can be seen especially in the fiction of Greene and Lodge, and in the poetry of Spenser, Grenville, Campion, Daniel, Drayton, and Jonson.

—Walter R. Davis

SIMPSON, Louis (Aston Marantz).   American.   Born in Jamaica, West Indies, 27 March 1923; became a U.S. citizen. Educated at Munro College, Jamaica, 1933–40, Cambridge Higher Schools Certificate 1940; Columbia University, New York, B.S. 1948, A.M. 1950, Ph.D. 1959. Served in the United States Army, 1943–45: Purple Heart and Bronze Star. Married 1) Jeanne Claire Rogers in 1949 (divorced, 1954), one son; 2) Dorothy Roochvarg in 1955, one son and one daughter. Editor, Bobbs-Merrill Publishing Company, New York, 1950–55; Instructor, Columbia University, 1955–59; Professor of English, University of California, Berkeley, 1959–67. Since 1967, Professor of English, State University of New York at Stony Brook. Recipient: American Academy in Rome Fellowship, 1957; Edna St. Vincent Millay Award, 1960; Guggenheim Fellowship, 1962, 1970; American Council of Learned Societies Grant, 1963; Pulitzer Prize, 1964; Columbia University Medal for Excellence, 1965; American Academy of Arts and Letters award, 1976. Lives in Port Jefferson, New York.

PUBLICATIONS

Verse

The Arrivistes: Poems 1940–1949.   1949.
Good News of Death and Other Poems.   1955.
A Dream of Governors.   1959.
At the End of the Open Road.   1963.
Five American Poets, with others, edited by Thom Gunn and Ted Hughes.   1963.
Selected Poems.   1965.
Adventures of the Letter I.   1971.
Searching for the Ox: New Poems and a Preface.   1976.

Plays

The Father Out of the Machine: A Masque, in Chicago Review, Winter 1951.
Andromeda, in Hudson Review, Winter 1956.

Fiction

Riverside Drive.   1962.

Other

James Hogg: A Critical Study.   1962.
Air with Armed Men (autobiography).   1972; as North of Jamaica, 1972.
Three on the Tower: The Lives and Works of Ezra Pound, T. S. Eliot, and William Carlos
    Williams.   1975.

Editor, with Donald Hall and Robert Pack, New Poets of England and America.   1957.
Editor, An Introduction to Poetry.   1967.

Reading List: Simpson by Ronald Moran, 1972.

*   *   *

Always more of a "paleface" than a "redskin" (to adopt Philip Rahv's famous categorization of American writers), Louis Simpson took some time to find his own poetic voice. His early poetry is heavily dependent on John Crowe Ransom, and much of the work of his first two volumes, The Arrivistes and Good News of Death, seems to derive from art rather than life. The exception comes with a remarkable group of war poems, especially "Carentan O Carentan" and "The Battle," which, with the exception of Randall Jarrell's, seem to me the best poems to have come from American poets' confrontation with World War II.

A Dream of Governors is a tired, "literary" volume, full of echoes of such poets as Nemerov, Hecht, and Wilbur, all of them more polished performers than Simpson himself. Reading it, you feel that Simpson's talent is all but dead. But At the End of the Open Road achieves a remarkable break-through. Gone are the formal posturings, the conventional subjects, the making of poems out of poems, that featured so heavily in the earlier volumes. It is as though Simpson has suddenly found his true subject, and with it an answerable style. Instead of trying to be like other poets, he is now content to be himself: he lets his Jewishness into the poetry, his sense of being something of an outcast, but an outcast who nevertheless knows he belongs to America, and who therefore sets out to celebrate his country, whenever he can find it and whatever it may prove to be. As the title of the volume hints, Simpson turns, as so many American poets have found themselves turning, to Walt Whitman. The Whitman he responds most deeply to is the poet who could embrace multitudes, engage contradictions, responsibly accept irresponsibility: whose gigantic achievement was to perceive the noble folly of American dreams. "All the grave weight of America/Cancelled! Like Greece and Rome./The future in ruins." Those lines come from "Walt Whitman at Bear Mountain," one of Simpson's best poems.

Most of the poems of At the End of the Open Road are written in an informal, loose-limbed manner, which more powerfully and convincingly convey the sense of a personal voice than the earlier poems had managed to do. And where Simpson does return to a more formal mode, as in the extraordinarily fine, wittily melancholic "My Father in the Night Commanding No," he does it without leaning on any other poet. Some of the finest poems in this remarkable volume are ones where Simpson broods on the inescapable fact of his Jewishness. He prods at it like an aching tooth, fascinated by it, yet fearing the pain it causes. The best of these is undoubtedly "A Story about Chicken Soup."

In Adventures of the Letter I, Simpson attempted to make further use of the style he had discovered for himself: musing, wryly observant, quizzical, contemplative. I think of it as a volume in which Simpson is marking time. There are no poems in it as good as the best of the previous volume; and yet it is an utterly readable, enjoyable piece of work by a poet who, having found his own voice, can be relied on not to bore. Like Whitman, Simpson has become at the very least a good companion.

—John Lucas

SITWELL, Dame Edith.   English.   Born in Scarborough, Yorkshire, 7 September 1887; sister of the poets Sir Osbert Sitwell, *q.v.*, and Sir Sacheverell Sitwell, *q.v.* Educated privately at her father's house, Renishaw Hall, Derbyshire. Visiting Professor, Institute of Contemporary Arts, London, 1957. Recipient: Royal Society of Literature Benson Medal, 1934; Foyle Poetry Prize, 1958; Guinness Poetry Award, 1959. Litt.D.: University of Leeds, 1948; D.Litt.: University of Durham, 1948; Oxford University, 1951; University of Sheffield, 1955; University of Hull, 1963. Honorary Associate, American Institute of Arts and Letters, 1949. Vice-President, 1958, and Companion of Literature, 1963, Royal Society of Literature. D.B.E. (Dame Commander, Order of the British Empire), 1954. *Died 9 December 1964.*

PUBLICATIONS

Collections

   Fire of the Mind (selections), edited by Elizabeth Salter and Allanah Harper, 1976.

Verse

   The Mother and Other Poems.   1915.
   Twentieth-Century Harlequinade and Other Poems, with Osbert Sitwell.   1916.
   Clowns' Houses.   1918.
   The Wooden Pegasus.   1920.
   Façade, music by William Walton.   1922.
   Bucolic Comedies.   1923.
   The Sleeping Beauty.   1924.
   Troy Park.   1925.
   Poor Young People and Other Poems, with Osbert and Sacheverell Sitwell.   1925.
   Elegy on Dead Fashion.   1926.
   Poem for a Christmas Card.   1926.
   Rustic Elegies.   1927.
   Five Poems.   1928.
   Gold Coast Customs.   1929.
   Collected Poems.   1930.
   In Spring.   1931.
   Epithalamium.   1931.
   Five Variations on a Theme.   1933.
   Selected Poems, with an Essay.   1936.
   Poems New and Old.   1940.
   Street Songs.   1942.
   Green Song and Other Poems.   1944.
   The Weeping Babe: Motet for Soprano Solo and Mixed Choir, music by Michael
      Tippett.   1945.
   The Song of the Cold.   1945; revised edition, 1948.
   The Shadow of Cain.   1947.
   The Canticle of the Rose: Selected Poems 1920–1947.   1949.
   Poor Men's Music.   1950.
   Façade and Other Poems.   1950.
   Selected Poems.   1952.
   Gardeners and Astronomers.   1953.

Collected Poems. 1954.
(Poems). 1960.
The Outcasts. 1962; augmented edition, as *Music and Ceremonies,* 1963.

Plays

The Sleeping Beauty (masque), music by Leighton Lucas (produced 1936).
The Last Party (radio play), in *Twelve Modern Plays,* edited by J. Hampden. 1938.

Fiction

I Live under a Black Sun. 1937.

Other

Children's Tales from the Russian Ballet. 1920; as *The Russian Ballet Gift Book,* 1922.
Poetry and Criticism. 1925.
Alexander Pope. 1930.
Bath. 1932.
The English Eccentrics. 1933; revised edition, 1957.
Aspects of Modern Poetry. 1934.
Victoria of England. 1936.
Trio: Dissertations on Some Aspects of National Genius, with Osbert and Sacheverell
    Sitwell. 1938.
English Women. 1942.
A Poet's Notebook. 1943; revised edition, 1950.
Fanfare for Elizabeth. 1946.
A Notebook on William Shakespeare. 1948.
The Queens and the Hive. 1962.
Taken Care Of: An Autobiography. 1965.
Selected Letters, 1919–1964, edited by John Lehmann and Derek Parker. 1970.

Editor and Contributor, *Wheels.* 6 vols., 1916–21.
Editor, *The Pleasures of Poetry: A Critical Anthology.* 3 vols., 1930–32.
Editor, *Edith Sitwell's Anthology.* 1940.
Editor, *Look! The Sun* (anthology of poetry). 1941.
Editor, *Planet and Glow-Worm: A Book for the Sleepless.* 1944.
Editor, *A Book of Winter.* 1950.
Editor, *The American Genius: An Anthology of Poetry, with Some Prose.* 1951.
Editor, *A Book of Flowers.* 1952.
Editor, *The Atlantic Book of British and American Poetry.* 1958.
Editor, *Poems of Our Time 1900–1960* (supplement only). 1959.
Editor, *Swinburne: A Selection.* 1960.

Bibliography: *A Bibliography of Edith, Osbert, and Sacheverell Sitwell* by Richard Fifoot,
1963; revised edition, 1976.

Reading List: *The Three Sitwells* by R. L. Mégroz, 1927; *A Celebration for Sitwell: Essays*
edited by José Garcia Villa, 1948; *Triad of Genius* by M. Wykes-Jones, 1953; *Sitwell: The
Hymn to Life* by G. Singleton, 1961; *Sitwell: A Critical Essay* by Ralph J. Mills, Jr., 1966;

The Last Years of a Rebel: A Memoir of Sitwell by Elizabeth Salter, 1967; *Sitwell: The Symbolist Order* by J. D. Brophy, 1968; *A Nest of Tigers: Edith, Osbert, and Sacheverell Sitwell in Their Times* by John Lehmann, 1968.

*   *   *

During her lifetime, there were vehement differences of opinion about the worth of Edith Sitwell's poetry. Since her death it has attracted little serious criticism. She was her own worst enemy, courting attention by almost mountebank behaviour, deliberately provoking attack and then reacting with insolence or even spite. Yet she was not a charlatan, as her detractors alleged. She was a dedicated poet, passionately interested in revitalising the language of poetry through technical innovations.

She and her two equally remarkable brothers belonged to the artistic avant-garde of the early 1920's, on whom Diaghilev's Russian Ballet made an ineradicable impression. Edith Sitwell's earlier poems are highly stylised, indeed deliberately artificial. Their rhythms reflect those of the dance, their dominant imagery is pastoral or fairy-tale. *Façade*, in which she collaborated with William Walton, has had a more than ephemeral success. The lyrics on the printed page may seem, at best, engaging trivia; spoken or chanted, the verbal patterns offset by the musical, their artistic value is doubled.

Edith Sitwell's poetry was always inventive. Her feeling for individual words was sensuous. For her they possessed texture, colour, and weight as well as sonority. She valued poems as artefacts, and her own for two decades were remarkable for surface brilliance and ingenuity rather than for any depth of feeling, far less intensity of thought. World War II however had a profound effect on her. The volumes published during the 1940's contain poems far more serious and moving than their predecessors. The three Poems for an Atomic Age, particularly "The Shadow of Cain," are remarkable expressions of anguish, as is the rather earlier "Still Falls the Rain."

Edith Sitwell's approach to poetics, as to criticism and biography, was essentially non-academic. Her biographical study of Pope manifested a sympathetic appreciation of his artistry and wit at a time when his poetry was still undervalued. *A Poet's Notebook* affords a good insight into her mind, revealing the eclecticism of her taste and her serious (if highly idiosyncratic) engagement with major as well as minor English and French writers. She was able to recognise creative promise in the living, and launched Dylan Thomas into the literary world of London. A fastidious writer of prose, she developed in *English Eccentrics* biographical themes that suited her admirably. For she was, though too self-consciously, an eccentric, a non-conformist, prepared at all times to assert her own convictions. She deliberately cultivated an aristocratic stance (to which she was entitled by birth), and enhanced her Gothic beauty with spectacular clothes. Many were alienated by her theatricality and offended by her arrogance. Nevertheless, she took her art extremely seriously, and at her best could communicate an original vision with a fine command of rhythm, imagery, and diction.

—Margaret Bottrall

SITWELL, Sir (Francis) Osbert; 5th baronet, 1942. English. Born in London, 6 December 1892; brother of the poets Dame Edith Sitwell, *q.v.*, and Sir Sacheverell Sitwell, *q.v.* Educated at Eton College. Served as a Captain in the Grenadier Guards, 1912–18, and fought in France; invalided home, 1916. With his brother Sacheverell, and others, organized the Exhibition of Modern French Art, London, 1919. Justice of the Peace, Derbyshire, 1939; Chairman, Management Committee, Society of Authors, London, 1944–45, 1946–48, 1951–53; Trustee, Tate Gallery, London, 1951–58. LL.D.: University of St. Andrews, Scotland, 1946; D.Litt.: University of Sheffield, 1951. Fellow, and Companion of Literature, 1967, Royal Society of Literature. Honorary Associate, American Academy of Arts and Letters, 1950; Honorary Fellow, Royal Institute of British Architects, 1957. C.B.E. (Commander, Order of the British Empire), 1956; C.H. (Companion of Honour), 1958. *Died 4 May 1969.*

PUBLICATIONS

Verse

Twentieth-Century Harlequinade and Other Poems, with Edith Sitwell.   1916.
The Winstonburg Line: 3 Satires.   1919.
Argonaut and Juggernaut.   1919.
At the House of Mrs. Kinfoot: Consisting of Four Satires.   1921.
Out of the Flame.   1923.
Poor Young People and Other Poems, with Edith and Sacheverell Sitwell.   1925.
England Reclaimed: A Book of Eclogues.   1927; *Wrack at Tidesend: A Book of Balnearics,* 1952; *On the Continent: A Book of Inquilinics,* 1958; complete version, as *Poems about People; or, England Reclaimed,* 1965.
Miss Mew.   1929.
Collected Satires and Poems.   1931.
Three-Quarter Length Portrait of Michael Arlen.   1931.
A Three-Quarter Length Portrait of Viscountess Wimborne.   1931.
Mrs. Kimber.   1937.
Selected Poems Old and New.   1943.
Four Songs of the Italian Earth.   1948.
England Reclaimed and Other Poems.   1949.

Plays

All at Sea: A Social Tragedy for First-Class Passengers Only, with Sacheverell Sitwell (as *For First Class Passengers Only,* produced 1927).   1927.
Gentle Caesar, with Rubeigh J. Minney.   1942.
Demos the Emperor: A Secular Oratorio.   1948.

Fiction

Triple Fugue (stories).   1924.
Before the Bombardment.   1926.
The Man Who Lost Himself.   1929.
Dumb-Animal and Other Stories.   1930.
Miracle on Sinai: A Satirical Novel.   1933.
Those Were the Days: Panorama with Figures.   1938.
Open the Door! A Volume of Stories.   1941.
A Place of One's Own.   1941.
The True Story of Dick Whittington: A Christmas Story of Cat-Lovers.   1945.

Alive — Alive Oh! and Other Stories.   1947.
Death of a God and Other Stories.   1949.
Collected Stories.   1953.
Fee Fi Fo Fum! A Book of Fairy Stories.   1959.
A Place of One's Own and Other Stories.   1961.

Other

Who Killed Cock Robin? Remarks on Poetry, On Criticism, and, as a Sad Warning, The Story of Eunuch Arden.   1921.
Discursions on Travel, Art, and Life.   1925.
C. R. W. Nevinson.   1925.
The People's Album of London Statues, illustrated by Nina Hamnett.   1928.
Dickens.   1932.
Winters of Content: More Discursions on Travel, Art, and Life.   1932.
Brighton, with Margaret Barton.   1935.
Penny Foolish: A Book of Tirades and Panegyrics.   1935.
Trio: Dissertations on Some Aspects of National Genius, with Edith and Sacheverell Sitwell.   1938.
Escape with Me! An Oriental Sketch-Book.   1939.
Sing High! Sing Low! A Book of Essays.   1944.
A Letter to My Son.   1944.
Left Hand, Right Hand! An Autobiography: Left Hand, Right Hand!   1944 (as *The Cruel Month*, 1945); *The Scarlet Tree*, 1946; *Great Morning!*, 1947; *Laughter in the Next Room*, 1948; *Noble Essences or Courteous Revelations, Being a Book of Characters*, 1950.
Winters of Content and Other Discursions on Mediterranean Art and Travel.   1950.
The Four Continents, Being More Discursions on Travel, Art, and Life.   1954.
Tales My Father Taught Me: An Evocation of Extravagant Episodes (autobiography).   1962.
Pound Wise (essays).   1963.
Queen Mary and Others (essays).   1974.

Editor, with Margaret Barton, *Sober Truth: A Collection of Nineteenth-Century Episodes, Fantastic, Grotesque, and Mysterious.*   1930.
Editor, with Margaret Barton, *Victoriana: A Symposium of Victorian Wisdom.*   1931.
Editor, *Belshazzar's Feast*, music by William Walton.   1931.
Editor, *Two Generations* (writings by Georgiana Caroline Sitwell and Florence Alice Sitwell).   1940.
Editor, *A Free House! or, The Artist as Craftsman, Being the Writings of W. R. Sickert.*   1947.

Bibliography: *A Bibliography of Edith, Osbert, and Sacheverell Sitwell* by Richard Fifoot, 1963; revised edition, 1976.

Reading List: *The Three Sitwells* by R. L. Mégroz, 1927; *Sitwell* by Roger Fulford, 1951; *Triad of Genius* by M. Wykes-Jones, 1953; *A Nest of Tigers: Edith, Osbert, and Sacheverell Sitwell in Their Times* by John Lehmann, 1968.

*   *   *

Sir Osbert Sitwell's early works showed talent but an uncertain sense of direction. As a poet, with a taste for the grotesque and odd but not for direct satire, and lacking a lyrical voice, he came a poor third to his sister Edith and his brother Sacheverell. A novel like *Before the Bombardment* and a set of stories like *Triple Fugue* owed perhaps, as Evelyn Waugh suggested, something to the grotesque fantasies of Ronald Firbank but there was something morose about the humour, and even a certain glum pity.

It was not until the set of five autobiographies, named after the opening volume *Left Hand, Right Hand*, and published after the Second World War, that Sir Osbert's gifts expressed themselves richly and fully. In his father, Sir George Reresby Sitwell, he had to his hand, or from the facts of memory created, one of the great comic characters in English fiction, and in the loyal valet Henry Moat a sort of Sancho Panza to Sir George's Don Quixote. It is interesting how the treatment of Sir George becomes more and more affectionate as the autobiography progresses. Sir George was not at all an evil man, but he was completely self-centred, though with some interests, like that in ornamental gardens, which his children shared. He was incapable of even trying to grasp anybody else's point of view. But Sir Osbert gradually comes to see that the pain he inflicted on his family was not deliberate and that he compensated, in a way, as they grew older, by presenting them with the delight of a living legend. The richness of Sir Osbert's own sense of scene and character and his brilliant gift for digression give him in the end a legendary quality himself.

—G. S. Fraser

SITWELL, Sir Sacheverell; 6th baronet, 1969. Born in Scarborough, Yorkshire, 15 November 1897; younger brother of the poets Dame Edith Sitwell, *q.v.*, and Sir Osbert Sitwell, *q.v.* Educated at Eton College; Balliol College, Oxford. Served in the Grenadier Guards in World War I. Married Georgia Doble in 1925; two sons. With his brother Osbert, and others, organized the Exhibition of Modern French Art, London, 1919. Justice of the Peace, 1943; High Sheriff of Northamptonshire, 1948–49. Freeman, City of Lima, Peru, 1960. Lives in Towcester, Northamptonshire.

PUBLICATIONS

Verse

The People's Palace.   1918.
The Parrot.   1923.
Doctor Donne and Gargantua: First Canto.   1921; Canto the Second, 1923; Canto the Third, 1926; The First Six Cantos, 1930.
The Hundred and One Harlequins.   1922.
The Thirteenth Caesar and Other Poems.   1924.
Poor Young People and Other Poems, with Edith and Osbert Sitwell.   1925.
Exalt the Eglantine and Other Poems.   1926.
The Cyder Feast and Other Poems.   1927.
Two Poems, Ten Songs.   1929.
Canons of Giant Art: Twenty Torsos in Heroic Landscapes.   1933.
Collected Poems.   1936.
Selected Poems.   1948.
Tropicalia.   1972.

To Henry Woodward. 1972.

Agamemnon's Tomb. 1972.

Rosario d'Arabeschi, Basalla ("as the Moors call it") and Dionysia, A Triptych of Poems, The Strawberry Feast, Ruralia, To E. S., Variations upon Old Names of Hyacinths, Lily Poems, The Archipelago of Daffodils, A Charivari of Parrots, Flowering Cactus, A Look at Sowerby's English Mushrooms and Fungi, Auricula Theatre, Lyra Varia, The House of the Presbyter, Nigritian, Twelve Summer Poems of 1962, Doctor Donne and Gargantua (Cantos Seven and Eight), Badinerie, An Indian Summer, Temple of Segesta, L'Amour au Théâtre Italien, A Notebook on My New Poems, Nymphis et Fontibus, and Nymphaeum, A Pair of Entr'actes for August Evenings, A Second Triptych of Poems, Harlequinade, Brother and Sister: A Ballad of the Paralelo Tropicalia, Little Italy in London. 29 vols., 1972–77.

J. S. Bach, Liszt, Domenico Scarlatti, from "Credo; or, An Affirmation." 1976.

Plays

All at Sea: A Social Tragedy for First-Class Passengers Only, with Osbert Sitwell (as *For First Class Passengers Only,* produced 1927). 1927.

Ballet: *The Triumph of Neptune,* 1926.

Other

Southern Baroque Art: A Study of Painting, Architecture and Music in Italy and Spain of the 17th and 18th Centuries. 1924.

All Summer in a Day: An Autobiographical Fantasia. 1926.

German Baroque Art. 1927.

A Book of Towers and Other Buildings of Southern Europe. 1928.

The Gothick North: A Study of Medieval Life, Art, and Thought (The Visit of the Gypsies, These Sad Ruins, The Fair-Haired Victory). 1929.

Beckford and Beckfordism: An Essay. 1930.

Far From My Home: Stories: Long and Short. 1931.

Spanish Baroque Art: With Buildings in Portugal, Mexico, and Other Colonies. 1931.

Mozart. 1932.

Liszt. 1934; revised edition, 1955.

Touching the Orient: Six Sketches. 1934.

A Background for Domenico Scarlatti, 1685–1757; Written for His Two Hundred and Fiftieth Anniversary. 1935.

Dance of the Quick and the Dead: An Entertainment of the Imagination. 1936.

Conversation Pieces: A Survey of English Domestic Portraits and Their Painters. 1936.

Narrative Pictures: A Survey of English Genre and Its Painters. 1937.

La Vie Parisienne: A Tribute to Offenbach. 1937.

Roumanian Journey. 1938.

Edinburgh, with Francis Bamford. 1938.

German Baroque Sculpture. 1938.

Trio: Dissertations on Some Aspects of National Genius, with Edith and Osbert Sitwell. 1938.

The Romantic Ballet in Lithographs of the Time, with Cyril W. Beaumont. 1938.

Old Fashioned Flowers. 1939.

Mauretania: Warrior, Man, and Woman. 1940.

Poltergeists: An Introduction and Examination Followed by Chosen Instances. 1940.

Sacred and Profane Love. 1940.

Valse des Fleurs: A Day in St. Petersburg and a Ball at the Winter Palace in 1868. 1941.
Primitive Scenes and Festivals. 1942.
The Homing of the Winds and Other Passages in Prose. 1942.
Splendours and Miseries. 1943.
British Architects and Craftsmen: A Survey of Taste, Design, and Style During Three Centuries 1600 to 1830. 1945; revised edition, 1946.
The Hunters and the Hunted. 1947.
The Netherlands: A Study of Some Aspects of Art, Costume and Social Life. 1948; revised edition, 1974.
Morning, Noon and Night in London. 1948.
Theatrical Figures in Porcelain: German 18th Century. 1949.
Spain. 1950; revised edition, 1951.
Cupid and the Jacaranda. 1952.
Truffle Hunt with Sacheverell Sitwell. 1953.
Fine Bird Books 1700–1900, with Hanasyde Buchanan and James Fisher. 1953.
Selected Works. 1953.
Portugal and Madeira. 1954.
Old Garden Roses: Part One, with James Russell. 1955.
Selected Works. 1955.
Denmark. 1956.
Great Flower Books 1700–1900: A Bibliographical Record of Two Centuries of Finely-Illustrated Flower Books, with Wilfrid Blunt and Patrick M. Synge. 1956.
Arabesque and Honeycomb. 1957.
Malta. 1958.
Austria. 1959.
Lost in the Dark Wood (vol. 1 of *Journey to the Ends of Time*). 1959.
Bridge of the Brocade Sash: Travels and Observations in Japan. 1959.
Golden Wall and Mirador: From England to Peru. 1961.
The Red Chapels of Banteai Srei, and Temples in Cambodia, India, Siam, and Nepal. 1962; as *Great Temples of the East,* 1963.
Monks, Nuns, and Monasteries. 1965.
Southern Baroque Revisited. 1967.
Baroque and Rococo. 1967.
Gothic Europe. 1969.
For Want of a Golden City (autobiography). 1973.
The Netherlands. 1974.
Notebook on "Twenty Canons of Giant Art." 1976.
A Note for Bibliophiles. 1976.
A Study of J. S. Bach's Organ Preludes and Fugues. 1977.

Editor, *Gallery of Fashion 1790–1822, from Plates by Heideloff and Ackermann.* 1949.
Editor, *Great Houses of Europe,* photographs by E. Smith. 1961.

Bibliography: *A Bibliography of Edith, Osbert, and Sacheverell Sitwell* by Richard Fifoot, 1963; revised edition, 1976.

Reading List: *The Three Sitwells* by R. L. Mégroz, 1927; *Triad of Genius* by M. Wykes-Jones, 1953; *A Nest of Tigers: Edith, Osbert, and Sacheverell Sitwell in Their Times* by John Lehmann, 1968; *Sitwell: A Symposium* edited by Derek Parker, 1975; *Hand and Eye* edited by Geoffrey Elborn, 1977.

*   *   *

Sir Sacheverell Sitwell is possibly the most productive but also the least obtrusive of the Sitwell trio, Edith, Osbert, and Sacheverell, of whom he was the youngest. His two earliest prose books, *Southern Baroque Art* and the poetic autobiographical fantasia *All Summer in a Day*, show his great gift, in which he perhaps excelled both his brother and sister, of combining picturesque but precise description with the evocation of a mood. He is a tremendous traveller, from Mauretania to Japan, and from Denmark to Spain, and anybody who has covered the same ground will find that Sir Sacheverell (he inherited the family baronetcy on the death of his brother Osbert) sharpens his own memory, and gives it more exactness. But travel is only one of his interests; he has written books on musicians as various as Offenbach and Mozart, on old garden roses, on British architects and craftsmen, on theatrical figures in porcelain, and a bibliographical study, written with collaborators, of great flower books. If one has a criticism of his enormous output in prose it is that though his eye and ear are magically alert he has never shown much curiosity about human character. The world for him is a raree-show, of which men and women are a very minor part. Yet he uses music, landscape, flowers, and architecture to evoke recurrent though evanescent human moods. Since his *Selected Poems* of 1948, the changes in poetic fashion have reduced publication of his verse. But a small press in Northamptonshire has published over 20 small volumes since 1972. They have probably had few readers, but they show an advance on his earlier work. He is a writer who awaits revaluation and rediscovery.

—G. S. Fraser

SKELTON, John.   English.   Born, probably in Yorkshire, c. 1460. Educated at Cambridge University (possibly at Peterhouse), B.A. possibly 1479; probably also at Oxford University (Poet Laureate of Oxford, 1488, and of Cambridge, 1505; Laureate, University of Louvain, 1492). At the end of his life claimed to be married to a woman in Diss, Norfolk, by whom he had had several children. Official court poet, 1488; tutor to Prince Henry, later King Henry VIII, 1494–1502; Orator Regius, 1512; enjoyed the patronage of Cardinal Wolsey and the Countess of Surrey (mother of the poet); ordained, 1498: Rector of Diss from 1502; satirized Wolsey in his verse, 1515–22. *Died 21 June 1529.*

PUBLICATIONS

Collections

Poetical Works, edited by Alexander Dyce.   2 vols., 1843; augmented by F. J. Child, 3 vols., 1856.
Complete Poems, edited by Philip Henderson.   1931; revised edition, 1964.
Poems, edited by R. S. Kinsman.   1969.

Verse

The Bowge of Court.   1499.
A Ballad of the Scottish King.   1513.

The Tunning of Elinor Rumming. 1521.
Speak Parrot. 1521.
A Goodly Garland or Chaplet of Laurel. 1523.
Divers Ballads and Ditties Salacious. 1527.
Against a Comely Coystrowne. 1527.
A Replication Against Certain Young Scholars. 1528.
Colin Clout. 1530.
Philip Sparrow. 1545.
Why Come Ye Not to Court? 1545.

Play

Magnificence. 1533; edited by J. Farmer, 1910.

Other

Certain Books. 1545.
Pithy, Pleasant, and Profitable Works, edited by John Stow. 1568.
Speculum Principis, edited by F. M. Salter, in *Speculum*. 1934.

Translator, *The Bibliotheca Historica of Diodorus Siculus*, edited by F. M. Salter and H.
   L. R. Edwards. 2 vols., 1956–57.

Reading List: *Skelton, Laureate* by William Nelson, 1939; *Skelton: Poet Laureate* by Ian A.
Gordon, 1943; *Skelton: The Life and Times of an Early Tudor Poet* by H. L. R. Edwards,
1949; *Skelton and Satire* by Arthur R. Heiserman, 1961; *Skelton: Contribution à l'Histoire
de la Prérenaissance Anglaise* by Maurice Pollet, 1962, translated by John Warrington, 1971;
La Poesia di Skelton by Edwige Schulte, 1963; *Skelton's Poetry* by Stanley E. Fish, 1965;
Skelton's "Magnyfycence" and the Cardinal Virtue Tradition by William O. Harris, 1965;
Skelton by Nan Cooke Carpenter, 1968.

*   *   *

Because he failed to understand the forces shaping early Renaissance England – the growth
of the modern monarchy, the need to reform the church from within, the development of
humanist scholarship and appreciation of classical prose style, the study of Greek – John
Skelton's verse seems to lash out intemperately, while paradoxically calling for temperance in
government, morality, and scholarship. This intemperance in the service of order gives his
verse its characteristic flavor, as various litigious or obsessed personae struggle to rebuke or
restrain others and, ultimately, themselves. The speakers so vigorously convey the passion
they ostensibly wish to control that it becomes their own: "He is so fyers and fell;/He rayles
and he ratis,/He calleth them doddypatis;/He grynnes and he gapys,/As it were jack napis./
Such a madde bedleme/For to rewle this reame" (*Why Come Ye Nat to Courte?*). The
pretense of quoting from one of Wolsey's tirades with "doddypatis" forces the speaker and
reader momentarily to experience Wolsey's anger. This mood of scarcely controlled
vituperation appears from the beginning of Skelton's career in the rhyme royal stanzas of the
elegy for the Earl of Northumberland (1489), which excoriates the Judas-like plotting of the
earl's retainers. Skelton's obsessiveness may stem from his sense of divine mission as heir to
both Apollo (or Skelton's favorite Latin poet Juvenal) and various Old Testament prophets.
   Skelton's obsessiveness dominates the brilliant *Bowge of Courte*, a variant of the medieval
dream vision. Drede, the appropriately named poet tempted aboard an imposing ship named
the Bowge of Courte (the wages or rewards of court), must finally leap overboard to escape

the lethal onslaught of the sinister allegorical figures who resent his competition. The fear and other allegorized qualities that Drede tries to fight (Disceyte, Suspycyon) give the poem its tone of unbearable obsession, lightened but not negated by Skelton's ironic humor. When Drede awakes from his Kafkaesque nightmare, he is teasingly ambivalent about its meaning and implies that life at court is not susceptible to rational control, a resolution less didactic than in the traditional dream allegory.

Though Skelton remained a brilliant manipulator of the iambic pentameter or looser four-stress line in rhyme royal stanzas throughout his career, some time before the composition (c. 1505) of *Phyllyp Sparowe* he developed his signature verse form, the Skeltonic, a line of generally two, sometimes three, accented and any number of unaccented syllables. The lines exhibit structural alliteration, parallelism, and, most important, rhyme-runs of up to fourteen lines, though couplets are frequent. The result, a rush of sound and sense in which individual lines count for little, suits his uncontrolled protagonists. Diverse theories have attempted to derive the form from origins as varied as the Latin sequence, the leonine hexameter, and Anglo-Saxon verse. That all these theories have some plausability suggests that the Skeltonic is the product of an eclectic imagination. Its closest rhythmical analogues are the verses of the 14th-century alliterative revival (the long four-beat lines tended to break in half); and the Skeltonic's combination of rhythm and rhyme parallels the stanzas of the Wakefield Master. Thus, within the body of medieval English verse with its fusion of native stress and continental syllabic traditions, there was a body of poetry resembling the Skeltonic. Because of these roots in the traditional rhythm of English verse, the Skeltonic can convey the illusion of direct speech and also, more surprisingly, multi-levelled irony, pathos, and expressionistic intensity.

Utilizing all these effects, the first part of *Phyllyp Sparowe* dramatizes a convent student's attempt to accept the loss of her pet sparrow, slain by the convent cat. Starting with tags from the Catholic Office for the Dead, the poem seems both a direct expression of the girl's uncomprehending grief, intensified by her desire for hyperbolic vengeance against all cats, and an elaborate parody of the mass, ironically inappropriate from the lips of a child. Occasionally, as with all Skelton personae, his voice fuses with that of his character to raise questions about the innocence the poem had been demonstrating: "To Jupyter I call,/Of heven emperyall,/That Phyllyp may fly/Above the starry sky,/To treade the pretty wren/That is our Ladyes hen./Amen, amen, amen!" After describing an elaborate bird mass and displaying her familiarity with the names of all the writers in the classical, medieval, and Renaissance pantheons (while protesting her lack of learning), young Jane accepts her loss by composing a Latin epitaph for the bird. The second part of the poem, "The Commendacyons," is a lengthy praise of Jane, as the poet presumably both stimulates and calms his own obsession with the erotic appeal of the adolescent girl. The poem, perhaps Skelton's finest, admirably controls the complex tones of the two voices.

Almost as successful is *The Tunnyng of Elinour Rummyng* (written c. 1517), an expressionistic picture of an alewife and her transcendantly vulgar female patrons. The genius of the poem is that, as the male speaker piles on detail after repetitious detail, his own involvement overcomes his disgust at the (doubly) infectious atmosphere: "Theyr thrust was so great/They asked never for mete/But 'Drynke, styll drynke,/And let the cat wynke!/Let us wasshe our gommes/From the drye crommes!' " The speaker's periodic pauses seem the exhaustion of real participation and prepare for the final: "For my fyngers ytche!/I have written to myche/Of this mad mummynge/Of Elinour Rummynge."

Some characteristic Skelton poems like "Against the Scottes" are primarily invectives and contributed to his reputation of boorish tastelessness and to the tradition of an unconventional private life preserved in the anonymous *Merie Tales by Maister Skelton* (1567). The most brilliant invective, "A Devoute Trentale" (for one of his less loved parishioners), celebrates in English and Latin Skeltonics the demise of John Jayberd, "incola de Dis" (a pun on the deceased's past and present domains), and epitomizes him wittily: "Senio confectus,/Omnibus suspectus,/Nemini dilectus,/Sepultus est emong the weedes:/God forgyve him his mysdeedes." More indecent are the flytings against Garnesche, a court rival, which stress his low origins and unattractive person. These same traits appear later in the anti-Wolsey poems *Collyn Clout* and *Why Come Ye Nat to Courte?* which for many years established Skelton as a satirist and were often quoted in histories of the period.

The attack on Wolsey really begins in *Magnyfycence* (written 1515–16?), a generalized treatment of the danger to Henry VIII from advisors who advocate costly and immoral novelty. Perhaps the first secular morality, *Magnyfycence* focuses on wealth as the index to happiness, but its climactic stress on Prince Magnyfycence's conversion by Adversity, Goodhope, and Redress brings it close to the religious pattern. Despite metrical versatility and lively comic villains like Folly and Fancy, *Magnyfycence* is too long and undramatic to sustain much interest, and the protagonist displays too little suffering or insight to support his conversion and the theme of the work.

Collyn Clout (written 1521–22?) dramatizes, in the guise of attacks on ecclesiastical corruption, the speaker's struggle with his awareness of the futility of such attacks: "What can it avayle/To dryve forth a snayle/Or to make a sayle/Of a herynges tayle?/To ryme or to rayle,/Eyther for delyte/Or elles for despyte?" More ominous is his knowledge that the "polluted" language of criticism can threaten religion itself. The poem never convincingly resolves the protagonist's frustration but presents an arresting portrait of anxiety, like versified Nashe.

Speke, Parrot, a long poem in several parts, was especially popular in the 1930's when critics thought its allusiveness made it a kind of Renaissance *Waste Land*. The poem uses its pattern of Old Testament symbolism to mount an attack on Wolsey's abuses of power at home and abroad – "Hys wolvys hede, wanne, blo aß lede,/gapythe over the crown" – a power stemming from Wolsey's inability to transcend his low origins, which make him treat human beings like merchandise: "So bolde a braggyng bocher, and flesshe sold so dere." Skelton's unilluminated conservatism shines through wittily in his attack on the impracticality of the New Learning: "But our Grekis theyr Greke so well have applyed,/That they cannot say in Greke, rydynge by the way,/'How, hosteler, fetche my hors a botell of hay.' " And the protagonist's final attempt to "speke now trewe and playne" makes clear that the poem's seeming complexity resulted from Parrot's caution about forthright utterance. As in all Skelton's supposed satires, he lacks the ability to select a meaningful detail that illuminates both a defect and its implied remedy though he compensates with a protagonist exaggerated to expressionistic proportions. Veering between an attack on Wolsey and the plight of the poet-reformer, the poem is a flawed but intriguing work.

Why Come Ye Nat to Courte?, a less complex dramatization of anger at Wolsey's one-man rule of church and state, succeeds primarily when the anger overreaches itself in finding outrageous and sometimes irrelevant expression. The bizarrely ingenious linking of Wolsey's sexual indiscretions (presumably the cause of his diseased eye) with his spiritual blindness, shocks, yet says nothing about the issues motivating the speaker's animosity. Like Collyn, the protagonist either maliciously or ignorantly attributes even Wolsey's possibly salutary reforms to willful malice or ignorance. Thus, the speaker exhibits the same outrageousness he attributes to Wolsey and undercuts any real satiric thrust.

"The Garlande of Laurell" (written 1523), a variant of the dream vision, seems more muted that most of Skelton's work, as the poet dreams of his ultimately triumphant evaluation at the Court of Fame. The poem's strength lies in its witty view of reputation, a prefiguring of the distinction between true and false fame in "Lycidas." One of the poem's envoys requests both a prebend and protection from Wolsey: "Inter spemque metum," a wish foreshadowing the theme of reconciliation in "A Replycacyon" (1527–29), which begins with a dedication to Wolsey and ends with an envoy stressing the poet's link with "hys noble grace,/That caused you to devyse/This lytel enterpryse." Despite the possible political motives for its composition, the poem, an attack on two Cambridge scholars forced to recant publicly their Lutheran activities, exhibits all the vigor and occasionally questionable taste of the flytings, as it excoriates the penitents. Like *Collyn Clout*, the poem concludes with a stress on the futility of writing verse designed to educate or improve its readers: "For be ye wele-assured/That frensy nor jelousy,/Nor heresy will ever dye." But the poem has insufficiently developed this theme to give the lines any impact. The force in "A Replycacyon," however self-serving its origins, that links it with the body of Skelton's best poetry is the continuing belief that "God maketh his habytacion/In poetes which excelles,/ And sojourns with them and dwelles."

—Burton Kendle

SLESSOR, Kenneth. Australian. Born in Orange, New South Wales, 27 March 1901. Educated at Mowbray House School, Chatswood; North Shore School, Sydney, 1910–19; Sydney Grammar School. Married 1) Noela Senior in 1922 (died 1945); 2) Pauline Wallace in 1951 (marriage dissolved, 1961), one son. Reporter for *The Sun*, Sydney, 1920–24, 1926; a Founding Editor, *Vision*, 1923–24; staff member of *Punch*, Melbourne, and the *Melbourne Herald*, 1925; staff member, 1927, Associate Editor, 1936, and Editor, *Smith's Weekly*, Sydney, and Editor-in-Chief of Smith's Newspapers, 1939; Official War Correspondent for the Australian Forces in the U.K., the Middle East, Greece, and New Guinea, 1940–44; Leader Writer and Literary Editor of *The Sun*, Sydney, 1944–57; Editor of *Southerly*, Sydney, 1956–61; Leader Writer for the *Daily Telegraph*, Sydney, 1957–69. Member of the Advisory Board, Commonwealth Literary Fund, from 1953, and the National Literature Board of Review, from 1968. O.B.E. (Officer, Order of the British Empire), 1959. *Died in 1971.*

PUBLICATIONS

Verse

> *Thief of the Moon.*   1924.
> *Earth-Visitors.*   1926.
> *Trio*, with Harley Matthews and Colin Simpson.   1931.
> *Darlinghurst Nights.*   1931.
> *Cuckooz Contrey.*   1932.
> *Five Bells: XX Poems.*   1939.
> *One Hundred Poems, 1919–1939.*   1944; revised edition, as *Poems*, 1957.

Other

> *Portrait of Sydney.*   1951.
> *The Grapes Are Growing: The Story of Australian Wine.*   1963.
> *Life at the Cross* (on King's Cross, Sydney).   1965.
> *Canberra.*   1966.
> *Bread and Wine: Selected Prose.*   1970.

> Editor, with Jack Lindsay, *Poetry in Australia.*   1923.
> Editor, *Australian Poetry.*   1945.
> Editor, with John Thompson and R. G. Howarth, *The Penguin Book of Australian Verse.*   1958.

Reading List: *Slessor* by Max Harris, 1963; *Slessor* by Graham Burns, 1963; *Slessor* by Clement Semmler, 1966; *Critical Essays on Slessor* edited by A. K. Thomson, 1968; *Slessor* by Herbert C. Jaffa, 1971.

*   *   *

Kenneth Slessor's considerable reputation in Australia as a poet rests on a collection of 104 poems containing what he wished to preserve. After 1947 he ceased to write verse, because, he said, he had nothing more to say. Slessor is given most of the credit for having introduced modernism into Australian poetry, and, along with his contemporary FitzGerald, he certainly announced many of the themes to be developed by younger writers: time, history, voyages, symbolic landscape. Slessor is also pre-eminently the poet of the city of Sydney and its harbour near which he lived most of his adult life. His excursions into the countryside produce little but images of horror and sterility.

Much of his work in the early 1920's was influenced by his association with the artist Norman Lindsay and his son Jack in literary enterprises intended to bring about a cultural renascence in Australia, free from "decadent" European modernism as well as from nationalism. The basis of these ideas was a woolly kind of Nietzscheanism, a rather frenzied vitalism which found curiously static expression in Norman Lindsay's drawings of satyrs and centaurs. Slessor's poems "Thieves' Kitchen," with its romantic abstractions, and "Marco Polo," with its decorative gestures and its undergraduate finale, for all their rhythmic energy are hardly less factitious than the drawings, though pieces like "Heine in Paris" and "Nuremburg" show a genuine individuality and a luxuriant imagination. Slessor's preoccupation with historical subjects was mainly a form of escape from an unsatisfactory present; history was not a process of which he was a living part and which required understanding. All Slessor's dissatisfactions with the modern world, his distress at the eternal flux of life, his sense of the frustration of man's aspirations, issue simply in rage or lamentation. There is no attempt to reason out an explanation why the world has come to be the way it is, no suggestion that poetry might contribute its mite towards the mitigation of human misery. A late poem like "Gulliver," for example, a horrifying indictment of man trapped in the trivialities of modern life, differs from the youthful "Marco Polo" only in its surface realism, its conversational tone, its physical immediacy. The yearning to be "anywhere but here" is the same.

The difference between Slessor and the poet he most resembles, Thomas Hardy, is instructive. Among the poets known to have influenced Slessor, Tennyson, de la Mare, Housman, and T. S. Eliot, Hardy's name is never mentioned. But his debt to Hardy is acknowledged in a short story Slessor wrote for the magazine *Vision* in 1923; it is clear that he took the image of the face trapped behind a pane of glass, which haunts his verse from first to last, from Hardy's "The Face at the Casement" on which he based his story. Hardy took a dim view of man's estate: man seemed to be nothing but the puppet of blind forces, a spectacle to make the gods yawn (as in Slessor's "The Old Play"). One may not like the metaphysic Hardy constructed to deal with the universe he saw, but at least it made possible a way of life not in danger of collapsing into dandyism. Slessor concurs with Hardy's pessimism, his nostalgia, but he has no countervailing argument: it is a concurrence only in mourning. Slessor remained a romantic throughout his career, but what appealed to him in romanticism was its grotesque, flamboyant aspects and a certain mindless sensuality, not its confrontation with a vision of what man might be.

Nevertheless, in spite of reservations about the intellectual content of Slessor's poems, his contribution towards liberating the language of Australian poetry can hardly be over-estimated, and, in spite of the contradictions of the *Vision* program (a national re-birth without nationalism), Slessor developed new lyrical energies in proliferating images and exploring rhythmical possibilities with a zest that denies the elegiac mood characteristic of so much of his verse. He and FitzGerald set new standards in poetry, Slessor in his dedication to technical perfection, FitzGerald in his insistence on solid content and precise thinking.

It is not surprising that an elegy is the peak of Slessor's achievement: the long poem *Five Bells* which re-lives the drowning of an artist friend in Sydney Harbour. All Slessor's preoccupations are gathered up in this poem: his favourite image, the pane of glass, which becomes the port-holes of space through which the dead man is desperately trying to communicate with the living: his other favourite image, the sea, whose eternal movement represents the flux, the destructive aspect of time; the harbour, which represents some sort of permanence within this flux; the sense of human alienation, of fruitful contacts, frustrated by separation or death; of self-alienation, the figure at the window watching a life in which he can never take part. The poem opens with the sound of ship's bells in the harbour marking the watches against a memorable vision of the water at night:

> Deep and dissolving verticals of light
> Ferry the falls of moonshine down. Five bells
> Coldly rung out in a machine's voice. Night and water
> Pour to one rip of darkness, the Harbour floats
> In air, the Cross hangs upside down in water.

The bell recalls the image of the dead Joe and starts off a series of agonised attempts to reconstruct his life and find a meaning in it. All Slessor can remember in the end are little disconnected episodes and the poem comes slowly to an end, not with the conclusion that there is nothing to know but that the poet himself is inadequate to the effort of knowing it. Like all good elegies, *Five Bells* is at once a cry of grief for a particular being and a lament for the general human condition. Protest against death is Slessor's most constant theme, but his anguish does not lead him into nihilism: he does not prefer non-being to the pain of knowing he must die. Slessor's defence against the charge of nihilism can be seen in the last two lines of "South Country," which indicates that death, the norm, is threatened by life, not the other way round: "Something below pushed up a knob of skull,/Feeling its way to air."

The poem "Sleep" reveals Slessor's facility in image-making. Here we find a single idea under the control of one dominating image, and the result is a perfect unity of form and concept. One of the last poems, "Beach Burial," is even more memorable, a triumph of vowel and consonantal music and rhythmical fitness, as well as a most moving and humble tribute to the drowned merchant seamen of the Second World War. *Bread and Wine*, a collection of his best journalistic pieces, includes some fine examples of his work as a war correspondent, as well as his rare literary criticism. The excellence of his prose makes one regret that so much of his talent was expended on ephemeral journalism.

—Dorothy Green

SMART, Christopher. English. Born in Shipbourne, near Tunbridge, Kent, 11 April 1722. Educated at Durham Grammar School, 1733–39; Pembroke College, Cambridge, matriculated 1739, B.A. 1742, M.A. 1747. Married Anna Maria Carnan in 1753; two daughters. Fellow of Pembroke College, 1745–53, and Praelector in Philosophy and Keeper of the Common Chest, Cambridge University, 1746–47 (awarded Seatonian Prize, at Cambridge, 5 times, 1750–53, 1755); confined for a short period in Bedlam, 1751; left Cambridge to become a writer in London, 1755: worked for the bookseller John Newbery for whom he edited, as Mary Midnight, *The Midwife*, 1751–53, and various other periodicals; Co-Editor, *Universal Visitor*, 1756–59; confined to Bedlam, 1763; impoverished during his later years; died in a debtor's prison. *Died 21 May 1771.*

PUBLICATIONS

Collections

Collected Poems, edited by Norman Callan.   2 vols., 1949.
Poems (selection), edited by Robert Brittain.   1950.
Religious Poetry, edited by Marcus Walsh.   1972.

Verse

The Horatian Canons of Friendship, Being the Third Satire of the First Book of Horace Imitated.   1750.
On the Eternity of the Supreme Being.   1750.
A Solemn Dirge, Sacred to the Memory of Frederic, Prince of Wales.   1751.
The Nut-Cracker.   1751.
On the Immensity of the Supreme Being.   1751.
Poems on Several Occasions.   1752.
On the Omniscience of the Supreme Being.   1752.
The Hilliad: An Epic Poem, book 1.   1753.
On the Power of the Supreme Being.   1754.
On the Goodness of the Supreme Being.   1756.
Hymn to the Supreme Being on Recovery from a Dangerous Fit of Illness.   1756.
Mrs. Midnight's Orations and Other Select Pieces.   1763.
A Song to David.   1763; edited by J. B. Broadbent, 1960.
Poems.   1763.
Poems on Several Occasions.   1763.
Ode to the Earl of Northumberland, with Some Other Pieces.   1764.
The Psalms of David (with *Hymns and Spiritual Songs for the Fasts and Festivals of the Church of England*).   1765.
The Parables of Our Lord and Saviour Jesus Christ, Done into Familiar Verse for the Use of Younger Minds.   1768.
Hymns for the Amusement of Children.   1771(?); edited by Edmund Blunden, 1947.
Rejoice in the Lamb [Jubilate Agno]: A Song from Bedlam, edited by W. F. Stead.   1939; edited by W. H. Bond, 1954.

Plays

The Grateful Fair; or A Trip to Cambridge (produced 1747?).
The Judgment of Midas, in *Poems.*   1752.
Hannah: An Oratorio, music by John Worgan (produced 1764).   1764.
Abimelech: An Oratorio, music by S. Arnold (produced 1768).   1768.
Providence: An Oratorio.   1777.

Other

Mother Midnight's Comical Pocket-Book.   1753.

Editor, *An Index to Mankind; or, Maxims Selected from the Wits of all Nations.*   1751.
Editor, with others, *The Student; or, Oxford and Cambridge Monthly Miscellany.*   2 vols., 1750–51.

Editor, *The Muses' Banquet; or, A Present from Parnassus.*   2 vols., 1752.

Editor, *Be Merry and Be Wise; or, The Dream of the Jests, and the Marrow of Maxims, for the Conduct of Life.*   1753.

Editor, with Richard Rolt, *The Universal Visitor and Memorialist for the Year 1756.*   1756.

Editor, *A Collection of Poems for the Amusement of Children Six Foot High* and *Three Feet High.*   2 vols., 1756.

Editor, *The Nonpareil; or, The Quintessence of Wit and Humour* (selections from *Midwife; or, Old Woman's Magazine*).   1757.

Translator, *Carmen Cl. Alexandri Pope in S. Caeciliam, Latine Redditum.*   1743.

Translator, *The Works of Horace Translated Literally into English Prose.*   2 vols., 1756.

Translator, *The Fables of Phaedrus* (in verse).   1765.

Translator, *The Works of Horace Translated into Verse with a Prose Interpretation.*   4 vols., 1767.

Bibliography: *A Bibliography of the Writings of Smart* by G. J. Gray, 1903.

Reading List: *Smart: A Biographical and Critical Study* by E. G. Ainsworth and C. E. Noyes, 1943; *Poor Kit Smart* by Christopher Devlin, 1961; *Smart* by Geoffrey Grigson, 1961; *Smart as a Poet of His Times: A Reappraisal* by Sophia Blaydes, 1966; *Smart: Scholar of the University* by Arthur Sherbo, 1967; *Poetry of Vision: Five Eighteenth-Century Poets* by P. M. Spacks, 1967; *The Poetry of Smart* by Moira Dearnley, 1968; *Smart* by Frances E. Anderson, 1974.

*   *   *

After a notable though brief academic career at Cambridge, Christopher Smart became a professional writer in London, where he achieved a modest reputation composing verse in mostly minor and conventional modes. His collection of *Poems on Several Occasions* contains odes, lyrics, ballads, a masque, Latin versions of Pope and Milton, and a blank-verse georgic poem, "The Hop-Garden." The most significant works of these early London years are the poems on the attributes of the Supreme Being with which Smart five times won the Seatonian Prize of Cambridge University (1750–55). These are Miltonic blank verse exercises in conventional religious sublimity, in which Smart had yet to find his own form and voice, but they surpass the usual level of prize poetry, and already introduce Smart's favourite theme of the grateful chorus of nature in praise of its Creator.

Confinement in the madhouse allowed Smart to escape some of the restrictions of demand and tradition, and create the distinctive religious verse which is his main achievement. Much recent attention has focussed on the *Jubilate Agno*, written on a daily basis from 1759 to 1763, though not published until 1939. The *Jubilate* is an antiphonal poem, formed on the model of Hebrew poetry, and particularly of the Psalms. "Let" verses calling man and the creatures to praise are echoed by more imaginative and personal "For" verses: "Let Chesed rejoice with Strepsiceros, whose weapons are the ornaments of his peace. For I preach the very GOSPEL of CHRIST without comment & with this weapon shall I slay envy" (B1.9). It may be (the incompleteness of the surviving manuscript demands caution) that the *Jubilate* has an overall prophetic scheme, the replacement of Israel by the English as the chosen race; but the responsive structure breaks down early in the poem and the later parts, though not incoherent, have partly the character of a journal, an imaginative exercise in mnemonics by a learned man striving to preserve the stock of his knowledge.

Less ambiguous is Smart's accomplishment in the religious verse written in the madhouse and published in the early 1760's. In these poems Smart developed for himself a distinctive high lyric style, using varied but relatively simple stanzaic forms as defining framework for a poetic language characteristically compressed, metaphoric and allusive. Smart's masterpiece is *A Song to David*, a poem of energetic and committed devotion in which he writes in praise of, and identifies himself with, David the psalmist, "the great Author of The Book of Gratitude," the model of the inspired poet-priest. After describing the virtues of David and the subjects of his divine verse, the *Song* moves into "an exercise upon the decalogue" which uses many parts of the Bible including the New Testament, presents David as the leader of the natural chorus of Adoration in an extended passage which is Smart's finest expression of the theme, and concludes with a rhetorical climax which brings together David, Christ and Smart:

> Glorious – more glorious is the crown
> Of Him that brought salvation down
>   By meekness, call'd thy Son;
> Thou at stupendous truth believ'd,
> And now the matchless deed's atchiev'd,
>   DETERMINED, DARED, and DONE.

The *Song* is constructed with what Smart himself called "exact Regularity and Method," its subjects organised in numerically balanced stanza groups. The *Hymns and Spiritual Songs for the Fasts and Festivals of the Church of England* are a collection of liturgical poems which resemble the *Song* in their careful structure and condensed and figurative style. The best hymns of the cycle ("New Year," "St. Mark," and "The Nativity of Our Lord and Saviour Jesus Christ," for example) are religious lyrics of high quality. The more sophisticated poetic character and orthodox Anglican theology of Smart's *Hymns* differentiate them from the popular hymns of Smart's century. With the *Hymns* were published his monumental, and inevitably more mechanical, *Translation of the Psalms of David*, in which the Psalter is versified, and thoroughly christianized. Though it is not certain whether Smart's *Hymns* were intended to be sung, the *Psalms* were "adapted to the Divine Service," and music was written specially for them by William Boyce and others.

The production of Smart's last years is more various. Biblical stories are the basis of the two oratorios *Hannah* and *Abimelech*; *Hannah* dramatises the adoration theme with some success. The *Poetical Translation of the Fables of Phaedrus* and the versification of the parables were written for the new reading public of children. The verse translation of the works of Horace is an ambitious attempt to write English poetry in the style of Horace's "unrivalled peculiarity of expression." The *Hymns for the Amusement of Children* distil into a language of expressive simplicity the themes of praise and gratitude.

Smart is a difficult case for critical judgment, a considerable poet who commanded no following. The spiritual, formal, and stylistic distinctness of his major religious lyrics seems to have discouraged a contemporary readership, and in his own time, and later, his madness has been too much taken into account. Reliable evaluation will depend on fuller consideration of the published religious verse, and the inaccessible verse Horace.

—Marcus Walsh

SMITH, A(rthur) J(ames) M(arshall).   American.   Born in Montreal, Quebec, Canada, 8 November 1902; emigrated to the United States, 1930; naturalized, 1941. Educated at McGill University, Montreal (Editor, *McGill Literary Supplement*), B.Sc. in arts 1925, M.A. 1926; University of Edinburgh, 1926–28, Ph.D. 1931. Married Jeannie Dougal Robins in 1927;

one son. Assistant Professor, Ball State Teachers College, Muncie, Indiana, 1930–31; Instructor, Doane College, Crete, Nebraska, 1934–35; Assistant Professor, University of South Dakota, Vermillion, 1935–36. Instructor, 1931–33, since 1936 Member of the English Department, and since 1960 Professor of English and Poet-in-Residence, Michigan State University, East Lansing; now retired. Visiting Professor, University of Toronto, 1944–45, University of Washington, Seattle, 1949, Queen's University, Kingston, Ontario, 1952, 1960, University of British Columbia, Vancouver, 1956, Dalhousie University, Halifax, Nova Scota, 1966–67, Sir George Williams University, Montreal, Summers 1967, 1969, State University of New York at Stony Brook, 1969, and McGill University, 1969–70. Recipient: Guggenheim Fellowship, 1941, 1942; Governor-General's Award, 1944; Rockefeller Fellowship, 1944; Lorne Pierce Medal, 1966; Canada Centennial Medal, 1967; Canada Council Medal, 1968. D.Litt.: McGill University, 1958; LL.D.: Queen's University, 1966; Dalhousie University, 1969; D.C.L.: Bishop's University, Lennoxville, Quebec, 1967. Lives in East Lansing, Michigan.

PUBLICATIONS

Verse

News of the Phoenix and Other Poems.   1943.
A Sort of Ecstasy: Poems New and Selected.   1954.
Collected Poems.   1962.
Poems: New and Collected.   1967.

Other

Some Poems of E. J. Pratt: Aspects of Imagery and Theme.   1969.
Towards a View of Canadian Letters: Selected Critical Essays 1928–1972.   1973.

Editor, with F. R. Scott, *New Provinces: Poems of Several Authors.*   1936.
Editor, *The Book of Canadian Poetry.*   1943.
Editor, *Seven Centuries of Verse: English and American, from the Early English Lyrics to the Present Day.*   1947.
Editor, *The Worldly Muse: An Anthology of Serious Light Verse.*   1951.
Editor, with M. L. Rosenthal, *Exploring Poetry.*   1955; revised edition, 1973.
Editor, with F. R. Scott, *The Blasted Pine: An Anthology of Satire, Invective and Disrespectful Verse, Chiefly by Canadian Writers.*   1957; revised edition, 1967.
Editor, *The Oxford Book of Canadian Verse: In English and French.*   1960; revised edition, 1965.
Editor, *Masks of Fiction: Canadian Critics on Canadian Prose.*   1961.
Editor, *Masks of Poetry: Canadian Critics on Canadian Verse.*   1962.
Editor, *Essays for College Writing.*   1965.
Editor, *The Book of Canadian Prose.*   2 vols, 1965–73.
Editor, *100 Poems: Chaucer to Dylan Thomas.*   1965.
Editor, *Modern Canadian Verse: In English and French.*   1967.
Editor, *The Collected Poems of Anne Wilkinson and a Prose Memoir.*   1968.
Editor, *The Canadian Century* (anthology).   1975.

Reading List: *Ten Canadian Poets* by Desmond Pacey, 1958; *The McGill Movement: Smith,*

F. R. Scott, and Leo Kennedy edited by Peter Stevens, 1969; *Odysseus Ever Returning* by George Woodcock, 1970.

*   *   *

Though almost his whole academic life was lived in the United States, A. J. M. Smith has been one of the most influential figures in the Canadian modernist movement, as an editor and anthologist, as a critic, and as a poet. In the *McGill Literary Supplement* and the *McGill Fortnightly Review* he and F. R. Scott, while still students between 1924 and 1927, virtually launched the evolution that took Canadian poetry out of the colonial into the cosmopolitan stage; and as early as 1928, in a historic article in the *Canadian Forum* entitled "Wanted – Canadian Criticism," Smith put forward the argument that to be mature in a creative sense, a culture needed also a tradition of criticism. Over the years he has done a great deal to create that tradition in the essays on Canadian poets and on their cultural ambiance which in 1973 he collected in *Towards a View of Canadian Letters*.

But Smith's essays are hardly more than an iceberg's tip in considering his importance as a critic, which is much more substantially expressed in the series of notable anthologies in which he revealed the nature of Canadian poetry as an identifiable tradition. These begin with *New Provinces*, in which he and F. R. Scott gathered in 1936 the work of the few modernist poets then working in Canada. A few years later, Smith published *The Book of Canadian Poetry*, which he specifically entitled "a critical and historical anthology"; this was the first work that went through the whole of Canadian poetry from its colonial beginnings and performed an act of critical evaluation which established the important Canadian poets and their dominant manners and themes. Selection itself was, in this pioneer collection, a critical act; few people have disputed the canon of significant Canadian poetry which Smith established in *The Book of Canadian Poetry* and reinforced in successive editions. In 1960 he published *The Oxford Book of Canadian Verse*, the first definitive anthology of poems in Canada's two major languages, and in 1967 *Modern Canadian Verse: In English and French*. In all these volumes the selection was reinforced by perceptive commentary, and, if Smith's anthologies are not unquestioningly accepted as the definitive statements on the development of poetry in Canada, they have greatly influenced trends in literary history and critical evaluation alike.

As a poet Smith (who began to attract international attention during the 1930's when his work was published in journals like *New Verse*) is an artist whose self-criticism has been almost fanatical. His four volumes of highly metaphysical poetry, beginning with *News of the Phoenix* and ending with *Poems: New and Selected*, are rigorously chosen, and in every case except the first book contain old poems carefully revised, as well as new ones; the *Collected Poems* honed down the canon to a hundred pieces, all that Smith wished to keep from more than thirty years writing poetry.

Comparing these poems which appear again and again in different versions, one has the impression that Smith is a poet little bound by time. He began to attract attention in the 1930's, but Yeats and the Sitwells seem his natural siblings rather than the Auden-Spender circle. And if the world Smith creates in his poems is autonomous in time – a kind of poetic Laputa that might dip down as easily in the seventeenth century as in the twentieth – it seems equally free in place.

Admittedly, there are a very few poems which seem to declare a parochial preference. Smith proclaims his intention

> To hold in a verse as austere
> As the spirit of prairie and river,
> Lonely, unbuyable, dear,
> The North, as a need and for ever.

But even in his rather imagistic poems on Canadian landscapes the result has little of guidebook topography; rather, the glimpse one receives is of a detached and personal world, so that the familiar cedar and firs and wild duck calls in a poem like "The Lonely Land" lead us into a country in feeling as mythological as any painted by Poussin for the encounter of Gods and mortals:

> This is a beauty
> of dissonance
> this resonance
> of stony strand
> this smoky cry
> curled over a black pine
> like a broken
> and wind-battered branch
> when the wind
> bends the tops of the pines
> and curdles the sky
> from the north.

Smith's aims are spareness, clarity, balance, the austerity of a latter-day classicism enriched by the discoveries of the Symbolists and the Imagists. Unlike the wildly intuitive versifier he celebrated in "One Sort of Poet," Smith never sings, "*Let it come! Let it come!*" His poems are carefully worked to the last safe moment of polishing. One is aware of the unending search for words that are "crisp and sharp and small," for a form as "skintight" as the stallions of his "Far West." Occasionally the visions clarified through Smith's bright glass are too sharp for comfort, the detachment too remote for feeling to survive. More often, they are saved by the dense impact of the darker shapes that lie within the crystal, the "shadows I have seen, of me deemed deeper/That backed on nothing in the horrid air."

It is this enduring sense of the shapeless beyond shape that gives Smith's best poems their peculiar rightness of tension, and make his austerities so rich in implication.

—George Woodcock

SMITH, Stevie (Florence Margaret Smith). English. Born in Hull, Yorkshire, 20 September 1902. Educated at Palmers Green High School, London, and the North Collegiate School for Girls. Secretary to Neville Pearson, Newnes Publishing Company, London, 1923–53. Occasional writer and broadcaster for the BBC. Member, Literature Panel, Arts Council of Great Britain. Recipient: Cholmondeley Award, 1966; Queen's Gold Medal for Poetry, 1969. *Died 8 March 1971.*

PUBLICATIONS

Collections

Collected Poems, edited by James MacGibbon.   1975.

Verse

A Good Time Was Had by All.   1937.
Tender Only to One: Poems and Drawings.   1938.
Mother, What Is a Man? Poems and Drawings.   1942.
Harold's Leap.   1950.
Not Waving But Drowning: Poems.   1957.
Selected Poems.   1962.
The Frog Prince and Other Poems.   1966.
The Best Beast: Poems.   1969.
Scorpion and Other Poems.   1972.

Fiction

Novel on Yellow Paper; or, Work It Out for Yourself.   1936.
Over the Frontier.   1938.
The Holiday.   1949.

Other

Some Are More Human than Others: Sketch-Book.   1958.
Cats in Colour.   1959.

Editor, *T. S. Eliot: A Symposium for His 70th Birthday.*   1958.
Editor, *The Batsford Book of Children's Verse.*   1970; as *The Poet's Garden,* 1970.

Reading List: *Ivy and Stevie: Ivy Compton-Burnett and Stevie Smith: Conversations and Reflections* by Kay Dick, 1971.

*   *   *

Stevie Smith was primarily a poet of the odd, the disconcerting, the unexpected. She seems to have formed her characteristic style as early as the 1930's, though it was not until the publication of her *Selected Poems* and a selection in the Penguin Modern Poets series in the early 1960's that she reached a substantial audience. She was adept at playing one emotion off against another within a poem – quirkiness of a wild-eyed eccentricity against plain common sense, levity against loneliness, sharpness against dreaminess. There is much humour, and often zany comedy, in her work, but at the same time a sense of isolation and blankness, and a preoccupation with death.

Her verse forms and her language may strike some readers as naive; they take elements from nursery rhymes, from banal songs, from hymns, and play sly and outrageous tricks with them. In fact she was a sophisticated artist, and her effects are calculated. She can show asperity and a kind of gleeful malice, and the force of these is made the stronger by the child-like stumbling or sing-song with which she displays them.

Religion and the religious life fascinated and repelled her. Apart from hymns, she was soaked in the Authorised Version of the Bible, and was indignant about what she took to be the commonplace flatness of the *New English Bible.* Within the range of her distinctive poetic voice, she was very varied, sustaining a gruesome narrative (as in "Angel Boley"), facing death with poignant cheerfulness (as in "Black March" and "Scorpion"), or simply using words with playful lunacy, as in "Tenuous and Precarious" ("two Romans"). Her best-known poem, "Not Waving, But Drowning," is a small classic of elegiac gaiety and sardonic stoicism. Her three novels (especially *Novel on Yellow Paper*) have their admirers, and they share characteristics with her verse; but it is as a poet that she is remembered, and is likely to go on being so.

—Anthony Thwaite

SMITH, Sydney Goodsir. Scottish. Born in Wellington, New Zealand, 26 October 1915. Educated at the University of Edinburgh; Oriel College, Oxford, M.A. Taught English to the Polish Army in Scotland for the War Office. Married; two children. Joined the British Council, Edinburgh, 1945; worked as a free-lance writer, journalist and broadcaster. Recipient: Atlantic-Rockefeller Award, 1946; Festival of Britain Scots Poetry Prize, 1951; Thomas Urquhart Award, 1962. *Died in January 1975.*

PUBLICATIONS

Collections

Collected Poems. 1976.

Verse

Skail Wind. 1941.
The Wanderer and Other Poems. 1943.
The Deevil's Waltz. 1946.
Selected Poems. 1947.
Under the Eildon Tree: A Poem in xxiv Elegies. 1948.
The Aipple and the Hazel. 1951.
So Late in the Night: Fifty Lyrics 1944–1948. 1952.
Cokkils 1953.
Omens: Nine Poems. 1955.
Orpheus and Euridice: A Dramatic Poem. 1955.
Figs and Thistles. 1959.
The Vision of the Prodigal Son. 1960.
Kynd Kittock's Land. 1965.
Girl with Violin. 1968.
Fifteen Poems and a Play. 1969.
Gowdspink in Reekie. 1974.

Play

The Wallace: A Triumph (produced 1960). 1960.

Fiction

Carotid Cornucopius: Caird o the Cannon Gait and Voyeur o the Outluik Touer: A Drammatick, Backside, Bogbide, Bedride or Badside Buik, by Gude Schir Skidderie Smithereens. 1947.

Other

A Short Introduction to Scottish Literature. 1951.

Editor, *Robert Fergusson 1750–1774: Essays by Various Hands to Commemorate the Bicentenary of His Birth.* 1952.
Editor, *Gavin Douglas: A Selection of His Poetry.* 1959.
Editor, with J. Delancey Ferguson and James Barke, *The Merry Muses of Caledonia,* by Robert Burns. 1959.
Editor, with others, *Hugh MacDiarmid: A Festschrift.* 1962.
Editor, *Bannockburn: The Story of the Battle and Its Place in Scotland's History.* 1965.
Editor, *A Choice of Burns's Poems and Songs.* 1966.

Reading List: "The Poetry of Smith" by Norman MacCaig in *Saltire Review 1,* April 1954; *Smith* by Hugh MacDiarmid, 1963; Essay by Thomas Crawford, in *Studies in Scottish Literature* edited by G. Ross Roy, 1969.

*   *   *

Sydney Goodsir Smith, after MacDiarmid, is in some ways the most powerful poet of the Scottish Renaissance Movement using only the Scots tongue. It was not indigenous to him, and in daily life he spoke what could only be described as Oxford English, though warmed by an aroused concern not usually associated with such a sound.

Like most post-Burns Scots-writing poets, Smith thus fabricated his language, a process not fully developed in his first book, *Skail Wind.* By the time of *The Deevil's Waltz,* however, he was beginning to master his language, ridding himself of the thick sound-play which marred his earlier verses. There were already signs of the strong lyric side to his talent, as in "Largo," in which the feeling of impotence against impersonal forces is symbolised by the last fishing-boat sailing from the Fife harbour:

> And never the clock rins back,
> The free days are owre;
> The warld shrinks, we luik
> Mair t'oor maisters ilka hour....

Smith's mature work is mostly love-poetry. Love and thought, sex and emotion, illumine a single total experience, for Smith as for Burns before him.

> I loe* ma luve in a lamplit bar   *love
> Braw on a wuiden stool,
> Her knees cocked up and her neb* doun   *nose
> Slorpan a pint o yill.*   *ale

His supreme achievement, *Under the Eildon Tree,* ranks with MacDiarmid's *A Drunk Man Looks at the Thistle.* Using the myth of Thomas the Rhymer, the poet laments the loves of some of the world's great lovers as reflected through his own experience of the passion.

Allusions to mythology and world literature abound, but are skilfully woven into the texture of the verse in the Poundian manner. Smith's series of elegies, both moving and funny, give the impression of absolute word-rightness that comes only with a masterpiece.

> Ah, she was a bonnie cou!
> Saxteen, maybe sevinteen, nae mair,
> Her mither in attendance, *comme il faut*
> *Pour les jeunes filles bien élevées,*
>   Drinkan like a bluidie whaul tae!
> Wee briests, round and ticht and fou *   *full
> Like sweet Pomona in the orange grove;
> Her shanks were lang, but no ower lang, and plump,
>   A lassie's shanks,
> Wi the meisurance o'Venus –
>   Achteen inch the hoch* frae heuchle-bane* til knap,   *thigh; hip bone
>   Achteen inch the cauf frae knap* til cuit*   *knee-cap; ankle
> As is the true perfection calculate
> By the Auntients efter due regaird
> For this and that....

His difficulty in later years arose from the youthfully orientated nature of his favourite subject, although the plight of a meths-drinker and the peculiarities of his much-loved Edinburgh also moved his muse to memorable heights. Sometimes, when writing in strict forms, he would allow a rhythmic falter. He is also one of the few twentieth-century poets who almost totally eschewed imagery, relying on word-manipulation, description, and the association of ideas to gain his effects.

His play *The Wallace*, written for an Edinburgh International Festival, proved to be a patriotic exercise too dependent on rhetoric for lasting conviction, while his Joycean prose-fantasy in Scots, *Carotid Cornucopias*, though clever and amusing, is prevented by the evident artificiality of the language from touching those depths of associative meaning achieved in its model *Ulysses*.

—Maurice Lindsay

SNODGRASS, W(illiam) D(ewitt). American. Born in Wilkinsburg, Pennsylvania, 5 January 1926. Educated at Geneva College, Beaver Falls, Pennsylvania, 1943–44, 1946; University of Iowa, Iowa City, 1949–55, B.A. 1949, M.A. 1951, M.F.A. 1953. Served in the United States Navy, 1944–46. Married 1) Lila Jean Hank in 1946 (divorced, 1953), one daughter; 2) Janice Wilson in 1954 (divorced, 1966), one son and one step-daughter; 3) Camille Rykowski in 1967. Instructor in English, Cornell University, Ithaca, New York, 1955–57, University of Rochester, New York, 1957–58, and Wayne State University, Detroit, 1959–67. Since 1968, Professor of English and Speech, Syracuse University, New York. Visiting Teacher, Morehead Writers Conference, Kentucky, Summer 1955, and Antioch Writers Conference, Yellow Springs, Ohio, Summers 1958–59. Recipient: Ingram Merrill Foundation Award, 1958; Longview Award, 1959; Poetry Society of America Special Citation, 1960; Yaddo Resident Award, 1960, 1961, 1965; National Institute of Arts and Letters grant, 1960; Pulitzer Prize, 1960; Guinness Award, 1961; Ford Foundation Fellowship, for drama, 1963; Miles Award, 1966; National Endowment for the Arts grant,

1966; Academy of American Poets Fellowship, 1972; Guggenheim Fellowship, 1972. Member, National Institute of Arts and Letters, 1972; Fellow, Academy of American Poets, 1973. Lives in Erieville, New York.

PUBLICATIONS

Verse

> *Heart's Needle.*   1959.
> *After Experience: Poems and Translations.*   1968.
> *Remains.*   1970.
> *The Führer Bunker: A Cycle of Poems in Progress.*   1977.

Other

> *In Radical Pursuit: Critical Essays and Lectures.*   1975.

> Editor, *Syracuse Poems 1969.*   1969.

> Translator, with Lore Segal, *Gallows Songs,* by Christian Morgenstern.   1967.

Bibliography: *Snodgrass: A Bibliography* by William White, 1960.

*   *   *

In his essay "A Poem's Becoming" (*In Radical Pursuit*), W. D. Snodgrass charts the evolution of his verse from the the densely composed, ambiguous lyrics of his early years at the University of Iowa to a style of "becoming," in which a dramatic action unfolds through the speaker's intimate disclosures and self-revelations. But throughout his transitions to a freer mode of lyric delivery, he has remained a technically conservative poet, writing most work in tightly rhymed patterns and in set metrical rhythms.

Although the craftsmanship of *Heart's Needle* and *After Experience* is at once lustrous and immaculate, Snodgrass is chiefly to be noted for having given voice to the inner life of the average middle-class American who came to maturity during World War II. Like Lowell, whom he studied under, Snodgrass bases the speaker in his poems on his own life, from service in the war to graduate student days in Iowa to teaching posts around the country. His poems, however, are a careful selection of experiences that capture the disappointments, vicissitudes, and angst of a whole generation of Americans. The most emphatic theme of *Heart's Needle* and *After Experience* is a sense of an increasingly depersonalized identity as social life grows more rationalized.

Heart's Needle begins with the disenchantments of returning veterans, who, in "Returned to Frisco, 1946," reenter civilian life

> free to prowl all night
> Down streets giddy with lights, to sleep all day,
>
> Pay our own way and make our own selections;
> Free to choose just what they meant we should....

With this hint at authoritarianism, Snodgrass chronicles the life of the post-war American who carries pent-up, even violent, emotions under a carefully trained surface. Some of these poems have their speaker worry that he has grown too fearful and timid, as in "Home Town," where he has pursued, then eluded a bold, young girl:

> Pale soul, consumed by fear
> of the living world you haunt,
> have you learned what habits lead you
> to hunt what you don't want;
> learned who does not need you;
> learned you are no one here?

The lovely, complex music of the final sequence, "Heart's Needle," captures this likeable, confused new Everyman as he struggles to remain parent to his young daughter. Snodgrass gives these ten poems his richest, most daringly metaphorical speech.

After Experience continues the Everyman chronicle of *Heart's Needle*, but this volume is less carefully structured and often less resonant in its language. Many of the poems take up themes of captivity, terror, potential violence, and disaster. Typical is "Lobsters in the Window," with its moving depiction of the near-frozen lobster seen through a restaurant window:

> He's fallen back with the mass
> Heaped in their common trench
> Who stir, but do not look out
> Through the rainstreaming glass,
> Hear what the newsboys shout,
> Or see the raincoats pass.

The closing section of the volume features skilful translations of a number of poets, particularly Rilke.

—Paul Christensen

SNYDER, Gary (Sherman).   American.   Born in San Francisco, California, 8 May 1930. Educated at Reed College, Portland, Oregon, B.A. in anthropology 1951; Indiana University, Bloomington, 1951–52; University of California, Berkeley, 1953–56; studied Buddhism in Japan, 1956, 1964, 1965–68. Married 1) Alison Gass in 1950 (divorced, 1951); 2) the poet Joanne Kyger in 1960 (divorced, 1964); 3) Masa Uehara in 1967; two children. Held various jobs, including seaman and forester, 1948–56; Lecturer in English, University of California, Berkeley, 1964–65. Recipient: Bollingen Foundation Research Grant for Buddhist Studies, 1965; National Institute of Arts and Letters prize, 1966; Frank O'Hara Prize, 1967; Guggenheim Fellowship, 1968; Pulitzer Prize, 1975. Lives in California.

PUBLICATIONS

Verse

Riprap.   1959.
Myths and Texts.   1960; revised edition, 1978.

Hop, Skip, and Jump.   1964.
Nanoa Knows.   1964.
Riprap and Cold Mountain Poems.   1965.
Six Sections from Mountains and Rivers Without End.   1965; augmented edition, 1970.
Three Worlds, Three Realms, Six Roads.   1966.
A Range of Poems.   1966.
The Back Country.   1967.
The Blue Sky.   1969.
Sours of the Hills.   1969.
Regarding Wave.   1970.
Manzanita.   1971.
Anasazi.   1971.
The Fudo Trilogy: Spell Against Demons, Smokey the Bear Trilogy, The California Water Plan.   1973.
Turtle Island.   1974.

Other

Four Changes.   1969.
Earth House Hold: Technical Notes and Queries to Fellow Dharma Revolutionaries.   1969.
On Bread and Poetry: A Panel Discussion, with Lew Welch and Philip Whalen.   1976.
The Old Ways (essays).   1977.

Bibliography: in *Schist 2,* Summer 1974.

Reading List: "Snyder Issue" of *In Transit,* 1969.

*   *   *

Gary Snyder's writing is the chronicle of an itinerant visionary naturalist. His poetry contains few technical innovations, but consolidates the Imagist ideas of Pound and Williams and the free forms of Olson and the Beat poets. The poetry is wholly absorbed in the chronicle of the poet's wanderings, his religious training in Japan, and his mythic and cultural perception of nature and experience.

Snyder organizes most of his poetry according to experience rather than theme. In *Riprap,* the crisp, taciturn Imagist poems narrate his days as "look out" and "choker" in the remote reaches of the American northwest, and then his first trip to Japan on merchant tankers. The charm of these poems lies in the frank, modest, often tender lyric nature of the young observer, as in "Piute Creek":

> No one loves rock, yet we are here.
> Night chills. A flick
> In the moonlight
> Slips into Juniper shadow:
> Back there unseen
> Cold proud eyes
> Of cougar and Coyote
> Watch me rise and go.

Cold Mountain Poems contains translations of the Chinese poet, Han-Shan, in which Snyder shows skill as an interpreter and cunning in the choice of a poet like himself in vision and inclination. Han-Shan was a mountain recluse, whose regard for the mystery of nature is intense but not ponderous.

Myths and Texts, written before *Riprap* but not published until 1960, is the best orchestrated and developed of his works. By dividing the book into three parts, "Logging," "Hunting," and "Burning," Snyder creates an initiation ritual for his persona, who enters nature as a destroyer (working for logging companies), then as hunter, who must understand his prey to succeed, and who returns from these encounters awed by the power and will of nature. The themes of his early books establish the lines of development of his succeeding works. In *The Back Country*, he narrates experience from early years in Washington and Oregon, his departure for Japan in 1956, his later return to California. The volume has some notational lyrics, but the concision and intensity of most of the poems are deeply effective and dramatic.

Earth House Hold, a collection of prose, powerfully states the depth of his regard for the natural world and shows the maturing intellectual and spiritual subtlety of his mind over the twenty years it records. Snyder, now a cult figure of the ecology movement, carefully traces the evolution of his thought from jottings of natural phenomena to notes for the making of tribal culture in the post-industrial era. An able prose writer, Snyder is both factual and commanding as a theorist of a new pastoral ideology.

Regarding Wave and *Turtle Island* continue the chronicle of the poet through family life and residence in the United States, where environmental abuse has stirred him to a lyricism of greater and greater activism. The final passages of *Turtle Island* are a series of prose tracts on conservation addressed directly to the reader.

—Paul Christensen

SOMERVILLE, William. English. Born in Colwich, Staffordshire, 2 September 1675. Educated at Winchester College, 1690–94; New College, Oxford, 1694–96; Middle Temple, London, 1696. Married Mary Bethel in 1708 (died, 1731). Fellow, New College, until 1705; thereafter spent his life as a country squire at the family seat of Edstone, Warwickshire. *Died 17 July 1742.*

PUBLICATIONS

Collections

   Poetical Works. 2 vols., 1766.

Verse

   The Two Springs: A Fable. 1725.
   Occasional Poems, Translations, Fables, Tales. 1727.
   The Chace. 1735; revised edition, 1749.
   Hobbinol; or, The Rural Games: A Burlesque Poem in Blank Verse. 1740.
   Field Sports. 1742.
   A Collection of Miscellaneous Poems, edited by F. G. Waldron. 1802.

Bibliography: "Somerville's The Chace, 1735" by J. D. Fleeman, in *Publications of the Bibliographical Society of America 58*, 1964.

*   *   *

The verse of that Warwickshire squire and one-time Oxford fellow, William Somerville, reflects the literary and sporting interests of a well-educated country gentleman. Johnson went so far as to say "he writes very well for a gentleman." Some occasional poems addressed to Addison or referring to Marlborough must have been written about 1712, but the rest of Somerville's early verse, collected into *Occasional Poems* is not easy to date. It consists of unremarkable odes, addresses, epistles, fables, imitations of Horace, and salacious tales in octosyllabic couplets on such subjects as "The Night-Walker Reclaim'd" or "The Inquisitive Bridegroom." His gift for burlesque is admirably shown in a spirited and facetious piece of minor Augustan mock-epic in heroic couplets, "The Bowling-Green"; but more interesting, in view of his later development, is the imitation of John Philips's burlesque Miltonic blank verse in Somerville's poem written as early as 1709, "The Wicker-Chair," which was eventually revised and published with a dedication to Hogarth, under the title of *Hobbinol; or, The Rural Games; A Burlesque Poem*. Here Somerville has certainly followed the advice he gave to Thomson to "read Philips much," for *Hobbinol* very deliberately combines the country-subject of *Cyder* with the comedy of *The Splendid Shilling* in a mock-heroic description, at perhaps too great a length, of village sports. Somerville exposes the boorishness of the country fellow at play, but not without a touch of the John Bullish, roast-beef patriotism of his age and some genuine admiration for "the British freeholders, who, when dressed in their holiday clothes ... eat and drink as plentifully, and fight as heartily, as the greatest hero in the Iliad" (Preface to *Hobbinol*).

Somerville's best poem is his blank-verse didactic piece *The Chace*. This relates the history of the chase and describes in plain, vivid terms the techniques of hunting the fox, stag, hare, otter, and other creatures; it provides detailed instructions upon such matters as the construction of kennels and the breeding of hounds; it reflects upon the psychology of bitches and the mystery of the scent; and intersperses all this with moral and patriotic digressions, and with romantic, exotic excursions describing such pursuits as "the Asiatic way of hunting" and "the ancient way of hunting the tiger with a mirror." Somerville brought into currency the definition of hunting as "the sport of kings; image of war without its guilt"; and by his references to heroic poetry and tactful echoes of Virgil's *Georgics* he contrives to dignify hunting by associating it with patriotism, sociability, health, and even virtue. Though *The Chace* can have few readers today, it was very popular for a century after first publication, and was the favourite reading of Surtees' Mr. Jorrocks. Somerville's last poem, *Field Sports*, is a languid supplement to *The Chace*, describing hawking and angling – "the more polite entertainments of the field."

—A. J. Sambrook

SORLEY, Charles Hamilton.   Scottish.   Born in Aberdeen, 19 May 1895. Educated at King's College Choir School, Cambridge, 1904–08; Marlborough College, 1908–13; studied in Germany, 1914. Commissioned 2nd Lieutenant in the Suffolk Regiment, 1914, and rose to the rank of Captain: trained troops in England, 1914–15; served in France and Belgium, 1915; killed in action at Hulluch. *Died 13 October 1915.*

PUBLICATIONS

Verse

Marlborough and Other Poems.   1916; revised edition, 1916.
(Poems).   1931.

Other

Letters from Germany and from the Army, edited by W. R. Sorley.   1916.
The Letters of Sorley, with a Chapter of Biography, edited by W. R. Sorley.   1919.

Reading List: *The Ungirt Runner: Sorley, Poet of World War I* by Thomas B. Swann, 1965 (includes bibliography); in *Heroes' Twilight* by Bernard Bergonzi, 1965; *Out of Battle: Poetry of the Great War* by Jon Silkin, 1972.

*   *   *

Charles Hamilton Sorley was the only young English poet of the 1914–18 war who had more than a superficial knowledge of pre-war Germany, where he had spent several months after leaving Marlborough College and before taking up his place at Oxford. Right from the start he detested the mendacious vulgarity of anti-German propaganda, and saw the conflict between England and Germany as a fratricidal struggle. In what was probably his last poem, the sonnet that begins "When you see millions of the mouthless dead," Sorley accepts the triumph of death over all who had once been loved: "None wears the face you knew./Great death has made all his for evermore."

Sorley's reputation as a poet depends on a handful of poems inspired by his love of the Marlborough downs and by his reaction to the war. They do not compare in quality with the finest poems of Owen, Rosenberg, and Blunden, but they are remarkable achievements for a man of Sorley's age who had experienced only a few weeks' fighting before his death in action, and before the bloody slaughter in the mud of Flanders that shocked Owen and his fellow poets into maturity.

Sorley's poems, first published in *Marlborough and Other Poems,* are much better known than his letters, which are still in print nearly sixty years after their publication in 1919. Yet his letters display more unmistakably than his poems Sorley's remarkable intellectual power and moral insight. They reveal the complexity and ambiguity of his feelings about the war, as well as an ability to convey the horror and excitement aroused by the spectacle of carnage, and give an inkling of what he might have achieved had he lived.

—John Press

SOUSTER, (Holmes) Raymond.   Canadian.   Born in Toronto, Ontario, 15 January 1921. Educated at University of Toronto schools; Humberside Collegiate Institute, Toronto, 1938–39. Served in the Royal Canadian Air Force, 1941–45. Married Rosalie Lena Geralde in 1947. Since 1939, Staff Member, and currently Securities Custodian, Canadian Imperial Bank of Commerce, Toronto. Editor, *Direction,* Sydney, Nova Scotia, 1943–46: Co-Editor,

Contact,Toronto, 1952–54; Editor, *Combustion*,Toronto, 1957–60. Chairman, League of Canadian Poets, 1968–72. Recipient: Governor-General's Award, 1965; President's Medal, University of Western Ontario, 1967; Centennial Medal, 1967. Lives in Toronto.

PUBLICATIONS

Verse

> *Unit of Five,* with others, edited by Ronald Hambleton.   1944.
> *When We Are Young.*   1946.
> *Go to Sleep, World.*   1947.
> *City Hall Street.*   1951.
> *Cerberus,* with Louis Dudek and Irving Layton.   1952.
> *Shake Hands with the Hangman.*   1953.
> *A Dream That Is Dying.*   1954.
> *For What Time Slays.*   1955.
> *Walking Death.*   1955.
> *Selected Poems,* edited by Louis Dudek.   1956.
> *Crêpe-Hanger's Carnival: Selected Poems 1955–58.*   1958.
> *Place of Meeting: Poems 1958–60.*   1962.
> *A Local Pride.*   1962.
> *12 New Poems.*   1964.
> *The Colour of the Times: The Collected Poems.*   1964.
> *Ten Elephants on Yonge Street.*   1965.
> *As Is.*   1967.
> *Lost and Found: Uncollected Poems.*   1968.
> *So Far So Good: Poems 1938–1968.*   1969.
> *The Years.*   1971.
> *Selected Poems.*   1972.
> *Change-Up: New Poems.*   1974.
> *Rain Check.*   1975.
> *Extra Innings.*   1977.

Fiction

> *The Winter of the Time.*   1949.
> *On Target.*   1973.

Other

> Editor, *Poets 56: Ten Younger English-Canadians.*   1956.
> Editor, *Experiment: Poems 1923–1929,* by W. W. E. Ross.   1958.
> Editor, *New Wave Canada: The New Explosion in Canadian Poetry.*   1966.
> Editor, with John Robert Colombo, *Shapes and Sounds: Poems of W. W. E. Ross.*   1968.
> Editor, with Douglas Lochhead, *Made in Canada: New Poems of the Seventies.*   1970.
> Editor, with Richard Woollatt, *Generation Now* (textbook).   1970.
> Editor, with Douglas Lochhead, *100 Poems of Nineteenth Century Canada* (textbook).   1973.

Editor, with Richard Woollatt, *Sights and Sounds* (textbook).   1973.
Editor, with Richard Woollatt, *These Loved, These Hated Lands* (textbook).   1974.

Reading List: "Groundhog among the Stars" by Louis Dudek, in *Canadian Literature*, Autumn 1964; "To Souster with Vermont" by Hayden Carruth, in *Tamarack Review*, Winter 1965.

*   *   *

Raymond Souster represents the second generation of modern Canadian poets, the poets who rejected the influence of the English poets of the 1930's who had dominated their predecessors, and looked to American poets like Ezra Pound and William Carlos Williams, less as models than as guides to the acquisition of a way of speaking proper to their experience as North Americans. What distinguishes Souster from the poets with whom he shared that direction in the 1940's, such as Irving Layton and Louis Dudek, is the modesty of presence and the quietness of voice he has adopted. His work is entirely lacking in the histrionics of being a poet.

There are other items of traditional poetic baggage Souster has abandoned in his efforts to write a poetry of direct experience. He avoids not only metrical forms but also recondite allusions, archaisms, even symbolism − everything, in other words, that can impede his search for the pure image, or even the pure imageless voice that can convey truly an experience or an emotion.

Souster's poems tend to be short, colloquial in diction, frequently epigrammatic, aiming at the sharp and often ironic insight into a specific situation that expands in the mind to an insight into existence itself. He has been writing with such consistent regularity over the past thirty years that his books offer many examples of the kind of self-contained yet resonantly allusive poem which, at his best, he creates. A good example, for its combination of brevity and intensity, is the six-line poem "The Six-Quart Basket":

> The six-quart basket
> one side gone
> half the handle torn off
>
> sits in the centre of the lawn
> and slowly fills up
> with the white fruits of the snow.

Other poems are less lucid because their feeling is darker, and, for all Souster's evident enjoyment of the bright surface of the earth and the occasional haunting nostalgia of his poems, the dominant mood that underlies them is perhaps best summed up in his own lines:

> life isn't a matter of luck
> of good fortune, it's whether
> the heart can keep singing
> when there's really no reason
> why it should

—George Woodcock

SOUTHEY, Robert. English. Born in Bristol, 12 August 1774. Educated at Westminster School, London; Balliol College, Oxford; also studied law. Married 1) Edith Fricker in 1795 (died, 1837); 2) Caroline Ann Bowles in 1839. Involved with Coleridge in an abortive scheme for a "pantisocracy" in America, 1794; visited Spain and Portugal, 1800; settled near Wordsworth at Greta Hall, Keswick, 1803, and worked as a translator and journalist; contributor to the *Quarterly Review* from 1808. Poet Laureate, 1813 until his death. *Died 21 March 1843.*

PUBLICATIONS

Collections

> *Poetical Works.* 10 vols., 1860.
> *Poems,* edited by Edward Dowden. 1895.
> *Select Prose,* edited by Jacob Zeitlin. 1916.

Verse

> *Poems,* with Robert Lovell. 1795.
> *Joan of Arc: An Epic Poem.* 1796; revised edition, 2 vols., 1798, 2 vols., 1806, 1812.
> *Poems.* 2 vols., 1797–99; revised edition of vol. 1, 1797.
> *Thalaba the Destroyer.* 2 vols., 1801.
> *Madoc.* 1805.
> *Metrical Tales and Other Poems.* 1805.
> *The Curse of Kehama.* 1810.
> *Roderick, The Last of the Goths.* 1814.
> *Odes to the Prince Regent, the Emperor of Russia, and the King of Prussia.* 1814.
> *The Minor Poems.* 3 vols., 1815.
> *The Poet's Pilgrimage to Waterloo.* 1816.
> *The Lay of the Laureate: Carmen Nuptiale.* 1816.
> *A Vision of Judgement.* 1821; edited by R. E. Roberts, 1932.
> *A Tale of Paraguay.* 1825.
> *All for Love, and The Pilgrim to Compostella.* 1829.
> *Poetical Works.* 1829.
> *The Devil's Walk,* with Coleridge, edited by H. W. Montagu. 1830.
> *Selections from the Poems,* edited by I. Moxon. 1831; as *The Beauties of the Poems,* 1833.
> *Poetical Works.* 10 vols., 1837–38.
> *Oliver Newman: A New England Tale, with Other Poetical Remains,* edited by H. Hill. 1845.
> *Robin Hood: A Fragment, with Other Fragments and Poems,* with Caroline Southey. 1847.

Play

> *The Fall of Robespierre,* with Coleridge. 1794.
> *Wat Tyler: A Dramatic Poem.* 1817.

Fiction

The Doctor.   7 vols., 1834–47 (vols. 6 and 7 edited by J. W. Warter); edited by J. W. Warter, 1848.

Other

Letters Written During a Short Residence in Spain and Portugal, with Some Account of Spanish and Portuguese Poetry.   1797; revised edition, 2 vols., 1808.
Letters from England.   3 vols., 1807; edited by Jack Simmons, 1951.
History of Brazil.   3 vols., 1810–19.
The History of Europe.   4 vols., 1810–13.
Omniana; or, Horae Otiosiores, with Coleridge.   2 vols., 1812; edited by Robert Gittings, 1969.
The Origin, Nature, and Object of the New System of Education.   1812.
An Exposure of the Misrepresentations and Calumnies in Mr. Marsh's Review of Sir George Barlow's Administration at Madras.   1813.
The Life of Nelson.   2 vols., 1813; revised edition, 1814, 1830.
A Summary of the Life of Arthur Duke of Wellington.   1816.
The Life of Wesley and the Rise and Progress of Methodism.   2 vols., 1820; edited by M. H. Fitzgerald, 1925.
The Expedition of Orsua and the Crimes of Aguirre.   1821.
Life of John Duke of Marlborough.   1822.
History of the Peninsular War.   3 vols., 1823–32.
The Book of the Church.   2 vols., 1824.
Vindiciae Ecclesiae Anglicanae: Letters to Charles Butler, Comprising Essays on the Romish Religion and Vindicating the Book of the Church.   1826.
Sir Thomas More; or, Colloquies on the Progress and Prospects of Society.   2 vols., 1829.
Essays Moral and Political.   2 vols., 1832.
Selections from the Prose Works, edited by I. Moxon.   1832; as *The Beauties of the Prose Works,* 1833.
Lives of the British Admirals.   5 vols., 1833–40; vol. 1 as *The Early Naval History of England,* 1835; edited by D. Hannay, as *The English Seamen,* 1904.
The Life of the Rev. Andrew Bell, vol. 1.   1844.
Select Biographies: Cromwell and Bunyan.   1844.
Common Place Book, edited by J. W. Warter.   4 vols., 1849–51.
Selection from the Letters, edited by J. W. Warter.   1849.
Correspondence with Caroline Bowles, edited by Edward Dowden.   1881.
Southey: The Story of His Life Written in His Letters, edited by J. Dennis.   1887.
Journal of a Tour in the Netherlands in the Autumn of 1815.   1902.
Letters: A Selection, edited by M. H. Fitzgerald.   1912.
The Lives and Works of the Uneducated Poets, edited by J. S. Childers.   1925.
Journal of a Tour in Scotland in 1819, edited by C. H. Herford.   1929.
Journals of a Residence in Portugal 1800–01, and a Visit to France 1838, edited by Adolfo Cabral.   1960.
New Letters, edited by Kenneth Curry.   2 vols., 1965.

Editor, and Contributor, *The Annual Anthology.*   2 vols., 1799–1800.
Editor, with Joseph Cottle, *The Works of Chatterton.*   3 vols., 1803.
Editor, *Palmerin of England,* by Francisco de Moraes, translated by Anthony Munday.   1807.
Editor, *Horae Lyricae,* by Isaac Watts.   1834.

Editor, *The Works of William Cowper: Poems, Correspondence, and Translations, with a Life of the Author.*   15 vols., 1835–37.

Translator, *On the French Revolution*, vol. 2, by Mr. Necker.   1797.
Translator, *Amadis of Gaul*, by Vasco Lobeira.   4 vols., 1803.
Translator, *Chronicle of the Cid.*   1808.
Translator, *The Geographical, Natural, and Civil History of Chili*, by Abbé Don J. Ignatius Molina.   1808.
Translator, *Memoria Sobre a Litteratura Portugueza.*   1809.

Reading List: *Life and Correspondence* by C. C. Southey, 6 vols., 1849–51; *The Early Life of Southey 1774–1803* by William Haller, 1917 (includes bibliography); *Southey* by Jack Simmons, 1945; *Southey and His Age*, 1960, and *Southey*, 1964, both by Geoffrey Carnall; "The Published Letters of Southey: A Checklist," in *Bulletin of the New York Public Library*, March 1967, and *Southey*, 1975, both by Kenneth Curry; *Southey: The Critical Heritage* edited by Lionel Madden, 1972.

*   *   *

Robert Southey is now remembered mainly as a mediocre associate of Coleridge and Wordsworth, or as the fatuously self-applauding poet laureate of Byron's *Vision of Judgment*, apostate revolutionary and diligent manufacturer of books in verse and prose. Not that his work is forgotten altogether: indeed, a modified form of his version of "The Story of the Three Bears" has become one of the most familiar texts in the language, and publishers still find it worth reprinting his *Life of Nelson*. But the few acknowledged successes seldom kindle interest beyond themselves.

As a poet he is exceptionally versatile. There are irregular odes, a heroic epistle from the Fair Rosamond in the manner of Pope's "Eloisa to Abelard," sublime compositions on Biblical topics, sportive trifles on a pig and on gooseberry pie, sentimental sonnets, burlesque sonnets and elegies by the fictitious Abel Shufflebottom, lugubrious sapphics, sententiously reflective poems in blank verse, and ballads and metrical tales. In various "monodramas" he enters vehemently into the defiance of isolated and imperilled characters. In "English Eclogues" (1798–9) Southey makes his own particular experiment to discover, as Wordsworth put it, how far the language of conversation in the middle and lower classes of society is adapted to the purposes of poetic pleasure: at their best they achieve a pleasantly sardonic crispness.

The turmoil of his emotional life, of which one has tantalising glimpses in the brief record he left of some of his dreams, is nearly always firmly repressed. He wrote to escape from his emotions, not to explore them. Something slips out in his fascination with traditional stories of the Devil and his interventions in human affairs, and while most of his ballads on this theme are more humorous than terrifying, there is no mistaking the element in them of sheer nightmare. As the Devil comes to claim the old woman of Berkeley, the frenzied endeavours of piety are paralysed: "the choristers' song that late was so strong,/Grew a quaver of consternation." More commonly, Southey tells tales in which the Devil or his representatives are thwarted, as in that notable tour-de-force "The Young Dragon"; but salvation is always a miracle.

The characteristic animation of Southey's poetry is most perfectly expressed in the "rhymes for the nursery" on the cataract of Lodore, but it is equally apparent in his exotic verse narratives *Thalaba the Destroyer* and *The Curse of Kehama*, written to illustrate the Arabian and Hindu mythologies respectively. Their irregular verse and bizarre subjects were more congenial to him than the more orthodox materials of his other long poems: *Joan of Arc*, *Madoc*, and *Roderick, The Last of the Goths*. In these large compositions the poetry tends to be lack-lustre and featureless, giving less scope for alluring fantasies of invulnerability.

Southey's deepest need was to feel invulnerable, whether in the Arabia or India of his imagination, or in his secluded life in the Lake District. His most satisfying poetry contrives to juxtapose the pleasures of domestic seclusion with the perils of an ugly world, as in the poem on the Battle of Blenheim, when an old man and two children reflect upon the dreadful slaughter many years after the event. Longer poems in a similar vein are *The Poet's Pilgrimage to Waterloo* and *A Tale of Paraguay*.

He took his role as poet very seriously, the more so when appointed Poet Laureate in 1813. He saw himself as commissioned to keep up the spirit of the country in her battles, and carry on a crusade against sedition and a heartless political economy. In the 1790's he had been equally vehement on the radical side, and *Wat Tyler*, a verse play written in 1794 but not published until it appeared in 1817 in a pirated edition, denounces the aristocracy with a splendid zest. His later political views must be studied in his prose writings, notably in some of the articles he wrote for the *Quarterly Review*, where the intensity of his indignation can generate an eloquence resembling the water coming down at Lodore. The *Colloquies on the Progress and Prospects of Society* are a temperate summing up of his convictions, developed in conversations with the ghost of Sir Thomas More, with a reassuring background of Lakeland scenery.

One of Southey's pleasantest characteristics is the wide-ranging curiosity which informs an unusually comprehensive survey of English society in *Letters from England*, finds its most wayward expression in his eccentric novel *The Doctor*, and spices his laborious histories of Brazil (1810–19) and of the Peninsular War (1823–32), not to mention the *Life of Wesley and the Rise and Progress of Methodism*. The celebrated *Life of Nelson* is on a smaller scale than these other works, and the constraint perhaps makes the book less attractive to those who enjoy Southey in a more outrageous vein. His private correspondence suffers from no such inhibitions: it supplies vivid materials for anyone who wants to understand the emotional climate of early nineteenth-century Britain.

—Geoffrey Carnall

SOUTHWELL, Robert. English. Born in Horsham St. Faith, Norfolk, in 1561. Educated by English jesuits in Douai; also studied in Paris and Rome; Jesuit novice, Rome, 1578; ordained priest, 1584; returned to England, with Father Garnet, as missionaries, 1586: sheltered by various Catholic families, and became chaplain to the Countess of Arundel. Betrayed, and imprisoned in the Tower of London, 1592–95, and then executed. Canonized, Roman Catholic Church, 1970. *Died 21 February 1595*.

PUBLICATIONS

Collections

  Prose Works, edited by W. J. Walter. 1828.
  Poems, edited by J. H. McDonald and Nancy Pollard Brown. 1967.

Verse

> *Saint Peter's Complaint; Other Poems.*   1595; revised edition, 1595, 1602; edited by W.
> J. Walter, 1817.
> *Moeniae; or, Certain Excellent Poems and Spiritual Hymns.*   1595.

Other

> *An Epistle of Comfort to the Reverend Priests.*   1587(?); edited by Margaret Waugh,
> 1966.
> *Mary Magdalen's Funeral Tears.*   1591.
> *The Triumphs over Death; or, A Consolatory Epistle.*   1595; edited by J. W. Trotman,
> 1914.
> *A Humble Supplication to Her Majesty.*   1595 (1601?); edited by R. C. Bald, 1953.
> *A Short Rule of Good Life.*   1596(?); edited by Nancy Pollard Brown, in *Two Letters
> and Short Rules of a Good Life,* 1972.
> *Spritual Exercises and Devotions,* edited by J. M. de Buck, translated by P. E.
> Hallett.   1931.

Bibliography: *The Poems and Prose Writings of Southwell: A Bibliographical Study* by J. H.
McDonald, 1937.

Reading List: *Southwell* by R. Bastian, 1931; *The Life of Southwell* by Christopher Devlin,
1956; *The Poetry of Southwell* by Joseph D. Scallon, 1975.

*   *   *

For his short, heroic life Robert Southwell provides an explanation in *An Epistle of
Comfort:* "When England was Catholic, it had many glorious confessors. It is now for the
honour and benefit of our country that it be also well stored with the number of martyrs."
For his poetry, he offers a programme in his prefatory epistle to *Saint Peters Complaint,*
deploring the unworthy subjects of secular poets and proposing "to weave a new webbe in
their owne loome."

His subject-matter is always religious, sometimes Biblical, sometimes gnomic, sometimes
introspective. Within this range, he draws on a variety of metrical and rhetorical patterns,
and his writing is informed by a curious mixture of influences: Ignatian meditation, the
Italian poetry both secular and religious which he read during his Jesuit training in Rome, the
popular English collections such as *Tottel's Miscellany* which he would refine to higher use.
In the ballad stanzas of "The Burning Babe" he combines apparent naivety, a startling vision,
and ingeniously fused conceits for love, pain, and purification. In the sequence of lyrics on
the Virgin Mary he develops the paradoxes proper to her story. In "Looke home" he works
with a quiet series of definitions: "Mans mind a myrrour is of heavenly sights,/A breefe
wherein all marvailles summed lye." Nourished on meditation, Southwell can unite emotion
with the exercise of a subtle mind, expressed with colloquial force or simplicity. In "Sinnes
heavy load," he attributes Christ's fall to the ground (in Gethsemane or on the way to
Calvary) solely to "my sinne"; "But had they not to earth thus pressed thee,/Much more they
would in hell have pestred mee."

The longest of his poems, *Saint Peters Complaint,* grew slowly through at least four
versions, beginning as a partial translation of Luigi Tansillo's *Le Lagrime di San Pietro* and
ending as a dramatic monologue, passionate and analytical, in 132 stanzas. Together with
Mary Magdalens Funerall Teares, in prose, this work introduced into England the "literature
of tears" of the Counter-Reformation, a line of penitential writing taken up by authors from

Lodge and Nashe to major metaphysical and baroque poets of the seventeenth century, including Herbert, Crashaw, and Vaughan.

In the half-century after Southwell's execution, at least twenty editions of his various poems appeared, both evidence and vehicle for his influence on seventeenth-century writers. His prose was equally popular, and like his verse it has immediate, and not merely historical, interest. The sweetness and the rigour of his mind are expressed in beautifully cadenced sentences, as in *An Humble Supplication to Her Majestie*, and in *An Epistle of Comfort* he writes movingly of the plight of English Catholics, or in *A Short Rule of Good Life* he counsels scrupulous attention to detail, whether in devotion or in dress.

—Kay Stevenson

SPENCER, Bernard. English. Born in Madras, India, 30 November 1909. Educated at Marlborough College; Corpus Christi College, Oxford. Reviewer for the *Morning Post* and *Oxford Mail*; subsequently a schoolteacher: Classics Master at Westminster School, London; helped Geoffrey Grigson to edit *New Verse* in the late 1930's, and, with Lawrence Durrell and Robin Fedden, edited *Personal Landscape*, Middle East, 1942–45; joined the British Council, 1940; Lecturer, Institute of English Studies, Salonika; served five years in Egypt, two years in Italy; Director of Studies, British Institute, Madrid, 1948–49; served at London headquarters, 1950–53, Madrid, 1954, Athens, 1955, London, 1956–58, Spain and Turkey, 1959–62, and in Vienna, 1962–63. *Died 12 September 1963.*

PUBLICATIONS

Verse

    Aegean Islands and Other Poems.   1946.
    The Twist in the Plotting: Twenty Five Poems.   1960.
    With Luck Lasting.   1963.
    Collected Poems.   1965.

Other

    Editor, with Stephen Spender, *Oxford Poetry 1930.*   1930.
    Editor, with R. Goodman, *Oxford Poetry 1931.*   1931.
    Editor, with others, *Personal Landscape.*   1945.

    Translator, with Lawrence Durrell and Nanos Valaortis, *The King of Asine and Other Poems,* by George Seferis.   1948.

Reading List: articles by John Betjeman and Lawrence Durrell, in *London Magazine,* 1963–64.

*   *   *

Although Bernard Spencer was a contemporary of Auden, MacNeice, and Spender and, like them, was a frequent contributor to *New Verse*, he brought out no collection of poems before the appearance of *Aegean Islands* in 1946. While sharing the contemptuous hostility displayed by Auden and his friends towards the idiocy and cruelty of capitalism, Spencer was less concerned than they with the social pattern of Britain, perhaps because of his sojourn on the shores of the Mediterranean in the late 1930's and during the war. He was one of the moving spirits in the publication of *Personal Landscape*, a periodical devoted largely to the work of writers whom the chances of war had brought to Egypt as civilians or as members of the armed forces.

Spencer is essentially a lyrical poet, keenly responsive to the landscapes and seascapes in which he found himself. He loved the Mediterranean, the lands of the olive and the grape, where it was still possible to follow a way of life not distorted by the demands of industrialism and the dictates of greed. But he was too acute and honest an observer to pretend that the traditional culture of the Mediterranean could survive, uninfected by war and revolution. Bernard Spencer's two later collections, *The Twist in the Plotting* and *With Luck Lasting*, celebrate the sensuous properties of the world in which he rejoiced, but recognize, with sad irony, the despoiling of landscapes and lives by human wickedness and folly. In "The Rendezvous" he revisits a city made hideous by slogans of hate:

> And true
> to loves love never thought of, here
> with bayonet and with tearing fence,
> with cry of crowds and doors ̦slammed to,
> waits the once known and dear, once chosen
> city of our rendezvous.

He deserves to be more widely read than at present and to be recognized as one of the most gifted poets of his generation.

—John Press

SPENDER, Stephen (Harold). English. Born in London, 28 September 1909; son of the writer Harold Spender. Educated at University College School, London; University College, Oxford. Served as a fireman in the National Fire Service, 1941–44. Married 1) Agnes Marie Pearn in 1936; 2) Natasha Litvin in 1941, one son and one daughter. Editor, with Cyril Connolly, *Horizon* magazine, London, 1939–41; Counsellor, UNESCO Section of Letters, 1947; Co-Editor, 1953–66, and Corresponding Editor, 1966–67, *Encounter* magazine, London; Contributor, *Art and Literature*, 1964–66. Elliston Lecturer, University of Cincinnati, 1953; Beckman Professor, University of California, Berkeley, 1959; Visiting Professor, Northwestern University, Evanston, Illinois, 1963; Clark Lecturer, Cambridge University, 1966; Visiting Professor, University of Connecticut, Storrs, 1968–70; Mellon Lecturer, Washington, D.C., 1968; Northcliffe Lecturer, University of London, 1969; Visiting Lecturer, University of Florida, Gainesville, 1976. Since 1970, Professor of English Literature, University College, University of London. Consultant in Poetry, Library of Congress, Washington, D.C., 1965–66. Honorary Member, Phi Beta Kappa, Harvard University, Cambridge, Massachusetts; Fellow, Institute of Advanced Studies, Wesleyan University, Middletown, Connecticut, 1967. Recipient: Queen's Gold Medal for Poetry, 1971. D.Litt.: University of Montpellier; Loyola University, Chicago. Honorary Fellow,

University College, Oxford, 1973. Honorary Member, American Academy of Arts and
Letters, 1969. C.B.E. (Commander, Order of the British Empire), 1962. Lives in London.

PUBLICATIONS

Verse

Nine Experiments by S. H. S., Being Poems Written at the Age of Eighteen.   1928.
20 Poems.   1930.
Poems.   1933; revised edition, 1934.
Vienna.   1934.
The Still Centre.   1939.
Selected Poems.   1940.
Ruins and Visions.   1942.
Spiritual Exercises (To Cecil Day Lewis).   1943.
Poems of Dedication.   1947.
Returning to Vienna 1947: Nine Sketches.   1947.
The Edge of Being.   1949.
Collected Poems 1928–1953.   1955.
Selected Poems.   1964.
The Generous Days: Ten Poems.   1969; augmented edition as The Generous Days,
    1971.

Plays

Trial of a Judge (produced 1938).   1938.
Danton's Death, with Goronwy Rees, from a play by Georg Büchner (produced
    1939).   1939.
To the Island (produced 1951).
Mary Stuart, from the play by Schiller (produced 1957).   1959.
Lulu, from the play by Frank Wedekind (produced 1958).
Rasputin's End, music by Nicholas Nabokov.   1963.

Fiction

The Burning Cactus (stories).   1936.
The Backward Son.   1940.
Engaged in Writing, and The Fool and the Princess.   1958.

Other

The Destructive Element: A Study of Modern Writers and Beliefs.   1935.
Forward from Liberalism.   1937.
The New Realism: A Discussion.   1939.
Life and the Poet.   1942.
Jim Braidy: The Story of Britain's Firemen, with William Sansom and James
    Gordon.   1943.
Citizens in War – and After.   1945.
Botticelli.   1945.

937

European Witness (on Germany).   1946.
Poetry since 1939.   1946.
World Within World: The Autobiography of Spender.   1951.
Europe in Photographs.   1951.
Shelley.   1952.
Learning Laughter (on Israel).   1952.
The Creative Element: A Study of Vision, Despair, and Orthodoxy among Some Modern Writers.   1953.
The Making of a Poem (essays).   1955.
The Imagination in the Modern World: Three Lectures.   1962.
The Struggle of the Modern.   1963.
Ghika: Paintings, Drawings, Sculpture, with Patrick Leigh Fermor.   1964.
The Magic Flute: Retold.   1966.
The Year of the Young Rebels.   1969.
Love-Hate Relations: A Study of Anglo-American Sensibilities.   1974.
Eliot.   1975.
The Thirties and After.   1978.

Editor, with Louis MacNeice, *Oxford Poetry 1929*.   1929.
Editor, with Bernard Spencer, *Oxford Poetry 1930*.   1930.
Editor, with John Lehmann and Christopher Isherwood, *New Writing, New Series I* and *II*.   1938–39.
Editor, with John Lehmann, *Poems for Spain*.   1939.
Editor, *A Choice of English Romantic Poetry*.   1947.
Editor, *Selected Poems*, by Walt Whitman.   1950.
Editor, with Elizabeth Jennings and Dannie Abse, *New Poems 1956*.   1956.
Editor, *Great Writings of Goethe*.   1958.
Editor, *Great German Short Stories*.   1960.
Editor, *The Writer's Dilemma*.   1961.
Editor, with Donald Hall, *The Concise Encyclopedia of English and American Poets and Poetry*.   1963; revised edition, 1970.
Editor, with Irving Kristol and Melvin J. Lasky, *Encounters: An Anthology from Its First Ten Years*.   1963.
Editor, *Selected Poems*, by Abba Kovner and Nelly Sachs.   1971.
Editor, *A Choice of Shelley's Verse*.   1971.
Editor, *D. H. Lawrence: Novelist, Poet, Prophet*.   1973.
Editor, *The Poems of Percy Bysshe Shelley*.   1974.
Editor, *W. H. Auden: A Tribute*.   1975.

Translator, *Pastor Hall*, by Ernst Toller.   1939.
Translator, with J. L. Gili, *Poems*, by García Lorca.   1939.
Translator, with J. B. Leishman, *Duino Elegies*, by Rainer Maria Rilke.   1939; revised edition, 1948.
Translator, with J. L. Gili, *Selected Poems*, by García Lorca.   1943.
Translator, with Frances Cornford, *Le Dur Désir de Durer*, by Paul Eluard.   1950.
Translator, *The Life of the Virgin Mary (Das Marien-Leben)* (bilingual edition), by Rainer Maria Rilke.   1951.
Translator, with Frances Fawcett, *Five Tragedies of Sex* (includes *Spring's Awakening, Earth-Spirit, Pandora's Box, Death and Devil, Castle Wetterstein*), by Frank Wedekind.   1952.
Translator, with Nikos Stangos, *Fourteen Poems*, by C. P. Cavafy.   1977.

Bibliography: *Spender: Works and Criticism: An Annotated Bibliography* by H. B. Kulkarni, 1977.

Reading List: *Spender, MacNeice, Day Lewis: A Critical Essay* by Derek Stanford, 1969; *Spender and the Thirties* by Andrew K. Weatherhead, 1974; *"The Angry Young Men" of the Thirties: Day Lewis, Spender, MacNeice, Auden* by Elton E. Smith, 1975.

* * *

Stephen Spender's crucial epoch was the "pink decade," 1930–39, in which intellectuals began by hoping for revolutionary achievements from Soviet Communism and ended (with the Berlin-Moscow Non-Aggression Concordat) with the disillusioned admission that Russia was subject to the same compromises as other sovereign states. A profoundly personal poet, Spender diagnosed England's loss of personal belief (*The Destructive Element*) as the disease that produced the observable symptoms of decaying cities, factories abandoned or short-handed, widespread unemployment (*Trial of a Judge*), corrupt and ineffectual political leadership (canto 2, *Vienna*), and aristocratic stupidity ("The Cousins," 1936). Indeed, even the most enlightened leaders were fumbling and distracted ("Exiles from Their Land," *The Still Centre*), and individual illness was only a fractured segment of the vast malaise of the age ("The Dead Island," 1936). So sensitive an individualist that boarding school was unmitigated purgatory, Spender urged his liberal friends to surrender to the discipline of communism because it was the only force capable of defeating fascism (*Forward from Liberalism*). Invoking the sanction of Joseph Conrad and Henry James in his criticism, he warned writers that, although reality is dangerous to idealists, it is the final test of relevant, revolutionary art. Later he admitted he could no longer accept the Party's dogmatic dismissal of all non-communist writers as having nothing relevant to say.

In both his personal and political life, Spender has always been obsessed with relationship: person to person, person to group. Thus the autobiographic statement of his development tended to become the record of a coming revolutionary world conflict. But he often seems to have been left with opposing convictions: the 1920's was the last age in which an individual, by himself, could influence history; yet, by the end of the 1930's, he was reluctant to choose between East and West, socialism and capitalism. He simply wanted the freedom to be and to express his uniquely gifted self. Thus his poetry often took the two-sided form of compulsive compassion for the suffering of others, coupled with a masochistic insistence on sharing that suffering.

Without the playful and mordant wit of MacNeice and Auden, his poetry has always risen on Romantic wings and engaged the sympathy of its audience by its touching idealism.

—Elton E. Smith

SPENSER, Edmund. English. Born, probably in East Smithfield, London, c. 1552. Educated at Merchant Taylors' School, London, 1561–69; Pembroke Hall, Cambridge (sizar, i.e., poor scholar), 1569–76, B.A. 1573, M.A. 1576. Married 1) Machabyas Chyld in 1579 (died by 1591); 2) Elizabeth Boyle in 1594. Secretary to John Young, Bishop of Rochester, 1578–79; entered the household of the Earl of Leicester, 1579, and became acquainted with Sidney; appointed Secretary to Lord Grey of Wilton, Lord Deputy of Ireland, 1580, and thereafter held various official posts in Ireland; in return for services was given Kilcolman Castle in Cork, where he settled in 1586; visited London with Ralegh, 1589; revisited London, 1596; made Sheriff of Cork, 1598; Kilcolman burned down, 1598, and he returned to London. *Died 16 January 1599.*

PUBLICATIONS

Collections

> *Works: A Variorum Edition,* edited by Edwin Greenlaw, and others. 10 vols.,
> 1932–58.

Verse

> *The Shepherd's Calendar, Containing Twelve Eclogues Proportionable to the Twelve
> Months.* 1579.
> *The Faerie Queene, Disposed into Twelve Books, Fashioning XII Moral Virtues* (6 books
> completed). 2 vols., 1590–96; revised edition, with *Mutability Cantos,* 1609; edited
> by A. C. Hamilton, 1977.
> *Complaints, Containing Sundry Small Poems of the World's Vanity.* 1591.
> *Daphnaida: An Elegy upon the Death of the Noble and Virtuous Douglas
> Howard.* 1591; revised edition, in *Four Hymns,* 1596.
> *Amoretti and Epithalamion.* 1595; *Epithalamion* edited by E. Welsford, with *Four
> Hymns,* 1969.
> *Colin Clout's Come Home Again.* 1595.
> *Four Hymns.* 1596; edited by E. Welsford, with *Epithalamion,* 1969.
> *Prothalamion; or, A Spousal Verse in Honour of the Double Marriage of Lady Elizabeth
> and Lady Katherine Somerset.* 1596.

Other

> *A View of the Present State of Ireland,* in *The History of Ireland,* edited by J.
> Ware. 1633; edited by W. L. Renwick, 1970.
> *Three Proper and Witty Familiar Letters; Two Other Very Commendable Letters,* with
> Gabriel Harvey. 1580.

> Translator, *Axiochus,* by Plato. 1592.

Bibliography: *A Critical Bibliography of the Works of Spenser Printed Before 1700* by F. R.
Johnson, 1933; *Two Centuries of Spenserian Scholarship 1609–1805* by J. Wurtsbaugh,
1936; *Spenser: An Annotated Bibliography 1937–1972* by Waldo F. McNeir and Foster
Provost, 1975.

Reading List: *The Life of Spenser* by A. C. Judson, in *Works,* 1945; *Spenser and the Faerie
Queene* by Leicester Bradner, 1948; *The Allegorical Temper* by Harry Berger, Jr., 1957; *The
Allegory of the Faerie Queene* by M. P. Parker, 1960; *Spenser and the Numbers of Time* by
Alastair Fowler, 1964; *Spenser's Image of Nature: Wild Man and Shepherd in the Faerie
Queene* by D. Cheney, 1966; *The Poetry of the Faerie Queene* by Paul J. Alpers, 1967, and
Spenser: A Critical Anthology edited by Alpers, 1969; *Spenser's Anatomy of Heroism: A
Commentary on the Faerie Queene* by Maurice Evans, 1970; *The Faerie Queene: A
Companion for Readers* by Rosemary Freeman, 1970; *The Prophetic Moment: An Essay on
Spenser* by Angus Fletcher, 1971; *A Preface to Spenser* by Helena Mennie Shire, 1978.

*   *   *

"The best poets are astronomical poets."
Gabriel Harvey

Spenser made for Elizabethan England the heroic poem hoped for by each emergent nation-state of renaissance Europe. He brought to the reading Englishman, in print and in his own tongue, fresh and lovely verses – and a chance to participate in the new poetry from Italy, its great themes, its philosophy of love, its re-envigorated sense of language. (Sir Philip Sidney had written earlier in "the sweet new style" – but his poems remained unprinted, a private pleasure among friends.)

Spenser had won himself a fine education by his own talents; as scholar and poet he must make his career. By 1579 in the household of Lord Leicester, the Queen's favourite, he published – if under a pseudonym – *The Shepheardes Calender*. This major poem of sparkling originality gave a virtuoso display of verse-rhythms and forms in a language no longer plain-style Tudor, but coloured by country speech or rising to eloquence in words from poetry abroad. It was a pastoral – but with a difference. A series of eclogues like Vergil's were now given cosmic form, being fashioned as a calendar of months, each month with its traditional character and zodiac sign; and there were pictures (woodcuts) – another innovation. Thus a calendar made of poetry interpreted in universal terms the year 1579 as it passed, its crises and its personalities. The work was an immediate success. But the poet had carried pertinence of comment too far. Offence was taken in high places and the poet was removed from the scene – to Ireland.

Spenser was appointed Secretary to the Lord Governor of Ireland, whose thankless task it was to keep peace in the portion of that island under English settlement and to defend it from the determined efforts of the native Irish to end that colonisation. Elizabeth would not adequately support her Deputy and would not recognise the dire threat of Irish "rebels" now supported by Catholic powers in Europe. As civil servant – and later as himself settler and land-holder – Spenser wrote his first-hand experiences, his informed anxieties of some sixteen-years' residence, into a political treatise *A Vue of the Present State of Ireland*. The mounting danger he announced in 1596 was not heeded. General rebellion two years later proved him justified – but destroyed his home. He returned to London to die.

Spenser's heroic poem *The Faerie Queene* was planned on a grand scale in his Cambridge days: from the court of Gloriana (figuring Elizabeth) twelve Knights should ride out, each champion of a Virtue, each on a quest to overcome that Virtue's vicious foes. At some point he foreclosed his plan to a sequence of seven Books. As Alastair Fowler has argued, he gave to a recognised *genre* a new cosmic form, the seven days of the week each under its planet. Knight, Virtue and the terrain through which his adventures lead him all "belong" in their character to the Book's number and planet.

This sense of an indwelling potency or significance in each phenomenon of nature making up a vast harmonious whole (the sacral universe) is a sense we have lost – but can recapture through study and alert response to the poem's persuasive power. Artistic involvement in cosmic form is itself "formative": we participate in harmony. We progress with the Knight through his Book, learning to tell false from true, to defeat enticements or menaces by evil powers, to discern and to will the good to prevail. So we today can be fashioned "in virtuous and gentle discipline" as Spenser intended. All the time there are clues to historical events, which provide instances of profound issues under discussion. *The Faerie Queene* Books I to III, printed in 1590, won Spenser fame and a royal pension – but no post in England. Later Books conceived from Ireland under Elizabeth's misgovernment show a darkening image of the Queen, as lady of the Book. As Defender of the Faith she had shone in Una of Book I, Of Holinesse. As Astraea, heavenly maid of Justice, she has departed from the earth in Book V and she appears ambiguously in figures of female tyranny and qualified mercy. The Quest is for Irena – peace and Ireland, inbuilt irreconcileables. The Irish colouring deepens in the Book of Courtesie – and of "the savage man." The fragment of Book VII shows the enemy of cosmic harmony, mutability in nature and rebellion in man, arraigned before a council of Olympian gods – on Arlo Hill, visible from Spenser's Irish domain. Though the issues of this

941

Elizabethan heroic poem are with us today sometimes in identical gear, luckily so is the vision of cosmic harmony, mankind and the graces dancing to the poet's piping, vouchsafed us still.

Spenser's major poems on love are similarly illuminating and "formative": love is the creating principle of the universe, flowing from God to man and returning upwards in aspiration towards true love through perception of true beauty. His last printed volume was *Fowre Hymnes* of such love and beauty. His single eclogue, *Colin Clout's Come Home Againe*, treats of varieties of love, of incestuous lust, and of never ending devotion for his own beloved, of false and true in sophisticated love-service of the sovereign lady, Elizabeth. His sonnet sequence, *Amoretti*, traces the psychic discipline of courtship on the outline of his own for Elizabeth Boyle, his second wife. It culminates in a celebration of marriage, *Epithalamion*, an ode. Here cosmic rhythm at its zenith of solar power at midsummer informs the record of the marriage day and night, a dance of the hours in a polyphonic pattern of number symbolism and delightful sounds. The modern reader is drawn in to participate fully as he learns to discern the harmony of intellectual concepts. (No other sonnet sequence had this climax of marriage, of cosmic joy and harmony.)

Prothalamion, his last poem, celebrates the espousal of two noble sisters, held at Essex House on Thames-side (where Spenser had served Lord Leicester). The brides made their way there by water and they are figured as swans, while the swan image also voices the poet's farewell singing. Symbolism of number in line and stanza gives cosmic orientation. Venus's blessing is asked for the brides and cosmic harmony is conjured between Cynthia/ Elizabeth and Lord Essex, for the moment in royal displeasure.

The minor poems offer "complaints" on mutability (a renaissance concern), a beast-fable mirroring personalities at court, several gracious trifles for presentation to noble patronesses and a fabled apology – written long since to Leicester, now dead – for that early offence.

Spenser made the experience of poetry universal in a new way. We can perceive the "profit and delight" it offers and learn to share it.

—Helena Mennie Shire

STAFFORD, William (Edgar). American. Born in Hutchinson, Kansas, 17 January 1914. Educated at the University of Kansas, Lawrence, B.A. 1936, M.A. 1947; University of Iowa, Iowa City, Ph.D. 1954. Conscientious Objector during World War II; active in Pacifist organizations, and since 1959 Member, Oregon Board, Fellowship of Reconciliation. Married Dorothy Hope Frantz in 1944; two daughters and two sons. Member of the English Department, 1948–54, 1957–60, and since 1960, Professor of English, Lewis and Clark College, Portland, Oregon. Assistant Professor of English, Manchester College, Indiana, 1955–56; Professor of English, San Jose State College, California, 1956–57. Consultant in Poetry, Library of Congress, Washington, D.C., 1970–71. United States Information Agency Lecturer in Egypt, Iran, Pakistan, India, Nepal, and Bangladesh, 1972. Recipient: Yaddo Foundation Fellowship, 1955; National Book Award, 1963; Shelley Memorial Award, 1964; National Endowment for the Arts grant, 1966; Guggenheim Fellowship, 1966; Melville Cane Award, 1974. D.Litt.: Ripon College, Wisconsin, 1965; Linfield College, McMinnville, Oregon, 1970. Lives in Portland, Oregon.

Publications

Verse

>   *West of Your City.*   1960.
>   *Traveling Through the Dark.*   1962.
>   *Five American Poets,* with others, edited by Thom Gunn and Ted Hughes.   1963.
>   *Five Poets of the Pacific Northwest,* with others, edited by Robin Skelton.   1964.
>   *The Rescued Year.*   1966.
>   *Eleven Untitled Poems.*   1968.
>   *Weather.*   1969.
>   *Allegiances.*   1970.
>   *Temporary Facts.*   1970.
>   *Poems for Tennessee,* with Robert Bly and William Matthews.   1971.
>   *Someday, Maybe.*   1973.
>   *That Other Alone.*   1973.
>   *In the Clock of Reason.*   1973.
>   *Going Places.*   1974.
>   *Stories That Could Be True: New and Collected Poems.*   1977.

Other

>   *Down in My Heart* (experience as a conscientious objector during World War II).   1947.
>   *Friends to This Ground: A Statement for Readers, Teachers, and Writers of Literature.*   1967.
>   *Leftovers, A Care Package: Two Lectures.*   1973.
>
>   Editor, with Frederick Candelaria, *The Voices of Prose.*   1966.
>   Editor, *The Achievement of Brother Antoninus: A Comprehensive Selection of His Poems.*   1967.
>   Editor, with Robert H. Ross, *Poems and Perspectives.*   1971.

Reading List: "Stafford Issue" of *Northwest Review,* Spring 1974, and of *Modern Poetry Studies,* Spring 1975.

*   *   *

   William Stafford's poetry exemplifies the best of what is left of American transcendentalism. Like Emerson and Thoreau, he regards the human imagination as "salvational," and many of his poems are about the capacity of the imagination to derive meaning and awe from the world. Like the transcendentalists Stafford also regards the natural world as a possible model for human behavior:

>   The earth says every summer have a ranch
>   that's minimum: one tree, one well, a landscape
>   that proclaims a universe – sermon
>   of the hills, hallelujah mountain,
>   highway guided by the way the world is tilted.

943

But, although in Stafford's poems Nature ("the landscape of justice") evinces both a glimmer of consciousness and a strict propriety of process, it contains few prescriptions definite enough to be useful guides to human behavior. It provides only distant analogues. Nor is Nature a comforting maternal presence. If there be any one lesson which the human species might draw from natural process, it is humility, to know your place, to have local priorities. Stafford has an organic conception of poetry, which also recalls the transcendentalists. For him, poetry is a manifestation of the "deepest [truest] place we have":

> They call it regional, this relevance –
> the deepest place we have: in this pool forms
> the model of our land, a lonely one,
> responsive to the wind. Everything we own
> has brought us here: from here we speak.

Composition is thus, for Stafford, a means of bringing to light the dark processes of the self:

> I do tricks in order to know:
> Careless I dance,
> then turn to see
> the mark to turn God left for me.

The style of Stafford's poems is quiet and colloquial. Few of them are very long. Throughout his poetry, certain words recur with an intensionally symbolic meaning. The most prominent of these words are "dark," "deep," "cold," "far," "God," and "home." Many of his earlier poems are rhymed, some heavily, some with slant or touch rhyme. His earlier work shows a fondness for sprung rhythm rather than quantitative metric. Since 1960 his work has grown steadily more relaxed in form and more rhetorically inventive. Typical of such inventiveness is the poem "Important Things":

> Like Locate Knob out west
> of town where maybe the world
> began. Like the rusty wire
> sagged in the river for a harp
> when floods go by.
> Like a way of talking, the slur
> in hello to mean you and God
> still think about justice.
> Like being alone, and you are
> alone, like always.
> You always are.

—Jonathan Holden

STANLEY, Thomas. English. Born in Cumberlow, Hertfordshire, baptized 8 September 1625. Educated at Pembroke Hall, now Pembroke College, Cambridge, matriculated 1639, M.A. 1642. Married Dorothy Enyon; nine children. After several years spent travelling on the Continent he retired to lodgings in the Middle Temple, London; his wealth allowed him to live as a man of letters and classical scholar and to act as patron to numerous writers; after collapse of the Royalist cause in 1649, continued this way of life in Cumberlow. Fellow of the Royal Society, 1663. *Died 12 April 1678.*

PUBLICATIONS

Collections

Poems and Translations, edited by Galbraith Miller Crump.   1962.

Verse

Poems and Translations.   1647; as *Poems*, 1651.
Psalterium Carolinum.   1657.

Other

*The History of Philosophy, Containing the Lives, Opinions, Actions, and Discourses of the
    Philosophers of Every Sect.*   3 vols., 1655–62.

Bibliography: "Stanley: A Bibliography of His Writings in Prose and Verse" by M. Flower, in *Transactions of the Cambridge Bibliographical Society,* 1950.

*   *   *

Thomas Stanley's main achievements are scholarly, but he was also a poet and translator, and as such, he has a place among the Cavalier lyrists, together with his cousin Lovelace and his friends Shirley and Hall.

Stanley's importance as a translator is partly historical, for his choice of subjects such as Anacreon and Marino reflects the interests of his age. His graceful translations are not conspicuously different from his own compositions, employing similar conceits and paradoxes and the same vocabulary of hearts, flames, roses, ashes, stars, and snow. The majority of Stanley's own poems are brief lyrics describing or addressed to a mistress whose love he seeks, enjoys, or with quiet bitterness forgoes. These surpass not only his dull excursion into political comment, *Psalterium Carolinum*, but also his "Register of Friends" and other pieces addressed to male acquaintances, which – for all the value Stanley sets on friendship – do not contain particularly memorable verse. Yet his love-lyrics, metrically skilled and neatly constructed as they are, lack urgency, and while the plaintive cadences or muted Platonism of individual pieces can be moving, read as a whole the collection gives the impression of underlying languor. A poem to his friend Hammond contains an open statement of preference for emotional non-involvement, which bears out the impression given by his poetry as a whole. When translating he tends to tone down passages which display a vigour or physicality not found in his own poems, of which Saintsbury remarked with truth in his edition (*Minor Poets of the Caroline Period*, 1921): "There is a very little of the *exercise* about them." Moreover, while Stanley's phraseology or material is at times reminiscent of some of his contemporaries, the converse is hardly true, for no strongly marked identity can be found in his work; nor does he ever achieve one of those golden moments that lift so many of the minor poets of this age temporarily above themselves in one or two poems of exceptional felicity.

Inasmuch as any personality at all emerges from the poems, it is a slightly schizoid one, that prefers to avoid vulnerability by suppressing feeling, and suffers the inevitable consequence of emotional flattening, a stoical dreariness devoid of hope. Hence while most of his poems make their impact through the prettiness of the conceit on which they are based, or the neatness of the conclusion, or the swell and fall of the verse which Stanley can contrive so admirably, a number of his most effective pieces draw their strength from a grim preference for suppression, a strongly willed refusal to participate, to be involved, to live. "The Divorce," "The Repulse," "The Exequies," "Despair" – which rejects both pain and any possibility of joy – and the heavily ominous "Expectation" are among the poems which show this attitude most clearly. For all the charm of his lighter lyrics it is in these sombre pieces that Stanley is most moving, for here the withholding of his full energies ceases to be a trivialising inhibition, and becomes instead a source of genuine tension and power.

—Margaret Forey

STEAD, C(hristian) K(arlson).   New Zealander.   Born in Auckland, 17 October 1932. Educated at Mount Albert Grammar School; University of Auckland, B.A. 1954, M.A. (honours) 1955; University of Bristol (Michael Hiatt Baker Scholar), Ph.D. 1961. Married Kathleen Elizabeth Roberts in 1955; two daughters and one son. Lecturer in English, University of New England, Armidale, New South Wales, 1956–57. Lecturer in English, 1959–61, Senior Lecturer, 1962–63, Associate Professor, 1964–67, and since 1967 Professor of English, University of Auckland. Chairman, New Zealand Literary Fund Advisory Committee. Recipient: Poetry Awards Incorporated prize, 1955; Winn-Manson Katherine Mansfield Award, for fiction and for essay, 1960, and Fellowship, 1972; Nuffield Travelling Fellowship, 1965; Jessie McKay Award, 1972; New Zealand Book Award, 1975. Lives in Auckland.

PBLICATIONS

Verse

> *Whether the Will Is Free: Poems 1954–62.*   1964.
> *Crossing the Bar.*   1972.
> *Quesada: Poems 1972–1974.*   1975.

Fiction

> *Smith's Dream.*   1971.

Other

> *The New Poetic: Yeats to Eliot.*   1964.

> Editor, *New Zealand Short Stories: Second Series.*   1966.

946

Editor, *Measure for Measure: A Casebook.*   1971.
Editor, *The Letters and Journals of Katherine Mansfield: A Selection.*   1977.

Reading List: essay by Roy Fuller, in *London Magazine,* July 1964; by James Bertram in *Islands 2,* 1972.

*   *   *

C. K. Stead's *The New Poetic* illustrates his robust, clear-eyed criticism and special skill in the analysis of a text. Many consider Stead's chief distinction as a writer is as a critic. The most substantial of his prose writings is *Smith's Dream,* a kind of political novel set in a New Zealand that has become dominated by a Fascist dictator who is supported by a strong American military presence. The author's interest is in events rather than the springs of action, personal or political, and he shows considerable narrative skill. The tale has been made into the film *Sleeping Dogs.*

As a poet Stead is not prolific but through his three volumes of verse he has established a solid reputation in his country. *Whether the Will Is Free* is apprentice work strongly influenced by the poets he has chosen for models. The best-known of these early poems is "Pictures from a Gallery Underseas." Stead's poetry has the qualities of good expository prose, clarity, firmness of exposition, and a strong sense of organisation. Its inspiration is often literary but the language has the vitality of common speech and a natural rhythm. The poems in *Crossing the Bar* are poems of statement rather than exploration. He comments on American politics, the nature and importance of poetry, literary events like Auden's sixtieth birthday. There are, too, personal poems like the moving "A Small Registry of Births and Deaths" on his experience of fatherhood. Caesar is a dominant figure in the book. From him the poet has learnt his style, his Rome anticipates modern America: "What Wolf began, Eagle accomplishes." A good deal of Stead's political thinking is summed up in a striking statement of the consequences of political miscalculation: "Minerva had a mouse in mind./It was a weasel, tore her beak." Caesar the victorious soldier is Stead himself fighting that campaign with his "Enemy, brother, Lucifer/My own self" whose outcome is poetry.

The title sequence of *Quesada* is an extended allusion to the questing Don Quixote. The style of the volume is more relaxed than that of the other books, and more open to experience. Confessedly secular in outlook and without a mythopoeic imagination Stead writes verse that frequently lacks any sense of the mystery of life, something essential to the truest poetry. The deficiency is to some extent compensated for when he writes in the Romantic mode of the earlier part of this last volume. Besides the image of Quesada, romantic and compassionate, the book contains an admirable evocation of the South of France.

—F. M. McKay

STEPHENS, James.   Irish.   Born in Dublin in 1882. No formal education; self-taught. Worked as a clerk in a solicitor's office; Founder, with Padraic Colum and Thomas MacDonagh, *Irish Review,* 1911; lived as a free-lance writer, and campaigned for the creation of the Irish Free State. Recipient: Polignac Prize, 1912; Irish Tailltean Gold Medal, 1923. *Died 26 December 1950.*

Collections

  A Stephens Reader, edited by Lloyd Frankenberg.   1962; as *A Selection*, 1962.
  Letters, edited by Richard J. Finneran.   1974.

Verse

  Where the Demons Grin.   1908.
  Insurrections.   1909.
  The Lonely God and Other Poems.   1909.
  The Hill of Vision.   1912.
  Songs from the Clay.   1915.
  The Adventures of Seamus Beg, The Rocky Road to Dublin.   1915.
  Green Branches.   1916.
  Reincarnations.   1918.
  Little Things and Other Poems.   1924.
  A Poetry Recital.   1925.
  Collected Poems.   1926; revised edition, 1954.
  Optimist.   1929.
  Theme and Variations.   1930.
  Strict Joy.   1931.
  Kings and the Moon.   1938.

Play

  Julia Elizabeth (as *The Marriage of Julia Elizabeth*, produced 1911).   1929.

Fiction

  The Charwoman's Daughter.   1912; as *Mary, Mary*, 1912.
  The Crock of Gold.   1912.
  Here Are Ladies (stories).   1913.
  The Demi-Gods.   1914.
  Hunger: A Dublin Story.   1918.
  Deirdre.   1923.
  In the Land of Youth.   1924.
  Etched in Moonlight (stories).   1928.

Other

  The Insurrection in Dublin.   1916.
  Irish Fairy Tales (juvenile).   1920.
  Arthur Griffith, Journalist and Statesman.   1924(?).
  On Prose and Verse (essays).   1928.
  James, Seumas, and Jacques: Unpublished Writings, edited by Lloyd
    Frankenberg.   1964.

Editor, *The Poetical Works of Thomas MacDonagh.* 1916.
Editor, with E. L. Beck and R. H. Snow, *Victorian and Later English Poets.* 1934.

Bibliography: *Bibliographies of Modern Authors 4* by Iolo A. Williams, 1922.

Reading List: *Stephens, Yeats, and Other Irish Concerns* by G. B. Saul, 1954; "Stephens Issue" of *Colby Library Quarterly 9,* 1961; *Stephens: His Work and an Account of His Life* by Hilary Pyle, 1965; *The Fenian Chief: A Biography of Stephens* by Desmond Ryan, 1967; *Stephens: A Critical Study* by Augustine Martin, 1977.

*   *   *

James Stephens's work as a poet may be divided into three distinct groupings. The earliest verse is one of social themes, often developed in direct speech and owing an acknowledged debt to Browning. It is very much of its period, carrying the concern of Colum and O'Sullivan for the people of contemporary Ireland into a cityscape. These realist poems are to be found in *Insurrections,* his first published book of verse. In *Insurrections* are to be found also his first visionary poems, and the beginnings of his obsession for Blake, something he derived from his older friend, the poet and painter, George Russell (AE). *The Hill of Vision* is, in fact, cloaked in Blakean imagery and ideas. It still bears, however, a vigorous Stephens imprint and a remarkable grasp of the use of satire and of humour, both of which his subsequent excursions into theosophy and Indian philosophy were to stifle. Thus the final books of verse, *Strict Joy* and *Kings and the Moon,* are composed of mystic meditations or emotional outbursts celebrating the Absolute, which are devoid of poetic tension and of the imaginative ideas and colourful idioms that characterize his earlier work. His generally most satisfying body of verse – translations from or developments of the themes of three Gaelic poets, O Bruadair, O Rahilly and Raftery, which he gathered under the heading *Reincarnations* – brings his colloquial and spiritually inspired styles together in a wealth of expressive imagery, which he uses with a triumph of economy.

The development of his prose parallels that of his poetry. *The Charwoman's Daughter,* a charmingly related idyll set in Dublin streets, marries a stern realism, with which he and his fellows were attempting to present 20th-century Ireland, with a not too rigid symbolism based on Blakean concepts. *The Crock of Gold,* his most popular book, takes his Blakean ideology a step further, moving the setting out of Dublin into rural Ireland, and perhaps excelling *The Charwoman's Daughter* in the magic and personality of its narrative. *The Demi-Gods,* not such a success, substitutes theosophical ideas for those of Blake. His two sets of short stories are self-consciously intellectual, and the medium seems to have inhibited his gift for relaxed narrative. This found further outlets, however, in his eye-witness account of the rising in 1916, *The Insurrection in Dublin;* in his retellings of Irish legends published in three volumes, of which *Irish Fairy Tales* is the most perfect; and in the series of original broadcasts which he recorded for the BBC in London during World War II.

—Hilary Pyle

STEVENS, Wallace. American. Born in Reading, Pennsylvania, 2 October 1879. Educated at Harvard University, Cambridge, Massachusetts, 1897–1900; New York University Law School, 1901–03; admitted to the New York Bar, 1904. Married Elsie V. Kachel in 1909; one daughter, Holly. Worked as a Reporter for the New York *Herald Tribune,* 1900–01; practised law in New York, 1904–16; joined the Hartford Accident and

Indemnity Company, Connecticut, 1916: Vice-President, 1934–55. Recipient: Harriet Monroe Poetry Award, 1946; Bollingen Prize, 1950; National Book Award, 1951, 1955; Pulitzer Prize, 1955. Member, National Institute of Arts and Letters, 1946. *Died 2 August 1955.*

PUBLICATIONS

Collections

> *Letters*, edited by Holly Stevens.   1967.
> *The Palm at the End of the Mind: Selected Poems and a Play*, edited by Holly Stevens.
>   1971.

Verse

> *Harmonium.*   1923; revised edition, 1931.
> *Ideas of Order.*   1935.
> *Owl's Clover.*   1936.
> *The Man with the Blue Guitar and Other Poems.*   1937.
> *Parts of a World.*   1942.
> *Notes Toward a Supreme Fiction.*   1942.
> *Esthetique du Mal.*   1945.
> *Description Without Place.*   1945.
> *Transport to Summer.*   1947.
> *Three Academic Pieces: The Realm of Resemblance, Someone Puts a Pineapple Together,*
>   *Of Ideal Time and Choice.*   1947.
> *A Primitive Like an Orb.*   1948.
> *The Auroras of Autumn.*   1950.
> *Selected Poems*, edited by Dennis Williamson.   1952.
> *Selected Poems.*   1953.
> *Collected Poems.*   1954.

Plays

> *Carlos among the Candles* (produced 1917).   In *Opus Posthumous*, 1957.
> *Three Travelers Watch a Sunrise* (produced 1920).   In *Opus Posthumous*, 1957.
> *Bowl, Cat, and Broomstick*, in *Quarterly Review of Literature 16*, 1969.

Other

> *Two or Three Ideas.*   1951.
> *The Relations Between Poetry and Painting.*   1951.
> *The Necessary Angel: Essays on Reality and the Imagination.*   1951.
> *Raoul Dufy: A Note.*   1953.
> *Opus Posthumous* (miscellany), edited by Samuel French Morse.   1957.

Bibliography: *Stevens: A Descriptive Bibliography* by J. M. Edelstein, 1973.

Reading List: *The Shaping Spirit: A Study of Stevens* by William Van O'Connor, 1950; *The Comic Spirit of Stevens* by Daniel Fuchs, 1963; *The Clairvoyant Eye: The Poetry and Poetics of Stevens* by Joseph N. Riddel, 1965; *The Act of the Mind: Essays on the Poetry of Stevens* edited by Roy Harvey Pearce and J. Hillis Miller, 1965; *On Extended Wings: Stevens' Longer Poems* by Helen H. Vendler, 1969; *Stevens: Poetry as Life* by Samuel French Morse, 1970; *Introspective Voyager: The Poetic Development of Stevens* by A. Walton Litz, 1972; *Stevens* by Lucy Beckett, 1974; *Stevens: The Poems of Our Climate* by Harold Bloom, 1977; *Souvenirs and Prophecies: The Young Stevens* by Holly Stevens, 1977.

*   *   *

Wallace Stevens is a poet who combined a long poetic career with another career, that of a business executive. The career that concerns us here – that of poet – produced a large body of work that circles around a lifelong consideration from which all his best poems radiate. Each poem is one testimony to an encompassing vision of what Stevens judges to be the prime obligation of a modern poet. That obligation leaves its mark on comparatively brief and early poems like "Peter Quince at the Clavier," "Sunday Morning," and "Thirteen Ways of Looking at a Blackbird" and continues in later and quite extensive works like *Transport to Summer* and *Ideas of Order*. Stevens is, early and late, concerned with a purification of the human intellect and sensibility – in the first place, the intellect and sensibility of the poet who is writing, and, in the second place, the intellect and the sensibility of the reader who responds to what the poet has written.

The purification takes place as service to a set of ideas – "ideas of order" in Stevens' phrase – that are ignored or, at best, served badly and intermittently in the culture to which Stevens belongs. Our sensibility has been corrupted by habits of thought that seduce the poet and his readers from a prime duty. Poet and reader have the chance, if they but respond rightly to the world which constantly surrounds them and indeed bombards them with endless impressions, to take in special sensations (the colors of light on the sea, the taste of cheese and pineapple, a musical cadence) and set them down in words. These sensations are most pure at a special time of the year (summer) and in southern climes where light and color are most intense. The sensations are adulterated by many things, by winter and northern climes, for example. Even more crucial in Stevens' account are the betrayals that are built into human culture, the dogmas and traditions and forms of artistic expression that are conventional and hackneyed. Stevens can speak bitterly of "statues" that dominate public squares and inhibit the innocent and intense sensory responses of the people who walk there.

Implied by this emphasis is a psychology – a theory of human perception – that is basically nominalistic. What is real and worthy of reverence – the poet's reverence and his readers' – is, for example, the contact the eye makes with a certain slant of light which is never the equivalent of some past contact with a slant of light. It is a mistake to move from several such special moments to any general conception about "shades of light." Each moment of perception must be preserved in its uniqueness, and the poet must, ideally, move no farther from that moment than the carefully selected set of words that allow him to make a verbal record. Stevens – a poet quite well-informed in such matters – is aware of the traps into which other poets and other human beings have fallen. In *Harmonium*, there is an "Invective Against Swans." Stevens writes: "The soul, o ganders, flies beyond the parks/And far beyond the discords of the wind." Here the "soul" has a vertigo that takes it beyond "parks" (and their clusters of rare and unique sensations) and beyond the manifestly rich "discords of the wind." The "soul" treacherously detaches the human sensibility from its proper and health-giving ground: the never-ending moments of intense sensation. The "soul" carries the human sensibility into a context of religious and social ideas that have at best a tenuous connection with "parks" and "discords of the wind."

The positive aspect of Stevens' reiterated warning appears in such lines as the following from "Credences of Summer" in *Transport to Summer*. Here, Stevens suggests, is sound belief: "The rock cannot be broken. It is the truth./It rises from land and sea and covers

951

them." That is, the rock is — and remains — the source of acute physical perception. It is a natural object, far removed from any piece of stone that human hands have chipped at and made into a "statue" — is a memorial of some past event or an expression of human dogmas. A few more lines refine this particular statement, one that resembles countless others in Stevens' work. The "rock of summer" (a "rock of winter" is apparently inferior) is not "A hermit's truth nor symbol in hermitage." A "hermit's truth" is what the gander soul flutters toward. Stevens continues:

> It is the visible rock, the audible,
> The brilliant mercy of a sure repose,
> On this present ground, the vividest repose,
> Things certain sustaining us in certainty.

Brief annotation — and all of Stevens' work stimulates such effort — would indicate that it is the actual rock that is esteemed, not the idea, Platonic or otherwise, of "rock." From the visible rock the errant "soul" gains a sure and not a treacherous "repose." And the rock is a "present ground" and, as such, the source of the only certainty that a poet and his reader can have confidence in.

Such lines indicate a perspective that extends throughout Stevens' work like a prairie landscape, insistent and unaltering. The lines, elegant in expression and charged with authority, invite each person to be a "center" into which are gathered separate moments of "vividest repose." Not the ersatz "repose" of some religious or political certainty. Not, even, the "repose" that some poets, retreating from politics and dogma, try to discover in personal relations, intense and unshakable. For the fierce outcry which is Matthew Arnold's only comfort on the "darkling plain" of "Dover Beach" — "Ah, love, let us be true/To one another!" — Stevens would have scarcely more patience than he has for "statues." As he observes in *Parts of a World*:

> Words are not forms of a single word.
> In the sum of the parts, there are only the parts.
> The world must be measured by eye ...

To the villainous "gander soul," the whole is always greater than the sum of its parts and testimony to principle, to some inclusive order that lies in a divine mind or, at least, at the very roots of things. The "single word" (or Word, as Christians would say) is a delusion. Words serve the eye, and the eye takes in what aspect a "rock of summer" has at a particular moment.

As Stevens' large body of work indicates, such labor can be lifelong. It can exclude — and does — elements of existence that have counted for other poets and that, from Stevens' point of view, have corrupted them and those who read them. Stevens' "center" (the poet's awareness and perhaps his readers') is a clear crystal which sensation reaches — reaches and passes through with as little refraction as possible.

—Harold H. Watts

STEWART, Douglas (Alexander). Australian. Born in Eltham, New Zealand, 6 May 1913. Educated at New Plymouth Boys High School; Victoria University College, Wellington. Married Margaret Coen in 1946; one daughter. Literary Editor, *The Bulletin*,

Sydney, 1940–61; Literary Adviser, Angus and Robertson, publishers, Sydney, 1961–73. Recipient: *Encyclopaedia Britannica* Award, 1968; Wilke Award, for non-fiction, 1975. O.B.E. (Officer, Order of the British Empire). Lives in Sydney.

PUBLICATIONS

Verse

Green Lions. 1937.
The White Cry. 1939.
Elegy for an Airman. 1940.
Sonnets to the Unknown Soldier. 1941.
The Dosser in Springtime. 1946.
Glencoe. 1947.
Sun Orchids. 1952.
The Birdsville Track and Other Poems. 1955.
Rutherford and Other Poems. 1962.
The Garden of Ships: A Poem. 1962.
(Poems). 1963; as *Selected Poems,* 1969, 1973.
Collected Poems, 1936–1967. 1967.

Plays

Ned Kelly (produced 1944). 1943.
The Fire on the Snow and The Golden Lover: Two Plays for Radio. 1944.
Shipwreck (produced 1948). 1947.
Four Plays (includes *The Fire on the Snow, The Golden Lover, Ned Kelly, Shipwreck*). 1958.
Fisher's Ghost: The Historical Comedy (produced 1961). 1960.

Radio Plays: *The Fire on the Snow,* 1941; *The Golden Lover,* 1943; *The Earthquake Shakes the Land,* 1944.

Fiction

A Girl with Red Hair and Other Stories. 1944.

Other

The Flesh and the Spirit: An Outlook on Literature. 1948.
The Seven Rivers (on angling). 1966.
The Broad Stream (criticism). 1975.
Norman Lindsay: A Personal Memoir. 1975.

Editor, *Coast to Coast: Australian Stories.* 1945.
Editor, with Nancy Keesing, *Australian Bush Ballads.* 1955.
Editor, with Nancy Keesing, *Old Bush Songs and Rhymes of Colonial Times, Enlarged and Revised from the Collection of A. B. Paterson.* 1957.

Editor, *Voyager Poems*. 1960.
Editor, *The Book of Bellerive,* by Joseph Tischler. 1961.
Editor, (*Poems*), by A. D. Hope. 1963.
Editor, *Modern Australian Verse: Poetry in Australia II*. 1964.
Editor, *Selected Poems,* by Hugh McCrae. 1966.
Editor, *Short Stories of Australia: The Lawson Tradition*. 1967.
Editor, with Nancy Keesing, *The Pacific Book of Bush Ballads*. 1967.
Editor, with Nancy Keesing. *Bush Songs, Ballads, and Other Verse*. 1968.
Editor, with Beatrice Davis, *Best Australian Short Stories*. 1971.
Editor, *The Wide Brown Land: A New Selection of Australian Verse*. 1971.
Editor, *Australia Fair*. 1976.

Reading List: *Stewart* by Nancy Keesing, 1965; *Stewart* by Clement Semmler, 1975.

*   *   *

Douglas Stewart is one of the most prolific and versatile of Australian writers. Well-known as a poet and radio playwright, he has also written short stories, essays, and biography. His account of the Sydney *Bulletin*, whose Red Page he edited from 1940 to 1960, is lively, informative, and graceful, and an important contribution to local literary history.

Stewart's *Collected Poems* assembled the best of his verse from 1936 onwards. Though he is a New Zealander by birth, few native Australians have developes Stewart's feeling for Australian landscape and animal life. His relationship with the natural world has been in turns egocentric, anthropomorphic, even animistic, but in the later poems it has become fraternal and non-attached. Where once he would have wished an insect to look at the world as a man would, he now tries to see the world, not merely as an insect would see it, which would be affectation, but through the eyes of an insect without surrendering the vision of a man. Courtesy is what distinguishes Stewart's attitude to the non-human world, and the reserve which is part of his own nature is scrupulously respected in other creatures, as the volume *Sun Orchids* makes clear. The mood of his verse is primarily one of good humour and well-being, and, in a darkening world living on the edge of a balance of terror, such a mood strikes many readers as superficial and evasive. The long narrative poem *Rutherford*, for instance, in spite of some fine passages, never really comes to grip with the central moral problem of post-Baconian science, while the weight of the verse suggests that the author shares the fuzzy optimism of his hero. Against this, however, should be set the magnificent ballad-sequence, *Glencoe*, with its fine structural coherence, its dramatic appropriateness and the timeless urgency of its theme: the wanton spirit of senseless faction in mankind which guarantees the suffering of the innocent. The main part of the sequence ends with one of Stewart's finest lyrics, the lament "Sigh, wind in the pine", with its grim warning:

> Oh life is fierce and wild
> And the heart of the earth is stone,
> And the hand of a murdered child
> Will not bear thinking on.
>
> Sigh, wind in the pine, ,
> Cover it over with snow;
> But terrible things were done
> Long, long ago.

The poem was written not long after another massacre: Hiroshima.

Those who deny Stewart the capacity for reflection must take *Glencoe* into account. They must also consider that his reflective exercises are as a rule conducted far below the surface of his poems, as the early poem "The River" makes plain: what he sees he has no objection to sharing, what he really thinks or feels, he seems to regard as largely his own business. His principal gift as a poet is the ability to transfigure the commonplace, to catch a moment of heightened experience and endow it with a history. The facility with which he seizes the poetic moment has sometimes led him into verbosity through over-exercise, and in some of his occasional verse there is a sense of strain. At times indeed he can degenerate into producing a kind of poetic "chirruping." Stewart's preoccupation with an immediate moment of intense awareness has tended to obscure the metaphysical base from which he works, expressed in paradoxical images of fire and snow, heat and cold, which perhaps hint at a struggle between the rational and the irrational in his own nature. Flame and snow come together in "Day and Night with Snow" (an early poem) and in "Flowering Place" (one of his most recent), while variants of the same image crop up in "Spider Gums," "The River," and "Flower of Winter." There is nothing static about this symbolism: fire is as much an image of destruction as it is of the continuity of life; snow, as much an image of potentiality, of steadfastness, as of death. His grasp of this archetypal imagery seems to be intuitional rather than intellectual, but for a lyrist, this is hardly a disadvantage.

The lack of intellectual rigour, however, becomes something of an obstacle in his prose work, especially in the literary criticism, in spite of its general good sense. His criticism, in *The Flesh and the Spirit* and *The Broad Stream*, belongs to the same impressionist genre, without being as captious or exhibitionist, as that of his more famous predecessor on the *Bulletin*, A. G. Stephens. It is intuitional, idiosyncratic, intensely subjective, capable of crystallising the essentials of a work under scrutiny, but liable to the temptations of large, arresting generalisations which will not stand up to close analysis because they take little account of what is extra-literary. It is never dull, always stimulating, often prejudiced, on occasions brilliant, and like much of the verse, often humorous.

Stewart's plays, written mainly for radio and all in verse, are strangely static: there is a much more genuinely dramatic element in the *Glencoe* ballads, or the poem "Terra Australis" than in *Fire on the Snow* or *Ned Kelly*. It is odd, for instance, that a dramatist should always choose situations which involve the characters in so much merely waiting around and talking. *Fire on the Snow*, about Scott's last expedition, unlike *Ned Kelly* and *Shipwreck*, is in addition devoid of human conflict; the enemy is nature, and endurance the only possible response. Written for radio, it is not a play for the theatre at all; and even *Ned Kelly*, which lends itself more easily to the stage, almost founders from excessive verbalisation. *Shipwreck* is a more shapely drama, in which the tendency to lyric expansion is kept under control. Even so, there is too much reliance at certain points on clumsy reporting of off-stage events. This play, however, is securely founded on a real moral conflict: whether a captain is justified in making a dangerous journey to bring help to his shipwrecked crew and passengers, when he must leave them on the verge of mutiny under precarious control. *Shipwreck* is perhaps the strongest and most interesting of Stewart's plays. But *The Golden Lover*, on a New Zealand theme, is the most endearing. It dramatises the difficulty of choosing between dream and reality, between unearthly, intense love and domestic security; and in the Maori girl Tawhai, her lumpish husband Ruarangi, and Whana, the "golden lover" from the people of the Mist, Stewart has succeeded in creating three of his most convincing characters. As with *Ned Kelly*, however, the ending is left ambiguous; or rather it seems to be ambiguous until we reflect that the voices of commonsense have been given all the best tunes. It is difficult to avoid the conclusion, when one considers all the plays together, that the one value Stewart unequivocally endorses is sheer survival.

It is in the prose, finally, especially in the biographical writing on Kenneth Slessor and Norman Lindsay, that doubts make themselves felt about Stewart's ultimate seriousness. The weight given to the superficial picturesqueness of some of the figures he admires, the flavour of old boy nostalgia for Bohemia, seem to sort ill with the realities of the life the world has known since Hiroshima. Nevertheless, it is possible that the generally light-hearted and circumspect temper of Stewart's writing may conceal a deep ineradicable pessimism, even disgust, about human nature, and that he has turned away to the natural world, content only with the surface pleasures of human society. Two passages in *Shipwreck* may crystallise his view of humanity; when Heynorick, the "observing" butler says suddenly, echoing Hamlet – "The appalling things that happen between sky and earth/Where the beast called man walks upright!" – and when Pelsart tells the condemned sailor: "I cannot pity you, prisoner; but, sometimes, my friends,/I am sorry for the race of men, trapped on this planet."

—Dorothy Green

STICKNEY, Trumbull. American. Born in Geneva, Switzerland, 20 June 1874. Spent his childhood in Europe; tutored by his father. Educated at Walton Lodge, Clevedon, Somerset, 1886; Cutler's School, New York City, 1890; Harvard University, Cambridge, Massachusetts, 1891–95 (Editor, *Harvard Monthly*), B.A. (magna cum laude) 1895; the Sorbonne, Paris, Doctorat ès Lettres, 1903. Instructor in Greek, Harvard University, 1903–04. *Died 11 October 1904.*

PUBLICATIONS

Collections

  Homage to Stickney (selected verse), edited by James Reeves and Seán Haldane. 1968.
  The Poems, edited by Amberys R. Whittle. 1972.

Verse

  Dramatic Verses. 1902.
  Poems, edited by George Cabot Lodge, John Ellerton Lodge, and William Vaughn Moody. 1905.

Other

  Les Sentences dans la Poésie Grecque d'Homère à Euripide. 1903.

  Translator, with Sylvain Lévi, *Bhagavadgita.* 1938

Reading List: *The Fright of Time: Stickney* by Seán Haldane, 1970; *Stickney* by Amberys R. Whittle, 1973.

*   *   *

One of that group of gifted Americans who came to early maturity in the 1890's only to have their lives snuffed out before the first decade of the new century was completed,

Trumbull Stickney is memorable on several counts. As an accomplished Greek and Sanskrit scholar and one of the first intellectual cosmopolitans to attempt a career in American letters, he exhibits a cultural impulse which is to be later followed more extensively by writers like Pound and Eliot. Further, along with William Vaughn Moody and George Cabot Lodge, he aimed at resuscitating verse-drama, and his work in this genre (*Prometheus Pyrphoros* and two fragments based on the lives of the Emperor Julian and the young Benvenuto Cellini) points forward to later efforts in the century. And, powerfully under the influence of Browning, he produced a number of "dramatic scenes" ("Kalypso," "Oneiropolos," "Lodovico Martelli," "Requiescam," etc.), although his instincts for dramatic conflict and psychological subtlety seem less vigorous than his evident delight in historical reconstruction.

It is perhaps the lyrical quality of his writing that suggests the most promise in his work. Almost suffocated in the cloying rhetoric of the *fin de siècle*, heavy with twilight and rose-dust and a fatigued embrace of futility, Stickney's lyrics frequently manage a new, if wistful, vitality to the clichés of Romantic decadence. In poems like "Chestnuts in November," "At Sainte-Marguerite," "Mt. Lykaion," and in isolated passages from "Eride," Stickney's tempered musicality sustains the conventional formal structures, raising these poems above the level of similar lamentations which the Mauve Decade manufactured in wholesale lots. And in poems like "With thy two eyes look on me once again," "Leave him now quiet by the way," and, especially, "Mnemosyne," a quiet strength joins with a precise sense of rhythmical phrasing to produce verse which possesses an autonomy of statement and genuine eloquence. It is futile to speculate on what might have been, but in half a dozen poems Stickney's success was authentic and undeniable. As graceful as Santayana's verse but more concretely sensual, with an intellectual structure as sturdy as the early Robinson's but more personal and direct in tone, Stickney's achievement illustrates the highest ambitions of his generation, while implying a technique that may compensate for the weaknesses of its gentility.

—Earl Rovit

STRODE, William. English. Born at Shaugh Prior, near Plympton, Devon, c. 1601. Educated at Westminster School, London (King's Scholar); entered Christ Church, Oxford, 1617, B.A. 1621, B.D. 1631, D.D. 1638. Married the sister-in-law of Bishop Skinner; one daughter. Public Orator, and Proctor, Oxford University, 1628. Ordained, 1628: Chaplain to Richard Corbett, Bishop of Oxford; held livings of East Bradenham, Norfolk, 1632–37; Blackbourton, Oxfordshire, from 1638; Badley, Northamptonshire, 1638–42; South Stoke, Oxfordshire, from 1641. *Died 11 March 1645.*

PUBLICATIONS

Collections

Poetical Works, edited by Bertram Dobell.   1907.

Play

The Floating Island (produced 1636).   1655; in *Poetical Works*, 1907.

Other

A Sermon Concerning Death and the Resurrection.   1644.
A Sermon Concerning Swearing.   1644.
A Sermon at a Visitation at Lynn.   1660.

Reading List: "The Poetry of Strode" by H. Morris, in *Tulane Studies in English, 1957; A Critical Edition of the Poetical Works of Strode* edited by Margaret Forey, unpublished B. Litt. thesis, 1966.

*   *   *

The poetry of William Strode was popular in his time, and was printed anonymously in miscellanies to the end of the century; the virtual extinction of his reputation after his death is probably largely due to the lack of any contemporary edition of his verse, much of which is still unpublished. His main affinities are with the courtly lyrists – indeed some of his poems have often been ascribed to Carew – and he shows interest in trying his hand at currently fashionable modes of writing, such as the mock-song and the "sic vita" poem; but, though he never attempted an original poem of any length, in some respects his range is wide, and another poet whom he often resembles is one very different from Carew, namely his patron Bishop Corbett. Strode shares Corbett's enjoyment of popular culture, and writes sympathetically of ordinary people and everyday events. His lively ballads and colloquial accounts of local affairs are humorous rather than witty; his tone is normally rollicking and genial, as in his thanks to a friend "For your good looks [i.e., welcoming expression] and for your claret,/For often bidding, 'Do not spare it,' " or his rueful complaint to his shoemaker, "How is't I pay to you/One groat for ev'ry toe in Spanish shoe?" Yet Strode was also capable of great delicacy, as in the recurrent bird-imagery which adds softness and even a touch of warmth to the gently falling snow in his most successful piece, the charming "I saw fair Cloris walk alone." Elsewhere the homeliness and simplicity of his imagery, his delight in what is neat and seemly, the spontaneity and naturalness of his manner, and the gentle dignity of his most successful treatments of serious topics give his work individuality and quiet charm. Unfortunately the quality of his poems is uneven, and such faults as flatness, forced wit, confused syntax, or the metrical weakness of his favourite enjambed couplets, mar pieces which contain fine lines or passages. Nevertheless his poetry deserves more attention than it has received. The sermons on the whole are of less value, though parts of *On Death and the Resurrection* are quietly moving.

Strode is also of interest as an anti-Puritan satirist. The influence of his staunchly Parliamentarian family (which included one of the Five Members, and was related by marriage to Pym), may be seen in the kindlier pieces, but his attack on Puritan hypocrisy in "The Town's New Teacher" – described by Firth in *Transactions of the Royal Historical Society*, 1912, as the best example of its kind – is scathing. Equally bitter, but less successful, was Strode's allegorical play *The Floating Island*, performed before the king in 1636. Strode was no dramatist, and although the performance was marked by Inigo Jones's introduction of movable wings to the English stage, the tedious piece was a failure with the court. However, the timing of its attack on Burton, Bastwick, and Prynne, whom Laud was shortly to arrest, makes it of some historical importance, since it was under Laud's aegis that the play was produced.

—Margaret Forey

SUCKLING, Sir John. English. Born in Whitton, Middlesex, baptized 10 February 1609. Educated at Trinity College, Cambridge, 1623–26, left without taking a degree; Gray's Inn, London, 1626–27. Inherited large estates on the death of his father, 1627, and attended court, 1627–29; travelled on the continent, returned to England and knighted, 1630; served in the English embassy to Gustavus Adolphus, 1631; returned to England, 1632, and became a court poet and attendant to Charles I; with his followers took up the King's cause in the first Bishops War, 1639, and served as a captain of carabineers in the second Bishops War, 1640; Member of the short Parliament, 1640; took part in the "Army Plot," 1641: when the plot was discovered, forced to flee to Paris, where he died. *Died in 1641.*

PUBLICATIONS

Collections

    Works, edited by Thomas Clayton and L. A. Beaurline. 2 vols., 1971.
    Cavalier Poets, edited by Thomas Clayton. 1978.

Plays

    The Sad One (produced 1632?). In *Last Remains,* 1659.
    Aglaura (produced 1637; revised version, produced 1638). 1638.
    The Goblins (produced 1637–41?). In *Fragmenta Aurea,* 1646.
    The Discontented Colonel. 1642; as *Brennoralt* (produced 1639–41?), in *Fragmenta Aurea,* 1646.

Other

    A Letter Written to the Lower Houses of Parliament. 1641.
    A Letter Found in the Privy Lodgings at Whitehall. 1641.
    Fragmenta Aurea (miscellany). 1646.
    Last Remains. 1659.

Bibliography: in *Works* 1971.

*   *   *

In comparison with other luminaries at the court of Charles I such as William Davenant, Richard Lovelace, and Edmund Waller, Sir John Suckling was clearly the most naturally gifted, versatile, and undisciplined. His posthumous collection *Fragmenta Aurea* contains four plays, numerous love lyrics, verse satires, several political and religious tracts, and almost fifty personal letters, many of them as well-written and interesting as Byron's. An excellent critic, he was an avid reader of Shakespeare, Jonson, and Donne, but his own careless verses only rarely reflect their patience with language. In such occasional sparks of lyricism as his famous song from *Aglaura* ("Why so pale and wan, fond lover?") he is a worthy disciple of Jonson, but such flashes of genius are rarely sustained.

Suckling's play *Aglaura* was performed at court in 1637 by the King's Men, and when it failed to please as a tragedy Suckling gave the last act a happy ending and showed it again the following year to great royal applause. *The Goblins* is Suckling's only comedy and possibly his best play for its lively presentation of a band of Robin Hood bandits. In 1639 he returned to tragedy with *Brennoralt*, a thinly-disguised political allegory attacking the Scots. His unfinished tragedy, *The Sad One* is, like his other plays, slipshod in construction and inconsistent in characterization, but occasionally illuminated by brilliant dialogue and graceful songs.

Suckling's best-known verses are "A Ballad upon a Wedding" and his satiric poem "The Wits" ("A Sessions of the Poets"), in which he wittily portrays poets like Jonson, Carew, and Davenant competing for the laurel. His love poems are typical of his generation of cavalier lyrists – cynical, witty, derisively anti-Petrarchan in the manner of the young Donne's "Go and catch a falling star," but without Donne's complex metaphors and iron-hard language. The love lyrics were calculated to convey the impression of a cynical rake, a pose belied by many of Suckling's personal letters and his eminently earnest anti-Socinian treatise "An Account of Religion by Reason."

—James E. Ruoff

SURREY, Earl of; Henry Howard.   English   Born, probably in Kenninghall, Norfolk, c. 1516; eldest son of Thomas Howard, Duke of Norfolk. Educated by the scholar John Clerke, and possibly at Christ Church, Oxford. Married Lady Frances Vere in 1535. Cup-Bearer to Henry VIII: accompanied Henry to France, 1532–33; Earl Marshal at the trial of Anne Boleyn, 1536; Steward of Cambridge University, 1541; served with the army in Scotland, 1542; Field Marshal of the English army on the Continent, 1544; Commander at Boulogne, 1545–46, defeated at St. Etienne, and replaced by the Earl of Hertford, 1546; recalled to England, and condemned and executed on charge of quartering royal arms. Knighted, 1536; Knight of the Garter, 1541. *Died 21 January 1547.*

PUBLICATIONS

Collections

> *Poems,* edited by F. M. Padelford.   1920; revised edition, 1928.
> *Poems,* edited by Emrys Jones.   1964.

Verse

> *An Excellent Epitaph of Sir Thomas Wyatt.*   1542.
> *The Fourth Book of Virgil, Drawn into a Strange Metre.*   1554.
> *Certain Books of Virgil's Aenaeis.*   1557; edited by F. H. Ridley, 1963.
> *Songs and Sonnets* (Tottel's miscellany; 40 poems by Surrey).   1557.

Reading List: *Surrey* by Edwin Casady, 1938; *The Elizabethan Love Sonnet* by J. W. Lever, 1959; *Two Tudor Portraits: Surrey and Lady Katherine Grey* by Hester W. Chapman, 1960;

" 'Love that doth raine': Surrey's Creative Imitation" by W. O. Harris, in *Modern Philology* *66*, 1969.

*   *   *

When Surrey's poems were printed alongside Wyatt's in Tottel's miscellany in 1557, his were given pride of place because they suited the taste of the time and the compiler's ideas of correctness. Nearly all the critics during the next three centuries agreed that Surrey was Wyatt's superior, largely because of the smoothness of his versification. In the present century, paradoxically because of the renewed interest in Donne, Wyatt's reputation has grown steadily and Surrey's has as steadily declined. Yet, although Wyatt is doubtless the better poet, acknowledged by Surrey as his master, the pupil is by no means negligible.

Much of his work can be seen as a continuation of Wyatt's. Wyatt, for example, had versified the Penitential Psalms, setting them in a narrative framework of David's love for Bathsheba. Surrey at the end of his short life, when his enemies were plotting against him, wrote verse paraphrases of five chapters of *Ecclesiastes* and of four Psalms. It is easy to see why he chose Psalm 55: "My foes they bray so loud, and eke threpe on so fast,/Buckled to do me scathe, so is their malice bent." Surrey also followed Wyatt in translating a number of Petrarch's sonnets, sometimes diverging from the originals (as Wyatt had done), e.g., "The soote season that bud and blome furth brings," but more usually sticking close to the Italian. His versification was more musical than Wyatt's and he would not have rhymed "suffer" with "banner" as Wyatt did. Yet Wyatt succeeded in making original poems, as when he adapted a Petrarchan sonnet to express his grief on the execution of his friend and patron, Thomas Cromwell; and Surrey's generally read like translations. The two poets can be directly compared in one instance, since they translated the same sonnet, Wyatt's "The longe love that in my thought doeth harbar" and Surrey's "Love that doth raine and live within my thought." Wyatt has revitalised the imagery; but Surrey's is more immediately accessible and closer to the original.

Surrey, however, was able sometimes to use translation as a means of self-expression, especially his feeling for nature, as in the opening of one of the sonnets:

> Alas, so all thinges nowe doe holde their peace,
> Heaven and earth disturbed in no thing;
> The beastes, the ayer, the birds their song doe cease;
> The nightes chare the starres aboute dothe bring.
> Calme is the sea, the waves worke lesse and lesse;
> So am not I, whom love alas doth wring.

The other love poems are written in various styles. Eight of them, like most of the Biblical paraphrases, are written in Poulter's Measure – a metre in which Wyatt had contrived to write the most unreadable of his poems. Most of Surrey's, it must be confessed, are somewhat wooden, but in one or two he scores a modest success by his use of simple and unaffected language. One of the best – supposed to be spoken by a woman – begins:

> Good ladies, you that have your pleasure in exyle,
> Stepp in your foote, come take a place, and mourne with me awhyle;
> And such as but their lords do sett but lytle pryce,
> Let them sitt still, it stills them not what chaunce come on the dyce.

One of Surrey's love poems, partially translated, is in *terza rima*, the form used by Wyatt in his satires and psalms. But the ones that have worn best, to judge by their frequent appearance in modern anthologies, are the short lyrics in stanza form. They were not intended, as Wyatt's obviously were, to be set to music; but they are closer in spirit to English songs than to his Italian models. One of them, expressing the feelings of a wife whose husband is on the seas, contains two echoes from Serafino but they have been assimilated into the very English poem:

> When other lovers in armes acrosse
> Rejoyce their chief delight,
> Drowned in teares to mourne my losse
> I stand the bitter night
> In my window, where I may see
> Before the windes how the cloudes flee.
> Lo, what a mariner love hath made me!

The same poem ends with the colloquial line: "Now he comes, will he come? alas, no, no!"

It is important to remember that Surrey was just thirty when he died, and that much of his best verse was written on subjects other than love. The poem he wrote in Windsor Castle in 1537 effectively contrasts his imprisonment with the happier years he spent there as a companion to the Duke of Richmond. Perhaps his finest poem is the elegy on Wyatt, written in 1542, in which his admiration for his mentor's integrity, courage, and piety brings out a reflection of those qualities in himself. It is perhaps the finest English elegy before "Lycidas." The satirical poem on London, written after his arrest for riotous behaviour, shows that alongside his pride and piety was a lack of self-control; but his translations of Horace and Martial, written in a direct and masculine style, show that his beliefs and ideals, if not always his conduct, were approximating to those of Wyatt.

It is not known when his translation of the *Aeneid* II and IV was written: it was his most influential, and probably his most important, work. It owes something to Gavin Douglas's translation, but unlike that it is written in blank verse – apparently the first to be written in English. He realised that rhyme would give a wrong impression of Virgil's epic. Surrey's verse is usually end-stopped, and his translation lacks narrative drive; but he manages the speeches effectively and he has many felicitous phrases.

His success with the speeches was the main reason why Elizabethan dramatists, unlike the French, avoided rhymed tragedies, and why Milton chose blank verse for *Paradise Lost* instead of the stanzaic form of Spenser, Tasso, and Ariosto, or the couplets of Cowley's biblical epic. Surrey was also responsible in some of his sonnets for the invention of the English form (three quatrains and a couplet) which Shakespeare gratefully followed.

—Kenneth Muir

SWIFT, Jonathan. English. Born in Dublin, Ireland, 30 November 1667, of English parents. Educated at Kilkenny Grammar School, 1674–82; Trinity College, Dublin, 1682–88. Married Esther (Stella) Johnson in 1716 (died, 1728). Companion and Secretary to Sir William Temple at Moor Park, Farnham, Surrey, 1689–91, 1691–94, 1695–99; ordained in the Anglican Church, in Dublin, 1695, and held first living at Kilroot, Northern Ireland, until 1698; Chaplain to the Earl of Berkeley, Lord Lieutenant of Ireland, 1700; vicar of Laracor; Prebend, St. Patrick's Cathedral, Dublin, 1701; editor of several volumes of Temple's works during the 1700's; aligned with the Tory ministry of Oxford and Bolingbroke, 1710: lived in London, wrote political pamphlets, and contributed to *The Examiner*, 1710–14; Dean of St. Patrick's Cathedral, Dublin, from 1713; a leader of the Irish resistance movement from 1724; visited London, 1726, 1727, but otherwise resided in Dublin until his death. D.D.: University of Dublin, 1701. *Died 19 October 1745.*

Collections

>Poems, edited by Harold Williams.   3 vols., 1937.
>Prose Works, edited by Herbert Davis.   14 vols., 1939–68.
>Gulliver's Travels and Other Writings, edited by Louis A. Landa.   1960.
>The Correspondence, edited by Harold Williams.   5 vols., 1963–65.
>A Tale of a Tub and Other Satires, edited by Kathleen Williams.   1975.
>Selected Poems, edited by C. H. Sisson.   1977.

Verse

>Baucis and Philemon, Imitated from Ovid.   1709.
>Part of the Seventh Epistle of the First Book of Horace Imitated.   1713.
>The First Ode of the Second Book of Horace Paraphrased.   1713.
>The Bubble.   1721.
>Cadenus and Vanessa.   1726.
>Miscellanies in Prose and Verse, with others.   4 vols., 1727–32.
>Horace, Book I, Ode XIV, Paraphrased.   1730.
>The Lady's Dressing Room, to Which Is Added A Poem on Cutting Down the Old Thorn at Market Hill.   1732.
>An Elegy on Dicky and Dolly.   1732.
>The Life and Genuine Character of Doctor Swift, Written by Himself.   1733.
>On Poetry: A Rhapsody.   1733.
>An Epistle to a Lady.   1734.
>A Beautiful Young Nymph Going to Bed, Written for the Honour of the Fair Sex.   1734.
>An Imitation of the Sixth Satire of the Second Book of Horace, completed by Pope.   1738.
>Verses on the Death of Dr. Swift.   1739.

Fiction

>A Tale of a Tub, Written for the Universal Improvement of Mankind, to Which Is Added an Account of a Battle Between the Ancient and Modern Books in St. James's Library.   1704; revised edition, 1710; edited by G. C. Guthkelch and D. N. Smith, 1958.
>Travels into Several Remote Nations of the World, by Captain Lemuel Gulliver.   1726; revised edition, 1735; edited by Angus Ross, 1972.

Other

>A Discourse of the Contests and Dissensions Between the Nobles and the Commons in Athens and Rome.   1701; edited by F. H. Ellis, 1967.
>Predictions for the Year 1708.   1708.
>A Project for the Advancement of Religion and the Reformation of Manners.   1709.
>A New Journey to Paris.   1711.
>The Conduct of the Allies.   1711.
>Some Remarks on the Barrier Treaty.   1712.
>A Proposal for Correcting, Improving, and Ascertaining the English Tongue.   1712.

Mr. Collin's Discourse of Free-Thinking. 1713.

The Public Spirit of the Whigs. 1714.

A Proposal for the Universal Use of Irish Manufacture. 1720.

Fraud Detected: or, The Hibernian Patriot, Containing All the Drapier's Letters to the People of Ireland. 1725; as *The Hibernian Patriot,* 1730.

A Short View of the Present State of Ireland. 1728.

A Modest Proposal for Preventing the Children of Poor People from Being Burthen to Their Parents or the Country. 1729.

An Examination of Certain Abuses, Corruptions, and Enormities in the City of Dublin. 1732.

The Works. 1735.

A Complete Collection of Genteel and Ingenious Conversation. 1738; edited by E. Partridge, 1963.

Some Free Thoughts upon the Present State of Affairs Written in the Year 1714. 1741.

Three Sermons. 1744.

Directions to Servants. 1745.

The Last Will and Testament of Swift. 1746.

Brotherly Love: A Sermon. 1754.

The History of the Four Last Years of the Queen. 1758.

Editor, *Letters Written by Sir William Temple and Other Ministers of State.* 3 vols., 1700–03.

Editor, *Miscellanea: The Third Part,* by William Temple. 1701.

Editor, *Memoirs: Part III,* by William Temple. 1709.

Bibliography: *A Bibliography of the Writings of Swift* by H. Teerink, 1937, revised edition, edited by Arthur H. Scouten, 1963; *A Bibliography of Swift Studies 1945–1965* by J. J. Stathis, 1967.

Reading List: *The Mind and Art of Swift* by Ricardo Quintana, 1936; *The Sin of Wit* by Maurice Johnson, 1950; *Swift: The Man, His Works, and the Age* by Irvin Ehrenpreis, 2 vols. (of 3), 1962–67; *Swift and the Satirist's Art* by E. W. Rosenheim, Jr., 1963; *Swift and the Age of Compromise* by Kathleen Williams, 1968, and *Swift: The Critical Heritage* edited by Williams, 1970; *Swift: A Critical Introduction* by Denis Donoghue, 1969; *Swift* edited by C. J. Rawson, 1971, and *Gulliver and the Gentle Reader* by Rawson, 1973.

*   *   *

Swift began as a poet, and wrote many poems throughout his life. His poetic achievement has been overshadowed by his major prose satires, but deserves to be recognised. After a brief early period of Cowleyan odes, Swift abandoned "serious" or "lofty" styles (both terms are his own), and became one of the masters in a great English tradition of "light" verse, informal but far from trivial, which includes the works of Skelton, Samuel Butler, Prior, Byron, and Auden. Byron admired him especially, and said he "beats us all hollow." Swift seldom wrote what he called "serious Couplets," avoiding a form which his friend Pope was bringing to a high refinement of precision and masterfulness. He preferred looser and more popular metres, and most often the loose octosyllabic couplet chiefly associated with Butler's *Hudibras,* a poem Swift greatly admired. These looser forms reflected the disorders of life, rather than seeming to subdue or iron out these disorders within the reassuring contours of a style which overtly proclaimed the author's triumphant and clarifying mastery. Even the few poems which, exceptionally, Swift wrote in the heroic couplet, the "Description of the Morning" and the "Description of a City Shower," tend to flatten that eloquently patterned metre into an idiom of bare realistic notation, registering the chaotic and unstructured energies of common city scenes rather than any sense of the satirist's control.

These two poems also parody some conventions of grand poetic description, and Swift's impulse to undercut the loftier orderings of "serious" poets runs through virtually all his work as a poet. The celebrated "excremental" poems ("The Lady's Dressing Room," "A Beautiful Young Nymph Going to Bed," "Strephon and Chloe," "Cassinus and Peter") are among other things parodies of the false idealisations of love-poetry. The famous plaintive cry that "Celia, Celia, Celia shits," which occurs in two of the poems and has shocked healthy-minded readers like D. H. Lawrence and Aldous Huxley, has this dimension of parody, although more than mere parody is at work. The words are too playful to support any simple view that Swift hated the human body or was a misogynist. Through his foolish Strephons, Swift mocks those who cannot accept the physical facts and seek refuge in idealising poeticisms. But he also tells us that the body is ugly and perishable, and that in matters of love and of friendship the moral and intellectual virtues are a sounder guide. These themes also run through many non-scatological poems which he wrote to women friends, notably the moving and tender poems to Stella and the archly self-justifying "Cadenus and Vanessa."

The latter, a defence of his role in a one-sided love-affair, is one of several autobiographical poems which Swift, at various periods, wrote as apologies for some aspect of his private or public life. Of these, the most interesting are "The Author upon Himself" and *Verses on the Death of Dr. Swift*. The latter is perhaps his best-known poem, a comprehensive and in many places light-hearted and low-key defense of his literary and political career, rising towards the end to a pitch of self-praise which some readers have found distasteful. *An Epistle to a Lady* is a revealing poem about Swift's unwillingness to write in a "lofty Stile"; and *On Poetry: A Rapsody* whose title implies a similar point, is in the main an angry and witty account of the world of bad poets and hireling politicians.

In the 1730's Swift also wrote a series of angry poems on Irish affairs, of which "The Legion Club" is the best known. These attacks on prominent public men in Ireland sometimes have the force to ritual curses, and are perhaps the only places where Swift attempts what is often (and almost always wrongly) attributed to him, a Juvenalian grandeur of denunciation.

Swift's earliest major work is the prose *Tale of a Tub* (published 1704, but begun about 1696 and largely written by 1700), a brilliantly inventive and disturbing display of his satiric powers. It is the last and greatest English contribution to the long Renaissance debate on the relative merits of the Ancients and the Moderns. Through a deliberately diffuse and all-embracing parody, the *Tale* mimics the laxity, muddle, and arrogance of Modern thought, both in religion and in the various branches of literature and learning. This parody is sometimes very specific, as when Dryden's garrulous self-importance, or the mystical nonsense of some "*dark* Author" like Thomas Vaughan, is mocked. But it extends beyond specific examples to the whole contemporaneous republic of bad authors and to all deviant religions, which for Swift meant mainly the dissenting sects and Roman Catholicism. The cumulative force of its many-sided and probing irony reaches even further, however, transcending parody altogether and turning into a comprehensive anatomy of modern culture and indeed of human folly in general. Many readers, from Swift's time to our own, have felt that its effect was so destructive as to undermine even those things to which Swift claimed to be expressing loyalty, including the Church of England and indeed religion itself. Swift defended himself against such charges, but they stuck, and were to damage his career as a churchman. Whether or not Swift's defense is wholly accepted, the work shows Swift's deep and characteristic tendency to put his most powerful energies into the destructive or critical side of his vision, leaving the positive values to emerge by implication from the wreckage. The *Tale* was published with two accompanying pieces, *The Battle of the Books* and the *Discourse Concerning the Mechanical Operation of the Spirit*. The first extends the *Tale*'s satire on learning, the second on religious abuses.

In the years after 1704, Swift wrote a number of tracts on matters of religion and ecclesiastical politics. Of these, the "Argument Against Abolishing Christianity," has exceptional distinction as an ironic *tour de force*, subtle, inventive, slippery and playful, yet charged with an urgency of purpose and a sense of cherished values under threat.

During the period of Swift's early fame, 1710–14, Swift became a protégé of Harley and wrote many political tracts in support of his Tory ministry and of the controversial Peace of Utrecht. Harley put him in charge of the *Examiner*, for which he wrote some of his best brief polemical pieces, notably against the Duke of Marlborough, hero of the war against France. Of his other political writings in this period perhaps the most important is *The Conduct of the Allies*. Swift was one of the members of the Scriblerus club, a group of satirical wits associated with Harley (now Earl of Oxford), whose other regular members were Pope, Gay, Arbuthnot, and Thomas Parnell. The Club mostly met in 1714, and was effectively dispersed after Queen Anne's death in that year and the consequent collapse of the Tory administration. But the Club's activities not only resulted in the collectively composed *Memoirs of Martinus Scriblerus* (which Pope published much later, in 1741), but also influenced other writings by individual Scriblerians, including *Gulliver's Travels* (1726), and Pope's *Dunciad* (1728). In 1713, Swift became Dean of St. Patrick's Cathedral in Dublin, the highest preferment he could achieve in the Church. He regarded it as a blow to his hopes, and thought of his native Ireland as a place of exile.

After the Queen's death in 1714, he remained in Ireland for almost the whole of his life, and became actively involved in Irish political affairs. His Irish writings of the 1720's and (to a lesser degree) the 1730's earn him his honoured place as a defender of Ireland's rights. He was one of a series of great Anglo-Irishmen who fought to relieve Ireland's wrongs at the hands of the English oppressor: the list includes Charles Stewart Parnell and W. B. Yeats. The most important literary text among Swift's Irish writings is *A Modest Proposal*, an ironic pamphlet advocating the selling of Irish infants for food as a means of helping the economy. This *Proposal* is the climax of a whole series of tracts, which includes *A Proposal for Universal Use of Irish Manufacture*, the *Drapier's Letters*, and *A Short View of the State of Ireland*, in which the economic and political weaknesses of Ireland are bitterly exposed, and remedies suggested. The common view that these works are mainly or entirely anti-English is only partially true. It is becoming increasingly recognised that Swift was also concerned to expose the Irish for their failure to help themselves: their slavish temperament, economic fecklessness, commercial disreputability, the draining of the country's resources by absentee landlords. These criticisms underlie *A Modest Proposal*, which is more accurately read as a cry of exasperation against Irishmen of all classes and parties than as an attack on the English oppressor (although it is that too). Swift disliked the Irish while feeling called upon to defend their political rights. He thought of himself as English, accidentally "dropped" in Ireland by birth and kept there by an unhappy turn in his career. But he fought powerfully for Irish interests, achieved some practical successes (especially with the *Drapier's Letters*), and became and has remained a national hero.

Gulliver's Travels was published in 1726. It bears strong traces of Swift's involvement in Irish affairs. But its reach is, of course, much wider. Like *A Tale of a Tub*, it has a framework of parody (in this case mainly of travel-books), but its principal satiric concerns, unlike those of the *Tale*, are not in themselves enshrined in the parody. Neither work deals merely with bad books, and both are concerned with a fundamental exploration of the nature of man. But in the *Tale*, the follies of unregulated intellect and impulse are directly expressed in the kind of book and the features of style which Swift mimics, whereas in *Gulliver's Travels* the travel-book format is mainly a convenient framework for a consideration of human nature which is only marginally concerned with the character of travel-writers.

In the first two books, an allegory of human pride begins to establish itself. The tiny Lilliputians of Book I are a minuscule and self-important replica of the society of England; the giants of Book II demonstrate that in the eyes of larger creatures we ourselves seem as ludicrous as the Lilliputians seem to us. The two Books have a complementary relationship which is forceful and clear: a neat balancing of narrative structures which supports and illustrates the basic satiric irony, and is able to accommodate a wide range of detailed satiric observation about English and European mores and institutions.

966

This exceptionally tidy structural arrangement gives way in the rest of the work to something more complex and less predictable. Book III takes us to a miscellany of strange lands, all of them inhabited by humans of normal size, and between them illustrating particular social and political institutions (repressive government, insane and inhumane scientific research projects, wild follies of intellect). If the schematic relationship between Books I and II is not continued, much of Book III adds to or develops the exposure of particular human characteristics and institutions which had begun in the earlier books. But towards the end of Book III a new note is struck. Gulliver visits the land of the Struldbruggs, who have the gift of immortality but without perpetual youth. The horror which these hideous creatures arouse as they decay into increasing senility is no longer primarily concerned with moral culpability. It is a portrayal of certain grim features of the human situation which are independent of good and evil.

In Book IV satire becomes absolute, transcending all mere particularities of vice and folly of the kind encountered so far. The savage Yahoos have most of the vices and follies satirised earlier, but they embody a sense of the radical ugliness of the human animal, in his moral and his physical nature, which amounts (or so it seems to many readers) to a more fundamental disenchantment. The Houyhnhnms, the horse-shaped rulers of the humanoid Yahoos, are by contrast absolutely reasonable and virtuous, as the Yahoos are absolutely irrational and vicious. Swift said that he wished to disprove the traditional definition of man as a "rational animal," and he did so partly by enshrining an ideal rationality in a beast commonly named in philosophical discourse as an example of the non-rational animal: the horse. Swift's analysis has usually been considered a bleak and disturbing one, although some recent critics have held that Swift really believed that man both was and ought to be a creature who came somewhere between Yahoo and Houyhnhnm, a liberal and humane though fallible creature of the sort exemplified by the good Portuguese captain, who appears briefly near the end. This latter view seems to me misguided.

—C. J. Rawson

SWINBURNE, Algernon Charles. English. Born in London, 5 April 1837. Educated in France; Eton College, 1849–53; Balliol College, Oxford, 1856–60, left without taking a degree. Visited Landor in Florence, 1864; was associated with Rossetti and the Pre-Raphaelites. Lived with Theodore Watts-Dunton at Putney, in semi-retirement, from 1879. *Died 10 April 1909.*

PUBLICATIONS

Collections

Complete Works, edited by Edmund Gosse and T.J. Wise. 20 vols., 1925–27.
A Swinburne Anthology: Verse, Drama, Prose, Criticism, edited by Kenelm Foss. 1955.
Letters, edited by Cecil Y. Lang. 6 vols., 1959–62.
A Choice of Swinburne's Verse, edited by Robert Nye. 1973.

Verse

Poems and Ballads. 1866; second series, 1878; third series, 1889.
A Song of Italy. 1867.
Ode on the Proclamation of the French Republic. 1870.
Songs Before Sunrise. 1871.
Songs of Two Nations. 1875.
Songs of the Springtides. 1880.
Specimens of Modern Poets: The Heptalogia; or, The Seven Against Sense (parodies). 1880.
Studies in Song. 1880.
Tristram of Lyonesse and Other Poems. 1882.
A Century of Roundels. 1883.
A Midsummer Holiday and Other Poems. 1884.
Poetical Works, Including Most of the Dramas. 1884.
Select Poems. 1886.
Cleopatra. 1886(?).
Siena. 1890(?).
A Sequence of Sonnets on the Death of Browning. 1890.
Astrophel and Other Poems. 1894.
The Tale of Balen. 1896.
A Channel Passage. 1899.
A Channel Passage and Other Poems. 1904.
Poems. 6 vols., 1904.
Selected Lyrical Poems. 1906.
The Ballade of Truthful Charles and Other Poems. 1910.
Border Ballads, edited by T. J. Wise. 1912; edited by William A. MacInnes, as *Ballads of the English Border*, 1925.
Lady Maisie's Bairn and Other Poems. 1915.
Poems from Villon and Other Fragments. 1916.
Posthumous Poems, edited by Edmund Gosse and T. J. Wise. 1917.
Rondeaux Parisiens. 1917.
The Italian Mother and Other Poems. 1918.
The Ride from Milan and Other Poems. 1918.
The Two Knights and Other Poems. 1918.
A Lay of Lilies and Other Poems. 1918.
Queen Yseult. 1918.
Undergraduate Sonnets. 1918.
Lancelot, The Death of Rudel, and Other Poems. 1918.
The Queen's Tragedy. 1919.
Hyperion and Other Poems, edited by Georges Lafourcade. 1928.
A Roundel of Retreat. 1960.
Will Drew and Phil Crewe and Frank Fane. 1962(?).

Plays

The Queen-Mother, and Rosamond. 1860.
Atalanta in Calydon. 1865.
Chastelard. 1865.
Bothwell, Act One. 1871; complete version, 1874.
Erechtheus. 1876.
Mary Stuart. 1881.
Marino Faliero. 1885.

Locrine (produced 1899).   1887.
The Sisters.   1892.
Rosamund, Queen of the Lombards.   1899.
Tragedies.   5 vols., 1905.
The Duke of Gandia.   1908.
Pasiphaë, edited by Randolph Hughes.   1950.

Fiction

Love's Cross Currents: A Year's Letters.   1901; unexpurgated edition, edited by
   Francis Jacques Sypher, 1974.
The Chronicle of Queen Fredegond.   1909.
Lucretia Borgia, edited by Randolph Hughes.   1942.
Lesbia Brandon, edited by Randolph Hughes.   1952.

Other

Notes on Poems and Reviews.   1866; edited by Clyde K. Hyder, 1966.
Byron.   1866.
An Appeal to England.   1867.
William Blake.   1867.
Christabel and the Poems of Coleridge.   1869.
Under the Microscope.   1872.
Le Tombeau de Théophile Gautier.   1873.
George Chapman.   1875.
Essays and Studies.   1875.
Note on the Muscovite Crusade.   1876.
A Note on Charlotte Brontë.   1877.
A Study of Shakespeare.   1880.
A Study of Victor Hugo.   1886.
Thomas Middleton.   1887.
The Whippingham Papers, with others.   1888.
A Study of Ben Jonson.   1889.
Studies in Prose and Poetry.   1894.
Dead Love and Other Unedited Pieces.   1901.
Percy Bysshe Shelley.   1903.
The Age of Shakespeare.   1909.
Shakespeare.   1909.
Three Plays of Shakespeare.   1909.
Les Fleurs du Mal and Other Studies.   1913.
Charles Dickens.   1913.
A Study of Les Misérables, edited by Edmund Gosse.   1914.
Pericles and Other Studies.   1914.
Théophile.   1915.
Félicien Cossu: A Burlesque, edited by Edmund Gosse.   1915.
Ernest Clouët: A Burlesque, edited by Edmund Gosse.   1916.
Contemporaries of Shakespeare, edited by Edmund Gosse and T. J. Wise.   1919.
Autobiographical Notes.   1920.
Columbus.   1944.
Le Prince Proletaire.   1963.
The Influence of the Roman Censorship on the Morals of the People.   1964.
New Writings, edited by Cecil Y. Lang.   1964.

Swinburne Replies, edited by Clyde K. Hyder. 1966.
Swinburne as Critic, edited by Clyde K. Hyder. 1972.

Editor, *A Selection from the Works of Lord Byron.* 1866.
Editor, *Christabel and Lyrical and Imaginative Poems,* by Coleridge. 1869.

Bibliography: in *Complete Works,* 1927.

Reading List: *La Jeunesse de Swinburne,* 1928, and *Swinburne: A Literary Biography,* 1932, both by Georges Lafourcade; *Swinburne's Theory of Poetry* by Thomas E. Connolly, 1964; *The Crowns of Apollo: Swinburne's Principles of Literature and Art* by Robert L. Peters, 1965; *Swinburne: A Critical Biography* by Jean Overton Fuller, 1968; *Swinburne: The Critical Heritage* edited by Clyde K. Hyder, 1970; *Swinburne's Poetics: Theory and Practice* by Meredith B. Raymond, 1971; *Swinburne* by Ian Fletcher, 1973; *Swinburne: The Portrait of a Poet* by Philip Henderson, 1974.

*   *   *

When the strident red-headed imp invaded the prim Victorian drawing room gleefully shouting shocking indecencies and blasphemies in new and compelling poetic rhythms, many Victorians shuddered and drew back. Hardly since Byron had such a scandalously outré figure usurped the literary scene. But others, particularly the young Pre-Raphaelite set, welcomed this new dithyrambic voice of revolt. When, half a century later, Algernon Charles Swinburne, now a staid, secluded, irascible little old gentleman infatuated with babies and Jacobean quartos and virtually imprisoned by his solicitor-friend Watts-Dunton at No. 2, The Pines, Putney, left the scene, he was almost universally respected by the literary establishment. In between these two extremes lay an extraordinarily rich and productive career as lyrist, playwright, narrative poet, critic, writer of fiction, and controversialist.

Tired of the prudish pieties of Tennyson, the melancholy Stoicism of Arnold, and the too-vigorous romantic optimism of Browning, Swinburne early became and long continued a cogent poet of revolt. In the face of the Tennysonian domestic ideal, he hymned the cruelty and deadliness of love and became the laureate of what Mario Praz has called the sado-masochistic Victorian "Romantic agony." Though the eroticism often seems curiously detached, from the early plays in *The Queen-Mother, and Rosamond* through *Atalanta in Calydon* and poems such as "Dolores," "Faustine," and "Laus Veneris" in *Poems and Ballads,* to the long dramatic trilogy on Mary Queen of Scots, kisses are bloody, pain is pleasure, passion leads to death, and such lethal ladies as Lucretia Borgia, Mary Stuart, the Empress Faustina, and Venus of the Tannhauser legend are prime heroines. Though heard before in Keats, these were new accents in Victorian poetry.

Swinburne's religious and political radicalism, also shocking in its day, is less interesting now. It is still stimulating to hear (as in "Hymn to Proserpine") Venus exalted over the Virgin, the "roses and raptures of vice" over the "lilies and languors of virtue." Though it no longer seems blasphemous, Swinburne's pessimism, his celebration in such poems as "The Garden of Proserpine" and "A Forsaken Garden" of the fact that death waits for all, that there is no immortality, and that even death will eventually die, is still compelling. But his long autobiographic monologue "The Triumph of Time" and his attempt at philosophic poetry in "Hertha" now seem insubstantial; and his rhapsodic or vituperative Hugoesque and Mazzinian political poems in *Songs Before Sunrise* and *Studies in Song* have faded with the liberal causes – Italian independence, protest against Napoleon III – which gave them birth.

In his criticism Swinburne was far less of a rebel. His critical poems and essays are both historically important and enduringly suggestive. His near deification of Hugo, Landor, and minor writers like Sir Henry Taylor can be discounted as friendly prejudice. His praise of Baudelaire, significant in its time, is probably overblown. But his book on Blake was one of the first to call attention to that neglected poet and was also one of the earliest strong Victorian statements of an art-for-art's-sake theory of criticism. Like his interest in Baudelaire and his critical essays on pictorial art, it points forward toward Pater and Wilde. Controversial in its time, Swinburne's effort in *A Study of Shakespeare* to date the plays by stylistic analysis is now largely ignored, but his critical rediscovery and comment on then forgotten Elizabethan and Jacobean dramatists such as Chapman importantly carry on the work of Charles Lamb. His later dramatic criticism, however, is marred by too eulogistic a tone and by his squabbles with Furnivall and others.

But Swinburne is not primarily a philosophic or critical writer. His basic greatness lies in his technical innovation and skill. Swinburne gave English poetry a music that it had never before heard. He blows new notes, to paraphrase a remark by Tennyson, through forms popular with other Victorians. Thus in *Atalanta in Calydon* and *Erechtheus* he skillfully refashions with his new verbal music the then fashionable imitation of Greek tragedy. The nineteenth-century Elizabethan Revival had popularized poetic closet drama on sixteenth-century models; in *The Queen-Mother*, *Chastelard*, and parts of the excessively long *Bothwell* Swinburne turns the form into something peculiarly his own, introducing new mood, new stylization, new "Pre-Raphaelite" effects. Like Keats, Tennyson, Rossetti, and Morris, Swinburne effectively adapts the literary ballad, though he remains closer than they to the original popular ballad. Reacting strongly against Tennyson's injection of modern allegory into Arthurian poetic romance, Swinburne writes, with at least fair success, his own more direct narrative poems on Tristram of Lyonesse and on Balen and Balan. He handles adroitly the sonnet (especially the sonnet of literary criticism), the roundel (*A Century of Roundels*), and the ballade.

Swinburne's greatest originality and success, however, is in the sound and movement of his verse. With their compelling rhythms, their alliteration, their verbal creation of mood, choruses such as "When the Hounds of Spring" and "Before the Beginning of Years" in *Atalanta* have a masterly musical quality that is all Swinburne's own. It is not surprising that on the appearance of *Poems and Ballads* Oxford undergraduates went through their courts chanting the sensuously throbbing lines of "Dolores." In a poem such as "Faustina" repetition is used with extraordinary effectiveness. The famous couplet (from "Hymn to Proserpine") "Thou has conquered, O pale Galilean; the world has grown grey with thy breath;/We have drunken of things Lethean, and fed on the fullness of death" is endlessly quotable not only for its radical sense but even more because of its felicitously balanced phrases, alliterations, internal rhymes, and rhythmic vigor. Equally memorable for their dirgelike, melancholy sonority and double rhymes are such stanzas as the celebrated one from "The Garden of Proserpine" that begins "From too much love of living" and ends "even the weariest river/Winds somewhere safe to sea." The rhetoric of many of the plays, too, though rarely dramatic, has a telling slow, rich power, especially when Swinburne mingles echoes from the Old Testament with Pre-Raphaelite eroticism.

Too often, alas, Swinburne becomes intoxicated with his own words. Few of the poems have strong organization; most are amalgamations of repetitious images and phrases held together by rhythm, alliteration, and rhyme alone. They have little logical progression; stanzas can sometimes be transposed at will. Both in prose and poetry Swinburne is far too prolix. As he himself recognizes in his delightful self-parody in his *Specimens of Modern Poets*, pulsing rhythm, constant alliteration, too emphatic rhyming, and torrential wordiness often obfuscate meaning with the result that the reader is borne nowhere on endless waves of words. This is Swinburne's main fault. But in his best works – both in prose and poetry – rhythm, rhyme, alliteration, and wording combine impressionistically into a verbal music that itself becomes the "meaning."

Despite flashes of vivid description and bars of the old music, the poems on nature that Swinburne at the urging of Watts-Dunton produced in his later years rarely strike fire. The later plays are lifeless. The sentimental poems on babies had best be forgotten. Though they have been praised by Randolph Hughes and others and are interesting as biographical and psychological documents, the prose fictions such as *Lesbia Brandon* and *Love's Cross*

Currents are in my judgment of no importance. Swinburne's juvenilia and pornographic writings such as *The Whippingham Papers*, though they too help to round out the figure of the man, do not add to his literary stature. His letters, however (edited by Cecil Lang in an excellent collected edition), are fascinating. Yet, like Wordsworth's, Swinburne's reputation must finally rest partly on the breadth, quantity, and historical importance of his work; partly on his criticism; but primarily on a small canon of tremendously effective early lyrics and lyrical dramas. Though of major importance, his work (as Arnold said of Wordsworth's) needs stringent selection.

—Curtis Dahl

SYLVESTER, Joshua(h). English. Born in the Medway region of Kent in 1563. Educated at the school of Adrian à Saravia, Southampton, 1573–76. Married to Mary Sylvester; five or six children. Businessman and merchant; later associated with the Earl of Essex; Groom to the Chamber of Prince Henry, 1606; Secretary to the merchant adventurers, and lived at Middleburg, 1613–18. *Died 28 September 1618.*

PUBLICATIONS

Collections

Works, edited by A. B. Grosart.   2 vols., 1880.

Verse

A Canticle of the Victory Obtained by Henry the Fourth at Ivry, from Du Bartas.   1590.
The Triumph of Faith, The Sacrifice of Isaac, The Ship-Wreck of Jonas, A Song of the Victory, from Du Bartas.   1592.
The Profit of Imprisonment: A Paradox, from Odet de la Noue Lord of Teligni.   1594.
Monodia: An Elegy in Commemoration of Dame Helen Branch, Widow.   1594.
The Second Week or Childhood of the World.   1598.
Bartas His Divine Weeks and Works.   1605; revised edition, 1621; edited by Susan Snyder, 2 vols., 1978.
Posthumous Bartas: The Third Day of His Second Week.   1606.
Posthumous Bartas: The Fore-Noon of the Fourth Day of His Second Week.   1607.
Lachrimae Lachrimarum.   1612; with *Other Elegies*, 1613.
The Parliament of Virtues Royal, from Jean Bertaut and others.   1614; *Second Session,* 2 vols., 1615.
The Sacred Works.   1620.
The Maiden's Blush; or, Joseph, from Girolamo Fracastoro.   1620.
The Wood-Man's Bear.   1620.
Panthea; or, Divine Wishes and Meditations.   1630.

Play

Nebuchadnezzer's Fiery Furnace, edited by M. Rösler.   1936.

Other

Translator, *A Panegyric of Henry the Fourth,* by Pierre Matthieu, with *The Heroic Life of Henry the Fourth* by E. Grimeston.   1612.

Reading List: *Du Bartas en Angleterre* by H. Ashton, 1908; *Milton's Use of Du Bartas* by G. C. Taylor, 1934.

*   *   *

Preceded by Sir Philip Sidney and King James, among others, Joshua Sylvester turned into English the ambitious religious poetry of the French Protestant, Guillaume de Salluste du Bartas (1544–1590), and published the most complete translation of his *Sepmaines* as *Bartas His Devine Weekes and Workes*, which ran through half a dozen editions by the mid-seventeenth century. The first "week," in seven "days" and seven books, expands the first chapter of Genesis through surveys of knowledge from mineralogy to morality. Thus, in the Third Day, on the division of the Earth and Sea, the poet proposes to discuss both the "Bounds of the ocean's rage" and "Why it is salt," along with "Mines, Metals, Gemms of price:/Right use of Gold: the Load-stone's rare effects:/The Country-life preferr'd in all respects." The second, unfinished week undertakes the entire sacred history of the world, and proceeds in four "days" from Adam through David.

As Sylvester turns the hexameters of du Bartas into thousands of heroic couplets, there are inevitably some anticipations of eighteenth-century moral essays in verse. Thus the *Devine Weekes* sometimes suggests Pope in epigrammatic neatness and in moral stance, as in scorn for mortals who proudly speculate in theology until "th'Author's praise they in themselves eclipse."

Milton and the young Dryden were among Sylvester's readers, although Dryden in his later years scorned the verse as "fustian." Admirers of the translation are apt to appreciate precisely those qualities which Sylvester and du Bartas share: large enthusiasm, quaint simile, exuberant diction. Sylvester can parallel du Bartas' wordplay as deftly as in turning "Bruyant, courant, errant, terrible, horrible, rible," into "They jumble, tumble, rumble, rage, and rave." His additions to du Bartas are usually no more than adaptation of references to French history or geography so that they become familiarly English.

Although he wrote a substantial volume of devotional, complimentary, satiric, and (somewhat obscurely) autobiographical verse of his own, Sylvester's positive reputation rests on his translations. His original compositions are seldom reprinted, read, or praised, despite the ingenuity of anagrams, the visual allure of shaped poems, or the enticement of such titles as "Tobacco Battered and the Pipes Shattered (about their Ears that idlely Idolize so base and barbarous a Weed; or at least-wise over-love so loathsome Vanitie)."

—Kay Stevenson

SYMONS, Arthur (William). English. Born in Milford Haven, Pembrokeshire, 28 February 1865. Educated at private schools abroad. Married Rhoda Bowser in 1901. Member of the Rhymers Club, London, and a friend of Wilde, Dowson, and Yeats. Journalist: on the staff of the *Athenaeum*, 1891, *Saturday Review*, 1894, and *Academy*: contributor to the *Yellow Book*: Editor of its successor, *The Savoy*, 1896. *Died 22 January 1945.*

PUBLICATIONS

Collections

Poetry and Prose (selection), edited by R. V. Holdsworth.   1974.

Verse

Days and Nights.   1889.
Silhouettes.   1892.
London Nights.   1895.
Amoris Victima.   1897.
Images of Good and Evil.   1899.
The Loom of Dreams.   1901.
Poems.   2 vols., 1902.
Lyrics.   1903.
A Book of Twenty Songs.   1905.
The Fool of the World and Other Poems.   1906.
Knave of Hearts 1894–1908.   1913.
Lesbia and Other Poems.   1920.
Love's Cruelty.   1923.
From Catullus, Chiefly Concerning Lesbia.   1924.
Jezebel Mort and Other Poems.   1931.
Amoris Victimia (selection of verse and prose).   1940.

Plays

The Minister's Call, from the story "A Modern Idyll" by Frank Harris (produced 1892).
The Dead City, from a play by Gabriele D'Annunzio.   1898.
Gioconda, from the play by Gabriele D'Annunzio.   1901.
Francesca da Rimini, from the play by Gabriele D'Annunzio.   1902.
The Fool of the World: A Morality (produced 1906).   1906.
Cleopatra in Judea (produced 1907).   In *Tragedies,* 1916.
Electra, from the play by Hoffmansthal (produced 1908).
The Dawn, from a play by Emile Verhaeren.   1915.
Tragedies (includes *The Death of Agrippina, Cleopatra in Judea, The Harvesters*).   1916.
The Toy Cart, from a work by Sudraka (produced 1916).   1919.
Tristan and Iseult.   1917.
Cesare Borgia, Iseult of Brittany, The Toy Cart.   1920.

Other

An Introduction to the Study of Browning.   1886; revised edition, 1906.
Studies in Two Literatures.   1897.
Aubrey Beardsley.   1898; revised edition, 1908.
The Symbolist Movement in Literature.   1899; revised edition, 1908.
Cities.   1903.
Plays, Acting, and Music.   1903; revised edition, 1909.
Studies in Prose and Verse.   1904.
Spiritual Adventures.   1905.
Studies in Seven Arts.   1906.
Cities of Italy.   1907.
Great Acting in English.   1907.
William Blake.   1907.
London: A Book of Aspects.   1909.
The Romantic Movement in English Poetry.   1909.
Dante Gabriel Rossetti.   1910.
Figures of Several Centuries.   1916.
Cities and Sea-Coasts and Islands.   1917.
Colour Studies in Paris.   1918.
Charles Baudelaire.   1920.
Studies in Elizabethan Drama.   1920.
Dramatis Personae (essays).   1923.
The Café Royal and Other Essays.   1923.
Collected Works.   9 vols., 1924.
Notes on Conrad with Some Unpublished Letters.   1925.
Studies on Modern Painters.   1925.
Eleonora Duse.   1926.
Parisian Nights (essays).   1926.
A Study of Hardy.   1927.
Studies in Strange Souls.   1929.
From Toulouse-Lautrec to Rodin with Some Personal Impressions.   1929.
Confessions: A Study in Pathology.   1930.
A Study of Wilde.   1930.
Mes Souvenirs.   1931.
Wanderings.   1931.
A Study of Pater.   1932.
The Memoirs of Symons: Life and Art in the 1890's, edited by Karl Beckson.   1977.

Editor, *Essays,* by Leigh Hunt.   1887.
Editor, *A Selection from the Poems of Mathilde Blind.*   1897.
Editor, *The Confessions of St. Augustine.*   1898.
Editor, *The Poetical Works of Mathilde Blind.*   1900.
Editor, *Ten Plays,* by Massinger.   1904.
Editor, *A Sixteenth Century Anthology.*   1905.
Editor, *Poems,* by Coleridge.   1905.
Editor, *A Pageant of Elizabethan Poetry.*   1906.
Editor, *Poems,* by Keats.   1907.
Editor, *The Hellenics and Gebir,* by Walter Savage Landor.   1907.
Editor, *Poems of John Clare.*   1908.
Editor, *A Book of Parodies.*   1908.
Editor, *Poems,* by Shelley.   1926.

Translator, *L'Assommoir,* by Emile Zola.   1894.

Translator, *The Child of Pleasure* (verse only), by Gabriele D'Annunzio.   1898.
Translator, *Poems in Prose,* by Baudelaire.   1905.
Translator, *Les Fleurs du Mal, Petits Poèmes en Prose, Les Paradis Artificiels,* by Baudelaire.   1925.
Translator, *Queen Ysabeau,* by Villiers de l'Isle-Adam.   1925.
Translator, *The Adventures of Giuseppe Pignata.*   1925.
Translator, *The Letters of Baudelaire to His Mother, 1833–1866.*   1928.
Translator, *The Woman and the Puppet,* by Pierre Louÿs.   1935.

Reading List: *Symons* by T. E. Welby, 1925; *Symons: His Life and Letters,* 1962, and *Symons: A Critical Biography,* 1963, both by Roger Lhombreaud; *Symons* by John M. Munro, 1969.

*   *   *

Arthur Symons is almost the type-case of the highly professional all-round man of letters whose significance it is to be judged as part of a scene or period rather than as an individual. He was a copious poet, throughout a long working life, but his best poems – a handful of mellifluous erotic nocturnes, concerned with his obsession with young dancers and singers – can all be found in *Silhouettes* and *London Nights.* After that there is little but polished emptiness. The brief period when he edited the eight numbers of the periodical *The Savoy* shows a flair for finding brilliant contributors whose reputations have outlasted his own: Verlaine, Yeats, Conrad, Shaw, Beerbohm, and Beardsley are among them. He was a prolific translator, reviewer, writer of causeries and of topographical essays. But probably his most important role is to be seen in his book *The Symbolist Movement in Literature* which both Yeats and Eliot acknowledged to have influenced them profoundly.

Symons was a pioneer in bringing to the attention of English and American writers the work of such French poets as Mallarmé, Verlaine, Rimbaud, and Laforgue. He knew many of them personally, attended some of Mallarmé's famous Tuesdays, and took the initiative in inviting Verlaine to lecture in England. As an indefatigable go-between for what was variously described as the modern, the decadent, and the symbolist or symbolical, Symons has his place in the history of ideas and of style.

But apart from this function, best remembered in *The Symbolist Movement in Literature,* there is another work by Symons, too little known partly because it has never been properly available: his *Confessions* (sub-titled "A Study in Pathology"), an account of his mental collapse in Italy in 1908, when he was thrown into prison in Ferrara, and from which he emerged to spend the next few years in mental hospitals in England. It is a horrifying account of delusions and cruelty and, ironically, is the only work of real interest he achieved between that year, 1908, and his death in January 1945.

—Anthony Thwaite

TAGORE, Sir Rabindranath. Indian. Born in Calcutta, 6 May 1861; son of Maharshi Tagore, grandson of Prince Tagore. Educated privately; University College, University of London, 1878–80. Married Mrinalinidebi in 1884; one son and one daughter. Managed family estates at Shileida from 1885; founded the Santiniketan, a school to blend Eastern and Western philosophical/educational systems, Bolpur, Bengal, 1901, which later developed into an international institution called Visva-Bharti; visited England, 1912; contributed regularly to the *Visvabharati Quarterly*; delivered the Hibbert Lectures, Oxford University, 1930. Began painting, 1929: exhibitions in Moscow, Berlin, Munich, Paris, and New York. Recipient: Nobel Prize for Literature, 1913. D.Lit.: University of Calcutta; Hindu University, Benares; University of Dacca; Osmania University, Hyderabad; D.Litt.: Oxford University. Knighted, 1915; resigned knighthood in 1919 as protest against British policies in the Punjab. Wrote in Bengali and translated his own works into English. *Died 7 August 1941.*

PUBLICATIONS (in English)

Collections

    A Tagore Reader, edited by Amiya Chakravarty.   1961.

Verse

    Gitanjali.   1912.
    The Gardener.   1913.
    The Crescent Moon: Child-Poems.   1913.
    Fruit-Gathering.   1916.
    Lover's Gift, and Crossing.   1918.
    Poems.   1922.
    The Curse at Farewell, translated by Edward Thompson.   1924.
    Fireflies.   1928.
    Fifteen Poems.   1928.
    Sheaves: Poems and Songs, edited and translated by Nagendranath Gupta.   1929.
    The Child.   1931.
    The Golden Boat, translated by Chabani Bhattacharya.   1932.
    Poems, edited by Krishna Kripalani.   1942.
    A Flight of Swans, translated by Aurobindo Bose.   1955.
    Syamali, translated by Sheila Chatterjee.   1955.
    The Herald of Spring, translated by Aurobindo Bose.   1957.
    Wings of Death: The Last Poems, translated by Aurobindo Bose.   1960.
    Devouring Love, translated by Shakuntala Sastri.   1961.
    A Bunch of Poems, translated by Monika Varma.   1966.
    One Hundred and One.   1967.
    Last Poems, translated by Pritish Nandy.   1973.
    Later Poems, translated by Aurobindo Bose.   1974.

Plays

    The Post Office, translated by Devabrata Mukerjee (produced 1913).   1914.
    Citra.   1914.
    The King of the Dark Chamber.   1914.

Malini, translated by Kshitish Chandra Sen (produced 1915). In *Sacrifice and Other Plays*, 1917.
The Cycle of Spring. 1917.
Sacrifice and Other Plays (includes *Malini; Sanyas, or, The Ascetic; The King and the Queen*). 1917.
Sacrifice (produced 1918). In *Sacrifice and Other Plays*, 1917.
The King and the Queen (produced 1919). In *Sacrifice and Other Plays*, 1917.
The Fugitive. 1918.
The Mother's Prayer (produced 1920). 1919.
Autumn Festival (produced 1920).
The Farewell Curse, The Deserted Mother, The Sinner, Suttee (produced 1920).
The Farewell (produced 1924).
Three Plays (includes *Muktadhara, Natir Puja, Candalika*), translated by Marjorie Sykes. 1950.

Fiction

Glimpses of Bengal Life (stories). 1913.
The Stone and Other Stories, translated by C. F. Andrews and others. 1916.
Mashi and Other Stories. 1918.
The Parrot's Training. 1918.
The Home and the World, translated by Surendranath Tagore. 1919.
The Wreck. 1921.
Gora. 1924.
Broken Ties and Other Stories. 1925.
Two Sisters, translated by Krishna Kripalani. 1943.
Farewell My Friend, with The Garden, translated by Krishna Kripalani. 1946.
Four Chapters, translated by Surendranath Tagore. 1950.
More Stories from Tagore. 1951.
Binodini, translated by Krishna Kripalani. 1959.
The Runaway and Other Stories, edited by Somnath Maitra. 1959.
Caturanga, translated by Asok Mitra. 1963.
Lipika, translated by Indu Dutt. 1969.
The Broken Nest, translated by Mary M. Lagos and Supriya Sen. 1971.

Other

Sadhana: The Realisation of Life. 1913.
Stray Birds (aphorisms). 1916.
My Reminiscences, translated by Surendranath Tagore. 1917.
Letters. 1917.
Nationalism. 1917.
Personality: Lectures Delivered in America. 1917.
Greater India (lectures). 1921.
Thought Relics. 1921.
Creative Unity. 1922.
The Visvabharati, with C. F. Andrews. 1923.
Letters from Abroad, edited by C. F. Andrews. 1924; revised edition, as *Letters to a Friend*, 1928.
Talks in China. 1925.
Lectures and Addresses, edited by Anthony X. Soares. 1928.
City and Village. 1928.

The Religion of Man. 1932.
Collected Poems and Plays. 1936.
Man (lectures). 1937.
My Boyhood Days. 1940.
Eighty Years, and Selections. 1941.
A Tagore Testament. 1953.
Our Universe, translated by Indu Dutt. 1958.
Letters from Russia, translated by Sasadhar Sinha. 1960.
Tagore, Pioneer in Education: Essays and Exchanges Between Tagore and L. K. Elmhirst. 1961.
A Visit to Japan, translated by Shakuntala Shastri. 1961.
Towards Universal Man. 1961.
On Art and Aesthetics. 1961.
The Diary of Westward Voyage, translated by Indu Dutt. 1962.
On Rural Reconstruction. 1962.
The Cooperative Principle. 1963.
Boundless Sky (miscellany). 1964.
The Housewarming and Other Selected Writings, edited by Amiya Chakravarty. 1965.

Reading List: *Tagore, Poet and Thinker* by Mohinimohana Bhattarcharya, 1961; *The Lute and the Plough: A Life of Tagore* by G. D. Khanolkar, 1963; *Ravindranath's Poetry* by Dattatuaya Muley, 1964; *Rabindranath* by Sati Ghosh, 1966; *Tagore: His Mind and Art* by Birenda C. Chakravorty, 1971.

*   *   *

The complexity of Rabindranath Tagore's genius and the extraordinary range of his intellectual and artistic interests have been noted by scholars in India and the West alike. While hailed primarily as a poet, Tagore excelled as a dramatist, essayist, novelist, short story writer, and, in non-literary endeavors, as painter, philosopher, educator, musician, social reformer, and ambassador of good will to cultures as diverse as China, the United States, and Latin America. Tagore's creative versatility serves to confirm his own belief that most great artists function at higher levels of awareness, often experiencing a natural, spontaneous urge for total Self-realization, which in Vedanta (the highest aspect of Hindu philosophy) is called Unity Consciousness.

This principle of unity (*Sahitya*) is the focal point of Tagore's aesthetic philosophy; derived from the root *Sahit*, meaning "to be with," the word *Sahitya* is the Sanskrit term for both "unity" and "literature." In his book *Sahitya* (1908) Tagore emphasizes that man's sense of oneness with the rest of creation is the root of all aesthetic delight; the poet is essentially restating the Vedantic view of art, which holds that artistic expression has its basis in states of consciousness and that the highest creative expression can only follow from the artist's own direct experience of pure consciousness (*Turiya*). In *Sahityer Pathe* (1926) the poet states, "Aesthetic delight is such a sense of harmony beyond the object that it does not delay in merging with our consciousness. In this case the revelation of the truth of the object is the same as the revelation of my consciousness" (p. 45). The distinguishing characteristic of all great artists, according to Tagore, is their ability to enlarge their own consciousness to the point that it becomes one with the Universal Self, thereby intuiting or reflecting all other selves.

In this regard Tagore considers the writing of poetry to be a spiritual discipline, a kind of *via purgativa*. Thus he shares the Hindu view of art as *Sadhana* – the process of spiritual training which transforms consciousness in such a way that the artist (individual self) can no longer be separated from his art (Universal Self). In *The Cycle of Spring* (1917) Tagore states: "The secret of all art lies in self-[as opposed to Self] forgetfulness. The poet or artist sets free the poet or artist in us" (p. 77). Tagore emphasizes the ability of art to raise the consciousness of not only the artist, but the perceiver as well: "True art withdraws our thoughts from the mere machinery of life, and lifts our souls above the meanness of it. It releases the self from the restless activities of the world and takes us out of the noisy sickroom of ourselves" (ibid).

Critics generally recognize three major stages in the poetic development of Tagore: 1) "romantic" poetry expressing a vague longing for essence transcending the mutability of matter (pre-*Gitanjali*, 1878–1908); 2) "mystic" poetry describing the synthesis of matter and spirit (*Gitanjali*, 1909–1915); 3) "realist" poetry defining the role of duality in the human experience (post-*Gitanjali*, 1916–1941). Tagore's early poetry, of which *Chitra* is a good example, consists largely of verse narrative, miscellaneous poems, songs, and poetic drama. *Gitanjali*, for which Tagore was awarded the Nobel Prize in 1913, consists primarily of his prose translations of selected lyrics from the 1910 Bengali version of *Gitanjali* and *Gitalipi*. *Gitanjali*, which literally means "Song Offerings," is a long, free-verse poem which depicts the author's growth of consciousness from "drunk delight" (*Ananda*) in creation as a child, at the start of the poem, to the acceptance of and thus transcendence of the cycle of birth-and-death (*Samsara*) when he is an old man at the end. Tagore's later poetry, from *Fruit-Gathering* (1916) on, far exceeds his earlier poetry both in volume and quality. Tagore left much of his later work untranslated, but what we do have in English reveals a poet keenly aware of the fragmentation experienced by modern man, yet confident in man's ability to achieve unity through the creative processes and the evolution of his awareness.

—Gail and H.A. Mirza

TATE, Allen. American. Born in Winchester, Kentucky, 19 November 1899. Educated at Georgetown Preparatory School, Washington, D.C.; Vanderbilt University, Nashville, Tennessee, B.A. 1922. Married 1) the novelist Caroline Gordon, in 1924; 2) the poet Isabella Stewart Gardner in 1959; 3) Helen Heinz in 1966; has three children. Member of the Fugitive Group of Poets: Founding Editor, with John Crowe Ransom, *The Fugitive*, Nashville, 1922–25; Editor, *Sewanee Review*, Tennessee, 1944–46; Editor, Belles Lettres series, Henry Holt and Company, New York, 1946–48. Lecturer in English, Southwestern College, Memphis, Tennessee, 1934–36; Professor of English, The Woman's College, Greensboro, North Carolina, 1938–39; Poet-in-Residence, Princeton University, New Jersey 1939–42; Lecturer in the Humanities, New York University, 1947–51. Since 1951, Professor of English, University of Minnesota, Minneapolis: Regents' Professor, 1966; Professor Emeritus, 1968. Visiting Professor in the Humanities, University of Chicago, 1949; Fulbright Lecturer, Oxford University, 1953, University of Rome, 1953–54, and Oxford and Leeds universities, 1958–59; Department of State Lecturer at the universities of Liège and Louvain, 1954, Delhi and Bombay, 1956, the Sorbonne, Paris, 1956, Nottingham, 1956, and Urbino and Florence, 1961; Visiting Professor of English, University of North Carolina, Greensboro, 1966, and Vanderbilt University, 1967. Member, Phi Beta Kappa Senate, 1951–53. Since 1948 Fellow, and since 1956 Senior Fellow, Kenyon School of English (now School of Letters, Indiana University, Bloomington). Constutant in Poetry, Library of Congress, Washington, D.C., 1943–44. Recipient: Guggenheim Fellowship, 1928, 1929; National Institute of Arts and Letters grant, 1948; Bollingen Prize, 1957; Brandeis University Creative Arts Award, 1960; Gold Medal of the Dante Society, Florence, 1962; Academy of American Poets Fellowship, 1963; Oscar Williams-Gene Derwood Award, 1975; National Medal for Literature, 1976. Litt.D.: University of Louisville, Kentucky, 1948; Coe College, Cedar Rapids, Iowa, 1955; Colgate University, Hamilton, New York, 1956; University of

Kentucky, Lexington, 1960; Carleton College, Northfield, Minnesota, 1963; University of the South, Sewanee, Tennessee, 1970. Member, American Academy of Arts and Letters; President, National Institute of Arts and Letters, 1968. Since 1964, Member, Board of Chancellors, Academy of American Poets. Lives in Sewanee, Tennessee.

PUBLICATIONS

Verse

The Golden Mean and Other Poems, with Ridley Wills. 1923.
Mr. Pope and Other Poems. 1928.
Ode to the Confederate Dead, Being the Revised and Final Version of a Poem Previously Published on Several Occasions: To Which Are Added Message from Abroad and The Cross. 1930.
Three Poems. 1930.
Robert E. Lee. 1932.
Poems 1928–1931. 1932.
The Mediterranean and Other Poems. 1936.
Selected Poems. 1937.
Sonnets at Christmas. 1941.
The Winter Sea: A Book of Poems. 1944.
Poems 1920–1945: A Selection. 1947.
Poems 1922–1947. 1948.
Two Conceits for the Eye to Sing, If Possible. 1950.
Poems. 1960.
The Swimmers and Other Selected Poems. 1970.
Collected Poems 1919–1976. 1977.

Play

The Governess, with Anne Goodwin Winslow (produced 1962).

Fiction

The Fathers. 1938. revised edition, 1960.
The Fathers and Other Fiction. 1976.

Other

Stonewall Jackson: The Good Soldier: A Narrative. 1928.
Jefferson Davis: His Rise and Fall: A Biographical Narrative. 1929.
Reactionary Essays on Poetry and Ideas. 1936.
Reason in Madness: Critical Essays. 1941.
Invitation to Learning, with Huntington Cairns and Mark Van Doren. 1941.
Sixty American Poets, 1896–1944: A Preliminary Checklist. 1945.
On the Limits of Poetry: Selected Essays, 1928–1948. 1948.
The Hovering Fly and Other Essays. 1949.
The Forlorn Demon: Didactic and Critical Essays. 1953.

The Man of Letters in the Modern World: Selected Essays, 1928–1955.   1955.
Collected Essays.   1959.
Essays of Four Decades.   1968.
Modern Literature and the Lost Traveller.   1969.
The Translation of Poetry.   1972.
The Literary Correspondence of Donald Davidson and Tate, edited by John T. Fain and
    T. D. Young.   1974.
Memoirs and Opinions 1926–1974.   1975.

Editor, with others, *Fugitives: An Anthology of Verse.*   1928.
Editor, with Herbert Agar, *Who Owns America? A New Declaration of
    Independence.*   1936.
Editor, with A. Theodore Johnson, *America Through the Essay: An Anthology for
    English Courses.*   1938.
Editor, *The Language of Poetry.*   1942.
Editor, *Princeton Verse Between Two Wars: An Anthology.*   1942.
Editor, with John Peale Bishop, *American Harvest: Twenty Years of Creative Writing in
    the United States.*   1942.
Editor, *Recent American Poetry and Poetic Criticism: A Selected List of
    References.*   1943.
Editor, *A Southern Vanguard* (the John Peale Bishop memorial anthology).   1947.
Editor, *The Collected Poems of John Peale Bishop.*   1948.
Editor, with Caroline Gordon, *The House of Fiction: An Anthology of the Short
    Story.*   1950; revised edition, 1960.
Editor, with Lord David Cecil, *Modern Verse in English, 1900–1950.*   1958.
Editor, with John Berryman and Ralph Ross, *The Arts of Learning.*   1960.
Editor, *Selected Poems of John Peale Bishop.*   1960.
Editor, with Robert Penn Warren, *Selected Poems,* by Denis Devlin.   1963.
Editor, *T. S. ELiot: The Man and His Work: A Critical Evaluation by Twenty-Six
    Distinguished Critics.*   1966.
Editor, *The Complete Poems and Selected Criticism of Edgar Allan Poe.*   1968.
Editor, *Six American Poets: From Emily Dickinson to the Present: An
    Introduction.*   1972.
Translator, *The Vigil of Venus.*   1943.

Bibliography: *Tate: A Bibliography* by Marshall Fallwell, Jr., 1969.

Reading List: *The Last Alternatives: A Study of the Works of Tate* by M. K. Meiners, 1963;
Tate by George Hemphill, 1964; *Tate* by Ferman Bishop, 1967; *Rumors of Morality: An
Introduction to Tate* by M. E. Bradford, 1969; *Tate: A Literary Biography* by Radcliffe
Squires, 1971, and *Tate and His Works: Critical Evaluations* edited by Squires, 1972.

*   *   *

   Allen Tate is always associated with the Fugitives, the small group of Southern poets who
were led by John Crowe Ransom of Vanderbilt University of Nashville during the early
1920's. But Tate was always his own man, and as a young Fugitive he found it necessary to
reject much in the South; by 1924 he was living in New York City. Certainly Southern
literary culture offered nothing that he could imitate directly, though his sense of the age led
him to the French symbolists and hence back to Poe, about whom he was to write three of his
most important essays. His best poem before 1925 is his version of Baudelaire's
"Correspondences." This seems as important as his friendship with his first master, Ransom,
because it allowed him access to the mainstream of modern poetry.

In New York City, married to the novelist Caroline Gordon, Tate was on close terms with many writers of his generation, especially Hart Crane, and he could easily be put among the second generation of modernists (if we put Eliot, Pound, and Joyce in the first generation). It may well be that his regional sense was sharpened by his residence in the East and then Paris for six years. At any rate, by 1926 he was writing the first version of his most ambitious early poem, "Ode to the Confederate Dead." The recently published correspondence between Tate and his Fugitive friend Donald Davidson shows him at that time occupying a kind of intermediary position between Davidson, who was writing *The Tall Men*, a long poem about Tennessee, and Crane, who was working on *The Bridge*, a visionary poem about America. Almost by instinct Tate shunned the "epical" treatment of experience. Where his Southern quality emerges most convincingly is in the elevation of tone that was characteristic of the rhetoricians of this region. In a sense the Old South was organized by the voices of the preacher and the politician, and this legacy of public speaking descended to many of the writers of the modern Southern Renascence.

The 1930's was the Agrarian period for the old Fugitive group, and Tate was frequently involved in the controversies that grew out of this movement, which coincided with an extraordinary outburst of literary achievement in the South. But his main energy went into his poetry, and his *Selected Poems* is one of the best collections of poetry in the decade. This volume contains the final version of the "Ode to the Confederate Dead," a distinguished meditative poem called "The Mediterranean," and a dozen shorter poems of great power and considerable range, such as "Emblems," "The Cross," and "The Wolves."

Meanwhile he was becoming one of the most important American critics; his first volume, *Reactionary Essays on Poetry and Ideas*, fully established his position. As critic he has always taken a large view of literary culture, but many of his influential early essays were written about such contemporaries as Crane, Archibald MacLeish, and John Peale Bishop. Certain theoretical essays have become classics of modern criticism: "Tension in Poetry," "Techniques of Fiction," "The Hovering Fly," and "A Southern Mode of the Imagination." These have generated as much discussion as anything written during the last generation in the United States. Perhaps the finest essays are two on Poe and Dante, "The Angelic Imagination" and "The Symbolic Imagination," published in 1951 at a time when he was writing some outstanding poems. Tate's criticism, in fact, is very much the work of a poet and often provides the setting for his verse.

Another work in prose that is closely related to Tate's verse of the 1930's is his novel *The Fathers*, which has been even more admired in recent years than it was when it was first published. Influenced in its technique by Ford Madox Ford's *The Good Soldier* ("the masterpiece of British fiction in this century"), the novel dramatizes with a great poetic intelligence the destruction of a Virginia family at the beginning of the Civil War. The critic Radcliffe Squires has shown the extent to which Allen Tate drew on the history of his own family for the subject.

The last phase of Tate's poetry started during the early 1940's, though it was long anticipated. It includes the splendid satire "Ode to Our Young Pro-Consuls of the Air," an attack on the modern religion of the state; his very title proposes an analogy between America and Rome. This in a sense was preparatory for the long poem "Seasons of the Soul" and a later group of poems in *terza rima*, including "The Swimmers" and "The Buried Lake," his most impressive work of all. In these late poems Tate has set his experience (his own, his family's, his region's) against a background of Christian experience represented most fully by Dante, and has "imitated" Dante's verse more closely than any other American poet has done. Brilliant and sometimes restless, Allen Tate has been more than a fine poet: he has helped to set the standards for the literary community in the United States.

—Ashley Brown

TAYLOR, Bayard. American. Born in Kennett Square, Chester County, Pennsylvania, 11 January 1825. Educated at Bolmar's Academy, West Chester, Pennsylvania, 1837–40; Unionville Academy, Pennsylvania, 1842. Married 1) Mary Agnew in 1850 (died, 1850); 2) Marie Hansen in 1857, one daughter. Teacher at Unionville Academy, 1842; apprenticed to the printer of the West Chester *Village Record*, 1842–44; travelled in Europe, as correspondent for the *Saturday Evening Post* and *United States Gazette* of Philadelphia, and the New York *Tribune*, 1844–46; Publisher, *Pioneer* newspaper, Phoenixville, Pennsylvania, 1846–47; Columnist, *Literary World*, New York, 1847–48; Manager, Literary Department, New York *Tribune*, 1848, and covered the California gold rush for the *Tribune*, 1849; travelled in the Middle and Far East, 1851–53, and lectured throughout the United States on his travels, 1854–56; travelled in Europe, 1856–58; settled on a farm, Cedarcroft, near his native village, 1858; served as a correspondent in Washington for the *Tribune*, 1862; Secretary, later Chargé d'Affaires, American Legation, St. Petersburg, Russia, 1862–63; returned to Cedarcroft, and worked on his translation of *Faust*, 1863–70; Non-Resident Professor of German, Cornell University, Ithaca, New York, 1870–77; United States Ambassador to Germany, 1878. *Died 19 December 1878.*

PUBLICATIONS

Collections

> *The Dramatic Works.* 1880.
> *The Poetical Works.* 1880.

Verse

> *Ximena; or, The Battle of Sierra Morena and Other Poems.* 1844.
> *Rhymes of Travel, Ballads, and Poems.* 1849.
> *A Book of Romances, Lyrics, and Songs.* 1851.
> *Poems of the Orient.* 1854.
> *Poems of Home and Travel.* 1855.
> *Poems.* 1856.
> *The Poet's Journal.* 1862.
> *The Poems.* 1864.
> *The Picture of St. John.* 1866.
> *The Golden Wedding: A Masque.* 1868.
> *The Ballad of Abraham Lincoln* (juvenile). 1870.
> *Lars: A Pastoral of Norway.* 1873.
> *Home Pastorals, Ballads, and Lyrics.* 1875.
> *The National Ode.* 1877.

Plays

> *The Masque of the Gods.* 1872.
> *The Prophet.* 1874.
> *Prince Deukalion.* 1878.

Fiction

Hannah Thurston. 1863.
John Godfrey's Fortunes. 1864.
The Story of Kennett. 1866; edited by C. W. La Salle, II, 1973.
Joseph and His Friend. 1870.
Beauty and the Beast, and Tales of Home. 1872.

Other

Views A-Foot; or, Europe Seen with Knapsack and Staff. 1846.
Eldorado; or, Adventures in the Path of Empire. 1850.
A Journey to Central Africa. 1854.
The Lands of the Saracen. 1854.
A Visit to India, China, and Japan in the Year 1853. 1855; revised edition, edited by G.
   F. Pardon, 1860.
Northern Travel. 1857.
Travels in Greece and Russia. 1859.
At Home and Abroad. 2 vols., 1859–62.
Colorado: A Summer Trip. 1867.
By-Ways of Europe. 1869.
A School History of Germany. 1874.
Egypt and Iceland in the Year 1874. 1874.
The Echo Club and Other Literary Diversions. 1876.
Boys of Other Countries: Stories for American Boys. 1876.
Studies in German Literature. 1879.
Critical Essays and Literary Notes, edited by Marie Hansen-Taylor. 1880.
Life and Letters, edited by Marie Hansen-Taylor and H. E. Scudder. 2 vols., 1884.
Unpublished Letters in the Huntington Library, edited by John R. Schultz. 1937.
Correspondence of Taylor and Paul Hamilton Hayne, edited by Charles Duffy. 1945.

Editor, *Hand-Book of Literature and Fine Arts.* 1852.
Editor, *Cyclopedia of Modern Travel.* 1856.
Editor, *Frithiof's Saga,* by Esaias Teghér, traslated by William Lewery Blackley. 1867.
Editor, *Travels in Arabia.* 1871.
Editor, *Japan in Our Day.* 1872.
Editor, *Travels in South Africa.* 1872.
Editor, *The Lake Regions of Central Africa.* 1873.
Editor, *Central Asia.* 1874.
Editor, *Picturesque Europe.* 1877.

Translator, *Faust,* by Goethe. 2 vols., 1870–71; edited by Stuart Atkins, 1972.
Translator, *A Sheaf of Poems,* edited by Mary Taylor Kiliani. 1911.

Reading List: *Tayor* by Albert H. Smyth, 1896 (includes bibliography); *Taylor: Laureate of the Gilded Age* by Richmond Croom Beatty, 1936; *The Genteel Circle: Taylor and His New York Friends* by Richard Cary, 1952; *Taylor and German Letters* by John T. Krumpelmann, 1959; *Taylor* by Paul C. Wermuth, 1973.

*   *   *

Although he wished to be remembered for his poetry, Bayard Taylor supported himself by writing travel literature, and it is for these works, as well as his translation of *Faust*, that we remember him today. The titles of his many travel books, most of which were widely read during the nineteenth century, reveal the vast extent of Taylor's travels: *A Journey to Central Africa*, *Lands of the Saracen*, *India, China, and Japan*, *Northern Travel*, *Travels in Greece and Russia*, and *Egypt and Iceland*, among other works too numerous to list here. Ironically, however, Taylor was at his best when writing about his homeland. His book on the California gold rush, *Eldorado*, which he wrote for Horace Greeley's *New York Times*, is one of the earliest and most engaging accounts; and *Colorado*, which he wrote while on a summer trip to the West, is a classic of American overland adventure. Rarely controversial, always factual, and seldom boring, Taylor's books appealed to the sensibilities of a nineteenth-century American audience which was eager to learn more about foreign culture and exotic lands, including the American West.

With the onset of the Civil War, the market for travel literature declined, and, to earn a living, Taylor began writing novels. His models were Dickens and Thackeray, and his plots were overly melodramatic and excessively contrived, but, despite their conventionality, Taylor's novels provide a value insight into the tastes and spirit of the times which demanded felicitous endings, purity from its heroines, and a proper respect for social decorum. They also bridge the gap between the romanticism of the first half of the nineteenth century and the realism of the second. *Hannah Thurston*, for example, is about a bluestocking suffragette turned housewife and mother, who finds true happiness and freedom in the values of the home; and *The Story of Kennett*, with its quaint and descriptive portrayal of life in a rural Pennsylvania town, anticipates the local color movement of the 1870's, 1880's and 1890's.

Taylor's poems, like his travel books and his novels, demonstrate more than a modicum of literary talent but suffer from a self-conscious desire to please. He had an astute ear for music, and his verse is technically quite proficient, but it lacks the universal tensions which make for good poetry. Nonetheless, his most famous poem, "The Bedouin Song," is far from his best; and such poems as "The Summer Camp," "Hylas," "Daughter of Egypt," and "Hassan and His Mare" deserve more recognition than they have received. *The Poet's Journal* and *The Picture of St. John* are especially deserving of attention because they constitute Taylor's attempt to write long narrative verse about his own experiences, vaguely disguised. His most popular collection of poetry, *Poems of the Orient*, displays a refreshing and aesthetically pleasing sense of exoticism. A collected edition of Taylor's poems was published during his lifetime; his masques and closet dramas were published after his death.

Throughout his life, Taylor maintained a genuine admiration for German culture. His second wife was German, and he was for many years non-resident professor of German literature at Cornell University. Taylor's interest in Germany appears in many of his works, but more especially in *Studies in German Literature*, which was for many years one of the best introductions to the field, and in his translation of *Faust*, whose copious scholarly annotations and faithful reproduction of the meter of the original make it to this day one of the finest available translations of Goethe's masterpiece.

—James A. Levernier

TAYLOR, Edward. American. Born in Sketchley, Leicestershire, in 1642. Lost a teaching position in Bagworth, Leicestershire, for failing to subscribe to the Act of Uniformity, 1662; may then have attended Cambridge University; emigrated to Massachusetts Bay Colony, 1668; attended Harvard University, Cambridge, Massachusetts, B.A. 1671. Married 1) Elizabeth Fitch in 1674 (died, 1689); 2) Ruth Wyllys. Congregational Minister, Westfield, Massachusetts, 1671 until his retirement, 1725. M.A.: Harvard University, 1720. *Died 24 June 1729.*

PUBLICATIONS

Collections

The Poetical Works, edited by Thomas H. Johnson.   1939.
The Poems, edited by Donald E. Stanford.   1960; *Selection,* 1963.

Verse

Metrical History of Christianity (transcript), edited by Donald E. Stanford.   1962.

Other

Christographia (sermons and meditations), edited by Norman S. Grabo.   1962.
The Diary, edited by Francis Murphy.   1964.
Treatise Concerning the Lord's Supper (sermons), edited by Norman S. Grabo.   1966.

Bibliography: *Taylor: An Annotated Bibliography 1668–1970* by Constance J. Gefvert, 1971.

Reading List: *Taylor* by Norman S. Grabo, 1961; *Taylor* by Donald E. Stanford, 1965; *The Will and the Word: The Poetry of Taylor* by William J. Scheick, 1974; *The Example of Taylor* by Karl Keller, 1975.

*   *   *

It should be remembered as we read the poetry of Edward Taylor that he was for over fifty years the village parson of a small New England frontier town, Westfield in western Massachusetts. The ministry was his vocation; poetry was his avocation. The religious experience of the Puritan Calvinist was his abiding concern as a preacher and it was the subject matter of all his extant poems. His library, impressive for its time and place, had many religious books, some of them rare and expensive, but only one volume of verse in English, the poems of Anne Bradstreet. Yet Taylor wrote poetry all of his mature life, and today he is considered the major poet of New England Calvinistic Congregationalism just as Jonathan Edwards, who lived two generations later, is considered its paramount preacher, and this position Taylor has attained in spite of the fact that he published nothing during his life time.

Taylor's reputation as a poet rests on (to quote verbatim his own title page as it appears on his undated manuscript) *Gods Determinations touching his Elect: and The Elects Combat in their Conversion, and Coming up to God in Christ together with the Comfortable Effects thereof* and on his (to quote Taylor's manuscript page again) *Preparatory Meditations before my Approach to the Lords Supper. Chiefly upon the Doctrin preached upon the Day of administration.*

The manuscript of *Gods Determinations* was prepared with particular care and may have been intended for publication, a supposition strengthened by the aim and content of the work. *Gods Determinations* is a series of poems in the form of dramatic dialogues interspersed with narrative and expository passages which explain and justify God's ways in bringing a few selected men ("the elect") to salvation. Its purpose, apparently, was to convert those members of the Puritan community who felt themselves unable to accept full communion in the church because they had not experienced the reception of God's saving grace. Hence a great deal of the poem is taken up with a dramatization of the various ways in which God's grace operates among sinning men.

987

Gods Determinations opens with a "Preface" which describes the creation in Calvinistic terms. The physical universe as well as all its inhabitants, including man, was created out of nothing by an Omnipotent God who may return it to nothing if he pleases. "The Effects of Mans Apostacy" follows, describing the Fall and the terror of natural man when he finds God his enemy. The tone of the verse and the theology are similar to that of Jonathan Edwards's later famous sermon "Sinners in the Hands of an Angry God." With the third poem, a dialogue between Justice and Mercy, personified attributes of God, the dramatic struggle for the redemption of the elect begins with Justice playing the role of divine avenger who punishes and terrifies man and Mercy playing the role of divine comforter who offers salvation to those who confess their sins and come into the church. Satan and Christ join the struggle and the ensuing action is seen as a series of military engagements in which Satan is eventually defeated by the combined efforts of Justice and Mercy. At the end of the poem the elect are depicted as riding to Glory in Christ's coach.

Much of the poem, in style and content, is "dated." However, Satan's methods of tempting the sinner to abandon hope, methods derived in part from William Ames's *Cases of Conscience*, are subtle and sophisticated, and they reveal an understanding of the psychology of guilt that is still of interest to the modern reader. Also, there are passages written in a vigorous, colloquial, and highly figurative style which are worth noting, particularly the famous query in the opening lines referring to the creation: "Who in this Bowling Alley bowld the Sun?"

The *Preparatory Meditations* is a body of remarkable devotional verse consisting of more than two hundred poems written over a period of more than forty years, from 1682 to 1725. Because of their style, which is reminiscent of the so-called Metaphysical Poets (particularly Herbert but also occasionally Donne, Crashaw, and Vaughan) they have in recent years attracted the attention of scholars, for in the age of Pope he was writing like Donne. But his Meditations are of more than mere historical interest. His recurrent and moving expression of the experience of Saving Grace establishes him as the most important religious poet in American literature and worthy of comparison not only with Donne and Herbert but also with Gerard Manley Hopkins.

The purpose of each Meditation was to prepare the pastor for administering the Lord's Supper, a sacrament by means of which the soul of the participant was united to Christ; therefore a number of the Meditations express the almost mystical exaltation of the union of the human with the divine, as in "The Experience":

> Most strange it was! But yet more strange that shine
> Which filld my Soul then to the brim to spy
> My Nature with thy Nature all Divine
> Together joyn'd in Him thats Thou, and I.

The structure of the poems varies, but more frequently it is three-fold with the opening lines expressing despairing personal awareness of original sin followed by joyful contemplation of Saving Grace made possible through faith in Christ and concluding with the hope that the poet will be one of the elect who will achieve salvation. These poems are in the tradition of the Christian meditative practice of self-examination best exemplified among the Roman Catholics by Loyola, but by the seventeenth-century common among protestant divines such as Richard Baxter, author of *The Saints Everlasting Rest* (1650), a book with which Taylor was probably familiar and which may have influenced his own meditative methods. The meditant fixes his attention on some point of doctrine, analyzes it by means of his understanding, and as a result of comprehending it is moved by feelings of love, hope, joy, etc. The doctrine in Taylor's Meditations is usually stated in a Biblical text which is quoted in the title of the poem, the favorite source of quotation for Taylor being the *Song of Songs* or, as Taylor called it, *Canticles*. Taylor frequently makes use of Christian allegory, symbolism, typology, and a figurative style derived chiefly from the Bible (especially from the *Song of Songs* and *Revelation*) and from Herbert. A widely variant vocabulary is employed with words ranging from the humble life of the farmer – "I'le Wagon Loads of Love, and Glory bring" to abstruse theological terminology. Complicated conceits with terms and images from widely disparate fields of experience are juxtaposed and yoked by violence together in the metaphysical style (as defined by Samuel Johnson). At its best the style is direct and forceful, but at its worst bizarre, over-rhetorical, and rhythmically awkward. Yet in reading the *Preparatory Meditations* as a whole, one gains the impression that they were written by a humble, extremely pious, sincere Puritan for whom the experience of God's grace was profound and overwhelming.

Taylor composed and preached innumerable sermons during his long pastorate but the manuscripts of only a few have survived, the more important being available in *Christographia*, a series of fourteen sermons preached in Westfield from 1701–1703 on the mystery of the union of the divine and human natures of Christ, and in *Treatise Concerning the Lord's Supper* (eight sermons preached in 1694), in which he argues that the Lord's Supper should be confined to the regenerate elect only. These sermons are, then, an attack on the practice of Solomon Stoddard (the grandfather of Jonathan Edwards) who in his Northampton Church was using the sacrament as a converting ordinance and inviting all who led a Christian life to partake. In this as in other matters Taylor expressed the views of the conservative faction of the Congregational Church of New England.

Taylor also wrote a number of occasional poems, the most interesting of which are the charming "Upon a Wasp Child with Cold" and the striking "Upon the Sweeping Flood." He composed a long poem of over twenty thousand lines and of doubtful literary merit on the persecutions and martyrdoms of the Christians from the earliest times through the reign of Queen Mary of England, *Metrical History of Christianity*. He also wrote elegies on his contemporaries, the best being those on his first wife and on Samuel Hooker, pastor of the church of Farmington, Connecticut. But by far his best poetry is to be found in *Gods Determinations* and in the *Preparatory Meditations*.

—Donald E. Stanford

TEASDALE, Sara. American. Born in St. Louis, Missouri, 8 August 1884. Educated privately. Married Ernst B. Filsinger in 1914 (divorced, 1929). Lived in Europe and the Middle East, 1905–07; settled in New York City, 1916. Recipient: Pulitzer Prize, 1917; Poetry Society of American Annual Prize, 1917. *Died 29 January 1933.*

PUBLICATIONS

Collections

Collected Poems.   1937.

Verse

Sonnets to Duse and Other Poems.   1907.
Helen of Troy and Other Poems.   1911; revised edition, 1922.

Rivers to the Sea. 1915.
Love Songs. 1917.
Vignettes of Italy: A Cycle of Nine Songs for High Voice. 1919.
Flame and Shadow. 1920; revised edition, 1924.
Dark of the Moon. 1926.
Stars To-Night: Verses New and Old for Boys and Girls. 1930.
A Country House. 1932.
Strange Victory. 1933.

Other

Editor, *The Answering Voice: One Hundred Love Lyrics by Women.* 1917; revised
edition, 1928.
Editor, *Rainbow Gold: Poems for Boys and Girls.* 1922.

Bibliography: by Vivian Buchan, in *Bulletin of Bibliography 25,* 1967.

Reading List: *Teasdale: A Biography* by Margaret Haley Carpenter, 1960.

*   *   *

Sara Teasdale, whose verse suggests, in her own phrase, "a delicate fabric of bird song," is
one of America's most charming lyrists. Well-received and popular for some fifteen years
after *Love Songs* (1917) took the Pulitzer Prize for poetry, she was posthumously, and
unjustly, somewhat underrated by the time *Collected Poems* appeared in 1937.

Miss Teasdale's first book of consequence was her third, *Rivers to the Sea,* in which signs
of the mature poet became clearly evident. Happily, the best of her early work was
incorporated into the body of *Love Songs,* whose seemingly artless musicality informs a most
lucid lyricism. *Flame and Shadow* marks, if anything, an advance in emotional depth and
"natural falterings"; but *Dark of the Moon,* while gracefully competent, appears somewhat
anticlimactic in its minor accents: the book of a "woman seemingly poured empty." The first
posthumous collection, *Strange Victory,* has, however, some of its author's most memorable
pieces – in "All That Was Mortal," "Grace Before Sleep," "Advice to a Girl," and others.

Miss Teasdale's verse, repeatedly concerned with the stars, often reflective of her travels,
always simple in technique and verse form and natural in statement, dewlike and fragile in
quality, and gentle in its acceptance of sorrow (though never bathetic), poses no intellectual
problems. Constantly preoccupied with beauty, as idea and as evocation, it offers instead
quietly ironic, but joyful, acceptance of life, exquisiteness of feminine perception, and most
delicate artistry. All of which does not deny that Miss Teasdale has occasionally "reached into
the black waters whose chill brings wisdom," poems like "Wood Song" and numerous
others being the memorable evidence.

—George Brandon Saul

TENNYSON, Alfred, Lord.   English.   Born in Somersby, Lincolnshire, 6 August 1809.
Educated at Louth Grammar School and at home; Trinity College, Cambridge (Chancellor's
Medal for poetry, 1829), 1828–31; encouraged by the "Apostles" group at Cambridge to

become a poet. Married Emily Sarah Sellwood in 1850; two sons. Lived at Farringford, Isle of Wight, from 1853, and at Aldworth, Surrey, from 1869. Poet Laureate, 1850 until his death. Created Baron Tennyson, 1884. *Died 6 October 1892.*

PUBLICATIONS

Collections

(Works), edited by Hallam Tennyson. 9 vols., 1907–08.
Poems. 1912; revised edition, as *Poems and Plays*, 1953.
The Poems, edited by Christopher Ricks. 1969.

Verse

Poems by Two Brothers, with Charles Tennyson. 1827; edited by Hallam Tennyson, 1893.
Poems, Chiefly Lyrical. 1830; revised edition, 1842; edited by Clyde de L. Ryals, 1966.
Poems. 1832.
The Lover's Tale. 1832; revised edition, 1879; complete version, 1879.
Poems. 2 vols., 1842; revised edition, 1853; edited by A. M. D. Hughes, 1914; edited by Christopher Ricks, 1968.
The Princess: A Medley. 1847; revised edition, 1850, 1851, 1853.
In Memoriam. 1850; edited by Robert H. Ross, 1974.
Ode on the Death of the Duke of Wellington. 1852; revised edition, 1853.
The Charge of the Light Brigade. 1855.
Maud and Other Poems. 1855; revised edition, 1856, 1859.
Idylls of the King (4 idylls). 1859; others published in *The Holy Grail and Other Poems*, 1869, *Gareth and Lynette*, 1872, and *Tiresias and Other Poems*, 1885; complete version, 1889.
(Poems), edited by J. D. Campbell. 1862; as *Suppressed Poems 1830–1862*, edited by J. C. Thomson, 1904.
Ode for the Opening of the International Exhibition, music by William Sterndale Bennett. 1862.
A Welcome to Alexandra Princess of Wales. 1863.
Enoch Arden and Other Poems. 1864.
A Selection from the Work. 1865.
The Victim. 1867.
The Window; or, The Loves of the Wrens. 1867.
A Welcome to Marie Alexandrovna. 1874.
Ballads and Other Poems. 1880.
Hands All Round: A National Song, music by C. Villiers Stanford. 1882.
Early Spring. 1883.
Tiresias and Other Poems. 1885.
An Ode Written for the Opening of the Colonial and Indian Exhibition 1886, music by Arthur Sullivan. N.d.
Locksley Hall Sixty Years After. 1886.
Carmen Saeculare: An Ode for the Jubilee of Queen Victoria, music by C. Villiers Stanford. 1887.
Demeter and Other Poems. 1889.
The Death of Oenone, Akbar's Dream, and Other Poems. 1892.

Patriotic Poems. 1914.
*Unpublished Early Poems,*edited by Charles Tennyson. 1931.

Plays

Queen Mary (produced 1876). 1875.
Harold. 1877.
The Falcon (produced 1879). With *The Cup,* 1884.
The Cup (produced 1881). 1884.
The Promise of May (produced 1882). 1883; in *Locksley Hall Sixty Years After,* 1886.
Becket (as arranged by Henry Irving, produced 1893). 1884.
The Foresters, Robin Hood, and Maid Marian (produced 1893). 1892.
The Devil and the Lady, edited by Charles Tennyson. 1930.

Other

Tennyson and William Kirby: Unpublished Correspondence, edited by Lorne
Pierce. 1929.

Editor, *Gordon Boys' Morning and Evening Hymns,* music by Lady Tennyson, edited by
Dr. Bridges. 1885.

Bibliography: *A Bibliography of the Writings of Tennyson* by Thomas J. Wise, 2 vols., 1908
(includes forged editions); *Tennyson: An Annotated Bibliography* by Charles Tennyson and
Christine Fall, 1967.

Reading List: *Tennyson: A Memoir* by Hallam Tennyson, 1897; *Tennyson,* 1949, and *Six
Tennyson Essays,* 1954, both by Charles Tennyson; *Tennyson: The Growth of a Poet* by
Jerome H. Buckley, 1960; *Critical Essays on the Poetry of Tennyson* edited by John Killham,
1960; *Tennyson Laureate* by Valerie Pitt, 1962; *The Pre-Eminent Victorian: A Study in
Tennyson* (biography) by Joanna Richardson, 1962; *Tennyson: A Biographical and Critical
Study* by Christopher Ricks, 1972; *Tennyson's Major Poems* by James Kincaid, 1975; *The
Poetry of Tennyson* by A. Dwight Culler, 1977; *Tennyson, Poet and Prophet* by Philip
Henderson, 1978.

*   *   *

Alfred Tennyson's life and work almost span the century, and encompass numerous
aspects of the Victorian period and its literature. With his sensibility closely responsive to the
doubts, needs, enthusiasms, and certitudes of the age, Tennyson eventually became a
pervasive influence on it, as a best seller, Laureate, and friend of the Queen. Not the rigidity
and fixity often mistakenly attributed to the Victorians, but the unending struggle to keep
humane values in view characterises the poems as a whole.

The possibility of faith was a central preoccupation for Tennyson and his contemporaries,
primarily in a Christianity based on the literal truth of the Gospels, but also faith in all other
authority which, along with Christianity, seemed shaken by geological, historical, biological,
and social studies. Tennyson directly confronts the problem of how to create poetry of stature
which retains certain elements of romantic poetry, including a capacity for commitment,
affirmation, and grandeur, yet takes account of the thrust of realism, scientific knowledge,
and social problems. To this end the variety of serious, notably sustained, virtuoso poetic
experiments in form, subject, and language is directed. Ranging through dialect, dialogue,
monodrama, lyric, domestic idyl, elegy, and epic, the poems tackle a prodigious diversity of

subjects including the nature and limits of perfection in Greek and Arthurian heroes and heroines, the condition of England, the role of the artist and of art, women in society, evolution, faith, love, death, and mortality. The resultant poetry yields a superb rendering of doubt and its dignity as well as a mystical Christianity which transcends it.

Many of the earlier poems are dialectical, concerning themselves variously with the presentation of alternative perspectives. Dialogue poems such as "Supposed Confessions of a Second-Rate Sensitive Mind" and "The Two Voices," paired or companion poems such as "All Things Will Die"/"Nothing Will Die" and "Ulysses"/"Tithonus," poems in which the dominant situations are overshadowed by their antitheses such as "The Lady of Shalott," "The Lotos-Eaters," and "The Palace of Art," and framed poems such as "Morte d'Arthur" come into this category. This dramatic juxtaposition of dual or multiple views remains a characteristic strategy to define truth in the later poetry. It is a structural element in various degrees and forms even in long poems such as *The Princess* (which might be said to be defeated by the excess of perspectives it offers), *In Memoriam*, and *Maud*, as well as in the pair of Locksley Hall poems composed thirty years apart. While it has been argued that Tennyson is not a "great thinker," it should be recognised that Tennyson's characteristic dialectical mode makes the poetry very much a poetry of ideas. At the same time, while his poems can be prodigiously and meticulously inclusive, certain poems finally transcend and reject the dilemma created by their multiplicity.

Tennyson's greatest achievement is *In Memoriam*, the series of 131 elegies written over seventeen years and published in 1850 anonymously. The two-volume *Poems* of 1842 had established Tennyson as a major young poet (he regarded his sales as "sensational"), and the laudatory reception of *In Memoriam* proved sufficient to effect his election as Laureate in that same year, upon Wordsworth's death. *In Memoriam*, like many other of Tennyson's best poems (including *Maud*, "Ulysses," and "Morte d'Arthur"), germinated in late 1833 following the death at 22 of Arthur Hallam, Tennyson's close friend and support from Cambridge and his sister Emily's fiancé. But the tone of *In Memoriam*, and its preoccupation with death and love, despair, and faith, are manifest in earlier poems such as "Supposed Confessions," "The Two Voices" (originally called "Thoughts of a Suicide"), "Mariana," and many lesser known works which predate Hallam's death, which suggests that Tennyson's achievement in the poem resulted from ripeness and practice as well as genius and long gestation. Beginning with a funeral and ending with a marriage, the poem was described by Tennyson as "a kind of *Divina Commedia*," but to a friend he confessed "It's too hopeful, this poem, more than I am myself." But the happiness in the Epilogue is hard won, and the bulk of the poem charts "the low beginnings of content." The looseness of structure (Tennyson permitted F. T. Palgrave to publish a selection of the elegies in a different order), the breadth of Tennyson's "subject" of loss, and his prodigious technical fluency combine to make *In Memoriam* one of the most moving and inclusive long poems in English.

Repetition in all its aspects (which includes the dialectical patterns noted above) is a technique common to all of Tennyson's poetry, but in *In Memoriam* the play of diction, rhythms, themes, and imagery is particularly rich, subtle, and expansive. Tennyson achieves an exquisite and largely sustained balance between his eye for details of nature and his preoccupation with universal matters as in "Sad Hesper" (cxxi), between personal and common grief as in "I cannot see the features right" (lxx), and between art and life as in "I held it truth, with him who sings" (i). Although the narrator of *In Memoriam* is somewhat dramatised (Tennyson said that the "I" is mankind), the poem avoids problems of tone and voice evident in *The Princess* and *Maud*, and the archaic language and setting of the *Idylls* which proved an impediment to full expression there. In the conception and execution of *In Memoriam* Tennyson eluded all such weaknesses. It is the kind of high poetry at which his earlier poetry aimed; it perfectly expresses the tensions voiced in "Ulysses," "Though much is taken, much abides," the tensions in the individual and in Victorian society.

Critics disagree considerably about the nature and quality of Tennyson's achievement in *Maud*. None denies the presence of outstanding individual lyrics, and few dispute the percipiency of the "mad" section. Rather it is the unity of the poem which critics feel variously is seriously undermined by the violently shifting perspectives, voices, and tone; the ways in, and degree to which details of Tennyson's personal experience and problems have contributed to the unsatisfactory nature of the poem are usefully discussed by Ralph Rader (*Tennyson's Maud*, 1963) and J. Wordsworth (*Essays in Criticism*, 1975). The conclusion of the poem in which the private problems of the protagonist, the public problems of the society at (corrupt) peace, and the failure of love are all resolved in a cleansing war (the Crimea!) may seem initially repugnant, but Tennyson's thirst for nobility, his familiarity with the heroic past as a model for his present hopes, and his position as Laureate-author of the resounding Wellington ode (1852) – to say nothing of the careful identification of the nobility of war with the grandeur of Maud throughout the poem – make the conclusion understandable and aesthetically defensible, if imperfect. Tennyson himself insisted that the narrator was dramatised, calling the poem "a little Hamlet," *Maud; or, The Madness*, and in 1875 a "Monodrama"; perhaps comparison with some of Browning's grotesque narrators is helpful here. Many old themes appear in *Maud*, but the intensity of the language of sexual affirmation both recalls and surpasses "The Gardener's Daughter" (written 1833/34), and its despair is more untrammeled than *In Memoriam*'s.

At about the time *Maud* was published Tennyson decided on the final shape of *Idylls of the King*, a poem which he had been contemplating since the 1830's and the death of Arthur Hallam. But his intention to pursue King Arthur, which he regarded as the "greatest of all poetical subjects" weakened when John Sterling attacked "Morte d'Arthur" in the *Quarterly* on the publication of *Poems* (1842), and the first instalment only appeared in 1859. With three more following in 1869, 1872, and 1885, the twelve books announced and properly ordered by Tennyson in 1872 were complete. While it is true that the sumptuous imagery that the medieval court setting allowed might resemble the escapism of the Soul in "The Palace of Art," it is equally true that a full reading reveals a poem which traces the rise and fall of the ideal in society, the nature of the hero and the psychology and variety of betrayal and corruption, and the indignity of sin and the stature derived from the struggle to resist or overcome it. It pursues the themes of passion and social analysis found in *Maud*, but, perhaps because of the protection the period setting offered, they are even darker in the *Idylls*: the bulk of the passion is adulterous or cruel, the chaos of disorder destroys the Round Table, and the final battles merely affirm Arthur's mystical perfection in his death. The golden age (of Maud's love) shrinks notably in the *Idylls*, with Arthur's perception of Camelot shown continually to the reader as mistaken; finally (in "Guinevere") he is robbed even of his memory of "the golden days before thy sin": "For which of us, who might be left, could speak/ Of the pure heart, nor seem to glance at thee?" Tennyson emerges from his quest for nobility and heroism with a corrupted vision not only of feudal society but of the ideal court, with Galahad and Arthur alone intact, and with the stature of Guinevere and Lancelot recoverable only through humility and penitence. Where the poem does suffer from its medievalism is in its language which too often loses a direct relation to experience in the inversions, archaisms, and extended similes; it rings false then, making one recall Bagehot's estimate of Tennyson work as "ornate." It is perhaps significant that, for all the pessimism of the poem, Tennyson still perceived the promise of Arthur, and dedicated the poem to the Queen, contending to the last the multiplicity of truth: "Poetry is like shot silk with many glancing colours."

—Laurel Brake

THOMAS, Dylan (Marlais). Welsh. Born in Swansea, Glamorganshire, 27 October 1914. Educated at Swansea Grammar School. Worked with a documentary film unit during World War II. Married Caitlin Macnamara in 1936; two sons and one daughter. Reporter, *South Wales Daily Post*, Swansea, 1931–32. Free-lance writer from 1933. Visited the United States, giving poetry readings, 1950, 1952, 1953. Recipient: Foyle Poetry Prize, 1953. *Died 9 November 1953.*

PUBLICATIONS

Collections

    Selected Letters, edited by Constantine FitzGibbon. 1966.
    Collected Prose. 1969.
    Selected Writings, edited by J. P. Harries. 1970.
    The Poems, edited by Daniel Jones. 1971; revised edition, 1974.
    Selected Poems, edited by Walford Davies. 1974.

Verse

    18 Poems. 1934.
    Twenty-Five Poems. 1936.
    The Map of Love: Verse and Prose. 1939.
    The World I Breathe (includes stories). 1939.
    New Poems. 1943.
    Deaths and Entrances. 1946.
    Twenty-Six Poems. 1950.
    In Country Sleep and Other Poems. 1952.
    Collected Poems 1934–1952. 1952; as *The Collected Poems,*1953.
    Two Epigrams of Fealty. 1954.
    Galsworthy and Gawsworth. 1954.

Plays

    Return Journey (broadcast 1947). In *New Directions: Five One-Act Plays in the Modern Idiom*, edited by Alan Durband, 1961.
    The Doctor and the Devils, from the Story by Donald Taylor (film-script). 1953.
    Under Milk Wood: A Play for Voices (produced 1953). 1954.
    The Beach of Falesá (film-script). 1963.
    Twenty Years A-Growing: A Film Script from the Story by Maurice O'Sullivan. 1964.
    Me and My Bike: An Unfinished Film-Script. 1965.
    The Doctor and the Devils and Other Scripts (includes *Twenty Years A-Growing, A Dream of Winter, The Londoner*). 1966.

    Screenplays: *Balloon Site 568*, 1942; *Wales*, 1942; *New Towns for Old*, 1942; *Our Country*, 1944; *When We Build Again*, 1945; *The Three Weird Sisters*, with Louise Birt and David Evans, 1948; *No Room at the Inn*, with Ivan Foxwell, 1948.

    Radio Play: *Return Journey*, 1947.

Fiction

> *Portrait of the Artist as a Young Dog.*   1940.
> *A Prospect of the Sea and Other Stories and Prose Writings,* edited by Daniel Jones.   1955.
> *Adventures in the Skin Trade.*   1955; as *Adventures in the Skin Trade and Other Stories,* 1955.
> *Rebecca's Daughters.*   1965.
> *Two Tales: Me and My Bike, and Rebecca's Daughters.*   1968.
> *The Outing.*   1971.
> *The Followers.*   1976.
> *The Death of the King's Canary,* with John Davenport.   1976.

Other

> *Selected Writings,* edited by John L. Sweeney.   1946.
> *Quite Early One Morning: Broadcasts.*   1954.
> *Conversations about Christmas.*   1954.
> *Letters to Vernon Watkins,* edited by Vernon Watkins.   1957.
> *Miscellany: Poems, Stories, Broadcasts.*   1963.
> *The Colour of Saying: An Anthology of Verse Spoken by Dylan Thomas,* edited by Ralph N. Maud and Aneirin Talfan Davies.   1963; as *Dylan Thomas's Choice: An Anthology of Verse Spoken by Dylan Thomas,* 1964.
> *Miscellany Two: A Visit to Grandpa's and Other Stories and Poems.*   1966.
> *The Notebooks,* edited by Ralph N. Maud.   1967; as *Poet in the Making: The Notebooks of Thomas,* 1968.
> *Twelve More Letters.*   1970.
> *Early Prose Writings,* edited by Walford Davies.   1971.
> *Living and Writing,* edited by Christopher Capeman.   1972.
> *Miscellany Three.*   1978.

Bibliography: *Thomas: A Bibliography* by J. Alexander Rolph, 1956; *Thomas in Print* by Ralph Maud and Albert Glover, 1970, *Appendix, 1969–1971* by Walford Davies, 1972.

Reading List: *The Poetry of Thomas* by Elder Olson, 1954; *A Reader's Guide to Thomas* by William York Tindall, 1962; *Dylan: Druid of the Broken Body* by Aneirin Talfan Davies, 1964; *The Life of Thomas* by Constantine FitzGibbon, 1965; *Thomas: A Collection of Critical Essays* edited by C. B. Cox, 1966; *Thomas: New Critical Essays* edited by Walford Davies, 1972; *The Country of the Spirit* by Rushworth M. Kidder, 1973; *Thomas: Poet of His People* by Andrew Sinclair, 1975, as *Thomas: No Man More Magical,* 1976; *Thomas: A Biography* by Paul Ferris, 1977.

*   *   *

Dylan Thomas is one of the most original voices in British poetry since Yeats and Eliot. While Thomas wrote compelling autobiographical stories and a splendid radio play, *Under Milk Wood,* his major achievement is as a poet. He saw himself as an heir to the English Romantic tradition, a tradition that he evoked in his poetry as an alternative to the classicism of Eliot and the political consciousness of Auden, the other major voice to appear in the 1930's.

Critics spoke of his spontaneity as a means of explaining his difficult imagery and syntax. However, Thomas was a craftsman who, in an obsessive quest for the meaning he sought, rewrote every line countless times: "My lines, *all* my lines, are of the tenth intensity. They are not the words that express what I want to express. They are the only words I can find that come near to expressing a half" (quoted by Constantine FitzGibbon). For Thomas, poetry was a means of self-definition and of self-discovery. Thomas's major subject was his own emotional life; he used his poems to define his private passions and attitudes rather than to respond to public events ("My poetry is, or should be, useful to me for one reason: it is the record of my individual struggle from darkness towards some measure of light ..."). He also believed that his poems about his own emotions described struggles and conflicts that readers would recognize as their own.

Thomas's early poems are informed by a pantheistic view of the universe; God is not a personality but a ubiquitous presence throughout the universe. In "The Force That Through the Green Fuse Drives the Flower" (1933), Thomas defines how the destructive and constructive forces of the natural world are in a vital relationship. In this poem, the speaker marvels how each positive aspect is balanced by a corresponding negative aspect:

> The force that through the green fuse drives the flower
> Drives my green age; that blasts the roots of trees
> Is my destroyer.
> And I am dumb to tell the crooked rose
> My youth is bent by the same wintry fever.

Thomas's early poems consist of images organized around a concept. As he wrote to his friend and fellow Welsh poet Vernon Watkins, "A poem by myself *needs* a host of images because its centre is a host of images.... Each image holds within it the seed of its own destruction, and my dialectical method, as I understand it, is a constant building up and breaking down of the images that comes out of the central seed, which is itself destructive and constructive at the same time." In his early work Thomas was intoxicated by the sound and feel of words; quite often sound partially subsumes sense and obscurity results.

Both the Welsh bardic tradition and Welsh nonconformity were important influences on Thomas. The latter shaped his concern with sin and salvation in both his religious and ostensibly secular poems. In "Vision and Prayer" and "Altarwise by Owl-light," the intense sonnet sequence that recalls seventeenth-century religious poetry, Thomas expresses his hope if not his faith in Christ's intervention on man's behalf. Thomas did much of his work as a poet between July 1931 and November 1934 in Swansea, Wales. The poems written in this period are the basis of his first two volumes, *18 Poems* and *Twenty-five Poems*; and many of his later poems were based on notebook versions of poems written then. Throughout his career he wrote about Wales and the people he knew there. The poverty and hopelessness of Swansea young men in the depression inform "I See the Boys of Summer." Among his most moving poems are "After the Funeral," his elegy for his aunt, Ann Jones, and the poem to his dying father, "Do Not Go Gentle into That Good Night."

Perhaps Thomas's masterpiece is "A Winter's Tale," a poem that is part of a great burst of creativity in 1944–45, the period when he also wrote "A Refusal to Mourn," "Fern Hill," and "Poem in October." Thomas's later poems have more of a traditional narrative shape, and are more logical, controlled, and ultimately clearer. "A Winter's Tale" is the central work in *Deaths and Entrances*, a book that established his reputation as a major figure. In this poem Thomas shows how not only the poet, but every man can achieve personal salvation through his imagination. That the creative imagination is part of each man derives from Thomas's Nonconformist upbringing. Thomas wrote of the vitality of the imagination at a time when poetry and indeed civilization seemed threatened by World War II, and when he was deeply worried about his own and his father's health in addition to his own economic situation. The man at prayer is Thomas himself who, while living through a private and historical winter, feared personal and cultural death as well as the atrophy of his poetic energies. That this lonely man becomes one with the bird – symbol of poetic creativity and the imaginative process – shows how any man can overcome self-doubt and anxiety.

Persistent lung trouble, hypochondria, and alcoholism no doubt contributed to the preoccupation with death in his poetry. His series of remarkable birthday poems, "Twenty-four Years," "Poem in October," and "Poem on his Birthday," becomes increasingly concerned with his own death which he knew was fast approaching. This obsession belies his frequent testimony within the poems that he has come to terms with death. Yet if Thomas's poems regret the inevitable passing of his vitality, they also celebrate not only his passions and joys, but the variety and splendor of God's creation. In the November 1952 note to his *Collected Poems*, Thomas wrote: "These poems, with all their crudities, doubts, and confusions, are written for the love of Man and in Praise of God, and I'd be a damn' fool if they weren't."

—Daniel R. Schwarz

THOMAS, (Philip) Edward. English. Born in London, 3 March 1878. Educated at Battersea Grammar School, London; St. Paul's School, London; Lincoln College, Oxford. Corporal in the Artists' Rifles in World War I; killed in action at Arras, 1917. Married Helen Noble in 1899; one son and two daughters. Journalist: reviewer for *Daily Chronicle* and often periodicals; encouraged by Robert Frost, began writing verse 1914, and wrote most of his poetry during acitve service. *Died 9 April 1917.*

PUBLICATIONS

Collections

The Prose (selection), edited by Roland Gant.   1948.
Poems and Last Poems, edited by Edna Longley.   1973.
Thomas on the Countryside: A Selection of His Prose and Verse, edited by Roland Gant.   1977.
Collected Poems, edited by R. George Thomas.   1978.

Verse

Six Poems.   1916.
An Annual of New Poetry, with others.   1917.
Poems by Edward Thomas – "Edward Eastaway."   1917.
Last Poems.   1918.

Fiction

The Happy-Go-Lucky Morgans.   1913.

Other

The Woodland Life.   1897.
Horae Solitariae (essays).   1902.
Oxford.   1903; revised edition, 1922.
Rose Acre Papers.   1904.
Beautiful Wales.   1905; as *Wales*, 1924.
The Heart of England.   1906.
Richard Jefferies: His Life and Work.   1909.
The South Country.   1909.
Rest and Unrest (essays).   1910.
Feminine Influence on the Poets.   1910.
Windsor Castle.   1910.
Celtic Stories.   1911.
The Isle of Wight.   1911.
Light and Twilight (essays).   1911.
Maurice Maeterlinck.   1911.
The Tenth Muse.   1911.
Swinburne: A Critical Study.   1912.
Borrow: The Man and His Books.   1912.
Lafcadio Hearn.   1912.
Norse Tales.   1912.
The Icknield Way.   1913.
The Country.   1913.
Pater: A Critical Study.   1913.
In Pursuit of Spring.   1914.
Four-and-Twenty Blackbirds (juvenile).   1915; as *The Complete Fairy Tales*, 1966.
The Life of the Duke of Marlborough.   1915.
Keats.   1916.
A Literary Pilgrim in England.   1917.
Cloud Castle and Other Papers.   1922.
The Last Sheaf.   1928.
The Childhood of Thomas: A Fragment of Autobiography.   1938.
The Friend of the Blackbird.   1938.
Letters to Gordon Bottomley, edited by R. George Thomas.   1968.
The Diary, 1st January–8th April 1917, edited by Roland Gant.   1977.

Editor, *The Poems of John Dyer*.   1903.
Editor, *The Pocket Book of Poems and Songs for the Open Air*.   1907.
Editor, *The Book of the Open Air*.   2 vols., 1907–08.
Editor, *Some British Birds*.   1908.
Editor, *British Butterflies and Other Insects*.   1908.
Editor, *The Hills and the Vale*, by Richard Jefferies.   1909.
Editor, *The Plays and Poems of Christopher Marlowe*.   1909.
Editor, *The Pocket George Borrow*.   1912.
Editor, *This England: An Anthology from Her Writers*.   1915.
Editor, *The Flowers I Love*.   1916.

Reading List: *Thomas: A Biography and a Bibliography* by R. P. Eckert, 1937; *The Life and Letters of Thomas* by John Moore, 1939; *Thomas* by Henry Coombes, 1956; *Thomas* by Vernon Scannell, 1962; *Thomas: A Critical Biography* by William Cooke, 1970; *Thomas* by R. George Thomas, 1972; *Thomas: A Poet for His Country* by Jan Marsh, 1978.

*   *   *

The diffident, tentative rhythms of Edward Thomas's poetry, full of qualification and obliquity, forever modulating into conditional and subjunctive, are the reflex of what he described in a 1908 review as "a centrifugal age, in which principles and aims are numerous, vague, uncertain, confused, and in conflict." Like his mentor, the nature-mystic Richard Jefferies, he is always "listening, lying in wait,/For what [he] should, yet never can remember," aware of the ephemeral nature of those epiphanies which endow the moment with value ("truths I had not dreamed,/And have forgotten since their beauty passed"), seeking to penetrate to some inapprehensible core of meaning contained within the shifting forms of experience, but repeatedly brought to the admission which ends "The Glory": "I cannot bite the day to the core." His poems are frequently poised – "The Signpost" or "The Bridge" – at some transit point, some "moment brief between/Two lives," in a twilight latent with forfeit possibilities. He is recurrently engaged on a journey with no clear destination, pursuing, in "The Other," his own elusive identity, or, in "Lob," a lost spontaneity symbolized by the autochthonous figure who epitomizes the threatened but irrepressible creativity of the English land, language, and people. Much of his pastoral poetry is tinged with an elegiac sadness, even when he is affirming the capacity of this England to abide, "out of the reach of change" ("Haymaking").

Thomas felt himself to be "a superfluous man," living on the margins of a society with which he could not identify, appalled by the suburbanization of that "South Country," that "Heart of England," which was his spiritual home and locale of all his writing, turning in scepticism and revulsion from the easy assurances and insistent warmongering of many of his contemporaries. At times, this leads to a sense of metaphysical dispossession and exile, as in "Home":

> I would go back home again
> Now. Yet how should I go?
>
> This is my grief. That land,
> My home, I have never seen....

But Thomas's mood is essentially that for which he praised John Davidson in 1903 – "alert, determined despair, not that comatose despair which is contented with itself, but a despair that is nervous and interested, and so strenuous that it serves some men as well as hope." Though he despised the motives that went into the Great War, he nevertheless looked to it as some kind of release from the "captivity," the "evil dream" of his life. Most of his poetry was indeed written in the two years between enlistment and his death at Arras in 1917. But, beyond this, the War seemed an answer to a dilapidated civilization, turning "young men to dung," but also replacing "the old house,/Outmoded, dignified,/Dark and untenanted" with a new one in which true community might be restored. Though Thomas acknowledged that he was a product of the old house, he affirmed, too, in "Gone, Gone Again," his hope for the new:

> I am something like that;
> Only I am not dead,
> Still breathing and interested
> In the house that is not dark....

For all his fear of becoming an "isolated, self-considering brain" there can be few collections of poetry with a higher proportion of narratives of encounter and conversation, more vocatives or simple celebrations of the unique quiddity, the richness and enigma of other lives – men, women, and children, birds, beasts, and flowers – revealing a tender and respectful affection which affirms the creatureliness of all life.

—Stan Smith

THOMAS, R(onald) S(tuart). Welsh. Born in Cardiff, in 1913. Educated at the University of Wales, B.A. in classics 1935; St. Michael's College, Llandaff. Ordained deacon, 1936, priest, 1937; Curate of Chirk, 1936–40, and of Hanmer, 1940–42; Rector of Manafon, 1942–54; Vicar of St. Michael's, Eglwysfach, 1954–67. Since 1967, Vicar of St. Hywyn, Aberdaron, with St. Mary, Bodferin. Recipient: Heinemann Award, 1955; Queen's Gold Medal for Poetry, 1964; Welsh Arts Council Award, 1968, 1976. Lives in Gwynedd, Wales.

PUBLICATIONS

Verse

The Stones of the Field.   1946.
An Acre of Land.   1952.
The Minister.   1953.
Song at the Year's Turning: Poems 1942–1954.   1955.
Poetry for Supper.   1958.
Judgement Day.   1960.
Tares.   1961.
The Bread of Truth.   1963.
Pietà.   1966.
Not That He Brought Flowers.   1968.
H'm.   1972.
Selected Poems 1946–1968.   1973.
What Is a Welshman?   1974.
Laboratories of the Spirit.   1975.
Frequencies.   1978.

Other

The Mountains.   1968.
Young and Old (juvenile).   1972.

Editor, The Batsford Book of Country Verse.   1961.
Editor, The Penguin Book of Religious Verse.   1963.
Editor, Selected Poems, by Edward Thomas.   1964.
Editor, A Choice of George Herbert's Verse.   1967.
Editor, A Choice of Wordsworth's Verse.   1971.

Reading List: Thomas by R. G. Thomas, 1964; "Thomas Issue" of Poetry Wales, Winter 1972.

*   *   *

Born one year before Dylan Thomas, R. S. Thomas has emerged as the most significant Anglo-Welsh poet since the death of the younger man. His concerns appear regional; there is a cyclical preoccupation throughout his career with relationships: the poet and his vocation (he is an Anglican priest), the educated man and the land-wise peasant, the poet-priest and his country. It becomes clear as one reads his work that the regional is a starting point for the universal.

His verse is, as Glyn Jones says, "lucid, sparing, austere," sometimes even bleak. There is nothing here of the nostalgic warmth of his namesake, little, it would seem, of the easy celebration that some critics affirm as the essence of Dylan Thomas. He is much more a poet of the unresolved, perhaps unresolvable, tensions with which an adult sensiblilty has to cope. That he is an Anglican priest who had to learn Welsh as a second language in order to work in Welsh-speaking parishes, that he is an educated man with a care for the uneducated, an urban man amongst countrymen, that he has a wry acceptance of his own inadequacies, a fierce conscience that examines his own motives and thinks them no better than other men's — all these things make him a type of our modern dilemma. His verse, sharply focussed on the here and now, accepts without question the implications of time and eternity. His Welsh peasant is, like Alun Lewis' "landless soldier lost in war," a figure for humanity.

—John Stuart Williams

THOMPSON, Francis.   English.   Born in Preston, Lancashire, 13 December 1859. Studied for the priesthood at Ushaw College 1870–76; studied medicine at Owens College, Manchester, for 6 years, left without a degree. Came to London 1888, and lived as a tramp and became a drug addict; rescued by the magazine editor Wilfrid Meynell and his wife Alice, who recognized his talent and helped him for the rest of his life; lived mainly in lodgings in London, with intervals in Sussex and Wales. *Died 13 November 1907.*

PUBLICATIONS

Collections

Works, edited by Wilfrid Meynell.   3 vols., 1913.
Poems, edited by Wilfrid Meynell.   1937.

Verse

Poems.   1893.
Sister-Songs: An Offering to Two Sisters.   1895.
New Poems.   1897.
Little Jesus.   1897.
Victorian Ode for Jubilee Day.   1897.
Ode to English Martyrs.   1906.
Poems.   1911.
Uncollected Verses.   1917.
The Mistress of Vision.   1918.
Youthful Verses.   1928.
The Man Has Wings: New Poems and Plays, edited by Terence L. Connolly.   1957.

Other

> *The Life and Labours of Saint John Baptist de la Salle.* 1891.
> *Health and Holiness.* 1905.
> *Shelley.* 1909.
> *Saint Ignatius Loyola,* edited by J. H. Pollen. 1909.
> *A Renegade Poet and Other Essays.* 1910.
> *Sir Leslie Stephen as a Biographer.* 1915.
> *Literary Criticisms Newly Discovered and Collected,* edited by Terence L. Connolly. 1948.
> *Minor Poets Newly Discovered and Collected,* edited by Terence L. Connolly. 1949.
> *The Real Robert Louis Stevenson and Other Critical Essays,* edited by Terence L. Connolly. 1959.

Bibliography: *A Critical Bibliography of Works by and about Thompson* by M. P. Pope, 1959.

Reading List: *An Account of Books and Manuscripts of Thompson* by Terence L. Connolly, 1937; *Thompson: La Vie et l'Oeuvre d'un Poète* by P. Danchin, 1959; *Thompson, Man and Poet* by J. C. Reid, 1959; *Thompson* by P. H. Butter, 1961; *Thompson: A Critical Biography* by Paul van K. Thomson, 1961; *Strange Harp, Strange Symphony: The Life of Thompson* by John E. Walsh, 1968.

*   *   *

Most of Francis Thompson's poetry was written in the two years or so after his rescue from the London streets, when it came bursting out, sometimes in uncontrolled flood ("Sister Songs"), once at least finding fit form (*Hound of Heaven*); in the mid-1890's, when he was writing more intellectual meditations on religious subjects, influenced by Patmore; and towards the end of the decade when his relationship with Katie King produced a freshet of moving love poems.

Though few of his poems are without lines which lift the heart, few are completely satisfying wholes. One is "Arab Love-Song," at once a sensuous love poem and a call from the divine lover to the soul. Every word counts, and the images work well together on both levels of meaning. Seldom did Thompson sustain such density and economy throughout a whole poem. This, like the less completely successful but still moving "Ad Amicam" sonnets, belongs to the Katie King period. Another good love poem is "Love Declared," unusually for Thompson a poem of love's fulfilment. The "Narrow Vessel" series, in which the earlier "Love Declared" is inappropriately placed, does not quite succeed in making an account of his shy relationship with a girl in Wales bear the weight of the theme – of the soul's failure to answer the demands of love. Nor does the "Love in Dian's Lap" series, connected with Alice Meynell, rise, except intermittently, to the height of the theme – of human love frustrated leading to love of God. Art does not quite marry lived experience with the meaning seen in it. The best of the poems to children is perhaps "Daisy," and of the short religious poems the splendid "The Kingdom of God."

The bulk of his valuable poetry is in the long odes, with their great rhythmical inventiveness and richness of imagination. The greatest is *The Hound of Heaven,* expressing with wonderful speed and urgency the terror of the soul's flight and the majestic instancy of God's pursuit – a living God, for once. It has a clear line of development, and its élan carries us through the weaknesses which are even here present – e.g., in the middle of the third section. More representative is "Ode to the Setting Sun" – exciting, in parts splendid, but repetitious and insufficiently controlled. His development can be seen by comparing this early outburst with the more coherent, less moving, "Orient Ode" – Patmore-influenced, though still highly original, a meditation on the sun expressed in bold, complex images – or with the better, shorter, and more deeply felt "Contemplation."

Thompson's early prose (e.g., *Shelley*) was too mannered and rhetorical; but in his last ten years he made his living by writing witty, lucid, highly intelligent, and knowledgeable reviews and critical articles in a style often eloquent and seldom too ornate for the purpose. These five hundred or more items show him, even in decline, as no mere feckless dreamer.

— P. H. Butter

THOMSON, James.   Scottish.   Born in Ednam, Roxburghshire, baptized 15 September 1700. Educated at Jedburgh Grammar School; University of Edinburgh, matriculated 1715; studied for the ministry. Abandoned his studies and went to London, 1725: Tutor to Thomas Hamilton, afterwards Earl of Haddington; Companion and Tutor to Charles Talbot, the future Lord Chancellor's son, 1730–33; Secretary of Briefs, 1733–37; appointed Surveyor-General of the Leeward Islands, 1744. Received a pension from the Prince of Wales, 1738–48. *Died 27 August 1748.*

PUBLICATIONS

Collections

> *Works*, edited by George Lyttelton.   4 vols., 1750.
> *Complete Poetical Works*, edited by J. L. Robertson.   1908.
> *Letters and Documents*, edited by Alan D. McKillop.   1958.

Verse

> *Winter.*   1726, revised edition, 1726, 1730; *Summer,* 1727, revised edition, 1730;
>   *Spring,* 1728, revised edition, 1731; complete version, as *The Seasons,* 1730, revised
>   edition, 1730, 1744, 1746; edited by A. J. Sambrook, with *The Castle of Indolence,*
>   1972.
> *A Poem Sacred to the Memory of Sir Isaac Newton.*   1727.
> *Britannia.*   1729; revised edition, 1730.
> *A Poem to the Memory of Mr. Congreve.*   1729.
> *The Four Seasons and Other Poems.*   4 vols., 1735.
> *Ancient and Modern Italy Compared, Being the First Part of Liberty.*   1735; *Greece,*
>   1735; *Rome,* 1735; *Britain,* 1736; *The Prospect,* 1736; complete version, as *Liberty,*
>   1738.
> *A Poem to the Memory of Lord Talbot, Late Chancellor of Great Britain.*   1737.
> *The Castle of Indolence.*   1748; edited by J. A. Sambrook, with *The Seasons,* 1972.
> *Poems on Several Occasions.*   1750.

Plays

The Tragedy of Sophonisba (produced 1730).   1730.
Agamemnon (produced 1738).   1738.
Edward and Eleonora.   1739.
Alfred: A Masque, with David Mallet, music by Thomas Arne (produced 1740).   1740;
    revised version (produced 1751), 1751; as *Alfred the Great,* 1753.
Tancred and Sigismunda (produced 1745).   1745.
Coriolanus (produced 1749).   1749.

Other

Works.   1736; revised edition, 2 vols., 1744.

Reading List: *The Background of Thomson's Seasons* by Alan D. McKillop, 1942; *Thomson: Poet of the Seasons* by Douglas Grant, 1951; *The Varied God: A Critical Study of Thomson's Seasons,* 1959, and *The Poetry of Vision,* 1967, both by Patricia M. Spacks; *The Unfolding of the Seasons* by Ralph Cohen, 1970.

*   *   *

Winter is a religious-sublime poem in which James Thomson's descriptions of the terrible beauties of that season prompt the poet to reflect upon the power of God. Thomson added poems on the other seasons, written like *Winter* in blank verse and Miltonic diction, and revised and expanded them all repeatedly, until the final version of *The Seasons* (1746) was over fourteen times as long as the first version of *Winter.* In this process of growth *The Seasons* assumed a somewhat more secular character. Since Thomson regarded Nature as the work of God and Newton as the great interpreter of this work, he inevitably brings a great deal of imaginatively exciting new science into his poem, but this tends to concentrate the reader's attention upon second causes, rather than upon the First Cause. *The Seasons* under revision also grows more and more to resemble the *Georgics,* as Thomson draws upon Virgil's practical advice on husbandry, his myths, his exotic excursions, his anthropomorphic mock-heroic accounts of beasts, and, above all, his great patriotic rhapsodies. Like all English readers of the *Georgics,* Thomson is moved by Virgil's appealing myth of the innocence, felicity, vigour, patriotism, and piety of the husbandman's life. In the later stages of revision Thomson brings in ever-longer geographical excursions to describe the wonders of Nature in the Arctic and the tropics; he brings in longer reflections upon society and history; and he interpolates sentimental stories to add a human interest which he may have thought was lacking at first. However, there is a more significant human interest. Thomson's poem describes external nature, but it is, as Wordsworth said, "written nobly from himself." The subject is not so much religion, science, philosophy, history, and nature as a mind responding to these things. The unity of this apparently shapeless poem is in the movement of Thomson's own mind, and the poet is his own subject; standing alone, he finds in the shapes and sounds of unconscious external nature the self-conscious life of his own thought and feeling. Down to the middle of the nineteenth century *The Seasons* was probably the best-known of all English poems after *Paradise Lost.* Until the effect of Wordsworth's poetry came to be widely felt, it was the dominant influence upon English nature poetry, and did much to shape what is sometimes called the "romantic" view of external nature.

Thomson's occasional lyrical poems are unremarkable, except for his "Hymn on Solitude" (written 1725) which is one of the earliest and finest of eighteenth-century imitations of Milton's "L'Allegro" and "Il Penseroso." The blank-verse *Poem Sacred to the Memory of Sir Isaac Newton* blends panegyric, patriotism, religion, and science; its best lines are a dramatic, subtly personified, account of the spectrum. *Britannia*, also in blank verse, is a piece of anti-Walpole invective which rises to imaginative vision only in the lines on the wreck of the Spanish Armada "where loud the Northern Main/Howls thro' the fractur'd *Caledonian Isles*." The social, political, patriotic, and party interests of *Britannia* reappear in the series of five much longer blank-verse poems (1735–6) collected under the title of *Liberty*, in which Thomson dutifully, but not very animatedly, traces the progress of civilization through Europe from ancient times to modern. Here, as always in Thomson, there is imaginative vitality when landscape description is used to evoke states of mind and feeling; but for the most part the poet seems to be only half engaged with his subject. *Liberty* was a fruit of that same mistaken ambition which led Thomson to devote most of his energies to the writing of high-minded and languid heroic tragedies: *Sophonisba, Agamemnon, Edward and Eleonora, Tancred and Sigismunda*, and *Coriolanus*. He also wrote, in collaboration with David Mallet, the masque *Alfred* in which first appeared Thomson's best known lyric – "Rule Britannia."

The *Castle of Indolence*, in two cantos, is one of the happiest eighteenth-century imitations of Spenser. In the opening of the first canto Thomson richly evokes a dreamy, honeyed, languorous drowsiness where the Castle becomes the symbol of one kind of poetic imagination and Indolence becomes the poet's dream; but in the remainder of the poem Thomson elaborates an allegory in which the Castle is destroyed by the Knight of Arts and Industry. Indolence is condemned, and progress is praised in its various moral, intellectual, social, and material forms. It looks as if Thomson – consciously or not – is dramatizing a conflict between the moralizing, didactic public poet who was responsible for most of his writings, and the inward-looking visionary who wrote the most imaginative descriptions in *The Seasons*.

—A.J. Sambrook

THOMSON, James. Pseudonym: "B.V." Scottish. Born in Port Glasgow, 23 November 1834. Educated at the Royal Caledonian Orphan Asylum, London, 1843–50; Military Training College, London, 1850, 1852–54; trained as an army schoolmaster. Assistant Regimental Headmaster, Ballincolig, County Cork, 1851–52; Army Teacher in Devonshire, Dublin, Aldershot, Jersey, and Portsmouth, 1856 until discharged for a breach of discipline, 1862; moved to London, 1862; worked as a lawyer's clerk and subsequently, as "B.V.," as a journalist; Contributor to the *National Reformer*, 1860–75; mining agent in the United States, 1872; War Correspondent in Spain for the New York *World*, 1873; contributor to a tobacconists' trade monthly, *Cope's Tobacco Plant*, London, 1875–81. *Died 3 June 1882.*

PUBLICATIONS

Collections

Poems, Essays, and Fragments, edited by J. M. Robinson.   1892.
Poetical Works, edited by Bertram Dobell.   2 vols., 1895.
Poems and Some Letters, edited by Anne Ridler.   1963.
The Speedy Extinction of Evil and Misery: Selected Prose, edited by William David Schaefer.   1967.

Verse

The City of Dreadful Night and Other Poems.   1880.
Vane's Story, Weddah and Om-el-Bonain, and Other Poems.   1881.
A Voice from the Nile and Other Poems.   1884.

Other

A Commission of Inquiry on Royalty.   1876.
The Story of a Famous Old Jewish Firm.   1876; augmented edition, 1884.
The Devil in the Church of England, and The One Thing.   1876.
The Pursuit of Diva Nicotine.   1878.
Essays and Phantasies.   1881.
Shelley: A Poem, with Other Writings Relating to Shelley, to Which Is Added an Essay on
    the Poems of William Blake.   1884.
Satires and Profanities, edited by G. W. Foote.   1884.
Selections from Original Contributions to "Cope's Tobacco Plant."   1889.
Biographical and Critical Studies, edited by Bertram Dobell.   1896.
On George Meredith.   1909.
Walt Whitman: The Man and the Poet, edited by Bertram Dobell.   1910.

Translator, Essays, Dialogues, and Thoughts, by Giacomo Leopardi.   1905.

Reading List: The Laureate of Pessimism by Bertram Dobell, 1910; Thomson: A Critical
Study by Imogene B. Walker, 1950; Thomson by Charles Vachot, 1964; The Pessimism of
Thomson in Relation to His Times by Kenneth H. Byron, 1965; Thomson: Beyond "The City"
by William David Schaefer, 1966 (includes bibliography).

                              *   *   *

    James Thomson wrote under the initials "B.V." for "Bysshe Vanolis," a tribute to Shelley
and to the German Romantic poet and novelist Hardenberg who had called himself
"Novalis." This cryptogrammatic form of self-description is in keeping with an acute sense of
estrangement experienced by Thomson in his dealings with his fellow men. Running through
all his work it reaches its culmination in the isolated central figure of his best-known poem,
"The City of Dreadful Night."
    Of the many and complex factors combining to create this melancholy isolation several are
the direct result of his experience of London. A constant inner debate as to how far he should
or could identify with the urban crowd was accompanied by repeated struggles to leave the
city, but in these he was always defeated by economic circumstances. A background of two
serious bereavements in his early years contributed to his development of a philosophy of
unrelenting atheistic pessimism.
    The poems "Doom of a City" (1857) and "Vane's Story" (1864) both treat the problem of
the poet's isolation from other men. A prose work, "A Lady of Sorrow" (1862–63), shows
the urban wanderer, beset by a sense of loss, projecting his grief onto the city landscape until
it becomes transformed into a series of hallucinatory images. Although in the mid-1860's he
also attempted popular idylls about the lighter side of London life, "Sunday up the River" and
"Sunday at Hampstead," there is even here an undercurrent of bitterness. His poem "Blake,"
written at the same time, presents his predecessor as the archetypal wanderer in the desolate
city:

> There were thousands and thousands of human kind
>   In this desert of brick and stone;
> But some were deaf and some were blind,
>   And he was alone.

"The City of Dreadful Night," published in *The National Reformer* in 1874, was praised by George Eliot for its "distinct vision and grand utterance." Although the poem is allegorical, one extended metaphor in which Thomson's philosophy of pessimism is represented by the image of the nightmare city, the texture of language used is not densely metaphorical but clear and straightforward. A number of features of the poem symbolise Thomson's experience of the real city, creating at the same time an uncanny supernatural effect. In his selection of recognisable detail combining with the strange and unfamiliar, he emerges as one of the few nineteenth-century English poets to follow the Coleridgean rather than the Wordsworthian strain in *Lyrical Ballads*. The city is never visited by the sun, the streets are empty, the place is engulfed in silence:

> The Street-lamps burn amidst the baleful glooms,
>   Amidst the soundless solitudes immense
> Of rangèd mansions dark and still as tombs.
>   The silence which benumbs or strains the sense
> Fulfills with awe the soul's despair unweeping:
> Myriads of habitants are ever sleeping,
>   Or dead, or fled from nameless pestilence!

In a combination of powerful symbolism with challenging intellectual concepts Thomson produced a poem unique in English nineteenth-century writing. It is perhaps significant that it was the American, Herman Melville, a writer greatly admired by Thomson who described the poem as "the modern book of Job."

—Bridget O'Toole

TICKELL, Thomas. English. Born in Bridekirk, Cumberland, in 1686. Educated at Queen's College, Oxford, matriculated 1701, B.A. 1705, M.A. 1709. Married Clotilda Eustace in 1726; two sons and two daughters. Fellow, Queen's College, 1710–26; Professor of Poetry, Oxford University, 1711; moved to London and associated with Addison, through whose influence he entered diplomatic service: employed by Addison when Secretary to the Lord Lieutenant of Ireland, 1714, and made Under-Secretary by Addison when Secretary of State, 1717; Secretary to the Lord Justices in Ireland, 1724–40. *Died 23 April 1740.*

PUBLICATIONS

Collections

Poetical Works, edited by Thomas Park. 1807.

Verse

Oxford.   1707.
A Poem to the Lord Privy-Seal on the Prospect of Peace.   1713.
An Imitation of the Prophecy of Nereus, from Horace, Book 1, Ode XV.   1715.
The First Book of Homer's Iliad.   1715.
An Epistle from a Lady in England to a Gentleman at Avignon.   1717.
An Ode Occasioned by the Earl Stanhope's Voyage to France.   1718.
An Ode to the Earl of Sunderland at Windsor.   1720.
Kensington Garden.   1722.
To Sir Godfrey Kneller, at His Country Seat.   1722.
Lucy and Colin: A Song Written in Imitation of William and Margaret.   1725.
A Poem in Praise of the Horn-Book.   1728.
On Her Majesty's Re-Building the Lodgings of the Black Prince and Henry V and Queen's
    College, Oxford.   1733.

Other

Editor, The Works of Addison.   4 vols., 1721.

Reading List: Tickell and the Eighteenth-Century Poets by R. E. Tickell, 1931.

                         *   *   *

Thomas Tickell began his poetical career with Oxford of which Bonamy Dobrée in English
Literature in the Early Eighteenth Century says that its decasyllabic couplets "conduct one
gravely round a tour of the sights of Oxford, with the expected references to the great men,
especially the poets, who had lived there." Other works include occasional pieces, and
political poems like Epistle from a Lady in England to a Gentleman at Avignon (which
favoured the Hanoverian Succession) and "The Prospect of Peace." But it is chiefly as the
loyal friend of Addison that he is remembered. His translation of the first book of Homer's
Iliad earned him the emnity of Pope. Pope suspected, apparently with some reason, that
Addison was encouraging Tickell to enter into competition with his own projected translation
of Homer. After Addison's death Tickell edited his works, and produced his "Elegy on the
Death of Mr. Addison." Johnson, in the Lives of the Poets, says "neither he nor Addison ever
produced nobler lines than are contained in the third and fourth paragraphs; nor is a more
sublime or more elegant funeral-poem to be found in the whole compass of English
literature." Edmund Gosse, in Ward's English Poets, was probably nearer the mark when he
said, "In it a sublime and public sorrow for once moved a thoroughly mediocre poet into
utterance that was sincere and original." It is certainly true that Tickell's personal feeling
breaks through the formality of this poem, and redeems it from the triviality of much
eighteenth-century funerary writing:

                What mourner ever felt poetic fires?
                Slow comes the verse, that real woe inspires:
                Grief unaffected suits but ill with art,
                Or flowing numbers with a bleeding heart.

Kensington Garden is fanciful mock-heroic poem of some charm, though Johnson
criticised Tickell for mixing Greek gods with Gothic fairies. To some extent this poem

belongs to the same world as Pope's *Rape of the Lock*, though falling a long way below that masterpiece. *Lucy and Colin* is of interest as one of the earliest examples of the eighteenth-century fashion for sentimental exploitation of the traditional ballad form – a fashion which was to have important consequences for the Romantic movement.

—John Heath-Stubbs

TIMROD, Henry. American. Born in Charleston, South Carolina, 8 December 1828. Educated at German Friendly Society School and Cotes' Classical School, 1836–40; Franklin College, later University of Georgia, 1845–46; read law in the office of James L. Petigru, Charleston, 1847–49. Served in the Confederate Forces during the Civil War, 1862 (discharged for health reasons, 1862). Married Kate Goodwin in 1864; one son. Schoolmaster and tutor in various Southern plantation families before the outbreak of the Civil War, 1850–61; Assistant Editor, Charleston *Mercury*, 1863; Associate Editor, and part-owner, *South Carolinian*, Columbia, 1864 until 1865 when Sherman's troops sacked the town; Assistant Private Secretary to Governor J. L. Orr, 1867. *Died 7 October 1867.*

PUBLICATIONS

Collections

> *The Essays*, edited by Edd Winfield Parks. 1942.
> *The Collected Poems: A Variorum Edition*, edited by Edd Winfield Parks and Aileen Wells Parks. 1965.

Verse

> *Poems.* 1859.
> *The Poems*, edited by Paul Hamilton Hayne. 1873.
> *The Uncollected Poems*, edited by Guy A. Cardwell. 1942.

Other

> *The Last Years of Timrod 1864–1867: Including Letters to Paul Hamilton Hayne and Letters about Timrod by William Gilmore Simms, John R. Thompson, John Greenleaf Whittier, and Others*, edited by Jay B. Hubbell. 1941.

Reading List: *Timrod* by Edd Winfield Parks, 1964.

*   *   *

Had it not been for the Civil War, Henry Timrod, although the best Southern poet of his time except for Poe, could be almost unknown today. In view of his reputation as chief of the Southern poets of the War – he is characterized in such rebarbative phrases as "Laureate of the Confederacy" and "Harp of the South" – his life and thought are rich in ironies.

There was nothing of the Cavalier about his ancestry, and he was not a zealous propagandist for the region or for slavery. Like a number of other antebellum Southern writers, he was often at odds with his section and its culture; a strain of astrigent candor ran through his excellent essays. Although Charleston was the publishing center of the South, Timrod describes the region as a literary backwater, archaic in taste, unformed in judgment, materialistic, prosaic, uninterested in intellectual and poetic knowledge. He opposed Southernism in literature and emphasized that poetry must belong to the world.

To some of the older generation of Charleston literary men, Timrod seemed extavagantly avant-garde: his principal heroes and models were Wordsworth and Tennyson. His theory and practice were tempered, however, by classicist ideas and habits. He insisted that after inspiration must come artistry; that excessive subjectivity spoils verse; and that poetry must be true and ethical. His apprentice verses show him industriously experimenting in forms and meters, and variant versions of mature poems indicate that he was an assiduous reviser. Sidney Lanier wrongly held that Timrod possessed a dainty artless art but never had time to learn the craft of the poet. His lyricism is most successful when most considered: his verse lacks spontaneity, intensity, and figurative imagination; his ideas and metrics are unoriginal. He was in a large sense an occasional poet whose delight in words and skill with meters could produce simply structured, controlled verses remarkably free of the sentimental verbosity and crudity of form that are characteristic of his Southern contemporaries.

Amative and nature poetry make up the bulk of Timrod's verse, but the critical consensus is right in judging his war poetry, most of which stresses the losses and sorrows of the conflict, to be his best. Most memorable are "Ethno-genesis," "The Cotton Boll," "Carolina," "A Cry to Arms," "Charleston," and his Magnolia Cemetery ode.

Nearly all of Timrod's verses were first published in Southern newspapers and magazines, usually for no pay. *The Southern Literary Messenger*, of Richmond, and *Russell's Magazine*, of Charleston, were the most important of the miscellanies to which he made regular contributions. Friends guaranteed the costs of the one slim volume of his verse that appeared during his lifetime. Posthumous collections more than double the number of poems contained in that first volume.

—Guy A. Cardwell

TOLSON, Melvin B(eaunorus). American. Born in Moberly, Missouri, 6 February 1898. Educated at Lincoln High School, Kansas City, Missouri, graduated 1918; Fisk University, Nashville, Tennessee, 1918–20; Lincoln University, Oxford, Pennsylvania, 1920–23, B.A. 1923; Columbia University, New York, M.A. 1940. Married Ruth Southall in 1922. Teacher at Wiley College, Marshall, Texas, 1924–47; Professor of English and Drama, Langston University, Oklahoma, 1947–66. Poet-in-Residence, Tuskegee Institute, 1965. Mayor of Langston after 1954. Recipient: Omega Psi Phi Award in Creative Literature, 1945; National Institute of Arts and Letters award, 1966. D.L.: Lincoln University, 1954.; D.H.L.: Lincoln University, 1965. Poet Laureate of Liberia, 1947; appointed permanent Breadloaf Fellow in Poetry, 1954. *Died 29 August 1966.*

PUBLICATIONS

Verse

Rendezvous with America.   1944.
Libretto for the Republic of Liberia.   1953.
Harlem Gallery: Book I, The Curator.   1965.

Play

The Fire in the Flint, from a work by Walter White (produced 1952).

Reading List: Introduction by Karl Shapiro to Harlem Gallery, 1965; Tolson by Joy Flasch, 1972.

*   *   *

On the basis of his first volume of poetry, *Rendezvous with America*, it would hardly have been possible to predict the kind of poet Melvin Tolson was to be a decade later. A poet who writes "I gaze upon her silken loveliness/She is a passion-flower of joy and pain/On the golden bed I came back to possess" does not show particular promise. Likewise the lines "America is the Black Man's country/The Red Man's, the Yellow Man's/The Brown Man's, the White Man's" are not suggestive of the great lines yet to come.

There are, however, certain characteristics of the earlier poetry which were to be developed in such a way as to become hallmarks of the later poetry, more its essence than ornament. The second stanza, for example, of "An Ex-Judge at the Bar" is in style and content very much like a good deal of Tolson's later poetry and untypical of the rather commonplace character of much of the first volume. That stanza, "I know, Bartender, yes, I know when the Law/Should wag its tail or rip with fang and claw./When Pilate washed his hands, that neat event/Set for us judges a Caesarean precedent," is in tone typically Tolsonian. The juxtaposition of the formal and the informal, the classical and the contemporary, the familiar and the unusual accounts in large measure for the unique character of Tolson's best poetry.

Such juxtapositions are more pronounced in *Libretto for the Republic of Liberia*, where, in addition, the "gift for language" noted in Allen Tate's introduction to the volume, becomes apparent. The effect of the juxtaposition of the learned encyclopedic references and the most abstruse vocabulary with commonplace references, vocabulary, and rhyme, managed within a highly traditional form, is pyrotechnic. The occurrence in the same context of French, German, Latin, Hebrew, Swahili, Arabic, Spanish, and Sanskrit references with commonplace activities, occupations, facts, and events created a system of tensions not unlike the dynamic of forces holding an atom or a galaxy together. Each element threatens to go off on its own; yet as long as the balance of forces remains constant, the system functions. Tolson, by virtue of an extraordinary mind and intelligence, keeps a vast array of disparate elements in constant relationship. His poetry is, therefore, coherent, and the primary effect it arouses is of the containment and control of vast reserves of energy.

This bears on Karl Shapiro's controversial statement in his introduction to *Harlem Gallery*, Tolson's final volume, that "Tolson writes in Negro." It is not at bottom the language which prompted Shapiro's observation. Rather, it is the intellectual disposition of the tension between two worlds that finds its manifestation in the language. Tolson belongs (and this

1012

distinguishes him from Eliot, Pound, and Hart Crane, whom he read avidly) to an Afro-American world and an American-European world, and he knows these worlds in intricate detail. The balance he sustains between them is the source of his power. Few understand him because few know both worlds as well, and few are as totally committed as he to such a high universal standard of values.

—D. B. Gibson

TOWNSHEND, Aurelian. English. Born, possibly in Norfolk, c. 1583. Nothing is known of his early life and education. Married in 1622; three sons and two daughters. Steward to Sir Robert Cecil, afterwards Earl of Salisbury; a friend of Ben Jonson; accompanied Lord Herbert of Cherbury on a tour abroad, 1608; resident in London in the 1620's and was prominent as a court poet: probably held the post of gentleman of the privy chamber; succeeded Ben Jonson as composer of court masques, 1631–32; granted freedom from arrest for debt by the House of Lords, 1643; possibly in the service of the Earl of Dorset at Knole in 1640's. *Died c. 1651.*

PUBLICATIONS

Collections

   Poems and Masks, edited by E. K. Chambers.   1912.
   Poems and Masques, edited by Cedric C. Brown.   1977

Plays

   Albion's Triumph (produced 1632).   1632.
   Tempe Restored (produced 1632).   1632.

*   *   *

Although poems have turned up since E. K. Chambers's edition of 1912, the canon of Aurelian Townshend's verse is still small, and many surviving datable poems come from his middle and later years. Clearly, some lyrics must precede the time at which he was chosen to write verses for court masques in 1631/2, but there is little sign that Townshend saw himself publicly as a notable poet, even after he was taken up by the Caroline court and found serviceable for dramatic and celebratory verses. Only his masques and a few occasional poems were printed in his lifetime. A few lyrics found their way into songbooks from 1651 onwards. Otherwise, the verse survives in manuscript anthologies.

   The songs in *Albions Triumph* and *Tempe Restored* are neat but lack the variety of tone or declamatory energy of Jonson or Carew. The opening verses of *Albions Triumph* are laboured. Those who have noticed Townshend have usually commented on an individual lyrical quality in his poetry, and it is true that one or two of his non-lyrical poems (e.g., the elegy on the Countess of Bridgewater) have flat passages. Even at his best and wittiest,

Townshend rarely surprises in sentiment: the best of his occasional and celebratory verse is a decorous and direct, if sometimes conceited, expression of the obvious.

Nevertheless, in the poem on Venetia Digby he proclaimed that he delighted "most in unusual ways." Perhaps a striving for originality can be found in his attempt to emulate the display of Donne, for example in "The Paradox" and "Hide not thy love." These longer poems achieve distinguished lines and stanzas that are Donne-like, though finally they lack the dramatic compression, immediacy, and calculated obliqueness of Donne. Townshend's originality may also be seen in the variety of genuinely lyrical measures and forms he tries. Some poems which seem rhythmically overdetermined to the mere reader, or awkward because of disparate stanza-forms, were written with an eye chiefly on the conventions of song-writing and song-setting. Fortunately, the music for eight songs survives. Seven were set by Henry Lawes. Within lyrical kinds, Townshend's range is broad and indicates Caroline courtly fashion, from the delicate parody of Herrick's "Amidst the myrtles" ("Thou shepherd whose intentive eye") to the stout bacchanalian ditty, "Bacchus, I-acchus," a chorus-song written for the court revival of Cartwright's *The Royal Slave*. There are signs also that his range could have extended further outside the lyrical: his verse-letter to Carew on the death of Gustavus Adolphus convinces in the closing heroic and elegiac imagery, nicely set off by the opening section of relaxed colloquialism. At his finest Townshend judges well the tone for aristocratic and courtly occasions. The success of "Victorious Beauty" as a poem addressed to a noble patroness lies in the balance between witty impudence and subservient social grace. In this kind of delicacy Townshend is strikingly representative of the more refined manners of the Caroline court.

—Cedric C. Brown

TRAHERNE, Thomas. English. Born in Hereford c. 1638. Educated at Brasenose College, Oxford, B.A. 1656, M.A. 1661, B.D. 1669. Took holy orders: Rector of Credenhill, Herefordshire, 1657; Chaplain to Sir Orlando Bridgeman, Lord Keeper of the Great Seal, 1667. *Died 27 September 1674.*

PUBLICATIONS

Collections

> *Centuries, Poems, and Thanksgivings*, edited by H. M. Margoliouth. 2 vols., 1958.
> *Poems, Centuries, and Three Thanksgivings*, edited by Anne Ridler. 1966.

Verse

> *Poems of Felicity*, edited by H. I. Bell. 1910.
> *Poetical Works, Now First Published from the Original Manuscripts*, edited by Bertram Dobell. 1903.
> *Felicities* (includes prose), edited by Arthur Quiller-Couch. 1934.

Other

Roman Forgeries. 1673.
Christian Ethics; or Divine Morality Opening the Way to Blessedness. 1675; edited by
G. R. Guffey and C. L. Marks, 1968.
A Serious and Pathetical Contemplation of the Mercies of God. 1699; edited by Roy
Daniells, 1941.
Hexameron; or, Meditations on the Six Days of Creation, in A Collection of Meditations
and Devotions. 1717; edited by G. R. Guffey, 1966.
Centuries of Meditations, Now First Published from the Author's Manuscript, edited by
Bertram Dobell. 1908; edited by J. Farrar, 1960.
Of Magnanimity and Charity, edited by J. R. Slater. 1942.

Reading List: Traherne by Q. Iredale, 1935; Traherne by G. I. Wade, revised edition, 1946;
Three Metaphysical Poets by Margaret Willy, 1961; The Paradise Within: Studies in
Vaughan, Traherne, and Milton by Louis J. Martz, 1964; Traherne: Mystic and Poet by K. W.
Salter, 1964; The Mystical Poetry of Traherne by A. L. Clements, 1969; Mystical Symbolism
in the Poetry of Traherne by Alison J. Sherrington, 1970; The Expanded Voice: The Art of
Traherne by Stanley Stewart, 1970; The Temple of Eternity: Traherne's Philosophy of Time
by Richard D. Jordan, 1972.

*   *   *

When Thomas Traherne's work was rediscovered, by chance, two-and-a-half centuries
after his death, its author was at first thought to be Henry Vaughan. There are striking
resemblances in the style and spirit of their work, and in their irradiating imagery of light,
and, above all, in the affinity of their attitude towards childhood.

For Traherne, as for Vaughan, "The first Impressions are Immortal all" ("Dumnesse"). In
poems like "The Salutation," "Eden," "Wonder," and "Shadows in the Water," and his prose
masterpiece Centuries of Meditations, we are reminded also of Blake and Wordsworth. The
same luminous intensity of vision evokes the child's innocence of "the Dirty Devices of this
World," the freshness of his delight, and that sense of limitless horizons which made "All
Time ... Eternity, and a Perpetual Sabbath." Perceiving the kinship between the "Infant-eye"
view of the universe, with its intuitions of a world beyond the visible one, and the mystic's
intimations of harmony and happiness, Traherne believed that these held the key to the most
fundamental realities of human life and its relationship with God. Only through regaining
that wisdom "unattainable by Book," and becoming "as it were a little Child again," could a
man enjoy the world in communion with his Creator: through those praises which, Traherne
declared, are "the Marks and Symptoms of a Happy Life ... the very End for which the
World was created."

"Enjoy" is perhaps the most frequent verb in Traherne's work. Its objects are marvellously
comprehensive, ranging from sea, sky, stars, and the "lovely lively air" to Blake's grain of
sand and "evry Spire of Grass"; from the diverse personalities of his fellow men to the simple
fulfilment of daily material needs. In his profound conviction of the interdependence of the
worlds of sense and spirit, each enriching and intensifying the other, the senses are seen – in
the metaphor of "News" – as ambassadors, bringing tidings from a foreign country which
houses man's true treasure. To this "Christian epicurean," as he termed himself, an ascetic
rejection of the divinely planned universe seemed a denial of that desire implanted in him as
positive proof of his immortal soul and its destination. Savouring life to the utmost on both
planes, the natural and the transcendental, Traherne is indeed – in his own phrase –
"Felicity's perfect Lover."

Traherne's is a poetry of scattered felicities: his impetuous, exuberant urgency tends too often to spill over into repetitive diffuseness. Apart from a handful of completely achieved pieces, he lacks as a poet the verbal discipline of his spiritual autobiography, *Centuries of Meditations.* Here, as nowhere else, he achieves a harmonious fusion of form with content, of the sonorous splendours of the older style with the vigorous simplicity of the new. This eloquent and impassioned testament to his creed of dedicated joy places Traherne among the masters of English religious prose.

—Margaret Willy

TRUMBULL, John. American. Born in Westbury, Connecticut, 24 April 1750. Educated at Yale University, New Haven, Connecticut (Berkeley Scholar), 1763–70, B.A. 1767, M.A. 1770; studied law in John Adams's law office in Boston, 1773; admitted to the Connecticut Bar, 1773. Married Sarah Hubbard in 1776; seven children. Schoolteacher, Weathersfield, Connecticut, 1770–71; contributed essays (as "The Correspondent") to the *Connecticut Journal,* 1770–73; Tutor at Yale University, 1771–73; practised law in New Haven and Hartford, Connecticut, 1774–1825; Treasurer of Yale University, 1776–82; Member of the Hartford City Council, 1784–93; State's Attorney for Hartford, 1789–95; Member, General Assembly of Connecticut, 1792, 1800–01; Judge, Connecticut Supreme Court, 1801–19, and Supreme Court of Errors, 1808–19. Literary leader of the "Hartford Wits" in the 1780's and 1790's. LL.D.: Yale University, 1818. Member, American Academy of Arts and Sciences, 1791. *Died 11 May 1831.*

PUBLICATIONS

Collections

The Works, edited by Theodore Sizer. 1950; supplement, *The Autobiography,* 1953.
The Satiric Poems, edited by Edwin T. Bowden. 1962.

Verse

An Elegy on the Death of Mr. Buckingham St. John. 1771.
The Progress of Dulness. 3 vols., 1772–73.
M'Fingal: A Modern Epic Poem, Canto First. 1775; *M'Fingal in Four Cantos,* 1782; edited by Benson J. Lossing, 1864.
The Poetical Works. 2 vols., 1820.
The Anarchiad, with others, edited by Luther G. Riggs. 1861.

Other

An Essay on the Use and Advantages of the Fine Arts. 1770.
Biographical Sketch of the Character of Governor Trumbull. 1809.

Reading List: *Trumbull, Connecticut Wit* by Alexander Cowie, 1936 (includes bibliography); *Trumbull* by Victor E. Gimmestad, 1974.

*   *   *

John Trumbull is best remembered as spokesman for the group of writers known as the "Connecticut" or "Hartford Wits." This group, which included Joel Barlow, Timothy Dwight, and David Humphreys, among others, was active during the years following the Revolutionary War. Most of its members, Trumbull included, were educated at Yale and were extremely conservative in their political and literary views. They appreciated Neoclassical decorum, and, from their center at Hartford, Connecticut, they used their literary talent to exert pressure on the nation to stem the rise of Jeffersonian democracy, which they feared, and to create a strong federal government.

A lawyer by profession, Trumbull was also devoted to the arts. He composed verses at the age of four and passed the entrance exam to Yale when he was only seven. He possessed a keen mind and a shrewd wit, which he used to his advantage when he wrote satire. He was a master of the octosyllabic line, and he delighted in writing hudibrastic verse. For poetic models, he emulated the works of Pope, Swift, and Dryden. More concerned with ideas than with emotions, Trumbull valued restraints and disliked emotion. Needless to say, he did not appreciate the Romantics, especially Wordsworth and Coleridge, who he felt placed expression before reason and subjectivity before objectivity.

Trumbull possessed a genuine gift for humor. At his best when writing burlesque or satire, Trumbull found more serious verse difficult to sustain. Like his contemporaries, he considered the ode and the elegy superior in literary merit to satire, and although he frequently tried to write in these forms, his "Ode to Sleep: An Elegy on the Times," and *An Elegy on the Death of Mr. Buckingham St. John* are among his least interesting poems. More engaging is *The Progress of Dullness*, a three part satirical epic, written while Trumbull was studying for his master's degree at Yale, which ridicules outmoded educational practices and which calls for a more useful system of instruction than that which Trumbull experienced as an undergraduate.

His most famous poem, *M'Fingal*, earned Trumbull the title of "Poet of the Revolution." Written in the tradition of Dryden's *Mac Flecknoe*, it is a mock heroic epic about the raucous adventures of a Tory squire named M'Fingal who tries to prevent a group of patriots from giving further support to the Revolutionary War and is himself tarred and feathered in the process. During the Revolutionary War, *M'Fingal* was used to stir up popular sentiment against the British, and it was even printed in England, where its literary merit drew the praise of critics who were impartial enough to disassociate their political allegiances from their critical pronouncements. In America, the popularity of *M'Fingal* continued long after it ceased to be useful as anti-British propaganda. Today it is recognized as one of the finest political verse satires written in America prior to the Civil War.

Trumbull is also remembered for his essays. Like his verse, Trumbull's essays are best when they satirize institutions and events. Favorite among these are education, the clergy, and, of course, the British, whom he never really despised but was always ready to satirize. He patterned his prose style, which is witty and extremely polished, after that of Addison and Steele, whom he very much admired.

—James A. Levernier

TUCKERMAN, Frederick Goddard. American. Born in Boston, Massachusetts, 4 February 1821. Educated at Bishop Hopkins' School, Burlington, Vermont, 1833–37; Harvard College, Cambridge, Massachusetts, 1837–38, and Harvard Law School, Cambridge, 1839–42; admitted to the Suffolk County, Massachusetts Bar, 1844. Married Hannah Lucinda Jones in 1847 (died, 1857); three children. Briefly practised law; retired to Greenfield, Massachusetts, 1847, and lived there for the remainder of his life. *Died 9 May 1873.*

PUBLICATIONS

Collections

The Complete Poems, edited by N. Scott Momaday. 1965.

Verse

Poems. 1860.

Reading List: *Tuckerman* by Samuel A. Golden, 1966.

*   *   *

Because Frederick Goddard Tuckerman's poetry was rescued from near-oblivion only fairly recently, a natural temptation for the critic is to fan the excitement generated by that rescue by overstating the value of the poetry. This temptation should be avoided, for much of Tuckerman's poetry is pedestrian.

Tuckerman's narrative poems are often merely inflated anecdotes. Many poems are maimed by Tuckerman's tepid sermonizing. Sometimes his diction is ornate and tediously archaic, and his syntax awkward, even puzzling. Several sonnets are poorly constructed; the climax is followed by a number of distractingly anti-climactic lines. In his perceptive book on Tuckerman, Samuel A. Golden summarizes part of Tuckerman's world view. For the poet, "man's certainty rests in God." Unfortunately, Tuckerman's expressions of his religious faith are almost always inadequately documented, verbally bland, and so, quite unconvincing.

Nonetheless, the excitement caused by the rediscovery of Tuckerman's work is justified. Five sonnet sequences and "The Cricket" – all inspired by the death, after childbirth, of Tuckerman's wife – represent his finest efforts. Both the content and the form of these poems are, at their best, of a high quality.

In the nineteenth century most American poets regarded nature from a wholly sentimental point of view. Tuckerman tempered his view. As his sonnets make clear, he, too, believed that nature was a part of God's cosmic scheme. Unlike his contemporaries, however, he did not proceed to interpret nature for the benefit of his readers. Instead, he admitted that he did not comprehend the ways of nature. Nor did nature provide Tuckerman with an all-encompassing comfort. "The Cricket" and the sonnets report that he gained solace from nature only after severely qualifying the degree of solace he hoped to gain.

Equally interesting, although Tuckerman – like his Transcendentalist peers – sometimes yearned to merge with nature, he chose to resist this impulse. He also came to realize that it was impossible to fulfill such an impulse. While the Transcendentalists found nature (indeed, the whole universe) to be wondrously like their own personalities, Tuckerman found nature to be quixotic, contradictory, enigmatic, and fundamentally separate from himself.

Finally, in "The Cricket" and the first two sonnet sequences especially, Tuckerman's stylistic weaknesses are far outweighed by many fine phrases, metaphors, and long descriptive passages enhanced by skillful rhythms and rhyming. In "The Cricket," for instance, Tuckerman speaks of dead friends with "faces where but now a gap must be" and of death as the "crowning vacancy." He describes a night of love in terms of "wringing arms . . ./Closed eyes, and kisses that would not let go." His best sonnets also display a superb blending of form and content.

—Robert K. Johnson

TUPPER, Martin (Farquhar). English. Born in Marylebone, London, 17 July 1810. Educated at Charterhouse School, London, 1821–26; Christ Church, Oxford, matriculated 1828, B.A. 1832, M.A. 1835; Lincoln's Inn, London, 1832–35; called to the Bar, 1835, but never practised. Married Isabella Devis in 1835; had several children. Inherited Albury House, near Guildford, Surrey, 1840, and lived there for the remainder of his life; visited America, 1851, 1876. Recipient: Prussian Gold Medal for Science and Art, 1844. D.C.L.: Oxford University, 1847. Granted Civil List pension, 1873. Also an inventor: Fellow of the Royal Society, 1845. *Died 29 November 1889.*

PUBLICATIONS

Verse

Sacra Poesis. 1832.
Geraldine: A Sequel to Coleridge's Christabel, with Other Poems. 1838.
Proverbial Philosophy: A Book of Thoughts and Arguments, Originally Treated. 1838; revised edition, 4 vols., 1876(?).
A Thousand Lines Now First Offered to the World We Live In. 1845.
Hactenus. 1848.
The Loving Ballad to Brother Jonathan. 1848.
King Alfred's Poems Turned into English Metres. 1850.
Ballads for the Times. 1850; revised edition, 1852.
Complete Poetical Works. 1850.
Half a Dozen No-Popery Ballads. 1851.
A Hymn for All Nations. 1851.
A Dirge for Wellington. 1852.
Half a Dozen Ballads for Australian Emigrants. 1853.
A Batch of War Ballads. 1854.
A Dozen Ballads for the Times about Church Abuses. 1854.
A Dozen Ballads for the Times about White Slavery. 1854.
Lyrics of the Heart and Mind. 1855.
Three Hundred Sonnets. 1860.
Cithara: A Selection from the Lyrics. 1863.
Our Canadian Dominion: Half a Dozen Ballads about a King for Canada. 1868.
Twenty-One Protestant Ballads. 1868.

A Creed. 1870.
Fifty of the Protestant Ballads. 1874.
Select Miscellaneous Poems. 1874.
Jubilate! An Offering for 1887. 1887.

Plays

Alfred: A Patriotic Play. 1858.
Raleigh: His Life and Death. 1866.
Washington. 1876.
Three Five-Act Plays and Twelve Dramatic Scenes. 1882.

Fiction

The Crock of Gold: A Rural Novel. 1844.
Heart: A Social Novel. 1844.
The Twins: A Domestic Novel. 1844.
Stephan Langton. 1858.
Rides and Reveries of the Late Mr. Aesop Smith. 1858.

Other

A Modern Pyramid to Commemorate a Septuagint of Worthies (poems and essays). 1839.
Probabilities: An Aid to Faith. 1847.
Surrey, with J. Tudor. 1849.
Complete Prose Works. 1850.
Farley Heath (miscellany). 1850.
Paterfamilias's Diary of Everybody's Tour. 1856.
On Rifle-Clubs. 1859.
Plan of the Ritualistic Campaign. 1865(?); as *The Anti-Ritualistic Satire,* 1868.
A Selection from the Works. 1866.
Autobiography. 1886.

Editor, *An Author's Mind: The Book of Title-Pages.* 1841.

Translator, *La Bannière sur le Char de la Victoire,* by John Sullivan. 1866.
Translator, *Elégie sur la Mort de Lord Palmerston,* by John Sullivan. 1866.
Translator, *A Victor Hugo,* by John Sullivan. 1885.

Reading List: *Tupper and the Victorian Middle-Class Mind* by Ralf Buchmann, 1941; *Tupper: His Rise and Fall* by Derek Hudson, 1949.

*   *   *

Martin Tupper became a byword in his later years for a writer of bad verse, and this blanket of critical disapproval has obscured the better qualities of a life of constant philanthropical activity. His enormously successful *Proverbial Philosophy* went through fifty English editions and four separate series between 1838 and 1880 and was adopted as a new *Pilgrim's Progress* for the early Victorians. Tupper's own word for its form, which he derived from Solomon, was "rhythmics" rather than poetry; he conceived his book primarily as a religious and moral work, though eventually (and paradoxically) he influenced all writers of free verse from Whitman to Eliot.

Tupper was educated at Charterhouse and Christ Church, Oxford, where he became a friend of Gladstone. He was not without talent or humour; there are felicitous passages in his work and hints in his translations of King Alfred's poems of a distinction that generally eluded him. Tupper was betrayed by his own restless energy and lack of self-criticism which prompted him to produce patriotic and evangelical verse on every conceivable occasion. In 1850, when his *Proverbial Philosophy* had long been a favourite with Queen Victoria and Prince Albert, he was a candidate for the laureateship bestowed on Tennyson (and would have made a punctual though inferior performer).

He was seen at his best as a local and national patriot in the house at Albury, Surrey, which he inherited in 1840 and occupied for forty years. His local novel *Stephan Langton* was written with the deliberate object of making "our country classic ground," and may be thought to have succeeded as it was kept in print for over a century. Many Surrey readers have accepted the truth of the episodes at Friday Street, St. Martha's, and above all at "the Silent Pool" in Albury, though they are historically quite untrustworthy. Tupper is also remembered in Surrey for preserving Albury old church; for his rediscovery of the Romano-Celtic temple on Farley Heath, properly investigated a century later; and as the chief propagandist of the local and national volunteer revival of 1859. The motto of the volunteers, "Defence not Defiance," came from one of his poems.

Towards the end of his life, when he was the butt of the critics and his private investments had failed, Tupper was grateful for a civil list pension. He was forced to leave Albury and died at Upper Norwood, but was buried in the churchyard of Albury "new" church. Having goaded him for so long, the newspapers found friendly things to say of him after his death. Tupper was unfairly treated, but was a born protestant martyr who ran himself on to the sword.

—Derek Hudson

TURBERVILE, George. English. Born in Whitchurch, Dorset, c. 1543. Educated at Winchester School (scholar); New College, Oxford; resided at one of the Inns of Court, 1562. Married in 1574. Fellow of New College, 1561; Secretary to Thomas Randolph, Ambassador to Russia, 1568–69; retired to an estate in Shapwick, Dorset, 1577. *Died c. 1597.*

PUBLICATIONS

Collections

Poems, edited by John Erskine Hankins. 1952.

Verse

The Eclogues of Mantuan Turned into English. 1567; edited by Douglas Bush, 1937.
The Heroical Epistles of Ovid, with Aulus Sabinus' Answers. 1567; edited by F. S. Boas, 1928.

Epitaphs, Epigrams, Songs, and Sonnets, with a Discourse of the Affections of Tymetes to Pyndara. 1567; edited by J. P. Collier, 1867.
A Plain Path to Perfect Virtue Devised by Mancinus. 1568.

Other

Tragical Tales Translated out of Sundry Italians, with Some Other Broken Pamphlets and Epistles Sent to Certain of His Friends in England, at His Being in Moscovia. 1576(?); edited in part by L. E. Berry and R. O. Crummery, in *Rude and Barbarous Kingdom,* 1969.

Editor, *The Book of Falconry or Hawking.* 1575.
Editor, *The Noble Art of Venery or Hunting.* 1575(?); edited version, 1908.

Reading List: *Life and Works* by John Erskine Hankins, 1940; Introduction by Richard J. Panofsky to *Epitaphes, Epigrams, Songs, and Sonets,* 1977.

*   *   *

George Turbervile belonged to the energetic generation of young writers who set about at the start of Elizabeth's reign to build a vernacular library for England by the wholesale importation of ancient and foreign works. Scion of a prominent Dorsetshire family, he was educated at important centers of the New Learning, Winchester School and New College, Oxford. A facility for making verses put him much in demand among his fellows as a source of love letters; Turbervile made it the basis of a prolific career as a poet and translator. He englished a variety of works, from Ovid's *Heroicall Epistles* through *A Plaine Path to Perfect Vertue* by Mancinus to a pair of elegant treatises on falconry and hunting compiled "out of the best aucthors." He favored English schoolboys with a useful version of Mantuan's eclogues, and his versifications of melodramatic Italian novelle catered to still another segment of Elizabethan taste.

The volume of "Tragicall Tales" also contained a miscellany of original work, including reports on a 1568 trip to Muscovy that Hakluyt reprinted. The bulk of Turbervile's own poetry appeared in his *Epitaphes, Epigrams, Songs, and Sonets*. A bookish poet, he loaded his verses with his learning. The copious enlargement and over-precious rhetorical artifice that passed for stylistic elegance in his day are likely to displease a modern ear – as they already displeased Turbervile's younger contemporaries less than two decades later. Whether reciting Ovid at length to his mistress, expanding apothegms by grammar-school schemes, or praising deceased nobles by comparing them to every god in the pantheon, Turbervile too often smothers his poems with pedantry. Only when pursuing a different stylistic ideal, such as the clarity of the song set to music or the efficiency of the epigram, does he merit Yvor Winters's praise as "one of the most minute stylists of the century." Among his imitations of poems from the Greek Anthology are to be found Turbervile's most readable and appealing productions.

Like many poets of his generation who were affected by the ethical tone of their humanist education, Turbervile experienced some discomfort with poetic love. He insisted on the inconsequentiality of his love poems, calling them trifles and toys, and he reached toward an urbane detachment from the follies of conventional *amour*. When he strung a number of poems together into a continuous narrative and offered it to his young readers as "a Glasse &

Myrror for them to gaze vpon" to teach them "to flee that fonde and filthie affection of poysoned & vnlawful loue," he discovered the characteristic Elizabethan mode of love poetry, the amatory sequence, and was the first to commit one to print.

Turbervile experimented with dozens of verse forms, and with subjects, tones, and stylistic devices of every description. Though his work was rapidly superseded by that of later poets, he laid down a broad foundation for them to build upon, and his contribution has too frequently been overlooked.

—William E. Sheidley

TUSSER, Thomas.   English.   Born in Rivenhall, Essex, c. 1524. Trained as a singer: chorister at Wallingford College, Berkshire, then at St. Paul's Cathedral, London; educated at Eton College; King's College, and Trinity Hall, Cambridge. Married twice; second wife, Amy Moon, by whom he had three sons, one daughter. Resided at court as musician to Lord Paget for ten years; thereafter settled as a farmer at Cattiwade, Suffolk; after death of his first wife lived variously in Norfolk, Essex, and London, and then Cambridge: matriculated as a servant of Trinity Hall. Died in debtor's prison, London. *Died 3 May 1580.*

PUBLICATIONS

Verse

   A Hundred Good Points of Husbandry.   1557; augmented edition, with *A Hundred Good Points of Huswifery,* 1570; augmented edition, as *Five Hundred Points of Good Husbandry United to as Many of Good Huswifery,* 1573; augmented edition, 1580; edited by W. Payne and S. J. Herrtage, 1878; 1571 text edited by Dorothy Hartley, 1931.

*   *   *

Thomas Tusser's fame rests entirely upon one extremely popular farmer's almanac in doggerel verse, first published in 1557 by Richard Tottel as *A Hundred Good Points of Husbandry* and thereafter much augmented. Its final version, as *Five Hundred Points of Good Husbandry* in 1573, contains additional illustrations, a section of good housewifery, and autobiographical verses of Tusser's experiences as a farmer in Suffolk. *Five Hundred Points* provides practical advice on planting, tillage, forestry, animal husbandry, home economics, and weather. Like Benjamin Franklin's Poor Richard, Tusser embellishes his instructions with gossipy antecdotes, jokes, pious truisms, and homespun observations on men and manners. An execrable poet, Tusser endeared himself to generations of readers for his sustained tone of rustic common sense and congeniality rather than for any aesthetic qualities, yet his work clearly illustrates that before the Industrial Revolution ordinary people found poetry and the most practical subjects entirely compatible. Among the most popular books of the sixteenth century, *Five Hundred Points* was reprinted almost consistently down to the modern period, with introductions by Sir Walter Scott in 1810 and Rudyard Kipling in 1931.

—James E. Ruoff

VAN DOREN, Mark (Albert). American. Born in Hope, Illinois, 13 June 1894. Educated at the University of Illinois, Urbana, A.B. 1914, A.M. 1915; Columbia University, New York, Ph.D. 1920. Served in the Army during World War I. Married Dorothy Graffe in 1922; two sons. Instructor, 1920–24, Assistant Professor, 1924–35, Associate Professor, 1935–42, and Professor of English, 1942–59, Columbia University; also, Lecturer at St. John's College, Annapolis, Maryland, 1937–57. Literary Editor, 1924–28, and Film Critic, 1935–38, *The Nation*, New York; Participant in the radio program Invitation to Learning, CBS, 1940–42. Visiting Professor of English, Harvard University, Cambridge, Massachusetts, 1963. Recipient: Pulitzer Prize, 1940; Columbia University's Alexander Hamilton Medal, 1959; Hale Award, 1960; National Conference of Christians and Jews Brotherhood Award, 1960; Huntington Hartford Creative Award, 1962; Emerson-Thoreau Award, 1963. Litt.D.: Bowdoin College, Brunswick, Maine, 1944; University of Illinois, Urbana, 1958; Columbia University, 1960; Knox College, Galesburg, Illinois, 1966; Harvard University, 1966; Jewish Theological Seminary of America, New York, 1970; L.H.D.: Adelphi University, Garden City, New York, 1957; Mount Mary College, Milwaukee, Wisconsin, 1965; Honorary Fellow: St. John's College, 1959; Honorary M.D.: Connecticut State Medical Society, 1966. Member, American Academy of Arts and Letters. *Died 10 December 1972.*

PUBLICATIONS

Verse

> *Spring Thunder and Other Poems.* 1924.
> *7 P.M. and Other Poems.* 1926.
> *Now the Sky and Other Poems.* 1928.
> *Jonathan Gentry.* 1931.
> *A Winter Diary and Other Poems.* 1935.
> *The Last Look and Other Poems.* 1937.
> *Collected Poems 1922–1938.* 1939.
> *The Mayfield Deer,* 1941.
> *Our Lady Peace and Other War Poems.* 1942.
> *The Seven Sleepers and Other Poems.* 1944.
> *The Country Year.* 1946.
> *The Careless Clock: Poems about Children in the Family.* 1947.
> *New Poems.* 1948.
> *Humanity Unlimited: Twelve Sonnets.* 1950.
> *In That Far Land.* 1951.
> *Mortal Summer.* 1953.
> *Spring Birth and Other Poems.* 1953.
> *Selected Poems.* 1954.
> *Morning Worship.* 1960.
> *Collected and New Poems 1924–1963.* 1963.
> *The Narrative Poems.* 1964.
> *That Shining Place: New Poems.* 1969.
> *Good Morning: Last Poems.* 1973.

Plays

> *The Last Days of Lincoln* (produced 1961). 1959.

Never, Never Ask His Name (produced 1965).   In *Three Plays*, 1966.
Three Plays (includes *Never, Never Ask His Name, A Little Night Music, The Weekend That Was*).   1966.

Fiction

The Transients.   1935.
Windless Cabins.   1940.
Tilda.   1943.
The Short Stories.   1950.
The Witch of Ramoth and Other Tales.   1950.
Nobody Says a Word and Other Stories.   1953.
Home with Hazel.   1957.
Collected Stories.   3 vols., 1962–68.

Other

Henry David Thoreau: A Critical Study.   1916.
The Poetry of John Dryden.   1920; revised edition, 1931; as *John Dryden: A Study of His Poetry*, 1946.
American and British Literature since 1890, with Carl Van Doren.   1925; revised edition, 1939.
Edwin Arlington Robinson.   1927.
Dick and Tom: Tales of Two Ponies (juvenile).   1931.
Dick and Tom in Town (juvenile).   1932.
Shakespeare.   1939.
Studies in Metaphysical Poetry: Two Essays and a Bibliography, with Theodore Spencer.   1939.
The Transparent Tree (juvenile).   1940.
Invitation to Learning, with Huntington Cairns and Allen Tate.   1941.
The New Invitation to Learning.   1942.
The Private Reader: Selected Articles and Reviews.   1942.
Liberal Education.   1943.
The Noble Voice: A Study of Ten Great Poems.   1946; as *Great Poems of Western Literature*, 1966.
Nathaniel Hawthorne.   1949.
Introduction to Poetry.   1951.
Don Quixote's Profession.   1958.
The Autobiography.   1958.
The Happy Critic and Other Essays.   1961.
The Dialogues of Archibald MacLeish and Van Doren, edited by Warren V. Busch.   1964.
In the Beginning, Love: Dialogues on the Bible, with Maurice Samuel, edited by Edith Samuel.   1973.
The Book of Praise: Dialogues on the Psalms, with Maurice Samuel, edited by Edith Samuel.   1975.

Editor, *Samuel Sewall's Diary.*   1927.
Editor, *A History of the Life and Death, Virtues and Exploits of General George Washington*, by Mason Locke Weems.   1927.
Editor, *An Anthology of World Poetry.*   1928; selection, as *An Anthology of English and American Poetry*, 1936.

Editor, *The Travels of William Bartram.* 1928.

Editor, *Nick of the Woods; or, The Jibbenainosay: A Tale of Kentucky,* by Robert Montgomery Bird. 1928.

Editor, *A Journey to the Land of Eden and Other Papers,* by William Byrd. 1928.

Editor, *An Autobiography of America.* 1929.

Editor, *Correspondence of Aaron Burr and His Daughter Theodosia.* 1929.

Editor, with Garibaldi M. Lapolla, *A Junior Anthology of World Poetry.* 1929.

Editor, *The Life of Sir William Phips,* by Cotton Mather. 1929.

Editor, with Garibaldi M. Lapolla, *The World's Best Poems.* 1932.

Editor, *American Poets, 1630–1930.* 1932; as *Masterpieces of American Poets,* 1936.

Editor, *The Oxford Book of American Prose.* 1932.

Editor, with John W. Cunliffe and Karl Young, *Century Readings in English Literature,* 5th edition. 1940.

Editor, *A Listener's Guide to Invitation to Learning, 1940–41, 1941–42.* 2 vols., 1940–42.

Editor, *The Night of the Summer Solstice and Other Stories of the Russian War.* 1943.

Editor, *Walt Whitman.* 1945.

Editor, *The Portable Emerson.* 1946.

Editor, *Selected Poetry,* by William Wordsworth. 1950.

Editor, *Introduction to Poetry.* 1951; as *Enjoying Poetry,* 1951.

Editor, with others, *Riverside Poetry: 48 New Poems by 27 Poets.* 1956.

Editor, *100 Poems.* 1967.

*   *   *

Mark Van Doren's poetry, which consists of over a thousand poems in *Collected and New Poems* and other volumes, including a posthumous collection, *Good Morning,* constitutes one of the more prolific and accomplished bodies of work by an American poet in the 20th century. While the sheer bulk has often astonished and sometimes dismayed critics, it represents, as Richard Howard has observed, "not so much an embarrassment as an embodiment of riches."

Van Doren was originally hailed by T. S. Eliot and others as a master of rural verse and conveniently placed in the tradition of Robert Frost. He soon demonstrated, however, a distinctive voice that deepened through a sustained middle period culminating in his first *Collected Poems* (1939) and which grew in variety of subject matter and range for over three more decades after he received the Pulitzer Prize in 1940. Influenced by John Dryden as a young scholar, Van Doren belongs in a group that might include Hardy, early Yeats, Graves and, in specifically American ways, Emily Dickinson, Edwin Arlington Robinson, and Frost. Allen Tate once wisely concluded, after also suggesting "a trace of William Browne (epigrams and *Britannia's Pastorals,* 1613), traces of Ben Jonson, more than a trace of Robert Herrick" that all of them might "add up to Mark Van Doren who is like nobody else."

Singularly devoid of the common French influences in modern verse, Van Doren also eschewed confessional or analytic tendencies. He treated his principal subjects, the cosmos, love, finality, family matters, and particularly children, animals, paradox, and knowledge in a lucid manner that transcends simplistic notions of modernity and personal sensibilities. There is a passionate intelligence lurking behind many of the poems that somehow never intrudes. Indeed, it is a subtle presence that calls forth different interpretations on subsequent readings, though there is never intentional obscurity.

His poetic corpus, apart from substantial accomplishments in other literary fields, contains an intricate world of pleasures, observations, and intellectual insights. As a master craftsman,

Van Doren would make an excellent case study for the continuity of English lyric and narrative verse. He also personifies a humanistic and metaphysical approach that is American at its core, a kind of Emersonian individualism with contemporary concerns. Taken together, his work over a half-century illustrates the American literary presence at its best with a poetry that, as one critic observed, never having been in fashion, will never go out of fashion.

—William Claire

VAUGHAN, Henry. Welsh. Born in Newton-by-Usk, Llansaintfraed, Brecknockshire, 17 April 1622. Privately educated at Llangattock, 1632–38, then at Jesus College, Oxford, matriculated 1638, left without taking a degree; studied law in London, then medicine, and qualified as a physician. Served in Colonel Price's Royalist Company, as a surgeon, 1645. Married 1) Catherine Wise c. 1646 (died, 1653), three daughters and one son; 2) his first wife's sister Elizabeth Wise c. 1655, three daughters and one son. Practised medicine in Brecknock. 1645–50, and in Newton-by-Usk, 1650 until the end of his life. *Died 23 April 1695.*

PUBLICATIONS

Collections

Works, edited by L. C. Martin. 2 vols., 1914; revised edition, 1957.
Complete Poems, edited by Alan Rudman. 1976.

Verse

Poems, with the Tenth Satire of Juvenal Englished. 1646.
Silex Scintillans; or, Sacred Poems and Private Ejaculations. 1650; revised edition, 1655.
Olor Iscanus: A Collection of Some Select Poems and Translations. 1651.
Thalia Rediviva: The Pass-Times and Diversions of a Country-Muse, in Choice Poems on Several Occasions, with Some Learned Remains. 1678.

Other

The Mount of Olives; or, Solitary Devotions. 1652.

Editor, *Flores Solitudinis: Certain Rare and Elegant Pieces Collected in His Sickness and Retirement.* 1654.

Translator, *Hermetical Physic,* by Henry Nolle. 1655.

Bibliography: *A Comprehensive Bibliography of Vaughan* by E. L. Marilla, 1948, *Supplement* by Marilla and James D. Simmonds, 1963.

Reading List: *Vaughan: A Life and Interpretation* by F. E. Hutchinson, 1947; *Vaughan* by E. W. Williamson, 1953; *Vaughan: Experience and Tradition*, 1959, and *The Unprofitable Servant in Vaughan*, 1963, both by Ross Garner; *Of Paradise and Light: A Study of Vaughan's Silex Scintillans* by E. C. Pettet, 1960; *Three Metaphysical Poets* by Margaret Willy, 1961; *On the Mystical Poetry of Vaughan*, 1962, and *Masques of God: Form and Theme in the Poetry of Vaughan*, 1972, both by R. A. Durr; *The Paradise Within: Studies in Vaughan, Traherne, and Milton* by Louis J. Martz, 1964.

*   *   *

Henry Vaughan's phrase about one who "sees Invisibles" epitomizes his own mystical insight and exaltation. In all his mature work the influence of George Herbert, in subject, spirit, and even language, is pervasive and profound. Yet Vaughan is no mere imitator of the man he acknowledged as master in his poetry and religious life alike. Lacking Herbert's sense of form and verbal economy, Vaughan at his best soars to a lyrical rapture which is distinctively his own.

On all his books after the first, Vaughan inscribes himself with the title of "Silurist" — a reference to the ancient tribe of Silures which had once inhabited the south-eastern district of his native Wales. His early verse is not remarkable, consisting mainly of derivative love-songs in the manner of contemporaries like Donne. Throughout the 1650's he was publishing various prose translations and contemplative works. His volume *Thalia Rediviva*, sub-titled "The Pastimes and Diversions of a Countrey-Muse," includes an "Elegiac Eclogue" between two shepherds, possibly written for the death in 1648 of his younger brother William, and afterwards adapted for that, in 1666, of Thomas his twin.

According to a mutual friend, Henry and Thomas Vaughan resembled each other as closely in spirit as in body: "Not only your *faces*, but your *wits* are *Twins*." Both brothers were keenly interested in the art of alchemy, and published translations and prose treatises on Hermeticism. The traditions of this occult philosophy, which attracted other seventeenth-century writers like Donne and Sir Thomas Browne, furnished Henry Vaughan with various apt and fruitful analogies for his poems.

It is, however, essentially as a Christian poet that Vaughan seeks to communicate his apprehensions of spiritual reality. In his greatest work, *Silex Scintillans*, two contrasting themes are clearly defined. One is a desolating sense of alienation from God, caused by man's "black self-wil" and "hard, stonie heart." A prisoner in "sad captivity" on earth, the exiled spirit yearns for its true home, now "so far/That he hath quite forgot how to go there." Although disgusted with "impure, rebellious clay" and the "dark Confusions" it houses, Vaughan does not regard material substance as intrinsically evil. Otherwise he could not have expressed that frank and lyrical delight in nature which forms the other main theme of *Silex Scintillans*.

The mounting, exultant surge of praise in "The Morning Watch" expresses the central idea of prayer as "the world in tune." In many other poems Vaughan sees the wonders of creation as the outward proof and pledge of God's power and love, actively proclaiming that Presence which animates and illumines it. For him the visible, finite beauties of cloud and flower, "purling Corn," "primros'd" spring path, and the snow that "*Candies* our Countries wooddy brow," which he celebrates with such delicate precision and felicity of phrase, are divinely infused embodiments of invisible and infinite Beauty which show man "heaven … and point him the way home." God's "wondrous Method" in ordering the universe is echoed in man's spiritual processes. One of Vaughan's favourite images for the soul is that of a flower or plant: shaken by the storms of sin, thirsting for dew and aspiring upwards "as flow'rs do to the Sun"; or sensing, like the child in "The Retreate," "through all this fleshly dresse/Bright *shootes* of everlastingnesse."

It is, Vaughan believes, in that "first, happy age;/An age without distast and warrs," before the spirit is separated from its source or has "walkt above/A mile, or two, from its first love," that man is nearest the state of his primal innocence. He laments that, distracted by the world's insistent claims and clamour, "I find my selfe the lesse, the more I grow." In poems like "Childe-hood," "Looking Back," and "The Retreate" – the most perfect and poignant expression of that regret – he yearns no less passionately than Wordsworth in the Immortality Ode to regain the lost clarity and purity of vision which were his when he "Shin'd in [his] Angell-infancy."

The verb is characteristic. Images of light irradiate Vaughan's most memorable poems as symbols of spiritual illumination. "The World," with its famous opening,

> I saw Eternity the other night
> Like a great *Ring* of pure and endless light,
>   All calm, as it was bright,

opposes the light of God to the darkness of mundane preoccupations. God's "deep, but dazling darkness," in "The Night," is matched in "They are all gone into the world of light!" by the metaphor of death as "the Jewel of the Just,/Shining nowhere, but in the dark," and sight of the dead walking "in an Air of glory,/Whose light doth trample on my days." Many lesser-known poems, too, make light synonymous with man's experience of God, whose "beams, and brightnes" are invoked to

> brush me with thy light, that I
> May shine unto a perfect day....
> Rove in that mighty, and eternall light
>   Where no rude shade, or night
> Shall dare approach us.

Vaughan is, however, a disconcertingly uneven writer. Too many of his poems are as trite and commonplace in sentiment and expression as the average hymn; and his capacity to sustain a single poem at a consistently satisfying level is comparatively rare. Yet where he does (to adapt his title image) strike sparks from the flint, the illumination is unforgettable. These isolated splendours which haunt the inward ear, as much as the impact of such unified and wholly realized poems as "Man," "The Retreate," and "The Morning Watch," assure Vaughan his permanence among the English religious poets.

—Margaret Willy

VAUX, Thomas; 2nd Baron Vaux of Harrowden. English. Born in Harrowden, Northamptonshire, in 1510; eldest son of the first Baron Vaux; succeeded to the barony, 1523. Educated at Cambridge University. Married Elizabeth Cheney; two sons and two daughters. Served with Cardinal Wolsey in France, 1527, and with Henry VIII, in Calais and Boulogne, 1532; attended the House of Lords, 1530–55; Captain of the Isle of Jersey until 1536. Knight of the Bath, 1533. *Died in October 1556.*

PUBLICATIONS

Collections

Poems, edited by Larry P. Vonalt.   1960.

*   *   *

Thomas, Lord Vaux, is of the period of Wyatt and Surrey, and is a good example of the "courtly maker" of the day. Though only fifteen poems definitely ascribed to him have survived, Vaux has enjoyed a considerable posthumous reputation. His work appeared in the most popular Elizabethan anthologies, two poems in Tottel's *Miscellany*, the rest in *The Paradise of Dainty Devices*. Many were set to music; two had the additional exposure of the stage, most notably "The Aged Lover Renounceth Love," three muddled stanzas of which are sung by the gravedigger in *Hamlet*. Praised by Puttenham in 1586 for "the facillitie of his meetre" and the precision of his style, Vaux has held the respect of critics for his simplicity, polish, and evident religious sincerity. In 1939 Yvor Winters claimed Vaux as "a distinguished representative" of the native plain style, and in that guise he has experienced a mild but durable revival over the past several decades.

Vaux wrote on amatory and penitential subjects. Despite an occasional fine line or image – e.g., "Like as the hart that lifteth up his ears/To hear the hound ..." or "The days be long that hang upon desert" – some of his love poems fail to cohere under the burden of the miscellaneous conceits with which they are adorned. Others are successfully held together by clever chains of imagery or are redeemed by elegance and wit. The mysterious obscurity of three poems on false blame hints of a particularity unusual in Vaux, but a particularity that rather cripples than invigorates their emotional power. In "The Assault of Cupid" Vaux turns to the richer vein of medieval love allegory, creating something of a spoof by substituting for the stately interplay of abstractions a spirited account of modern warfare, complete with pikemen and guns that fill the air with smoke.

A different medieval flavor distinguishes "The Aged Lover," which not only details the usual reminders of death but also confronts, as in a mirror, the poet's aging self: gray hair, bald pate, wrinkles, cough, bent spine, and failing poetic inspiration. To this harrowing meditation on the passage of time Vaux adds his favorite moral theme of guilt and repentance for past and not yet relinquished follies. But he is not always unremittingly sober in the moral poems. "Of a Contented Mind," for example, elaborates a bitter Stoic thought, only to conclude with a wink, "I can be well content/The sweetest time of all my life to deem in thinking spent."

A master of technique, Vaux expressed that mastery by working within the confines of conventional themes and genres. In his poems one never hears a distinct voice, such as that of Wyatt, chafing against traditional values and responses; rather, Vaux offers the impersonal, classic voice of the tradition itself, in its pure, controlled, and full expression.

—William E. Sheidley

VERY, Jones.   American.   Born in Salem, Massachusetts, 28 August 1813; spent much of his childhood at sea with his father, a ship's captain. Educated at Fisk Latin School, Salem, 1832–34; Harvard University, Cambridge, Massachusetts, 1834–36 (Junior and Senior Bowdoin Prize), A.B. 1836; Tutor in Greek at the university and entered the Harvard Divinity School, 1836; forced to resign because of erratic behavior caused by his mystical experiences, 1838. Spent a month in McLean Asylum, Somerville, Massachusetts, 1838;

enjoyed the patronage of Emerson, 1838–c. 1840; licensed to preach by the Cambridge Association of Ministers, 1843: held temporary pastorates in Eastport, Maine, and North Beverly, Massachusetts; returned to Salem, 1848, and thereafter lived a retired life with his sisters. *Died 8 May 1880.*

PUBLICATIONS

Collections

Selected Poems, edited by Nathan Lyons.   1966.

Other

Essays and Poems.   1839; revised edition, edited by James Freeman Clarke, as *Poems and Essays,* 1886; edited by Kenneth W. Cameron, as *Poems,* 1965.

Reading List: *Very: Emerson's "Brave Saint"* by William Irving Bartlett, 1942 (includes bibliography); *Very: The Effective Years 1833–1840* by Edwin Gittleman, 1967.

*   *   *

A curious example of single-minded Quietism, Jones Very occupies a special place in 19th-century American poetry. He wrote over 700 poems, most of these produced between 1833 and 1840 – the tumultuous years in which Very resolved his youthful religious doubts and reconciled himself to the eccentricities of his dominating mother and the loss of his sea-captain father. Dramatically realizing the Transcendentalist equation of self-reliance with God-reliance, Very experienced a transfiguring conversion in which he attained a second birth through the agency of the Holy Spirit. True, most of these poems tend to be repetitive, conventional in thought and expression, tedious, oblivious to drama, the play of language, humor, or the ambiguities of human experience. In his best poems, however, Very's voice can be as piercing as a knife-blade. Writing from the perspective of one who knows himself to be the passive instrument of a Higher Will, Very triumphs in lean enunciations of Being rather than explorations of Becoming. Characteristically using mild variations on the form of the Shakespearian sonnet and deeply imbued with the diction and syntax of the Bible, his utterance sometimes rises above its own awkwardness and penchant for bland abstractions to achieve an intense purity of religious awareness. Even though his successful poems are overly dependent on the Christian paradox of total submission as a condition of total fulfillment, the results are unsentimental and wholly persuasive.

His "nature poetry" and his literary essays could perhaps have been written by any gifted young man swept up in the enthusiasm of Channing's Unitarianism and Emerson's *Nature.* But some dozen or so meditational sonnets (e.g., "The Hand and Foot," "The Absent," "Morning," "The Presence," "The Journey," "The Eagles") succeed in translating literally the Transcendentalist exhortations to discover an inner divinity into spiritual declarations of considerable power. At first extravagantly praised by Emerson, Alcott, Margaret Fuller, and Elizabeth Peabody, Very became something of an embarrassment due to the fanatic rigidity with which he judged all deviations from his way to salvation as well as the monochromatic mediocrity of much of his verse. From 1843 until his death, his literary production was almost entirely restricted to not particularly distinguished sermons.

—Earl Rovit

WALCOTT, Derek (Alton). Jamaican. Born in Castries, St. Lucia, West Indies, 23 January 1930. Educated at St. Mary's College, St. Lucia; University of the West Indies, Kingston, Jamaica, B.A. 1953. Married; three children. Taught at St. Mary's College and Jamaica College. Formerly, Feature Writer, *Public Opinion*, Kingston, and *Trinidad Guardian*, Port-of-Spain. Since 1959, Founding Director, Trinidad Theatre Workshop. Recipient: Rockefeller Fellowship, for drama, 1957; Guinness Award, 1961; Heinemann Award, 1966; Cholmondeley Award, 1969; Order of the Humming Bird, Trinidad and Tobago, 1969; Obie Award, for drama, 1971. Lives in Trinidad.

PUBLICATIONS

Verse

    Twenty-Five Poems. 1948.
    Epitaph for the Young. 1949.
    Poems. 1953.
    In a Green Night: Poems 1948–1960. 1962.
    Selected Poems. 1964.
    The Castaway and Other Poems. 1965.
    The Gulf and Other Poems. 1969.
    Another Life. 1973.
    Sea Grapes. 1976.
    Selected Poems, edited by O. R. Dathorne. 1977.

Plays

    Henri Christophe: A Chronicle (produced 1950). 1950
    Henri Dernier: A Play for Radio Production. 1951.
    Sea at Dauphin (produced 1954). 1954.
    Ione: A Play with Music (produced 1957). 1954.
    Drums and Colours (produced 1958). In *Caribbean Quarterly 1* and *2*, 1961.
    Ti-Jean and His Brothers, music by André Tanker (produced 1958). In *The Dream on Monkey Mountain and Others Plays*, 1971.
    Malcochon; or, Six in the Rain (produced 1959). In *The Dream on Monkey Mountain and Other Plays*, 1971.
    The Dream on Monkey Mountain (produced 1967). In *The Dream on Monkey Mountain and Other Plays*, 1971.
    In a Fine Castle (produced 1970).
    The Dream on Monkey Mountain and Other Plays (includes *Ti-Jean and His Brothers, Malcochon, Sea at Dauphin*, and the essay "What the Twilight Says"). 1971.
    The Charlatan, music by Galt MacDermot (produced 1974).
    The Joker of Seville, and O Babylon! 1978.

Reading List: *Walcott: "Another Life"* by Edward Baugh, 1978.

*   *   *

    The first and simplest pleasure offered by Derek Walcott's poetry is the sense of being alive and out-of-doors in the West Indies: sand and salt on the skin, sunlight and space and the open beach, sea-grapes and sea-almonds, liners and islands, where always "The starved eye devours the seascape for the morsel of a sail,/The horizon threads it infinitely."

Walcott was a painter before he was a poet, and as a youth set off with a friend around his native island of Santa Lucia to put it on canvas and thus create it in the imagination. Later he found he could do the work of creation better with words and metaphor, and that this too was needed:

> For no-one had yet written of this landscape
> that it was possible, though there were sounds
> given to its varieties of wood.

Walcott has kept his painter's eye, and is especially aware of effects of light. He often compares life with art ("Tables in the trees, like entering Renoir"), as indeed he often quotes or echoes lines from the English Metaphysicals, Tennyson, Eliot, Dylan Thomas, and others. These things, taken together with the high polish of his verse, have sometimes led to accusations of virtuoso artificiality and preciosity. But, though there may be some lapses which deserve such strictures, it is precisely the successful transmuting of life into art which makes Walcott's achievement so important.

At his best he fuses the outward scene with inward experience and with a form of English words, resonant within the tradition of literature in English but also appropriate to the particular occasion, all in one single act of perception. In so doing he enhances and illustrates (in the Renaissance sense of that word) the landscape and the human lives that are found on the islands. It is not surprising, perhaps, that he should be such a good love poet, for the experience of love has this same quality of enhancing places: "But islands can only exist/If we have loved in them."

Love, the creation of a centre of consciousness, and a relationship of security with the place one lives are particularly important in societies where a history of slavery, cultural deprivation, colonial dependency, and, latterly, tourism have combined to reinforce the more generalized modern feelings of alienation and contingency. Walcott's work may therefore be quite as socially important as that of more obsessively socially-orientated West Indian writers.

Walcott by no means ignores the well-known dilemmas of the West Indian situation. In "Ruins of a Great House" he works out in a complex fashion his relationship with men like Ralegh, "ancestral murderers and poets," with England and the English language, and with the earlier history of a ruined plantation house. Here and elsewhere he is aware that he has one white grandfather, who like many others "drunkenly seeded their archipelago." When the Mau Mau insurrection in Kenya occurs, he cannot give murderers on either side his blessing though "poisoned with the blood of both," and when he sees television film of the Biafran war he notes "The soldiers' helmeted shadows could have been white." In general his aim seems to be not to make rhetoric out of the past, but to transcend it: "All in compassion ends/So differently from what the heart arranged."

Walcott is also a successful and prolific playwright, the founder-director of the Trinidad Theatre Workshop, a travelling group of players who move around the Caribbean. Whereas the poetry is almost entirely in standard English, the plays are largely in the creole idiom of the West Indies. A further linguistic complication is that the popular language of Walcott's home island is a Creole French (as on Jean Rhys's home island of Dominica) and the French phrases and songs of the islands also find their way in quotation, and, with their special intonations, into his work.

In his best-known play, *Dream on Monkey Mountain*, Makak the charcoal-burner lives in utter degradation, dreams he is king of a united Africa, yet has to go on living in the everyday world. "The problem," Walcott said in an interview (*New Yorker*, 26 June 1971), "is to recognize our African origins but not to romanticize them." Generally, one feels that Walcott has little sympathy for exploitation of the past by modern ideologists, even if they are negro ideologists, and some of his bitterest lines are reserved for post-independence politicians.

Against their power and rhetoric he sets out on a subtler and more revolutionary course:

> I sought more power than you, more fame than yours,
> I was more hermetic, I knew the commonweal,
> I pretended subtly to lose myself in crowds
> knowing my passage would alter their reflection

and at the same time to redeem the past

> Its racial quarrels blown like smoke to sea.
> From all that sorrow, beauty is our gain
> Though it may not seem so
> To an old fisherman rowing home in the rain.

—Ned Thomas

WALLER, Edmund.   English.   Born in Coleshill, Hertfordshire, now Buckinghamshire, 3 March 1606. Educated at Eton College; King's College, Cambridge, matriculated 1620, may have left without taking a degree; admitted member of Lincoln's Inn, London, 1622. Married 1) Anne Banks in 1631 (died, 1634); 2) Mary Bracey in 1644 (died, 1677). Wealthy landowner: inherited large estate at Beaconsfield, Buckinghamshire, 1616. Served in Parliament: Member for Amersham, 1621, Ilchester, 1624, Chipping Wycombe, 1626, and Amersham, 1628–29, and St. Ives, in the Long Parliament, 1640; defended episcopacy, and conducted the impeachment of Sir Francis Crawley, 1641; opposed raising of troops by Parliament, 1642; appointed commissioner to treat with Charles I at Oxford, 1643; involved in an attempt to seize the City of London for Charles ("Waller's Plot"), 1643: expelled from Parliament, 1643, imprisoned in the Tower of London, 1643–44, then banished from the country; lived in France, 1644 until the banishment was revoked by the House of Commons, 1651; returned to England, appointed a commissioner of trade, 1655; elected to Parliament as Member for Hastings, 1661, and sat in the House of Commons until his death. Member of the Royal Society, 1661. *Died 21 October 1687.*

PUBLICATIONS

Collections

Works in Verse and Prose, edited by E. Fenton.   1729.
Poems, edited by G. Thorn Drury.   2 vols., 1893.

Verse

To the King's Most Excellent Majesty.   1642.
Poems.   1645; *Second Part,* 1690.
A Panegyric to My Lord Protector.   1655.

Upon the Late Storm, and the Death of His Highness.   1658.
The Passion of Dido for Aeneas, with Sidney Godolphin.   1658.
To the King, upon His Majesty's Happy Return.   1660.
To My Lady Morton.   1661.
A Poem on St. James's Park.   1661.
To the Queen, upon Her Majesty's Birthday.   1663.
Instructions to a Painter.   1666.
Of the Lady Mary.   1677.
A Poem on the Present Assembling.   1679.
A Poem upon the Present Assembly of Parliament.   1685.
Divine Poems.   1685.

Plays

Pompey the Great, with others, from a play by Corneille (produced 1664).   1664.
The New Masque for The Maid's Tragedy by Beaumont and Fletcher.   1683(?).
The Maid's Tragedy, from the play by Beaumont and Fletcher (produced 1689).   In
Poems, 1690.

Other

The Works of Waller in This Parliament.   1644.
The Life and Death of William Laud.   1645.

Reading List: *Towards an Augustan Poetic: Waller's "Reform" of English Poetry* by A. W.
Allison, 1962; *The Poetry of Limitation: A Study of Waller* by W. L. Cherniak, 1968.

*   *   *

To the generation of poets that succeeded him, Edmund Waller appeared one of the most
important writers of the seventeenth century. Dryden, in his preface to Walsh's *Dialogue
Concerning Women,* 1691, even said that if Waller had not written "none of us could write."
Although Waller also anticipated the Augustan age in attitudes and diction, it was primarily
his versification that made him so important an influence on Dryden and later on Pope. It was
Waller who, together with Denham, first made conspicuous and extensive use of a balanced,
end-stopped couplet, discarding the slackly-rhymed enjambed couplet, often metrically
rough, favoured in the early part of the century. He makes frequent use of parallel or
antithetical phrases: "A prince with such advantages as these,/Where he persuades not, may
command a peace"; "The valiant Duke! whose early deeds abroad/Such rage in fight and art
in conduct showed./His bright sword now a dearer interest draws,/His brother's glory and
his country's cause." Syntactical patterning is also achieved by inversion: "Light was the
wound, the prince's care unknown." Diction is abstract, Latinate and elevated – where
Donne had said "Till age snow white hairs on thee," Waller speaks of "the violation/Of
coming years." Epithets are appropriate, not startling. The result is poetry essentially
civilised, showing manners, order, control. It is better suited to public occasions than to
intimate exchanges, and Waller employed it frequently in celebrating public events. The
blandness of his style extended to his matter: though his successors were to use his shapely
couplet for satiric purposes, Waller himself devoted it to heroic panegyric. As times changed,
his subject-matter changed; praise of Cromwell was succeeded by praise of Charles II; the
tone and style, however, remained constant.

Yet the poems that influenced the Augustans are not those which have survived. Greater masters of the couplet followed and eclipsed his achievements in versification, and Waller is now remembered mainly as the author of the exquisite lyric, "Go, lovely rose." Even here, where his subject-matter was most Caroline, we find him using effects that Pope was later to adopt and transform, for "Tell her that wastes her time and me" gains its poignancy from the zeugma which replaces the expected "her time and mine," so drawing attention to the double meaning of "waste." Other lyrics derived from the Caroline tradition have retained their power: "On a girdle," "To a very young lady," and "It is not that I love you less." "Of the last verse in the book," which Waller wrote in his eighties, treats of old age and approaching death with a grave dignity quite unlike the graceful playfulness of the earlier lyrics. The theme is summarised in its most famous couplet: "The soul's dark cottage, battered and decayed,/Lets in new light through chinks that time has made." Augustan in its powerful generalisations, impressive in its dignified serenity, Waller's last poem shows a life not conspicuous for nobility attaining a noble close.

—Margaret Forey

WALSH, William. English. Born in Abberley, Worcestershire, in 1663, and lived on the family estate there for all of his life. Educated at Wadham College, Oxford, matriculated 1678, but did not take a degree. Whig Member of Parliament for Worcestershire, 1698, 1701, 1702, and for Richmond, Yorkshire, 1705–08; Gentleman of the Horse in Queen Anne's household; a friend and literary adviser of Alexander Pope. Died 18 March 1708.

PUBLICATIONS

Collections

Works in Prose and Verse.   1736.

Verse

Letters and Poems Amorous and Gallant.   1692.
A Funeral Elegy upon the Death of the Queen.   1695.
Ode for the Thanksgiving Day.   1706.

Play

Squire Trelooby, with Congreve and Vanbrugh, from a play by Molière (produced 1704).   Revised version by James Ralph published as *The Cornish Squire,* 1734.

Other

A Dialogue Concerning Women, Being a Defence of the Sex.   1691.

Reading List: articles by Phyllis Freeman, in *Bodleian Quarterly Review*, 1934, and *Review of English Studies*, 1948, 1957.

*   *   *

William Walsh was a late member of that seventeenth-century "mob of gentlemen who wrote with ease." He had the reputation among his contemporaries of an amiable beau; and the bulk of his verse consists of light, pretty, but languid amatory verses, written in a variety of lyrical forms, including – a relatively uncommon one in his day– the sonnet. A collection of these verses together with some elaborately gallant love-letters published in 1692 (*Letters and Poems, Amorous and Gallant*) carried a preface in which Walsh condemns Petrarchan conceits and Donne-like wit, praises controlled and precise workmanship, and argues for propriety, good sense, and elegance. This preface treats of pastoral, too, where Walsh accepts the neo-classical view that pastoral must represent a golden age of truth, sincerity and innocence. His own four pastoral eclogues and his pastoral elegy "Delia," to the memory of Mrs. Tempest, are wholly conventional.

Walsh's political verse shows more vigour. As a zealous Whig he was provoked by some violently Jacobite Messianic poems hailing Queen Anne's accession to write, in his "The Golden Age Restor'd" (1703), a neat, ironic, insolently urbane satire upon the Tories, in which, like some of the poets he attacks, he takes Virgil's fourth eclogue as his model. His imitation of Horace Book III, Ode iii (1705) adapts Horace's vision of Roman greatness to praise the memory of William III.

Walsh, Congreve, and Vanbrugh each wrote one act of a farce adapted from Molière's *Monsieur de Pourceaugnac* under the title *Squire Trelooby*, acted in 1704, of which the text is now lost (but see *Philological Quarterly*, 1968, pp. 145–56). A poem "In Defence of Painting" where Walsh claims that art and reason must compensate for the defects of nature was sent to Dryden in 1686 but not published until 1951 (see *Modern Language Notes*, pp. 518–23). Dryden befriended Walsh, contributed a preface to his prose *Dialogue Concerning Women, Being a Defence of the Sex* and, in his own postscript to the translation of Virgil (1697), declared that Walsh was "without Flattery ... the best critic of our Nation"; but there is hardly enough in the surviving letters and other writings (whether or not one includes the Preface to the Pastorals in Dryden's Virgil which has sometimes been attributed to Walsh) to justify such a high estimate. However, Pope submitted his own juvenile pastorals to Walsh for correction, adopted some of Walsh's notions in his "Discourse on Pastoral Poetry," probably conceived the *Essay on Criticism* under Walsh's influence, and certainly ends that poem with high praise of Walsh as "the Muse's Judge and Friend." It was Walsh who asked Pope to make "correctness" his study and aim. Johnson's judgement remains true, that Walsh "is known more by his familiarity with greater men, than by anything done or written by himself."

—A. J. Sambrook

WARD, Ned (Edward Ward). English. Born in Oxfordshire in 1667. Married; one daughter. In early life visited the West Indies; afterwards a publican in Moorfields, London; moved to Fulwood's Rents, where he kept a punch shop and tavern, possibly the King's Head, next door to Gray's Inn, 1699–1731; also a journalist: edited *The Weekly Comedy*, 1699; *The Infallible Astrologer*, with Tom Brown, 1700–01; and *The London Terraefilius*, 1707–08. Pilloried for attacks on the government, 1705. *Died 20 June 1731.*

Verse

The Poet's Ramble after Riches; or, A Night's Transactions upon the Road
    Burlesqued. 1691.
The Miracles Performed by Money. 1692.
Sot's Paradise; or, The Humours of a Derby Ale-House, with a Satire upon the
    Ale. 1698.
Ecclesia et Factio: A Dialogue Between Bow-Steeple Dragon and the Exchange
    Grasshopper. 1698.
O Raree-Show, O Pretty-Show; or, The City Feast. 1698.
The Insinuating Bawd and the Repenting Harlot. 1699.
The Cockpit Combat; or, The Baiting of the Tiger. 1699.
A Walk to Islington, with a Description of the New Tunbridge Wells and Sadler's Music
    House. 1699.
The Wealthy Shop-Keeper; or, The Charitable Citizen. 1700; revised edition, as The
    Character of a Covetous Citizen, 1702.
A Journey to Hell; or, A Visit Paid to the Devil. 3 vols., 1700–05; as The Infernal Vision,
    n.d.
Bribery and Simony; or, A Satire upon the Corrupt Use of Money. 1703.
All Men Mad; or, England a Great Bedlam. 1704.
The Dissenting Hypocrite or Occasional Conformist. 1704.
Helter Skelter; or, The Devil upon Two Sticks. 1704.
The Libertine's Choice; or, The Mistaken Happiness of the Fool in Fashion. 1704.
Honesty in Distress, But Relieved by No Party. 1705.
A Satire Against Wine, with a Poem in Praise of Small Beer. 1705.
A Trip to Germany; or, The Poet Turned Carbineer. 1705.
The Rambling Fuddle-Caps; or, A Tavern Struggle for a Kiss. 1706.
Hudibras Redivivus; or, A Burlesque Poem on the Times. 2 vols., 1707.
Marriage Dialogues; or, A Poetical Peep into the State of Matrimony. 1708; as
    Matrimony Unmasked, 1710; revised edition, as Nuptial Dialogues and Debates, 1723.
The Modern World Disrobed; or, Both Sexes Stript of Their Pretended Virtue (prose and
    verse). 1708; as Adam and Eve Stripped of Their Furbelows, 1710.
The Forgiving Husband and Adultress Wife; or, A Seasonable Present to the Unhappy
    Pair in Fenchurch-Street. 1709.
Vulgus Britannicus; or, The British Hudibras. 1710.
Don Quixote Translated into Hudibrastic Verse. 2 vols., 1711–12.
The Poetical Entertainer; or, Tales, Satires, Dialogues, etc., Serious and Comical. 5
    vols., 1712.
The Quack Vintners; or, A Satire upon Bad Wine. 1712.
The History of the Grand Rebellion. 3 vols., 1713–15.
The Field Spy; or, The Walking Observator. 1714.
The Mourning Prophet; or, Faction Revived by the Death of Queen Anne. 1714.
The Hudibrastic Brewer; or, A Preposterous Union Between Malt and Meter. 1714.
The Republican Procession; or, The Tumultuous Cavalcade: A Merry Poem. 1714;
    revised edition, 1714, 1727.
The Lord Whiglove's Elegy, with a Pious Epitaph upon the Late Bishop of
    Addlebury. 1715.
St. Paul's Church; or, The Protestant Ambulators. 1716.
British Wonders. 1717.
The Vanity of Upstarts. 1717.
The Delights of the Bottle; or, The Complete Vintner. 1720.

The Northern Cuckold; or, The Garden House Intrigue. 1721.

The Merry Travellers; or, A Trip upon Ten-Toes from Moorfields up to Bromley, Intended as The Wandering Spy. 1721.

The Parish Guttlers; or, The Humours of a Select Vestry. 1722.

The Wandering Spy; or, The Merry Travellers, part 2. 1722.

The Wandering Spy; or, The Merry Observator. 6 vols., 1724.

News from Madrid: The Spanish Beauty; or, The Tragi-Comical Revenge. 1726.

Apollo's Maggot in His Cups; or, The Whimsical Creation of a Little Satirical Poet: A Lyric Ode. 1729.

Durgen; or, A Plain Satire upon a Pompous Satirist. 1729; as The Cudgel; or, A Crab-Tree Lecture, 1742.

To the Right Honourable Humphrey Parsons. 1730.

Fiction and Satirical Prose

The School of Politics; or, The Humours of a Coffee-House. 1690; revised edition, 1691.

Female Policy Detected; or, The Arts of a Designing Woman Laid Open. 1695.

The London Spy. 2 vols., 1698–99; revised edition, 1703, 1704, 1706, 1753; edited by K. Fenwick, 1955.

A Trip to Jamaica; with a True Character of the People of the Island. 1698.

A Hue and Cry after a Man-Midwife. 1699.

A Frolic to the Horn-Fair with a Walk from Cuckold's Point Through Deptford and Greenwich. 1699.

Modern Religion and Ancient Loyalty: A Dialogue. 1699.

A Trip to New-England, with a Character of the Country and the People, both English and Indians. 1699.

The World Bewitched: A Dialogue Between Two Astrologers and the Author. 1699.

The Dancing School with the Adventures of the Easter Holidays. 1700.

The English Nun; or, A Comical Description of a Nunnery. 1700.

The Reformer: Exposing the Vices of the Age in Several Characters. 1700.

The Grand Mistake; or, All Men Happy If They Please. 1700(?).

Labour in Vain; or, What Signifies Little or Nothing. 1700.

Laugh and Be Fat; or, An Antidote Against Melancholy. 1700.

The Metamorphosed Beau; or, The Intrigues of Ludgate. 1700.

The Pleasures of Single Life or the Miseries of Matrimony. 1700(?).

The Rambling Rakes; or, London Libertines. 1700.

A Step to the Bath, with a Character of the Place. 1700.

A Step to Stir-Bitch-Fair, with Remarks upon the University of Cambridge. 1700.

Aesop at Paris, His Life and Letters. 1701.

Battle Without Bloodshed; or, Martial Discipline Buffooned by the City Train-Bands. 1701.

The Revels of the Gods; or, A Ramble Through the Heavens. 1701.

Three Nights Adventures or Accidental Intrigues. 1701.

The Rise and Fall of Madam Coming Sir. 1703.

The Secret History of the Calves-Head Club; or, The Republican Unmasked. 1703; revised edition, 1706; as The Whig's Unmasked, 1713.

Female Dialogues; or, Ladies' Conversations. 1704.

Fair Shell but a Rotten Kernel; or, A Bitter Nut for a Facetious Monkey. 1705.

A Comical View of London and Westminster; or, The Merry Quack, with A Legacy for the Ladies; or, Characters of the Women of the Age, by Tom Brown. 1705.

The Barbeque-Feast; or, The Three Pigs of Peckham, Broiled under an Apple-Tree. 1706.

The Wooden World Dissected in the Character of a Ship of War. 1706.
Mars Stript of His Armour; or, The Army Displayed in All Its True Colours. 1708.
The Wars of the Elements; or, A Description of a Sea Storm. 1708.
The History of the London Clubs; or, The Citizen's Pastime. 2 vols., 1709; as *The Secret History of the Clubs,* 1709; revised edition, as *A Complete and Humorous Account of All the Remarkable Clubs and Societies,* 1756.
The Tory Quaker; or, Aminadab's New Vision of the Fields. 1717.
The Dancing Devils; or, The Roaring Dragon: A Dumb Farce. 1724.
The Amorous Bugbears; or, The Humours of a Masquerade. 1725.
The Bachelor's Estimate; or, The Expenses of a Married Life. 1725.
A Fiddler's Fling at Roguery. 1730.

Other

A Collection of the Writings. 1700.
The Writings. 4 vols., 1703–09.
Five Travel Scripts Commonly Attributed to Ward, edited by H. W. Troyer. 1933.

Translator, *A Seasonable Sketch of an Oxford Reformation,* by J. Allibond. 1717.

Reading List: *Ned Ward of Grubstreet: A Study of Subliterary London in the Eighteenth Century* by H. W. Troyer, 1946 (includes bibliography).

*   *   *

Ned Ward is one of the best examples of the late Restoration journalist, attempting rather successfully to enliven literary English by incorporating colloquial idiom and vulgar imagery. He was satirical poet, prose humorist, low-life reporter, Tory propagandist. In his verse he was greatly influenced by Samuel Butler, whose manner he vulgarized in *Hudibras Redivivus,* so scurrilous in its attacks on the Whigs that it earned Ward two stands in the pillory. The quality of his verse, direct and aggressive, and the cynicism with which he wrote are both illustrated in these lines from *Hudibras Redivivus*:

> For he that writes in such an Age,
> When Parties do for Pow'r engage,
> Ought to chuse one Side for the Right,
> And then, with all his Wit and Spite,
> Blacken and Vex the Opposite.
> Scurrility's a useful Trick,
> Approv'd by the most Politic;
> Fling Dirt enough, and some will stick.

Though Ward's verse-writing led him into competition with Pope and to being satirized in *The Dunciad,* to which he replied in his own way in *Durgen* and *Apollo's Maggot in His Cups,* he is best known and most influential for his prose journalism, which at times was inventive enough to approach fiction. His best work was undoubtedly contained in the *London Spy,* a series of eighteen monthly numbers which consist mainly of reportage of London low life, pungently written, with a great deal of slang interspersed, and decorated with metaphors of startling vulgarity and vigour. Ward's personal experience was broad. He travelled widely for a man of his day, making a visit to the Caribbean, described in *Trip to Jamaica,* and another to the American colonies that gave him the material for *Trip to New England,* but he was most at home in London, where he kept a tavern for several years, watching his customers and listening to their ways of speaking. Taverns, prisons, brothels, London parks at ambiguous nightfall, all feature prominently in his descriptive reports.

There seems little doubt that – just as his later series of periodical essays, *The Humours of a Coffee-House*, not only predated but also influenced *The Tatler* – the vivid descriptions of low life in the *London Spy* helped create a style of reportage and a taste among readers for verisimilitude in describing the seamier aspects of social life, both of which Defoe later used for his own purposes in such novels as *Moll Flanders* and *Captain Singleton*. The *London Spy* is still good reading for anyone interested in low-life reportage and in the relationship between literary and colloquial writing, but Ward's importance is mainly historical – that of a vigorous pioneer in the craft of journalism and, less directly, in the development of a viable tradition of realism in fiction.

—George Woodcock

WARNER, William. English. Born in London in 1558. Educated at Magdalen Hall, Oxford; studied law. Practised as an attorney in London; a friend of Marlowe and Drayton. *Died 9 March 1609.*

PUBLICATIONS

Verse

> *Albion's England: Books 1–4.* 1586; *Books 1–6,* 1589; *Books 1–9,* 1592; *Books 1–12,* 1596; *Books 1–13,* 1602; *Books 14–16,* 1606.

Play

> *Menaechmi,* from the play by Plautus (produced 1592?). 1595; edited by Geoffrey Bullough, in *Narrative and Dramatic Sources of Shakespeare,* 1957.

Fiction

> *Pan His Syrinx or Pipe: Seven Tragical and Comical Arguments.* 1584; revised edition, as *Syrinx; or, A Sevenfold History,* 1597; edited by W. A. Bacon, 1950.

* * *

William Warner, much praised and often quoted in his own day, owed his reputation entirely to *Albion's England,* his long narrative poem of myth, history, fiction, and moral truths told in rollicking and, frequently, halting "fourteeners":

> I tell of things done long ago, of many things in few:
> And chiefly of this clyme of ours, the accidents pursue.
> Thou high director of the same, assist my artlesse pen,
> To write the gests of Bruton's stout, and actes of English men.

First published in four books (1586), the poem was augmented in several subsequent editions up to 1606, when it reached its final state of sixteen books and a prose abstract. Its last contemporary re-issue in 1612 marked not only a quarter-century of popular success against comparable verse histories (e.g., Samuel Daniel's *Civil Wars* and Michael Drayton's *Mortimeriados*) but also the end of the genre itself in an age grown philosophically skeptical and culturally and politically more sophisticated. Warner's work had appealed to the same instincts in its readership as did the immensely popular *A Mirror for Magistrates* – pride in nation, an interest in its past, and the enjoyment of a good tale. *Albion's England* first appeared only a year before the last sixteenth-century edition of *A Mirror for Magistrates*, and it was current during the surge of national pride occasioned by the defeat of the Armada – these facts seem to have been enough to insure its success throughout the century. Warner's *Pan His Syrinx* is a lengthy prose romance comprised of seven interwoven exotic tales whose style, influenced by John Lyly's *Euphues*, left no legacy. His reputation, which had been secured only by his long poem, waned as the genre of verse "history" became less central to English culture. Perhaps Drayton's kind assessment (in "To Henry Reynolds") written some years after Warner's death, remains acute:

> Then *Warner* though his lines were not so trim'd,
> Nor yet his Poem so exactly lim'd
> And neatly joynted, but the Criticke may
> Easily reproove him, yet thus let me say;
> For my old friend, some passages there be
> In him, which I protest have taken me,
> With almost wonder, so fine, cleere, and new
> As yet they have bin equalled by few.

—Frank Fabry

WARREN, John Byrne Leicester. See **de TABLEY, Lord**.

WARREN, Robert Penn. American. Born in Guthrie, Kentucky, 24 April 1905. Educated at Guthrie High School; Vanderbilt University, Nashville, Tennessee, B.A. (summa cum laude) 1925; University of California, Berkeley, M.A. 1927; Yale University, New Haven, Connecticut, 1927–28; Oxford University (Rhodes Scholar), B.Litt. 1930. Married 1) Emma Brescia in 1930 (divorced, 1950); 2) the writer Eleanor Clark in 1952, one son and one daughter. Member of the Fugitive Group of poets: Co-Founding Editor, *The Fugitive*, Nashville, 1922–25; Assistant Professor, Southwestern College, Memphis, Tennessee, 1930–31, and Vanderbilt University, 1931–34; Assistant and Associate Professor, Louisiana State University, Baton Rouge, 1934–42, and Founding Editor, *Southern Review*, Baton Rouge, 1935–42; Professor of English, University of Minnesota, Minneapolis, 1942–50; Professor of Playwriting, 1950–56, and Professor of English, 1962–73, Yale University; now Professor Emeritus. Consultant in Poetry, Library of Congress, Washington, D.C., 1944–45; Jefferson Lecturer, National Endowment for the Arts, 1974. Recipient: Caroline Sinkler

Award, 1936, 1937, 1938; Houghton Mifflin Literary Fellowship, 1939; Guggenheim Fellowship, 1939, 1947; Shelley Memorial Award, 1943; Pulitzer Prize, for fiction, 1947, for poetry, 1958; Screenwriters Guild Robert Meltzer Award, 1949; Sidney Hillman Prize, 1957; Edna St. Vincent Millay Memorial Prize, 1958; National Book Award, for poetry, 1958; Bollingen Prize, for poetry, 1967; National Endowment for the Arts grant, 1968; Henry A. Bellaman Prize, 1970; Van Wyck Brooks Award, for poetry, 1970; National Medal for Literature, 1970; Emerson-Thoreau Medal, 1975. D.Litt.: University of Louisville, Kentucky, 1949; Kenyon College, Gambier, Ohio, 1952; University of Kentucky, Lexington, 1955; Colby College, Waterville, Maine, 1956; Swarthmore College, Pennsylvania, 1958; Yale University, 1959; Fairfield University, Connecticut, 1969; Wesleyan University, Middletown, Connecticut, 1970; Harvard University, Cambridge, Massachusetts, 1973; LL.D.: University of Bridgeport, Connecticut, 1965. Member, American Academy of Arts and Letters; Chancellor, Academy of American Poets, 1972. Lives in Fairfield, Connecticut.

PUBLICATIONS

Verse

Thirty-Six Poems. 1935.
Eleven Poems on the Same Theme. 1942.
Selected Poems 1923–1943. 1944.
Brother to Dragons: A Tale in Verse and Voices. 1953.
Promises: Poems 1954–1956. 1957.
You, Emperors and Others: Poems 1957–1960. 1960.
Selected Poems: New and Old 1923–1966. 1966.
Incarnations: Poems 1966–1968. 1968.
Audubon: A Vision. 1969.
Or Else: Poem/Poems 1968–1974. 1974.
Selected Poems 1923–1975. 1977.

Plays

Proud Flesh (in verse, produced 1947; revised [prose] version, produced 1948).
All the King's Men (produced 1959). 1960.

Fiction

Night Rider. 1939.
At Heaven's Gate. 1943.
All the King's Men. 1946.
Blackberry Winter (stories). 1946.
The Circus in the Attic and Other Stories. 1947.
World Enough and Time: A Romantic Novel. 1950.
Band of Angels. 1955.
The Cave. 1959.
Wilderness: A Tale of the Civil War. 1961.
Flood: A Romance of Our Times. 1964.
Meet Me in the Green Glen. 1971.
A Place to Come To. 1977.

Other

John Brown: The Making of a Martyr.   1929.
I'll Take My Stand: The South and the Agrarian Tradition, with others.   1930.
Understanding Poetry: An Anthology for College Students, with Cleanth Brooks.   1938;
    revised edition, 1950, 1960.
Understanding Fiction, with Cleanth Brooks.   1943; revised edition, 1959.
A Poem of Pure Imagination: An Experiment in Reading, in *The Rime of the Ancient
    Mariner,* by Samuel Taylor Coleridge.   1946.
Modern Rhetoric: With Readings, with Cleanth Brooks.   1949; revised edition, 1958.
Fundamentals of Good Writing: A Handbook of Modern Rhetoric, with Cleanth
    Brooks.   1950; revised edition, 1956.
Segregation: The Inner Conflict in the South.   1956.
Remember the Alamo!   1958.
Selected Essays.   1958.
The Gods of Mount Olympus.   1959.
The Legacy of the Civil War: Meditations on the Centennial.   1961.
Who Speaks for the Negro?   1965.
A Plea in Mitigation: Modern Poetry and the End of an Era.   1966.
Homage to Theodore Dreiser.   1971.
John Greenleaf Whittier's Poetry: An Appraisal and a Selection.   1971.
A Conversation with Warren, edited by Frank Gado.   1972.
Democracy and Poetry.   1975.

Editor, with Cleanth Brooks and J. T. Purser, *An Approach to Literature: A Collection of
    Prose and Verse with Analyses and Discussions.*   1936; revised edition, 1939, 1952.
Editor, *A Southern Harvest: Short Stories by Southern Writers.*   1937.
Editor, with Cleanth Brooks, *An Anthology of Stories from the Southern Review.*   1953.
Editor, with Albert Erskine, *Short Story Masterpieces.*   1954.
Editor, with Albert Erskine, *Six Centuries of Great Poetry.*   1955.
Editor, with Albert Erskine, *A New Southern Harvest.*   1957.
Editor, with Allen Tate, *Selected Poems,* by Denis Devlin.   1963.
Editor, *Faulkner: A Collection of Critical Essays.*   1966.
Editor, with Robert Lowell and Peter Taylor, *Randall Jarrell 1914–1965.*   1967.
Editor, *Selected Poems of Herman Melville.*   1971.
Editor, with Cleanth Brooks and R. W. B. Lewis, *American Literature: The Makers and
    the Making.*   2 vols., 1974.

Bibliography: *Warren: A Bibliography* by Mary Nancy Huff, 1968.

Reading List: *Warren: The Dark and Bloody Ground* by Leonard Casper, 1960; *Warren* by
Paul West, 1964; *Warren: A Collection of Critical Essays* edited by John Lewis Longley, Jr.,
1965; *A Colder Fire: The Poetry of Warren,* 1965, and *The Poetic Vision of Warren,* 1977,
both by Victor H. Strandberg; *Web of Being: The Novels of Warren* by Barnett Guttenberg,
1975.

*   *   *

Robert Penn Warren is a distinguished American writer in at least three genres: the novel,
poetry, and the essay. Although he has lived outside the South since 1942, he has so
consistently written novels, essays, and poetry on southern subjects, in southern settings, and
about southern themes that he must be regarded still as a southern writer. Over much of his
work there is a typically southern brooding sense of darkness, evil, and human failure, and he

employs a Gothicism of form and an extravagance of language and technique of a sort often associated with writing in the southeastern United States. Warren is a profoundly philosophical writer in all aspects of his work. Writing of Joseph Conrad, he once said, "The philosophical novelist, or poet, is one for whom the documentation of the world is constantly striving to rise to the level of generalization about values ... for whom the urgency of experience ... is the urgency to know the meaning of experience." The description fits him well.

In Warren's principal work in the novel and poetry, there is a persistent obsession with time and with history, a sense of man's imperfection and failure, and an awareness that innocence is always lost in the acts of achieving maturity and growth. His characters are usually men who destroy themselves through seeking an absolute in a relative universe. From John Brown, the subject of his first book, a biography, to Percy Munn, the protagonist of *Night Rider*, to Willie Stark of *All the King's Men*, to Jeremiah Beaumont of *World Enough and Time*, to Lilburn Lewis in the poem-play *Brother to Dragons*, to Jed Tewksbury in *A Place to Come To* — Warren's protagonists repeat this pattern of the obsessive and ultimately self-destructive search for the impossible ideal.

His work usually rests on actual events from history or at least on actual historical situations — *Night Rider* on the Kentucky tobacco wars, *At Heaven's Gates* on a Nashville political murder, *All the King's Men* on the career of Huey Long, *World Enough and Time* on an 1825 Kentucky murder, *Band of Angels* and *Wilderness* on the Civil War, *The Cave* on Floyd Collins's cave entombment, *Flood* on the inundating of towns by the Tennessee Valley Authority, *A Place to Come To* to at least some extent on his own experiences as a college teacher, although the story can hardly be considered autobiographical. The poem *Brother to Dragons* is based on an atrocious crime committed by Thomas Jefferson's nephews. This concern with history and the individual implications of social and political events is also present in his non-fiction, such as *Segregation: The Inner Conflict in the South*, *The Legacy of the Civil War*, and *Who Speaks for the Negro?* These works, too, deal with fundamental issues of southern history.

In order to present the philosophical meaning of his novels and poems, Warren uses highly individualized narrators, such as Jack Burden in *All the King's Men*; special techniques of narrative point of view, as in *World Enough and Time*; frequently a metaphysical style; the illumination of events through contrast with enclosed and frequently recollected narratives, as in *Night Rider* and *All the King's Men*; and highly melodramatic plots which become elaborate workings out of abstract statements, as in *Band of Angels*.

His poetry reiterates essentially the same view of man. He began as an undergraduate at Vanderbilt University writing poetry with the Fugitive poetry group — John Crowe Ransom, Allen Tate, and Donald Davidson — and he continued to write a relatively fixed form, tightly constructed, ironic lyric verse until about 1943. Between 1943 and 1953 he concentrated predominantly on the novel. With *Brother to Dragons* he returned to poetic expression, and since that time has written extensively in both poetic and novelistic forms. The verse forms that he has used since 1953 have been much looser, marked by broken rhythms, clusters of lines arranged in patterns dictated by emotion, and frequent alternations in the level of diction. Behind his poetry, as behind his fiction, there is usually an implied, if not explicit, narrative pattern. This narrative pattern is often historical, as in "The Ballad of Billy Potts," *Brother to Dragons*, or *Audubon*. In his recent verse, Warren contrasts man's weaknesses and imperfections with the enduring stars, with time, and with eternity.

As a critic and teacher, Warren has had a profound influence on the study and criticism of literature. His textbook *Understanding Poetry*, written with Cleanth Brooks, a presentation of poetry in New Critical terms emphasizing the poem as an independent work of art, went a long way toward creating a revolution in how literature was taught in American colleges. He has written many other textbooks and critical studies such as his *Homage to Theodore Dreiser*, *John Greenleaf Whittier's Poetry*, and *Democracy and Poetry*.

Warren is still very active; during his 72nd year he published *Selected Poems 1923–1975* and a distinctive and distinguished novel, *A Place to Come To*. Warren's work in all genres is marked by a high concern with language, a depth of philosophical statement, a firm and rigorous commitment to a moral-ethical view of man, and a willingness to experiment often beyond the limits of artistic safety with the forms in which he works. Warren is a peculiarly indigenous American writer of great intelligence and of significant accomplishment. He can, with justice, be called our most distinguished living man of letters.

—C. Hugh Holman

WARTON, Joseph. English. Born in Dunsfold, Surrey, baptized 22 April 1722; elder brother of Thomas Warton, *q.v.* Educated at Basingstoke Grammar School, Hampshire; Winchester College, 1735–40; Oriel College, Oxford, matriculated 1740, B.A. 1744, M.A. 1759, B.D. and D.D. 1768. Married 1) Mary Daman in 1748 (died, 1772), three sons and three daughters; 2) Charlotte Nicholas in 1773, one daughter. Took holy orders, 1744, and served as Curate to his father at Basingstoke, 1744–45; subsequently served as Curate at Chelsea, London; appointed Rector of Winslade, 1748; Travelling Chaplain with the Duke of Bolton, 1751; contributed to *The Adventurer*, 1753–56; Rector of Tunworth, 1754–55; Second Master, 1755–66, and Headmaster, 1766–93, Winchester College; Rector of Wickham, Hampshire, 1783–1800, and Upham, Hampshire, 1790–1800; retired to Wickham on leaving Winchester. Member, Literary Club, 1773. *Died 23 February 1800.*

PUBLICATIONS

Collections

> *Poems,* in *British Poets 68,* edited by Thomas Park.   1822.
> *The Three Wartons: A Choice of Their Verse,* edited by Eric Partridge.   1927.

Verse

> *The Enthusiast; or, The Lover of Nature.*   1744.
> *Odes on Various Subjects.*   1746.
> *An Ode Occasioned by Reading West's Translation of Pindar.*   1749.
> *An Ode to Evening.*   1749.

Other

> *Ranelagh House: A Satire in Prose.*   1747.
> *An Essay on the Writings and Genius of Pope.*   2 vols., 1756–82.

> Editor, *Poems on Several Occasions,* by Thomas Warton, the Elder.   1748.
> Editor and Translator, *The Works of Virgil in Latin and English.*   4 vols., 1753.
> Editor, *Sidney's Defence of Poetry.*   1787.
> Editor, with others, *The Works of Pope.*   9 vols., 1797.

Reading List: *Biographical Memoirs of Warton* (includes letters) by John Wooll, 1806; *The Ascendancy of Taste: The Achievement of Joseph and Thomas Warton* by Joan Pittock, 1973.

* * *

Joseph Warton's poem *The Enthusiast*, published when he was only 22, celebrates in Miltonic blank verse the new preference for the irregularities of nature over rigid classical forms. While still at school Warton had been friendly with William Collins, with whom he planned to publish a volume of odes. In the event Warton's *Odes on Various Subjects* were preferred by Dodsley to those of Collins, presumably because they were more congenial to the taste of the time. The odes were frequently reprinted throughout the century. In the Preface to the *Odes* Warton complained that "the fashion of moralizing in verse has been carried too far," insisting that invention and imagination alone characterise true poetry. From 1753, Warton was responsible for the papers on literary criticism in *The Adventurer*; and in the same year appeared the work on which Warton placed his hopes of preferment, an edition of the works of Virgil. This included his own translations of the *Eclogues* and *Georgics*. In his *Essay on the Writings and Genius of Pope*, Warton pursued his campaign against the didactic and satiric verse modes popularised by Pope (a second volume was not published until 1782), and he edited Pope's works in nine volumes. Most of the material incorporated in the notes came from the *Essay*. At the time of his death Warton was engaged in preparing an edition of Dryden.

As a member of the Literary Club Warton was acquainted with Johnson, Burke, Garrick, Reynolds in the leading literary coterie of the mid-century. In later life he corresponded with Wilkes on friendly terms. His correspondence, part of which was published in Wooll's *Biographical Memoirs*, and in manuscript in the Bodleian and in the British Library, reveals an enthusiastic, ambitious, and kindly personality, an indefatigable seeker in the field of literary enterprises.

—Joan Pittock

WARTON, Thomas. English. Born in Basingstoke, Hampshire, 9 January 1728; younger brother of Joseph Warton, *q.v.* Educated at Basingstoke Grammar School; Trinity College, Oxford, matriculated 1744, B.A. 1747, M.A. 1750, B.D. 1767. Took holy orders, 1748; Fellow of Trinity College, 1751 until his death: Professor of Poetry, 1757–67, and Camden Professor of History, 1785–90, Oxford University; Rector of Kidlington, 1771. Member, Literary Club, 1782. Fellow, Society of Antiquaries, 1771. Poet Laureate, 1785 until his death. *Died 21 May 1790.*

PUBLICATIONS

Collections

> *Poetical Works*, edited by R. Mant. 2 vols., 1802.
> *Poetical Works of Goldsmith, Collins, and Warton*, edited by George Gilfillan. 1854.
> *The Three Wartons: A Choice of Their Verse*, edited by Eric Partridge. 1927.

Verse

> *The Pleasures of Melancholy.*   1747.
> *The Triumph of Isis.*   1749.
> *Newmarket: A Satire.*   1751.
> *Ode for Music as Performed at Oxford 1751.*   1751.
> *Mons Catharinae prope Wintoniani.*   1774.
> *Poems.*   1777; as *Poems on Various Subjects,* 1791.
> *Verses on Reynolds's Painted Window at New College Oxford.*   1782.
> *Verses Left under a Stone.*   1790(?).
> *The Hamlet: An Ode.*   1859.

Other

> *A Description of Winchester.*   1750.
> *Observations on the Faerie Queene of Spenser.*   1754.
> *A Companion to the Guide, and a Guide to the Companion: A Supplement to All Accounts of Oxford.*   1760(?).
> *The Life of Sir Tho. Pope.*   1772.
> *The History of English Poetry.*   3 vols., 1774–81; edited by W. C. Hazlitt, 4 vols., 1871; *An Unpublished Continuation,* edited by R. M. Baine, 1953.
> *Specimen of the History of Oxfordshire.*   1781; as *A History of Kidlington,* 1783.
> *An Enquiry into the Authenticity of the Poems Attributed to Rowley.*   1782.
> *Essays on Gothic Architecture,* with others.   1800.
> *Correspondence of Thomas Percy and Warton,* edited by M. G. Robinson and Leah Dennis, constitutes *Percy Letters,* vol. 3.   1951.

> Editor, *The Union; or, Select Scots and English Poems.*   1753.
> Editor, *Inscriptionum Romanorum Metricarum Delectus.*   1758.
> Editor, *The Life and Literary Remains of Ralph Bathurst.*   2 vols., 1761.
> Editor, *The Oxford Sausage; or, Select Poetical Pieces.*   1764.
> Editor, *Anthologiae Graecae.*   1766.
> Editor, *Theocrite Syracusii quae Supersunt.*   2 vols., 1770.
> Editor, *Poems upon Several Occasions by Milton.*   1785; revised edition, 1790.

Reading List: *Warton: A Biographical and Critical Study* by Clarissa Rinaker, 1916 (includes bibliography); *The Ascendancy of Taste: The Achievement of Joseph and Thomas Warton* by Joan Pittock, 1973.

*   *   *

Thomas Warton was one of the most celebrated figures of eighteenth-century Oxford. His versatility and resourcefulness as a minor poet are evident in his popular *Pleasures of Melancholy* and his defence of Oxford in *The Triumph of Isis*, as well as in the facetious verses he composed for *The Oxford Sausage*. His *Verses on Reynolds's Painted Window* uniquely illustrate the mental agonies and doubts which the violent shifting of aesthetic values imposed on men like Warton. In 1785 he was appointed Poet Laureate, but his lack of success in versifying on royal topics excited the mockery of Peter Pindar and the compilers of *The New Rolliad.*

Warton was a principal agent in obtaining the degree of M.A. for Johnson, and was a prominent member of the Literary Club. His enthusiasm for early poetry, in particular that of Spenser and Milton, imparts a freshness and originality to his work which makes it of greater intrinsic interest than that of his brother Joseph. His *Observations on the Faerie Queene of Spenser* displays a high level of critical and scholarly imagination, and his substantial correspondence with Thomas Percy reveals his passionate interest in early literature and his wealth of antiquarian information.

Warton's *History of English Poetry*, despite its faults, established for the first time a British literary tradition in which the focal achievement is the work of the Elizabethans. His edition of Milton's minor poems is itself a kind of conclusion to his observations in the *History*, for it is preoccupied with the ways in which the imagination of a great poet employs fiction and allegory from various sources to create works of classic importance. Warton's love of poetry and his critical acumen are expressed with imagination and authority in his contribution to the Chatterton controversy, *An Enquiry into the Authenticity of the Poems Attributed to Rowley*. Characteristically, his lectures as Poetry Professor dealt with the delight of Greek literature, a novel topic at that time.

—Joan Pittock

WATKINS, Vernon (Phillips). Welsh   Born in Maesteg, Glamorganshire, 27 June 1906. Educated at Swansea Grammar School; Repton School; Magdalene College, Cambridge, 1924–25: studied modern languages. Served in the Home Guard, 1939–41, and the Royal Air Force, 1941–45. Married Gwendolyn Mary Davies in 1944; four sons and one daughter. Clerk, Lloyds Bank, Swansea, 1925–41, 1946–65. Visiting Lecturer in Modern Poetry, University of Washington, Seattle, 1964, 1967; Calouste Gulbenkian Fellow in Poetry, University College, Swansea, 1965–66. Recipient: Guinness Prize, 1957. D.Litt.: University of Wales, Cardiff, 1966. Fellow, Royal Society of Literature, 1951. *Died 8 October 1967.*

PUBLICATIONS

Verse

> *Ballad of Mari Lwyd and Other Poems.*   1941.
> *The Lamp and the Veil.*   1945.
> *The Lady with the Unicorn.*   1948.
> *Selected Poems.*   1948.
> *The Death Bell: Poems and Ballads.*   1954.
> *Cypress and Acacia.*   1959.
> *Affinities.*   1962.
> *Selected Poems 1930–1960.*   1967.
> *Arrival in East Shelby.*   1968.
> *Fidelities.*   1968.
> *Uncollected Poems.*   1969.
> *Ballad of the Outer Dark.*   1977.
> *The Influences.*   1977.

Other

Selected Verse Translations, with an Essay on the Translation of Poetry, edited by Ruth
    Pryor.   1977.

Editor, *Letters to Vernon Watkins*, by Dylan Thomas.   1957.
Editor, *Landmarks and Voyages: Poetry Supplement*.   1957.

Translator, *The North Sea*, by Heinrich Heine.   1955.

Bibliography: *Two Swansea Poets: Dylan Thomas and Watkins*, 1969.

Reading List: *Watkins 1906–1967* edited by Leslie Norris, 1970; *Watkins* by Roland
Mathias, 1974; *Watkins and the Spring of Vision* by Dora Polk, 1977; "Watkins Issue" of
Poetry Wales 12 edited by J. P. Ward, 1977.

                                   *   *   *

Vernon Watkins has been celebrated more by fellow Welshmen than by the metropolitan
critics of English literature. Yet his poetry, though rooted in the landscape of South Wales,
especially the Gower peninsula, is not narrowly provincial, but has a European breadth in its
range of reference. This is further reflected in fine translations of Heine's *The North Sea*,
Homer, Dante, and many French and German lyrics; Hölderlin is a particular inspiration in
his own poetry. Not a native Welsh-speaker (though his parents were), Watkins draws little
of specifically Welsh literature into his work apart from the myth of Taliesin, the prototype of
the poet-seer with the gift of inspiration and the capacity for self-transformation, who is the
focus of several poems. His own metaphysical vision, shaped early by Blake and later by
Yeats, is replete with visual and sensory detail. Through the verbal re-creation of a loved
place or the accurate observation of, say, a hero, a foal, fruit blossom, or snow that is whiter
than sea-foam, he seeks to reveal the truths of eternity mediated by the accidents of time. A
sense of serene thankfulness, achieved through the conquest of grief and pain, suffuses much
of his work, e.g., "Peace in the Welsh Hills":

> Here, where the earth is green, where heaven is true
> Opening the windows, touched with earliest dawn,
> In the first frost of cool September days,
> Chrysanthemum weather, presaging great birth,
> Who in his heart could murmur or complain:
> "The light we look for is not in this land"?
> That light is present, and that distant time
> Is always here, continually redeemed.

Philosophically, Watkins's poetry represents a struggle to reconcile elements of Neo-
Platonism with the traditional insights of Christianity. Within these thematic limits there is a
slow maturing of thought throughout his substantial published work. His poems largely lack
the immediacy of contemporary allusion and fashionable subject-matter.
    Watkins's attention to the craft of his verse is meticulous; many of his poems have gone
through dozens of drafts before reaching their final form. In the introduction to *Dylan
Thomas: Letters to Vernon Watkins* he declares his method of working to be "from music and
cadence towards the density of physical shape." He experimented with a large variety of
metres, rhymed and unrhymed, stanza forms, and poetic types. His diction remains generally
reflective and hieratic, with some infusion of the colloquial and the plain, especially in his
ballads. Although his work consists mainly of short lyric forms, several extended pieces – the

"Ballad of Mari Lwyd," the rhapsodic "Sea-Music for My Sister Travelling," the transmuted chronicle of a visit to Yeats in "Yeats in Dublin," the posthumously published masque *The Influences* (Yeatsian through and through) – demonstrate a more ambitious mood, which is perhaps ultimately less successful, because too diffuse.

—David Blamires

WATSON, Thomas. English. Born in London c. 1557. Possibly educated at Oxford University; studied law in London. Married a Miss Smith. Visited Paris, 1581, and met Sir Francis Walsingham, thereafter his patron; returned to England and became a prominent figure in London literary society; in his last years employed in the household of William Cornwallis, probably as a tutor. *Died* (buried) *26 September 1592.*

PUBLICATIONS

Collections

   Poems, edited by E. Arber.   1870.

Verse

   The Hecatompathia; or, A Passionate Century of Love.   1582; edited by S. K. Heninger, Jr., 1964.
   An Eclogue upon the Death of Sir Francis Walsingham.   1590 (also a Latin version *Meliboeus,* 1590).
   The First Set of Italian Madrigals Englished.   1590; edited by E. H. Fellowes, in *English Madrigal Verse,* 1967.
   Amintae Gaudia (in Latin).   1591; translated by I. T. as *An Old Fashioned Love,* 1594.

Other

   Compendium Memoriae Localis.   1585(?).
   A Gratification unto John Case for His Book in Praise of Music.   1586(?); edited by M. C. Boyd, in *Elizabethan Music and Musical Criticism,* 1940.

   Translator, *Antigone* (in Latin), by Sophocles .   1581.
   Translator, *Tebani Helenae Raptus* (in Latin), by Coluthus.   1586.
   Translator, *Amyntas* (in Latin), by Tasso.   1587; translated by Abraham Fraunce, 1587; both versions edited by W. F. Staton, Jr., and F. M. Dickey, 1967.

Reading List: *Primi Studi su Watson,* 1964, and *Watson e la Tradizione Petrarchista,* 1969, both by C. G. Cecioni.

*   *   *

Thomas Watson, translator and poet, friend to such Elizabethan worthies as John Lyly, Christopher Marlowe, and Thomas Nashe, enjoyed a high reputation during his lifetime for his knowledge of ancient and Continental languages and for his poetry written in the Petrarchan manner. Today Watson is little read, but he remains interesting to the student of cultural change and the literary historian. His major work, *Hecatompathia; or, A Passionate Century of Love*, a collection predominantly of eighteen-line "sonnets," published about the time that Sidney was writing his sonnet cycle, *Astrophel and Stella*, antedates by a decade the vogue of sonneteering in England. His *Italian Madrigals Englished*, a substantial anthology of contemporary Italian art-songs with English adaptations to the Italian text (together with two pieces "composed after the Italian vaine" by William Byrd), is one of two such collections which appeared in England just prior to the assimilation and naturalization of Italian polyphonic music by English composers. Though Watson was no inventive genius – nearly his entire canon is comprised of translations, paraphrases, and adaptations – his use of up-to-date Continental poetry and music to underpin his own creative abilities, limited though they were, helped to stimulate and form an audience for the creative activity that so distinguishes the last decade of the sixteenth century in England.

In addition to Watson's general influence upon the literary and musical taste of his time, he occupies a place of some importance in the history of lyric poetry as a reformer of English prosody, and, were it not for the more obvious technical achievements of Sidney's *Astrophel and Stella*, Watson's reputation would be higher than it is. Yet when we recall that the verses of the early Elizabethan poets are characterized by a metrical rigidity, an unfailing *caesura*, inevitable end-stopping, and non-functional alliteration, we can better realize by how far Watson's supple line (in imitation of Petrarch's) could transcend them, as in *Hecatompathia*, 39:

> When first these eyes beheld with great delight
> The phoenix of this world, or second sun,
> Her beams or plumes bewitched all my sight,
> And love encreas'd the hurt that was begun,
> Since when my grief is grown so much the more
> Because I find no way to cure the sore.

From the evidence of his most influential work Watson appears to have been as interested in educating his readers as he was in writing poetry. Each of the *Hecatompathia* poems is prefaced with a notation (sometimes of considerable length) in which the poet acknowledges a source, points out a classical allusion, notes the similarity of this or that motif to a classical or Continental work, narrates a myth, or explains his method. By thus calling attention to the significance of historical knowledge to an appreciation of his poems, Watson seems as much the humanist who would use art to unite past with present as the poet intent upon anatomizing the vagaries of love.

Of Watson's Latin translations (Sophocles's *Antigone*; Tasso's *Aminta*, an activity which earned him the respect of his most learned contemporaries, little need be said except to note that the act of translation again points to the humanistic bent of this scholar-poet who did not stay at Oxford for his degree. His obvious commitment to the Latin language chimes with his intention to educate the readers of his "passions" to the continuities of the literary tradition.

—Frank Fabry

WATSON, Sir William. English. Born in Burley-in-Wharfedale, Yorkshire, 2 August 1858; grew up in Liverpool. Educated at a school in Southport. Married Maureen Pring in 1909; two daughters. Visited America several times on lecture tours. LL.D.: University of Aberdeen, 1904. Knighted, 1917. *Died 11 August 1935.*

PUBLICATIONS

Collections

    The Poems.   1936.

Verse

    The Prince's Quest and Other Poems.   1880.
    Epigrams of Art, Life, and Nature.   1884.
    Wordsworth's Grave and Other Poems.   1890.
    Shelley's Centenary.   1892.
    Lachrymae Musarum and Other Poems.   1893.
    The Eloping Angels: A Caprice.   1893.
    Odes and Other Poems.   1894.
    The Father of the Forest and Other Poems.   1895.
    Ode for the Centenary of the Death of Burns.   1895.
    The Purple East: A Series of Sonnets on England's Desertion of Armenia.   1896.
    The Lost Eden.   1897.
    The Year of Shame.   1897.
    The Hope of the World and Other Poems.   1898.
    Collected Poems.   1898.
    New Poems.   1902.
    Ode on the Day of the Coronation of King Edward VII.   1902.
    Selected Poems.   1903.
    For England: Poems Written During Estrangement.   1904.
    Poems, edited by J. A. Spender.   2 vols., 1905.
    Sable and Purple with Other Poems.   1910.
    The Muse in Exile.   1913.
    The Man Who Saw and Other Poems Arising Out of the War.   1917.
    Retrogression and Other Poems.   1917.
    The Superhuman Antagonists and Other Poems.   1919.
    Ireland Arisen.   1921.
    Ireland Unfreed.   1921.
    A Hundred Poems Selected from Various Volumes.   1922.
    Poems Brief and New.   1925.
    Selected Poems.   1928.

Play

    The Heralds of the Dawn.   1912.

Other

Excursions in Criticism, Being Some Prose Recreations of a Rhymer.   1893.
Pencraft: A Plea for Older Ways.   1917.

Editor, *English Lyrics,* by Alfred Austin.   1890.
Editor, *Lyric Love: An Anthology.*   1892.

Reading List: *Watson* by J. G. Nelson, 1966.

*   *   *

The name of Sir William Watson is now almost forgotten. His presence lingers in the pages of comprehensive poetry anthologies of the Victorian period, where indulgent editors usually find space to print a couple of his poems, usually "Shelley's Centenary" and "Wordsworth's Grave." Devotees of the 1890's will remember him as the writer who presented John Lane, publisher of the notorious *Yellow Book*, with the ultimatum that either Aubrey Beardsley's illustrations of sin-wasted succubae should no longer be accepted for the journal or his own contributions would cease. Such was his reputation at the time that Lane immediately capitulated, and dismissed Beardsley from his position as art editor, recognising that the ultimate success of the journal rested more firmly on Watson's conventional literary talents than on the bizarre eroticism of his now more highly esteemed contemporary.

From first to last Watson's poetry remained virtually the same: noble sentiments expressed in measured Miltonic cadences, formal, stiff, redeemed from pomposity by an occasional flash of anger or biting sarcasm. Watson's poetry is, in fact, less notable for its craft than for its high moral concerns and the evident sincerity with which they are expressed. In 1890 he set forth his poetic criteria in "Wordsworth's Grave," praising the Lake poet's ability to sing "a lofty song of lowly weal and dole," and comparing him to Watson's own contemporaries whose verses, he said, either "deaden with ignoble sloth" or "deafen with shrill tumult," being an apparent reference to the decadents on the one hand and the so-called activists such as Kipling and Newbolt on the other. Watson's political no less than his poetical sympathies were firmly rooted in the past, and in his poem "After the Titans" he criticised his political contemporaries:

> Men light and slight, on narrower scale designed,
> Offspring and image of the change we trace
> In art, arms, action, manners, morals, mind –
> The burly oak departing, in its place
> The lissom willow, swaying to the wind.

Especially critical of moral lapses in high places, Watson criticised the British government in "Ver Tenebrosum" for supporting the Egyptians against the Sudanese in 1885, and, in *The Purple East*, for not intervening on behalf of the Armenians who were being massacred by the Turks. Later, in *For England*, he again attacked the government, this time for their opposition to the Boers in South Africa.

Eventually, Watson was forced to recognise that his was a lone crusade on behalf of moral justice, but he clung to his belief in Britain's noble destiny, and in his stately "Ode on the Day of the Coronation of King Edward VII" (1907) expressed the hope that his country would live to be:

> Saluted in the hearts of men as she
> Of high and singular election, set
> Benignant in the sea;
> That greatly loving freedom loved to free,
> And was herself the bridal and the embrace
> Of strength and conquering grace.

Even at this date, however, Watson realised that he was out of step with his times, and his last years were clouded with disappointment. Frustrated by his inability to find a public which would respond to his fervid romantic idealism, and lamenting the moral decline into which he believed Britain had fallen, he looked forward to death almost as a release. As he expressed it in "The False Summer" (*Poems Brief and New*):

> The summer that begrudged its honey,
> And promised boons it never gave,
> Now in its lean, mean parsimony,
> Departs into its dirgeless grave.
> Come, honest Winter! Thou at least
> Wilt not thy lack of heart conceal,
> Or bid me to a monarch's feast
> To mock me with a beggar's meal.

—John M. Munro

WATTS, Isaac.   English.   Born in Southampton, Hampshire, 17 July 1675. Educated at Southampton Grammar School, until 1690, and at a nonconformist academy in Stoke Newington, London, 1690–94. Wrote first hymn c. 1695, and thereafter wrote more than 600 hymns throughout his life; tutor in the family of Sir John Hartopp, Stoke Newington, 1696–1702; non-conformist minister: Assistant Pastor, 1699–1702, and Pastor, 1702–48, Mark Lane, London; because of ill-health turned over part of his pastoral duties to an assistant in 1713, and lived the remainder of his life with his friends Sir Thomas and Lady Abney at their homes at Theobalds and Stoke Newington. D.D.: University of Edinburgh, 1728. *Died 25 November 1748.*

PUBLICATIONS

Collections

> *Works*, edited by D. Jennings and F. Doddridge.   6 vols., 1753; revised edition, edited
>   by G. Burder, 6 vols., 1810–11.

Verse

> *Horae Lyricae: Poems Chiefly of the Lyric Kind.*   1706; revised edition, 1709; edited by
>   Robert Southey, 1834.

Hymns and Spiritual Songs.   1707; revised edition, 1709; edited by S. L. Bishop, 1962.
Divine Songs Attempted in Easy Language for the Use of Children.   1715; revised
   edition, 1740; as *Divine and Moral Songs for Children,* 1787.
The Psalms of David Imitated.   1719.

Other

An Essay Against Uncharitableness.   1707.
A Guide to Prayer.   1715; edited by Harry Escott, 1948.
The Art of Reading and Writing English.   1721.
Sermons on Various Subjects.   3 vols., 1721–27.
The Christian Doctrine of the Trinity.   1722.
*Death and Heaven; or, The Last Enemy Conquered and Separate Spirits Made
   Perfect.*   1722.
Three Dissertations Relating to the Christian Doctrine of the Trinity.   1724.
Logic.   1725.
*The Knowledge of the Heavens and the Earth Made Easy; or, The First Principles of
   Astronomy and Geography.*   1726.
A Defense Against the Temptation of Self-Murder.   1726.
An Essay Towards the Encouragement of Charity Schools.   1728.
A Caveat Against Infidelity.   1729.
Cathecisms; or, Instructions in the Principles of the Christian Religion.   1730.
*An Humble Attempt Towards the Revival of Practical Religion among Christians and
   Particularly Protestant Dissenters.*   1731.
Philosophical Essays on Various Subjects.   1733.
Reliquiae Juveniles: Miscellaneous Thoughts in Prose and Verse.   1734.
The Redeemer and the Sanctifier.   1736.
Humility Represented in the Character of St. Paul.   1737.
A New Essay on Civil Power in Things Sacred.   1739.
The Doctrine of the Passions Explained and Improved.   1739.
The Improvement of the Mind; or, A Supplement to the Art of Logic.   1741.
The World to Come; or, Discourses on the Joys and Sorrows of Departed Souls.   2 vols.,
   1745.
Useful and Important Questions Concerning Jesus.   1746.
The Glory of Christ as God-Man Displayed in Three Discourses.   1746.
Evangelical Discourses on Several Subjects.   1747.
*The Rational Foundation of a Christian Church and the Terms of Christian
   Communion.*   1747.
Discourses on the Love of God and Its Influence on All Passions.   1760 (4th edition).
A Treatise on the Education of Children and Youth.   1769 (2nd edition).
Nine Sermons Preached in 1718–19, Now First Published.   1812.

Reading List: *The Hymns of Wesley and Watts: Five Informal Papers* by B. L. Manning,
1942; *Watts: His Life and Works* by A. P. Davis, 1943 (includes bibliography); *Watts* by Erik
Routley, 1961; *Watts, Hymnographer: A Study of the Beginnings, Development, and
Philosophy of the English Hymns* by Harry Escott, 1962.

*   *   *

Though Isaac Watts wrote a large number of spiritual works in prose, and a *Logic* which
remained in use for a hundred years after his death, his most notable literary achievement is
as a writer of hymns, and as a major originator of the English hymn tradition. At the

beginning of the eighteenth century, the Church of England and most of the Protestant sects (Watts himself was an Independent) used metrical versions of the Psalms rather than hymns in worship. Watts was not the first but was certainly the most influential advocate for the replacement of the Psalms, arguing in his "Short Essay Toward the Improvement of Psalmody" suffixed to his *Hymns and Spiritual Songs* that "when we sing, especially unto God, our chief design is, or should be, to speak our own hearts and our words to God," and that we must therefore sing composures suitable to our own case. Watts claimed that the Psalms, based on Hebrew culture and an Old Testament morality, could not satisfy the needs of contemporary Christian devotion. Watts therefore planned a system of evangelical hymnody, containing both christianised psalms and original hymns.

Watts's *Hymns and Spiritual Songs* are divided into three sections, the first based on particular scriptural texts, the second of "mere human composure," and the third "Prepared for the Holy Ordinance of the Lord's Supper." In this collection appear some of the finest and best-known English hymns, including "There is a land of pure delight," "Come, let us join our cheerful songs," and "When I survey the wondrous cross." Intended for the social worship of all classes, stating important points of doctrine clearly, and keeping the major topics of belief in the mind of the congregation, the *Hymns* are consciously unpoetic in style. Watts speaks in his Preface of suiting the metaphors "to the level of vulgar capacities," of aiming at plainness of sense and regularity of rhythm, of rejecting the "beauties" of poetry. Watts normally uses a familiar imagery of Protestant belief, metaphors articulating meaning explicitly. Occasionally some of the more sophisticated stylistic and formal features of the seventeenth-century devotional lyric appear in Watts's writing; "When I survey the wondrous cross," for example, is a meditation, stanza four of which is omitted in most hymn books because of the vivid, punning metaphor of Christ on the cross: "His dying crimson, like a robe,/Spreads o'er his body on the tree." Generally, however, those of his hymns which contained "expressions ... not suited to the plainest capacity," and therefore not fitted to congregational use, were set apart by Watts, and published rather in his *Horae Lyricae*. *Horae Lyricae* contains three books, one of poems "sacred to devotion and piety," a second including pieces in such distinctly literary forms as odes, epistles, and epigrams, and a third of elegies and epitaphs, "sacred to the memory of the dead." The more literary nature of this work is confirmed both by the important critical Preface, in which Watts argues for the turning of poetry to divine subjects, and by the fact that Samuel Johnson chose to represent Watts only by this collection in the *Works of the English Poets*.

A decade later, Watts undertook an evangelical version of the Psalms of David, "imitated in the language of the New Testament, and applied to the Christian state and worship." The intention was to make the Psalms once more an appropriate vehicle for Christian devotion, christianised, simplified in style, purged of the distinctively judaic, adapted to an eighteenth-century English context. Some of Watts's finest and most familiar "hymns" are in fact to be found in his version of the Psalms, notably "Our God, our help in ages past" and "Jesus shall reign where'er the sun."

The *Divine Songs Attempted in Easy Language for the Use of Children* is a collection of pedagogical and catechismal, rather than devotional, poetry, and lies outside Watts's system of hymnody. The Christian message is presented here more generally, avoiding, for the most part, the theological particularity which may be found in the *Hymns* and *Psalms*. Style is simplified further, "to the level of a child's understanding," and indeed to the point of being liable to parody: Lewis Carroll's "'Tis the voice of the lobster" and "How doth the little crocodile" are both based on poems by Watts in this collection. Yet here too Watts offered an influential model, reflected not only in eighteenth-century children's poetry, but also, formally at least, in William Blake's *Songs of Innocence*, though Blake would not have found acceptable the authoritarian and conventional morality of Watts's *Songs*.

Few poets have had a greater effect on the culture of the English-speaking world than Watts, yet the nature of his religious poetry poses difficulties for the critic, for whom it was not designed. Watts has more often been admired for his exemplary life (as by Samuel Johnson in his *Life* of Watts), or for his unquestionable historical importance, than for his specifically artistic merits. Yet the simplicity and restraint of Watts's writing are themselves the result of an artistic process of selection and exclusion, and are in themselves a poetic virtue. The exact economy of Watts's style makes his best hymns classic and authoritative statements of an important aspect of popular religious belief and experience.

—Marcus Walsh

WEBB, Francis (Charles). Australian. Born in Adelaide, South Australia, 8 February 1925. Educated at Christian Brothers schools, Chatswood and Lewisham; University of Sydney. Served in the Royal Australian Air Force in Canada, during World War II. Worked for various Canadian publishers. Recipient: Commonwealth Literary Fund Fellowship, 1960. *Died in 1973.*

PUBLICATIONS

Verse

A Drum for Ben Boyd. 1948.
Leichhardt in Theatre. 1952.
Birthday. 1953.
Socrates and Other Poems. 1961.
The Ghost of the Cock. 1964.
Collected Poems. 1969.

Reading List: "The World of Webb" by Sylvia Lawson, in *Australian Letters,* 1961; "The Poetry of Webb" by Vincent Buckley, in *Meanjin,* 1963.

*   *   *

Of the younger modern Australian poets of this century, Francis Webb, on the publication of his *A Drum for Ben Boyd* became one of the two leading figures, with David Campbell. Webb's early death cut his achievement short. Webb spent much of his adult life in mental hospitals and a good deal of his poetry undoubtedly attempts to convey experiences peculiar to what are called psychotic states of mind. It is inevitable, therefore, that he should have enjoyed a kind of *succès de scandale* on that account. But much of his poetry is genuinely visionary poetry, the result of a more than ordinarily lucid and energetic way of seeing, of an imagination and a sensibility of greater scope and intensity than usual.

It would be a mistake to see in Webb's early poems, written before his illness, the preoccupations with night, death, dream, eccentricity, solitude, silence, obscure terrors, and rejections that merely bespeak the alienated mind. What most characterises his verse is its immense vitality, its positiveness. Even its privacies are not egocentric. These are not poems of withdrawal, but of reaching out; in contrast to many more "normal" poets, Webb did not "live the life of monologue." Poetry for him was a means of keeping in touch with reality; his early poem, "Compliments of the Audience," is an affirmation of faith in images, which, he argues, are all that emerge to testify to reality from the blackness of memory, the blurred barrenness of thought. *A Drum for Ben Boyd*, a sequence of poems by various speakers giving their different impressions of the merchant-adventurer Boyd, was a remarkable performance for a young man of 22, especially since, in an era of historic poems, it questioned the validity of historiography. His second long poem, *Leichhardt in Theatre*, was no less challenging, and contains perhaps the central symbol of Webb's belief system: the "nomad horseman energy." Other preoccupations which bind the work as a whole together are his interest in music, in painting, and in everything to do with the sea. He gives special importance to laughter, as his last long poem, *Ghost of the Cock*, demonstrates, and the clown image is a recurrent one. Leichhardt, for instance, is presented as part-clown, part-hero.

Webb's greatest technical strength lies in his appeal to the ear. He handles the language as a musician handles tones and produces a rich concourse of sound which carries its own meaning, even if the mind is slow to interpret it. This gift is most in evidence perhaps in the volume *Socrates*, which also shows him in full possession of his visionary world. All his key experiences come together in this book: his Catholic faith, war-time flying, music, the sea, his own illness, his need for monastic solitude. There is much of the "desert father" in Webb's verse: his passionate nature made it necessary for him to turn all women into the Virgin, all children into the infant Christ. The poem "For Ethel" is the nearest we get to any sense of an earthly, particular woman. It is in a poem about a new-born child that Webb comes closest to intimate human contact, with all his senses sharpened, particularly the sense of touch: it is one of the most beautiful of all contemporary Nativity poems, as the opening stanza suggests:

> Christmas is in the air.
> You are given into my hands
> Out of quiet, loneliest lands.
> My trembling is all my prayer.
> To blown straw was given
> All the fullness of heaven.

Webb was too rich and complex a poet to yield himself to short analysis. Perhaps some glimpse of the man and the poet is revealed in his lines about Socrates, musing on the relationship between his soul and his body, as the "chains" of earthly ties are about to be loosed:

> Chains grapple with me gently, as old friends,
> The subtle iron lends its tinklings to my move.
> And it is all of love; for I see Andromeda musing,
> Given back to entire music, swathed in frail silver links:
> They chime, climb or sink with gain or fail of pulse,
> And all about, incurious hulls and the long, long flutes of the sea.

—Dorothy Green

WESLEY, Charles. English. Born in Epworth, Lincolnshire, 18 December 1707; younger brother of the founder of Methodism, John Wesley. Educated at Westminster School, London, 1716–26 (King's Scholar, 1721; Captain of the School, 1725); Christ Church, Oxford, matriculated 1726, B.A. 1730, M.A. 1733; joined with other students in strict method of religious observance and study: nicknamed "methodists." Married Sarah Gwynne in 1749; eight children. Involved in the Methodist movement, under his brother's lead, from 1730: ordained deacon and priest, 1735; accompanied his brother to Georgia as Secretary to the governor, James Oglethorpe, 1735–36; involved in study, Oxford, 1736–38; believed himself "converted" 1738; involved in evangelical work in London, 1738–39; settled at Bristol, and preached through the West of England and Wales, 1730–56; because of ill-health retired to Bath and gave up active ministry, 1761; diverged from his brother on various points of doctrine from 1762; settled in London, 1771, and occasionally preached in London until the end of his life. Composed nearly 9,000 hymns, of which 500 are still in use. *Died 29 March 1788.*

PUBLICATIONS

Collections

Poetical Works of John and Charles Wesley. 13 vols., 1868–72.
Representative Verse, edited by Frank Baker. 1962.

Verse

Hymns and Sacred Poems. 2 vols., 1749.

Other

Sermons, edited by S. Wesley. 1816.
Journal, edited by T. Jackson. 2 vols., 1849.
The Early Journal, 1736–39, edited by John Telford. 1909.

Bibliography: *A Bibliography of the Works of John and Charles Wesley* by R. Green, 1896.

Reading List: *The Evangelical Doctrines of Wesley's Hymns* by J. E. Rattenbury, 1941; *Wesley as Revealed in His Letters,* 1948, and *Wesley's Verse,* 1964, both by Frank Baker; *The Hymns of Wesley: A Study of Their Structure* by R. N. Flew, 1953; *Wesleys Hymnen* by E. Mayer, 1957; *Singer of a Thousand Songs: A Life of Wesley* by E. Myers, 1965.

*   *   *

The 8989 extant hymns of Charles Wesley echo the essence of the Evangelical Revival of eighteenth-century England. Certainly, not every poem evidences the same degree of quality, but together the hymns convey the intensity of the poet's deep personal feelings. Few subjects or occasions escaped his notice: his own conversion and marriage; domestic upheavals from panics, earthquakes, religious riots, rumored invasions; festivals of the Church and doctrines of the faith; scenes from the paraphrases of Scripture; deaths of friends; the education of children; the effects of local surroundings. As with his elder brother John, Charles Wesley spent little time contemplating and transmitting abstract themes; instead, he emphasized the personal and the concrete. His lines thus reflected the experiences of thousands of believers and an equal number of those struggling to believe.

Although Wesley's hymns demonstrate the influence of a variety of British poets upon the hymnodist – from Shakespeare to Edward Young – the content and language of Scripture remained his principal source. Thus, in "Waiting for the Promise," we see:

> Fainting soul, be bold, be strong;
> Wait the leisure of thy Lord:
> Though it seem to tarry long,
> True and faithful is His word.

Wesley's contemporaries would have recognized the words of Psalm 27:16, from Coverdale's prose version in the *Book of Common Prayer*: "O tarry thou the Lord's leisure," indicating that Methodism's bard continued to hold to his Anglican upbringing and education. No doubt, that is true; yet, Wesley must not be relegated to a mere paraphraser of Scriptures, a versifier who combined experience with emotionalism and pumped both into the liturgy of the Methodist service. Instead, he must be remembered as a legitimate, devotional poet who established the idea that a hymn is indeed a poem. John Wesley, in the preface to *A Collection of Hymns for the Use of the People Called Methodists* (1780), set forth what still stands as the most accurate assessment of his brother's poetry: "In these hymns there is no doggerel, no botches, nothing put in to patch the rhyme, no feeble explatives. ... Here are... both the purity, the strength and the elegance of the ENGLISH language: and at the same time the utmost simplicity and plainness, suited to every capacity." The Methodist patriarch challenged critics to judge "whether there is not in some of the following verses, the true Spirit of Poetry: such as cannot be acquired by art and labour; but must be the gift of nature." He concluded that through labor "a man may become a tolerable imitator.... But unless he is born a Poet, he will never attain the genuine SPIRIT OF POETRY."

Despite his brother's exuberance, Charles Wesley met with only limited success and acceptance outside of Methodism. Today, there is little doubt of the overall popularity and the wide poetic and hymnodic acceptability of such pieces as "All praise to Him who dwells in bliss"; "Christ the Lord is risen to-day"; "Christ, whose glory fills the sky"; "Come, let us join our friends above"; "Come, Thou long-expected Jesus"; "Hail the day that sees Him rise"; "Hark! how all the welkin sings"; "Hark, the herald-angels sing"; "Lo! He comes, with clouds descending"; "Love Divine, all loves excelling"; "Jesu, Lover of my soul." However, by mid-eighteenth century, English congregational song had been nurtured by the common metres and generalized experiences from the voices of Protestant Dissent: Watts, Doddridge, Gibbons, and Hart. Wesley's specific experiences, his departure from the simple metres of the old Psalmody, his enthusiastic and controversial spirit – all appeared foreign to the tastes of Britons unfamiliar with the influences and teachings of Wesleyan Methodism.

Not until the late nineteenth century, when Methodism finally emerged from the abuse and contempt initiated by contemporary rivals of the Wesleys, did Charles Wesley's devotional poetry achieve the recognition it deserves. Essentially, the major pieces were seen to reflect the poet's sincere faith arising from his far-ranging loyalties and desires to interpret Christian experience. The hymns transmit that faith because he relied upon what people knew and felt, upon the essence of their own values. Culturally superior to the majority of persons whom he addressed, Wesley intentionally held back his own knowledge and, instead, wove his reactions and concerns through Scriptures, attempting to educate his readers with essential theological lessons. In the end, there remains little doubt as to the purpose and direction of a new voice who spoke with and for certain eighteenth-century Britons seeking God in times of trouble:

Weary of all this wordy strife,
　　These notions, forms, and modes, and names,
To Thee, the Way, the Truth, the Life,
　　Whose love my simple heart inflames,
　　Divinely taught, at last, I fly,
　　With Thee, and Thine to live, and die.

　　　　　　　　　　　　　　　　　　—Samuel J. Rogal

WHEATLEY, Phillis.　American.　Born in Africa, possibly Senegal, c. 1753; sold as a slave to the John Wheatley family in Boston in 1761. Educated in the Wheatley family. Married John Peters, a freed slave, in 1778; three children. Sent to England for her health, 1773, and was received in London society; returned to Boston in the same year to care for Mrs. Wheatley; separated from the Loyalist Wheatleys by the Revolutionary War; thereafter her health deteriorated; died in poverty. *Died 5 December 1784.*

PUBLICATIONS

Collections

　　Poems (includes letters), edited by Julian D. Mason, Jr.　1966.

Verse

　　An Elegiac Poem on the Death of George Whitfield.　1770.
　　To Mrs. Leonard.　1771.
　　To the Rev. Mr. Pitkin.　1772.
　　To Thomas Hubbard.　1773.
　　Poems on Various Subjects, Religious and Moral.　1773.
　　An Elegy to Mary Moorhead.　1773.
　　An Elegy to Samuel Cooper.　1784.
　　Liberty and Peace.　1784.

Reading List: *Wheatley: A Critical Attempt and Bibliography* by Charles Frederick Heartman, 1916; *Bid the Vassal Soar* (on Wheatley and George Moses Horton) by Merle A. Richmond, 1974.

　　　　　　　　　　　*　　*　　*

　　Phillis Wheatley's poetry is characterized by its adherence to form, in particular the heroic couplet, and conformity to neo-classical ritual in language and content. Thematically, she wrote to God's goodness, as opposed to His wrath, and she stressed that salvation is the most important goal in life. Her exposure to history, Classical literature, and myths is obvious in her poetry.

Wheatley's verses were didactic, pious, conventional, and predictable in that she wrote a significant number of occasional poems – for commemorating an event, perhaps, or for lamenting a death. Her tone fits the poems, however, and there is revealed in them a genuine adaptation to the subject-at-hand. She incorporates the Popean politeness into her verses as well as other features of his style – antithesis, the mid-line pause, and apostrophe.

Underneath the instructive tone and religious themes is the note of genuine religious joy based on her salvation from "The land of errors ... those dark abodes." Some critics have argued that Phillis Wheatley lost contact with her blackness; rather, she accomodated her blackness to a form she selected freely to use for expressing herself artistically – the heroic couplet. In all of Phillis Wheatley's poetry there rings an affirmation for life, even when she clearly identifies her race in what seems shame for her past enslavement. Her efforts to project herself away from the individual to the universal was part of the artistic detachment imposed by the form of poetry she loved, and the Puritan world in which she lived and believed. Her total output seems small only if one forgets her origins, her brief life, and the possibility that her husband sold or lost many of her works after her death. From poverty and slavery emerged a remarkable poet who sang "What songs should rise, how constant, how divine!"

—Margaret Perry

WHEELWRIGHT, John (Brooks).   American.   Born in Boston, Massachusetts, in 1897. Educated at Harvard University, Cambridge, Massachusetts; Massachusetts Institute of Technology, Cambridge: studied architecture. Practised as an architect in Boston. Editor, *Poems for a Dime* magazine. Official of the New England Poetry Society. *Died 15 September 1940.*

PUBLICATIONS

Collections

Collected Poems, edited by Alvin H. Rosenfeld.   1972.

Verse

Rock and Shell: Poems 1923–1933.   1933.
Mirrors of Venus: A Novel in Sonnets, 1914–1938.   1938.
Political Self-Portrait.   1940.
Selected Poems.   1941.

Other

Editor, *A History of the New England Poetry Club.*   1932.

*   *   *

John Wheelwright published three books during his lifetime, but none received sufficient notice to give him reputation while alive. Wheelwright was not the average Socialist scribbler of the Depression era, but a "proper Bostonian" of impeccable ancestry: on his father's side, he claimed his radical blood from the first Wheelwright, an emigré from England in 1636, who preached religious tolerance until he was banished from the Bay Colony. On his mother's side, he descended from John Brooks, an early governor of Massachusetts.

The contradictions explicit in such ancestry, radicalism, and political authority, were manifest in Wheelwright's own character and poetry. He taunted Boston Brahmins with his eccentric behavior in public and declared his allegiance to the proletariat, whose Depression plight he championed in many poems. All the while he accepted his upper-class status and remained much of his life an official of the doughty New England Poetry Society.

Wheelwright was an erratic craftsman in his poems, even though he emphasized his technique in long prose commentaries that accompanied his three published books. Many poems are long-winded, prosaic, and loosely framed. But occasionally his poems spring out with unanticipated lyric genius, as in "Train Ride" (*Political Self-Portrait*). His "sonnet novel" *Mirrors of Venus*, generally over-wrought, includes his masterful elegy "Father":

> Come home. Wire a wire of warning without words.
> Come home and talk to me again, my first friend. Father,
> come home, dead man, who made your mind my home.

Wheelwright's work often takes the form of rambling poetic tracts, where he is an interpreter of what he felt to be the reshaping of America. As he wrote at the end of *Political Self-Portrait*, "The main point is not what noise poetry makes, but how it makes you think and act, – not what you make of it; but what it makes of you." Although this is unfair to the musical grace of much of his language, it is pointed and correct essentially about his intentions for his poetry.

His first book, *Rock and Shell*, shows the poet searching for some premise of unity in his experience, especially in the powerful opening poem, "North Atlantic Passage," which joins prose and poetry together. Spiritual loneliness is followed by sexual loneliness in this carefully plotted book. *Mirrors of Venus* is, as one critic described it, his *In Memoriam* to his friend Ned Couch, but sags generally from its weight of technical embellishments.

Political Self-Portrait is his best book; here he has found a balance between the wrought textures of language and loosely plotted ideological arguments. The poems are longer, more discursive, but intensely dramatic as they register a diffident, sensitive conscience faced with social unheaval and coming war. The poems are rich in imagery, raw in angry, direct language, but dignified overall by the depth of the speaker's convictions. Some of these poems have lost their edge now, but many, including "Collective Collect," "Bread-Word Giver," and "Train Ride" are lasting expressions of faith in humanity. "Dusk to Dusk," included in the recent *Collected Poems*, has an even shriller tone of indignation than *Political Self-Portrait*, and its structure seems driven to fragments by the unleashed energies of this unusual poet.

—Paul Christensen

WHETSTONE, George. English. Born in London c. 1544. Courtier: spent his inheritance in extravagant living, and thereafter supported himself by writing and soldiering: served as an officer in the army, fighting against the Spanish in the Low Countries, 1572–74; accompanied Sir Humphrey Gilbert on his expedition to Newfoundland, 1578–79; visited Italy, 1580; accompanied the English forces to Holland, 1585–86, and fought at the Battle of Zutphen, 1586. *Died c. 1587.*

Verse

The Rock of Regard (includes fiction).   1576; edited by J. P. Collier, 1870.
A Remembrance of George Gascoigne.   1577; edited by E. Arber, with *Notes of Instruction* by George Gascoigne, 1868.
A Remembrance of Sir Nicholas Bacon.   1579; edited by A. Boswell, in *Frondes Caducae 1,* 1816.
A Remembrance of Sir James Dier.   1582 (?); edited by A. Boswell, in *Frondes Caducae 1,* 1816.
A Remembrance of Thomas, Late Earl of Sussex.   1583; edited by A Boswell, in *Frondes Caducae 1,* 1816.
A Mirror of the Life of Francis, Earl of Bedford.   1585; edited by T. Park, in *Heliconia 2,* 1815.

Play

Promos and Cassandra, from a story by Giraldi Cinthio (produced 1578).   1578; edited by Geoffrey Bullough, in *Narrative and Dramatic Sources of Shakespeare,* 1958.

Fiction

An Heptameron of Civil Discourses.   1582; as *Aurelia the Paragon of Pleasure,* 1593.

Other

A Mirror for Magistrates of Cities; A Touchstone for the Times.   1584; as *The Enemy to Thriftiness,* 1586.
The Honourable Reputation of a Soldier.   1585.
The English Mirror.   1586.
The Censure of a Loyal Subject, edited by Thomas Churchyard.   1587; edited by J. P. Collier, in *Illustrations of Early English Popular Literature 1,* 1863.
Sir Philip Sidney His Honourable Life.   1587; edited by A. Boswell, in *Frondes Caducae 1,* 1816.

Reading List: *Whetstone: Mid-Elizabethan Gentleman of Letters* by T. C. Izard, 1942.

*   *   *

Although George Whetstone wrote voluminously in a variety of genres – conduct books, travel accounts, pastorals, moral treatises, and amorous verse complaints – he is remembered chiefly as author of the ten-act tragicomedy *Promos and Cassandra,* which provided Shakespeare with his principal source for *Measure for Measure.* Whetstone's own source was the fifth novel of the eighth decade of Giraldi Cinthio's *Hecatomithi* (1565). Although Whetstone in his preface describes his play as a "history" and a "comical discourse," it is the first English play to deal seriously with a domestic conflict, and is thus a significant landmark in the development of domestic drama. Of slender poetic talent, Whetstone wrote the play in limping poulter's measure, followed his source closely, and maintained a humorless tone. In writing *Measure for Measure*, Shakespeare found little to appropriate from Whetstone except the bare bones of the plot, and even here Shakespeare wisely altered certain details to suit his own purposes. Four years after writing the play, Whetstone reworked it into a prose tale, *An Heptameron of Civil Discourses*. This change of genre enabled Whetstone to embellish the original story with lengthy digressions on one of his favorite subjects, the customs and manners of Italian nobility.

Whetstone's earliest work, *The Rock of Regard* (1576), consists of several prose tales with verse "complaints" of dissolute women like Cressida. Some of the verses are vigorous and brilliant, particularly his "Invective Against Dice." This work indicates that penchant for didacticism characteristic of such later works as *The Enemy to Unthriftiness*, essentially a sermon inveighing against vices, and *The English Mirror*, a systematic analysis in prose of a catalogue of wicked and worthy behavior. Another prose work, *The Honourable Reputation of a Soldier*, is a conduct book worthy of note for its firm, direct style and its psychological treatment of military life. One of Whetstone's last works was *The Censure of a Loyal Subject*, a dialogue castigating the condemned conspirators of the Babington Plot. In summary, Whetstone's strength as a writer would appear to be in his prose style, which is often vigorous and occasionally vivid when not dulled by sermonizing.

—James E. Ruoff

WHITMAN, Walt(er). American. Born in West Hills, Huntington, Long Island, New York, 31 May 1819. Educated in schools in Brooklyn, New York, 1825–30. Office Boy/Clerk in a lawyer's office, a doctor's office, and, in 1830, a printing office; began newspaper work on the Long Island *Patriot and Star*, 1831–34; schoolteacher on Long Island, 1836–41; Founder and Editor, *The Long Islander*, Huntington, 1838; Compositor, *Long Island Democrat*, 1839; worked as a newspaper man in New York, and as editor of the *Aurora*, *Tatler* and *Democrat*, 1840–46; Editor, Brooklyn *Daily Eagle*, 1846–47; Editor, New Orleans *Crescent*, 1848; Editor, Brooklyn *Freeman* (Free Soil Party paper), 1848–49; gave up newspaper work and, living with his parents, worked as a part-time carpenter while writing verse, 1850–54; free-lance journalist, 1855–62: Editor, Brooklyn *Daily Times*, 1857; served as a nurse in the Civil War, in Washington, D.C., 1862–65; Clerk in the Bureau of Indian Affairs, Washington, 1865; worked in the Attorney-General's Office, Washington, 1865 until he suffered a paralytic stroke, 1873; lived with his brother in Camden, New Jersey; travelled to the Far West and Canada, 1879–80; bought a house in Camden, 1884, and lived there for the remainder of his life. *Died 26 March 1892.*

PUBLICATIONS

Collections

The Collected Writings, edited by Gay Wilson Allen and Sculley Bradley. 1961–
The Complete Poems, edited by Francis Murphy. 1975.

Verse

Leaves of Grass.   1855; revised edition, 1856, 1860, 1867, 1870, 2 vols., 1876, 1881,
    1889, 1891, 1897; manuscripts edited by Fredson Bowers, 1955, Harry W. Blodgett,
    1959, and Arthur Golden, 2 vols., 1968.
Drum-Taps.   1865; with *Sequel to Drum-Taps*, 1866.
Poems, edited by W. M. Rossetti.   1868.
Passage to India.   1870.
After All, Not to Create Only.   1871.
As a Strong Bird on Pinions Free.   1872.
November Boughs (includes prose).   1888.
Good-Bye My Fancy.   1891.
Pictures: An Unpublished Poem, edited by Emory Holloway.   1927.

Fiction

Franklin Evans; or, The Inebriate.   1842; edited by Emory Holloway, 1929.
The Half-Breed and Other Stories, edited by Thomas O. Mabbott.   1927.

Other

Democratic Vistas.   1870.
Memoranda During the War.   1875–76.
Specimen Days and Collect.   2 vols., 1882–83; revised edition, as *Specimen Days in
    America,* 1887.
Complete Poems and Prose 1855–1888.   1888–89.
Complete Prose.   1892.
Autobiographia.   1892.
In Re Walt Whitman, edited by Horace L. Traubel and others.   1893.
Calamus: Letters, edited by Richard M. Bucke.   1897.
The Wound Dresser (letters), edited by Richard M. Bucke.   1898.
Notes and Fragments, edited by Richard M. Bucke.   1899.
An American Primer, edited by Horace L. Traubel.   1904.
Diary in Canada, edited by William Sloane Kennedy.   1904.
Lafayette in Brooklyn.   1905.
Criticism: An Essay.   1913.
The Gathering of Forces (essays), edited by Cleveland Rogers and John Black.   2 vols.,
    1920.
Uncollected Poetry and Prose, edited by Emory Holloway.   2 vols., 1921.
Rivulets of Prose: Critical Essays, edited by Carolyn Wells and Alfred F.
    Goldsmith.   1928.
Whitman's Workshop, edited by Clifton J. Furness.   1928.
A Child's Reminiscence, edited by Thomas O. Mabbott and Rollo G. Silver.   1930.
I Sit and Look Out (essays), edited by Emory Holloway and Vernolian Schwarz.   1932.
Whitman and the Civil War: A Collection of Original Articles and Manuscripts, edited by
    Charles I. Glicksberg.   1933.
New York Dissected (essays), edited by Emory Holloway and Ralph Adimari.   1936.
Whitman's Backward Glances, edited by Sculley Bradley and John A.
    Stevenson.   1947.
Faint Clews and Indirections, edited by Clarence Gohdes and Rollo G. Silver.   1949.
Whitman Looks at the Schools, edited by Florence Bernstein Freedman.   1950.

Whitman of the New York Aurora, edited by Joseph Jay Rubin and Charles H. Brown. 1950.
Whitman's Civil War, edited by Walter Lowenfels. 1960.
Whitman's New York: From Manhattan to Montauk (essays), edited by Henry M. Christman. 1963.
Camden Conversations, edited by Walter Teller. 1973.

Bibliography: by Oscar Lovell Triggs, in *Complete Writings 10*, 1902; "Whitman's Journalism: A Bibliography" by William White, in *Walt Whitman Review*, September 1968.

Reading List: *Whitman* by Frederick Schyberg, translated by Evie Allison Allen, 1951; *The Solitary Singer: A Critical Biography*, 1955, revised edition, 1967, and *A Reader's Guide to Whitman*, 1970, both by Gay Wilson Allen; *Whitman Reconsidered*, 1955, and *Whitman*, 1961, both by Richard Chase; *Leaves of Grass One Hundred Years After* edited by Milton Hindus, 1955; *The Evolution of Whitman* by Roger Asselineau, 2 vols., 1960; *The Presence of Whitman* edited by R. W. B. Lewis, 1962; *Whitman: A Collection of Critical Essays* edited by Roy Harvey Pearce, 1962; *A Century of Whitman Criticism* edited by Edwin H. Miller, 1969; *The Foreground of Leaves of Grass* by Floyd Stovall, 1974.

*   *   *

The life and work of Walt Whitman are in some measure a metaphor for America. Whitman began sounding his "barbaric yawp" over the roofs of the world when the youthful United States was a power of little consequence among nations. He was scorned or ignored at first, but gradually his *Leaves of Grass* compelled attention to its democratic message. By the time Whitman died his poetry had become a force to reckon with in the world.

Whitman's considerable apprenticeship as a newspaper writer and editor before 1855 gives no warning of a major poet in the making. His early poetry is undistinguished, and his prose is only competent journalism. But somehow Whitman found his inspiration and his vocation as poet. Emerson was probably the dominant influence, for in his essay "The Poet" he had called for a great American poet: "I look in vain for the poet whom I describe." And he added that "we have yet had no genius in America" who "knew the value of our incomparable materials." Whitman, for his part, later said: "I was simmering, simmering, simmering; Emerson brought me to a boil."

In response to a presentation copy of the first edition of *Leaves of Grass* in 1855 Emerson wrote Whitman: "I find it the most extraordinary piece of wit and wisdom that America has yet contributed ... I greet you at the beginning of a great career." The first edition was a slender volume of 95 pages that Whitman had had to publish himself, but it contained one of the great poems of the English language, the long, untitled poem that later, after revisions and additions, was called "Song of Myself." What Emerson had read when he opened the volume to the beginning of the poetry was

> I celebrate myself,
> And what I assume you shall assume,
> For every atom belonging to me as good belongs to you.

Thus began Whitman's mystic vision of equality, national purpose, and international brotherhood, "hoping to cease not till death," as he added in a line written later. The work did go on as long as he lived, and preparations for the final edition of his lifetime, arranged in the way he wanted his literary executors to print future editions, were in progress at the time he died.

The first edition is the work of the somewhat brash, 36-year-old Brooklyn carpenter-poet. But by the time the third edition appeared in 1860, Whitman had matured and deepened his human sympathies. Also the book had grown from the original 12 poems to 100 and contained the so-called "sex poems" that made Whitman anathema to proper Victorians. These are the "Children of Adam" poems dealing with heterosexual love and the "Calamus" poems treating homosexual affection. Many of them are tender, beautiful poems worth close study. But the most important new poem was "Out of the Cradle Endlessly Rocking," one of Whitman's greatest lyrics. It blends theme, symbol, and reminiscence in a free-verse form that Whitman had absolutely mastered. This edition, moreover, gives us a clear insight into Whitman's growth as a poet. It is an articulated whole, with a beginning, middle, and end, and one can begin to see the shape of *Leaves of Grass* in its final form. The most prominent themes of the third edition are love and death; both appear in the first two editions, but here they take on a tragic significance, and in Whitman's struggle with these themes he becomes a major poet.

Whitman's experiences in Washington as a volunteer nurse and his visits to Virginia battlefields during the Civil War provided the material for *Drum-Taps*, later incorporated into *Leaves of Grass*. This is the best collection of war poetry produced by any American writer on the Civil War. "Come Up from the Fields, Father" and "Vigil Strange I Kept on the Field One Night" are vivid, poignant examples. Shortly after *Drum-Taps* appeared, Lincoln's assassination inspired Whitman's memorable elegy "When Lilacs Last in the Dooryard Bloom'd." This poem employs the symbols of star (Lincoln), lilac (love), and bird (poet's soul) in 16 stanzas of beautiful free verse and begins:

> When lilacs last in the dooryard bloom'd,
> And the great star early droop'd in the western sky in the night,
> I mourn'd, and yet shall mourn with ever-returning spring.

But at the end the poet is reconciled to the loss of the wartime leader. The star, the lilac, and the bird singing in the swamp will remind him annually of "the dead I loved so well."

The fifth edition of *Leaves of Grass* came out in 1870, and in it the main order of the book became settled. It opens with the "Inscriptions," follows with "Starting from Paumanok," and ends with "Songs of Parting." Published as an annex to this edition was another of Whitman's best-known poems, "A Passage to India," a poem in which his vision of universal fraternity is clearly shown. It begins by celebrating the joining of east and west by the transcontinental railroad, the Suez Canal, and the Atlantic cable and goes on to envision these engineering feats as part of "God purpose" for "The people to become brothers and sisters."

An edition of 1881 was to have been brought out by James R. Osgood and Co. of Boston, but the district attorney of Boston threatened prosecution and Whitman was forced to find another publisher. A bolder Philadelphia firm issued the book without incident, for by this time Whitman, "The good gray poet," as his friend William O'Connor had dubbed him during the Washington years, was becoming a national figure and living down the early notoriety. In this edition the poems received their final revisions and titles ("Song of Myself" appears here for the first time) and permanent positions. Whitman continued to write until he died, but later editions print the later poems as annexes.

Although Whitman's poetry is the reason for his literary stature, he also wrote a considerable body of prose. The preface to the 1855 edition is an important statement; also noteworthy is the preface to *As a Strong Bird. Democratic Vistas*, however, is his major prose work. It is a collection of essays that are more a glimpse into the future of democracy than an analysis of the present. It tempers Whitman's usual buoyant optimism with a frank admission that the American democracy of 1871 (the period of the Grant Administration and the "Gilded Age") was not perfect. But he did not lose his faith in the ultimate success of the American experiment. Another prose work of interest is the informal autobiography that he published under the title *Specimen Days*.

Whitman is the first American poet to achieve a truly international reputation. Although Baudelaire discovered Poe before anyone ever had heard of Whitman, the Pre-Raphaelites in England soon discovered Whitman, and William Michael Rossetti edited an edition of *Leaves of Grass* in 1868. British interest in Whitman helped to convince Americans that the poet was not a charlatan, and from that modest beginning his reputation has spread like eddies from a rock dropped in still water. Jan Christian Smuts wrote a book on him in 1895, a study of his prosody was published in Italy in 1898, and an important French study appeared in 1908.

Although Whitman claimed he was not interested in technique, the sizable number of extant manuscripts show that he labored over his poems, making many cuts, additions, emendations. The variant readings of successive editions likewise reveal the poet as reviser. His form, however, has given critics trouble over the years. He said: "My form has strictly grown from my purports and facts, and is the analogy of them." His purpose was to present his vision and his experience, and it is not surprising that some readers have seen in his work the raw material of poetry rather than finished poems. The chief structural device is parallelism: repetition of idea, repetition of syntax, repetition of sound. Some 41% of the 10,500 lines of *Leaves of Grass* contain initial reiteration. One notes also that run-on lines are a rarity, and the first person singular is used extensively.

The influences on Whitman's free verse seem to have been public address, the Bible, and music. Not only was Emerson an inspiration in Whitman's finding his vocation as poet, but Emerson's essays, written as lectures, contain many of the same rhetorical devices that Whitman uses. Whitman as a young man wrote speeches and at one time had thought of making a career as a public speaker. The parallelism and coordinate structure of the Bible, which Whitman knew well, also may have influenced his style, though this is hard to document. Finally, the impact of music must be accorded a place in Whitman's development. The repetition of themes, the use of *recitative* and *aria* support Whitman's own statement: "But for the opera I could never have written *Leaves of Grass*."

—James Woodress

WHITTIER, John Greenleaf. American. Born in Haverhill, Massachusetts, 17 December 1807. Educated at local schools; studied art at Haverhill Academy, 1827; teacher there, 1827–28. Editor, various country newspapers, 1826–32; engaged in the anti-slavery campaign as editor of various reform journals and as polemicist, 1833–60; settled at Amesbury, Massachusetts, 1836: after the Civil War lived in semi-retirement, devoting himself to verse. *Died 7 September 1892.*

PUBLICATIONS

Collections

> *The Writings,* edited by Horace E. Scudder. 7 vols., 1888–89; revised edition, 1894.
> *The Poetical Works,* edited by W. Garrett Horder. 1919.
> *Letters,* edited by John B. Pickard. 3 vols., 1977.

Verse

> *Moll Pitcher.* 1831; revised edition, 1840.
> *Mogg Megone.* 1836.
> *Poems Written During the Progress of the Abolition Question, 1830–1838.* 1837.

Poems. 1838.
Moll Pitcher, and The Minstrel Girl. 1840.
Lays of My Home and Other Poems. 1843.
The Song of the Vermonters. 1843.
Miscellaneous Poems. 1844.
Ballads and Other Poems. 1844.
The Stranger in Lowell. 1845.
Voices of Freedom. 1846.
Poems. 1849.
Songs of Labor and Other Poems. 1850.
Poetical Works. 1853.
The Chapel of the Hermits and Other Poems. 1853.
A Sabbath Scene. 1854.
The Panorama and Other Poems. 1856.
The Sycamores. 1857.
The Poetical Works. 2 vols., 1857.
Home Ballads and Other Poems. 1860
In War Time and Other Poems. 1864.
National Lyrics. 1865.
Snow-Bound: A Winter Idyl. 1866.
The Tent on the Beach and Other Poems. 1867.
Among the Hills and Other Poems. 1869.
Poetical Works. 2 vols., 1870.
Ballads of New England. 1870.
Miriam and Other Poems. 1871.
The Pennsylvania Pilgrim and Other Poems. 1872.
Hazel-Blossoms. 1875.
Mabel Martin: A Harvest Idyl. 1876.
Favorite Poems. 1877.
The Vision of Echard and Other Poems. 1878.
The King's Missive and Other Poems. 1881.
The Bay of Seven Islands and Other Poems. 1883.
Early Poems. 1885.
Saint Gregory's Guest and Recent Poems. 1886.
Poems of Nature. 1886.
Narrative and Legendary Poems. 1888.
At Sundown. 1890.
Legends and Lyrics. 1890.
A Legend of the Lake. 1893.
The Demon Lady. 1894.

Other

Legends of New England. 1831.
Justice and Expediency. 1833.
Narrative of James Williams. 1838.
The Supernaturalism of New England. 1847; edited by Edward Wagenknecht, 1969.
Leaves from Margaret Smith's Journal. 1849.
Old Portraits and Modern Sketches. 1850.
Literary Recreations and Miscellanies. 1854.
Prose Works. 2 vols., 1866.
Works. 1874.
Complete Works. 1876.

Whittier on Writers and Writing: The Uncollected Critical Writings, edited by Edwin
Cady and Harry Hayden Clark.   1950.

Editor, *The Journal of John Woolman.*   1872.
Editor, *Child Life: A Collection of Poems.*   1873.
Editor, *Child Life in Prose.*   1874.
Editor, *Songs of Three Centuries.*   1876; revised edition, 1877.

Bibliography: *A Bibliography of Whittier* by Thomas F. Currier, 1937.

Reading List: *Life and Letters of Whittier* by Samuel T. Pickard, 1894, revised edition, 2 vols.,
1907; *Whittier: Bard of Freedom* by Whitman Bennett, 1941; *Whittier: Friend of Man* by
John A. Pollard, 1949; *Whittier* by Lewis Leary, 1961; *Whittier: An Introduction and
Interpretation by* John B. Pickard, 1961; *Whittier: A Portrait in Paradox* by Edward
Wagenknecht, 1967; *Whittier's Poetry: An Appraisal and a Selection* by Robert Penn
Warren, 1971; *Life of Whittier* by William J. Linton, 1972.

*   *   *

In the "Proem," a poem which introduced his collected works, John Greenleaf Whittier
scrutinized his life and poetic achievement in these lines:

> The rigor of a frozen clime,
> The harshness of an untaught ear,
> The jarring words of one whose rhyme
> Beat often Labor's hurried time,
> Or Duty's rugged march, through storm and strife,
> are here.

The honesty of these sparse lines is characteristic. Reared as a poor farm boy in a non-
conformist Quaker faith, he had little education and was primarily a sectional romantic poet
in his early years. Fortunately his enlistment in the abolitionist cause in 1833 converted the
aspiring young lyricist into a radical propagandist, politician, and part-time editor whose
verses championed the rights of slaves and democratic principles. The twenty years of
abolitionist work reforged Whittier's vapid sentimentalism into a powerful weapon for the
oppressed and strengthened his regard for moral action. By the 1850's Whittier's reform
work was over, and in his remaining years his writing showed him as a religious humanist,
striving for moral perfection and inner spirituality rather than social and political reform.

Like most of the "schoolroom" poets, Longfellow, Lowell, Holmes, and others, Whittier's
themes were few and limited: the value of domestic emotions, the innocence of childhood,
the necessity of social equality, and the nobility of ethical action. However, unlike these other
popular poets, Whittier drew upon his native roots for inspiration. In his best poems Whittier
displayed a mastery of local color techniques, a competent use of rural imagery, and the
everyday language of the Merrimack farmer. His instinctive handling of native materials
conveyed his inner love for the environment that molded, and his understanding of the
traditions that inspired, him. Still his poetry suffered from the diffusion and sentimentality
inherent in the tradition of public rhetoric in which he wrote. Perhaps no other established
nineteenth-century American poet wrote so much poor verse, but the miracle is that by the
most exacting poetical standards his best remains so good.

Aside from a few nature poems like "The Last Walk in Autumn," an occasional
Abolitionist poem like "Ichabod," and selections from his religious poems, Whittier's ballads
and genre pieces represent his finest poetical achievement. They contain some of the best
examples of native folklore written in America. His ballads, especially, express his lifelong

interest in colonial history, the Quakers, local legends, and folk superstitions; and they are remarkably true to the graphic realism and dramatic intensity of traditional folk balladry. His best ballads take incidents like a skipper who had betrayed his own townspeople, a witch who prophesied death, or the terrifying actions of specter warriors, bed-rocks them with exact physical detail, and then concentrates on the dramatic moment of conflict. "Telling the Bees" skillfully handles a local superstition with childlike detail to hide the chilling reality of nature's destruction; "The Garrison of Cape Ann," "The Palatine," and "The King's Missive" rework historical incidents; "Amy Wentworth," "The Countess," and "The Witch of Wenham" narrate pastoral romances; while the often-parodied "Barbara Frietchie" was accepted by a war-wearied nation as an expression of their personal conviction that the Union must be preserved. Whittier's finest ballad, "Skipper Ireson's Ride," was based on an old Marblehead song about women tarring and feathering a fishingboat captain. The ballad opens *in medias res*, plunging directly into the wild tumult and chaos of mob action as the skipper is pushed through Marblehead. Finally Ireson cries out his remorse, and with "half scorn, half pity" the women free him. The final refrain changes "Old" Floyd Ireson to "Poor" Floyd Ireson and becomes a mournful dirge forever accusing and dooming Ireson, besides emphasizing the hollowness of the women's revenge.

Similarly, Whittier's genre poems elevated the ordinary details of Essex County life into a universal expression of boyhood innocence, agrarian simplicity, and pastoral romance that caught the pathos and beauty of a dying rural tradition. In poems like "Maud Muller," "In School-Days," "Among the Hills," and "Memories," Whittier idealized and typified the district school days, the harvest-filled autumn days, and the barefoot-boy days to capture the romantic aspirations of a responsive American public. "Cobbler Keezar's Vision," "Abraham Davenport," "To My Old Schoolmaster," and others contain some of Whittier's best rustic anecdotes as well as realistic and humorous sketches of the Yankee character. Whittier's particular skill in recreating the past is seen most fully in his one sustained triumph, *Snow-Bound*. In this poem Whittier expresses the value of family affections by the symbolic development of a fire-snow contrast and by the skillful interweaving of present reality with past memories. His artistic handling of structure, careful development of the fire image, and graphic depiction of the family and outside visitors make this a minor masterpiece of nineteenth-century poetry. In this poem Whittier captured the essence of the New England mind and placed himself in the direct line of American expression that stretches from Anne Bradstreet to Robert Frost.

Although Whittier's poems fall far short of the poetic imagination and philosophical depth of major American poets such as Whitman, Poe, Dickinson, and Emerson, his verses exhibit more spiritual illumination and downright "grit" than the polished verses of Longfellow and the other minor poets. Despite the severe criticism of his poetry in the twentieth century, Whittier's place in American literature seems secure. He will continue to be read and enjoyed as long as people respond to their traditions and demand honest expression of their fundamental democratic and religious feelings.

—John B. Pickard

WIGGLESWORTH, Michael. American. Born in England, probably in Yorkshire, 18 October 1631; emigrated with his parents to the Massachusetts Bay Colony, 1638. Educated at Harvard University, Cambridge, Massachusetts, graduated 1651. Married 1) Mary Reyner in 1655 (died, 1659), one daughter; 2) Martha Mudge in 1679 (died, 1690), six children; 3) Sybil Sparhawk Avery in 1691, one son. Fellow and Tutor at Harvard University, 1652–54; ordained to the ministry of the Puritan Church, 1656, and thereafter served as Minister to the church at Malden, Massachusetts; also studied and practised medicine; Fellow at Harvard University, 1697–1705. *Died 27 May 1705.*

Publications

Collections

The Day of Doom with Other Poems, edited by Kenneth B. Murdock.   1929.

Verse

The Day of Doom.   1662(?); revised edition, 1666.
Meat Out of the Eater.   1670; revised edition, with *Riddles Unriddled,* 1689.
Riddles Unriddled: or, Christian Paradoxes.   1689.

Other

The Diary, edited by Edmund S. Morgan.   1965.

Reading List: *Sketch of the Life of Wigglesworth, with a Fragment of His Autobiography, Some of His Letters, and a Catalogue of His Library* by John W. Dean, 1863, revised edition, 1871; *No Featherbed to Heaven: A Biography of Wigglesworth* by Richard H. Crowder, 1962.

                              *   *   *

Michael Wigglesworth's first major publication, *The Day of Doom* – a best-seller for a century – was a jeremiad of 224 eight-line stanzas presenting in vivid detail the Calvinist notion of the events of the Final Judgment. The writer's purpose was not to write fine poetry but to provide uncomplicated facts in easy rhyme. For generations children recited from memory the entire poem, which devotes a few stanzas to the rewards of the saved but many more to the pleas, sentencing, and punishment of the damned. In the same volume with *The Day of Doom* Wigglesworth published several other poems setting forth Puritan doctrine, pleading with the reader to turn from wickedness and avoid everlasting punishment (e.g., "A Short Discourse on Eternity" and "Vanity of Vanities"), verses couched in sermonic phrases, jogging along in well-worn meters without much variety. The imagery, already familiar to his church-going readers, was nevertheless vigorously pictorial as the poet strove to convert the sinners.

Another jeremiad, "God's Controversy with New-England," showed the reader that because of the general evil-doing of the colonists God was right in inflicting illness and drought on the region. The verse forms here change from ballad structure ("fourteeners") to six-line iambics to quatrains as Wigglesworth pleads the cause for spiritual renewal.

The other large work he called *Meat Out of the Eater,* a series of ten meditations and "A Conclusion Hortatory" demonstrating "the Necessity, End, and Usefulness of Afflictions." "Riddles Unriddled," clusters of verses constituting nine paradoxes, uses a little more variety in verse form in an attempt to fit structure to meaning. For example, the first paradox, "Light in Darkness," consists of ten "Songs," some in the form of medieval debates. The poet moves from ballad form in one "Song" to six-syllable lines in couplet rhyme in another. The other paradoxes likewise are composed of a number of separate poems, illustrating such themes as "Strength in Weakness" and "In Confinement Liberty."

In a twelve-year span (1662–1673) – during a period when he was physically too weak to preach from his Malden pulpit – Wigglesworth wrote nearly all his extant poetry, and in a surprising variety of forms: lyric, dramatic, narrative, descriptive, didactic and hortatory, and autobiographical. Though not a major poet, he made a serious contribution to Puritan

Calvinist doctrine, preserving in not unreadable verse the ideas that his readers were hearing from the pulpit Sunday after Sunday.

Wigglesworth's *Diary* was edited by Edmund S. Morgan. He transcribed and made available to modern readers the frequent passages in shorthand. The *Diary* fully discloses the poet's constant struggle with his conscience, his soul warring against powerful drives inside his frail flesh. A couple of college orations (including "The Praise of Eloquence") have been preserved and are sometimes anthologized. Written in "plain style," they are obviously class assignments discussing the elements of effective oratory.

—Richard H. Crowder

WILBUR, Richard (Purdy). American. Born in New York City, 1 March 1921. Educated at Amherst College, Massachusetts, B.A. 1942; Harvard University, Cambridge, Massachusetts, M.A. 1947. Served in the United States Army, 1943–45. Married Charlotte Ward in 1942; one daughter and three sons. Member of the Society of Fellows, 1947–50, and Assistant Professor of English, 1950–54, Harvard University; Associate Professor of English, Wellesley College, Massachusetts, 1955–57. Since 1957, Professor of English, Wesleyan University, Middletown, Connecticut. General Editor, Laurel Poets series, Dell Publishing Company, New York. State Department Cultural Exchange Representative to the U.S.S.R., 1961. Recipient: Guggenheim Fellowship, 1952, 1963; American Academy in Rome Fellowship, 1954; Pulitzer Prize, 1957; National Book Award 1957; Edna St. Vincent Millay Memorial Award, 1957; Ford Foundation Fellowship, for drama, 1960; Melville Cane Award, 1962; Bollingen Prize, for translation, 1963, and for verse, 1971; Sarah Josepha Hale Award, 1968; Brandeis University Creative Arts Award, 1970; Prix Henri Desfeuilles, 1971; Shelley Memorial Award, 1973. L.H.D.: Lawrence College, Appleton, Wisconsin, 1960; Washington University, St. Louis, 1964; D.Litt.: Amherst College, 1967. Member, American Academy of Arts and Sciences; since 1974, President, American Academy of Arts and Letters; Chancellor, Academy of American Poets. Lives in Cummington, Massachusetts.

PUBLICATIONS

Verse

> *The Beautiful Changes and Other Poems.* 1947.
> *Ceremony and Other Poems.* 1950.
> *Things of This World.* 1956; one section reprinted as *Digging to China*, 1970.
> *Poems 1943–1956.* 1957.
> *Advice to a Prophet and Other Poems.* 1961.
> *The Poems.* 1963.
> *Prince Souvanna Phouma: An Exchange Between Richard Wilbur and William Jay Smith.* 1963.
> *Complaint.* 1968.
> *Walking to Sleep: New Poems and Translations.* 1969.
> *Seed Leaves: Homage to R. F.* 1974.
> *The Mind-Reader: New Poems.* 1976.

Plays

The Misanthrope, from the play by Molière (produced 1955).   1955; revised version,
   music by Margaret Pine (produced 1977).
Candide (lyrics only, with John LaTouche and Dorothy Parker), book by Lillian
   Hellman, music by Leonard Bernstein, from the novel by Voltaire (produced
   1956).   1957.
Tartuffe. from the play by Molière (produced 1964).   1963.
School for Wives, from a play by Molière (produced 1971).   1971.
The Learned Ladies, from a play by Molière.   1978.

Other

Loudmouse (juvenile).   1963.
Opposites (juvenile), illustrated by the author.   1973.
Responses: Prose Pieces 1948–1976.   1976.

Editor, *A Bestiary* (anthology).   1955.
Editor, *Complete Poems of Poe.*   1959.
Editor, with Alfred Harbage, *Poems of Shakespeare.*   1966; revised edition, as *The
   Narrative Poems, and Poems of Doubtful Authenticity,*   1974.
Editor, *Selected Poems,* by Witter Bynner.   1978.

Translator, *The Funeral of Bobo,* by Joseph Brodsky.   1974.

Bibliography: *Wilbur: A Bibliographical Checklist* by John P. Field,   1971.

Reading List: *Wilbur* by Donald L. Hill, 1967; *Wilbur: A Critical Essay* by Paul F.
Cummins, 1971.

*   *   *

Richard Wilbur's first volume of poems surprised its early readers in 1947: there was none
of the standard theorizing about history or large "modern" issues and only occasional
reflections of the poet's experiences in the war; instead, the poet of *The Beautiful Changes*
spoke openly of beauty, unabashedly expressing his delight in the sights and sounds and
movements of the world and demonstrating a dazzling virtuosity at recreating them in his
verse. He also revealed his delight in wit, imaginative play, and even games. One of the
poems was entitled simply "&," and his delights are joined in some lines from "Grace":

> One is tickled again, by the dining-car waiter's absurd
> Acrobacy – tipfingered tray like a wind-besting bird
> Plumblines his swinging shoes, the sole things sure
> In the shaken train.

In addition to the high spirits, the poems often almost exemplified elegance, poise, and good
manners.
   A number of those qualities and subjects came to seem even more startling in the years
which followed. From the beginning up to *The Mind-Reader*, Wilbur's poetry has shown
notable continuities. He has remarked that in his later poems he tends to move towards "a
plainer and more straightforward" way of writing and, also, from poems that use a "single
meditative voice balancing argument and counter-argument, feeling and counter-feeling" to

more "dramatic" ones (such as "Two Voices in a Meadow" or "The Aspen and the Stream") that may use two opposing voices. Readers may also detect a general deepening of feeling and a clearer personal voice as well as some unpredictable developments. But most of the earlier qualities remain, and there continue to be signal exclusions: no confessional poetry and no free verse (Wilbur wrote that in the fairy story about the genie which could be summoned out of a bottle, he had always assumed that the genie gained his strength from being *in* the bottle).

It is unlikely that anyone could have predicted, however, that the poet who showed an almost Keatsian responsiveness to the sensuous should become the translator of Molière into extraordinary English couplets. In retrospect, it is clearer that Molière represents part of what Wilbur is, as well as what he admires: a humane voice of uncommonly rational common-sense; a user of language that is both familiar and chaste; a witty enemy of the pompous, the gross, and the fanatic; and a juggler, a master of poise and point. Nor could one have anticipated "Junk," the liveliest recreation of Anglo-Saxon meters and feeling since Pound, or the scathing Miltonic sonnet to Lyndon Johnson, or the tenderness of the translations from Charles d'Orléans, Voltaire, and Francis Jammes, or the effectiveness of "A Christmas Hymn," or the moving elegy for Dudley Fitts.

Neither could one have quite anticipated "Walking to Sleep," an extraordinary exploration of the paths, strategems, surprises, and terrors that lie between waking and sleep, nor "The Mind-Reader," although both long poems extend one of Wilbur's most persistent themes in his more obviously personal lyrics: the processes, reflections, and creations of the mind. Wilbur once remarked, "A good part of my work could, I suppose, be understood as a public quarrel with the aesthetics of Edgar Allan Poe." His continuous concern is evidenced by his edition of Poe's poems and a number of substantial essays on both the prose and the verse: three of the sixteen provocative and lucid essays in *Responses: Prose Pieces 1948–1976* concern Poe. He once wrote, "There has never been a grander conception of poetry [than Poe's], nor a more impoverished one." As that sentence suggests, the quarrel continues because Wilbur finds it so difficult to make a decision once for all. His ambivalence (at the simplest level, his fascination with the intellectual, the perfectly beautiful and purely harmonious, and his almost simultaneous reaction away from such an ideal in an acceptance and love for the imperfect human and material reality that we can know here and now) is the theme of a number of his best poems. "A World Without Objects Is a Sensible Emptiness" is one of many that balances the soul's longing for purity and perfection with, almost simultaneously with the moment of ascension towards the empyrean, a counter movement as it accepts and rejoices in the body and its world. Wilbur's poetry often seems that of a natural Platonist who keeps learning to accept the Incarnation. "The Writer" movingly recognizes that the literary "flight" has its origins as well as final resting place in human suffering and love.

If Robert Frost has an authentic living heir, it is probably Wilbur – particularly as the poet of the short lyric in strict and familiar meters who speaks in the middle voice, wittily and movingly, to a wide audience. There are, however, important differences: Wilbur's voice is usually more obviously that of an urban man in contrast to the characteristic voice of the countryman which Frost so carefully crafted; and Frost never devoted such care to the attempt to translate, self-effacedly, the poetry of others, nor did he write for the public theater. But the most important difference is probably in their spirits. Frost did not share with anything like Wilbur's conviction the notion that "Love Calls Us to the Things of This World." It may have been, in part at least, that conviction which enabled Wilbur to make imaginatively convincing his "Advice to a Prophet" concerning how we might be persuaded not to destroy our earth.

—Joseph H. Summers

WILKINSON, Anne (Cochran Boyd). Canadian. Born in Toronto, Ontario, 21 September 1910. Educated privately. Married Frederik R. Wilkinson in 1932 (divorced, 1953); two sons and one daughter. Co-Founding Editor, *Tamarack Review*, Toronto, 1956. *Died 10 May 1961.*

PUBLICATIONS

Collections

Collected Poems, and a Prose Memoir, edited by A. J. M. Smith.   1968.

Verse

Counterpoint to Sleep.   1951.
The Hangman Ties the Holly.   1955.

Other

Lions in the Way: A Discursive History of the Oslers.   1956.
Swann and Daphne (juvenile).   1960.

*   *   *

Anne Wilkinson's work is beautifully of a piece, and part of the impressive effect her poetry makes on the reader is the result of the precision and firmness of her literary identity. All the poems, however varied, strike one as issuing from a single source. She brings to mind the name of Hopkins, not in any passive or imitative way but in the intensity and singularity of her sensibility. Her disinterestedness is quite pure, her eye bent without distraction upon the object, and yet the savour of inimitable individuality, of the presence of the author in every syllable, is unmistakable. She is capable of taking a single image, as in her exquisite poem "Lens," and of deriving from it a substantial poem. But all the generation is from within, so that there is no sense of the softness or accretion of pointless apposition – as there is in her weaker production. The pose in "Lens," as in all her best work, is perfect because of the clarity and force, almost the ferocity, of the vision.

She is fascinated by the variety and the continuity of sense-experience, by its blending and blurring of the physical and the psychological, by its organic relationship with the vegetable world at one end of the scale ("Still Life," "A Poet's-Eye View," "Summer Acres") and at the other by its extension into the psychic world ("The Puritan," "After Reading Kafka," "To a Psycho-Neurotic"). Such activity of the senses in the poet produces, as we see, for example, in Wordsworth's *The Prelude*, a world of exceptional presence and brilliance, the mind of the poet being in its creativity almost the opposite to the mere registering instrument advanced by Locke as a mental model. The more vital the subject in fact, the more powerful the object. Thus for Anne Wilkinson even the formless flow of time is something ferocious, "Time is tiger." The external world appears as "The striped, discerning tiger"; the poet's relations with it as dangerous and terrifying, as in "Poem of Anxiety":

When night's at large in the jungle
I go fearful
Lest I kiss or claw his eye.
Too whoo, too whit, who's who
When all the jungle reeks?

To say that Anne Wilkinson's poetry is saturated with sense-experience is to say that she is infatuated with existence, the senses being for her the immediate and subtlest entrance into life. This is why her best work gives the reader the sense of sharing an entranced experience of pure existence. It is this model or shape of perfection she struggles to make the rest of living, and even the act of dying, conform to, just as it is the inwardness and sincerity with which the effort is made that confers on her poetry an extraordinary distinction and integrity.

There are two initiating and sustaining conceptions in Anne Wilkinson's poetry: a deep conviction about the unity of existence, which does not exclude a fine sense of its manifold distinctions; and a vibrant joy in the face of existence, which can go with the most intimate experience of grimness and pain. The first never puffs into grandiosity, the second does not slump into complacency because the poetry is marked by qualities tending constantly to work for poise and actuality, wit, continuity, palpability. It is this recovering, connecting, particularizing, palpable tradition of poetry, a line joining Robert Graves to Gerard Manley Hopkins and Keats to Donne, which Anne Wilkinson represents so strongly in Canadian literature.

If poetry as illumination of the present is the burden of the first part of the poem "Lens," poetry as the recovery of the past is that of the second. The augmentation of being becomes the rescuing of it. The imagery of eye, lens, and light turns into one of film and dark room where "the years/Lie in solution." It is because of man's unbroken connection with his own beginnings, human, animal, natural, that the poet's imagination can sharpen into needlepoint precision what lies vaguely latent in the consciousness:

A stripe of tiger, curled
And sleeping on the ribs of reason
Prints as clear
As Eve and Adam, pearled
With sweat, staring at an applecore....

—William Walsh

WILLIAMS, William Carlos. American. Born in Rutherford, New Jersey, 17 September 1883. Educated at a school in Rutherford, 1889–96; Chateau de Lancy, near Geneva, Switzerland, and Lycée Condorcet, Paris, 1897–99; Horace Mann High School, New York, 1899–1902; University of Pennsylvania, Philadelphia, 1902–06, M.D. 1906; did two years internship at hospitals in New York City, 1906–08, and post-graduate work in paediatrics at the University of Leipzig, 1908–09. Married Florence Herman in 1912; two sons. Practised medicine in Rutherford, 1910 until he retired in the mid 1950's. Editor, *Others*, 1919; Editor, with Robert McAlmon, *Contact*, 1920–23; Editor, with Nathanael

West, *Contact*, 1932. Appointed Consultant in Poetry, Library of Congress, Washington, D.C., 1952, but did not serve. Recipient: Loines Award, 1948; National Book Award, 1950; Bollingen Prize, 1952; Academy of American Poets Fellowship, 1956; Brandeis University Creative Arts Award, 1958; National Institute of Arts and Letters Gold Medal, 1963; Pulitzer Prize, 1963. LL.D.: State University of New York at Buffalo, 1956; Fairleigh Dickinson University, Teaneck, New Jersey, 1959; Litt.D.: Rutgers University, New Brunswick, New Jersey, 1948; Bard College, Annandale-on-Hudson, New York, 1948; University of Pennsylvania, 1952. Member, National Institute of Arts and Letters. *Died 4 March 1963.*

PUBLICATIONS

Collections

   The Williams Reader, edited by M. L. Rosenthal.   1966.

Verse

   Poems.   1909.
   The Tempers.   1913.
   Al Que Quiere!   1917.
   Kora in Hell: Improvisations.   1920.
   Sour Grapes.   1921.
   Spring and All.   1923.
   Go Go.   1923.
   The Cod Head.   1932.
   Collected Poems, 1921–1931.   1934.
   An Early Martyr and Other Poems.   1935.
   Adam & Eve & the City.   1936.
   The Complete Collected Poems 1906–1938.   1938.
   The Broken Span.   1941.
   The Wedge.   1944.
   Paterson, Book One.   1946; *Book Two,* 1948; *Book Three,* 1949; *Book Four,* 1951; *Book Five,* 1958; *Books I–V,* 1963.
   The Clouds.   1948.
   The Pink Church.   1949.
   Selected Poems.   1949.
   The Collected Later Poems.   1950; revised edition, 1963.
   The Collected Earlier Poems.   1951.
   The Desert Music and Other Poems.   1954.
   Journey to Love.   1955.
   Pictures from Brueghel and Other Poems.   1962.

Plays

   Betty Putnam (produced 1910).
   A Dream of Love (produced 1949).   1948.
   Many Loves (produced 1958).   In *Many Loves and Other Plays,* 1961.
   Many Loves and Other Plays: The Collected Plays (includes *A Dream of Love; Tituba's Children; The First President,* music by Theodore Harris; *The Cure*).   1961.

Fiction

A Voyage to Pagany. 1928.
A Novelette and Other Prose 1921–1931. 1932.
The Knife of the Times and Other Stories. 1932.
White Mule. 1937; In the Money: White Mule, Part II,1940; The Build-Up, 1952.
Life along the Passaic River (stories). 1938.
Make Light of It: Collected Stories. 1950.
The Farmers' Daughters: The Collected Stories. 1961.

Other

The Great American Novel. 1923.
In the American Grain. 1925.
The Autobiography. 1951.
Williams' Poetry Talked About, with Eli Siegel. 1952; revised edition, edited by
    Martha Baird and Ellen Reiss, as The Williams-Siegel Documentary, 1970, 1974.
Selected Essays. 1954.
John Marin, with others. 1956.
Selected Letters, edited by John C. Thirlwall. 1957.
I Wanted to Write a Poem: The Autobiography of the Works of a Poet, edited by Edith
    Heal. 1958.
Yes, Mrs. Williams: A Personal Record of My Mother. 1959.
Imaginations: Collected Early Prose, edited by Webster Schott. 1970.
The Embodiment of Knowledge, edited by Ron Loewinsohn. 1974.
Interviews with Williams: Speaking Straight Ahead, edited by Linda W.
    Wagner. 1976.

Translator, Last Nights of Paris, by Philippe Soupault. 1929.
Translator, with Raquel Hélène Williams, The Dog and the Fever, by Francisco de
    Quevedo. 1954.

Bibliography: Bibliography of Williams by Emily Mitchell Wallace, 1968.

Reading List: Williams by Vivienne Koch, 1950; Williams: A Critical Study by John
Malcolm Brinnin, 1963; The Poems of Williams, 1964, and The Prose of Williams, 1970, both
by Linda W. Wagner; The Poetic World of Williams by Alan Ostrom, 1966; Williams: A
Collection of Critical Essays edited by J. Hillis Miller, 1966; An Approach to Paterson by
Walter Peter Scott, 1967; The Music of Survival by Sherman Paul, 1968; Williams: The
American Background by Mike Weaver, 1971; The Inverted Bell: Modernism and the
Counterpoetics of Williams by Joseph N. Riddell, 1974; Williams: The Knack of Survival in
America by Robert Coles, 1975; Williams: Poet from Jersey by Reed Whittemore, 1975.

*   *   *

William Carlos Williams is one of the leading figures of American modernist poetry
whose recent recognition critically supports the impact his poems and fiction had throughout
the modern and contemporary periods. Williams was a writer's writer in that his reputation
existed chiefly among other writers – Ezra Pound, H. D., Marianne Moore, Hart Crane,
Wallace Stevens, John Dos Passos, Ernest Hemingway – at least until New Directions began
publishing his work in the late 1930's. Most of Williams's first dozen books were privately

printed or subsidized. Some were collections of poems; others were an innovative mixture of poetry and prose, or of prose-poem form. Regardless of apparent genre, Williams wrote consistently in a mode based on the rhythms of the speaking voice, complete with idiomatic language, colloquial word choice, organic form and structure, and an intense interest in locale as both setting and subject.

This most American of poets was born of mixed parentage, and part of his fascination with the identification of – even the definition of – the American character may have stemmed from his own feeling of dislocation. His short early poems as well as his collection of essays on American historical figures, *In the American Grain*, present personae and scenes germane to the United States: "a young horse with a green bed-quilt/on his withers shaking his head," "A big young bareheaded woman/in an apron," "Flowers through the window/lavender and yellow//changed by white curtains." The fact that these scenes and characters are presented with neither apology nor psychological justification emphasized the aesthetic position that the thing was its own justification. Whether echoing James Dewey, Henri Bergson, or William James, Williams's innate pragmatism led him to a concentration on the unadorned image (as a means to universal understanding, truth) that opened many new directions in modern poetry. Williams did not use the image as symbol, a substitute for a larger idea; he was content to rest with the assumption that the reader could duplicate his own sense of importance for the red wheelbarrows and green glass between hospital walls, and thereby dismiss the equivocation of symbolism. As he said so succinctly in *Paterson*, "no ideas but in things."

Allied with the notion of presentation was the corollary that the author was to be as invisible as possible, so as not to dilute the effect of the concrete object or character. Not until his later poems did Williams change that tenet, but the strikingly personal "The Desert Music" and "Asphodel, That Greeny Flower" benefit from his use of a more personal stance toward the materials. Through the writing of his five-book epic poem, *Paterson*, through the 1940's to 1958, Williams was moving toward a kind of self-revelation, albeit unevenly. The epic concerns a poet-doctor-city persona named Paterson, tracing some events of the poet-doctor's life through an intense juxtaposition of scene, image, and memory. The technique of placing one image or scene against another, often without verbal transition, resembled the montage effect in the art contemporary with Williams; troubling as it was to his readers thirty years ago, it became the *modus operandi* for many contemporary writers, a way of increasing speed, of covering more images and sources of imagery, in the context of a rapidly-moving poem.

Williams established many new principles in the writing of his poetry – his confidence that the common American was an apt source of character, his joy in re-creating natural speech, his experimentation with a structure and line that would allow the flexible and fluid pace of speech to be presented – but his prose was also influential. From the 1923 *Spring and All*, when he combined aesthetic theory with such famous poems as "The Red Wheelbarrow," "To Elsie," and "At the Ballgame," to the trilogy of a family establishing itself in American business culture (the Stetchers in *White Mule*, *In the Money*, and *The Build-Up*), Williams turned away from the established conventions in order to present sharply, idiomatically, the gist of his drama. Much of his prose is carried through dialogue that makes Hemingway's seem contrived and redundant; most of his fiction has no ostensible plot. Moving as far from artifice as possible, his prose was criticized repeatedly for being artless; but contemporary readers have found the organic emphasis on language-structure-character an important direction for their own writing. "The Burden of Loveliness," "Jean Beicke," "The Use of Force" are stories often anthologized, provocative in their presentation of convincing characters whose human conditions proceed without drama, but – in Williams's handling – always with sympathy.

That Williams was a practicing physician until the mid 1950's adds some interest to his use of apparently real people in his fiction and poetry. The authenticity of his knowledge about people is undeniable, and he speaks movingly in his autobiography about the reciprocity between being a doctor (a pediatrician by specialization, but a general practitioner for all intents) and a writer. Working from insights that a more reclusive person might not have had, Williams was able to portray accurately many elements of the American culture that had not been treated in the literature of the twentieth century (Eliot's Prufrock would not have come to Williams's New Jersey office). Disturbed as he often was about his lack of time to write, he nevertheless acknowledged that his busy life was a rich one; and his writing after his retirement (a condition which occurred chiefly because of a severe stroke) frequently returned to subjects and characters from that more active life. The stories about Williams's writing during his rushed days as physician are apocryphal: pulling his car off the road while on his way to make a house call so that he could scribble a poem on a prescription blank; equipping his office desk with a hidden typewriter so that he could flip the machine in place between patients. His production as writer in the midst of his full days as doctor is amazing, but what made that production possible was his personal intent: he considered himself primarily a poet; his aim and direction in life were toward success in writing. No hurried schedule could prevent his implementing that dream.

Williams's poems are not all affirmative pictures of American character and scene; in fact, much of his writing during the 1930's and 1940's is bleak and despairing, and the early books of *Paterson* reflect that disillusionment with what had earlier appeared to be inexhaustible American promise. The late books of *Paterson*, however, supply Williams's own hard-won answers: love, even if foolhardy; virtue; knowing oneself; doing what one can; creating. These are hardly new answers, but their lack of innovation does not lessen their impact. Like Dante traveling through the Inferno, Paterson-Williams takes us into blind alleys (his poems are realistic because we see wrong answers as well as right ones, and sometimes no answers at all), only to move up through Limbo to a kind of modern-day heaven, a place with the answers at least implied in passages like

> Through this hole
> at the bottom of the cavern
> of death, the imagination
> escapes intact.
> It is the imagination
> which cannot be fathomed.
> It is through this hole
> we escape....

From this resolution, it is only a step to the gentle poise of the last poems. One of the most striking poems of his Pulitzer prize-winning book, *Pictures from Brueghel*, is "Asphodel," the love poem to his wife of nearly fifty years, which speaks of "love, abiding love." "Death/is not the end of it," Williams writes, comparing love to "a garden which expands ... a love engendering/gentleness and goodness." Williams contrasts the quiet assurance of this love with "Waste, waste!/dominates the world. It is the bomb's work." And his love is broadened to include his total response to life, as he declares proudly toward the end of the poem:

> Only the imagination is real!
> I have declared it
>   time without end.
> If a man die
>   it is because death
>   has first
> possessed his imagination....
>
> But love and the imagination
>   are of a piece
>   swift as the light
> to avoid destruction....

Williams's impact on modern American poetics might appear to have been largely technical, for all the discussion of his use of the local, the triadic line, the idiom; but in the last analysis readers and fellow writers probably respond as well to the pervasive optimism of the doctor-poet's view, and to the openness with which he shared his life and his reactions with his readers. One may forget the rationale for Williams's triadic line division; but one does not forget his candor and his affirmation.

—Linda W. Wagner

WILMOT, John. See **ROCHESTER, 2nd Earl of**.

WINCHILSEA, Countess of; Anne Finch, née Kingsmill.   English.   Born in Sidmonton, Hampshire, c. 1661. Educated privately. Married Heneage Finch in 1684 (4th Earl of Winchilsea, 1712). Maid of Honour to Mary of Modena, the consort of James II: after downfall of the Stuarts retired to the country with her husband. *Died 5 August 1720.*

PUBLICATIONS

Collections

> *Poems,* edited by Myra Reynolds.   1903.
> *Poems* (selection), edited by J. Middleton Murry.   1928.

Verse

> *The Spleen: A Pindaric Ode,* with *A Prospect of Death,* by John Pomfret.   1709.
> *Free-Thinkers: A Poem in Dialogue.*   1711.
> *Miscellany Poems on Several Occasions.*   1713.

*   *   *

The Countess of Winchilsea is a minor poet who for generations has endeared herself to her readers, partly by the freshness, delicacy, and originality of her talent, partly by the personal touches that abound in her verses.

Wordsworth was so struck by her "Nocturnal Reverie" that he wished a selection of her poems might be published. Gosse secured the inclusion of a few specimens in Ward's *English Poets,* and there Matthew Arnold discovered her and was impressed. Most anthologies of 18th-century poetry print a few of her pieces. The scholarly edition by Myra Reynolds, draws on manuscript as well as printed sources, and reveals the range of her literary activities. Pindaric odes, fables in the manner of La Fontaine, satires, even a tragedy, besides verse epistles, songs, and meditative lyrics, flowed from her pen. Many are commonplace; but when the best are assembled, they add up to something unusual and attractive.

Anne Kingsmill, as she was before her marriage to Heneage Finch, later Earl of Winchilsea, was a Maid of Honour to Mary of Modena, James II's consort. The downfall of the Stuarts meant a life of retirement in the country for Anne and her husband, but this was no disaster. Not only were they devoted to one another, as her poems show, but neither of them depended on urban pleasures. Lady Winchilsea asked nothing better than "an Absolute Retreat," in which she could enjoy "contemplations of the mind" and the joys of friendship. For someone of her epoch, her delight in landscape, her feeling for birds and beasts, trees and flowers, was unusually deep and sensitive. This no doubt commended her to Wordsworth. Her diction, too, is pure, and her best poems have a spontaneous air about them.

Unlike the later 18th-century Bluestockings, the Countess of Winchilsea was not a lady of formidable learning, but she resembled them in being a defender of a woman's right to cultivate her mind and express herself in print. In several poems she protests against the conventions that condemned women to "the dull manage of a servile house." She insists on developing her own gifts, "Nor will in fading silks compose/Faintly the inimitable Rose." *The Spleen*, from which these lines are taken, is at least as interesting an account of depression as Matthew Green's more famous, and later, treatment of the same subject.

—Margaret Bottrall

WINTERS, (Arthur) Yvor. American. Born in Chicago, Illinois, 17 October 1900. Educated at the University of Chicago, 1917–18; University of Colorado, Boulder, B.A., M.A. 1925; Stanford University, California, Ph.D. 1935. Married the writer Janet Lewis in 1926; one son and one daughter. Instructor in French and Spanish, University of Idaho, Pocatello, 1925–27; Instructor, 1928–37, Assistant Professor, 1937–41, Associate Professor, 1941–49, Professor of English, 1949–51, and Albert Guerard Professor of Literature, 1961–66, Stanford University. Founding Editor, *The Gyroscope*, Los Altos, California, 1929–30; Western Editor, *Hound and Horn*, 1932–34. Fellow, Kenyon School of English, Gambier, Ohio, 1948–50. Recipient: National Institute of Arts and Letters grant, 1952; Brandeis University Creative Arts Award, for poetry, 1959; Harriet Monroe Poetry Award, 1960; Guggenheim Fellowhip, 1961; Bollingen Award, 1961; National Endowment for the Arts grant, 1967. Member, American Academy of Arts and Sciences. *Died 25 January 1968.*

PUBLICATIONS

Verse

The Immobile Wind. 1921.
The Magpie's Shadow. 1922.
The Bare Hills. 1927.
The Proof. 1930.

The Journey and Other Poems. 1931.
Before Disaster. 1934.
Poems. 1940.
The Giant Weapon. 1943.
Three Poems. N.d.
To the Holy Spirit. 1947.
Collected Poems. 1952; revised edition, 1960.
The Early Poems. 1966.

Fiction

The Brink of Darkness. 1932.

Other

Notes on the Mechanics of the Poetic Image: The Testament of a Stone. 1924.
The Case of David Lamson: A Summary, with Frances Theresa Russell. 1934.
Primitivism and Decadence: A Study of American Experimental Poetry. 1937.
Maule's Curse: Seven Studies in the History of American Obscurantism. 1938.
The Anatomy of Nonsense. 1943.
Edwin Arlington Robinson. 1946; revised edition, 1971.
In Defense of Reason. 1947; revised edition, 1960.
The Function of Criticism: Problems and Exercises. 1957.
On Modern Poets. 1959.
The Poetry of W. B. Yeats. 1960.
The Poetry of J. V. Cunningham. 1961.
Forms of Discovery: Critical and Historical Essays on the Forms of the Short Poem in English. 1967.
Uncollected Essays and Reviews, edited by Francis Murphy. 1976.
Hart Crane and Winters: Their Literary Correspondence, edited by Thomas Parkinson. 1978.

Editor, *Twelve Poets of the Pacific.* 1937.
Editor, *Selected Poems*, by Elizabeth Daryush. 1948.
Editor, *Poets of the Pacific, Second Series.* 1949.
Editor, with Kenneth Fields, *Quest for Reality: An Anthology of Short Poems in English.* 1969.

Bibliography: *Winters: A Bibliography* by Kenneth A. Lohf and Eugene P. Sheehy, 1959.

Reading List: *The Complex of Winters' Criticism* by Richard Sexton, 1974; "Winters Rehearsed and Reconsidered" by René Wellek, in *Denver Quarterly 10*, 1975.

*   *   *

The poetry of Yvor Winters falls into two phases, the Imagist phase (1920–28), and the Post-Symbolist phase (1929–68). During the first period Winters was writing markedly cadenced, imagistic free verse under the influence of William Carlos Williams, Ezra Pound, Glenway Wescott, H.D., and American Indian poetry. The influence was technical: that is, Winters learned to write his free verse by studying carefully selected poems he admired by these authors, but his own poems were not merely imitative. He developed a style of his own of great emotional intensity, brilliantly perceptive and even hypersensitive to the point of being hallucinative. The literary and autobiographical background of these early years is described by Winters in his Introduction to *The Early Poems*, in which he states that his philosophical position at that time was solipsistic and deterministic, a position which he later rejected. Some of the most remarkable of these verses are evocative of the life and landscape of New Mexico where Winters was recuperating from tuberculosis. At the same time, Winters was studying the mechanics of the image and how it was most effectively employed not only by the Imagists but by Coleridge, Browning, Hopkins, Robinson, Stevens, Emerson, and the French Symbolists.

In his late twenties Winters became impatient with the limitations of so-called free verse; he began to suspect that he could gain a greater emotional and intellectual range by the employment of the conventional iambic line as it occurs in the heroic couplet, the sonnet, in tetrameter and pentameter quatrains, and in other forms. *The Proof*, though it opens with poems written in the imagist manner, contains in the closing pages a number of verses in traditional iambic meters. The eight poems in *The Journey* are all in heroic couplets which show the influence not only of Dryden and Pope but also of the freely run-over couplets of Charles Churchill. One of the best of these, "On a View of Pasadena from the Hills," was directly influenced by Robert Bridges's 1899 poem in iambic pentameter couplets, "Elegy: The Summer-House on the Mound."

In his early thirties Winters was re-reading the poetry of Bridges, Hardy, Robinson, Stevens, Paul Valéry, and T. Sturge Moore with increasing admiration. All these poets (including Stevens in his best poem, "Sunday Morning") wrote in conventional prosody, a fact which strengthened Winters's conviction that free verse and imagism were temporary aberrations from the main tradition of Anglo-American verse. At this time he was forming the tastes and principles to be found in his critical essays, which were to attract considerably more attention than his poetry. In *Primitivism and Decadence* he analyzed the technical innovations of the "new poetry," and, although he admired a few free verse poems by H.D., Williams, Stevens, and Marianne Moore, he concluded that on the whole the experimentalist movement had been a failure. By the time he was writing the poetry that appeared in *The Giant Weapon* and in the *Collected Poems* of 1952 he had developed his critical theory concerning the nature of poetry, applied in a series of essays eventually published under the titles *In Defense of Reason*, *The Function of Criticism*, and *Forms of Discovery*. The gist of his theory is that a successful poem is a statement in words about human experience which communicates by means of verse – as distinct from prose, which is less precisely rhythmical than verse and therefore less effective in expressing emotion – appropriate feeling motivated by an understanding of the experience. In this kind of poetry full use is made of both the denotative and connotative significance of words. This theory is obviously operating in all the poetry of Winters's mature years.

Late in his career Winters began referring to what he called the post-symbolist style of the best American poetry of the twentieth century. In his essay "Poetic Styles Old and New" (1959), after a discussion of the two major styles of the Renaissance, the plain and the ornamental, he said in describing post-symbolism, "It ought to be possible to embody our sensory experience in our poetry in an efficient way, not as ornament, and with no sacrifice of rational intelligence." Sensory experience communicated by fresh and original imagery charged with rational significance occurs in Winters's best poems from about 1930 on, including "The Slow Pacific Swell" (1931), "Sir Gawaine and the Green Knight" (1937), and "A Summer Commentary" (1938).

A few dominant and closely related themes, explored in Winters's verse from the beginning of his career until the end, give to his work a remarkable coherence and unity. Among these are a recurrent examination of the relationship between the rational mind and the poetic sensibility which may enrich it or destroy it, a theme which derives from his own experience and also from the poetry of T. Sturge Moore. In his earliest verse the sensibility is dominant to the point of rational disintegration, and even as late as 1955 Winters was writing in his "At the San Francisco Airport": "The rain of matter upon sense/Destroys me momently." Achievement of balance between intellect and sensibility is the subject of "A Summer Commentary" and "Sir Gawaine and the Green Knight"; it is implicit in his allegorical poems on Greek subjects such as "Heracles," "Theseus," "Orpheus," and others. His concern with threats to the preservation of one's identity motivated a number of poems on death and the ravages of time, the most powerful of which are "For My Father's Grave," "To the Holy Spirit," "The Cremation," "A Leave-Taking," and "Prayer for My Son."

Winters is considered one of the most intellectual of all American poets. Yet he was keenly alive to the beauties of the sensory world as well as to its dangers. His purpose was "To steep the mind in sense/Yet never lose the aim." Consequently much of his poetry is remarkable for its freshly perceived descriptive detail of the natural world as in "The California Oaks" and "Time and the Garden." Finally it should be noted that Winters is the only twentieth-century poet of consequence who mastered the technique of free verse as practised by the Imagists and then abandoned it for conventional prosody, although he did not abandon what he had learned about the effective use of imagery. His poetry and his criticism present a significant case history of revolution and counter-revolution in modern poetry.

—Donald E. Stanford

WITHER, George. English. Born in Bentworth, Hampshire, 11 June 1588. Educated at Magdalen College, Oxford, 1604–06; entered Lincoln's Inn, London, 1615. Imprisoned for *Abuses Stript and Whipt*, 1613–14, and for *Wither's Motto*, 1621. Served as a captain of horse in the First Bishops' War, 1639; sold estate to raise a regiment for the Puritan cause, 1642: Governor of Farnham Castle, 1642, captured by the Royalists but released at Denham's request; Justice of the Peace for Hampshire, Surrey, and Essex, 1642–58; Major-General of the forces in Surrey, 1643; briefly imprisoned for *Justitiarius Justificatus*, 1646; Commissioner for the sale of the King's goods, 1653; Master of the Statute Office, 1655; lost positions and property at the Restoration; imprisoned for unpublished satire against Parliament, *Vox Vulgi*, 1660–63. *Died 2 May 1667.*

PUBLICATIONS

Collections

Miscellaneous Works. 6 vols., 1872–73. (10 other volumes of reprints of Wither's works also published by the Spenser Society).
Poetry, edited by F. Sidgwick. 2 vols., 1902.

Verse

Prince Henry's Obsequies; or, Mournful Elegies upon His Death. 1612.
Epithalamia; or, Nuptial Poems. 1612.
Abuses Stript and Whipt, The Scourge: Epigrams. 1613.
A Satire, Dedicated to His Most Excellent Majesty. 1614.
Fidelia. 1615.
The Shepherd's Hunting. 1615; edited by William B. Hunter, Jr., in *The English Spenserians,* 1977.

Exercises upon the First Psalm, Both in Prose and Verse. 1620.

Works, Containing Satires, Epigrams, Eclogues, Sonnets, and Poems. 1620.

The Songs of the Old Testament, Translated into English Measures. 1621.

Wither's Motto: Nec Habeo, Nec Careo, Nec Curo. 1621.

Juvenilia. 1622; revised edition, 1633; selection, as *Extracts from Juvenilia,* edited by A. Dalrymple, 1785; revised edition, as *Juvenilia,* edited by J. M. Gutch, 4 vols., 1820.

Fair-Virtue, The Mistress of Phil'arete. 1622.

The Hymns and Songs of the Church. 1623.

Britain's Remembrancer. 1628; selections, as *Mr. Wither His Prophecy,* 1642, *Wither's Remembrancer,* 1643, *Mr. Geo. Wither Revived,* 1683.

The Psalms of David Translated into Lyric Verse. 1632.

A Collection of Emblems, Ancient and Modern. 4 vols., 1635.

Halleluiah; or, Britain's Second Remembrancer. 1641; selections included in *Wither's Remembrancer,* 1643.

Campo-Musae; or, The Field-Musings of Captain George Wither. 1643.

The Great Assizes Holden in Parnassus by Apollo. 1645.

Vox Pacifica: A Voice Tending to the Pacification of God's Wrath. 1645.

What Peace to the Wicked? 1646.

Amygdala Britannica. 1647.

Carmen Expostulatorium. 1647.

Carmen-Ternarium Semi-Cynicum. 1648.

A Si Quis; or, Queries. 1648.

Prosopopoeia Britannica: Britain's Genius, or Good-Angel, Personated. 1648.

The Tired Petitioner. 1648; edited by J. M. French, in *Four Scarce Poems,* 1931.

A Thankful Retribution. 1649.

An Alarum from Heaven; or, A Memento to the Great Council. 1649.

Vaticinium Votivum; or, Palaemon's Prophetic Prayer. 1649.

Carmen Eucharisticon: A Private Thank-Oblation. 1649.

Three Grains of Spiritual Frankincense. 1651.

The British Appeals, with God's Merciful Replies. 1651.

A Timely Caution. 1652.

The Dark Lantern, Containing a Dim Discovery; The Perpetual Parliament. 1653.

Westrow Revived. 1653.

Three Private Meditations. 1655.

The Protector. 1655.

Vaticinium Causuale. 1655.

Boni Ominis Votum: A Good Omen to the Next Parliament. 1656.

The Sudden Flash Timely Discovering Some Reason Wherefore the Style Protector Should Not Be Deserted by These Nations. 1657.

A Cause Allegorically Stated. 1657.

Epistolium-Vagum-Prosa-Metricum; or, An Epistle at Random. 1659.

A Cordial Confection, to Strengthen Their Hearts Whose Courage Begins to Fail. 1659.

Salt upon Salt, Made Out of Certain Ingenious Verses upon the Late Storm and the Death of His Highness Ensuing. 1659.

Speculum Speculativum; or, A Considering Glass, Being an Inspection into the Present and Late Sad Condition of These Nations. 1660.

Furor-Poeticus Propheticus. 1660.

A Triple Paradox, Affixed to a Counter-Mure Raised Against the World, the Flesh, and the Devil. 1661.

An Improvement of Imprisonment, Disgrace, Poverty, into Real Freedom, Honest Reputation, Perdurable Riches. 1661.

Verses Intended to the King's Majesty. 1662.

Tuba-Pacifica, Seasonable Precautions. 1664.

A Memorandum to London, Occasioned by the Pestilence. 1665.
Sighs for the Pitchers. 1666.
Echoes from the Sixth Trumpet. 1666; as *Nil Ultra; or, The Last Works,* 1668; as *Fragmenta Prophetica; or, The Remains,* 1669.
Vaticinia Poetica. 1666.
Divine Poems (By Way of Paraphrase) on the Ten Commandments. 1688.
A Strange and Wonderful Prophecy. 1689.
Wither's Redivivus. 1689.
A Paraphrase of the Ten Commandments. 1697.
Select Lyrical Passages, Written about 1622, edited by E. Brydges. 1815.
Vox Vulgi: A Poem in Censure of the Parliament of 1661 (sic), edited by W. D. Macray. 1880.
The History of the Pestilence 1625, edited by J. M. French. 1932.

Other

A Preparation to the Psalter. 1619.
The Scholar's Purgatory. 1625(?).
Read and Wonder: A War Between Two Entire Friends, the Pope and the Devil. 1641.
Se Defendendo: A Shield, and Shaft, Against Detraction. 1643.
Mercurius Rusticus; or, A Country Messenger. 1643.
Letters of Advice, Touching the Choice of Knights and Burgesses for the Parliament. 1644.
The Speech Without Door. 1644.
Prophecy of the Downfall of Antichrist. 1644.
To the Most Honourable the Lords and Commons: Petition. 1646.
Justitiarius Justificatus: The Justice Justified. 1646.
Opobalsamum Anglicanum: An English Balm, Lately Pressed Out of a Shrub and Spread upon These Papers. 1646.
Major Wither's Disclaimer. 1647.
Articles Presented Against This Parliament. 1648.
Respublica Anglicana; or, The History of Parliament in Their Late Proceedings. 1650.
The Modern States-Man. 1653.
To the Parliament of the Common-Wealth: The Humble Petition of G. W. 1654.
The Petition and Narrative of Wither. 1659.
Fides-Anglicana; or, A Plea for the Public-Faith of These Nations. 1660.
Predictions of the Overthrow of Popery. 1660.
The Prisoner's Plea. 1661.
Joco-Serio, Strange News, of a Discourse Between Two Dead Giants. 1661.
Parallelogrammaton: An Epistle to the Three Nations of England, Scotland and Ireland. 1662.
A Proclamation in the Name of the King of Kings, to All the Inhabitants of the Isles of Great Britain (includes verse). 1662.
Meditations upon the Lord's Prayer. 1665.
The Grateful Acknowledgement of a Late Trimming Regulator. 1668.

Translator, *The Nature of Man,* by Nemesius. 1636.

Reading List: "Wither: The Poet as Prophet" by Allan Pritchard, in *Studies in Philology,* 1962; *The Later Career of Wither* by C. S. Hensley, 1969; *The Spenserian Poets* by Joan Grundy, 1969.

*   *   *

George Wither was a voluminous poet who went on writing long after his poetic light was extinguished. His later works, produced in the mistaken belief that he was God's prophet, chosen to denounce the coming reign of Antichrist, can mostly be dismissed as "poetical prosings." It is on his earlier works, up to and including *Britain's Remembrancer* (1628), that his reputation as a poet must rest. These too are effusions: Wither despised "method" and had a fatal facility for producing smooth and quite readable but seemingly interminable couplets. But unlike the later outpourings, these poems have genuine charm and interest.

Fair-Virtue could be described as Wither's *Testament of Beauty*: in it he engagingly expatiates on his love of beauty in woman, virtue, Nature, and poetry itself. *Fidelia*, a verse-epistle from a forsaken woman, is delicately feminist in its sympathies, and is well, sometimes movingly, written. *The Shepherd's Hunting*, a dramatization in pastoral form of his imprisonment in the Winchilsea, addressed to his friends and fellow-poets, notably William Browne, is an appealing piece of self-portraiture. His imprisonment arose out of the publication of *Abuses Stript and Whipt*, a collection of satires, vigorously attacking vice and immorality in all the estates of the realm. Despite the satiric persona Wither adopts, the spirit and manner of this work are closer to the moral essayist than the satirist, and this is even more apparent in the enormously popular *Wither's Motto*. Here Wither simply takes the stage and holds forth about himself and his opinions, painting a self-satisfied portrait of a man humble but content. The portrait is intended to be a model for others: if in Wither's eyes poetry both delights and teaches, the delight is in the first place for himself (coming from the sheer joy of "making") and the teaching for his reader. Didacticism and self-expression were the two poles on which his work always turned. *Britain's Remembrancer* both teaches and preaches: it finds in the Plague of 1625 an opportunity to combine vivid, detailed description with an exhaustive analysis of the abuses of the day, for which the Plague is seen as a punishment. This poem is valuable to historians, as indeed are parts of the later polemics, for its social and political comment. As the watch-dog of liberty, Wither's incessant barking is irritating but sometimes not entirely unjustified.

Other works deserving to be remembered are Wither's prose work, *The Scholar's Purgatory*, a lively account of the confrontations between author and printer (i.e., the Stationers' Company); his *Epithalamia* for Princess Elizabeth, which has a pleasing freshness; his *Hymns and Songs of the Church* and, still more, his *Haleluiah*, which provides the reader with hymns for every conceivable occasion, written in simple language, employing a variety of stanzas, and indicative of a tender, pastoral concern and sympathetic heart. His fine *Collection of Emblems* is a valuable cultural document of the times. Most memorable, and indeed remembered, of all, are his delightful lyrics, "Shall I wasting in despair," "I loved a lass, a fair one," and "So, now is come our joyfullest Feast."

—Joan Grundy

WORDSWORTH, William. English. Born in Cockermouth, Cumberland, 7 April 1770. Educated at Hawkshead Grammar School, Lancashire; St. John's College, Cambridge, 1787–91, A.B. 1791. Lived in France during the early period of the Revolution, 1791–92: involved with Annette Villon, who bore him a daughter; married Mary Hutchinson in 1802, five children. Lived with his sister Dorothy at Racedown, Dorset, 1795–97; settled with Dorothy at Alfoxden, Somerset, near Coleridge at Nether Stowey, 1797; toured Germany with Dorothy and Coleridge, 1798–99; settled with Dorothy at Grasmere, in the Lake

District, 1799, and remained there for the rest of his life; came into a legacy from his father, 1802; quarrelled with Coleridge, 1810; appointed Stamp Distributor for Westmorland, 1813; reconciled with Coleridge and toured the Rhineland with him, 1828. D.C.L.: University of Durham, 1838; Oxford University, 1839. Poet Laureate, 1843 until his death. *Died 23 April 1850.*

PUBLICATIONS

Collections

Poetical Works, edited by Ernest de Selincourt and Helen Darbishire. 5 vols., 1940–49; revised edition of vols. 1–4, 1952–58.
Prose Works, edited by W. J. B. Owen and Jane W. Snyder. 3 vols., 1974.
The Cornell Wordsworth, edited by Stephen Parrish. 1975–
Complete Poems, edited by John O. Hayden. 2 vols., 1976.

Verse

An Evening Walk: An Epistle in Verse. 1793.
Descriptive Sketches. 1793.
Lyrical Ballads with a Few Other Poems, with Coleridge. 1798; revised edition, as *Lyrical Ballads with Other Poems,* 2 vols., 1800; 1800 text edited by R. L. Brett and A. R. Jones, 1963; 1798 text edited by W. J. B. Owen, 1967.
Poems. 2 vols., 1807.
The Excursion, Being a Portion of the Recluse. 1814.
The White Doe of Rylstone; or, The Fate of the Nortons. 1815.
Poems. 2 vols., 1815.
Thanksgiving Ode, January 18, 1816, with Other Short Pieces. 1816.
Peter Bell: A Tale in Verse. 1819.
The Waggoner. 1819.
The River Duddon: A Series of Sonnets, Vaudracour and Julia, and Other Poems. 1820.
Miscellaneous Poems. 4 vols., 1820.
The Little Maid and the Gentlemen; or, We Are Seven. 1820(?).
Ecclesiastical Sketches. 1822.
Memorials of a Tour on the Continent 1820. 1822.
Poetical Works. 4 vols., 1824; revised edition, 1827, 1836–42, 1845, 1846, 1849–50.
Epitaph. 1835.
Yarrow Revisited and Other Poems. 1835.
The Sonnets. 1838.
England in 1840! 1840(?).
Poems on the Loss and Re-Building of St. Mary's Church, Cardiff. 1842.
Select Pieces from the Poems. 1843.
Grace Darling. 1843.
Verses Composed at the Request of Jane Wallas Penfold. 1843.
The Prelude; or, Growth of a Poet's Mind: An Autobiographical Poem. 1850; edited by Ernest de Selincourt, 1926, revised by Helen Darbishire, 1959; 1805 text edited by de Selincourt, 1933, revised by Stephen Gill, 1970; both texts edited by J. C. Maxwell, 1976.
The Recluse. 1888.

Play

The Borderers, in *Poetical Works.* 1842.

Other

Concerning the Relations of Great Britain, Spain, and Portugal to Each Other and to the Common Enemy at This Crisis. 1809.
A Letter to a Friend of Robert Burns. 1816.
A Description of the Scenery of the Lakes in the North of England. 1822.
Letters of the Wordsworth Family from 1787 to 1855, edited by W. Knight. 3 vols., 1907.
Wordsworth and Reed: The Poet's Correspondence with His American Publisher 1836–50, edited by L. N. Broughton. 1933.
The Letters of William and Dorothy Wordsworth, edited by Ernest de Selincourt. 5 vols., 1935–39; revised by Chester L. Shaver and others, 4 vols., 1967–78.
Some Letters of the Wordsworth Family, Now First Published, edited by L. N. Broughton. 1941.
Pocket Notebook, edited by G. H. Healey. 1942.

Bibliography: *Wordsworth Criticism: A Guide and Bibliography* by J. V. Logan, 1947, supplemented by *Wordsworthian Criticism 1945–59* by E. F. Henley and D. H. Stam, 1960, revised edition, 1965; *The Cornell Wordsworth Collection: A Catalogue* by G. H. Healey, 1957.

Reading List: *Wordsworth* by Herbert Read, 1930, revised edition, 1949; *The Mind of A Poet: A Study of Wordsworth's Thought* by Raymond D. Havens, 1941; *Wordsworth and the Vocabulary of Emotion* by Josephine Miles, 1942; *Wordsworth and Other Studies* by Ernest de Selincourt, 1947; *The Poet Wordsworth* by Helen Darbishire, 1950; *Wordsworth: A Reinterpretation* by F. W. Bateson, 1954, revised edition, 1956; *Wordsworth's Poetry 1787–1814* by Geoffrey H. Hartman, 1964; *Wordsworth: The Chronology of the Early Years 1770–1799*, 1967, and ... *the Middle Years 1800–1815*, 1975, both by Mark L. Reed; *Imagination and Fancy: Complementary Modes in the Poetry of Wordsworth* by J. Scoggins, 1967; *Tradition and Experiment in Wordsworth's Lyrical Ballads* by Mary Jacobus, 1976; *Wordsworth: Language as Counter-Spirit* by Francis Fergusson, 1977.

*   *   *

William Wordsworth is always thought of as the pre-eminent poet of nature, though he declared himself that his subject was "the Mind of Man –/My haunt, and the main region of my song." It is true that his chief concern is with man, but he does express a belief in the regenerative power of nature to such an extent that there is some truth in the popular belief. What is not true is that Wordsworth, because of this belief, is a facile optimist who turns his eyes away from human misery. He portrays suffering humanity in many of his poems, showing a variety of causes: poverty, separation, bereavement, neglect. As Geoffrey Hartman has written "those famous misreaders of Wordsworth who say he advocates rural nature as a panacea should be condemned to read *The Excursion* once a day."

Wordsworth's eye for human unhappiness is the sharper because he has such a powerful and authentic vision of the ideal life. It is authentic because it is based on the poet's own experience and observation, and it includes a "natural" life which is based on much more than a love for the country. It is found in the experience of a child who, like Wordsworth himself, is allowed a large measure of freedom; in the lives of shepherds and independent farmers, whose work is satisfying and meaningful; and in the lives of all those who are able to love their fellow human beings, whose benevolent instincts are not thwarted by oppression, wrong habits, or an acceptance of false or trivial values. Throughout his poetry Wordsworth is the enemy of the glittering, the fashionable, and the temporary; and one feature of his belief in "nature" is a concentration on those things which would render men's feelings "more sane, pure and permanent" (letter to John Wilson, June 1802). The result is that he concentrates on the simplest and most elemental passions of the human heart: the love of a mother for her idiot child, the compassion due to the aged and the poor, a mother's grief for her lost baby. It is this consistent, austere aim to portray universal and simple emotions which lies behind the much misunderstood Preface to the 1800 edition of *Lyrical Ballads*, in which Wordsworth states as his aim the tracing of "the primary laws of our nature." It is this which is responsible for his choice of "low and rustic life," since he believed that there "the essential passions of the heart" spoke more plainly, were more simple, and were more durable. To this must be added his belief (deduced from his own experience, and fully articulated in *The Prelude*) that a mind which has been influenced by a simple and natural benevolence can survive adverse circumstances and unwholesome influences. Moments when he feels reassured in this belief, as he encounters a particularly beautiful or striking moment, are among the most memorable passages of Wordsworth's poetry, for instance in "Lines Written a Few Miles above Tintern Abbey."

In his earliest published poems, *An Evening Walk* and *Descriptive Sketches*, Wordsworth shows both his concern with simple human states and his awareness of natural beauty. Drawing on eighteenth-century traditions of the picturesque, in *An Evening Walk*, and transcending them in *Descriptive Sketches*, he gives word-paintings of Lake District and Alpine scenes respectively; yet in both poems he is also concerned with suffering humanity. In *An Evening Walk* the peaceful description is interrupted by a harrowing portrait of a homeless widow (her soldier-husband has been killed at Bunker's Hill in the American war) whose starving and frozen children die in her arms; and in *Descriptive Sketches* the sublime scenery of the Alps is contrasted with the miseries of the impoverished and oppressed Swiss.

Descriptive Sketches was written for the most part in France in 1792, and its plea for freedom indicates Wordsworth's political enthusiasm at this time for the French Revolution. His disillusion with its later stages, and his separation from his French mistress and their child, were the two chief causes of the poet's unhappiness in the years which followed his return to England in December 1792. For a time he found help in the writings of the political philosopher William Godwin, only to find that Godwin's view of man took too little account of man's deepest affections; and although critics no longer believe that Wordsworth had some kind of "breakdown" at this time, it is clear that in the years that followed he was given new faith in himself as a poet, and in mankind generally, by the love of his sister Dorothy and the friendship with Coleridge. The poetry of these years includes *The Borderers*, a verse drama of considerable psychological insight but insufficient dramatic force, which shows a good man betrayed into a great crime and subjecting another man to the same process; and "The Ruined Cottage," which shows the destruction of an innocent family by famine, sickness and war. "The Ruined Cottage" was later incorporated into Book I of *The Excursion*, with the addition of some consoling reflections; in its original form (printed by Jonathan Wordsworth in *The Music of Humanity*, 1969) it is Wordsworth's most powerful narrative of wretchedness and neglect. The understatement of its blank verse narrative allows the gradual unfolding of the tragedy to develop with a slow, accumulating force. To it was added the fragment describing the pedlar (later the Wanderer) in which the poet expresses clearly and confidently his belief in the One Life of nature (a concept derived from Coleridge) and in the ability of man to gain power from nature and to suffer with those who suffer.

Lyrical Ballads continues these themes. On the one hand there are the compassionate poems ("The Thorn," "Simon Lee," "Goody Blake and Harry Gill") dealing with misery, neglect, and old age, but on the other hand there are poems of love and care ("The Idiot Boy") and those which celebrate the harmony between man and nature ("To my Sister," "Expostulation and Reply," "The Tables Turned"). In "Tintern Abbey," the last-written and last-placed poem of the collection, Wordsworth describes the power of memory to recreate the scene, and the power of the mind to "see into the life of things"; as an expression of the sublime feelings awakened by nature, the central passage (beginning "And I have felt") is unsurpassed.

The winter of 1798–99, spent with Dorothy in Germany, is notable on two counts: the composition of the "Lucy poems," and the first attempt at what later became *The Prelude*. The "Lucy Poems," four elegiac lyrics (a fifth was composed later), describe a beautiful young girl, a child of nature: the poems celebrate her loss and her perfection, in simple language and lyric metres which nevertheless allow a complexity of response. In the first, two-part *Prelude*, the poet describes his childhood and schooltime, and the "spots of time" which act as a renovating power in later years. Between 1799 and 1805 Wordsworth extended *The Prelude* to thirteen books, including his experiences in Cambridge, the Alps, London, and France, and celebrating the loss and restoration of his imaginative power. The poem has individual passages of great beauty and energy, in which specific interactions between man and nature are shown (boat-stealing, skating, hooting to the owls, crossing the Alps, the climbing of Snowdon): these are notable, not only for their vividness, but for their variety of tone and effect. But the strength of *The Prelude* is not only in individual passages, but also in its structure: it is an epic, closely modelled on *Paradise Lost*, showing the "heroic argument" of the developing human mind. The ecstatic childhood gives way to a sober maturity, and the close-knit rural community is left behind for Cambridge and London; but what is lost is balanced by a gain in understanding and human feeling, so that, when the poet's faith in himself is restored at the end, he has a more mature and compassionate awareness of human demands. The loss of the childhood paradise thus becomes an individual "fortunate fall."

A similar process of loss and gain is found in the "Immortality Ode," where the memory of childhood serves to emphasise that its radiance has gone; yet this is replaced by an awareness of mortality, a faith that looks through death, and a philosophic mind. The "Immortality Ode" ends with thanks to "the human heart by which we live," and Wordsworth's poetry of this period is constant in its recognition of the claims of human nature. In "Resolution and Independence" he is cured of self-pity by his meeting with the leech-gatherer, a man of patience and fortitude; and in "Peele Castle" he bids farewell to "the heart that lives alone."

Wordsworth's other great achievements in the years after *Lyrical Ballads* were his sonnets, in which again he follows his great master, Milton. Wordsworth's sonnets are not so abrupt, complex, or dense as Milton's: their most notable characteristic is an arresting line, the thought of which is then developed with economy and beauty. Figurative language, especially the simile, is used to great effect, and Wordsworth uses the tight structure of the sonnet to express single ideas with a marvellous clarity and finality.

The major philosophical poem which Wordsworth published during his lifetime was *The Excursion*. It has been described by Geoffrey Hartman as a dinosaur, dying of its own weight, and although it addresses itself to matters of great importance, such as human despondency and bereavement, it does so in a way which lacks the intensity and excitement of the earlier poetry. And, with a few exceptions, the publication of *The Excursion* marks the end of Wordsworth's effective career as a poet. In the last forty years of his life he applied himself, for the most part, to conventional subjects, and treated them in a conventional way. It is idle to speculate on the causes of this decline; it is rather a matter for rejoicing that during the great decade (ending with *Poems*, 1807) Wordsworth wrote so powerfully about man in society and man in relation to nature, the unchanging passion of the human heart.

—J. R. Watson

WOTTON, Sir Henry. English. Born in Broughton Malherbe, Kent, 30 March 1568. Educated at Winchester School; New College, Oxford, 1584, moved to Queen's College, Oxford, B.A. 1588; Middle Temple, London, 1595. Courtier and diplomat: travelled on the Continent, 1588–95; returned to England and became Secretary to the Earl of Essex, 1595–1601; lived in Italy, 1601–03; knighted, 1603; Ambassador to Venice. 1604–12, 1616–19, 1621–24, and went on additional diplomatic missions to France, 1612, The Hague, 1614, and Vienna, 1620; Member of Parliament for Appleby, 1614, and Sandwich, 1625; Provost of Eton College, 1624–39; ordained deacon, 1627. *Died in December 1639.*

PUBLICATIONS

Collections

>   *Poems*, edited by Alexander Dyce.   1843.
>   *Poems by Wotton and Others*, edited by J. Hannah.   1845.

Other

>   *The Elements of Architecture.*   1624; edited by F. Hard, 1968.
>   *Ad Regem e Scotia Reducem Wottoni Plausus et Vota.*   1633.
>   *A Parallel Between Robert Late Earl of Essex and George Late Duke of Buckingham.*   1641; edited by E. Brydges, 1814.
>   *A Short View of the Life and Death of George Villiers Duke of Buckingham.*   1642.
>   *A Panegyric of King Charles.*   1649.
>   *Reliquiae Wottonianae: or, A Collection of Lives, Letters, Poems*, edited by Izaak Walton.   1651; revised edition, 1654, 1685; *A Philosophical Survey of Education; or, Moral Architecture, and The Aphorisms of Education*, edited by H. S. Kermode, 1938.
>   *The State of Christendom; or, A Discovery of Many Hidden Mysteries of the Times.*   1657.
>   *Letters to Sir Edmund Bacon.*   1661.
>   *Letters and Dispatches, 1617–1620*, edited by George Tomline.   1850.

Reading List: *Life and Letters of Wotton* by L. P. Smith, 2 vols., 1907; *Wotton, with Some General Reflections on Style in English Poetry* by H. H. Asquith, 1919.

*   *   *

Although he sometimes appears in library catalogues as "Sir Henry Wotton, *poet*," it is by hardly more than a dozen poems that he merits the label. Friend of Izaak Walton (who was later to write his biography), ambassador to Venice, and in his last years provost of Eton College, Wotton is relished for his letters, his treatise on architecture, his humane though unfinished *Philosophical Survey of Education; or, Moral Architecture*, and a handful of anthology pieces, notably "You Meaner Beauties of the Night," written for Elizabeth of Bohemia.

Reliquiae Wottonianae, edited by Izaak Walton, is as charming a collection of works and fragments as its long subtitle promises: "A Collection of Lives, Letters, Poems; with Characters of Sundry Personages, and Other Incomparable Pieces of Language and Art."

Unfinished as it is, the treatise on education is admirable and moving as an early attempt to base an educational system on sympathetic observation of "the Naturall Capacities and Inclinations of Children."

Wotton's enthusiasm in *The Elements of Architecture* for "the secret power of proportion" informs his poems as surely as it shapes his appreciation of Italian buildings and his ideal of the English country house. While the group of poems he produced is small, poise and polish, a pervasive classical spirit, characterize his moral verse, the delicacy of his best known lyric, and the precise quietness of his epitaph for the wife of his nephew, Sir Albertus Morton: "He first deceased; she for a little tried/To live without him, liked it not, and died." Drummond of Hawthornden reports that Ben Jonson had by heart "The Character of a Happy Life," and, dates apart, Wotton would qualify as a most authentic son of Ben.

—Kay Stevenson

WRIGHT, Judith. Australian. Born in Armidale, New South Wales, 31 May 1915. Educated at New England Girls School, Armidale; University of Sydney, B.A. Married J. P. McKinney; one daughter. Secretary, J. Walter Thompson, advertising agency, Sydney, 1938–39; Secretary, University of Sydney, 1940–42; Clerk, Australian Universities Commission, Brisbane, 1944–46; Statistical Research Officer, University of Queensland, Brisbane, 1946–49. Since 1967, Honours Tutor in English, University of Queensland. Commonwealth Literary Fund Lecturer, Australia, 1949, 1962; Guest Delegate, World Poetry Conference, Canada, 1967; Creative Arts Fellow, Australian National University, Canberra, 1974. Co-Founder and President, Wildlife Preservation Society of Queensland, 1962–65. Recipient: Grace Leven Prize, 1949, 1972; Commonwealth Literary Fund Fellowship, 1964; *Encyclopaedia Britannica* Award, 1964; Fellowship of Australian Writers Robert Frost Medal, 1975. D.Litt.: University of Queensland, 1962; University of New England, Armidale, 1963. Fellow of the Australian Academy of the Humanities, 1970. Lives in North Tamborine, Queensland.

PUBLICATIONS

Verse

    The Moving Image. 1946.
    Woman to Man. 1949.
    The Gateway. 1953.
    The Two Fires. 1955.
    Birds. 1962.
    (Poems). 1963.
    Five Senses: Selected Poems. 1963.
    City Sunrise. 1964.
    The Other Half. 1966.
    Collected Poems 1942–1970. 1971.
    Alive. 1973.
    Fourth Quarter. 1978.
    The Double Tree: Selected Poems 1942–1976. 1978.

Fiction

The Nature of Love.   1966.

Other

The Generations of Men.   1959.
King of the Dingoes (juvenile).   1959.
Range the Mountains High (juvenile).   1962.
Shaw Neilson (biography and selected verse).   1963.
Charles Harpur.   1963.
The Day the Mountains Played (juvenile).   1963.
Country Towns (juvenile).   1964.
Preoccupations in Australian Poetry.   1965.
The River and the Road (juvenile).   1966; revised edition, 1971.
Henry Lawson.   1967.
Conservation as an Emerging Concept.   1971.
Because I Was Invited (essays).   1976.

Editor, *Australian Poetry 1948.*   1948.
Editor, *A Book of Australian Verse.*   1956; revised edition, 1968.
Editor, *New Land, New Language: An Anthology of Australian Verse.*   1957.
Editor, with A. K. Thomson, *The Poet's Pen.*   1966.
Editor, *Witnesses of Spring: Unpublished Poems,* by Shaw Neilson.   1970.

Reading List: *Critical Essays on Wright* edited by A. K. Thomson, 1968; *Wright* by A. D. Hope, 1975.

*   *   *

Judith Wright has such an awareness of time and place that she seems to look beyond these categories. "The Cycads" (*The Moving Image*), whose "smooth dark flames flicker at time's own root," is a fair representative of this attitude. She sees Australia as an age-old country, but it is also her "blood's country." These poems have a firmly realised local habitation in New England, its landscape, history, and early life, particularly in her recognition of the inescapable association of man and the land where he finds himself. In her most famous poem, "Bullocky," she celebrates an early worker, compelled and driven mad by his environment, but his bones are now everlastingly part of it.

This ability for genuinely fundamental perceptions appears again in *Woman to Man* which records the primitive and elemental awareness of woman in several of its poems dealing with such experiences as conception, pregnancy, and parturition, what A. D. Hope has called "the continuous epic of generation." Relying much on Blake's idea of the double-vision, she grapples in *The Gateway* and in *The Two Fires* with the problem of time, the life that grows from the birth, and, beyond that, with Blakean influences, the doors of eternity, the first steps towards a later recognition of the ability of the five senses to "gather into a meaning/all acts, all presences/ ... a rhythm that dances/and is not mine."

Another influence at work in this period, and later, is T. S. Eliot, whose *Four Quartets* no doubt seemed relevant both to Wright's struggles with the problems of time and also with those which she was conscious of having – "My speech inexact, my note not right" – with language. She was wrestling with philosophical difficulties.

Birds is a return to what she calls the "reverence of the heart." She had became co-founder and president of the Wild Life Preservation Society of Queensland, and *Birds*, a book of light-weight poems, probably represents a necessary breathing-space before the next phase.

Five Senses suggests reassurance and reconciliation. The troubles of the 1950's give way to a sense of fulfilment, aptly represented by the poem "For My Daughter," growing up, growing away, the mother ready to accept the new relationship. Likewise, "Turning Fifty" (*The Other Half*) reflects a mood of acceptance; and "Shadow," the new section in *Collected Poems 1942–1970*, speaks of completeness as she elegises her husband: "Growing beyond your life into your vision,/at last you proved the circle and stepped clear." *Alive* concerns itself with her own process of ageing, but, just as in the 1950's the atomic bomb had troubled her, so in this collection and in "Shadow" she was disturbed by Vietnam and the spoliation of the Australian natural environment. Her later work, competent though it generally is, is rarely so richly satisfying as her first two collections. It does not have that intuitive metaphysical depth that characterises the earlier work.

She has written extensively in the field of literary criticism; *Preoccupations in Australian Poetry* and *Because I Was Invited* collect her best work. The latter also contains many of her articles on conservation. She also wrote short stories and novels for children. As a critic, she is no systematiser but rather a defender of what she likes; she has made a case particularly for such early Australian poets as Harpur, Baylebridge, and Shaw Neilson, who are all too easily underrated.

—Arthur Pollard

WYATT, Sir Thomas. English. Born at Allington Castle, Kent, in 1503. Educated at St. John's College, Cambridge, matriculated 1515, B.A. 1518, M.A. 1520. Married the Hon. Elizabeth Brooke in 1520 (separated, 1526). Courtier of King Henry VIII: Clerk of the King's Jewels, 1524–31; sent on a diplomatic mission to France, 1526; accompanied Sir John Russell, Ambassador to the Papal Court, 1527; Marshal of Calais Castle, 1528–32; Justice of the Peace, Essex, 1532; Privy Councillor, 1533; imprisoned in connection with charges of adultery with Anne Boleyn, then pardoned, 1536; knighted, and appointed Sheriff of Kent, 1537; Ambassador to Spain and to the Emperor Charles V, 1537–39; on embassy in France and Holland, 1539–40; charged with treason, as an ally of Cromwell, imprisoned in the Tower, tried and acquitted, 1541; granted lands at Lambeth, London, by the king, 1541, and appointed High Steward of the king's manor at Maidstone, Kent, 1542. *Died 11 October 1542.*

PUBLICATIONS

Collections

Collected Poems, edited by Kenneth Muir and Patricia Thomson. 1969.
Collected Poems, edited by Joost Daalder. 1975.

Verse

> Certain Psalms Commonly Called the VII Penitential Psalms, edited by J.
>   Harington. 1549.
> Songs and Sonnets (Tottel's miscellany; 97 poems by Wyatt). 1557.
> Unpublished Poems by Wyatt and His Circle, edited by Kenneth Muir. 1961.

Other

> Translator, Plutarch's Book of the Quiet of Mind. 1528; edited by C. R. Baskervill,
>   1931.

Reading List: Humanism and Poetry in the Early Tudor Period by H. A. Mason, 1959; Wyatt
by Sergio Baldi, 1961; Life and Letters of Wyatt by Kenneth Muir, 1963; Wyatt and His
Background by Patricia Thomson, 1964, and Wyatt: The Critical Heritage, edited by
Thomson, 1974; The Canon of Wyatt's Poetry by Richard Harrier, 1975.

                                   *   *   *

Unfortunately for modern readers, some aspects of Sir Thomas Wyatt's poetry remain
problematic for lack of sure scholarly knowledge. Although many of his lyrics may have
been set to music, only one contemporary accompaniment has been discovered; and the
principles of Tudor scansion and pronunciation have by no means been finally ascertained.
Such matters are of more than academic interest, for they have a bearing on the vexed
question of Wyatt's metrical technique, which in its turn must affect our estimate of his poetic
stature. Some of Wyatt's importance, moreover, is primarily historical. In translating from a
number of Italian originals (including Ariosto and Petrarch) he regained for English poetry
something of the cosmopolitan scope it had enjoyed in Chaucer's time. In pioneering the
development of the English sonnet, he carried out a labour whose significance is at once
apparent, even if later sonneteers such as Sidney and Spenser based their work less on the
foundations laid by Wyatt than on a fresh recourse to foreign models.

A critical estimate of Wyatt's poetry must concentrate, however, on its intrinsic merits. In
this respect the sonnets are much less important than the lyrics or "ballets," of which there
are over 120, and whose stanzaic form is richly varied. It is in these lyrics, for the most part
brief and song-like in construction, that we find displayed Wyatt's characteristic gifts; and
here there is less evidence of the metrical uncertainty which is apt to interfere with our
enjoyment of the more formal pieces. The following lines, from one of Wyatt's Petrarchan
versions, illustrate the irregularities which typically beset the sonnets:

> My plesaunt dayes they flete away and passe,
> But daily yet the ill doeth chaunge into the wours;
> And more then the halfe is runne of my cours.

The most ingenious reader cannot make these last two lines scan. And the argument that such
lines represent a deliberate departure from the iambic norm meets with the justifiable retort
that a norm is precisely what Wyatt fails to establish. He never confidently controls either the
stress-pattern or the syllabic foundation of his verse, and the resultant uncertainty
undermines many of his efforts after rhythmic delicacy. But we can not dismiss the sonnets
out of hand, for even here there are numerous brief passages suggestive of Wyatt's
originality, and couched in his graphic and forceful idiom; and occasionally, as in the
Petrarchan translation "My galy, charged with forgetfulness," an entire poem is sustained at
this level, to memorable effect.

Apart from the sonnets, we must mention briefly a number of other works, including a set of penitential Psalms and three Satires, two Horatian and one original. This latter gives us an attractive picture of Wyatt sitting "in Kent and Christendome/Emong the muses where I rede and ryme."

It is in the ballets, however, as we have suggested, that Wyatt is at his best. The most famous of these – "They fle from me that sometyme did me seke," "Ons as methought fortune me kissed," "My lute awake!" – are written in a poetic medium capable of expressing a wide variety of feeling and of achieving cadences of haunting gravity: "But all is torned thorough my gentilnes/Into a straunge fasshion of forsaking." Even the less inspired of the short lyrics have an ease of movement which avoids all suggestion of the mechanical. The formal conventions – the use, for instance, of refrain – are turned to the poet's own purpose, just as the conventional ethics and rhetoric of courtly love are charged with a personal urgency which gives them fresh life.

For the achievement of Wyatt's best lyrics is not primarily technical. Technique is the servant: the poems are controlled by a rare dramatic and psychological intelligence whose insights transcend the limitations of the particular code of love in whose context Wyatt wrote. Although the situations are familiar – the lover communes with himself about the progress of his suit, or reproaches his mistress for her cruelty, or proclaims his own fidelity – their treatment often involves an unexpected emotional complexity. Consider, for instance, the irony and compassion implicit in the lines beginning "There was never nothing more me payned," where the poet upbraids himself for his hardheartedness, while recognising that he will undoubtedly continue to give his mistress cause for her grief. And where the feeling is simpler, it may be given superbly direct expression: "And wilt thou leave me thus?/Say nay, say nay, for shame...."

The lyrics we have mentioned, and others like them, are unmistakably Wyatt's: no-one else could have written them, and English poetry would be the poorer without them. It is this personal and unique voice which speaks to us still today, and this, for the general reader if not for the specialist, must outweigh considerations of Wyatt's historical importance. Wyatt is one of the enduring love-poets of the language.

—James Reeves

WYLIE, Elinor (Hoyt). American. Born in Somerville, New Jersey, 7 September 1885; brought up in Philadelphia and Washington, D.C. Educated at Miss Baldwin's School, Bryn Mawr, and Holton Arms School, Washington, D.C. Married Philip Hichborn in 1905 (died, 1911), one son; left her husband to elope with Horace Wylie, 1910, and moved to England with him as Mr. and Mrs. Waring; returned to the United States after Wylie's divorce, 1915, and married him, 1916 (divorced, 1923); moved to New York in 1921, and became a prominent figure in New York literary circles; married the poet William Rose Benét, q.v., in 1923; thereafter lived in New York and London; Poetry Editor of *Vanity Fair*, New York, 1923–25; Editor, Literary Guild, New York, 1926–28. Recipient: Julia Ellsworth Ford Prize, 1921. *Died 16 December 1928.*

PUBLICATIONS

Collections

Collected Poems, Collected Prose, edited by William Rose Benét. 2 vols., 1932–33.

Verse

> *Incidental Numbers.* 1912.
> *Nets to Catch the Wind.* 1921.
> *Black Armour.* 1923.
> *(Poems),* edited by Laurence Jordan. 1926.
> *Trivial Breath.* 1928.
> *Angels and Earthly Creatures: A Sequence of Sonnets.* 1928.
> *Angels and Earthly Creatures* (collection). 1929.
> *Nadir.* 1937.
> *Last Poems,* edited by Jane D. Wise. 1943.

Fiction

> *Jennifer Lorn: A Sedate Extravaganza.* 1923.
> *The Venetian Glass Nephew.* 1925.
> *The Orphan Angel.* 1926; as *Mortal Image,* 1927.
> *Mr. Hodge and Mr. Hazard.* 1928.

Reading List: *Wylie: The Portrait of an Unknown Lady* by Nancy Hoyt, 1935; *Wylie* by Thomas A. Gray, 1969.

*   *   *

Elinor Wylie's prestigious social background, striking personality, beauty, elegance, and conversational gifts, with the romantic aura of her daring break with conventional society when she eloped with Horace Wylie, made her a symbolic figure to many persons caught up in the "American poetic renaissance." Consequently, judgments of her writings were for some years infused with feelings about the writer. Thomas Gray's monograph of 1969 discusses widely differing views of her achievement.

In the essay "Jewelled Bindings" (1923), Wylie saw herself and a few other contemporary lyric poets as "enchanted by a midas-touch or a colder silver madness into workers in metal and glass ... in crisp and sharp-edged forms." They choose "short lines, clear small stanzas, brilliant and compact." Such standards produced her most widely known poems: the 3-quatrain "Let No Charitable Hope" that climaxes with "In masks outrageous and austere/ The years go by in single file;/But none has merited my fear,/And none has quite escaped my smile"; "The Eagle and the Mole," with its fastidious trimeter: "Avoid the reeking herd ..."; the art-for-art's-sake poem "Say not of Beauty she is good,/Or aught but beautiful"; and the exquisite "Velvet Shoes": "Let us walk in the white snow/In a soundless space...."

This preference for the delicately sensuous or even impalpable characterized many of her poems – "I love the look, austere, immaculate,/Of landscapes drawn in pearly monotones" – and her first two "novels." *Jennifer Lorn: A Sedate Extravaganza* appealed to a public that was seeking relief from the ugly realities. Set in the late 18th century in the realms of aristocracy and wealth in England and India, it is a long catalogue of lovely, delicate objects; what plot it has concerns the fragile, fainting Jennifer and – the spine of the story – her husband Gerald, the exact, cool aesthete. It has been compared to a tapestry, and among the *mille fleurs* are many phrases and lines from 18th-century literature. Wylie's wide reading in this period showed itself also in the amusing *Venetian Glass Nephew.* Her long and perhaps abnormal admiration for Shelley brought about *The Orphan Angel,* in which the libertarian poet is rescued from drowning and accompanies a Yankee sailor to America and across the continent. This trend toward more realistic treatment continued in *Mr. Hodge and Mr. Hazard,* a satirical allegory on the stifling of the late romantics by the Victorians.

Mary Colum, who ranks Wylie as "one of the few important women poets in any literature," observes, "She seemed to write little out of a mood or out of a passing emotion ... but nearly always out of complex thought...." (*Life and the Dream*, 1947). Many found her poems cold; the fastidious speaker seeks isolation and death. A last group of sonnets, however, shows a capacity for love: "And so forget to weep, forget to grieve,/And wake, and touch each other's hands, and turn/Upon a bed of juniper and fern." H. Lüdecke (in *English Studies 20*, December 1938) finds her not a "great" poet but a "rare" poet: "Refinement is her essential characteristic as an artist."

—Alice R. Bensen

YEATS, William Butler. Irish. Born in Sandymount, County Dublin, 13 June 1865; son of the artist John Butler Yeats, and brother of the artist Jack Butler Yeats; lived in London, 1874–83. Educated at Godolphin School, Hammersmith, London; Erasmus Smith School, Dublin; studied art in Dublin, 1883–86; left art school to concentrate on poetry. Married Georgie Hyde-Lees in 1917; one son and one daughter. Lived mainly in London, spending part of each year in Ireland, 1890–1921: a Founder of the Rhymers Club, London, and member of the *Yellow Book* group; met Lady Gregory, 1896, and thereafter spent many of his summer holidays at her home in Sligo; Co-Founder, with Lady Gregory and Edward Martyn, Irish Literary Theatre, later Abbey Theatre, Dublin, 1899: Director of the Abbey Theatre, 1904 until his death; Editor of *Beltaine*, 1899–1900, *Samhain*, 1901–08, and *The Arrow*, 1906–09; settled with his family in Ireland, 1922: Senator of the Irish Free State, 1922–28. Recipient: Nobel Prize, 1923. D.Litt.: Oxford University, 1931; Cambridge University; University of Dublin. *Died 28 January 1939.*

PUBLICATIONS

Collections

Letters, edited by Allan Wade. 1954.
Poems, Prose. Plays, and *Criticism* (selections), edited by A. Norman Jeffares. 4 vols., 1963–64
Variorum Edition of the Plays, edited by Russell and C. C. Alspach. 1966.
Variorum Edition of the Poems, edited by Peter Allt and Russell Alspach. 1967.

Verse

Mosada: A Dramatic Poem. 1886.
The Wanderings of Oisin and Other Poems. 1889.
The Countess Kathleen and Various Legends and Lyrics. 1892.
Poems. 1895; revised edition, 1899, 1901, 1904, 1908, 1912, 1913, 1927, 1929.
The Wind among the Reeds. 1899.
In the Seven Woods, Being Poems Chiefly of the Irish Heroic Age. 1903.
Poems 1899–1905. 1906.
Poetical Works: Lyrical Poems, Dramatic Poems. 2 vols., 1906–07.
Poems, Second Series. 1909.
The Green Helmet and Other Poems. 1910; revised edition, 1912.
A Selection from the Poetry. 1913.
A Selection from the Love Poetry. 1913.
Poems Written in Discouragement 1912–13. 1913.
Nine Poems. 1914.
Responsibilities: Poems and a Play. 1914.
Responsibilities and Other Poems. 1916.
The Wild Swans at Coole, Other Verses, and a Play in Verse. 1917; revised edition, 1919.
Nine Poems. 1918.
Michael Robartes and the Dancer. 1921.
Selected Poems. 1921.
Later Poems (Collected Works 1). 1922.
Seven Poems and a Fragment. 1922.
The Cat and the Moon and Certain Poems. 1924.

October Blast.   1927.
The Tower.   1928.
Selected Poems, Lyrical and Narrative.   1929.
The Winding Stair.   1929.
Words for Music Perhaps and Other Poems.   1932.
The Winding Stair and Other Poems.   1933.
Collected Poems.   1933; revised edition, 1950.
Wheels and Butterflies.   1934.
The King of the Great Clock Tower: Commentaries and Poems.   1934.
A Full Moon in March.   1935.
Poems.   1935.
New Poems.   1938.
Last Poems and Two Plays.   1939.
Selected Poems, edited by A. Holst. 1939.
Last Poems and Plays.   1940.
The Poems.   2 vols., 1949.

Plays

The Countess Kathleen (produced 1899).   In *The Countess Kathleen and Various
Legends and Lyrics,* 1892; revised version as *The Countess Cathleen,* 1912.
The Land of Heart's Desire (produced 1894).
The Shadowy Waters (produced 1904).   1900; revised version, in *Poems,* 1906.
Diarmuid and Grania, with George Moore (produced 1901).   1951; edited by Anthony
Farrow, 1974.
Cathleen ni Hoolihan (produced 1902).   1902.
The Pot of Broth (produced 1902).   In *The Hour Glass and Other Plays,* 1904.
Where There Is Nothing (produced 1904).   1902; revised version, with Lady Gregory,
as *The Unicorn from the Stars* (produced 1907), 1908.
The Hour Glass: A Morality (produced 1903).   1903; revised version (produced 1913),
in *The Mask,* April 1913.
The King's Threshold (produced 1903).   1904; revised version (produced 1913), in
Poems, 1906.
The Hour Glass and Other Plays, Being Volume 2 of Plays for an Irish Theatre (includes
Cathleen ni Houlihan and *The Pot of Broth*).   1904.
On Baile's Strand (produced 1904).   In *Plays for an Irish Theatre 3,* 1904; revised
version, in *Poems,* 1906.
Deirdre (produced 1906).   In *Plays for an Irish Theatre 5,* 1907.
The Golden Helmet (produced 1908).   1908; revised version, as *The Green Helmet*
(produced 1910), 1910.
At the Hawk's Well; or, Waters of Immortality (produced 1916).   In *The Wild Swans at
Coole,* 1917.
The Dreaming of the Bones (produced 1931).   In *Two Plays for Dancers,* 1919.
Two Plays for Dancers (includes *The Dreaming of the Bones* and *The Only Jealousy of
Emer*).   1919.
The Player Queen (produced 1919).   1922.
Four Plays for Dancers (includes *At the Hawk's Well, The Only Jealousy of Emer, The
Dreaming of the Bones, Calvary*).   1921.
Plays in Prose and Verse (Collected Works 2).   1922.
Plays and Controversies (Collected Works 3).   1923.
King Oedipus, from the play by Sophocles (produced 1926).   1928.
The Resurrection (produced 1934).   1927.

Oedipus at Colonus, from the play by Sophocles (produced 1927).   In *Collected Plays*, 1934.
Fighting the Waves (produced 1929).   In *Wheels and Butterflies*, 1934.
The Words upon the Window Pane.   1934.
Collected Plays.   1934; revised edition, 1952.
Nine One-Act Plays.   1937.
The Herne's Egg.   1938.
The Herne's Egg and Other Plays (includes *A Full Moon in March* and *The King of the Great Clock Tower*).   1938.
Purgatory and *The Death of Cuchulain*, in *Last Poems and Two Plays*.   1939.

Fiction

John Sherman and Dhoya.   1891.
The Secret Rose (stories).   1897.
The Tables of the Law; The Adoration of the Magi.   1897.
Stories of Red Hanrahan.   1905.

Other

The Celtic Twilight: Men and Women, Dhouls and Fairies.   1893; revised edition, 1902.
Literary Ideals in Ireland, with AE and John Eglinton.   1899.
Is the Order of R.R. and A.C. to Remain a Magical Order?   1901.
Ideas of Good and Evil.   1903.
Discoveries: A Volume of Essays.   1907.
Collected Works.   8 vols., 1908.
Poetry and Ireland: Essays, with Lionel Johnson.   1908.
Synge and the Ireland of His Time.   1911.
The Cutting of an Agate.   1912; revised edition, 1919.
Reveries over Childhood and Youth.   1915.
Per Amica Silentia Lunae.   1918.
Four Years.   1921.
The Trembling of the Veil.   1922.
Essays (Collected Works 4).   1924.
A Vision.   1925; revised edition, 1937; edited by George Mills Harper and W. K. Hood, 1978.
Early Poems and Stories (Collected Works 5).   1925.
Estrangement, Being Some Fifty Thoughts from a Diary Kept in 1909.   1926.
Autobiographies (Collected Works 6).   1926.
The Death of Synge and Other Passages from an Old Diary.   1928.
A Packet for Ezra Pound.   1929.
Stories of Michael Robartes and His Friends.   1932.
Letters to the New Islands, edited by Horace Reynolds.   1934.
Dramatis Personae.   1935.
Dramatis Personae 1896–1902.   1936.
Essays 1931 to 1936.   1937.
The Autobiography.   1938; revised edition, as *Autobiographies*, 1955.
On the Boiler (essays, includes verse).   1939.
If I Were Four-and-Twenty.   1940.
Pages from a Diary Written in 1930.   1940.
The Senate Speeches, edited by Donald Pearce.   1960.
Reflections, edited by Curtis Bradford.   1970.

Ah, Sweet Dancer: Yeats and Margaret Ruddock: A Correspondence, edited by Roger McHugh. 1970.
Uncollected Prose, edited by John F. Frayne and Colton Johnson. 2 vols., 1970–74.
Interviews and Recollections, edited by E. H. Mikhail. 1977.
The Correspondence of Robert Bridges and Yeats, edited by J. Finneran. 1977.

Editor, *Fairy and Folk Tales of the Irish Peasantry.* 1888; as *Irish Fairy and Folk Tales*, 1893.
Editor, *Stories from Carleton.* 1889.
Editor, *Representative Irish Tales.* 1891.
Editor, *Irish Fairy Tales.* 1892.
Editor, with E. Ellis, *The Works of Blake.* 3 vols., 1893.
Editor, *The Poems of Blake.* 1893.
Editor, *A Book of Irish Verse.* 1895; revised edition, 1900.
Editor, *A Book of Images Drawn by W. Horton.* 1898.
Editor, *Twenty-One Poems*, by Lionel Johnson. 1905.
Editor, *Some Essays and Passages*, by John Eglinton. 1905.
Editor, *Sixteen Poems*, by William Allingham. 1905.
Editor, *Poems of Spenser.* 1906.
Editor, *Twenty-One Poems*, by Katharine Tynan. 1907.
Editor, *Poems and Translations*, by J. M. Synge. 1909.
Editor, *Selections from the Writings of Lord Dunsany.* 1912.
Editor, with F. Higgins, *Broadsides: A Collection of Old and New Songs.* 2 vols., 1935–37.
Editor, *The Oxford Book of Modern Verse 1892–1935.* 1936.
Editor, *The Ten Principal Upanishads*, translated by Shree Purohit Swami and Yeats. 1937.

Bibliography: *A Bibliography of the Writings of Yeats* by Allan Wade, 1951, revised edition, 1958, additions by Russell Alspach, in *Irish Book 2*, 1963; *Yeats: A Classified Bibliography of Criticism* by K. P. S. Jochum, 1978.

Reading List: *The Poetry of Yeats* by Louis MacNeice, 1941; *Yeats: The Man and the Masks*, 1948, and *The Identity of Yeats*, 1954, revised edition, 1964, both by Richard Ellmann; *The Golden Nightingale: Essays on Some Principles of Poetry in the Lyrics of Yeats* by Donald Stauffer, 1949; *Yeats: The Tragic Phase: A Study of the Last Poems* by V. Koch, 1951; *Prolegomena to the Study of Yeat's Poems* and *Plays* by G. B. Saul, 2 vols., 1957–58; *Yeats the Playwright: A Commentary on Character and Design in the Major Plays* by Peter Ure, 1963; *Between the Lines: Yeats's Poetry in the Making* by Jon Stallworthy, 1963; *Yeats's Vision and the Later Poems* by Helen Vendler, 1963; *Yeats: A Collection of Critical Essays* edited by John Unterecker, 1963; *Yeats's Golden Dawn* by George Mills Harper, 1974; *A Commentary on the Collected Plays of Yeats* by A. Norman Jeffares and A. S. Knowland, 1974; *Yeats's Early Poetry: The Quest for Reconciliation* by Frank Murphy, 1975; *Yeats: The Critical Heritage* edited by A. Norman Jeffares, 1976.

*   *   *

William Butler Yeats wrote his early poetry out of a love of a particular place, Sligo, in the West of Ireland, with its folklore, its belief in the supernatural, and its legends. He found material for his own mythology in translations of the Gaelic tales into English. These tales of the Red Branch cycle and the Fenian cycle became tinged in his handling with *fin de siècle* melancholy, with what was called the Celtic twilight. His first long poem, "The Wanderings of Oisin," was founded upon Gaelic pagan legends and gave an account of Oisin visiting three islands in the other-world. In "The Rose" his poems developed this use of Gaelic material, and his Rose symbolism showed the effect of his editing Blake and his interest in the occult tradition, as well as the effect of his love for Maud Gonne. *The Wind among the Reeds* contains more elaborate poetry, intense, at times obscurely allusive, drawing upon Gaelic mythology and Rosicrucian images ("The Secret Rose"), defeatist in its romantic poems (the devotion of "He wishes for the Cloths of Heaven"), and filled with a delicate melancholic beauty.

He began to change this style; *In the Seven Woods* contains more personal, realistic poems ("The Folly of Being Comforted," "Adam's Curse"). *The Green Helmet* records the emptiness of love, now Maud Gonne had married (there is exalted celebration of her beauty in "No Second Troy" and "Words"). He reflects on how he seemed to have lost spontaneity ("All Things can tempt me from this craft of verse"). His *Collected Works* had appeared in 1908; but he found a new kind of poetic voice in *Responsibilities*; this is the antithesis of his early work; stripped of decoration and mystery it is savagely satiric in its defence of art against the philistines. He draws images of aristocratic patronage from Renaissance Italy, he contrasts contemporary Ireland with the past, filled with brave leaders ("September 1913"), he reflects on Irish ingratitude ("To a Shade"), and in his poems on beggars and hermits transmits enjoyment of coarse vitality. And yet there is still the magnificence of vision in "The Cold Heaven." "A Coat" repudiates the celtic "embroideries out of old mythologies"; now he is walking naked. *The Wild Swans at Coole* continues his praise of Maud Gonne ("The People" and "Broken Dreams"); his elegy on Major Robert Gregory and "An Irish Airman Forsees His Death" mark a new capacity for elevating the personal into heroic stature; and his three poems "Ego Dominus Tuus," "The Phases of the Moon," and "The Double Vision of Michael Robartes" reflect his interest in putting his thoughts into order, into some kind of system. This found its best poetic expression in "The Second Coming" of *Michael Robartes and the Dancer* which also contained his poems (notably "Easter 1916") on the Rising. Other poems record his marriage, and "A Prayer for My Daughter" attacks the intellectual hatred of Maud Gonne.

These two volumes showed Yeats emerging from the wintry rages of *Responsibilities* into a new appreciation of beauty balanced against tragedy. His own life had blossomed: marriage, children, his tower in the west of Ireland, the Nobel Prize for poetry, membership of the Irish Senate – and, above all, the writing of *A Vision* which gave him a "system of symbolism," a structure for his thought, and the confidence to write fully of his interests – he was now a sufficient subject for his poetry. And how superbly he wrote in *The Tower* of his ideas on life, on death. "Sailing to Byzantium," "The Tower," "Meditations in Time of Civil War," "Nineteen Hundred and Nineteen," "Leda and the Swan," "Among School Children," and "All Soul's Night" have a lofty but passionate authority about them. He was discovering his own intellectual ancestry among the eighteenth-century Anglo-Irish, expressed in "Blood and the Man" and "The Seven Sages" of *The Winding Stair*. Here, too, are the extremes of "vacillation," the contemplation of death after life in "Byzantium," and the noble poems on his friends Eva Gore-Booth and Con Markiewicz, and on Lady Gregory at Coole Park in 1929 and again in 1931 – "we were the last romantics," he cried, realising "all is changed." This note is there in *A Full Moon in March*, where "An age is the reversal of an age"; and, as Yeats grows older, the brilliant metaphysical compression of "The Four Ages of Man" strikes a note which runs through *Last Poems*, which records heroic stances in the face of coming death – of civilization and the self. There are, of course, as ever, the poems on love, the celebration of his friends ("The Municipal Galley Revisited" and "Beautiful Lofty Things"), the despairing recognition of the foul rag and bone shop of the heart, the recording of his own views on Ireland, on poetry, and on himself in "Under Ben Bulben" and, most movingly, in "The Man and the Echo."

Yeats began writing plays in his teens – heroic plays with little dramatic content. But he left conventional modes behind with *The Countess Cathleen*, written for Maud Gonne, and with the aim of blending pagan legend with Christian belief. Yeats revised this play extensively, as he did *The Shadowy Waters*, a study of the heroic gesture, carried by somewhat cryptic symbolism. He also wrote some short plays for the Irish National Dramatic Society, notably the revolutionary *Cathleen ni Houlihan*. *The King's Threshold* marks a change in Yeats's heroes from passivity to more active roles – Seanchan the poet hero in this play (founded upon a middle-Irish story) asserts the place of poetry in public life. Yeats was also deeply interested in Cuchulain, the hero of the Red Branch cycle of stories, and in *On Baile's Strand* he used the story of Cuchulain unwittingly killing his own son. In *Deirdre* he conferred a lofty dignity upon Deirdre's suicide after the heroic gesture made by her and Naoise when they realise they are doomed. In *The Golden Helmet*, rewritten in verse as *The Green Helmet*, Yeats used an old Irish tale as basis for an ironical farce, another "moment of intense life." The strangeness of Yeats's imagination and his very real capacity for farce emerged in *The Player Queen*, which is most effective on stage and extends the theories which were first elaborated in the prose work *Per Amica Silentia Lunae*.

Yeats found the Abbey Theatre was not suitable for the plays he wanted to write: his *Four Plays for Dancers* arose in part out of his interest in the Japanese Noh drama to which Ezra Pound had introduced him. He wanted to do without an orthodox theatre, and so the ritual of music and dancing aided the mysterious art he sought. *At the Hawk's Well* and *The Only Jealousy of Emer* develop the Cuchulain mythology, while *The Dreaming of the Bones* blends supernatural with political themes. *Calvary* is more complex, and depends upon *A Vision*'s ideas. A later play, *Resurrection*, is far more effective, being intense and economic in its presentation of abstract ideas against a turbulent background. His versions of *King Oedipus* and *Oedipus at Colonus* capture the essence of the Greek tragedies with success, and his sense of dialogue and neat construction make *The Words upon the Window Pane* a *tour de force*, communicating via a glance the agony in Swift's spirit. After *The King of the Great Clock Tower*, *A Full Moon in March*, and *The Herne's Egg*, another examination of the limitations of the hero's role, came *Purgatory*, a brilliant evocation of the history of a ruined house and its family, bound in a murderous cycle. *The Death of Cuchulain* written just before Yeats's death in 1939 examines the proud disdain of his hero for death.

Yeats wrote a large number of articles and reviews up to the end of the century; these were mainly on Irish writing. His first extended prose work was *John Sherman and Dhoya*, fiction which gave his youthful impressions of Sligo. The essays in *The Celtic Twilight* portrayed the traditional beliefs and scenery of the West of Ireland in limpid prose, but *The Secret Rose* contained more complex stories, a mixture of symbolism and mysticism written in that "artificial elaborate English" which was popular in the 1890's. His mannered prose appeared in *The Tables of the Law* and *The Adoration of the Magi*. By the turn of the century he changed his prose style, revised *The Celtic Twilight* and some of the stories in *The Secret Rose*. *Ideas of Good and Evil* contained essays written earlier in his complex style. The need for propaganda for the Abbey Theatre further simplified his style, and he was influenced by Lady Gregory's use of the idiomatic language of country people in her translations from the Irish.

In his autobiographical writings Yeats created an evocative, richly patterned record of his own unique experience, and of his family and his friends. His diaries, some of which were published in *Estrangement*, show his attempts to achieve unity. And his thought, based on most diverse sources, appeared in *A Vision* which contains many witty as well as profound passages as he got "it all in order." His prose became more flexible, ranging between complexity and simplicity – "The Bounty of Sweden" is a good example. Some of his senate speeches are excellent pieces of rhetoric. His introduction to *The Words upon the Window-Pane* (1934) shows his capacity for imaginative meditation and creative criticism. The many introductions he wrote to the work of writers he admired contain a lofty generosity. On the other hand, his airing of opinions – and prejudices – in *On the Boiler* has an engaging touch of the outrageous. His intellectual curiosity, his originality, and his ability to convey his ideas attractively appears in his correspondence, notably in his youthful letters to Katharine Tynan and his later unreserved, lively letters to Mrs. Shakespeare. His criticism is beginning to be appreciated more fully as the complexity and strength of his mind are understood.

—A. Norman Jeffares

1109

YOUNG, Andrew (John).   Scottish.   Born in Elgin, 29 April 1885. Educated at the Royal High School, Edinburgh; University of Edinburgh, M.A. 1908; New College, Edinburgh; ordained a minister of the United Free Church of Scotland. Worked with the Y.M.C.A. in France during World War I. Married Janet Green in 1914; one son and one daughter. Joined the Church of England, 1939, and after a few months at Wells Theological College became Curate of Plaistow, West Sussex, 1940; Vicar of Stonegate, Sussex, 1941 until his retirement, 1959. Canon of Chichester Cathedral, 1948–71. Recipient: Royal Society of Literature Benson Medal, 1939; Heinemann Award, 1946; Queen's Gold Medal for Poetry, 1952; Duff Cooper Memorial Prize, 1960. LL.D.: University of Edinburgh, 1951. Fellow of the Royal Society of Literature. *Died 25 November 1971.*

Publications

Collections

   Complete Poems, edited by Leonard Clark.   1974

Verse

   Songs of Night.   1910.
   Cecil Barclay Simpson: A Memorial by Two Friends, with D. Baillie.   1918.
   Boaz and Ruth and Other Poems.   1920.
   The Death of Eli and Other Poems.   1921.
   Thirty-One Poems.   1922.
   The Bird-Cage.   1926.
   The Cuckoo Clock.   1928.
   The New Shepherd.   1931.
   Winter Harvest.   1933.
   The White Blackbird.   1935.
   Collected Poems.   1936.
   Speak to the Earth.   1939.
   The Green Man.   1947.
   Collected Poems.   1950.
   Into Hades.   1952.
   Out of the World and Back: Into Hades and A Traveller in Time.   1958.
   Quiet as Moss: Thirty Six Poems (juvenile), edited by Leonard Clark.   1959.
   The Collected Poems, edited by Leonard Clark.   1960.
   Burning as Light: Thirty Seven Poems (juvenile), edited by Leonard Clark.   1967.

Plays

   The Adversary (includes *Rizpah*).   1923.
   Nicodemus: A Mystery, music by Imogen Holst.   1937.

Other

   A Prospect of Flowers.   1945.
   A Retrospect of Flowers.   1950.

A Prospect of Britain. 1956.
The Poet and the Landscape. 1962.
The New Poly-Olbion: Topographical Excursions, with an Introductory Account of the Poet's Early Days. 1967.
The Poetic Jesus. 1972.
Meditations on Some Poems, edited by Leonard Clark. 1977.

Reading List: *Young, Prospect of a Poet: Tributes by 14 Writers* edited by Leonard Clark, 1957, and *Young* by Clark, 1964.

*   *   *

Andrew Young belongs to that rural company of parson-poets which has included, among others, Barnes, Crabbe, Hawker, and, in our own day, the Welsh poet R. S. Thomas. But he differs from all these in not being mainly parochial. He takes his place as a significant nature poet alongside Thomson, Clare, Wordsworth, and Blunden, though, again, he is different from each of these. He had his own way of saying things.

Young is a superb miniaturist; he wrote about the natural phenomena of the British countryside, and also about literary figures, archaeology, the Christian religion, and his nationwide travels in search of wild flowers, with strict economy and intensity. A visionary – as illustrated by his long poem *Out of the World and Back* – a scholar, and a probing theologian, Young had the rare gift of being able to write about common things with profundity, so that his readers are made aware of the macrocosm within the microcosm. He packed much thought and feeling into a small space.

Although he was a writer for over 50 years, his style – with the exception of his long poem – did not greatly change. Having found what he could do best of all, he saw no reason to express himself in newer accents, so that his poems were never in, or out, of fashion. They will continue to hold our attention because of their purity, craftsmanship, imaginative content, and meditative quality. Mostly short, they are traditional in form, owing much to Tennyson, Hardy, and Housman. But they have Young's individual voice and eye, are often ironical, witty, and fanciful, with emotions controlled. Walter de la Mare said of him that he "watches words as a cat watches a mouse." He employed a concentrated technique and was himself a man of few words; his powers of observation, though, were immediate and accurate. He could shock into surprise and wonder by a few simple statements of fact, and by his skilful use of contrast and figurative language.

Young's prose writings, especially those about wild flowers and topography, are full of fascinating, out-of-the-way knowledge, but all spiced with good humour and written with a light touch. A Scot by birth and nurture, no writer was more English. No poet wrote with such enthusiasm and grace about the flora and fauna of the British countryside, the landscape and the changing scenes, and few with so mystical an awareness of the passage of the soul of man from earth to the regions beyond.

—Leonard Clark

YOUNG, Edward. English. Born in Upham, Hampshire, baptized 3 July 1683. Educated at Winchester School; New College, and Corpus Christi College, Oxford, Bachelor of Civil Laws, 1714, Doctor 1719. Married Lady Elizabeth Lee in 1731 (died, 1741); one stepdaughter and one son. Law Fellow, All Souls College, Oxford, 1708; moved to London: member of Addison's circle; Tutor/Companion to the Marquis of Wharton in Ireland, 1716, and later Tutor to the Marquis of Exeter; took holy orders, 1724, and appointed Royal Chaplain, 1727; Rector of Welwyn, Hertfordshire, 1730 until his death; Clerk to the Closet of the Princess Dowager of Wales, 1761. *Died 5 April 1765.*

PUBLICATIONS

Collections

Complete Works, edited by J. Nichols.   2 vols., 1854.
Correspondence, edited by Henry Pettit.   1971.
(Selected Poems), edited by Brian Hepworth.   1975.

Verse

An Epistle to Lord Lansdown.   1713.
A Poem on the Last Day.   1713.
An Epistle to the Lord Viscount Bolingbroke, Sent with A Poem on the Last Day.   1714.
The Force of Religion; or, Vanquished Love: A Poem.   1714.
On the Late Queen's Death, and His Majesty's Accession to the Throne.   1714.
A Paraphrase on Part of the Book of Job.   1719.
A Letter to Mr. Tickell Occasioned by the Death of Joseph Addison.   1719.
The Universal Passion.   7 vols., 1725–28; revised edition, as *Love of Fame: The Universal Passion, in Seven Characteristical Satires,*   1728.
Poetic Works.   1726.
Cynthio.   1727.
Ocean: An Ode Occasioned by His Majesty's Late Royal Encouragement of the Sea-Service, to Which Is Prefixed An Ode to the King, and A Discourse on Ode.   1728.
Imperium Pelagi: A Naval Lyric Written in Imitation of Pindar's Spirit, Occasioned by His Majesty's Return September 1729 and the Succeeding Peace.   1730; as *The Merchant, 1730.*
Two Epistles to Mr. Pope Concerning the Authors of the Age.   1730.
The Foreign Address: or, The Best Argument for Peace, Occasioned by the British Fleet, and the Posture of Affairs when the Parliament Met 1734.   1735.
Poetical Works, edited by E. Curll.   2 vols., 1741.
The Complaint; or, Night-Thoughts on Life, Death, and Immortality: Night the First to *Night the Eighth.*   8 vols., 1742–45; *The Consolation* [Night the Ninth] *and Some Thoughts Occasioned by the Present Juncture,* 1746; complete version (nine nights), 1750.
A Sea Piece Containing the British Sailor's Exultation and His Prayer Before Engagement, Occasioned by the Rumour of War.   1755.
The Poetical Works.   4 vols., 1757.
Resignation.   1761; revised edition, 1762.

Plays

Busiris, King of Egypt (produced 1719).   1719.
The Revenge (produced 1721).   1721.
The Brothers, from a play by Thomas Corneille (produced 1753).   1753.

Other

A Vindication of Providence: or, A True Estimate of Human Life, in Which the Passions Are Considered in a New Light (sermon).   1728.
An Apology for Princes; or, The Reverence Due to Government (sermon).   1729.
The Centaur Not Fabulous, in Five Letters to a Friend on the Life in Vogue.   1755; augmented edition, 1755.
An Argument Drawn from the Circumstances of Christ's Death for the Truth of His Religion (sermon).   1758.
Conjectures on Original Composition in a Letter to the Author of Sir Charles Grandison.   1759; edited by E. J. Morley, 1918.

Bibliography: *Young: A Handlist of Critical Notices and Studies* by Francesco Cordasco, 1950.

Reading List: *Le Poète Young* by Walter Thomas, 1901 (includes bibliography); *The Life and Letters of Young* by H. C. Shelley, 1914; *Das Pseudoklassizistische und Romantische in Youngs Night Thoughts* by K. Laux, 1938; *Young and the Fear of Death* by C. V. Wicker, 1952; *Young: Versuch einer Gedanklichen Interpretation auf Grund der Frühwerke* by Erich König, 1954; *Young* by I. St. J. Bliss, 1969.

*   *   *

Edward Young, the contemporary of Addison, is also the precursor of the Romantics. He is yet another of those mid-eighteenth-century figures who mark the progress to what is yet to be.

His early work such as, for example, *The Force of Religion: or, Vanquish'd Love*, is cast in heroic couplets. This is a narrative poem on the last days of Lady Jane Grey, but its dramatic qualities make it not surprising that Young tried his hand at work for the stage. *Busiris*, though it proved a success on the stage, is as turgid and flat as most tragedies of its day, and it cannot be said that *The Revenge* is any better. Well-constructed though both of them are, there are too much rhetoric and inflated feeling and too little real passion and sense of relentless overwhelming circumstances for them to be convincing.

Young practised that fashionable mode of the time, the satire in heroic couplets. *Love of Fame: The Universal Passion* appeared in seven parts. It covers a variety of topics – human vanity, the state of contemporary learning, women, the praise of war, and the corruption of courts, but, despite its title, it lacks both an organising principle and a coherent plan. Young's satires are fluent and stand precursor to much of Pope's best work, especially in their character-sketches, though Young is more genial and more general than Pope.

The sadness of personal bereavement may have led Young to his greatest and longest work, *The Complaint; or, Night-Thoughts*, in which he turned to blank verse. It is by this poem that he is now chiefly remembered though not always to his credit. The poem grew, one *Night* following upon another, and, as it grew, each *Night* grew longer. Young had already treated apocalyptic themes in *The Last Day*. Now at the climax of a long development in the poetry of melancholy which issued also in Gray's *Elegy*, Young employs an occasion of deepest personal trouble as a point of departure to consider "the nature, proof and importance of personal immortality" (Heading of *Nights* VI and VII).

He uses the moral argument; he appeals to cosmological evidence; he is still in the Augustan fashion reasoning his way to faith; but, more and more, feeling keeps breaking in. Indeed, *Night-Thoughts*, far from being a gloomy poem, is a poem of triumph, of death as "the crown of life," giving, if life has been lived aright, the entry to immortal bliss. Even cosmology teaches the same lesson; night is not darkness but a plenitude of burning wonders of God's creation. Young, the Christian, moves on, however, to emphasise the God of history and especially the Christ of the Incarnation and the Passion. On the Cross "There hangs all human hope: that nail supports/The falling universe: that gone, we drop." He sees life as a time of probation and hence he considers the infidelity of his interlocutor, Lorenzo, to be senseless. Immortality is all, and in the seventh *Night* he seeks by a series of psychological arguments – man's misery here, his enlightened self-love, his fundamental sense of aspiration – to suggest the likelihood of everlasting life. The intuitive and assertive element in this is important. It shows Young's relationship with the Evangelicals and reminds us of the pre-Romantic position which he will assume again in *Conjectures on Original Composition*.

This work was preceded by the prose treatise *The Centaur Not Fabulous*, in which Young attacked the infidelity and, even more, the immoralities of the day. Like others of its author's output, it shows a sincerity which, unfortunately, loses something of its impact as a result of prolixity. The *Conjectures* departs from that tradition of authority and "imitation" that marks neo-classicism, lauds originality, the literary equivalent of "enthusiasm" in religion, and emphasises "natural genius." In adumbrating his theories Young also suggests the two levels of the creative mind, the conscious and ordinary and the unconscious and inscrutable.

—Arthur Pollard

ZUKOFSKY, Louis.   American.   Born in New York City, 23 January 1904. Educated at Columbia University, New York, M.A. in English 1924. Married Celia Thaew in 1939; one son. Teacher of English and Comparative Literature, University of Wisconsin, Madison, 1930–31; Visiting Assistant Professor, Colgate University, Hamilton, New York, 1947; Member of the Faculty, 1947–55, and Associate Professor, 1955–66, Polytechnic Institute of Brooklyn, New York. Poet-in-Residence, San Francisco State College, 1958; Guest Professor, Graduate School, University of Connecticut, Storrs, Fall 1971. Recipient: National Endowment for the Arts grant, 1966, 1968. *Died 12 May 1978.*

PUBLICATIONS

Verse

> *First Half of "A" – 9.*   1940.
> *55 Poems.*   1941.
> *Anew.*   1946.
> *Some Time/Short Poems.*   1956.
> *Barely and Widely.*   1958.
> *"A" 1–12.*   1959.
> *16 Once Published.*   1962.
> *I's, Pronounced "Eyes".*   1963.
> *After I's.*   1964.
> *Found Objects 1962–1926.*   1964.
> *Iyyob.*   1965.
> *All: The Collected Short Poems, 1923–1958.*   1965.
> *"A" Libretto.*   1965.
> *All: The Collected Short Poems, 1956–1964.*   1966.
> *Little: A Fragment for Careenagers.*   1967.
> *"A" – 14.*   1967.
> *"A" 13–21.*   1969.
> *All: The Collected Shorter Poems, 1923–1964.*   1971.
> *"A" – 24.*   1972.
> *"A" 22 and 23.*   1975.
> *"A."*   1979.

Play

> *Arise, Arise.*   1973.

Fiction

> *It Was.*   1961.
> *Ferdinand, Including It Was.*   1968.
> *Little.*   1970.

Other

> *Le Style Apollinaire,* translated by René Taupin.   1934.

5 *Statements for Poetry.*   1958.
Bottom: On Shakespeare.   1963.
Prepositions: The Collected Critical Essays.   1967.
Autobiography.   1970.

Editor, *An "Objectivists" Anthology.*   1932.
Editor, *A Test of Poetry.*   1948.

Translator, *Albert Einstein,* by Anton Reiser.   1930.
Translator, with Celia Zukofsky, *Catullus: Fragmenta,* music by Paul
    Zukofsky.   1969.
Translator, with Celia Zukofsky, *Catullus.*   1969.

Bibliography: *A Bibliography of Zukofsky* by Celia Zukofsky, 1969.

Reading List: *At: Bottom* by Cid Corman, 1966; "Zukofsky Issue" of *Grosseteste Review,*
Winter 1970, and of *Maps 5,* 1974; by Peter Quartermain, in *Open Letter Second Series,* Fall
1973; by Barry Ahearn, in *Journal of English Literary History,* Spring 1978.

                                    *   *   *

If William Carlos Williams, by writing about roses as though no-one had written about
them before, freed the American language from its heavy dependence on English antecedents
and associations, Louis Zukofsky, by stripping words of their meaning or by overloading
them so that no single meaning comes through, showed writers like Robert Creeley and
Robert Duncan (and others) how to let the movement of words generate a play and discovery
of meaning by paying attention to their music so that the language might *sing.* It is a trick he
learned from Apollinaire (about whom he wrote a book in 1932) and from Spinoza, who
insisted that a thing is said to be free if it "exists by the mere necessity of its own nature and is
determined in its actions by itself alone." For Zukofsky, the poem is an object.
    Here is one of his poems:

                                        FOR
                                    Four tubas
                                         or
                                  two-by-four's.

Zukofsky's Brooklyn accent emphasises the palindromic echoes of "four tubas" and "tuba-
fours"; the aural rhyme of "or" with "four" and the visual rhyme of "or" with the title, and
the ambiguity of the apostrophe, all reflect a mind which not only delights in puns but also
takes absolutely literally Pound's dictum that poetry is made up of sight, sound, intellection,
and rhythm. The complexities of meaning are established through tentative possibilities of
relationship which are never fully realised in the poem: the romantic, lyric implications of
the title, the mundane quality of the last line, the echoing of the final "by" back to the
meaning of the "ba" of the first line, the ambiguity of the prepositions, all of whose meanings
have relevance to the structure of a poem which, highly comic yet at the same time moving,
draws attention to the neglected minutiae of the language: prepositions, conjunctions,
articles. The poetry is in the words, rather than in the ideas.
    Thus, in *"A,"* his long poem in 24 movements which explore most traditional verse forms
(*"A"*-7 is a sonnet-cycle, *"A"*-9 is a double canzone, *"A"*-21 is a Roman comedy), Zukofsky
plays on the possibilities of the indefinite article (as, earlier − in 1926 − he had written "Poem
Beginning 'The' ") while interweaving personal, political and aesthetic themes round two
central figures: Bach and Shakespeare (music and poetry). If themes are stated, they are stated

so that they may play against one another ("Words rangeless, melody forced by writing," in "*A*"-6), and much of the poem's complex play occurs as the result of pitting one specialised vocabulary or context against another – as, in "*A*"-9, modern physics is pitted against Marx, Cavalcanti, and Spinoza. Similarly, Zukofsky may pit one language against another, as in the opening of "*A*"-15 (English echoing the Hebrew sound of passages from the Book of Job), or in his "translation" of *Catullus*, where the English, repeating the sound of the Latin, comes to be seen, in its knotted turbulence, from "outside itself." Such work, innovative, difficult, often bewildering, and controversial, has nevertheless been influential: some readers, many of them poets, consider Zukofsky to rank with Pound and Joyce among twentieth-century writers.

—Peter Quartermain

NOTES
ON
ADVISERS
AND
CONTRIBUTORS

ALCOCK, Peter. Senior Lecturer in English, Massey University, Palmerston North, New Zealand; Associate Editor of *World Literature Written in English* and bibliographer for *Journal of Commonwealth Literature*. Member of the Executive Committee, Association for Commonwealth Literature and Language, 1968–77. **Essays:** Blanche Baughan, Denis Glover.

ALEXANDER M. J. Lecturer in English, University of Stirling, Scotland. Author of *The Earliest English Poems*, 1966, and Beowulf, 1973. **Essays:** Hilaire Belloc; Beowulf Poet; Laurence Binyon; Rupert Brooke; Marianne Moore.

ALLEN, Walter. Novelist and Literary Critic. Author of six novels (the most recent being *All in a Lifetime*, 1959); several critical works, including *Arnold Bennett*, 1948; *Reading a Novel*, 1949 (revised, 1956); *Joyce Cary*, 1953 (revised, 1971); *The English Novel*, 1954; *Six Great Novelists*, 1955; *The Novel Today*, 1955 (revised, 1966); *George Eliot*, 1964; *The Modern Novel in Britain and the United States*, 1964; and travel books, social history, and books for children. Editor of *Writers on Writing*, 1948, and *The Roaring Queen* by Wyndham Lewis, 1973. Has taught at several universities in Britain, the United States, and Canada; past editor of the *New Statesman*. **Essay:** Rudyard Kipling.

ANDERSON, W. E. K. Headmaster, Shrewsbury School, Shropshire. Editor of *The Journal of Sir Walter Scott*, 1972. **Essay:** Sir Walter Scott.

ASTLE, David. Principal Lecturer in Communication Studies, Sheffield City Polytechnic. **Essays:** Lascelles Abercrombie; Roy Fuller.

AUBERT, Alvin. Associate Professor of English, State University of New York, Fredonia; Publisher and Editor of *Obsidian: Black Literature in Review*. Author of *Against the Blues* (verse), 1972. **Essays:** James Weldon Johnson.

BAREHAM, T. Senior Lecturer in English, New University of Ulster, Coleraine. Author of *George Crabbe: A Critical Study*, 1977, *A Bibliography of Crabbe* (with S. Gattrell), 1978, and articles on Shakespeare and Malcolm Lowry. **Essays:** Sir Richard Blackmore; Robert Bloomfield; William Lisle Bowles; George Crabbe; Stephen Duck; Sir Samuel Garth, Samuel Rogers.

BATESON, F. W. Emeritus Fellow and Tutor in English Literature, Corpus Christi College, Oxford. Formerly, Founding-Editor of *Essays in Criticism*. Author of many books, including *English Comic Drama 1700–1750*, 1929; *English Poetry and the English Language*, 1934 (revised, 1973); *English Poetry: A Critical Introduction*, 1950 (revised, 1966); *Wordsworth: A Re-interpretation*, 1954; *A Guide to English Literature*, 1965 (revised, 1976); *Essays in Critical Dissent*, 1972; *The Scholar Critic*, 1972. Editor of *Pope's Epistles to Several Persons*, 1951 (revised, 1961), and *Selected Poems of Blake*, 1957.

BELLMAN, Samuel Irving. Professor of English, California State Polytechnic University, Pomona. Author of *Marjorie Kinnan Rawlings*, 1974, and articles on Hawthorne and other writers. **Essay:** Edwin Markham.

BENSEN, Alice R. Professor Emerita of English, Eastern Michigan University, Ypsilanti. Author of *Rose Macaulay*, 1969. **Essays:** Charlotte Mew; Elinor Wylie.

BERGONZI, Bernard. Senior Lecturer in English, University of Warwick, Coventry. Author of *Descartes and the Animals*, 1954; *The Early H. G. Wells*, 1961; *Heroes' Twilight*, 1965; *The Situation of the Novel*, 1970; *T. S. Eliot*, 1971; *Gerard Manley Hopkins*, 1977;

Reading the Thirties, 1978. Contributor to *The Observer, Times Literary Supplement,* and other periodicals. **Essays:** Roy Campbell; Philip Larkin.

BERGONZI, Gabriel. Free-lance writer and lecturer. **Essay:** Alice Meynell.

BERRY, Francis. Professor of English, Royal Holloway College, University of London. Author of several books of verse, the most recent being *Ghosts of Greenland,* 1966, and of critical works including *Poets' Grammar,* 1958, *Poetry and the Physical Voice,* 1962, and studies of Herbert Read, Shakespeare, and John Masefield. **Essays:** Matthew Arnold; Lord Byron; Arthur Hugh Clough; Sir John Denham; Edward FitzGerald; John Masefield.

BIRNEY, Earle. See his own entry.

BLAMIRES, David. Member of the Department of German, University of Manchester. Author of *Characterization and Individuality in Wolfram's "Parzifal,"* 1966, and *David Jones, Artist and Writer,* 1971. Co-Editor of *Studies in Medieval Literature and Languages,* 1973. **Essays:** David Jones; Vernon Watkins.

BODE, Walter. Editor in the Chemistry Department, University of California, Berkeley; Assistant Editor of *San Francisco Theatre Magazine,* and free-lance theatre and film critic. **Essay:** Ogden Nash.

BOTTRALL, Margaret. Biographer and Critic. University Lecturer, Department of Education, and Senior Tutor, Hughes Hall, Cambridge University, until 1972. Author of *George Herbert,* 1954, and *Every Man a Phoenix: Studies in Seventeenth-Century Autobiography,* 1958. Editor of *Personal Records,* 1961, and *Songs of Innocence and Experience,* by Blake, 1970. **Essays:** Richard Crashaw; John Hookham Frere; Lord Herbert of Cherbury; John Keble; Edith Sitwell; Anne Finch, Countess of Winchilsea.

BOWDEN, Mary Weatherspoon. Co-ordinator of a scholarly edition of Freneau's works. Author of *Philip Freneau,* 1976, and of articles on Washington Irving. **Essay:** Philip Freneau.

BRAKE, Laurel. Member of the Department of English, University College of Wales, Aberystwyth. **Essays:** William Morris; Alfred, Lord Tennyson.

BRATTON, J. S. Lecturer in English, Bedford College, University of London. Author of *The Victorian Popular Ballad,* 1975. **Essay:** Thomas Hood.

BROER, Lawrence R. Associate Professor of English, University of South Florida, Tampa. Author of *Hemingway's Spanish Tragedy,* 1973, and of many essays and reviews in journals. Editor of *Counter Currents,* 1973, and *The Great Escape of the '20's,* 1977, and Co-Editor of *The First Time: Initial Sexual Experiences in Fiction,* 1974. **Essays:** Stephen Vincent Benét; William Rose Benét.

BROWN, Ashley. Professor of English, University of South Carolina, Columbia; Contributor to *Sewanee Review, Shenandoah, Southern Review, Spectator,* and other periodicals. Editor of *The Achievement of Wallace Stevens* (with R. S. Haller), 1962, *Modes of Literature* (with John L. Kimmey), 1968, and *Satire: An Anthology* (with Kimmey), 1977. **Essays:** John Peale Bishop; Allen Tate.

BROWN, Cedric C. Member of the Department of English Language and Literature, University of Reading, Berkshire. Editor of *The Poems and Masques of Aurelian Townshend,* 1977. **Essay:** Aurelian Townshend.

BROWN, Lloyd W. Member of the Department of Comparative Literature, University of Southern California, Los Angeles. **Essays:** Louise Bennett; Edward Brathwaite.

BROWN, Terence. Member of the Faculty, Trinity College, Dublin. Author of *Louis MacNeice: Sceptical Vision*, 1975. Editor of *Time Was Away: The World of Louis MacNeice* (with Alec Reid), 1974. **Essays:** Padraic Colum; Aubrey De Vere; W. R. Rodgers.

BUTTER, P. H. Regius Professor of English, University of Glasgow. Author of *Shelley's Idols of the Cave*, 1954; *Francis Thompson*, 1961; *Edwin Muir*, 1962; *Edwin Muir: Man and Poet*, 1966. Editor of *Alastor, Prometheus Unbound, and Other Poems*, by Shelley, 1971, and *Selected Letters of Edwin Muir*, 1974. **Essays:** Edwin Muir; Percy Bysshe Shelley; Francis Thompson.

CALHOUN, Richard J. Alumni Professor of English, Clemson University, South Carolina; Co-Editor, *South Carolina Review*. Editor of *A Tricentennial Anthology of South Carolina Literature* (with John C. Guilds), 1971, *James Dickey: The Expansive Imagination*, 1973, and *Two Decades of Change* (with E. M. Lander, Jr.), 1975. **Essay:** James Dickey.

CAMPBELL, Ian. Lecturer in English Literature, University of Edinburgh. Author of *Thomas Carlyle*, 1974, and of articles on Scottish literature since 1750. Associate Editor of the Duke-Edinburgh edition of *Carlyle Letters*, and editor of Carlyle's *Reminiscences* and *Selected Essays*. **Essay:** Allan Ramsay.

CARDWELL, Guy A. Professor of English Emeritus, Washington University, St. Louis. Author of *Twins of Genius*, 1953, *Der Amerikanische Roman*, 1954, *Charleston Periodicals*, 1960, and of articles, poems, and stories in periodicals. Editor of *The Uncollected Poems of Henry Timrod*, 1942; *Readings from the Americas*, 1947; *Discussions of Mark Twain*, 1963; *Life on the Mississippi*, by Twain, 1968. **Essay:** Henry Timrod.

CARNALL, Geoffrey. Reader in English Literature, University of Edinburgh. Author of *Robert Southey and His Age*, 1960, *Robert Southey*, 1964, and *The Mid-Eighteenth Century* (with John Butt), a volume in the Oxford History of English Literature, 1978. **Essay:** Robert Southey.

CARPENTER, Frederic I. Author of *Emerson and Asia*, 1930; *Emerson Handbook*, 1953; *American Literature and the Dream*, 1955; *Robinson Jeffers*, 1962; *Eugene O'Neill*, 1964; *Laurens van der Post*, 1969. Has taught at the University of Chicago, Harvard University, and the University of California, Berkeley. **Essay:** Robinson Jeffers.

CHRISTENSEN, Paul. Assistant Professor of Modern Literature, Texas A. & M. University, College Station. Author of *Old and Lost Rivers* (verse), and *Charles Olson: Call Him Ishmael*, 1978. **Essays:** A. R. Ammons; John Ashbery; John Berryman; Robert Bly; Louise Bogan; Robert Creeley; E. E. Cummings; Stanley Kunitz; Denise Levertov; James Merrill; W. S. Merwin; Frank O'Hara; Charles Olson; Kenneth Rexroth; W. D. Snodgrass; Gary Snyder; John Wheelwright.

CLAIRE, William. Director of the Washington Office, State University of New York. Founding Editor and Publisher, *Voyages: A National Literary Magazine*, 1967–73. Author of *Publishing in the West: Alan Swallow*, and of two books of verse, *Strange Coherence of Our Dreams* and *From a Southern France Notebook*. Contributor to many periodicals, including *Antioch Review*, *American Scholar*, *The Nation*, *New Republic*, and the *New York Times*. **Essay:** Mark Van Doren.

CLARK, John R.   Professor and Chairman, Department of English, University of South Florida, Tampa. Author of *Form and Frenzy in Swift's "Tale of a Tub,"* 1970, and of many essays, reviews, and translations in periodicals. Editor of *Satire – That Blasted Art* (anthology), 1971, and of the satire issue of *Seventeenth-Century News*, 1975. **Essays:** Earl of Dorset; John Oldham; Matthew Prior.

CLARK, Leonard.   Author and Editor of many books of verse, fiction, and non-fiction for children and adults, including *Collected Poems and Verses for Children*, 1975, *Winter to Winter and Other Poems*, 1977, and studies of Alfred Williams, Walter de la Mare, and Andrew Young. Inspector of Schools in Devon, Yorkshire, and London, 1936–70. Frequent contributor of verse, essays, and reviews to periodicals. **Essays:** Kathleen Raine; Andrew Young.

CLUCAS, Garth.   Free-lance writer, currently engaged in research at Linacre College, Oxford. **Essays:** Geoffrey Dutton; Geoffrey Hill.

COCKSHUT, A. O. J.   G. M. Young Lecturer in Nineteenth-Century Literature, Oxford University. Author of *Anthony Trollope: A Critical Study*, 1955; *Anglican Attitudes*, 1959; *The Imagination of Charles Dickens*, 1961; *The Unbelievers: English Agnostic Thought, 1840–90*, 1964; *The Achievement of Walter Scott*, 1969; *Truth to Life*, 1974. **Essay:** Coventry Patmore.

COHN, Ruby.   Professor of Comparative Drama, University of California, Davis; Editor of *Modern Drama*, and Associate Editor of *Educational Theatre Journal*. Author of *Samuel Beckett: The Comic Gamut*, 1962; *Currents in Contemporary Drama*, 1969; *Edward Albee*, 1970; *Dialogue in American Drama*, 1971; *Back to Beckett*, 1973; *Modern Shakespeare Offshoots*, 1976.

COLLINS, William J.   Member of the English Department, University of California, Davis. Free-lance music critic and the author of a forthcoming book on Maria Callas and Renata Tebaldi. **Essay:** Stephen Collins Foster.

CORCORAN, Neil.   Member of the Department of English, University of Sheffield. **Essays:** Conrad Aiken; Robert Lowell; Delmore Schwartz.

CRAIK, T. W.   Professor of English, University of Durham. Author of *The Tudor Interlude*, 1958, and *The Comic Tales of Chaucer*, 1964. Joint General Editor of *The Revels History of Drama in the English Language*, and editor of plays by Massinger, Marlowe, and Shakespeare. **Essay:** Thomas Sackville.

CROSSAN, Greg.   Lecturer in English, Massey University, Palmerston North, New Zealand. Author of *A Relish for Eternity* (on John Clare), 1976. New Zealand Contributor to *Annual Bibliography of English Language and Literature*. **Essay:** Felicia Hemans.

CROWDER, Richard H.   Professor Emeritus of English, Purdue University, Lafayette, Indiana. Fulbright Lecturer, University of Bordeaux, 1963–65. Author of *Those Innocent Years* (on James Whitcomb Riley), 1957, *No Featherbed to Heaven: Michael Wigglesworth*, 1962, and *Carl Sandburg*, 1964. Joint Editor, *Frontiers of American Culture*, 1968. **Essays:** Carl Sandburg; Michael Wigglesworth.

CURNOW, Allen.   See his own entry.

DAHL, Curtis.   Samuel Valentine Cole Professor of English, Wheaton College, Norton, Massachusetts. Author of *Robert Montgomery Bird*, 1966, and of articles on William Cullen

Bryant, Edward Bulwer-Lytton, and Benjamin Disraeli. **Essays:** William Cullen Bryant; Algernon Charles Swinburne.

DANIELS, William. Professor of English, Southwestern at Memphis College, Tennessee. Author of articles on George William Russell and Yeats in *Dublin University Review,* Irish University Review, and *Eire-Ireland.* **Essay:** George William Russell.

DAVIS, Walter R. Professor of English, University of Notre Dame, Indiana. Author of *A Map of Arcadia,* 1965, and of articles on Surrey, Lodge, Spenser, Drayton, Bacon, and Browne. Editor of *The Works of Thomas Campion,* 1967, *Idea and Act in Elizabethan Fiction,* 1969, and *Twentieth Century Interpretations of "Much Ado about Nothing,"* 1969. **Essays:** John Cleveland; Richard Lovelace; Sir Philip Sidney.

DAVISON, Dennis. Senior Lecturer in English, Monash University, Melbourne. Author of *The Poetry of Andrew Marvell,* 1964, *Dryden,* 1968, and *W. H. Auden,* 1970. Editor of *Selected Poetry and Prose,* by Marvell, 1952, *Restoration Comedies,* 1970, and *The Penguin Book of Eighteenth-Century Verse,* 1973. **Essay:** Guy Butler.

DONNO, Elizabeth Story. Professor of English, Columbia University, New York; Editor of *Renaissance Quarterly.* Editor of *Metamorphosis of Ajax* by Sir John Harington, 1962; *Elizabethan Minor Epics,* 1963; *The Complete Poetry of Andrew Marvell,* 1972; *An Elizabethan in 1582: The Diary of Richard Madox,* 1976; *Marvell: The Critical Heritage,* 1977. **Essay:** Michael Drayton.

DOWDEN, Wilfred S. Professor of English, Rice University, Houston. Author of *Joseph Conrad: The Imaged Style,* 1970. Editor of *The Letters of Thomas Moore,* 2 vols., 1964. **Essay:** Thomas Moore.

DOYLE, Charles. Professor of English, and Director of the Division of American and Commonwealth Literature, University of Victoria, British Columbia. Author (as Mike Doyle) of several books of poetry, the most recent being *Going On,* 1974, and of critical studies of New Zealand poetry, R. A. K. Mason, and James K. Baxter. Editor of *Recent Poetry in New Zealand,* 1965. **Essays:** James K. Baxter; R. A. K. Mason; Al Purdy.

DOYNO, Victor A. Associate Professor of English, State University of New York, Buffalo. Editor of *Parthenophil and Parthenophe,* by Barnabe Barnes, 1971. **Essay:** Barnabe Barnes.

DRAPER, R. P. Professor of English, University of Aberdeen, Scotland. Author of two books on Lawrence, and editor of *Lawrence: The Critical Heritage,* 1970, and *Hardy: The Tragic Novels: A Casebook,* 1975. **Essay:** D. H. Lawrence.

DUNLAP, Rhodes. Member of the Department of English, University of Iowa, Iowa City. Editor of *The Poems of Thomas Carew,* 1949. **Essays:** Thomas Carew; William Habington.

ELLIOTT, Brian. Reader in Australian Literary Studies, University of Adelaide. Author of *Leviathan's Inch* (novel), 1946; *Singing to the Cattle and Other Australian Essays,* 1947; *Marcus Clarke,* 1958; *The Landscape of Australian Poetry,* 1967. Editor of *Coast to Coast: Australian Stories 1948,* 1949, and *Bards in the Wilderness: Australian Poetry to 1920* (with Adrian Mitchell), 1970. **Essays:** Charles Harpur; Andrew Barton Paterson.

FABRY, Frank. Professor of English, University of South Florida, Tampa; Assistant Editor of *Seventeenth-Century News.* Author of articles on Sidney and on satire in *Renaissance Quarterly, English Literary Renaissance,* and *Seventeenth-Century News.* **Essays:** Richard Barnfield; Nicholas Breton; William Warner; Thomas Watson.

FAULKNER, Peter. Member of the Department of English, University of Exeter, Devon. Author of *William Morris and W. B. Yeats*, 1962; *Yeats and the Irish Eighteenth Century*, 1965; *Humanism in the English Novel*, 1976; *Modernism*, 1977. Editor of *William Morris: The Critical Heritage*, 1973, and of works by Morris. **Essays:** Elizabeth Barrett Browning; Walter Savage Landor.

FLETCHER, Ian. Reader in English Literature, University of Reading, Berkshire. Author of plays and verse, and of *Walter Pater*, 1959 (revised, 1970); *A Catalogue of Imagist Poets*, 1966; *Beaumont and Fletcher*, 1967; *Meredith Now*, 1971; *Swinburne*, 1972. Editor of anthologies of verse and drama, and of works by Lionel Johnson, Victor Plarr, and John Gray. **Essays:** Oliver St. John Gogarty; T. Sturge Moore; Shaw Neilson.

FOREY, Margaret. Examiner and part-time teacher; currently editing a work by William Strode. Formerly Lecturer at the University of Durham. Author of "Cleveland's 'Square Cap': Some Questions of Structure and Date" in *Durham University Journal*, 1974. **Essays:** Edward Benlowes; Richard Corbett; Thomas Stanley; William Strode; Edmund Waller.

FOSTER, Edward Halsey. Associate Professor and Director of the American Studies Program, Stevens Institute of Technology, Hoboken, New Jersey. Author of *Catharine Maria Sedgwick*, 1974; *The Civilized Wilderness*, 1975; *Josiah Gregg and Lewis Hector Garrard*, 1977; *Susan and Anna Warner*, 1978; and of articles on American literature and American studies. Editor of *Hoboken: A Collection of Essays* (with Geoffrey W. Clark), 1976. **Essay:** Fitz-Greene Halleck.

FOSTER, John Wilson. Associate Professor of English, University of British Columbia, Vancouver; Book Review Editor of *The Canadian Journal of Irish Studies*. Author of *Forces and Themes in Ulster Fiction*, 1974. **Essays:** Margaret Atwood; Patrick Kavanagh.

FRASER, G. S. Reader in Modern English Literature, University of Leicester. Author of several books of verse, the most recent being *Conditions*, 1969; travel books; critical studies of Yeats, Dylan Thomas, Pound, Durrell and Pope; and of *The Modern Writer and His World*, 1953, *Vision and Rhetoric*, 1959, and *Metre, Rhythm, and Free Verse*, 1970. Editor of works by Keith Douglas and Robert Burns, and of verse anthologies. **Essays:** George Barker; William Empson; Frederick Locker-Lampson; Ezra Pound; Sir Osbert Sitwell; Sir Sacheverell Sitwell.

FRENCH, Warren. Professor of English and Director of the Center for American Studiies, Indiana University-Purdue University, Indianapolis; Member of the Editorial Board, *American Literature* and *Twentieth-Century Literature*; series editor for Twayne publishers. Author of *John Steinbeck*, 1961; *Frank Norris*, 1962; *J. D. Salinger*, 1963; *A Companion to "The Grapes of Wrath*,"1963; *The Social Novel at the End of an Era*, 1966; and a series on American fiction, poetry, and drama, *The Thirties*, 1967, *The Forties*, 1968, *The Fifties*, 1971, and *The Twenties*, 1975.

GABIN, Jane S. Teaching Assistant in English, University of North Carolina, Chapel Hill. Author of an article on Dudley Buck; has directed a recital of the music and poetry of Sidney Lanier. **Essays:** John Gould Fletcher; Richard Hovey; Sidney Lanier.

GALL, Sally M. Adjunct Assistant Professor of English, New York University. Distinguished Visiting Professor, Drew University, Madison, New Jersey. Author of articles on M. L. Rosenthal, Ramon Guthrie, and Sylvia Plath in *Modern Poetry Studies* and *American Poetry Review*. **Essay:** Ramon Gurthrie.

GERBER, John C. Chairman of the Department of English, State University of New York,

Albany; Member of the Editorial Board, *Resources for American Literary Study*. Formerly Chairman of the Department of English, University of Iowa. Author of *Factual Prose* (with Walter Blair), 1945; *Literature*, 1948; *Writers Resource Book*, 1953; and other works on writing and speaking. Editor of *Twentieth-Century Interpretations of "The Scarlet Letter*,"1968, and *Studies in Huckleberry Finn*, 1971; General Editor of the Iowa-California edition of the works of Mark Twain. **Essay:** Ralph Waldo Emerson.

GÉRIN, Winifred. Biographer and Critic. Author of *Anne Brontë*, 1959; *Branwell Brontë*, 1961; *The Young Fanny Burney*, 1961; *Charlotte Brontë*, 1967; *Horatia Nelson*, 1970; *Emily Brontë*, 1971; *The Brontës*, 2 vols., 1973; *Elizabeth Gaskell: A Biography*, 1976. Editor of *Five Novelettes* by Charlotte Brontë, 1971. **Essay:** Emily Brontë.

GIBSON, D. B. Professor of English, Rutgers University, New Brunswick, New Jersey. Author of *The Fiction of Stephen Crane*, 1968. Editor of *Five Black Writers*, 1970, *Black and White: Stories of American Life*, 1971, and *Modern Black Poets*, 1973. **Essay:** Melvin Tolson.

GILL, Roma. Member of the Department of English, University of Sheffield. Editor of *The Plays of Christopher Marlowe*, 1971, *William Empson: The Man and His Work*, 1974, and of works by Middleton and Tourneur. **Essays:** Giles Fletcher, the Elder; Christopher Marlowe.

GLASRUD, Clarence A. Professor of English Emeritus, Moorhead State University, Minnesota; Advisory Editor, *Studies in American Fiction*; Member of the Board of Publications, Norwegian-American Historical Association. Author of *Hjalmar Hjorth Boyesen: A Biographical and Critical Study*, 1963. Editor of *The Age of Anxiety*, 1960. **Essay:** Oliver Wendell Holmes.

GLEN, Duncan. Head of Graphics, Preston Polytechnic, Lancashire; Editor of *Akros*, a literary magazine. Author of several books of verse, the most recent being *Gaitherings: Poems in Scots*, 1977, and of *Hugh MacDiarmid and the Scottish Renaissance*, 1964, *The Individual and the Twentieth-Century Scottish Literary Tradition*, and other critical works. Editor of *Selected Essays of MacDiarmid*, 1969, and *MacDiarmid: A Critical Survey*, 1972. **Essay:** Hugh MacDiarmid.

GORDON, Ian A. Professor of English, University of Wellington, 1936–74; also taught at the University of Leeds and the University of Edinburgh. Author of *John Skelton*, 1943; *The Teaching of English*, 1947; *Katherine Mansfield*, 1954; *The Movement of English Prose*, 1966; *John Galt*, 1972. Editor of *English Prose Technique*, 1948, and of works by William Shenstone, John Galt, and Katherine Mansfield. **Essay:** William Shenstone.

GORDON, Lois. Professor of English and Comparative Literature, Fairleigh Dickinson University, Teaneck, New Jersey. Author of *Strategems to Uncover Nakedness: The Dramas of Harold Pinter*, 1969, and of articles on Richard Eberhart, Randall Jarrell, Faulkner, T. S. Eliot, and Philip Roth. **Essays:** Richard Eberhart; Randall Jarrell.

GRAHAM, Desmond. Lecturer in English Literature, University of Newcastle upon Tyne; Poetry Reviewer, *Stand* magazine. Author of *Introduction to Poetry*, 1968, and *Keith Douglas: A Biography*, 1974. Editor of *The Complete Poems of Keith Douglas*, 1978. **Essays:** Keith Douglas; Sidney Keyes.

GREEN, Dorothy. Member of the Faculty, Humanities Research Centre, Australian National University, Canberra. Author of books of verse including *The Dolphin*, 1967, and of articles on Australian literature. **Essays:** Christopher Brennan; Rosemary Dobson; Robert D. FitzGerald; Mary Gilmore; Henry Kendall; Kenneth Mackenzie; Kenneth Slessor; Douglas Stewart; Francis Webb.

GREEN, Roger Lancelyn. Author of more than 50 books including fiction and verse for children and adults, retellings of folk and fairy tales, and critical studies of Andrew Lang, A. E. W. Mason, Lewis Carroll, J. M. Barrie, Mrs. Molesworth, C. S. Lewis, and Rudyard Kipling; also editor of works by these authors and others, and translator of plays by Sophocles. **Essay:** Andrew Lang.

GRUNDY, Joan. Reader in English Literature, Royal Holloway College, University of London. Author of *The Spenserian Poets*, 1969. Editor of *The Poems of Henry Constable*, 1960. **Essays:** Henry Constable; Giles Fletcher, the Younger; Phineas Fletcher; Norman Nicholson; George Wither.

GURR, Andrew. Professor of English Language and Literature, University of Reading, Berkshire. Author of *The Shakespearean Stage*, 1970. Editor of several plays by Beaumont and Fletcher. **Essay:** Allen Curnow.

HAMILTON, Harlan W. Professor Emeritus of English, Case Western Reserve University, Cleveland. Author of *Doctor Syntax: A Silhouette of William Combe*, 1969, and articles on Johnson and Combe in *English Studies Today*, *Western Humanities Review*, and *PMLA*. **Essays:** William Combe; John Pomfret.

HARMON, Maurice. Lecturer in Anglo-Irish Literature, University College, Dublin; Editor of *Irish University Review*. Author of *Sean O'Faolain*, 1967, *The Poetry of Thomas Kinsella*, 1974, and *Select Bibliography of Anglo-Irish Literature and Its Backgrounds*, 1977. Editor of *Irish Poetry after Yeats: Seven Poets*, 1978. **Esssays:** Austin Clarke; Seamus Heaney.

HASSLER, Donald M. Associate Professor of English, Kent State University, Kent, Ohio. Author of *Erasmus Darwin*, 1972. **Essays:** Erasmus Darwin; Anna Seward.

HEATH-STUBBS, John. Writer and Lecturer. Author of several books of verse, the most recent being *The Watchman's Flute*, 1978, a book of plays, and of *The Darkling Plain: A Study of the Later Fortunes of Romanticism*, 1950, *Charles Williams*, 1955, and studies of the verse satire, the ode, and the pastoral. Editor of anthologies and works by Shelley, Tennyson, Swift, and Pope; translator of works by Giacomo Leopardi, Alfred de Vigny, and others. **Essays:** Mark Akenside; Alfred Austin; William Barnes; Wilfrid Scawen Blunt; Charles Churchill; Samuel Taylor Coleridge; Hart Crane; Ernest Dowson; William Drummond; William Mickle; Ambrose Philips; Christina Rossetti; Dante Gabriel Rossetti; Thomas Tickell.

HEWITT, Geof. Poet and Editor; Contributing Editor, *New Letters*, Kansas City, Missouri. His most recent book of verse is *Stone Soup*, 1974. Editor of the poems of Alfred Starr Hamilton and of verse anthologies. **Essay:** Muriel Rukeyser.

HOFFMAN, Daniel. Professor of English, University of Pennsylvania, Philadelphia. Author of several books of verse, the most recent being *Able Was I Ere I Saw Elba*, 1977, and of critical works including *The Poetry of Stephen Crane*, 1957; *Form and Fable in American Fiction*, 1961; *Poe Poe Poe Poe Poe Poe Poe*, 1972; *Barbarous Knowledge: Myth in the Poetry of Yeats, Graves, and Muir*, 1973. Editor of anthologies and of works by Crane and Robert Frost. **Essays:** Robert Graves; Edgar Allan Poe.

HOLDEN, Jonathan. Member of the English Department, Stephens College, Columbia, Missouri. Author of *Design for a House* (verse), 1972, and of poetry for *Antioch Review*, *North American Review*, and other periodicals. **Essay:** William Stafford.

HOLMAN, C. Hugh. Kenan Professor of English, Chairman of the Division of Humanities, and Special Assistant to the Chancellor, University of North Carolina, Chapel Hill; Editor of *Southern Literary Journal.* Author or co-author of several books, including five detective novels, *The Development of American Criticism,* 1955; *The Southerner as American,* 1960; *Thomas Wolfe,* 1960; *Seven Modern American Novelists,* 1964; *The American Novel Through Henry James: A Bibliography,* 1966; *Three Modes of Modern Southern Fiction,* 1966; *Roots of Southern Writing,* 1972; *The Loneliness at the Core,* 1975. Editor of works by Thomas Wolfe, William Gilmore Simms, and others. **Essay:** Robert Penn Warren.

HUDSON, Derek. Free-lance Writer and Editor. Author of books on Winthrop Mackworth Praed, Thomas Barnes, Norman O'Neill, Charles Keene, Martin Tupper, James Pryde, Lewis Carroll, Joshua Reynolds, Arthur Rackham, and others, and on journalism and topography. Editor of anthologies and of the diary of Henry Crabb Robinson. **Essay:** Martin Tupper.

HUDSPETH, Robert N. Associate Professor of English, Pennsylvania State University, University Park. Author of *Ellery Channing,* 1973. Currently editing the letters of Margaret Fuller. **Essay:** William Ellery Channing.

HUGHEY, Ruth. Professor Emeritus of English, Ohio State University, Columbus. Author of *John Harington of Stepney, Tudor Gentleman,* 1971, and of articles on Harington, Elizabeth Grymeston, and Elizabeth I. Editor of *The Correspondence of Lady Katherine Paston,* 1941, and *The Arundel Harington Manuscript of Tudor Poetry,* 2 vols., 1960. **Essay:** Sir John Harington.

JAMES, Louis. Senior Lecturer in English and American Literature, University of Kent, Canterbury. Author of *The Islands in Between,* 1968, and *Fiction for the Working Class Man 1830–1850,* 1974.

JEFFARES, A. Norman. Professor of English Studies, University of Stirling, Scotland; Editor of *Ariel: A Review of International English Literature,* and General Editor of the Writers and Critics series and the New Oxford English series; Past Editor of *A Review of English Studies.* Author of *Yeats: Man and Poet,* 1949; *Seven Centuries of Poetry,* 1956; *A Commentary on the Collected Poems* (1958) and *Collected Plays* (1975) *of Yeats.* Editor of *Restoration Comedy,* 1974, and *Yeats: The Critical Heritage,* 1977. **Essays:** William Cowper; William Butler Yeats.

JOHNSON, Robert K. Professor of English, Suffolk University, Boston. Author of articles on Richard Wilbur, Wallace Stevens, T. S. Eliot, and William Carlos Williams. **Essays:** Robert Frost; Archibald MacLeish; Howard Nemerov; Frederick Goddard Tuckerman.

JOSEPH, M. K. Professor of English, University of Auckland. Author of several books of verse, most recently *Inscription on a Paper Dart,* 1974; three novels, most recently *A Soldiers Tale,* 1976; and of *Byron the Poet,* 1964. Editor of *Frankenstein* by Mary Shelley, 1969. **Essay:** William Falconer.

JOYNER, Nancy C. Member of the Department of English, Western Carolina University, Cullowhee, North Carolina. **Essays:** Laura Riding; Edwin Arlington Robinson.

KALLICH, Martin. Professor of English, Northern Illinois University, De Kalb. Author of *The Psychological Milieu of Lytton Strachey,* 1961; *The American Revolution Through British Eyes* (with others), 1962; *Heav'n's First Law: Rhetoric and Order in Pope's Essay on Man,* 1967; *Oedipus: Myth and Drama* (with others), 1968; *The Other End of the Egg: Religious*

Satire in Gulliver's Travels, 1970; *The Association of Ideas and Critical Theory in 18th-Century England,* 1970; *Horace Walpole,* 1971; *The Book of the Sonnet* (with others), 1972. **Essay:** John Scott.

KELLNER, Bruce. Associate Professor of English, Millersville State College, Pennsylvania. Author of *Carl Van Vechten and the Irreverent Decades,* 1968; *The Wormwood Poems of Thomas Kinsella,* 1972; *The Poet as Translator,* 1973; *Alfred Kazin's Exquisites: An Excavation,* 1975. Editor of *Selected Writings of Van Vechten about Negro Arts and Letters,* 1978. **Essays:** Henry Wadsworth Longfellow; Robert Service.

KELLY, Richard. Professor of English, University of Tennessee, Knoxville. Editor of *Tennessee Studies in Literature,* 1970–76. Author of *Douglas Jerrold,* 1970, *Lewis Carroll,* 1970, and *Great Cartoonists of Nineteenth-Century Punch,* 1978. Editor of *The Best of Mr. Punch: The Humorous Writings of Douglas Jerrold,* 1970. **Essay:** Edward Lear.

KEMP, Peter. Lecturer in English and American Literature, Middlesex Polytechnic, London. Author of *Muriel Spark,* 1974. **Essay:** Siegfried Sassoon.

KENDLE, Burton. Associate Professor of English, Roosevelt University, Chicago. Author of articles on D. H. Lawrence, John Cheever, and Chekhov. **Essays:** Sir John Davies; John Skelton.

KINNAMON, Keneth. Professor and Associate Head of the English Department, University of Illinois, Urbana-Champaign. Author of *The Emergence of Richard Wright,* 1972. Editor of *Black Writers of America: A Comprehensive Anthology* (with Richard K. Barksdale), 1972, and of *James Baldwin: A Collection of Critical Essays,* 1974. **Essay:** Langston Hughes.

LEARY, Lewis. Kenan Professor of English, University of North Carolina, Chapel Hill. Author of *Idiomatic Mistakes in English,* 1932; *That Rascal Freneau: A Study in Literary Failure,* 1941; *The Literary Career of Nathaniel Tucker,* 1951; *Mark Twain,* 1960; *Twain's Letters to Mary,* 1961; *John Greenleaf Whittier,* 1962; *Washington Irving,* 1963; *Norman Douglas,* 1967; *Southern Excursions,* 1971; *Faulkner of Yoknapatawpha County,* 1973; *Soundings: Some Early American Writers,* 1975; *American Literature: A Study and Research Guide,* 1976. Editor of works by Freneau and Twain, and several collections of essays.

LESTER, G. A. Lecturer in English Language and Medieval Literature, University of Sheffield. Author of *The Anglo-Saxons,* 1976. **Essay:** Cynewulf.

LEVERNIER, James A. Assistant Professor of English, University of Arkansas, Little Rock. Contributor to *ESO: A Journal of the American Renaissance, Research Studies, The Markham Review, Explicator,* and other periodicals. Editor of *An Essay for the Recording of Illustrious Providences* by Increase Mather, 1977, and *The Indians and Their Captives* (with Hennig Cohen), 1977. **Essays:** Ebenezer Cooke; Kenneth Fearing; Louise Imogen Guiney; Charles Fenno Hoffman; Francis Hopkinson; Joaquin Miller; Bayard Taylor; John Trumbull.

LEWIS, Peter. Lecturer in English, University of Durham. Author of *The Beggar's Opera* (critical study), 1976, and articles on Restoration and Augustan drama and modern poetry. Editor of *The Beggar's Opera* by John Gay, 1973, and *Poems '74* (anthology of Anglo-Welsh poetry), 1974. **Essays:** Basil Bunting; John Gay.

LINDSAY, Maurice. Director of the Scottish Civic Trust, Glasgow, and Managing Editor of *The Scottish Review*. Author of several books of verse, the most recent being *Walking Without an Overcoat*, 1977; plays; travel and historical works; and critical studies, including *Robert Burns: The Man, His Work, The Legend*, 1954 (revised, 1968), *The Burns Encyclopedia*, 1959 (revised, 1970), and *A History of Scottish Literature*, 1977. Editor of the Saltire Modern Poets series, several anthologies of Scottish writing, and works by Sir Alexander Gray, Sir David Lyndsay, Marion Angus, and John Davidson. **Essays:** John Armstrong; James Beattie; Robert Burns; Thomas Campbell; John Davidson; William Dunbar; Sir David Lyndsay; Harold Monro; Sydney Goodsir Smith.

LIVESAY, Dorothy. See her own entry. **Essay:** Isabella Valancy Crawford.

LODGE, David. Reader in English, University of Birmingham. Author of five novels (the most recent being *Changing Places*, 1975); *Language of Fiction*, 1966; *The Novelist at the Crossroads*, 1971; and studies of Graham Greene and Evelyn Waugh. Editor of novels by Jane Austen, George Eliot, Hardy, and *Twentieth Century Literary Criticism: A Reader*, 1972.

LOHOF, Bruce A. Associate Professor and Chairman of the Department of History, University of Miami; Joint Editor of the *Indian Journal of American Studies*, and member of the editorial board of *Journal of Popular Culture*. Former Senior Fulbright-Hays Scholar and Director of the American Studies Research Centre, Hyderabad, India. Author of articles for *Social Studies Bulletin, Industrial Archaeology, Centennial Review*, and other periodicals, and of papers for the American Studies Association and the Popular Culture Association. **Essay:** Timothy Dwight.

LUCAS, John. Professor of English and Drama, Loughborough University, Leicestershire; Advisory Editor of *Victorian Studies, Literature and History*, and *Journal of European Studies*. Author of *Tradition and Tolerance in 19th-Century Fiction*, 1966; *The Melancholy Man: A Study of Dickens*, 1970; *Arnold Bennett*, 1975; *Egilssaga: The Poems*, 1975; *The Literature of Change*, 1977; *The 1930's: Challenge to Orthodoxy*, 1978. Editory of *Literature and Politics in the 19th Century*, 1971, and of works by George Crabbe and Jane Austen. **Essays:** Philip James Bailey; Matthew Green; Ebenezer Jones; John Westland Marston; William Mason; Kenneth Patchen; John Wilmot, Earl of Rochester; Louis Simpson.

LYLE, A. W. Lecturer in English, University of Sheffield. **Essays:** Alexander Barclay; William Browne; George Gascoigne; Joseph Hall.

MACKERNESS, E. D. Member of the Department of English Literature, University of Sheffield. Author of *The Heeded Voice: Studies in the Literary Status of the Anglican Sermon 1830–1900*, 1959, *A Social History of English Music*, 1964, and *Somewhere Further North: A History of Music in Sheffield*, 1974. Editor of *The Journals of George Sturt 1890–1927*, 1967. **Essay:** Thomas Campion.

MacLAINE, Allan H. Professor of English, University of Rhode Island, Kingston. Author of *The Student's Comprehensive Guide to the Canterbury Tales*, 1964, *Robert Fergusson*, 1965, and of articles on Burns. **Essays:** Gavin Douglas; Robert Fergusson; Thomas Gray.

McDIARMID, Matthew P. Member of the Department of English, University of Aberdeen, Scotland. Author of articles on Scots writers for the *Scottish Historical Review* and other periodicals. Editor of works by John Barbour, James I, and Robert Fergusson. **Essays:** John Barbour; Blind Hary; Sir Richard Holland.

1131

McKAY, F. M.   Member of the Department of English, Victoria University of Wellington, New Zealand. Author of *New Zealand Poetry: An Introduction*, 1970. Editor of *Poetry New Zealand*, 1971. **Essays:** Alistair Campbell; Eileen Duggan; C. K. Stead.

MINER, Earl.   Townsend Martin Professor of English and Comparative Literature, Princeton University, New Jersey. Author of *Dryden's Poetry*, 1967; *An Introduction to Japanese Court Poetry*, 1968; *The Metaphysical Mode from Donne to Cowley*, 1969; *The Cavalier Mode from Jonson to Cotton*, 1971; *Seventeenth-Century Imagery*, 1971; *The Restoration Mode from Milton to Dryden*, 1974; *Japanese Linked Poetry*, 1978. **Essays:** Samuel Butler; Charles Cotton; John Dryden.

MIRZA, Gail.   Free-lance Writer and Translator; Joint Editor of the *Journal of Humanistic and Interdisciplinary Studies*. Author of a work on Juan Ramón Jiménez, Tagore, and Yeats. **Essay** (with H. A. Mirza): Sir Rabindranath Tagore.

MIRZA, H. A.   Teacher of Literature and Interdisciplinary Studies, University of Connecticut, Storrs; Joint Editor of the *Journal of Humanistic and Interdisciplinary Studies*. Author of articles on literature, philosophy, psychology, and East-West studies. **Essay** (with Gail Mirza): Sir Rabindranath Tagore.

MITCHELL, Jerome.   Professor of English, University of Georgia, Athens. Fulbright Guest Professor, University of Bonn, 1972–73; former editor of *South Atlantic Bulletin*. Author of *Thomas Hoccleve: A Study in Early 15th-Century English Poetic*, and *The Walter Scott Operas*, 1977. **Essay:** Thomas Hoccleve.

MONTEIRO, George.   Professor of English, Brown University, Providence, Rhode Island. Editor of *Henry James and John Hay: The Record of a Friendship*, 1965; *Poems* by Emily Dickinson, 1967; *The Scarlet Letter* by Hawthorne (with Hyatt H. Waggoner), 1968; *The Poetical Works of Longfellow*, 1975. **Essay:** John Hay.

MOORE, Catherine E.   Associate Professor of English, North Carolina State University, Raleigh. **Essay:** Anna Barbauld.

MOORE, Rayburn S.   Professor of English and Chairman, Division of Language and Literature, University of Georgia, Athens; Member of the Editorial Board, *Georgia Review*. Author of *Constance Fenimore Woolson*, 1963, *Paul Hamilton Hayne*, 1972, and many articles and reviews. Editor of *The Major and Selected Short Stories of Woolson*, 1967. **Essays:** Thomas Holley Chivers; Paul Hamilton Hayne.

MORPURGO, J. E.   Professor of American Literature, University of Leeds. Author and editor of many books, including the *Pelican History of the United States*, 1955 (third edition, 1970), and volumes on Cooper, Lamb, Trelawny, Barnes Wallis, and on Venice Athens, and rugby football. **Essay:** Edmund Blunden.

MUIR, Kenneth.   Professor Emeritus of English Literature, University of Liverpool; Editor of *Shakespeare Survey*, and Chairman, International Shakespeare Association. Author of many books, including *The Nettle and the Flower*, 1933; *King Lear*, 1952; *Elizabethan Lyrics*, 1953; *John Milton*, 1955; *Shakespeare's Sources*, 1957; *Shakespeare and the Tragic Pattern*, 1959; *Shakespeare the Collaborator*, 1960; *Introduction to Elizabethan Literature*, 1967; *The Comedy of Manners*, 1970; *The Singularity of Shakespeare*, 1977; *Shakespeare's Comic Sequence*, 1978. Editor of several plays by Shakespeare, and of works by Wyatt and Middleton; translator of five plays by Racine. **Essays:** William Blake, Andrew Marvell; Henry Howard, Earl of Surrey.

MUNRO, John M.   Professor of English, American University of Beirut, Lebanon. Author of *English Poetry in Transition*, 1968; *Arthur Symons*, 1969; *Decadent Poetry in the 1890's*, 1970; *The Royal Aquarium: Failure of a Victorian Compromise*, 1971; *James Elroy Flecker*, 1976; *A Mutual Concern*, 1977; and other books. Editor of *Selected Poems of Theo. Marzials*, 1973. **Essays:** Lord de Tabley; James Elroy Flecker; Sir William Watson.

NESBITT, Bruce.   Member of the Department of English, Simon Fraser University, Burnaby, British Columbia. Author of *Earle Birney*, 1975. **Essays:** Archibald Lampman; Dorothy Livesay; E. J. Pratt; F. R. Scott.

NEW, W. H.   Associate Professor of English, University of British Columbia, Vancouver; Associate Editor of *Canadian Literature* and *World Literature Written in English*. Author of *Four Hemispheres*, 1971, and *Malcolm Lowry*, 1971.

NIVEN, Alastair.   Member of the Department of English Studies, University of Stirling, Scotland. Author of *D. H. Lawrence: The Novels*, 1978. **Essay:** Gabriel Okara.

NORDLAND, Brady.   Free-lance Writer and Researcher. **Essay:** S. T. Dobell.

NORTON-SMITH, J.   Reader in English Language and Literature, University of Dundee, Scotland; Editor of *Reading Medieval Studies* and General Editor of Brill's Medieval and Renaissance Authors series. Author of *Six Poems and Six Drawings* (with Fritz Janschka), 1972, and *Geoffrey Chaucer*, 1974. Editor of *Poems* by John Lydgate, 1966. *The Kingis Quair* by James I, 1971, and *The Quare of Jelusy*, 1975. **Essays:** James I, King of Scotland; John Lydgate.

O'DONNELL, Thomas F.   Professor of English, State University of New York, Brockport. Author of *Harold Frederic* (with Hoyt C. Franchere), 1961, and of articles on American writers, especially those of New York State, for *American Transcendental Quarterly* and other periodicals. Joint Editor of *A Bibliography of Harold Frederic*, 1975, and editor of works by Frederic, James Kirke Paulding, and Adriaen Van Der Donck. **Essays:** Anne Bradstreet; Joseph Rodman Drake.

OLIVER-MORDEN, B. C.   Teacher at the Open University and the University of Keele. Editor of the 18th-Century section of *The Year's Work in English 1973*. **Essays:** William Collins; Oliver Goldsmith; Laurie Lee; George Lyttelton; James Macpherson; William Bell Scott.

O'TOOLE, Bridget.   Member of the Faculty, New University of Ulster, Coleraine. **Essays:** Ebenezer Elliott; James (B. V.) Thomson.

PATRIDES, C. A.   Professor of English Literature, University of Michigan, Ann Arbor. Formerly, Professor of English, University of York, England. Author of *Milton and the Christian Tradition*, 1966, and *The Grand Design of God: The Literary Form of the Christian View of History*, 1972. Editor of *Approaches to Paradise Lost*, 1968; *The Cambridge Platonists*, 1969; *History of the World* by Sir Walter Ralegh, 1971; *English Poems* by George Herbert, 1974; *Selected Prose* by Milton, 1974; *Major Works* by Sir Thomas Browne, 1977; *Approaches to Marvell*, 1978. **Essay:** Sir Walter Ralegh.

PEARCE, Roy Harvey.   Professor of English, University of California at San Diego. Author of *Colonial American Writing*, 1951, *The Savages of America*, 1953 (revised, 1965), and *The Continuity of American Poetry*, 1961. Co-Editor of the Centennial Edition of the Writings of Hawthorne, and of anthologies of essays on Hawthorne and Whitman.

PEARSALL, Derek. Professor, Centre for Medieval Studies, University of York. Author of *Gower and Lydgate*, 1969, *Lydgate*, 1970, and *Old English and Middle English Poetry*, 1977. Editor of *Medieval Literature and Civilisation* (with R. A. Waldron), 1969, *Landscapes and Seasons of the Medieval World* (with Elizabeth Salter), 1973, and *Piers Plowman* by William Langland, 1978. **Essays:** Gawain Poet; John Gower; William Langland; Layamon.

PERKINS, George. Professor of English, Eastern Michigan University, Ypsilanti. Author or editor of *Writing Clear Prose*, 1964; *Varieties of Prose*, 1966; *The Theory of the American Novel*, 1970; *Realistic American Short Fiction*, 1972; *American Poetic Theory*, 1972; *The American Tradition in Literature* (with others), fourth edition, 1974.

PERRY, John J. Member of the Department of English, State University of New York, Brockport. **Essays:** Alexander Hume; Sir Charles Sedley.

PERRY, Margaret. Assistant Director for Reader Services, University of Rochester Libraries, New York; Contributing Editor, *Afro-American in New York Life and History*. Author of *A Bio-Bibliography of Countée P. Cullen*, 1971, *Silence to the Drums: A Survey of the Literature of the Harlem Renaissance*, 1976, and of several short stories published in periodicals. **Essays:** Countée Cullen; Phillis Wheatley.

PETERSEN, Kirsten Holst. Member of the Commonwealth Literature Division of the English Department, University of Aarhus, Denmark; reviewer for *Danida*. Editor of *Enigma of Values* (with Anna Rutherford), 1975. **Essay:** John Pepper Clark.

PICKARD, John B. Associate Professor of English, University of Florida, Gainesville. Author of *Whittier: An Introduction and Interpretation*, 1961, and *Emily Dickinson*, 1967. Editor of *Legends of New England* by Whittier, 1965, and *The Letters of Whittier*, 3 vols., 1975. **Essays:** James Russell Lowell; John Greenleaf Whittier.

PINION, F. B. Former Sub-Dean and Reader in English Studies, University of Sheffield; Editor of the *Thomas Hardy Society Review*. Author of *A Hardy Companion*, 1968; *A Jane Austen Companion*, 1973; *A Brontë Companion*, 1975; *A Commentary on the Poems of Hardy*, 1976; *Hardy: Art and Thought*, 1977. Editor of *Two on a Tower* by Hardy, and of Hardy's complete short stories. **Essay:** Thomas Hardy.

PITTOCK, Joan. Member of the Department of English, University of Aberdeen, Scotland. Author of *The Ascendancy of Taste: The Achievement of Joseph and Thomas Warton*, 1973. **Essays:** Joseph Warton; Thomas Warton.

POLLARD, Arthur. Professor of English, University of Hull, Yorkshire. Author of *Mrs. Gaskell, Novelist and Biographer*, 1965, and *Anthony Trollope*, 1978. Editor of *The Letters of Mrs. Gaskell* (with J. A. V. Chapple), 1966; *The Victorians* (Sphere History of Literature in English), 1970; *Crabbe: The Critical Heritage*, 1972; *Thackeray: Vanity Fair* (casebook), 1978. **Essays:** John Byrom; John Langhorne; James McAuley; Judith Wright; Edward Young.

PRESS, John. Area Officer, British Council, Oxford. Author of three books of verse – *Uncertainties*, 1956, *Guy Fawkes Night*, 1959, and *Troika* (with others), 1977 – and several critical books, including *Rule and Energy*, 1963, *A Map of English Verse*, 1969, *The Lengthening Shadows*, 1971, and *John Betjeman*, 1974. **Essays:** Sir John Betjeman; Robert Bridges; Donald Davie; W. H. Davies; David Gascoyne; Robert Herrick; Louis MacNeice; Charles Hamilton Sorley; Bernard Spencer.

PYLE, Hilary. Free-lance writer. Author of *Jack B. Yeats: A Biography*, 1970. **Essay:** James Stephens.

QUARTERMAIN, Peter. Associate Professor of English, University of British Columbia, Vancouver. Author of "Louis Zukofsky: Re Location" in *Open Letter*, 1973; and "Romantic Offensive: *Tish*" in *Canadian Literature*, 1977. **Essays:** Robert Duncan; Allen Ginsberg; Louis Zukofsky.

RAWSON, C. J. Professor of English, University of Warwick, Coventry; Joint Editor of *Modern Language Review* and *Yearbook of English Studies*, and General Editor of the Unwin Critical Library. Author of *Henry Fielding*, 1968; *Fielding and the Augustan Ideal under Stress*, 1972; *Gulliver and the Gentle Reader*, 1973; *Focus: Swift*, 1978. Editor of *Fielding: A Critical Anthology*, 1973, and *Yeats and Anglo-Irish Literature: Critical Essays* by Peter Ure, 1973. **Essays:** Thomas Parnell; Jonathan Swift.

RAY, David. Professor of English, University of Missouri, Kansas City; Editor of *New Letters*, Kansas City. His most recent book of verse is *Gathering Firewood: New Poems and Selected*, 1974. Editor of *The Chicago Review Anthology*, 1959, *Richard Wright: Impressions and Perspectives* (with Robert M. Farnsworth), and of verse anthologies. **Essay:** Horace Gregory.

REDEKOP, E. H. Associate Professor of English, University of Western Ontario, London. Author of *Margaret Avison*, 1970. **Essay:** Margaret Avison.

REDSHAW, Thomas Dillon. Associate Editor of *Eire-Ireland*, and teacher of the College of St. Thomas, St. Paul, Minnesota. Author of *Heimaey*, 1974, and of verse in periodicals. Editor of *The Collected Poems of Thomas MacGreevy*, 1971. **Essay:** John Montague.

REES, Joan. Member of the Department of English Language and Literature, University of Birmingham. Author of *Samuel Daniel*, 1964, *Fulke Greville: A Critical Biography*, 1971, and *Jane Austen, Woman and Writer*, 1976. Editor of *Selected Writings* by Greville, 1973. **Essays:** Samuel Daniel; Sir Fulke Greville.

REEVES, James. Author of more than 50 books, including verse (*Collected Poems*, 1974), plays, and books for children; critical works include *The Critical Sense*, 1956, *Understanding Poetry*, 1965, *Commitment to Poetry*, 1969, *Inside Poetry* (with Martin Seymour-Smith), 1970, and *The Reputation and Writings of Alexander Pope*, 1976. Editor of many collections and anthologies, and of works by D. H. Lawrence, Donne, Clare, Hopkins, Robert Browning, Dickinson, Coleridge, Graves, Swift, Johnson, Marvell, Gray, Whitman, and others; translator of fairy tales. Died, 1978. **Essays:** Thomas Lovell Beddoes; George Darley; Emily Dickinson; Sir Thomas Wyatt.

REILLY, John M. Associate Professor of English, State University of New York, Albany: Advisory Editor, *Obsidian: Black Literature in Review*, and *Melus*. Author of the bibliographical essay on Richard Wright in *Black American Writers* and of articles on Wright and other Afro-American writers, and on detective fiction, in *Colorado Quarterly*, *Phylon*, *CLA Journal*, *Journal of Black Studies*, *Armchair Detective*, *Journal of Popular Culture*, and other periodicals. Editor of *Twentieth-Century Interpretations of "Invisible Man,"* 1970, *Richard Wright: The Critical Reception*, 1978, and of the reference book *Detective and Crime Writers*, 1980.

RHODES, H. Winston. Professor of English (retired), University of Canterbury, Christchurch. Formerly, Editor of *New Zealand Monthly Review*. Books include *New Zealand Fiction since 1945*, 1968, *Frank Sargeson*, 1969, and six edited volumes of Rewi Alley's prose and verse.

ROGAL, Samuel J. Associate Professor of English, Mary Holmes College, West Point, Mississippi. Author of articles on hymns and sacred music, John Wesley, George Eliot, Pope, and Milton, in *The Serif, Eighteenth-Century Life, Nineteenth-Century Fiction, Milton Quarterly*, and other periodicals. **Essay:** Charles Wesley.

ROGERS, Pat. Professor of English, University of Bristol. Author of *Grub Street: Studies in a Subculture*, 1972, and *The Augustan Vision*, 1974. Editor of *A Tour Through Great Britain* by Daniel Defoe, 1971, *Defoe: The Critical Heritage*, 1972, and *The Eighteenth Century*, 1978. **Essays:** William Diaper; John Philips; Alexander Pope.

ROTHSTEIN, Eric. Professor of English, University of Wisconsin, Madison. Author of *George Farquhar*, 1967, and *Restoration Tragedy: Form and the Process of Change*, 1967. Co-Editor of *The Augustan Milieu: Essays Presented to Louis A. Landa*, 1970. **Essay:** Christopher Anstey.

ROVIT, Earl. Professor of English, City College of New York. Author of *Herald to Chaos: The Novels of Elizabeth Madox Roberts*, 1960; *Ernest Hemingway*, 1963; *The Player King*, 1965; *Saul Bellow*, 1967; *A Far Cry*, 1967; *Crossings*, 1973. **Essays:** Trumbull Stickney; Jones Very.

RUIHLEY, Glenn Richard. Member of the Department of English, Eastern Michigan University, Ypsilanti. Author of *The Thorn of a Rose: Amy Lowell Reconsidered*, 1975. Editor of *A Shard of Silence: Selected Poems* by Lowell, 1957. **Essays:** Amy Lowell; Edgar Lee Masters; Edna St. Vincent Millay.

RUOFF, James E. Associate Professor of English, City College of New York. Author of *Elizabethan Poetry and Prose*, 1972, *Crowell Handbook of Elizabethan and Stuart Literature*, 1973, and *Major Shakespearean Tragedies* (with Edward G. Quinn), 1973. **Essays:** Thomas Churchyard; Abraham Cowley; Sir John Suckling; Thomas Tusser; George Whetstone.

RUTENBERG, Daniel. Member of the Department of Humanities, University of South Florida, Tampa. **Essay:** Austin Dobson.

SAFFIOTI, Carol Lee. Assistant Professor of English, University of Wisconsin – Parkside, Kenosha. **Essay:** Sterling Brown.

SALGĀDO, Gāmini. Professor of English, University of Exeter, Devon. Author of *Eyewitnesses of Shakespeare: Firsthand Accounts of Performances, 1590–1890*, 1975, and *The Elizabethan Underworld*, 1977. Editor of *Sons and Lovers: A Collection of Critical Essays*, 1969, *Cony Catchers and Bawdy Baskets*, 1973, works by D. H. Lawrence and Shakespeare, and collections of Jacobean and Restoration plays. **Essay:** Ben Jonson.

SAMBROOK, A. J. Reader in English, University of Southampton, Hampshire. Author of *A Poet Hidden: The Life of Richard Watson Dixon*, 1962, and *William Cobbett: An Author Guide*, 1973. Editor of *The Scribleriad*, 1967, *The Seasons and The Castle of Indolence* by James Thomson, 1972, and *Pre-Raphaelitism: Patterns of Literary Criticism*, 1974. **Essays:** Robert Blair; John Cunningham; Richard Watson Dixon; James Grainger; David Mallet; Lady Mary Wortley Montagu; Richard Savage; William Somerville; James Thomson; William Walsh.

SAUL, George Brandon. Professor Emeritus of English, University of Connecticut, Storrs; Contributing Editor, *Journal of Irish Literature*. Author of fiction (*The Wild Queen*, 1967), verse (*Hound and Unicorn*, 1969, and *Adam Unregenerate*, 1977), and of critical works, including *Prolegomena to the Study of Yeats's Poems* (1957) and *Plays* (1958), *Traditional*

Irish Literature and Its Backgrounds, 1970, and *In Praise of the Half-Forgotten: Essays*, 1976. Also a composer. **Essay:** Sara Teasdale.

SCHWARZ, Daniel R. Associate Professor of English, Cornell University, Ithaca, New York. Author of articles on T. S. Eliot, Conrad, Hardy, and Dylan Thomas, in *Studies in the Novel, Modern Fiction Studies, Twentieth-Century Literature*, and other periodicals. **Essay:** Dylan Thomas.

SCOBIE, Brian W. M. Member of the Faculty, School of English, University of Leeds. **Essay:** Robert Henryson.

SEELYE, Catherine. Free-lance writer. **Essays:** Eugene Field; Vachel Lindsay.

SELL, Roger D. Member of the Department of English, Abo Academy, Finland. Editor of *The Shorter Poems of Sir John Beaumont*, 1974. **Essay:** Sir John Beaumont.

SEWELL, Brocard. Lecturer in English, Mount Carmel College, Niagara Falls, Ontario; Priest of the Carmelite Order (English Province). Former Editor of *Aylesford Review*. Author of *Montague Summers: A Memoir*, 1966; *Footnote to the Nineties*, 1968; *The Vatican Oracle*, 1970; *Olive Custance*, 1975; *Cecil Chesterton*, 1975. **Essay:** Robert Stephen Hawker.

SHADY, Raymond C. Member of the English Department, St. John Fisher College, Rochester, New York. Editor of *Love's Mistress* by Thomas Heywood, 1977. **Essay:** John Marston.

SHEIDLEY, William E. Associate Professor of English, University of Connecticut, Storrs. Co-Editor of the journal *Children's Literature*, 1974–77. Author of articles on Marlowe, George Turbervile, Barnabe Googe, and Shakespeare in *Concerning Poetry, Journal of English and Germanic Philology, Studies in Philology*, and *Modern Language Quarterly*. **Essays:** Barnabe Googe; George Turbervile; Thomas Vaux.

SHIRE, Helena Mennie. Fellow of Robinson College, Cambridge. Former Senior Research Fellow in the Arts, Carnegie Trust for the Universities of Scotland. Author of *Song, Dance and Poetry of the Court of Scotland under King James VI*, 1969, and *A Preface to Spenser*, 1978. **Essays:** Sir Robert Ayton; Alexander Montgomerie; Edmund Spenser.

SHUCARD, Alan R. Associate Professor of English, University of Wisconsin – Parkside, Kenosha. Author of two books of verse – *The Gorgon Bog*, 1970, and *The Louse on the Head of the Lord*, 1972. **Essays:** Gwendolyn Brooks; Paul Laurence Dunbar; Robert Hayden.

SILKIN, Jon. Founder and Joint Editor, *Stand* magazine, and Co-Founding Editor, Northern House publishers, both in Newcastle upon Tyne. Author of several books of verse, the most recent being *The Little Time-Keeper*, 1976, and of *Out of Battle: Poetry of the Great War*, 1972. Editor of several anthologies of poetry, and translator of *Against Parting* by Nathan Zach, 1968. **Essays:** Sir Herbert Read; Isaac Rosenberg.

SIMPSON, Peter. Member of the Department of English, University of Canterbury, Christchurch, New Zealand. **Essays:** Mary Ursula Bethell; A. R. D. Fairburn; William Pember Reeves.

SINGH, Amritjit. Academic Associate, American Studies Research Centre, Hyderabad, India; Joint Editor of *The Indian Journal of American Studies*. Author of *The Novels of the Harlem Renaissance: Twelve Black Writers*, 1976, and of articles for Indian and American periodicals. Co-Editor of the bibliographies *Indian Literature in English*, 1977, and *Afro-American Poetry and Drama*, 1977. **Essay:** Claude McKay.

SIVARAMAKRISHNA, M.   Reader in the Department of English, Osmania University, Hyderabad; Editor of *Tenor* magazine. Author of many articles on English and American literature. **Essays:** Dom Moraes; Sarojini Naidu.

SKLOOT, Floyd.   Director of Program Services, Illinois Capital Development Board, Springfield. Author of *Vigil* (verse), 1978, and of poetry, fiction, and essays in *Shenandoah, Southern Poetry Review, Transatlantic Review, Eire-Ireland,* and *Journal of Education Finance.* **Essay:** Thomas Kinsella.

SMALL, Ian C.   Member of the Department of English Language and Literature, University of Birmingham. **Essay:** Lionel Johnson.

SMITH, A. J. M.   See his own entry. **Essay:** Ralph Gustafson.

SMITH, Elton E.   Professor of English and Bible, University of South Florida, Tampa. Author of *"The Two Voices": A Tennyson Study,* 1964; *William Godwin* (with Esther Marian Greenwell Smith), 1965; *Louis MacNeice,* 1970; *"The Angry Young Men" of the Thirties,* 1975; *Charles Reade,* 1977. **Essays:** C. Day Lewis; Stephen Spender.

SMITH, Stan.   Lecturer in English, University of Dundee, Scotland. Author of the forthcoming book *A Superfluous Man* (on Edward Thomas), and of articles on modern literature for *Critical Quarterly, Literature and History, Irish University Review, Scottish International Review,* and other periodicals. **Essays:** W. H. Auden; William Ernest Henley; Ted Hughes; Alfred Noyes; Sylvia Plath; Theodore Roethke; Edward Thomas.

SOLOMON, Harry M.   Associate Professor of English, Auburn University, Alabama. Author of *Sir Richard Blackmore* (forthcoming), and of articles on Shaftesbury, Swift, and others for *Southern Humanities Review, Keats-Shelley Journal, Studies in English Literature,* and other periodicals. **Essays:** William King; Katherine Philips.

SPEAR, Hilda D.   Lecturer in English, University of Dundee, Scotland. Author of *Remembering, We Forget* (on the poetry of World War I), 1978, the biographical and bibliographical sections of *The Pelican Guide to English Literature 5,* 1957, and of articles on Charles Stuart Calverley, Wilfred Owen, Siegfried Sassoon, Isaac Rosenberg, and Ford Madox Ford. Editor of *The English Poems of Calverley,* 1974, and *The Mayor of Casterbridge* by Thomas Hardy, 1978. **Essays:** Richard Harris Barham; Charles Stuart Calverley; Winthrop Mackworth Praed.

STALLWORTHY, Jon.   James Wendell Anderson Professor of English, Cornell University, Ithaca, New York. Deputy Academic Publisher, Oxford University Press, 1974–77. Author of several books of verse, the most recent being *The Apple Barrel,* 1974, two studies of Yeats's poetry, and *Wilfred Owen,* 1974. Editor of two anthologies of verse and of a casebook on Yeats's last poems; translator of an anthology of Polish poetry and of *The Twelve and Other Poems* by Alexander Blok, 1970. **Essay:** Wilfred Owen.

STANFORD, Donald E.   Professor of English, Louisiana State University, Baton Rouge; Editor of *The Southern Review.* Author of *New England Earth,* 1941, and *The Traveler,* 1955. Editor of *The Poems of Edward Taylor,* 1960; *Nine Essays in Modern Literature,* 1965; *Selected Poems of Robert Bridges,* 1974; *Selected Poems of S. Foster Damon,* 1974. **Essays:** Edward Taylor; Yvor Winters.

STEAD, C. K.   See his own entry.

STEVENSON, Kay.   Lecturer in Literature, University of Essex, Colchester. **Essays:** William Alabaster; Francis Quarles; Robert Southwell; Joshua Sylvester; Sir Henry Wotton.

STOREY, Graham. University Lecturer, and Fellow of Trinity Hall, Cambridge. Editor or Joint Editor of *The Journals and Papers of Hopkins*, 1959, *Letters of Charles Dickens* (Pilgrim Edition), vols., 1–3, 1965–69, and *Hopkins: A Selection*, 1967. **Essay:** Gerard Manley Hopkins.

SUMMERS, Joseph H. Professor of English, University of Rochester, New York. Author of *George Herbert: Religion and Art*, 1954, *The Muse's Method: An Introduction to Paradise Lost*, 1962, and *The Heirs of Donne and Jonson*, 1970. Editor of *Selected Poems* by Andrew Marvell, 1961, *The Lyric and Dramatic Milton*, 1965, and *Selected Poetry* by George Herbert, 1967. **Essays:** Elizabeth Bishop; George Herbert; Henry King; Richard Wilbur.

SUTHERLAND, James. Emeritus Professor of Modern English Literature, University College, London. Formerly, Editor of *Review of English Studies*. Author of many books, including *Leucocholy* (poems), 1926; *The Medium of Poetry*, 1934; *Defoe*, 1937; *A Preface to Eighteenth Century Poetry*, 1948; *The English Critic*, 1952; *On English Prose*, 1957; *English Satire*, 1958; *English Literature in the Late Seventeenth Century*, 1969; *Daniel Defoe: A Critical Study*, 1971. Editor of plays by Rowe, Dekker, Shakespeare, and Dryden, *The Dunciad* by Pope, 1943, and *The Oxford Book of Literary Anecdotes*, 1975.

SWEETSER, Wesley D. Professor of English, State University of New York, Oswego. Author of *Arthur Machen*, 1964, *A Bibliography of Machen* (with A. Goldstone), 1965, and *Ralph Hodgson: A Bibliography*, 1974. **Essays:** Alfred Domett; Ralph Hodgson; George Meredith.

TAYLOR, Donald S. Member of the English Department, University of Oregon, Eugene. Editor of *The Complete Works of Thomas Chatterton*, 2 vols., 1971. **Essay:** Thomas Chatterton.

TAYLOR, Myron. Associate Professor of English, State University of New York, Albany. Author of articles on Shakespeare in *The Christian Scholar*, *Studies in English*, and *Shakespeare Quarterly*. **Essay:** John Milton.

THOMAS, Ned. Lecturer in English, University College of Wales, Aberystwyth; Founding Editor of *Planet* magazine. Author of *George Orwell*, 1965, and *The Welsh Extremist: Essays on Modern Welsh Literature and Society*, 1971. **Essay:** Derek Walcott.

THWAITE, Anthony. Free-lance Writer, and Co-Editor of *Encounter* magazine, London. Author of several books of verse, the most recent being *A Portion for Foxes*, 1977; travel books; a book for children; and critical works, including *Contemporary English Poetry*, 1959 and *Poetry Today*, 1973. Co-Editor of two anthologies of English verse and translator of *The Penguin Book of Japanese Verse* (with Geoffrey Bownas), 1964. **Essays:** A. E. Housman; Stevie Smith; Arthur Symons.

TIBBLE, Anne. Free-lance Writer. Author of *African Literature*, 1964, *The Story of English Literature*, 1970, *The God Spigo* (novel), 1976, two volumes of autobiography, and books on Helen Keller, Gertrude Bell, Gordon, and John Clare. Editor of works by Clare. **Essays:** John Clare; Christopher Okigbo; Okot p'Bitek.

TRAVERSI, Derek A. Professor of English Literature, Swarthmore College, Pennsylvania. Author of *An Approach to Shakespeare*, 1938 (revised, 1968); *Shakespeare: The Last Phase*, 1954; *Shakespeare: From Richard II to Henry V*, 1957; *Shakespeare: The Roman Plays*, 1963; *T. S. Eliot: The Longer Poems*, 1976. **Essays:** Geoffrey Chaucer; T. S. Eliot; William Shakespeare.

TURNER, Richard C. Assistant Professor of English, Indiana University-Purdue University, Indianapolis. **Essay:** Adrienne Rich.

TYDEMAN, William M. Senior Lecturer in English, University College of North Wales, Bangor. Author of *The Theatre in the Middle Ages*, 1978, and of the chapter on the earlier 16th century in *Year's Work in English Studies*, 1971–74. Editor of *English Poetry 1400–1580*, 1970, and of casebooks on Wordsworth and Coleridge. **Essay:** Stephen Hawes.

WADDINGTON, Raymond B. Professor of English, University of Wisconsin, Madison; Member of the editorial boards of *Sixteenth Century Journal* and *Literary Monographs*. Author of *The Mind's Empire: Myth and Form in George Chapman's Narrative Poems*, 1974, and of articles on Shakespeare, Chapman, Milton, and others. Co-Editor of *The Rhetoric of Renaissance Poetry*, 1974. **Essay:** George Chapman.

WAGNER, Linda W. Professor of English, Michigan State University, East Lansing. Author of *The Poems* (1964) and *Prose* (1970) *of William Carlos Williams*; *Denise Levertov*, 1967; *Hemingway and Faulkner: Inventors, Masters*, 1975; *Introducing Poems*, 1976; *John Dos Passos*, 1978. **Essays:** Anne Sexton; William Carlos Williams.

WALL, Alan. Free-lance Writer. **Essays:** Thom Gunn; Edgell Rickword.

WALSH, George. Publisher and Free-lance Writer. **Essay:** Manmohan Ghose.

WALSH, Marcus. Lecturer in English, University of Birmingham. Editor of *The Religious Poetry of Christopher Smart*, 1972. **Essays:** John Dyer; Samuel Johnson; Christopher Smart; Isaac Watts.

WALSH, William. Professor of Commonwealth Literature and Chairman of the School of English, University of Leeds. Author of *Use of Imagination*, 1958; *A Human Idiom*, 1964; *Coleridge*, 1967; *A Manifold Voice*, 1970; *R. K. Narayan*, 1972; *V. S. Naipaul*, 1973; *Patrick White's Fiction*, 1978. **Essays:** Earle Birney; A. D. Hope; John Keats; A. M. Klein; Anne Wilkinson.

WARNER, Alan. Professor of English, New University of Ulster, Coleraine. Author of *A Short Guide to English Style*, 1961, *Clay Is the Word* (on Patrick Kavanagh), 1973, and *William Allingham*, 1975. **Essay:** William Allingham.

WATSON, J. R. Member of the Department of English, University of Leicester. Author of *Picturesque Landscape and English Romantic Poetry*, 1970. Editor of *Browning: "Men and Women" and Other Poems: A Casebook*, 1974, and *Victorian Poetry* (with N. P. Messenger), 1974. **Essay:** William Wordsworth.

WATTS, Harold H. Professor of English, Purdue University, Lafayette, Indiana. Author of *The Modern Reader's Guide to the Bible*, 1949; *Ezra Pound and the Cantos*, 1951; *Hound and Quarry*, 1953; *The Modern Reader's Guide to Religions*, 1964; *Aldous Huxley*, 1969. **Essays:** Hilda Doolittle; Wallace Stevens.

WEALES, Gerald. Professor of English, University of Pennsylvania, Philadelphia; Drama Critic for *The Reporter* and *Commonweal*. Author of *Religion in Modern English Drama*, 1961; *American Drama since World War II*, 1962; *A Play and Its Parts*, 1964; *The Jumping-Off Place: American Drama in the 1960's*, 1969; *Clifford Odets*, 1971. Editor of *The Complete Plays of William Wycherley*, 1966, and, with Robert J. Nelson, of the collections *Enclosure*, 1975, and *Revolution*, 1975. **Essay:** James Whitcomb Riley.

WELCH, Robert. Lecturer in English Literature, University of Leeds. Author of *A Guide to Animal Farm*, 1978, *Anglo-Irish Poetry, 1800–1900*, 1978, and of articles on Anglo-Irish literature in *Irish University Review, Studies, Eire-Ireland*, and other periodicals. **Essays:** Sir Samuel Ferguson; James Clarence Mangan.

WHEELER, Thomas. Professor of English, University of Tennessee, Knoxville. Author of *Paradise Lost and the Modern Reader*, 1974, and of articles on Milton and Thomas More. **Essays:** Joseph Beaumont; Sidney Godolphin.

WILLIAMS, John Stuart. Head of the Communications Department, South Glamorgan Institute of Higher Education, Cardiff. Author of four books of verse, the most recent being *Banna Strand*, 1975. Editor of three verse anthologies. **Essays:** Alun Lewis; R. S. Thomas.

WILLY, Margaret. Free-lance Writer and Lecturer. Author of two books of verse – *The Invisible Sun*, 1946, and *Every Star a Tongue*, 1951 – and several critical works, including *Life Was Their Cry*, 1950; *Three Metaphysical Poets: Crashaw, Vaughan, Traherne*, 1961; *Three Women Diarists: Celia Fiennes, Dorothy Wordsworth, Katherine Mansfield*, 1964; *A Critical Commentary on "Wuthering Heights,"* 1966; *A Critical Commentary on Browing's "Men and Women,"*1968. Editor of two anthologies and of works by Goldsmith. **Essays:** Robert Browning; Walter de la Mare; John Donne; Thomas Traherne; Henry Vaughan.

WOODCOCK, George. Free-lance Writer, Lecturer, and Editor. Author of verse (*Selected Poems*, 1967), plays, travel books, biographies, and works on history and politics; critical works include *William Godwin*, 1946; *The Incomparable Aphra*, 1948; *The Paradox of Oscar Wilds*, 1949; *The Crystal Spirit* (on Orwell), 1966; *Hugh MacLennan*, 1969; *Odysseus Ever Returning: Canadian Writers and Writing*, 1970; *Mordecai Richler*, 1970; *Dawn and the Darkest Hour* (on Aldous Huxley), 1972; *Herbert Read*, 1972; *Thomas Merton*, 1978. Editor of anthologies, and of works by Charles Lamb, Malcolm Lowry, Wyndham Lewis, and others. **Essays:** Bliss Carman; Irving Layton; Charles Mair; P. K. Page; Charles G. D. Roberts; Duncan Campbell Scott; A. J. M. Smith; Raymond Souster; Ned Ward.

WOODRESS, James. Professor of English, University of California, Davis; Editor of *American Literary Scholarship*. Author of *Howells and Italy*, 1952; *Booth Tarkington*, 1955; *A Yankee's Odyssey: The Life of Joel Barlow*, 1958; *Willa Cather: Her Life and Art*, 1970; *American Fiction 1900–1950*, 1974. Editor of *Voices from America's Past* (with Richard Morris), 1961, and *Eight American Authors*, 1971. **Essays:** Joel Barlow; Karl Shapiro; Walt Whitman.

WRIGHT, Judith. See her own entry.

YOUNG, T. D. Gertrude Conaway Vanderbilt Professor of English, Vanderbilt University, Nashville. Author of *Jack London and the Era of Social Protest*, 1950; *The Literature of the South*, 1952 (revised, 1968); *Donald Davidson: An Essay and a Bibliography* (with M. Thomas Inge), 1965; *American Literature: A Critical Survey*, 1968; *John Crowe Ranson: Critical Essays and a Bibliography*, 1968; *Ransom*, 1970; *Davidson* (with Inge), 1971. Editor of *The Literary Correspondence of Davidson and Tate* (with John T. Fain), 1974. **Essays:** Donald Davidson; John Crowe Ransom.